The UN Security Council
in the Twenty-First Century

A project of the International Peace Institute

The UN Security Council in the Twenty-First Century

edited by
Sebastian von Einsiedel
David M. Malone
Bruno Stagno Ugarte

LYNNE
RIENNER
PUBLISHERS

BOULDER
LONDON

Published in the United States of America in 2016 by
Lynne Rienner Publishers, Inc.
1800 30th Street, Boulder, Colorado 80301
www.rienner.com

and in the United Kingdom by
Lynne Rienner Publishers, Inc.
3 Henrietta Street, Covent Garden, London WC2E 8LU

Library of Congress Cataloging-in-Publication Data
The UN security council in the twenty-first century / edited by Sebastian
von Einsiedel, David M. Malone and Bruno Stagno Ugarte.
    pages cm
    Includes bibliographical references and index.
    ISBN 978-1-62637-258-0 (hardcover : alk. paper)
    ISBN 978-1-62637-259-7 (pbk. : alk. paper)
    1. United Nations. Security Council. I. Einsiedel, Sebastian von, 1972–
JZ5006.7.U52 2015
341.23'23—dc23

                                                         2015034322

British Cataloguing in Publication Data
A Cataloguing in Publication record for this book
is available from the British Library.

Printed and bound in the United States of America

 The paper used in this publication meets the requirements
of the American National Standard for Permanence of
Paper for Printed Library Materials Z39.48-1992.

    5 4 3 2 1

Contents

Foreword, Terje Rød-Larsen   ix
Preface   xi
Acknowledgments   xiii

1 Introduction, *Sebastian von Einsiedel, David M. Malone,*
  and Bruno Stagno Ugarte   1
2 The UN Security Council: Decisions and Actions,
  Peter Wallensteen and Patrik Johansson   27

Part 1 Competing Interests on the Security Council

3 The United States in the Security Council, *Stephen John Stedman*   57
  3.1 Commentary: The Permanent One's Search for
    Maximum Flexibility, *David Bosco,* 75
4 China in the Security Council, *Zhu Wenqi and Leng Xinyu*   83
5 Russia in the Security Council, *Dmitri Trenin*   105
6 France and the United Kingdom in the Security Council,
  Thierry Tardy and Dominik Zaum   121
7 Power Dynamics Between Permanent and Elected Members,
  Colin Keating   139
8 Council Reform and the Emerging Powers, *Kishore Mahbubani*   157
9 Working Methods: The Ugly Duckling of
  Security Council Reform, *Christian Wenaweser*   175
10 The Security Council at Seventy: Ever Changing or
  Never Changing? *Edward C. Luck*   195

Part 2 Addressing Thematic Issues

11 Humanitarian Action and Intervention, *Thomas G. Weiss*   217
12 Promoting Democracy, *Francesco Mancini*   235

13 Acting on Human Rights, *Joanna Weschler*   259

14 Responding to Terrorism, *Peter Romaniuk*   277

15 Confronting Organized Crime and Piracy, *James Cockayne*   299

16 Weapons of Mass Destruction: Managing Proliferation,
    Waheguru Pal Singh Sidhu   323

Part 3 Enforcing Council Mandates

17 The Use of Force: A System of Selective Security, *Adam Roberts*   349

18 Robust Peacekeeping and the Limits of Force,
    Jean-Marie Guéhenno   373

19 The Security Council and NATO, *Herman Schaper*   393

20 The Role of Sanctions, *Sue Eckert*   413

Part 4 Evolving Institutional Factors

21 Relations with the UN Secretary-General, *Simon Chesterman*   443

22 Special Representatives of the Secretary-General, *Connie Peck*   457

23 Collaborating with Regional Organizations, *Bruno Stagno Ugarte*   475

24 Groups of Friends, *Teresa Whitfield*   491

25 International Courts and Tribunals, *Eran Sthoeger*   507

Part 5 Key Country Cases

26 The Arab-Israeli Conflict, *Markus E. Bouillon*   529

27 Iraq, *David M. Malone and Poorvi Chitalkar*   551

28 The Balkans, *Mats Berdal*   569

29 Somalia, *John L. Hirsch*   595

30 Sudan, *Heiko Nitzschke*   615

31 Afghanistan, *Francesc Vendrell*   643

32 The Democratic Republic of the Congo, *Tatiana Carayannis*   661

33 Côte d'Ivoire, *Arthur Boutellis and Alexandra Novosseloff*   681

34 Libya, *Alex J. Bellamy and Paul D. Williams*   699

35 Syria, *Salman Shaikh and Amanda Roberts*   717

    35.1 Commentary: The Council's Failure on Syria,
        Raghida Dergham, 741

Part 6 The Security Council and International Order

36 The Security Council and Peacekeeping, *Richard Gowan* 749
37 The Security Council and International Law, *Ian Johnstone* 771
38 The Security Council and the Changing Distribution of Power,
    Bruce Jones 793
39 The Security Council in a Fragmenting World, *Jeremy Greenstock* 815
40 Conclusion: The Security Council and a World in Crisis,
    *Sebastian von Einsiedel, David M. Malone, and
    Bruno Stagno Ugarte* 827

Appendixes

1 Security Council–Mandated UN Peacekeeping Operations
   and Observer Missions, 1945–2014 878
2 Security Council–Mandated UN Political Missions, 1989–2014 891
3 Non-UN Peace or Enforcement Operations Mandated
   by the Security Council, 1945–2014 899
4 Security Council–Mandated Sanctions Regimes, 1945–2014 905
5 Vetoes Cast in the UN Security Council, 1989–2014 918

List of Acronyms 921
Bibliography 929
The Contributors 957
Index 963
About the Book 999

Foreword

Terje Rød-Larsen,
President, International Peace Institute

THE INTERNATIONAL PEACE INSTITUTE (IPI) IS PLEASED TO
present *The UN Security Council in the Twenty-First Century,* edited by
Sebastian von Einsiedel, David M. Malone, and Bruno Stagno Ugarte.

Ten years ago IPI, then known as the International Peace Academy,
under the leadership of David Malone, produced a thirty-nine-chapter study
of the Security Council that would become a standard text on the subject for
countless students, scholars, and practitioners of international affairs. It was
thus with great pleasure that we agreed to partner with David and his colleagues Sebastian von Einsiedel and Bruno Stagno Ugarte, both long-time
friends of IPI, on the production of this new volume—not a second edition
of the original classic text, but an entirely new book. Encyclopedic in scope,
this new book features the most knowledgeable authors in the field.

The book follows a long course of work on the Security Council at IPI
during the past decade, including work on the Council's approach to counterterrorism and in-depth studies of the Council and civil war. In 2010, IPI
published the first of two studies that gathered insights from IPI's comprehensive Security Council Compliance Database, which documents all Security Council resolutions adopted in the context of civil wars between 1989
and 2006 and tracks the parties' compliance. Most recently, IPI has returned
to the study of sanctions, publishing three reports on the topic in 2014: one
on the Council's current approach to drawing down sanctions and two
addressing the issue of improving implementation.

The UN Security Council in the Twenty-First Century covers a comprehensive range of topics and country cases. The book encompasses both
broad themes and detailed procedures, from the great power politics of the
Council's five permanent members to the specific evolution of Security
Council working methods, and from the Arab-Israeli conflict to Syria and

the Democratic Republic of the Congo (to name just three of the many cases covered). It provides both historical analysis and contemporary insight. In addition, it features useful appendixes that will benefit both scholars and practitioners; these include lists of all UN peacekeeping operations since 1948 and all Security Council sanctions regimes imposed between 1945 and 2014.

With this kind of breadth and depth of study, this volume will contribute to a better understanding of the Security Council for many years to come. We are grateful to the authors and editors for all of their work on the project.

IPI also owes a debt of thanks to all of its generous donors, who fund our research and make publications like this one possible. In particular, IPI would like to thank the Carnegie Corporation and the governments of Germany and Singapore for their support of this project.

Preface

IN EARLY 2004, ONE OF THE THREE COEDITORS OF THIS BOOK, David M. Malone, published a multiauthor volume on the United Nations Security Council with Lynne Rienner Publishers titled *The UN Security Council: From the Cold War to the Twenty-First Century.* That book, appearing at a time when the relevance of the United Nations was questioned by many in the aftermath of the US-led invasion of Iraq, traced the body's evolution and operations from the end of the Cold War to the early 2000s. It has since become a standard reference volume on the Council, widely used in universities and other research communities, as well as among UN delegates, UN Secretariat officials, and NGOs. The book's success prompted Lynne Rienner, in early 2013, to approach Malone to suggest a new edition. By then, not only had the Security Council experienced significant change in its dynamics, internal operations, and role in international affairs, but it was arguably once again facing a fundamental crisis of relevance, in light of its weak responses to the Syrian civil war, recurrent crises in UN peacekeeping operations, and a resurgence of great power rivalry, causing concern that the UN might fall back into Cold War paralysis.

The significant evolution of the Security Council since 2004 and the altered context in which it operates a decade later made clear that, rather than a revised edition of the earlier book, an entirely new book was called for. Malone consequently sought out two coeditors, Sebastian von Einsiedel and Bruno Stagno Ugarte, and together we recast both the structure and content the 2004 volume.

By slicing and dicing the Security Council in many different ways, looking at its decisions, activities, and operations, the competing interests of its members, the substantive themes of its work, and its institutional development, this new volume assesses the body's objectives and performance in the post–Cold War era and in particular since the turn of the millennium. We aim to offer multiple perspectives on the body. As coeditors, we bring different viewpoints to the subject matter, shaped by our different backgrounds and experiences with respect to the Council. David Malone, a Canadian career diplomat, former president of the International Peace Institute, and current rector of United Nations University, sat on the Security Council in the early 1990s and has published widely on multilateral security. Bruno Stagno Ugarte served as Costa Rica's permanent representative to the UN from 2002 to 2006 and subsequently as foreign minister while Costa Rica was a member of the Council from 2008 to 2009. He recently headed Security Council Report, an NGO monitoring and reporting on the Security Council, and today leads the global advocacy activities of Human Rights Watch. Sebastian von Einsiedel, a former staffer at UN headquarters in the office of the Secretary-General, in the Department of Political Affairs, and in the UN political field mission in Nepal, is director of United Nations University's Center for Policy Research and has written numerous articles on UN security issues.

This book is a multidisciplinary and multinational product with forty-nine authors from twenty-three countries. It features a mix of senior-level practitioners, a number of whom have served on the Council as diplomats or sought to implement its mandates as UN officials; political scientists, international lawyers, and journalists; and members of the NGO community who interact frequently with the Council. With such diversity among the contributors, the chapters necessarily look at the Council from different angles. The book's authors often differ in their assessments of important episodes in the Council's recent history, in particular with respect to Libya and Syria and to the roles and motivations of key member states in those cases. As editors, we have welcomed this diversity of views, but encouraged the authors to engage with, or at least consider, alternative arguments.

—*the Editors*

Acknowledgments

WE ARE DEEPLY INDEBTED TO A NUMBER OF KEY INDIVIDUALS and institutions without whose help this volume would not have been possible. We are particularly grateful to the International Peace Institute (IPI), which again agreed to host this project, and to several of its members who became actively involved in producing the volume. Special thanks go to Francesco Mancini, IPI's former senior director of research and one of this book's contributors, who enthusiastically oversaw the project at IPI; Adam Lupel, IPI's excellent director of research and publications, who provided helpful advice and guidance; and François Carrel-Billiard, Taimi Strehlow, Anette Ringnes, and Beatrice Agyarkoh, who provided invaluable institutional support to the project in numerous ways. Bianca Selway provided valuable research assistance in updating the appendixes at the end of the volume. Throughout the project, Terje Rød-Larsen, IPI's president, has been an invaluable supporter.

This volume would not have been possible without the support of generous contributions, in particular from the government of Germany, the government of Singapore, and the Carnegie Corporation of New York. We are particularly grateful to Ambassador Peter Wittig, who so ably represented Germany in the Security Council in the turbulent two-year period of 2011–2012, for being a champion of this book.

Thanks to IPI and this project's funders, the editors and the authors of this book's chapters were able to meet in New York in 2013 at the Whitney family's beautiful Greentree estate. We are most grateful to the Greentree Foundation for its support. The authors' meeting helped us to forge a common approach to the book, shed light on the evolution of the Council's treatment of the key issues, identify trends we believe to be genuinely important, and focus on the implications of those trends for the future role of the Council and the UN in the sphere of international security. We are particularly grateful to key Council ambassadors who took the time to join us for selected sessions, considerably enriching the discussion with frank assessments and insightful analyses of the Council and its flaws: Martin Briens, the French deputy permanent representative to the UN; Mark Lyall Grant, the UK's permanent representative to the UN; Gert Rosenthal, Guatemala's permanent representative to the UN and his country's former foreign minister; Hardeep Singh Puri, former permanent representative of India to the UN; and Christophe Eick, minister plenipotentiary at the German permanent mission to the UN. Their insights are reflected, one way or another, throughout the book.

We thank the authors, with whom we have been engaged in a spirited dialogue throughout the life of this project. We are most indebted to them for their significant commitment of time and effort in contributing to the volume and for their patience in enduring and responding to multiple comments in several rounds of redrafting. While we are deeply grateful to them all, we would like to single out three authors who have been particularly involved beyond their individual chapter contributions: Jean-Marie Guéhenno, by providing an insightful keynote address on what the changing nature of violence in contemporary conflict means for the Security Council; and Bruce Jones and Heiko Nitzschke, whose comments on various chapters and continuous advice on the book's structure have done much to shape it.

We also thank Richard Gowan, John L. Hirsch, Francesco Mancini, Heiko Nitzschke, and Teresa Whitfield for joining us at a lengthy brainstorming session in the final phases of producing the manuscript. At that session we were also joined by two longtime observers of the Council from the media, James Traub and Colum Lynch, whose insightful writing on the Council and the UN at large has done so much to foster a wider understanding of the inner workings of the United Nations. Anthony Yazaki and Alexandra Ivanovic provided helpful research and copyediting support, for which we are very grateful. Sam Daws, a legend in his own time at a still young age for his encyclopedic knowledge of the Council, has always been available to all of his friends, many of them authors and editors of this volume, for advice and information.

We also want to thank our respective home institutions for being so supportive in allowing us to pursue this project in parallel to our respective day jobs. All three of us changed jobs in the course of this project: halfway through the production of this book, David Malone left his position as president of Canada's International Development Research Centre to become rector of United Nations University (UNU) and a UN under-secretary-general; Bruno Stagno Ugarte moved from Security Council Report, where he served as executive director, to lead Human Rights Watch's global advocacy efforts; and Sebastian von Einsiedel, who was a staff member of the

UN Secretariat's Department of Political Affairs when he embarked on this project, moved temporarily to New York University's Center for International Cooperation, which generously hosted him while we were working on this book, and toward the end of this project joined UNU. Without the strong support of our employers, and their patience with the distractions such an ambitious project can sometimes impose, volumes like these would be difficult to achieve. In particular, Sebastian von Einsiedel and David Malone greatly appreciate the enthusiastic support of the UNU Council, particularly that of its chair, Mohamed Hassan, for policy-relevant research.

Finally, we thank Lynne Rienner for publishing this book and for initiating this project in the first place. Her dedication to UN-focused scholarship is exceptional and deserves much credit.

—the Editors

1

Introduction

*Sebastian von Einsiedel, David M. Malone,
and Bruno Stagno Ugarte*

IN 2004, WHEN THE PREDECESSOR VOLUME TO THIS BOOK WAS published, the UN Security Council was widely seen as being at a cross-roads. The UN had recently embarked on major new peacekeeping oper-ations in Kosovo, East Timor, Sierra Leone, and the Democratic Republic of the Congo (DRC), but its ability to address the shortcomings that had led to disastrous peacekeeping failures in Somalia, Srebrenica, and Rwanda in the early 1990s remained uncertain. The dustup among the Council's permanent five members (P5) around the Kosovo crisis in 1999, leaving lasting scars in Moscow, still reverberated, and disagree-ment persisted over the circumstances under which humanitarian suffer-ing would trump national sovereignty, calling for coercive action. The September 11, 2001, terrorist attacks in the United States temporarily restored unity in the Security Council, leading to robust responses, including recognition of the right of the United States to self-defense in these circumstances, which provided cover for its Afghanistan interven-tion, and the establishment of far-reaching, globally binding counterter-rorism norms. For a brief period, there was hope that the P5 could forge a lasting strategic partnership around counterterrorism. But that unity soon dissipated due to the toxic diplomatic struggle preceding the 2003 US-led intervention in Iraq, which was fought in the name of the "war on terror." At the time, the very relevance of the Council, and the UN, was widely questioned: supporters of the Iraq invasion lamented the Council's inability to enforce its own resolutions and address new threats, whereas opponents criticized the Council for failing to prevent the United States from waging a war they saw as illegal. And there was concern that the

Council faced a future in which it was confined to mandating mop-up operations after US-led military interventions.

Today, the Security Council is arguably facing an even deeper crisis of relevance. The record of UN peacekeepers, increasingly deployed by the Council into situations where there is "no peace to keep," in Darfur, the DRC, and South Sudan, has raised questions about their ability to bring stability to conflict-ridden countries and act effectively on civilian protection mandates. Council-mandated multinational operations have fared no better, with Afghanistan and Iraq going through renewed cycles of violence, seeming to show the limits of third-party postconflict statebuilding—even when that third party is led by a major power willing to invest significant resources. Celebrations over the Council's authorization to implement the Responsibility to Protect (R2P) doctrine through the use of force in Libya in 2011 appeared premature when deep divisions emerged among the P5 over the manner in which the North Atlantic Treaty Organization (NATO) implemented its mandate to protect civilians from slaughter by the Muammar Qaddafi regime. These divisions extended to Syria, where the Council's inability to agree on any meaningful response to the escalating civil war is widely seen as the Council's biggest failure since the Rwandan genocide. Meanwhile, the outbreak of the Ukrainian crisis in 2014 has evoked the specter of a new Cold War, raising fears the Council will be thrown back into the state of near paralysis it had been in for nearly forty-five years. Also reinforcing the sense that the Council may be entering a new era is the perception of US retrenchment. The dominant fear in 2004 that the Council could be rendered obsolete by US unilateralism has since been replaced by concern that Washington, the main driver of the Council's liberal interventionism since the end of the Cold War, has lost its desire and will to lead forceful action within (and even outside) a UN framework.

Meanwhile, the Council's own procedures have become increasingly sclerotic and stylized as the embattled P5 are criticized ever more loudly by the membership at large and circle the wagons around their own privileges, some enshrined in the UN Charter, others invented through practice over the years.[1]

Looking at the UN Security Council today, one may thus easily become disillusioned by its shortcomings, ineffectiveness, and episodic failures. And there is indeed much to criticize in the Council's performance across different areas. However, if one traces its evolution and impact since its inception, and in particular since the end of the Cold War, it also becomes clear that the Council has been highly adaptable and innovative, in both procedural and substantive terms. It has creatively interpreted the UN Charter to redefine dramatically the notion of sovereignty, expand its authority, refine Charter tools, and develop new instruments. Maybe most important, along the way it has consolidated its position as the ultimate arbiter on the legitimacy of the use of force other than self-defense. While some of the Council's innovations (such as the invention of peacekeeping) date back to the Cold War, most of them occurred in the 1990s. As the focus of this volume is on the period since the turn of the millennium, this introductory chapter will offer an overview of the historical background against which most of the rest of the volume is situated.

Origins and Cold War

Conceived by the Allies during the last year of World War II, and founded in the war's immediate aftermath at the San Francisco Conference in 1945, the UN's main purpose was to prevent a future world war. To that end, member states committed themselves in Article 1(1) of the UN Charter to "take effective collective measures for the prevention and removal of threats to the peace." While the Charter does not contain the term "collective security"—because, in the words of Michael Howard, "it smelled of the failures of the 1930s"[2]—the concept is nevertheless firmly enshrined in Chapters I, V, and VII of the Charter. As the primary UN organ concerned with the maintenance of international peace and security, the Security Council can invoke the collective security mechanisms of the Charter, including the coercive measures of Chapter VII, when it determines the existence of a threat to international peace and security.

In its design, the Security Council was meant to fix the flaws that had rendered ineffective its predecessor body, the Council of the League of Nations. Most important, the major powers of the day, World War II's victors, were endowed with special rights (permanent membership and the veto, first and foremost) and responsibilities, which were to ensure the lasting presence of these major powers, with their military capacities for possible enforcement action, in the new system.

Originally counting eleven members (the membership was enlarged to fifteen in 1965 through the addition of four nonpermanent members), the Security Council was imbued by the Charter with two sets of powers that differentiate it from any other intergovernmental organ. The first one was the power to take decisions that are legally binding on concerned member states. Indeed, contrary to widely held perception, the Charter, according to Article 25, commits concerned member states to carry out *all* decisions the Council adopts, not just those under Chapter VII. The second power unique to the Council is its authority, under Chapter VII, to enforce its decisions through various sanctions and embargoes (Article 41) as well as through the use of military force (Article 42). The Charter also foresaw the establishment of a standby system under which member states would make available earmarked military forces for Council-mandated operations. However, no member state showed any interest in entering into such arrangements, dooming the UN to this day to rely on self-appointed groups of states for enforcement action.[3]

In any case, the advent of the Cold War just a few years after the establishment of the new world organization rendered the new collective security system largely ineffective for the following four decades. Before 1990, the Security Council explicitly authorized military action under Chapter VII in only two instances. The first such authorization occurred in 1950, to reverse a North Korean invasion into South Korea, and then only because the Soviet Union—to its later regret—had boycotted the Security Council at the time. The second instance was the robust peacekeeping mission deployed in the Congo in the early 1960s (ONUC). This episode constitutes a notable exception to the UN's inability to intervene forcefully in any of this period's many internal violent conflicts due to the standoff between the United States and the Soviet Union, which often supported opposing parties in what were in many respects proxy wars between them. But the Congo intervention cost the life of the UN's much admired second Secretary-General, Dag Hammarskjöld, and brought the organization close to financial ruin, confirming to many that the Council should aim to avoid the use of force. (Precipitating a crisis over the funding of UN peacekeeping, France and the Soviet Union challenged their related assessments of dues for ONUC.) Mandatory sanctions were imposed by the Council in only two instances during the Cold War, against Southern Rhodesia in 1966 and South Africa in 1977. But these were exceptions that were only made possible by the universally condemned racial policies of the white minority regimes there.

With enforcement action largely ruled out by Cold War constraints, the Council nevertheless maintained a certain relevance by making creative use of the Charter's less intrusive Chapter VI provisions, which allow the Council to "investigate any dispute" and "recommend appropriate procedures or methods of adjustments." Building on Chapter VI (but falling short of Chapter VII), the Council deployed two military observer missions in the late 1940s, one to Palestine (UNTSO) and one to Kashmir (UNMOGIP), providing an early template of what later evolved into peacekeeping. Dubbed by Hammarskjöld a "Chapter VI ½" instrument, peacekeeping is actually not mentioned in the UN Charter, which did not prevent the Council from deploying fourteen further peacekeeping or military observer missions to defuse mostly interstate conflicts between 1958 and 1990.[4] (It should be noted that the first proper peacekeeping operation, meaning one involving lightly armed troops, was UNEF I, which was deployed in 1956 in the context of the Suez crisis, and was mandated by the General Assembly instead of the Security Council. The Council was deadlocked on the issue, not least because France and the UK were belligerents, alongside Israel and against Egypt.) In doing so, the Council managed to play an often overlooked "role in the mitigation and containment of conflicts which, it was feared, would otherwise bring the superpowers into more direct confrontation."[5]

Early Post–Cold War Euphoria

Mikhail Gorbachev's ascent to power in the Soviet Union in 1985 and the initiation of his reformist *perestroika* program a year later heralded the end of the Cold War. One important signal of the decisive thaw in the super-power standoff was a noticeable improvement in the climate among the P5 in the second half of the 1980s. In 1986, John Thomson, the UK permanent representative to the UN, took the initiative to call together his fellow P5 ambassadors, at his residence away from UN headquarters, for an informal discussion on how they could contribute to an early end of the murderous Iran-Iraq War.[6] The others welcomed this initiative and a system of regular P5 informal meetings soon took hold. These meetings helped anticipate and defuse conflicts among the five and allowed them to exchange notes on their national positions regarding various crises of the hour, if not formally to coordinate their positions. This newfound trust paid off a year later when, after having been publicly challenged by Secretary-General Javier Pérez de Cuellar to tackle a resolution to the Iran-Iraq War, Security Council proposals for a ceasefire, monitored by a small UN observer mission, made serious headway.[7] The post–Cold War era had started at the UN.

A celebrated *Pravda* article by Gorbachev of September 17, 1987, sought the "wider use of . . . the institution of UN military observers and UN peacekeeping forces in disengaging the troops of warring sides, observing ceasefires and armistice agreements," and called for the P5 to become "guarantors" of international security.[8]

While P5 cooperation required some time to take root,[9] the much improved climate among the permanent members could soon be gauged by the sharp decline in the use of the veto: only 12 substantive vetoes were invoked from January 1990 to June 2003, compared to 193 during the first forty-five years of the UN's history. Veto threats remained highly relevant, as the Council's dealings on Bosnia in 1993–1995, Kosovo in 1999, and Iraq in early 2003 made clear, but very few issues seriously divided the P5 after 1987. Meanwhile, the ability and disposition of the P5 to cooperate with each other seriously diminished the margin for maneuver of elected Council members, who were soon grumbling that they were systematically marginalized, a complaint lent more weight by a tendency of the Secretariat to consult privately with some or all of the P5 before advancing recommendations to the Council as a whole.

Converging perspectives among the P5 on a number of violent conflicts around the world, particularly on the need to disentangle the superpowers from them, allowed the Council to initiate action toward settlements. Between 1988 and late 1989, it established five peacekeeping and observer forces to assist settlement of the Iran-Iraq War (UNIIMOG); the crises in Afghanistan (UNGOMAP), Angola (UNAVEM I), and Namibia (UNTAG); and interlinked conflicts within Central America (ONUCA).

While the end of the Cold War had to some extent already unlocked the Council's potential to contribute to the resolution of serious problems of international peace and security by drawing on newfound cooperation between the superpowers, the Council's approach to conflicts remained relatively cautious until the Iraqi invasion and annexation of Kuwait in August 1990.

These events led the Council to impose a comprehensive trade embargo on Baghdad only four days later (Resolution 661), and in November of that year to authorize the use of force by a US-led coalition of member states.[10] These steps, along with the Council's decisions following the March 1991 liberation of Kuwait, including disarmament obligations imposed on Baghdad as well as measures adopted to encourage protection of Iraqi minorities and to provide humanitarian assistance to the Kurdish population, were important not only in their own right but also because they proved precedential and consequential in many respects and would continue to move the Council for years to come.[11]

The success of the coalition's military campaign against the Saddam Hussein regime induced what in retrospect appears to have been an unwarranted era of euphoria about a "new world order," at the center of which a reinvigorated Security Council would have the potential and capabilities to address conflicts worldwide. Having successfully tackled a conceptually straightforward challenge to international peace and security in the form of Iraq's attack on Kuwait, the Council then waded into the murkier waters of civil wars and of intercommunal strife.

The Council's initial record of successfully managing the unwinding of conflicts in El Salvador, Cambodia, and Mozambique that had been fueled by the Cold War, provided reason for optimism. Presaging later complex peace operations, these missions, all deployed in 1992, were trendsetting in two ways: first, unlike most of their Cold War predecessors, they were deployed to help settle civil wars instead of serving as "plate-glass windows" deployed along international borders; and second, they had significantly broader mandates than their Cold War predecessors, with large civil components tending to the political, human rights, civil affairs, electoral, humanitarian assistance, and policing tasks of the missions.[12] (Civilian leadership of large UN peacekeeping operations had been initiated with great success in Namibia in 1989–1990 by Martti Ahtisaari, later president of Finland.) The missions in El Salvador, Cambodia, and Mozambique also reflected the Council's growing engagement in democracy promotion, as well as the tendency to see elections both as a means of effecting a "new deal" in postconflict countries in which power could be shared with former combatants in rough proportion to electoral results, but also as an exit strategy for the missions. The success of these three missions benefited from strong UN leadership on the ground, adequate resourcing, and a strongly engaged and supportive Security Council.[13] However, they also benefited from a permissive environment that was all too absent in later UN operations, including a robust political settlement among conflicting parties who ultimately shared a desire for peace, (relatively) functional state institutions, and small territories.

Building on an emerging view in much of the world that the Council was at last coming into its own, the first-ever Security Council summit was convened on January 31, 1992, to discuss new orientations and activities for the Council. Secretary-General Boutros Boutros-Ghali, who had just assumed the UN's top job, was asked to submit "analysis and recommendations on ways of strengthening and making more efficient within the framework and provisions of the Charter the capacity of the United Nations for preventive diplomacy, for peacemaking and for peace-keeping."[14] Boutros-Ghali responded with a wide-ranging, thoughtful, and ambitious document, *An Agenda for Peace.* This report advocated, among other things, for consideration in certain circumstances of a "preventive deployment" of UN peacekeepers to forestall hostilities known to be looming, and, when circumstances warranted, the use of force by the UN itself rather than by coalitions of member states.[15] *An Agenda for Peace* noted that peacekeeping had been carried out "hitherto" with the consent of all parties, hinting that this might not be necessary in the future. It seemed to assume a quantum leap in the willingness by member states to support robust UN action in the peace and security field.

The Council, too, seemed to believe that because enforcement of its decisions against Iraq had been successfully carried out, the constraints on and limitations of UN peacekeeping had fallen away. In the barely thirty-one months that followed Resolution 686 on the end of hostilities in the Gulf region on March 2, 1991, the Council accelerated the pace of its work by adopting 185 resolutions and launching fifteen new peacekeeping and observer missions as compared to 685 resolutions and seventeen missions in the previous forty-six years of UN history.[16] Along the way, the peacekeeping budget increased from $240 million in 1986 to $2.7 billion in 1993, and the number of troops in the field from 10,000 to almost 55,000.[17]

Similarly, starting with the sanctions imposed on the Saddam Hussein regime in 1990, the Council also moved rapidly in the early post–Cold War years to impose a dizzying array of sanctions regimes to coerce conflicting parties to comply with Council decisions and international law as well as to deny them access to arms and resources. From 1991 to 2000, the Security Council imposed twelve different sanctions regimes, not only against states but increasingly also against nonstate actors such as the Khmer Rouge, UNITA in Angola, the RUF in Sierra Leone, and the Taliban in Afghanistan. Along the way, the Council moved away from comprehensive trade embargoes (imposed in the early 1990s on Iraq, the former Yugoslavia, and Haiti) toward ever more targeted sanctions on diplomats, as well as bans on travel, financial transactions, air flight, and arms, once the humanitarian costs of sanctions regimes in Iraq and Haiti became widely known. The ability of regimes in countries struck by sanctions to enrich themselves greatly by controlling black markets in prohibited products also took some time to sink in.

The Sobering Effect of the Triple Peacekeeping Disasters

As Mats Berdal has pointed out, the large increase in the deployment of peacekeeping missions meant they soon "dominated the day-to-day business of the Council in a manner unprecedented in the Cold War years . . . and created severe strains on the organization's limited capacity for mounting, managing, and sustaining operations."[18] These strains, together with the application of insufficient or inappropriate resources, wishful thinking, and a flight from reality, largely account for the UN's triple peacekeeping disasters in Bosnia, Somalia, and Rwanda, unfolding during the years 1993–1995, which brought lasting shame on the UN and a sudden end to the first boom period of peacekeeping in the post–Cold War era.

In Rwanda, a cost-conscious Security Council, having deployed an understaffed and underequipped mission to implement a peace agreement, decided to cut and run when the genocide broke out, leaving hundreds of thousands of Rwandans to their fate. (The UN Secretariat shoulders a significant degree of blame in the episode by failing to share essential information with the Council about possible planning for a genocide and for failing at least to try to press the Council into action.)[19] In Bosnia, the Council resorted to rhetorical posturing when its mission, UNPROFOR, ran into difficulties on the ground, equipping it with a robust Chapter VII mandate, including to protect civilians in so-called safe areas, without providing the necessary military hardware and political support to fulfill that promise. This led to disaster in Srebrenica, where thousands of civilians who had sought refuge in one of the safe areas were slaughtered.[20] In Somalia, the Council, whose initial mission (UNOSOM I) of just 500 soldiers was unable to protect the delivery of humanitarian aid, first mandated a robust US-led multinational mission (UNITAF), which was later replaced by a 28,000-strong UN peacekeeping mission (UNOSOM II). The Council, in the spirit of Boutros-Ghali's interventionist peace agenda, authorized the

mission under Chapter VII to take military action against any faction threatening the ceasefire, thus breaking with the well-established peacekeeping
principles of impartiality and minimum use of force. The mission soon
found itself at war with a powerful militia, culminating in the "Black Hawk
Down" episode in which eighteen US soldiers were killed and leading
eventually to the ignominious withdrawal of the mission.[21]

The peacekeeping failures in Rwanda, Bosnia, and Somalia had two
lasting consequences at the UN. First, they led to a retrenchment of UN
peacekeeping. Excluding successor, follow-up, and replacement operations
for the previously established missions in Yugoslavia, Angola, and Haiti,
the Council established only one new peacekeeping operation with "boots
on the ground" between January 1, 1995, and January 1, 1999, the relatively short-lived MINURCA in the Central African Republic in 1998. It
was not until 1999 and 2000 that the deployment of a new generation of
peacekeeping operations in Kosovo, East Timor, Sierra Leone, and the
DRC pointed to a resurgence of this tool. Overall, the number of Council
resolutions addressing civil war situations dropped from over seventy in
1993 to below thirty in 2000.[22]

The second legacy, specifically reflecting lessons from Bosnia and
Somalia, was a widely accepted notion that the UN was ill-suited to wage
war. Member states concluded that transition from peacekeeping to peace
enforcement represented more than "mission creep," and started viewing
the two types of operations as fundamentally different, one requiring consent (by the warring parties) and impartiality (of the peacekeepers), the
other requiring robust forces to confront one or several belligerent groups,
even if in defense of a Council mandate conceived as neutral relative to
the parties to the conflict. (This "black-and-white" view may have made
the UN excessively risk-averse, however, as in complex conflict theaters
there can be consent by the main warring factions and impartiality, but
there may still be the need for forceful action against other spoilers.)
Boutros-Ghali, in his 1995 *Supplement to An Agenda for Peace* (more of a
reassessment than an addendum), concluded: "Neither the Security Council nor the Secretary-General at present has the capacity to deploy, direct,
command or control [enforcement] operations except perhaps on a very limited scale. . . . It would be folly to attempt to do so at the present time when
the Organization is resource-starved and hard pressed to handle the less
demanding peacemaking and peacekeeping responsibilities entrusted to it."[23]

Consequently, the Security Council increasingly left enforcement of
its decisions to "coalitions of the willing" such as Operation Uphold
Democracy in Haiti, 1994–1995; IFOR and then SFOR in Bosnia, since
1995; MISAB in the Central African Republic, 1997; INTERFET in East
Timor, 1999; and ISAF in Afghanistan, early 2002.[24] It also alternately
both worried about and supported in qualified terms enforcement activi-

ties by regional bodies, notably ECOMOG, the military arm of the West African economic cooperation arrangement ECOWAS, in Liberia and Sierra Leone.

The Shifting Limits of Sovereignty

The UN's deepening involvement in civil wars led to an increasing tension with the traditional cornerstones of UN collective security: sovereignty and noninterference. In his *Agenda for Peace,* the Secretary-General had already acknowledged that the new security environment forced the UN to look inside the borders of a state. Reiterating that "respect for [the state's] fundamental sovereignty and integrity are crucial to any common international progress," he cautioned that "the time of absolute and exclusive sovereignty, however, has passed: its theory was never matched by reality."[25]

It was also the Security Council that, driven by its three Western permanent members (P3), did more than any other actor on the international scene to erode traditional conceptions of state sovereignty. Broadening its understanding of "threats to peace," the Council in the early 1990s increasingly invoked collective security measures under Chapter VII of the UN Charter in response to developments that beforehand would have been considered to fall outside the realm of collective action.[26] The first such case was Resolution 688 of April 5, 1991, in which the Council implicitly invoked Chapter VII, stating that massive cross-border flows of Kurdish refugees from northern Iraq posed a threat to international peace and security in the region.[27] Other instances of Chapter VII action in response to largely internal developments with only tenuous effects on international peace and security include the 1992–1993 intervention during a humanitarian catastrophe in Somalia, the UN's efforts from 1992 to 1995 to end the civil war in Bosnia-Herzegovina, and the authorization of a multinational force in 1994 to restore democratically elected president Jean-Bertrand Aristide in Haiti.

Further qualifying the concept of sovereignty, and enlarging its own authority, was one of the Council's most consequential innovations in international relations, namely the creation of the International Criminal Tribunals for the Former Yugoslavia (ICTY) and Rwanda (ICTR) in 1993 and 1994 respectively. While the slow proceedings of the tribunals were initially much criticized, these steps by the Council greatly intensified pressure for a more universal International Criminal Court (ICC), a statute for which was adopted at a diplomatic conference in Rome in 1998. These new international tribunals were the main manifestations of what Anne-Marie Slaughter has termed the progressing "individualization of international law"—that is "the process by which we have taken the black box of the state and made it gradually transparent to focus on individuals rather than states as unitary political entities."[28] However, the UN's expanded role in peace and security was accepted only reluctantly by many member states, in particular from the developing world. They were highly critical of the UN's increasing interference in the name of international peace and security in what had traditionally been internal matters. Self-critical introspection over the genocide in Rwanda and vows of "never again" notwithstanding, humanitarian intervention and the limits of sovereignty remained highly controversial issues in the Security Council, often inducing paralysis rather than action vis-à-vis armed conflicts and humanitarian crises.

Serious tensions in the Council around issues relating to state sovereignty and legitimation of the use of force resurfaced over conflicting objectives and approaches among the P5 to the situation in Kosovo. Things came to a head in the 1999 Kosovo war, when NATO's bombing campaign against Serbia in the absence of a Security Council authorization proved hugely controversial not only among a number of UN member states but also among some international lawyers and humanitarian experts.[29] When the Secretary-General, in his speech before the General Assembly that same year, welcomed the "developing international norm in favour of intervention to protect civilians from wholesale slaughter,"[30] the reaction among many countries from the Group of 77 (G-77), a grouping of developing countries, ranged from cool to hostile. This highlighted the urgent need to establish consensus on this question and to provide intellectual underpinning for it.

An answer to the key question "When is it right to fight?"[31] was attempted in the influential report "The Responsibility to Protect" by the International Commission on Intervention and State Sovereignty, commissioned by Canada in 2000.[32] The Responsibility to Protect (R2P) concept interprets sovereignty not just as a shield against outside interference but also as an obligation of states to shield their respective populations from humanitarian disasters. If states fail to live up to this responsibility, it shifts to the international community, possibly requiring, in the last instance, the use of force. Member states, building on the thoughtful report of the UN's High-Level Panel on Threats, Challenges, and Change at the 2005 World Summit, subsequently endorsed the so-called R2P concept, committing "to take collective action . . . through the Security Council . . . on a case-by-case basis." That latter clause, highlighting the Council's nature as a political rather than principled body, proved crucial, as its willingness to apply the norm remained highly selective in the following years.

During the 1990s, the Security Council proved increasingly willing to interpret dangers to international peace and security more broadly, and repeatedly turned its attention to socioeconomic issues and their interrelationship to security. The Council adopted resolutions on, among other things, illicit flows of small arms and light weapons to Africa (Resolution 1209 of 1998), civilians in armed conflict (Resolution 1296 of 2000), HIV/AIDS (Resolution 1308 of 2000), and gender in postconflict peacebuilding (Resolution 1325 of 2000). However, this change in Council deliberations was not driven by any new, formal doctrine or procedures. Instead, many nonpermanent members tended to use their two-year stint on the Council in order to identify and spotlight nontraditional security threats. Despite the cries of critics arguing that the Council had become a "theme park" dedicating precious time to issues with little operational relevance, the trend has proved enduring.

September 11, Terrorism, and the Iraq War

When the terrorist attacks of 9/11 hit Washington, D.C., and New York, the Security Council was still reeling from its divisions over Kosovo, and many of its members were concerned over the unilateralist signals emanating from the recently elected George W. Bush administration. The attacks led to an unprecedented unity and resolve in the Security Council, where delegates were visibly shaken by the destruction terrorism had wrought just a few dozen blocks away from the Council chamber. The Council, before 9/11, had already been far more active in countering terrorism than it is sometimes given credit for, having earlier imposed sanctions on Libya, Sudan, and the Taliban regime in Afghanistan for failing to comply with Council demands to hand over individuals suspected of participation in international terrorist acts.[33]

But 9/11 proved to be a game changer. Only a day after the attacks, the Council passed Resolution 1368, condemning the attacks and recognizing "the inherent right of individual or collective self-defence in accordance with the Charter."[34] For the first time, the Security Council invoked Article 51 against an attack from a nonstate entity, al-Qaeda, providing a legal basis for the US invasion of Afghanistan two months later. On September 28 the Council adopted what still remains perhaps its most groundbreaking (in terms of ambition rather than effect) resolution ever—Resolution 1373—which imposed significant binding obligations on all states to, among other things, enhance legislation, strengthen border controls, coordinate executive machinery, and increase international cooperation in combating terrorism.[35] Resolution 1373 also created the Counter-Terrorism Committee (CTC), which the Council complemented soon thereafter with the Counter-Terrorism Executive Directorate (CTED), to monitor compliance of all states with the resolution. While the CTC got off to a brisk start under the energetic leadership of UK ambassador Jeremy Greenstock, it rapidly proved to be more of a "process" response to events than a substantively effective initiative. It lacked teeth to decide on whether and how to deal with states clearly not in compliance with Council decisions.[36] This did not prevent complaints against the Council for turning itself into a global legislator, because Resolution 1373 included provisions from international treaties related to terrorism that had not yet entered into force. (That complaint grew louder when the Council, three years later, adopted a similar resolution—Resolution 1540—imposing globally binding obligations on member states to prevent the spread of weapons of mass destruction to non-state actors.)

However, the unity of purpose the Council demonstrated after 9/11 soon began to fray as the Bush administration began to set its sights on Iraq, arguing, among other things, that the modern terrorist threat made weapons of mass destruction in the hand of rogue regimes unacceptable. The question of how to implement the sanctions and disarmament demands that had been imposed on Iraq in 1990–1991 had, over the course of the 1990s, increasingly become a point of contention among the P5. Starting in 1994, Russia and France—later joined by China—began to argue ever more loudly in favor of a road map toward lifting the sanctions. They also became increasingly critical of the aggressive tactics of the inspection commission (UNSCOM) mandated by the Security Council to verify Iraq's compliance with disarmament obligations.[37] This culminated in Operation Desert Fox in December 1998, a US-UK bombing campaign against alleged weapons sites in Iraq without explicit UN approval, which served as a final blow to the original Gulf War coalition of 1991 and resulted in consensus within the Security Council on the Iraq situation.[38]

Scars thus already ran deep in the Council when the Bush administration embarked on a major push, starting in the fall of 2002, to get the UN body to endorse robust disarmament action vis-à-vis Iraq. That push proved initially successful, yielding a robust resolution (1441) that afforded Iraq "a final opportunity to comply with its disarmament obligations," obliging it to declare all of its weapons and imposing a resumed inspections process. Any false statements or omissions by Iraq, or a failure to cooperate fully with the resolution, would trigger the requirement for the Council to "convene immediately." Despite the fact that the inspection regime was able to conduct its work largely unhindered by Iraq and did not turn up any evidence of an active weapons of mass destruction (WMD) program, Washington continued to insist that Iraq was in noncompliance and called for military disarmament. Russia, France, and China, however, were unconvinced and publicly threatened to veto any draft resolution that would authorize the use of force. This was, as the situation unfolded, unnecessary, as by the time the Bush administration decided to give up on such a resolution, it was clear that it would not have received the necessary nine votes for it to pass. On March 20, 2003, the United States, supported by the United Kingdom and some others, initiated its second war against Iraq, this time, however, in the absence of approval by the Security Council or the company of a significant coalition.[39]

While public opinion might have proved relieved that the UN had not authorized this fool's errand, it seems to have blamed the Council for having failed to prevent the 2003 war from occurring. Compounding the fiasco was a management and financial scandal, breaking in slow motion later in 2003 and throughout 2004, relating to the Council-mandated oil-for-food program intended to alleviate the humanitarian impact of UN sanctions in Iraq, a development that profoundly undermined two years of Kofi Annan's otherwise successful second term as Secretary-General.[40] Overall, despite the Council's lead in settling the Iran-Iraq War through a peace plan it advanced in 1987 and its success in reversing by military means Saddam Hussein's 1990 aggression against Kuwait, Iraq remains the ultimate petri dish for study of Council dysfunction and delusion.[41]

What these episodes reveal is that the Council is above all a political body, driven by what Kieran Prendergast, former UN under-secretary-general for political affairs, describes as "expediency."[42] Relentless reactivity and short-term thinking have caused the Council often to take very shortsighted decisions as well. The most convenient options for P5 members on any given day may win out over carefully developed analyses and plans advanced by others. As the chapters in this book will show, this remains as true today as it was in the 1990s.

Academic Context and Resources

It is hard enough to take a snapshot of the Council at any given time, due to its long, multifaceted agenda, opaque proceedings, and uncertain impact on international relations. Partly for this reason, throughout the 1990s the Council had been studied primarily through the lens of international law, one particular crisis, or one individual's memoirs. Sidney Bailey and Sam Daws's magisterial volume on the Council's procedures, which also covers with great acuity a number of substantive issues, served for a long time as the principal reference tool for students of the Council and—recently updated—continues to do so to this day.[43] The commentary on the UN Charter by Bruno Simma et al., first published in 1995 and now in its third edition, is an essential resource for any student of the Council.[44] Other brief but incisive overviews were offered by Brian Urquhart and the late Anthony Parsons in the early 1990s, but by the early 2000s these were already mostly of historical interest.[45] Important contributions to the understanding of the Council were made throughout the 1990s and beyond by international law scholars, such as Thomas Franck, Jose Alvarez, Simon Chesterman, Adam Roberts, and others, shedding light on the Council's impact on international criminal justice and the laws of war.[46] Specific areas of Council activity such as peace-keeping, sanctions, or Council reform were examined in sectoral studies by Mats Berdal and Spyros Economides,[47] David Cortright and George Lopez,[48] and Bruce Russett.[49] Ian Hurd[50] and Ian Johnstone[51] shed considerable, original light on considerations of legitimacy in the Council's record and of the power and uses of deliberation in the Council setting for member states.

Highly publicized diplomatic clashes in the Council around the 1999 Kosovo crisis and the 2003 Iraq War fanned wider interest in the body, leading to more systematic treatments. A compelling compilation of articles, *The United Nations Security Council and War,* edited by Vaughan Lowe, Adam Roberts, Jennifer Welsh, and Dominik Zaum, is strongly recommended.[52] So is Bruce Cronin and Ian Hurd's more theoretically minded book on the Security Council's international authority[53] and Jared Genser and Bruno Stagno Ugarte's volume on the Council and human rights.[54] Meanwhile, a handful of single-author volumes have been published in recent years, including by Edward Luck[55] and David Bosco,[56] who provide easily accessible introductions to the Council's role in international politics. In 2006, David Malone wrote about the Council's interaction with Iraq over a twenty-five-year period, in a single-author volume, kicking off with the Iran-Iraq War in 1980.[57] Relative to later years, he drew on valuable ideas of James Cockayne with respect to the Council's weak capacity to manage complex regulatory-legal frameworks (such as the sprawling and vexed humanitarian, sanctions, and disarmament processes it launched in Iraq) rather than operating in the political-military mode of decisionmaking to which it was more accustomed and better suited. The present volume builds on all of this literature and includes many of the individuals involved in these different projects, but also draws on much other research.

Our approach is not theoretically driven. That said, what all authors of this book have in common is a belief that the Council matters. In that sense, most if not all of them would probably subscribe to a thought tradition that has been termed "liberal institutionalism" in international relations theory, namely the notion "that cooperation in world politics can be enhanced through the construction and support of multilateral institutions based on liberal principles"[58] and that in turn, the behavior and choices of powerful states can be altered (and occasionally constrained) by the existence of international institutions (and the norms and rules they are based on). This volume will provide ample evidence of application of these notions.

The shaping power of institutions notwithstanding, any longtime student of the Council would find it hard not to acknowledge the enduring relevance of some basic tenets of the so-called realist tradition, according to which international relations is marked by a constant struggle among self-interested nation-states for power and influence. Indeed, major crises in the post–Cold War era, from Kosovo to Iraq, Syria, Ukraine, and the Middle East, remind us that the Council is a body dominated by major powers, whose national interests continue to shape Council deliberations. In that sense, the Council today displays elements of continuity with what was described so admirably by Andrew Boyd in *Fifteen Men on a Powder Keg* in the early 1970s, but in a completely altered geopolitical setting.[59]

Indeed, as this book will highlight, the Council's composition, powers, and voting arrangements as enshrined in the UN Charter reflect the concept of a great power concert that the main framers of the UN Charter had in mind in 1945, when the victors of World War II—the United States, Russia, China, the United Kingdom, and France—were accorded permanent membership and veto rights in the body.

Structure of the Book

This foregoing history of the Security Council's decisions from 1945 to 2003 provides the backdrop against which this book's chapters are written. Complementing our introduction and helping to frame the rest of the volume is Chapter 2 by Peter Wallensteen, one of the world's foremost thinkers on violent conflict, and his colleague Patrik Johansson, who look at key trends in Security Council decisions and actions over the past two and a half decades, drawing from a wealth of data on Council decisionmaking assembled at the University of Uppsala.

Part 1, "Competing Interests on the Security Council," reflects the editors' assessment that it is the national interests of powerful states, and in particular those of the P5, that remain the key drivers of Council decisions. This part suggests that the P5's interrelationships and relative power in the international system have evolved significantly over time, with important consequences for the way they use and approach the Council. Chapters in this part also provide examples of how the deliberative process of multilateral Council diplomacy has at times shaped and constrained the P5's choices. This part includes separate chapters on each of the P5, with the exception of France and the UK, whose positions on and approach within the Council we considered similar enough to justify covering them in a single chapter. We have deliberately chosen to select authors from the respective P5 countries to write these chapters, as we felt they would be best positioned to explain—rather than criticize—what drives each permanent member's Council diplomacy. (For Chapter 6, on France and the UK, we brokered an Anglo-French coauthor arrangement.)

Opening Part 1, Stanford University political scientist and former senior UN official Stephen Stedman, in Chapter 3, dissects the ambiguous (some might say schizophrenic) approach of Washington toward the Council, torn between the desire to have the body legitimize and generate support for its foreign policy goals, and the reluctance to make necessary compromises or accept any constraints along the way. In Chapter 3.1 in a brief complementary commentary on the "permanent one," David Bosco, a US legal scholar and columnist on US multilateralism, argues that the US approach to the Council can best be understood as a search for "maximum flexibility." Chapter 4, on China's role in the Council, by Chinese scholars Zhu Wenqi and Leng Xinyu, highlights the flexibility Beijing displayed in the Council for the first fifteen years of the post–Cold War era, but also explains why and how China has become more assertive in the Security Council as its global influence and interests have grown. Dmitri Trenin, a leading Russian international affairs analyst, explains in Chapter 5 how Moscow's evolving approach to the Council has been largely determined by its changing relations with the West. He argues that from Moscow's perspective it is the United States that, in the post–Cold War era, has repeatedly led assaults on world order (in Kosovo, Iraq, and Libya), inducing Russia's leadership to abandon the idea of a partnership with the West and to see the Council primarily as a tool to rein in unconstrained Western use of force. (This may help explain, yet not excuse, why Moscow proceeded to launch a major assault on world order by illegally annexing the Crimea and supporting separatist rebels in eastern Ukraine, which occurred after Trenin submitted his chapter.) Thierry Tardy and Dominik Zaum, prominent UN experts of France and the UK, argue in Chapter 6 that the two countries compensate for their relative decline in the international system through skillful and highly active Council diplomacy, working hard to make a case for their permanent seats, which may be increasingly contested by emerging powers who want to join the select club, and which do not sit particularly well with EU pretensions to a common foreign policy (compounded by occasional French and UK procedural and sometimes political arrogance vis-à-vis other EU members on Council business).

The remaining four chapters in Part 1 address how the unique position of the P5 has shaped their interaction with the ten elected Council members (E-10), emerging powers, and aspirants for permanent seats, as well as how the P5 engage with the reform pressures arising from these dynamics. In Chapter 7, Colin Keating, who admirably represented New Zealand on the Council during the turbulent period of 1993–1994 and later enjoyed a front-row seat on Council action as founding head of the research nongovernmental organization (NGO) Security Council Report, illuminates how the structure and culture of the Security Council magnifies the differences in power between its members with the veto (including the continuity of knowledge imbuing the P5 with a sense of "institutional exceptionalism") and those without. While the elected Council members' margin of maneuver was always circumscribed, Keating explains how, since the early 2000s, the E-10 have become more marginalized, essentially relegating them to the role of rubberstamping decisions reached among the P5 or choosing between positions of contending members of the P5. In Chapter 8, Kishore Mahbubani, who proved during his time as Singapore's ambassador to the UN in the early 2000s that even small countries can play an ambitious role on the Council, shares Keating's concerns about P5 dominance. However, unlike Keating, he sees the solution in enlarging the club of veto-holding permanent members, a failure of which, in his view, would eventually condemn the Council to irrelevance. In Chapter 9, Christian Wenaweser, Liechtenstein's ambassador to the UN and one of the longest-serving permanent representatives in New York, equally laments the P5's stranglehold on the Council, but argues that the debate around Council reform has focused excessively on enlargement of the body, neglecting the possibly more important dimension of its working methods, reform of which would address (in part) the Council's lack of transparency and accountability. His chapter includes a compelling insider's account of his ultimately unsuccessful efforts on the front lines of a campaign for reform of Council working methods as one of the founders of the so-called Small Five initiative. In Chapter 10, Edward C. Luck, eminent UN scholar and former special adviser of the Secretary-General on the Responsibility to Protect, is more sanguine than either Keating, Mahbubani, or Wenaweser about the Council's current composition, its ability to adapt, and the opportunities of the E-10 to positively influence Council decisionmaking. Less concerned about P5 collusion than about the growing risk of P5 disunity, he warns against overambitious reform efforts that could damage the "concert of power" nature of the Council.

Part 2 of the volume, "Addressing Thematic Issues," focuses on how evolving norms and threats have shaped the Council's decisionmaking and actions over the past quarter century. In Chapter 11, Thomas G. Weiss, one of the foremost experts on the UN and humanitarian norms and action, traces the normative and ideational development in this field over the past quarter century and highlights the factors that circumscribe the consistent application of humanitarian values by the Council. In Chapter 12, Francesco Mancini, former director of research at the International Peace Institute in New York, surveys how and why democracy promotion became so prominent in the Council's operations during the 1990s yet is facing increasing headwinds since the early 2000s. Joanna Weschler, director of research at Security Council Report and former head of Human Rights Watch's UN office, explains in Chapter 13 why the Council, despite making important headway in factoring human rights into its work since the end of the Cold War, remains inconsistent and often disappoints in its human rights record. In Chapter 14, Peter Romaniuk, an expert on multilateral counterterrorism activity, tracks the Council's shifting approach to counterterrorism, explaining why the Council's strong resolve in the aftermath of the 9/11 attacks ultimately did not live up to its promise. James Cockayne, a rising star among scholars of organized crime, shows in Chapter 15 how the Council has been highly innovative in devising responses to the growing threat of organized crime and piracy, but also suggests that these experiments in international law enforcement face significant conceptual and operational challenges in a political body such as the Council. In Chapter 16, Waheguru Pal Singh Sidhu, Indian scholar of the UN and of weapons of mass destruction, assesses the Council's track record on nuclear nonproliferation throughout its seventy-year history, focusing on the Council's handling of the cases of Iraq, North Korea, Libya, Iran, and Syria, as well as its approach to nonstate actors on this issue.

Part 3 of the book, "Enforcing Council Mandates," focuses on the Council's enforcement actions under Articles 41 and 42 of the UN Charter. In Chapter 17, Adam Roberts, Oxford professor emeritus and dean of British international relations scholars, surveys the remarkably rich record of the Council in authorizing UN peacekeeping forces, regional peacekeeping forces, and coalitions of the willing to use force, arguing that its inconsistency and shortcomings suggest a system of "selective" rather than "collective" security. In Chapter 18, Jean-Marie Guéhenno, president of the International Crisis Group and former UN under-secretary-general for peacekeeping operations, illuminates the doctrinal, strategic, and operational challenges the UN faces when its peacekeepers are deployed to protect civilians in active conflict situations while having to adhere to the peacekeeping principles of consent, impartiality, and minimum use of force. In Chapter 19, Herman Schaper, who served as Dutch ambassador to both NATO and the UN, traces the evolving and at times tortured relationship between these two organizations since their origins in the 1940s, and, looking at the cases of Bosnia, Afghanistan, and Libya, explains why NATO has emerged as the UN's enforcer of choice since the end of the Cold War. In Chapter 20, Sue Eckert, former US assistant secretary of state and leading sanctions scholar, shows how the evolution of UN sanctions from a blunt hatchet (comprehensive trade embargoes) into a scalpel (targeted sanctions), and their employment in the service of a wide range of objectives against a wide range of actors, confronts the Council with increasing challenges of strategic coordination and management.

Part 4, "Evolving Institutional Factors," explores the Council's relationships with five key actors that are central to the Council's life. The most visible and important of these relationships is of course that with the UN Secretary-General, covered here in Chapter 21 by Simon Chesterman, dean of law at the National University of Singapore. Dependent on P5 support for election and reelection, endowed with a certain autonomy relative to the Council anchored in Article 99 of the Charter, yet confronted with pressures—in particular from the P5—to act more as "secretary" than "general," the Secretary-General faces a particularly difficult balancing act in his relations with the P5 members, especially when they are divided. In Chapter 22, Connie Peck, drawing on years of research she conducted as founding head of the preventive diplomacy program at UNITAR, turns the focus to the special representatives of the UN Secretary-General, who are responsible for overseeing the UN's peace operations in the field, and whose success often depends on how deftly they manage their relations with the Council. Bruno Stagno Ugarte, coeditor of this volume, shows in Chapter 23 that even though the Council's interaction with regional and subregional organizations evolved from a struggle for primacy during the Cold War to one of cooperation during the post–Cold War era, their relationship remains difficult due to competing interests and differing institutional cultures. In Chapter 24, longtime UN observer and mediation expert Teresa Whitfield shines a light on the changing role of Groups of Friends in the life of the Council. A much-used instrument throughout the 1990s for the Council to maximize leverage and involve knowledgeable non-Council members into its work, Groups of Friends have evolved significantly in their role and influence since the early 2000s, with new Groups of Friends having moved toward either a Contact Group model featuring comparatively little interaction with the Council, or a thematic model encouraging the Council's engagement with crosscutting questions. In Chapter 25, on international courts tribunals, a promising young legal scholar, Eran Sthoeger, focuses on the dynamics and relationship between the Council and the international tribunals it has helped set up in Rwanda, the former Yugoslavia, Sierra Leone, and Lebanon, as well as the International Criminal Court, to which it has already referred two situations.

Part 5, "Key Country Cases," offers a set of ten case studies and a commentary assessing the Council's decisionmaking and its results in specific countries that have featured prominently in the Council's life over the past two decades. In Chapter 26, longtime UN staffer and Middle East expert Markus E. Bouillon explores the Council's involvement in the Middle East going back to 1947, noting that while the Council has often played a useful role as a crisis manager, divisions among its permanent members have prevented it from assuming leadership in efforts to settle the Arab-Israeli conflict. In Chapter 27, David M. Malone, coeditor of this book, and Poorvi Chitalkar, from the Global Centre on Pluralism in Canada, look at a quarter century of Council decisionmaking on Iraq, which shaped the body's track record like no other issue. In Chapter 28, Mats Berdal, one of academia's leading voices on civil wars, surveys the Council's struggles throughout the 1990s to respond to the wars of succession in the former Yugoslavia, focusing in particular on the divisive questions arising from the use of force in Bosnia. In Chapter 29, John L. Hirsch, who served as a US ambassador and senior diplomat in various positions in Africa in the 1980s and 1990s, traces the highs and lows of over twenty years of Council engagement in Somalia, which yielded temporary success in the early 1990s, but also revealed the Council's limitations during its confrontation with committed warlords, and documents recent reengagement with the country driven by growing concerns over terrorism and piracy. In Chapter 30, Heiko Nitzschke, member of Germany's permanent mission to the UN in New York covering Security Council issues and a former UN staffer in Sudan, provides a chapter that assesses the multifaceted yet often fraught Council decisionmaking on Sudan since the 1990s, from its early steps to confront Khartoum over its sponsorship of terrorism to its later parallel efforts to resolve the north-south and Darfur crises in the country. Chapter 31, Francesc Vendrell's account of the Council's engagement with Afghanistan from the mid-1990s onward, combines dispassionate analysis with firsthand accounts that draw on his experience as both the UN's and the European Union's chief diplomat in the troubled country. In Chapter 32, Africa scholar and UN expert Tatiana Carayannis looks at the Council's long engagement with the DRC. Initially remaining only a bystander after the outbreak of civil war in 1996, even though the war had its roots in the Rwandan genocide and the Council-mandated response thereto, the Council became ever more deeply involved after deploying a peace operation in 1999, leading Congo to become "the de facto laboratory for the Council's response to complex conflicts," with various experiments in peace enforcement. In Chapter 33, French peacekeeping experts Arthur Boutellis and Alexandra Novosseloff trace the (often French-driven) involvement of the Council in Côte d'Ivoire, extending over a decade, that culminated in 2011 in robust action to enforce the results of contested elections in the name of the protection of civilians.

The last three chapters of Part 5 deal with the Council's efforts to respond to the upheavals brought about by the Arab Spring. In Chapter 34, Alex Bellamy and Paul D. Williams, both leading experts on R2P and on peace operations, shine a light on Council dynamics around one of the most controversial episodes in the Council's recent history: its authorization of the use of force against the Qaddafi regime in 2011 and the much contested implementation of that mandate by NATO. The controversy around Libya complicated Council members' unsuccessful efforts to find a common approach to the escalating civil war in Syria, which is analyzed in great detail in Chapter 35 by Salman Shaikh and Amanda Roberts, with the former drawing on his insights into regional dynamics as head of the Brookings Institution's Doha Office and the latter from her perch as senior research analyst covering Syria for Security Council Report. Complementing this is Chapter 35.1, an analytical commentary from Lebanese journalist Raghida Dergham, longtime UN correspondent of *al-Hayat,* who laments the fecklessness of the P5 as well as other key players.

Finally, Part 6, "The Security Council and International Order," explores the wider implications of Council decisionmaking for peace and security, international law, and global order. In Chapter 26, peacekeeping expert and scholarly pundit Richard Gowan traces the resurgence of peacekeeping since 1999, arguing that peacekeeping mandates and their implementation, rather than being a simple reflection of P5 preferences, are often the result of significant compromise and improvisation that results from competing interests of Council members, regional players, troop-contributing countries, and host nations, as well as unforeseen developments in volatile crises. International legal scholar and UN expert Ian Johnstone, in Chapter 37, on the Council and international law, demonstrates how the Council has expanded its original field of competence, increasingly acting over the past two decades as a lawmaker, as a quasi-judicial body, and as an enforcer of international law, raising important questions with respect to its accountability and legitimacy. In Chapter 38, Bruce Jones, a leading voice on multilateral security issues and global order at the Brookings Institution, explores how changing great power relations and the rise of emerging powers will affect the Council's ability to engage in conflict management and humanitarian action and to address a range of emerging threats. In Chapter 39, Jeremy Greenstock, who served as the UK's ambassador on the Security Council in the early 2000s, argues that the Council's crisis management function has been complicated by the growing difficulty in reaching multilateral consensus in a world with an ever greater number of states, a proliferation and fragmentation of multilateral decisionmaking processes, multiple power centers, and a growing tendency of governments to cater to their domestic audience in international negotiations. Yet the Council also benefits from built-in incentives that draw the great powers toward pragmatic approaches to problem solving, even after major international disputes. Finally, in Chapter 40 the coeditors summarize major developments and trends the Council has undergone since the turn of the millennium, highlighting its achievements and shortcomings and the challenges it faces in adapting to a changing world.

In the Appendixes, we offer five tables that we hope will give readers easily accessible overviews of major Council decisions (or, in the case of vetoes, major nondecisions). The first table lists all UN peacekeeping operations and observer missions the Council has mandated since its inception, starting with UNTSO in 1948. The second table includes all Council-mandated political missions, which have been broadly defined as "UN civilian missions that are deployed for a limited duration to support Member States in good offices, conflict prevention, peacemaking and peacebuilding."[60] While the General Assembly mandated a number of such missions in the late 1940 and 1950s, the Security Council only started using this tool in the post–Cold War era and with increasing frequency since the start of the new millennium, although this trend seems to have ebbed as of late. The third table looks at peacekeeping and enforcement operations mandated by the Council since 1945 that were carried out by coalitions of the willing or regional organizations. The fourth table lists all sanctions regimes imposed by the Security Council, and the final table lists all the vetoes cast by any of the P5 in the post–Cold War era.

Notes

1. Deference to the P5 extends even to their near-automatic inclusion in other UN-elected and UN-appointed bodies, as well as to a presumption of their precedence over that of other countries in UN protocol, all of which could be challenged by other member states but rarely has been. Thus, complaints about the P5 by other states in the absence of any serious challenge to their privileges extending way beyond the Security Council itself, often strike observers as pointlessly whiny.

2. Michael Howard, "The Historical Development of the UN's Role in International Security," in *United Nations, Divided World: The UN's Roles in International Relations,* edited by Adam Roberts and Benedict Kingsbury (Oxford: Clarendon, 1993).

3. Edward Luck, *UN Security Council: Practice and Promise* (London: Routledge, 2006), pp. 25–26.

4. See Appendix 1 in this volume.

5. Mats Berdal, "The Security Council and Peacekeeping," in *The United Nations Security Council and War: The Evolution of Thought and Practice Since 1945,* edited by Vaughan Lowe, Adam Roberts, Jennifer Welsh, and Dominik Zaum (Oxford: Oxford University Press, 2008), p. 179.

6. For an account of evolving dynamics within the Council, particularly among the P5, from 1986 to 1990, see Cameron Hume, *The United Nations, Iran, and Iraq: How Peacemaking Changed* (Bloomington: University of Indiana Press, 1994), especially pp. 81–82, 88–102.

7. United Nations, press release, UN Doc. SG/SM/3956, January 13, 1987, p. 5.

8. Mikhail S. Gorbachev, "Reality and the Guarantees of a Secure World," in *FBIS Daily Report: Soviet Union,* September 17, 1987, pp. 23–28.

9. David M. Malone, interviews with Alexander M. Belonogov, permanent representative of the Soviet Union to the UN, 1986–1990, and John Thomson, permanent representative of the UK to the UN, 1982–1987, conducted in Ottawa, March 20, 1996, and Princeton, April 15, 1996, respectively.

10. United Nations Security Council Resolution 678 (November 29, 1990), UN Doc. S/RES/678.

11. A number of the measures adopted by France, the United Kingdom, the United States, and their allies, particularly in northern Iraq (to protect, through a no-fly zone, and provide assistance to the Kurds), were initiated without explicit Security Council authorization. These measures were, however, not then seriously challenged within the Council. Some of the humanitarian activities of Operation Provide Comfort were eventually taken over by the UN.

12. See Michael C. Williams, *Civil-Military Relations and Peacekeeping* (London: Routledge, 1998).

13. See Blanca Antonini, "El Salvador," and Aldo Ajello and Patrick Whitman, "Mozambique," in *The UN Security Council: From the Cold War to the 21st Century,* edited by David M. Malone (Boulder, CO: Lynne Rienner, 2004).

14. United Nations Security Council, "The Responsibility of the Security Council in the Maintenance of International Peace and Security," UN Doc. S/23500, January 31, 1992, p. 1.

15. United Nations Secretary-General, *An Agenda for Peace, Preventive Diplomacy, Peacemaking and Peace-Keeping,* UN Doc. A/47/277, June 17, 1992.

16. During this period, the UN launched the following new peacekeeping operations and observer bodies: UNIKOM in Kuwait (1991); MINURSO in Western Sahara (1991); ONUSAL in El Salvador (1991); UNAVEM II in Angola (1991); UNAMIC in Cambodia (1991); UNPROFOR in the former Yugoslavia (1992); UNTAC in Cambodia (1992); UNOSOM in Somalia (1992); ONUMOZ in Mozambique (1992); UNOSOM II in Somalia (1993); UNOMUR in Uganda and Rwanda (1993); UNOMIG in Georgia (1993); UNOMIL in Liberia (1993); UNMIH in Haiti (1993); and UNAMIR in Rwanda (1993). In addition, the Council authorized the US-led UNITAF in Somalia (1992); and an UNPROFOR presence, in effect a preventive deployment, in Macedonia (1992).

17. Simon Chesterman, "Blue Helmet Blues," *Security Dialogue* 34, no. 3 (September 2003): 369.

18. Berdal, "The Security Council and Peacekeeping," p. 191.

19. See Gérard Prunier, *The Rwanda Crisis: History of a Genocide* (New York: Columbia University Press, 1995); Michael Barnett, "The UN Security Council: Indifference and Genocide in Rwanda," *Cultural Anthropology* 12, no. 4 (1997): 551; Matthew Vaccaro, "The Politics of Genocide: Peacekeeping and Disaster Relief in Rwanda," in *The UN, Peacekeeping, American Policy, and the Uncivil Wars of the 1990s,* edited by William J. Durch (New York: St. Martin's, 1996); Howard Adelman and Astri Suhrke, "Rwanda," in *The UN Security Council: From the Cold War to the 21st Century,* edited by David M. Malone (Boulder, CO: Lynne Rienner, 2004), pp. 483–489; Romeo Dallaire, *Shake Hands with the Devil: The Failure of Humanity in Rwanda* (New York: Carroll and Graf, 2004).

20. United Nations Secretary-General, *Report to the Secretary-General Pursuant to General Assembly Resolution 53/35: The Fall of Srebrenica,* UN Doc. A/54/549, November 15, 1999; Mats Berdal, "Bosnia," in Malone, *The UN Security Council,* pp. 451–466.

21. See John L. Hirsch and Robert Oakley, *Somalia and Operation Restore Hope: Reflections on Peacemaking and Peacekeeping* (Washington, DC: US Institute of Peace, 1995); Mark Bowden, *Black Hawk Down: A Story of Modern War* (New York: Atlantic Monthly, 1999); Chesterman, "Blue Helmet Blues," pp. 373–374.

22. James Cockayne, Christoph Mikulaschek, and Chris Perry, "The UN Security Council and Civil War: First Insights from a New Dataset" (New York: International Peace Institute, September 2010): 6.

23. United Nations Secretary-General, *Supplement to* An Agenda for Peace: *Position Paper of the Secretary-General on the Occasion of the Fiftieth Anniversary of the United Nations,* report of the Secretary-General pursuant to General Assembly Resolution 53/35, UN Doc. A/50/60, January 3, 1995, p. 18, www.un.org/documents/ga/docs/50/plenary/a50-60.htm.

24. See Oliver Ramsbotham and Tom Woodhouse, *Encyclopedia of International Peacekeeping Operations* (Santa Barbara, CA: ABC-CLIO, 1999).

25. United Nations Secretary-General, *An Agenda for Peace: Preventive Diplomacy, Peacemaking, and Peacekeeping,* report of the Secretary-General pursuant to the statement adopted by the Summit Meeting of the Security Council on 31 January 1992, UN Doc. A/47/277-S/24111, June 17, 1992, para. 17.

26. Simon Chesterman, *Just War or Just Peace? Humanitarian Intervention and International Law* (Oxford: Oxford University Press, 2001).

27. The question of whether United Nations Security Council Resolution 688 is indeed a Chapter VII resolution is debated among international lawyers. See Chesterman, *Just War or Just Peace?* pp. 124–133, 196–201.

28. Anne-Marie Slaughter, "Luncheon Address: Rogue Regimes and the Individualization of International Law," *New England Law Review* 36, no. 4 (2002): 815.

29. Simon Chesterman, *Just War or Just Peace?;* Thomas G. Weiss, "The Humanitarian Impulse," in Malone, *The UN Security Council.*

30. United Nations Secretary-General Kofi Annan, speech before the UN General Assembly, New York City, 54th Session, 4th Plenary Meeting, UN Doc. A/54/PV.4, September 20, 1999, http://daccess-dds-ny.un.org/doc/UNDOC/GEN /N99/858/23/PDF/N9985823.pdf?OpenElement.

31. Gareth Evans, "When Is it Right to Fight?" *Survival* 46, no. 3 (Autumn 2004): 59–82.

32. International Commission on Intervention and State Sovereignty, "The Responsibility to Protect" (Ottawa: International Development Research Centre, 2001).

33. Edward Luck, "Tackling Terrorism," in *The UN Security Council.*

34. Washington rejected an initial offer by France, then presiding over the Council, to recommend the Council authorize reprisals, as the United States believed that it had no need for such authorization under the circumstances.

35. Eric Rosand, "Security Council Resolution 1373, the Counter-Terrorism Committee, and the Fight Against Terrorism," *American Journal of International Law* 97 (April 2003): 333–341.

36. Eric Rosand and Sebastian von Einsiedel, "9/11, the 'War on Terror,' and the Evolution of Counter-Terrorism Institutions," in *Cooperating for Peace and Security: Evolving Institutions and Arrangements in a Context of Changing U.S. Security Policy,* edited by Bruce D. Jones, Richard Gowan, and Shepard Forman (Cambridge: Cambridge University Press, 2010).

37. David Malone, "Goodbye UNSCOM: A Sorry Tale in US-UN Relations," *Security Dialogue* 30, no. 4 (December 1999): 400–401.

38. David Malone, *The International Struggle over Iraq: Politics in the United Nations Security Council, 1980–2005* (Oxford: Oxford University Press, 2006).

39. Simon Chesterman and Sebastian von Einsiedel, "Dual Containment: The United States, Iraq, and the U.N. Security Council," in *September 11, 2001: A Turning Point in International and Domestic Law,* edited by Paul Eden and Thérèse O'Donnell (Ardsley, NY: Transnational, 2005).

40. Independent Inquiry Committee into the United Nations Oil-for-Food Programme, "Report on the Management of the Oil-for-Food Programme," September 2005.

41. See the concluding chapter in Malone, *The International Struggle over Iraq.*

42. Quoted in Malone, *The International Struggle over Iraq,* pp. 160–165.

43. Sidney Bailey and Sam Daws, *The Procedure of the UN Security Council* (Oxford: Oxford University Press, 1998).

44. Bruno Simma, Daniel-Erasmus Khan, Georg Nolte, and Andreas Paulus, eds., *The Charter of the United Nations: A Commentary,* 3rd ed. (Oxford: Oxford University Press, 2012).

45. Brian Urquhart, "The UN and International Security After the Cold War," and Anthony Parsons, "The UN and the National Interests of States," in *United*

Nations, Divided World: The UN's Roles in International Relations, edited by Adam Roberts and Benedict Kingsbury (Oxford: Clarendon, 1993).

46. Thomas M. Franck, *Recourse to Force: State Action Against Threats and Armed Attacks* (Cambridge: Cambridge University Press, 2002); Jose E. Alvarez, "Judging the Security Council," *American Journal of International Law* 90, no. 1 (January 1996): 1–39; Simon Chesterman, *Just War or Just Peace?;* Roberts and Kingsbury, *United Nations, Divided World.*

47. Mats Berdal and Spyros Economides, eds., *United Nations Interventionism, 1991–2004* (Cambridge: Cambridge University Press, 2007).

48. David Cortright and George A. Lopez, *The Sanctions Decade: Assessing UN Strategies in the 1990s* (Boulder, CO: Lynne Rienner, 2000).

49. Bruce Russett, ed., *The Once and Future Security Council* (New York: St. Martin's, 1997).

50. Ian Hurd, *After Anarchy: Legitimacy and Power in the United Nations Security Council* (Princeton: Princeton University Press, 2007).

51. Ian Johnstone, *The Power of Deliberation: International Law, Politics, and Organizations* (Oxford: Oxford University Press, 2011).

52. Lowe et al., *The United Nations Security Council and War.*

53. Bruce Cronin and Ian Hurd, eds., *The UN Security Council and the Politics of International Authority* (London: Routledge, 2008).

54. Jared Genser and Bruno Stagno Ugarte, eds., *The United Nations Security Council in the Age of Human Rights* (Cambridge: Cambridge University Press, 2014).

55. Edward Luck, *UN Security Council: Practice and Promise* (London: Routledge, 2006).

56. David L. Bosco, *Five to Rule Them All: The UN Security Council and the Making of the Modern World* (New York: Oxford University Press, 2009).

57. Malone, *The International Struggle over Iraq.*

58. Robert Keohane, "Twenty Years of Institutional Liberalism," *International Relations* 26, no. 2 (June 2012): 125.

59. Andrew Boyd, *Fifteen Men on a Powder Keg* (London: Methuen, 1971).

60. United Nations Secretary-General, *Overall Policy Matters Pertaining to Special Political Missions,* report of the Secretary-General, UN Doc. A/68/223, July 29, 2013, p. 2.

2

The UN Security Council: Decisions and Actions

Peter Wallensteen and Patrik Johansson

THE CHARTER OF THE UNITED NATIONS ENTRUSTS THE SECURITY Council with the primary responsibility for maintaining international peace and security. It is up to the Council to make the idea of collective security timely, effective, and dependable. Failure to meet expectations has implications for the standing of the UN as such, and might lead others to fill the void—major powers, other international organizations, or regional bodies. In the absence of Council action, the UN may still play a role in peacemaking by the activation of other organs of the UN (notably the General Assembly and the Secretary-General). However, the moment the Council exerts its authority, all others are expected to fall in line.

During the first forty-five years of its existence, the Security Council's ability to act for the collective interest in peace and security was severely limited by the Cold War, which divided its permanent members. The Council was sidelined, but other UN bodies were activated at times, such as the Secretary-General (notably during the times of Dag Hammarskjöld) or the General Assembly (which actually set up the first UN peacekeeping operation, the UN Emergency Force [UNEF] in 1956).[1] Conversely, the end of the Cold War has been followed by a dramatic increase in Council activity and, with that, an increased UN involvement in conflict management and peace processes. This development is reflected in the number and types of adopted resolutions, as well as in changes in the use of the veto.

A quarter century after the end of the Cold War, it is possible to discuss overall trends in Security Council decisions and actions, to compare patterns since 1990 to those of the Cold War period, and to analyze formative decisions by the post–Cold War Security Council.

We first look at overall trends in Security Council decisionmaking. We illustrate differences between the Cold War and the post–Cold War period with tables and graphs, and analyze the use of Chapter VII, the use of the veto, and the number of resolutions on different issue areas over time. We then take a look at the regional aspects of Council action. Next we address thematic resolutions, discuss the consistency (or inconsistency) of Council decisionmaking, and relate the activity of the Security Council to the decrease in the incidence of armed conflict since the end of the Cold War. We conclude the chapter by drawing some conclusions from the analysis.

Trends in Security Council Decisions

The primary way for the Security Council to act is through its decisions, the resolutions. Other forms of decisionmaking, notably the presidential statements and press releases, are also important aspects of Security Council action. However, in this chapter we focus on resolutions, as most of them include decisions, which, unlike presidential and press statements, entail a legal commitment and, according to Article 25, are binding on member states (see Chapter 37). Thus we use the frequency of resolutions as an indicator of Council activity as well as international concern for particular issues.[2]

Council resolutions, whether under Chapter VI or Chapter VII of the UN Charter, reflect a consensus or near consensus among Council members and create an expectation that resolutions will be implemented by all member states. If united, Council members can potentially command significant respect and influence in the world as a whole, in particular when they activate their respective networks and use their influence for the implementation of their decisions. The Council's five permanent members alone account for 60 percent of the world's total defense spending.[3] This military preponderance of the P5 is complemented by considerable economic resources, which could be mustered to back up Council decisions, at least in theory. The Council's potential authority also benefits from the fact that the handful of powerful UN member states aspiring to ascend to permanent member status—Germany, Japan, India, and Brazil—which, like the P5 have a vested interest in preserving the standing of the Council, are frequently elected as nonpermanent members of the Council.[4] In principle, the Council could thus employ significant leverage on any given issue if its members' interests and objectives are aligned. A review of the voting statistics will provide us with some initial indication on how the Council has used this authority over time.

All Resolutions

From 1946 through 2014, the Security Council adopted a total of 2,195 resolutions, 646 before 1989 and 1,549 since 1990, reflecting the explosion of

Council activity in the post–Cold War era.[5] The shift becomes even more striking if we look at the most weighty Council decisions, those adopted under Chapter VII. During the forty-four-year period 1946–1989, the Council adopted a total of 21 Chapter VII resolutions, compared to the well over 600 since 1990—thirty times as many Chapter VII resolutions in half the time. This means that on average, the annual number of Chapter VII resolutions since 1990 is higher than the total figure of such resolutions during the Council's previous history.

Further, with the exception of China, the permanent Council members made significantly greater use of their veto power during the Cold War than after. From 1946 to 1989, there were a total of 232 vetoes, preventing the adoption of 192 draft resolutions (on several occasions, more than one permanent member voted against the same draft resolution). After the end of the Cold War, thirty-two vetoes have prevented the adoption of twenty-seven draft resolutions. These developments are summarized in Table 2.1. Figure 2.1 plots resolutions and vetoes year by year since 1946.

Both Table 2.1 and Figure 2.1 illustrate the dramatic increase in Council activity and the concurrent decline in the use of the veto since the end of the Cold War. The year 1990 constitutes a formative year, with a marked increase in the number of resolutions adopted per year, which, since 1992, has never fallen below forty (compared with a Cold War yearly average of fifteen resolutions). Furthermore, we can observe a remarkable intensification in the resort to Chapter VII. This requires some further elaboration.

Use of Chapter VII

Under Chapter VII of the UN Charter, the Council can decide on enforcement measures in response to threats to the peace, breaches of the peace, and acts of aggression. Not all Chapter VII resolutions contain enforcement measures, but the extraordinary powers vested in the Security Council through Chapter VII prompt special attention to this category of resolutions.[6]

As Figure 2.1 illustrates, the increase of Chapter VII resolutions is even more striking than the trend in the overall numbers. Having adopted

Table 2.1 Security Council Resolutions and Vetoes, Cold War and Post–Cold War Periods, 1946–2014

	Resolutions	Chapter VII Resolutions	Vetoes Cast	Vetoed Drafts
1946–2014	2,195	685	267	221
1946–1989	646	21	232	192
1990–2014	1,549	664	35	29

Figure 2.1 Security Council Resolutions and Vetoes, Annual Data, 1946–2014

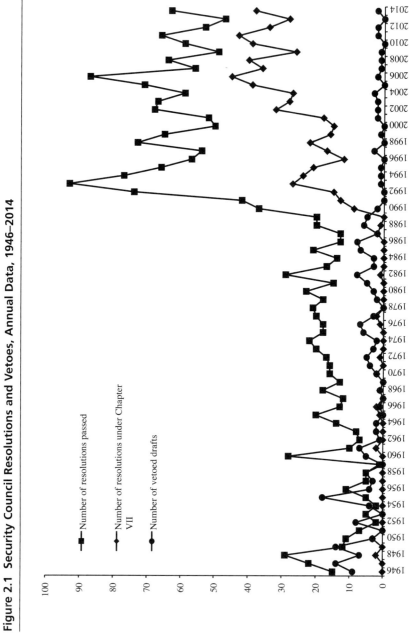

on average one Chapter VII resolution every other year during the Cold War, the Council since 1990 has adopted one such resolution every two weeks. There are several possible reasons for this increase.

One explanation is the increased attention to civil wars in the post–Cold War era. During the Cold War this was regarded as interference in internal affairs, and thus many civil wars were kept off the agenda. Since then, however, a large number of internal armed conflicts have entered the Council's agenda.[7] By invoking Chapter VII, the Council effectively emphasizes the threat that certain civil wars pose to international peace and security.

A second explanation for the increase in the use of Chapter VII is that there are new issues on the agenda that are seen as particularly threatening to international peace and security and require immediate collective action. Resolutions on, for example, international terrorism and nonproliferation are often adopted under Chapter VII, signaling the strong commitment of the Council on these particular issues.

Third, available resources do not always match the needs for decisive action in the various conflicts on the Council's agenda. In such situations, the Council has occasionally resorted to Chapter VII language to convey resolve even in the absence of agreement on substantive action (see Chapter 28). Fourth, since the mid-1990s the Security Council's agenda has been dominated by conflicts located in Africa, a region where great power interests are limited, making the invocation of Chapter VII easier than in other regions (see, for example, Figure 2.7 later).

Finally, there is the principle of "parallelism of form," which means that a decision made under Chapter VII can only be amended by another decision under Chapter VII.[8] As Chapter VII decisions become more common, as well as more detailed, more follow-up decisions are needed, and these will also have to be made under Chapter VII. It has been argued that the resort to Chapter VII indicates that the Security Council considers a situation to be of special importance. This might have been particularly true during and immediately after the Cold War, but in light of the dramatic increase in the resort to Chapter VII over the past two decades, this seemingly reasonable argument needs to be questioned. It is not only the absolute number of Chapter VII resolutions that has increased. Since the end of the Cold War, Chapter VII resolutions also constitute an ever-increasing share of all Security Council resolutions. Each year since 2005, Chapter VII resolutions have constituted more than half of all Security Council resolutions, often closer to two-thirds. This development is illustrated in Figure 2.2.

An inflationary resort to Chapter VII carries the risk of undermining the signaling value of Chapter VII and may affect the compliance rate.[9]

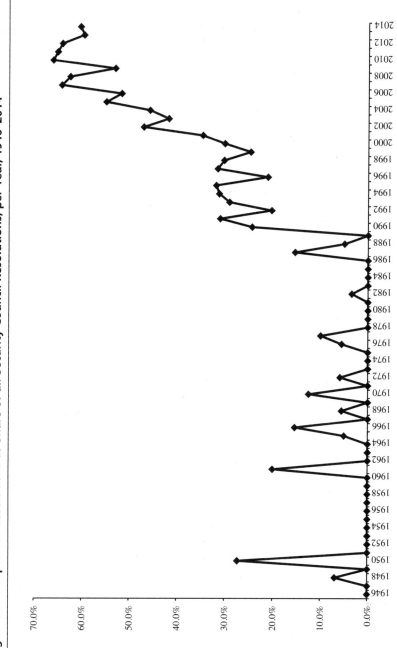

Figure 2.2 Chapter VII Resolutions as Share of all Security Council Resolutions, per Year, 1946–2014

Theoretically, the "teeth" of Chapter VII may wear down if used too often and with too little impact, ultimately with possible detrimental effects for the standing of the Council. Exploiting the signaling value of Chapter VII by using tough language as a substitute for tough action can work only so many times before the Council's credibility is questioned. At the same time, decisions that do not refer to Chapter VII may be interpreted to mean that the situation under consideration is of lesser importance. This speaks in favor of a cautious application of Chapter VII and of reserving its use for the gravest threats and where, if need be, enforcement measures are likely to be implemented.

Figure 2.3 gives data on twenty of the country situations that have received the greatest attention by the Security Council. It shows that conflicts brought onto the Council's agenda during the Cold War period, such as Cyprus, Namibia, and Western Sahara, were addressed primarily without resort to Chapter VII. Even in the case of South Africa, where Chapter VII was used to impose mandatory sanctions, only 4 percent of resolutions were adopted under Chapter VII.[10]

This stands in sharp contrast to several post–Cold War conflicts where the overwhelming majority of resolutions have been adopted under Chapter VII. Examples in Figure 2.3 include Iraq (82 percent of resolutions under Chapter VII), Sudan (86 percent), Somalia (90 percent), and Côte d'Ivoire (98 percent). An exception to the post–Cold War pattern is the situation in Georgia, which has generated a significant number of resolutions, but none under Chapter VII.

The Arab-Israeli conflict remains on the Council's agenda sixty-five years after the first resolution was adopted, but it is still addressed without resort to Chapter VII, as can be seen in Figure 2.3. Nearly 15 percent of all Security Council resolutions since 1946 concern this situation—but they include only three Chapter VII resolutions. In Resolutions 54 (1948) and 62 (1948), the Security Council determined that the situation in Palestine constituted a threat to international peace and security, and in Resolution 611 (1988) it made the same determination with respect to the Israeli aggression against Tunisia (a commando raid killing the Palestine Liberation Organization's [PLO] second in command, Khalil al-Wazir, in Tunis).

In the cases of Georgia and Palestine, the influence of two of the permanent members, Russia and the United States, respectively, is visible. These are conflicts that they consider to be of vital interest, and thus they are prepared to prevent resolutions that are too demanding on their own allies. Controlling whether Chapter VII is used or not is one way for the permanent members to make resolutions compatible with their own interests. Another and more obvious way is to use the veto, to which we now turn.

34

Figure 2.3 Resolutions and Vetoes on Selected Country Situations, in Categories Used by the UN, 1946–2012

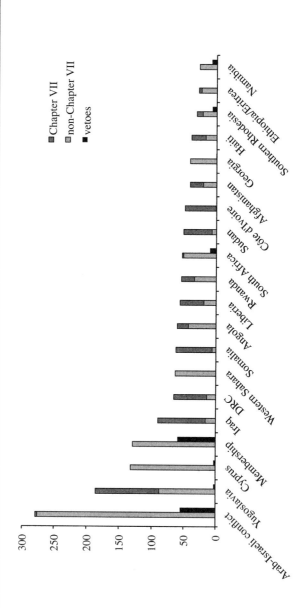

Use of the Veto

The five permanent members of the Security Council—China, France, Russia, the United Kingdom, and the United States—have the power to veto the adoption of resolutions. According to the UN Charter (Article 27), decisions by the Security Council require "an affirmative vote of nine members including the concurring votes of the permanent members." According to developed practice, the concurring votes of the permanent members are not required; a resolution is adopted even if one or more permanent members abstain from voting. But by casting a negative vote, each permanent member can block any Council decision.

In the following analysis of veto patterns, we consider only those vetoed draft resolutions that garnered the required number of positive votes and therefore would have passed in the absence of a negative vote by a permanent member. Further, negative votes cast in closed sessions, such as votes regarding the appointment of a new Secretary-General, are not included. These limitations are common practice in statistical analyses of the veto.[11]

As seen in Table 2.1, from 1946 through 2012, the permanent members cast a total of 264 vetoes, thereby preventing the adoption of 219 draft resolutions. The distribution of vetoes cast is: Soviet Union/Russia, 123; the United States, 83; the United Kingdom, 30; France, 18; and China, 10.[12]

Figure 2.4 shows that the Soviet Union cast the most vetoes during the first twenty years, and the United States from the 1970s through the 1990s. Half of the Soviet Union's vetoes until 1970 concerned the issue of membership. With China represented by the Republic of China (Taiwan) at this time, the Soviet Union was often alone in opposing proposals for new members that the other permanent members favored. Conversely, proposals favored by the Soviet Union regularly failed to achieve the required number of positive votes, meaning that negative votes cast by the other permanent members did not register as vetoes. In fact, from 1946 to 1970, the Soviet Union cast forty-eight vetoes against the admission of new members. During the same period, more than twenty negative votes regarding the admission of new members were cast by other permanent members, none of which counted as a formal veto—the single exception being China's negative vote against the membership of Mongolia in 1955.

The United States cast its first veto in 1970 (along with the United Kingdom's fourth), against a draft resolution condemning the UK for refusing to use force to overthrow the white minority government in Southern Rhodesia.[13] The subsequent increase in US vetoes is partly explained by the Israeli occupation of the West Bank, the Gaza Strip, and other areas in 1967, adding a new dimension to the structure of the Arab-Israeli conflict (over 40 percent of US vetoes from 1970 to 1989 concerned this conflict), and partly by the People's Republic of China (PRC) taking over the Chi-

Figure 2.4 Vetoes Cast by the Permanent Members, Yearly Average per Ten-Year Period, 1946–2012 (last period seven years)

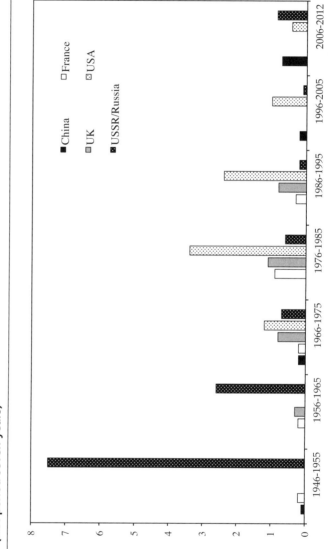

nese seat on the Security Council in 1971, affecting the balance of power within the Council.

The decline in vetoes since the end of the Cold War indicates the rise of a more cooperative approach of the Security Council. Indeed, as Figure 2.1 shows, this has also resulted in a sustained record of a large annual number of joint decisions.

This does not mean, however, that the veto has disappeared or become obsolete. All actors know that it is available, and even a limited use of the veto is a way to signal this fact. The United States regularly uses its veto to prevent resolutions considered too harsh against Israel, but allows the adoption of less committing resolutions on the Israeli-Palestinian conflict. Likewise, by the end of 2012, China and Russia had accepted half of the draft resolutions on Syria, but prevented what they perceived as unbalanced or far-reaching formulations.

The veto power was introduced to ensure the collaboration of the five major powers after World War II, effectively preventing the new organization from taking measures against their vital interests. It was argued in San Francisco that the veto was consistent with political realities, that it was a necessary condition for the creation of the United Nations, and that the organization would break down in the event that enforcement action were undertaken against a permanent member.[14] This argument is logical and at times the United Nations has been on the brink of collapse, particularly with the votes in the Council in 1950, when the West used the Soviet absence to pursue its own course in the Korean War. No permanent member has since then been absent from the Council's deliberation. The Soviet decision to return to its seat signified that it saw the value of the United Nations and did not want to allow it to become a Western-dominated body. The price may have been that the Soviet Union was the country using the most vetoes of any, as just noted. In a remarkable way, the veto may have saved the United Nations.

It seems that once an issue is on the formal agenda, it is hard to remove. Consequently, permanent members have on several occasions used the veto to keep certain country situations off the agenda. As previously discussed, a permanent member can also attempt to make a resolution less demanding, by preventing the Council from using Chapter VII. Either of these two types of action is more likely if a permanent member is involved in the conflict as a primary party, or is supporting an ally. Still, even when defending the interests of an ally, the issue can be of greater importance to the permanent member than to those other states wanting to react to a certain situation. There may then be a realization that no substantive resolution will be accepted, so there is no use proposing one.

During the Cold War era, the People's Republic of China vetoed two draft resolutions,[15] while the Soviet Union's record included 114 vetoes.

Only on one occasion did the two cast negative votes against the same draft.[16] Voting patterns have changed significantly since then, with China having vetoed seven draft resolutions and Russia nine since 1990, with five of those vetoes having been cast jointly in the course of the past decade: on Burma in 2007, Zimbabwe in 2008, and three times on Syria in 2011–2012. (China is thus the only permanent member that has increased its use of vetoes since the end of the Cold War, although it continues to prefer not to be isolated in the use of its veto.) As Chapter 4 in this volume suggests, the recent convergence of Chinese and Russian vetoes seems to indicate a joint effort to balance US dominance in world affairs as well as a concerted pushback by both countries against what they see as a Western-driven assault on state sovereignty by broadening the understanding of what constitutes a threat against international peace and security. It remains to be seen to what degree this reflects larger trends in international affairs with lasting effects on Council dynamics.

The Western powers vetoed in concert several times during the Cold War. Conversely, since 1990 France and the United Kingdom have not used their veto at all; they have merely abstained on a few occasions. In other words, all sixteen US vetoes since 1990 have been lone vetoes.

Issue Areas Addressed by the Council

Figure 2.5 provides an overview of the number of resolutions in different issue areas over time. Again, the post–Cold War increase is clearly visible.

The analysis shows that the Security Council did not address intrastate conflicts until the 1960s, with the single exception of the Spanish question addressed in three resolutions in 1946. In 1990, as the post–Cold War rise in Council activity accelerated, the main issue was Iraq's invasion of Kuwait, but several resolutions also concerned the Arab-Israeli conflict and the situation in Central America. Since 1991, a majority of resolutions each year have concerned intrastate conflicts. Distinguishing between those intrastate conflicts over government and those over territory, we find that during the 1990s the increased Council attention to intrastate conflict concerned both types of conflict. Since 2002, however, less and less attention has been paid to intrastate conflicts over territory, while the number of resolutions addressing intrastate conflicts over government has remained high. In fact, in each year since 2003, intrastate conflicts over government have attracted more resolutions than all other issue areas together, reflecting the fact that from 2003 to 2012, 85 percent of war years[17] have concerned conflicts over government.

However, a number of the most deadly conflicts over the past quarter century have not entered the Council's agenda at all.

Figure 2.5 Number of Resolutions in Different Issue Areas, Yearly Average per Ten-Year Period, 1946–2012 (last period seven years)

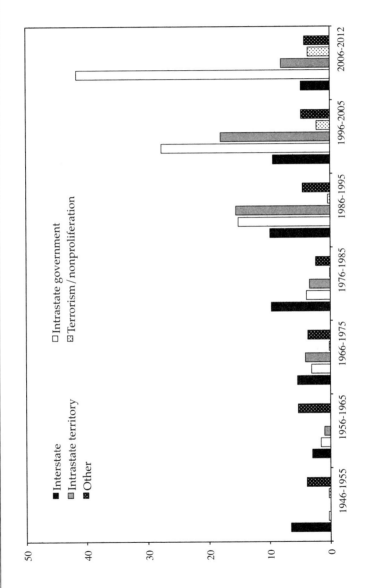

Regional Aspects of Council Action

Regional Distribution of Council Resolutions

In Figure 2.6, presenting the overall geographical distribution of Council resolutions, European concerns (primarily Yugoslavia; see Figure 2.3) received a lot of attention. However, by the end of the 1990s, European conflicts were receiving less attention from the Council. Since then, the agenda has been dominated by African conflicts.

In some cases, the Council's attention to a region has been related to a single issue. For example, from 1993 to 2012, the Security Council adopted forty-eight resolutions dealing with the Americas, of which thirty-nine were on Haiti, indicating that the Council considered the issue to be highly important. Prior to this there was almost no attention by the Council to this region, although the early 1990s also saw the establishment of the UN Observer Group in Central America (ONUCA) and the UN Observer Mission in El Salvador (ONUSAL).[18]

There is a similar pattern for Europe, where the situation in Cyprus was the one standing out for a long time. From the first resolution of 1964 through 1991, the Security Council adopted eighty-one resolutions on European issues—eighty of which addressed Cyprus.[19] The Security Council continued to adopt resolutions regarding Cyprus after 1991, but as just indicated, this agenda item then had to compete with other European issues on the agenda.

When the same analysis is limited to Chapter VII, the post–Cold War focus on Africa becomes even more significant, as is shown in Figure 2.7. In fact, more than two-thirds of all Chapter VII resolutions over the period 2003–2012 deal with African issues, which, as noted earlier, can be partly explained by Africa being a region where great power interests are limited. However, the relative frequency with which Chapter VII is invoked with respect to Africa is not a recent development. Indeed, more than half of the (few) Chapter VII resolutions adopted during the Cold War dealt with Africa, most importantly with Southern Rhodesia.

Regional Arrangements

Chapter VIII of the UN Charter deals with "regional arrangements," which was referred to in only a handful of Council resolutions during the Cold War. However, since 1990, about a quarter of all Security Council resolutions have mentioned regional organizations, in general or by name. Even more interesting, this has often been in resolutions that are taken under Chapter VII. Also since 1990, over 40 percent of all resolutions (and over 50 percent of all Chapter VII resolutions) have dealt with Africa. It is no surprise therefore than half of all Security Council resolutions referring to regional organizations have concerned African conflicts.

Figure 2.6 Number of Resolutions on Different Regions, Yearly Average per Ten-Year Period, 1946–2012 (last period seven years)

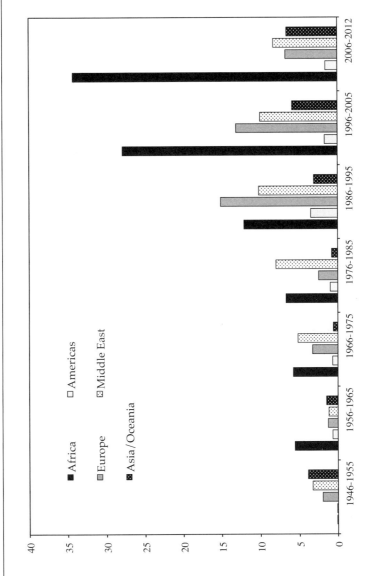

Figure 2.7   Number of Chapter VII Resolutions on Different Regions, Yearly Average per Ten-Year Period, 1946–2012 (last period seven years)

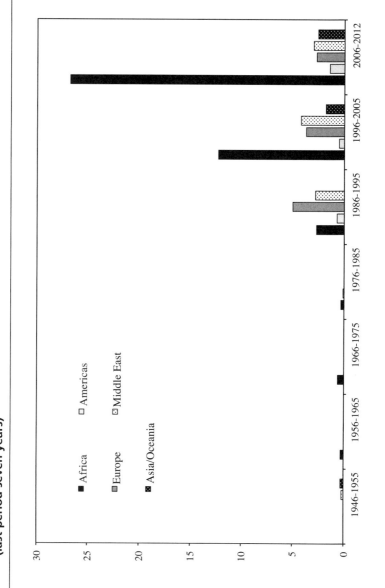

From the UN's perspective, there are distinct advantages in cooperating with regional organizations. They can be tasked with carrying out some of the mandates, they can contribute troops to UN operations, and they often enjoy "unique leverage . . . and have strong networks with important national and regional actors and can often contribute to a more refined analysis."[20] The Economic Community of West African States (ECOWAS) has been active in conflicts in West Africa, often with military means. Together with the African Union (AU), it is probably the most capable African organization and fits the criteria of a regional organization in the UN sense. In a way, this has given space for the concept of "African solutions to African problems." However, there is also a record of hybrid operations, notably between the UN and the AU. Lately, also the European Union (EU) has been interested in participating in such operations.[21]

The importance of UN cooperation with regional and subregional organizations in Africa stands in an interesting contrast to UN responses to the wars in the Middle East and Central Asia, where there has only been little such cooperation, and only recently. The UN-mandated operation in Afghanistan, for instance, does not have a regional organization of, say, Central or South Asia, to turn to. Until recently, Arab regional organizations have been reluctant to cooperate with the UN or other organizations. However, the transformations and upheavals brought about by the Arab Spring have led to an intensification of cooperation between the UN and the Arab League, reflecting a convergence of interests between key Arab states and key permanent Council members with respect to the crises in Libya and Syria. This manifested itself in prominent references to the Arab League in Council resolutions on the crisis of Libya in 2011 as well as on Syria in 2012, where the UN and the Arab League deployed a joint special envoy.

NATO too, even though not recognized as a regional collective security organization within the meaning of Chapter VIII but as a collective defense organization, has over the years been repeatedly tasked by the Security Council with robust peacekeeping and peace enforcement mandates. Its Council-mandated deployments in the Balkans in the 1990s, in Afghanistan since shortly after September 11, 2001, and in Libya in 2011 make NATO the main contributor to non-UN multinational military operations, contributing an average of 70 percent of troops since the turn of the century (see Chapter 19). However, it is seldom explicitly referred to in the Council's declarations.

There is reason to speak of an emerging division of labor. UN peace operations have been concentrated to Africa, where 70 percent of UN troops have been deployed since 2000.[22] At the turn of the millennium, some 80 percent of non-UN troops in peace operations were deployed in Europe (primarily in the former Yugoslavia), but since 2008 the focus has shifted to Central and South Asia (primarily Afghanistan), where 80 percent have been deployed over the past few years.[23]

Thematic Issues in Council Action

Not all resolutions, however, address a specific geographic area. Some decisions concern institutional matters, such as the Council's very first resolution, 1 (1946), on the Military Staff Committee. Resolution 272 (1969) dealt with the International Court of Justice; and Resolution 635 (1989) was about the marking of explosives. Some resolutions have concerned the refinement of particular measures available to the UN, notably 1327 (2000), on UN peace operations, and 1459 (2003), on the Kimberley Process Certification Scheme, a sanctions-promoting measure.

Other resolutions have taken up new themes that require UN attention, notably 1325 (2000), on women, peace, and security, which was followed by further resolutions on gender-related themes; and there are several significant resolutions on children in armed conflict, for instance 1539 (2004) and 1612 (2005). In fact, since 1946, more than a hundred resolutions have developed these and other general agenda items. It appears that such items have become more common, which points to a broader set of concerns of the UN as well as the need to deepen its involvement and attention to certain instruments and themes.

Two important resolutions in this category are 1373 (2001), "Threats to International Peace and Security Caused by Terrorist Acts," and 1540 (2004), "Non-Proliferation of Weapons of Mass Destruction." The first one was adopted in the aftermath of the 9/11 attacks, imposing on all member states a series of obligations (including legal ones) to more effectively counter the terrorist threat, and created a Security Council committee to monitor implementation of the resolution. The second momentous resolution was 1540 of April 2004, which, among other things, obliges all states to adopt appropriate laws and develop and maintain effective controls to prevent nonstate actors' access to weapons of mass destruction (WMD) (see Chapter 37).

These resolutions are often referred to as examples of the Security Council acting as legislator: they create legal obligations through the adoption of thematic Chapter VII resolutions rather than through multilateral treaty negotiations, challenging the notion of legislative equality of member states. They could also be seen as preventive in character, as they aim at preventing—rather than simply responding to—terrorism or WMD proliferation. Furthermore, both these resolutions contain decisions of an open-ended nature, meaning that the permanent members can reject any attempt to modify them (the "reverse veto"). The Council has thus designated certain issues as too important to allow individual member states to decide on their own how to address them.[24]

These two resolutions demonstrate the power that is vested in the UN. If the permanent members and the Council are united, the innocent-sounding Article 25 actually means that obligations of the Charter, when it says that members "agree to accept and carry out" the Council's decisions, override the obligations of all other conventions and treaties. Thus, for the full membership, it is important who is represented on the Council. The permanent members are able to block decisions on their own, but to make positive decisions there is a need, as we have seen, of nine votes. Even if united, the permanent members need the support of at least four other, elected Council members.

Consistency of Council Action

In order to fulfill its responsibilities under the Charter, the Council needs to be perceived as legitimate by the UN member states. Inconsistent and biased treatment of different conflicts undermines such legitimacy. An important aspect of this inconsistency is Council inaction. Several major armed conflicts were left unattended by the Security Council during the Cold War. Examples include Afghanistan, Mozambique, Burma/Myanmar,[25] Sudan, Uganda, and the Vietnam War, all of which were active at war-level intensity (at least a thousand battle-related deaths per year) for at least ten consecutive years at some time during the Cold War. During the past quarter century, too—despite the increased activity of the Security Council—several major armed conflicts have failed to attract the attention of the Council. Examples include Algeria, Chechnya, Colombia, Mindanao, Sri Lanka, and the Kurdish issue in Turkey.

In other cases the Security Council has reacted disturbingly late. The war between Iran and Iraq in the 1980s had lasted for eight years and resulted in between 500,000 and 1 million casualties and the displacement of 1–2 million people, within and outside the two countries, before the Security Council could agree in Resolution 598 (1988) that the war constituted a threat to international peace and security under Chapter VII.[26] By the mid-1990s, when the Security Council adopted Resolution 1054 (1996) relating to Sudan, civil war had ravaged the country for about twenty of its forty years as an independent state. More than 1 million people had been killed, 400,000 Sudanese were refugees in neighboring countries, and 4 million were internally displaced persons (IDPs)—the largest IDP population in the world at the time.[27] And when the first Chapter VII resolution on Afghanistan was adopted, Resolution 1267 (1999), the armed conflict in that country had been active at war-level intensity every single year since 1978.

Table 2.2 shows that the Security Council has failed to adopt any resolution on ten of the twenty-five most deadly conflicts of the post–Cold War era. Another two—Nepal and Syria—have not been considered threats to peace and security. Conversely, some of the conflicts that have received the most attention by the Council are not among the most deadly conflicts. Examples include Côte d'Ivoire and Haiti (see Figure 2.3), which never reached war-level intensity, but were addressed for other reasons.

Table 2.2 The Twenty-Five Armed Conflicts with the Highest Accumulated Number of Battle-Related Deaths, 1989–2012

Conflict[a]	Battle-Related Deaths	Total Years Active (Years at War Level)[b]	Additional Fatalities, Nonstate Violence	Additional Fatalities, One-Sided Violence	Total UNSC Resolutions (Chapter VII)
1 Eritrea-Ethiopia (Badme)	98,192	3 (3)	[c]	[c]	28 (4)
2 Afghanistan	94,446	23 (21)	1,685	7,664	41 (20)
3 Sri Lanka (Eelam)	57,168	19 (16)	621	3,034	0
4 Sudan	44,793	24 (17)	18,326	14,912	48 (42)
5 Ethiopia (Eritrea)	43,470	3 (3)	[c]	[c]	0
6 Ethiopia	41,901	3 (3)	6,165	2,332	0
7 Turkey (Kurdistan)	26,555	24 (8)	0	1,174	0
8 Somalia	25,119	17 (9)	10,702	1,503	63 (57) [d]
9 Iraq-Kuwait	22,848	2 (2)	0	1,149	0
10 Pakistan	19,387	9 (5)	2,669	2,122	0
11 India (Kashmir)	19,287	24 (11)	0	3,277	0
12 Iraq	18,288	15 (7)	3,207	7,505	90 (74)
13 Russia (Chechnya)	17,601	12 (5)	244	2,842	0
14 Colombia	16,662	24 (7)	2,294	2,583	0
15 Syria	15,897	2 (1)	89	3,261	3 (0)
16 Democratic Republic of the Congo	15,324	10 (5)	12,265	66,983	61 (51)
17 Congo	14,176	5 (2)	0	1,365	0
18 Uganda	11,802	22 (4)	1,692	5,718	0
19 Bosnia-Herzegovina (Serb)	11,633	4 (4)	0	12,578	129 (79)[e]
20 Sierra Leone	10,572	10 (2)	40	6,184	41 (16)

Conflict[a]	Battle-Related Deaths	Total Years Active (Years at War Level)[b]	Additional Fatalities, Nonstate Violence	Additional Fatalities, One-Sided Violence	Total UNSC Resolutions (Chapter VII)
21 Nepal	9,908	11 (4)	30	2,365	8 (0)
22 Rwanda	9,199	16 (5)	0	510,449	62 (26)
23 Chad	8,724	18 (2)	412	3,934	6 (6)
24 Burundi	8,597	16 (4)	100	7,062	19(6)[d]
25 Iraq-Coalition	8,202	1 (1)	0	0	0

Sources: Battle-related deaths and active-conflict years from Uppsala Conflict Data Program (UCDP) and Peace Research Institute Oslo (PRIO), 2013, available at www.pcr.uu.se/research/ucdp/datasets/ucdp_prio_armed_conflict_dataset. Additional fatalities from UCDP, One-Sided Violence Dataset, and UCDP, Non-State Conflict Dataset.

Notes: The ranking of conflicts is based on battle-related deaths as registered in the UCDP-PRIO Armed Conflict Dataset. This dataset does not include nonstate conflicts and one-sided violence, which are treated by the UCDP as separate forms of violence. Fatalities due to nonstate conflicts and one-sided violence are not necessarily associated with the armed conflicts in the table, but if such fatalities are significant in a country experiencing armed conflict, it increases the need for Security Council action. Therefore, they are presented in separate columns. It should also be noted that the content of Security Council resolutions does not always refer to a single conflict in the UCDP dataset.

a. The UCDP Armed Conflict Dataset distinguishes between conflicts over government and conflicts over territory. Where conflicts are over territory, that territory is indicated in parentheses. Where there are no parentheses, the conflict is over government.

b. Active conflicts are defined here as those exceeding twenty-five battle deaths per year. They are defined as "war-level" for years in which they exceed 1,000 battle deaths. While many of the conflicts listed started before 1989, the number of years active presented in the table is calculated for the period 1989–2012.

c. For Ethiopia, as three conflicts were taking place in the country during the period 1989–2012, the additional fatalities due to nonstate and one-sided violence are included in relation with the conflict over government on line 6. This doesn't mean, however, that these additional fatalities are associated with this particular conflict.

d. Resolutions pertaining to the three conflicts Iraq, Iraq-Kuwait, and Iraq-Coalition are presented in the Iraq category.

e. For many of the resolutions on Bosnia-Herzegovina (Serb), the conflict relates both to Bosnia and to other conflicts in the former Yugoslavia.

The inconsistency of attention and resolve in Security Council decisionmaking has been the object of much criticism, most recently by Saudi Arabia, which withdrew its candidacy to the Council in 2013 after having been elected to that body.[28] However, the Council has consistently steered clear of "objective" criteria for involvement, and managed to preserve "its birthright of sole and plenary discretion in such matters."[29] This is evident, for example, in the complete lack of cross-references between different situations on the Council's agenda—each case is constantly judged on its own merits.

The inconsistency with respect to issues can partly be explained by the way conflicts enter or are deterred from entering the Council agenda. First, whereas governments are often reluctant to allow the United Nations or other international organizations to intervene in internal conflicts, rebel organizations have instead often hoped for such attention. However, going against this we can also suggest that the higher the degree of prolonged involvement by neighbors in a conflict (for instance, in the DRC, Liberia, and Somalia), the more likely there is Council involvement. Regional and global considerations can stimulate action that overrides the wishes of a government. Ultimately, the outcome will depend on the ability of a government to muster support from one of the permanent members in preventing a conflict from entering the Council agenda. In practice, major power interests in combination with sovereignty concerns have often trumped the impulse for international action based on concerns over humanitarian plight or the threat of regional diffusion of conflict.

Second, dealing with interstate conflicts was the original reason for the creation of the UN, and thus we would expect such conflicts more or less automatically to come to the agenda. This certainly is true for the few interstate wars in this post–Cold War period, notably Iraq in 2003 (Iraq versus the United States and allies) and Eritrea versus Ethiopia. The India-Pakistan conflict over Kashmir remains the most important exception.

Third, whereas Russia prefers to keep the Security Council out of conflicts it is involved in, most obviously Chechnya and South Ossetia, the United States prefers to act through the Council in the conflicts it is involved in, most importantly Afghanistan and Iraq. Similar preferences characterize their otherwise shared concern for the issue of terrorism. The United States has promoted Council involvement in its struggle against al-Qaeda, while Russia and China have chosen to treat such challenges in Chechnya and Xinjang as internal affairs. Other conflicts with a terrorism dimension, such as Colombia, Sri Lanka, and Kurdistan, which do not directly involve any permanent member, have not been addressed by the Council other than as part of the general counterterrorism agenda.

Thus there remains an inconsistency with respect to the issues that enter the agenda. The members of the Security Council make their joint assessment of this, and the outcome may vary. However, once an issue is on the agenda, there is also a matter of what type of actions will be taken. Will similar conflicts be judged in the same way and thus be exposed to the same type of reaction? This is a large question that we leave for future study.

Council Action and the Decline of Armed Conflict

It remains a little-known fact that, as seen in Figure 2.8, after a steady rise in the incidence of armed conflicts from the end of World War II onward, all the way through to the early 1990s, the number of armed conflicts declined by 40 percent between 1992 (fifty-two) and 2003 (thirty-one), and has since remained smaller than in the early 1990s, despite a few ups and downs. It is safe to assume that the end of the Cold War (together with the concomitant fueling of proxy wars by the superpowers) is the most important factor explaining this decline.[30] However, it has been suggested by a number of researchers that the upsurge of international activism in peace-making, peace enforcement, peacekeeping, and peacebuilding—much of it driven by the UN Security Council—constitutes an important element in the decline in the frequency of armed conflict since the peak years.

This relationship is suggested by the fact that the constant increase in resolutions following the end of the Cold War (which can be seen in Figure 2.1) coincides with a steady decrease of international conflict. Interestingly, the decrease in the number of civil wars is not a result of better prevention (indeed, the conflict onset rate throughout the 1990s was almost twice higher than that during the 1980s) but of the fact that significantly more conflicts were ended than new ones started, pointing not to better effectiveness in international efforts at preventing wars but better effectiveness at ending them.[31]

And indeed, there is a pattern of the UN becoming involved when an armed conflict turns into a peace process. When governments as well as rebels want to negotiate, using the UN or other international organizations seems to be a particular pattern. In the past two decades, only a few peace agreements have been negotiated entirely outside the UN framework, notably those of South Africa in the early 1990s and in Nepal in 2006. As the total of peace agreements has increased remarkably since the end of the Cold War, peace processes have become a particular UN concern. This is a matter of being involved not only in the peacemaking itself, but also in accompanying measures, such as peacekeeping operations and sanctions.[32]

The Uppsala Conflict Data Program has registered 141 armed conflicts (with at least twenty-five battle-related deaths per year) since the end of the Cold War. At the end of 2012, there were thirty-two ongoing conflicts, including six wars. Stated differently, this means that 109 armed conflicts

50

Figure 2.8 Armed Conflicts by Intensity, 1946–2012

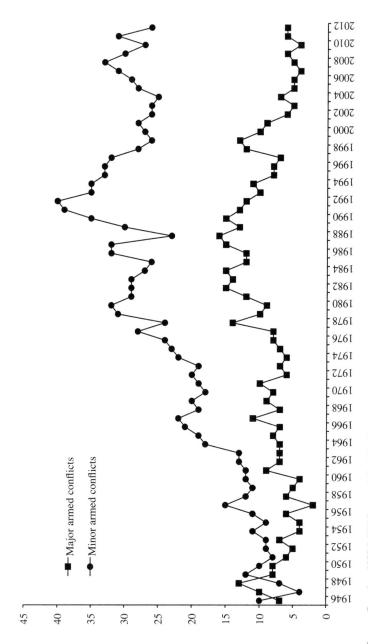

Source: Based on UCDP-PRIO Armed Conflict Dataset.

have ended since the end of the Cold War. The United Nations has been involved in many, but far from all, of these conflicts and their endings. Of the thirty-two conflicts ongoing in 2012, only twelve[33] were subject to at least one Security Council resolution during the year, including four of the six wars. This is, of course, not the full story of UN involvement, as the Secretary-General deployed his good offices in several other conflicts. Taking this into account, we could say the Council and the UN in various ways were involved in about half of all ongoing armed conflicts from a security perspective.

Conclusion

In this chapter we have demonstrated the remarkable resurgence of the UN Security Council as an actor in matters pertaining to international peace and security in the post–Cold War era. This can be seen in the number of resolutions that constitute the data for the analysis. These resolutions demonstrate the high degree of cooperation among the permanent members, resulting in constructive engagement in a series of armed conflicts. In fact, this chapter points out that UN action is particularly geared toward supporting peace processes in internal armed conflicts.

We find that the increased use of Chapter VII, the most intrusive measure at the disposal of the Council, reflects the Council's evaluation of serious threats to international security. By the end of the period studied in this chapter, more than half of all annual resolutions referred to Chapter VII. However, we have some reservations about this and suggest a more cautious application.

The investigation of the voting patterns also points to a selection effect, where the interests of the permanent members in particular areas do affect the Council's actions, whether direct or via allies. Often, national governments are also able to prevent conflicts from entering the agenda of the Council. There are, however, instances where global concerns have been overriding such more narrow concerns. Still, this means that only about half of all armed conflicts have resulted in resolutions by the Council.

The use of the veto has declined, testifying to such working relations in the Council. Still, this state of affairs may not last and there are indicators of possible shifts ahead, most noticeable in closer coordination between China and Russia in the past decade as reflected in an increased use in the joint veto, which may presage global political realignments. Also, the United States has often found itself alone, particularly in matters relating to the Israeli-Palestinian conflict.

We have also shown that there are distinct geographical patterns. The Council has been particularly concerned with conflicts in Africa. A possibility is that Africa is the region with the least tensions among major powers and thus more joint action is forthcoming. At the same time, the persistence of conflicts in Africa may suggest that the Council's actions are not sufficiently highly motivated or effective to deal with this problem. We also note an increasing tendency to resort to or leave issues to regional organizations in this region particularly.

Finally, we have shown that the Council since its inception has used its position also to broaden the agenda for international peace and security. This was particularly marked during the first decade of the new millennium, when it took up issues of terrorism, nonproliferation of weapons of mass destruction, as well as matters of gender and children, in relation to armed conflicts. Only in the sphere of the international Responsibility to Protect (R2P) has this generated a backlash, illustrated in particular by the inability to resort to Chapter VII action on Syria.

Notes

1. United Nations General Assembly Resolution 1000, A/RES/1000 (November 5, 1956).

2. We are, of course, aware of the possibility that many decisions on a particular issue not only may reflect urgency and action, but also could mean that the Council has a difficulty in formulating a coherent strategy. Thus, the crisis in former Yugoslavia took considerable attention, but also included inadequate action, leading to further needs for decisions. This in turn reflected deep divisions, not least between the United States and its European allies.

3. A total of $1,056 billion out of a total of $1,753 billion in 2013, according to Stockholm International Peace Research Institute, *Yearbook 2013: Armaments, Disarmaments, and International Security,* www.sipri.org/yearbook/2013.

4. For instance, Brazil and Japan have both served as elected members ten times, more than any other member state. They are followed by Argentina (nine times); Colombia, India, and Pakistan (seven); Canada and Italy (six); and Belgium, Germany, and Panama (five).

5. Manuel Fröhlich describes a similar increase over the past few decades regarding the appointment of special representatives of the Secretary-General. Manuel Fröhlich, "The Special Representatives of the United Nations Secretary-General," in *Routledge Handbook of International Organization,* edited by Bob Reinalda (London: Routledge, 2013), pp. 231–243.

6. There is no agreed-upon definition of what constitutes a Chapter VII resolution, and observers disagree in some cases. We use Patrik Johansson's definition in "The Humdrum Use of Ultimate Authority: Defining and Analysing Chapter VII Resolutions," *Nordic Journal of International Law* 78, no. 3 (2009): 310. "A Security Council Resolution is considered to be 'a Chapter VII resolution' if it makes an explicit determination that the situation under consideration constitutes a threat to the peace, a breach of the peace, or an act of aggression, and/or explicitly or implicitly states that the Council is acting under Chapter VII in the adoption of some or all operative paragraphs."

7. James Cockayne, Christoph Mikulaschek, and Chris Perry, "The United Nations Security Council and Civil War: First Insights from a New Dataset" (New York: International Peace Institute, September 2010).

8. Erika de Wet, *The Chapter VII Powers of the United Nations Security Coun-*

cil (Portland: Hart, 2004), pp. 251–252. An exception to the principle of "parallelism of form" is Resolution 460 (December 21, 1979), UN Doc. S/RES/460, which terminated the sanctions against Southern Rhodesia. The resolution explicitly states that the measures against Southern Rhodesia were imposed under Chapter VII, but does not refer to Chapter VII in its decision to terminate those measures.

9. The study of compliance, therefore, is an urgent field for research on the UN. However, current research, such as the International Peace Institute's data on Security Council compliance, is yet too limited to allow any general conclusions. Also, the Targeted Sanctions Consortium has data evaluating compliance with sanctions decisions. Of course, the effectiveness of UN sanctions has been much debated. For a recent study of individual targeting, see Peter Wallensteen and Helena Grusell, "Targeting the Right Targets? The UN Use of Individual Sanctions," *Global Governance* 18, no. 2 (April–June 2012): 207–230.

10. Southern Rhodesia is an exception: 29 percent of the thirty-one resolutions were adopted under Chapter VII.

11. See, for example, Global Issues Research Group, "Table of Vetoed Draft Resolutions in the United Nations Security Council, 1946–2002" (London: Foreign and Commonwealth Office, 2003); Anjali V. Patil, "The UN Veto in World Affairs, 1946–1990: A Complete Record and Case Histories of the Security Council's Veto" (Sarasota: UNIFO, 1992).

12. Discounting vetoes on admission of new members, the distribution is Soviet Union, seventy; the United States, seventy-seven; the United Kingdom, thirty; France, eighteen; and China, eight. The last time a permanent member voted against the admission of a new member to the United Nations was the US vote against membership for the Socialist Republic of Vietnam in 1976. The application for membership by the Palestinian Authority in 2011 was resisted by the United States but was never put to a vote in the Security Council. Instead the General Assembly made the State of Palestine a permanent observer nonmember state in November 2012. See www.un.org/en/members/nonmembers.shtml.

13. United Nations Security Council, "Burundi, Nepal, Sierra Leone, Syria, and Zambia: Draft Resolution," UN Doc. S/9696, March 11, 1970.

14. Patil, "The UN Veto in World Affairs," p. 13.

15. In addition, the Republic of China used the veto once, in 1955, against the membership of Mongolia. The Republic of China (Taiwan) held the Chinese seat in the Security Council until 1971, when it was replaced by the People's Republic of China (mainland China).

16. Or more specifically, against a proposed amendment to a draft resolution on the Middle East, subsequently vetoed by the United States when voted upon as a whole.

17. War years are defined as the number of conflicts active at war-level intensity (at least 1,000 battle-related deaths per year) per year, added together for all years of the period.

18. This was first demonstrated in the issue of Guatemala in 1954, which the United States insisted should be dealt with by the Organization of American States, while the UN Secretary-General, Dag Hammarskjöld, wanted to have it as a UN issue, not the least as it would require an obvious US involvement. See Peter Wallensteen, *Peace Research: Theory and Practice* (London: Routledge, 2011), chap. 12.

19. The exception is Resolution 395, which dealt with tensions between Greece and Turkey in relation to the Aegean Sea. See United Nations Security Council Resolution 395, S/RES/395 (August 25, 1976).

20. United Nations Department of Political Affairs, *2012 Annual Report,* May 2013, p. 11, www.un.org/wcm/webdav/site/undpa/shared/undpa/pdf/DPA%20Annual%20Report%202012.pdf.

21. For a recent analysis, see Anders Bjurner and Peter Wallensteen, eds., *Regional Organizations in Peacemaking: Challengers to the UN?* (London: Routledge, 2014).

22. Regional organizations, most importantly the European Union and the African Union, have contributed to non-UN police missions since 2003. Non-UN police staff are also deployed primarily in Europe and Africa. Still, the UN remains the dominant actor, with seven times the number of police staff compared to all non-UN police operations together since 2010.

23. Contributions to and deployment of UN and non-UN peace operations are based on the *Annual Review of Global Peace Operations,* issues 2006–2013, published by the Center on International Cooperation, and we have used the Stockholm International Peace Research Institute's Multilateral Peace Operations Database (the original source of the *Annual Review*) to backdate these figures to 2000. Following the example of the *Annual Review,* we have excluded the massive multinational operation in Iraq when calculating percentages.

24. Anette Ahrnens, "A Quest for Legitimacy: Debating UN Security Council Rules on Terrorism and Non-Proliferation" (Lund: Lund University, Department of Political Science, 2007), pp. 158–159.

25. In Burma/Myanmar, both the conflict over government and the territorial conflict over the Kachin region were active at war-level intensity for at least ten consecutive years during the Cold War period.

26. In addition, from 1980 to 1991, the Security Council adopted another fifteen resolutions relating to the Iran-Iraq War, but Resolution 598, S/RES/598 (July 20,1988), was the only one adopted under Chapter VII.

27. It is worth noting in this context that what eventually prompted the Security Council to act under Chapter VII, in Resolution 1054 (April 26, 1996), UN Doc. S/RES/1054, was the failure of the Sudanese government to extradite three persons suspected of involvement in an assassination attempt against Egyptian president Hosni Mubarak in 1995. The first Chapter VII resolution addressing armed conflict in Sudan as a threat to international peace and security was Resolution 1556 (July 30, 2004), UN Doc. S/RES/1556.

28. See also Adam Roberts and Dominik Zaum, *Selective Security: War and the United Nations Security Council Since 1945,* Adelphi Paper no. 395, International Institute for Strategic Studies (London: Routledge, July 2008); Aidan Hehir, "The Permanence of Inconsistency: Libya, the Security Council, and the Responsibility to Protect," *International Security* 38, no. 1 (2013): 137–159.

29. Jared Schott, "Chapter VII as Exception: Security Council Action and the Regulative Ideal of Emergency," *Northwestern Journal of International Human Rights* 6, no. 1 (2007): 24–80.

30. This was discussed in a comprehensive way in Human Security Centre, *Human Security Report 2005: War and Peace in the 21st Century* (New York: Oxford University Press, 2005).

31. World Bank, "World Development Report 2011: Conflict, Security, and Development" (Washington, DC, 2011).

32. Peter Wallensteen, *Understanding Conflict Resolution* (London: Sage, 2012), chap. 9.

33. Counting "Sudan–South Sudan (border)" and "Sudan–South Sudan (Abyei)" as two different conflicts, and "Mali" and "Mali (Azawad)" as two different conflicts, makes it twelve instead of ten. They were all addressed in Security Council resolutions during 2012.

Part 1

Competing Interests on the Security Council

3

The United States in
the Security Council

Stephen John Stedman

FOR ITS FIRST FORTY-FIVE YEARS THE UNITED NATIONS SECURITY
Council was an institution where great powers would gather to say no to
collective security. The Council existed mostly to profess resolve for the
righteousness of one's positions, but not pass resolutions. The United States
was satisfied with using the Council as a negative instrument of foreign
policy and treated the Council as a place to exercise its veto on behalf of its
interests or the interests of key allies. The Council was a bit player in the
US foreign policy pageant, only occasionally taking central stage during
crises. Its deliberations seldom shaped US policy, nor was it an important
vehicle for pursuing US foreign policy goals.

This relationship has changed over the past twenty-five years in complex, unexpected ways. Since 1990, every US president and their foreign
policy teams have wanted a Security Council that can say yes—to sanctions, to the use of humanitarian force, and to the use of force in pursuit of
key security interests. But while US policymakers now value the imprimatur of a Security Council resolution, it is never clear how much and at
what expense. The United States has never accepted the Council as the sole
arbiter of whether it is legal for it to use force, and US unilateral use of
force is usually accompanied by complicated legal justification as to why
the United States can act alone. And while legal scholars acknowledge that
bad legal justifications are better than no legal justification, the point is
made—an absence of a Security Council resolution has never stopped the
United States from using force when it believes its interests are at stake.

But here's the rub: such a stance is more justifiable if the Council is an
institution that can only say no. Since the 1990s, when the Council began to

57

say yes to collective security, US unilateralism has garnered much more scrutiny. At the same time, US reengagement with the Council occurs during an era of tremendous asymmetrical power in the international system. The United States now often wants a Council that says yes, but it still does not accept that it must be restrained if the Council says no. US hegemony means that the United States can always act forcefully on its own should it so desire. And even when the Council says yes, the United States tends to reserve to itself the role of arbiter of what a Council's yes means. When it comes to the Council, it cannot be said that the United States plays well with others.

Power and its distribution in the international system best explain the role of the Security Council in US foreign policy, and as the distribution of power has changed since 1990, the importance of the Security Council for the United States has risen. But because the Council was largely moribund for its first forty-five years, any US president who would like to make the Council more central to its foreign policy faces several ongoing challenges. The first challenge is a reputational one based on forty-five years of Council paralysis and of the disdain of the United States for the Council. The Council's poor image in the political circles of Washington ensures that many US politicians deride the Council out of habit. At the same time, the US history of weak commitment to the Council and of using force to depose regimes it doesn't like ensures that other UN member states and their publics approach any US initiative at the Council with intense scrutiny and skepticism. The second challenge is that between 1945 and 1990, US foreign policy makers and the US bureaucracy were trained to prioritize bilateral and alliance diplomacy. A world in which the Council matters requires a different foreign policy operating system than one in which it is irrelevant. And US policymakers always hold the Council's relevance in doubt. The third challenge is a basic one of collective action: the imprimatur of a Council resolution may bring positive, diffuse benefits, but the process of getting a resolution passed incurs transaction costs and sometimes alteration of goals.

Thus this constant dilemma for US foreign policy in the past twenty-five years: the legality of Security Council mandates and resolutions has some value, but at the cost of freedom of action and compromise on preferences to forge Council approval, and reputational cost should the Council say no and the United States then choose to act anyway.

The United States and a Security Council That Says No

Any in-depth examination of the United States and the Security Council should begin with a simple fact: for most of its life the Council has been of tangential importance to the aims and conduct of US foreign policy. This is borne out in the WikiLeaks cable trove, of which, among 251,287 released classified cables, only 6,532 (or 2.6 percent) discussed the UN Security Council—this according to the US State Department's own labeling system. The trove spans the end of 1966 to early 2010, during which time human rights garnered 49,044 cables, and terrorism 28,801 cables. The overwhelming number of cables, 145,451 to be exact, dealt with US external political relations, which reflects the number and importance of America's bilateral relations.[1]

Although the data remain to be systematically analyzed, one would expect the number of cables focused on the Security Council to have increased after the end of the Cold War. It would be surprising if the number of such cables were not clustered around high-visibility crises that thrust the Council into the limelight, and it would be interesting to see the yearly average of such cables, to see if they correlate at all with the professed multilateralism of different US presidencies. But taken at face value, what the number reveals seems right and accords with much of what has been written about US foreign policy. As one recent historian of global governance observes, "One can read entire histories of American foreign policy in the Cold War without coming across a single reference to the United Nations."[2]

Those few histories that do try to make the UN a central part of US foreign policy tend to suffer from what social scientists refer to as selection bias; by looking only at US engagement with the UN, one can convince oneself and maybe others of a central role for the UN in US policy. It is only by looking at the totality of America's diplomacy—its bilateral relations, its important military allies and alliances, and its attention to international financial institutions—that one gets proper perspective.

At the founding of the United Nations in 1945, US president Harry S. Truman declared, "We all have to recognize—no matter how great our strength—that we must deny ourselves the license to do always as we please."[3] But within a year the Cold War rendered the UN Security Council paralyzed. Given what was at stake in the superpower competition, the United States quickly lost interest in the Security Council as an instrument for collective action. When the Soviet Union boycotted the Council in 1950, the United States cleverly took advantage and received Council authorization for war in Korea. But this was an exception. The return of the Soviet Union to the Council resulted in few resolutions and many vetoes. For several years in the 1950s, Council vetoes outnumbered resolutions by as many as four to one.[4] In the first twenty years of the Council, the Soviet Union vetoed 106 resolutions, and effectively convinced the other permanent members of the futility of Council action.[5]

A hobbled Security Council proved a feeble constraint on unilateral use of force, especially by the great powers themselves, usually played out in military interventions to prop up friendly regimes or change hostile ones. A provocative book coauthored by one of the deans of UN studies notes that the language used by the Soviet Union in crushing political rebellions by nominally sovereign states in Eastern Europe could have been written by US State Department lawyers justifying US military intervention in Central America.[6]

By the 1960s the United States seemed content that the Council was principally an organ that could say no rather than yes. Between 1945 and 1965 the United States did not exercise its veto power a single time. All of the sixty-nine US vetoes of Council resolutions during the Cold War took place between 1966 and 1990. Collective security for the United States meant NATO and regional alliances. From the 1970s onward, the most important utility of the UN Security Council for the United States was the veto against resolutions deemed hostile to Israel, a key US ally. From 1971 to 1990, the United States vetoed twenty-eight resolutions critical of Israel.

Postponing the Realist Moment, 1990–1996

With the end of the Cold War, US interest in the Security Council surged. President George H. W. Bush and his closest foreign policy advisers, James Baker and Brent Scowcroft, quite deliberately turned to the Council for a unified collective response to Iraq's invasion of Kuwait. In the immediate aftermath of the war, the Security Council provided the legal basis for humanitarian intervention in the Kurdish areas of northern Iraq. At the same time, the Bush administration engaged with the Council in order to address a series of regional conflicts that were overlaid with Cold War tensions: Cambodia in Southeast Asia, Namibia in southern Africa, and Nicaragua and El Salvador in Central America. The Bush administration's foreign policy use of the Security Council stemmed from a belief that the end of America's superpower competition with the Soviet Union created an opening for collective security; that the United Nations could prove useful diplomatically in ending protracted conflicts; and that action routed through the Council would increase global burden-sharing and reduce America's security responsibilities.

These first forays of a revitalized collective security proved stunningly successful. The Gulf War was short, its aim limited, and its costs paid largely by others, especially Kuwait, Saudi Arabia, Japan, and Germany.[7] Negotiations produced peace agreements for Cambodia and El Salvador; US diplomacy enabled the United Nations to implement a comprehensive agreement and elections for an independent Namibia, and to innovate with new uses and missions for its peacekeepers.

For a brief period, the Council seemed transformed into an institution that would always say yes. Moreover, there seemed to be uncritical acceptance that a Security Council that would say yes was an unquestioned boon for US foreign policy and for the United Nations. The belief in such a convergence stemmed from a basic misunderstanding about the end of the Cold War: that the bipolar distribution of power that had structured international conflict and cooperation had been replaced by a world in which power and its distribution no longer mattered. In short, for a bright shining moment, idealism trumped realism. Few stopped to ask what unipolarity might mean for the Security Council and its ability to provide collective security on a sustainable basis. Ironically, it would be a new Democratic US administration that would reveal that, at least for the United States, unipolarity was still accompanied by a profound ambivalence about the Security Council as an instrument of US foreign policy.

The quick successes of the Council under George H. W. Bush yielded long-term unexpected, unintended consequences that ensured that America's relationship to the Security Council in the 1990s and beyond would be fraught with tension. The most important issue for the United States was how to deal with Iraq and the aftermath of the Gulf War: in particular, how and under what circumstances Iraq would be brought into normal standing with the Council. A second issue was UN peacekeeping: when and how missions should be deployed, and whether and when the United States should contribute troops to UN-mandated and UN-led missions. A third issue was humanitarian intervention—whether and how the Council should respond to mass killing and atrocity. Common to all these issues was the use of force: when and how it should be deployed. A fourth conflictual issue was sanctions: when and how to apply them and, just as important, when to remove them.

US diplomacy with the Council in the 1990s is now shrouded in myth. Given how badly relations deteriorated between the United States and the Council after the US invasion of Iraq in 2003, it is tempting to believe that President Bill Clinton's foreign policy strongly supported collective security and Council-based multilateralism. But this would be incorrect. The first Clinton administration scapegoated the United Nations for its own failure in Somalia in 1993; beggared the UN peacekeeping missions in Bosnia and Rwanda, all but ensuring their catastrophic failure; did the same for Sierra Leone at the end of the 1990s but was saved by intervention by British special forces; actively supported withdrawal of peacekeepers in the face of genocide in Rwanda; and gradually usurped the Council's prerogatives in addressing noncompliance by Saddam Hussein toward Council resolutions. US unilateralism toward Iraq began well before the George W. Bush administration.

The Clinton administration was often frustrated by the constraints that international order pose on great powers, and easily fell into multilateralism à la carte. An in-depth historical examination of the United States, the

United Nations, and Iraq in the 1990s accuses the Clinton administration of "creeping unilateralism."[8] The original enforcers of the no-fly zone over Iraq were the United States, the United Kingdom, and France, but France dropped out in 1995 because of disagreement over the sanctions regime against Iraq. It was Clinton, not his successor, who proclaimed the goal of regime change in Iraq. And it was the Clinton administration in 1998 that forced the original arms inspectors out of Iraq and, along with the UK, bombed Iraq without new Security Council approval.

Central to the relationship between Clinton and the Council are three cases of failure—Somalia, Rwanda, and Bosnia—and a case of perceived failure that was transformed into catastrophic failure, Iraq. US policymakers (and the American public) blamed the UN for these failures, but the United States in various degrees was complicit in all of them. At the heart of these failures was a misunderstanding about international power and how it could have and should have shaped international cooperation at the end of the Cold War.

When Bill Clinton was inaugurated in 1993, the United Nations seemed poised to realize its potential, long stifled by the Cold War. Between 1989 and 1993 there were more new peacekeeping missions than in the previous forty years. International leaders seemed content to put problem after problem to the Council. At the time, the Council and the UN Secretary-General, Boutros Boutros-Ghali, were more than willing to take up these responsibilities. At the end of 1992, Boutros-Ghali released an ambitious vision for an activist and interventionist UN, titled *An Agenda for Peace.* This was all done in the naive and mistaken belief that member states were actually going to provide the resources, will, and determination to implement that vision. From the United Nations, there was an eagerness to take on new tasks, a willingness to expand its activities, without understanding that US commitment would make or break the organization.

And the lack of commitment almost broke UN peacekeeping. The response of the Clinton administration to the surge in peacekeeping operations it inherited was to underfund them. Because the United States was the largest financial contributor to new missions, the Clinton administration consistently demanded that the UN Secretariat lowball troop, cost, and risk estimates. In the case of UN-protected areas of Bosnia and the UN mission in Rwanda, the result was genocide. The response of the administration was to scapegoat the UN and the peacekeepers, in the strange belief that the failures of the organization would not reflect upon the Council itself.

In his first speech at the General Assembly in 1993, President Clinton foreshadowed his administration's ambivalence about a Security Council that could say yes: "If the American people are to say yes to UN peacekeeping, the United Nations must know when to say no."[9] One of the more disingenuous remarks by a US president at the United Nations, it managed to hide several important facts: that the United Nations does not exist apart from its member states, of which the United States is the most powerful; that it is the Security Council that authorizes peacekeeping missions; that the United States had said yes to every one of the new missions during the expansion of peacekeeping in the early 1990s; that one way that the United Nations says no is through Security Council vetoes by its five permanent members, of which the United States is one and can block any mission it doesn't like. This then was Clinton's response to a Security Council that could say yes: not too often and on the cheap, and when it goes wrong, it's the fault of a disembodied UN and not the Council.

President Clinton's speech at the General Assembly came six days before what has become known as the Battle of Mogadishu, made famous in the book and subsequent movie *Black Hawk Down*. The battle between the guerrilla fighters of Somali warlord Mohamed Farah Aidid and US special forces transfixed the American public. The Clinton administration was quick to blame the United Nations for the calamity, but in fact the battle was the culmination of a series of incremental commitments and decisions made by the Clinton administration. One of its first decisions upon inheriting the intervention from the Bush administration was to decrease the overall US military presence at the same time that the UN took on the much more fundamental and challenging tasks of nation- and statebuilding. When carrying out those tasks inevitably prompted violence by Aidid, whose power was threatened, the United States escalated the conflict. Every major military decision on how and whom to fight in Somalia was taken by the United States, not the United Nations. The force commander of the second UN Operation in Somalia (UNOSOM II) was Jonathan Howe, a US admiral and former deputy national security adviser for President George H. W. Bush.

In the aftermath of the Battle of Mogadishu, the Clinton administration reassessed that it had little interest in Somalia, a decision that affected the UN in two ways. First, it led to an interagency process that produced Presidential Decision Directive 25, which set out conditions for US support for UN peacekeeping missions. What was meant originally to be a directive on when US troops should be used in peacekeeping became instead a directive on when the United States should support Security Council authorization for new missions, even if they did not involve US troops. In short order, the United States became the Council's gatekeeper for new missions. This, in turn, had direct consequences for UN response to the genocide in Rwanda in April 1994. Deeming that the conditions on the ground were unconducive to peacekeeping, US ambassador to the UN Madeleine Albright argued to the Council that the existing UN mission should be withdrawn. Exemplary of the hold of bilateral interests on US Council behavior, the overriding goal for the US mission to the UN was to provide cover to enable its NATO ally,

Belgium, to withdraw its troops from the UN Assistance Mission in Rwanda (UNAMIR), a small, embattled peacekeeping force.[10]

Blaming the UN Secretariat or the Security Council for one's own failings has been a constant temptation for US politicians in the post–Cold War era, irrespective of political party. Kofi Annan used to joke that *SG* stood for "scapegoat," not "Secretary-General." But in an era when the United States wants a Council that can say yes, and actually wants the UN to be effective, blaming the Council or the organization simply further discredits both in the eyes of legislators and those among the public who already believe them to be useless.

The Realist Moment Arrives, 1996–2001

By 1996 and the end of the first Clinton administration, the effects of US unipolarity seeped into the workings of the Council. The United States essentially vetoed a second term for Boutros-Ghali. In its diplomacy to end the war in Bosnia, the United States eschewed UN involvement and sought a minimal role for the organization in the implementation of the Dayton Accords. The United States sought a Council that would say yes to what it wanted on Iraq, but when the Council refused to go along, the United States went ahead anyway. The United States had usurped enforcement of Council resolutions on Iraq. The administration publicly linked the end of sanctions to the removal of Saddam Hussein. In 1999, knowing that a Security Council resolution authorizing force to protect Kosovars from Serbian attack would be vetoed by Russia, the United States and NATO went to war against Serbia without Council authorization, a military intervention deemed by a panel of respected international experts as "legitimate but not legal."[11]

Keeping with US Council diplomacy of the previous two decades, the Clinton administration used its veto on any resolution involving Israeli interests, a trend that would continue in the George W. Bush and Barack Obama administrations. Indeed, it can be said that whatever positive action various US administrations sought from the Council after the Cold War, the United States has consistently said no to Council resolutions on Israel and Palestine. All but one of the sixteen vetoes that the United States has exercised since 1992 has involved the Middle East, and in all those cases the United States has found itself largely isolated in the Council.

The Clinton skepticism toward peacekeeping also continued. Although the administration worked closely with the Council and then–Secretary-General Kofi Annan to create favorable legal and political conditions for an Australian forceful deployment to stop massacres in East Timor in 1999, it continued to depress cost and force estimates for new missions, especially in Africa. In 2000, after trumpeting the recommendations of the Brahimi

Report, on the future of UN peacekeeping—in particular, the recommendation that the Council should never deploy a mission without adequate
troops, resources, and mandate—US ambassador Richard Holbrooke pronounced the Council's new mission to the Democratic Republic of the
Congo as the first post-Brahimi mission, guided by its wisdom. Yet the
Council's authorization provided 5,500 troops for a territory larger than the
size of France, with questionable consent of the warring parties, in a broken
state consumed by ongoing violence. In 2000, when rebels took 500 peacekeepers hostage in Sierra Leone, and the mission teetered on the brink of
disaster, the Clinton administration's preferred policy option was not to
deploy deadly force but to send former US senator Jesse Jackson Sr. as a
special envoy. The Clinton administration never believed that the failure of
peacekeeping might reflect badly on the Council, or if it did, it didn't care.
This in spite of the hard work of a US ambassador, Richard Holbrooke, to
make the Council and the UN relevant and effective.

There is no published history of the US ambassadors to the UN, and little analysis of their role. But in looking at the three Clinton ambassadors,
Madeleine Albright in the first term, and Bill Richardson and Richard Holbrooke in the second, there is a basic distinction in how different appointees
approach their jobs. With Albright, the ambassadorship was a platform for
her own career and she had little willpower to avoid scapegoating and belit-
tling the organization, even when US policy was complicit in failure. For
Richardson and Holbrooke, no less ambitious, there seemed a much greater
discipline in avoiding cheap shots at the organization, and a greater willingness to be an advocate for greater Council responsibility and greater
resources to the United Nations.

The United States and Creeping Multilateralism at the Council, 2001–2008

The foreign policy team of George W. Bush came to office hostile to international law and intent on freeing itself from international constraint: its
unilateralism neat, not diluted. Upon taking office it set out to repudiate
much of the international architecture and arrangements that the United
States had been instrumental in establishing fifty-five years earlier.

The Bush administration's stated goal was primacy, and the imperative
to ensure it would face no international challengers well into the twenty-
first century. Its acolytes coined the term "lawfare," meant to convey that
international law, treaties, and conventions were weapons of the weak used
to constrain the United States, and therefore were to be opposed. Among
the Bush team's first actions were repudiation of the Anti–Ballistic Missile
Treaty, the Rome Statute of the International Criminal Court, and the Comprehensive Nuclear Test Ban Treaty.

The terrorist attacks of September 11, 2001, complicated the administration's antipathy to the United Nations, because the Security Council and the Secretariat proved themselves useful in dealing with Afghanistan. The Security Council promptly and roundly condemned the attacks, and gave the United States freedom in crafting its military response. The Council gave legality to US use of force, invoking Article 51, and the right of self-defense in UN Security Resolution 1368. The US administration sought and received UN help in creating the Bonn process, which in short order crafted a transitional government in Afghanistan. Although the United States embraced international help in mediation, policing, and transitional governance assistance, it excluded the UN, and many of its NATO allies, from any military role.

There was little dissent from the Council concerning US actions toward Afghanistan. This would change with revelations of the conduct of US security operations, including US treatment of prisoners, indefinite detention at Guantanamo, and the use of torture and rendition. Even so, if these had been the totality of Council concerns, it is unlikely they would have created much opposition to the United States, for the simple reason that many Council members turned a blind eye to rights abuses in the fight against terrorism, and other member states would have been implicated in the abuses.

The issue that blew the Council apart was Iraq. The United States had long usurped for itself the right to use force to compel Iraqi compliance with Council resolutions. As mentioned, it was the Clinton administration that had first voiced regime change as the goal of US foreign policy. The attacks of September 11 provided an opening for members of the Bush administration to go after Saddam Hussein. The Pentagon, unhappy with the Central Intelligence Agency (CIA) and the professional intelligence apparatus, created its own office for intelligence that single-mindedly put forward a story of Iraqi complicity with the September attacks, sought any evidence that could possibly make the case, and bullied much of the professional intelligence community to agree. When the Pentagon crafted its version of 9/11, involving Saddam Hussein as instigator, whom it also claimed clandestinely possessed nuclear, chemical, and biological weapons he had hidden from UN inspectors, only the US State Department's Bureau of Intelligence and Research demurred.

In order to appease its top ally, the United Kingdom, the Bush administration worked the Council hard to get a resolution authorizing an invasion of Iraq. When the Council, skeptical of US intelligence, more trustful of UN inspectors, and genuinely disturbed at the likely revolutionary consequences that the invasion would cause for the greater Middle East, refused to authorize, the United States, with about fifty allies went to war anyway. Having sought a Council yes, the United States refused to take no as an answer.

Summer of 2003 was the nadir for US relations with the Council. There was serious talk within Washington, D.C., that the United States should walk away from the United Nations altogether. Such talk failed to gain traction as the Bush administration realized that it still needed the United Nations—to mediate among rival factions within Iraq and to help create arrangements and institutions that would enable it to leave Afghanistan. Moreover, unlike the Clinton administration, which grudgingly approved UN peacekeeping operations in Africa, the Bush administration became a robust supporter of UN peacekeeping missions, which greatly expanded from 2001 to 2008. Under President Bush, the United States was willing to shoulder more expensive missions, larger deployment of troops, and more coercive missions. Partly because of the newfound tendency to see failed states as petri dishes for terrorism, the Bush administration embraced UN peacekeeping as a cheap, sometimes catchall solution to Africa's civil wars and internal violence.

Given the dramatic break between the United States and the Council on Iraq, one might have predicted a return to pre–Cold War US attitudes toward the Council—that it could only say no, and that its only function was as a place to exercise the veto to protect vital interests. This certainly was the preference of John Bolton, George Bush's second-term choice to be US ambassador to the Council. In his memoirs, Bolton portrays the ideal ambassador to the UN as the nation's litigator, always putting forward a strong case for US national interests.[12] Such a role makes sense only if the Council were theater, where one makes speeches for the benefit of one's domestic audience and international friends.

However, what is striking by the end of the Bush second term is the high-profile issues that the United States brought to the Council—Iran, North Korea, Lebanon, and Afghanistan. In part this was driven by the hope that the United Nations could be a useful tool in exiting the quagmires of Iraq and Afghanistan. But one also senses that the administration had learned that unilateralism provided little traction for its toughest foreign policy challenges. Very late in the game, the Bush foreign policy team discovered the virtues of the Council and burden-sharing, when the issues were tough, US policy was stymied, and the burden to share was failure.

President Obama: Getting to Yes?

Barack Obama's election as president of the United States raised the hopes (and fears) of many foreign policy observers that the United States would vigorously engage with international institutions and take a lead in trying to strengthen them. Both candidate Obama's campaign statements in 2008 and his own writings expressed a desire for robust, effective international institutions that reflected the current distribution of power and could address contemporary threats and challenges.

Upon coming to office, President Obama did not share his two predecessors' initial ambivalence or hostility to the Security Council. Indeed, the administration not only desired a Security Council that could say yes, but sought to conduct its foreign policy with the benefit of international legality and the legitimacy derived from strong multilateral and collective agreement on threats and responses. By appointing Susan Rice, a close confidant who shared Obama's worldview, as his ambassador to the UN and as a member of the cabinet, Obama ensured that the Security Council would play an unprecedented role in US foreign policy.

The administration sought nothing less than a change in how foreign policy was conducted. The Security Council was not to be an afterthought or a box to be checked. It was supposed to be a positive instrument in the service of US foreign policy. America's bilateral relations were to be harnessed to elicit action at the Security Council. Given that in most administrations the Council is only occasionally important to the pursuit of major policy aims, this proved more difficult to the administration than it imagined at the start. As one US National Security Council (NSC) staffer opined to me early on, "We don't have the muscle memory for working through the Security Council."

The task then was to see the Council as an integral part of foreign policy, and to figure out how bilateral diplomacy in capitals can get Security Council action. This was not universally popular with many regional bureaus at the State Department and embassies, who felt that too much of their time was spent trying to win support for multilateral initiatives at the expense of their bilateral account.

Obama's foreign policy, certainly in the first two years, was reactive and crisis-driven, focused primarily on Iraq, Iran, and Afghanistan. One early exception was its "reset" with Russia, to a large degree motivated by the desire to get Russian support for tougher sanctions against Iran in the Council. Administration rhetoric expressed a desire for US foreign policy to engage China, and for the emerging powers of India, Brazil, South Africa, Indonesia, and others to generate greater international cooperation against transnational threats. This desire to engage the emerging powers and make them reliable, responsible international partners, and the administration's inability to rise above day-to-day firefighting in hotspots such as South Asia and the greater Middle East, provide the larger context for understanding the administration's views on the UN Security Council.

Despite President Obama's past rhetoric, his administration showed little interest in reforming the Council. Indeed, it would be more accurate to say that because the administration was so focused on crises, it actually feared that attempts to reform or transform the Council would detract time, attention, and resources from where they were most needed—the here and now. This was certainly the case with Security Council expansion. As one State Department official told me, "The antagonism and polarization are not worth it when we are working hard on current sensitive issues."

There was begrudging acceptance by some in the administration that the Security Council should better reflect the world as it is today, and that there would be value in having new major powers on the Council, but only if they were willing to contribute to the Council's mission of maintaining peace and security in a manner commensurate with their new position. But among the most skeptical and resistant to engaging on the issue were diplomats at the US mission to the UN, who judged that the result of any expansion would be a dilution of US power on the Council, and a diminishment in the body's effectiveness and efficiency. Indeed, many within the administration were unhappy with the behavior of Brazil and Turkey (and to a lesser degree Nigeria) on the Security Council in 2010, and felt that if this was a preview of giving emerging powers greater say on the Council, then they wanted no part. One person on the NSC confided to me that "the current Council is not making for a good forward looking experience."

The Obama administration's use of the Council to pursue key policy goals paid off on several key issues. The Council achieved unprecedented unity on Iran and the need to bring it back into standing within the nonproliferation treaty, and few would have predicted the level of agreement achieved on sanctions within the Council. The Council continued its activism on Africa, deploying new missions to war-torn countries, bolstering existing missions, and innovating with more forceful deployments. The most surprising Security Council resolutions invoked the Responsibility to Protect in justifying use of force in Libya and Côte d'Ivoire. While the latter mostly went unnoticed, the former brought to the fore old tensions around the United States seeking forceful action from the Council. Having won a resolution to use force to protect civilians, the United States immediately came under criticism for seeking regime change in Libya—a charge supported by Obama's own remarks within hours of the resolution that "Qaddafi must go."

Nonetheless, it is important to understand that Obama's foreign policy was not enthusiastic about military intervention.[13] His overwhelming priority in his first term was to end US engagement in wars in Iraq and Afghanistan. On Libya, the administration was fearful of incremental military involvement, and therefore it insisted on a tougher, more comprehensive mandate on Libya than what was on offer from its allies. Moreover, the administration succeeded in limiting its military liability in the intervention.

This context is important for understanding US diplomacy in the Council over Syria. Forceful intervention by the Council was a nonstarter, because Russia and China decided to veto even resolutions that contained no enforcement measures. But in a strange way an intransigent Council was useful to the administration. Obama's advisers were divided among themselves on their goals, strategy, and tactics. It was easy for the United States to rail against Council timidity toward Syria, but a Council eager to act would have essentially called a US bluff. What the Council offered the administration was a potential diplomatic route to containing the conflict. While it is easy today to dismiss the possibility of a negotiated settlement of the war, the first mediation by former UN Secretary-General Kofi Annan yielded a US and Russian approved communiqué in July 2012 that, had it been energetically seized upon by both the United States and Russia, could have put Syria on a path to transition—a path that two years later would still be blocked. Whether because of election-year politics in the United States, a basic lack of trust between US and Russian diplomats, Russian "buyer's remorse" at the prospect of an uncertain process that might oust Bashar al-Assad, or all of the above, the United States and Russia immediately walked away from the communiqué amid mutual recriminations.

The administration's doggedness and success of working the Council in the first term makes its biggest foreign policy debacle that much more puzzling: its handling of allegations of chemical weapon use by the Assad regime in Syria in August 2013. Perhaps because it was at a time of transition between Ambassadors Rice and Powers, or perhaps because the president's rhetorical "red line" on the use of chemical weapons made a year earlier drove policy, the administration jumped too quickly to a threat of unilateral force. While the administration knew that Russia would veto any Council resolution to use force against Assad, it did little to shape an agenda and debate that could have legitimized a coercive response. Instead it insisted that it could use force without a Council mandate. The administration seemed stunned when David Cameron, the UK prime minister, lost a motion in Parliament to endorse the use of force against Assad. While French president François Hollande advocated military attacks, much of French and European public opinion was opposed. Overnight the global debate and agenda became what should be done about the United States and its threat of force against Assad, not what should be done about Assad's gassing of his own people.

Several things were striking about the episode. First, by claiming for itself the unilateral right to use force to police international treaties and resolutions, the Obama administration replicated the Clinton administration's tendency to relegate to itself how Council resolutions would be enforced. Second, Obama's quick-draw approach to threatening force while UN inspectors were still on the ground seemed warily reminiscent of the US-Iraq experience of a decade earlier. Third and similarly, the Obama administration seemed to think that its own evidence was sufficiently trustworthy and robust to trump whatever the UN inspectors would find. This despite a global erosion in trust in the United States, and in the wake of the Edward

Snowden leaks about surveillance of allied leaders and citizens. Fourth, the administration largely sought solace in referring to the legitimacy of the use of force as opposed to its legality—a practice usually followed by those who want to mask that their legal case is weak.

This last point needs elaborating. For most Americans, if asked about the legality of the president using military force, they will likely respond with an answer rooted in domestic law and precedence. They are much more likely to refer to the War Powers Act and the role of Congress in making war legal, than to international law and the Security Council. Even when asked specifically about the role of the Council in authorizing force, the American public are much more reticent than citizens of other countries to believe that one should seek Council approval on going to war. Yet between 2006 and 2010, American opinion on this shifted slightly. In 2004, when asked whether the United States should have Security Council approval before using force, 48 percent of the American public said no, and only 41 percent said yes. In 2011, these numbers shifted, with 45 percent saying yes and 44 percent saying no.[14]

Conclusion

Every US president in the post–Cold War era has desired a Security Council that can say yes. In the 1990s the United States wanted a Council that could say yes, and then worried about a Council that said yes too often—the worry being that if the Council were profligate with peacekeeping missions, then it would be a drag on the US budget. Even the George W. Bush administration, which came to office ideologically skeptical of the Council, tried hard and fudged evidence to get the Council to authorize the president's invasion of Iraq in 2003. But every US president in the post–Cold War era has also sought to act unilaterally in the face of a Council that would say no or did say no. Only President Obama, when facing a Council that would say no to use force to punish Syria for use of chemical weapons, pulled back from the unilateral use of force, and that stemmed as much from domestic opposition as from international opposition.

The Security Council has become a more interesting and active institution in the past twenty-five years because power in the international system has changed, with profound implications for US foreign policy and international institutions that require US engagement to be effective. Within a decade of the end of the Cold War, unipolarity and US dominance went from something to cheer to something to fear. The Council went from embrace of US power in the early 1990s to outright opposition in 2003, to intermittent cooperation and conflict today.

With unipolarity came a United States freed to pursue a more value-driven foreign policy. The promotion of democratic values has been part of every US president's agenda in the post–Cold War era, and US foreign policy has been much more activist in advocating military force as a response to humanitarian tragedy. The Council has often acceded to this agenda. In the past twenty-five years, the Council has approved over sixty peacekeeping operations, usually in the service of ending civil war, and usually featuring elections as part of a peace process.

It is striking then how much the Council has moved away from its founding in realist principles of sovereignty and noninterference, and embraced a broader humanitarian agenda on peace and security. But as long as it is a Council with permanent members who have a veto, it will always be a Council that, on occasion, will say no to US initiatives. When the Council says no now, it is largely for two reasons. The first is the traditional reason for saying no—because an initiative threatens perceived vital interests of one of the five permanent members. The second is for prudential reasons, when the Council believes that the use of force will be much more unpredictable and dangerous than the United States believes, as in Iraq in 2003. The biggest failure of US foreign policy in 2003 was not that the United States didn't get Council approval for its war in Iraq, for it also did not get approval from some of its closest allies. Its biggest failure was its decision to go to war.

There is a theory that governments seek Security Council authorization to go to war not for the legitimacy of a Council decision, but for the reassurance it gives that war is the right policy.[15] In hindsight the Council's refusal in 2003 looks prescient, and that prescience casts a long shadow that will affect any power that decides to go to war in the absence of a Council resolution. If the war against Iraq had not happened, or if it had turned out differently, it is doubtful that so much popular opposition would have erupted against President Obama's threat of unilateral force against Syria in 2013.

One of the enduring fears of US foreign policy makers is that international law will somehow constrain the United States against its will or interests. This raises the question of whether, in a post–Cold War era of presidents trying to work through the Security Council, valuing a Council that says yes, and seeking that yes when use of force is sought, successive presidents will find themselves prisoners of the expectation that the Council must be part of their foreign policy and that Council resolutions and international law are needed to use force.

Every president can make arguments based on the legitimacy of unilateral action, but legitimacy is not an unlimited well, and indeed a good case can be made that there has been a shift even in American attitudes that legitimacy is inferior to legality. It is plausible that every time the United States decides to eschew the Council, it reduces the future likelihood that the Council will be sympathetic toward future US initiatives, and that Americans will buy arguments based on legitimacy and not the legality of use of force. US allies and their publics are already skeptical of a defense of force based solely on legitimacy. Thus the great unknown: as US administrations continue to work through the Council, and seek a Council that can say yes, will the American public come to expect that even in the use of military force, the United States should obtain Council approval?

But perhaps this might all be moot if, as some fear, we are entering an era of confrontation between the United States and Russia. Some might believe that in the aftermath of Russia's military seizure and annexation of Crimea in March 2014, we will return to a Council that can only say no. But if, as suggested here, the distribution of international power determines Council dynamics, this seems unlikely. Russia's invasion of Ukraine does not change the structure of power in the international system. Unlike the Soviet Union, which was patron to clients throughout the world, Russia exerts little global influence. It still has vital interests and will use the Council to protect them. But this does not mean a return to the pre-1990 Council. The test will be whether the Council can continue to act on Africa, can continue to authorize and adequately fund peacekeeping, and can continue to forge consensus, even at what appears a glacial pace, on tough cases such as Iran.

Notes

1. WikiLeaks, "Secret US Embassy Cables," https://wikileaks.org/cablegate.html.

2. Mark Mazower, *Governing the World: The History of an Idea* (New York: Penguin, 2012), pp. 214–215.

3. Quoted in Stephen C. Schlesinger, *Act of Creation: The Founding of the United Nations* (Boulder, CO: Westview, 2003), p. 292.

4. Gareth Evans, *Co-operating for Peace: The Global Agenda for the 1990s and Beyond* (St. Leonard's, Australia: Allen and Unwin, 1993), p. 21.

5. All data on Security Council resolutions here and in subsequent paragraphs can be found at www.globalpolicy.org/component/content/article/102/40069.html.

6. Thomas M. Franck and Edward Weisband, *Word Politics: Verbal Strategy Among the Superpowers* (New York: Oxford University Press, 1971).

7. Andrew Bennett, Joseph Lepgold, and Danny Unger, "Burden-Sharing in the Persian Gulf War," *International Organization* 48, no. 1 (1994): 39–75.

8. David M. Malone, *The International Struggle over Iraq: Politics in the UN Security Council, 1980–2005* (Oxford: Oxford University Press, 2006).

9. Bill Clinton, "Remarks to the 48th Session of the United Nations General Assembly," September 27, 1993, www.state.gov/p/io/potusunga/207375.htm.

10. Jared Cohen, *One Hundred Days of Silence: America and the Rwanda Genocide* (Lanham: Rowman and Littlefield, 2007), pp. 82–85.

11. Independent International Commission on Kosovo, *The Kosovo Report: Conflict, International Response, Lessons Learned* (New York: Oxford University Press, 2000).

12. John Bolton, *Surrender Is Not an Option* (New York: Threshold, 2007).

13. Bruce Jones, "Libya and the Responsibilities of Power," *Survival* 53, no. 3 (2011): 51–60.

14. The 2004 figures are from Andrew Kohut and Bruce Stokes, *America Against the World* (New York: Times Books, 2006); the 2011 figures are from Bruce Stokes and Pew Research Center, "UN Approval Before Using Military Force Lacks Widespread Global Agreement," August 2013, www.pewresearch.org/fact-tank /2013/08/30/un-approval-before-using-military-force-lacks-widespread-global -agreement.

15. Erik Voeten, "The Political Origins of the UN Security Council's Ability to Legitimize the Use of Force," *International Organization* 59, no. 3 (2005): 527–557.

3.1

Commentary:
The Permanent One's Search
for Maximum Flexibility

David Bosco

IN THE WANING DAYS OF WORLD WAR II, THE UNITED STATES helped design a UN Security Council with remarkable power and authority. Forty-five years later, after Iraq's invasion of Kuwait, the United States was decisive in reviving the Council from its Cold War slumber. Since then, the United States, often dubbed "the permanent one," has championed several important expansions of Council power and authority. Yet the central role of the United States in creating a powerful Council is only one part of the story. Viewed more broadly, US policy toward the Council and its authority has often been opportunistic and instrumental. I argue in this chapter that the US approach can be best explained as the pursuit of maximum diplomatic flexibility. Particularly since 1990, the Council has been a valuable diplomatic tool for the United States. Yet even as successive US administrations have advanced an array of innovative Council tools and strategies, they have worked to ensure that the Council remains an instrument of US power rather than a restraint on it.

Expansion of the Council's Powers

Since 1990 the United States has frequently sought to expand the Council's powers and solidify its authority, particularly regarding internal conflicts. Shortly after the successful Gulf War, the George H. W. Bush administration sought Council approval for several interventions that dealt with primarily civil conflicts, including Iraqi repression of its Kurdish and Shiite populations, mass starvation in Somalia, and political discord in Haiti. As Frederick Rawski and Nathan Miller have argued, "the United States was the driving force behind the authorization of intervention in Somalia in 1992 and Haiti in 1994, identifying humanitarian crises and disruptions to democracy, respectively, as threats to international peace and security—a radical redefinition of the concept."[1] This assertive push by the Council into internal affairs had substantial support from other Western Council members, but US leadership was critical.

Around the same time, the United States engineered one of the more ambitious innovations in the Council's history. In response to atrocities in the Balkans, Washington urged the Council to create an international criminal justice mechanism to investigate and prosecute crimes committed on the territory of the former Yugoslavia. The idea of the Council creating a court met with considerable skepticism, including from some of Washington's closest allies on the Council. But US support for the idea prevailed. According to a former aide, then–UN ambassador Madeleine Albright "drove the Security Council toward approval" of the plan.[2] Soon thereafter, and also with US leadership, the Council used the same approach to create a court with a mandate to investigate atrocities committed in Rwanda.[3] These ad hoc tribunals created the important precedent of the Council, on its own, adding to the world's multilateral architecture. The UN Charter makes clear that the Council may create subsidiary bodies, but few had anticipated that this authority would be construed so broadly.

In the aftermath of the terrorist attacks of September 11, 2001, the United States organized another significant expansion of Council power, this time by directing states to adopt certain domestic legislation. The Bush administration, as it sought to craft an international response to global terrorism, drafted a resolution (1373) requiring all states to, among other things, prevent the flow of funds to terrorist organizations, enhance legislation, strengthen border controls, coordinate executive machinery, and increase international cooperation in combating terrorism. Three years later, again at the behest of the United States, the Council required all member states to enact domestic legislation to curtail the transfer of weapons of mass destruction to nonstate actors.[4] In both cases, the Council established reporting requirements for all states to demonstrate compliance. Those unprecedented mandates—never before had the Council required all states to create national legislation—generated concern that the Council was seriously overstepping its authority. A number of observers noted that the Council's post-9/11 actions—driven by the United States—had propelled the body from its traditional role as guardian of international peace and security into a function as a global legislator.[5]

This level of US innovation and energy at the Council was not inevitable. At distinct moments, US policymakers have made the conscious decision to employ the Council rather than other, more ad hoc mechanisms. The record since 1990 suggests that even US administrations that are ideologically skeptical of the United Nations have seen little danger—and significant advantage—in expansions of the Council's powers. As former State Department legal adviser Michael Matheson has argued, "because the United States can prevent any adverse action by the Council, there is much less reason to fear that resort to the Council would create legal precedents for future action against U.S. interests."[6]

The extraordinary privilege of the veto power also means that the United States has little interest in undermining the Council's unique place within the international architecture. There has been occasional discussion, particularly among US conservatives, of bypassing the United Nations by seeking to promote a "league of democracies," perhaps based around NATO. During his 2008 presidential bid, Senator John McCain argued that such a league would allow a likeminded concert of nations to act when the United Nations could not, and he explicitly framed the initiative as a way of avoiding Russian and Chinese opposition.[7] Other conservatives, notably Richard Perle, have gone further, arguing that the United States should seek the UN's marginalization and assertively challenge the Council's legitimizing function. The Bill Clinton administration's reliance on NATO rather than UN authorization during the 1999 Kosovo conflict raised the prospect that Washington might seek to develop a legal doctrine of humanitarian intervention without Council approval. But Washington has ultimately realized that preserving the Council's formal preeminence is in its interests. Even during its moments of most intense frustration with the body, such as in the run-up to the 2003 Iraq War, Washington has continued its broad support for the Council's work, and after the Iraq conflict quickly sought to reengage the body.

The Council à la Carte

Unsurprisingly, US innovation in developing the Council's tools and its determination to preserve the Council's unique place has not, however, resulted in a policy of employing the Council consistently. Instead, US support for an active Council role in managing crises varies widely depending on the political and strategic context, domestic political considerations, and the expected voting dynamics on the Council itself. The United States has also resisted any restrictions, even informal ones, on the use of the veto power.

In several areas close to its interests, the United States has actively sought to limit the Council's role. This tendency is perhaps most pronounced on the Israel-Palestine dispute. All recent US administrations have opposed the Council assuming a more prominent role in this area. US opposition to a Council role is not surprising given the scant support its positions have received, even among traditionally supportive Council members. Given this reality, the nearly constant US position has been that significant Council involvement on Palestine is not productive and that direct negotiations between the parties are the key to a solution. For the most part, the United States has assumed a defensive posture when Israel-Palestine issues have come before the Council. Using its veto if necessary, Washington has typically fended off resolutions it deems hostile to Israel, without seeking to involve the Council substantively in the peace process. Following that established pattern, the Obama administration made clear its willingness to veto a Palestinian bid for full membership in the organization.[8]

That veto power is, of course, the ultimate method for preventing the Council from acting in ways that Washington opposes. Since 1989, the United States has used the veto power more frequently than any other P5 member. Recent administrations have used the veto power more sparingly, and almost exclusively on draft resolutions related to the Israel-Palestine conflict. The United States has also deployed its power to block Council action in situations that do not count as formal uses of the veto. Perhaps the most sustained exercise of this unilateral blocking power came during the Clinton administration, when Madeleine Albright repeatedly, and unilaterally, blocked the reappointment of Boutros Boutros-Ghali as Secretary-General in 1996.

Along with other P5 members, the United States has defended the veto and insisted that any reforms to the Council not alter it. When Switzerland and other members of the Small Five (S5) group attempted to create guidelines for Council behavior, including the use of the veto, the United States reacted sharply. As part of a document submitted as a General Assembly resolution in March 2012, the S5 recommended that P5 members "explain . . . the reasons for resorting to a veto or declaring its intention to do so."[9] Under strong pressure from the United States and other P5 members, the S5 ultimately withdrew the resolution. The Swiss ambassador was reportedly told by P5 members that the Council's procedure "is the sole and exclusive domain of the Security Council."[10] Washington also kept its distance from a 2013 French initiative designed to discourage Council members from using the veto in situations of mass atrocity. While the United States has been highly critical of Russian and Chinese vetoes in the context of Syria, it has been cautious about endorsing any broad restrictions—even nonbinding ones—on how P5 members employ the veto.[11]

"We Are Prepared to Act Alone"

Even as it has expressed its determination to maintain the veto power, the United States has insisted that the absence of Council backing for US policies is not itself a restriction on US freedom of action. The United States has consistently maintained that the Council's role in legitimizing the use of force does not restrict US military action. All recent US strategy documents have articulated the right of the United States to unilaterally defend its vital interests—and not just its territory. The Clinton administration's National Security Strategy declared: "If our most important national interests are at stake, we are prepared to act alone."[12] The George W. Bush administration stated it would "not hesitate to act alone, if necessary, to exercise our right of self-defense by acting preemptively."[13] In the wake of the costly and controversial Iraq War, the Obama administration came closest to acknowledging restrictions on US freedom of action. Its strategy document provided that "the United States must reserve the right to act unilaterally if necessary to defend our nation and our interests, yet we will also seek to adhere to standards that govern the use of force."[14] The document left unclear whether those "standards" referred solely to law governing conduct during hostilities or whether they included Council approval. During Senate confirmation hearings, UN ambassador-designee Samantha Power returned to a more traditional formulation that clarified the US position: "There's no question that internationally, a Security Council authorization is helpful. But from the standpoint of American interests, it is U.S. national security interests and the needs of the American people that are paramount."[15] For all the differences in tone toward the United Nations, the Obama administration has ended up where previous administrations have in terms of the US military's freedom of action.

This approach on the use of force has been evident in the way in which Washington has approached its counterterror operations. Since the 9/11 attacks, US administrations have kept Council involvement to a minimum on matters related to US military operations against Islamic extremists. In the immediate aftermath of the 9/11 attacks, the United States sought and received recognition from the Council of its right to operate in self-defense.[16] Since then, Washington has kept the Council at arm's length regarding these operations. The United States has not sought Council approval for its drone strikes in Pakistan, Yemen, and other countries. It did not seek approval for the cross-border raid into Pakistan that killed Osama bin Laden or even notify the Council of its action after the fact. Instead, the United States has sought to situate these activities as a continuing exercise in self-defense that does not require Council involvement.

The United States and Council Reform

The perennial issue of Security Council reform has offered the United States an opportunity to help reshape the Council's membership to reflect the new power realities of the world. US leaders have consistently chosen not to engage actively in this effort. Instead, the United States has made clear through its actions that it is content with the glacial pace of negotiations.

Since the early 1970s, the United States has expressed broad support for expanding Council membership to certain states while insisting that any reform must leave the veto power untouched. The United States has also supported the candidacy of certain members for new permanent seats. In June 1993, the Clinton administration voiced support for Japanese and German membership.[17] The George W. Bush administration backed only Japan's candidacy. While continuing to support Tokyo, President Obama also spoke out in favor of a permanent Council seat for India.[18]

Yet no US administration has sought to advance the process. US officials have often bypassed Council reform when listing their reform priorities for the UN and have repeatedly expressed concern that expansion might render the Council less effective.[19] This approach has been largely consistent across administrations. As Kara McDonald and Stewart Patrick have noted, the Obama administration has offered only small tweaks to the position of previous administrations, including its India endorsement and its stated intention not to link Council reform with other UN reform issues.[20] (Washington's lack of emphasis on Council expansion is not unique among the P5, with Russia and China at least equally keen to keep membership limited.)

Conclusion

The record of the past two decades suggests that the United States has been remarkably innovative in expanding the Council's powers while also insisting on certain sharp limits to the Council's international role and adopting a very conservative approach regarding the veto and Council reform. In effect, Washington has sought to expand Council authority without giving any substantial ground on central questions regarding control of the body. A key question for the broader UN membership is whether this state of affairs is acceptable. Some diplomatic rhetoric suggests mounting frustration with the Council's structure and performance. Saudi Arabia described its unprecedented decision in late 2013 to decline a Council seat for which it had been elected as a form of protest at the Council's dysfunction. Other states, notably the Small Five, have expressed frustration in other ways. If this dissatisfaction with the Council somehow coalesces, it might force the United States to alter course. Until that moment, however, Washington's maximum-flexibility approach to the Council will continue.

Notes

1. Frederick Rawski and Nathan Miller, "The United States in the Security Council: A Faustian Bargain?" in *The UN Security Council: From the Cold War to the 21st Century,* edited by David M. Malone (Boulder, CO: Lynne Rienner, 2004), p. 359.

2. David Scheffer, *All the Missing Souls: A Personal History of the War Crimes Tribunals* (Princeton: Princeton University Press 2012), p. 22.

3. See United Nations Security Council Resolution 955, S/RES/1540 (November 8, 1994).

4. See United Nations Security Council Resolution 1540, S/RES/1540 (April 28, 2004).

5. See, for example, Paul C. Szasz, "The Security Council Starts Legislating," *American Journal of International Law* 96, no. 4 (2002): 901–905.

6. Michael J. Matheson, *Council Unbound: The Growth of UN Decision Making on Conflict and Post-Conflict Issues After the Cold War* (Washington, DC: US Institute of Peace, 2006), p. 239.

7. See Liz Sidoti, "McCain Favors a League of Democracies," *Washington Post,* April 30, 2007.

8. See, for example, James Hider and Roger Boyes, "Palestinians on Collision Course with US over Statehood Bid," *The Times,* September 15, 2011.

9. United Nations General Assembly, "Enhancing the Accountability, Transparency, and Effectiveness of the Security Council," UN Doc. A/66/L.42/Rev.2, May 15, 2012, www.un.org/Docs/journal/asp/ws.asp?m=A/66/L.42/Rev.2.

10. Rita Emch, "Swiss Withdraw UN Draft Resolution," *SWI,* May 18, 2012, www.swissinfo.ch/eng/swiss-withdraw-un-draft-resolution/32719648.

11. For an analysis of Council dynamics on proposals for restraining the use of the veto power, see United Nations Association of the United Kingdom, "UN Security Council and the Responsibility to Protect: Voluntary Restraint of the Veto in Situations of Mass Atrocity," London, 2014, www.una.org.uk/sites/default/files/Briefing%20-%20Veto%20code%20of%20conduct_0.pdf.

12. Bill Clinton, "A National Security Strategy of Engagement and Enlargement" (Washington, DC: White House, July 1994), p. i, http://nssarchive.us/NSSR/1994.pdf.

13. George W. Bush, "The National Security Strategy of the United States of America" (Washington, DC: White House, September 2002), p. 6, http://nssarchive.us/NSSR/2002.pdf.

14. Barack Obama, "National Security Strategy" (Washington, DC: White House, May 2010), p. 22, http://nssarchive.us/NSSR/2010.pdf.

15. US Senate Committee on Foreign Relations, "Hearing on the Nomination of Samantha Power," July 17, 2013, www.foreign.senate.gov/hearings/2013/07/17/nomination-1.

16. See United Nations Security Council Resolution 1368 (September 12, 2001), UN Doc. S/RES/1368, which condemned the attacks and recognized the "inherent right of self-defense."

17. Julia Preston, "U.S. Seeks to Expand U.N. Security Council; Permanent Seats for Germany, Japan Face French, British Opposition," *Washington Post,* June 10, 1993, p. 1.

18. White House Office of the Press Secretary, "Remarks by President Obama to the Joint Session of the Indian Parliament," New Delhi, November 8, 2010, www.whitehouse.gov/the-press-office/2010/11/08/remarks-president-joint-session-indian-parliament-new-delhi-india.

19. R. Nicholas Burns, "On United Nations Reform," testimony before the Senate Foreign Relations Committee, Washington, DC, July 21, 2005, http://2001-2009.state.gov/p/us/rm/2005/49900.htm.

20. Kara C. McDonald and Stewart Patrick, *UN Security Council Enlargement and US Interests,* Special Report no. 59 (New York: Council on Foreign Relations, December 2010).

4

China in the Security Council

Zhu Wenqi and Leng Xinyu

CHINA IS THE ONLY ASIAN PERMANENT MEMBER OF THE SECU-
rity Council and the only member loosely defined as a developing country.
In 1971 the People's Republic of China, with Beijing as its capital,
replaced the Republic of China. At the time, the country was at grips with
the Cultural Revolution and hardly engaged in international relations.
Since 1971, China has progressed from a near-rejectionist stance within
the Council, which took the form of unwillingness to participate in many
processes, including, initially, some votes, to that of a world power participating actively in the Council's life, where China's representatives,
although disinclined to take the lead on either contemporary security
crises or the thematic discussions among member states, today are fluent
and influential.

We begin this chapter with a brief sketch of the normative foundations
of Chinese foreign policy and the central importance accorded to the principle of state sovereignty and nonintervention. We then assess Beijing's
evolving role in the Security Council over the past four decades. We trace
the PRC's changing attitude toward the UN, from a stance of passive
resistance in the 1970s toward an increasingly participatory and constructive engagement in the 1990s, when it did not let its attachment to sovereignty and nonintervention stand in the way of the emergence of an
activist Council whose core business became crisis management in internal
conflicts. We then analyze China's Council diplomacy over the past two
decades in the specific areas of peacemaking, peacekeeping, counterterrorism, nuclear nonproliferation, as well as human rights crises and the
Responsibility to Protect.

An analysis of China's decisionmaking in the Council shows the growing importance of the Security Council in its foreign policy and Beijing's increasing investment in Council-mandated operations, most notably in the area of peacekeeping, where it has become an important troop contributor. Analysis also suggests that, over the past decade, China has become increasingly assertive in the Council—casting six vetoes in the Council between 2007 and 2014. We challenge overly simplistic characterizations of China's Council diplomacy as primarily driven by either principle or economic interests. Instead, we paint a more subtle picture of a China that is often struggling to reconcile strongly held principles with international relationships and manifold—sometimes conflicting—interests that have grown and become more complex as the country has emerged as a major global economic and political power.

Principles Underpinning Chinese Foreign Policy

Since its founding in 1949, the People's Republic has considered state sovereignty to be the most sacrosanct principle of international law—a natural consequence of the country's long history of vulnerability to interference by foreign powers. In addition to mutual respect for sovereignty and territorial integrity, Chinese premier Zhou Enlai advanced the principles of mutual nonaggression, noninterference in internal affairs, equality and mutual benefit, and peaceful coexistence as the foundation of Chinese foreign relations. These so-called Five Principles of Peaceful Coexistence[1] would serve as an enduring normative underpinning of Beijing's foreign policy.

The coexistence principles would also have influence beyond China's own internal decisionmaking processes. Most significant, third world leaders wove them into the declaration of the 1955 Asian-African Conference in Bandung, laying the basis for the later establishment of the Non-Aligned Movement (NAM), which China staunchly supported during the Cold War and beyond.[2]

Two decades later, the Five Principles figured prominently in Vice Premier Deng Xiaoping's 1974 address to the UN General Assembly, during which he elaborated upon Mao Zedong's theory of the three worlds.[3] Deng affirmed China's solidarity with the third world[4] and its unequivocal rejection of hegemony, asserting that "the Chinese Government and people firmly support all oppressed peoples and oppressed nations in their struggle to win or defend national independence, develop the national economy and oppose colonialism, imperialism and hegemonism."[5]

Sixty years after the PRC's founding, the fundamentals of Chinese foreign policy reflect remarkable continuity, as apparent in the Information Office of the State Council's September 2011 white paper, *China's Peaceful Development,* which reaffirms the Five Principles and lists as China's "core interests": "state sovereignty, national security, territorial integrity, and national reunification; China's political system established by the Constitution and overall social stability; and the basic safeguards for ensuring sustainable economic and social development."[6]

While the principles and fundamental goals of Chinese foreign policy remained constant, strategies to achieve them have evolved. Throughout the Cold War and during the early 1990s, China displayed much skepticism vis-à-vis international organizations as tools of the powerful, and limited its participation in multilateral institutions, including the UN Security Council. Since the mid-1990s, however, the United Nations has played a growing role in Chinese foreign policy thinking. China came to appreciate the fact that the UN Charter is based on the same principles as its own foreign policy. Its ideological affinity with NAM countries would ensure that China would find itself generally in the voting majority in the General Assembly. More important, Beijing, often echoing positions adopted by Russia and France, came to value the Security Council, and its own position therein as a permanent member, as an institutional expression of "multipolarity," oft-invoked by Chinese leaders signifying their growing concern with the dominance of the United States in world affairs after the end of the Cold War.[7] Council membership was one venue through which China could attempt to counterbalance the unfettered power of the United States. Finally, China grew attached to the veto (and the threat thereof) as a key instrument in the defense of vital foreign policy objectives, in particular with respect to Taiwan and Tibet. Accordingly, foreign policy concepts advanced by China's leaders since the late 1990s, from the "new security" concept first proposed by Foreign Minister Qian Qichen in 1997 and later elaborated by President Jiang Zemin, to the "harmonious world" concept put forward by President Hu Jintao, advance the idea of effective multilateralism with a central role for the United Nations.[8]

It should therefore not come as a surprise that US China scholar David Shambaugh notes that "interestingly, the Chinese government and scholars have become some of the world's strongest advocates of the United Nations."[9] This is also reflected in the "marked improvement," over the past decades, of the quality of diplomats Beijing sends to New York, who tend to be widely praised for their professionalism.[10]

Reflecting a gradual departure from Deng Xiaoping's maxim enunciated in the early 1990s that "China should maintain a low profile and never take the lead," China's evolving foreign policy doctrine also indicates China's intention to assume more international responsibility commensurate with its increasing weight in global politics. The following section examines China's growing engagement with the UN Security Council and use of the veto in the post–Cold War period though the lens of its national interests.

China's Changing Engagement with the Council

The Early Years

The People's Republic of China has shifted from an excluded actor in the world's global collective security body to one that is increasingly prominent. The slow transformation of the PRC's engagement is an outcome not only of shifting international alignments but also of developments within China that have altered its relative position within the world system.

During the Cold War, Western powers initially precluded the PRC from assuming the Chinese seat on the Security Council. As part of its containment policy, the United States refused to recognize the People's Republic as China's legitimate government, instead providing steadfast support to the Taiwan-based Republic of China (ROC). Despite objections from the Soviet Union, the ROC remained China's representative at the UN for more than two decades after its expulsion from the mainland by the People's Liberation Army (PLA).[11]

By 1970, however, the United States found it increasingly difficult to isolate China and was preparing a strategic rapprochement with Beijing. Decolonization gave birth to newly independent states that quickly sought membership in the United Nations; indeed, the number of UN member states more than doubled as European empires gave way to national liberation movements. The UN General Assembly's growing third world majority finally pushed through Resolution 2758 in 1971, which expelled the ROC and transferred its UN seat to the People's Republic.

Upon entry into the UN, China began to challenge the existing UN system and denounced it throughout most of the 1970s. Yet despite its radical rhetoric, and in light of its relatively weak position in the international system at the time, Beijing adopted a very passive stance in the Security Council, often declining to participate in debates, mostly abstaining in voting when it chose to participate, and making sparse use of the veto. Indeed, among the permanent five members, China has exercised the veto power the least frequently by a large margin—only twice during the Cold War (both times in 1972) and a mere eight times since 1990, as depicted in Table 4.1.

Beijing's restraint during that period may be explained by China's "inexperience and the need to watch and learn how the institution worked" as well as by the fact that few of its economic or political interests were affected by Council decisions.[12] Instead, the PRC preferred to "use its rhetorical power to support the NAM . . . and to use the UN as a conduit through which to forge formal diplomatic ties with states." The PRC seems to have been rather effective in this aim, as almost sixty countries changed their recognition from Taipei to Beijing during the 1970s.[13]

During the 1980s, China continued its passive stance but developed a more positive attitude toward the UN, reflecting the ascent of reformist leaders in Beijing around Deng Xiaoping in the late 1970s whose historic decision to pursue "reform and opening-up" led to significant moderniza-tion and integration of China into the international system. China also muted its pro-NAM rhetoric and criticism of superpower hegemony, while increasing its participation in voting as part of Deng's "independent foreign policy of peace." In that decade, China's voting affinity with the United States increased by almost 30 percent.

The First Post–Cold War Decade

China's progressive integration into the international institutional order, its growing realization of the benefits of such integration, and the possible effects of its multilateral socialization became increasingly visible at the end of the Cold War, when China did not stand in the way of the emergence of a more activist Security Council and despite its principled objections of a Western-backed expansion of the Security Council's interpretation of what falls within the scope of "threats to international security."

An early indication of China's constructive attitude came when China voted in favor of all eleven resolutions concerning the Iraq-Kuwait conflict and abstained on Resolution 678, which authorized the allies to "use all necessary means" against Iraqi forces to restore peace and security.[14] (In explaining China's abstention, Minister Qian Qichen argued that the resort to military action might have a negative impact on world peace and security in the long term and upon Iraq's neighboring states in the short term.)

Displaying remarkable pragmatism and flexibility, China often chose to abstain on a considerable number of draft resolutions that clashed with its strict interpretation of sovereignty and nonintervention and mandated coer-cive action in response to a number of situations that had been previously considered as falling within of internal affairs of a state.[15] China thus went along with Security Council decisions to use force to respond to the human-itarian disaster in Somalia in 1992–1993, to mandate coercive measures including sanctions and eventually to restore a democratically elected gov-ernment in Haiti in 1993–1994, and to protect safe areas in Bosnia and Herzegovina in 1993. In most of these cases, China did not receive imme-diate compensation for its laissez-faire approach in the Council.

China, despite its aversion to sanctions, rooted in lingering resentments over having itself been a target of such measures in the 1950s as well as following the 1989 Tiananmen incident, went along with the establishment of twelve separate sanctions regimes throughout the 1990s, the majority of them in response to situations of internal conflict, as in the former Yugoslavia, Somalia, Cambodia, Liberia, Haiti, Angola, Rwanda, and Sierra Leone.

Beijing also supported one of the most remarkable expansions of the Council's authority, namely the mandating of two ad hoc tribunals to try the

Table 4.1 China's Vetoes in the Security Council, 1972–2014

	Issue Discussed	Stated Reasons	Other P5 Negative Votes
August 8, 1972	UN membership of Bangladesh	Bangladesh in violation of UN resolutions[a]	None
September 10, 1972	Israel's invasion of Syria and Lebanon	Draft "failed to condemn" Israel "for aggressive acts" against Syria and Lebanon[b]	Soviet Union
January 10, 1997	UN military observers to Guatemala	Guatemalan government invited Taiwan Authority to signing ceremony of peace agreement[c]	None
February 25, 1999	UN peacekeeping mission in Macedonia	UNPREDEP accomplished its mandate[d]	None
January 12, 2007	Sanctions on Myanmar	Myanmar issue is mainly the internal affair of a sovereign state and does not constitute a threat to international or regional peace and security[e]	Russian Federation
July 11, 2008	Sanctions on Zimbabwe	Imposing sanctions would adversely affect the negotiating process[f]	Russian Federation
October 4, 2011	Syrian situation	Draft resolution violated principle of noninterference; threat of sanctions risks exacerbating conflict	Russian Federation
February 4, 2012	Syrian situation	Draft resolution placed "undue emphasis" on pressuring the Syrian government	Russian Federation
July 19, 2012	Syrian situation	Draft resolution counterproductive; puts pressure on only one party, which would derail a political settlement and thus threaten regional stability[g]	Russian Federation

continues

Issue Discussed	Stated Reasons	Other P5 Negative Votes
Syrian situation	International Criminal Court (ICC) referral undermines trust among conflict parties as well as peace negotiations and violates Syria's judicial sovereignty and the principle of complementarity.	Russian Federation
May 22, 2014		

Notes: a. According to Joel Wuthnow, China attempted to assist its ally Pakistan in using Bangladesh's independence as a bargaining chip for its prisoners in India. See Joel Wuthnow, "Beyond the Veto: Chinese Diplomacy at the UN," PhD thesis, Columbia University, 2011, p. 32.
b. Ibid.
c. United Nations Security Council, "Provisional Verbatim Record of the 3730th Meeting," S/PV.3730, January 10, 1997 (statement of China's Ambassador Qin Huasun, p. 20).
d. United Nations Security Council, "Provisional Verbatim Record of the 3982nd Meeting," S/PV.3982, February 25, 1999 (statement of China's Ambassador Qin Huasun, pp. 6–7).
e. United Nations Security Council, "Provisional Verbatim Record of the 5619th Meeting," S/PV.5619, January 12, 2007 (statement of China's Ambassador Wang Guangya, p. 3).
f. United Nations Security Council, "Provisional Verbatim Record of the 5933rd Meeting," S/PV.5933, July 11, 2008 (statement of China's Ambassador Wang Guangya, p. 13).
g. United Nations Department of Political Information, "Security Council Fails to Adopt Draft Resolution on Syria That Would Have Threatened Sanctions, Due to Negative Votes of China, Russian Federation," SC/10714, July 19, 2012.

international crimes committed in the civil war in the former Yugoslavia and the Rwandan genocide. Although China questioned the invocation of Chapter VII of the UN Charter as appropriate in establishing the International Criminal Tribunal for the Former Yugoslavia (ICTY) and the International Criminal Tribunal for Rwanda (ICTR),[16] it voted in favor of Resolutions 808 and 827 (setting up the ICTY), and abstained on Resolution 955 (setting up the ICTR), but not without noting that the "special circumstances" of these cases should "not constitute any precedent."[17] China also supported the ICTY's and the ICTR's functioning by dispatching judges and other legal personnel. And while in 1998 China promised to veto the establishment by the Security Council of another ad hoc tribunal in Cambodia because of Phnom Penh's opposition to such a measure, early in the following decade it supported the Secretary-General's request to conclude an agreement with the Sierra Leonean government to establish the Special Court of Sierra Leone (SCSL) and expressed no qualms when Resolution 1688 invoked Chapter VII in its demand for the surrender or transfer of former Liberian president Charles Taylor to that court.[18]

Mats Berdal has observed with respect to China's stance in the context of Security Council action in response to the civil war in Bosnia and Herzegovina—which may also hold true for other cases—that "Chinese voting behavior reflected concerns other than the effect that [its] policies might have had on the course of the conflict and the UN's involvement in it" and instead "was primarily designed, through abstentions rather than vetoes, to register Chinese disquiet with the UN's growing involvement in the internal affairs of member states."[19] Again and again, after the Council adopted enforcement measures in response to humanitarian emergencies or civil conflict, China publicly criticized and disassociated itself from these steps and was at pains to highlight the "unique and exceptional" circumstances of each situation, lest precedent be created. Lacking the leverage to counter Western interventionism, it was still keen to uphold—at least rhetorically—what it saw as the bedrock of international law: nonintervention and the sanctity of sovereignty.

However, on the rare occasions when China saw its own sovereignty and territorial integrity threatened, it did make use of its veto power. It showed a steadfast readiness to sacrifice peacekeeping operations and their host countries' stability when the latter crossed Beijing's nonnegotiable red line: respect for its "One China" policy. In Haiti, in early 1996, China threatened to veto the extension of the UN Mission in Haiti (UNMIH) because of Port-au-Prince's recognition of Taiwan, and only relented under pressure from other Latin American countries and after succeeding in reducing the mission's troop strength to levels widely considered as too low to fulfill its mandate. In 1997, China broke its twenty-six-year avoidance of the veto and barred the extension of the UN Verification Mission in

Guatemala (MINUGUA) because of the Guatemalan government's diplomatic ties to Taiwan and its decision to invite Taiwan's foreign minister to attend the signing of the peace accords a month earlier. However, China allowed the mission's mandate to be renewed a few days later, following Guatemala's commitment to stop supporting moves to put Taiwan's UN's status on the agenda of the General Assembly and a threat by Mexico to resort to the "Uniting for Peace" formula and have the mission mandated by the General Assembly.[20] The "One China" policy was also at the heart of Beijing's February 1999 veto against extending the Macedonian-based UN Preventive Deployment Force (UNPREDEP), which was widely seen as an effective measure to prevent spillover from the unrest in Kosovo into this neighboring country. Unlike Haiti and Guatemala, which had recognized Taiwan in 1956 and 1960 respectively, Macedonia recognized the ROC in January 1999 in return for a lucrative investment deal with Taipei, mistakenly gambling that Beijing would bow to US pressure not to wield the veto.[21] While China was widely criticized for this move, the intended deterrent effect seems to have been effective, as no fragile country has recognized the ROC since.

Peacekeeping
China's involvement in UN peacekeeping may be, as one recent study on China and the United Nations asserted, "the field in which Beijing has moved furthest toward engagement with the organization."[22] Prior to 1981, it refused to even participate in UN Security Council voting on peacekeeping issues or to contribute to the world body's peacekeeping budget.[23] Beijing's stance began to soften during the 1980s, when it started to cast approving votes on the mandating of peace operations,[24] although initially it did not participate in such missions.

This changed in 1989, when China sent twenty military observers to participate in the monitoring of elections in Namibia by the UN Transition Assistance Group (UNTAG). The following year, the People's Liberation Army sent five military observers to join the UN Truce Supervision Organization (UNTSO) in the Middle East. Two years later, it dispatched a 400-strong engineering corps to the UN Transitional Authority in Cambodia (UNTAC), which was the first time that China deployed an organic military unit on a peacekeeping mission.

China's operational involvement in peacekeeping started to grow in 2000, and since 2004 China has ranked consistently among the top twenty troop contributors, contributing between 1,000 and 2,150 men and women—mostly offering engineering, transport, and medical support—deployed under the blue flag.[25] As of June 2014, China was the fourteenth largest troop contributor, with 2,193 police and military personnel serving in UN peacekeeping operations, some 700 more than all its fellow permanent members combined.[26] Eighty percent of those troops were deployed in African countries, roughly equivalent to the ratio of total UN peacekeepers deployed on the continent. In total, by the end of 2012, according to the State Council's Information Office, 22,000 Chinese military personnel had served in twenty-three UN peacekeeping missions.[27] And with an assessed contribution of 6.6 percent of the UN's peacekeeping budget, China is the sixth largest funder of peacekeeping operations.[28] A recent study on China's recent involvement in peacekeeping conducted by the Stockholm International Peace Research Institute (SIPRI) concluded that "Chinese peacekeepers are consistently rated among the most professional, well trained, effective and disciplined in UN peacekeeping operations."[29]

Remarkably, although China has long insisted on upholding the three well-established peacekeeping principles of consent, impartiality, and nonuse of force except for self-defense and, over the past two decades, has consistently voiced its discomfort with "robust peacekeeping," it seems to have recently developed a more flexible attitude in this respect. In late 2014, with the deployment of an infantry battalion to South Sudan, China for the first time contributed combat troops to a UN peacekeeping mission, the mandate of which contained enforcement elements under Chapter VII of the UN Charter.[30]

China's growing role in peacekeeping is part and parcel, according to the SIPRI study, of "the country's overall efforts, since the late 1990s, to raise its profile in the international community as a constructive and responsible power." Participation in UN peace operations is seen as a way to enhance the country's soft power by "projecting a benign and 'harmonious' image beyond its borders" and to "softly balance US and other Western influence while gradually but more firmly establishing China's status as a great power," while also providing valuable experience to the PLA in humanitarian relief and disaster response operations.[31]

Counterterrorism

Throughout the 1990s, China displayed a degree of skepticism vis-à-vis efforts to muster robust Council action in response to acts of terrorism, reflecting its general dislike of sanctions as well as its assessment that this was primarily a US concern and not a significant threat to international peace and security warranting coercive measures. Accordingly, China only reluctantly went along with the imposition of sanctions and worked to weaken their severity—against Libya in 1992 and 1993 (in response to Tripoli's involvement in the Lockerbie bombing) and Sudan in 1996 (in response to Khartoum's failure to extradite suspects involved in an assassination attempt against President Hosni Mubarak the year before).[32]

Sharing many other countries' concern about radical Islamist terrorist groups, China supported sanctions against the Taliban in 1999, whose ascent to power, in neighboring Afghanistan in 1996, Beijing watched with great concern. Yet China did make clear its misgivings when the sanctions regime was strengthened the following year, and chose to abstain in the vote, referring to collateral damage on civilian life.

However, the terrorist attacks of September 11, 2001, proved a turning point for the Council on counterterrorism, leading to a convergence on the issue among the P5 and to a series of remarkably robust counterterrorism resolutions, all adopted unanimously. China, from the start, argued that counterterrorism activities should take place within the framework of the Security Council, reflecting concerns about an increasingly unilaterally minded Washington.[33] On September 12, 2001, China voted in favor of Resolution 1368. China also voted in favor of Resolution 1373, which, adopted under Chapter VII, imposed a wide range of binding counterterrorism obligations on all member states, including burdensome reporting requirements to the Security Council. Over the following decade, China has shown continued support for—albeit little initiative in shaping—the Council's counterterrorism regime set up under Resolution 1373.

Nonproliferation of Weapons of Mass Destruction

While less pronounced than in the field of counterterrorism, there is also a significant overlap of interests among the permanent five members of the Security Council in the area of nonproliferation of weapons of mass destruction in recent years. This manifested itself in particular through progressively strengthened sanctions regimes against Iran and North Korea, the two countries who ended up on the Council agenda because of their noncompliance with the terms of the Nuclear Non-Proliferation Treaty (NPT).

Newfound Council resolve on nonproliferation matters may seem surprising in light of the Council's past disagreements over how to pursue Iraq's disarmament, with China and Russia advocating from at least 1997 onward that the UN inspection regime should be dismantled and sanctions lifted, as Iraq had fulfilled international demands. The divide culminated in 2003, with Russia, France, and Germany vigorously opposed to the US-led Iraq War, justified by Washington with proliferation concerns. It is noteworthy, however, that China, in challenging US intentions, assumed a more low-profile approach than did, for example, France.

While interests among the P5 overlap, they are not identical and China has specific—and sometimes conflicting—interests vis-à-vis North Korea and Iran, both of which are important in explaining China's dilemma in participating in decisionmaking in the Security Council. The North Korean nuclear crisis is of particular sensitivity to China. On the one hand, the Democratic People's Republic of Korea (DPRK) is China's oldest and closest ally, alongside which it fought against the United States in the Korean War. Also, China is heavily invested in the stability of the regime in

Pyongyang, as it shares a 1,400-kilometer border with North Korea (almost half the size of the US-Mexico border) and any destabilization of its southern neighbor, North Korea, would risk triggering northbound refugee flows. China is also home to a sizable group of ethnic Koreans. On the other hand, China's trade, investment, and relations with South Korea dwarf those with North Korea,[34] and Beijing is increasingly concerned about an unpredictable neighbor armed with nuclear weapons, which, if not reversed, could in turn trigger nuclearization of China's regional adversaries, Japan and South Korea.

When the DPRK withdrew from the Non-Proliferation Treaty in 2003, the Council stayed largely mute, because of China's preference for quiet diplomacy and its preference for keeping its immediate sphere of interest away from the Council agenda. Negotiations with the DPRK took place in an ad hoc multilateral framework, the Six-Party Talks. However, with the escalation of the nuclear crisis, the center of gravity moved toward the Council. (The Six-Party Talks were discontinued in 2009.) When the DPRK launched a long-range missile test in July 2006, the Council issued a condemnation, but China was able to prevent Chapter VII measures. When, later that year, the DPRK launched its first nuclear test, even China realized the need to up the ante and joined a unanimous Council resolution imposing sanctions on North Korea. And when the DPRK launched further nuclear tests in 2009 and 2013 (the latter one a mere 130 kilometers from China's border), China grew increasingly concerned and impatient with the DPRK, voting in both cases for reinforced sanctions.

As in North Korea, China also had to reconcile divergent interests with respect to the Iran nuclear crisis. China and Iran harbor mutual feelings of civilizational affinity rooted in trade relationships, cultural exchanges, and military alliances going back centuries.[35] They share concerns over US hegemony and unbalanced international distribution of power in the post–Cold War world and are strongly attached to the sovereignty principle. Moreover, as of 2011, China is Iran's largest trading partner, and Iran is China's third largest oil supplier, providing 10 percent of its ever-growing consumption.[36] At the same time, China, having become in the fall of 2013 the world's biggest net importer of oil, is increasingly invested in stability in the wider Middle East. It is also keenly aware of the priority Washington attaches to preventing a nuclear Iran and the potential for military confrontation should these efforts fail.

Unlike the North Korea nuclear crisis, on which multilateral negotiations took place outside a Council framework, negotiations with Iran were conducted in a P5+1 setting, involving the permanent five Council members plus Germany. Indeed, between 2006 and 2013, the Council adopted six resolutions, five under Chapter VII, and four of which imposed and expanded sanctions. Remarkably, China voted in favor of all those resolutions, including the ones on which important elected Council members, such as Turkey, Brazil, or Indonesia, abstained or voted against. That said, China was supportive of and engaged in the resumption of nuclear talks with Iran, which yielded an interim agreement in November 2013.[37]

Human Rights and the Responsibility to Protect

The aspect of China's Council diplomacy that has tended to attract the most attention—and criticism—in the West over the past decade or so is its approach to gross human rights abuses and war crimes. Beijing seems to have become more assertive in recent years in defense of the sovereignty principle, as signified by the increase in its use of the veto power. In the eyes of some Western scholars, the Chinese position to reinforce sovereignty is likely motivated by a number of factors, including China's growing economic, political, and military clout; its heartfelt attachment to long-held principles and discomfort with liberal norms;[38] its suspicion that the human rights agenda is nothing but a smokescreen to advance Western interests; its growing trade relations, drive for energy security, and access to natural resources, particularly in Africa; and the emergence of a resurgent Russia, with whom China shares misgivings about US dominance in world politics and with whom it has forged a geostrategic axis giving each other cover in the Security Council.[39]

China's positioning in the Council during the 1999 Kosovo crisis indicated its growing willingness to oppose US-driven interventions outside the framework. It made clear its opposition to any military intervention and, together with Russia, threatened to veto any resolution authorizing the use of force against Serbia (Russia's ally, not China's), a threat made all the more credible by China's veto of the UNPREDEP extension a few months earlier.

The failure of the Security Council to reach consensus on the Kosovo crisis led to much introspection in the UN on how to reconcile the sovereignty principle with humanitarian imperatives. The result was the new concept of the Responsibility to Protect (R2P), which was adopted by the UN at the 2005 World Summit and according to which the international community has an obligation to act if a state is unwilling or unable to protect its own population from war crimes. China did not endeavor to impede the adoption of the concept but stressed that any "collective action" could only be invoked by the Security Council and only "on a case-by-case basis."[40] Subsequently, China accepted Security Council resolutions drawing on R2P. Its tentative support at a high level of abstraction for the concept notwithstanding, China continued to harbor serious reservations about R2P and Security Council action in response to human rights abuses. China's veto of the 2007 United States and United Kingdom–backed draft resolution condemning Myanmar for human rights abuses generally, and condemning its counterinsurgency campaign against minorities in particular, was a reminder of this fact. It was China that led the opposition to efforts to sanction Myanmar, shedding its usual reticence in the Council. Contrary to the view held in the West that economic interests featured prominently in Beijing's stance (in particular large Chinese investments in oil, mining, and gas), China was more concerned that the resolution, had it gone through, would have significantly lowered the threshold for Council action in response to internal policies of member states in the name of the R2P doctrine in the absence of actual conflict, and would have sent the wrong signal toward minorities in Myanmar vying for autonomy.[41] Also, China was convinced that sanctioning—and further isolating—the Myanmar regime was the wrong approach to bring about positive change in Myanmar, a stance that seems to have been validated by developments on the ground since.

There are also commentators in the West observing that natural resources likely figured also into China's veto of the 2008 draft resolution to impose sanctions on resource-rich Zimbabwe, involving an arms embargo as well as an asset freeze and travel bans on regime elites.[42] However, given the negligible size of China's trade and investment relationship at the time, this argument is not convincing; China's primary motivation to block the resolution is best explained by growing concern vis-à-vis the Council's increasingly broad interpretation of "threats to international peace and security" warranting Council intervention even in situations where the nature of political instability was purely domestic and where regional ramifications were absent.

China's stance on the Darfur situation is probably the one that attracted the most attention in the West in recent years. By the time the Security Council got involved in the Darfur crisis in 2004, a gruesome civil war had led to the displacement and death of a very large number of the local population. Over the coming three years, China, under the shadow of its veto power, would follow a pattern of pressuring the United States and others to significantly weaken any sanctions-related draft resolution and then abstaining in the vote, citing concerns about potentially destabilizing effects and adverse humanitarian consequences, as well the undermining impact on international mediation efforts.[43] These concerns were legitimate, but critics pointed to Beijing's relationship with Khartoum and China's oil dependence on Sudan, which by 2002 became China's fourth largest supplier, accounting for 10 percent of China's imports that year.[44] However, for those who believe China's policy to be monolithic, Beijing, to the great shock of Khartoum, ultimately abstained on rather than voting against Resolution 1593 in 2005, which referred the situation in Darfur to the International Criminal Court. This resolution eventually led to the indictment of several leading figures in the Khartoum government, not least President Omar al-Bashir.

With the 2008 Olympics around the corner, China may also have factored concerns about its international reputation into its Council decision-making on Darfur. In 2007, China strongly encouraged President Bashir to consent to the deployment of a hybrid peacekeeping mission, the UN-AU Mission in Darfur (UNAMID), which Khartoum had steadfastly refused up to this point, and to which China eventually contributed over 300 troops, becoming the first non-African country deploying troops to Darfur. China may also have been sensitive to the concerns about Darfur expressed by numerous African leaders during the November 2006 China-Africa summit in Beijing. President Bashir visited Beijing in June 2011, which implied that China did not think it was under legal obligation to cooperate on immunity matters with the ICC as a nonstate party.

In light of China's unease with Chapter VII measures in the cases of Darfur, Myanmar, and Zimbabwe, China's acceptance through abstention of military protection measures mandated by the Council in response to the Muammar Qaddafi regime's use of force against the uprising in Libya in early 2011 is all the more remarkable. Beijing first voted in favor of a resolution that imposed sanctions on Tripoli and referred the Libya case to the ICC (Resolution 1970) and later abstained, alongside Russia, Germany, India, and Brazil, on a resolution that permitted the first-ever Council-mandated military operations against an internationally recognized government for humanitarian reasons (Resolution 1973). It should be noted that China did so despite huge economic losses in Libya[45] and the fact that around 30,000 of its citizens were residing in the country. Soon after the NATO-initiated military operations against Libya, China as well as the other members of the BRICS group (Brazil, Russia, India, and South Africa), all of which happened to be Council members at the time, came to regret their support for Resolution 1973. Only days into the NATO campaign, China joined India and Russia in demands for a ceasefire and suggested that allied forces had exceeded the UN's mandate by imperiling civilians in Libya.[46] These concerns only grew as NATO's military operations were extended to target Tripoli and shifted their emphasis from civilian protection to forcing regime change, moving the operation well beyond what was understood by a number of Council members to be authorized by Resolution 1973.

A clear feeling of having been misled by NATO in Libya led China, acting mostly hand-in-hand with Russia, to adopt a more uncompromising position with respect to the Syrian civil war. Between October 2011 and May 2014, China and Russia jointly vetoed four consecutive draft resolutions on Syria. Even though none of them would have imposed any sanctions on the Syrian regime, China rejected the drafts with reference to Syrian sovereignty, arguing that they were counterproductive and would derail any possibility of a political settlement by placing "undue emphasis on pressuring the Syrian Government for a prejudged result of the dialogue."[47]

Indeed, China was deeply suspicious of the West's efforts to once again push for regime change under the guise of the R2P doctrine.[48]

From China's perspective, the West failed to provide sufficient evidence that the Bashar al-Assad regime was indeed responsible for the alleged atrocities and voiced concern that a position that was premised on the departure of the Assad regime would undermine the neutrality of the Council. Unlike Russia, China had no strategic interests in Syria. Both Moscow and Beijing were genuinely concerned, however, about the spread of violent Islamic extremism. The increasingly chaotic Western approach to Syria, particularly as of mid-2013, may have given rise to genuine worry that the fallout of misguided policies could spell serious consequences for an entire region bordering both on the Russian Federation and on China. Ultimately, at a moment of internal political drama for both the United Kingdom and United States on Syria that undermined the authority of the leaders of both countries on this issue, Moscow was able to bring the Council together in September 2013 to a position of unanimous support for the internationally supervised destruction of Syria's stock of chemical weapons.[49]

China's position concerning R2P issues seems perplexing to the West, and commentators often fail to appreciate the different circumstances that motivate China's positions in different situations. In general, economic and geopolitical interests have weighed less in China's decisionmaking than is generally assumed. While China unequivocally subscribed to the R2P concept at the 2005 World Summit, it is genuinely concerned that an excessively broad interpretation of the doctrine may erode the nonintervention clause of the UN Charter and allow Council action that does not meet the criteria set out by the 2005 World Summit for R2P's application (and set out by the 2001 report of the International Commission on Intervention and State Sovereignty, which developed the R2P concept in the first place).[50] In China's eyes, these criteria had not been met in the cases of Myanmar, Zimbabwe, Darfur, and Syria.

Conclusion

China's Security Council diplomacy has significantly evolved since the end of the Cold War. During the 1990s, China's stance in the Council, a continuation of its stance adopted during the 1980s, was restrained. When it entertained concerns about the course of action proposed by others, it generally abstained from voting and outlined its preoccupations orally rather than through the use of its veto power. However, while China's approach during much of the 1980s was largely inconsequential due to the Council's overall low profile induced by Cold War paralysis, its restraint during the 1990s made it an enabler of the Western-driven transformation of the Council into an interventionist organ mandating a wide range of highly intrusive measures in a significant number of civil wars. The only instances in which China chose to use its veto power occurred in situations in which host countries of peacekeeping operations entertained excessively close relations with (or decided to recognize) Taiwan.[51]

Since the turn of the millennium, China has become increasingly active and assertive in the Security Council, both in defending its own interests as well as in displaying a greater readiness to challenge Western agendas. This manifested itself most clearly in the dramatic increase of China's use of the veto; between 2007 and 2014, China, jointly with Russia, cast six vetoes in the Council, compared with the four vetoes it cast in the preceding thirty-five years. It also, in private, threatened use of the veto on a number of other occasions, preventing or watering down sanctions measures, most notably in the case of Darfur.

Increase in confidence in the diplomatic arena, a natural byproduct of China's rise to great power status, is part of the story. However, its ever-closer association with Russia in the Council since the turn of the millennium, largely rooted in concern by both countries over Western initiatives, is also notable. Beijing's inclination to be more proactive in the Council was thus reinforced by a Russia that was both resurgent and increasingly alienated by and suspicious of the United States.

The most reliable predictor of China's positions within the Council is, not surprisingly, its pattern of diplomatic and economic relationships globally. Those have grown dramatically since the late 1990s, with China having become the world's largest exporter in 2010, the second largest economy in 2011, and the largest importer of oil in 2013. China is immeasurably more important to most countries of the world than it was only twenty years ago, and the contribution of the outside world to China's prosperity and long-term economic prospects is also much greater.

Not all signs point in the direction of increasing confrontation in the Council between East and West. China's increasing commercial interests around the world also mean that it is increasingly invested in stability in a number of regions, compelling it at times to exert pressure, including through the Security Council, on friends whose uncompromising or reckless behavior risks bringing about serious escalation of conflict or crisis. Its Council votes in favor of sanctions against Iran and North Korea are cases in point. Finally, China's growing engagement in peacekeeping underlines its appreciation of soft power as well as its desire to be, and to be seen as, a responsible stakeholder in collective security. According to Rosemary Foot, this also reflects China's engagement in the multilateral arena more broadly: "China's reasonably productive involvement in international organizations has been important to it materially but has also been perceived as a way for it to signal that it is a responsible great power engaged in a peaceful rise and vital domestic reform."[52]

However, China's overall profile in the Council remains deliberately understated relative to its global heft. Indeed, in 2013, China did not act as a penholder on any situation-specific or thematic matter on the Council's agenda, compared to the United States leading on fifteen items, the United Kingdom on ten, France on nine, and Russia on two.[53] As we look to the future, China can be expected to adhere strongly to the principles of nonintervention. While Beijing is increasingly looking outward, its primary focus in the foreseeable future will remain China's internal development, and its foreign policy is unlikely to see a drastic reorientation in years to come. This means that China will remain reluctant to have the Council mandate coercive measures, under Chapter VII of the Charter. With its positions on the Council deeply rooted in traditional culture and thinking, China will continue to follow in its Council diplomacy Confucius's famous maxim: "Do not do unto others what you do not want done to yourself."

Notes

1. The Five Principles of Peaceful Coexistence first appeared in written form in the Preamble to the Agreement (with exchange of notes) on Trade and Intercourse Between the Tibet Region of China and India, which was signed on April 29, 1954.

2. The concept of "nonalignment" emerged from India in the early 1950s, but the Indian prime minister was initially skeptical of the political third force (between the superpower blocs) that the nonaligned movement eventually became after the Bandung and Belgrade conferences of 1955 and 1961 respectively.

3. In contrast to the US conceptualization, the first world consisted of the imperialist superpowers (both the United States and Soviet Union); the second world, other developed states; and the third world, the globe's nonaligned countries.

4. The PRC's positioning as a part of the developing world, rather than the socialist bloc, was in part a response to Soviet-US rapprochement unfolding in a context of worsening tensions between the United States and China over the Taiwan issue during the 1950s. The souring of Sino-Soviet relations culminated with the withdrawal of Soviet advisers and aid in 1960 and China's withdrawal, as an "associated observer," from the Warsaw Pact the following year.

5. Deng Xiaoping, "Speech on the Sixth Special Session," United Nations General Assembly, 26th Session, New York, April 6, 1974.

6. People's Republic of China, Information Office of the State Council, "China's Peaceful Development," Beijing, September 2011, http://ag.china -embassy.org/eng/xwfw/t866863.htm.

7. John Garver, "Sino-Russian Relations," in *China and the World: Chinese Foreign Policy Faces the New Millennium,* edited by Samuel S. Kim (Boulder, CO: Westview, 1998), pp. 116–118.

8. See Chinese Foreign Ministry, "China's Position Paper on the New Security Concept," August, 6, 2002, www.fmprc.gov.cn/ce/ceun/eng/xw/t27742.htm. See also President Hu Jintao, "Build Towards a Harmonious World of Lasting Peace and Common Prosperity," speech at the 2005 United Nations World Summit, New York, September 15, 2005, www.fmprc.gov.cn/ce/ceun/eng/zt/shnh60/t212915.htm.

9. David Shambaugh, *China Goes Global: The Partial Power* (Oxford: Oxford University Press, 2013), pp. 24–25.

10. Michael Fullilove, "China and the United Nations: The Stakeholder Spectrum," *Washington Quarterly* 43, no. 3 (2011): 68.

11. As Beijing's early ally, the Soviet Union actually boycotted the Council in January 1950 in opposition to the continued occupancy of China's seat by the Republic of China. The Soviet Union quickly returned to the Council as its absence paved the way for the approval of a US-led intervention on the Korean Peninsula opposing China's ally, North Korea.

12. Joel Wuthnow, "Beyond the Veto: Chinese Diplomacy at the UN," PhD thesis, Columbia University, 2011, p. 23.

13. Ibid., p. 34.

14. Thomas G. Weiss, *Military-Civilian Interactions: Humanitarian Crises and the Responsibility to Protect* (Oxford: Rowman and Littlefield, 2005), p. 89.

15. Samuel S. Kim, "China and the United Nations," in *China Joins the World: Progress and Prospects,* edited by Elizabeth Economy and Michael Oksenberg (New York: Council of Foreign Relations, 1999).

16. United Nations Security Council, "Provisional Verbatim Record of the 3453rd Meeting," S/PV.3453, November 8, 1994 (statement of China's Ambassador Li Zhaoxing, p. 11).

17. Cited in Wayne Sandholz, "Creating Authority by the Council: The International Criminal Tribunals," in *The UN Security Council and the Politics of International Authority,* edited by Bruce Cronin and Ian Hurd (New York: Routledge, 2008), p. 137.

18. United Nations Security Council, "Statement by the President of the Security Council," S/PRST/2007/23, June 28, 2007, para. 3.

19. Mats Berdal, "Bosnia," in *The UN Security Council: From the Cold War to the 21st Century,* edited by David M. Malone (Boulder, CO: Lynne Rienner, 2004), pp. 457–458.

20. Paul Lewis, "China Lifts U.N. Veto on Guatemala Monitors," *New York Times,* January 21, 1997, www.nytimes.com/1997/01/21/world/china-lifts-un-veto-on-guatemala-monitors.html.

21. Czeslaw Tubilewicz, *Taiwan and Post-Communist Europe: Shopping for Allies* (London: Routledge, 2007), pp. 138–139.

22. Fullilove, "China and the United Nations," p. 69.

23. Susan Tieh, "China in the UN: United with Other Nations?" *Stanford Journal of East Asian Affairs* 4, no. 1 (2004): 19–28.

24. Wuthnow, "Beyond the Veto," p. 34.

25. United Nations Department of Peacekeeping Operations, "Troop and Police Contributors Archive: 1990–2012," www.un.org/en/peacekeeping/resources/statistics/contributors_archive.shtml.

26. United Nations Department of Peacekeeping Operations, "Ranking of Military and Police Contributions to UN Operations," June 30, 2014, www.un.org/en/peacekeeping/contributors/2014/jun14_2.pdf.

27. State Council of China, Information Office, "Diversified Employment of China's Armed Forces," Beijing, April 2013, pt. 5.

28. United Nations Secretary-General, "Implementation of General Assembly Resolutions 55/235 and 55/236," A/67/224/Add.1, December 27, 2012.

29. Bates Gill and Chin-Hao Huang, *China's Expanding Role in Peacekeeping: Prospects and Policy Implications,* Policy Paper no. 25 (Stockholm: Stockholm International Peace Research Institute, November 2009), p. vii.

30. "China Sends First Infantry Battalion for UN Peacekeeping," *Xinhua,* December 22, 2014, http://news.xinhuanet.com/english/china/2014-12/22/c_133871006.htm.

31. Gill and Huang, *China's Expanding Role in Peacekeeping,* pp. 12–16.

32. See Chapter 14, on terrorism, and Chapter 30, on Sudan, in this volume.

33. United Nations Security Council, "Provisional Verbatim Record of the 4370th Meeting," S/PV.4370, September 12, 2001 (statement by Permanent Representative of China Wang Yingfan, p. 5).

34. Shambaugh, *China Goes Global,* p. 100.

35. John Garver, "China-Iran Relations," speech at the Woodrow Wilson Center for International Scholarship, Washington, DC, July 14, 2005, www.wilsoncenter .org/event/iran-china-relations.

36. US Energy Information Administration, "Overview Data for China," May 30, 2013, www.eia.gov/countries/country-data.cfm?fips=CH.

37. Qin Gang, official statement, November 11, 2013, www.mfa.gov.cn /mfa_chn/fyrbt_602243/jzhsl_602247/t1097841.shtml.

38. Shambaugh, *China Goes Global,* p. 131; Garver, "Sino-Russian Relations," pp. 114–132.

39. Shambaugh, *China Goes Global,* p. 83.

40. Interview with UN officials involved in the negotiations in New York, May 2013. See also United Nations General Assembly, "2005 World Summit Outcome," A/RES/60, October 24, 2005.

41. International Crisis Group, "China's Myanmar Dilemma," Brussels, September 14, 2009, p. 3, www.crisisgroup.org/~/media/Files/asia/north-east-asia/177 _chinas_myanmar_dilemma.pdf.

42. Wuthnow, "Beyond the Veto," pp. 274–275.

43. See, for example, "China Threatens to Veto UN Darfur Draft," *Reuters,* September 15, 2004. See also Wuthnow, "Beyond the Veto," pp. 222–272.

44. Yitzhak Shichor, "Speak Softly and Carry a Big Stick: Non-Traditional Chinese Threats and Middle Eastern Instability," in *China's Rise: Threat or Opportunity,* edited by Herbert Yee (London: Routledge, 2011), p. 116.

45. In the aftermath of Resolution 1973, fifty investment and commercial contracts valued at $18.8 billion were affected or suspended. See "'Premature' for Firms to Go Back into Libya," *China Daily,* August 30, 2011, www.china.org.cn /business/2011-08/30/content_23309819.htm.

46. Emily O'Brien and Andrew Sinclair, "The Libyan War: A Diplomatic History, February–August 2011" (New York: Center on International Cooperation, August 2011), pp. 12–13.

47. United Nations Security Council, "Provisional Verbatim Record of the 6711th Meeting," S/PV.6711, February 4, 2012 (statement by China's Ambassador Li Baodong, p. 9). See also United Nations Security Council, "Provisional Verbatim Record of the 6627th Meeting," S/PV.6627, October 4, 2011 (statement by China's Ambassador Li Baodong, p. 5).

48. United Nations Security Council, "Provisional Verbatim Record of the 6711th Meeting," S/PV.6711, February 4, 2012 (statement by China's Ambassador Li Baodong, p. 9).

49. United Nations Security Council, Resolution 2118, S/RES/2118 (September 27, 2013).

50. International Commission on Intervention and State Sovereignty, "The Responsibility to Protect" (Ottawa: International Development Research Centre, December 2001), para. 4.18; United Nations High-Level Panel on Threats, Challenges, and Change, *A More Secure World: Our Shared Responsibility,* UN Doc. A/59/565, December 2, 2004, para. 207.

51. While a number of authors have argued that China has become more tolerant in accepting peacekeeping countries' relations with Taiwan, it is more likely that

host countries of peacekeeping operations have learned to keep their distance from Taipei, lest they provoke a Chinese veto.

52. Rosemary Foot, "US-China Interactions in Global Governance and International Organizations," in *Tangled Titans: The United States and China,* edited by David Shambaugh (Lanham: Rowman and Littlefield, 2013), p. 363.

53. Security Council Report, "February 2013 Monthly Forecast: Chairs of Subsidiary Bodies and Pen Holders for 2013," January 31, 2013, www.securitycouncil report.org/monthly-forecast/2013-02/subsidiary_chairs_and_pen_holders _for_2013.php.

5

Russia in the Security Council

Dmitri Trenin

RUSSIA'S ATTITUDE TOWARD THE UNITED NATIONS, AND PAR-
ticularly its Security Council, is a reflection of Moscow's views of the
global order, and of Russia's national interests. These views are based on
the notion of a stable balance among the world's most powerful nations,
including Russia, and their joint leadership in tackling international issues.
Moscow regards the veto power on collective decisions that it enjoys at the
Council as a guarantee that its national interests will be safely protected, at
least legally. The status of a permanent, veto-wielding member of the
Council also gives Russia the prestige of a global power, which it has been
struggling to uphold following the breakup of the Soviet Union.

Moscow realizes, of course, that the system designed and put in place
seven decades ago faces a challenge from those who are not privileged by
it. Rhetorically, Russia endorses the need for UN reform, while it is prepared to watch competing ideas concerning rebuilding the world body clash
and battle one another to a standstill. Moscow itself is more concerned with
the world's most powerful country, the United States, and the security
alliance it leads, NATO, circumventing the UN Security Council to intervene militarily in situations in which Russia and China oppose such intervention. Keeping the United States within the United Nations framework
has thus become one of Moscow's major foreign policy goals.

I begin this chapter with a brief description of Russia's foreign policy
legacy from the Soviet period, and the immediate post–Cold War era. I then
place Russia's attitudes toward the Council into the wider perspective of
Moscow's foreign policy universe, and discuss the interests that lie behind
Russia's staunch defense of traditional international law. Having thus

framed the issue, I proceed to address Moscow's positions on key international issues, such as peacekeeping, counterterrorism and other transnational security issues, and nonproliferation. Given the sharp divisions within the Council on some of these issues, I seek to describe the nature of the controversies between Russia, on the one hand, and the United States and its allies, on the other; and also the nature of diplomatic cooperation between Russia and China. Finally, I look at Russia's position on the issue of UN reform. In concluding the chapter, I suggest that the Russian stance on Security Council–related issues is rooted in the fundamental principles of Moscow's foreign policy, closely tied to its national interests, and is unlikely to change in the foreseeable future.

The Soviet Legacy

The starting point of any analysis of contemporary Russian foreign policy, including its approach to the United Nations, needs to be an understanding that the Russian Federation sees itself as a new incarnation of the historical Russian state started some 1,150 years ago and, more immediately, as a successor state of the Soviet Union. The link is perhaps most vividly symbolized by the Russian Federation immediately inheriting, in December 1991, the Soviet Union's permanent seat on the UN Security Council. In addition to its arsenal of nuclear weapons, permanent membership in the Security Council has been a key attribute of Russia's continuing great power status in the world after the end of the Cold War and the breakup of the Soviet Union. This allowed Russia to punch above its weight on the global scene, particularly through the 1990s. To put it simply, Russia likes the UN because of the Council, and it likes the Council because of its status as a permanent, veto-wielding member. By contrast, Russia usually attaches far less importance to the UN General Assembly, a merely consultative forum with no enforcement powers in which it does not enjoy a privileged position.

Russia's Approach to the Council
in Light of Evolving East-West Relations

At the close of the Cold War confrontation, Soviet and then Russian leaders hoped for much more cooperative, even alliance-type relations with the United States and Western Europe. General-Secretary Mikhail Gorbachev's groundbreaking speech at the United Nations in December 1988 laid down that approach. Not only did Gorbachev, having just entered into a major nuclear arms control agreement with Washington, announce conventional troop cuts, but he also came up with a wholly new philosophy of international relations, built on cooperative security. Just over three years later,

President Boris Yeltsin's participation in the 1992 first-ever Security Council meeting at the heads-of-state level seemed to symbolize the new state of the world. In that view, the UN, and particularly its Security Council, were to be transformed from a crucible of permanent confrontation and crude conflict management to a body that actually resolved issues for the benefit of the international community.

This era of high hopes did not last very long. Russia's approach to the Security Council was essentially informed by its evolving relations with the West. Already by the mid-1990s, it became clear to Moscow that hopes of Russia's progressive integration into the West were unrealistic; that the interests of the Western powers and Russia diverged on a number of issues; and that world politics, even in the postconfrontation era, was still a power game. Even though 1995 saw Russia's participation, under US/NATO command, in the IFOR operation in Bosnia, mandated under the US-negotiated Dayton agreement, the dynamic had already changed.

Relations with the United States reached a new low with the enlargement of NATO to include several of Moscow's former Warsaw Pact allies in Central and Eastern Europe, agreed upon shortly thereafter. Russian elites interpreted this move as both a no-confidence vote in a post-Soviet Russia, and an attempt to put pressure on them. The conflict over Kosovo in 1999, in which NATO launched an air war against the Federal Republic of Yugoslavia, led to a brief rupture in Russia's relations with NATO, and caused more lasting damage by reviving the notion, in the minds of political and military leaders in Moscow, of the United States as a threat to Russia. The NATO operation was undertaken without UN approval; what protected Russia from a similar fate, some Russians reasoned, was its nuclear weapons arsenal.

Ever since the first bombings of Serbian forces in Bosnia in the mid-1990s, Moscow has been wary of US moves to use force at will in various situations around the world. The Russians tried to counter this perceived militarization of US foreign policy and the domination of military force in global politics at a time when US power was unmatched and the buzzword was "unipolarity." Seen from Moscow, US military might was no longer held in check by a rival power, and military force—described as coercive diplomacy—once again became a usable policy instrument. Pursuant to this, Russia threatened to veto any Security Council resolution that would endorse the US-led use of force in Kosovo. This made the 1999 NATO war against Yugoslavia illegal, in terms of international law, but cast Russia, in Western eyes, in the role of a spoiler.

The situation changed again when Moscow made fresh efforts at rapprochement with the West, and the United States in particular, in the wake of the terrorist attacks of September 11, 2001. Less than three weeks after the attacks, the Security Council unanimously passed Resolution 1373, which imposed binding counterterrorist obligations on all UN member states. Not only did Russia subsequently support the US operation Enduring Freedom in Afghanistan, aimed at destroying al-Qaeda and dislodging the Taliban from power, but Moscow also assisted Washington with intelligence and encouraged its allies in Afghanistan, the so-called Northern Alliance, to fight alongside US forces against the common enemy, the Taliban. In terms of actual support given to the United States in Afghanistan in 2001, Russia was probably second only to the United Kingdom, which contributed ground troops to the US-led operation.

With the Taliban defeated and al-Qaeda disabled, the administration of President George W. Bush lost interest in Russia from 2002 onward, and focused instead on preparing to invade Iraq. Moscow was clearly unhappy with Saddam Hussein's dodgy tactics toward UN weapons inspectors looking for WMD-related activities in Iraq. Russia voted for strongly worded Council resolutions urging Saddam to cooperate with the United Nations. Moscow, however, resolutely rejected the use of force against Baghdad, which was also opposed by Paris and Berlin (with Germany a nonpermanent Council member at the time). When the US-led invasion occurred in the absence of an authorization by the UN Security Council in March 2003, this, to the Russians, was a second major breach of the world order after Kosovo.

This led to a general hardening of Moscow's foreign policy, including in the Security Council, where Russian representatives became less restrained in their use of the veto. Russia finally left the West's political orbit, where it had stayed after the fall of the Soviet system, and began to assert its strategic independence. This process was accompanied by steadily rising tensions between Russia and the West, especially over NATO's bid to include Ukraine and Georgia, and culminated in a short war in the Caucasus in August 2008, when Georgian forces attacked the breakaway region of South Ossetia, provoking Moscow's military response. At that point, Russian-Western relations plunged to their lowest point since the mid-1980s.

In 2009, the US foreign policy "reset" toward Russia during President Barack Obama's first term evoked hopes of closer international collaboration between Moscow and the West. Vladimir Putin, who had assumed the position of prime minister in 2008 after having served a maximum of two consecutive terms as president, allowed President Dmitri Medvedev to try to resolve politico-military issues of tension between Moscow and Washington, such as the controversy over the planned US/NATO ballistic missile defense system in Europe, and to reach out to Western countries to form "modernization alliances" with them. It was in this context that Russia cooperated with the United States in the Security Council on strengthening sanctions against Iran through Resolution 1929 (2010) and joined the West in condemning Libya's Muammar Qaddafi, whose rule was threatened by a rebellion, and then decided, in March 2011, to abstain on a Security Council resolution authorizing a Western-led military operation to establish a no-fly zone in Libya.

The failure of the "Medvedev round" to achieve a qualitative improvement of Russian-Western relations—Moscow's third unsuccessful attempt to construct an acceptable relationship with the United States since the end of the Cold War—has resulted in a new hardening of Moscow's policy toward the West, which, with Putin's reelection to the presidency in 2012, was again formally directed by him. In particular, Putin has rebalanced Moscow's foreign policy with a greater emphasis on Eurasian integration with several former Soviet republics, and greater outreach to the Asia Pacific region. The Ukraine crisis, which broke out in early 2014, led to a new confrontation between Russia and the United States and an estrangement between Russia and the European Union. As a result, Moscow moved even closer to Beijing.

The UN Security Council in the Russian Foreign Policy Universe

The Russian foreign policy concept adopted in 2013 identifies the United Nations as the main regulator of international relations. From Russia's perspective, it is the UN Security Council that, in the current era, best epitomizes world governance. All the importance of economics and finance notwithstanding (and none of that importance is lost on Russia's leaders), security, to them, remains the pinnacle of high politics. In Moscow's view, the global community should be ideally organized on the basis of a consensus of its most powerful members—the P5 "coequals"—including Russia, of course. Other international bodies, from the Group of Eight (G8) and the Group of 20 (G-20) to the Shanghai Cooperation Organization (SCO) and the BRICS—are also deemed important, but the Security Council sits at the top of their hierarchy.

The overtly "polycentric" nature of the Security Council and the formal equality of its five permanent members reflect, however imperfectly, the multipolarity of the existing world order. To be effective, the Council, in Moscow's view, should be able both to prevent any one power—in reality, the United States—from establishing its global hegemony, or practicing unconstrained use of force, and to provide a platform for bargaining and cooperation among the world's top league players. The Council's responsibility in matters of world peace and security, Moscow argues, should not be diluted or usurped by US-dominated Western institutions such as NATO. This explains vehement Russian objections to references in NATO's 2010 Strategic Concept suggesting a global role for the alliance. Russians tend to insist that their notion of the unique role of the Council most closely reflects the original United Nations concept of collective decisionmaking on the basis of the UN Charter.

Understanding the special function and procedure of the Council, the Russian government has been appointing its best diplomats to serve as its UN ambassadors. With the exception of a brief interlude from 2004 to 2006, the Russian Federation, in the past two decades, has been represented in New York by only two people: Sergey Lavrov, who served from 1994 to 2004 before becoming foreign minister, a position he occupies to this day, and Vitaly Churkin, who has served since 2006. Between them, Lavrov and Churkin have crafted a new style of Russian diplomacy: they are highly professional, extremely well-briefed, articulate, and reasonably open, but also clearly enjoy a good argument and are ever-ready to defend Russia's national interest and its leadership's point of view. Unlike in the days of the Cold War, it is Russia's ambassador in New York rather than in Washington or elsewhere on a bilateral mission who is the most outspoken and best-known Russian Federation foreign ministry official after the minister himself. Russian UN-mission diplomatic personnel are initiated in New York to the world of global politics.

International Law, the Use of Force, and the World Order

Unlike its Soviet predecessor, the Russian Federation has been a strong supporter of international law, as understood by the founders of the United Nations in 1945. Moscow, since the end of the Cold War, has defended the principles of state sovereignty, territorial integrity, and noninterference in internal affairs of other states. In particular, the Russians have insisted that military force can only be used with the consent of the UN Security Council, and that any use of force without Council approval is illegal. Russia especially strongly condemned the use of force by NATO against the Federal Republic of Yugoslavia in 1999, and by the United States and Britain against Iraq in 2003. Russia's position on Syria since 2011 has also been guided by Moscow's rejection of foreign military interference and outside political meddling in the affairs of a sovereign UN member state.

This does not suggest that Moscow has suddenly turned pacifist. Russia itself used military force in 2008 against Georgia, in response to the Georgian president Mikheil Saakashvili's attempt to regain control over a tiny rebel province, South Ossetia, during which a number of Russian peacekeepers, deployed there under a 1992 ceasefire agreement, were killed. With the bulk of the Western media branding Russia, rather than Georgia, as the aggressor, Russia sent in regular forces to protect the South Ossetian population and to secure the province, and temporarily occupy parts of Georgia proper. With the Council unable to meet promptly, the ceasefire agreement was eventually negotiated by the presidents of Russia and France, then holding the EU presidency.

Even though it briefly used the argument itself in South Ossetia, Russia rejects the notion of humanitarian intervention as hypocritical, and disagrees with the argument that, under certain circumstances, state sovereignty may be interfered with in the name of higher values. While not wishing to appear backward-looking and totally wedded to norms and principles formulated seven decades ago, Russia professes its readiness to engage in a dialogue to modernize international law. Significantly, it did endorse the concept of the Responsibility to Protect at the 2005 World Summit. However, it insisted at the time that no international action involving the use of force should be undertaken without an explicit decision by the UN Security Council.

The position taken by the Russian leadership under Presidents Yeltsin, Putin, Medvedev, and again Putin agrees not only with Moscow's post-Soviet international philosophy of supporting traditional international law, in particular with regard to state sovereignty and noninterference in internal affairs of other countries, but also the realities of power relations. Considerably smaller and much weaker than before, Russia has to rely more on international legal arrangements, rather than brute force, to protect and promote its interests. Russia may be said to have turned legalist. It needs to ensure, however, not only that its direct interests are well protected by legal means, but also that no precedent is created by the international community, such as outside support for a regime change or a military intervention, which might do damage to Russia's interests later.

As the 2011 Libya experience suggests, Russia does not necessarily shy away from allowing very forceful Council-based action, but it is adamant that the terms of the mandate be fully observed and that operations under the mandate actually remain under the Council's full control. NATO's failure, in Russia's view, to live up to those requirements, provoked Moscow's vehement reaction, which soon thereafter made itself felt in the Syrian context. Russian officials have little time for arguments in support of the legality of NATO's actions in Libya: to them, the operation was guided by the political, geopolitical, and business motives of those who had initiated it. Mindful of both the Libyan experience and the earlier case of pre-2003 Iraq, Moscow not only blocked any action leading to intervention in Syria or supporting a regime change in Damascus, but also vetoed any language that it feared might later be construed to justify military action, on the basis of noncompliance with past Council demands—a tactic used by the George W. Bush administration in the run up to the invasion of Iraq.

Contrary to popular belief, the Russian government's position on Syria since the beginning of the uprising in 2011 has not been primarily informed by Russia's specific interests on the ground in Syria, such as an alleged geopolitical alliance, an alliance that, in reality, has been dead for twenty-five years; the arms trade, which requires subsequent debt write-offs; or the (rather modest) naval resupply facility at Tartus. Instead, Russia's position on Syria is motivated primarily by a concern about the global order: the use of force and, secondarily, Moscow's assessment of the Syrian opposition (before the rise of the Islamic State) as being dominated by religious extremists who, should they manage to topple the regime of Bashar al-Assad, would turn Syria into a terrorist base.

When faced in 2013, after the chemical weapons attack near Damascus, with the real prospect of US military strikes against Syria, Russian diplomats scrambled to engineer an agreement with Damascus and Washington that would result in Syria's chemical disarmament, under the auspices of the Organisation for the Prohibition of Chemical Weapons. For Moscow, supporting the effort of the Obama administration to disengage the US military from conflict areas around the world was worth the effort. The elimination and liquidation of the Syrian chemical weapons arsenal have also been viewed in Moscow as a step toward a diplomatic solution to the war in Syria, in the format of a UN-backed conference in Geneva (which finally took place in January 2014), Russia's preference all along.

Not all situations are similar. Despite the strong disagreements with the West over Syria, Russia supported in 2013 the French-led military offensive in Mali. It has also supported more muscular rules of engagement for the UN force in the Democratic Republic of the Congo, adopted in 2013. In some cases, Russia has taken time to decide on its final position. Thus it originally opposed in 2011 the French-backed UN peacekeeping mission in Côte d'Ivoire, taking sides in a domestic conflict in that country, but later relented and allowed the UN peacekeepers to assist in consolidation of power in the hands of one of the competing local factions.

When Russia itself had to use military force, as it did during the operation to take control of Crimea following the victory of the Maidan Uprising that toppled Ukrainian president Viktor Yanukovych in February 2014, the Kremlin justified its actions in the name of Russia's national security interests and the need to defend ethnic Russians from triumphant Ukrainian nationalists. Moscow charged the Europeans with the failure of the negotiated solution to the political crisis in Kiev, which they had brokered. Russian officials also drew parallels between Moscow's actions in Crimea and its support for anti-Maidan militants in eastern Ukraine, on the one hand, and NATO's handling of the Kosovo crisis, on the other. The message was clear: if the West was unwilling to take Russia's security interests into account, Russia would take matters into its own hands.

Peacekeeping

In the wake of the end of the Cold War, as old conflicts suddenly reopened, Russia took part in UN-mandated peacekeeping operations in a number of areas, from the Balkans to the Middle East to Africa. Russia's biggest involvement was in Bosnia-Herzegovina, where in 1995, to help implement the Dayton Accords, it even put its forces under NATO's Supreme Allied Commander, a US general. Although successful in operational and rewarding in professional terms, this experience was later judged as diminishing Russia's prestige, never to be repeated. When Russia in 1999 took part in peacekeeping in Kosovo, it insisted on a national sector. That operation began in an atmosphere of deep division between Russia and the NATO countries, which almost led to a collision between their forces on the ground.

Elsewhere, Russia's peacekeeping presence was relatively small, often notional. Of some interest was the deployment of an engineer battalion to Lebanon in the wake of the 2006 war between Hezbollah and Israel. The battalion was composed of Russian servicemen of Chechen origin. By that time, however, Russia had reduced the scope of its peacekeeping efforts outside the former Soviet Union. In 2003, it withdrew from SFOR and KFOR operations in Bosnia-Herzegovina and Kosovo, respectively, to focus on the management of post-Soviet conflicts.

From 1993, Russia sought, and failed, to get UN status for its own third-party peacekeeping operations in the former Soviet Union, particularly in Tajikistan, Moldova, and the South Caucasus, including in Abkhazia and South Ossetia. This status was never conferred on Russia, but peacekeeping operations in Moldova and Georgia did get a measure of international legitimacy. They were based on agreements to which Chişinău and Tbilisi (until the 2008 war) were parties; they operated in parallel with observers from the UN (in Abkhazia) and the Organization for Security and Cooperation in Europe (OSCE) (in South Ossetia); and they were embedded in the diplomatic process. Eventually, they were phased out almost completely. In Tajikistan, Abkhazia, and South Ossetia, Russian forces were transformed into military bases. Only in Moldova's Transnistria region did they continue to function as peacekeepers.

Since 2008, the Russian navy has been taking part in UN-sponsored international anti-piracy activities off the coast of East Africa. Russia has also supported UN peacekeeping operations in Chad, the Central African Republic, and South Sudan, where it sent helicopter pilots, military observers, and police. From Moscow's perspective, however, these activities mostly fall too far from Russia's national interests, and thus are not deemed to be worth the effort of deploying troops on the ground. This attitude underlies Moscow's basic approach: international relations are essentially about competition among the world's major powers. The current Russian leadership feels no compunctions about putting its national interests above anything else.

Transnational Threats

Russia is directly affected by a wide range of transnational threats, including drugs, terrorism, and organized crime. It mostly has to deal with these issues using its domestic resources, but is seeking ways to enhance its leverage using the UN. On the issue of drug trafficking, Moscow's biggest concern is Afghanistan, the source of much of the heroin consumed in Russia. According to some estimates, each year twice as many Russians die from the effects of Afghanistan-produced drugs than the total of the casualties sustained by the Soviet Union during its ten-year Afghan war. Since the defeat of the Taliban in 2001, Russian officials claim, the flow of drugs to Russia from Afghanistan has grown manyfold. Moscow has been disappointed with the inability of both Kabul and the International Security Assistance Force (ISAF) to stem drug production in Afghanistan, and Moscow has been pressing other Council members to adopt a robust Chapter VII mandate to counter drug production in Afghanistan, which Russia insists is a threat to international peace and security. Moscow's pressure, however, has so far come to no avail, and has led to tensions between Russia, on one hand, and the United States/NATO, on the other. However, in a demonstration exercise, Russia in October 2010 staged a onetime joint operation with the United States against four Afghan drug laboratories. This example, however, did not lead to any sustained collaboration. Russia, of course, has cooperated with a host of other countries in sharing information about drug shipments, seizing such shipments, and disrupting drug networks. Yet it is Afghanistan that remains topmost on Moscow's mind.

Terrorism, since the 1990s, has been another scourge plaguing Russia. Originally linked to the conflict in Chechnya, and still centered in Russia's Northern Caucasus, terrorist groups there soon developed international links, including with al-Qaeda and its affiliates. At the Security Council, Russia pushed for the adoption of robust counterterrorism resolutions, and supported the creation of the Counter-Terrorism Committee and other bodies that monitor the sanctions against groups and individuals affiliated to al-Qaeda and the Taliban. Yet Russia's own war on terror is often met with skepticism in the West, where Moscow's methods are viewed as heavy-handed. Chechnya's former separatist leaders, whom Russia accuses of links with terrorists, have been given asylum in the West. The Boston Marathon bombing of 2013, however, demonstrated that Caucasus-linked terrorism can also be a threat to countries other than Russia.

The tumultuous 1990s gave rise to organized crime in Russia, which at some point—before the recentralization of the state early in the new millennium—wielded a lot of power inside the country. With postcommunist Russia joining the world, Russia's borders, previously tightly shut, were opened, and the initial weakness of the state allowed transborder criminal activities to thrive. Russian criminal groups also established connections with criminals in other countries, and vice versa, posing a common threat. Russia has been actively seeking, and obtaining, international cooperation in extraditing criminals from other countries. Since 2012, the Russian government has been trying to "discipline" the country's elites, making them declare their property abroad and prohibiting officials from keeping financial assets abroad. In 2013, Moscow also moved against its state-owned companies using tax havens, until recently a common practice.

Nuclear Nonproliferation

Russia, still a nuclear superpower and a cofounder of the Nuclear Non-Proliferation Treaty regime, sees itself as a guardian of global strategic stability. Since the 1960s, it has consistently opposed efforts by non–nuclear weapon states to acquire or produce nuclear weapons, possibly with one exception: India. In 1998, Russia took India's emergence as a nuclear power relatively calmly, given New Delhi's well-known principled stance on the issue and in recognition of the long-standing close political relationship between the two countries. Pakistan's nuclear weapons program, by contrast, had long been viewed with concern in Moscow due to the pervasive political instability in Pakistan and the rise in Islamist extremism in that country.

Moscow's approaches to the Iranian and North Korean nuclear issues are different from those of the Western powers, but the goal is the same: no nuclear weapons for those countries. On Iran, the goal is still achievable, but, the Russians believe, only if Iran and the international community find a common ground on the parameters and monitoring of Iran's uranium enrichment program, which would not have a weapons component, and agree on security safeguards for the world, and security guarantees for Iran. From the Russian standpoint, imposing sanctions on Iran is a dual-edged sword: while some Council-imposed sanctions—which Russia has supported—may help push Iran closer to compromise, isolating Iran altogether would only empower Iranian hardliners and undercut pragmatists.

Moscow has also been consistently skeptical of US, Israeli, and occasionally French alarmism over Iran's nuclear weapons progress, seeing Tehran's project as relatively slow-moving compared to those of the countries that eventually developed their nuclear weapons, and thus allowing room for diplomacy. Many Russians suspect that such alarmism mainly serves to support the case for military action against Iran, which Moscow believes could lead to disastrous consequences. Moscow flatly rejects the possibility of ever granting Council approval to use force against Iran, basically ensuring that any US or Israeli military action against Iran would be illegal under international law, should it ever occur. From the Russian perspective, the most promising way of dealing with Tehran is through the P5+1 talks, which bring together the P5 plus Germany. Moscow had privately encouraged Washington to engage Tehran bilaterally, outside the P5+1 framework, which the Obama administration actually did in 2013. The Ukraine crisis notwithstanding, Russia continued to cooperate with the other P5+1 nations in working toward a final agreement with Iran in 2014–2015.

On North Korea, Russia takes a broadly similar stance, though Pyongyang has progressed much further than Iran toward nuclear weapons and missile technology. Russia opposes military action on the Korean Peninsula, which is situated close to Russia's borders in the Far East. Instead, it favors a combination of incentives and disincentives to push the North Koreans back to the Six-Party Talks (of which Russia is one of the parties) and to make the parties realize what they are missing in terms of economic opportunities by being obstinate. Russians of course were not amused in 2006 when a North Korean missile landed by mistake within Russia's exclusive economic zone off Vladivostok. In 2009 and 2013, Moscow strongly condemned North Korean provocative missile launches and nuclear tests, and voted at the Council for sanctions against Pyongyang, but as in the Iran case it then opposed introducing more sanctions on top of those approved.

It is clear that if the efforts aimed at preventing or rolling back nuclear proliferation in Iran and North Korea are to succeed, close collaboration among the P5 is a must. Precisely this, however, has been in short supply since the mid-1990s.

The Security Council's Internal Divisions

For the reasons explained, Russia is interested in an effective Security Council, kind of a global Politburo or a board of directors of World Inc. Making Western actions that Russia opposes at the Council illegal in the sense of international law is small comfort to Moscow. Should the United States develop a habit of acting outside the UN framework, the world according to the Kremlin would be a less secure place. Russia, of course, is not shy about using its veto right to protect its principles, wedded as they are to Moscow's wider interests.

Steeped in the culture of great power competition and its accompanying controversy, the Russians are not allergic to being in a minority of one, even though the price of this is usually high in terms of international public opinion. However, Russian officials regard public opinion to be constantly shifting and too vulnerable to manipulation to be a solid factor in decision-making. Like the weather, public opinion is constantly changing, whereas national interests form the landscape of world politics. Where possible, however, Moscow has sought partners for its contrarian moves: France and Germany in the case of Iraq in 2003; China and other BRICS countries, more recently, such as in the case of Syria.

Russo-Chinese Cooperation on the Security Council

Russo-Chinese interaction in the Security Council requires special attention. Russian and Chinese representatives in New York often vote together, and occasionally use their veto jointly against Western-supported draft resolutions, most spectacularly on Syria in 2012–2013, where they opposed what they saw as a one-sided Western approach placing all the blame for the violence on the Assad regime. Moscow and Beijing also built a common front in other cases, such as allegations of human rights abuse against Zimbabwe and Myanmar, where they sought to uphold the principle of non-interference in domestic affairs of other countries. Both sets of principles, of course, are closely tied to Russia's and China's national interests, as their leaders interpret them. The Russo-Chinese tandem, however, should not be mistaken for an alliance, a reincarnation of the Moscow-Beijing bloc of the 1950s. True, Beijing and Moscow have managed to markedly improve their relations after a bitter split in the early 1960s and the almost three decades of a cold war between them. The current Sino-Russian relationship is good and appreciably solid. Within it, however, each partner is being essentially pragmatic, and focused on its own interests. What unites the Chinese and the Russians is their rejection of US global supremacy, and promotion of a more balanced international system.

Evidently, China's behavior at the Council has been very different from Russia's. Since the 1990s, the Chinese—in stark contrast to the Russians—have been pursuing more low-profile policies, and have avoided casting their veto where China's interests are not directly affected. Beijing could also reap the benefits of Moscow's much more vocal opposition to US policies—one veto is enough to block Council action—without having to expose itself by using its own veto. Thus, in the run-up to the US/UK invasion of Iraq, China thought it wiser to keep a low profile and let Russia and France take the heat for openly opposing the use of force. More recently, however, Beijing has started loosening the self-imposed restraint and taking more overt stances, most significantly by openly siding with Russia on the subject of Syria. Even though the West, in particular the Germans, sought to mollify China's opposition to condemning the Syrian regime, these attempts have not delivered the results desired.

Having China siding with Russia at the UN Security Council, and even de facto accepting Moscow's leadership, strengthens Russia's hand internationally. However, Russia does not have to bribe China to support its stance at the Council. At this juncture, China's interests regarding the structure and functioning of the world order happen to coincide with Russia's. This basic coincidence of interest is likely to last for the foreseeable future.

UN Reform

For Moscow, the concept of a world order as enshrined in the UN Charter and the UN architecture, with the Security Council at its pinnacle, is one that suits its interests very well. Russia gives a nod to the calls stressing the need to reform the United Nations, but is clearly interested in preserving the primary role of the Security Council, and Russia's own permanent, veto-wielding position within it. Russian officials insist that no reform, however small, should come at the expense of the status, rights, and privileges currently exercised by the five permanent members. Consensus among the P5 is deemed to be key to the effectiveness of the Council. In principle, Russia does not oppose adding new permanent members to better reflect the current distribution of power and influence in the world. It helps that Moscow has no particular phobias with regard to the major aspirants, such as Germany, Japan, India, or Brazil, but it is adamant that the role of the Council in maintaining peace and security around the world be strengthened, not weakened, as a result, and that the veto right of the permanent members be preserved and not extended to any new permanent members. This only reaffirms the central point: for Russia, the United Nations is above all about the Security Council, and the Council's prime value to Moscow lies in Russia holding permanent membership with the veto right.

Russian officials reject criticism that Moscow's frequent use of the veto destroys consensus among the permanent members and renders the Security Council dysfunctional. For Russia, it is such actions as the 2003 invasion of Iraq, undertaken without a Council mandate, that undermine the international system and global security. The Kremlin posits Russia, one of the principal founding members of the United Nations, as the guardian of international law and thus a pillar of global stability. Essentially, this is a very conservative attitude. Russian diplomacy at the United Nations is highly professional; it attaches a lot of interest to procedural details; and it possesses a long institutional memory and is very much history-conscious. At the same time, Russia has cast itself more in the role of a defender of the existing system—and, critics would add, its own privileges under it—than a proponent of innovation, an originator of new ideas, or an intellectual leader for the international community.

Outlook

Russian official documents consistently refer to the United Nations as the main regulator and coordinator of global politics. All its deficiencies and shortcomings notwithstanding, the UN is believed to have no alternative in the present-day world. It is also endowed with unique legitimacy, far superior to that of any other international body. When Russian officials refer to the UN in such terms, however, they primarily mean the UN Security Council, not the General Assembly. It is the Council that Moscow appreciates most about the UN system. It sees the Council as the best instrument available to debate and occasionally decide, but at the very least to legally block any action detrimental to the Russian interests on the matters of international peace and security.

Russian leaders, of course, are realists enough not to place their security in the hands of the Security Council alone. They are seeking to upgrade Russia's own military strength, cooperate more closely with its nominal allies in the Collective Security Treaty Organization (CSTO), and use Moscow's wide web of political relations with all the key international players. These range from strategic stability relations with the United States and the Russia-NATO Council to the Shanghai Cooperation Organization and the BRICS group to the G-8/20, in all of which Russia is a member.

This stance will continue as far as one can see. Russia's de facto strategic independence, regained in the mid-2000s, has become more pronounced over the past decade. With the Eurasian Economic Union, formally launched in 2015, Russia hopes to again lead a bloc of like-minded countries. The Russo-Chinese partnership will continue to develop, but it will fall far short of an alliance. As long as Russia and China share key interests regarding global security governance, they will stick together. Moscow, however, will try to stay away from Beijing's quarrels with neighbors and steer clear of potential Sino-American conflicts. In the future, the level of Russia's cooperation with the Western countries at the UN Security Council will depend, as before, on the general state and direction of Russian-American and, to a lesser degree, Russian-European relations.

Russia's leaders realize, of course, that what makes for a great power in the twenty-first century is not simply a combination of nuclear weapons and Security Council membership. They are painfully aware that without relaunching the economy and attending to the health and education of its people, Russia will be history's loser. Should this happen, Russia's Security Council membership will be reduced to the defense of a status no longer supported by the realities of the new millennium. Conversely, should Russia be able to use its current economic crisis to diversify its economy and strengthen its scientific and technological capacity, its UN diplomacy will acquire a much stronger material base and enhance Russia's impact on twenty-first century global developments.

6

France and the United Kingdom in the Security Council

Thierry Tardy and Dominik Zaum

AS PERMANENT MEMBERS OF THE UN SECURITY COUNCIL, FRANCE and the United Kingdom share many common features, in terms of both their respective foreign and defense policies, and their conception of their role within the supreme UN political body.

France and the UK are both postcolonial, medium-sized, nuclear powers, and members of the European Union and NATO. They have developed similar strategic cultures that combine a certain attachment to some rules and principles of global governance, and a propensity and capability to take part in multilateral or national military operations overseas. Notably, since the end of World War II, the foreign policies of France and Britain have been driven by the necessity to manage relative decline in power. In this process, their permanent position at the UN Security Council has been perceived both as a remnant of past grandeur and as a means to continue to shape the international political agenda to their own benefit.

France and Britain have generally been considered to be the most active members of the Council. This activism has to a certain extent been aimed at justifying their seat in the select club, to demonstrate that because of their contribution they deserve the privilege to be a permanent part of the world's most important mechanism of global security governance.

Indeed, since the end of the Cold War, be it in the Balkans, in sub-Saharan Africa, or in Libya, or on issues such as peacekeeping, nonproliferation, or sanctions, France and the UK have played a prominent role in the Council in terms of drafting resolutions, leading debates, and shaping the agenda. In doing so, they also have displayed a high level of convergence in the Security Council in terms of positions and votes. Occasional differences do occur, as was the case over Iraq in 2003 or with some recurrence on the Israel-Palestine issue. Furthermore, the overlap between France's policy in sub-Saharan Africa—its former colonies in particular—and the continued prominence of this region on the agenda of the Council has placed France in a position notably distinct from that of Britain, which has not pursued its security interests through the Council to the same extent. However, France and the UK by and large share the same vision of the role of the Council in security governance as well as of its utility for their own global positioning.

In this chapter we offer a comparative analysis of the French and British policies within the UN Security Council. We show the similarities in their approach to and positions in the Council, and draw on key substantive issues over the past decade—Iraq, Iran, Libya, sub-Saharan Africa, peace-keeping, terrorism—to highlight both their common features and occasional differences. The first section outlines why the Security Council matters for French and British foreign policies and addresses similarities and differences. The second section looks at how France and the UK engage with the Council, probing both the depth of their involvement and key processes through which they engage the Council. In the third section, we examine how the two countries have approached key challenges posed to the Security Council, in particular the issue of reform and the rise of new powers, especially when they sit on the Council. Finally, we summarize the issues and briefly evaluate the extent to which France's and Britain's engagement in the Council have been successful with regard to advancing their own security interests and promoting key goals of the UN Charter.

Why the Council Matters for French and British Foreign Policy: Similarities and Differences

The UN Security Council is of similar strategic importance to France's and the UK's identity and role on the international scene. This importance has to do with both "being" and "doing" in international politics, in the sense that their permanent seat simultaneously confers an international status that neither France nor Britain would be in a position to enjoy were they not part of the club, and offers an irreplaceable platform of expression of their respective foreign policies and action on the international scene.

First, the permanent seat with its veto power provides status. It provides both states a privileged position in the society of states, as it guarantees them a say in all UN-discussed issues irrespective of real clout or interest in the matter. For Gaullist France, which has always been obsessed with its status, being recognized as one among the five biggest powers has long been an end in itself; it has provided "prestige and moral position," which are two "attributes of power."[1] Britain is arguably more reconciled with its middle-power status, and the postwar sense that it is indisputably one of the great powers has gradually given way to latent insecurity about its position on the Council,[2] and a perceived need to support its claim to a permanent seat through strong engagement. There is also a recognition that its ability to "punch above its weight" is both driven and enabled by its continued status as a permanent member. A Council that is a prominent part of the international security architecture, and a permanent seat on the Council, are therefore, for the UK as for France, ends in themselves.[3] In addition, both countries have used their status as permanent members to secure key senior positions for their nationals in the main peace and security departments of the UN Secretariat, where France has fielded subsequent heads of the Department of Peacekeeping Operations (DPKO) since 1997 and where an Englishman was in charge of the Department of Political Affairs (DPA) from 1993 to 2005.

Interestingly enough, the circumstances in which France and the UK gained status as permanent members of the Security Council differed. Great Britain, as one of the four victorious powers of World War II, was part of all talks on the establishment of the UN and strongly contributed to the drafting of the Charter; that it would become a member of the Security Council was undisputed.[4] By contrast, not only was France absent from the big conferences that laid the grounds for the creation of the UN, but at both the Dumbarton Oaks conference (August–October 1944) and the Yalta conference (February 1945), the United States and the Soviet Union were cautious about a French permanent seat on the Council, while the British pushed for it. Only after Yalta was France formally offered a permanent seat.[5]

Subsequently, both France's and the UK's presence in the club has in a way compensated for their inexorable decline in power. The illusion of grandeur was maintained through the permanent and veto-yielding seat, and later reinforced through both countries' ascension to nuclear power status.

With the end of the Cold War, the balance between "being" and "doing" slightly shifted as France and Britain became increasingly active within the revitalized Council, with the UK organizing the first Security Council summit at the level of heads of state and government, in 1992,[6] and both countries contributing significantly to UN peacekeeping operations in the early post–Cold War years, especially in the Balkans. Two aspects matter here. The first is the position of permanent member as a vehicle or instrument of foreign policy: France and Britain, as countries that both have had a long diplomatic tradition and continue to be among the few countries in the world with global diplomatic networks and ambitions, being part of a body that has become "central to the life of international diplomacy"[7] is essential. The other aspect is their position within the Council as a source of responsibility, which in turn creates a necessity to act. Indeed, being a permanent member has significantly shaped the foreign policies of Britain and France by putting them in the limelight of international politics and consequently requiring them to articulate their own positions on a wide range of issues. These two elements matter for France and Britain in a way that they do not for the other three permanent members. Against this backdrop, the two countries have developed in the Council a proactive policy with expertise and leading roles on many thematic, regional, or country-specific issues, to support their contention that they deserve their permanent seats.[8] No other foreign policy instrument provides France or the UK a similar position on the world scene. The only one that comes close is their nuclear status, but its utility in terms of international influence and visibility is too contested to offer the same kind of benefits.[9]

These similarities in outlook have been complemented by the parallel convergence in their respective strategic cultures and conception of the role of coercion in international relations, as illustrated by cases as diverse as Bosnia and Herzegovina in the 1990s, Kosovo in 1998–1999 (on which the Security Council was notably sidelined by NATO), Afghanistan since 2001, and Libya in 2011. Furthermore, both countries have been leading the Council's engagement with conflicts in Africa, peacekeeping,[10] and sanctions, among other issues. In recent years, Britain has been in the lead on Cyprus, Darfur, Libya, Nepal, Sierra Leone, Somalia, and Yemen, while France has been in the lead on Burundi, the Central African Republic, Chad, Côte d'Ivoire, the Democratic Republic of the Congo, Lebanon, Mali, and Syria. The two countries are also members of collective drafting groups, such as the ones dealing with Western Sahara, Haiti, and the Balkans.

Over the past three decades, Britain and France have proposed and supported (alone, together, or with others) an average of almost two-thirds of the draft resolutions subsequently adopted by the Council (discussed later). On most issues, the two countries operate as allies, backing each other on their respective agendas: in over 800 draft resolutions tabled at the Council since 2000, France and the UK diverged only eleven times in their votes, with one of them abstaining if the other one was in favor (see Table 6.1). In over half of the cases, the draft resolutions on which their votes diverged concerned the Palestinian question and were vetoed by the United States. This is not to say that they would systematically agree on a given issue, but their alliance of necessity would in most cases trump possible divergences. This has been illustrated in two cases, Somalia and Mali, for which the UK and France are respectively in the lead; although discrepancies have been expressed in particular on Somalia, where France was reluctant to endorse some aspects of the UN and AU policies pushed by the UK,[11] in the end reciprocal support prevailed.[12]

In this broad picture, the overlap between security developments in sub-Saharan Africa and the French policy in this region has made France more visible at the Council than the UK; put differently, French political and security interests in Africa are reflected more consistently in the Council's agenda than are British geographical or thematic interests, notwith-standing Somalia. To a certain extent, be it in Chad, Côte d'Ivoire, the DRC, or Mali, the Council's involvement can be seen as legitimizing French policy in the region. In some cases, the Council may also be used as a burden-sharing tool or as part of an exit strategy, for example through the establishment of a UN peacekeeping operation, as in Mali or in the Central African Republic.

In this context of general convergence, the two countries do differ on certain issues debated at the Security Council. These divergences tend to

Table 6.1 French and UK Diverging Votes on UN Security Council Resolutions, 2000–2013

	Resolutions Passed	Resolutions Vetoed	French/UK Divergent Votes	Resolutions on Which Votes Diverged
2000	50	0	0	n.a.
2001	52	2	1	S/2001/1199 of December 14, on the Palestinian question; draft resolution vetoed by United States (France in favor, UK abstained)
2002	78	2	0	n.a.
2003	66	2	5	1487 of June 12 on peacekeeping[a] (France abstained, UK in favor) 1497 of August 1 on Liberia (France abstained, UK in favor) 1506 of September 12 on Libya (France abstained, UK in favor) S/2003/891 of September 16 and S/2003/980 of October 14 on the Palestinian question; both draft resolutions vetoed by United States (France in favor, UK abstained)
2004	59	3	2	S/2004/240 of March 25 and S/2004/783 of October 5 on the Palestinian question; both draft resolutions vetoed by United States (France in favor, UK abstained)

continues

Table 6.1 continued

	Resolutions Passed	Resolutions Vetoed	French/UK Divergent Votes	Resolutions on Which Votes Diverged
2005	71	0	0	n.a.
2006	87	2	2	S/2006/508 of July 13 and S/2006/878 of November 11 on the Palestinian question; both draft resolutions vetoed by United States (France in favor, UK abstained)
2007	56	1	0	n.a.
2008	65	1	0	n.a.
2009	48	1	0	n.a.
2010	59	0	1	1958 of December 15 on Iraq (France abstained, UK in favor)
2011	66	2	0	n.a.
2012	53	2	0	n.a.
2013[b]	29	0	0	n.a.

Notes: a. The issue of contention was the impunity of the peacekeepers from the International Criminal Court.

b. Until July 31, 2013.

reflect different assessments of particular issues, or long-term policies vis-à-vis a country or region. Typically, Iraq in 2003 was a case of strategic dissonance over the threat assessment posed by a particular situation, while shedding light on a longer-term trend of British alignment with the United States. Since the Iraq episode, British convergence with the United States at the expense of a "British-French axis" was manifested at the Council in a series of votes on the Israel-Palestine issue, on which the UK abstained—while France voted in favor—on draft resolutions vetoed by the United States.[13] There is also Britain's propensity to consult with the United States, which France does not observe to the same degree. Such alignment should not be overstated, though, especially in the context of a comparative analysis of the British and French policies at the Council, which reveals a Franco-British axis that is not necessarily weaker than the US-UK alignment.

Indeed, over the past three decades, the French and the British have displayed a broad convergence of views and acted in tandem on issues such as Libya, the International Criminal Court (ICC),[14] or Syria,[15] on which the British position has arguably been closer to that of France than that of the United States.[16] Most notably and exceptionally, on February 18, 2011, the UK voted together with France in favor of a draft resolution on the settlement issue in Palestinian territories, which was vetoed by the United

States.[17] This had already happened twice, in 2002 on Bosnia-Herzegovina and already on Palestine.[18] On strategic issues where the French and the British are very closely aligned, such as Libya or Syria, the Security Council is also seen as a vehicle to engage the United States, without which the Franco-British ability to shape events remains limited. Apart from these issues, France and the UK have differed on issues such as Cyprus and Western Sahara, where their respective alliances mean that they find themselves on opposite sides of the diplomatic table. More recently, France and the UK have also to an extent competed for the Council's attention and devotion of resources to conflicts or peacekeeping operations in countries in their respective spheres of influence, a dynamic that has grown somewhat more intense in the context of the global financial crisis.

Finally, despite their different approaches to and visions for the EU, both countries see the EU's role at the Security Council in similar terms. For neither country does the EU have a place on the Council beyond what it has already obtained in terms of delivering statements. They do encourage the engagement of the Council with other international and regional organizations, including the EU (e.g., through peace operations), yet they have (in common with the other permanent members) not supported a role for such organizations on the Council. While the EU has asserted greater weight in international organizations over the past two decades,[19] and is even able, through its "upgraded" observer status within the UN, to "present and promote the EU's positions" at the UN General Assembly,[20] it has not been able to play this role in the Security Council. Both France and the UK have consistently refused to be perceived as EU representatives at the Council, even though there is a degree of coordination among EU members on their positions—not least because such a perception could fuel proposals for replacing their permanent seats with a "European" one. Often the French and British have even found themselves at odds with other EU members, thus undermining ambitions to create a common foreign and security policy. In this context, France has been a keener supporter of EU-led peace operations endorsed by the Council (e.g., Operation Artemis in the DRC in 2003, or the EU force in Chad and the Central African Republic in 2008–2009) than the UK, and is less suspicious about an EU role and presence within the UN in general, yet this has not been extended to a desire to strengthen an EU representation on the Council.

Engagement in the Council

Leading the Council's Agenda
As noted earlier, France and the UK are the most active members of the Security Council. Four indicators of their active engagement stand out.

First, in their role as so-called penholders, both France and the UK are leading Council engagement on key issues on the Council's agenda. As Table 6.2 highlights, they lead as penholders, together with the United States, on the vast majority of issues on the Council's agenda—in marked contrast to Russia, which leads on two issues, and China, which leads on none. When one unpacks these figures, a more differentiated picture emerges, yet one that further underlines the depth of the two countries' engagement. As of early 2015, Britain and France lead on four of the five countries with the biggest UN peacekeeping forces (Darfur, the DRC, Lebanon, and Mali), as well as on what were arguably among the most controversial and prominent issues on the Council's agenda in 2012 and 2013, such as Libya, the Sahel, and Syria—though it is noteworthy that the United States leads on prominent and contested nonproliferation issues, especially Iran and North Korea. When comparing the issues where the UK and France hold the pen, it appears that France is more explicitly focused on countries and regions where it has strong historical and colonial links and ongoing security interests (such as sub-Saharan Africa or Lebanon) than is the UK, which leads on thematic issues (such as civilians in armed conflict, and the role of women in peace and security) largely eschewed by France.

Second, their prominent role with regard to key issues on the Council's agenda is reflected in their involvement in drafting key resolutions. A look at the resolutions passed since January 2010 highlights that, with two exceptions, France and the UK have been sponsors or cosponsors, and therefore involved in the drafting, of all resolutions that have established new peacekeeping operations in the Democratic Republic of the Congo, UNISFA in Sudan, UNMISS in South Sudan, and UNOCI in Côte d'Ivoire; of resolutions establishing special political missions (UNSMIL in Libya); and of resolutions establishing or extending sanctions regimes.[21]

Third, both countries have headed a substantially larger number of Security Council visiting missions than other permanent members. The Council has regularly used such field visits since the end of the Cold War for fact-finding purposes, to underline the Council's engagement in a conflict or region, or to impress the Council's position on conflict parties.[22] French-led missions have almost exclusively focused on Central Africa and the Great Lakes region, while British missions have (despite a strong emphasis on West Africa) a wider geographic focus.

Finally, since 1989, neither country has used their veto—in contrast to the other three permanent members. Traditionally, both countries have been averse to being the sole state casting a veto—France has done so only twice (in 1947 and 1976), and Britain five times, in the 1960s and 1970s, but exclusively in the context of the Rhodesian question.[23] In March 2003, the Jacques Chirac administration explicitly stated that it would vote against any resolution that would seek authorization of the use of force against

129

Table 6.2 Engagement in Security Council Work

	China	France	Russian Federation	United Kingdom	United States	United Nations Total
Penholder for issues on Security Council agenda (2014)	0	9	2	10	15	47[a]
Vetoes (1990–2014)	8	0	11	0	16	36
Vetoes (2008–2014)	5	0	7	0	1	13
Last time veto was used (as of December 31, 2014)	May 22, 2014	Dec. 23, 1989	May 22, 2014	Dec. 23, 1989	Feb. 18, 2011	
Headship/coheadship of Security Council missions (1990–2013)	0	8	0	9	5	41[b]
Peacekeeping operations Operations participated in (2013)	9	7	8	3	5	14
Police and troops deployed (December 2014)	2,181	922	75	289	127	104,062
Leadership positions (March 2013)[c]	1	1	0	1	4	40
Contribution to peacekeeping budget (2012–2013)	$286 million	$549 million	$144 million	$597 million	$1.9 billion	$7.3 billion

Notes: a. On three issues, Contact Groups/Groups of Friends (all with UK and French participation) were penholders, and on ten issues nonmember states were penholders.

b. The remaining missions were headed by nonpermanent members.

c. Leadership positions include special representatives and deputy special representatives of the Secretary-General, force commanders, and police commanders.

Iraq.[24] Ironically, it was the initial insistence of the British—or at least of Prime Minister Tony Blair—on the need for such an explicit authorization that made accommodation between the United States and France on this issue impossible. In the end, however, the inability of the United Kingdom and the United States to secure nine votes in favor of their draft resolution meant that it was never put to a vote. Arguably, one of the reasons for France and the Britain not using the veto is that it would highlight the privileges that permanent membership accords them, and the degree to which these privileges are at odds with their actual power. It would threaten to erode both the legitimacy of the Council (in which both countries have a greater interest than do their fellow permanent members) and, more importantly, the legitimacy of their claim to a permanent seat.

While all of these four aspects are strong indicators of the active engagement of both countries in the Security Council's business, it is also worth highlighting that there are areas where their engagement—similar to that of other permanent members—is more limited. While the UK and France—like the other P5—are deeply engaged in different sanctions regimes, neither country chairs any of the sanctions committees or any of the other subsidiary organs of the Council, and neither involves itself with the day-to-day management of the committees (with the exception of the Informal Expert Group on Civilians in Armed Conflict, chaired by the UK, which also chaired the Counter-Terrorism Committee for the first two years after the attacks of September 11, 2001). This has been traditionally left to the nonpermanent members. Similarly, as highlighted in Table 6.2, while both countries are major financial contributors to the peacekeeping budget, their actual involvement in UN-led peacekeeping operations is very limited, partly as a result of their shared analysis of their ill-defined commitment to the UN operations in the former Yugoslavia in the early 1990s and the traumas that followed. However, their levels of participation differ slightly: French contributions to UN operations have been higher than the UK's mainly because of France's contingent in UNIFIL in Lebanon.[25] Most notably, France has sustained a high level of military deployment in support of UN peace operations, such as in Côte d'Ivoire and Mali, or through the EU in the Democratic Republic of the Congo and Chad. The situation in the Central African Republic further attests to France's activism in security management, with both a French and an EU operation (to which France contributes most of the troops) present in that country, and an open push for a UN peacekeeping mission to take over for the two operations. In all these cases, France is keen to operate in accordance with UN Security Council resolutions—many of which France itself drafts—yet outside the UN command-and-control structure. Although at times pursued reluctantly, those interventions provide France visibility at the Security Council and make it a driving force of a policy motivated by a mix of narrowly defined security interests (antiterrorism in Mali) and a broader commitment to stability in areas that fall within France's sphere of influence. This is something the UK has not done since the deployment of a small force in support of UNAMSIL in Sierra Leone in 2000, not least because substantial UK deployments in Afghanistan and Iraq arguably made it difficult for the British armed forces to deploy in substantial numbers elsewhere during the first decade of the twenty-first century.

Conceptualizing and Making UN Policy

The importance of the UN Security Council for British and French foreign and security policy is also reflected in key national security documents. In the UK, the National Security Strategy published by the coalition government in October 2010 identifies the UK's permanent membership on the Council as central to the UK's ability to project power and influence internationally.[26] Furthermore, its 2011 strategy to address and prevent conflict in weak and fragile countries, the Building Stability Overseas Strategy, highlights the importance of the UN framework, including the Security Council, for such efforts. It also conveys a sense that the UK, as a permanent member, has a particular responsibility to support the Council's work in this regard.[27]

Similarly, most French foreign and security policy documents highlight the centrality and legitimacy of the Security Council within the international security architecture, as well as the strategic importance of France's permanent position. Interestingly enough, though, while the 2008 French white paper on national defense and security was explicit on the merits of the United Nations and its Security Council in the maintenance of international peace and security,[28] as well as on the responsibility that being a permanent member confers to France, the 2013 white paper is far more laconic. This reflects a certain skepticism vis-à-vis the UN as a possible framework of French security policy, in a context where the operations in Libya and Mali have raised the merits of swift coercive action over those of long-term peacekeeping.

Who, then, is responsible for Security Council policy in the two countries, and what are the processes through which policy is developed? While both countries tend to have very senior diplomats heading their missions in New York, with a lot of weight in their respective bureaucracies and often with a close link to their respective ministers, they are career diplomats and do not tend to have the autonomy that, for example, some US permanent representatives have had, who have often been appointed to political positions with cabinet rank.

In the UK, the Foreign and Commonwealth Office (FCO) leads on UN policy, even if political direction on high-profile issues (e.g., Iraq in 2002–

2003, Libya in 2011, and Syria in 2012–2013) comes from the prime minister's office or the new National Security Council. As with most policy
processes, Britain's UN policy, including the drafting of resolutions, is an
iterative process, and involves a range of geographic and thematic departments and posts within the FCO, as well as at times other parts of the government, such as the Ministry of Defense or Department for International
Development. Within the FCO, which leads on the technical aspects of different resolutions, drafting can be quite dispersed between London and the
UK mission in New York (with a greater role for the mission on issues for
which the UK is penholder), and across thematic departments in London.
Drafting of resolutions is mainly done in London, and coordinated on most
aspects of Council policy by the Department of International Organizations,
with specialized thematic departments—such as on peacekeeping, human
rights, and proliferation—often leading the drafting of relevant resolutions.
In particular, in discussions of changes to the mandates of peacekeeping
operations, or about transition from peacekeeping to special political missions or UN country teams, staff from the embassies, or from the country
offices of the Department for International Development, in the affected
countries increasingly provide inputs based on their better understanding of
local dynamics and sensitivities.

In France, the Ministry of Foreign Affairs has the lead on UN policy.
The Directorate for the United Nations, International Organizations,
Human Rights, and Francophonie defines and coordinates the French
position on all UN-related issues, in close cooperation with France's permanent mission in New York—which drafts resolutions when France is
penholder—and other regional and thematic directorates in Paris (such as
the Africa Directorate, the Middle East and North Africa Directorate, and
the European Union Directorate). On matters of strategic importance,
such as Iraq in 2003 or Libya in 2011, the office of the president becomes
the focal point of decisionmaking. Under the Nicolas Sarkozy administration, a tendency toward centralization of decisionmaking had placed the
Elysée at the centre, which is less the case under the François Hollande
presidency. In New York, the seniority of the permanent representative
makes him (to date, never a woman in this office) a key actor of policy
elaboration and implementation. He is the one toward whom all other
actors converge, and knows best the margin of maneuver of France within
the Council. On issues that may imply a military deployment (ranging
from peacekeeping to more coercive activities or even wars) of French
troops in particular, the Ministry of Defense is also directly involved. In
the same vein, the Ministry of Economy and Finance plays its role in
debates related to sanctions.

One interesting difference between France and the UK, which also
seems to have affected their respective positions toward different peace-

keeping operations, is the accounting for their budgetary contributions to the UN. In France, both the country's contributions to the overall UN budget and to the peacekeeping budget come directly from the budget of the Ministry of Foreign Affairs, and increases in these contributions—for example because of the establishment of new peacekeeping operations—therefore have direct, cumulative effects on France's resources. In the UK, by contrast, the contribution to the peacekeeping budget is separate and comes directly from the treasury reserve, and changes in the budget do therefore not directly affect the FCO's resources. Unsurprisingly, the FCO has arguably been more sanguine about peacekeeping costs and the size of missions in recent years, not least because overall costs to the UK have largely stayed below the allocated budget. While the UK's share of the general UN budget comes directly from the FCO, this is unlikely to see the sudden large increases not uncommon in the peacekeeping budget, even if it includes the increasingly prominent and sizable special political missions (such as UNMIN in Nepal, or UNSMIL in Libya).

Security Council Reform:
The Necessity to Remain at the Center

Dramatic changes in the character of international society, in particular changes in the international balance of power and the rise of emerging powers like Brazil, India, and Japan, have fueled demands for Security Council reform. With the emergence of forums like the G-20, the structure and membership of the Council have arguably come to be seen as archaic, raising fears that it might be increasingly sidelined as issues are taken up by alternative groupings that are seen to better reflect the contemporary realities of power.

These changes in the international order have undoubtedly informed French and British interests in Council reform; for both countries, ensuring the Council's centrality must in return guarantee their own role, and therefore reform—meaning enlargement—is no longer perceived as a threat. Yet their attitudes toward reform have also been shaped by two further considerations. On the one hand, their declining status in the international balance of power, and the overrepresentation of Western European states on the Council, mean that any Council reform that would put all permanent seats up for discussion would threaten the current position of France and the UK on the Council. On the other hand, as long as it does not threaten their own position, any reform strengthening the legitimacy of the Council, and affirming its role at the center of the international security architecture, presumably serves France's and the UK's interests, as it strengthens their ability to project power and influence internationally. As Council reforms have largely been framed in terms of enlargement, rather than replacement, and in terms of reforming working methods, both states have generally been the most supportive of reform efforts among the P5.

One exception to this support for reform has been resistance to occasional proposals that the two countries should give up their respective permanent seats in favor of a shared or pan-European one—a proposal mooted informally by the Italian foreign minister in the early 1990s, and then by the European Parliament.[29] Both countries have, unsurprisingly, fervently rejected any such proposal, regardless of the feasibility or acceptability to other permanent members of the membership of a regional organization.

During the stalled reform efforts that started with the 2004 report of Secretary-General Kofi Annan's High-Level Panel on Threats, Challenges, and Change, both countries have supported permanent membership for the so-called Group of Four (G4) (Brazil, India, Japan, and Germany), as well as greater African representation among the permanent members, and even issued a joint statement to that end at the 2008 and 2009 Anglo-French summits.[30] At their 2008 summit, the two countries also introduced the idea of an intermediate reform, with an extended membership for key aspirant states, and the possible conversion of these seats into permanent ones following a review process. While the proposal gathered some support among member states, it failed to break the deadlock in the reform discussions. Notably, France also proposed that permanent members should refrain from using the veto in Responsibility to Protect situations in response to the Council's divisions over Syria,[31] a proposal that initially appeared in the 2001 report of the International Commission on Intervention and State Sovereignty, and that was rooted in a "code of conduct" for the use of the veto mooted by French foreign minister Hubert Védrine in one of the commission's roundtable discussions.[32]

Proposals for working-method reforms have also been initiated by nonpermanent members, such as the so-called Small Five (Costa Rica, Jordan, Liechtenstein, Singapore, and Switzerland). France and the UK have been publicly supportive of such efforts, and expressed concern about the prominence of informal consultations in the Council, and the concomitant lack of transparency. Behind the scenes, however, both countries have generally joined their fellow permanent members in resisting and scuttling substantial reforms of the Council's working methods, as over S5 efforts to pass a General Assembly resolution calling on the P5 to refrain from using the veto in situations of genocide, war crimes, and crimes against humanity, in May 2012.[33] Most important, Paris and London were defending a principled position whereby the General Assembly was not the appropriate forum for defining the working methods of the Council. To the extent that France and the UK have supported or even initiated reforms, such as the introduction of horizon-scanning briefings by the DPA to the Council, these reforms do not make any concessions with regard to P5 dominance, but are merely informal exercises of the Secretary-General's power under Article 99 of the Charter to bring to the Council's attention matters that may threaten international peace and security. Their public support for modest working-method reforms has been largely driven by their desire to be seen as being "on the right side" of the argument on Council reform and blunt criticisms of the Council, because of their interest in a Council widely recognized as legitimate and relevant, and because most working-method reforms do not generally challenge their more tenuous claims to a permanent seat.

The rhetoric of reform has so far left the structure and membership of the Council largely unaffected. Similarly, neither reform rhetoric nor the reality of a changing international order has dramatically changed British and French diplomacy around the horseshoe table. Despite emphasizing the need to engage with the emerging powers (and a strong emphasis of British ministers from the prime minister down on greater economic and political cooperation with emerging powers, especially the democratic ones) at the Council, the UK and France continue to fall back almost instinctively to negotiations with first their fellow "P1" member, the United States, and then broadening discussions to the P5 and ultimately the wider Council membership.[34] Nonpermanent members, and especially European ones, may play an increasing role at early stages of debates, yet neither the greater international role of the emerging powers, nor their unprecedented presence on the Council in recent years (between 2010 and 2012, all G4 members and the leading African contenders for a permanent Council seat were at some point elected members), has been reflected in greater engagement or sustained joint policy initiatives with them. Furthermore, the Libyan episode, with India, Brazil, and most importantly Germany abstaining on Security Council Resolution 1973 (2011), authorizing the use of force against the Muammar Qaddafi regime, and the Indian and Brazilian resistance to strengthening the sanctions regime against Iran, have not played in favor of the candidates' claim to a permanent seat. The embrace and support for change in the Council by France and the UK is therefore carefully circumscribed and strongly informed by a desire to shore up key aspects of the status quo.

Conclusion

To evaluate the role of France and the UK on the Council, one can ask two specific questions. First, how has their permanent membership affected the role and workings of the Security Council? Second, has their permanent membership served their wider political and security interests?

With regard to the first, the discussion in this chapter suggests that, overall, the presence of France and the UK on the Council has helped to enhance its role in international politics. Both countries have a strong interest in a Security Council that is perceived as legitimate and that remains close to the center of international politics, as this enhances their own standing in the international society of states. Both have generally sought to keep the Council engaged, and through the Council keep other great powers involved in collective efforts to address threats to international peace and security. Their strategic culture has shaped their interests in a more interventionist UN, and with it an interest in strengthening the organization's capacities to that end.

With regard to the second question, the chapter suggests that permanent membership has served both countries' interests very well, helping them to maintain a privileged position in international society that exceeds their military and economic clout. In the early decades of the Cold War, an active Council (and UN more generally) was at times seen as threatening core colonial interests of both France and the UK. This is no longer the case, for two reasons. First, the norms and institutions advanced by the UN (including the Council) broadly reflect liberal principles that are also central to French and British policy. An active Council is therefore no threat to the core interests and values of France and Britain. Second, given their limited ability to autonomously project force and engage in sustained military campaigns, an active Security Council does not pose a major constraint on their foreign and security policies. Both France and the UK are therefore in a way comfortable with their seat, and there is little doubt that the benefits to them outweigh the costs and constraints it imposes. This arguably contrasts with the stance of the other three permanent members, who either feel more constrained in their policy choices by the Council, or do not always share the norms it promotes and see its activism as a threat to core principles of international order.

France and the UK are widely recognized as the two most active members of the Security Council, and the ones that publicly profess the greatest interest in reforming and strengthening the institution. As this chapter has shown, however, this activism is a reflection of their perceived weakness. Despite strong public commitment to reform, both countries also have a major stake in maintaining key elements of the status quo, clearly circumscribing the kind of reforms they seek, and their activism in the Council has helped to ward off changes that would threaten their permanent presence (though given the very limited interest in reforms by the other three permanent members, these boundaries have hardly been tested). For the Council, however, activism driven by relative weakness is arguably preferable to defensive obstinacy, unabated passivity, or supreme-power arrogance.

Notes

1. Marie-Claude Smouts, "France and the UN System," in *The United Nations System: The Policies of Member States,* edited by Chadwick F. Alger, Gene M. Lyons, and John E. Trent (Tokyo: United Nations University Press, 1995), p. 188.

2. Adam Roberts, "Britain and the Creation of the United Nations," in *Still More Adventures with Britannia: Personalities, Politics, and Culture in Britain*, edited by William Roger Louis (London: Tauris, 2003), p. 233.

3. Mats Berdal, "The UN Security Council: Ineffective but Indispensable," *Survival* 45, no. 2 (2003): 12.

4. Roberts, "Britain and the Creation of the United Nations."

5. David L. Bosco, *Five to Rule Them All: The UN Security Council and the Making of the Modern World* (New York: Oxford University Press, 2009), pp. 26–27.

6. David Hannay, *New World Disorder: The UN After the Cold War—An Insider's View* (London: Tauris, 2008), pp. 77–83.

7. Edward Luck, *UN Security Council: Practice and Promise* (London: Routledge, 2006), p. 5.

8. In 2004, Kishore Mahbubani presented France and the UK as "the two most active members of the Council among the P-5." See Kishore Mahbubani, "The Permanent and Elected Council Members," in *The UN Security Council: From the Cold War to the 21st Century,* edited by David M. Malone (Boulder, CO: Lynne Rienner, 2004), p. 258.

9. See Paul Williams, "The United Kingdom," and Thierry Tardy, "France," in *Providing Peacekeepers: The Politics, Challenges, and Future of UN Peacekeeping Contributions,* edited by Alex Bellamy and Paul Williams (Oxford: Oxford University Press, 2013).

10. In 2009, France and the United Kingdom launched an initiative to improve the overall effectiveness of peacekeeping operations and in particular their political and military direction. See Franco-British nonpaper on peacekeeping, January 2009, www.franceonu.org/IMG/pdf_09-0116-FR-UK_Non-Papier_-_Peacekeeping_2_-2.pdf; United Nations Security Council, "Statement by the President of the Security Council," UN Doc. S/PRST/2009/24, August 5, 2009.

11. Interview with a French official, Paris, April 18, 2003.

12. Interview with French officials, New York, February 15, 2013.

13. This happened in September 2003, October 2003, July 2006, and November 2006, for Draft Resolutions S/2003/891 (September 16), S/2003/980 (October 14), S/2006/508 (July 12), and S/2006/878 (November 10), respectively. See United Nations Security Council, "Provisional Verbatim Record" of the following meetings, respectively: 4828th (UN Doc. S/PV.4828, September 16, 2003), 4842nd (UN Doc. S/PV.4842, October 14, 2003), 5488th (UN Doc. S/PV.5488, July 12, 2006), and 5565th (UN Doc. S/PV.5565, November 10, 2006).

14. See Jean-Marc de la Sablière, *Dans les Coulisses du Monde* (Paris: Robert Laffont, 2013), pp. 308–314.

15. See Colum Lynch, "Syrian Shadow Boxing," *Foreign Policy,* August 3, 2012.

16. Interview with French officials, New York, February 15, 2013.

17. United Nations Security Council, "Provisional Verbatim Record on the 6484th Meeting," UN Doc. S/PV.6484, February 18, 2011.

18. See vote on Bosnia-Herzegovina, June 30, 2002, and vote on Palestine, December 20, 2002, for Draft Resolutions S/2002/712 and S/2002/1385, respectively. See United Nations Security Council, "Provisional Verbatim Record" of the following meetings, respectively: 4563rd (UN Doc. S/PV.4563) and 4681st (UN Doc. S/PV.4681).

19. Article 34(2) of the 2007 Lisbon Treaty states that "Member States which are also members of the United Nations Security Council will concert and keep the other Member States and the High Representative fully informed. Member States which are members of the Security Council will, in the execution of their functions,

defend the positions and the interests of the Union, without prejudice to their responsibilities under the provisions of the United Nations Charter."

20. See United Nations General Assembly Resolution A/65/L.64/Rev.1 (May 3, 2011).

21. The exceptions are Resolution 1990 (June 27, 2011), UN Doc. S/RES/1990, establishing the UN Interim Security Force for Abyei (UNISFA), and Resolution 2048 (May 18, 2012), UN Doc. S/RES/2048, imposing sanctions on Guinea Bissau.

22. Jeremy Greenstock, "The Security Council in the Post–Cold War World," in *The United Nations Security Council and War: The Evolution of Thought and Practice Since 1945,* edited by Vaughan Lowe, Adam Roberts, Jennifer Welsh, and Dominik Zaum (Oxford: Oxford University Press, 2008), pp. 255–256.

23. See Lowe et al., *The United Nations Security Council and War,* app. 5, tab. 3.

24. Notably, a vote against would not have been a veto in the absence of at least nine votes in favor.

25. France also contributed to the UN Operation in Côte d'Ivoire (UNOCI) and the UN Mission in the Central African Republic and Chad (MINURCAT).

26. Her Majesty's Government, "A Strong Britain in an Age of Uncertainty: The National Security Strategy" (London: Her Majesty's Stationery Office, October 2010), p. 4, www.gov.uk/government/uploads/system/uploads/attachment_data/file /61936/national-security-strategy.pdf.

27. See Department for International Development, Foreign and Commonwealth Office, and Ministry of Defense, "Building Stability Overseas Strategy" (London: Her Majesty's Stationery Office, July 2011), p. 32.

28. See, in particular, La Documentation Odile Jacob, "La Sécurité Collective au XXIè Siècle," in *Livre Blanc sur la Défense et la Sécurité Nationale* (Paris: Odile Jacob, 2008).

29. See Peter Wilenski, "The Structure of the UN in the Post–Cold War Period," in *United Nations, Divided World,* edited by Adam Roberts and Benedict Kingsbury (Oxford: Oxford University Press, 1993), p. 442; European Parliament resolution on the reform of the United Nations, P6_TA(2005)0237, June 9, 2005. The proposal was recently revived by two scholars: Daniel Deudney and Hanns W. Maull, "How Britain and France Could Reform the UN Security Council," *Survival* 53, no. 5 (2011): 107–128.

30. "Joint UK-France Summit Declaration," March 27, 2008; "UK-French Summit: Declaration on Global Governance and Development," July 6, 2009, www.franceonu.org/france-at-the-united-nations/press-room/speaking-to-the -media/press-releases/article/6-july-2009-uk-french-summit.

31. "Statement of the Permanent Representative of France at the UN Security Council," New York, November 26, 2012.

32. See International Commission on Intervention and State Sovereignty, "The Responsibility to Protect: Research, Bibliography, Background" (Ottawa: International Development Research Centre, December 2001), p. 380, http://responsibility toprotect.org/ICISS%20Report.pdf.

33. For a detailed discussion, see Chapter 9, on Security Council reform, in this volume.

34. For a very critical view of this process, see Chinmaya Gharekan, *The Horseshoe Table: An Inside View of the UN Security Council* (Delhi: Pearson Longman, 2006).

7

Power Dynamics Between Permanent and Elected Members

Colin Keating

DECISIONMAKING IN INTERNATIONAL ORGANISATIONS TENDS to mirror the power relationships of their members. Some international organisations—the World Trade Organisation and the United Nations are good examples—are set up in part with the objective of establishing a "rules-based" environment that acts to level, or at least moderate, the power asymmetries among the members. But within the United Nations, the structure and the culture of the Security Council seem to result in precisely the opposite dynamic. They actually accentuate or magnify the differences in power among its members.

The reason for this situation lies in the decisions taken in San Francisco in 1945 to seat the five victors of World War II as permanent members of the Security Council and to give them the power of veto over Council decisions.

For more than forty years during the Cold War, the power dynamic set up as a result of those 1945 decisions led to a persistent failure by the Security Council. In most cases that arose, the Council was unable to act in accordance with its mandate to respond to threats to international peace and security. Also during that period, the elected members of the Council often suffered marginalisation as a result of ideological pressure to support the positions of one or more of the permanent members.

To accommodate the author, the spelling in this chapter is inconsistent with that in the rest of the book.

At the end of the Cold War, it seemed as if there might be an opportunity for a different kind of power dynamic to evolve and for the Security Council to operate more as was intended by the Charter, as a genuinely collective international security tool. In the early 1990s, political cohesion among the P5 was generally very positive. And elected members found a refreshing degree of freedom to express opinions, take initiatives, and even lead on important agenda items.

The first half of the 1990s was also a period in which the Security Council saw the least number of vetoes in its history.[1] As the representative of New Zealand on the Security Council in 1993–1994, I certainly felt for a time that there was a possibility that the culture that had dominated the Council for the previous four decades could evolve positively and that, in the new political context, the legal differences between permanent and elected members need not dominate the normal dynamics within the Council and the veto could be confined to extraordinary cases.

This optimism encountered some serious setbacks. On Bosnia, the P3 (France, the United Kingdom, and the United States) were seriously divided over whether the Council should authorise a more forceful policy to protect civilians. Because each of them had the power of veto, this regularly resulted in stalemated discussions and a Council that appeared increasingly inept and ineffective. In this sense, the underlying power of the veto was a day-to-day reality.[2] Moreover, one could see this underlying power beginning to be employed for reasons far removed from protecting vital national security interests. An example is the case of the so-called safe areas established in 1993. The P5 very reluctantly reached consensus on this policy, under pressure from the elected members. But the policy was seriously compromised due to lack of UN military capacity on the ground. The low number of authorised peacekeepers—only a fraction of what was recommended by the Secretary-General—was driven by the underlying veto power, used in this case for nakedly financial reasons.

The failure of the Council to act decisively on the Rwandan genocide in 1994 was one of the most important setbacks. The use of P5 power by several permanent members was responsible for this lack of action. At various points, China, the UK, and ultimately the United States obstructed efforts by myself as president of the Council, in the month the genocide broke out, and by other elected members, to get the Council to recognise that the situation was indeed genocide and to respond by reinforcing the UNAMIR peacekeeping mission. And most disturbing, that power was used in the absence of any requirement to protect a vital national security interest of any P5 member.[3]

The period of excellent Russian cooperation in the Council also became much more conditional and much more focused on national interest when it became clear that, apart from Georgia and a small presence in Tajikistan, the United States would not agree to UN peacekeeping being available to help stabilise threats to international peace and security in the former Soviet Union.

More than twenty years have now passed since the end of the Cold War, and it is timely to examine how the dynamics in the Security Council between permanent members and elected members have evolved. How is the Council currently operating? And what has happened in terms of the culture? Has the Council adapted to modern realities to deliver better outcomes for the United Nations membership as a whole?

In order to fully understand the present, however, it is important to understand the past. So I begin this chapter with a fresh look at the real impact of what was decided in San Francisco in 1945. I then consider the quite radical developments relating to the Security Council that have occurred over the past two decades and the role of the permanent members in this and the adverse impact on elected Council members.

Finally, a note of caution is also in order. It is true that the power asymmetries in the Security Council and the veto are a real source of frustration among many at the United Nations. And it is a fact that lack of agreement in the Council has many times led to unnecessary human suffering and real anger. But it is equally true that some representatives (and sometimes the media) dwell excessively on this problem, as if it were the only source of failure in the Council. And sometimes the role of the P5 is used simplistically as a political justification for opposing other necessary and worthwhile reforms that would mitigate human suffering. It needs to be remembered that there are many issues (indeed the majority of its agenda items) on which the Security Council and its permanent members do eventually reach consensus. And there have been some positive developments in the past two decades. So a balanced assessment is required.

In the final sections of this chapter, I examine some of the positive changes that have occurred in Security Council practice during this period, and I assess the current culture of the Security Council and the modern dynamics between permanent and elected members.

What Was the Real Impact of the San Francisco Decisions?

In order to fully appreciate the significance of the decisions taken in San Francisco in 1945 regarding permanent membership of the Security Council and the veto, it is helpful to step back and think about the issue in terms of the wider context of international law that prevailed at that time.

Prior to 1945, the fundamental rule in international law was that a sovereign state could only be bound (i.e., legally compelled to comply) by a rule or decision if it consented to that rule or decision—or, in the case of an adjudication, if it had consented in advance that the ruling would be binding. There were some exceptions relating to customary international law, but in general a new rule could only be generated in a treaty, which only became binding when a state had signed and ratified it. And decisions by international organisations were at most only recommendatory and could not bind without explicit consent.

In many respects, this is still the fundamental rule of international law. But in 1945 in San Francisco, there was a fundamental change. The UN Charter gave the Security Council power, in situations where it determined that there was a breach of the peace or a threat to international security, to make binding decisions that all members of the United Nations were obliged to implement.[4]

The reason behind this revolutionary change flowed from the catastrophic experience of World War II, and the failure of the League of Nations in the lead-up to that conflict to stem the drift to global war. The inability of the League, under the then-existing framework of international law, to compel Mussolini's Italy to halt its aggression against Ethiopia,[5] was seen as evidence of the need for a new and more powerful collective security framework that could compel states to comply with its decisions and take enforcement measures if necessary.

It is important to emphasise just how revolutionary this new framework in international law for peace and security really was. Now, instead of each of the 193 member states effectively having a unilateral right to exempt itself from collective decisions by withholding consent, a small Council could impose decisions on all, by majority vote. In today's terms, this means that a mere nine states (the number of affirmative votes necessary for a resolution to be adopted) can agree binding decisions that the other 184 have a binding legal obligation to implement.

But in terms of the way that the Security Council works in practice, it is even more important to understand that while the rules were changed fundamentally in 1945, this does not impact on all 193 states but only 188 of them. Because of the power of veto—the right to withhold consent—the five permanent members still, in essence, enjoy the benefits of the preexisting international law. Nothing can bind them without their consent. Or as the Charter says: "Decisions of the Security Council . . . shall be made by an affirmative vote of nine members including the concurring votes of the permanent members."[6] So while the international community as a whole has moved into a new legal and political era involving much more demanding accountability and legal responsibility, five states—China, France, Russia, the United Kingdom, and the United States—effectively still live in the pre-1945 legal world.

The unique status of the P5 in practice is much more significant than their formal legal entitlements would suggest. Permanence gives continuity of knowledge and experience, which is a huge competitive advantage, especially when five elected members retire every year. So each year, one-third of the Council membership is newly elected and facing a steep learning curve.

In practice, the veto often does not need to be exercised. Indeed, it often only needs to be hinted at to effectively change the negotiating context on a resolution. Some call this the "closet veto"—the veto that is exercised in practice but never seen on the record. The power of the P5 also has a psychological element. This derives in part from the economic and military power of the P5 members and the dependence in one way or another of many states on the bilateral goodwill of P5 members. But it is also due, in no small part, to a kind of institutional exceptionalism exhibited by the P5 both as to the substance of many issues and as to procedure—and especially about their role in the Council. This exceptionalism is often manifested in their jealous protection of their prerogatives. And it seems to me that this exceptionalism has its origin in the 1945 decision to allow the P5 to continue to enjoy the old rules of the game—while everyone else has to play according to new and much more onerous rules.

When it is put this way, it is easier to understand the growing demand in the United Nations at large for reform of the Security Council, and the growing resentment of the status quo. This has also, however, generated the unhealthy development of a growing number of emerging powers demanding to be given the same status as the P5.

Developments to Expand the Role and Scope of the Security Council

The unease about the Security Council becomes all the more understandable in light of the rapid evolution of the role, scope, and power of the Council witnessed in recent history. The past quarter century has seen a quite remarkable sequence of developments relating to the collective management of international peace and security by the Security Council and the threshold for the exercise of the powers of the Security Council.

In 1945 the Council was set up to manage threats to the peace arising between states. However, the Council now routinely seeks to manage conflicts or threats of conflict within states. Indeed the vast bulk of the Council's work is now devoted to internal conflicts—something that would have been inconceivable in 1945.

The Charter sets a threshold for determining when the Security Council can act. This threshold is whether a situation is likely to endanger "the maintenance of international peace and security."[7] It is clear that the definition of what constitutes a threat to international peace and security is now extremely wide, and potentially encompasses almost any situation involving internal conflict except situations where one of the P5 chooses to withhold its consent. The selective exercise of this power has been evident in cases such as Syria (three joint vetoes by Russia and China in 2011–2012) and Palestine (fourteen lone vetoes by the United States between 1990 and 2014), and this dynamic has also increased the overall level of concern in some quarters about whether the Security Council can really be trusted to exercise its enhanced powers properly.

But the expansion of the power of the Security Council in recent years has gone well beyond the threshold question. The Council has also now widened the scope of the measures it employs so that they can relate not just to states, but can also be targeted at individuals. This has occurred in two ways. Most significant, the Council has adopted binding legal decisions, which impose individual criminal responsibility in certain cases. It has done this by establishing international criminal tribunals[8] and, in two cases (Darfur and Libya), by referring situations to the International Criminal Court. In addition, the Council has expanded the scope of its sanctions power to also directly impose targeted financial measures, travel bans, and arms embargoes against named individuals and companies.[9] These are radical developments in terms of institutional power.

The scope of the intervention by the Security Council has also broadened in other major ways. The Council now routinely mandates "multidimensional" UN peacekeeping operations (which are legally subordinate bodies of the Council) with very wide and sometimes quite intrusive responsibilities. These tasks often include disarming and demobilising combatants, conducting operational policing, protecting civilians, reforming security sector institutions, developing human rights and rule of law institutions, organising and supporting elections, and generally trying to address the root causes of conflict. The costs of these missions by 2014 amounted to over $8 billion per year—four times the cost of all of the rest of United Nations activity put together. By any standard this is a revolutionary expansion of the Council's role and influence.

Most states seem to accept that the wider definition of the role of the Council and the expansion of its scope of activity represent an important and necessary modernisation of the role of the United Nations. This can be inferred from the fact that, every year, the General Assembly approves, by consensus, the budgets for Security Council missions to address these kinds of wider conflicts. There have also been several occasions (most recently in 2012 on Syria)[10] when the vast majority of members of the United Nations

General Assembly have responded to the failure of the Security Council to act in certain cases of internal conflict and actually called for stronger UN engagement.

Impact on the Role of the Elected Members

The dynamics between the elected members of the Council and the permanent members have also evolved quite significantly over the past two decades. As indicated earlier, it was not unusual in the early 1990s for elected members to take initiatives on major substantive items and to strongly contest the policy options on other items where a member of the P5 had the lead. This was certainly the New Zealand experience in 1993–1994 on issues as diverse as Rwanda, Somalia, Bosnia, Haiti, and North Korea's nuclear programme. In the years that followed, other elected members, such as Ireland, Slovenia, Singapore, and Norway, were able to play important roles—including in the case of Norway taking initiatives on highly controversial issues such as the Middle East.

But by the mid-2000s the dynamic had changed. The case of North Korea is a good example. In 1993–1994, the nuclear crisis was managed collectively within the Council with regular meetings in informal consultations, and Council members like New Zealand, from the Asia Pacific region, were able to play an active and equal role at all stages of the debate and to input substance to the negotiations. By contrast, when the issue returned to the Council in 2006,[11] the dynamic was much more closed. Substance was negotiated among the P5, sometimes backed by direct interaction between P5 members, on the one hand, and Japan and South Korea, on the other, usually on a bilateral basis. All of the meaningful discussion took place outside the collective Council consultations. Mostly, the elected members of the Council were faced with previously cooked decisions and were given no opportunity to input effectively to the negotiations.

The same dynamic progressively dominated the Council's handling of many other controversial issues, including for instance Lebanon and Iran. And it is inconceivable today that an elected member could play an independent leadership role on the Palestine issue in the way that Norway did. In many respects, on major issues the Council has become either a vehicle for political theatre, when the P5 cannot agree, or a tool for the ratification and formalisation of decisions already taken privately by the P5.

None of this could have happened, however, without the concurrence or passivity of the elected members of the Council. There is a sixth veto in the Security Council—the collective no-vote of at least seven elected members, which can prevent a draft resolution from obtaining the nine affirmative votes that are necessary under Article 27 for its adoption.

It was never politically easy in the Security Council in the early 1990s to stand up against the momentum of one or more P5 members seeking an outcome. But neither was it politically impossible.

It seems that during the 2000s this equation changed radically for most elected members. The reasons for this are unclear. It may be that it was the fallout from the terrorist attacks on the World Trade Centre in 2001 and President George W. Bush's famous "You are either with us or against us" speech,[12] or perhaps it was the crisis in the Security Council in 2002 and 2003 over the Iraq War. Certainly the elected Council members that withheld the votes to authorise the invasion of Iraq in 2003 came under sustained and intense bilateral pressure. And this pressure was also felt in an intense personal sense by several of the ambassadors of the elected members. It is entirely possible that in light of that experience, it was felt in many capitals that the political cost of standing up to the P5 in the Security Council had become too high.

Certainly the evidence is clear that the level of control of the Council by the P5 expanded during this period and was matched by an increasing marginalisation of the elected members. It is also significant to note that the increased dominance of the P5 even began to infect the procedural handling of issues in the Security Council. This development is particularly bizarre since there is one thing that Article 23 of the Charter does make clear: there is no veto on procedural matters.

One particularly significant development on procedure occurred in the early 2000s. There is no record of exactly when. In the 1990s it had been the practice (which accords with the Provisional Rules of Procedure) that the monthly programme of work would be in the hands of the Council presidency. This meant that for ten out of fifteen months, the procedural control of the Council was in the hands of an elected member. Some of course chose not to make use of that power, but the possibility of its use was an important check in the system. New Zealand proved this during its Council presidency in April 1994 on Rwanda.[13] However, by the mid-2000s the practice had radically changed. The monthly programme of work is now submitted for active approval by all Council members. This undercuts the power of the presidency and introduces a veto on one of the most significant practical procedural questions: what will be discussed and when.[14] It is now commonplace for P5 members to use this veto to control the Council and exclude discussion of items that they find inconvenient.

A second procedural area in which the creeping expansion of P5 power has been seen relates to the day-to-day work of the Council in overseeing the UN field operations it has established. These include both peacekeeping operations and political missions, and this work (often routine and technical) has become the main activity of the Council. Over the past decade, the procedural context has progressively shifted away from one in which there was no recognised ownership of these agenda items by any single country and any member could present draft resolutions or propose initiatives, to a situation where the P5 members now have the lead on most resolutions relating to peacekeeping missions. This seems to have been formalised by the anointment of recognised "penholders,"[15] who are almost always P5 members and who claim the exclusive responsibility for drafting of resolutions and leading discussion on almost all of the agenda items. This development has not only crowded out the space for elected members, but has also been institutionalised in a way that tends to entrench the procedural and substantive power of the P5.

A further and even more important procedural evolution has been the shift of many negotiations on the substance of Council resolutions and statements right out of the Council altogether. A decade or more ago, all resolutions and statements were introduced for initial discussion in informal consultations at the level of ambassador. Several rounds of negotiations at that level were the norm. Sometimes particular paragraphs that required technical drafting would be referred to a more junior level for more intensive work and would then be reported back to the informal consultations. But there was never any doubt that the negotiations were collectively owned by the fifteen permanent representatives.

Today that approach is not the norm. It is much more normal for substantive work to be initiated and led by the P5 penholder at much more junior levels and never discussed in informal consultations at senior levels until an agreed text has been reached. Often this involves the P5 "experts" having a first cut at the drafting before the text is circulated to others. It is quite common for decisions to be negotiated at the junior level in "round robin" e-mails without any meetings at all. This tends to increase the marginalisation of the elected members. Because of the "penholder" phenomenon, most of the initiators of these e-mail negotiations are junior or mid-level P5 diplomats. They are called "experts" but rarely do they have any expertise at all in the relevant subject area. However, because of the resource asymmetry between P5 diplomats and the diplomats representing most elected members, the penholder has a decided advantage. Moreover, whereas in the past smaller delegations could compensate by bringing to bear the weight of their experienced ambassadors in informal consultations, the current decision-reaching format usually results in such ambassadors being presented with a series of fait accompli. A further development, which intensifies this problem, is the innovation of the so-called silence procedure: "silence is deemed to be consent" and the penholder diplomat will circulate a text and set a deadline of sometimes only a matter of hours by which all fourteen other members are deemed to have accepted the text unless they raise objections.

Most P5 members will say that the introduction of these procedural developments is solely for the purpose of efficiency. But workload is scarcely an excuse. The Council in recent years has been averaging a little over 80 decisions a year. By contrast, during the period of much more open, flexible, and collegial decisionmaking in the early 1990s, the Council was averaging well over 150 decisions a year.[16] And it is perhaps not merely a coincidence that the collateral damage from this "greater efficiency" is the negative impact on the role and capacity of elected members.

Another practice that also inflicts significant collateral damage on the elected members relates to the policy for appointing the chairs of Council subsidiary bodies, such as sanctions committees and Council working groups. The permanent members traditionally decline to take these roles. (However, France did chair the Council Working Group on Children in Armed Conflict for a number of years, and the UK the Counter-Terrorism Committee in the early years after its establishment.) This reluctance is understandable. These roles often require the selected ambassador to commit very significant personal time as well as significant mission staff capacity to service committee work. In my own case, in 1993–1994, my role as chair of a sanctions committee consumed on average two hours a day, seven days a week, on very technical process matters. This was time that was not available for contributing to the larger policy work of the Council and was a severe handicap. By contrast, the P5 ambassadors had that many more hours available. This unfair burden-sharing still rankles elected members today. And the issue becomes especially contentious because the P5 have traditionally decided among themselves which elected member will be assigned to chair which committee.[17]

This is an example of a procedural issue that under the Charter should be decided by a majority vote without any veto. Yet the five veto holders have in practice become the deciders, effectively excluding their elected colleagues from any meaningful participation.

Participation in Council meetings (and, equally important, in informal meetings of members of the Council) by nonmembers of the Council is another contentious procedural issue, and one that can often significantly influence the quality and political sustainability of Council decisions. The Charter, in Articles 31, 32, and 44, seemed to envisage a relatively liberal regime in which nonmembers of the Council, whether as parties, as affected states, or as troop contributors, would routinely participate in the Council's work. The General Assembly in 1949 indicated that, in its view, these decisions were indeed procedural and not subject to the veto.[18] But in practice the P5 have employed a very restrictive interpretation of these rights. And even worse, affected states are only given the floor once the decision affecting them has been effectively negotiated. Some elected members have tried to suggest that a more respectful policy in which the Council would first hear the affected countries (or regional organisations such as the African Union) and then engage them (albeit without the right to vote) in the process would often deliver better outcomes. But even in cases where elected members as a whole have agreed with this principle, P5 insistence has usually prevailed, because elected members are politically reluctant to force a procedural vote.

It is worth stressing that it is not just the very small countries that struggle with the Council's working methods. From 2010 to 2013, the elected members of the Council included Germany, Japan, India, Brazil, South Africa, Nigeria, Turkey, and Mexico. But it is fair to say that this previously unseen concentration of "heavyweights" had only minimal if any impact on the power relationships between the P5 and the elected members, and on the overall quality of the Council's output relative to other recent periods. Many representatives of these countries have subsequently expressed frustration at their collective inability to loosen the P5 stranglehold.

Some Positive Developments

It is important to acknowledge that the picture is not all bad. One important evolution that has emerged in parallel to the changes described here is the extraordinary growth in the thematic focus of the Security Council. Few would have anticipated in 1945 (or even in 1990) that the Security Council would carve out a leading role in building global norms.

The thematic decisions of the Security Council now cover a broad range of issues that are relevant to conflict situations, either causes of new conflict, drivers of existing conflict, or impediments to the restoration of international peace and security and peacebuilding.[19] The highlights include key humanitarian and human rights issues such as protection of civilians; children in armed conflict; justice, rule of law, and impunity; women, peace, and security; and sexual violence in conflict.

But the scope also extends to the tools for preventing and managing conflict, and addressing the root causes of conflict, such as preventive diplomacy and mediation; peacekeeping, peacebuilding, and postconflict stabilisation; disarmament, demobilisation, and reintegration; security sector reform; stemming the proliferation of small arms and light weapons and weapons of mass destruction; natural resource management; sanctions; and cooperation with regional organisations. The Council also increasingly addressed nontraditional security threats, including piracy, terrorism, illicit cross-border trafficking and organised crime, and climate change.

The impetus for the evolution of the thematic work of the Council has often come from elected members and from the Secretary-General. The thematic work has received wide support and encouragement from civil society and the media. It seems that many elected members came to recognise in the early 2000s that the stranglehold of the P5 on most of the conventional business of the Council meant that they would struggle to achieve prominence during a two-year term. As a result, many resorted to taking up a thematic issue during their presidency month to gain profile.

Mostly, the P5 grudgingly tolerated this evolution. But there were often private expressions of scorn by P5 members, claiming that all the country in question wanted was a media opportunity for its politicians. In a sense, this was true at the outset, but over time the incremental process of thematic decisionmaking progressively built up a normative framework. The tactic of seeking a report by the Secretary-General also played an important role in both sustaining the momentum but also in ensuring that any future debates on the same issue would be grounded in information and data provided by the Secretariat. It also gave the Secretariat the opportunity to have policy input by way of generic recommendations, around which consensus can be more easily achieved in thematic debates than in the more politicised debates around specific conflict situations. And the net result was an evolving corpus of agreed language and norms that could then be leveraged back into the discussions on country-specific issues.

As time went on, even P5 members came alive to the political profile opportunities offered by thematic debates and resolutions. And there have been some notable P5 contributions, including by the UK on peacekeeping and climate change, by France on children in armed conflict, by the United States on nuclear nonproliferation and sexual violence in conflict (which the UK subsequently also championed), and by Russia on piracy. But overall there is still a sense of reserve by the P5 and on some occasions quite vigorous pushback, such as by Russia on the sexual violence and gender initiatives and by China on the extension of the framework relating to children to countries that are not on the Council agenda.

A second area of positive development, which needs to be recorded, is the effort that has been made to improve transparency in the work of the Council. Information technology has helped a lot, by ensuring that the Secretariat and member states are easily able to notify the wider membership in a timely way of upcoming meetings.

The past decade has also seen an increase in the amount of time spent by the Council in public sessions, hearing briefings from the Secretary-General, or other key sources of information including, from time to time, nongovernmental or even civil society sources.[20] But this progress is significantly offset by the development, mentioned earlier, of so much of the real negotiation now taking place outside the UN complex—thereby much reducing transparency.

A third positive development is the effort that has been made by the Council to record in an accessible way some of the process that governs its day-to-day work.[21] This effort (often referred to by way of shorthand as the "Note 507" process or the "Working Methods Handbook")[22] helps empower newly elected Council members by teaching them the informal "rules of the game." Progress in developing and expanding the content of Note 507 has been very slow and painful. It has suffered from constant pushback by the P5. But the achievements that have been made are largely a credit to the efforts by Japan to sustain momentum over two separate terms on the Council.

In the same vein, the work of the Secretariat to streamline processes and information about sanctions committees[23] is also a significant development, as are the Secretariat's efforts to update and make available online the history of formal Security Council practice in the "Repertoire of Practice."[24]

A fourth positive development has been the achievement by a small number of elected members to be recognised as penholders on country-specific issues. In 2013, Australia (on Afghanistan) and Togo (on Guinea-Bissau) were the only recognised penholders among the elected Council members on country-specific issues. South Africa (on Timor-Leste) and Germany (on Afghanistan) had previously held the pen on country-specific issues.[25] Elected members are more often able to secure a recognised leadership role on regional or thematic issues—especially where there is a working group or committee to be chaired (e.g., Rwanda on conflict prevention in Africa, or Togo on West Africa).

Another positive development, which began in the early 1990s, was the emergence of a new format for meetings between Council members and nonmember states that were parties to a conflict. The format was also used for meetings with individuals who could shed light on conflict situations. The format came to be known as the "Arria style" meeting—named after the ambassador of Venezuela, Diego Arria, who convened the first such event. The format proved helpful and was used quite often in the 1990s. In 1996, for instance, it was used more than twenty times. However, by 2002 the practice of using the Arria format to consult with states affected by conflict lapsed completely. It seems that this was a result of P5 determination to narrow the range of Council activity and perhaps also to limit the opportunities for elected members to initiate policy via this route. The Arria format became essentially restricted to meetings with NGOs. They focused on thematic agenda items, and attendance by ambassadors (other than from the sponsoring country) virtually disappeared. By 2010–2011, the use of the format had virtually disappeared altogether, with at most two to three such meetings per year. It is pleasing to note, though, that the number of such meetings have subsequently seen some increase.

With respect to the issue of participation by states affected by Council decisions and other stakeholders, the restricted use of the Arria format in 2001–2002 left the Council without any effective institutional tool for providing meaningful participation by states affected by conflict and by other interested stakeholders. This may have helped to stimulate the sense in the wider UN membership that there was a significant problem with Council working methods. However, it was not until 2009, in the context of the humanitarian crisis in Sri Lanka, that the Council moved to address this weakness. The inability to take up the issue of the Sri Lanka conflict in formal sessions, because of P5 differences, led to the format now known as the "informal interactive dialogue," whereby Council members can discuss substance with stakeholders.[26] But the process is still relatively rare. Decisions to use it are ad hoc and variable and always constrained by the threat of P5 blockage, even though such decisions are by any definition procedural and not formally subject to the veto.

Last, it needs to be said that despite the formidable obstacles that have evolved in Council process and in the power dynamics between elected and permanent members, a number of small countries have demonstrated in recent years that it is nevertheless still possible to assert a leadership role. Austria, Costa Rica, Denmark, Guatemala, and Uganda are some of several countries that have distinguished themselves in this regard.

Conclusion

The structure of the Security Council and the culture that this has engendered were almost certain to result in a situation in which the power asymmetries between the permanent and the elected members would be magnified. But the real impact of this was concealed during the Cold War period, due to the ideological differences that mostly rendered the Security Council irrelevant.

The post–Cold War experience of a rapid expansion in Security Council power and activity, both in scope and in depth, has raised the political stakes considerably—as well as the financial impact of many Council decisions. All this has contributed to further tilting the balance in the Council in favour of the permanent members and against the elected members. The emergence in the past decade or so of some very divisive and controversial issues on which P5 members have had very strong views has also raised the political stakes and impacted on the dynamics within the Council. In such cases P5 members have used bilateral leverage on elected members sufficiently often that for some elected members their role in the Council can become very constrained.

It would be wrong to say that the political dynamics arising from the role of the P5 make the Council dysfunctional. That would fly in the face of the evidence of the generally positive impact that the Council, working with the UN system as a whole, has had on a very large number of situations over the past two decades. And although the results are meagre to date, it would be wrong to say that all of the P5 are always set against reform of the Council's working methods. There has been limited progress.

And the UK and France have at times shown commendable leadership in looking to improve the ways in which the Council works.

However, the current situation is clearly suboptimal in terms of outcomes and clearly not sufficiently adapted to the needs of the modern world. Structures, processes, and rules on participation designed for the world of 1945 are simply inadequate in the current world and especially in light of the expanded scope of the Security Council's role and power.

This governance deficit is driving the widespread political challenge to the credibility and legitimacy of the institution as a whole. Saudi Arabia's decision in October 2013 to reject a term on the Security Council is the tip of an iceberg of discontent.[27]

Can this problem be turned around? There is broad support for change. Reform of the Security Council has been under active discussion for over twenty years. But it has stalled because of opposition to the demands by a small number of emerging powers that they should become additional permanent members. Many think that this will inevitably exacerbate the current power dynamic. Separate initiatives on reform of the Council's working methods have also been attempted, but without significant progress to date.

Perhaps the most promising approach is a proposal for an "intermediate solution"[28] under which a new category of members would be established for the group of countries whose size, power, and global role are approaching that of some of the P5. This group is a good bit wider than the current aspirants for new permanent status. Under the proposal, the members would still have to stand for election, but would be entitled to serve for an extended period. The accountability that comes with the need for reelection would contribute to building a new "centre" in the Security Council, an intermediate role between the current group elected for only two-year terms and the old permanent members.

And equally important, there are the beginnings of movement within the P5 on the question of the veto. In October 2013, the foreign minister of France, Laurent Fabius, proposed an innovative approach to constrain the exercise of the veto.[29] In this regard members of the Council might usefully revisit the recommendations on the veto made by the General Assembly in Resolution 267 of April 14, 1949. In that resolution the Assembly proposed a limitation on the exercise of the veto in terms not dissimilar from those proposed by Foreign Minister Fabius.[30]

Despite these developments, there is still a very long way to go before the international community can realistically hope to accomplish a formal reform that will really adapt both the structures and the culture of the Security Council to the needs of the twenty-first century. It is therefore all the more important, in the interim, that the members of the Council holding office—both elected and permanent—intensify the work to modernise the working methods of the Council within the current context. Much could be done in that regard if the political will is generated. Whether this can happen will depend very much on the cohort of elected members over the coming years and the quality of the partnership that they can generate with the permanent members on these issues.

Notes

1. Security Council Report, "In Hindsight: The Veto," November 2013 Monthly Forecast, October 31, 2013, www.securitycouncilreport.org/monthly-fore cast/2013-11/in_hindsight_the_veto.php.

2. Colin Keating, "The Role of the UN Security Council," in *Responding to Genocide: The Politics of International Action,* edited by Adam Lupel and Ernesto Verdeja (Boulder, CO: Lynne Rienner, 2013), pp. 185–188.

3. A detailed analysis of this tragic case can be found in Colin Keating, "Rwanda: An Insider's Account," in *The UN Security Council: From the Cold War to the 21st Century,* edited by David M. Malone (Boulder, CO: Lynne Rienner, 2004), pp. 500–512.

4. United Nations, *Charter of the United Nations,* San Francisco, June 26, 1945, Article 25.

5. George W. Baer, *Test Case: Italy, Ethiopia, and the League of Nations* (Stanford: Hoover Institution, 1976).

6. United Nations, *Charter of the United Nations,* Article 27(3).

7. United Nations, *Charter of the United Nations,* Articles 34 and 39.

8. International Criminal Tribunals for the Former Yugoslavia and Rwanda in Resolution 827, S/RES/827 (May 25, 1993), and Resolution 955, S/RES/955 (November 8, 1994), respectively; as well as Special Tribunal for Lebanon in Resolution 1757, S/RES/1757 (May 30, 2007).

9. See, for example, targeted measures against individuals in Libya in United Nations Security Council Resolution 1970, S/RES/1970 (February 26, 2011).

10. See General Assembly Resolution 66/253, A/RES/66/253 (February 16, 2012).

11. United Nations Security Council, "Letter Dated 4 July 2006 from the Permanent Representative of Japan to the United Nations Addressed to the President of the Security Council," S/2006/481, July 5, 2006.

12. "You Are Either with Us or Against Us," CNN, November 6, 2001, http://edition.cnn.com/2001/US/11/06/gen.attack.on.terror.

13. Keating, "Rwanda," pp. 500–512.

14. See Security Council Report, "Security Council Working Methods: A Work in Progress," Special Research Report no. 1, March 30, 2010, http://www.security councilreport.org/special-research-report/lookup-c-glKWLeMTIsG-b-5906427.php, and "Security Council Transparency Legitimacy and Effectiveness," Special Research Report no. 2, October 18, 2007, www.securitycouncilreport.org/special -research-report/lookup-c-glKWLeMTIsG-b-3506555.php.

15. Security Council Report, "In Hindsight: Penholders," September 2013 Monthly Forecast, August 29, 2013, www.securitycouncilreport.org/monthly -forecast/2013-09/in_hindsight_penholders.php.

16. Security Council Report, "Security Council Statistics in 2012," February 2013 Monthly Forecast, January 31, 2013, www.securitycouncilreport.org/monthly -forecast/2013-02/security_council_statistics_in_2012.php.

17. Security Council Report, "December 2013 Monthly Forecast: In Hindsight—Appointment of Chairs of Subsidiary Bodies," November 27, 2013, www.security councilreport.org/monthly-forecast/2013-12/in_hindsight_appointment_of _chairs_of_subsidiary_bodies.php.

18. United Nations General Assembly Resolution 267, A/RES/267 (April 14, 1949) .

19. Security Council Report, "Thematic and General Issues," www.security councilreport.org/thematic-general-issues.php.

20. See data provided in the summaries of the Security Council's work produced annually by the UN Department of Political Affairs' Security Council Affairs Division. See, for instance, United Nations, "Highlights of Security Council Practice 2014," New York, January 2015, www.un.org/en/sc/inc/pages/pdf/highlights/2014 .pdf.

21. United Nations Security Council, "Note by the President of the Security Council," S/2006/507, July 19, 2006; S/2007/749, December 19, 2007; S/2008/847, December 31, 2008; and S/2010/507, July 26, 2010.

22. United Nations Security Council, "Working Methods Handbook," www.un .org/en/sc/about/methods.

23. United Nations Security Council, Sanctions Committee, "Security Council Sanctions Committee: An Overview," www.un.org/sc/committees.

24. "Repertoire of the Practice of the Security Council," www.un.org/en/sc /repertoire.

25. Security Council Report, "February 2013 Monthly Forecast: Chairs of Subsidiary Bodies and Pen Holders for 2013," January 31, 2013, www.securitycouncil report.org/monthly-forecast/2013-02/subsidiary_chairs_and_pen_holders _for_2013.php.

26. Security Council Report, "Update Report no. 5: Sri Lanka," April 21, 2009, www.securitycouncilreport.org/update-report/lookup-c-glKWLeMTIsG-b -5113231.php.

27. "Saudi Arabia Officially Rejects U.N. Security Council Seat," *Al Arabiya News,* November 13, 2013, http://english.alarabiya.net/en/News/middle-east/2013 /11/13/Saudi-Arabia-officially-rejects-U-N-Security-Council-seat.html.

28. Permanent Mission of the Principality of Liechtenstein to the United Nations, "Explanatory Memorandum: Intermediate Model for the Enlargement of the Security Council," February 26, 2010, www.globalpolicy.org/security -council/security-council-reform/50115-proposal-on-security-council-reform -elements-for-the-immediate-model.html.

29. Laurent Fabius, "Suspending the Right to Veto in the Event of Mass Crimes," *France Diplomatie,* October 4, 2013, www.diplomatie.gouv.fr/en/french -foreign-policy-1/united-nations/events-2136/events-2013/article/suspending-the -right-to-veto-in.

30. United Nations General Assembly Resolution 267, A/RES/267 (April 14, 1949).

8

Council Reform and the Emerging Powers

Kishore Mahbubani

THE UN SECURITY COUNCIL WAS FORMED IN 1945 WITH FIVE permanent members. After almost seventy years, there has been no change in the composition of the P5. As we are moving into an era of major shifts of geopolitical power, with several new powers emerging, if, after a hundred years, there is no change in P5 composition by 2045, one result will be clear: the Council will lose its credibility. The P5 therefore face a Hobson's choice in the next three decades: they can retain either their composition or their credibility. They cannot have both.

I have three goals in this chapter. First, I explain why the Security Council must include new emerging powers as permanent members to retain its credibility. As Kofi Annan told the UN General Assembly in 2003, "If you want the Council's decisions to command greater respect, particularly in the developing world, you need to address the issue of its composition with greater urgency."[1] Second, I explain why Security Council reform is inherently difficult. Third, I suggest a win-win-win solution that will finally break the reform logjam and allow the entry of new emerging powers. In short, contrary to conventional wisdom among many scholars and diplomats, Security Council reform is not impossible.

The Case for Reforming Permanent Membership

One big lesson I learned when I served on the Security Council for two years in 2001 and 2002 as Singapore's ambassador to the UN is that few in the world outside the organization understand the roles and real powers of the P5. Fortunately, just before I served on the Council, a Chilean diplomat alerted me that while in theory the body has fifteen members (five permanent members and ten elected), in practice it has five members and ten observers. This was a profound insight. The P5 almost totally dominate and run the Council. This is why the composition of the permanent members matters so much: if they do not reflect the great powers of today, the Council will increasingly make flawed decisions, as it has begun to do.

The P5 dominate the Security Council primarily through their use of the veto. Since the veto is rarely used in formal votes (and its use has been declining in formal votes: of the 265 vetoes cast since 1946, only 32 were cast between 1990 and 2013),[2] many observers have fallen prey to the illusion that nowadays there is no significant difference in the powers of the permanent and the elected members. The truth is that while the formal veto is rarely used, the informal veto is used almost every day, especially in the frequent and more important informal consultations among Council members. Many elected members are also inclined to self-censor, refraining from proposing or suggesting any new initiative if they sense it will encounter any kind of P5 opposition.

A brief anecdote will illustrate how this works. When I presided over the Council in May 2002, I received a request from the International Court of Justice (ICJ) to give a public briefing on its work to the Council. I thought that this was an excellent idea, and I supported it. However, when this ICJ proposal was discussed in the Council, the US delegation opposed a public briefing, for reasons I cannot recall. Technically, the question of whether to have such a briefing was a "procedural" one, in which the P5, according to the UN Charter, have no veto right.[3] However, the US delegation argued that any discussion on whether the public briefing was a "procedural" or a "substantive" issue was in itself a substantive issue, a decision on which would require at least nine affirmative votes in the Council and no negative votes from any of the permanent members. As a result of this implicit threat from the United States to exercise its veto power, the other Council members conceded and agreed to hold a closed-door, private ICJ briefing. Effectively, this meant that a veto for a "substantive" issue was also applied to a "procedural" issue, therefore undermining the intent of the UN Charter. It is hard to understand how it would have undermined any US national interests to allow the ICJ to give the briefing in public.[4]

Since such informal vetoes are exercised behind closed doors, few observers are aware how often this happens and how it distorts decision-making. The veto is clearly a flawed instrument. Yet despite its flaws, it is indispensable. The main reason why the UN has survived for seven decades and why the League of Nations collapsed after less than three decades is that the UN, unlike the League, gave the great powers a vested interest in keeping it alive through the privilege of the veto. And even though the US government has frequently criticized and even occasionally demonized the

UN, it has never threatened to leave it. The veto is too valuable an asset to give up easily. As Inis Claude wisely observed in his classic work *Swords into Plowshares,* the veto ensured "that all of the great powers would accept their place in the leadership corps of the new organization; in this [it was] successful, and this fact was perhaps the major basis for the hope that the United Nations would prove more effective than the League."[5]

As long as our world has great powers, we should preserve the veto. However, if the veto is to fulfill its real goal of anchoring the great powers in the UN system, the veto must be wielded by today's or tomorrow's great powers, not yesterday's great powers. This is the fundamental reason why the composition of the permanent membership must be changed. If the emerging powers are not provided the veto and see no interest in supporting or implementing the decisions of the Security Council, the body will lose its relevance, its credibility, and, most dangerously, its legitimacy. There is one nightmare scenario that the P5 should seriously contemplate. If a new great power, like India, were to announce unilaterally that it would no longer accept Council decisions as binding, there is nothing the P5 could do to enforce its decisions on India. Hence, it will not be long before the Council faces a Hobson's choice: retain its composition or retain its credibility.

There can be no doubt that among the P5, three represent today's powers (the United States, China, and Russia) while two represent yesterday's powers (the United Kingdom and France). The best way to illustrate how much the relative positions of the great powers have changed is to look at the top ten largest economies in 1980 and compare them with the projected top ten economies in 2030 to indicate the degree to which economic power will have shifted to emerging powers in a fifty-year period. The 1980 list included, in order of economic power, the following countries: the United States, Japan, the Soviet Union, West Germany, France, the United Kingdom, Italy, Canada, and China. The 2030 list is likely to feature China, the United States, India, Japan, Russia, Brazil, Germany, Mexico, the United Kingdom, and France.[6] Hence, India, Japan, Brazil, Germany, and Mexico will have larger economies than the United Kingdom and France, yet will not be represented in the Council. The United Kingdom and France can argue that they have global military power-projection capabilities that would trump their diminishing economic status. But the relative size of their military budgets has also shrunk. From 1988 to 2012, the military expenditures of the United Kingdom and France declined from 3.6 percent and 4.0 percent of gross domestic product (GDP) to 2.3 percent and 2.5 percent respectively.[7] More important, the United Kingdom and France have implicitly acknowledged that they have no legitimacy to use the veto. This is why they have consciously avoided using it since 1989, as they well know that a political explosion would result from a unilateral veto by them.

Privately, both British and French diplomats have admitted to me that their permanent membership is in peril and hence they must earn their legitimacy daily through extraordinary performance in the Council.

An even more dangerous flaw in the P5 composition is that two regions (Africa and Latin America) are not represented at all in the Council, while Asia, with nearly 60 percent of the world's population, is severely under-represented. By contrast, although the European Union constitutes 7 percent of the world population, Western European countries control 40 percent of the permanent Council seats.

So far, there has been a fairly high degree of compliance with Council decisions, which is in itself a remarkable achievement. In theory, countries comply because they are legally obliged to do so under Article 25 of the UN Charter, which states that "the Members of the United Nations agree to accept and carry out the decisions of the Security Council in accordance with the present Charter." In practice, they also do so because Council decisions are perceived to be legitimate.

However, some examples of past noncompliance illustrate how future problems of compliance could arise. In 1992, the Council imposed a set of aviation, diplomatic, and travel sanctions as well as an arms embargo on Libya in response to the Muammar Qaddafi regime's support of terrorist groups responsible for the infamous Lockerbie bombing in 1988 and the bombing of UTA Flight 772 in 1989. According to international law, all nations were obliged to comply. However, the Organization of African Unity (OAU), the African Union's predecessor, was enraged by what it perceived to be an unfair decision. The OAU passed a resolution at its 1998 summit stating that it would not enforce certain sanctions, openly flouting a Council decision. Yet instead of penalizing the OAU, the P5 realized that they had no power to do so and remained silent in the face of this defiance.

A small incident that happened in 2001 illustrates how the Council will have difficulty imposing its will on future great powers. In that year, the Irish delegation tried to propose "informal consultations" on a major threat to international peace and security, the situation in Kashmir. Initially, the majority of Council members agreed with Ireland. However, after a week of ferocious lobbying by India in key capitals, the Council members' support for Ireland's initiative evaporated, and when two P5 members, the United States and the United Kingdom, conceded to India's pressures, Kashmir was not discussed. And it has not been discussed ever since.

As the P5 increasingly represent a smaller and smaller share of the global economy, it is inevitable that the emerging powers will become more and more critical of the P5 and its composition. Indeed, if the United States and China (the two largest economies in the world) are excluded from the equation, the three remaining P5 members control only 8.5 percent of the global economy. Yet they control 60 percent of the P5 seats, illustrating how unrepresentative of today's global power structure the Council's composition has become.

Resentment toward the P5 is thus likely to rise, all the more so as the P5 use their privileged position to promote their national interests rather than the global interests "in accordance with the Purposes and Principles of the United Nations," as the UN Charter calls for. There are several egregious examples that can be cited here. When the Council had to renew the mandate of the UN Preventive Deployment Force in 1999, China decided to veto it not because UNPREDEP had failed in its mission, but because Macedonia had established diplomatic relations with the government in Taiwan. Similarly, the United States vetoed a resolution in 2011 condemning Israel for building more illegal settlements in the West Bank, even though there was absolutely no doubt that what Israel did was wrong. Indeed, every other Council member voted in favor of the resolution. Meanwhile, Russia matched this record of China and the United States when it vetoed the Council resolution extending the UN mission in Georgia in 2009.

These are only a few egregious examples of national interests of the P5 members trumping their global responsibilities. A full audit would add countless further cases. I had a full firsthand experience of this when I chaired the Sanctions Committee on Liberia from 2001 to 2002. The P5 delegations, especially those of the United States and the United Kingdom, would arbitrarily add names to the lists of people against whom sanctions would be applied. When I pressed the delegations to explain why these names were inserted, the only response I received was: "We have received instructions from our capital to do so." There was a complete absence of due process. This issue rose to prominence following the establishment of the Council's Sanctions Committee Pursuant to Resolution 1267 (1999) to implement sanctions on individuals and entities associated with al-Qaeda and the Taliban, which came to be successfully challenged in European courts. Landmark cases of individuals contesting their inclusion in the sanctions lists include the 2005 *Kadi* case in the European Court of Justice (ECJ)[8] and the 2010 *al-Ghabra* case in the UK's Supreme Court,[9] in both of which the courts ruled in favor of the plaintiff.

Another clear demonstration of the corruption practiced by the P5 was demonstrated over the Iraq sanctions process. To ensure that the Iraqi people did not suffer from sanctions, humanitarian supplies were allowed to be sent to the Iraqi people. In theory, the contracts to provide the humanitarian supplies were supposed to be allocated on commercial merit. In practice, the P5 followed an approach of "if you scratch my back, I'll scratch yours, but if you claw my back, I'll claw yours." As a result, it was not surprising that a majority of contracts were awarded to companies from the P5 countries. Under the infamous oil-for-food program, Saddam Hussein gave preference to buyers from oil companies from some P5 countries whose governments might have had a say in easing sanctions. These contracts were then approved by the Security Council, with several quiet and private trade-offs among the P5.[10] As more such evidence of corruption surfaces, it will further undermine the legitimacy of the P5. Demands for change will become more insistent.

Obstacles to Reform

The flaws in the Security Council's composition have given rise to global clamors for change, in response to which the P5 members have declared that they are, in principle, in favor of Council reform, including adding emerging powers to the permanent membership (although they differ on which emerging powers should be elevated to that status). However, these public declarations of support notwithstanding, the P5 harbor serious reservations about the desirability of Council reform.

They have been able to disguise their lack of support for reform because there is a natural political logjam created between the aspirants to permanent membership and their most prominent detractors, traditionally the aspirants' regional rivals. Hence, for every Brazil that stakes a claim to permanent membership, there is an Argentina that says, "Why not me?" The same is true for India and Pakistan, Japan and South Korea, Germany and Italy, Nigeria and South Africa.

As a result of such competition, the UN has not been able to move ahead on Council reform, even though from time to time significant momentum was generated. In 1997, when the Malaysian ambassador to the UN, Tan Sri Razali Ismail, was president of the UN General Assembly, he came close to pushing through an Assembly resolution that would have expanded Council membership by five more permanent members and four more elected members. The five additional permanent members would have consisted of one developing member state from Africa, one from Asia, one from the Latin America and the Caribbean, and two from industrialized states. The four nonpermanent members would have included one African state, one Asian, one Eastern European, and one Latin American and Caribbean.[11]

In reaction to this determined push by Ambassador Razali, an informal "Coffee Club" (named after its members' weekly meetings over coffee on Tuesday mornings)[12] was created, which included several countries that felt they would be disadvantaged by this reform. It was led by the ambassadors of Italy and Pakistan, Paulo Fulci and Ahmad Kamal respectively. However, it also included countries like Spain, Argentina, Canada, Mexico, and South Korea.

Similarly, an equally strong push for Council reform spearheaded by Brazil, Germany, India, and Japan (the so-called Group of Four) was made in 2005. The G4 tabled a draft resolution in the General Assembly that proposed adding six new permanent members without veto power (two African, two Asian, one Latin American and Caribbean, and one from the category "Western Europe and Other") and four nonpermanent members (one from Africa, one from Asia, one from Eastern Europe, and one from Latin America and the Caribbean) to the Council.[13] The Coffee Club, later renamed the "Uniting for Consensus" group, responded with a counterproposal that would add ten nonpermanent seats for two-year terms.[14] Complicating the debate, the African states were insistent that the African seats envisioned in the G4 proposal hold veto power.

All these public disputes between the aspirant member states and their detractors have created the impression that the main obstacle to Council reform is this natural gridlock. However, even if a two-thirds majority in the General Assembly would unite behind an expansion of permanent members, it would likely face stiff opposition from the P5, who, despite their many disagreements over certain issues, are happy to keep their club closed and small. Indeed, when the G4 draft resolution began to gain momentum, China launched a ferocious campaign to halt it. It suspended the leave of all of its diplomats in that year to mount a strong global campaign against Japan. Although the United States supported the Japanese bid, it joined the Chinese campaign because it saw Council enlargement as running counter to its interests.[15] Indeed, a senior official in the Bill Clinton administration told me that by the late 1990s, Washington, D.C., had come to the conclusion that Council enlargement would only make the role of the United States on the Council more difficult, saying that, given how tough it was to get agreement among fifteen members, "can you imagine how much harder it would get with twenty members?"

This US opposition to Council reform enjoys bipartisan support. According to a confidential cable released by WikiLeaks, Zalmay Khalilzad, ambassador to the UN under the George W. Bush administration, wrote that the United States "should quietly allow discontent with P5 veto prerogatives to ensure the veto is not extended to new members while joining Russia and China in stoutly defending existing P5 vetoes."[16] His remarks were clearly cynical. The United States would actually like to stoke unhappiness over the P5 veto to ensure that no new power gets it, while knowing full well that the US veto cannot be taken away without US consent. But the second limb of Ambassador Khalilzad's statement is equally revealing of a powerful new political reality: the United States can only work with Russia and China, but not with the United Kingdom and France, to protect veto privileges. Why is that?

The simple answer is that, as indicated earlier, the United Kingdom and France recognize that they no longer enjoy the political legitimacy to exercise the veto or to stand in the frontlines defending it. This is why neither the United Kingdom nor France has exercised the official veto since the end of the Cold War. They know well that if they were to do so, this would severely undermine their increasingly flimsy claim to permanent membership. At the same time, the decision not to exercise the official veto is a shrewd one. They can still exercise the "unofficial" veto in informal consultations, and they do so frequently. So they can enjoy the very special privilege of permanent Council membership without paying a political price. In short, one must never underestimate the political shrewdness of the P5 members.

We can, however, question their wisdom. There is no doubt that the P5, in fighting to retain their current composition, are defending the indefensible. If the United States, China, and Russia were truly wise, instead of being merely cunning, they should realize that their interests differ from those of the United Kingdom and France. The world is questioning the permanent-membership credentials of the United Kingdom and France, not theirs. Hence, if these three powers are to retain their legitimacy over the long term rather than the short term, they should accept the new political reality that the interests of the P5 are no longer convergent. The United States, Russia, and China should have a vested interest in retaining the legitimacy of permanent membership and increasing that membership. The United Kingdom and France are desperate to avoid change.

This is not the only area where the interests of the P5 are changing. Hitherto, the United States has been the chief opponent of Council expansion in any form, as it has believed (probably correctly so) that any addition of new members would constrain the United States more than it would constrain the other permanent members. The United States is clearly the biggest elephant in the room, and will remain the biggest elephant for quite a while. In 1980, according to the International Monetary Fund (IMF), the US share of the global economy, in terms of purchasing power parity (PPP), was 25 percent, while that of China was 2.2 percent. However, in 2014, the US share of the global economy in PPP terms fell to 16.1 percent, while China's rose to 16.3 percent.[17] Justin Lin, the former chief economist of the World Bank, has predicted that by 2030, the size of the Chinese economy will be twice that of the United States in PPP terms.[18] In short, the United States must begin to prepare itself psychologically and politically to be the second biggest elephant in the room. In anticipation of this inevitable change, President Bill Clinton, in 2003, wisely conveyed this advice to the American people:

> If you believe that maintaining power and control and absolute freedom of movement and sovereignty is important to your country's future, there's nothing inconsistent in [the United States continuing to behave unilaterally]. [The United States is] the biggest, most powerful country in the world now.

We've got the juice and we're going to use it. . . . But if you believe that we should be trying to create a world with rules and partnerships and habits of behavior that we would like to live in when we're no longer the military po- litical economic superpower in the world, then you wouldn't do that. It just depends on what you believe.[19]

In short, by the time the United States becomes number two, it may actually be in its national interests to have added a few more members who could help it constrain the new biggest elephant in the room, China. By then the United Kingdom and France will be too weak to help the United States balance China. By contrast, India and Brazil would be strong and confident enough to provide a more evenly balanced Security Council.

It is vital to emphasize this point, because no change will come to the Council until the United States decides it is in its national interests to do so. In my new book, *The Great Convergence,* I have tried to build on Bill Clin- ton's wise advice and have argued that the time has come for US leaders and thinkers to realize that it is now in the national interests of the United States to strengthen multilateral institutions, including the Security Council.[20] Fortunately, it is also in the interests of other emerging powers, including China and India, Brazil and Nigeria, to do the same. This great convergence of interests will therefore open a political window for Council reform. To illustrate the argument of convergence, I use a simple metaphor to explain how our world has been fundamentally transformed. In the past, the system of nations could be compared to separate boats, with captains and crews taking care of each boat, and with rules designed to ensure that the boats did not collide. This was what the rules-based order of 1945 was all about. Today, after rapid globalization and the literal shrinking of the globe, its 7 billion people no longer live on 193 separate boats. Instead, they live in 193 separate cabins on the same boat. However, the problem with this boat is that we have captains and crews taking care of each cabin, but no captain or crew taking care of the boat as a whole. Once we absorb this metaphor, we will begin to understand how the new global challenges, from financial crises to pandemics, from global climate change to global terrorism, cross national borders effortlessly. Fortunately, many of the world's leaders understand that they must meet more often to handle these global challenges. Hence, there has been a proliferation of meetings of global leaders, from the G-20 and the Asia Pacific Economic Cooperation (APEC) forum, to theme-specific summits on climate change and nuclear security. The wisdom that global leaders have demonstrated in increasing the frequency of their face-to-face interaction must now be carried to its logical conclusion: they must work equally hard to reform and strengthen global institutions. Hence it is only a matter of time before the political window opens for Council reform.

A Win-Win-Win Solution

When that window opens, the biggest obstacle to success will come from the absence of a political formula that could be broadly acceptable, especially to the middle powers that have sufficient size and political clout to block Council reform. And it is perfectly understandable why these middle powers have been blocking reform. The aspirants to permanent membership (including Germany, India, Brazil, Japan, Nigeria, and South Africa) have asked the other middle powers and small states to virtually commit political suicide by voting to increase their political clout and stature by granting them permanent membership. It is perfectly reasonable for middle powers and small states to avoid committing political suicide. This is one key reason why no expansion of permanent membership has taken place despite two decades of determined efforts by the aspirant states.

If they hope to succeed in the next two decades (and it may well take this long), the aspirants must work on a formula that will also provide incentives for middle powers to reform Council composition. In short, if India, Brazil, and Nigeria want Pakistan, Argentina, and South Africa to vote for their permanent membership, it is vital to ensure that the near-losers also end up as near-winners. This is why I have proposed in my book *The Great Convergence* a new 7-7-7 formula for Council reform: seven permanent members (with veto rights), seven semipermanent members, and seven elected members. It is important that membership not exceed twenty-one, as the United States has made it absolutely clear that its preference is to have no more than twenty members in a reformed Council.

How would the seven permanent members be selected? The United States, China, and Russia would retain their historical claims. The UK and France would logically give up their seats to a single European seat representing Europe's common foreign and security policy. The three remaining seats would then be allocated to Africa, Asia, and Latin America. It would be fair for Asia to get two out of seven seats, since Asia is home to 55 percent of the world's population. Because China and India are each home to more than one-seventh of the world's population, it would make logical sense for each to get one seat out of seven permanent seats. Securing agreement on how to allocate the seven permanent seats would not be difficult. The logical seven candidates would be the EU, the United States, China, India, Russia, Brazil, and Nigeria.

This list raises some obvious questions. Why include India instead of Japan, and Nigeria instead of South Africa? Brazil's claim to the Latin American seat cannot be challenged. It is far larger than any of its Latin American counterparts in population and GDP. By contrast, Japan's GDP used to be much larger than India's. This strengthened its claim to a permanent Council seat. However, few noticed that the size of India's GDP surpassed Japan's in PPP terms in 2011. With demographic decline being

Japan's destiny, and with India emerging as one of the world's youngest countries, there is no doubt that India is on track to become a more powerful country than Japan in all indicators. Also, unlike Japan, whose foreign policy is subservient to that of the United States, India stands out as an independent actor on the world scene, willing to stand up to the United States.[21] This is why more developing countries support India's case over Japan's.

The choice between Nigeria and South Africa is harder to make. South Africa has a larger GDP than does Nigeria, and is perceived to be better-governed. Hence it would seem to be a stronger candidate than Nigeria. But the governance travails of South Africa have been rising. When Goldman Sachs economist Jim O'Neill, who coined the term "BRIC" (Brazil, Russia, India, China), was asked to predict the next few emerging economies, he created a new acronym, "MINT" (Mexico, Indonesia, Nigeria, Turkey).[22] He chose Nigeria over South Africa as having better economic prospects in the long term. More important, Nigeria's population is 170 million, more than three times that of South Africa's 51 million.

Since the "permanent" members of the Council enjoy enormous privileges, this quite naturally leads to enormous resentment from those countries that feel they are equally deserving. A simple way to reduce the resentment is to attach significant responsibilities to these enormous privileges. Two such responsibilities come quickly to mind. First, while all the permanent members should continue to pay their UN dues on the well-established principles of "capacity to pay," each permanent member should pay a premium to reflect their privileged status. Hence, each permanent member should pay a minimum of 5 percent of the UN budget. If any of them claim that they are unable to make such a minimum payment (which, as of the 2015–2016 budget, would be an inconsequential sum of $267 million a year), they should automatically disqualify themselves from taking on the global responsibilities that a permanent member should take on. Second, the permanent members should also agree to serve as the ultimate "police departments" and "fire departments" of the world in the field of international peace and security. Hence, if genocide were about to break out in Rwanda or Burundi, Sudan or Syria, the new permanent members should see it as their constitutional responsibility to respond to such crises. The natural resentment of their privileged status will dissipate when it is made clear that permanent members also bear heavy burdens.[23]

Franklin Delano Roosevelt once said, "Great power involves great responsibility."[24] When the great powers were assigned the veto in 1945, there was also a clear expectation that they would have to take on great responsibilities to match the great privileges they received as veto-wielding powers. As Inis Claude writes, one of the objectives of middle powers and small states during the establishment of the Security Council "was to gain assurance that the most powerful members would initiate and support positive collective action within and on behalf of the organization in times of crisis."[25]

The second challenge would be to select a pool of twenty-eight "precertified" countries who could take turns occupying the seven semipermanent seats, serving two-year terms on a rotating basis. By getting an automatic return to the Council every eight years instead of having to wait, as is currently the case for some countries, for decades (the current formula of competition among all 188 states has meant that even a relatively heavyweight country like India was kept out of the Council for two decades, from 1992 to 2011), this category of twenty-eight countries would effectively enjoy semipermanent status. Many of them know what a real privilege this would be, as most of them have had to spend a small fortune financially and politically to get reelected to the Council every few years. Under this model, their frequent return to the Council would be guaranteed. I have no doubt that there will be some disagreement about how to allocate these semipermanent seats among the regional groups. However, the best criteria for selecting deserving members for the twenty-eight semipermanent members would be a country's share of global population and global economy. At the same time, since the UN works on the basis of regional groupings, the twenty-eight slots could be allocated like this: nine seats for Asia Pacific, seven seats for Africa, seven seats for Western Europe, four for Latin America, and one for Eastern Europe, reflecting their relative weights in the new political order. And importantly, the prospect of semipermanent seats would help to win over the near-losers in the competition for new permanent seats.

Any formula for Council reform must also gain the support of the two-thirds majority in the General Assembly, which mostly comprises relatively small states. Unlike the middle powers, who are always scrambling to get reelected to the Council every few years to demonstrate that they are significant powers, the interests of the small states are different. They have a greater interest in an effective Security Council that helps to preserve peace and prevent aggression. Hence, reform leading to a stronger and more credible Council is in their national interests. These small states also command the largest share of votes in the General Assembly. If they do not support a formula for reform, there will be no reform. Hence, all these small states should also get seven elected seats in the revised Council. In theory, the 160 remaining states that will have to compete for these seven seats will be seen as "losers." But in practice, they will be winners, because in the past there has never been a level playing field in the competition for the ten non-permanent Council seats, as many of the middle powers have served frequently in the Security Council, such as Brazil (ten times), Egypt (five times), and Japan (nine times), crowding out small states such as Singapore (one time), the United Arab Emirates (one time), and Guyana (two times), who as a result serve very rarely. The creation of semipermanent seats for the middle powers may, paradoxically, create more political space for representation by the small states in a new, twenty-one-member Security Council.[26]

This twenty-one-member Council would be superior to the current fifteen-member Council in many ways. It would enjoy greater "representational" legitimacy, since a much larger percentage of the world's population would participate in its deliberations. Also, since geopolitics is also about geography, it would be an obvious improvement to have at least one permanent member from each of the regional groups. Each region has its own geopolitical dynamics. The permanent member or members from each region would be under pressure to represent that region's interests. All this could help to promote greater geopolitical stability. Equally important, the middle powers of the world, which have hitherto resented their exclusion from the Security Council and which resent the enormous effort they have to put into getting reelected once a decade or so, would feel happier at the prospect of automatically rejoining the Council every eight years. The middle powers would also be winners. The smaller states should also benefit from this new formula, since they would not have to compete with the middle powers for the scarce number of elected Council seats.[27]

It is important to emphasize and explain the advantages of the 7-7-7 formula compared to earlier proposals for Council reform. It creates winners at all levels, including middle powers that have adamantly blocked Council reform in the past. The only real losers will be the United Kingdom and France. But they will be compensated in other ways. First, they will give up their permanent seats in favor of a common European seat in which they will be major participants (and they can reach a private agreement with their European partners to have a "permanent" presence in a permanent European seat). Second, they will not have to worry about trying to defend the legitimacy of a Security Council that is "frozen" in the old order. France and the United Kingdom would gain little by being permanent members of an organization that is progressively losing its legitimacy.[28]

The other big advantage of the 7-7-7 formula is that it is dynamic. It can and should be reviewed every ten years. Hence, if the economy of any middle power does exceptionally well and it is qualified to join the group of twenty-eight on the basis of the stipulated criteria, it could well claim a semipermanent seat. This principle of creating mechanisms for constant review and change in major international organizations would represent a major leap forward in human history, because all major international organizations, including the Council, the IMF, and the World Bank, have hitherto stoutly resisted mechanisms for constant review. Yet as we move into a world of even more rapid changes and major shifts of power, it would be fatal for any international organization not to have mechanisms for constant review. Indeed, provisions for change should be an essential requirement for all international organizations.[29]

Despite the inherent appeal of the 7-7-7 formula, we should not expect early movement on Council reform. Apart from the continuing resistance of the P5, especially the United States, there are also two regions that block reform, Africa and Europe.

The G4 reform proposal put forward by Japan, Germany, India, and Brazil floundered in 2005 primarily because of the inability of the African group to support it. While this proposal foresaw two permanent seats for African member states, it would have come without veto rights, which the African group insisted should be extended to any new permanent member "so long as it exists." In principle, this is a reasonable position. All the efforts by Nigeria and South Africa to moderate the African position failed, even though Nigerian president Olusegun Obasanjo had explicitly warned African leaders that the failure to compromise on the question of the veto would "certainly frustrate the reform efforts."[30] If Africa were to support the 7-7-7 formula, they would end up the biggest winners, as their presence in the Council would increase from two nonpermanent seats to one permanent seat (with veto), seven semipermanent rotating seats, and three elected seats.

The other regional group that will ultimately have difficulty reaching agreement is the European Union. On the surface, the disagreement is between the United Kingdom, France, and Germany on the one hand (as the United Kingdom and France support permanent membership for Germany) and Italy, Spain, Poland, and some other EU members (who feel that permanent membership for Germany would further downgrade their political status in Europe and globally) on the other. Underneath the surface, there are deeper challenges that will emerge. The late ambassador Richard Holbrooke, who once served as US ambassador to the UN, said to me what many Americans believe but few dare to utter: that Europe has been overrepresented in the Council. The world at large would find it completely unacceptable that the EU, home to only 5 percent of the world's population, could have so many permanent members. Over time, Germany will realize that its quest for individual permanent membership is impossible. It will also come to realize that the United Kingdom and France are cynically supporting Germany's permanent membership quest because they get all the credit from Germany for overt support while getting quiet self-satisfaction from the knowledge that Germany will never succeed.

Fortunately, Germany has a back door that it can use to gain effective permanent membership. It would thus be logical for the EU to be represented with a single permanent member's seat, since it has, at least in theory, a common foreign and security policy. If Germany wants to stop its Sisyphean labor of pushing a huge boulder up a hill and instead take on the far easier task of pushing a boulder down a hill following the laws of political gravity, it should abandon its quest for individual permanent membership and push for a single EU seat. This would put Germany's position in line with that of the vast majority of EU members. At the same time, given Germany's growing domination of EU decisionmaking as a result of its enormously strong economic position, it is natural that it would exert significant influence in the Council through an EU permanent seat.

There can be no denying that France and the United Kingdom will resist and fight the 7-7-7 formula, as they will have to give up their position in the privileged P5 club. However, under the formula, the EU, with only 5 percent of the world's population, would still field, at any given time, one to two (or close to 25 percent) of the seven semipermanent member seats, meaning that in addition to the EU permanent seat, Germany, France, the United Kingdom, Italy, Spain, and Poland would still be returning to the Council in their purely national capacities every eight years. If indeed the EU is developing a common strategic worldview with the adoption of its common foreign and security policy, it should come to realize that the 7-7-7 formula preserves the European overrepresentation in a key global body. At some time, the United Kingdom and France will have to show the wisdom of supporting long-term European interests over short-term national interests.

Indeed a lot of wisdom will have to be shown by many leading capitals in the world if we are to succeed in our common global interest in reforming the Security Council and preparing it for its critical twenty-first-century roles. In the short run, the "losers" will fight hard to prevent any change to the current composition. But if the current composition gradually but steadily erodes the standing and legitimacy of the Council, it is inevitable that the rising and emerging powers will see the wisdom of the 7-7-7 formula and work toward it. Winston Churchill once quipped that "you can always count on Americans to do the right thing—after they've done everything else." Over the past two decades, we have tried all the alternatives. Hence, in the next two decades, we should naturally gravitate toward the correct solution.

Notes

1. United Nations General Assembly, "Official Verbatim Record of the 58th Session of the 7th Plenary Meeting," A/58/PV.7, September 23, 2003.

2. United Nations, Dag Hammarskjöld Library Research Guides, "Security Council: Veto List," http://research.un.org/en/docs/sc/quick/veto.

3. United Nations, *Charter of the United Nations,* San Francisco, June 26, 1945, Article 27(2).

4. Kishore Mahbubani, *The Great Convergence: Asia, the West, and the Logic of One World* (New York: PublicAffairs, 2013), p. 236.

5. Inis L. Claude Jr., *Swords into Plowshares: The Problems and Progress of International Organization* (New York: Random, 1971), p. xx.

6. PricewaterhouseCoopers, *The BRICs and Beyond: Prospects, Challenges, and Opportunities,* January 2013, www.pwc.com/en_GX/gx/world-2050/assets/pwc-world-in-2050-report-january-2013.pdf.

7. Stockholm International Peace Research Institute (SIPRI), "SIPRI Military Expenditure Database," www.sipri.org/research/armaments/milex/milex_database.

8. EUR-Lex, *Yassin Abdullah Kadi and Al Barakaat International Foundation v. Council of the European Union and Commission of the European Communities,* Joined Cases C-402/05 P and C-415/05 P, September 3, 2008, http://eur-lex.europa.eu/legal-content/EN/TXT/?qid=1420817388053&uri=CELEX:62005CJ0402.

9. Supreme Court of the United Kingdom, Judgment: *HM Treasury vs. al-Ghabra,* January 27, 2010.

10. Independent Inquiry Committee into the United Nations Oil-for-Food Programme, "Manipulation of the Oil-for-Food Programme by the Iraqi Regime" (New York: Council on Foreign Relations, October 2005), https://web.archive.org/web/20130823070841/http://www.iic-offp.org/documents/IIC%20Final%20Report%2027Oct2005.pdf.

11. United Nations General Assembly, "Report of the Open-Ended Working Group on the Question of Equitable Representation on and Increase in the Membership of the Security Council and Other Matters Related to the Security Council," 51st Session, Supplement no. 47, UN Doc. A/51/47, 1997, Annex I.

12. Francesco Paolo Fulci with Antonia Anania, "Ottobre Nero al Palazzo di Vetro," *Caffe Europa,* November 10, 2000, www.caffeeuropa.it/attualita/107attualita-fulci.html.

13. United Nations General Assembly, "Afghanistan, Belgium, Bhutan, Brazil, Czech Republic, Denmark, Fiji, France, Georgia, Germany, Greece, Haiti, Honduras, Iceland, India, Japan, Kiribati, Latvia, Maldives, Nauru, Palau, Paraguay, Poland, Portugal, Solomon Islands, Tuvalu and Ukraine: Draft Resolution," A/59/L.64, July 6, 2005.

14. United Nations General Assembly, "Draft Resolution on Reform of the Security Council," A/59/L.68, July 21, 2005.

15. "China and US 'Unite' over UN Bid," BBC, August 4, 2005, http://news.bbc.co.uk/2/hi/americas/4746459.stm.

16. Zalmay M. Khalilzad, "USUN Views on Security Council Reform," December 29, 2007, www.wikileaks.org/plusd/cables/07USUNNEWYORK1225_a.html.

17. International Monetary Fund, "World Economic Outlook Database," April 2015, www.imf.org/external/pubs/ft/weo/2015/01/weodata/index.aspx.

18. Justin Yifu Lin, *Demystifying the Chinese Economy* (New York: Cambridge University Press, 2012), p. 16.

19. Bill Clinton, "Global Challenges," speech at Yale University, October 31, 2003.

20. Mahbubani, *The Great Convergence.*

21. As was demonstrated by the Devyani Khobragade case in late 2013 and early 2014.

22. Jim O'Neill, "Who You Calling a BRIC?" *Bloomberg View,* November 13, 2013, www.bloomberg.com/news/2013-11-12/who-you-calling-a-bric-.html.

23. Mahbubani, *The Great Convergence,* pp. 240–241.

24. Franklin Delano Roosevelt, quoted in "F.D.R. and the Stuff of His War," *New York Times,* February 3, 2006, www.nytimes.com/2006/02/03/arts/design/03fdr.html?pagewanted=all&_r=0.

25. Claude, *Swords into Plowshares,* p. 82.

26. Mahbubani, *The Great Convergence,* pp. 242–243.

27. Ibid., p. 243.

28. Ibid., pp. 244–245.

29. Ibid., p. 245.

30. Olusegun Obasanjo, quoted in Jonas von Freiesleben, "Reform of the Security Council," in *Managing Change at the United Nations* (New York: Center for UN Reform Education, 2008), p. 7.

9

Working Methods: The Ugly Duckling of Security Council Reform

Christian Wenaweser

THE MERE MENTION OF SECURITY COUNCIL REFORM TRIGGERS strong reactions even among the most hardened UN diplomats, ranging from eye-rolling to outright sarcasm. After two decades of consecutive New York–based processes, everybody knows that the effort is as deadlocked as ever. In addition to being unproductive, efforts to enlarge the Council—the most controversial aspect of Council reform, which tends to generate the fiercest rhetoric and most uncompromising positions—have also undermined the prospect of the arguably more promising efforts to reform the working methods of the Council. The fact that for the past two decades the official reform processes have pursued both goals in parallel has ultimately hindered the prospects of improving the way the Council operates, as I will show in this chapter.

Many states that have no clear stake in the efforts to enlarge the Council have consistently emphasized the importance of the way in which the Council conducts its business and how this relates to the rest of the membership—as it is mandated to act on their behalf. They have argued that, whether the Council will be enlarged or not, their time of service on the Council would always be limited to rare two-year stints as one of the body's elected members. At the same time, for the past quarter century, the Council has continuously expanded its activities in areas of work that affect some or all member states that are not part of the body's decisionmaking process, for instance by imposing universally binding obligations; imposing sanctions that all states are bound to implement; or by mandating peacekeeping operations, the troops and funding for which are largely provided by countries that are not part of the relevant negotiations. Interaction with and access for non-Council members to these processes seems therefore of paramount importance—not least to secure the acceptance of Council decisions and to ensure their implementation. Many states have become increasingly dissatisfied with the quality of some of the resolutions they were asked to implement, because these resolutions either seemed ineffective, served the interests of just a few powerful member states, or, in some cases, were in conflict with international law.[1]

States have therefore increasingly expressed their frustration with the Council's work modalities, which have not been able to keep up with the substantial expansion of the Council's role. For many, the Council remains secretive in its proceedings and decisionmaking, inaccessible to those it should work with and irresponsive to requests from the outside.

The Beginnings: No Binding Rules

At its very first meeting on January 17, 1946, the Security Council adopted its Provisional Rules of Procedure, which were amended several times during the same year.[2] The last change to the provisional rules was made in 1982,[3] even though much has changed in the Council's practice in the decades since. The fact that the rules of the Council are still provisional has been the subject of much criticism, and their finalization has become a routine demand in discussions on the work of the Council. The fact that the Council is the only UN organ without adopted rules of procedure is to many evidence that its work is conducted with no transparency and predictability, which favors the five permanent members (P5), who have the comparative advantage of institutional memory. Nevertheless, the Council has shown no interest in updating its provisional rules or even adopting them. The rules are therefore both incomplete, in that they do not reflect changes in the Council's practice made in the past three decades, but also difficult to rely on, as they are only provisional.

Key Innovations Since the End of the Cold War

For a very long time, the Council did not undertake any systematic effort to review its working procedures. It was only in 1993 that it established a body formally in charge of this task, the Informal Working Group on Documentation and Other Procedural Questions (IWG). But it was a half-hearted move, because the IWG has always been chaired by the Council presidency of the month. Given all the other tasks of the presidency, this was a recipe for inaction. Nevertheless, the Council on occasion has certainly been innovative in the way it operates, including in response to new challenges. The 1990s in particular were a productive era in this respect. The end of the Cold War offered new opportunities and led to a rapid expansion of the Council's work into new areas. The establishment of international criminal tribunals,[4] thematic discussions of threats to international peace and security, the significant expansion of the reach of the UN's sanctions committees, and the creation of new types of peacekeeping operations all fall into this period. Some of these changes resulted in innovations in the working methods of the Council.

Arria Formula

One of the most important of these innovations was the so-called Arria formula. First applied in 1992 by Venezuelan Council ambassador Diego Arria in the context of the war in Bosnia, the formula makes it possible for the Council to meet with individuals with expertise who could be of particular interest for its work. It also assists the Council in obtaining real-time information from the field.[5] The design of the formula is simple. The discussion is not an official meeting and does not take place in the Council chamber. Rather, it is held upon invitation of one Council member (usually not the presidency member), often with all member states invited to participate, while usually only Council members have the right to speak.[6] The formula has been applied for different purposes, while interaction with nonstate actors is still the primary one.[7] It is generally considered an important step in the opening of the Council to the outside, and advocates of improvements to working methods have usually called for its more frequent use. The Arria formula also illustrates that elected members can be instrumental in bringing about changes from within the Council.

Security Council Missions

The practice of the Council to visit countries for different purposes (e.g., fact-finding, supporting peace agreements, and mediation efforts) also picked up in frequency in the early 1990s.[8] The vast majority of these visits have been to African countries (situations in Africa regularly make up the bulk of the Council's agenda). Since 2001, Council visits have usually been carried out with the participation of all Council members. They are generally considered a positive tool that allows the Council to better assess the situation, to engage directly with players on the ground, and to have a direct impact on the situation. But there has also been criticism of the way in which the Council decides on the destination of these field missions,[9] on the agenda of these trips,[10] and on their budgetary aspects.[11] While few will question the potential value of such field visits, their modalities could likely be significantly improved.

Open Thematic Debates

The Council's practice of discussing thematic questions in an open format also began in the 1990s. Open thematic debates quickly became a tool for elected members in particular to increase their profile on the Council by advancing its agenda on key crosscutting challenges. As a result, the Council has produced an impressive body of work in areas such as protection of civilians; women, peace, and security; and children and armed conflict. While these issues remain to this day firmly established aspects of its work, the Council has also faced criticism when venturing occasionally into areas that have but a tenuous link with the peace and security agenda—climate change, illicit cross-border trafficking, or pandemics—leading at times to complaints about "encroachment" of the Council into areas of work that are the natural domain of the General Assembly. In recent years, states have more frequently complained about the ritualistic nature of open debates and their lack of impact on an actual outcome.[12]

Wrap-Up Sessions

The format of the "wrap-up session" was first introduced in March 2000, under the presidency of Bangladesh.[13] The purpose of the format is to provide an interactive discussion among Council members to assess the body's performance during the preceding month, with the rest of the membership allowed to follow the debate. After the initial success of the format and the peak of its popularity in 2002, wrap-up sessions became unpopular thereafter, but were seeing a bit of a renaissance as of 2013.[14] The format has been considered useful by proponents of greater transparency and accountability.

"Horizon Scanning"

A "horizon scanning" is an informal briefing given to the Council by the Department of Political Affairs. It is thus a soft application of the Secretary-General's competence under Article 99 of the UN Charter to bring matters to the attention of the Council that may threaten international peace and security. The format allows the Secretariat to bring emerging crisis situations to the Council's attention and thus to facilitate early response and preventive action. It emerged in 2010 upon the initiative of the UK and enjoyed early, but also somewhat short-lived, success. After horizon scannings quickly became a monthly fixture in the work of the Council at first, criticism arose, and the format lost popularity.[15] Like other Council discussions, horizon-scanning meetings have quickly morphed from an interactive exchange into the reading of prepared statements. Also, a number of permanent Council members as well as countries referenced in the briefings became increasingly uncomfortable with a format that could be perceived as putting issues on the Council's agenda, without it having taken a decision to this effect.[16] At the time of writing, the format was unlikely to become a permanent and regular feature of the Council's working methods, even though it has great potential. Issues such as piracy and the situation in northern Mali or in Yemen were first discussed as part of this format and have since proven to require long-term attention of the Council.

Informal Interactive Dialogue

The informal interactive dialogue was a format created in 2009 to allow the Security Council to discuss the unfolding crisis in Sri Lanka—a situation not on the agenda of the Security Council—after attempts to raise it under "any other business" had been blocked.[17] Just like the Arria formula, the format is not a formal meeting of the Council, not announced in the *UN Journal,* and not held in the Council chamber—and it is understood that it will not result in any outcome. While clearly an insufficient response to the situation in Sri Lanka,[18] it was at the same time welcomed as a creative tool to give the Council more flexibility. More recently, it was used in the Council's dialogue with the International Criminal Court (ICC), in the context of the regular briefings of the ICC's chief prosecutor on the Court's activities in Libya.[19]

On occasion, the Council has thus indeed been innovative in creating new formats, but many of these tools have remained underutilized and applied inconsistently.

Efforts to Reform in Connection with Enlargement

The Open-Ended Working Group

In addition to the changes the Council has made over time to its proceedings, there have consistently been initiatives from the outside to recommend improvements in this respect. The earliest examples date back to the early days of the UN, when the General Assembly adopted a number of little-known resolutions on the question of working methods.[20] In 1993, the General Assembly established an Open-Ended Working Group to deal with all matters related to Security Council reform.[21] While primarily set up to address the increasing calls for enlargement, the group also had the mandate to consider working methods,[22] and over the following years produced an impressive menu of proposed measures for their improvement—always with the goal of comprehensive reform. While these early years turned out to be the only productive era in the long life of the group, its work inspired the one comprehensive proposal for Council reform in the 1990s, the Razali proposal.

Brave New World: The Razali Proposal

The proposal informally submitted by Razali Ismael (Malaysia) during his tenure as the president of the fifty-first session of the General Assembly in 1997 is memorable in that it is the only proposal by a General Assembly president for a comprehensive reform of the Council.[23] While the proposal is best known for its approach to expansion—suggesting the creation of five new permanent seats without the veto right—its ambitious recommendations for reform of working methods are no less remarkable. To this effect, it suggests measures such as consultations between members of the Security Council and the countries most affected by its decisions, invitations to nonmembers to participate in informal consultations, the holding of "frequent orientation debates" before the Council takes decisions, clarification of what constitutes a procedural matter, and more frequent advisory opinions from the International Court of Justice.[24] This list of measures drew on discussions in the Open-Ended Working Group[25] and, as a whole, offered an ambitious reform agenda. Even more remarkable is a measure related to the use of the veto: in order to balance the provision that the five new permanent members would not be accorded veto power, Razali sought to "discourage the use of the veto, by urging the original permanent members of the Security Council to limit the exercise of their veto power to actions taken under Chapter VII of the Charter." The suggested political bargain was thus to withhold the veto right for new permanent members while limiting its use for original ones.[26]

The Razali proposal illustrates both the quality of work done on working methods during the early years of the Open-Ended Working Group and the willingness of the UN membership at the time to move forward on these issues—including on the use of the veto. However, the proposal was in the end not put to a vote in the General Assembly, as its chances of success seemed uncertain. Thereafter, the dynamic in the Open-Ended Working Group diminished significantly, and the following years saw little movement.

The G4 Initiative

The absence of any forward movement after a decade of efforts to reform the Council led to mounting frustration especially among those states that had aspirations to a permanent seat on the Council. And geopolitical realities had shifted, with the argument for permanent seats for Germany and Japan largely based on economic power and, in light of their relative economic decline, generally considered somewhat less compelling than in the early 1990s. Brazil and India, on the other hand, were viewed as emerging powers and therefore seen as increasingly credible contenders. The 2005 World Summit presented the perfect opportunity for these states to push for a solution. Originally meant to focus on the UN's development agenda, it soon became clear that it would turn into a comprehensive reform event in light of the crisis the UN found itself after the divisions over the 2003 US-led intervention in Iraq.[27] Coming together under the label "G4,"[28] Germany, Japan, Brazil, and India presented an enlargement proposal that suggested the creation of six new permanent seats, combined with four new nonpermanent ones.[29] The G4 proposal was similar to the Razali proposal in not demanding the exercise of veto rights for the new permanent members until a review could decide on the matter. But it differed from its predecessor in assigning an additional permanent seat to the African Group. The initiative created a strong dynamic and triggered powerful reactions. The Uniting for Consensus Group, led by Italy and composed of numerous regional rivals of aspirants to permanent seats (e.g., Pakistan, Argentina, Mexico, and the Republic of Korea),[30] opposed the effort vigorously from the beginning and hastily put together a counterproposal. The P5 were split on the proposal, with France and the UK eventually supporting it,[31] and China, Russia, and the United States opposed. The African Group, after much negotiation and summit meetings,[32] finally came together in a position that seemed close to that of the G4 on the surface, but in fact made it impossible for African states to support it, given the proposed creation of six permanent seats with a veto right and five new nonpermanent seats. The insistence on the veto in particular was a no-go not just for the permanent members, but also for large parts of the nonpermanent membership. With the failure of the G4 to rally African states behind their proposal, the effort faltered well before the World Summit took place in September 2005.

This process in the run-up to the 2005 summit illustrated not only the difficulty of enlarging the Security Council, but also that the proponents of enlargement proposals were not willing to make a serious effort to advance the reform of working methods. The G4, in trying to enhance support for their proposal, made significant concessions to the detriment of an ambitious approach to working methods, in particular on the use of the veto. Similarly, the counterproposals by the Uniting for Consensus Group and the African Group were woefully inadequate already in their original versions. An uncomfortable reality was thus revealed to the proponents of reform of working methods: any proposal to enlarge the Council would be a challenge to the institutional supremacy of the P5, and thus nobody would be willing to compound that challenge by adding on far-reaching reform proposals on working methods of the Council.

Going It Alone: The Rise and Fall of the S5

This realization led to the creation of the Small Five (S5) in late 2005.[33] The group, composed of Costa Rica, Jordan, Liechtenstein, Singapore, and Switzerland, was driven by the belief that accountability, legitimacy, and transparency of the Council's work were as important to its quality as enlargement. Having seen that working methods were treated as an afterthought by all the enlargement models, the S5 decided to advance working methods on their own track.[34] The group moved expeditiously to put together a set of measures for consideration by the Security Council, which it soon tabled in the format of a draft resolution of the General Assembly.[35] In the ensuing consultations, the S5 made it clear that states should prepare for a vote, while indicating openness to direct engagement with the Security Council.

The permanent members showed a differentiated reaction, with adamant opposition by China, Russia, and the United States. They not only rejected the measures put forward by the S5, but also argued that the resolution was beyond the legal authority of the Assembly. The Charter, they argued, did not foresee supremacy of the Assembly over the Council, so recommendations on the Council's procedures were not within the competence of the Assembly. The S5 argued that Article 10 of the UN Charter provided a solid legal basis for recommendations on Council reform coming from the General Assembly—and that this had been accepted by everyone in the long history of the Open-Ended Working Group.[36] The two European permanent members adopted a more sophisticated approach and tried to get control of the debate, in order to avoid a possibly divisive vote. The United Kingdom in particular offered constructive engagement on the ideas put forward by the S5—with the exception of measures dealing with the veto. As a result, the hitherto dormant Informal Working Group on Documentation was brought to life and given a permanent chair.[37] Japan, as the first chair, engaged in intense informal consultations with the S5 with a twofold goal: first, to get an ambitious set of measures agreed in the Council, and second, to avoid a vote on the S5 resolution in the General Assembly. It was clear that the arguments of the S5 had hit a nerve. Most states reacted positively to the initiative, which was generally perceived to enjoy strong support,[38] even though there was some unease over the prospect of a vote. The efforts within the IWG eventually led to the adoption of Presidential Note 507 by the Council, containing a wide range of measures on working methods, strongly inspired by the S5 proposals, that were intended to enhance transparency as well as interaction with non-Council members. The topics covered ranged from briefings and documentation to the role of subsidiary organs and the drafting of resolutions.[39] The moment for the S5 initiative had been well chosen: through an effort of about half a year, the Council had made more progress on working methods than in the past two decades combined—at least on paper.

The Emperor's New Clothes: Intergovernmental Negotiations

While the S5 focused on monitoring the way in which the Council implemented the measures in Presidential Note 507, the enlargement effort was taken up again. The G4 constituency was increasingly showing signs of weakening, but was still able to agree on some procedural issues. Also, it was now complemented by a number of mainly developing states, under the leadership of India, that came together under the label "L.69," after the draft resolution in the General Assembly that they had submitted. This group was a spin-off of the G4, with the main substantive difference that over time it argued that the creation of new permanent seats would not be an effective reform unless accompanied by the veto right. These two groups had come to the conclusion that the Open-Ended Working Group needed to be replaced by a negotiating process. The Uniting for Consensus Group, as well as some of the P5, resisted, but in the end there was consensual agreement on a framework for negotiations. General Assembly Decision 62/557 set a new framework for the discussions on Council reform, for all intents and purposes replacing the Open-Ended Working Group.[40] Before long, though, it became clear that the much-anticipated beginning of this new phase in Council reform was essentially a relabeling of the circular process of years past. The "negotiations" were a recycling of known positions and characterized by procedural maneuvers. Working methods found their way into the new mandate, though as part of a rather odd couple: one of the five "key issues" identified in the mandate was "size of an enlarged Security Council and working methods of the Council."[41] The S5 had seemingly achieved their goal for this exercise. With a clear marker in the negotiating mandate, the group would continue to pursue its objectives on three different tracks: directly with the Council, through the General Assembly, and in the framework of the process established under Decision 62/557. Nevertheless, the decision would come back to haunt the group.

Waiting for Implementation

While the S5 saw Presidential Note 507 as not going far enough, they considered it a good step in the right direction—if implemented. Yet here lay the problem. The S5 were interested in working with the Council on the implementation of the measures contained in Note 507, but this interest was not reciprocated. In the following years, the S5 met just once with the Informal Working Group on Documentation, the Council body in charge of working methods, for a lively but ultimately inconsequential exchange. There was a fundamental difference of opinion. The S5 and large parts of the UN membership considered Note 507 to be a commitment of the Council to concrete measures to enhance transparency and interaction with the wider membership.[42] The Council, led by the P5, on the other hand, treated it as a menu to choose from. As a consequence, implementation of the measures remained inconsistent and incomplete and was left to the discretion of the presidency of the respective months. Efforts of the S5 to discuss mechanisms for systematic implementation within the IWGD were unsuccessful. Rather than promoting consistent implementation, the Council worked to add other reform measures: an update of Presidential Note 507 was adopted in 2010,[43] with the additions focusing on technical issues,[44] and did not address many of the questions that had been a high priority for the S5, such as the use of the veto. In fact, the question was never discussed in the IWG, in keeping with the stated belief of some of the P5 that the use of the veto did not fall in the area of working methods. So, four years after the adoption of the original version of Presidential Note 507, the picture from an S5 perspective was mixed at best: a technical update, poor implementation, no recognizable effort leading to systematic implementation, and continued lack of political will in the Council.

The Long Road to a Second Resolution

In 2011, after five years of existence, the S5 were thus facing a dilemma. On the one hand, the group had created a brand whose work was widely respected. In the enigmatic world of Security Council reform, the S5 stood out as perhaps the only group whose purpose was not primarily driven by national self-interest.[45] At the same time, the group found itself at a crossroads, unable to move forward on substance. The discussions on Council reform were as circular as ever, the Council itself was showing no interest to advance the agenda, and systematic implementation of even limited reform reflected in Note 507 was a distant prospect. To increase the pressure, the S5 decided to submit another draft resolution to the General Assembly, and a first draft was informally circulated to the wider membership in March 2011.[46]

It contained three invitations to the Security Council. First, to enhance implementation of Note 507 and to report thereon to the Assembly. Second, to consider the measures contained in the annex to the resolution. And third, to report to the Assembly on measures taken pursuant to this consideration. The annex to the resolution contained twenty-one measures covering a number of areas and ranging from the very technical to the highly political.[47] For many, the recommendation to the P5 to refrain from the use of a veto to block Council action aimed at preventing or ending genocide, war crimes, and crimes against humanity was central—a recommendation that became even more topical against the background of the two double vetoes cast in 2011 by Russia and China on the situation in Syria.

The S5 had agreed that a decision on possible tabling of the draft resolution would be made on the basis of the reactions of the membership. The response, however, was rather muted and gave only limited indication of the level of support it might enjoy. The proposed measures dealing with the use of the veto elicited much reaction. Some members were of the view that these measures were the political core of the resolution, but others cautioned that they might constitute a deal-breaker for the P5.[48] There was also some discomfort with the idea of taking the working methods out of the framework established by Decision 62/557, dealing with comprehensive Council reform. Most states adopted a wait-and-see attitude, reluctant to take a public position on a controversial proposal that risked angering powerful member states. By contrast, the P5 made no secret of their opposition to the text.

As the weeks and months passed, the S5 began discussing the possibility of tabling the text for formal consideration by the Assembly. This, the proponents argued, was necessary to maintain the relevance of the group and to have a concrete political impact.[49] But the more skeptical voices within the S5 argued that tabling a resolution would risk endangering the group's constructive engagement with the Council, which had resulted in a number of ongoing projects—including regular meetings with the incoming Council presidencies and the ten elected members (E10), improvements of the format of the annual report of the Security Council, and lessons learned on peacekeeping missions—that needed to be intensified.[50] The S5 also discussed the purpose of tabling. Some S5 members hoped that the Council would respond constructively by engaging with the group, and perhaps adopt its own text, just as it had done in 2006 with Note 507. Others were not thrilled at the prospect of repeating this scenario, as they expected a similar outcome: a commitment on paper to which the Council would not live up. Those latter S5 members were of the view that a formal decision by the Assembly was necessary to make the Council take the matter more seriously.[51] In the end, the group agreed on tabling the draft resolution, with the option of pushing for a vote at a later stage and in the face of the possible defection of the more impatient members of the group.

The expectation of the S5 that formally submitting the draft resolution would lead to more concrete reactions was met, at least to a point. States offered their comments, some of which were incorporated into the text. Most notably, the provision that would have allowed the P5 to cast a no vote without giving this the effect of blocking a decision was deleted from the text, as it was argued by some that this was not possible without amending the UN Charter.[52] While overall the draft resolution found strong substantive support, there were increasing expressions of concern that the text adopted a "piecemeal approach" by addressing only one part of the mandate on Security Council reform (working methods), but not the others (in particular enlargement). The counterargument by the S5 was simple: Security Council enlargement was a onetime act that would, under whatever enlargement model, require amendments to the Charter. But reform of working methods was an ongoing process—after all, the resolution suggested establishing a dialogue between the Council and the wider membership and was outside any amendment exercise. In addition, enlargement would always dominate the discussion on Council reform and inevitably lead to compromises made at the expense of working methods. Nevertheless, the S5 made a big effort to alleviate these concerns, for instance removing the term "working methods" from the title of the draft resolution as yet another assurance that the text was without prejudice to comprehensive Council reform.[53]

Going for a Vote?

With the opposition of the P5 so unequivocal, the S5 focused on securing as much support as possible for a vote. Generally, the response to these efforts was positive and numerically the support for the S5 was growing.[54] But resistance also became more forceful—and more coordinated. With the exception of the P5, very few states openly opposed the text. However, delinking the resolution from the overall dynamics on enlargement that had always hobbled Security Council reform proved impossible. The Uniting for Consensus Group led the chorus of those who—while professing support in principle for the substance of the resolution—began opposing its adoption due to its projected impact on Council reform as a whole. A vote on the S5 text, they feared, would break the taboo of voting on Council reform. Quite tellingly, the G4 and most of the L.69 constituency supported the S5 text. The initiative was now drawn into the destructive vortex of Security Council enlargement dynamics.

The African states were a numerically and politically important group for the outcome of a vote. While they were unified, at least on paper, by the Ezulwini consensus on the question of enlargement, they had no clear position on reform of working methods. A sizable number of African states expressed their intention to vote for the S5 text. Others, however, were uncomfortable, either due to their proximity to positions of the Uniting for Consensus Group, or simply because they feared that the vote would make public an open secret: that, in truth, the African states were deeply divided on the question of Council reform. Combined, these elements led to an African position that was playing for time—time that the S5 did not have.

The permanent members had long before concluded that the only good outcome would be to have the S5 proposal go away. They therefore embarked on a coordinated campaign to undermine the prospects of a vote. Those with strong influence in Africa worked intensely in that region to minimize support for the S5 initiative. They also increased their pressure on the S5. A week before the vote was to be held, the permanent representatives of the P5 jointly summoned their S5 counterparts for a meeting held at the US permanent mission, at which they voiced their strong opposition to the S5 text, warned of the consequences of a possible vote, and urged the withdrawal of the resolution.[55] A lively exchange ensued, but at no point during the meeting did the P5 offer a compromise or show interest in negotiating, contrary to what some among the S5 had expected. The meeting was essentially a joint demarche. This headwind notwithstanding, the S5 continued their lobbying, with considerable success, and everything seemed to be leading toward a showdown in the General Assembly plenary on May 16, 2012.

Legal Opinion on Majority Required

The campaign against the S5 resolution focused increasingly on its alleged linkage to Council enlargement. This, the opponents felt, would give the best leverage to undermine a text that otherwise found strong support. In addition to arguing that separate reform of working methods would harm the prospects of enlargement, this linkage also offered a procedural tool: it could now be argued that the text formed an integral part of Council reform and therefore fell under the provisions of General Assembly Resolution 53/30, which requires enlargement decisions to be adopted by the same margin as is required for the entry into force of Charter amendments, meaning two-thirds of the membership. This would mean that the S5 resolution would have to garner a minimum of 129 yes votes in order to pass. By contrast, the S5 had always argued that only a simple majority was required for adoption, because it had been established practice in the Assembly to take decisions by simple majority, even on issues that were considered "important."[56] In addition, Resolution 53/30 explicitly dealt with decisions implying Charter amendment—and because the S5 text had no such implications, the issue was seemingly moot.[57] However, those advocating the opposing view referred to General Assembly Decision 62/557, which made working methods part of the overall mandate on Security Council reform, including enlargement, for which Resolution 53/30 stipulated a two-thirds majority, which should therefore apply across the board—that is, also to the S5 text—even though it had nothing to do with enlargement. Support for this view eventually came from unexpected quarters: the president of the Assembly, put under considerable pressure to issue a ruling on the question, referred the matter to the Legal Counsel of the United Nations. Her response confirmed that it was well within the competence of the Assembly to decide on this matter. But, in convoluted reasoning, the Legal Counsel also came to the conclusion that "it would appear that the . . . resolution falls within the purview of . . . resolution 53/30 . . . and General Assembly decision 62/557,"[58] implying the need for a two-thirds majority. That the Legal Counsel would so clearly come down on one side of the discussion came as a surprise to many. The P5 proceeded to disseminate the letter widely[59] and intensified the pressure on the president to rule in accordance with the advice from the Legal Counsel.

Withdrawal

Several factors thus came together to undermine support for the S5 resolution and prospects for a vote: strong pressure on countries that had expressed support for the text, an informal legal opinion that could set the bar very high for the resolution to be passed, and finally an announcement from the African Group that they would ask for consideration to be deferred in order to hold more consultations. Time was clearly not on the side of the

S5. Much of its support came from small states whose backing could be jeopardized as a result of P5 lobbying in capitals. Faced with these multiple challenges, the S5 finally withdrew the draft resolution.[60] Shortly thereafter, the group was disbanded, putting an end to six years of consistent advocacy for improving working methods of the Council.

Accountability, Coherence, and Transparency

The withdrawal of the S5 resolution and the end of the group were significant setbacks for efforts to improve working methods of the Council from the outside. The issue did not go away, however. In May 2013, on the initiative of Switzerland, the Accountability, Coherence, and Transparency (ACT) Group was established to essentially pursue the same goals as the S5 did, with a number of marked differences. The ACT Group has decided to stay away from the discussions on Security Council reform and not to engage at all in the intergovernmental negotiations. And it is numerically bigger than was the S5, composed of twenty-three states from all regions of the world. In addition, it intends to adopt a more decentralized modus operandi, with the lead on substantive issues distributed over a number of subgroups.[61] At the time of writing, the work of the group was still in its early stages. The group is likely to focus initially on small and incremental change in its different areas of work. Time will tell whether the ACT Group will be able to replicate one of the strengths of the S5 group: the ability to act quickly and effectively. The diverse membership may make the process of finding agreement more difficult.

On the whole, the S5 era was certainly productive and put the issue of working methods permanently on the agenda. But it was incomplete and in particular left one question unanswered: whether states would be willing to vote on a General Assembly resolution that makes concrete recommendations to the Security Council about how to carry out its work. Sooner or later, the ACT Group will face the question of whether to take up this challenge. Only the adoption of a resolution would put the Council to the test of how it would respond to such a formal call from the membership.

Conclusion

There can be no doubt that the Security Council needs to do more to adjust to the new challenges it faces and to create more ownership among the membership for the decisions it takes. The effectiveness of the Council depends to a large extent not only on the quality of its decisions, but also on the willingness of states to implement them. Council members themselves, including permanent members, often admit this much. But there has never been a radical change in the corporate culture of the Security Council. Proceedings continue to be dominated by the permanent members, who have the enormous advantage of institutional memory. As part of this culture, the Council reserves the right to apply its proceedings very much on an ad hoc basis, which leads to significant frustration among the membership as a whole, often also among the elected members.

Along the same lines, permanent members in particular argue that changes to the working methods can only come from within. The Council, the argument goes, is the master of its own proceedings, and only measures agreed among Council members have a chance of actually being implemented. This of course contradicts the consensual mandates on Security Council reform of the past two decades that have consistently tasked the General Assembly to make suggestions on working methods, along with enlargement. Nevertheless, the argument still carries much weight in practice and has in the more recent past prevented any Assembly decision on the Council's working methods.

The second attempt of the S5 to present such a resolution made it clear that the inclusion of working methods in the larger context of Security Council reform is a poisoned chalice. The enlargement question to which working methods have been linked is politically so charged and so controversial in nature that many states may continue to oppose formal recommendations by the Assembly to the Council on issues of working methods, unless there is a simultaneous decision on enlargement. The real impediment to reform via the General Assembly is therefore not just the permanent members, but also the states that attach more importance to protecting their stakes on Council enlargement than to concrete improvements on working methods. This is all the more deplorable because Council enlargement may well remain an elusive goal for many years to come, while the need to improve working methods could increase further. It will require a significant change in the collective mind-set of the membership to allow the ugly duckling of working methods to spread its wings and become the beautiful swan of real change in the Council's corporate culture that it can and should be.

History illustrates that the Council can be innovative in equipping itself with new tools and mechanisms. But it is unlikely to open itself up to the rest of the membership unless pressured to do so. Many of the most significant recent advances in the Council's procedures originated outside the Council—through external pressure, monitoring, and suggestions, which are therefore proven tools to advance the agenda on working methods.

A test for the Council's ability to reform may well be imminent. The 2013 French initiative to suggest a code of conduct on the use of the veto picked up a central theme of the proposals put forward by the S5.[62] If indeed brought to a successful conclusion, this initiative would be a most significant development in the domain of working-methods reform and indeed the first-ever indication that permanent members are willing to commit themselves to restrictions with respect to the use of the veto. It remains to be seen whether this initiative will bear fruit—and to what extent pressure from outside the Council will help it to do so.

Notes

1. The most notorious example was United Nations Security Council Resolution 1422 (July 12, 2002), UN Doc. S/RES/1422, renewed one year later in Resolution 1487 (June 12, 2003), UN Doc. S/RES/1487, applying Article 16 of the Rome Statute of the International Criminal Court in a manner widely considered to violate both the Rome Statute and the UN Charter.

2. For the evolution of the Provisional Rules of Procedure, see United Nations Security Council, "Provisional Rules of Procedure," UN Doc. S/96/Rev. 7, 1983, www.un.org/en/sc/about/rules.

3. This change added Arabic as the sixth official language of the Council.

4. The International Criminal Tribunal for the Former Yugoslavia (ICTY), in United Nations Security Council Resolutions 808, S/RES/808 (February 22, 1993), and 827, S/RES/827 (May 25, 1993); and the International Criminal Tribunal for Rwanda (ICTR), in Resolution 955, S/RES/955 (November 8, 1994).

5. On the importance of such information for the discussions on the Rwanda genocide, see Colin Keating, "Rwanda: An Insider's Account," in *The UN Security Council: From the Cold War to the 21st Century,* edited by David M. Malone (Boulder, CO: Lynne Rienner, 2004).

6. On the historical evolution of the Arria formula, see, for example, James Paul, "The Arria Formula," *Global Policy Forum,* October 2003, www.globalpolicy .org/component/content/article/185/40088.html.

7. See United Nations Security Council, *Working Methods Handbook,* "Background Note on the 'Arria-Formula' Meetings of the SC Members," www.un.org/en /sc/about/methods/bgarriaformula. The Arria formula was also used to meet with the head of the Syrian National Coalition, Ahmad Jarba, on July 26, 2013.

8. The first field mission of the Council was undertaken in 1964, when it visited Cambodia and Vietnam. Between 1964 and 1992, however, there were fewer than a dozen missions. Thereafter, the Council visits became a regular tool, with some countries being visited on a regular basis (e.g., there was a country visit to the Democratic Republic of the Congo every year in the decade 2000–2010).

9. An invitation extended by the Dutch government to visit the legal institutions in The Hague (including the ad hoc tribunals established by the Council) has not been taken up, due mainly to resistance by Russia.

10. The terms of reference, which de facto constitute the agenda for the visit, were previously negotiated and allow states to block the discussion of certain topics. When visiting Sudan in 2006, the Council did not bring up the cooperation with the International Criminal Court, even though the Court was seized with the situation as a result to a referral by the Council in Resolution 1593 (March 31, 2005), UN Doc. S/RES/1593.

11. The costs for field visits are usually significant and covered by the regular budget of the United Nations. The actual costs are not usually disclosed, which has been criticized by the S5 group, among others.

12. Illustrated, among other things, through the fact that resolutions or presidential statements are usually adopted at the beginning of the meeting, followed often by dozens of speeches.

13. For a brief overview of the history of the format, see Security Council Report, "Security Council Working Methods: Tale of Two Councils," Special Research Report no. 3, March 25, 2014, www.securitycouncilreport.org/special -research-report/security-council-working-methods-a-tale-of-two-councils.php; Security Council Report, "Council Wrap-Up Session," *What's in Blue,* January 30, 2013, www.whatsinblue.org/2013/01/council-wrap-up-session.php.

14. In 2013, for instance, the presidencies of the Republic of Korea and Pakistan held wrap-up sessions.

15. For a brief overview, see Security Council Report, "In Hindsight: Horizon-Scanning Briefings," May 2013 Monthly Forecast, May 1, 2013, www.security councilreport.org/monthly-forecast/2013-05/in_hindsight_horizon-scanning_brief ings.php. Some P5 members and some countries mentioned in horizon-scanning briefings criticized the format.

16. This was the case in particular with respect to the discussions on Madagascar, Mali, the Maldives, and Mexico.

17. The format is also referred to as "informal interactive discussion" and also has some predecessors. See United Nations Security Council, *Working Methods Handbook,* "Informal Interactive Dialogues and Other Informal Meetings of the Security Council," www.un.org/en/sc/inc/pages/pdf/methods/dialogues.pdf.

18. On the response of the United Nations to the armed conflict in Sri Lanka, see Secretary-General's Internal Review Panel, *Report of the Secretary-General's Internal Review Panel on United Nations Action in Sri Lanka* (Petrie Report), November 2012, www.un.org/News/dh/infocus/Sri_Lanka/The_Internal_Review _Panel_report_on_Sri_Lanka.pdf.

19. The format allowed the prosecutor to engage in wider conversation with the Council that went beyond the Libya investigation as such—which in turn was the reason why some Council members showed little interest in applying the format again in the future.

20. United Nations General Assembly Resolutions 40(I) (December 13, 1946), UN Doc. A/RES/40(I); 117(II) (November 21, 1947), UN Doc. A/RES/117(II); and 267(III) (April 14, 1949), UN Doc. A/RES/267(III), dealing with the use of the veto, including the question of which issues should be considered procedural.

21. The exact title of the group is "Open-Ended Working Group on the Question of Equitable Representation on and Increase in the Membership of the Security Council and Other Matters Related to the Security Council," thus reflecting the comprehensive nature of the mandate of the group.

22. Its work was divided in two clusters: one dealing with enlargement and the other dealing with working methods.

23. Global Policy Forum, "Razali Reform Paper: Paper by the Chairman of the Open-Ended Working Group on the Question of Equitable Representation on and Increase in the Membership of the Security Council and Other Matters Related to the Security Council," www.globalpolicy.org/component/content/article/200/41310.html. As the proposal was never formally submitted, it does not exist as a UN document.

24. Paras. 9 and 10 of the Razali proposal.

25. The report of the Open-Ended Working Group during its fiftieth session contains five pages of proposals to improve the working methods of the Council. See UN Doc. A/50/47/Add.1, September 9, 1996, pp. 9–13.

26. There are no public records on the reactions from states to the proposal, as Razali consulted in "confessionals" with every member state bilaterally. It seems, however, that the main controversy revolved around the creation of new permanent seats, with the provisions on working methods playing a secondary role.

27. While the summit ultimately did not reform the Security Council, it laid the foundation for the creation of the Human Rights Council and the Peacebuilding Commission and forged agreement on the principle of Responsibility to Protect (R2P).

28. All efforts of the G4 to rally two African states behind the proposal and to thus expand it to a "G6" group failed.

29. The position was developed in the course of several AU summits and finalized as the "Ezulwini consensus," adopted in March 2005.

30. The Uniting for Consensus Group was the successor to the Coffee Club, which had in the 1990s been one of the main interest groups on Council reform.

31. After the G4 had agreed not to suggest the creation of new veto powers.

32. The African states first met at a regular summit meeting in Sirte (Libya) and, later in the summer of 2005, at a special summit meeting in Ezulwini (Swaziland). To this day, the official position of the African Group on Security Council reform is the "Ezulwini consensus."

33. The group first started operating informally, but was quickly dubbed "S5," in an ironic nod to the established term "P5." The S is usually understood to stand for "Small."

34. The S5 had different positions on the enlargement of the Council: Jordan and Singapore were declared supporters of the G4, Costa Rica a member of the Uniting for Consensus Group, while Liechtenstein and Switzerland were uncommitted. Throughout its existence, the group never discussed enlargement issues, only questions of inclusion of the working-methods dimension in the overall reform discussion.

35. United Nations General Assembly, "Costa Rica, Jordan, Liechtenstein, Singapore and Switzerland: Draft Resolution," UN Doc A/60/L.49, March 17, 2006.

36. The General Assembly had also adopted such resolutions (see endnote 20) in the past, sometimes with support from permanent members.

37. The fact that previously the working group's chairmanship had rotated on a monthly basis (always assumed by that month's presidency) meant that very few states even contemplated investing energy in the process during a time that was not only too short, but also burdened with numerous other tasks.

38. Ambassador Emyr Jones Parry, permanent representative of the United Kingdom, once noted that resolution might get 187 yes votes in the Assembly, but still not be implemented in the Council. The Russian Federation and the United States in particular emphasized the point that they would not implement the measures, irrespective of the level of support they enjoyed, due to the interference they constituted in the affairs of the Council.

39. The provisions on the drafting of resolutions illustrate very well the gap between the goals reflected in Note 507 and practical reality. Paragraphs 41 and 42 state among other things that "all members of the Security Council should be allowed to participate fully in the preparation of . . . resolutions" and that "the members of the . . . Council . . . continue to informally consult with the broader UN membership . . . when drafting . . . resolutions," though in practice elected members are often, for the most part, excluded from the relevant processes.

40. The resolution in fact did not abolish the Open-Ended Working Group, as the Uniting for Consensus Group in particular resisted such a measure. But the group has not met since and is de facto defunct.

41. The formulation would later be subject to heated discussion in the framework of the second draft resolution the S5 submitted to the General Assembly.

42. What may sound naive has its basis in fact in Note 507 itself. Paragraph 1 reads: "In efforts to enhance the efficiency and transparency of the Council's work,

as well as interaction and dialogue with non-Council members, the members of the Security Council are committed to implementing the measures described in the Annex to the present note."

43. In order to maintain what the Council considered a brand, the note was also given a document number, 507.

44. On communication with the Peacebuilding Commission, interaction with troop-contributing countries, and planning and reporting on Security Council missions, among other things. The note follows the same structure as S/2006/507 (July 19, 2006), with an additional chapter on Security Council missions.

45. Praise for the work of the S5 can be found in almost every record of discussions on Security Council reform. Even the permanent members of the Council informally expressed respect for the substantive work done by the group, while usually expressing their opposition to some of the procedural aspects.

46. First issued as UN Doc. A/66/L.42 on March 28, 2012.

47. Relationship with the General Assembly and other principal organs, effectiveness of decisions, subsidiary bodies, operations mandated and on-site missions carried out by the Council, governance and accountability, appointment of the Secretary-General, use of the veto.

48. This notwithstanding the fact that the permanent members expressed nothing but solid opposition to the text as a whole from the very beginning.

49. Jordan and Singapore in particular made it clear that they did not view their participation in the group as meaningful unless the group would be willing to mount the challenge of a General Assembly resolution.

50. Switzerland in particular favored such continued engagement with the Council.

51. The counterargument was also made repeatedly, ever since the creation of the S5, in particular by permanent members, that an Assembly resolution adopted with the no votes of the P5 would be irrelevant, as it would be ignored by the Security Council.

52. In the annex of Draft Resolution A/66/L.42/Rev. 2 (May 15, 2012), the measures were modeled after the change of practice that the Council has adopted over time in its interpretation of the term "concurring vote" in Article 27.3 of the UN Charter (the term "veto" famously not appearing in the Charter at all). While during the early years an abstention was considered not a "concurring" vote and therefore amounted to a veto, this practice was later changed. The S5 proposal would make it possible for permanent members to vote against a resolution while declaring that they concur with its adoption on the basis of the usual majority requirements.

53. New operative paragraph 4 in A/66/L.42/Rev. 2 (United Nations Security Council, "Costa Rica, Jordan, Liechtenstein, Singapore, and Switzerland: Revised Draft Resolution," May 15, 2012). The title now read "Enhancing the Accountability, Transparency, and Effectiveness of the Security Council."

54. At the time of withdrawal of the resolution, the S5 counted some 110 clear expressions of support for their text, with many of the other states undecided.

55. Meeting at the US Permanent Mission to the UN on May 9, 2012, with the vote in the General Assembly plenary scheduled for May 16. With three S5 permanent representatives out of town, only Liechtenstein and Switzerland were present at permanent-representative level on the S5 side, while all permanent representatives of the P5 countries were present.

56. On all the landmark decisions of the Assembly in the recent past, there was not even a discussion whether a two-thirds majority was applicable. See General Assembly Resolution 67/19 on the status of Palestine, adopted by a simple majority requirement, UN Doc. A/RES/67/19, November 29, 2012.

57. Preambular paragraph of Resolution 53/30 (November 23, 1998) reads: "mindful of Chapter XVIII of the Charter of the United Nations" (the chapter dealing with Charter amendments).

58. Letter dated May 14, 2012, from Patricia O'Brien, of the Legal Counsel of the United Nations, to Mutlaq al-Qahtani, chef de cabinet of the president of the General Assembly.

59. For some detail on this, see the statement by Singapore in the open debate of the Security Council, in United Nations Security Council, "Provisional Verbatim Record of the 6870th Meeting," UN Doc. S/PV.6870, November 26, 2012: "Member States learnt of that legal opinion, not from [the Office of Legal Affairs] or even from the President of the General Assembly, who had first raised the query. Instead, it was a permanent member who faxed and emailed OLA's legal opinion to all Member States the morning of the formal consideration of the draft resolution, with the admonition to all Member States to support a no-action motion on A/66/L.42/Rev.2 (United Nations Security Council, "Costa Rica, Jordan, Liechtenstein, Singapore, and Switzerland: Revised Draft Resolution," May 15, 2012). How did that P-5 mission procure the OLA's legal opinion, even before the President of the General Assembly himself had circulated it to the United Nations membership? What does that say about the P-5's real position on working methods of the Security Council? Do deeds match words?"

60. The permanent representative of Switzerland announced the withdrawal of the text in a speech to the plenary of the General Assembly on May 16, 2012.

61. Among others on transparency, peacekeeping, accountability, and the use of the veto.

62. See Laurent Fabius, "A Call for Self-Restraint at the UN," *International New York Times,* October 4, 2013, www.nytimes.com/2013/10/04/opinion/a-call-for -self-restraint-at-the-un.html.

10

The Security Council at Seventy: Ever Changing or Never Changing?

Edward C. Luck

TALK OF SECURITY COUNCIL REFORM PREDATES THE COUNCIL itself. No other topic at the UN's founding conference in San Francisco in the spring of 1945 elicited such animated exchanges as the shape, composition, powers, and decisionmaking procedures of the new Council.[1] Countries overrun or threatened by aggression in the ongoing world war wanted a global security body with real teeth, one that could and would stand up to the next round of aggressors. In the form of the Security Council, they got just such a global body, one with unprecedented powers, including for the authorization of coercive military action when other measures "would be inadequate or have proved to be inadequate."[2] With the granting of such wide powers, however, came equally urgent questions of governance and decisionmaking. Who would decide when these powers would be invoked and on what basis? How could Council members, especially permanent ones, be held accountable, and would the voices of nonmembers be heard in its deliberations? Why should five countries be granted, in perpetuity, not only membership in the Council, but also a veto over its decisions and actions? Whose security interests would be ultimately served, those of the privileged five or those of the larger United Nations membership?[3] The reform conversation today revolves around remarkably similar questions. Both that conversation and the objects of that conversation have proven remarkably durable. As the Council reaches the venerable age of seventy, neither that august body nor its detractors have faded in the least. There are three principal reasons:

1. More than any other body in the United Nations system, the Council matters. The Council's mandate—the maintenance of international peace and security—could not be more central, universal, or enduring. When the Council ceases to be controversial, in all likelihood it will have ceased to matter. It is a backhanded compliment to the centrality of the work of the Council that its composition and working methods continue to attract so much attention and that seats on it remain so coveted.

2. Because the Council has the capacity to do great good or harm, the member states, not to mention "we the peoples," have every reason to search for ways to make it more inclusive, transparent, accountable, and effective. Moreover, the core concerns expressed so passionately at the UN's founding about the inherent inequities in the Council's composition and decisionmaking rules have never been fully addressed. With time, global geopolitics has changed far more than has the Council. To critics, the logic of the decisions of 1945 appears more and more anachronistic with the passing years.

3. In other respects, the Council has demonstrated the capacity for change, responding both to shifts in the circumstances and challenges before it and to some of the more modest demands of its nonpermanent members and the larger United Nations membership. So, would-be reformers need not be totally discouraged about what might still be possible. Having spent quality time on the reform of several of the world body's other principal organs—the General Assembly, the Economic and Social Council (ECOSOC), the Trusteeship Council, and the Secretariat—I can attest to the relative disinterest their functioning inspires, as well as the comparatively slow pace at which the renovation of the other intergovernmental bodies has progressed. By any objective standard, the reform of the Security Council has proceeded, at best, at a magisterially deliberate pace, yet compared to its peer institutions it appears adaptable, even innovative.

I begin this chapter with a quick review of how the Council and its reform debate have evolved over time, contrasting the efforts at adaptation and innovation with those at structural reform. I note that the former steps are decided by the Council itself and the latter by the General Assembly and national capitals, as they require Charter amendment. I then argue that reformers should consider which features should be maintained, as well as which should be eliminated or revamped. In asking what is right about the Council, I identify two features that should be preserved, indeed strengthened, in any reform effort: (1) the concert of major military powers the Council embodies and facilitates, and (2) the fresh ideas and energies provided by the annual ebb and flow of its nonpermanent members from around the world. This two-tiered structure defines an inherent tension that at times seems counterproductive and dysfunctional and at other points dynamic and creative. I contend that getting this relationship right is the cornerstone of successful reform, but few proposals begin (or end) here.

I conclude that the key to strengthening the Council and its work lies in expanding the opportunities for nonpermanent members to make a difference, not in adding more permanent ones. In essence, the reform effort has stalled because in large part it has been asking the wrong questions and getting the wrong answers. I propose that the length of nonpermanent terms be increased from two to three years, that the number of nonpermanent seats be expanded from ten to fifteen (and the size of the Council from fifteen to twenty members), and that nonpermanent members be eligible to stand for election to a second consecutive term. Each of these measures, of course, would entail amendments to the Charter (Articles 23 and 27).

Adaptation vs. Reform

Before addressing specific ideas and proposals for reform, it should be noted that there are two ways to change the Security Council, one internal and one external. The members of the Council determine its agenda, subsidiary structures, rules, procedures, and working methods, not to mention its outcomes. According to Article 29 of the Charter, "the Security Council may establish such subsidiary organs as it deems necessary for the performance of its functions."[4] Likewise, Article 30 states that "the Security Council shall adopt its own rules of procedure, including the method of selecting its President." As discussed later, these are the areas in which there have been significant innovations, particularly over the past two decades. Council members, however, are not the sole masters over its structural or constitutional reform. Such changes would require Charter amendment and therefore could not be addressed by the Council itself. According to Article 108, any amendment to the Charter must be "adopted by a vote of two thirds of the members of the General Assembly and ratified in accordance with their respective constitutional processes by two thirds of the Members of the United Nations, including all the permanent members of the Security Council." Ultimately, any of the five permanent members could block a proposed Charter amendment by failing to ratify it in its capital—though this has never been done—but they have no veto over a General Assembly vote in favor of an amendment. In December 1963, for instance, the Assembly voted by an overwhelming margin to expand the Security Council from eleven to fifteen members and ECOSOC from eighteen to twenty-seven members despite the vocal opposition of the five permanent members.[5] No doubt influenced by the strong support for these measures by the non-aligned countries and by the competitive politics of the Cold War, one by one the permanent members acted in their capitals to ratify these expansions, which came into effect at the end of August 1965.

The readiness of any of the permanent members to block a second effort to expand the Council has not been tested since, as the proponents of the various proposals for an enlargement have not put any of the proposals to a vote in the General Assembly. As I discovered in working with General Assembly president Razali Ismail of Malaysia on his comprehensive plan for Security Council reform in 1996–1997, there were virtual vetoes in each region concerning which country would best "represent" the region as a new permanent member of the Council.[6] Until those intraregional rivalries are settled, the likelihood of adding new permanent members to the Council seems small.

The prospects for further evolution of working methods, on the other hand, are bright, despite the decidedly conservative stances of the permanent members. They tend to have disproportionate influence over the practices, procedures, and working methods of the Council, given their institutional knowledge and continuity. They tend to believe that the long-term health of the Council is part of their stewardship and legacy, and that they alone are in a position to understand and interpret precedent. Indeed, the Council still operates under its 1946 Provisional Rules of Procedure (S/96/Rev. 7). When the permanent members agree on modifying working methods, they are virtually immoveable, in part because changes in working methods are expected to be the product of consensus (at least among the P5), though there is no Charter requirement for unanimity on procedural matters. But the permanent members do not always see eye-to-eye on such questions. While their stances vary from item to item and from time to time, the Russian Federation and China tend to be less enthusiastic about change, the United Kingdom and France more bullish, and the United States more variable. Somewhat perversely, the lack of progress on structural reform may have persuaded some of the permanent members, most notably the United Kingdom and France, to demonstrate more public readiness to respond to the drive by the larger UN membership for greater transparency, accountability, and inclusiveness.

This unsettled conversation among the P5 has provided an opening for the nonpermanent members to push the internal reform agenda, with substantial success since the early 1990s. With the end of the Cold War, the possibilities for Council activism were expanding on many fronts. The incoming Bill Clinton administration, among others, was more open to considering new ways for the Council to decide and to act, as the benefits of Council effectiveness and the cost of its ineffectiveness became more apparent. In 1993, the Council established an Informal Working Group on Documentation and Other Procedural Questions (IWG), which has often been the focal point for building a Council-wide consensus on steps forward and for documenting progress to date. Initially the group was chaired by the monthly Council president, but this was changed in 2006 to have an annual chair to permit greater continuity in its work. That year, led by Japan, the IWG pulled together a number of previously agreed steps into a comprehensive presidential note (S/2006/507), followed by an updated presidential note four years later (S/2010/507). These were followed by a series of *Working Methods Handbooks*.[7]

The move toward greater transparency was bolstered by the pioneering work of the Global Policy Forum and other NGOs and, especially, by the establishment of the Security Council Report in 2004 to provide authoritative but independent reporting and analysis of developments within the Council and its work. In recent years, the Security Council Affairs Division of the UN Secretariat has been providing much more diverse and detailed information about trends in the Council's work on its website than had been available previously. Its annual "Highlights of Security Council Practice" has been especially helpful in that regard. Since 2010, moreover, the Council itself has held an annual debate on its working methods. From within the larger UN membership, the S5 group— Switzerland, Costa Rica, Jordan, Liechtenstein, and Singapore—led the drive for Council working-methods reform from 2005 to 2012, as related in Chapter 9 of this volume by Christian Wenaweser, one of the most active participants in the group. In May 2013, it was replaced by the ACT (Accountability, Coherence, and Transparency) Group, again led by Switzerland and including a cross-section of twenty-two (twenty-seven in 2015) small to medium-size member states.[8]

In addition to greater transparency, there has also been modest progress toward accountability and inclusiveness. The Council's annual report to the General Assembly, mandated by the Charter, has become a bit more analytical, and the debate it inspires somewhat more interactive. The president will often convene a wrap-up session at the end of the month, in addition to providing briefings about the upcoming program of work for the month, while the Council's daily program is now published in the *UN Journal*. Most nonpermanent members brief their regional and other groups regularly on current and upcoming events in the Council. There has been a substantial growth in the number of press statements, as well as an increasing recognition of the utility of interacting with civil society and NGOs on a more frequent basis.

Beginning with the need to hear a wider range of voices in the Balkans crises of the early to middle 1990s, the practice of convening informal Arria-formula meetings has multiplied the opportunity for interactive discussions with a much wider range of civil society representatives and area and thematic experts. The more frequent organization of visits to countries and areas of concern by the Council members has given them opportunities to get a better feel for developments on the ground and to hear from and relay messages to parties to a conflict and those most affected by it. The

Council has begun to use informal interactive dialogues as a way of addressing situations not on its formal agenda, and "informal informals" as a means of discussing controversial subjects away from UN headquarters. In recent years, UN officials dealing with human rights, humanitarian affairs, children and armed conflict, sexual and gender-based violence, and atrocity crimes have had far more access to the Council than in the past. For instance, by February 2012, Navi Pillay, then the UN high commissioner for human rights, had addressed the Security Council more times (eleven) than all of her predecessors combined (eight).[9]

So the Council is gradually, often grudgingly, changing the way it does business, in part because the evolving nature of its business has demanded it. More progress and more farsighted leadership by the permanent members are needed. Its informal consultations (consultations of the whole) are neither informal nor interactive, despite repeated efforts to get away from the reading of formal statements often drafted in capitals. There is a growing recognition that the Council needs to get better at assessing how peacekeeping and other missions are faring and how its decisions are being implemented, in order to make midcourse adjustments as needed. It needs to be more proactive and more adept at prevention, as well as at developing closer collaboration with the Peacebuilding Commission (PBC) and others dealing with postconflict reconstruction. It has developed closer ties with the African Union, but the larger and more strategic question of developing a sensible division of labor with regional and subregional arrangements needs further thought and more consistent practice. As discussed later, relations between permanent and nonpermanent members are still uneven at best, particularly when it comes to who holds the pen and who decides who will chair each subsidiary body. So, working-methods reform remains a work in progress. The pace has been plodding and uncertain. But when measured over the course of decades, the distance traveled to date becomes both more visible and more encouraging.[10]

What Should Be Preserved

Though the reform impulse usually begins with an inventory of what is wrong with the body in question, the "do no harm" rule should be accorded priority in this case. Before undertaking surgery on an organ whose health and productivity really matter to countries and populations alike, one would do well at the outset to weigh carefully what it does relatively well and which characteristics and functions should be preserved. The previous section highlighted two of these characteristics and functions: (1) the growing and diverse collection of tools and instruments the Council has at its disposal to carry out its work and decisions, and (2) the adaptability the Council has demonstrated over the years in terms of the issues it addresses, how it employs those tools and instruments, the way it deliberates and relates to nonmembers, and its machinery and subsidiary bodies.

Concert of Major Powers and the Unanimity Principle

More than any other intergovernmental body in history with a political and security mandate, the Council has served as a sustained concert of major military and security powers through good times and bad. At the time of the UN's founding, the value of maintaining this concert of world powers was recognized by small as well as large countries and by both colonial powers and those still colonized.[11] From the outset, the Council has provided a unique ongoing forum in which global powers can identify issues and initiatives of common interest, as well as quietly sort through and clarify competing and diverging perspectives (that is, when they do not succumb to the temptation of using it as a stage for public diplomacy and grandstanding). When the members do find common ground, the Council can also serve as an instrument for shaping multilateral strategies and measures for helping to maintain international peace and security, for assessing the effectiveness of agreed measures as they are implemented, and for adjusting their application as needed.[12] Chapters VI, VII, and VIII of the Charter provide a historically unprecedented array of tools from which the Council can choose to carry out its decisions.

The founders of the United Nations—the leading political figures, not just statesmen, of their time—were anything but naive. Even a cursory reading of the wartime exchanges among Stalin, Churchill, and Roosevelt and the hardheaded negotiations at the Dumbarton Oaks preparatory meetings would confirm that the common desire for effective postwar peace and security instruments was matched by keen appreciation of national interests and substantial doubts about the prospects for comity among the anti-Axis coalition once the war was won.[13] For this reason, Roosevelt thought it essential to hold the founding conference before the guns fell silent.[14]

The Charter and the provisions for the Security Council, therefore, were designed to survive stormy weather. For almost two-thirds of its history, it should be recalled, the relationships among the five permanent members were severely strained by intense Cold War rivalries and deep ideological divides. Today, it is commonplace to observe that there are no permanent alliances or divisions within the Council, as political configurations shift from one agenda item to the next. For the Council's first forty-five years, however, the relationships were far more rigid, the rhetoric far more polarizing, and the points of convergence far less frequent.[15] So the first characteristic to be preserved is the sense of concert that could once more become critical, even existential, should relationships among the major powers again begin to fray. It would be both ahistorical and shortsighted to design a fair-weather Security Council that would be unable to withstand unfavorable global geopolitical trends. Over the quarter century since the end of the Cold War, the Council has managed to address a few issues of truly global significance, such as nuclear proliferation and terrorism, but the bulk of its work has been devoted to keeping local and subregional conflicts from escalating and to trying to curb the human costs of conflict and war.[16] Reformers should consider what kind of a Council would be best equipped in the future to ease or handle situations, such as in the South China Sea, the Korean Peninsula, Ukraine, and the Middle East, on which the permanent members could be both divided and deeply invested.

Reformers have had little choice but to largely accept the unanimity principle (or veto) as a fact of life, beyond the reach of structural reform, given that the Charter amendment process gives the permanent members a de facto veto over any formal modification of the veto. This, of course, was the way they wanted it in 1945, and it is unlikely that the United Nations Charter would have been acceptable to the countries that convened the San Francisco Conference without it. At the same time, it is important to underscore that the breaking of unanimity—the casting of a veto, particularly a "lonely" one—is a political decision that can have political costs domestically and internationally (just as voting for an unpopular resolution can). Given the markedly less frequent employment of the veto since the end of the Cold War, those political costs may well be rising, at least internationally.[17] It is less clear whether this is true domestically as well, for instance in the cases of Russian vetoes on Syria and Ukraine or US ones on Israel. Moreover, the post–Cold War decline in the employment of the veto could well be reversed if geopolitical relations among the permanent members fray any further and if the gap between international political costs and domestic political gains should widen. This is a question not only of the willingness of a permanent member to cast a veto, but also of the readiness of other Council members to insist on a vote on a draft resolution that they know a permanent member objects to and is likely to veto. Behind the scenes, of course, a permanent member may try to control a drafting process by implying or suggesting that it might have to oppose certain elements of a text that are "unacceptable," because the culture of consensus remains strong in the Council for all of its members, permanent or elected.

Given these structural inhibitions and political dynamics, reformers have focused more in recent years on inducing the permanent members to voluntarily restrain their use of the veto than on compelling them to formally relinquish it. The possibility of voluntary restraint has been raised most pointedly and painfully in cases of large-scale loss of life through mass atrocities, such as in Syria. A wide range of civil society actors have sought to bring political pressure and moral suasion to bear in that and other situations, such as Darfur and the eastern Democratic Republic of the

Congo, to discourage any of the permanent members from blocking international action that could save many lives. As the Secretary-General has suggested, it would be best if the permanent members could informally agree among themselves not to employ the veto to block international response to unfolding mass atrocities, something that had previously been proposed by the International Commission on Intervention and State Sovereignty in 2001 and by the High-Level Panel on Threats, Challenges, and Change in 2004.[18] France launched a similar initiative at the General Assembly in the fall of 2013.[19] These steps would not be legally binding, but if they could alter practice over time, they could be quite significant. They sensibly treat restraints on the veto as a political, not a constitutional, matter, as one of policy, not reform. It would be problematic, in my view, to try to outlaw or restrict one of the core provisions of the Charter, one that has allowed the Council to survive difficult times so that it could be much more responsive and effective in the politically less restrictive times since the end of the Cold War. The other side of this coin, of course, is that granting veto power to additional countries in the name of equity and fairness could have markedly negative consequences for the Council's capacity to decide and take action in a timely manner in any number of situations, including those in which a large number of civilian lives are at risk. There is every reason to expect that the geographical areas of strategic interest to one of the permanent members would grow with the expansion of their numbers and geographical diversity. More areas and more potential crises would become essentially off limits to Council action. That would be a step backward for effectiveness in the name of reform.[20]

The Role of the Nonpermanent Members

The Council is not and was never intended to be, of course, simply a concert of big military powers. The Council gains much of its legitimacy from two facts: that the majority of its members are nonpermanent, serving two-year terms, and that they, unlike the permanent members, are elected by a two-thirds majority of the General Assembly. They are, in effect, selected by their peers. Though not always observed in practice, Article 23(1) states that they are to be selected with "due regard being specially paid, in the first instance to the contribution of Members of the United Nations to the maintenance of international peace and security and to the other purposes of the Organization, and also to equitable geographical distribution." Though the latter criterion is followed much more scrupulously than the former, both add to the sense that the Council, though neither democratic nor equitable in terms of its composition and decisionmaking principles, does roughly reflect a broad cross-section of member states. In 1965, Article 23(1) was amended to increase the number of nonpermanent members from six to ten, enlarging the Council's membership from eleven to the present fifteen members. That move served to increase the representative character of the Council within a rapidly growing UN membership, and few would argue that it has reduced the Council's efficiency or effectiveness. The relationship between permanent and nonpermanent members is discussed at greater length and depth by Colin Keating in Chapter 7 in this volume, but a few points related to reform choices are addressed here.

With five newly elected nonpermanent members joining the Council each January, as five leave, the Council's composition shifts every year with the turnover of one-third of its members. This pattern offers the opportunity for the influx of fresh ideas and renewed energy, with each new member having the chance to make an innovative and unique contribution to the Council's work. But the relatively brief stay of nonpermanent members also puts a premium on the institutional knowledge and reservoir of expertise that the permanent members have acquired over the years. Many representatives of countries departing the Council have commented that this advantage, more than the veto power, has allowed the permanent members to perpetuate their dominance over the more numerous nonpermanent members in the deliberations and work of the Council.[21]

Those nonpermanent members that have made the most impact during their term have tended to be those that were able to define and claim a niche or two in the Council's broad agenda early on, to stick with it, and to develop specialized expertise in those areas. In some cases, they have brought regional and local knowledge about crises and the actors who drive them in their neighborhoods. Their perspectives, experience, and understanding of the dynamics of those situations are most likely to shape the Council's approach toward places and conflicts in which the five permanent members are not highly engaged or deeply invested. Over the past decade, many nonpermanent members have left their mark on the Council's handling of thematic, rather than geographic, issues. Their interest in these matters has undoubtedly helped to account for the expansion in the Council's attention devoted to such issues as human rights; humanitarian affairs; rule of law; peacekeeping; children and armed conflict; women, peace, and security; sexual and gender-based violence; governance, peacebuilding, and security sector reform; civilian protection, atrocity prevention, and the Responsibility to Protect; climate change; the role of regional and subregional arrangements; and mediation and conflict prevention. Each nonpermanent member will serve as president of the Council once or twice for a one-month period—it rotates alphabetically—giving them both the opportunity and the burden of shaping the program of work for the month or months, and of considering whether to hold and then oversee a high-level event on a topic of their choice.

The contributions of nonpermanent members in two other respects should be borne in mind in any reform effort. One, the Council's infrastructure of subsidiary bodies grew substantially in the first decade of the twenty-first century, with the number of committees and working groups under the Council running around twenty-five to twenty-eight at any point (twenty-six at the end of 2013). Most of the Council's oversight and implementation work is carried out by these groups, whether on counterterrorism, nonproliferation, sanctions, peace operations, or thematic issues, as well as institutional matters and working methods. These are generally chaired by nonpermanent members and are committees of the whole (with all fifteen members participating). They almost always act by consensus, in essence giving the nonpermanent as well as permanent members a veto over their work. Though the representatives of elected members sometimes complain that their responsibility for leading the subsidiary bodies is a way of diverting their attention and energies away from the core work of the Council, these assignments also represent opportunities for each member, whatever its size, to make a difference by demonstrating leadership on one or more issues of enduring importance to the Council and to the implementation of its decisions. If the effectiveness of the Council is to be assessed not only by the wording of its resolutions but also by the difference it makes on the ground and over time, then the work of the subsidiary bodies should be considered central, not peripheral, to what the Council is and does.

Two, the nonpermanent members can play a substantial role in crafting Council resolutions, presidential statements, and press statements—though this has varied considerably from issue to issue and case by case. As Christian Wenaweser (Chapter 9) and Colin Keating (Chapter 7) usefully note, the question of who serves as "penholder"—who takes the lead in drafting resolutions and other Council decisions and statements—is one of the more contentious matters at this point in the evolution of Council working methods. The permanent members, especially the Western ones, have traditionally played the role of lead penholder more often than not. This remains the case today. In recent years, however, it has become more common either for a nonpermanent member to be the lead penholder, or for a permanent and a nonpermanent member to share this task as co-penholders. For 2014, penholders included seven of the ten elected members: Australia on Afghanistan; Nigeria on Guinea-Bissau, West Africa, and peace and security in Africa; Chile on the two international criminal tribunals (ICTR and ICTY); the Republic of Korea on nonproliferation and weapons of mass destruction; Luxembourg on children and armed conflict; Argentina on working methods; and Australia, Jordan, and Luxembourg on humanitarian issues related to Syria.[22] Nevertheless, the overall balance remains skewed toward those who have the experience that permanency brings, along with native skills in the UN's working languages (mostly English, some French). Of the thirty-six penholder positions listed by Security Council Report for 2014, twenty-seven (or three-quarters) were claimed by permanent members. The result is that there are a number of situations in which there is a mismatch between the permanent-member penholder and the elected-member committee chair.[23] Given the persistent imbalance between permanent and elected penholders, some nonpermanent members feel left out of the process of formulating the Council's stance, relegated as they are to voting on a resolution or decision they had little chance to help craft.

One of the most common comments by diplomats of countries leaving the Council is how quickly their two-year terms have flown by.[24] They usually speak of the frenetic pace of activity, the importance of personal relationships, the broad agenda and myriad activities, how long it takes to get to know the Council's culture and procedures, and how little time is left to make a real contribution. The strain is felt most acutely by smaller delegations, but representatives from larger ones often make similar comments. From these reflections, it apparently takes most delegates of incoming members a good six months—one-quarter of their term—to get acclimated and comfortable with the unique demands of life in the Council. Assuming that their delegation has identified a niche or two where they would like to leave their mark, this leaves eighteen months and one presidency to try to make a difference. Then they depart, in most cases not to return to the Council for decades. There is little chance, under the current system, for either individual elected members or a class of them to build a legacy that could last for any sustained period, as five new elected members, each with their own priorities and preferences, prepare to take their place. Under such a system, the permanent members are bound to define and dominate the life of the Council.

A Proposal

To give the nonpermanent members, individually and collectively, a better opportunity to contribute to the work of the Security Council, I propose that the Charter be amended as follows:

- The first sentence of Article 23(1) to read: "The Security Council shall consist of twenty Members of the United Nations."
- The third sentence of Article 23(1) to read: "The General Assembly shall elect fifteen other Members of the United Nations to be non-permanent members of the Security Council."
- The first sentence of Article 23(2) to read: "The non-permanent members of the Security Council shall be elected for a term of three years."
- The third sentence of Article 23(2) to read: "A retiring member shall be eligible for immediate re-election once to a second three-year term."

- Article 27(2) to read: "Decisions of the Security Council on procedural matters shall be made by an affirmative vote of twelve members."
- Article 27(3) to read: "Decisions of the Security Council on all other matters shall be made by an affirmative vote of twelve members."

Whether such a package of reforms would attract sufficiently wide political support to be adopted remains to be seen, since it is uncertain whether those member states still seeking permanent seats will ever become reconciled to the prospect of accepting anything less.[25] Yet these amendments could make the Council more representative of the UN's membership as a whole without becoming unmanageably large or losing the chemistry of a relatively compact body in which personal relationships matter and each member's voice and vote count. The Assembly would continue to elect five new members each year (ten the first year these amendments come into effect), but only one-third rather than the current one-half of the nonpermanent members would retire each year. This would ensure greater continuity among the elected members, while giving the incoming members more continuing members from which to seek advice and assistance. Alliances among some of the elected members on certain thematic or situation-specific issues, for instance, would have more time to develop and have an impact.

The three-year term would add twelve months or 50 percent to the tenure of an elected member. The additional twelve months, however, would be a 67 percent increase to the period an elected member could fully participate in the life of the Council following the first six months of getting acclimated and finding niches on which to focus. The longer term would give the nonpermanent members less justification to claim that they are just "tourists" when it comes to the core work of the Council.

The possibility of reelection would make those nonpermanent members interested in continuing more accountable. At present, not only are the permanent members permanently unaccountable, but most elected members do not expect to stand for another term for many years. It is currently too easy for them to claim that they would have tried to accomplish certain things but that the system—that is, the permanent members—would not give them sufficient time or voice to do so. Those seeking immediate reelection could point to those areas—whether related to the leadership of a subsidiary body, a substantive theme, or a particular conflict situation—in which their role would require and deserve another three years on the Council. For the larger United Nations membership, both the longer terms and the possibility of reelection would raise the stakes of the election process. To elect a weak member would be a three-year, not a two-year, mistake. The possibility of ensuring that a strong contributor to the work of the Council could have six consecutive years to make a difference, on the other hand, should provide a powerful incentive to elect countries that are prepared to make a positive difference over an extended period. This would raise, as well, the importance of the platforms on which candidates for Council membership are running. The fact that the Assembly would still only elect five new members each year would give time to focus attention on a limited number of candidates, in contrast to those proposals for adding ten or more members each year for two-year terms.

These amendments could begin to alter the relationships between permanent and nonpermanent members of the Security Council by making those relationships more collegial and less hierarchical or paternalistic. The permanent members would be outnumbered by the elected members by a three-to-one instead of a two-to-one margin. Even when united, the permanent members would have to gain the assent of seven instead of four elected members to decide nonprocedural or procedural matters. They could not be certain which of the nonpermanent members might be reelected, so they would presumably try to avoid alienating any of them. Likewise, the elected members would have more time to demonstrate the expertise and local knowledge that they could contribute to the Council's deliberations. Many of the crisis situations addressed by the Council last more than the current two-year terms, and the longer tenures would provide some members more opportunities to assist in efforts at conflict prevention, management, and resolution.

Permanent and elected members should both have an incentive to make the selection process for chairs of subsidiary bodies and for penholders (or co-penholders) more transparent and interactive, because mistaken assignments could have deeper and longer-term consequences. With an expansion from ten to fifteen nonpermanent members, the burden of chairing multiple committees and working groups should be eased, as the work would be shared by more members. Likewise, the extra effort required for the presidency would become less frequent with the larger membership. But with a 50 percent increase of months served in a single term and a 33 percent expansion of the overall Council membership, the chances of having two presidencies in a single term would actually grow for elected members. The frequency of permanent members holding the presidency would decrease, of course, from one-third to one-fourth of the time.

For those countries determined to gain the international recognition that permanent membership might bring, the prospect of battling for two consecutive three-year terms might appear to be a rather distant consolation prize. It should be more attractive, however, than the current necessity of mounting expensive campaigns every few years for another two-year term. In essence, under the proposed amendments they would have the opportunity of serving the equivalent of three two-year terms back to back, giving the chance to gain some of the experience, inside knowledge, and focused effort that they now lack. For instance, the contributions in recent years that Japan has made to the formulation of Council working methods, India to peacekeeping, Brazil to the Responsibility to Protect, Germany to the relationship between climate change and security, and South Africa and Nigeria to conflict resolution in Africa, could be extended for sufficient periods to make a lasting difference—the legacy that so many delegates departing the Council lament not having had time to accomplish. As already indicated, the battle for seats on the Council could well become more intense even with the proposed enlargement, but the gains of winning those longer-term seats should make the prize worth the struggle.

The proposed package of amendments has the attribute of simplicity.[26] That does not guarantee, of course, that they would be easy to attain in the current political climate. From the outset, the deliberations on Council reform have prized perceptions of equity over effectiveness. Most countries, other than the S5 and their successors, have paid relatively little attention to the Council's working methods. The proposed amendments are designed to complement the ongoing efforts inside and outside the Council to improve its working methods. Indeed, it is in the context of growing accountability, transparency, and inclusiveness that the proposed reforms would make the most difference. In similar terms, the efforts at improving working methods can have their maximum effect only if the Council's composition is changed to enhance the position of the nonpermanent members within the Council rather than increasing the ranks of those with permanent membership. What the Council needs is permanent accountability, not more permanent members.

Conclusion

Three points in conclusion. First, reform of the Council needs to be crafted carefully so as to avoid damage to the concert of major powers that has been essential both to its conception and to its value over the years. As discussed here, geopolitical trends suggest that this concert may become both more strained and more needed in the years ahead. It should not be taken for granted. As obnoxious as most member states and commentators find the insider dealings among the five permanent members behind closed doors to be, it is more alarming when the five find it hard to do business with each other and their unity splinters. That is a very real and present danger. In recent years, the elected members have had to try to build bridges among the five on some of the toughest crises before the Council, such as in Ukraine, Syria, Libya, and Sudan. Those attributes that encourage cooperation among the permanent members need to be strengthened, not weakened, through the reform process. "Do no harm" should be rule one in undertaking reform. Reform should be seen as a means of strengthening an institution, not as a punishment to its members.

Second, the calendar alone has not, and should not, dictate when the composition of the concert of world powers—as reflected in permanent membership in the Security Council—will be altered. Critics are right to question whether the choice in 1945 of which countries should be granted permanent seats should remain, immutable, for all time regardless of shifts in global power relationships. Should the same countries be included in the concert of powers as the Council turns seventy or, as Kishore Mahbubani pointedly asks in Chapter 8 in this volume, when it reaches the century mark in 2045? At some point, change in the membership of this exclusive club will have to come. So far, however, no proposed alternative roster has been able to command sufficiently wide support either globally or within the regions to be adopted. Each of the candidates, like the existing permanent members, has a mix of promising and less promising qualities, and most look like stronger candidates in economic than in political or military terms. Each faces opposition or competition from some of its neighbors. The notion of an Asian, African, or Latin American seat sounds better in theory than in practice, as no regional power can—or is prone to—represent the interests of all of its neighbors. Would anyone suggest, for instance, that Russia could represent the security concerns of Ukraine or the Baltic states; China those of Vietnam, Japan, or the Philippines; India those of Pakistan; or Nigeria those of South Africa or Egypt? The European Union may someday achieve a truly supranational status in foreign and security policy, but today it is far from that goal.

Finally, those resisting reform most should reflect on how much the world and its security needs have been transformed since 1945. The United Nations has remained relevant because it has been adaptable, even innovative. Moreover, change has, to date, been healthy for the Council. Both its expansion in 1965 and the continuing improvements in its working methods have, on balance, made it a more effective, credible, and legitimate actor on the world stage. If the next round of change is undertaken with similar care and balance, the Security Council could emerge as an even more effective force for peace and security in the challenging years ahead.

Notes

　1. For a detailed account, including of the events and negotiations leading to the founding conference, see Ruth B. Russell, *A History of the United Nations Charter: The Role of the United States, 1940–1945* (Washington, DC: Brookings Institution, 1958), pp. 646–687. For more lively accounts, see Townsend Hoopes and Douglas Brinkley, *FDR and the Creation of the U.N.* (New Haven: Yale University Press, 1997); Stephen C. Schlesinger, *Act of Creation: The Founding of the*

United Nations (Boulder, CO: Westview, 2003); David Bosco, *Five to Rule Them All: The UN Security Council and the Making of the Modern World* (Oxford: Oxford University Press, 2009). In a fresh, but not entirely persuasive, account, Mark Mazower has positioned the founding of the world body in the context of the colonial-independence struggle, in *No Enchanted Palace: The End of Empire and the Ideological Origins of the United Nations* (Princeton: Princeton University Press, 2009).

2. United Nations, *Charter of the United Nations* (San Francisco, June 26, 1945), Article 42.

3. To respond to these legitimate concerns, the delegates added Article 109 to the Charter, calling for a general Charter review conference by the General Assembly's tenth annual session. This provision assured member states wary of the veto and the privileges of permanent membership that those provisions were not necessarily set in stone for all time. Given the politics of the Cold War, however, the review conference was never held.

4. In parallel provisions, Article 22 gives the General Assembly sovereignty over the establishment of its subsidiary organs and Article 21 over its rules of procedure.

5. For more detailed accounts of these votes and the events that led to them, see Edward C. Luck, *UN Security Council: Practice and Promise* (London: Routledge, 2006), pp. 113–114.

6. There is no provision in the Charter for one member of the Council to represent any other member state. The idea of regional representation was discussed at the San Francisco founding conference, but not accepted. See United Nations, "United Nations Conference on International Organization: Verbatim Minutes of the Fourth Meeting of Commission III, 20 June 1945" (Washington, DC: US Government Printing Office, 1946), p. 798.

7. The latest, in 2012, was published by the United Nations in cooperation with the Permanent Mission of Japan to the United Nations.

8. See United Nations Security Council, "Letter Dated September 19 2013 from the Permanent Representative of Switzerland to the United Nations, Addressed to the President of the Security Council," UN Doc. S/2013/568, September 23, 2013; Volker Lehmann, "Reforming the Working Methods of the UN Security Council: The Next Act" (New York: Friedrich Ebert Stiftung, August 2013).

9. Felice D. Gaer and Christen L. Broecker, *The United Nations High Commissioner for Human Rights: Conscience for the World* (Leiden: Martinus Nijhoff, 2014), p. 21.

10. Security Council Report has produced three special research reports assessing progress to date: "Security Council Working Methods: A Work in Progress?" March 30, 2010; "Security Council Working Methods: A Tale of Two Councils?" March 25, 2014; and "Security Council Transparency, Legitimacy, and Effectiveness: Efforts to Reform Council Working Methods, 1993–2007," October 18, 2007. See also Luck, *Practice and Promise,* pp. 122–124; Edward C. Luck, "Reforming the United Nations: Lessons from a History in Progress," in *United Nations: Confronting the Challenges of a Global Society,* edited by Jean E. Krasno (Boulder, CO: Lynne Rienner, 2004), pp. 350–397.

11. For instance, in 1946, Jawaharlal Nehru commented that, while the veto power was "obviously undesirable," it reflected "the real facts prevailing in the world today." Warning of the risks that would be posed by the "secession by any of the major powers," he acknowledged that they occupy "a special position in the world today and if they fall out there is trouble the smaller powers cannot check."

Quoted in Srinath Raghavan, "The United Nations and the Emergence of Independent India," in *Charter of the United Nations,* edited by Ian Shapiro and Joseph Lampert (New Haven: Yale University Press, 2014), pp. 148–149.

12. As discussed later, while public attention tends to be focused on the struggle to find common ground among the Council's members, especially the permanent ones, on the wording of its resolutions, one of the Council's long-standing weaknesses has been follow-up and assessment of progress on implementing agreed resolutions. In recent years, there has been a conscious effort among Council members to take the renewal of peace operation mandates as an opportunity to reconsider and adjust the mandates to reflect results achieved and changing conditions on the ground in places like the eastern DRC, Somalia, and Mali. There has also been an effort to deepen the dialogue between members of the Council and troop- and police-contributing countries.

13. For a particularly insightful account, see Robert C. Hilderbrand, *Dumbarton Oaks: The Origins of the United Nations and the Search for Postwar Security* (Chapel Hill: University of North Carolina Press, 1990).

14. In his January 1945 State of the Union address, President Roosevelt noted: "The nearer we come to vanquishing our enemies the more we inevitably become conscious of differences among the victors." Quoted in Edward C. Luck, "A Council for All Seasons: The Creation of the Security Council and Its Relevance Today," in *The United Nations Security Council and War: The Evolution of Thought and Practice Since 1945,* edited by Vaughan Lowe, Adam Roberts, Jennifer Welsh, and Dominik Zaum (Oxford: Oxford University Press, 2008), pp. 78–79.

15. One of the important exceptions was the Suez crisis, in which the United States and the Soviet Union found themselves on the same side opposing the British and French military intervention in support of the Israeli occupation of much of the Sinai Peninsula. One of the products was the invention of United Nations peacekeeping as an inter-positional force that would give diplomacy time to work and the protagonists an excuse to step down their military confrontation.

16. The Council, in my view, accomplished much more in terms of keeping local conflicts local during the Cold War than it is commonly given credit. Both Moscow and Washington understood that there were places and conflicts in which their national interests were not and should not be heavily engaged. In such situations, the Council and other United Nations organs and instruments, including the Cold War innovation of peacekeeping, could be useful even as the East-West confrontation raged elsewhere. In that regard, Stalin proved prophetic when he cautioned his Western Allies at one of the wartime conferences "against what he termed a tendency on the part of small nations to create and exploit differences among the great powers in order to gain the backing of one or more of them for their own ends." In his words, "a nation need not be innocent just because it is small." James F. Byrnes, *Speaking Frankly* (New York: Harper and Brothers, 1947), pp. 64–65, quoted in Edward C. Luck, "Change and the United Nations Charter," in Shapiro and Lampert, *Charter of the United Nations,* p. 114.

17. According to the *2013 Highlights of Security Council Practice,* prepared by the UN Security Council Affairs Division (SCAD) in January 2014 (www.un.org/en/sc/inc/pages/pdf/highlights/2013.pdf), only five vetoes were cast between January 1, 2009, and December 31, 2013, including none in 2013. Over 90 percent of the draft resolutions on which votes were taken during that five-year period passed unanimously. In contrast, during the Council's first five years, 1946–1950, an annual average of ten vetoes were cast (ten times more frequently than during the 2009–2013 period). The Council has been averaging about one veto per year over

the almost quarter century since the end of the Cold War. Luck, *Practice and Promise,* fig. 1.1, p. 8.

18. International Commission on Intervention and State Sovereignty (ICISS), "The Responsibility to Protect" (Ottawa: International Development Research Centre, December 2001); United Nations High-Level Panel on Threats, Challenges, and Change, *A More Secure World: Our Shared Responsibility* (New York, December 2004). Secretary-General Ban Ki-moon, in his report *Implementing the Responsibility to Protect* (UN Doc. A/63/677, January 12, 2009, para. 61, pp. 26–27), states that "within the Security Council, the five permanent members bear particular responsibility because of the privileges of tenure and the veto power they have been granted under the Charter. I would urge them to refrain from employing or threatening to employ the veto in situations of manifest failure to meet obligations relating to the responsibility to protect, as defined in paragraph 139 of the Summit Outcome, and to reach a mutual understanding to that effect." I was the primary drafter of that report.

19. French president François Hollande, statement at the opening of the 68th General Assembly, United Nations, New York, September 24, 2013; and op-ed article by French foreign minister Laurent Fabius, "A Call for Self-Restraint at the U.N.," *International New York Times,* October 4, 2013, www.nytimes.com/2013 /10/04/opinion/a-call-for-self-restraint-at-the-un.html?_r=0. Under the French plan, the five permanent members would agree to "voluntarily regulate their right to exercise the veto" in the case of mass crime when fifty members of the General Assembly request the Secretary-General to determine the scope of the crime and he concludes its serious nature. According to Minister Fabius, however, "to be realistically applicable, this code would exclude cases where the vital national interests of a permanent member of the Council were at stake."

20. Several aspirants for new permanent seats have pledged that they would not use the veto for a number of years or until a Charter review conference is held, but such a pledge would also be nonbinding.

21. Every year since 2003, following the election of the new members of the Council, the government of Finland convenes a day-and-a-half workshop for the newly elected and continuing members of the Council to help acquaint the incoming members with the functioning, procedures, and agenda of the Council, as well as with some of the challenges it will face in the new year. This annual event has become the occasion for stocktaking at the ambassadorial level for all of the members, and for considering next steps in the long-term effort to improve the Council's working methods. In the following spring, the Council publishes the nonattribution report of the interactions at this "Hitting the Ground Running" workshop. These reports, prepared by me, are a useful source for understanding the evolution of Council working methods and of relations between the permanent and nonpermanent members. At several points in this chapter, I draw from comments made by delegates at these sessions.

22. Security Council Report, "February 2014 Monthly Forecast: Chairs of Subsidiary Bodies and Penholders for 2014," January 31, 2014, http://www.security councilreport.org/monthly-forecast/2014-02/chairs_of_subsidiary_bodies_and_pen holders_for_2014.php

23. Several additional ones rotate according to who heads Groups of Friends or other relevant groups.

24. The concluding session at the "Hitting the Ground Running" workshop is usually devoted to reflections and lessons learned by the outgoing members. This point is drawn from those sessions, as well as other discussions I have had with outgoing members over the years.

25. In his discussion of Council reform in Chapter 8 of this volume, Kishore Mahbubani outlines an intriguing and more comprehensive 7-7-7 proposal, which envisions seven permanent seats with veto power, seven semipermanent seats, and seven elected two-year seats. Most proposals put forward over the past two decades have, like that of Mahbubani, sought to include something for everybody, while the proposal I put forward in this chapter focuses on enhancing the position of the non-permanent members within the Council.

26. There is nothing as anachronistic in the Charter as the so-called enemy clauses. These should be eliminated as part of the next wave of amendments, such as those proposed here. The General Assembly's outcome document of the September 2005 World Summit (UN Doc. A/60/L.1, September 15, 2005, para. 177, p. 40), reflecting the consensus views of all the heads of state and government, resolved "to delete references to 'enemy states' in Article 53, 77, and 107 of the Charter."

Part 2

Addressing Thematic Issues

11

Humanitarian Action and Intervention

Thomas G. Weiss

HUMANITARIAN CONCERNS HAVE BECOME CENTRAL TO FOREIGN
and military policies, but aid agencies often lament that national interests
threaten their principles and impede realizing their objectives. In particular,
calculations about vital interests by government decisionmakers explain
military humanitarian interventions, which among other things are likely to
fail unless there is a demonstrated willingness to sustain casualties and stay
the course. I focus here on events and trends from the past quarter century
that circumscribe the chances that humanitarian values can be more often
and consistently respected over the next decade than in the past.

The end of the Cold War made possible UN decisions about international peace and security that were inconceivable during the first four
decades of the world organization's history. A key explanation for the sheer
expansion in activity by the Security Council was the humanitarian
"impulse," the visceral desire to help those in life-threatening distress during armed conflicts. Invariably for the humanitarian as for other arenas,
such urges translate into a limited political momentum and a sliding scale
of commitments. The humanitarian impulse reflects the stark reality of
world politics that permits coming to the rescue of some but not all war victims. When humanitarian and strategic interests coincide, a window of
opportunity opens for activating the humanitarian impulse in the Security
Council. Nothing demonstrates this fact more than the Responsibility to
Protect (R2P), which led to robust military action against Libya but painful
dithering in Syria.

In exploring implications of changes in the nature and scope of Security Council decisions resulting from the humanitarian impulse since the

217

1990s, I examine the landscape from four angles: legal, ethical, political, and military.

Legal Landscape: Why No Imperative?

International humanitarian law is spelled out in the 1949 Geneva Conventions and the 1977 Additional Protocols, the basis for emergency relief and civilian protection in war-torn countries. The humanitarian "imperative" is the clear preference of those who believe that helping and protecting individuals caught in the crosshairs of armed conflicts must be universal to be meaningful, and who are dismayed by inconsistent Security Council decisions. The humanitarian imperative entails an obligation to treat all victims similarly and react to all crises in the same way—in effect, to deny the relevance of politics, which consists of drawing lines, weighing alternatives, and distributing limited resources. Double standards, properly understood, relate to dissimilar treatment of similar cases; but cases are inevitably different. Humanitarian action is desirable but not obligatory. The humanitarian impulse is permissive. The humanitarian imperative would be peremptory.

The humanitarian impulse is the maximum to which the international community of states can aspire. It has been activated more often since the end of the Cold War than earlier, and perhaps even more frequently. Lest the ideal become the enemy of the good, however, we should agree that international action in some cases is better than in none.

The dramatic evolution in attitudes toward the limits of sovereignty— after centuries, it no longer provides cover for mass atrocities—affects the ability of aid agencies to come to the rescue. The growth in the weight of humanitarian concerns and values to sustain diplomatic and military action was already clear to Adam Roberts by the end of the first post–Cold War decade: "humanitarian issues have played a historically unprecedented role in international politics."[1] With the exception of Raphael Lemkin's advocacy for the 1948 Genocide Convention, no idea has moved faster or farther in the international normative arena than R2P since the formulation of this norm by the International Commission on Intervention and State Sovereignty (ICISS) in a 2001 report, *The Responsibility to Protect.*

Friends and foes point to the commission's central conceptual contribution: reframing sovereignty as contingent rather than absolute.[2] R2P breaks new ground in coming to the rescue, because in addition to the usual attributes of a sovereign state encountered in international relations and law courses and in the 1934 Montevideo Convention—people, authority, territory, and independence—there is another: a modicum of respect for human rights. The interpretation of privileges for sovereigns has made room for modest responsibilities as well. When a state is unable or manifestly unwilling to protect the rights of its population—and especially when it abuses citizens—that state's sovereignty is qualified, and it loses the accompanying claim to the right of nonintervention. Downgrading the principle of noninterference in domestic affairs in the face of mass atrocities remains, of course, controversial. Many states (including Russia, China, and states in parts of the global South) are wary about setting aside the foundation for international order and the UN Charter that is represented by R2P's move from the periphery to the center of international public policy debates.

While "normatively based challenges to the sovereign rights of states are hardly new in international history,"[3] nonetheless the Security Council was largely missing in action for humanitarian matters during the Cold War—a virtual humanitarian tabula rasa existed at the outset of the 1990s. No resolution mentioned the humanitarian aspects of any conflict from 1945 until the Six Day War of 1967, and the first reference to the International Committee of the Red Cross (ICRC) was not until 1978.[4] While in the 1970s and 1980s "the Security Council gave humanitarian aspects of armed conflict limited priority . . . the early nineteen-nineties can be seen as a watershed."[5] During the first half of that decade, twice as many resolutions were passed as during the first forty-five years of UN history, a pace that has continued. By definition, all of the decisions were in situations with humanitarian problems; but the vast majority of decisions were actually propelled by the dimensions of humanitarian concerns.

Often used loosely to mean any kind of effort to influence another state's foreign policy, "intervention" should be reserved for three categories of threatened or actual Security Council coercion against the expressed wishes of a target state or group of political authorities: sanctions and embargoes; international criminal prosecution; and military force. Acting without the consent of a state violates the UN Charter's most cited provision, Article 2(7), which suggests only rare occasions would justify Council decisions. At the same time, Stephen Krasner reminds us of the long-standing "organized hypocrisy" of intervention because major powers routinely do what they wish, a view that Thucydides summarized more briefly in the Melian Dialogue.[6] Yet the Security Council has approved resolutions authorizing all types of coercion in unprecedented numbers since the end of the Cold War. The last decade of the twentieth century witnessed the increased use of sanctions,[7] and international judicial pursuit also expanded with ad hoc tribunals established by the Council. And following the creation of the International Criminal Court (ICC), the Council has referred cases to the ICC, and it also recommended the creation of hybrid legal mechanisms (e.g., for Sierra Leone).[8] Both sanctions and international criminal justice continue today, as does the most severe kind of intervention and the focus here, the use of force by outside militaries, which was the most notable story that began in the 1990s.

The Security Council's decisions are based on the Charter's Article 39 and the power to "determine the existence of any threat to the peace." However, the Council's interpretation of the meaning of that existence by invoking Chapter VII for a number of situations with humanitarian dimensions, but with only the most tenuous of international security implications, helped set the stage for progressively qualifying sovereignty: to stem the flow of Kurdish refugees after the Gulf War (1991); to alleviate the Somalia humanitarian crisis (1992–1993); to impinge on decisionmaking in Bosnia (1992–1995); to restore the democratically elected government in Haiti (1994); and to respond to disintegrating authority in Albania (1997). Many critics resented the Security Council's powers of self-definition about what constituted a legitimate threat to international peace and security, and pointed to the supposedly diabolical machinations of the great powers. In mid-decade the Commission on Global Governance supported decisions motivated by the humanitarian impulse, but judged ill-advised the Security Council's continually stretching the definition to include complex humanitarian emergencies. The commission recommended "an appropriate Charter amendment permitting such intervention but restricting it to cases that constitute a violation of the security of people so gross and extreme that it requires an international response on humanitarian grounds."[9]

A minority of international lawyers suggested an emerging customary law on humanitarian intervention;[10] but most disagreed about the contention that it was "legitimate" albeit "illegal" and viewed Kosovo as an unfortunate departure that threatened the Charter regime and international society by setting aside the need for a Security Council imprimatur.[11] Legal interpretations notwithstanding, state behavior and expectations certainly changed as exceptions to the principle of nonintervention became less exceptional and respect for the humanitarian impulse grew. Beginning with northern Iraq and Somalia in the early 1990s, through Libya in 2011, UN-authorized actions were justified by an expressed humanitarian purpose often against the will of national governments.

Significant institutional innovations in the international handling of humanitarian challenges usually occur after the end of wars when new kinds of horrors shock consciences and expose the inadequacies of existing response mechanisms. The founding of the modern humanitarian system is usually dated to 1863, when Henri Dunant's revulsion with the carnage at Solferino led to the founding of the ICRC. The aftermath of World War I and the Russian Revolution led to the establishment of the International Office for Refugees and Save the Children. Similarly, World War II led to the creation of a host of agencies—including Oxfam, Catholic Relief Services, World Vision, and CARE, along with those in the United Nations family, including the UN Children's Fund (UNICEF) and the UN High Commissioner for Refugees (UNHCR). The French doctors' movement—beginning with Médecins sans Frontières—emerged when dissident staff revolted against ICRC institutional orthodoxy in the Nigeria-Biafra war.

The sea change in world politics beginning in the 1990s led to no transformation of existing legal or institutional machinery, however, only to the 1992 establishment of the UN's toothless Department of Humanitarian Affairs (DHA) and its 1997 successor, the Office for the Coordination of Humanitarian Affairs (OCHA).[12] The end of the Cold War initially led to new conflicts and crises, along with the eruption of long-simmering ones held in check during the era of acute East-West tensions. While the numbers of conflicts declined again from the early 1990s onward, the budgets of humanitarian organizations, including those of the UN, expanded in an unprecedented fashion—over a fivefold increase in humanitarian aid in the first post–Cold War decade, from about $800 million in 1989 to some $4.4 billion in 1999, with an additional quadrupling to $16.7 billion by 2010.[13] And at least 2,500 international NGOs are in the business even if only a tenth of them are truly significant.[14] The UN Development Programme (UNDP) estimates that there could be 37,000 international NGOs with some relevance for "the crisis caravan," and that on average a thousand international and local NGOs show up for any contemporary emergency.[15] That said, the indirect mortality rates in civil wars have declined since the early 1990s, mainly as a result of the increased work by humanitarians in war zones.[16]

Ethical Landscape: Shocking the International Conscience

Lively debates surrounded the right of the international community of states to intervene in internal affairs to protect civilians, with some observers contending that there even exists a duty to do so.[17] The proper conduct of military and civilian personnel in humanitarian operations also was subject to controversy. The ICISS's reframing of the central ethical issue is noteworthy—replacing the rights of outsiders to intervene with the rights of affected populations to assistance and protection and the responsibility of outsiders to come to the rescue. Moving away from the picturesque vocabulary of the "right to intervene" alters the debate in fundamental ways. First and foremost, the ICISS framework emphasizes the rights of those in need and the responsibility of outsiders to aid and protect them (when national authorities fail to do so)—and embarrassment when they do not.

Whatever one's views about the feasibility, desirability, and likely impact of "military force for human protection purposes" (the mouthful coined by the ICISS to replace "humanitarian intervention"), the dominant moral discourse about humanitarian action certainly has shifted. At the outset of the post–Cold War era, it was central in about 10 percent of articles in *Ethics & International Affairs,* for instance, whereas by the mid-1990s humanitarian action was the topic of almost a third, and by the end of the decade nearly half, of the journal's main articles. This emphasis continued in the new century with specific country cases, interpretations of R2P, and a 2011 roundtable on Libya.

Greater moral attention from policy- and decisionmakers does not guarantee peace on Earth, but it can help improve the fragile norms protecting the vulnerable. Many Security Council decisions had an ethical grounding, but Resolution 794, approving the US-led military effort in Somalia in December 1992, set a new standard for humanitarian hype—the "H" word was mentioned eighteen times. While there are no "pure" humanitarian motivations, the Somalia effort came close. Although the intervention in Libya subsequently was criticized for supposedly dubious humanitarian justifications, the international response was not about bombing for democracy, sending messages to Iran, implementing regime change, keeping oil prices low, or pursuing narrow geopolitical interests. Some of these results may have occurred, but the dominant justification was the protection of Libyan civilians.

Other operations are more suspect. For example, Washington's response in Afghanistan following September 11, 2001, resembled interventions in the 1970s by India in East Pakistan (Bangladesh), Tanzania in Uganda, and Vietnam in Kampuchea (Cambodia) in that self-defense and regime change were immediate justifications, but humanitarian benefits an important byproduct. Michael Walzer in 2002 called the latter three interventions "the most successful [ones] in the last thirty years."[18] Michael Ignatieff pointed to "bad neighborhoods" in which an al-Qaeda can flourish as a source of legitimate pleas for humanitarian intervention. This argument seemed far-fetched when attacks took place against US embassies in East Africa and the USS *Cole* but became far less problematic after 9/11 and the George W. Bush administration's declaration of war on terror. "Our current debate about humanitarian intervention continues to construe intervening as an act of conscience," Ignatieff wrote, "when in fact, since the 1990s began, intervening has also become an urgent state interest: to rebuild failed states so that they cease to be national security threats."[19]

Mixed motives are present when humanitarian intervention can be morally legitimate *and* justified in terms of national security. The humanitarian impulse has permeated foreign and defense policy as well as transformed conceptions of interests and parameters of policy- and decisionmaking. Lloyd Axworthy's convictions as foreign minister about the link between basic rights and international security sustained Canada's human security agenda and led him to launch the ICISS.[20] The belief that democratic states have a long-term national interest as well as moral responsibility to promote human rights was dubbed "good international citizenship" by Gareth Evans as Australia's foreign minister, long before he became an

ICISS cochair.[21] If we fast-forward to August 2011, when President Barack Obama established the Atrocity Prevention Board—an interagency mechanism to facilitate rapid reaction across the US government and prevent mass atrocities—the White House highlighted that the prevention of mass atrocities was not only a US moral responsibility but a core national security interest as well.[22]

The wake of the war on terrorism represents clear and present ethical dangers for humanitarians as well as civil libertarians. Less obvious is the possibility that appropriately framed vital interests can also coincide with the humanitarian impulse. In a less connected world, collapsing states and humanitarian disasters could be isolated and kept at arm's length. Responses, if any, were driven by moral imperatives, because there were few genuine implications for security. Now failed states and human catastrophes pose problems not only to the denizens of war zones and their immediate neighbors but also to peoples worldwide. Robust responses, including military ones, "are thus strategic and moral imperatives."[23]

An accurate scorecard for intervention is required. Keeping the "humanitarian" in humanitarian intervention necessitates a just-war focus on means and ends to help ensure informed discussions about the reality of the humanitarian impulse when vital interests are present. Even when there is a requirement to address extreme cases of suffering, one can never set aside the possibility of abuse or selective application. After September 11, the temptation to "take off the gloves" and set aside the laws of war in the pursuit of the war on terrorism should be resisted better than it has been.

Rhetorical and Political Landscape: From Humanitarian Intervention to R2P

Humanitarian intervention was among the most controversial topics within UN circles in the 1990s; Secretary-General Kofi Annan's "two sovereignties" and signature speeches on the issue attracted substantial hostility, especially from many governments in the global South.[24] An academic cottage industry resulted, and governments sponsored a host of policy initiatives: the Canadian-inspired ICISS was the most prominent, but earlier efforts included the Swedish initiative, the Independent Commission on Kosovo, and efforts by other governments, including the US Policy Planning Staff and reports from the Council on Foreign Relations along with major inquiries into the legal authority for intervention by the Dutch and Danish governments.[25]

As indicated earlier, the Security Council viewed a range of humanitarian disasters, especially those involving large exoduses of forcibly displaced persons, as within its mandate and a legitimate reason to authorize intervention. As civil wars became the standard bill-of-fare, rights trumped sovereignty in enough Council decisions that it was no longer fatuous to hope for what Francis Deng and Roberta Cohen had dared to dub "sovereignty as responsibility."[26] After so many Council decisions were justified mainly on humanitarian grounds, with only the most tenuous links to traditional notions about threats to international peace and security (Somalia is the clearest stretch), the Commission on Global Governance's 1995 recommendation for a Charter revision became moot.

Endorsed by the ICISS in its opening sentence, state sovereignty is not challenged but reinforced.[27] The Responsibility to Protect has taken root in today's international normative landscape, which explains its move from the prose and passion of a blue-ribbon commission toward a mainstay on the international agenda since the December 2001 release of the ICISS's report *The Responsibility to Protect.* The 2004 report of the High-Level Panel on Threats, Challenges, and Change, *A More Secure World: Our Shared Responsibility,* endorsed "the emerging norm." Shortly thereafter, Secretary-General Kofi Annan included it in his 2005 report *In Larger Freedom,* and the 2005 World Summit endorsed it.[28] Current Secretary-General Ban Ki-moon put forward a three-pillar approach to R2P at the outset of his first term—the protection responsibilities of the state, international assistance and capacity building, and timely and decisive response—and has publicly committed his administration to emphasizing R2P in his second term.[29] Perhaps most important, the Security Council subsequently has specifically referred to it in over a dozen resolutions—seventeen as of December 2013, including on the Great Lakes region (Resolution 1653), on protection of civilians (1674, 1894), Darfur (1706), Libya (1970, 1973, 2016, 2040), Côte d'Ivoire (1975), South Sudan (1996, 2109), Yemen (2014), Mali (2085, 2100), small arms (2117), and the Central African Republic (2121, 2127).

The ICISS coined "R2P" to move beyond the pitched battles of "humanitarian intervention," and more than 150 heads of state and government at the September 2005 World Summit agreed. Concerns of course differed: the P5 insisted upon case-by-case language and Security Council authority so as not to imply any automatic action; and they were uniformly against criteria that could have been used by "sovereignty hawks" to block intervention.

It is worth revisiting the concerns of the most vociferous defenders of state sovereignty in the global South. Beginning with the international response in northern Iraq in 1991, the moniker of "humanitarian intervention" had led to circular tirades about the agency, timing, legitimacy, means, circumstances, consistency, and advisability of using military force to protect human beings. Reticence and even hostility are understandable for anyone familiar with the number of sins justified by colonial powers under a "humanitarian" rubric. Countries that gained their independence in the second half of the twentieth century are unlikely to welcome outside military intervention merely because of a qualifying adjective. Moreover, they and others are uneasy about cavalierly setting aside the principle of nonintervention in domestic affairs, the basis for international society and a restraint on major powers.

Yet R2P's central insight is that sovereignty is conditional; it thus permits a conversation about the limits of state power even with the most ardent defenders of sovereign inviolability. After centuries of largely looking the other way, sovereignty no longer provides a shield for mass murder in the eyes of legitimate members of the international community of states. Every state has a responsibility to protect its own citizens from mass killings and other gross human rights violations. If any state, however, is manifestly unable or unwilling to exercise that responsibility, or actually is the perpetrator of mass atrocities, its sovereignty is qualified and temporarily set aside. Meanwhile the responsibility to protect civilians under siege devolves to other states, ideally acting through the Security Council (an absolute requirement according to the 2005 World Summit decision). Deploying military force is an option after alternatives have failed or are considered likely to do so. Military intervention to help the vulnerable is restricted by the summit's language to cases of "genocide, war crimes, ethnic cleansing and crimes against humanity." While many critics emphasize state responsibility and prevention in the hopes of avoiding military force, James Pattison has reminded us that "humanitarian intervention is *only one part* of the doctrine of the responsibility to protect, but . . . it *is* part of the responsibility to protect."[30]

R2P was refined and the norm's interpretation was bolstered by restricting the number of triggers. As such, it provides possible responses to the grossest violations of human rights that deeply offend any sense of common humanity. By restricting its application to the most heinous and conscience-shocking crimes rather than the garden variety of abuses, the 2005 agreement clarified the norm and advanced its universal aspirations. R2P can be helpful as a tool for civil society to mobilize international public opinion against any P5 member blocking intervention. Clearly civil society can have more of an impact in the United States, France, and the United Kingdom than in China and Russia.

Most observers agree that R2P's potential strength, like all norms, is demonstrated by its legitimate use; but its misuse also demonstrates its traction, because imitation is a form of flattery. As such, abusing the norm—for instance, the United States and the United Kingdom for the case of Iraq in 2003, Russia for the case of Georgia in 2008, and France with respect to Burma in 2008—also helped to clarify what it was not. R2P was not an acceptable rationalization for the war in Iraq after the original justifications (links to al-Qaeda and weapons of mass destruction) evaporated; nor for

Moscow's imperial aims in its weaker neighbor; nor for intervention in Burma after a cyclone when the government was hampering the delivery of emergency aid but not murdering its population.

The resilience of long-standing shibboleths about sacrosanct state sovereignty suggests a need for more pragmatic and less predictable country stances toward humanitarian affairs. Is rapid and complete localization the best strategy (that is, the Afghan model), or a more massive external presence with longer-term trusteeship (that is, the models for Bosnia, Kosovo, and East Timor)? Are the recommendations to strengthen the UN's military oversight as recommended by the Brahimi Report, on UN peace operations, not better seen as desperately needed by war-torn countries rather than as a possible invasion of sovereignty and a drain on development funds? Interestingly, if we fast-forward to 2013, both Mali and the Central African Republic specifically requested such interventions.

Political correctness and North-South posturing have long been the bane of the UN's existence,[31] which does not serve the individual or collective interests of vulnerable populations and states. Intriguingly, regular sessions of the General Assembly and annual (since 2009) interactive dialogues on R2P gave rise to what some saw as lingering buyer's remorse but actually was not, even in the global South.[32] At the sixty-sixth session of the General Assembly in fall 2011, Brazil, in response to NATO's intervention in Libya, proposed that "the international community, as it exercises its responsibility to protect, must demonstrate a high level of responsibility while protecting" (RWP).[33] Tautological and ambivalent and perhaps mischievous, the framing nonetheless reflected the norm's rhetorical and political traction. A prominent member of the global South predictably communicated discomfort about the use of military force for regime change. At the same time, an emerging Brazil also was obliged to have a foreign policy unequivocally supportive of human rights; it could not be among the usual R2P-spoiler suspects.

Military Landscape: Expectations and Capacities

There hardly has been too much but rather too little deployment of military force for human protection purposes.[34] The March 2011 NATO-led military action approved by the Security Council against Libya was the first-ever such authorization against a functioning de jure government and the first such use of substantial force since NATO's contested operation in Kosovo. Until Libya, the sharp end of the R2P stick was replaced by skittishness from diplomats, UN staff, scholars, and policy analysts. The Security Council observed a new high-water mark for R2P in Libya; but with high tides come high risks. Few doubted that harsh measures were necessary to forestall a massacre in Benghazi, yet a growing chorus of criticism subsequently arose over NATO supposedly stretching its protective mandate to achieve regime change and overthrow Muammar Qaddafi. The controversy continued in connection with Security Council paralysis about robust action in Syria, where the bloodshed and suffering inflicted by the Bashar al-Assad regime were far worse.

Rhetoric is one thing, tough decisions are another. Talk is cheap, action and especially military action is not. It is easier to condemn than agree about actions for the hardest cases. Moreover, after a Chapter VII decision to use "all necessary means" is made, the United Nations steps aside.

It is hardly surprising that the UN is no longer in the military enforcement business. Whether or not the Security Council adequately anticipated and appreciated the difficulties, too many UN-mandated or UN-controlled military activities in the early post–Cold War period encountered significant resistance and loss of life. Decisions about actions were not matched by decisions about resources (for instance, in the so-called safe areas in Bosnia, probably the least-safe places in the Balkans). Worst of all, in the face of casualties, the world organization cut and ran in Somalia and Rwanda and stood by and watched atrocities in Srebrenica.

By the end of the 1990s, the UN had essentially retired from direct command-and-control over serious military operations. The ambitions articulated by Secretary-General Boutros Boutros-Ghali in his 1992 *Agenda for Peace* were considerably subdued in his 1995 supplement to that document.[35] The world organization's comparative advantage was in peacekeeping. Acting on the humanitarian impulse, let alone peace enforcement, required not consent and impartiality but major-league military personnel.

The dominant military trend already at the outset of the 1990s was "subcontracting."[36] The devolution of responsibility for the enforcement of Chapter VII decisions, virtually all of which had a substantial humanitarian rationale, went to "coalitions of the willing." Instead of being the "doer" envisaged by the Charter, the Security Council often became the "approver" of operations conducted by others. What began as an experiment in the Gulf War ended up being the standard operating procedure in Somalia, the Balkans, Sierra Leone, Liberia, Haiti, and East Timor; and it has continued in hybrid operations in the DRC and Sudan and was even more obvious in Côte d'Ivoire, Libya, Mali, and the Central African Republic. The disparity between demand and supply—along with inadequate financing and diminished confidence—has meant that the world organization relies on regional organizations and ad hoc coalitions to ensure compliance with enforcement decisions.

In brief, not everyone can act on the humanitarian impulse. The nature of violence in contemporary war zones means that only the militaries of major powers, and not neutrals or smaller powers, need apply. Military clout often is more important than moral clout, as evidenced by "humanitarian bombing." Furthermore, certain kinds of heavy airlift capacity and sophisticated technology are absolutely essential, which are mainly available from NATO, and especially from the US Air Force.

The Security Council adopted new roles in acting upon the humanitarian impulse. Sometimes the world organization handed over responsibilities entirely, sometimes it was in the back (instead of the driver's) seat, and sometimes it worked in tandem with an array of regional organizations or with individual great powers (e.g., in Iraq, Côte d'Ivoire, Mali, and the Central African Republic). For these eventualities, there are at least three conceptual challenges for military doctrine.

The first is to fill doctrinal voids in operationalizing the humanitarian impulse. A number of specific challenges are distinct from those of either peacekeeping or war-fighting, the endpoints on a spectrum of international military action. What about challenges in between? How can protection be afforded to populations at risk? How can those who prey upon them be deterred? What drives the choice of military methods? Can air power alone protect civilians? If vital interests are involved as well, to what extent are boots on the ground and casualties acceptable?

Two related but distinct sets of objectives exist within the category of enforcement decisions: compelling compliance and providing protection.[37] The former, commonly referred to as "peace enforcement," requires vast military resources and political will. It involves the search for comprehensive political settlements leading to sustainable peace. It encompasses not only traditional peacekeeping tasks such as monitoring ceasefires but also complex ones whose success requires deadly force.

A lesser form of enforcement action, "coercive protection," is pertinent for the humanitarian impulse, but its various forms are rarely specified. Common ones consist of maintaining humanitarian corridors, disarming refugees, protecting aid convoys, and creating safe havens or protected areas. Prominent examples include the no-fly zone in northern Iraq and the so-called safe areas of Bosnia.

A particularly important dimension of this kind of operation is the force posture of intervening troops. Coercive protection is distinct from other efforts, which have military forces oriented in relation to other military forces. Peacekeeping involves monitoring military ceasefires or interpositioning forces between belligerents after a ceasefire; compelling compliance involves the potential use of force against conflicting parties or spoilers; and war-fighting involves combat against designated opponents. In contrast, coercive protection requires the inter-positioning of forces between civilians and potential attackers (not just armies but also militias and gangs). Since the introduction in 1999 of language about the protection of civilians in the mandate for the UN Assistance Mission in Sierra Leone

(UNAMSIL), even consensual UN peace operations now routinely author- ize traditional peacekeepers to use force to protect civilians before they become war victims.

Distinguishing tactical from strategic use of force is easier to write about than implement. The "grey area" of protecting civilians necessitates undertaking numerous tasks that militaries worldwide do not favor: the forcible disarmament of belligerents (especially in refugee camps like those in the mid-1990s in eastern Zaire); the meaningful protection of safe areas (the gruesome example of Srebrenica comes immediately to mind); and the protection of staff (as expatriates like Fred Cuny and Sergio Vieira de Mello and local officials alike would testify if they were alive).

Military doctrines have evolved slowly to specify ways to meet the needs for coercive protection of civilians, the real R2P challenge. One major exception is the Mass Atrocity Response Operations (MARO) proj- ect, intriguingly with Harvard University taking the lead rather than the US Defense Department.[38]

The second challenge results from the necessity to ensure more than a modicum of international accountability for operations that are approved by the UN but fall under another organization's operational control. In only a few armed conflicts—Georgia and West Africa—has the world organization monitored the activities of regional organizations acting as subcontractors for an internationally approved operation. If the UN's imprimatur for a coalition of the willing is to be meaningful, more accountability and trans- parency are necessary for subcontractors, which is the most pertinent pas- sage from the Brazilian RWP proposal. What kinds of monitors in which situations with which types of mandates would be helpful? What kinds of independent reports should go back to the Security Council before an ongo- ing mandate is renewed? Can international finance be used to secure, as a quid pro quo, independent monitoring?

The final challenge has met more progress in that military establish- ments are interested in humanitarian tasks that were formerly viewed as peripheral. No longer are politicians and humanitarians chasing a reluctant military and pleading for help. Military budgets, operational training, and officers' career paths benefit from humanitarian tasks. "Military humanitar- ianism" was once viewed as an oxymoron—indeed, some humanitarians still refuse to put the two words together—but it is an accurate depiction of a central capacity of contemporary armed forces. What was once feared as "mission creep" is not necessarily unwelcome. Former US national security adviser Condoleezza Rice acerbically remarked that the 82nd Airborne Division's comparative advantage was not in escorting schoolchildren; there are, however, numerous other tasks in operations motivated by the humanitarian impulse that require first-rate militaries.

No task is more fraught than a decision to deploy military force.[39] When used for human protection purposes, policy options follow after answers to the following questions:

- Are countries, and not merely Washington, able to move beyond the "Somalia syndrome" and the apparent necessity—and according to Robert Pape even a "moral duty"—for "near zero" casualties[40] for soldiers coming to the rescue? Is this calculation justified, no matter how many victims potentially could be rescued?
- Have prudential considerations been given their due, and are the imagined benefits of averted atrocities (which involve counterfactual speculation) persuasive enough to outweigh the visible and certain destructiveness of a forceful humanitarian intervention?
- Does an exit strategy address "mission creep" because the requirements for terminating an operation, including peacebuilding, inevitably are more ambitious than the initial aim to avoid or halt mass atrocities?
- Are there plausible responses for the inevitable criticisms of inconsistency across cases where intervention did not or cannot occur?
- Is there a plan for military burden-sharing and diplomatic support from the appropriate regional organizations?

Conclusion

The prominence of the humanitarian impulse has altered the legal, ethical, rhetorical, and military landscapes of Security Council decisionmaking. The nature and scope of enforcement decisions, on occasion, have heightened the relevance of humanitarian values in relationship to narrowly defined vital interests. The traction of the "H" adjective can be abused. For instance, the beat of war drums for Iraq had nothing to do with humanitarianism; such a veneer was only applied after the original justifications were exposed as fatuous. That war became a temporary conversation stopper for R2P and also resulted in major humanitarian problems. But the balance of experience over the past quarter century is clear: potential victims and perpetrators of genocide and ethnic cleansing may find that neighbors, ad hoc coalitions, or even single states are willing to come to the rescue. Sovereignty ain't what it used to be.

Politics and military capacity ultimately determine whether, when, where, and why to protect and assist vulnerable populations. However shocking to the conscience a particular emergency and however hard or soft the applicable public international law, when political will and a military capacity exist,[41] humanitarian space will open and war victims will be assisted and protected. In Libya the value-added of R2P was moral and legal legitimacy as well as political will and military capacity. Rather than speaking truth to power, R2P was speaking truth *with* power. There are countless other recent examples of crises that lacked one or more of the moral, legal, political, and military elements—Sri Lanka, Syria, Zimbabwe all jump to mind—and civilians paid the price.

Policy analyses and prescriptions tend to extrapolate from recent headlines. It is worth recalling Andrew Hurrell's criticism of social science as being mired in a "relentless presentism."[42] In the aftermath of the intervention on behalf of the Kurds, there was nothing that humanitarians could not do; the end of the Cold War signaled not only a UN renaissance but the birth of a new world order. Virtually to the day only three years later, in April 1994, we apparently could do nothing in the face of Rwanda's genocide. In 1999, depending on one's point of view, the humanitarian intervention vintage was either an *annus mirabilis* or *annus horribilis* because of Kosovo and East Timor. And then we fast-forward a decade to robust decisionmaking and action in Libya but inaction in Syria. Brazil formulated RWP as a result of Libya. The Security Council's attitude toward decisionmaking also appears to track closely immediate precedents. The rollercoaster ride is likely to continue.

Even when conscience-shocking events occur in faraway places that do not directly threaten vital interests, publics and pundits as well as politicians sometimes clamor that "something be done." If interests and humanitarian concerns overlap—if there is sufficient symmetry between the humanitarian impulse and strategic stakes—states may respond with robust enough action to protect civilians from the ravages of war and the thugs disguised as their leaders.

A greater-than-usual degree of modesty is in order. Modesty is a virtue not only for diplomats and military officials but for aid workers *and* social scientists as well. Many observers, and among them the most fervent and committed of humanitarians, would have us embrace the humanitarian imperative, the moral obligation to treat affected populations similarly and react to crises consistently. However, such a notion flies in the face of politics, which consists of weighing options and available resources, of making tough decisions about doing the greatest good or the least harm.

Hopefully, Libya was not an aberration. The lawlessness in that divided country was predictable, which the lack of Kosovo-like, postintervention peacebuilding—an integral part of the ICISS's recommendations—made inevitable. Paralysis in Syria was shameful, but it has not dashed hopes for decisive intervention elsewhere. Human abattoirs are not inevitable. We are capable of uttering no more Holocausts, Cambodias, and Rwandas—and occasionally mean it. Despite the growing traction of the R2P norm, the humanitarian imperative remains an aspiration, but the humanitarian impulse remains vital.

Notes

1. Adam Roberts, "The Role of Humanitarian Issues in International Politics in the 1990s," *International Review of the Red Cross* 81, no. 833 (March 1999): 19.

2. International Commission on Intervention and State Sovereignty (ICISS), "The Responsibility to Protect" (Ottawa: International Development Research Centre, December 2001). For interpretations by commissioners, see Gareth Evans, *The Responsibility to Protect: Ending Mass Atrocity Crimes Once and For All* (Washington, DC: Brookings Institution, 2008); Ramesh Thakur, *The United Nations, Peace, and Security: From Collective Security to the Responsibility to Protect* (Cambridge: Cambridge University Press, 2006). See also Alex J. Bellamy, *Responsibility to Protect: The Global Effort to End Mass Atrocities* (Cambridge: Polity, 2009); Anne Orford, *International Authority and the Responsibility to Protect* (Cambridge: Cambridge University Press, 2011); Aidan Hehir, *The Responsibility to Protect: Rhetoric, Reality, and the Future of Humanitarian Intervention* (Houndmills: Palgrave Macmillan, 2012). My interpretation is Thomas G. Weiss, *Humanitarian Intervention: Ideas in Action,* 3rd ed. (Cambridge: Polity, forthcoming).

3. S. Neil MacFarlane, *Intervention in Contemporary World Politics,* Adelphi Paper no. 350 (Oxford: Oxford University Press, 2002), p. 79.

4. Christine Bourloyannis, "The Security Council of the United Nations and the Implementation of International Humanitarian Law," *Denver Journal of International Law and Policy* 20, no. 2 (1992): 335–356.

5. Th. A. van Baarda, "The Involvement of the Security Council in Maintaining International Law," *Netherlands Quarterly of Human Rights* 12, no. 1 (1994): 140.

6. Stephen D. Krasner, *Sovereignty: Organized Hypocrisy* (Princeton: Princeton University Press, 1999).

7. David Cortright and George A. Lopez, eds., *The Sanctions Decade: Assessing UN Strategies in the 1990s* (Boulder, CO: Lynne Rienner, 2000).

8. Richard J. Goldstone and Adam M. Smith, *International Judicial Institutions,* 2nd ed. (London: Routledge, 2015).

9. Commission on Global Governance, *Our Global Neighbourhood* (New York: Oxford University Press, 1995), p. 90.

10. Christopher Greenwood, *Humanitarian Intervention: Law and Policy* (Oxford: Oxford University Press, 2001).

11. Michael Byers and Simon Chesterman, "Changing Rules About Rules? Unilateral Humanitarian Intervention and the Future of International Law," in *Humanitarian Intervention: Ethical, Legal, and Political Dilemmas,* edited by Jeff F. Holzgrefe and Robert O. Keohane (Cambridge: Cambridge University Press, 2003).

12. Thomas G. Weiss, "Humanitarian Shell Games: Whither UN Reform?" *Security Dialogue* 29, no. 1 (March 1998): 9–24.

13. Development Assistance Committee, *Development Cooperation Report 2000* (Paris: Organization for Economic Cooperation and Development, 2001), pp. 180–181.

14. Figures are drawn from a 2003 Office for the Coordination for Humanitarian Affairs (OCHA) roster that no longer is updated.

15. Linda Polman, *The Crisis Caravan: What's Wrong with Humanitarian Aid?* (New York: Holt, 2010), p. 10.

16. Human Security Report Project, *Human Security Report 2012: Sexual Violence, Education, and War—Beyond the Mainstream Narrative* (Vancouver: Human Security Press, 2012), www.hsrgroup.org/human-security-reports/2012/text.aspx.

17. See Mario Bettati and Bernard Kouchner, *Le Devoir d'Ingérence* (Paris: Denoël, 1987); Mario Bettati, *Le Droit d'Ingérence* (Paris: Odile Jacob, 1996).

18. Michael Walzer, "The Argument About Humanitarian Intervention," *Dissent* (Winter 2002): 29.

19. Michael Ignatieff, "Intervention and State Failure," *Dissent* (Winter 2002): 115.

20. Lloyd Axworthy, "Human Security and Global Governance: Putting People First," *Global Governance* 7, no. 1 (2001): 19–23.

21. Nicholas J. Wheeler and Tim Dunne, "Good International Citizenship: A Third Way for British Foreign Policy," *International Affairs* 74, no. 4 (1998): 847–870.

22. White House, Office of the Press Secretary, "Presidential Study Directive on Mass Atrocities/PSD-10," Washington, DC, August 4, 2011, www.whitehouse.gov/the-press-office/2011/08/04/presidential-study-directive-mass-atrocities.

23. Robert I. Rotberg, "Failed States in a World of Terror," *Foreign Affairs* 81, no. 4 (2002): 127.

24. Kofi A. Annan, *The Question of Intervention: Statements by the Secretary-General of the United Nations* (New York: United Nations Publications, 2000).

25. Independent International Commission on Kosovo, *The Kosovo Report: Conflict, International Response, Lessons Learned* (New York: Oxford University Press, 2000); Alton Frye, ed., *Humanitarian Intervention: Crafting a Workable Doctrine* (New York: Council on Foreign Relations, 2000); US Department of State, "Interagency Review of U.S. Government Civilian Humanitarian & Transition Programs" (Washington, DC: George Washington University National Security Archive, April 2000), www2.gwu.edu/~nsarchiv/NSAEBB/NSAEBB30/index.html; Advisory Council on International Affairs and Advisory Committee on Issues of Public International Law, "Humanitarian Intervention" (The Hague: AIV and CAVV, April 2000); Danish Institute of International Affairs, "Humanitarian Intervention: Legal and Political Aspects" (Copenhagen, October 1999).

26. Roberta Cohen and Francis M. Deng, "Normative Framework of Sovereignty," in *Sovereignty as Responsibility: Conflict Management in Africa,* edited by Francis M. Deng et al. (Washington, DC: Brookings Institution Press, 1996).

27. Thomas G. Weiss, "The Responsibility to Protect (R2P) and Modern Diplomacy," in *The Oxford Handbook of Modern Diplomacy,* edited by Andrew Cooper, Jorge Heine, and Ramesh Thakur (Oxford: Oxford University Press, 2013).

28. United Nations High-Level Panel on Threats, Challenges, and Change, *A More Secure World: Our Shared Responsibility* (New York: United Nations, December 2004), para. 203; United Nations Secretary-General, *In Larger Freedom: Towards Development, Security, and Human Rights for All,* UN Doc. A/59/2005, March 21, 2005; United Nations General Assembly, *2005 World Summit Outcome,* UN Doc. A/RES/60/1, October 24, 2005, paras. 138–140.

29. United Nations General Assembly, *Implementing the Responsibility to Protect: Report of the Secretary-General,* UN Doc. A/63/677, January 12, 2009.

30. James Pattison, *Humanitarian Intervention and the Responsibility to Protect: Who Should Intervene?* (Oxford: Oxford University Press, 2010), p. 250, emphasis in original.

31. Thomas G. Weiss, "Moving Beyond North-South Theatre," *Third World Quarterly* 30, no. 2 (2009): 271–284.

32. Rama Mani and Thomas G. Weiss, eds., *The Responsibility to Protect: Cultural Perspectives in the Global South* (London: Routledge, 2011). On decisionmaking about Libya and Syria with an emphasis on emerging powers of the global South, see Mónica Serrano and Thomas G. Weiss, *The International Politics of Human Rights: Rallying to the R2P Cause?* (London: Routledge, 2014).

33. United Nations General Assembly and Security Council, "Letter to the United Nations Addressed to the Secretary-General," UN Doc. A/66/551-S/2011/701, November 11, 2011, p. 1.

34. This chapter's discussions of Libya and Syria draws on and updates Thomas G. Weiss, "Humanitarian Intervention and US Policy," in *Great Decisions 2012* (New York: Foreign Policy Association, October 2012).

35. United Nations Secretary-General, *An Agenda for Peace,* UN Doc. A/RES/47/120, December 18, 1992, www.un.org/documents/ga/res/47/a47r120.htm; and *Supplement to* An Agenda for Peace, UN Doc. A/50/60-S1995/1, January 3, 1995, www.un.org/documents/ga/docs/50/plenary/a50-60.htm.

36. Thomas G. Weiss, ed., *Beyond UN Subcontracting: Task-Sharing with Regional Security Arrangements and Service-Providing NGOs* (London: Palgrave Macmillan, 1998).

37. Thomas G. Weiss and Don Hubert, *The Responsibility to Protect: Research, Bibliography, and Background* (Ottawa: International Development Research Centre, 2001), chap. 8.

38. Mass Atrocities Response Operations Project, *Mass Atrocity Response Operations: A Planning Handbook* (Cambridge: Harvard Kennedy School Carr Center for Human Rights Policy, May 2010), www.hks.harvard.edu/cchrp/maro/handbook.php.

39. This argument first appeared in Weiss, "Humanitarian Intervention and US Policy."

40. Robert Pape, "When Duty Calls: A Pragmatic Standard of Humanitarian Intervention," *International Security* 37, no. 1 (2012): 41–80.

41. Simon Chesterman, *Just War or Just Peace? Humanitarian Intervention and International Law* (Oxford: Oxford University Press, 2001).

42. Andrew Hurrell, foreword to Hedley Bull, *The Anarchical Society: A Study of Order in World Politics,* 3rd ed. (New York: Columbia University Press, 2002), p. xiii.

12

Promoting Democracy

Francesco Mancini

THE WORD "DEMOCRACY" DOES NOT APPEAR IN THE UN CHAR-
ter, nor is "democratization" one of the stated purposes of the world body.
As of 2013, according to Freedom House, over a third of UN members,
including two of the five Security Council's permanent members, were not
electoral democracies.[1] The UN Charter is silent on overall features of
domestic political organization, which it considers falling within the limitation of domestic jurisdiction cited in Article 2(7) of the UN Charter.[2] Consequently, the promotion of democracy remains somewhat contested at the
UN and is sometimes criticized by some members of the Non-Aligned
Movement as a mere smokescreen for Western countries to pursue their
interests and expand their influence. They instead prefer to emphasize the
need for democratizing the UN's decisionmaking processes.[3] The George
W. Bush administration's pursuit of spreading democracy by force in Iraq
has further complicated the politics of the Security Council's work in this
area.[4]

Yet, since the end of the Cold War, the UN Security Council has continuously—although not consistently—promoted democracy and propagated democratic elections as the basis for a governance template for countries on its agenda, and its members seem—by and large—to accept this
role. Since 1993, approximately a hundred resolutions referred to "democracy" as a form of governance that needs to be enhanced, strengthened, or
supported.[5] From 1999 to 2013, sixteen out of nineteen peacekeeping missions and fourteen out of sixteen field-based political missions launched by
the Council around the world included mandates calling for ensuring or
promoting elections and democracy.[6] In addition, 10 percent of Council-

mandated sanctions regimes have had as their primary stated objective the restoration of an elected government, and in several other cases, such as Angola, the Democratic Republic of the Congo, Liberia, and Libya, democracy promotion was a secondary objective. Democracy promotion also manifests itself in the Council's oft-made calls for free and fair elections, for acceptance of election results by all parties, and for the development of democratic institutions in countries on its agenda.[7]

In this chapter I aim to shed more light on an issue that has so far received very little attention.[8] First, I briefly describe the foundation of democracy promotion in international law. Then, I explore the evolution of democracy promotion in the Council's activities in chronological order, beginning with the Cold War era up to the latest intervention in Côte d'Ivoire. I then briefly describe the role of the UN system in promoting democracy, beyond the Council, and attempt an assessment of the actual impact of the Council on democratization. In concluding, I seek to explain why the Council has been engaging in democracy promotion, and why it is likely to continue doing so. In brief, I argue that there is no single reason why the Council engages in democracy promotion. I identify three, mutually reinforcing factors: (1) the acceptance of democratic institutions as legitimate counterparts in international relations and the belief, shared by many, that democratic regimes are more peaceful and stable (normative factor); (2) the pragmatic need to identify an agreed-upon measure for disengagement from postconflict countries—that is, free and fair elections (strategic factor); and (3) the accommodation of multiple agendas of member states (political factor). These factors have produced a rather idiosyncratic engagement with democracy promotion, characterized by case-by-case decisionmaking rather than a comprehensive and coherent strategic approach. This seems consistent with the Council's activities in many other areas and with its political prerogatives as highlighted by the Charter.

Democracy and International Law

Despite the caveats already mentioned, it cannot be argued that the promotion of democracy by the UN is outside the constitutional mandate of the organization. In fact, there is strong evidence indicating otherwise.[9] Although the Soviet bloc insisted that the term "democracy" be left out of the UN Charter, the concept found its way into other international agreements of the post–World War II period.[10] Indeed, the 1948 Universal Declaration of Human Rights—which was adopted by the General Assembly without dissent—stated in Article 21 that "the will of the people shall be the basis of the authority of government," and called for that will to be discerned through "periodic and general elections."[11] Although the Universal Declaration is not a legally binding document, it remains widely regarded as forming part of customary international law and the strongest basis of UN engagement in democracy promotion.[12]

The language of Article 21 was crystallized in binding treaty form in Article 25 of the International Covenant on Civil and Political Rights (ICCPR), which highlighted the right of individuals to participate in "genuine periodic elections," and entered into force in 1976.[13] Caught in the ideological confrontation of the Cold War, Article 25 would only gain traction in 1996, when the UN Human Rights Committee adopted General Comment 25, which laid the legal basis for the principles of democracy under international law and elaborated the meaning of "genuine periodic elections" to comprise provisions that would ensure "free and fair elections."[14] These provisions included, among others, freedom of expression, assembly, and association, as well as the freedom to support or oppose the government.

Despite this solid legal foundation, the issue of multiparty elections is not tackled in the treaty, and it leaves the door open to questionable interpretations by single-party states bound to the ICCPR. China, which has signed but not ratified the covenant, can also claim to meet the standards. Reflecting the degree to which the concept of democracy remained contested in the UN context, since the 1990s a series of General Assembly resolutions on the subject carry a "sovereignty caveat" and emphasize that "there is no single model of democracy."[15]

The 1993 Vienna Declaration and Program of Action was another step in establishing a link between democracy and human rights, declaring in paragraph 8 that "democracy, development, and respect for human rights and fundamental freedoms are interdependent and mutually reinforcing." And Resolution 1999/57, adopted with fifty-one votes by the Commission on Human Rights in 1999, embedded the "rights of democratic governance" into human rights law in the strongest way, with only two abstentions, from China and Cuba. This document gave rise to the emerging interpretation—forcefully advanced by international legal scholar Thomas Franck—that democracy not only is an individual entitlement, but also confers international legitimacy on governments coming to office by democratic means.[16] At the 2005 World Summit, all UN member states reaffirmed that "democracy is a universal value" and that "democracy, development and respect for all human rights and fundamental freedoms are interdependent and mutually reinforcing."[17]

Finally, it must be added that the decisionmaking process and language of the Council's resolutions under Chapter VII of the UN Charter also contribute to the development of a doctrine of democratic entitlement. Yet despite this patchwork of legal precedence, the right to democratic governance has not yet been enshrined into a more widely adopted legal instrument.[18]

Evolution of the Council's Engagement with Democracy Promotion

The Council has continued to expand its role in democracy promotion over time, to become today a primary actor particularly when it comes to promoting elections in postconflict countries. Freed from the constraints of the ideological gridlock of the Cold War, the Council in the 1990s increasingly pushed for elections as a benchmark for stability and to prevent relapse into conflict. As the demands on warring parties became deeper and more comprehensive (e.g., rule of law and reforms to promote democratic institutions), the democratization and peacebuilding agenda substantively overlapped. President George W. Bush's "freedom agenda" in the aftermath of the tragic events of September 11, 2001, undermined rather than advanced a democratic agenda, generating strong anti-Western rhetoric and wariness of the overall promotion of democracy by external actors. Despite the backlash, today the promotion of democracy remains a common task in peace operations.

The Cold War Era

From the UN's founding to the end of the Cold War, the Council did not expressly engage with the promotion of democracy, reflecting the political realities of the era. Minor exceptions included urging Indonesia to hold "democratic elections" in 1949 and India to hold a "democratic plebiscite" in 1957 on the future of Jammu and Kashmir.[19] More significant exceptions were the condemnation of apartheid in South Africa and Southern Rhodesia.[20] While the imposition of sanctions on Southern Rhodesia in 1968 was triggered by its white minority government's unilateral declaration of independence from the United Kingdom, the sanctions on South Africa that led to the arms embargo in 1977 were formally justified as means for dealing with the country's nuclear proliferation and continuing cross-border military operations.[21] If the former case could be treated as another instance of decolonization activity, the latter clearly related to the Council's concerns of threats to international peace and security. However, in 1980 the Council explicitly recognized "the legitimacy of the struggle of the South African people for the elimination of apartheid and for the establishment of a democratic society."[22] A precedent was established, but only the end of the Cold War allowed for an exponential expansion of the scope, intensity, and explicitness of the Council's role in democracy promotion.

The 1990s

The democratization of Eastern European countries after the collapse of the Soviet Union further expanded the so-called third wave of democratization.[23] In 1950 there were no more than 22 democracies, but by the end of the 1990s that number had risen to 120 (62 percent of the world).[24] In

December 1989, only one month after the fall of the Berlin Wall, the UN General Assembly passed a resolution asserting that political legitimacy requires democracy.[25] The number of requests for electoral assistance submitted to the UN skyrocketed from seven between 1989 and 1992 to a total of eighty-nine by 1995.[26] This new geopolitical and ideological environment allowed the Council to consider the issue of democracy in a new light.

Alongside this geopolitical shift, the rise of internal conflicts and destructive civil wars in the 1990s led the Council to define internal conflict as a threat to international peace and security, thus triggering its Chapter VII authority and allowing interventions in intrastate wars. Gregory Fox has noted that from the second UN Angola Verification Mission (UNAVEM II) in 1991 to the UN Mission of Support in East Timor (UNMISET) in 2002, "the Council authorized seventeen missions to postconflict states, virtually all with a mandate to oversee some aspect of a transition to democratic governance."[27]

The UN Transitional Authority in Cambodia (UNTAC), launched in March 1992, was the first major UN exercise in governance transition. However, democracy promotion was limited to the preparation, holding, and certification of elections. Not only was the UN certification of elections it had itself organized viewed as controversial, but it was also clear that elections were seen as "a de facto exit strategy."[28] In this early stage, the Council's decisionmaking prioritized legitimating governments through elections in a postconflict country, rather than a more comprehensive approach toward democracy and governance reform. At that time, for example, many in Cambodia regretted that "the UN did not acquire a mandate for UNTAC to train a national Cambodian army and police force."[29]

This limited engagement would change in 1993—a transformative year for democracy promotion in the Council. Urging Somalia to take steps "leading to the establishment of representative democratic institutions," the Council authorized a "pro-democracy" intervention without consent, since Somalia had no recognized or de facto government. This absence was probably crucial for the acquiescence of China in the Council, because there was no encroachment on the traditional notion of sovereignty. At the same time, it also provided "lawyers and diplomats with a handle for isolating the Somali case as a precedent for the armed promotion of democracy under the Council's auspices."[30]

That same year, the Council mandated comprehensive economic sanctions and a naval blockade, and, the following year, the use of force to restore to power Haiti's president Jean-Bertrand Aristide, who had been deposed in a military coup after having been elected in democratic elections monitored by the UN.[31] China voted in favor of the sanctions after strong lobbying from Latin American and Caribbean countries, while abstaining on Resolution 940 of July 1994, which authorized a multinational force appealing to its attachment to the peaceful settlement of conflict and the principle of nonintervention.[32] The Council's involvement in Haiti resulted from UN-monitored elections in the Caribbean country a year before the military coup. However, the geographical proximity of Haiti to the United States, which made Florida the primary landing site for a large number of Haitian refugees, was a strong driver for the forceful intervention to restore democracy. In addition, the renewed engagement with the promotion of democracy by the Organization of American States (OAS), based on the provisions of the 1991 Santiago Declaration, one of the strongest pro-democracy frameworks at the regional level, played an important role.[33] All these factors explained the uniqueness of the Haiti case in the forceful promotion of democracy, an experience that was replicated only thirteen years later in Côte d'Ivoire, under other extraordinary circumstances, as explained later. Still, sanctions were used with the primary or secondary purpose of promoting democracy through the restoration of an elected government or to coerce warring parties to respect democratically elected governments not only in Haiti, but also in Angola and Sierra Leone.[34]

The year 1993 may also be considered the beginning of an overlap between the democracy and peacebuilding agendas. The trend of elections becoming a main component of peacebuilding consolidated throughout the 1990s and continues to drive the Council's decisionmaking on democracy promotion today.[35] Resolutions on Angola, Bosnia and Herzegovina, Burundi, Cambodia, the Central African Republic, the DRC, El Salvador, Haiti, Mozambique, Nicaragua, Sierra Leone, Somalia, and Tajikistan all included language that urged elections or referenda, democratic processes, or reforms toward democratic governmental reconfiguration in the context of war, postconflict, or national reconciliation.[36]

From 1993 to 2000, the Council referred to "democracy" in fifty-three resolutions.[37] Indeed, as a study of the International Peace Institute showed, from 1993 the Council began a pattern of placing more demands on warring factions in countries undergoing or emerging from civil wars to address governance issues than demands dealing with military conduct.[38] The largest portion of demands—nearly a third of the total demands adopted—related to governance and internal political relations on matters ranging from reconfiguring local and national governments to elections, political dialogue, and the media.[39] In other words, the Council did not merely seek to end armed conflict: it encouraged civil-war parties to reach and implement reforms and put in place political and governance arrangements based on democratic processes that could sustain peace and prevent conflict relapse. The mandates became more intrusive and, in Fox's words, the Council saw democratic institutions "as mechanisms of self-policing that, if functioning properly, create incentives for domestic actors to avoid return to conflict, thereby relieving international actors such as the United Nations from assuming the burden."[40]

The broadest engagement with democracy promotion, well beyond elections, arguably took place in Kosovo (UNMIK) and East Timor (UNTAET) beginning in 1999. If a major limitation of UNTAC's mandate in Cambodia was the lack of democratic institutional engineering, the mandates of these new transitional administration missions made up for these shortcomings and included designs of governance institutions that were democratic in nature.[41] These interventions imposed de facto benevolent UN autocracies to help populaces prepare for independence and democratic governance and committed the Council to support, promote, and build democratic institutions into the new millennium. The controversial nature of these mandates was immediately evident, with many suggesting they resembled colonialism or military occupation.[42] Three years into UNMIK, the ombudsperson established by the Organization for Security and Cooperation in Europe (OSCE) to monitor, protect, and promote human rights in Kosovo, published a damning report stating that "UNMIK is not structured according to democratic principles, does not function in accordance with the rule of law, and does not respect important international human rights norms."[43] This assessment highlighted the inherent contradictions in the idea of creating a democratic state through a benevolent autocracy, or as Simon Chesterman suggested, it showed that this is an "inherently flawed enterprise" since "the means are inconsistent with the ends, they are frequently inadequate for those ends, and in many situations the means are irrelevant to the ends."[44]

In fact, despite the Council's increasing promotion of democracy in the 1990s, it would be misleading to give the impression that all UN member states were behind it. Many in the Non-Aligned Movement "saw Western pro-democracy positions as a guise for intervention or attempts to destabilize their regimes."[45] The deeply controversial debate around Secretary-General Boutros Boutros-Ghali's *Agenda for Democratization,* released in December 1996 as the Secretary-General was stepping down from office, is a good reminder of the arguments over the concept at the time.[46] While he made a strong case that democracy was a universal goal and a prerequisite for lasting peace and development, many member states felt the Secretary-General was overstepping his authority and took issue with its "pontificating and paternalistic"[47] tone of his democratization agenda, ultimately exposing the many "difficulties connected with making democracy the task of international organizations" and upsetting both Western powers and the global South.[48]

In 1997, the newly elected Secretary-General, Kofi Annan, in his first report to the General Assembly on the issue of democracy, selected governance as the central organizing concept for all UN system activities regarding democracy.[49] Shifting the focus from a normative approach to the techniques for optimizing institutional arrangements was a smart maneuver, which subsequently helped frame the conversation on democracy for the new millennium.

The New Millennium

The Millennium Declaration, in which every UN member state pledged to strengthen its capacity to implement the principles and practices of democracy, provides additional evidence of a more conciliatory atmosphere.[50] At this point, more than a hundred countries had signed the Warsaw Declaration of the Community of Democracies, a "Clinton era" initiative, and in 2002 that community endorsed the Seoul Plan of Action, which listed the essential elements of representative democracy and set forth a range of measures to promote it. Regional organizations in many parts of the world also continued to include democracy promotion as a core component of their work. Notably, the African Union's 2000 Constitutive Act included in its preamble the call for a consolidation of "democratic institutions and culture" and the power to suspend a member if its government comes to power through unconstitutional means (Article 30).

While the Council showed some support for the African Union's anti-coup framework, as eventually indicated in the May 2009 presidential statement condemning the resurgence of coups in Africa, it made clear it had no appetite to adopt such principled commitments of its own, given China's and Russia's skepticism toward sanctions and the insistence of all of the P5 to approach each case on its own merits.[51] Consequently, the Council's reactions to coups over the past two decades has been inconsistent, and condemnations have been more likely in response to coups in fragile and conflict-affected states in Africa than elsewhere.[52]

Still, in the new millennium, calls for democracy by the Council acquired more specificity. For instance, in 2000, Resolution 1325, on women, peace, and security, incorporated gender inclusivity and the political participation of women as a key component of democratic governance and elections.[53] This resolution influenced, for example, the 2012 mandate extension of the UN Organization Stabilization Mission in the DRC (MONUSCO), which called for timely, credible, and peaceful provincial and local elections, and "ensuring full and effective participation of women in the electoral process."[54] The 2011 mandate for the UN Mission in South Sudan (UNMISS) also emphasized "the participation of women in decision-making forums."[55]

A global pessimism about democratic prospects and an aversion to foreign-imposed democratic structures arose from President George W. Bush's "freedom agenda" and the subsequent use of democracy promotion to justify military intervention in Iraq, the harsh counterterrorism measures that undercut democratic principles, "the tendency to flinch when likely winners of elections were worrisome, such as in the Palestinian territories," and the failure to push for democracy in places like Egypt and Pakistan or in very poor countries such as Mali where there was no counterterrorism priority.[56] Democracy promotion by the Council suffered in this climate. The post–Cold War enthusiasm for democracy was further dampened by the turmoil in postinvasion Afghanistan and Iraq. For example, while in 2000 roughly 24 percent of the Council's presidential statements referred to the promotion of democratic institutions, by 2011 only 7 percent included such language.[57] Many also pointed out that the Bush administration's foreign policy after September 2001 was detrimental for those UN missions outside the scope of the counterterrorism agenda. The 2004 UN Operation in Côte d'Ivoire (UNOCI), for example, received far less attention and support from the Council than did the missions in Kosovo and Sierra Leone in the late 1990s.[58]

On the other hand, the global skepticism on democracy promotion did not have a clear-cut effect on the Council's dynamics. Ensuring or promoting democracy, strengthening democratic institutions, or securing free and fair elections have remained tasks for all missions approved under Chapter VII since 2002, as well as for the mandates of all special political missions (with the exception of UNAMID in Darfur and UNISFA in Abyei).[59] For example, in 2006, UNMIT in East Timor was tasked with supporting the government in "enhancing a culture of democratic governance," and in 2013, MINUSMA was instructed to "foster principles of democratic governance" in Mali.[60] Between 2005 and 2009, in a series of resolutions that continued to add electoral tasks to UNMIS in Sudan, the Council ended up with the most complex electoral assistance scheme mandated so far.[61] The Sudanese elections involved a population census, boundary delimitation, national voter registration, and the nominations for and preparations of three executive and nine legislative elections.[62]

Under drafting led by the United States, in 2002 and 2003 the mandates of the political missions in Afghanistan (UNAMA) and Iraq (UNAMI) also contained strong language both in support of the local governments' efforts to build constitutional democracy and in tasking the missions to assist in the institution-building process and in the organization of elections.[63] The Afghan experience illustrates the tensions that coexist in a Council's mandate that relies on the legitimacy of the host country's leadership to carry on political work, but also includes pro-democracy tasks, which might lead to confrontation with the government. A public controversy erupted within the mission over reported frauds in the 2009 Afghan presidential election, which the deputy special representative of the Secretary-General, Peter Galbraith, proposed to tackle directly, while the head of UNAMA, Kai Eide, decided to defer to the Afghan authorities, to avoid undermining the country's sovereignty.

This case, which ended with the removal of Galbraith from his position, put the spotlight on the limitation of elections in promoting democracy. The Security Council was working under the assumption that a credible election would strengthen the legitimacy of the government and consolidate the democracy. Instead, it "deepened disenchantment and undermined confidence in the democratic process."[64] This also explains why the UN Secretariat remains very reluctant to get involved in judging the fairness of elections, since declaring a government an illegitimate counterpart would impede it from carrying on the political mandate (indeed, since 2000 the UN is no longer involved in the election observation and certification business, today carried out by other international institutions, such as the OSCE, or civil society organizations, such as the Carter Center).

Elections generated troubles for the Council also in Côte d'Ivoire, when violence erupted after presidential elections were finally held in 2010 after a five-year delay, and the incumbent Ivorian president, Laurent Gbagbo, refused to step down. This was the deadliest incident of electoral violence in Africa since 1990.[65] Over 3,000 people were killed and up to 1 million displaced, until troops of the president-elect, Alassane Ouattara, in conjunction with UN and French troops, defeated and arrested Gbagbo.[66] The Council reacted robustly, authorizing the use of force and imposing targeted sanctions, as it did in Haiti in 1993–1994.[67] Although the intervention was carried out to fulfill the mandate of protecting civilians, the situation became particularly entangled for the Council, which—unusually—had given an explicit mandate to the special representative of the Secretary-General (SRSG) and the head of UNOCI to certify the outcome of the presidential elections (see Chapter 33 in this volume). The Council's decision to call the election result, as certified by the SRSG, dismissing the validity of the Ivorian Constitutional Council's decision to back Gbagbo, was "a significant step for those Council members formally committed to working on the basis of host state consent."[68] The recognition by the African Union and the Economic Community of West African States (ECOWAS) of Ouattara as president-elect provided important cover for such Council action in the absence of which China and Russia would have been unlikely to go along. Even so, then–Russian president Dmitry Medvedev accused "UN peacekeepers of taking sides in the Ivory Coast conflict and exceeding their mandate."[69]

As the current situation in the Arab world remains fluid, it is hard to assess whether it will impact on the Council's emphasis on democracy. So far, the Council's influence in the so-called Arab Spring has been rather limited, with the notable exception of Council action on Libya and in Yemen. One lesson, however, is clear: the reminder that democratization follows a very contorted path. The Council will hardly be a key player in democracy promotion in the Arab region, and it will continue its ad hoc engagement based upon particular interests of its members, in particular the so-called P3 (France, the United States, and the United Kingdom).

The Role of the UN in Democracy Promotion Beyond the Council

Either with the consent of the states involved or pursuant to the authority of the Council under Chapter VII, the United Nations has substantially expanded its role in governance reforms of postconflict countries during the past two decades.[70] Kofi Annan in his 2005 report *In Larger Freedom* asserted that "the United Nations does more than any other single organization to promote and strengthen democratic institutions and practices around the world."[71] It is beyond the scope of this chapter to analyze this broader role of the UN system, but it is here worth mentioning in brief the work of many UN bodies, which either overlap with the Council's decisions in those countries on the Council's agenda (e.g., in Afghanistan, Cambodia, Liberia, and East Timor) or act independently upon request of the host government (e.g., in Kyrgyzstan, Lesotho, Mexico, and Peru). In this context, democracy promotion includes electoral promotion and assistance; assisting local governments "to enhance the checks and balances that allow democracy to thrive, promoting human rights, rule of law and access to justice, ensuring freedom of expression and access to information by strengthening legislation and media capacities"; and "promoting women's participation in political and public life."[72] Many of these long-term democracy-related tasks mandated by the Council end up being carried out in collaboration with UN development agencies, which also continue to assist with governance issues once a peace operation leaves.

Probably the largest set of activities includes electoral assistance.[73] Since 1991, the Department of Political Affairs, through its Electoral Assistance Division, has provided electoral assistance in more than a hundred countries, including most of those on the Council's agenda. This division coordinates requests for electoral assistance and channels such requests to the appropriate office or program. It also maintains a roster of international experts who can provide technical assistance. The United Nations Development Programme remains the UN system's main provider of technical electoral assistance, which is delivered as part of its mandate to promote democratic processes at the country level—an area that receives approximately $1.5 billion each year.[74] Although the recently established Peacebuilding Commission and Peacebuilding Support Office prominently engage in post-conflict governance development with a strong emphasis on "national ownership," "women empowerment," and "human rights standards," it is interesting to note that democracy and democratization are conspicuously absent from their tasks and language. Since the commission and office were forged during the years of Bush's controversial "freedom agenda," member states might have wanted to stay away from these terms.

The office of the UN high commissioner for human rights is also active in this area, mainly through workshops for local legislators and parliaments. Through its field operations, the office can provide legal and expert advice on relevant issues "such as respect for participatory rights in the context of free and fair elections, draft legislation on national referenda and training activities."[75] The UN Democracy Fund (UNDEF), launched in 2005 by a joint initiative of the United States and India, provides funding to promote civil society in democratic processes—85 percent of its funds are required to go to nongovernmental organizations rather than to UN agencies or governments. UNDEF is today supported by over forty member states and has financed projects such as civic education, women's empowerment, and anticorruption in China, Egypt, India, and Russia among other countries.

Assessing the Council's Role in Democracy Promotion

To the best of my knowledge, there is no study that has tried to evaluate the impact of the Council in democracy promotion. However, a few lessons can be inferred from the broader literature on determinants of democratization. One caveat is necessary, though. According to data collection conducted by the International Peace Institute, the Council tends to address civil wars that occur in authoritarian countries, rather than in more democratic ones, with failed or very weak institutions and extremely poor socioeconomic conditions.[76] This, on the one hand, indicates that the Council ends up promoting democracy in the toughest cases. On the other hand, this seems to indicate that the Council sees weak, poor, and authoritarian states as bearing less legitimacy and therefore is more prone to infringe their sovereignty, rather than to indicate a deliberate strategy to link peacemaking to democracy promotion.[77]

With that said, in 2005, the UN Secretary-General claimed "steady progress achieved in building peace and democracy in some war-torn lands" as one of the successes of collective action in recent years.[78] Numbers, however, show a more nuanced picture when it comes to the Council's actions. In fact, Freedom House does register significant improvements in the status of political rights and civil liberties of those countries targeted by the Council's democracy promotion efforts, but also setbacks.[79] Of the nineteen countries in which the Council has played a role in democracy promotion since 2000 through peacekeeping or political missions, sanctions, transitional administrations, or a combination of those actions, only Sierra Leone has moved from "partly free" to "free" from the time of the intervention to 2013. Côte d'Ivoire, Haiti, Kosovo, Liberia, and Libya moved from "not free" to "partly free." Afghanistan, East Timor, Iraq, and Nepal registered marginal improvements within the "partly free" category. The Central African Republic, Chad, and Guinea-Bissau are worse off today than when the Council dispatched a peace operation. Countries that were targets of democracy promotion in the 1990s are not much better off. Angola, Cambodia, Rwanda, and Somalia are all still classified as "not free." In sum, six countries experienced substantive improvements, while four only marginal: not such a disappointing record, when one takes into account that many countries still ranking in the "not free" category are today much more stable and less violent and poor than prior to the Council's intervention, such as Angola, Cambodia, and Rwanda. Still, at least three challenges that undermine the Council's democracy promotion efforts can be identified.

The first is time. Democratization requires societal transformations that frequently happen "over a generational time period, to develop social consensus, and to allow [countries'] societies to absorb change and to develop their institutional capacities."[80] Establishing order through blue helmets, pushing for security sector reforms, funding civil society, and holding elections only to leave quickly thereafter "may suffice for short-term peacebuilding but does not suffice for democratization."[81] Some scholars, like Roland Paris, have criticized the UN strategy in postconflict countries of "quick elections, democratic ferment, or economic 'shock therapy,'" advocating for a more controlled and gradual approach to democratization, starting from the "immediate building of government institutions that can manage political and economic reforms."[82] The Council, however, tends to opt for timelines based more on "the international need for a quick exit strategy than by a real consideration of how much time [is] necessary to undertake all the preliminary steps required for successful elections."[83] So, for example, Cambodia and El Salvador were put on the same timeline, even though the latter had formal democratic structures already in place.

The second challenge relates to promoting democracy exogenously. The effectiveness of peacekeeping, for example, on democratization is open to debate. Michael Doyle and Nicholas Sambanis have suggested there is weak statistical evidence.[84] Jeffrey Pickering and Mark Pency have indicated a positive role of peacekeeping and peacebuilding missions in fostering democratization.[85] Bruce Bueno de Mesquita and George Downs did not find any positive effect.[86] Virginia Page Fortna has shown that peacekeeping has little effect in either direction, concluding that peacekeepers "can help foster democracy by providing stability, decreasing levels of mistrust and fostering democratic institutions, but this external presence is unaccountable politically and can crowd out the indigenous growth of democracy."[87] In the case of transitional administration, fundamental dilemmas exist, as mentioned earlier, stressing the contradictions involved in attempting "to establish the conditions for legitimate and sustainable national governance through a period of benevolent foreign autocracy."[88] As data from Freedom House show, Cambodia, Kosovo, and East Timor cannot be described as full democracies, despite arguable improvements from their early postconflict days.

The third challenge is the Council's strong emphasis on pushing for free and fair elections. Although it is evident that the holding of elections does not mean that a democracy has been established, recent research also suggests that "holding elections, even very flawed ones, creates a voting muscle memory that proves important when real elections finally occur."[89] However, pushing for early—and flawed elections—can backfire for the Council. Once a national leader gains legitimacy through UN-assisted elections, the host government may grow less inclined to support the presence of the UN. This was the case of the Democratic Republic of the Congo. Since President Joseph Kabila's election in 2006, he has resented the UN's influence on his country and has threatened to expel peacekeepers. And while the UN shepherded South Sudan's secession from Sudan in 2011, its government is now at odds with the UN over human rights and aid money.[90] Meanwhile, despite smoother-than-expected elections in Mali, the elected leader "could cite the country's 'honor' as a recurrent reason for refusing to implement unwelcome reforms backed by the UN, arguing that fighting international interference is necessary to defend their national pride."[91]

Conclusion

Since the end of the Cold War, the Council has made use of a full range of tools to promote democracy, from sanctions to offering electoral assistance through its peace operations. The Council has injected democracy promotion both in its Chapter VII deliberations—including through the use of force, peacekeeping operations, transitional administrations, and sanctions—and in special political missions. Assistance in constitutional development process has also been mandated, such as in Afghanistan, Cambodia, East Timor, and Namibia.[92]

The continuing pursuit of democracy promotion by the Council can be explained by a combination of elements. First, there is a normative factor—the acceptance of democratic institutions as legitimate counterparts in international relations and the belief, shared by a majority of Council members, in particular the so-called P3, that democratic regimes are more peaceful and stable. Indeed, the P3 and many Western democracies, which periodically served as nonpermanent members of the Council, include democracy promotion among their foreign policy goals.[93] The trauma of World War II could be a possible explanation for this belief in democracy as a means to maintain international peace and security. After all, these are the countries that stated in the preamble to the 1945 constitution of the UN Educational, Scientific, and Cultural Organization (UNESCO): "the great and terrible war which has now ended was a war made possible by the denial of the democratic principles."

Additionally, some scholars have also demonstrated that democracies' commitment to maintain peace with each other is "statistically significant from the perspective of social science."[94] The vast literature on "democratic peace theory" has shown that democracy leads to substantial peace dividends.[95] At the same time, when it comes to internal conflict, the evidence is more complex. Some studies have shown that countries in democratic transition are more prone to experience civil wars, a fact that seems confirmed by the rise of election-related violence and tensions in countries like Afghanistan, Côte d'Ivoire, and Iraq.[96] At the same time, well-established liberal democracies are less likely than any other type of regime to experience civil war.[97] A majority of the Council's members seem to share these conclusions.

The belief in a "democratic civil peace" is also reflected in the Council's practice of promoting democracy as an "exit strategy" in postconflict countries. The normative factor, therefore, merges with a strategic factor—the pragmatic need to identify an agreed-upon measure for disengagement from postconflict countries. Hence, "free and fair elections" become an attractive benchmark for mission exit from postconflict countries and for preventing relapse into violence.

Finally, there is a political factor, represented by the Council's tendency to accommodate multiple agendas of member states. Mandates are becoming more aspirational lists of tasks that accommodate the many interests of the Council's members. With peacekeeping missions including as many as 300 functions, the risk of democratization becoming yet another item on the "laundry list" of the Council's agenda is real.[98] This has led to what some have called the "Christmas tree" effect on peace operation mandates.[99] At the same time, the tug-of-war that is generated by the drafting of a resolution allows for many elements to slip in resolutions as part of the bargaining process among member states. For these reasons, the continuing presence of language on democracy promotion should not be seen as the crowning of a comprehensive strategy, but rather as the fruit of a political process.

This latter factor bears the question of how much the Council is committed to democracy promotion. Recent events, from the backlash of the US-driven "freedom agenda" to the ongoing transitions in the Arab world, have undermined the "early post–Cold War optimism about the inevitable triumph of democracy" and "the equally optimistic assumption" that the international community could engineer political and social transformation in other countries.[100] Combined with the effects of other geopolitical drivers of change, including the rise of China, Russian assertiveness, Washington's political gridlock and growing isolationist tendencies, the euro zone's comatose state, and successful "authoritarian growth," from China to Rwanda, the Council's interest in democratization might become less en vogue.[101]

On the other hand, it seems safe to argue that the Council will continue to uphold democracy. First, after two decades of practice, the perspective of holding elections has become a central element in the conflict resolution strategy of the Council—the strategic factor mentioned earlier. Successful electoral processes today provide an indicator to measure the degree of stability in a country and signal to the Council's members the possibility of beginning an exit strategy.[102] Second, France, the United Kingdom, and the United States—penholders of the large majority of the Council's resolutions—are nations sympathetic to democracy promotion and supportive of the UN's role in this area—the normative factor. Democratization has become standard language in the Council's resolutions on postconflict countries. Some permanent and nonpermanent Council members, who might be perceived as less sympathetic to democracy promotion, have willingly accepted mandates that include free and fair elections and support for democratic institutions, and no nation has publicly taken a stand against democratic principles.[103] This is, first, due to a very general definition of democracy and elections in international law. As mentioned at the beginning of this chapter, since the issue of multiparty elections is not tackled in any treaty, countries like China can claim to meet the democracy standards. Second, also as mentioned, the tendency to accommodate multiple agendas in the Council's resolutions will leave a space for democratization, as long as democracy promotion does not infringe upon some Council members' agenda—the political factor. Of course, the continuing emphasis on elections and democracy building will never be uncontroversial. The Council is periodically accused "of pursuing a Western agenda in postconflict countries, with a strong emphasis on democracy, human rights, and international justice rather than adapting to local power dynamics."[104]

In sum, elections, which remain key provisions of peace agreements, will continue to be seen as effective options for conflict cessation and relapse—and the foundation of eventual disengagement, even if the holding of elections doesn't necessarily mean achievement of democracy. The dual commitment to the promotion of the norms and values of democracy and the respect of sovereign equality of states no matter what their form of government—a dichotomy that still rests at the foundation of the world body—will remain at the roots of the Council's decisionmaking process.

Notes

I thank Andrea Ó Súilleabháin for her research assistance and early drafting support. I am also grateful to Sujit Choudhry and Michael Doyle for sharing with me their insights on the topic.

1. Freedom House, "Freedom in the World: Electoral Democracies," 2013, www.freedomhouse.org/sites/default/files/Electoral%20Democracy%20Numbers%2C%20FIW%201989-2013_0.pdf.

2. The preservation of domestic jurisdiction is at the center of Article 2(7) of the Charter of the United Nations, a caveat that was not included in the Covenant of the League of Nations. The article states that "nothing contained in the present Charter shall authorize the United Nations to intervene in matters which are essentially within the domestic jurisdiction of any state." The exception is, of course, the application of enforcement measures under Chapter VII.

3. See, for example, the statement delivered by the delegation of Malaysia to the United Nations on behalf of the Non-Aligned Movement at the General Assembly 60th Session's debate concerning the Secretary-General's report *In Larger Freedom: Towards Development, Security, and Human Rights for All* (UN Doc. A/59/2005, March 21, 2005) on April 28, 2005, para. 14. See also the 2000 Summit of the G77 foreign ministers, where they called for the "democratization" of the United Nations, press release (April 12, 2000), www.g77.org/summit/presrelease_041200e.htm.

4. For an analysis of the extent to which democracy promotion was discredited under the George W. Bush administration due to its close association with the Iraq War, see Thomas Carothers, *U.S. Democracy Promotion During and After Bush* (Washington, DC: Carnegie Endowment for International Peace, 2007), http://carnegieendowment.org/files/democracy_promotion_after_bush_final.pdf.

5. All data in this paragraph have been collected by me, with the exception of those on UN sanctions, which are available via the SanctionsApp, developed by the UN Targeted Sanctions Research Project, https://itunes.apple.com/gb/app/sanctions app/id658885419?mt=8.

6. Three peacekeeping missions (UNAMID in Darfur, UNISFA in the disputed Abyei area of Sudan, and UNMEE in Ethiopia and Eritrea) and two special political missions (UNSCO in Jerusalem and UNSCOL in Lebanon) did not include language on democracy promotion and/or election.

7. Despite the obvious linkages between human rights and democracy (as explored later), this chapter does not address this relationship. For an analysis of the Security Council's relationship with human rights law and human rights in general, see Joanna Weschler's discussion on human rights in Chapter 13 of this volume; and David P. Forsythe, *The UN Security Council and Human Rights: State Sovereignty and Human Dignity* (Berlin: Friedrich Ebert Stiftung, May 2012).

8. The study of the UN in promoting democracy is a rarefied field. Within it, the attention devoted to the role of the Security Council is conspicuously absent. For example, the chapter on "Democracy and Good Governance" in Thomas G. Weiss and Sam Daws, eds., *The Oxford Handbook on the United Nations* (New York: Oxford University Press, 2007), does not include the role of the Council. Similarly, Edward Newman and Roland Rich, eds., *The UN Role in Promoting Democracy* (New York: United Nations University Press, 2004), is surprisingly thin on the role of the Council, as is Anna K. Jarstad and Timothy D. Sisk, eds., *From War to Democracy: Dilemmas of Peacebuilding* (New York: Cambridge University Press, 2008). Many other volumes on the Security Council simply ignore the issue. Since 2000, no articles on the Security Council have been published in the *Journal of Democracy,* and other publications on democracy promotion are unhelpfully vague in identifying the agent as "UN system" or "international community." David M. Malone, ed., *The UN Security Council: From the Cold War to the 21st Century* (Boulder, CO: Lynne Rienner, 2004), remains the only volume with a dedicated chapter on the topic.

9. For a detailed legal treatment of the subject, see Tom J. Farer, "The Promotion of Democracy: International Law and Norms," in Newman and Rich, *The UN*

Role in Promoting Democracy; Gregory H. Fox and Brad R. Roth, "Democracy and International Law," *Review of International Studies* 27, no. 3 (2001): 327–352; Roland Rich, "Bringing Democracy into International Law," *Journal of Democracy* 12, no. 3 (July 2001): 20–34.

10. Daniele Archibugi, "Democracy at the United Nations," in *The Changing Nature of Democracy,* edited by Takashi Inoguchi, Edward Newman, and John Keane (Tokyo: United Nations University Press, 1995), pp. 244–245.

11. The abstaining states were Byelorussia, Czechoslovakia, Poland, Saudi Arabia, Ukraine, the Union of South Africa, the Soviet Union, and Yugoslavia. United Nations General Assembly, *Universal Declaration of Human Rights Preamble,* UN Doc. A/RES/217A(III), December 10, 1948.

12. See Office of the United Nations High Commissioner for Human Rights, "Digital Record of the UDHR," February 2009, www.ohchr.org/EN/NEWS EVENTS/Pages/DigitalrecordoftheUDHR.aspx.

13. The International Covenant on Civil and Political Rights is only binding on states that have ratified it. As of July 2013, 167 states are party to the covenant, constituting approximately 85 percent of UN membership. United Nations Treaty Collections, *International Covenant on Civil and Political Rights,* December 16, 1966, http://treaties.un.org/Pages/ViewDetails.aspx?src=TREATY&mtdsg_no=IV-4&chapter=4&lang=en.

14. Rich, "Bringing Democracy into International Law," p. 23.

15. See United Nations General Assembly Resolutions 45/161, A/RES/45/161 (February 22, 1991); 46/130, A/RES/46/130 (March 2, 1992); 47/130, A/RES /47/130 (February 22, 1993); 49/180, A/RES/49/180 (March 2, 1995); 50/172, A/RES/50/172 (February 27, 1996); 52/119, A/RES/52/119 (February 23, 1998); 54/168, A/RES/54/168 (February 25, 2000); 56/154, A/RES/56/154 (March 22, 2004); and 60/164, A/RES/60/164 (March 2, 2006).

16. Thomas Franck, "The Emerging Right to Democratic Entitlement," in *Democratic Governance and International Law,* edited by Gregory Fox and Brad Roth (Cambridge: Cambridge University Press, 2000).

17. United Nations General Assembly, *2005 World Summit Outcome,* A/RES/60/1, October 24, 2005, art. 135.

18. Roland Rick and Edward Newman, "Introduction: Approaching Democratization Policy," in Newman and Rich, *The UN Role in Promoting Democracy,* p. 8.

19. United Nations Security Council Resolutions 67, S/RES/67 (January 28, 1949); and 126, S/RES/126 (December 2, 1957).

20. For a more detailed description of the early engagement of the Security Council with democracy promotion, see Gregory H. Fox, "Democratization," in Malone, *The UN Security Council,* pp. 70–72.

21. Newman and Rich, *The UN Role in Promoting Democracy,* p. 35.

22. United Nations Security Council Resolution 473, S/RES/473 (June 13, 1980).

23. The term was coined by Samuel Huntington in his article published in the *Journal of Democracy* in 1991 and the subsequent book *The Third Wave: Democratization in the Late Twentieth Century* (Norman: University of Oklahoma Press, 1993). The "third wave" included the democratic transitions in Latin America in the 1980s and in Africa and the Asia Pacific in the late 1980s.

24. Freedom House, *Democracy's Century: A Survey of Global Political Change in the 20th Century* (Washington, DC, 1999).

25. United Nations General Assembly Resolution 44/146, A/RES/44/146 (December 15, 1989).

26. Laura Zanotti, *Governing Disorder: UN, Peace Operations, International Security, and Democratization in the Post–Cold War Era* (University Park: Pennsylvania State University Press, 2011), p. 4.

27. Gregory H. Fox, "International Law and the Entitlement to Democracy After War," *Global Governance* 9, no. 2 (2003): 179.

28. Aurel Croissant, "The Perils and Promises of Democratization Through UN Transitional Authority: Lessons from Cambodia and East Timor," *Democratization* 15, no. 3 (2008): 665.

29. Michael W. Doyle, Ian Johnstone, and Robert C. Orr, eds., *Keeping the Peace: Multidimensional UN Operations in Cambodia and El Salvador* (Cambridge: Cambridge University Press, 1997), p. 164.

30. Tom Farer, "The Promotion of Democracy: International Law and Norms," in Newman and Rich, *The UN Role in Promoting Democracy,* p. 50.

31. United Nations Security Council Resolution 867, S/RES/867 (September 23, 1993). Chapter VII was invoked the next year to strengthen the peace mission with United Nations Security Council Resolution 940, S/RES/940 (July 31, 1994).

32. See Sebastian von Einsiedel and David M. Malone, "Haiti," in Malone, *The UN Security Council,* pp. 470–473.

33. Organization of American States General Assembly Resolution 1080, OAS-AG/RES 1080 (XXI-0/91) (June 5, 1991).

34. For Angola, see United Nations Security Council Resolution 864, S/RES/864 (September 15, 1993). For Haiti, see United Nations Security Council Resolution 841, S/RES/841 (June 16, 1993). For Sierra Leone, see United Nations Security Council Resolution 1132, S/RES/1132 (October 8, 1997).

35. Charles T. Call and Susan E. Cook, "On Democratization and Peacebuilding," *Global Governance* 9, no. 2 (2003): 233–246.

36. More details on these cases are included in Fox, "Democratization," pp. 72–80.

37. Fox, "Democratization," p. 69.

38. James Cockayne, Christoph Mikulaschek, and Chris Perry, *The United Nations Security Council and Civil War: First Insights from a New Dataset* (New York: International Peace Institute, 2010), p. 1.

39. Ibid., p. 15.

40. Fox, "Democratization," p. 70.

41. In Kosovo, UNMIK's mandate had as one of its central goals the "development of provisional institutions for democratic and autonomous self-government"; United Nations Security Council Resolution 1244, S/RES/1244 (June 10, 1999), para. 11(c). In East Timor, the Council stressed the need for UNTAET to "carry out its mandate effectively with a view to the development of local democratic institutions"; United Nations Security Council Resolution 1272, S/RES/1272 (October 25, 1999), para. 8.

42. See, for example, Gerald B. Helman and Steven R. Ratner, "Saving Failed States," *Foreign Policy* 89 (Winter 1992): 3; Peter Lyon, "The Rise and Fall and Possible Revival of International Trusteeship," *Journal of Commonwealth and Comparative Politics* 31, no. 1 (1993): 96.

43. Ombudsperson Institution in Kosovo, *Second Annual Report 2001–2002* (addressed to Michael Steiner, special representative of the UN Secretary-General), July 10, 2002.

44. Simon Chesterman, *You, the People: The United Nations, Transitional Administration, and Statebuilding* (Oxford: Oxford University Press, 2005), p. 249.

45. Caroline E. Lombardo, "The Making of an Agenda for Democratization," *Chicago Journal of International Law* 2, no. 1 (2001): 259.

46. United Nations Secretary-General, *An Agenda for Democratization,* A/51/761, December 20, 1996, www.un.org/en/events/democracyday/pdf/An_agenda _for_democratization[1].pdf.

47. Boutros-Ghali's senior political adviser, Rosaria Green, cited in United Nations Secretary-General, *An Agenda for Democratization,* p. 320.

48. Zanotti, *Governing Disorder,* p. 43.

49. United Nations Secretary-General, *Support by the United Nations System of the Efforts of Governments to Promote and Consolidate New or Restored Democracies,* A/52/513, October 21, 1997.

50. "We will spare no efforts to promote democracy and strengthen the rule of law." United Nations General Assembly Resolution 55.2, A/RES/55.2 (September 8, 2000), para. 24.

51. Security Council Report, "Update Report no. 3: The Resurgence of Coups d'État in Africa," New York, April 15, 2009, p. 4, www.securitycouncilreport.org /update-report/lookup-c-glKWLeMTIsG-b-5106497.php.

52. The strongest reaction to coups d'état was in the case of Haiti in 1993–1994, as mentioned earlier. Otherwise, the Security Council acted prudently, issuing presidential statements condemning coups in Burundi in 1996 and Mauritania in 2008, issuing presidential statements expressing concerns about coups in Sierra Leone and Cambodia in 1997, releasing press statements in the cases of the Central African Republic and Guinea-Bissau in 2003 and Fiji in 2006, and simply ignoring all other cases. All in all, the Security Council reacted to twenty-five of thirty-four cases of coups from 1993 to 2013.

53. United Nations Security Council Resolution 1325, S/RES/1325 (October 31, 2000) called for the inclusion and protection of women through constitutions, electoral systems, and judiciaries, further calling for Security Council missions to take into account gender considerations and the rights of women.

54. United Nations Security Council Resolution 2053, S/RES/2053 (June 27, 2012).

55. United Nations Security Council Resolution 1996, S/RES/1996 (July 8, 2011).

56. Mark Lagon, *Promoting Democracy: The Whys and Hows for the United States and the International Community* (New York: Council on Foreign Relations, February 2011), www.cfr.org/democracy-promotion/promoting-democracy-whys -hows-united-states-international-community/p24090.

57. My calculation.

58. Maud Edgren-Schori, Débora García-Orrico, Pierre Schori, Shahrbanou Tadjbakhsh, and Gilles Yabi, eds., *Security Council Resolutions Under Chapter VII: Design, Implementation, and Accountabilities* (Madrid: Fride, 2009), p. xxx.

59. UNAMID's mandate included tasks on rule of law, governance, and human rights, based on paragraphs 54 and 55 of the report of the Secretary-General and the chairperson of the African Union Commission (United Nations Security Council, *Report of the Secretary-General and the Chairperson of the African Union Commission on the Hybrid Operation in Darfur,* UN Doc. S/2007/307/Rev.1, June 5, 2007).

60. For UNMIT, see United Nations Security Council Resolution 1704, S/RES/1704 (August 25, 2006); and for MINUSMA, see United Nations Security Council Resolution 2100, S/RES/2100 (April 25, 2013).

61. United Nations Security Council Resolutions 1590, S/RES/1590 (March 24, 2005); 1784, S/RES/1784 (October 31, 2007); 1812, S/RES/1812 (April 30, 2008); 1870, S/RES/1870 (May 20, 2009); and 1881, S/RES/1881 (August 6, 2009).

62. Adrian Morrice, "Sudan: 2010 General Elections," annex case study, in *Lessons Learned: Integrated Electoral Assistance in UN Mission Settings,* by Adrian Morrice, Francisco Cobos, and Mary O'Shea (New York: United Nations Development Programme, United Nations Department of Political Affairs, and United Nations Department of Peacekeeping Operations, January 30, 2012), p. 3.

63. For UNAMA, see United Nations Security Council Resolution 1401, S/RES/1401 (March 28, 2002); and for UNAMI, see United Nations Security Council Resolution 1500, S/RES/1500 (August 14, 2003).

64. Center on International Cooperation, *Annual Review of Global Peace Operations 2010* (Boulder, CO: Lynne Rienner, 2010), p. 29.

65. US Institute of Peace, *Prevention Newsletter*, September 2011 (Washington, DC, September 1, 2011), p. 4.

66. United Nations Secretary-General, *Twenty-Eighth Report of the Secretary-General on the United Nations Operation in Côte d'Ivoire,* UN Doc. S/2011/387, June 24, 2011, para. 40; United Nations High Commissioner for Refugees News Agency, "Escalating Violence Fuels Dramatic Rise in Displacement in Côte d'Ivoire," March 25, 2011, www.unhcr.org/4d8c950a9.html.

67. United Nations Security Council Resolutions 1962, S/RES/1962 (December 20, 2010); and 1975, S/RES/1975 (March 30, 2011).

68. For a detailed treatment of the Côte d'Ivoire's crisis, see Alex J. Bellamy and Paul D. Williams, "The New Politics of Protection? Côte d'Ivoire, Libya, and the Responsibility to Protect," *International Affairs* 87, no. 4 (2011): 825–850.

69. "UN Defends Role in Ivory Coast," *Voice of America,* April 15, 2011, www.voanews.com/content/un-defends-role-in-ivory-coast-119964269/157907.html. Michael J. Matheson, "United Nations Governance of Post-Conflict Societies," *American Journal of International Law* 95, no. 1 (January 2001): 76.

70. Michael J. Matheson, "United Nations Governance of Post-Conflict Societies," *American Journal of International Law* 95, no. 1 (January 2001): 76.

71. United Nations Secretary-General, *In Larger Freedom,* para.151.

72. See United Nations, "Global Issues: Democracy and the United Nations," www.un.org/en/globalissues/democracy/democracy_and_un.shtml.

73. Election monitoring was terminated in 2000 due to the potential tensions with the provision of electoral assistance.

74. United Nations Development Programme, "Fast Facts: Democratic Governance," September 2010, www.un.org/en/globalissues/democracy/pdfs/UNDPfastfactsFINAL.pdf.

75. See United Nations Office of the High Commissioner for Human Rights, "Rule of Law: Democracy and Human Rights," www2.ohchr.org/english/issues/rule_of_law/democracy.htm.

76. "Between 1989 and 2006, civil wars that were not addressed by Security Council resolutions tended to occur in states that were more democratic than those countries that experienced civil wars that did figure on the active agenda of the Security Council. Five of the forty-four post–Cold War civil wars broke out in countries assessed by Polity IV as 'democratic,' and none of these five conflicts was addressed by a Security Council resolution. At the same time, eleven out of the fourteen civil wars that took place in states with 'autocratic' governments did figure on the active agenda of the Security Council." Cockayne, Mikulaschek, and Perry, *The United Nations Security Council and Civil War,* pp. 25–26.

77. This is echoed in several research findings, including in Andreas Andersson, "Democracies and UN Peacekeeping Operations, 1990–1996," *International Peacekeeping* 7, no. 2 (Summer 2000): 1–22; Virginia Page Fortna, *Does Peacekeeping Work? Shaping Belligerents' Choices After Civil War* (Princeton: Princeton Univer-

sity Press, 2008), p. 36; Kimberly Zisk Marten, *Enforcing the Peace: Learning from the Imperial Past* (New York: Columbia University Press, 2004); Roland Paris, *At War's End: Building Peace After Civil Conflict* (Cambridge: Cambridge University Press, 2004).

78. United Nations Secretary-General, *In Larger Freedom,* para. 11.

79. Freedom House classifies the status of political regimes in each country as "free," "partly free," or "not free." It conducts this assessment by aggregating its political rights and civil liberties scores.

80. World Bank, *World Development Report 2011: Conflict, Security, and Development* (Washington, DC, 2011), p. 144, www-wds.worldbank.org/external /default/WDSContentServer/WDSP/IB/2011/05/18/000356161_20110518030905 /Rendered/PDF/589880PUB0WDR0000public00BOX358355B.pdf.

81. Jarstad and Sisk, *From War to Democracy,* p. 257.

82. Paris, *At War's End,* pp. 7–8.

83. Krishna Kumar, "Post-Conflict Elections and International Assistance," in *Post-Conflict Elections, Democratization, and International Assistance,* edited by Krishna Kumar (Boulder, CO: Lynne Rienner, 1998), pp. 5–9.

84. Michael Doyle and Nicholas Sambanis, *Making War and Building Peace: United Nations Peace Operations* (Princeton: Princeton University Press, 2006).

85. Jeffrey Pickering and Mark Peceny, "Forging Democracy at Gunpoint," *International Studies Quarterly* 50, no. 3 (September 2006): 539–560.

86. Bruce Bueno de Mesquita and George W. Downs, "Intervention and Democracy," *International Organization* 60, no. 3 (Summer 2006): 627–649.

87. Virginia Page Fortna, "Peacekeeping and Democratization," in Jarstad and Sisk, *From War to Democracy*, p. 74.

88. Chesterman, *You, the People,* p. 1.

89. Isobel Coleman and Terra Lawson-Remer, eds., *Pathways to Freedom: Political and Economic Lessons from Democracy Transitions* (New York: Council on Foreign Relations, 2013), p. 4.

90. Josh Kron and Nicholas Kulish, "For South Sudan and the U.N., a Relationship of Growing Distrust," *New York Times,* July 20, 2013, www.nytimes.com/2013 /07/21/world/africa/for-south-sudan-and-the-un-a-relationship-of-growing -distrust.html?pagewanted=all&_r=0.

91. Richard Gowan, "Diplomatic Fallout: Will the U.N. Respect or Offend Mali's National Pride?" *World Politics Review,* August 5, 2013, www.worldpolitics review.com/articles/13139/diplomatic-fallout-will-the-u-n-respect-or-offend-mali-s -national-pride.

92. Vijayashri Sripati, "UN Constitutional Assistance Projects in Comprehensive Peace Missions: An Inventory, 1989–2011," *International Peacekeeping* 19, no. 1 (February 2012), p. 93. More on constitution building can also be found in International Institute for Democracy and Electoral Assistance (IDEA), "Constitution Building After Conflict: External Support to a Sovereign Process," Stockholm, May 2011, www.idea.int/publications/constitution-building-after-conflict/upload/CB-after -conflict.pdf.

93. The US Agency for International Development (USAID) became the first major bilateral donor to include democracy as part of its portfolio when it launched its Democracy Initiative in 1990. But many other European governments include democracy promotion among their main priorities, including Finland, Norway, Sweden, and the UK. France also includes the consolidation of the rule of law and democracy among its priorities, although the emphasis varies according to different administrations. The European Commission also has a number of instruments that

support democratic governance beyond the EU's borders, at the core of which lies the European Instrument for Democracy and Human Rights (EIDHR).

94. Michael Doyle, *Liberal Peace* (New York: Routledge, 2012), p. 203.

95. It goes beyond the scope of this chapter to summarize the large debate on democratic peace theory. As references, see Michael Brown, Sean Lynn-Jones, and Steven Miller, eds., *Debating the Democratic Peace* (Cambridge: MIT Press, 2001).

96. See, for example, Jack L. Snyder, *From Voting to Violence* (New York: Norton, 2000); Edward D. Mansfield and Jack L. Snyder, *Electing to Fight: Why Emerging Democracies Go to War* (Cambridge: MIT Press, 2007).

97. Håvard Hegre, Tanja Ellingsen, Scott Gates, and Nils Petter Gleditsch, "Toward a Democratic Civil Peace? Democracy, Political Change, and Civil War, 1816–1992," *American Political Science Review* 95, no. 1 (March 2001): 16–33. Other studies in support of "democratic civil peace" include R. J. Rummel, *Power Kills: Democracy as Method of Nonviolence* (New Brunswick, NJ: Transaction, 1997); William Zartman, "Changing Forms of Conflict Mitigation," in *Global Transformation in the Third World,* edited by Robert Slater, Barry Schutz, and Steven Dorr (Boulder, CO: Lynne Rienner, 1993); Joshua Muravchik, "Promoting Peace Through Democracy," in *Managing Global Chaos: Sources of and Responses to International Conflict,* edited by Chester Crocker and Fen Osler Hampsen, with Pamela Aall (Washington, DC: US Institute of Peace, 1996).

98. Peacekeeping missions can include as many as 300 different tasks that fall under more than twenty broad categories, such as disarmament, demobilization, and reintegration (DDR); electoral assistance; peace process management; human rights monitoring; security sector reform; and rule of law. See Jake Sherman and Benjamin Tortolani, "Implications of Peacebuilding and Statebuilding in United Nations Mandates," in *Robust Peacekeeping: The Politics of Force,* edited by J. Nealin Parker (New York: Center on International Cooperation, 2009), p. 15, http://reliefweb.int/sites/reliefweb.int/files/resources/DD53B6D0F50388FD492576E9000 CC1FA-Full_Report.pdf.

99. The term "Christmas tree mandates" is borrowed from Ellen Margrethe Løj, former special representative of the Secretary-General to Liberia. See Louise Riis Andersen and Peter Emil Engedal, *Blue Helmets and Grey Zones: Do UN Multidimensional Peace Operations Work?* (Copenhagen: Danish Institute for International Studies, 2013), p. 26, www.diis.dk/files/media/publications/import/extra/rp2013 -29_lan_blue-helmets_web.pdf.

100. Marina Ottaway, "Promoting Democracy After Conflict: The Difficult Choices," *International Studies Perspectives* 4 (2003): 314–322.

101. For example, see Richard Gowan, "The Strategic Context: Peacekeeping in Crisis, 2006–2008," *International Peacekeeping* 15, no. 4 (August 2008): 453–469.

102. Paul Collier, *Wars, Guns, and Votes: Democracy in Dangerous Places* (New York: Harper Collins, 2009), pp. 79–89.

103. Roland Rich, "Crafting Security Council Mandates," in Newman and Rich, *The UN Role in Promoting Democracy,* p. 83.

104. See, for example, Richard Gowan, *Five Paradoxes of Peace Operations* (Berlin: ZIF, 2011), p. 3, www.zif-berlin.org/fileadmin/uploads/analyse/dokumente /veroeffentlichungen/Policy_Briefing_Richard_Gowan_Sep_2011_ENG.pdf.

13

Acting on Human Rights

Joanna Weschler

IN THIS CHAPTER I LOOK AT THE DYNAMICS IN THE COUNCIL'S collective approach to human rights. I show how human rights, though no longer a taboo for the Council, have not been fully embraced as part of the Council's outlook. The tension between the urge to act in the face of atrocities and interpretations of Article 2(7) of the UN Charter, addressing nonintervention in matters within domestic jurisdictions, has not been fully overcome. And despite considerable advances in the Council's conceptual discussions on the matter, the fundamental question as to when and under what conditions a pattern of systematic human rights violations reaches a point where peace and security are threatened, requiring consideration by the Council, remains open. The issue is further complicated by national political interests of key member states and concerns about sovereignty, which significantly influence the Council's approach to human rights on any given issue.

I also examine some of the changes of the UN human rights architecture over the past decade or so and trace the development of the Security Council's own tools to address human rights aspects of situations on its agenda.[1]

The Early Decades

The UN Charter was drafted when World War II drew to a close and its atrocities and contempt for human rights loomed large. "Promoting and encouraging respect for human rights" was included in Article 1 of Chapter I of the UN Charter as one of the purposes of the new organization. The

259

adoption of the Universal Declaration of Human Rights followed some three years later. By then, however, the Cold War was in full swing, with the permanent members of the Security Council often paralyzed into inaction by the veto. For decades, human rights violations were almost never mentioned by the Security Council. While the communist-bloc members were particularly insistent that human rights were outside the scope of the Council, almost all governments felt at best ambivalent about seeing that body enter a territory so widely perceived as a matter of state sovereignty.

But even during the Cold War decades, human rights were not entirely absent from the Council's work. Several resolutions contained human rights language, for instance with respect to the situation in Hungary in 1956 (Resolution 120), in the Congo in 1961 (Resolution 161), and in the Dominican Republic in 1965 (Resolution 203). In the late 1960s and 1970s a number of Council resolutions, mostly in the context of the decolonization of Africa, invoked the Universal Declaration of Human Rights and other human rights instruments. Several resolutions related to apartheid South Africa, up through the 1980s, contained strong human rights language, including calls for the release of political prisoners, stays of executions and clemency, and the condemnation of massacres, in addition to sanctions imposed against Southern Rhodesia and South Africa under Chapter VII of the Charter, largely in response to the apartheid system as such.[2] Yet, overall, human rights references remained the exception during the Cold War.

Things changed at the outset of the 1990s. Two factors account for the growing attention to human rights in the Council's conflict resolution efforts. First, Cold War paralysis gave way to cooperation among the great powers on many conflict situations, allowing for a significantly more activist Security Council. Second, the conflicts the Council was called upon to address changed from initially primarily international ones to—by the middle of the decade—almost exclusively internal ones. Internal conflicts in most cases have involved human rights violations at every stage. The Council, being famously the UN's most pragmatic body, soon came to the realization that in order to achieve lasting peace, human rights needed to be addressed as part of peacemaking, peacekeeping, and peacebuilding.

Key Moments in the Post–Cold War Period

Of course, human rights concerns did not become a commonly included feature in Council deliberations overnight, and progress in some areas was sometimes offset by backsliding in others, especially during the past decade.

April 1991 was when the Council, for the first time, decided explicitly that repression could amount to threats to international peace and security.

In Resolution 688 on Iraq, it condemned "the repression of the Iraqi civilian population in many parts of Iraq . . . the consequences of which threaten international peace and security in the region." China abstained, as did India, while Cuba, Yemen, and Zimbabwe voted against. Resolution 688 was groundbreaking: in it the Council gave itself a mandate to take severe human rights violations as an early-warning indicator of a conflict with international implications.

At its first ever summit, held on January 31, 1992, the Security Council in its final statement noted that "the absence of military conflicts amongst states does not in itself ensure international peace and security" and concluded that "human rights verification had become one of the tasks of United Nations peacekeeping."[3]

Receiving adequate human rights information, however, was a problem, because the Council had not yet developed the necessary working methods. The permanent five Council members had their own channels, but the elected ten often experienced frustration and felt they were not getting enough information about key events. Such was the backdrop when, in March 1992, that month's Council president, Venezuelan ambassador Diego Arria, was contacted by a Croat priest who had just come out of the Balkan conflict zone. Ambassador Arria wanted the priest to convey his eyewitness account to other members of the Council but, being unable to find a formal way, simply invited his fellow ambassadors to meet with the priest in the delegates' lounge. Some ten or eleven ambassadors attended, and clearly they were stunned by what they heard and were able to appreciate the critical importance of firsthand information.[4] That meeting was the first of what have since become known as "Arria formula" briefings, informal Council meetings where non-Council experts brief the Council on specific conflict situations.

However, for the Council to receive human rights information in formal meetings remained extremely controversial. In August 1992, some Council members invited a special rapporteur of the UN Commission on Human Rights to brief. Even though Max van der Stoel, the rapporteur on Iraq, was allowed to speak, four countries (China, Ecuador, India, and Zimbabwe) had their reservations noted in the record. India's ambassador was particularly passionate about the issue: "Deviation from the Charter, in which the nations of the world have reposed their faith and support, could erode that confidence and have grave consequences for the future of the Organization as a whole. . . . The Council . . . cannot discuss human rights situations per se or make recommendations on matters outside its competence."[5] Despite the different internal conflicts ongoing at the time— notably in the Balkans—human rights briefings remained very controversial. Van der Stoel was invited to brief on Iraq once again later that year, and Tadeusz Mazowiecki, special rapporteur on the former Yugoslavia briefed once (in November 1992, over the objection of China and Zimbabwe), but these three occasions in 1992 when the Council heard UN special rapporteurs on human rights in formal sessions have remained the only such examples to this day.

Two major human rights catastrophes in the mid-1990s—the Rwanda genocide and the massacres of Srebrenica and other UN "safe areas"—occurred literally under the Council's watch. Rwanda had been plagued by a civil war, with hundreds of civilians killed in a series of massacres and incidents since 1990, when peace accords were signed in Arusha in August 1993. The Council was to set up a mission to supervise the implementation of the agreement. An August 1993 report by the special rapporteur of the Commission on Human Rights on extrajudicial executions recommended that any transitional arrangements introduced in Rwanda should have human rights at their heart. However, the mandate of the UN Assistance Mission for Rwanda (UNAMIR), established in October 1993, in what was perhaps one of the more serious human rights mistakes in the Council's history, did not include any human rights component. The Council furthermore ignored a number of warning signs of an impending genocide. Not only did the Council fail to act preventively, but after the carnage started, following the April 6, 1994, downing of a presidential plane over Kigali, it even reduced the UN presence on the ground. The first references to specific human rights activities appeared in June 1994 when the Council, in Resolution 925, welcomed the visit to Rwanda of the newly appointed UN high commissioner for human rights, noted the appointment of the special rapporteur by a special session of the Commission on Human Rights, and asked the Secretary-General to ensure that UNAMIR extend close cooperation to the special rapporteur.

The second major human rights disaster of the mid-1990s occurred in 1995 in the former Yugoslavia. Council-created "safe areas" in Bosnia were overrun by the Serb forces and thousands of male inhabitants were hauled away and then slaughtered. Particularly appalling were the events in Srebrenica, where the Dutch UN peacekeeping battalion did not attempt to protect the local population and furthermore forced outside all the military-age male civilians who had sought refuge in the UN compound in Potocari. Several thousand were subsequently taken away by the Serb paramilitaries and never seen again. To have created the so-called safe areas without providing them with adequate military protection had been a fatal error. The big powers, under pressure from the opinion of their publics, had wanted to appear resolute in addressing the massive human rights violations. But they had not been resolute enough to back their words with soldiers and resources, unwilling as they were to put their troops at risk. In essence, the powers used the adoption of successive Security Council resolutions on the conflict as a series of fig leaves to cover their inaction. Mazowiecki, the human rights rapporteur, visited the area within days of the July 1995 massacres and, in an almost unprecedented move—by UN standards—resigned from his post upon his return, explaining that he no longer could be associated with the UN after it failed so horribly the people it was supposed to protect.[6] The Council waited until December 1995, after the signing of the Dayton peace accords, to pass a resolution in which it explicitly condemned the human rights violations committed and stressed the need to fully investigate the events.

The mass atrocities in Rwanda and Srebrenica played a role in the gradual acknowledgment of the need to establish closer links between the UN human rights machinery and its peace and security system. The General Assembly created the post of the high commissioner for human rights, the high-level official responsible for all UN human rights activities, in 1993. By happenstance, the first high commissioner, Ecuadorian ambassador José Ayala Lasso, took office a day before the onset of the Rwandan genocide. Proponents of the establishment of this post had hoped that such an official, with the rank of under-secretary-general, would be able to establish a working relationship with the Security Council. It took years, however, before this hope could be realized. The first holder of the post shied away from trying to press human rights issues into the Council's outlook (in fact, as an elected Council member in 1992, he had been one of the most vocal opponents of allowing a human rights rapporteur to brief the Council, arguing that "human rights per se do not fall within the competence of the Security Council").[7] Lasso's successor, former Irish president Mary Robinson, who served as high commissioner from September 1997 until September 2002, early on in her tenure launched an effort to establish direct contacts with the Council and, initial resistance notwithstanding, achieved a degree of success. Despite resistance from some Council members—China in particular because of a previous meeting between the high commissioner and the Dalai Lama—Robinson was able to address the Council on September 16, 1999, at the invitation of the Secretary-General during the semiannual Council debate on the protection of civilians. Other meetings and consultations followed. But any interaction with the high commissioner remained controversial, and acceptance of the value of the high commissioner's contribution to the Council's work has come slowly and occasionally suffered setbacks.

Between 2005 and 2009, the high commissioner for human rights was invited only sporadically and did not participate in the semiannual debates on the protection of civilians. This began to change in 2009 due to intense diplomatic efforts by certain nonpermanent members of the Council, most notably Austria. Austria chaired the Council in November 2009, when a periodic debate on protection was scheduled, and invited the high commissioner to speak at that debate. When the next regular debate was about to be held, in June 2010, Austria conducted informal consultations with other members of the Council—in particular Russia and China, which had been among the most reluctant—and obtained their consent for another invitation. Agreeing to invite the high commissioner to the subsequent debate, in November 2010, proved considerably easier, following which invitation of the high commissioner to all regular debates on the protection of civilians in armed conflict became more frequent. Perhaps more important, the high commissioner has increasingly been accepted and sought as an important resource for the Council on specific conflict situations, most notably Syria. During the decade between 1999 and 2009, the high commissioner had some sixteen direct interactions with the Council, whereas in the period from the beginning of 2010 through February 2014, there have been over thirty such interactions.

Institutional Design Changes

Speaking in Stockholm in January 2004 shortly before the tenth anniversary of the Rwandan genocide, then–Secretary-General Kofi Annan said: "We should also consider establishing a Special Rapporteur on the prevention of genocide, who would be supported by the High Commissioner for Human Rights, but would report directly to the Security Council—making clear the link, which is often ignored until too late, between massive and systematic violations of human rights and threats to international peace and security." On March 11, 2004, during the monthly lunch with Council members, Annan announced his decision to appoint a special adviser on the prevention of genocide who would act as an early-warning mechanism to the Secretary-General and, through him, to the Security Council, by calling attention to potential situations that could result in genocide; make recommendations to the Security Council on actions to prevent and halt genocide; and liaise with the UN system on activities for the prevention of genocide and work to enhance the UN's capacity to analyze and manage information relating to genocide or related crimes.[8] In July 2004, Annan appointed an Argentinean human rights lawyer and former political prisoner, Juan Méndez, to the post (the mandate was endorsed by the General Assembly in the outcome document of the 2005 World Summit). Méndez was succeeded in 2007 by Francis Deng of Sudan, and Deng, in 2012, by Adama Dieng of Senegal.

The mechanism went through several transformations and became a free-standing post of an under secretary-general, based in New York. Its effectiveness and visibility during most of this period, probably due to the institutional and personnel issues, has not been impressive. The potential, however, for helping the Security Council to play a more proactive and preventive role is still there.

By mid-2000, the top UN human rights body, the Commission on Human Rights, was in a deep credibility crisis, having become dominated by states more concerned with protecting one another from human rights scrutiny than protecting populations from human rights violations. In a report published in March 2005 in preparation for the World Summit later that year, Annan proposed to replace the commission with a new body, the Human Rights Council (HRC). Addressing the Commission on Human Rights on April 7, he elaborated: "My basic premise is that the main inter-governmental body concerned with human rights should have a status, authority and capability commensurate with the importance of its work. The United Nations already has councils that deal with its two other main purposes, security and development. So creating a full-fledged council for human rights offers conceptual and architectural clarity."[9]

Early versions of the proposal to establish the HRC emphasized the importance of institutional links between the new body and the Security Council. However, General Assembly Resolution 60/251, establishing the Human Rights Council in March 2006, did not specifically mention the Security Council, though it did acknowledge that peace and security and human rights were interlinked and mutually reinforcing.

From its establishment in 2006 until 2011, if the HRC was mentioned at all in Security Council discussions, it was mostly as part of an argument about why the Security Council should not deal with a particular issue because of it being the job of another council. Prior to 2011, only one Security Council resolution referenced the HRC. Things changed with the start of the Libya crisis in February 2011. The first Council meeting on Libya was a briefing by Secretary-General Ban Ki-moon on February 25, one day after the HRC had held its first special session on Libya. The Secretary-General referred to this session in his briefing. From that point on, the Council began to occasionally look at the HRC as a source of useful guidance or information rather than a periphery or an excuse for not addressing human rights itself. And HRC decisions and developments related to situations on the Security Council agenda have begun to be referenced in briefings to the Council by top UN officials and in Security Council resolutions.

The Council's Development and Use of Different Human Rights Tools

The Council has over the years developed a number of tools specifically to address human rights, and adapted some of its existing practices and procedures. Council-mandated field missions in conflict and postconflict areas constitute a key tool with a potential for significant and often quick impact on human rights. Yet despite the January 1992 Council summit statement proclaiming human rights verification among the tasks of UN peacekeeping, the Council was slow and inconsistent in including human rights in the mandates of the missions it established.

The first such component predated the 1992 Council summit. In Resolution 693 of May 20, 1991, the Council established the UN Observer Mission in El Salvador (ONUSAL) with the initial mandate to verify the compliance by the parties with the July 26, 1990, human rights agreement (which was a component of a peace process ending a civil war in the country). ONUSAL's tasks included active monitoring of the human rights situation, investigation of specific cases of alleged violations of human rights, promotion of human rights, making recommendations to eliminate violations of human rights, and a reporting requirement to the Security Council and the General Assembly.[10] The first mission to be set up after the summit, the UN Transitional Authority in Cambodia (UNTAC), established in Resolution 745 of February 28, 1992, also included a human rights component. But for the next several years, human rights components were rarely part of newly established missions. Neither the UN Protection Force (UNPROFOR) for the former Yugoslavia, established just prior to the summit, nor the UN Assistance Mission for Rwanda (UNAMIR), established in October 1993, had such components in their mandates, despite the fact that severe human rights violations were prevalent in both conflicts. Including a human rights component became more of a norm than an exception toward the late 1990s, starting with the UN Observer Mission in Angola (MONUA) in 1997.[11] Nearly all peacekeeping operations and special political missions established since have had human rights tasks in their mandates, including investigating specific cases, supporting local human rights initiatives, human rights monitoring, and regular reporting to the Council. Those that currently do not have a human rights component tend to be classic peacekeeping missions, established during the Cold War years, with predominantly military mandates. A notable exception in this context has been the UN Mission for the Referendum in Western Sahara (MINURSO), for which repeated attempts by different Council members to include human rights in its mandate have been thwarted by staunch opposition from Morocco, supported in this by at least one of the permanent members.

As James Cockayne shows in Chapter 15 of this volume, the Council over the past two decades has increasingly made use of criminal justice approaches to address peace and security challenges, including in the area of human rights. The international criminal tribunals it established—for the former Yugoslavia established in May 1993 (ICTY, Resolution 827) and for Rwanda in November 1994 (ICTR, Resolution 955)—not only constituted a new tool but were also groundbreaking explicit acknowledgments that accountability for the most egregious war crimes and crimes against humanity was key to the maintenance of peace and security and that individual responsibility for such crimes was of concern to the Council. The 1998 Rome Statute of the International Criminal Court (ICC) provided the Council with the possibility of referring to the ICC conflict situations in which atrocity crimes were suspected of having taken place, a tool the Council made use of in the cases of Sudan in 2005 and Libya in 2011. (The Council's relationship with international courts and tribunals is addressed by Eran Sthoeger in Chapter 25.)

Since the late 1990s, the Council has been holding periodic debates on thematic issues such as children and armed conflict, protection of civilians, rule of law, and sexual violence in conflict. Over the years, the periodic discussions of each of these themes led to the development—through the adoption of a series of resolutions and presidential statements—of a complex normative system on these matters. Given that each of the themes has a strong human rights aspect, the potential impact of this approach on human rights protection in places of the deployment of Council-authorized missions is considerable. However, the Council's application of the principles agreed upon in the abstract to concrete conflict situations has been at best inconsistent and it has failed to establish operational mechanisms with teeth to implement these norms.

One notable exception is the Council's thematic work on children and armed conflict and conflict-related sexual violence, where it created special tools that make the implementation of the relevant norms more likely. In November 2005, the Council established its Working Group on Children and Armed Conflict to review and comment on reports on children in armed conflict situations. A unique feature of this subsidiary body is that it occasionally reviews situations of children in armed conflicts that as such are not on the Council agenda. The working group has engaged with governments and has been issuing concrete recommendations aimed at alleviating conflict-related abuses of children.

In Resolution 1820, adopted in June 2008, the Council identified sexual violence—when used as a tactic of war—as an impediment to international peace and security. Then in September of the following year, it adopted Resolution 1888, which asked the Secretary-General to appoint a special representative to provide strategic leadership in efforts to address problems identified in Resolution 1820. Following the establishment of the office in February 2010, the subsequent representatives have engaged with the Council on several occasions.

In the late 1990s, the United Nations subjected itself to a thorough analysis of its own role in the tragedies of Rwanda and Srebrenica.[12] The Rwanda report by former Swedish prime minister Ingvar Carlsson in particular focused on the need to incorporate human rights information in the work of the Council. It recommended the UN "improve the flow of information on human rights issues. Information about human rights must be a natural part of the basis for decisionmaking on peacekeeping operations, within the Secretariat and by the Security Council."

The Arria-formula informal briefings described earlier have become a key means for obtaining human rights information, though the frequency of their usage for this purpose varies. Between 2000 and 2005, several rapporteurs of the Commission on Human Rights briefed the Council in this format, and so did representatives of human rights and humanitarian organizations, often coming from the field and sharing firsthand experience. In the next few years, human rights–focused Arria briefings were infrequent, but experienced something of a revival toward the end of the decade. In 2009, Mexico organized an Arria-formula briefing on the Council's role in "strengthening a UN integrated approach to human rights and counterterrorism," with former high commissioner for human rights Mary Robinson among the speakers. From 2011 through 2014, various elected members (Australia, Germany, Guatemala, Lithuania, Nigeria, Portugal and Rwanda) took the initiative to organize several human rights–related Arria briefings, including with members of the HRC's Independent International Commission of Inquiry on the Syrian Arab Republic; with the heads of the seventeen human rights components of UN missions; on the activities of the Lord's Resistance Army in Africa's Great Lakes region; and with the members of the UN Commission of Inquiry on Human Rights in the Democratic People's Republic of Korea.

In late 2010, the United Kingdom introduced what became known as the "horizon-scanning" briefings by the UN Secretariat. The goal was to provide the Council with information that might allow it to undertake better preventive action. These monthly briefings were held during all of 2011 and part of 2012 and provided the Council with early warning on a range of issues—some with considerable human rights concerns—such as Libya, Yemen, and the Tuareg activity in the north of Mali. Due to the unhappiness of some permanent Council members with a meeting format that leaves the choice of issues to the Secretariat and not the Council, the practice dwindled, with five briefings held in 2012, three in 2013, and none in 2014. A possible new context for the use of horizon scanning, and specifically in relation to human rights, could have been the December 2013 Secretary-General's "Rights Up Front Action Plan," reflecting the UN Secretariat's new commitment to early and preventive action to respond to human rights violations and prevent mass atrocities. Under the second action of the six-point plan, the Secretariat is mandated to provide member states "with candid information with respect to peoples at risk of, or subject to, serious violations of international human rights or humanitarian law." The horizon-scanning format may have been expected to be seen by the Secretariat as a useful tool with which to fulfill this mandate, though as of early 2015 this did not appear to be the case.

The UN Charter, in Article 34, gives the Council the proactive power to investigate "any situation which might lead to international friction," and its Provisional Rules of Procedure further elaborate that "the Security Council may appoint a commission or committee or a rapporteur for a specified question."[13] In a few cases, the Council resorted to this tool for the specific purpose of collecting information on grave breaches of human rights and humanitarian law. In October 1992, by Resolution 780, the Council established a commission of experts to examine such violations in the territory of the former Yugoslavia, and in July 1994, by Resolution 935, it set up a commission of experts on violations committed in Rwanda "to collect all available information, including that gathered by the Special Rapporteur, and to report to the Council on possible appropriate next steps." These two commissions led to the subsequent establishment of the ad hoc international criminal tribunals for the former Yugoslavia and Rwanda, in May 1993 and November 1994 respectively.

The Council has resorted to the establishment of commissions of experts to investigate possible grave human rights violations three times. On May 25, 2004, in a presidential statement, the Council decided to establish an international commission of inquiry "to investigate all human rights violations committed in Côte d'Ivoire since 19 September 2002, and determine responsibility." In Resolution 1564 of September 18, 2004, it established a commission of inquiry "in order immediately to investigate reports of violations of international humanitarian law and human rights law in Darfur by all parties." In Resolution 2127 of December 5, 2013, on the Central African Republic, it decided to establish an independent commission "to investigate reports of violations of international humanitarian law, international human rights law and abuses of human rights in the Central African Republic (CAR) by all parties since 1 January 2013." The results of the Côte d'Ivoire investigation have never been made public or taken up by the Council. The results of the Darfur investigation led to the Council's referral of Darfur to the ICC. The CAR investigation commission submitted its report to the Council in June 2014.

The Council occasionally welcomed or took note of the results of investigations into severe human rights violations committed in conflicts on its agenda, as reported by commissions established by the HRC or the Secretary-General (and the Council was briefed several times informally by the HRC commissioners investigating Syria).

A unique way for the Council to gather firsthand information has been, starting in 1993, through its field trips. Most of the over forty missions undertaken since have been to conflict areas with rampant human rights violations. More often than not, these missions have sensitized the participating ambassadors to human rights issues and made them more inclined to address these issues in their work on the Council. On some occasions, the missions have had tangible and direct human rights impact. Such was the case of the 1999 visit to East Timor, when the delegation literally helped to stop violence. In 2009, during a visit to the Democratic Republic of the Congo, in meetings with the country's president and prime minister, the delegation raised specific cases of sexual violence committed by five high-ranking officers of the DRC armed forces. Within weeks, all five officers were ordered to be relieved of their posts and judicial proceedings were initiated against three of them. However, the Council has been inconsistent in making human rights part of the scope of its visits, even when human rights violations are a prominent feature of the situation on the ground.

Sanctions, starting in the early 1990s, have become a preferred measure for the Council to address conflict. It has used them for a variety of goals, including changing the behavior of a government with respect to its own population; mitigating the impact of a conflict; restoring a democratically elected government; and addressing global security issues such as nuclear proliferation and terrorism.

During the past decade, the Council has on several occasions included human rights violations as grounds to impose sanctions. In Resolution 1572 (2004) on Côte d'Ivoire, the Council decided, for the first time, that a "person determined as responsible for serious violations of human rights" could be subject to a travel ban and an assets freeze. In 2005, through Resolution 1591, the Council added committing "violations of international humanitarian or human rights law" in Darfur as grounds for imposing individual sanctions. In 2006, when renewing sanctions on the DRC through Resolution 1698, the Council added child recruitment or use of child soldiers and committing sexual violence against children to the criteria for imposing sanctions on individuals. In Resolution 1807 on the DRC, in March 2008, it added sexual violence against women to the criteria. In Resolution 1970 on Libya, adopted in February 2011, the Council made "commission of serious human rights abuses" a criterion for imposing individual sanctions. In July 2011, in Resolution 2002, the Council decided to make child recruitment, targeting of civilians, and sexual violence additional criteria for imposing sanctions on individuals in Somalia and Eritrea. However, in most cases, these resolutions do not specify who will be subject to the sanctions, and for sanctions to apply to a particular individual, another decision, this time by the Council's sanctions committee, is needed. In some cases, it took the Council several years to apply these sanctions to specific persons. Only occasionally the resolutions imposing sanctions contained also the list of the individuals to be targeted by the measures.

There is a human rights irony in the history of targeted sanctions. They were invented to avoid harming entire populations with the imposition of sanctions by instead aiming at limiting the negative impact to (often high-level) individuals deemed most responsible for prolonging any conflict or committing abuses. But following the 2001 terrorist attacks on the United States, the targeted sanctions originally imposed by Resolution 1267 (1999) on the leadership of the Taliban in Afghanistan were extended through Resolution 1390 (2002) to apply worldwide and to a vaguely defined group of "members of the Al-Qaida organization and the Taliban and other individuals, groups, undertakings and entities associated with them." The "1267 list" grew from just a handful of well-identified individuals in prominent leadership positions to several hundred alleged terrorists about most of whom very little information was available. These broadly applicable measures lacked standards of evidence and remedies. Almost immediately, cases of mistaken identity came to light and several states—for example Germany, Sweden, Liechtenstein, and Switzerland—undertook years-long efforts to get their wrongly listed citizens or residents removed from the list. States, nongovernmental organizations, media, and some in the UN Secretariat started raising concerns about the Council violating the due process rights of targeted persons.

The fact that the Council for years essentially ignored these concerns led world leaders to the unusual step of including an admonition of the Council in the outcome document of the 2005 World Summit, calling for "fair and clear procedures" as well as humanitarian exemptions in the listing and delisting of individuals and entities on sanctions lists. In the next few years, also due to several law suits that were being brought around the world, the Council relented and made considerable modifications to its sanctions procedures, culminating in 2009 with the creation of the post of an ombudsperson—a mechanism safeguarding due process—to assist in considering requests for removals from the sanctions list.

Recent Dynamics

The approach of Council members to human rights has evolved considerably over the past two decades. It is safe to say that the great disinclination to receiving information regarding and discussing human rights has been overcome. Even the historically most reluctant permanent members—China and Russia—have on certain occasions explicitly sought briefings from the high commissioner for human rights (for example, China, in May 2012, issued an official invitation for the high commissioner to brief during an open debate on protection of civilians in armed conflict, and Russia successfully argued for the need to receive a briefing in consultations on Libya in July 2012).

But certain lines have remained difficult to cross for some members. A telling dynamic developed in the Council over the concept of Responsibility to Protect. Starting in 1999, the Council began adopting a series of far-reaching thematic resolutions on protection of civilians in armed conflict.

Several peacekeeping operations received an explicit mandate to protect civilians under imminent threat of physical violence. Yet Council members needed more than four months to agree to express in a resolution their commitment to the Responsibility to Protect, even though all their leaders had already done so in the outcome document of the 2005 World Summit.[14]

After failing to act in the face of genocide in Rwanda, and abdicating its responsibility to see its own resolutions implemented in the case of Srebrenica, the Council, starting in September 1999, took a more hands-on approach to East Timor, including an emergency visit, aimed at mitigating violence and preventing further violations. But this "never again" resolve seems to have dissipated gradually, with the Council showing itself impotent in the face of massive civilian killings in Sri Lanka in 2009 and the agony of the population of Syria ongoing since early 2011.

Furthermore, the Council continues to be divided on when massive human rights violations constitute a threat to international peace and security. Several resolutions with strong human rights language were vetoed in the past few years. These were the January 2007 draft resolution on Myanmar, the July 2008 draft resolution on Zimbabwe, and the October 2011, February 2012, July 2012, and June 2014 draft resolutions on Syria. In each case the vetoes were cast by China and Russia.[15]

In the first several years following the end of the Cold War, addressing human rights in the Council required a degree of activism on the part of pro–human rights Council members. At different points, different delegations made particular human rights issues their cause and worked proactively to overcome their diplomatic colleagues' reluctance to have the matter addressed. Elected members tended to be particularly activist in their approaches to conflicts with a strong human rights aspect. This dynamic has changed considerably in the past few years. One of the reasons may be the emergence of a relatively recent practice of appointing "penholders" within the Council for particular issues. The penholders are almost always permanent members (in most cases from among the P3: France, the United Kingdom, and the United States), and they take the lead on all substantive matters related to a particular situation, including but not limited to drafting all resolutions. The P3 usually agree on a given draft resolution among themselves and then negotiate it with China and Russia. The agreed text is then circulated to the elected members, usually quite close to the adoption date. The elected members are strongly discouraged from making amendments, because this might disturb the sometimes painstakingly achieved consensus among the P5. This system has serious human rights implications. Elected members wishing to strengthen human rights language in the draft may be pressured into abandoning the idea for the sake of the consensus. But more important is the fact that the penholder system creates a default situation in which when a crisis arises, all members, including the permanent ones, defer to the penholder. If the penholder is unwilling or unable to take initiative (for example because it is already dealing with another crisis on which it holds the pen), no other Council member tends to step forward.

Since the end of the Cold War, the Council has resorted on three occasions to a procedural vote to place a situation on its agenda because of severe human rights violations. The unique aspect of procedural votes is that the veto does not apply, which explains why they are very rare events. (Indeed, only fourteen such votes have been recorded since 1990.) In July 2005, the United Kingdom, supported by three non-Council members requested a briefing on Zimbabwe, after a wave of violent evictions by the army and the police left more than half a million people homeless. In September 2006, the United States requested a briefing on Myanmar because of reports of grave human rights violations. And in December 2014, ten Council members led by Australia expressed concern about the scale and gravity of human rights violations described in the February 7, 2014, report by the Commission of Inquiry established by the Human Rights Council and requested that the situation in the Democratic People's Republic of Korea (DPRK) be placed on the Council's agenda.[16] In all three cases, procedural votes were a mechanism employed by Western, or a Western-led coalition of, Council members to overcome an unwillingness of Russia and China to take on these issues and who indeed voted against placing these situations on the Council agenda. Whether the DPRK episode will follow the pattern set in the first two cases, where a procedural vote is followed by one or just a handful of formal meetings but is subsequently quietly dropped from the Council's agenda, remains to be seen.[17]

The Security Council is a political body and its members are more likely to be guided by national interests than human rights norms. Furthermore, the most powerful countries at certain times protect their allies from any Council action that could lead to political changes on the ground. Examples include China's stalling during the process of formulating the Council's response to Darfur between 2004 and 2007; Russia's adamant opposition to meaningful Council action on Syria between 2011 and 2013; the extension of a degree of protection to Rwanda by the United States in the context of Rwandan support for the March 23 Movement (M23) rebel force operating in the eastern DRC; and France's unflinching support for Morocco in the context of Western Sahara.

Conclusion

It would be naive to expect the Council to become a body guided primarily by human rights principles. But it is not naive to expect the Council to appreciate how human rights norms and action can be helpful in addressing every stage of its peace and security work. From violations of these norms being among the first warning signs of a brewing conflict, to insisting on the observance of the norms during a conflict to minimize damage to the population and infrastructure, to fostering an environment grounded in these norms in the postconflict phase in order to achieve lasting results, this should be an intricate part of the framework in which the Council makes its decisions.

Yet the Council's resort to these norms has been inconsistent. The use of the tools the Council has developed, including certain provisions in Council resolutions, has also been haphazard at times. This has been evident in years-long delays between a sanctions decision and its application in practice; in creating human rights components in some but not all peace and political missions; in focusing on human rights aspects of a given situation during some of the Council's field travels but not all; and in including references to zero-tolerance for sexual exploitation by UN personnel in some but not all mandate renewals.

At the end of my chapter on human rights in the 2004 edition of *The UN Security Council: From the Cold War to the 21st Century,* I wrote: "For the time being, the issue remains open on how effective the Council can or wants to be in decreasing or preventing suffering caused by human rights violations, but it appears that human rights are no longer likely to disappear from the Council's radar screen anytime soon."[18] Over a decade later, this remains true.

Notes

1. The chapter builds upon and occasionally borrows from Joanna Weschler, "Human Rights," in *The UN Security Council: From the Cold War to the 21st Century,* edited by David M. Malone (Boulder, CO: Lynne Rienner, 2004).

2. See Sydney D. Bailey, *The UN Security Council and Human Rights* (New York: St. Martin's, 1994).

3. United Nations Security Council, "Provisional Verbatim Record of the 3046th Meeting," UN Doc. S/PV.3046, January 31, 1992; United Nations Security Council, "Note by the President of the Security Council," UN Doc. S/23500, January 31, 1992.

4. Interview with Diego Arria, November 13, 2002.

5. United Nations Security Council, "Provisional Verbatim Record of the 3105th Meeting," UN Doc. S/PV.3105, August 11, 1992.

6. Tadeusz Mazowiecki, press conference in Geneva, July 27, 1995; Tadeusz Mazowiecki, "A Letter of Resignation," *New York Review of Books,* September 21, 1995.

7. United Nations Security Council, "Provisional Verbatim Record of the 3150th Meeting," UN Doc. S/PV.3150, December 18, 1992.

8. See "Outline of the Mandate for the Special Adviser on the Prevention of Genocide," annexed to United Nations Secretary-General, "Letter Dated 12 July 2004 Addressed to the President of the Security Council," S/2004/567, July 13, 2004.

9. United Nations Secretary-General Kofi Annan, "Address to the Commission on Human Rights," Geneva, April 7, 2005, www2.ohchr.org/english/bodies/chr/sessions/61/speeches.htm.

10. United Nations Secretary-General "Central America: Efforts Toward Peace," Report to the Security Council, S/22494, April 16, 1991.

11. Katarina Månsson, "A Communicative Act: Integrating Human Rights in UN Peace Operations—Dialogues from Kosovo and Congo," PhD thesis, National University of Ireland, 2008.

12. United Nations Security Council, "Letter Dated 15 December 1999 from the Secretary-General Addressed to the President of the Security Council," UN Doc. S/1999/1257, December 16, 1999; United Nations General Assembly, *Report of the Secretary-General Pursuant to General Assembly Resolution 53/35: The Fall of Srebrenica,* UN Doc. A/54/549, November 15, 1999.

13. United Nations, *Charter of the United Nations* (San Francisco, June 26, 1945), Provisional Rules of Procedure, Rule 28.

14. United Nations General Assembly Resolution 1, A/RES/60/1 (September 16, 2005); United Nations Security Council Resolution 1674, S/RES/1674 (April 28, 2006).

15. United Nations Security Council, "United Kingdom of Great Britain and Northern Ireland and United States of America: Draft Resolution," UN Doc. S/2007/14, January 12, 2007; United Nations Security Council, "Australia, Belgium, Canada, Croatia, France, Italy, Liberia, Netherlands, New Zealand, Sierra Leone, United Kingdom of Great Britain, and Northern Ireland and United States of America: Draft Resolution," UN Doc. S/2008/447, July 11, 2008; United Nations Security Council, "France, Germany, Portugal, and United Kingdom of Great Britain and Northern Ireland: Draft Resolution," UN Doc. S/2011/612, October 4, 2011; United Nations Security Council, "Bahrain, Colombia, Egypt, France, Germany, Jordan, Kuwait, Libya, Morocco, Oman, Portugal, Qatar, Saudi Arabia, Togo, Tunisia, Turkey, United Arab Emirates, United Kingdom of Great Britain, and Northern Ireland and United States of America: Draft Resolution," UN Doc. S/2012/77, February 4, 2012; United Nations Security Council, "France, Germany, Portugal, United Kingdom of Great Britain, and Northern Ireland and United States of America: Draft Resolution," UN Doc. S/2012/538, July 19, 2012; United Nations Security Council, "Albania, Andorra, Australia, Austria, Belgium, Botswana, Bulgaria, Canada, Central African Republic, Chile, Côte d'Ivoire, Croatia, Cyprus, Czech Republic, Democratic Republic of the Congo, Denmark, Estonia, Finland, France, Georgia, Germany, Greece, Hungary, Iceland, Ireland, Italy, Japan, Jordan, Latvia, Libya, Liechtenstein, Lithuania, Luxembourg, Malta, Marshall Islands, Mexico, Monaco, Montenegro, Netherlands, New Zealand, Norway, Panama, Poland, Portugal, Qatar, Republic of Korea, Republic of Moldova, Romania, Samoa, San Marino, Saudi Arabia, Senegal, Serbia, Seychelles, Slovakia, Slovenia, Spain, Sweden, Switzerland, The Former Yugoslav Republic of Macedonia, Turkey, Ukraine, United Arab Emirates, United Kingdom of Great Britain and Northern Ireland and United States of America: Draft Resolution," UN Doc. S/2014/348, May 22, 2014.

16. United Nations Security Council, "Letter Dated 5 December 2014 from the Representatives of Australia (and Other Member States) Addressed to the President of the Security Council," S/2014/872, December 5, 2014.

17. An item that has not been discussed for three years or more gets automatically deleted from Council agenda, unless any member state of the UN requests its retention.

18. Weschler, "Human Rights," p. 67.

14

Responding to Terrorism

Peter Romaniuk

IN INTRODUCING HIS CLASSIC TEXT, *SWORDS INTO PLOWSHARES,*
Inis Claude laments that there are no straightforward criteria for assessing
the effectiveness of the United Nations. As a result, observers are prone to
inflate their expectations and, inevitably, express disappointment. "The
problem," Claude writes, "is to achieve and then use a set of educated
expectations concerning the international organizations of our time."[1] In
this chapter I respond to the problem identified by Claude by describing
and analyzing the UN Security Council's response to terrorism. How has
the Council responded and in what ways does this response "educate our
expectations" about the Council? As this question implies, I view the Council's record here as particularly instructive, as there are few items on the
Council's past or current agenda where its record of action is so distinctive.
As Ed Luck noted in his chapter in the 2004 edition of this volume, the
"rapidity, unanimity and decisiveness" with which the Council responded to
the terrorist attacks on the United States of September 11, 2001, were
"without precedent."[2] In particular, the passage of Resolution 1373 (2001),
so broad in its scope and deep in its reach, stood in "stark contrast" to the
Council's "history of ambivalence and hesitation in the face of terrorism."[3]
Others, too, noted that the assertive use of institutions such as the Council
in this way would be instructive, providing a "fruitful test" or even a "natural experiment" for our understanding of international cooperation generally.[4] Analogous to the idea of a "crucial case" in the social sciences,[5] the
novelty of the Council's response to terrorism provides rare insight.

The chapter proceeds in three sections based on the three key lessons
that we can glean from the Council's counterterrorism actions over time.

The first lesson is the most familiar: outcomes in the Council are derivative of politics among its membership, especially the five permanent members. The Cold War had the effect of constraining Council action on terrorism and cooperation advanced modestly elsewhere (through the specialized agencies and General Assembly) in a piecemeal fashion, wherein treaties criminalizing certain terrorist acts were elaborated. But the second lesson is that the past is not determinative of Council action, and politics, under the right circumstances, can enable rather than constrain. The immediate post-9/11 years are an exceptional illustration of this. At that time, the Council acted assertively to introduce broad and sweeping counterterrorism mandates, taking steps to institutionalize its leadership position. Many observers revised their expectations upward and in 2004 Luck expressed "guarded optimism" that the Council might be "transformed into an unambiguous political force against terrorism."[6] But as Claude might have anticipated, those expectations were unfulfilled. On the one hand, this is unsurprising and represents a reversion to the mean—continuity, rather than change, from the past. But on the other hand, recent developments suggest that states have adapted to the post-9/11 exertion of Council influence on counterterrorism. Therefore, the third lesson pertains to how states and the broader multilateral system respond to an activist Security Council. That is, there have emerged multiple ways for states to advance their interests by either acting to keep the Council in check or seeking to leverage its authority. Unlike in the past, this has led to *more* multilateralism in the field of counterterrorism, rather than less, as states have shopped for—or created—forums to advance cooperation on favorable terms.

Readers will note the dialectical nature of these lessons. To put it most straightforwardly: for most of its history, Council action on terrorism was a nonstarter; after 9/11, the Council suddenly came to dominate the field; in turn this has yielded contestation, within the UN system and beyond it, to right-size the Council's response. In concluding, I note how these lessons should help us form "educated expectations" about the Council's future actions on counterterrorism and beyond.

The Security Council and Terrorism During the Cold War

Upon its founding in 1945, the new Security Council might have looked to its predecessor, the Council of the League of Nations, for some direction in responding to terrorism. The League's Council had shown some leadership on the issue by establishing, in December 1934, the Committee for the International Repression of Terrorism (CIRT), to develop a convention for this purpose. In an achievement unmatched since, CIRT successfully completed its task in 1937. The resulting two conventions (one to "prevent and punish" terrorism and the other to establish a tribunal for offenses committed under the first) even contained a definition of "terrorism" (although it is circular, as it includes the undefined phrase "state of terror"). The main convention attracted only twenty-four signatories, and a single ratification, before the League fell out of existence.[7]

The Security Council showed little interest in placing terrorism on its agenda. Although a reference to a "criminal group of terrorists in Jerusalem" was included in a 1948 resolution expressing shock at the assassination of the UN mediator in Palestine, Count Folke Bernadotte,[8] the new Council was otherwise reticent to identify acts as terrorism or respond to them. It was only in response to events—an increase in incidents of aerial hijacking over the course of the 1960s—that the Council acted, and modestly so. In 1970, the coordinated hijacking of four planes (attempts to hijack a fifth were unsuccessful) by the Popular Front for the Liberation of Palestine (PFLP) prompted a consensus resolution to call for the release of passengers and crew members taken hostage, and for all states to act to prevent future hijackings.[9] Even then, the main forum through which the international community responded to the increase in hijackings was the International Civil Aviation Organization (ICAO), which had negotiated three conventions on various aspects of aviation and airport security by 1971. Here we see the origins of the "piecemeal approach" to counterterrorism diplomacy wherein states, reticent about broad-based action against terrorism due to competing perceptions of the legitimacy of nonstate violence, nonetheless act to criminalize certain terrorist tactics. Nine multilateral legal instruments were negotiated outside the Council during the Cold War and three more were added between 1989 and 9/11.[10]

As this record suggests, the Council was an ineffective forum for counterterrorism diplomacy during this period. Cold War politics, filtered through the evolving crisis in the Middle East, were to blame. States from the Non-Aligned Movement and the communist bloc, sympathetic to the Palestinian and anticolonial causes, sought to preserve the legitimacy of national liberation movements; in contrast, the West sought to outlaw nonstate violence and was more sympathetic to Israel. Beginning in the early 1970s, the discussion of terrorism in the Council increasingly took on a zero-sum dynamic. In response to the May 1972 attack by the United Red Army of Japan at Lod airport in Israel, in which twenty-six passengers were killed, the Council held only informal consultations and issued a mere statement.[11] The response to the Black September Organization's taking of Israeli athletes as hostages at the summer Olympic Games in Munich later that year was more divisive. Rival draft resolutions emerged from non-aligned Council members (which failed to mention terrorism or even the Munich crisis), the United States (characterizing the issue in much starker terms), and Western European states (attempting a synthesis). The US draft was not put to a vote, but the other drafts drew tit-for-tat vetoes, including the first sole veto exercised by the United States. It was only then that Secretary-General Kurt Waldheim took steps to include terrorism on the agenda of the General Assembly, yielding the highly politicized debate in the Sixth Committee that has consistently given truth to the cliché that "one man's terrorist is another man's freedom fighter."[12]

There was some minor variation in Council politics on terrorism over the duration of the 1970s. In 1973, a resolution was adopted by consensus criticizing Israel for its mistaken interception of a Middle East Airways plane thought to be carrying PFLP leader George Habash.[13] But no resolution was issued following the Israeli raid on an Air France aircraft hijacked to Entebbe, Uganda, after PFLP terrorists had released non-Jewish passengers. Council members split over whether to criticize the hijackers or the Israelis for their apparent breach of Ugandan sovereignty. Here a US-UK draft resolution was eventually put to a vote but failed, as nine members either abstained or declined to participate.[14] Similarly, despite progress in the Sixth Committee toward a convention against the taking of hostages (a result of West German action in response to Munich), the Council proved a fruitless venue for the United States in seeking redress for the seizure of its embassy in Tehran in 1979.

The pattern of silence or division seemed to yield in the mid-1980s, again in response to events. The year 1985 was a "banner year" for international terrorists,[15] with a marked increase in attacks, fatalities, and states victimized (including the Soviet Union). In this climate, the Council responded to the *Achille Lauro* attack in October that year with a short but relatively integrative statement that condemned "terrorism in all its forms, wherever and by whomever committed," and deplored the "reported death of a passenger" (a reference to Jewish American tourist Leon Klinghoffer, who was shot and thrown overboard in his wheelchair).[16] In December, a consensus resolution condemned hijacking, hostage-taking, and terrorism in similar language, and urged further international cooperation, including the implementation of relevant international treaties.[17] This was in response to the hijacking of an EgyptAir flight by the Abu Nidal group, which led to the deaths of fifty-eight passengers after the plane caught fire during an attempted raid by Egyptian commandos at Luqa airport in Malta. Also in December, grenade and gun attacks on El Al passengers checking in at Rome and Vienna airports killed 17 and wounded 115 others. But this time some Council members sought language regarding the prospect of Israeli retaliation, and the final statement, following US intervention, called upon "all concerned to exercise restraint."[18] By early 1986, distributive bargaining, and the use of the veto, returned. The April bombing of a Berlin disco frequented by US service members, and the US air raids on Libya that followed, resulted in nine meetings. A draft resolution that condemned both terrorism ("whether perpetrated by individuals, groups or States") and the US air raids was vetoed by Britain, France, and the United States.[19] Here, as previously, Council inaction reflected that its membership sought to use it in conflicting ways: to respond to terrorism and to police the counterterrorism actions of other states.

In the final years of the Cold War, Council action on terrorism came to conform to the "piecemeal approach," with consensus resolutions on hostage-taking and the marking of plastic explosives. The former followed from the kidnapping and subsequent hanging by Hezbollah of a US national serving as part of the UN Truce Supervision Organization (UNTSO) and the UN Interim Force in Lebanon (UNIFIL).[20] The latter followed the destruction in 1988 of Pan Am flight 103 over Lockerbie, Scotland. Here, the Council urged ICAO to develop an "international regime for the marking of plastic or sheet explosives for the purpose of detection."[21] A convention on the topic was duly concluded through ICAO in 1991.

If the Council was a predictable creature of the Cold War, the collapse of the Soviet Union gave rise to optimism, as manifested in the January 1992 presidential note on "the responsibility of the Security Council in the maintenance of international peace and security." Meeting for the first time at the heads-of-state level, the members of the Council noted the "momentous change" in world politics and members expressed "their deep concern over acts of international terrorism," while emphasizing the "need for the international community to deal effectively with such acts."[22] Short of an unambiguous peace dividend, the Council found, in the course of the 1990s, new ways of responding to terrorism, including sanctions. The Council imposed a range of such measures against Libya, Sudan, and the Taliban for terrorism-related reasons over this period. The question of whether or not sanctions are effective has yielded significant scholarly and policy debates, and the use of sanctions by the Council is the focus of a separate chapter in this volume (Chapter 20). Suffice it to note here that these three cases reflect a mixed record.

Libyan involvement in the bombing of Pan Am Flight 103 over Lockerbie and the 1989 bombing of UTA Flight 772 over Niger prompted the Security Council to call for cooperation in establishing responsibility for the attacks (Resolution 731 of 1992, adopted unanimously). Such requests to Libya from France, Britain, and the United States had gone unheeded. But five members, including China, abstained when the Council voted to impose an initial aviation ban, an arms embargo, diplomatic sanctions, and a travel ban on Libyan nationals involved in terrorism (Resolution 748 of 1992). While Libya made some conciliatory gestures, a subsequent effort to impose further sanctions (tightening the aviation ban, restricting the provision of oil-transporting equipment, and freezing Libyan assets abroad) again attracted abstentions from China and three others (Resolution 883 of 1993). In terms of their implementation, these measures received mixed support. European states relied on Libyan oil exports, and by mid-1998 the Organization of African Unity announced its intention to stop complying with the sanctions. In the resulting negotiations, Libya agreed to hand over two suspects for trial under Scottish law in the Netherlands (a deal enshrined in Resolution 1192 of 1998). After the suspects arrived in The Hague (in April 1999) the sanctions were suspended. They were finally removed in 2003 after Libya accepted responsibility for the acts in question, disavowed terrorism, and agreed to compensate the victims (Resolution 1506 of 2003). France and the United States abstained from that resolution; the latter subsequently removed Libya from its list of "state sponsors of terrorism" in June 2006. So the case can be made that the sanctions had their intended effect here.[23]

For its part, Sudan had been designated by the United States as a "state sponsor of terrorism" in 1993 for serving as a "refuge, nexus and training hub for a number of international terrorist organizations."[24] (For further discussion, see Chapter 30). The Council imposed diplomatic sanctions and a travel ban on Sudanese government officials in 1996 following an assassination attempt in Addis Ababa on Egyptian president Hosni Mubarak by Egyptian extremists sheltering in Sudan (Resolution 1054 of 1996). Both China and Russia abstained on that occasion, and did so again when an aviation ban was threatened (Resolution 1070 of 1996). Against the backdrop of growing concern over the humanitarian consequences of the comprehensive sanctions in place against Iraq, a report on the likely impact of these measures in Sudan was enough to dissuade Council members from activating the tougher measures. Sudan all the while denied harboring terrorists. It admitted that it previously had an "open-door" policy that, "in the name of pan-Arabism, might have enabled some terrorists to enter the country easily," but said that steps had been taken to seek their removal.[25] Among those taking advantage of Sudan's "open door" was Osama bin Laden, who resided there between 1992 and 1996, after which he left for Afghanistan. The sanctions seemed to have some influence over Khartoum. The Council took note of Sudan's efforts to comply with Resolutions 1054 and 1070 and formally lifted the sanctions in 2001 (Resolution 1372). But the United States (which had bombed certain sites in Sudan in 1998 following the terrorist attacks on its embassies in Dar-es-Salaam and Nairobi in 1998) abstained on that occasion and continues to list Sudan as a "state sponsor of terrorism."

Among the pre-9/11 cases of counterterrorism sanctions imposed by the Council, those against the Taliban and al-Qaeda have attracted the most attention and remain in place (following numerous revisions) at the time of this writing. The evolution of these measures reflects a process of "institutional adaptation" that says much about the Council as a sanctioner and as a counterterrorist,[26] a theme I return to later. Despite the contemporary relevance of these measures, their origins were modest. The Council became increasingly concerned about Afghanistan over the course of the 1990s and turned to sanctions in October 1999 (Resolution 1267, adopted unanimously). The measures included targeted financial sanctions on individuals and entities to be identified by a sanctions committee (a subsidiary organ of the Council, established by the resolution) and an aviation ban. At the time, the aim was to dissuade the Taliban from allowing Afghan territory to be used to harbor terrorists, especially Osama bin Laden. In a subsequent resolution (1333 of 2000, with China and Malaysia abstaining), bin Laden and his associates were specifically targeted and the measures were expanded. Reflecting the limited impact of the sanctions, that resolution also created an expert committee to report implementation. This was later supplemented by a "sanctions enforcement and support team," comprising up to fifteen persons, to be deployed to states bordering Afghanistan (Resolution 1363 of 2000, adopted unanimously). Preparations toward the establishment of these bodies were interrupted by the attacks of 9/11.

Beyond the use of sanctions, the Council became more comfortable condemning terrorist violence over the 1990s, as indicated in a series of presidential statements and a unanimous resolution that condemned the 1998 bombings of the US embassies in Kenya and Tanzania.[27] In 1999, the Russians advanced an "antiterrorism manifesto" that consolidated and affirmed Council and UN action on terrorism to date, resulting in a unanimous resolution.[28] The statements made in the debate on that resolution, warm in their praise of the Russian initiative, reflect the apparent potential of the Council as a counterterrorism actor, even as the vestiges of the past remained (such as Malaysia's reference to the distinction between terrorism and legitimate struggles for national liberation).[29]

In sum, the Council entered the new millennium with a record of responding to terrorism that reflected the politics of the era. Under these conditions, regional and other actors were generally more effective at responding to the demand for cooperation against terrorism, which was in any case most advanced among groups of like-minded states or bilaterally.[30]

The Council as Counterterror Activist

In light of the controversies that have emerged since September 11, 2001— dissension over the war in Iraq, the excesses of the George W. Bush administration's global "war on terror," and related concern over apparent US unilateralism—it is important to remember that the US response to 9/11 gave significant prominence to multilateralism and also engendered consensus. Before Guantanamo Bay, Abu Ghraib, and the like—and before Secretary of State Colin Powell's now infamous PowerPoint presentation to the

Council about Saddam Hussein's alleged weapons of mass destruction—
there was the *Le Monde* headline "We Are All Americans." In the days after
the attacks, there were few people in Turtle Bay who believed that the
Council should not be central to a robust multilateral response. For example, in its first meeting after the attacks, on September 12, the president of
the Council, speaking in his capacity as representative of France, said:

> All together, we must say that nothing anywhere can ever justify resort to ter-
> rorism. All together, we must take the view that the monstrous acts commit-
> ted yesterday are a challenge to the international community as a whole. Yes,
> we stand with the United States in deciding upon any appropriate action to
> combat those who resort to terrorism, those who aid them and those who pro-
> tect them. A global strategy is needed. The Security Council is the principal
> organ entrusted with international peace and security. It should work on this
> in a spirit of urgency.[31]

And work urgently it did. On the day after the attacks, the Council
unanimously passed Resolution 1368, which recognized the "inherent right
of individual or collective self-defence in accordance with the Charter."
Within two weeks, the Council passed Resolution 1373, which transformed the Council as a forum for action against terrorism. Students of the
Council should read 1373 and analyze its record of implementation.
Emerging out of the unique political climate in the immediate wake of the
9/11 attacks, 1373 manifests five attributes of an activist Security Council
par excellence.

First, 1373 is broad in its scope. Drafted by the United States, the resolution consolidates and extends precedents for responding to terrorism
from across the multilateral system. For example, the operational paragraphs of 1373 give strong emphasis to measures against terrorist financing, reflecting the recently concluded Terrorist Financing Convention
(1999), which had yet to enter into force. States are called upon to become
parties to the existing international instruments, the provisions of which
appear throughout the resolution specifically (e.g., with references to explosives) and generally (by requiring states to "prevent the commission of terrorist acts"). Beyond piecing together the "piecemeal approach," 1373 also
expands the reach of multilateral counterterrorism to cover border control
measures, the issuance of identity and travel documentation, arms trafficking, and controls on weapons of mass destruction. Similarly, there is broad
language about cooperation and information-sharing in criminal investigations and in administrative and judicial matters, and the requirement to
criminalize terrorist acts. The resolution draws a link between international
terrorism and transnational organized crime, illicit drugs, money laundering, illegal arms trafficking, and illegal movements of nuclear, chemical,
biological, and related materials. Whereas the Council had wavered in the

past, 1373 defines a broad agenda, effectively providing a blueprint for counterterrorism policy at the national level.

Second, as result of being passed under Chapter VII of the Charter, 1373 *obliges* member states to act. This is no small point, given that many of the measures integrated into 1373 from elsewhere in the multilateral system were of a voluntary or nonbinding character. In addition, as the example of the Terrorist Financing Convention attests, 1373 includes measures that had not yet entered into force through treaty mechanisms. The authority of the Council is important here, as it throws into relief the labors of other organs in the multilateral system. The historical pattern of incremental progress in the development of multilateral counterterrorism measures was cast off overnight.

Third, through 1373 the Council acted to institutionalize its response. While the Council had increasingly experimented with subsidiary organs, especially in the form of sanctions committees, the Counter-Terrorism Committee (CTC, established in the resolution) achieved a lot more prominence. Resolution 1373 also created the obligation that member states report to the CTC, and experts, each with technical knowledge covering the various substantive requirements of 1373, were appointed to review the reports. Beyond this core task, by October 2001 the chair of the CTC, British permanent representative Jeremy Greenstock, had circulated a work plan that included the establishment of contact points (in member states and international organizations) with whom to liaise about implementation of the resolution; the circulation of guidance to states; the identification of "best practices," to give operational expression to the requirements of 1373; and the establishment of a role for the CTC in brokering technical assistance in support of compliance.[32] On the latter point, a November 2011 resolution underscored the Council's "determination to proceed with the implementation" of 1373 but noted that "many States will require assistance in implementing all the requirements."[33] So, beyond simply imposing requirements, the Council seemed to be putting in place mechanisms to follow through with them.

Fourth, 1373 had the effect of placing the Council at the center of the global response to terrorism, as it gave the CTC and its experts the mandate to reach out across the multilateral system. As noted earlier, many specialist and regional bodies had considered terrorism in the past. The difference is that, prior to 1373, states sought to advance counterterrorism in other multilateral forums *in spite of* the Council; after 1373, the full range of multilateral bodies were prompted to act *because of* the Council. To illustrate this, in March 2003 the CTC convened a meeting in New York that was attended by sixty-five international, regional, and subregional organizations, with follow-up meetings in Washington, D.C. (in October 2003, in cooperation with the Inter-American Committee Against Terrorism, an initiative of the Organization of American States) and Vienna (in March 2004, in cooperation with the Organization for Security and Cooperation in Europe and the UN Office on Drugs and Crime [UNODC]). Beyond the functional objective of better coordinating counterterrorism action, the ability of the Council (through the CTC) to play the role of facilitator was unprecedented.

A further example of the reach of 1373 pertains to counterterrorist financing measures. In October 2001, the world's leading anti-money-laundering body—the limited-membership Financial Action Task Force (FATF)—expanded its mandate and elaborated eight (later nine) "special recommendations" to suppress terrorist financing. The first special recommendation stated: "Countries should also immediately implement the United Nations resolutions relating to the prevention and suppression of the financing of terrorist acts, particularly United Nations Security Council Resolution 1373."[34] The role of the FATF as a standard-setter, and its mutual evaluation process, are described elsewhere; suffice it to note here that the task force is generally considered to be influential.[35] The citing of 1373 in the first special recommendation effectively meant that the FATF would be working for the Council, at least insofar as the terrorist financing aspects of 1373 were concerned. (The Council subsequently returned the favor: Resolution 1617 of 2005 strongly urges states to implement FATF standards on money laundering and terrorism financing.)

In sum, if the Council was easy to ignore on the topic of terrorism prior to 1373, after 1373 it was not. My fifth point here is that 1373 and the CTC seemed, initially at least, to have a real impact. Greenstock was effective in advancing work plans, appointing experts, and reporting to the Council. The experts made progress in reviewing member-state reports, identifying relevant "best practices," and liaising with partners and stakeholders. They initiated a matrix, compiling requests for technical assistance in implementing 1373 and endeavoring to match them with donors. A good amount of such assistance seemed to be flowing. Much was made of the fact that, by the end of May 2003, all member states had submitted at least one report to the CTC—a record that far exceeded levels of reporting to sanctions committees. This record of apparent achievement led some to observe that the Council had given rise to a "new paradigm" for the international community in responding to terrorism.[36]

This, then, is what an activist Security Council looks like. Driven by the United States and undergirded by P5 consensus, the contrast between the pre- and post-9/11 periods was like night and day. In retrospect, perhaps the most remarkable thing about 1373 is its ambition. While any rational observer at the time would have conceded that 1373 could not (and probably should not, in some cases) be implemented by the vast majority of member states, the fate of the resolution and the CTC was by no means foreordained. How long could this "new paradigm" last? To be sure, within a few years, impediments emerged. We can point to three main reasons for this.

First, as a product of the Council, 1373 lacked sufficient support from the broader UN membership. Indeed, it is enough for the Council to require member states to act in modest ways, but the intrusiveness and obligatory nature of 1373, with the prospect of being held to account by the Council, soon yielded accusations that it was acting as a legislature. After all, counterterrorism and national security are domains in which most states seek to preserve their decisionmaking autonomy. In addition to inviting unsought scrutiny, member states found the reporting regime to be burdensome. Similar reporting requirements imposed by related resolutions—the successors to 1267 (1999) and 1540 (2004) on nonproliferation—led to claims of "reporting fatigue," and that the CTC was engaged in little more than paper-shuffling. While most critics claimed that the CTC was doing too much, others made the opposite argument, noting that 1373 might have the unintended consequence of giving rise to human rights abuses in the name of counterterrorism. Therefore, critics argued, the CTC should act to preserve human rights in pursuing its mandate—a point acknowledged by Greenstock, who sought input from the UN's human rights institutions but without integrating the issue into the day-to-day work of the CTC. In these ways, it seems that ambition simply caught up with 1373 and the CTC. The membership was not ripe for a resolution like 1373. The assertive exercise of Chapter VII power cannot dissolve decades of contention about whether and how the UN should act in response to terrorism.

Second, 1373 and the CTC lacked sufficient support from within the Council itself, as members moved on to other issues and failed to nurture the broader consensus needed to maintain momentum. This is evident on the part of the United States, which did not consider—or did not care—how its divisive drive for an additional Council resolution authorizing the use of force against Iraq would impact its achievements on counterterrorism.[37] There remained relative consensus among the P5 that the Council should lead the UN's counterterrorism response. But, as an extraordinary resolution, 1373 required an extraordinary amount of political and diplomatic support, as well as resources, to enhance buy-in and implementation. This was not forthcoming.

Third, the decline in prominence of 1373 and the CTC within half a decade reflects the broader travails of the Council's counterterrorism agenda. Most notably, recall that the Council had imposed sanctions against the Taliban and al-Qaeda in 1999. Over time, these measures would attract controversy, deriving from the rapid expansion of the list of targets subject to the sanctions after 9/11 (with most names having been forwarded by Washington). Within a few years, this yielded a range of lawsuits, especially in Europe, wherein citizens took action against their own govern-ments for having their assets frozen without the opportunity to be heard. At the time, the Council had not yet devised a mechanism for listed individuals to petition for their removal from the list, while processes for adding names to the list remained permissive. Criticism of the sanctions grew steadily from within the UN system (i.e., from member states and human rights bodies) as well as from human rights advocates in civil society and acade-mia. As noted earlier, the Council's response is something of a case study in "institutional adaptation" that, to some extent, reflects the embeddedness of human rights norms within the UN system.[38] As the debate evolved (reflected in the reports of the monitoring team attached to the Council's sanctions committee), the Council introduced iterative reforms.[39] Still, against the background of human rights concerns surrounding the CTC, the Council faced a credibility problem, especially among states for whom multilateralism would have been a welcome balance to the Bush adminis-tration's global war on terror.

Under these circumstances, Greenstock's successor as CTC chair, Spanish ambassador Inocencio Arias, reported to the Council in January 2004 on "problems encountered in implementing 1373," noting that "implementation . . . is encountering serious problems, both at the [level of] States and at the [CTC]. These should be tackled in a comprehensive way due to the intimate interaction between them and the urgency of the task."[40] That frank report was followed within a month by a "proposal for the revitalization" of the CTC, which suggested reorganizing the expert staff as a "Counter-Terrorism Committee Executive Directorate" (CTED) attached to the CTC.[41] That proposal was in turn endorsed by Resolution 1535 (2004), which established the CTED. But an executive director of the CTED was not appointed until midyear, and an organizational plan did not emerge until August. With its budget dependent upon the General Assem-bly, the CTED did not become fully staffed until September 2005, and only became operational in December. Although the mandate of the CTC was expanded during this period—Resolution 1624 (2005) obliged states to prohibit incitement to terrorism—the autumn of 2005 was nothing like that of 2001 for the Security Council in regard to counterterrorism. If the immediate post-9/11 moment was politically enabling, the Council appeared to overplay its hand.

Responding to the Council's Response:
Multilateral Counterterrorism Today

The uptick in action after 9/11 provides an opportunity to observe how states and other actors within the UN system react when presented with an activist Council. The contemporary record suggests that the primary effect of the Council's assertiveness has been to prompt competing visions for multilateral counterterrorism. As the struggle over reforming the sanctions against the Taliban and al-Qaeda implies, the Council's response elicited resistance in some quarters. More generally, those seeking to temper the influence of the Council pursued cooperation in different forums. Among other states, however, there remains a demand for operational cooperation at the multilateral level, and some states have sought to leverage the Council's counterterrorism role while also advancing cooperation elsewhere, such as through the new Global Counter-Terrorism Forum (GCTF). As a result of all this forum-shopping, there is great vitality in multilateral responses to terrorism today. An activist Council has prompted active multilateralism.

For all the contention that the Council's response to terrorism has attracted over the years, it is worth recalling the extent of politicization in the General Assembly. It was there that Yasser Arafat had declared (in 1974) that the "justice of the cause determines the right to struggle," and negotiations over a Comprehensive Convention on International Terrorism had long remained deadlocked over a definition of "terrorism."[42] For this reason, passage of the UN's Global Counter-Terrorism Strategy in 2006 (annexed to Assembly Resolution 60/288 of 2006) is remarkable. The strategy contains four pillars. The second and third of these (on measures to prevent and combat terrorism, and to build states' capacities in this regard) are essentially repetitive of Council resolutions. But the first and fourth pillars (on measures to address "conditions conducive" to terrorism, and to respect human rights and the rule of law in countering terrorism) fill gaps in the Council's response. By virtue of its scope, and as a product of the Assembly, the strategy can lay claim to a broad base of legitimacy.

With that said, bringing the strategy into existence was no small feat. In 2002, Secretary-General Kofi Annan had initially elicited ideas regarding the strategic-level response of the UN system to the threat of terrorism.[43] These ideas reappeared in different forms in successive strategic documents that finally yielded the *Uniting Against Terrorism* report in April 2006, which placed the idea of a global counterterrorism strategy firmly on the agenda.[44] Later that year, following a delicate negotiation process led by Swedish foreign minister and Assembly president Jan Eliasson, the strategy emerged.[45] Despite the politicking, there is a sense in which the strategy serves everyone's interests. For the P5, the strategy could be framed as affirming the Council's mandates, without ceding the initiative to the Assembly. Regarding the latter point, while the strategy undertook to "institutionalize" the Counter-Terrorism Implementation Task Force (CTITF)—the systemwide coordination mechanism established by the Secretary-General a year earlier—within the Secretariat, no new resources would be devoted to this task. For everyone else, the strategy provided at least the possibility of qualifying the Council's role by broadening the counterterrorism agenda. For many member states, a vehicle for democratizing the UN's counterterrorism response was an overdue development.

Since the emergence of the Global Counter-Terrorism Strategy, a fundamental question among stakeholders has been how to articulate the Council and Assembly responses.[46] The CTITF was designed to achieve this, but has struggled to fulfill its coordination role (admittedly a very difficult task across thirty-one member entities in a UN system that is notoriously stovepiped). Tellingly, the position of head of the CTITF office remained vacant for some two years. All the while, the strategy has enjoyed strong support among many member states at the rhetorical level. But in practice, levels of awareness are generally low, reporting on strategy implementation is weak, and no systematic plan to advance it has been elaborated. For many, the strategy has come to symbolize "unrealized potential."[47]

As a result, the Council has endured as the ascendant counterterrorism actor in the UN system. Following the dilemmas of "revitalization," former Australian counterterrorism ambassador Mike Smith stabilized the CTED during his tenure as executive director (2007–2013). Two recent developments in the Council show its capacity for incremental innovations in dealing with terrorism. First, regarding the sanctions against the Taliban and al-Qaeda, the Council disaggregated the Taliban from al-Qaeda, creating two sanctions regimes (and two separate lists) in place of one.[48] The goal here is to facilitate reconciliation between Taliban members and the government of Afghanistan, the latter of which is given an enhanced role in interacting with the sanctions committee for the purposes of delisting reconciled individuals. Beyond updating the sanctions to reflect the possibility of Taliban reconciliation, these revisions were seen as symbolically important in supporting the Afghan government.

Second, in reacting to the interrelated crises in Libya, Mali, and the broader Sahel, the Council has shown the capacity to integrate counterterrorism into its response to regional security problems. After the Arab Spring reached Libya, the Council imposed sanctions against members of the Muammar Qaddafi regime in response to the use of force against civilians (Resolution 1970 of 2011). A raft of abstentions (from China, Russia, Brazil, Germany, and India) from a follow-up resolution (1973 of 2011) reflected discontent with the parameters of NATO's role in responding to the crisis. But the Council acted unanimously in requesting that the sanctions committee and its expert panel collaborate with the CTED and other relevant UN bodies to "assess the threats and challenges, in particular related to terrorism, posed by the proliferation of all arms and related materiel of all types, in particular man-portable surface-to-air missiles, from Libya, in the region" (Resolution 2017 of 2011, paragraph 5).[49] This creative deployment of the Council's counterterrorism assets, as it were, was further developed in response to territorial gains by armed Islamist groups in northern Mali in the first half on 2012. Resolutions 2056 (2012) and 2100 (2013) name the groups in question, noting their listing under the al-Qaeda sanctions regime that had by then been split from the Taliban sanctions regime. Resolution 2056 also requests that the Secretary-General develop an integrated strategy for the Sahel region "encompassing security, governance, development, human rights and humanitarian issues" (paragraph 28). The subsequent "United Nations integrated strategy for the Sahel" comprises a unique attempt at normative and operational integration.[50] While integrated missions for other purposes are nothing new across the UN system, this is the first time that counterterrorism has been woven into a regional-level plan to contain and prevent nonstate violence. The "integrated strategy" sets out a range of "indicative actions" for various actors in the UN system to pursue, and the UN counterterrorism-related entities—including the CTED, the CTITF, the monitoring team attached to the al-Qaeda and Taliban sanctions committees, and the UNODC—are prominent among them.

These developments suggest that, although the Global Counter-Terrorism Strategy was elaborated in the Assembly, the Council has been more inclined to act strategically on counterterrorism of late. Of course, the outcomes of these developments remain to be seen. Regarding the Taliban sanctions, the aforementioned monitoring team recently reported that the sanctions face a fundamental challenge in that the Taliban does not recognize the legitimacy of the Afghan government and views Pakistan and the United States as its key negotiating partners.[51] The sanctions, it suggests, must be better integrated with the range of other measures and actors pursuing the broader objectives of conflict resolution in Afghanistan. The security and development challenges facing the Sahel are likewise daunting. In these and other regions in crisis, of course, the Security Council is one actor among many seeking to advance the cause of peace and security. Although the Council's inaction regarding other contemporary emergencies (most notably Syria) reflects poorly on the institution, it has been more responsive in the face of evolving terrorist threats and has increasingly viewed terrorism as a part of broader security challenges.

At the same time, the Council has again been forced to share the limelight on multilateral counterterrorism recently. In a series of unusual developments, two new multilateral bodies in the same issue area were announced within three days (and a few New York City blocks) of each other in September 2011: the UN's Counter-Terrorism Centre (UNCCT) and the aforementioned GCTF. At the behest of the Saudis, the Global Counter-Terrorism Strategy had included an acknowledgment "that the question of creating an international centre to fight terrorism could be considered, as part of the international efforts to enhance the fight against terrorism" (paragraph 9 of the strategy's second pillar). The UNCCT emerged following a voluntary contribution of $10 million (over three years) from Saudi Arabia. The UNCCT is housed with the CTITF, which itself is now within the UN Secretariat's Department of Political Affairs (DPA). Governed by an advisory board (chaired by Saudi Arabia), the aim of the UNCCT is to build state capacity and international cooperation, and otherwise enhance implementation of the global strategy. In August 2013, Saudi Arabia contributed an additional $100 million (more than the annual budget of the entire DPA) to the UNCCT.[52] At the time of writing, no clear plan has been elaborated concerning how these funds will be spent, and the UNCCT's activities to date have mostly involved conferences on thematic issues emerging from the global strategy. But there is at least the potential for a center of gravity on counterterrorism to emerge within the UN but outside of the Council.

In contrast, the GCTF has wasted little time in defining its role, elaborating its agenda, and taking steps to implement it. The idea of a counterterrorism body outside the UN system had been floated occasionally over the years, to enhance practical cooperation at the multilateral level beyond what had been possible through the UN.[53] The forum endeavors to fill this gap. It comprises thirty founding member states (including the P5), a range of institutional partners (including the CTED, the Council's monitoring team attached to the al-Qaeda and Taliban sanctions committees, and the CTITF), and an administrative unit housed within the US State Department. Members and partners collaborate through thematic and regional working groups. Perhaps the forum's principal achievement has been the elaboration of declarations and memoranda. These documents duly cite UN treaties and resolutions, but they are often pitched at a more granular level (i.e., as specific "best practices") and cover emerging areas of counterterrorism practice. Regarding the latter, there is a strong emphasis—and a working group—on terrorism prevention ("countering violent extremism," or "CVE" in the contemporary parlance), alongside statements on criminal justice and the rule of law, kidnapping for ransom, community-oriented policing, the management of terrorist detainees, the rehabilitation and reintegration of terrorist offenders, and so on. Beyond articulating norms, the GCTF has yielded some institutional developments, including the establishment of a center of excellence for CVE in Abu Dhabi, a global fund for community engagement and resilience, and a planned International Institute for Justice and the Rule of Law, to be hosted in Malta.[54] Of course, there is a sense in which the existence and momentum of the GCTF attests to the ineffectiveness of the Council and the UN on this issue. As nimble as the Council has sometimes been on counterterrorism in the post-9/11 period, the forum enables like-minded states to advance cooperation far more efficiently. But on the flip side, UN bodies engender greater legitimacy than does a limited-membership organization. In this regard, initial relations between the GCTF and the UN seem to be complementary.

Within and beyond the UN, multilateral counterterrorism is now something of a crowded field, with multiple actors pursuing a range of mandates across related issue domains and levels of governance. We can surmise that many states have an interest in counterterrorism cooperation, but that they sometimes disagree about how to cooperate. The record described earlier attests to the role that the Council has played in bringing about this state of affairs. After the shock of 9/11, of course, it was always likely that international counterterrorism cooperation would increase. But the Council's intervention, in the form of Resolution 1373, triggered a series of developments that have shaped the form and substance of counterterrorism cooperation today. A pendulum analogy is tempting here: having swung in the direction of the Council, momentum on multilateral counterterrorism would inevitably move away from it. However, developments in this field are not so linear, and the willingness of states to shop for amenable forums, and to initiate new multilateral mechanisms, implies that more complex dynamics are at work. A more suitable metaphor is that of a "ripple effect," wherein the consequences of Council action have had a discernable and ongoing impact across the multilateral system as others have adapted to an activist Council.

Conclusion

Later in the passage I cited in the introduction, Claude notes: "What [international organizations] are 'supposed' to be or to do should be determined not by our wishes as to what they might be or do, but by our understanding of the possibilities that appear in the situation in which they are embedded and of the probabilities that are revealed by the patterns of utilization established by states, their ultimate owners and operators."[55] The historical "pattern of utilization" regarding the Council on counterterrorism can be briefly stated: politics constrain but sometimes enable Council action; the bold assertion of Council power will likely elicit a range of responses from states, including resistance and forum-shopping, manifesting competing visions of multilateralism. Recalling Claude again, this finding should "educate the expectations" of Council-watchers, and I expect that future debates about the limits of Council authority (legally and operationally) will be duly informed by the record on counterterrorism. As for the future of the Council as a counterterrorism actor, the broader dynamics of consensus and contestation suggest that the Council will neither become irrelevant nor be the indispensable multilateral counterterrorism organ, as had once seemed possible. Rather, among the range of stakeholders in multilateral counterterrorism today, the challenge for the Council is to define its role relative to others and to achieve a division of labor that leverages its comparative advantages without again overreaching. In this regard, decision-makers within the Council (especially the P5) and among its subsidiary organs should integrate the lessons of history as they advance the UN's counterterrorism agenda with partners inside (the CTITF and UNCCT, in particular) and outside (the GCTF) the United Nations.

Notes

1. Inis L. Claude Jr., *Swords into Plowshares: The Problems and Progress of International Organization* (New York: McGraw Hill, 1984), p. 8.

2. Edward C. Luck, "Tackling Terrorism," in *The UN Security Council: From the Cold War to the 21st Century,* edited by David M. Malone (Boulder, CO: Lynne Rienner, 2004), p. 85.

3. Ibid.

4. The former observation was made by Bob Keohane, "The Globalization of Informal Violence, Theories of World Politics, and the 'Liberalism of Fear,'" *Dialog-IO* 1, no. 1 (2002): 36; and the latter by Ken Stiles, "The Power of Procedures and the Procedures of the Powerful," *Journal of Peace Research* 43, no. 1 (2006): 38.

5. On "crucial cases," see Harry Eckstein, "Case Study and Theory in Political Science," in *Handbook of Political Science,* vol. 7, *Strategies of Inquiry,* edited by Fred I. Greenstein and Nelson W. Polsby (Reading, MA: Addison-Wesley, 1975).

6. Luck, "Tackling Terrorism," pp. 84–85.

7. See Geoffrey Marston, "Early Attempts to Suppress Terrorism: The Terrorism and International Criminal Court Conventions of 1937," *British Yearbook of International Law* 73 (2002): 293–313; Ben Saul, "The Legal Response of the League of Nations to Terrorism," *Journal of International Criminal Justice* 4, no. 1 (2006): 78–102.

8. United Nations Security Council Resolution 57, S/RES/57 (September 18, 1948).

9. United Nations Security Council Resolution 286, S/RES/286 (September 9, 1970).

10. These are listed at http://www.un.org/en/terrorism/instruments.shtml.

11. Sydney D. Bailey, "The UN Security Council and Terrorism," *International Relations* 11, no. 6 (1993): 537–538.

12. See M. J. Peterson, "Using the General Assembly," in *Terrorism and the UN: Before and After September 11,* edited by Jane Boulden and Thomas G. Weiss (Bloomington: Indiana University Press, 2004), pp. 178–181; Peter Romaniuk, *Multilateral Counterterrorism: The Global Politics of Cooperation and Contestation* (New York: Routledge, 2010).

13. United Nations Security Council Resolution 337, S/RES/337 (August 15, 1973).

14. See Bailey, "The UN Security Council and Terrorism"; Luck, "Tackling Terrorism."

15. US Department of State, "Patterns of Global Terrorism 1985," October 1986, www.higginsctc.org/patternsofglobalterrorism/1985pogt.pdf.

16. United Nations Security Council, "Note by the President of the Security Council," UN Doc. S/17554, October 9, 1985.

17. United Nations Security Council Resolution 579, S/RES/579 (December 18, 1985).

18. Luck, "Tackling Terrorism," p. 92; United Nations Security Council, "Note by the President of the Security Council," UN Doc. S/17702, December 30, 1985.

19. Bailey, "The UN Security Council and Terrorism," p. 549.

20. See United Nations Security Council Resolutions 618, S/RES/618 (July 29, 1988) and 638, S/RES/638 (July 31, 1989).

21. United Nations Security Council Resolution 635, S/RES/635 (June 14, 1989).

22. United Nations Security Council, "Note by the President of the Security Council," UN Doc S/23500, January 31, 1992.

23. For example, see David Cortright and George A. Lopez, *The Sanctions Decade: Assessing UN Strategies in the 1990s* (Boulder, CO: Lynne Rienner, 2000), pp. 120–121.

24. US Department of State, "Patterns of Global Terrorism 1996," April 1997, www.state.gov/www/global/terrorism/1996Report/overview.html.

25. United Nations Security Council, *Report of the Secretary-General Pursuant to Security Council Resolution 1070 (1996),* UN Doc. S/1996/940, November 14, 1996, paras. 13–14.

26. Rosemary Foot, "The United Nations, Counterterrorism, and Human Rights: Institutional Adaptation and Embedded Ideas," *Human Rights Quarterly* 29, no. 2 (2007): 489–514.

27. United Nations Security Council Resolution 1189, S/RES/1189 (August 13, 1998). Presidential statements on terrorism are available at www.un.org/en/terrorism/pres-statements.shtml.

28. United Nations Security Council Resolution 1269, S/RES/1269 (October 19, 1999).

29. United Nations Security Council, "Provisional Verbatim Record of the 4053rd Meeting," UN Doc. S/PV.4053, October 19, 1999.

30. Martha Crenshaw, *Terrorism and International Cooperation* (Boulder, CO: Westview, 1989).

31. United Nations Security Council, "Provisional Verbatim Record of the 4370th Meeting," UN Doc. S/PV.4370, September 12, 2001.

32. United Nations Security Council, "Letter Dated 19 October 2001 from the Chairman of the Counter-Terrorism Committee Addressed to the President of the Security Council," UN Doc. S/2001/986, October 19, 2001.

33. United Nations Security Council Resolution 1377, S/RES/1377 (November 12, 2001).

34. In February 2012, the recommendations of the Financial Action Task Force (FATF)—the "International Standards on Combating Money Laundering and the Financing of Terrorism and Proliferation"—were consolidated. See www.fatf-gafi.org/recommendations.

35. See William C. Gilmore, *Dirty Money: The Evolution of International Measures to Counter Money Laundering and the Financing of Terrorism* (Strasbourg: Council of Europe Publishing, 2011).

36. Curtis A. Ward, "Building Capacity to Combat International Terrorism: The Role of the United Nations Security Council," *Journal of Conflict Security Law* 8, no. 2 (2003): 289–305.

37. On the US position, see Eric Rosand and Sebastian von Einsiedel, "9/11, the War on Terror, and the Evolution of Multilateral Institutions," in *Cooperating for Peace and Security: Evolving Institutions and Arrangements in a Context of Changing U.S. Security Policy,* edited by Bruce D. Jones, Shepherd Forman, and Richard Gowan (New York: Cambridge University Press, 2010).

38. Foot, "The United Nations, Counterterrorism, and Human Rights."

39. The relevant reports and resolutions are available at www.un.org/sc/commit tees/1267. See also Sue Eckert's discussion of sanctions in Chapter 20 of this volume; and Thomas Gehring and Thomas Dörfler, "Division of Labor and Rule-Based Decision-Making Within the UN Security Council," *Global Governance* 19 (2013): 567–587.

40. United Nations Security Council, "Note by the President of the Security Council," UN Doc. S/2004/70, January 26, 2004, p. 15.

41. United Nations Security Council, "Letter Dated 19 February 2004 from the Chairman of the Security Council Committee Established Pursuant to Resolution 1373 (2001) Concerning Counter-Terrorism Addressed to the President of the Security Council," UN Doc. S/2004/124, February 19, 2004, www.un.org/en/sc/ctc/docs /founding/s-2004-124.pdf?m=S/2004/124.

42. For Arafat's address, see United Nations General Assembly, "Official Records of the 2282nd Plenary Meeting, Twenty-Ninth Session," UN Doc. A/PV.2282, November 13, 1974, corr. 1; M. J. Peterson, "Using the General Assembly"; Mahmoud Hmoud, "Negotiating the Draft Comprehensive Convention on International Terrorism," *Journal of International Criminal Justice* 4, no. 5 (2006): 1031–1043.

43. United Nations General Assembly and Security Council, *Report of the Policy Working Group on the United Nations and Terrorism,* UN Doc. A/57/273-S/2002/875, August 6, 2002.

44. United Nations Secretary-General, *Uniting Against Terrorism: Recommendations for a Global Counter-Terrorism Strategy,* UN Doc. A/60/825, April 27, 2006. The prior reports include: United Nations High-Level Panel on Threats, Challenges, and Change, *A More Secure World: Our Shared Responsibility,* UN Doc. A/59/565, December 2, 2004; United Nations Secretary-General, *In Larger Freedom: Towards Development, Security, and Human Rights for All,* UN Doc. A/59/2005, March 21, 2005.

45. "UN Adopts Global Counter-Terrorism Strategy," *Voice of America News,* September 8, 2006, www.voanews.com/content/a-13-2006-09-08-voa58/323408 .html.

46. See James Cockayne, Alistair Millar, David Cortright, and Peter Romaniuk, *Reshaping United Nations Counterterrorism Efforts: Blue-Sky Thinking for Global Counterterrorism Cooperation 10 Years After 9/11* (New York: Center on Global Counterterrorism Cooperation, 2012), http://globalcenter.org/wp-content/uploads /2012/07/Reshaping_UNCTEfforts_Blue-Sky-Thinking.pdf; James Cockayne, Alistair Millar, and Jason Ipe, *An Opportunity for Renewal: Revitalizing the United Nations Counterterrorism Program—An Independent Strategic Assessment* (New York: Center on Global Counterterrorism Cooperation, September 2010), www .globalcenter.org/wp-content/uploads/2012/07/Opportunity_for_Renewal_Final.pdf.

47. Cockayne, Millar, and Ipe, *An Opportunity for Renewal,* p. 43.

48. See United Nations Security Council Resolutions 1988, S/RES/1988 (June 17, 2011), and 1989, S/RES/1989 (June 17, 2011). See also Gehring and Dörfler, "Division of Labor."

49. In this regard, see United Nations Security Council, *Report of the Assessment Mission on the Impact of the Libyan Crisis on the Sahel Region,* UN Doc. S/2012/42, January 18, 2012. See also Naureen Chowdhury Fink, "Preventing Terrorism and Conflict in Libya: An Innovative Role for the United Nations?" *CTC Sentinel* 5, no. 2 (2012): 16–20 (West Point, NY: US Military Academy, Combating Terrorism Center).

50. United Nations Security Council, *Report of the Secretary-General on the Situation in the Sahel Region,* UN Doc. S/2013/354, June 14, 2013.

51. United Nations Security Council, *Second Report of the Analytical Support and Sanctions Implementation Monitoring Team Submitted Pursuant to Resolution 1988 (2011) Concerning the Taliban and Other Associated Individuals and Entities,* UN Doc. S/2012/971, December 31, 2012, paras. 11–12.

52. The DPA's regular budget for 2012–2013 was $81 million. See www.un.org /wcm/content/site/undpa/main/about/funding.

53. Alistair Millar and Eric Rosand, *Allied Against Terrorism: What's Needed to Strengthen the Worldwide Commitment* (New York: Century Foundation, 2006); Rosand and von Einsiedel, "9/11," p. 144.

54. On these developments, see the website of the Global Counter-Terrorism Forum, www.thegctf.org/web/guest/related-activities.

55. Claude, *Swords into Plowshares,* p. 16.

15

Confronting Organized Crime and Piracy

James Cockayne

ON NOVEMBER 30, 1943, FRANKLIN ROOSEVELT WAS IN TEHRAN celebrating Winston Churchill's sixty-ninth birthday with Josef Stalin. FDR gave Churchill a Persian vase, and as discussion turned to the postwar order, he passed an aide a pencil sketch of what was to become the United Nations (see Figure 15.1). The three circles represent, from left to right, the forty-member United Nations (later the General Assembly), with its socio-economic competences below it; the Executive Committee (later the Security Council); and the Four Police—the first time that the four Allied powers of World War II—the United States, the United Kingdom, the Soviet Union, and China—were represented as "police" of the postwar order.

The institutional home that emerged for these Four Police was the Security Council, with France joining the four others as a veto power in 1945. Yet the Security Council has come to act not only as a body policing order but also—as the great student of the Security Council, Thomas Franck, explained in 2002—as a kind of a "jury" enforcing international law. The Council's legal deliberations, Franck explained, are not so much like those of a "judge" rigidly enforcing the law with only passing consideration of social context and norms, but rather more like a "global jury," a group of sovereign countries appointed to assess the conduct of one of their peers, "not without feelings and biases, but whose first concern is to do the right thing by the norms under which we all live."[1] Yet something has changed since Franck made this assessment. As the Council has begun to deal with nonstate criminal activity, such as drug, diamond, mineral, and wildlife trafficking, and piracy, its deliberations suggest an approach to law enforcement that draws increasingly on domestic criminal justice discourse

299

Figure 15.1 FDR's Pencil Sketch of What the UN Might Look Like

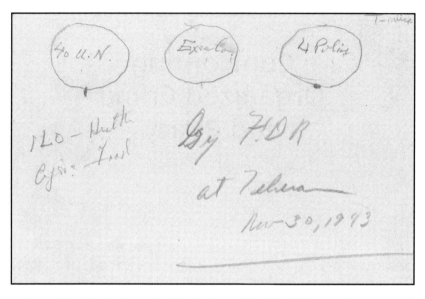

Source: Harry Hopkins Papers, Franklin D. Roosevelt Presidential Library and Museum, Hyde Park, New York, http://www.fdrlibrary.marist.edu/archives/pdfs/docsworldwar.pdf.

and techniques—including criminal investigation, trial, and punitive sanctions. The seeds of these experiments in international law enforcement were planted in the early 1990s, with action against Saddam Hussein that the United States promoted as a "police" action to enforce the "rule of law."[2] The criminal justice concepts spilled over from rhetoric into practice when the Council chose, in Resolution 687 (1991), establishing the postwar order for Iraq, to use its Chapter VII powers to create a judicial body to compensate civil damage claims. This was, as Rosalyn Higgins, later president of the International Court of Justice, said, "very, very different from anything we have expected of the Security Council before."[3] The Council soon realized that demanding investigation, criminal prosecution, and trial under Chapter VII was perhaps an even more useful, robust response short of Chapter VII military action, and used it as the basis of responses to terrorist incidents in Libya[4] and Ethiopia,[5] and to atrocities committed in the Balkans, Rwanda, Sierra Leone, Cambodia, and East Timor.[6]

The 1990s also saw Chapter VII sanctions regimes evolve away from trade embargoes imposed on whole states, and toward targeted sanctions attempting to cut off individuals and nonstate groups from financial and social participation in international society, almost like modern international outlaws. Although still—in the 1990s—framed as preventive rather than punitive measures, the Council's sanctions arrangements came increasingly to resemble the security-control orders used in some domestic criminal justice systems.[7] By 2014, the Council was no longer simply targeting criminal financing of armed groups for sanctions, but sanctioning certain business dealings with "criminal networks" themselves.[8]

Obstacles to Law Enforcement

The turn toward enforcement actions drawn from domestic criminal justice systems might be thought, therefore, to have set the Council up well to deal with the increasing threat that nonstate criminal activity has come to be seen to pose over the past two decades to international peace and security. By 2011, the UN Office on Drugs and Crime (UNODC) estimated transnational organized crime revenues at $870 billion per year, or equivalent to the sixteenth largest national economy in the world.[9] The 2005 World Summit outcome document adopted by the General Assembly expressed "grave concern at the negative effects on development, peace and security and human rights posed by transnational crime."[10] According to the 2011 report *Global Burden of Armed Violence,* of the 526,000 violent deaths in the previous year, only 55,000 could be attributed to armed conflict or terrorism; 396,000 deaths, however, were the result of intentional homicide, including interpersonal violence, gang violence, and economically motivated crime.[11] The 2011 *World Development Report* emphasized the ties between transnational crime, conflict, and conflict relapse.[12]

It is perhaps unsurprising, therefore, that the Security Council has begun to tackle criminal activity and violence related to conflicts already on its agenda. A recent survey suggests that almost three-quarters of current UN peace operations operate in environments significantly affected by organized crime. Of these, roughly half have mandates that pertain in some way to dealing with criminal activity, usually through support to host-state police institutions, small arms control, or protection of civilians. Few are mandated to tackle criminal groups directly.[13] In this chapter I explore how these mandates have emerged and been shaped, and in the process identify three obstacles that the Council has encountered.

First, sovereignty. The privilege of legally defining conduct as "criminal" and enforcing the resulting criminal law is at the heart of state sovereignty. The Council has faced stiff resistance, particularly from the developing world, when it has sought to tell states how to use their criminal justice powers. The best-known case of such resistance relates to the Council's "legislative" decision in Resolution 1373 (2001), adopted in the immediate aftermath of the attacks of September 11, 2001, imposing binding obligations on states to adopt certain domestic legislative measures to tackle terrorism, which had previously only been addressed through international treaty arrangements.[14] These legislative measures required states to criminalize certain "terrorist" conduct, and to use their law enforcement and administrative apparatus to enforce these new criminal norms. At least in that case, states largely agreed that such "terrorist" conduct was unacceptable. As we shall see, in dealing with other forms of conduct, such as trafficking, states have not always even been able to agree that it *should* be considered criminal. (The situation of trafficking in nuclear-related technology, considered in Chapter 16, was addressed by the Council through a similar "legislative" action, Resolution 1540 of 2004.) The Council has consequently faced less resistance to tackling criminal activity occurring where sovereignty is weakest: on the high seas (in dealing with piracy, long recognized as criminal under international law), in countries where the government has lost effective control over parts of its territory (most notably Afghanistan, the Central African Republic, the Democratic Republic of the Congo, Haiti, and Somalia), or in small countries of limited strategic interest to the great powers (such as Guinea-Bissau).

The second obstacle is limited access to law enforcement and judicial resources. Criminal violence flourishes where state capacity is weak. So in tackling such violence, the Security Council has had to look elsewhere for the resources to enforce its decisions. As we shall see, effective resources have not always proven easy to identify. States are reluctant to send their police abroad, and even when they have chosen to do so, police forces are traditionally not—unlike military forces—set up for foreign deployment. Transnational criminal networks are. So the Council's law enforcement forays have often found themselves outgunned. In West Africa, for example, some analysts put the profits from drug trafficking in some countries as being at GDP level.[15] Meanwhile, the UN's interagency response vehicle for building local transnational crime units, the West Africa Coast Initiative, has operated on small fractions of those sums.

The Council's efforts to fill the resulting resource and capacity gap have taken four forms. Most common, the Council has simply set down primary rules of conduct, and left it to other international actors to enforce these rules through their own military, criminal justice, customs, and financial enforcement systems, and through assistance to the affected state (including through the UNODC), in a *decentralized* fashion. In a second set of cases, notably relating to piracy, the Council has authorized *collective* enforcement of international law: using states' law enforcement, military, and judicial capacity, but still leaving it to states to coordinate the use of that capacity among themselves. In a third set of cases, including the DRC, Haiti, Kosovo, and Lebanon, the Council has experimented with the development of capacities for *direct* law enforcement: using UN personnel to investigate, analyze, police, try, and in some cases use military force (in peace operations) against criminal activity. And finally, in rare but increasingly frequent cases, especially relating to resource trafficking, the Council has also moved toward a *regulatory* approach. Here it prescribes not only primary rules of conduct, but also secondary rules about how nonstate actors, including business actors, must implement those primary rules, especially through "due diligence" in doing business with specific actors (e.g., in the DRC and Eritrea).

The third obstacle the Council has encountered in its experiments in international law enforcement is due process. As Franck recognized, the members of the Council are not "bound by the precise scruples underpinning the objectivity of judges"—or even modern criminal trial juries.[16] Yet the growing reliance on criminal justice *discourse* has increased international society's expectations that the Council's decisionmaking will meet modern expectations of criminal justice *practice.* Accordingly, as I explore later, the steps taken by states acting under Council Chapter VII authorization to police criminal activity—from terrorism to piracy—are increasingly being tested by state and regional courts against international due process, fair trial, and human rights standards. In some cases, such as the international response to piracy off Somalia, this has posed a major obstacle to the development of an effective law enforcement response to a significant criminal activity.

Organized Crime and Trafficking

Starting during the Cold War, UN Secretaries-General drew attention to specific trafficking issues relating to conflict situations already on the Council's agenda. For twenty years, UN peace operations in the Balkans, Central America, the DRC, Haiti, Somalia, and West Africa have all wrestled quietly with the impacts of criminal groups on conflict and peace processes.[17] Starting in the late 1990s, individual Council members also began warning of the threats posed by drug trafficking in Angola, Bosnia and Herzegovina, the DRC, Haiti, Iraq, Kosovo, Lebanon, Myanmar, and Somalia.[18]

It was the link between drug trafficking and terrorism, however, that moved the issue up the Council's agenda. Following the East Africa embassy bombings of 1998, and building on the approach used in dealing with terrorism in Libya and Sudan, Resolution 1267 (1999) demanded that the Taliban "cooperate with efforts to bring indicted terrorists [i.e., Osama bin Laden] to justice." The further measures imposed to encourage compliance by Resolution 1333 (2000), developed by the United States and Russia, included a ban on the sale of acetic anhydride, a heroin precursor, to Afghanistan, and a demand that the Taliban eliminate all illicit cultivation of the opium poppy.[19] The constraints this law enforcement approach potentially imposed on peace negotiations with the Taliban immediately attracted criticism from Secretary-General Kofi Annan.[20] That tension between impartial enforcement of the law and the bargaining sometimes required in keeping the peace remains present to this day in the Council's responses to organized crime and trafficking, for example in dealing with drug-trafficking political and military actors in Guinea-Bissau.

When the Council adopted Resolution 1373 (2001), which for the first time required all member states to domestically criminalize a certain form of conduct (terrorism), the Council retained the conceptual link between terrorism and organized crime developed in dealing with Afghanistan, describing the mixture of terrorist and criminal activities as a "serious challenge and threat to international security."[21] The counterterrorism bodies entrusted by the Council with implementation of Resolution 1373 (2001) have since routinely treated the potential links between terrorism and organized crime as falling within their purview; the UN Counter-Terrorism Executive Directorate, for example, has worked with states to build their border-management capacities and their criminal justice capacity to tackle money laundering.

Beginning in 2004, a "crescendo" of reporting from UNODC and the UN Office for West Africa (UNOWA) sounded the alarm regarding the corrupting influence the drug trade was having on West African political and security institutions.[22] Colombian and Venezuelan cocaine-trafficking networks had been building new routes to the European market through West Africa. The Council began to consider whether drug trafficking and organized crime might, in and of themselves, constitute threats to international peace and security—without any specific link to terrorism.[23] Between 2007 and 2009, the Council adopted a series of presidential statements and resolutions tasking UN bodies in the region with assisting local actors to tackle organized crime, ultimately describing it as a "threat to international peace and security"—absent any requirement of a demonstrated link to terrorism.[24] The Council then began to import the language developed in the West African context into commentary on the impact of drug trafficking on other situations on its agenda, notably Afghanistan and Haiti.[25] In presidential statements in late 2009 and early 2010, the Council committed for the first time to addressing the "world drug problem," not only through supply-side controls but through "common and shared responsibility"—code in drug-control circles for more holistic policies encompassing demand control, as well as eradication and supply controls. It also invited the Secretary-General to consider mainstreaming the issue of drug trafficking as a factor in conflict prevention strategies, conflict analysis, integrated mission assessment and planning, and peacebuilding support.[26]

The Sovereignty Obstacle

Chinese representatives were first to press the point that the Council's consideration of organized crime and trafficking should be limited to countries in conflict or postconflict situations, or at most to conflict prevention situations.[27] This gentle pushback became more robust, however, when the US delegation instigated an open debate in April 2012 titled "Threats to International Peace and Security: Securing Borders Against Illicit Flows."[28] The US representation argued that the Council should not address different forms of commodity trafficking in piecemeal fashion, but instead focus on efforts to strengthen national borders to deal with all trafficking.[29] China responded bluntly that "border management falls within the sovereignty of Member States," and that the Council should "avoid duplication of labor and disrupting the functions of other United Nations bodies."[30] Other member states clearly felt similarly. The Egyptian chair of the New York caucus of the Non-Aligned Movement wrote an open letter to the Council criticizing it for holding the debate and encroaching on state sovereignty.[31] During the Council debate, the Pakistani, Indian, and Cuban delegates all spoke loudly against the Council, engaging with the issue on these terms.[32] Australia, Germany, the UK, the EU, and the Secretary-General cautioned that hardening borders should not come at the expense of trade, migration, and development.[33]

Despite the differences within the Council, the United States was able to steer through a presidential statement requesting a "comprehensive survey and assessment of the UN's work" to assist states in countering illicit cross-border trafficking and movement.[34] Understanding the limits of the membership's appetite for Council activism in this area, the resulting report by the Secretary-General cautiously mapped the roles of twenty UN entities and three non-UN bodies—the International Organization for Migration (IOM), the World Customs Organization (WCO), and the International Criminal Police Organization (Interpol), without suggesting new major initiatives.[35] The role of the UN is explicitly envisaged as one of coordination and technical assistance to states—squarely within the paradigm of "decentralized" law enforcement. In that vein, the Secretary-General has established the internal Task Force on Transitional Organized Crime and Drug Trafficking, co-led by the UNODC and the UN's Department of Political Affairs, to coordinate UN action in these areas—primarily through assistance to states.[36]

Experiments with Private Enforcement

The enforcement of international counternarcotics prohibitions falls to states. The role of legitimate business is marginal, except perhaps in the area of anti–money laundering. But in some cases the Security Council has found that conflict actors and criminal networks have profited from trading licit goods, and has sought to create leverage over conflict actors by using sanctions mechanisms to prohibit trading of these goods with actors in a conflict area. In some of those cases, the Council has begun to experiment with an approach to law enforcement that draws on the informal enforcement power of private actors, notably commercial enterprises.

The trend began with the Council's attempts to constrain financing of the National Union for the Total Independence of Angola (UNITA) through trade in so-called conflict diamonds in the 1990s, which also found application in some West African conflicts of the period. These efforts led to the creation of the Kimberley Process Certification Scheme, intended to reduce illicit trade in diamonds through cooperation between states and the private sector, which the Council endorsed in 2003.[37] A decade later, the Council continues to look to the Kimberley Process as a partner in constraining conflict actors.[38]

Two years after its endorsement of the Kimberley Process, the Council—acting under Chapter VII—strongly urged member states to implement the "comprehensive, international standards" embodied in the Financial Action Task Force's recommendations on money laundering, designed to filter dirty money out of financial markets and prevent terrorist financing. The FATF's recommendations, while generated by an intergovernmental body, operate through due diligence carried out by private financial institutions.[39]

In November 2010, the Council went a step further, having one of its own creations generate guidance for private business actors, when it adopted "due diligence guidelines" prepared at its request by a group of experts monitoring implementation of sanctions on the DRC. These were intended to "mitigate the risk" of conflict in the eastern DRC arising from the provision of direct or indirect support to illegal armed groups, sanctions busters, and "criminal networks and perpetrators of serious violations of international humanitarian law and human rights abuses, including those within the national armed forces."[40] The Council indicated that sanctions could be imposed against any entity—meaning, including businesses—that failed to exercise due diligence in accordance with these guidelines. Soon after, these guidelines were given additional force when the US Congress adopted the Dodd-Frank Act, requiring industries to remove DRC suppliers from their supply chain.

The next year, in 2011, the Council adopted a similar due diligence scheme to remove Eritrean extractive enterprises from global supply chains, and extended the regime to the provision of financial services, including insurance and reinsurance, that would facilitate investment in the Eritrean extractive sector.[41] A subsequent 2012 resolution recognized that the "commerce" in charcoal through al-Shabaab–controlled areas of Somalia "may pose a threat to the peace, security, or stability of Somalia," and authorized a sanctions committee to impose targeted sanctions against "individuals *and entities* [i.e., charcoal-importing businesses in the Arabian Gulf] engaged in such commerce."[42] The resolutions of 2014 took a similar approach to entities involved in illicit trade in wildlife in the Central African Republic and the DRC.[43]

This is new ground for the Council. The emphasis on private business actors as implementers of international norms moves away from a "criminal justice" approach, and toward a more "regulatory" mode of enforcing international law.[44] The Council has moved from prescribing primary rules of conduct for states, to also prescribing primary rules of conduct for private business. These "guidelines" are strongly suggestive of secondary rules for states: rules about how they should themselves regulate business.

Experiments with Direct Enforcement

To date, Council experimentation with more direct UN involvement in enforcement has emerged along two main lines: fact-finding, and executive policing and military action.

Fact-Finding

The Council has charged a range of different bodies with fact-finding on specific trafficking and related criminal activities. Through their monitoring and reporting activities, panels of experts have sometimes played a prominent role in helping the Council understand and even adjust sanctions regimes to address criminal trafficking. This has included illicit gem and mineral trafficking in Angola, the Central African Republic, the eastern DRC, Eritrea, Liberia, and Sierra Leone; the illicit charcoal trade between Somalia and the Arabian Gulf; North Korean smuggling activities (including drug trafficking); and wildlife trafficking in the Central African Republic and the DRC. Yet the Council faces two challenges in further developing this tool.

First, due process. The more these processes begin to resemble judicial fact-finding mechanisms, the higher the probability that members of these panels and commissions will be sued for libel or defamation, or that the sanctions based on their investigations will be challenged on human rights grounds. This is not an abstract proposition. The report of a panel of inquiry established by the Secretary-General, at the request of the Security Council, to examine a massacre in Liberia in 1993, never saw the light of day, because of concerns about the reliability of its conclusions and the risks of defamation liability.[45] The publication of a report by a panel established in 2000 to deal with the exploitation of natural resources in the DRC aroused similar controversy.[46] And 2012 reporting by an expert group on Somalia suggesting governmental corruption also generated threats of litigation.[47]

Interestingly, fact-finding mechanisms dealing with criminal trafficking have not become nearly as professionalized as those dealing with atrocity crimes. Two decades of operation of international war crimes tribunals have created an influential epistemic community of lawyers and judges, who have had a dramatic influence on the way the UN system handles atrocity crimes. That community has successfully pushed for the articulation of UN investigation methods to serve both human rights bodies and war crimes tribunals.[48] It has created a "shadow" criminal trial, when the Council has backed atrocity investigations (for example in dealing with Darfur and terrorist bombings in Lebanon).[49] And its efforts have led to constraints on the Council's conflict management discretion that preclude the UN supporting offers of amnesty for war crimes. The absence of similar outcomes for dealing with economically linked transnational criminal activity may be said to be the result of the absence of any similarly professionalized community or institutionalized forces. As I have explored elsewhere, there are signs that the continuing lack of clarity about which criminal trafficking can legitimately be internationally amnestied may create instability in peace agreements where, as in Colombia, nonstate armed groups are deeply involved in organized crime.[50]

In fact, this international "trial" lobby's influence has even, on two occasions, extended into the area of organized crime broadly writ. First, in dealing with piracy, the Council has—as we shall see—considered a wide range of law enforcement solutions before ultimately, with input from the "international criminal justice" community, creating an international criminal trial process. Second, there is a case in which the international community has supported an internationalized criminal trial process to deal with organized crime groups: the International Commission Against Impunity in Guatemala (CICIG). But this had no Security Council involvement; it was supported entirely by the UN Secretariat.[51]

But the international community has previously considered broadening international trial mechanisms to cover some organized crime. The proposal in 1989 from Trinidad and Tobago that eventually led to the creation of the International Criminal Court contemplated the creation of a world drug-trafficking court. Trinidad tried to revive the idea in 2009 by having the crime of "drug trafficking" added to the ICC's Rome Statute. The idea was again picked up by several Council members at a Council retreat in 2011.[52] But further action on this idea seems unlikely in the near future, not least because of questions of cost, and ICC subject-matter jurisdiction.[53] Still, some organized criminal activity, such as human trafficking, may in some circumstances already fall within the Rome Statute.[54]

A second factor constraining the Council's use of fact-finding bodies to deal with criminal activity is the question of sovereignty. This is particularly acute in dealing with criminal networks—since it is not unheard of for government actors to participate in those networks, as the Council's recent sanctions on Guinea-Bissau officials make clear.[55] Its earlier resolutions dealing with resource trafficking in the eastern DRC likewise recognize the penetration of criminal networks into the Congolese armed forces.[56] Investigating criminal networks within government may threaten host-state consent and imperil UN staff safety. One can speculate that such reasoning may have influenced the Council's recent decision to ignore the Secretary-General's request to create a panel of experts to "investigate the identity and activities of those involved in transnational and organized crime in Mali and the subregion, with the possibility of imposing punitive, targeted sanctions."[57] Interestingly, however, the Council did subsequently impose sanctions on individuals and entities "providing support for armed groups or criminal networks" through trafficking of resources, including wildlife, in the Central African Republic—despite the presence in the country of a UN peacebuilding mission (BINUCA).[58]

Executive Policing and Military Action

Another area of Council experimentation with direct enforcement against organized crime is in executive policing and military action by peacekeeping forces. Such action has happened more by accident than design. The UN Mission in Kosovo (UNMIK), in particular, found itself dealing with criminal networks in the local police, judicial, and procurement institutions.[59] But since executive policing mandates are today comparatively rare, this area of practice has not grown significantly. Closely related, however, is the emerging question of military action by UN peace operations against organized crime groups. By far the most robust and successful action was taken by MINUSTAH against gangs in the *bidonvilles* of Haiti in 2007.[60] Operations by the Force Intervention Brigade charged by the Security Council with neutralizing M23, an armed group in the eastern DRC that was involved in illicit resource trafficking, were, at the time of writing, also viewed as relatively successful. Interestingly, they were led by the same Brazilian force commander as were the operations in Haiti. MINUSMA, in Mali, has however so far not been tasked with taking executive action against criminal networks in that country, despite acknowledgments by the Council of the relevance of trafficking to MINUSMA's broader stabilization role.

Some questions similar to those of executive policing and military action against criminal targets have arisen in the context of targeted sanctions. In the case of the sanctions lists for the Taliban and al-Qaeda, the Council's use of delisting as an incentive to encourage peace talks has laid bare that the original listing was politically motivated, rather than an exercise in justice. This may be no surprise to close observers of the Council, but the use of criminal justice machinery to implement the sanctions regime at the national level has led to expectations among the public—and in some judicial quarters—that listing and delisting meets judicial standards.

The line between politics and justice has arguably become even more blurred in the case of Guinea-Bissau. There the Security Council has listed political and military leaders for unconstitutional behavior. But the alleged involvement of some of those targets in drug trafficking (to which the Council has explicitly referred), the arrest of some of the targets by the US Drug Enforcement Administration, and the Council's own description of the sanctions as "punitive" raise a basic normative question, with real practical consequences. Are these sanctions intended to facilitate criminal justice, or just to create political leverage?

The larger question here is in which cases the Council will act as a jury, finding that the demands of justice should be tempered by political considerations, and in which cases will it act more like a judge, treating these actors not as partners for peace, but as targets for law enforcement—even military action. Such decisions go to the heart of the Council's political discretion. But the more it adopts the language of "criminal justice," the more it creates expectations that it will not act politically, but judicially—ignoring political exigencies and dealing out similar punishments to all who violate given legal norms. Its failure to ensure effective punitive action against those it has labeled as suspected criminals and even subjected to the criminal trial process—such as Sudanese president Omar al-Bashir—risks steadily eroding its legitimacy in the court of public opinion.

Piracy

The trajectory of the Security Council's response to maritime piracy has in many ways mirrored that relating to organized crime and trafficking. In both cases, the issue came onto the Council's agenda through conflict situations already there, with African situations figuring prominently. Over time, the criminal activity in question came to be considered a threat first to regional stability, and then to international peace and security in its own right. And ultimately, the Council decided to consider each issue in global context, through open, thematic debate.

The Somali piracy problem differed, however, from the Council's handling of organized crime and drug trafficking in four key respects. First, the legal definition of piracy as a crime in international law is clear and universally accepted, as is the right of every state to try and punish pirates. The same was not the case for "trafficking" or organized crime. Second, piracy involves conduct on the high seas, where the "sovereignty obstacle" to Council involvement was weak. To the extent that Somali piracy occurred on land, it has been characterized primarily as occurring within Somalia—at the time a collapsed state with a weak government whose consent could relatively easily be solicited by members of the Council. Sovereignty poses a clearer obstacle to Council action in dealing with many other terrestrial criminal activities—arguably including those aspects of piracy conspiracies that occur within stronger states, such as the organization of piracy ransom payments. Third, Somali piracy imposed direct, significant economic costs on the five permanent members of the Security Council, which few other criminal activities have. (The exceptions, perhaps, being drug trafficking and terrorism—which have been the other objects of significant Council attention.) And fourth, there were few incentives for the Non-Aligned Movement to object to Council action on piracy, unlike with other criminal activities. On the contrary, some NAM members—notably India—have found in the piracy issue an opportunity for strategic power projection, through participation in multilateral maritime enforcement activity in the Indian Ocean.

But the Council has, in a sense, also been a victim of its own success in this effort. In "solving" the piracy problem (a questionable conclusion itself, as we shall see), it has identified another: the absence of effective judicial capacity to enforce counter-piracy norms in accordance with global due process standards.

Experiments with Collective Enforcement

While Somalia has been on the agenda of the Security Council for two decades, it is only in the past decade that piracy has emerged onto the inter-national agenda. The collapse of central authority in Somalia in the 1990s led to the rise of local militias, some of whom graduated from protection of fishery stocks to the hijacking and ransoming of vessels passing through the major shipping lanes in the Gulf of Aden. By 2011 the costs of Somali piracy had reached $7 billion.[61]

Absent Council involvement, international law limited member states' rights of arrest of piracy suspects to the high seas. Under customary inter-national law and the 1982 UN Convention on the Law of the Sea, the polic-ing of armed robbery against ships within territorial waters, and the polic-ing of terrestrial involvement in piracy, are the responsibility of the territorial state. Yet Somalia, where most of the preparation and hostage-holding took place, lacked the necessary law enforcement and judicial capacity to bring its pirates to justice—the whole reason the issue was on the Council's agenda in the first place.[62] There was a lacuna, which the pirates were profitably exploiting.

The Council responded in June 2008, authorizing member states' use of force within Somalia's territorial waters (later extended also to Somalia's land territory).[63] It had learned lessons from its earlier experiences dealing with terrorism, taking several steps aimed "at fending off possible criticism

[for] acting as a 'legislator,'" including obtaining explicit Somali government consent, ensuring that the resolution did not radically alter international law (for example by specifically protecting existing third-party rights of innocent passage), and limiting the scope of the authorization in time and space.[64]

In contrast to their critical response to the Council's counterterrorism efforts in Resolution 1373 (2001), member states responded enthusiastically. Numerous multilateral naval operations were initiated: the EU's Operation Atalanta, two NATO operations (Allied Protector and Ocean Shield), a separate maritime task force (CTF 151) involving both NATO and non-NATO states (including Australia, New Zealand, Pakistan, the Republic of Korea, Singapore, Turkey, and Thailand), as well as operations by China, India, Iran, Japan, Malaysia, and Russia.[65] All of this activity required operational coordination, so in January 2009 member states set up the Contact Group on Piracy off the Coast of Somalia (CGPCS) outside the UN system, which was soon endorsed by the Council.[66] It is open to states, international organizations, and the private sector, and operates through five working groups, dealing with: (1) military coordination and regional maritime capacity development; (2) legal issues; (3) commercial shipping self-awareness and self-protection, including through promulgating best management practices and the Djibouti Code of Conduct; (4) public communications; and (5) efforts to identify and disrupt the financial networks of pirate leaders and their financiers.

The CGPCS has both similarities and differences to the Council's approach taken to other forms of organized crime. The involvement of private sector actors (such as shipping associations) in both the development and the implementation of CGPCS norms does echo the "private enforcement" approach developed by the Council in the resource-trafficking context. But whereas enforcement against most organized crime is decentralized, the CGPCS regime provides a coordination mechanism for collective enforcement. The UN Convention Against Transnational Organized Crime (a General Assembly legal instrument) creates no system similar to the CGPCS for collective decisionmaking about the strategic allocation of resources to fight organized crime. As commentators have pointed out, that is a central weakness in the global enforcement of international criminal law.[67] The CGPCS also develops secondary regulatory norms, such as the Djibouti Code of Conduct, designed to coordinate how different international actors (state and nonstate) implement the primary rules of conduct created by the Security Council. This somewhat resembles the approach taken by the Council in tasking expert bodies to develop "due diligence" guidelines to tackle illicit resource trafficking.

Still, as the Council learned, while the CGPCS has helped address problems of coordination, it cannot solve another problem that confronts the Council in its efforts to enforce international law: the limited supply of effective judicial capacity. In fact, the more the problems of coordination in naval interdiction were overcome, the more the problem of limited effective judicial capacity was revealed.

The Due Process Obstacle

It is one thing to authorize state navies to police international law far from home. It is quite another to ensure that those navies undertake these unaccustomed policing roles in a manner that meets the due process expectations of their home-state courts and regional human rights institutions.

States quickly began to treat the counter-piracy regime more as a basis for naval patrols in the Indian Ocean and Gulf of Aden than as a basis for arrest and prosecution of pirates. A Danish ship that captured ten pirates off Somalia in September 2008 let them loose on a Somali beach.[68] The British Foreign Office warned its military not to detain pirates, because of the cost and risk of violating international law.[69] By 2011, the US Congressional Research Service found that 90 percent of all pirates being detained off Somalia were not being brought to trial.[70]

The Council, and the CGPCS, recognized this problem and responded by trying to address the judicial capacity deficit. Resolution 1846 (2008) encouraged states to work together to build effective criminal justice capacity in the region.[71] The focus was on Kenya and the Seychelles, with legal arrangements put in place for detaining powers to transfer suspected pirates to those countries for trial,[72] but by mid-2010 there were also reports of pirates being handed over to Somali, Puntland, and Yemeni authorities, and discussions of prosecution arrangements between the EU and Mauritius, Mozambique, South Africa, Tanzania, and Uganda.

Building effective judicial capacity—and thus deterrence—was always going to take time. In the meantime, attacks rose, from 293 in 2008 to 406 in 2009, and the attack area expanded out into the Indian Ocean as pirates invested the proceeds of successful ransoms in larger, faster ships. In fact, the judicial capacity deficit was not shrinking, but growing. In 2009, the Kenyan high court found that Kenyan courts did not have jurisdiction to try piracy cases.[73] In 2010, a Dutch court found that pirates had spent so long aboard a ship while being transferred back to the Netherlands for trial that the standards set by the European Court of Human Rights for detention and trial had been violated.[74] And in November 2011, a court in Cologne ruled that Germany had violated the prohibition on torture and inhuman and degrading treatment (Article 3 of the European Convention on Human Rights, and Article 7 of the International Covenant on Civil and Political Rights) by transferring Somali pirates to Kenya.[75]

The Council began to consider whether it might need to create a specialized international piracy court to deal with the capacity deficit. Resolution 1918 (2010) asked the Secretary-General to report on the options, including mixed special chambers (like those used to try war crimes suspects in Bosnia and Cambodia), a regional tribunal, or an international tribunal.[76] In early 2011, former French foreign minister Jack Lang, appointed as a UN special adviser on the issue, recommended a Somalia-based solution: strengthened legislation and detention capacity, and the creation of a Somali extraterritorial jurisdiction court in Arusha, in Tanzania, later to be transferred to Mogadishu (similar to the Scottish court in the Netherlands that had ultimately tried the Lockerbie suspects), with two further special courts in Puntland and Somaliland.[77] Further investigation, however, identified significant legal, constitutional, human resources, and resourcing complications, and the Council's interest waned.[78] The idea of establishing specialized piracy courts within national jurisdictions, in contrast, has slowly gained favor.[79] Yet donors remain concerned about funding options. But the Council has encouraged the shipping industry to pay for effective judicial capacity in the region[80]—though to little effect. And local states see the emphasis on piracy chambers as potentially diverting resources from other domestic judicial needs, with no guarantee that such chambers would in fact be "full."[81]

Lessons Learned?

The question of where pirates should be tried began to appear moot, however, when piracy attacks began to decline significantly. In late April 2013 the US chair of the CGPCS effectively declared victory over Somali piracy, indicating that steps taken by the CGPCS—naval interdiction, increased ship security, detention, trial, and severe sentences—had so "de-glamorized" piracy in Somalia that the industry was collapsing.[82]

Certainly the CGPCS regime had generated a lot of enforcement activity. By 2011 there were over a thousand Somali piracy suspects detained in countries from Belgium to Yemen, from the United States to Malaysia.[83] But there are reasons to doubt that this decline is the result of a successful strategy of deterrence. As we have seen, most pirates are in fact not tried; they are released, for reasons of cost and legal constraints. There is no hard evidence that the factors cited by the chair of the CGPCS have indeed influenced the decisionmaking of Somali pirates. Moreover, the decline in attacks can also be explained by very different factors. International data make clear that the ransom obtained from each successful pirate attack rose steadily from an average of $600,000 per vessel in 2007 to $4.7 million per vessel in 2011.[84] There may simply be fewer attacks now because fewer are needed to sustain the piracy work force and their supporters and investors. And improvements in the economic and security situation within Somalia must also be considered: piracy recruits may now have safer, more attractive livelihood options on land.

Yet some actors in the Council seem to see the "success" of the Somali piracy response as a model for action against piracy in other regions. Piracy in the Gulf of Guinea has risen steadily in recent years: in 2010 there were forty-five attacks; in 2011, sixty-four.[85] In October 2011, the Council called for strengthened regional cooperation and welcomed an assessment mission by the UN Secretariat to recommend further steps. That mission warned, the following January, of "catastrophic" consequences of inaction.[86] In February the Council called on states to increase collective enforcement actions such as joint naval patrols, and regional law enforcement, with the UN playing a facilitative role. As the deputy secretary-general made clear later that year, the UN's response to piracy in the Gulf of Guinea specifically sought to "rely on the lessons learned from Somalia."[87]

Yet there are reasons to think that differences in the political contexts of Somalia and the Gulf of Guinea may limit the transferability of the Somali piracy-response model. In the Somali context, the transitional federal government was unable to control piracy, and consented to the Council authorizing collective enforcement action. In contrast, in the Gulf of Guinea context, the 2011 UN assessment mission heard from some interlocutors that there were "possible political motivations for some of the pirate attacks that may seek to use piracy as a weapon to affect political developments in specific regional States."[88] This was a reference to Nigeria. Piracy may be the latest manifestation of a deeply entrenched and criminalized war economy in the Niger Delta. Nigeria seems much less likely to support international involvement in responding to piracy than was Somalia.

On November 19, 2012, the Council held its first open debate on piracy as a global threat to international peace and security, notably instigated by a leading NAM country, India.[89] India's strong concern about piracy is not surprising: much of its trade passes through the Gulf of Aden, its nationals constitute 7 percent of the world's seafarers, and Indian nationals are the second largest group of Somali piracy hostages (after Filipinos).[90] Some speakers in this debate, notably the British permanent representative, recognized that piracy "is organized crime" thriving "in places where the rule of law is weak or has broken down."[91]

The British representative clearly had in mind the waters off Somalia and in the Gulf of Guinea. Other countries might point, however, to the London offices of the private security companies, shipping agents, and financial houses that participate in the payment of piracy ransoms. The Council has condemned the payment of such ransoms, but taken few operational steps to force states to enforce that condemnation.[92] The Council has contemplated the creation of an anti-piracy court with jurisdiction over "anyone who . . . intentionally facilitates piracy operations, including key figures of criminal networks involved in piracy who illicitly plan, organize, facilitate, or finance and profit from such attacks."[93] And France and Russia have both called for sanctions against such individuals.[94] Yet the shadow of the British veto is such that any such exercise of enforcement powers seems unlikely to follow such networks into British jurisdiction. Ultimately, exactly what constitutes "piracy" may not be so clearly agreed as the members of the Council had thought. Powerful states seem likely to be reluctant to allow the Council to have the last word on that question, demonstrating the enduring obstacle posed by sovereignty to the Council's involvement in international law enforcement.

Conclusion

The Security Council's approach to organized crime, trafficking, and piracy has drawn it into a variety of law enforcement experiments. The Council has moved furthest, fastest, where the criminal activity in question threatened P5 interests, the country was already on the Council's agenda, and no state with influence in the Council had a particular reason to limit such experimentation. The cases that have exhibited these traits so far have been drug trafficking in Afghanistan and Guinea-Bissau, piracy off the coast of Somalia, mineral trafficking from the DRC and Eritrea, and, most recently, wildlife trafficking in central Africa.

The sovereignty and resource obstacles have been particular drivers of Council experimentation. The limited willingness or capacity of states to deliver effective international law enforcement resources has forced the Council to look for alternative solutions, including creating international criminal justice mechanisms and, increasingly, encouraging the involvement of private sector actors. The "regulatory" approach that may be emerging, using outside expertise to help develop norms to be enforced following Council endorsement, offers an important supplement to the Council's repertoire, but also raises a series of questions around participation and voice in the development of these norms.

The Council also continues to struggle with integrating this "law enforcement" approach with a conflict management approach. This is a result of the "due process" obstacle thrown up by attempting to import criminal justice techniques from the domestic to the international plane. The Council's absolute political discretion is hard to reconcile with visions of "rule of law" born within the context of the *Rechtsstaat,* in which executive action is subject to judicial review and constrained by individual rights. The use of criminal justice discourse and techniques has created expectations that those treated as outlaws will be brought to justice; yet the

Council ultimately prefers, in some cases such as Afghanistan and Guinea-Bissau, to treat these actors not as targets for law enforcement, but as partners for peace. However politically wise, this risks creating perceptions of unequal treatment before the law among those whose expectations of justice have been stoked by Council rhetoric.

The simple reality is that the Security Council is a political body, not a forum for justice. It does not treat like cases alike. It may conclude that some instances of violence warrant not punishment, but conflict resolution, whether because of the traits of the case, or because of its own limited access to effective law enforcement capacity. In making such choices, the Council works not just like a "jury" of peers, with room for "feelings and biases," but—perhaps as FDR envisaged seven decades ago—like a community police force, exercising considerable operational and tactical discretion. The danger for the Council is that over time, an overreliance on criminal justice discourse may create a dangerous gap between its practice and public expectations of the Council as an enforcer of the international rule of law. An adjustment of rhetoric—and possibly also of practice—may be warranted.

Notes

1. Thomas M. Franck, *Recourse to Force: State Action Against Threats and Armed Attacks* (Cambridge: Cambridge University Press, 2002), pp. 186–187.

2. David M. Malone, *The International Struggle over Iraq: Politics in the UN Security Council, 1980–2005* (Oxford: Oxford University Press, 2006), pp. 67–68.

3. Rosalyn Higgins, *Problems and Process: International Law and How We Use It* (Oxford: Oxford University Press, 1994), p. 184.

4. See United Nations Security Council Resolutions 731, S/RES/731 (January 21, 1992); 748, S/RES/748 (March 21, 1992); 883, S/RES/883 (November 11, 1993); and 1192, S/RES/1192 (August 27, 1998). See also Michael Plachta, "The Lockerbie Case: The Role of the Security Council in Enforcing the Principle Aut Dedere Aut Judicare," *European Journal of International Law* 12 (2001): 125–140.

5. United Nations Security Council Resolutions 1044, S/RES/1044 (January 31, 1996); 1054, S/RES/1054 (April 26, 1996); and 1070, S/RES/1070 (August 16, 1996).

6. In creating or supporting the International Criminal Tribunal for the Former Yugoslavia, the International Criminal Tribunal for Rwanda, the Special Court for Sierra Leone, the Extraordinary Chambers in the Courts of Cambodia, and the Special Panels for Serious Crimes in East Timor.

7. James Cockayne, "Unintended Justice," in *International and Comparative Criminal Justice and Urban Governance: Convergence and Divergence in Global, National, and Local Settings,* edited by Adam Crawford (Cambridge: Cambridge University Press, 2011).

8. United Nations Security Council Resolution 2134, S/RES/2134 (January 28, 2014).

9. United Nations Office on Drugs and Crime (UNODC), *Estimating Illicit*

Financial Flows Resulting from Drug Trafficking and Other Transnational Organized Crimes (Vienna: October 2011), www.unodc.org/documents/data-and-analysis/Studies/Illicit_financial_flows_2011_web.pdf.

10. United Nations General Assembly Resolution 60/1 (October 24, 2005), UN Doc. A/RES/60/1, para. 111. See also paras. 112–115.

11. Geneva Declaration on Armed Violence and Development, *Global Burden of Armed Violence 2011* (Geneva, 2011), p. 4.

12. World Bank, *World Development Report 2011: Conflict, Security, and Development* (Washington, DC, 2011), https://openknowledge.worldbank.org/handle/10986/4389.

13. Walter Kemp, Mark Shaw, and Arthur Boutellis, *The Elephant in the Room: How Can Peace Operations Deal with Organized Crime?* (New York: International Peace Institute, June 2013), p. 12.

14. Stefan Talmon, "The Security Council as World Legislature," *American Journal of International Law* 99 (2005): 175–193.

15. UNODC, *Drug Trafficking as a Security Threat in West Africa* (Vienna, November 2008).

16. Thomas Franck, "Interpretation and Change in the Law of Humanitarian Intervention," in *Humanitarian Intervention: Ethical, Legal, and Political Dilemmas,* edited by Jeff L. Holzgrefe and Robert O. Keohane (Cambridge: Cambridge University Press, 2003), p. 229.

17. See the case studies in James Cockayne and Adam Lupel, eds., *Peace Operations and Organized Crime: Enemies or Allies?* (London: Routledge, 2011).

18. Security Council Report, "Drug Trafficking as a Threat to International Security," Update Report no. 1, December 4, 2009, www.securitycouncilreport.org/update-report/lookup-c-glKWLeMTIsG-b-5643641.php.

19. United Nations Security Council Resolution 1333, S/RES/1333 (December 19, 2000). See also United Nations Security Council, "Statement by the President of the Security Council," UN Doc. S/PRST/2003/7, June 18, 2003; United Nations Security Council, "Press Statement," UN Doc. SC/8850, October 9, 2006; United Nations Security Council Resolution 1817, S/RES/1817 (June 11, 2008).

20. Barbara Crossette, "Tough Sanctions Imposed on Taliban Government Split U.N.," *New York Times,* December 20, 2000, www.nytimes.com/2000/12/20/world/tough-sanctions-imposed-on-taliban-government-split-un.html.

21. United Nations Security Council Resolution 1373, S/RES/1373 (September 28, 2001), para. 4.

22. The term was used by Antonio Maria Costa, former executive director of the UNODC. See United Nations Security Council, "Provisional Verbatim Record of the 6277th Meeting," UN Doc. S/PV.6277, February 24, 2010, p. 21.

23. See James Cockayne and Phil Williams, *The Invisible Tide: Towards an International Strategy to Deal with Drug Trafficking Through West Africa* (New York: International Peace Institute, October 2009); James Cockayne, *Transnational Threats: The Criminalization of West Africa and the Sahel* (New York: Center on Global Counterterrorism Cooperation, December 2011).

24. United Nations Security Council Resolutions 1829, S/RES/1829 (August 4, 2008); 1876, S/RES/1876 (June 26, 2009); and 1885, S/RES/1885 (September 15, 2009); United Nations Security Council, "Statement by the President of the Security Council," UN Doc. S/PRST/2009/20, July 10, 2009; United Nations Security Council, "Provisional Verbatim Record of the 6212th Meeting," UN Doc. S/PV.6212, November 5, 2009; United Nations Security Council, "Statement by the President of the Security Council," UN Doc. S/PRST/2009/29, November 5, 2009.

25. See United Nations Security Council Resolutions 1890, S/RES/1890 (October 8, 2009); and 1892, S/RES/1892 (October13, 2009).

26. See United Nations Security Council, "Statement by the President of the Security Council," UN Doc. S/PRST/2009/32, December 8, 2009; United Nations Security Council, "Provisional Verbatim Record of the 6233rd Meeting," UN Doc. S/PV.6233, December 8, 2009; United Nations Security Council, "Statement by the President of the Security Council," UN Doc. S/PRST/2010/4, February 24, 2010; United Nations Security Council, "Provisional Verbatim Record of the 6277th Meeting," UN Doc. S/PV.6277, February 24, 2010.

27. United Nations Security Council, "Provisional Verbatim Record of the 6277th Meeting," UN Doc. S/PV.6277, February 24, 2010, p. 10; United Nations Security Council, "Provisional Verbatim Record of the 6668th Meeting," UN Doc. S /PV.6668, November 23, 2011, p. 25.

28. See United Nations Security Council, "Provisional Verbatim Record of the 6760th Meeting," UN Doc. S/PV.6760, April 25, 2012.

29. Ibid., pp. 18–19.

30. Ibid., p. 11.

31. United Nations Security Council, "Letter Dated 24 April 2012 from the Permanent Representative of Egypt to the United Nations Addressed to the President of the Security Council," UN Doc. S/2012/257, April 25, 2012.

32. United Nations Security Council, "Provisional Verbatim Record of the 6760th Meeting," S/PV.6760, April 25, 2012, pp. 8, 17, 29.

33. Ibid., pp. 12, 16, 25.

34. United Nations Security Council, "Statement by the President of the Security Council," S/PRST/2012/16, April 25, 2012.

35. United Nations Security Council, *Report of the Secretary-General on Illicit Cross-Border Trafficking and Movement,* UN Doc. S/2012/777, October 19, 2012.

36. See the briefing to the Council on this task force in United Nations Security Council, "Provisional Verbatim Record of the 6565th Meeting," UN Doc. S/PV.6565, June 24, 2011.

37. See United Nations Security Council Resolution 1459, S/RES/1459 (January 28, 2003).

38. See, for example, United Nations Security Council Resolution 2134, on the Central African Republic, S/RES/2134 (January 28, 2014).

39. See United Nations Security Council Resolution 1615, S/RES/1615 (July 29, 2005), para. 7.

40. United Nations Security Council Resolution 1952, S/RES/1952 (November 29, 2010).

41. United Nations Security Council Resolution 2023, S/RES/2023 (December 5, 2011).

42. United Nations Security Council Resolution 2036, S/RES/2036 (February 22, 2012), para. 23.

43. United Nations Security Council Resolutions 2134 (January 28, 2014), UN Doc. S/RES/2134; and 2136 (January 30, 2014), UN Doc. S/RES/2136.

44. On the "regulatory" mode, see James Cockayne and David Malone, "The UN Security Council: 10 Lessons from Iraq on Regulation and Accountability," *Journal of International Law and International Relations* 2, no. 2 (Fall 2006): 1–24.

45. But see Amos Wako, *The Carter Camp Massacre: Results of an Investigation by the Panel of Inquiry Appointed by the Secretary-General into the Massacre Near Harbel, Liberia, on the Night of 5–6 June 1993* (New York: United Nations, September 1993).

46. See United Nations Security Council, "Letter Dated 23 October 2003 from the Secretary-General Addressed to the President of the Security Council," UN Doc. S/2003/1027, October 23, 2003, paras. 9–32.

47. "Somalia Anger at Corruption Claims in Leaked UN Report," *BBC News,* July 17, 2012, www.bbc.com/news/world-africa-18878272.

48. See Navanethem Pillay, "Lecture on Human Rights Investigations and Their Methodology," February 24, 2010, http://unispal.un.org/UNISPAL.NSF/0/C9222 F058467E6F6852576D500574710.

49. In both cases, the Security Council mandated an investigation that led to the institution of criminal trial proceedings. In the case of Darfur, the situation was referred to the ICC; see United Nations Security Council Resolutions 1564, S/RES/1564 (September 18, 2004), and 1593, S/RES/1593 (March 30, 2005). In the case of Lebanon, a Special Tribunal for Lebanon was created; see United Nations Security Council Resolution 1595, S/RES/1595 (April 7, 2005) and 1757, S/RES /1757 (May 30, 2007).

50. James Cockayne, *Strengthening Mediation to Deal with Criminal Agendas,* Oslo Forum Paper no. 002 (Geneva: Centre for Humanitarian Dialogue, November 2013).

51. Andrew Hudson and Alexandra W. Taylor, "The International Commission Against Impunity in Guatemala: A New Model for International Criminal Justice Mechanisms," *Journal of International Criminal Justice* 8, no. 1 (2010): 53–74.

52. Anonymous official in the United Nations Secretariat.

53. The ICC declined in June 2013 to open an investigation into sexual abuse by Catholic priests in part on the grounds of lacking subject-matter jurisdiction.

54. See *Rome Statute* (Rome, July 17, 1998), Article 7(g).

55. See United Nations Security Council Resolution 2048, S/RES/2048 (May 18, 2012).

56. United Nations Security Council Resolution 1952, S/RES/1952 (November 29, 2010).

57. United Nations Security Council, *Report of the Secretary-General on the Situation in Mali,* UN Doc. S/2013/189, March 26, 2013, pp. 116–117.

58. United Nations Security Council Resolution 2134, S/RES/2134 (January 28, 2014). See also the very similar language in United Nations Security Council Resolution 2136 on the Democratic Republic of the Congo, S/RES/2136 (January 30, 2014).

59. See Cornelius Friesendorf, "Problems of Crime-Fighting by 'Internationals' in Kosovo," in Cockayne and Lupel, *Peace Operations and Organized Crime.*

60. James Cockayne, "The Futility of Force? Strategic Lessons for Dealing with Unconventional Armed Groups from the UN's War on Haiti's Gangs," *Journal of Strategic Studies* 37, no. 5 (2014): 736–769.

61. Oceans Beyond Piracy, *The Economic Costs of Somali Piracy 2011* (Broomsfield: One Earth Future Foundation, 2012), http://oceansbeyondpiracy.org /sites/default/files/economic_cost_of_piracy_2011.pdf.

62. See Tullio Treves, "Piracy, Law of the Sea, and Use of Force: Developments off the Coast of Somalia," *European Journal of International Law* 20, no. 2 (2009): 399–414.

63. United Nations Security Council Resolutions 1816, S/RES/1816 (June 8, 2008), para. 7; and 1851, S/RES/1851 (December 6, 2008), para. 6.

64. Treves, "Piracy." On the consent issue, see United Nations Security Council, "Letter Dated 12 May 2008 from the Permanent Representative of Somalia to the United Nations Addressed to the President of the Security Council," UN Doc.

S/2008/323, May 14, 2008; United Nations Security Council, "Provisional Verbatim Record of the 5902nd Meeting," UN Doc. S/PV.5902, June 2, 2008, pp. 2–5.

65. See, for example, United Nations Security Council, *Report of the Secretary-General Pursuant to Security Council Resolution 2020 (2011),* UN Doc. S/2012/783, October 22, 2012.

66. United Nations Security Council Resolution 1897, S/RES/1897 (November 30, 2009).

67. André Standing, *Transnational Organized Crime and the Palermo Convention: A Reality Check* (New York: International Peace Institute, 2011).

68. US Office of Naval Intelligence, "Worldwide Threat to Shipping, Mariner Warning Information" (Washington, DC, October 17, 2008), para. 10.

69. David B. Rivkin Jr. and Lee A. Casey, "Pirates Exploit Confusion About International Law," *Wall Street Journal,* November 19, 2008, www.wsj.com /articles/SB122705719422839565.

70. US Congressional Research Service, *Piracy off the Horn of Africa,* April 27, 2011, R40528.

71. United Nations Security Council Resolution 1846, S/RES/1846 (December 2, 2008).

72. See, for example, "Exchange of Letters for the Conditions and Modalities for the Transfer of Persons Having Committed Acts of Piracy and Detained by the European Union–Led Naval Force (EUNAVFOR), and Seized Property in the Possession of EUNAVFOR, from EUNAVFOR to Kenya," in OJ (2009) L79/49, annex to EU Council Decision 2009/293/CFSP, February 26, 2009.

73. Jon Bellish, "After a Brief Hiatus, Kenya Once Again Has Universal Jurisdiction over Pirates," *Blog of the European Journal of International Law,* October 24, 2012, www.ejiltalk.org/after-a-brief-hiatus-kenya-once-again-has-universal -jurisdiction-over-pirates/, in reference to the October 18, 2012, decision of the Kenyan Court of Appeal, in *In re Mohamud Mohammed Hashi, et al., Misc. Application 434 of 2009,* that "Kenya has jurisdiction to try piracy suspects whose alleged acts occurred beyond the country's territorial waters."

74. Rotterdam District Court Three-Judge Division for Criminal Cases, LJN: BM8116, Public Prosecutor's Office no. 10/600012-09, June 17, 2010, www.unicri .it/topics/piracy/database/Netherlands_2010_Crim_No_10_6000_12_09%20 Judgment.pdf.

75. Verwaltungsgericht Köln, "Urteil vom 11 November 2011," 25 K 4280/09, November 11, 2011.

76. United Nations Security Council Resolution 1918, S/RES/1918 (April 27, 2010), para. 4. The recommendations are contained in United Nations Security Council, *Report of the Secretary-General on Possible Options to Further the Aim of Prosecuting and Imprisoning Persons Responsible for Acts of Piracy and Armed Robbery at Sea off the Coast of Somalia . . . ,* UN Doc. S/2010/394, July 26, 2010.

77. United Nations Security Council, "Annex to the Letter Dated 24 January 2011 from the Secretary-General to the President of the Security Council: Report of the Special Adviser to the Secretary-General on Legal Issues Related to Piracy off the Coast of Somalia," UN Doc. S/2011/30, January 25, 2011.

78. United Nations Security Council Resolution 1976, S/RES/1976 (April 11, 2011), para. 26; United Nations Security Council, *Report of the Secretary-General on the Modalities for the Establishment of Specialized Somali Anti-Piracy Courts,* UN Doc. S/2011/360, June 15, 2011.

79. See, for example, United Nations Security Council Resolution 2015, S/RES/2015 (October 24, 2011).

80. United Nations Security Council Resolution 1976, S/RES/1976 (April 11, 2011), OP 27.

81. United Nations Security Council, *Report of the Secretary-General on Specialized Anti-Piracy Courts in Somalia and Other States in the Region,* UN Doc. S/2012/50, January 20, 2012.

82. "No Somali Pirate Hijacking," *The Guardian,* May 3, 2013, www.theguardian.com/world/2013/may/03/somali-pirate-hijacking.

83. United Kingdom House of Commons, Foreign Affairs Committee, "Piracy off the Coast of Somalia," 10th Report, December 20, 2011, www.publications.parliament.uk/pa/cm201012/cmselect/cmfaff/1318/131802.htm.

84. Ibid.

85. United Nations Security Council, "Provisional Verbatim Record of the 6723rd Meeting," UN Doc. S/PV.6723, February 27, 2012.

86. United Nations Security Council, "Letter Dated 18 January 2012 from the Secretary-General Addressed to the President of the Security Council," UN Doc. S/2012/45, January 19, 2012.

87. United Nations Security Council, "Provisional Verbatim Record of the 6865th Meeting," UN Doc. S/PV.6865, November 19, 2012, p. 2.

88. United Nations Security Council, "Letter Dated 18 January 2012 from the Secretary-General Addressed to the President of the Security Council," para. 60.

89. United Nations Security Council, "Provisional Verbatim Record of the 6865th Meeting," p. 9.

90. International Maritime Bureau and Oceans Beyond Piracy, *The Human Cost of Somali Piracy 2011* (Broomsfield: One Earth Future Foundation, June 2012), p. 18.

91. Ibid.

92. United Nations Security Council Resolution 2077, S/RES/2077 (November 21, 2012).

93. United Nations Security Council Resolution 2015, S/RES/2015 (October 24, 2011), para. 17.

94. United Nations Security Council, "Provisional Verbatim Record of the 6865th Meeting," pp. 5–6.

16

Weapons of Mass Destruction: Managing Proliferation

Waheguru Pal Singh Sidhu

OF THE MORE THAN 2,100 RESOLUTIONS PASSED BY THE UN Security Council in its seven-decade history, less than 50 (about 2 percent) pertain to weapons of mass destruction (WMD).[1] The majority of these were passed in the post–Cold War period and only a handful have been either operationalized or implemented; most of them address nuclear proliferation. Hence this chapter will focus primarily on nuclear weapons.

I argue that given the perceived centrality of nuclear weapons in maintaining world order during the Cold War and into the twenty-first century, coupled with the fact that the five permanent members of the Council are also the recognized nuclear weapon states, it is unsurprising that the Council has done very little to disarm these "official" nuclear arsenals (apart from feeble and ultimately doomed efforts in its early history). Instead, it concentrated on preventing proliferation beyond the P5 and preserving the existing nuclear order.

In the twenty-first century, the existing WMD (especially nuclear) order faces three sets of challenges: from states within the regime, from states outside the regime, and from nonstate actors. To address these challenges the Council has relied on norm creation, legislative action, negotiations, sanctions, and, increasingly, military action. While the Council has been relatively effective in establishing norms and rules against proliferation by nonstate actors, it has been less successful in curbing proliferation by states within the regime and woefully ineffective in preventing the proliferation by states outside the regime.

The Council's efforts have been marred by disunity, inconsistency, the underlying exceptionalism of the P5 to preserve their weapons while deny-

323

ing them to other states, and the growing indigenous capability of actual and potential proliferators. Significantly, once a state acquires nuclear weapons, the Council has been ineffective in reversing this reality; the only exception is South Africa, which was disarmed in the broader context of regime change. In the twenty-first century, military action is increasingly seen as the only way to reverse proliferation, but remains an unattractive option, given Council disunity and other factors.

I begin the chapter with a historical overview of the Council's role in addressing WMD issues through the Cold War, noting the early shift in the emphasis from disarmament to nonproliferation and the continued prominence given to the latter. Turning to the post–Cold War period, I focus on the Security Council's handling of the cases of Iraq, the Democratic People's Republic of Korea (DPRK), Libya, Iran, and Syria. I next examine the Council's approach to nonstate actors, and conclude with an evaluation of the Council's role in addressing WMD challenges in the twenty-first century.

The Early Years

During its first decade, the Council vigorously, though not unanimously, pursued disarmament objectives, albeit with very little success. Between 1947 and 1952 the Council passed a total of nine WMD-related resolutions, starting with Resolution 18 of February 13, 1947. This Council resolution accepted UN General Assembly Resolution 41(1) of December 14, 1946, on "principles governing the general regulation and reduction of armaments," but only selectively. The General Assembly resolution recommended that the Council "ensure the adoption of measures . . . for the prohibition of use of atomic energy for military purposes and the elimination from national armaments of atomic and all other major weapons adaptable now or in the future to mass destruction."[2] Instead, the Council established the UN Commission for Conventional Armaments (UNCCA) and excluded atomic and other WMD from its jurisdiction on the grounds that that these weapons fell within the competence of the already established UN Atomic Energy Commission (UNAEC).[3]

Subsequently, the Council did not give direction to the UNAEC either to create a draft convention or to push for measures to prohibit the use of atomic energy for military purposes, even though this was well within its mandate. Instead, it merely considered reports of the UNAEC and transmitted them to the General Assembly. However, even this routine did not garner unanimous support among the P5; the Soviet Union consistently abstained.

These early efforts at disarmament were doomed from the start, and their failure was directly related to the unfolding confrontation between the United States and the Soviet Union. Following the first successful nuclear test and the atomic bombing of Hiroshima and Nagasaki in 1945, the United States had emerged as the sole nuclear weapon state. It sought to preserve this monopoly through the so-called Baruch Plan. Predictably, the Soviet Union, which did not possess a nuclear weapon, rejected this plan, as "Stalin wanted to have the bomb and would accept no agreement that prevented him from having it."[4] Following the first nuclear test by the Soviet Union on August 29, 1949, any hopes for these early efforts to eliminate nuclear weapons vanished. Instead, both the UNAEC and the UNCCA were dissolved in January 1952, bringing the first and only serious Council efforts at disarmament to an inglorious end.[5]

Subsequently, the development of thermonuclear weapons by the United States and the Soviet Union, the nuclear tests by Britain (in 1952) and France (in 1960), interspersed with the Suez crisis and the Hungarian uprising (both in 1956) and the rising tide of the Cold War, rendered the Council impotent and further eroded any disarmament prospects. Following China's first nuclear test, in October 1964, and the prospect of at least a dozen other countries joining the nuclear club, the emphasis of the two superpowers and the Council shifted from futile disarmament efforts to preventing further proliferation and preserving the existing nuclear order.[6] This was the objective of Resolution 255 of June 19, 1968, which paved the way for the Nuclear Non-Proliferation Treaty (NPT); it was opened for signatures on July 1, 1968, to prevent further proliferation and create official nuclear weapon states.[7]

The resolution was an effort to woo countries to sign the NPT and give up the right to nuclear weapons in return for the most perfunctory of security guarantees. The resolution merely noted that a nuclear threat or use against a non–nuclear weapon state "would create a situation in which the Security Council, and above all its nuclear-weapon State permanent members, would have to act immediately in accordance with their obligations under the . . . Charter." It obfuscated the fact that such a nuclear threat was likely to come from the four nuclear-armed states in the Council, and that the Council would be unable or unwilling to act in such circumstances (as previous crises had proved). This resolution might have been aimed at China, the only nuclear weapon state outside the Council (as Taiwan held that seat until 1971). However, this was not reassuring enough for countries like India, which witnessed the Council's inaction (though some P5 members provided support) while it suffered a humiliating military defeat at the hands of China in 1962.

While the resolution appears to have assured countries already under US or Soviet nuclear protection as part of a military alliance, many nonnuclear and nonaligned countries were not convinced. Consequently, the resolution was passed with only ten votes and five abstentions, the latter by Algeria, Brazil, India, Pakistan, and, interestingly, even nuclear-armed

France (which had opted out of NATO's nuclear umbrella in 1966). From then onward the Council focused almost entirely on nonproliferation matters, both at the global level and the country level.

Cold War Foibles

During the Cold War, the Council's response to proliferation and indeed even WMD use was both inconsistent and ineffective. This was evident in its inaction following the 1974 Indian nuclear test; the mild reprimand of Israel's nuclear weapons program; and the Council's feeble admonitions of Iraq for the use of chemical weapons against Iran in the 1980s. The only exception was the successful response to South Africa's nuclear weapons program. India's "peaceful nuclear explosion"[8] on May 18, 1974—the first such detonation by a non-NPT state—was ignored by the Council, even though P5 members, notably the United States, condemned the test and took measures to curtail further proliferation by India and others.[9] The Council's inaction might partly be explained by the fact that the International Atomic Energy Agency (IAEA), established in 1957 to inhibit the use of nuclear technology for military purposes, did not refer the case to the Security Council (under Article XII.C of the IAEA statute) and partly by the fact that although India was not an NPT member, it used the cover of a "peaceful nuclear explosion," which was allowed even under the NPT. (Indeed "peaceful nuclear explosions" were in vogue between the 1960s and 1980s, and over 150 were conducted by the United States and the Soviet Union.)

In contrast, South Africa's nascent and clandestine nuclear weapons program was targeted in 1977 by Resolution 418, passed unanimously under Chapter VII of the UN Charter—the Council's first invocation related to WMD—which expressed grave concern at Pretoria being on the "threshold of producing nuclear weapons" and decided that "all States shall refrain from any cooperation with South Africa in the manufacture and development of nuclear weapons,"[10] even though South Africa, like India, was not an NPT member. While South Africa was the first country to face sanctions by the Council for its nuclear weapons program, these were part of a broader set of sanctions aimed at the apartheid regime.

Defying the Council, South Africa's nuclear weapons program continued and even received outside assistance, including, allegedly, from Israel. The first weapon was completed in 1982 and by 1989 Pretoria had built six nuclear warheads. In 1987—even as it was building up its nuclear arsenal, South Africa signaled its intensions to sign the NPT and, following intensive negotiations with the United States, the Soviet Union, Tanzania, and Zambia, signed the treaty as a non–nuclear weapon state in 1991. By the time South Africa held its first postapartheid elections in 1994, it had dismantled one partially completed and all six existing nuclear weapons under supervision of the IAEA.[11] It is unlikely that sanctions imposed under Resolution 418 were the dominant factor compelling South Africa to give up its arsenal. Instead it is likely that these sanctions contributed to the dismantling of the apartheid regime and along with it South Africa's nuclear weapons program. Thus regime change emerged as an important factor to counter future proliferation challenges.

Unlike South Africa's program, Israel's suspected nuclear weapons program was brought to the attention of the Council by a General Assembly resolution in 1978. The General Assembly urged the Council to adopt a resolution under Chapter VII for all states to "end all transfer of nuclear equipment or fissionable material or technology to Israel" and made particular mention of Israel's "military and nuclear collaboration with South Africa."[12] However, the Council did not oblige.

Following the Israeli attack on the Iraqi nuclear reactor at Osiraq on June 7, 1981, the IAEA referred the matter to the Council, which responded by unanimously passing Resolution 487, which strongly condemned Israel's military action and called upon Tel Aviv to "place its nuclear facilities under IAEA safeguards."[13] The resolution, which was not passed under Chapter VII, neither asked Israel to dismantle its weapons program nor imposed any sanctions. Since then there has been no Council resolution on Israel's nuclear weapons.[14] The Council also missed the opportunity to raise concerns about Iraq's nuclear program.

The Council's timid approach to Israel was probably prompted by the fact that Israel was not a signatory to the NPT and maintained ambiguity about its capability. Moreover, Israel's close military and political alliance with the United States and the significant technical and material support Israel's program received from the United States and France meant that any resolution aimed at disarming Israel's arsenal was likely to be vetoed.

Between 1984 and 1988, the Council's supine response was evident in the case of the deliberate use of chemical weapons by Iraq against Iran and its own population. It is estimated that these chemical attacks killed at least 60,000 (including Iraqi civilians in Halabja), and another 100,000 suffered the long-term consequences of these weapons.[15] The Council received several fact-finding mission reports and issued five presidential statements.[16] They all condemned Iraq's use of chemical weapons and asked Baghdad to respect the 1925 Geneva Protocol, as the 1993 Chemical Weapons Convention was being negotiated at the Conference on Disarmament in Geneva. (In fact, Iraq's attack provided a fillip for these negotiations.) In addition, the Council passed several resolutions between 1986 and 1988 that condemned the use of chemical weapons, called on countries to adopt strict control on the transfer of chemical precursors to countries believed to have used chemical weapons, and threatened to consider measures against errant parties.[17] Although unanimous, none of these were Chapter VII resolutions and thus provided no enforcement measures. Despite these statements and resolutions, Iraq was never specifically condemned and the Council took no action against Baghdad, primarily because France, the United Kingdom, and the United States were "reluctant for the Council to criticize the use of chemical weapons by Iraq."[18]

This acquiescence to Iraq's gross transgressions was primarily due to geopolitical considerations, which "conspired against an even-handed Security Council response"; additionally, the "balance of interests in the Council heavily favored Iraq."[19] These factors might also explain why the resolutions were not passed under Chapter VII. The Council's ineffective response to the Iraqi contraventions had two profound consequences on its role in dealing with WMD. First, it encouraged Saddam Hussein (and others in future) to contemptuously disregard or openly challenge the Council's resolutions and actions; and second, it compelled some Council members to unilaterally use force to enforce resolutions without authorization, which in turn had a detrimental effect both on Council unity and the curbing of proliferation. This set the stage for the Council's biggest triumph and tragedy in addressing WMD in the post–Cold War era in Iraq.

Post–Cold War Activism

The end of the Cold War raised great expectations that the Council might become more consistent and effective in managing proliferation issues.[20] While the P5 recognized that nonproliferation efforts might stand a better chance of success if there were some movement toward disarming their own nuclear arsenals, they were unable or unwilling to do so. This was evident at the Council's first-ever meeting at the heads-of-state level, on January 31, 1992, where it adopted a presidential statement that made only perfunctory references to the disarmament commitment of the P5 under the NPT. The statement categorically noted: "The proliferation of all weapons of mass destruction constitutes a threat to international peace and security. The members of the Council commit themselves to working to prevent the spread of technology related to the research for or production of such weapons and to take appropriate action to that end."[21]

The Council periodically passed similar resolutions to buttress the NPT, notably before crucial quinquennial reviews, as it did in 1995 through Resolution 984 (to support the indefinite extension of the NPT) and again through Resolution 1887 in 2009. While both resolutions referred to Article VI of the NPT (which urges nuclear weapon states to pursue good faith negotiations toward disarmament), this was an afterthought compared to the emphasis put on nonproliferation. Champions of disarmament were particularly disappointed when even Resolution 1887, the result of a historic summit meeting attended by fourteen heads of states and presided over by President Barack Obama (after his stirring April 2009 Prague speech), fell short.

Indeed, the Council's nonproliferation focus was exemplified by its hyperactivity and unexpected success in disarming Iraq; its helplessness in the face of provocative nuclear tests by India and Pakistan; its two-decade futile efforts to rein in the DPRK's nuclear ambitions; its inadvertent successes in reversing Libya's WMD program and dismantling Syria's chemical arsenal; and the ongoing tussle over Iran's nuclear program. However, the Council's endeavors were blighted by its own disunity and inconsistency, and by the ability of the proliferators to blunt the Council's diplomatic and coercive efforts by pointing to the P5's own WMD arsenals, exploiting the Council's lack of unity, and developing indigenous capabilities to build WMD.

The Iraq Challenge

Saddam Hussein's ill-advised invasion and occupation of Kuwait in 1990 set the stage for the Council's most successful and controversial nonproliferation and disarmament operation. Had Hussein not embarked on this political and military folly, it is quite likely that he might have got away with building nuclear weapons. (For details on the Council's response to the 1990–1991 crisis, see Chapter 27.)[22] Here it will suffice to note that the Council played a central role in the drama, and its response to the crisis "signaled a fundamental shift in the United Nations' capacity to act, promising a new decisiveness in the post–Cold War era."[23]

Iraq, although an NPT signatory, intensified its nuclear weapons program following Israel's 1981 attack on Osiraq.[24] Soon after its invasion of Kuwait in August 1990, Iraq "began a crash program intended to divert the safeguarded [highly enriched uranium] into building a nuclear weapon," and it was reported that by late 1990 Iraq had even "constructed a mockup of a nuclear weapon."[25] There were also concerns that Iraq might have tipped some of its ballistic missiles with chemical and biological weapons for use against Israel and the international coalition forces authorized by Resolution 678 to liberate Kuwait. The ensuing military campaign destroyed some, but not all, of Iraq's WMD capability, and also revealed the extent of its clandestine programs.

Following the end of hostilities, Resolutions 687, 707, and 715, all passed under Chapter VII, established a comprehensive disarmament and verification regime for the elimination, under international supervision, of Iraq's WMD and ballistic missiles with a range of more than 150 kilometers.[26] Such an intrusive mandate remains unique in the annals of the Council and was the direct result of the total military subjugation of Iraq.

The Council established the UN Special Commission (UNSCOM) to deal with Iraq's biological and chemical weapons programs and missiles, while the IAEA was to defang its nuclear weapons program. The entities were also to establish an ongoing monitoring and verification regime to ensure that Iraq did not reconstitute its WMD program. By late 1997, UNSCOM and the IAEA had not only disarmed Iraq and ensured that it had abandoned its WMD programs, but also obtained all the necessary information related to foreign assistance and technology used. However, efforts to establish the monitoring and verification regime were marred, on the one hand, by divisions among Council members, and on the other by increasing Iraqi brinkmanship. Russia and China, for instance, argued that the inspections and sanctions regime had served its purpose and should be dismantled to provide an incentive for Iraq to cooperate in establishing the long-term monitoring and verification regime. The United States and United Kingdom, however, asserted that Iraq's uncooperative behavior put it in "material breach" of Council resolutions, and that several outstanding issues still had to be resolved before the file could be closed, the monitoring and verification regime established, and sanctions lifted. In December 1998, these differences led the United States and United Kingdom to undertake military action—not authorized by the Council—to enforce compliance and ensure the return of UNSCOM to Iraq. The military operation had exactly the opposite result, leading effectively to UNSCOM's closure in 1999.

The UN Monitoring, Verification, and Inspection Commission (UNMOVIC), established in December 1999 by Resolution 1284 to complete the mandate of UNSCOM, proved to be an ill-fated successor. Resolution 1284 saw three permanent members—China, France, and Russia—abstain, and reflected a deeply divided Council. Consequently, despite the burden of sanctions and regular air strikes by the United States and United Kingdom, Iraq denied UNMOVIC entry for nearly three years. When UNMOVIC was finally allowed into Iraq in November 2002, its tenure lasted a mere four months before its staff had to be literally evacuated as the George W. Bush administration launched its preventive, nonproliferation, regime-change war in March 2003. Ironically, UNMOVIC's extraction occurred when Iraq was at its cooperative best.

Before its untimely operational demise (it was formally terminated only in 2007), UNMOVIC was able to establish that despite a gap of four years in inspections and monitoring, Iraq had not reconstituted its WMD programs. There is, perhaps, no better proof than the final report of the US-led Iraq Study Group, which concluded that Iraq's WMD capability was "essentially destroyed in 1991"; its ability to reconstitute the nuclear program progressively decayed after 1991; its chemical weapons program was not reconstituted; and its biological weapons program was abandoned in 1995.[27]

The Council's response to Iraq's WMD challenge holds several important lessons. First, it underlines that unanimity among P5 members is crucial to ensure results. The success of UNSCOM and the IAEA—despite weaknesses—was largely due to P5 consensus. Once that unity corroded in the late 1990s, the effectiveness of these entities rapidly eroded. Second, unauthorized military action by the United States and United Kingdom not only further weakened the Council's effectiveness, but also dented its legitimacy. Third, along with the unauthorized military action initiated by the Bush administration in 2003, the rationale for regime change under the guise of nonproliferation was deeply troubling to other Council members and the wider UN membership, who were generally averse to the violation of state sovereignty. Fourth, the ambiguity in the resolutions and the "lack of objective benchmarking" to determine whether Iraq had been disarmed led to disagreements between Iraq and the Council, but also within the Council.[28] Finally, the staffing of UNSCOM—its personnel were seconded from national agencies with their own agendas—put it at odds with the Iraqis and the IAEA. Worse, according to Hans Blix, UNSCOM's "dependence" on Western intelligence "seriously reduced [its] intended UN legitimacy" and it "was seen by many as an instrument in large measure controlled by the U.S., rather than a tool of the Security Council."[29]

Inadvertent Feat in Libya

Although suspicion that Muammar Qaddafi was pursuing clandestine WMD activities dates back to the early 1980s, none of the three Council resolutions—731, 748, and 883—passed against Libya between January 1992 and November 1993, to impose sanctions for its state sponsorship of international terrorism, raised these concerns (for details on the Libyan sanctions regime, see Chapter 14).

Curiously, while Libya started to cooperate on terrorism in the late 1990s, it actually stepped *up* its quest for developing and acquiring WMD. Despite several reports indicating Libya's nuclear and biological weapons activities, in violation of its treaty obligations, the Council did not take any steps, although the United States and France, which were seeking greater compensation for victims of Libya-sponsored terrorism, threatened to block the lifting of the UN sanctions. US officials argued this was on account of Libya's pursuit of WMD (though no Council resolution made any mention of this). Consequently, when sanctions were lifted on September 12, 2003, only the United States and France abstained but did not veto (presumably because they could not provide proof of Libya's WMD activities). The United States justified its abstention on Libya's past involvement in terrorism and pursuit of WMD, a theme it would repeat in the case of Iran.

The concerns of the United States were vindicated when within weeks of the sanctions being lifted a ship carrying centrifuge components bound for Libya was interdicted. This revealed not only Libya's quest for nuclear weapons but also the proliferation network of Pakistani nuclear scientist

Abdul Qadeer Khan. This interception, following a decade of isolation and embargoes, proved to be the last straw, breaking the sanctions-weary back of Libya. On December 19, 2003, Libya publicly renounced its WMD programs and Tripoli vowed to eliminate its chemical and nuclear weapons programs, adhere to its NPT and Biological Weapons Convention commitments, accede to the Chemical Weapons Convention, and limit the range and payloads of its missiles to conform to guidelines set by the Missile Technology Control Regime. The Council merely welcomed and encouraged Libya's decision through a presidential statement in April 2004. Unlike the Iraqi case, the Council did not set up a special commission to disarm Libya but left implementation to the IAEA and the Organisation for the Prohibition of Chemical Weapons (OPCW).

However, in January 2004, the United States and United Kingdom, in a separate and unusual operation—not mandated by the Council—removed nuclear weapon designs and stockpiles from Libya. Libyan officials informed the IAEA that this operation was "pursuant to mutual understandings with the UK and the USA, [under which] Libya had agreed to transfer to the USA sensitive design information, nuclear weapon–related documents, and most of the previously undeclared enrichment equipment, subject to Agency verification requirements and procedures."[30] In all, about twenty-five metric tons of nuclear components and documents were airlifted to the United States, including centrifuges from Pakistan. (Soon thereafter, Khan revealed that, for two decades, he had secretly provided North Korea, Libya, and Iran with technical and material assistance for making nuclear weapons.)[31] By 2010, even the uber-cautious US State Department's compliance report noted that Libya was meeting its Biological Weapons Convention and NPT obligations. In early 2011, the OPCW reported that Libya had destroyed about 54 percent of its chemical weapons stockpile. However, Resolution 1973 and the ensuing NATO-led military operation slowed this progress. Besides, the fate of Qaddafi's regime appears to have given cause to other regimes with nuclear ambitions, particularly the DPRK, to resist similar disarmament.

The DPRK Gauntlet

In 1993, following the IAEA discovery that Pyongyang had underreported its plutonium holdings, the agency asked for special inspections, which the DPRK refused. Instead, on March 12, 1993, it gave the three-month mandatory notice to withdraw from the NPT as per Article X of the treaty (the first such declaration by an NPT member) and notified the president of the Security Council accordingly. The IAEA Board of Governors, instead of dealing with the case in Vienna, also referred it to the Council.

In response, the Council passed Resolution 825 (with abstentions from China and Pakistan), which merely asked the DPRK to reconsider its withdrawal and encouraged member states to facilitate a solution. On June 11, one day before its notice of withdrawal would have taken effect, the DPRK suspended the withdrawal and agreed to cooperate with the IAEA. This was the result of diplomatic efforts by the United States and China (the abstention of the latter helped in engaging Pyongyang) to persuade the DPRK to step back. The ongoing UNSCOM inspections in Iraq following the 1991 war might also have given the DPRK reason to pause its escalatory approach.

While the DPRK did not leave the NPT, it continued to play a cat-and-mouse game with the IAEA and the Council through 1993—refusing to cooperate and then, in the face of a strongly worded Council statement, allowing inspections but provocatively removing fuel from a nuclear reactor before they could take place, which prompted another stern Council note. Things came to a head when the DPRK withdrew from the IAEA on June 13, 1994. Within days, former US president Jimmy Carter visited Pyongyang and paved the way for the so-called Agreed Framework, signed on October 21, 1994, between the United States and the DPRK. Although negotiated and signed outside the Council, the Agreed Framework was endorsed in a Council presidential statement on November 4, 1994.[32]

In retrospect, the Agreed Framework was seen as a sop to placate the DPRK and stood in contrast to the strict UNSCOM inspection regime being implemented in Iraq. The Council did not even consider military action against the DPRK because, unlike in the Iraq case, this would have been difficult to justify. Besides, according to US intelligence, the DPRK may have produced one or two nuclear weapons by January 1994, making a military intervention that much more dangerous and unappealing. Consequently, as the DPRK had not been militarily subjugated, it was unwilling to accept intrusive inspections. Finally, given the impending NPT review conference in 1995 (when the treaty would be extended indefinitely), the DPRK's gauntlet of withdrawing from the treaty had to be dealt with quickly, in case other states were tempted to followed suit.

By the late 1990s, the Agreed Framework began to unravel for a number of reasons, primarily related to the dynamics between Washington and Pyongyang. In fact, the Council was almost entirely out of the loop on the DPRK until 2003. Following George W. Bush's January 2002 State of the Union speech, in which he referred to the DPRK (along with Iraq and Iran) as an "axis of evil," relations between the United States and the DPRK deteriorated even further and the framework began to collapse.

On January 10, 2003, the DPRK announced its withdrawal from the NPT, effective January 11, arguing that it had satisfied the requirement under Article X when it originally announced its decision to withdraw on March 12, 1993, and suspended the decision one day before it would have become legally binding. A month later, the IAEA Board of Governors declared that the DPRK was "in further noncompliance" of its safeguard agreement and reported the matter to the Council. Discussing the issue only in informal consultations nearly two months after the referral, the Council chose not to take up the agenda item for another three years. This inaction was prompted by China and Russia, which opposed formal Council action in favor of quiet diplomacy. The United States, which was to hold trilateral talks with the DPRK and China in late April 2003, went along. Subsequently, the Six-Party Talks, among China, the DPRK, Japan, the Republic of Korea, Russia, and the United States, began in 2003 and sought to deal with the DPRK's proliferation and its exit from the NPT. Despite five rounds of these talks (between 2003 and 2005), Pyongyang neither returned to the NPT nor reversed its proliferation. Instead it declared on several occasions that it had built and possessed nuclear weapons. The DPRK's likely possession of nuclear weapons, coupled with China's desire to protect its oldest and closest ally, might explain why this case was mostly dealt with outside the Council, whereas the case of Iran (discussed later) was dealt with from within.

On July 4, 2006, the DPRK conducted a series of missile tests, including its longest-range missile, provoking the Council into unanimously passing Resolution 1695. Though not under Chapter VII—the result of a compromise between the United States, France, and Japan, who wanted the strongest language, and Russia and China, who sought less severity—the resolution was nonetheless sweeping in its scope. It called on the DPRK to "suspend all activities related to its ballistic missile programme, and in this context reestablish its preexisting commitments to a moratorium on missile launching."[33] As there is no international norm or treaty banning ballistic missile activity, this was tantamount to legislating a single-country law that would be difficult to enforce. Even the Missile Technology Control Regime (which the DPRK is not a party to) allows states to have missiles up to a 300-kilometer range. The Council also ignored similar missile launches by others and singled out the DPRK. According to one report, in 2006 alone eight countries—including China, France, Russia, and the United States—had launched more than twenty-eight ballistic missiles.[34] Thus the Council was holding the DPRK (and it would later hold Iran) to standards that the P5 did not uphold. (A similar bias was apparent in Resolution 1172 of June 6, 1998, against India's and Pakistan's nuclear tests. The Council urged both states to become parties to the nuclear Comprehensive Test Ban Treaty [CTBT] and participate in negotiations on a treaty banning the production of fissile material, even though neither the United States nor China were parties to the CTBT and were hesitant about a proposed Fissile Material Cut-Off Treaty.)

Predictably, Pyongyang, emboldened by Council inaction since 2003 and having withstood pressure from the Council's three permanent members during the five rounds of the Six-Party Talks, categorically declared that it would "not be bound" by the resolution. Instead, the DPRK taunted and mocked the Council with its first nuclear test, on October 9, 2006. The Council responded by unanimously adopting, under Chapter VII authority, Resolution 1718 on October 14, which imposed stringent arms and financial sanctions and established a sanctions committee.

In the face of a unified Council, a chastened and isolated DPRK came around, but not for long. It rejoined the Six-Party Talks and, in 2007, agreed to dismantle its nuclear weapons program and also shut down the Yongbyon reactor in exchange for economic aid. However, within a year, despite suffering the worst famine in a decade, Pyongyang reversed course, threatened to restart its nuclear program, and launched a three-stage rocket. The Council responded with a feckless presidential statement and the DPRK retorted by expelling the nuclear inspectors, boycotting the Six-Party Talks, and conducting another nuclear test, in May 2009. The Council then unanimously adopted Resolution 1874, condemning the DPRK's nuclear test, expanding the arms embargo, and authorizing inspection of cargo, as well as vessels on the high seas, bound to and from the DPRK. Pyongyang responded with a series of missile tests and declared the Six-Party Talks dead.

Between 2007 and 2009 the DPRK was also implicated in building a reactor at al-Kibar in Syria (revealed by an Israeli attack in September 2007) and proliferating nuclear technology to Myanmar; however, the Council did not act on either of these charges, nor on the succession process of Kim Jong-un, which was marked by a series of provocative actions that took place in 2010: the sinking of the South Korean warship *Cheonan,* the building of a new uranium enrichment plant, and the artillery barrage on a South Korean island. The change in leadership following the death of Kim Jong-il in 2011 did nothing to diminish the DPRK's defiance. In fact, the inauguration of Kim Jong-un was followed by the successful launch of a satellite onboard the Unha-3 rocket in December 2012, prompting the Council to pass Resolution 2087, which strengthened and expanded existing sanctions and froze the assets of additional DPRK individuals. Predictably, the DPRK replied with its third nuclear test, on February 12, 2013, and the Council responded with Resolution 2094, which strengthened existing sanctions by expanding the scope of materials covered and added additional financial sanctions, including blocking bulk cash transfers. However, the DPRK remained unrepentant.

Since the DPRK's case first came onto its agenda, the Council has failed to prevent the proliferation of Pyongyang's nuclear weapons and ballistic missiles, let alone reverse them. According to the February 2015 report of the sanctions committee, the panel saw "no evidence that the country intends to cease prohibited activities and found widespread evidence of resilience and adaptation in the . . . efforts to circumvent the measures imposed by the relevant resolutions."[35] Now that the DPRK has crossed the nuclear Rubicon, it appears unlikely that it will reverse course, despite the efforts of the Council.[36]

The Iranian Imbroglio

There is broad consensus that Iran's nascent nuclear weapons program dates back to the 1970s and was initiated by the Shah soon after Tehran joined the NPT. The program was more or less shelved after the 1979 Islamic Revolution. However, the experience of the decade-long war with Iraq, and Baghdad's use of chemical weapons, coupled with the indifference and ineffectiveness of the Council in holding Saddam Hussein responsible, played a significant role in Iran's decision to revive its nuclear capability.

In June 2003, the IAEA found that Iran had failed to report import of nuclear material and its processing, use, and storage in undeclared facilities. The fact that Iran pursued these activities in secret suggested that its nuclear program was moving toward weapons development. Iran argued that its program was peaceful, signed the more stringent Additional Protocol, and promised to suspend its enrichment program. The UK, France, and Germany (the so-called EU3) pressed Iran to keep its program suspended until the issues were resolved and ratify the Additional Protocol. However, while the IAEA reported that it had not seen any diversion for weapons or other explosive purposes, it was unable to conclude that there were no undeclared nuclear materials in Iran. The situation escalated when Iran resumed uranium enrichment and stopped implementing the Additional Protocol. This prompted the IAEA Board of Governors to report Iran to the Security Council in February 2006. (Interestingly, around the same time, three other countries—Egypt, the Republic of Korea, and Syria—were also engaging in undeclared activities and could also have been referred to the Council but were not, for a number of reasons.)[37]

The first Council resolution on the matter, 1696 (2006), mirrored the IAEA resolution, demanding that Iran suspend all enrichment-related and reprocessing activities until a negotiated solution that guaranteed the peaceful nature of Iran's nuclear program could be found, and urged Iran to win the confidence of the Council by resolving the outstanding issues. However, later, resolutions veered into legislating Iran-specific rules and included a series of progressively expansive sanctions targeting specific persons and entities. Resolution 1737 (2006) went further than the IAEA request and obligated Iran to suspend work on its heavy-water reactor. Similarly, Resolution 1929 (2010) ordered Tehran to refrain from "any activity related to ballistic missiles capable of delivering nuclear weapons." Subsequent resolutions progressively widened the scope of sanctions to impose a complete arms embargo, stringent financial sanctions, and a strict inspection regime of Iranian aircraft and vessels as well as cargo bound to or from Iran. In all, the Council adopted six Iran-related resolutions—five under

Chapter VII—the same number as for the DPRK, even though Pyongyang has nuclear weapons while Iran does not. Apart from the UN sanctions, the United States and its allies have also imposed their own set of sanctions. While these sanctions have inflicted a heavy burden on Iran's population, they have evidently not retarded its nuclear activities.[38]

Sanctions, however, represented only one track in a dual-track approach pursued by the Council. Diplomatic initiatives to resolve the Iranian nuclear issue have produced several proposals, but none have been acceptable to all the involved parties and the stalemate continues. In 2006, China, Russia, and the United States joined the EU3 in a so-called P5+1 format—a reference to the P5 plus Germany—to explore proposals with Iran. However, despite several on-again, off-again rounds of negotiations, there was no progress. Following the election of Hassan Rouhani as president of Iran in 2013, an interim nuclear deal was reached in November 2013, followed by the "Parameters for a Joint Comprehensive Plan of Action Regarding the Islamic Republic of Iran's Nuclear Program" in April 2015, but the prospects of a final agreement by the deadline of June 30, 2015, and its effective implementation remain uncertain.

Until the 2013 interim agreement, the proposal that came closest to being accepted by Iran was the Tehran Declaration of May 17, 2010, which was the result of a diplomatic initiative by Brazil and Turkey (both of whom were then on the Council). As per this agreement, 1,200 kilograms of low-enriched uranium would be transferred from Iran to Turkey in return for a supply of enriched uranium for the Tehran Research Reactor from the so-called Vienna Group (comprising three P5 members—France, Russia, and the United States—plus the IAEA). President Barack Obama had encouraged the Brazil-Turkey initiative in a letter on April 20, arguing that such an agreement "would build confidence and reduce regional tensions by substantially reducing Iran's [low-enriched uranium] stockpile."[39] However, the subsequent Tehran Declaration—perhaps the first instance of diplomatic success on the vexed Iran nuclear file—was summarily rejected by France, Russia, and the United States, partly on the grounds that it did not address Iran's production of 20 percent enriched uranium and its accumulation of a larger amount of low-enriched uranium, and partly because they saw it as a deliberate effort to countermand the P5-led efforts to bring Iran to task for the reported violations of its nuclear commitments.[40] Instead, in a shortsighted move that reflected P5 suspicions of initiatives taken by an elected member, the United States proposed, and the Council adopted, Resolution 1929 on June 9, 2010, which both Brazil and Turkey voted against, imposing stringent Chapter VII sanctions—similar to those on the DPRK—against Iran.

The outright rejection, by the United States and others, of the Tehran Declaration is all the more surprising, as it was not a radical new proposal and was similar to the earlier agreement that Iran had been discussing with the Vienna Group since October 2009. Moreover, Brazil in particular had kept the United States, Russia, and France informed at the highest levels, indicating that it was willing to work closely with the P5 to resolve the ongoing stalemate. Had there been an anti-P5 motive, the contours of the Tehran deal would have looked very different: Brazil might have offered to supply the enriched uranium directly, instead of reiterating that it be supplied by the Vienna Group.

Predictably, Resolution 1929 failed to affect Iran's behavior, for a couple reasons. First, the sanctions were significantly watered down to accommodate the interests of Russia and China (evident in additional sanctions imposed by the United States and its allies). Second, the resolution also lacked credence, as it was not passed unanimously. Apart from Brazil and Turkey (which voted against the resolution, objecting to its outright dismissal of the Tehran Declaration), even Lebanon abstained. What is clear is that to effectively address the issue of Iran's nuclear ambitions in the long run, there will need to be a convergence of P5 and non-P5 efforts. Neither effort is likely to succeed on its own, despite the recent entente between Tehran and Washington.

Postscript: Detoxing Syria

While P5 politics have prevented the Council from taking up Syria's nuclear file—which has been before the Council since July 2011—the use of toxins on August 21, 2013, near Damascus finally prompted a response to disarm Syria's chemical arsenal, albeit only after an agreement hammered out between the United States and Russia, outside the Council, narrowly averted a punitive US military attack (for which the Obama administration had difficulties obtaining congressional approval).

The mid-September 2013 US-Russia agreement ambitiously called for Syria (a nonsignatory to the Chemical Weapons Convention) to declare all of its chemical weapons stockpile and sites within a week; have international inspectors on the ground by November with unfettered access to all sites; and complete the elimination of all chemical weapons material by mid-2014—all this in the midst of a brutal civil war. The alacrity with which the agreement was achieved not only was prompted by the desire to avoid military confrontation by everyone, but also underlines the unwritten taboo against the use of WMD in the twenty-first century.

To carry out this expeditious dismantling, the United States and Russia rushed extraordinary procedures through the OPCW's executive council and also jointly pushed through Council Resolution 2118 on September 27, 2013, to support the process. Significantly, the resolution empowered the OPCW (with the UN providing political support) to disarm Syria's chemical arsenal rather than establishing an ad hoc commission of the Council to do so. This reflects lessons learned from the UNSCOM experience and is recognition of the OPCW's experience in dismantling the chemical arsenals of Albania, India, Libya, Russia, South Korea, and the United States, and hopefully is indicative of its technical capabilities to deal with Syria. Moreover, having the OPCW lead the process might help to circumvent the debilitating Council politics on Syria.

There was concern that the June 2014 timeline to disarm Syria's chemical weapons during a civil war was unrealistic. Even the United States and Russia are years behind in dismantling their own chemical arsenals. In Libya, the OPCW was able to destroy only 54 percent of the stockpile in seven years (until 2011), and this with the full cooperation of the Libyan regime. In contrast, Syria promptly signed the Chemical Weapons Convention, declared a stockpile of 1,300 metric tons of chemical weapons, and shared the location of dozens of production and storage sites, even though it did not provide written documentation. Whereas a complex operation involving more than a dozen countries accomplished the destruction of more than 98 percent of the weapons handed over by Syria in record time (even though the original deadline was not met), there have been accusations that Syria might not have revealed the entire extent of its program. Additionally, reports of the alleged use of chloride bombs by the Syrian regime and Damascus's reluctance to address them also strengthened these suspicions. At this time of writing in 2015 the Syrian chemical weapons chapter is far from closed.

Tackling Nonstate Actors

The brazen attacks of September 11, 2001, coupled with fears of future WMD terrorist attacks, and followed by the unmasking of the Khan network in 2004, set the stage for the Council's efforts to prevent WMD proliferation by nonstate actors. The result was Resolution 1540 of April 28, 2004, passed under Chapter VII, which is particularly innovative for three reasons. First, it seeks to deal exclusively with nonstate actors; second, it seeks to provide stopgap arrangements to plug existing loopholes in the present treaty-based regime; and third, it establishes binding rules for 193 member states without any of the non-Council members actually having agreed to these rules.

Resolution 1540 is far-reaching because it obliges all UN member states to "adopt and enforce appropriate effective laws which prohibit any non-State actor to manufacture, acquire, possess, develop, transport, transfer or use nuclear, chemical or biological weapons and their means of delivery" as well as to "take and enforce effective measures to establish domestic controls to prevent the proliferation of nuclear, chemical, or biological weapons and their means of delivery." It also envisages cooperative action and calls upon all states to promote dialogue and cooperation, including assistance in implementation of the resolution.

Although the United States proposed this resolution, in reflection of then–US undersecretary of state for arms control John Bolton's suspicions of multilateral institutions, it was initially reluctant to establish a formal Council committee to oversee its implementation and preferred individual member states, particularly itself, to take on this role. This was in contrast to its position on the need for an executive directorate to strengthen the UN's Counter-Terrorism Committee. Eventually, however, the US compromised and agreed to establishing a 1540 Committee, initially for only two years.[41]

While the resolution has been generally welcomed given that existing treaty-based regimes did not address this aspect of proliferation, there is widespread unease among the UN membership over the Council's tendency to legislate, circumventing the negotiated approach to developing treaty-based regimes. There is also concern about the ability of weak or poor states to implement these laws and enforce domestic control.[42] These reservations aside, the tenure of the 1540 Committee has now been extended until 2021. The Council thus recognizes that full implementation of the resolution by all states is a long-term task that will require continuous efforts at national, regional, and international levels. Further, Resolution 1977 (2011) provides for two comprehensive reviews, one after five years and one before the end of the mandate. Additionally, the 1540 Committee is also mandated to continue to strengthen its role in facilitating the provision of technical assistance and enhancing cooperation with relevant international organizations, as well as to continue to refine its outreach efforts and to institute transparency measures.

The efforts of the 1540 process are sought to be complemented by various ad hoc, non-UN-based initiatives, such as the Nuclear Security Summit process inaugurated by the United States in 2010 to encourage countries to voluntarily secure their nuclear materials, and the more contentious 2003 US-led Proliferation Security Initiative, which is designed to intercept suspicious cargo to and from states of proliferation concern. In fact, it was the latter initiative, through its interception of the German-owned freighter BBC *China,* carrying Malaysian-built centrifuge parts to Libya via Dubai, that exposed the Khan network and provided an impetus for Resolution 1540.[43]

Overall, Resolution 1540 is a partial success story in the Council's efforts to address nonstate-actor proliferation in that it establishes clear norms and requires states to legislate and regulate to prevent nonstate actors from obtaining WMD and the means to deliver them. However, the implementation of 1540 still remains uneven and far from complete. Apart from the lack of capacity of some states to actually report on the implementation of 1540 nationally, other states have deliberately misreported their

WMD holdings and steps taken to prevent WMD from falling into the hands of nonstate actors. A classic example is Syria, which in its 1540 declaration categorically denied possessing any WMD—including chemical weapons. Thus states could get away with false reporting, given the voluntary nature of these declarations and the inability of the 1540 Committee to independently verify them. However, a Chapter VII Council resolution, 2118 (2013), ironically on disarming Syria's chemical arsenal, includes a section that mandates all UN members to "inform immediately the Security Council of any violation of resolution 1540," thus empowering the 1540 Committee to verify all reports.[44]

Conclusion

In the twenty-first century, efforts particularly on the part of the P5 to prevent nuclear proliferation while seeking to preserve the existing nuclear and world order are starting to have diminishing returns. This might relate in part to the continuing relevance of nuclear weapons in underpinning the global order and the desire of new states to acquire these weapons to ensure their regime security; the lack of movement toward nuclear disarmament on the part of the P5 and the diminishing legitimacy of an unreformed Council in pursuing nonproliferation; the diminishing returns of imposing sanctions to change regime behavior; and the unattractiveness of the use of force to reverse proliferation.

The overarching and fundamental role of nuclear weapons aside, the inconsistency of the Council in applying norms to prevent proliferation has also proved detrimental. For instance, while Iraq was under sanctions and a strict inspection regime, the DPRK was simultaneously placated with the Agreed Framework, arrived at bilaterally and outside the Council, which probably emboldened the leadership in Pyongyang.

Moreover, the increasing dependence of the Council on sanctions to effect either regime change or at least change in the policies of a regime is proving to be regressive and detrimental, for a number of reasons. First, there is an assumption that countries seeking nuclear weapons can only build them by acquiring the necessary technological wherewithal and expertise from more industrialized countries in the West. While this was certainly the case for the early nuclear weapon proliferators, it is less so today.[45]

Second, even though most proliferating countries initially depended on key external elements for their nuclear programs, they were able to eventually establish indigenous nuclear weapon capabilities and insulate themselves against various sanction regimes. Thus, even with the establishment of the Nuclear Suppliers Group, a group of countries established in 1974 that seeks to contribute to nuclear nonproliferation through export controls, several other countries, including India, Pakistan, North Korea, and now Iran, acquired the necessary wherewithal to build nuclear weapons.

Third, the efforts of the Nuclear Suppliers Group were partly dented by the growing indigenous capabilities of the target countries and partly because of the networks that had sprung up to counter the group's guidelines. This is well borne out by the cases of Pakistan and the DPRK, both of which have become suppliers of nuclear weapons technology and missiles in their own right. For instance, Pakistan is known to have provided Iran with critical wherewithal, including reportedly a weapon design. Similarly, the DPRK is suspected of building a reactor, subsequently destroyed by Israel, to produce fissile material for Syria.

If efforts to prevent proliferation fail and new states acquire nuclear weapons, the Council is inevitably left with two unenviable options: either to accommodate the new state with nuclear weapons into the existing nuclear order, or to disarm the state's nuclear weapons and weapon capability through force. To exercise either of these options, a consensus at least among the P5 is essential. However, as recent cases have shown, such consensus is almost impossible to build, let alone sustain.

Notes

1. The UN Commission for Conventional Armaments (UNCCA) defines weapons of mass destruction as "atomic explosive weapons, radioactive material weapons, lethal chemical or biological weapons, and any weapons developed in the future which have characteristics comparable in destructive effect to those of the atomic bomb or other weapons mentioned above."

2. United Nations General Assembly Resolution 41(I), "Principles Governing the General Regulation and Reduction of Armaments," A/RES/41(I), December 14, 1946, para. 6.

3. The UNAEC was set up by the General Assembly Resolution 1(I), "Establishment of a Commission to deal with the Problems Raised by the Discovery of Atomic Energy," UN Doc. A/RES/1(I), January 24, 1946. This resolution was cosponsored by the United States and the Soviet Union, albeit for different reasons.

4. Bruce D. Larkin, *Designing Denuclearization: An Interpretive Encyclopedia* (New Brunswick, NJ: Transaction, 2008), p. 174.

5. United Nations General Assembly Resolution 502(VI), "Regulation, Limitation, and Balanced Reduction of All Armed Forces and All Armaments; International Control of Atomic Energy," UN Doc. A/RES/502(VI), January 11, 1952, dissolved the UNAEC and UNCCA and established under the direction of the Council the Disarmament Commission "for the elimination of all major weapons adaptable to mass destruction, and for the effective international control of atomic energy to ensure the prohibition of atomic weapons." Like its predecessors the Disarmament Commission has remained an ineffective and feckless body.

6. Nuclear weapons emerged as the principal guarantors of international peace and security, underpinning world order during the Cold War. It was the possession, or protection under the umbrella, of nuclear weapons that was widely regarded as one of the primary factors behind the long period of relative peace among great powers after World War II. See Waheguru Pal Singh Sidhu, "The Nuclear Disarma-

ment and Non-Proliferation Regime," in *Security Studies: An Introduction,* edited by Paul D. Williams (New York: Routledge, 2012), p. 410.

7. Jozef Goldblat, *Nuclear Non-Proliferation: A Guide to the Debate* (Stockholm: Stockholm International Peace Research Institute, 1985).

8. "Peaceful nuclear explosion," though indistinguishable from other nuclear explosions, were allowed under Article V of the NPT. Essentially they were nuclear explosions conducted for civilian or "peaceful" purposes, such as excavating canals, building reservoirs, and recovering natural resources. The International Atomic Energy Agency (IAEA) also promoted peaceful nuclear explosions. See the IAEA, "Peaceful Nuclear Explosions," www.iaea.org/sites/default/files /17203505359.pdf; and Comprehensive Test Ban Treaty Organization, "Peaceful Nuclear Explosions," http://www.ctbto.org/nuclear-testing/history-of-nuclear-testing/peaceful-nuclear -explosions/.

9. The US Congress passed the 1978 Nuclear Nonproliferation Act and Washington was instrumental in establishing the Nuclear Suppliers Group (NSG) in 1974. In addition to the United States, the original NSG members included Canada, West Germany, France, Japan, the Soviet Union, and the United Kingdom.

10. United Nations Security Council Resolution 418, S/RES/418 (November 4, 1977).

11. Zondi Masiza, "A Chronology of South Africa's Nuclear Program," *Nonproliferation Review* (Fall 1993): 35–55.

12. United Nations General Assembly Resolution 33/71A, "Military and Nuclear Collaboration with Israel," UN Doc. A/RES/33/71A, December 14, 1978. See also Peter Liberman, "Israel and the South African Bomb," *Nonproliferation Review* (Summer 2004): 1–35.

13. United Nations Security Council Resolution 487, S/RES/487 (June 19, 1981). See also International Atomic Energy Agency Director General, "Telegram Dated 12 January 1981 from the Director-General of the International Atomic Energy Agency to the President of the Security Council," S/14532, June 15, 1981.

14. Interestingly, another Israeli attack on a suspected facility in Syria in 2007 did not evoke any Council response. In fact, Syria did not report the attack and when the attack became public Damascus denied that the facility was a nuclear reactor. Only in 2011, following inspections, did the IAEA refer Syria to the Council for the undeclared nuclear facility. However, the divided Council has not considered the IAEA referral, even though it adopted Resolution 2118 in September 2013 to disarm Syria's chemical weapons stockpile.

15. Security Council Report, "The Security Council's Role in Disarmament and Arms Control: Nuclear Weapons, Non-Proliferation, and Other Weapons of Mass Destruction," Cross-Cutting Report no. 2, September 1, 2009, p. 14, www.security councilreport.org/cross-cutting-report/lookup-c-glKWLeMTIsG-b-5405331.php. See also Farhang Rajaee, ed., *The Iran-Iraq War: The Politics of Aggression* (Gainesville: University Press of Florida, 1993); Robin Wright, *Dreams and Shadows: The Future of the Middle East* (New York: Penguin, 2008), p. 438.

16. These were the "Note by the Secretary-General," UN Doc. S/16433, March 26, 1984; "Note by the President of the Security Council," UN Doc. S/16454, March 30, 1984; "Note from the President of the Security Council," UN Doc. S/17130, April 25, 1985; "Note by the President of the Security Council," UN Doc. S/17932 March 21, 1986; and "Note by the President of the Security Council," UN Doc. S/18863 May 14, 1987.

17. These were United Nations Security Council Resolutions 582, S/RES/582 (February 24, 1986); 612, S/RES/612 (May 8, 1988); and 620, S/RES/620 (August 26, 1988).

18. Security Council Report, "The Security Council's Role in Disarmament and Arms Control," p. 14.

19. David M. Malone and James Cockayne, "The UN in Iraq, 1980–2001," in *The Iraq Crisis and World Order: Structural, Institutional, and Normative Challenges*, edited by Ramesh Thakur and Waheguru Pal Singh Sidhu (Tokyo: United Nations University Press, 2006), pp. 18–19.

20. For an excellent assessment of these expectations, see David M. Malone, "An Evolving UN Security Council," in *Cooperating for Peace and Security*, edited by Bruce Jones, Shepard Forman, and Richard Gowan (Cambridge: Cambridge University Press, 2010), pp. 59–79.

21. United Nations Security Council, "Note by the President of the Security Council," UN Doc. S/23500, January 31, 1992.

22. See also David M. Malone, *The International Struggle over Iraq: Politics in the UN Security Council, 1980–2005* (Oxford: Oxford University Press, 2006).

23. Malone and Cockayne, "The UN in Iraq, 1980–2001," p. 21.

24. Al J. Venter, "How Saddam Almost Built His Bomb," *Middle East Policy* 51, no. 3 (February 1999): 52.

25. Christine Wing and Fiona Simpson, *Detect, Dismantle, and Disarm: IAEA Verification, 1992–2005* (Washington, DC: US Institute of Peace, 2013), p. 13.

26. For a detailed analysis of the Iraqi case, see Pascal Teixeira Da Silva, "Weapons of Mass Destruction," in *The UN Security Council: From the Cold War to the 21st Century*, edited by David M. Malone (Boulder, CO: Lynne Rienner, 2004), p. 206.

27. Central Intelligence Agency, "Comprehensive Report of the Special Advisor to the DCI on Iraq's WMD, with Addendums (Duelfer Report)," Langley, April 25, 2005.

28. Wing and Simpson, *Detect, Dismantle, and Disarm*, p. 30.

29. Hans Blix, *Disarming Iraq* (New York: Pantheon, 2004), p. 21.

30. IAEA Director-General, "Implementation of the NPT Safeguards Agreement of the Socialist People's Libyan Arab Jamahiriya," Doc. GOV/2004/12, February 20, 2004, http://fas.org/nuke/guide/libya/iaea0204.pdf.

31. William J. Broad, David E. Sanger, and Raymond Bonner, "How Pakistani Built His Network," *New York Times*, February 12, 2004. For additional details, see Christopher Clary, "Dr. Khan's Nuclear Walmart," *Disarmament Diplomacy Online* 76 (March–April 2004), http://www.acronym.org.uk/dd/dd76/76cc.htm.

32. United Nations Security Council, "Statement of the President of the Security Council," S/PRST/1994/64, November 4, 1994.

33. United Nations Security Council Resolution 1695, S/RES/1695 (July 15, 2006).

34. Hans M. Kristensen, "Nuclear Missile Testing Galore," *FAS Strategic Security Blog*, January 3, 2007, http://fas.org/blogs/security/2006/12/nuclear_missile_testing_galore.

35. United Nations Security Council, "Report of the Panel of Experts Established Pursuant to Resolution 1874 (2009)," S/2015/131, February 23, 2015, http://www.un.org/ga/search/view_doc.asp?symbol=S/2015/131.

36. For this perception, see "Israel PM Netanyahu Warns Iranians of 'Immortal Regime,'" *BBC News*, October 4, 2013, www.bbc.co.uk/news/world-middle-east-24395917.

37. Pierre Goldschmidt, "Safeguard Noncompliance: A Challenge for the IAEA and the UN Security Council," *Arms Control Today*, February 2010.

38. Paul K. Kerr, "Iran's Nuclear Program: Tehran's Compliance with International Obligations" (Washington, DC: Congressional Research Service, July 31, 2013).

39. Glenn Kessler, "U.S., Brazilian Officials at Odds over Letter on Iranian Uranium," *Washington Post,* May 28, 2010.

40. Waheguru Pal Singh Sidhu, "Iran: No Place for Cowboy Diplomacy," *Mint,* May 30, 2010, www.livemint.com/Opinion/JZ3kyRf9Bo3akwR6FSnpgI/Iran-no -place-for-cowboy-diplomacy.html.

41. Eric Rosand and Sebastian von Einsiedel, "9/11, the War on Terror, and the Evolution of Multilateral Institutions," in Jones, Forman, and Gowan, *Cooperating for Peace and Security,* pp. 147–148.

42. For contrasting views on UNSC Resolution 1540, see Daniel Joyner, "UN Security Council 1540: A Legal Travesty?" (Athens: University of Georgia, Center for International Trade and Security, August 2006); Seema Gahlaut, "UN Security Council 1540: A Principled Necessity" (Athens: University of Georgia, Center for International Trade and Security, August 2006).

43. Sharon A. Squassoni, Steve R. Bowman, and Carl E. Behrens, "Proliferation Control Regimes: Background and Status" (Washington, DC: Congressional Research Service, February 10, 2005), p. 15.

44. United Nations Security Council Resolution 2118, S/RES/2118 (September 27, 2013), para. 14.

45. Choe Sang-Hun, "North Korea Learning to Make Crucial Nuclear Parts, Study Finds," *New York Times,* September 23, 2013.

Part 3

Enforcing Council Mandates

17

The Use of Force: A System of Selective Security

Adam Roberts

SINCE THE END OF THE COLD WAR IN THE LATE 1980S, THE UN Security Council has authorized the use of force by several distinct types of actors: certain international military coalitions, UN peacekeeping forces, and also some non-UN peacekeeping forces. It has authorized force in a remarkably wide range of circumstances, and with varied purposes: to repel the invasion and annexation of a sovereign state, to protect the inhabitants of certain designated areas from grave threats, to restore order in a collapsed state, to combat terrorism and piracy, even to achieve regime change—the list goes on. Never before has there been such a period marked by repeated authorizations for, and uses of, armed force under the auspices of an international organization of global competence.

This record might easily seem to be a cause for celebration: at long last, the dispiriting decades when Cold War rivalries prevented the UN from taking decisive action in any crisis except over Korea in 1950 are now firmly behind us. Yet in fact the Security Council's record on the use of force in the post–Cold War years is far from being a success story. It is distinctly patchy. The Security Council system is best described not as one of "collective security," but rather as one of "selective security."[1] This term is not meant as either a manifesto or a criticism: it is a sober statement of fact. The selectivity that the term reflects is consistent with the UN Charter; it assumes many different forms; and its ramifications—some negative, some positive—will be explored.

Why is the record so patchy? The first and most obvious explanation is that in many situations—for a variety of reasons, by no means limited to the threat or use of the veto—the Security Council has failed to act. Sometimes it failed to discuss a situation at all, and sometimes, although it did discuss a situation, it could not agree on a course of action addressing the key issues at stake. In the period from 1945 to 1989, at a conservative count, there were 124 conflicts and crises in which the Council was inactive—just under three per year. Then in the period from 1990 to 2006 there were 28—just under two per year.[2] This indicates that, although the Council has been far more active in addressing conflicts in the post–Cold War era than it was before, it has still been highly selective. Even in cases where it has had significant involvement, it has often been unable to act effectively. For example, during the period of war and genocide in Rwanda in 1994, no countries on or outside the Council were willing to supply forces to protect the threatened Tutsi population; and in 1999 members of the Council disagreed about the use of force to end Serbian oppression in Kosovo.

A second explanation for the patchiness of the UN's record regarding the use of force is equally troubling. Even when forces have been authorized by the Council and are in place—whether in the context of enforcement or peacekeeping operations—their actual employment has been marked by difficulties, failures, and controversies. This problem, briefly summarized here, is discussed more fully at a later point in this chapter. Major international disagreements over how an authorization to use force was interpreted and implemented date back to the Cold War period. During the Korean War (1950–1953), there was a massive international row about whether the United States, at the head of a Council-authorized coalition to defend South Korea from invasion, was entitled to take certain controversial military actions. In the post–Cold War period there have been comparable disagreements—especially sharp in 2002–2003—revolving around the operational meaning of the authorizations given more than a decade earlier to the US-led coalition in respect of Iraq. And over Libya in 2011 there were poisonous international disagreements about how the NATO-led forces interpreted their mandate. There have also been extreme difficulties in carrying out UN mandates regarding the use of force during the conflicts in the former Yugoslavia in 1991–1995, in the Democratic Republic of the Congo since 1999, and in Afghanistan since 2002. In many cases in which the Council has authorized the use of force, there have been deep and enduring suspicions that certain powers were using the UN authorization for their own national interests.

These difficulties and failures help to explain why the post–Cold War era—despite being the period in which force has been authorized by the Council more frequently than ever before—has not seen as significant an amelioration of international relations as might have been anticipated. Certainly, state-led military interventions not authorized by the UN are by no means a thing of the past—witness the US-led invasion of Iraq in 2003, Russia's foray into Georgia in 2008, and Russia's unbadged military operations in Ukraine in 2014. A very few states—North Korea being the leading example—conspicuously reject key parts of the international order, especially the nuclear nonproliferation regime. Many more states clearly view the UN's contribution to their security as, at best, limited.

In short, the role of the Security Council in the post–Cold War years calls for rigorous analysis and sober reflection. Such reevaluation needs to take into account the changing facts of power, as the US role in the world is reconsidered, and new powers are emerging, especially in Asia. In this chapter I set the scene for fuller consideration in subsequent chapters of robust peacekeeping, sanctions, and NATO's role as a UN enforcer by focusing on seven issues: (1) the changing nature of conflict; (2) the Charter framework; (3) two main types of UN-authorized armed forces; (4) assessing UN peacekeeping and authorizations of force; (5) controversies surrounding UN-authorized uses of force; (6) the landscape of selective security; and (7) combining selectivity with legitimacy.

The Changing Nature of Conflict

The incidence and forms of conflict have changed in remarkable ways since 1945. There has been a significant decline of major interstate war—whether measured by number of wars or by casualties. At the same time, there has been a high incidence of intrastate conflicts, more commonly called civil wars. These include internationalized civil wars in which an outside power or powers have become directly involved. Here too there have been some signs of progress: there was a modest and uneven decline in the number of civil wars (and in the number of casualties in them) in the post–Cold War years, but then an increase again from 2009 onward.[3] Regarding the incidence and casualties of armed conflict generally, two leading specialists in this field wrote in 2013: "Overall, the 2000s has been the least conflict-ridden decade since the 1970s. A worrying finding, however, is that the number of internationalized intrastate conflicts continued to be at a high level for the fourth consecutive year."[4]

The decline in the incidence of international war has many causes. It takes place against a background of a more general decline in violence in modern societies over centuries, which can be attributed to the invention of printing, the establishment of states, the spread of commerce, the empowerment of women, and many other developments.[5] The decline in war in the past seven decades almost certainly owes something not just to long-term social trends, but also to particular factors: to memories of war—and especially of two world wars; to the development of nuclear weapons and the resulting focus on the concept of deterrence; to the increase in the number of democracies; to the benefits of globalization; to the growth of the international legal system; and indeed to the activities, values, and institutional framework of the United Nations. Even if all these factors are involved, there is no guarantee that the trends will necessarily continue: there have been periods before, such as the late nineteenth century, in which war was believed to be in decline.

The decline of international war does not necessarily mean that a capacity to deploy and use force has ceased to be important in international relations. Nor does it mean that the UN's main task is done. However, it does mean that the problems faced by the Security Council for most of its existence have been different from what was envisaged in 1945. The predominant overall process within the system of states since 1945 has been *fission*. The United Nations has grown from its original 50 to its present 193 members. The overwhelming majority of conflicts have been in postcolonial states—that is, in territories that were formerly under foreign rule, or were subordinate parts of the large socialist federations of the Soviet Union and Yugoslavia, and then achieved, or recovered, their independence as sovereign states.

Why is there so much conflict within, and sometimes between, postcolonial states? It is easy to blame it on the undoubted faults of the former colonial powers, or on alleged failings of their successors. However, a main cause is the sheer difficulty of establishing a stable political order, with an accepted constitutional system, legitimate borders both internal and external, confidence between different ethnic and religious communities, and good relations with neighbors. It is a striking fact that virtually all of the sixty-nine peacekeeping operations established by the UN between 1948 and 2014 were in postcolonial areas. A notable feature of many UN peacekeeping operations since 1988 is the extent of their involvement in postconflict reconstruction of societies and in assisting in processes of democracy building.

The conflicts in the postcolonial world have a character that makes them particularly difficult for outside powers or international organizations to address. In particular, many such conflicts, which generally have an element of civil war, raise such problems as whether or not, and if so in what circumstances, rebels are entitled to recognition and support; whether or not it is lawful and prudent to intervene militarily in a state without the consent of its government; and how to prevent competitive interventions by outside powers, with the risk of turning a civil war into an international one. And once an international organization is involved in civil-war situations, it faces a further set of problems: the blurring of lines between political and criminal violence; the necessity of collaborating with parties who may be discredited; and the difficulty of establishing a legitimate government to which it can transfer responsibilities at the end of an intervention.[6] With rare exceptions, the postcolonial wars of our era could hardly be more different from the classic case that has long been viewed as the trigger for bringing international security mechanisms into action: one in which the armed forces of one state commit an act of aggression by invading and occupying the territory of another state. Such clear-cut situations are a rarity today. It is natural that different states have different interests in a given war, and find it hard to agree on a common course of action. Or, sometimes, they may have no interests at stake, and therefore are reluctant to commit troops and lack staying power even when action may be needed. Moreover, as the experience of the post–Cold War era has confirmed, postconflict reconstruction of damaged societies is a fearsomely difficult task.[7]

In short, we are faced with a paradox. The success of international society in helping to get the problem of international war under control has been accompanied by a situation in which the UN is continuously engaged in addressing problems it was not created to deal with, and that indeed are notoriously hard to tackle—especially civil war, but also terrorist attacks and piracy.

The Charter Framework: Not Exactly Collective Security

The United Nations is commonly seen as an institution aimed at creating a system of collective security, but its architects clearly recognized the problems inherent in such a grand design. The term "collective security," which has a long lineage, is not mentioned in the Charter. It normally refers to a system, regional or global, in which each state in the system accepts that the security of one is the concern of all, and agrees to join in a collective response to threats to, and breaches of, the peace. That is not what we have, as reflected in the actual practice of the UN, and it is arguably not what the Charter envisages.

The UN Charter's overall approach (mainly laid down in Chapters VII and VIII) is, on the one hand, to establish a system with certain elements of collective security, and on the other to preserve the right of states to individual or collective self-defense, at least until the Security Council has taken necessary measures. The key provisions are in Chapter VII. The first article of this chapter, Article 39, states (in full): "The Security Council shall determine the existence of any threat to the peace, breach of the peace, or act of aggression and shall make recommendations, or decide what measures shall be taken in accordance with Articles 41 and 42, to maintain or restore international peace and security."

Other articles in Chapter VII confirm the Council's power to "take such action by air, sea, or land forces as may be necessary to maintain or restore international peace and security" and to do so "with the assistance of the Military Staff Committee."[8] So far, so good, from the point of view of collective security.

However, the Charter also contains some striking departures from a collective security system. The most important of these is Article 27, which gives each of the five permanent members of the Security Council a veto power. This ensures that the five cannot have the UN collective security system used against them, or indeed against a close ally. The General Assembly's "Uniting for Peace" resolution of November 3, 1950, which states that the Assembly is authorized to "make appropriate recommendations to Members for collective measures" in situations in which the Council fails to act, slightly modified the veto's effectiveness, at least in theory. But in practice, as Dominik Zaum has written, "it has failed to strengthen the UN as an instrument of collective security."[9]

Some other Charter provisions also indicate that the framers of the Charter were not putting all their eggs in the collective security basket. For example, Article 39 recognizes implicitly the power of the Security Council *not* to act in a particular crisis; Article 48 envisages the possibility of military action being taken by some (rather than all) UN member states; and Article 51 famously says, in part: "Nothing in the present Charter shall impair the inherent right of individual or collective self-defence if an armed attack occurs against a Member of the United Nations." Thus a system was established in which, from that day to this, a global organization of general competence has been superimposed on an older system of states, with neither trumping the other.

Two Main Types of UN-Authorized Armed Forces

Although the UN Security Council has authorized the use of armed forces in a variety of situations, it has authorized types of force and systems of command that differ from what was envisaged in the UN Charter. These departures from the script reflected profound and enduring realities. When confronted by situations requiring the large-scale use of force, the Council has not generally commanded substantial military action as anticipated in some provisions of Chapter VII. The perennial proposals for the Council to have standing military forces at its disposal were not realized.[10] Instead, the Council's primary methods for dealing with urgent security problems have fallen into two main categories—peacekeeping, and authorizations to use force—the distinction between which was never absolute.

Peacekeeping

Despite not being mentioned in the Charter, peacekeeping has become a symbol of the UN itself. The traditional principles of UN peacekeeping forces: they are composed of contingents from many different countries; they act impartially between belligerents, with their consent, and with the purpose of ensuring the implementation of a ceasefire or peace agreement; they operate under direct UN command and control; and they have been enjoined to keep the use of force to a minimum, usually for defense of the peacekeeping mission itself.

In the years since 1990, the Security Council has authorized fifty-one UN peacekeeping operations—a striking number compared to the eighteen such operations established in the years 1945–1990; and the Council has tended to authorize its peacekeeping forces, especially those in volatile postconflict situations, to use force not merely for self-defense, but also for certain other purposes, such as protecting threatened civilians and implementing the terms of a peace agreement. Sometimes its resolutions regarding the functions of UN peacekeeping operations have explicitly referred to Chapter VII of the UN Charter, and have authorized certain uses of force to implement the mandate.[11] The mixed experience of the UN in attempting to combine peacekeeping with a role involving a combat capability or even the actual use of armed force, which is a central subject in any overall assessment of the UN and the use of force, is discussed at relevant points later in this chapter, and is also surveyed in this volume by Jean-Marie Guéhenno (Chapter 18) and Richard Gowan (Chapter 36).

Authorization of States, Coalitions, and Regional Bodies to Use Force

In addition to its notable emphasis on UN peacekeeping forces, since 1990 the Council has also authorized a large number of forces not under direct UN command and control. This approach has often been adopted in situations in which something more than classic UN peacekeeping was needed. The result was the deployment of military forces in a wide variety of roles ranging from peacekeeping to combat. Council resolutions implicitly or explicitly authorized the use of armed forces by states, coalitions, or regional bodies, rather than under the command of the UN as such. Such resolutions authorizing non-UN forces are compatible with certain provisions in Chapter VII of the Charter (e.g., Articles 48 and 53), and have routinely referred to Chapter VII.[12] UN authorization of limited use of force by states has also become a common method for enforcing sanctions, air exclusion zones, and other restrictions on particular states and activities. There were twenty-seven such authorized military operations between 1950 and 2007,[13] and there have been more since. Examples of such authorizations to states, in most cases as leaders of coalitions, include:

- The United States in Korea (1950), Iraq-Kuwait (1990), Somalia (1992), and Haiti (1994).
- The United Kingdom in naval sanctions versus Rhodesia (1966).
- France in Rwanda (1994), Côte d'Ivoire (2003), the Democratic Republic of the Congo (2003), and Mali (2013).

• Italy in Albania (1997).
• Australia in East Timor (1999).

There has also been an increasing tendency for the Council to provide a measure of authorization or approval to certain actions of regional bodies and alliances, as distinct from individual states. Most of these actions have involved some combination of peacekeeping and use of force. Examples include:

• NATO in the former Yugoslavia: the Implementation Force (IFOR) in 1995–1996, and the Stabilization Force (SFOR) in 1996–2004.
• The European Union in the former Yugoslavia: the European Union Force (EUFOR Althea) since 2004.
• NATO in Afghanistan: the International Security Assistance Force (ISAF), led in 2002–2003 by individual NATO member countries, and, from 2003 to 2014, by NATO itself.
• The Economic Community of West African States (ECOWAS) in Côte d'Ivoire and Liberia: the ECOWAS Mission in Côte d'Ivoire (MICECI) and the ECOWAS Mission in Liberia (ECOMIL), both established in 2003.
• The African Union (AU) in Sudan and Somalia: the AU Mission in Sudan (AMIS), established in 2004, and the UN-AU Mission in Darfur (UNAMID) since 2007.

Sometimes the Council's authorizations have been to groupings of states that were not precisely defined—partly to leave open the possibility of other states joining, and partly because command-and-control arrangements were complex, ambiguous, or still being worked out. Thus in regard to the problem of piracy off the coast of Somalia, successive resolutions from 2008 onward have given authorization to a variety of states and regional bodies to "take part in the fight against piracy and armed robbery."[14] In the crisis in Libya in March 2011, the Council authorized "Member States that have notified the Secretary-General, acting nationally or through regional organizations or arrangements, and acting in cooperation with the Secretary-General, to take all necessary measures . . . to protect civilians and civilian populated areas."[15] This was in effect an authorization to NATO, and to the United States as the country taking the leading part in the subsequent military operations in Libya.

The causes of the increase in the number of authorizations to use force are numerous and cannot be systematically covered here. One significant element in many but by no means all cases is concern about refugee flows. In a single decade, from 1991 to 2000, there were at least nine crises in which humanitarian issues, including actual or potential refugee flows, were referred to prominently in Council resolutions, after which military action was authorized either by the Council itself or (in two cases) by major Western states. In all cases the reluctance of neighboring countries to accept large numbers of refugees contributed to the general willingness to treat situations producing large refugee flows as threats to international peace and security, calling for Council action.[16] In the twenty-first century the Council has continued to be preoccupied with refugee flows, the biggest of which has been the flight of more than 3.9 million from Syria since 2011. However, mainly because of differences between the major powers, the Council has been unable to address the Syrian conflict effectively.

The development of international law has contributed to the range of issues that can involve the Council in crises. In many fields—including human rights, the laws of war, the law of the sea, and the nonproliferation of nuclear weapons—there is a growing framework of norms to which the great majority of states subscribe. But this raises a question: What action is appropriate if a state is deemed to be in violation of important norms, and does this provide a justification for intervention? And sometimes, as for example over Iran's nuclear program, it may be reasonable to ask: Is it really better to treat this as an international legal question, which might imply a punitive mode, or to treat it as an adjustment in the balance of power, which may call for counterbalancing by other states? The question is of course simplistic: both ways of framing the issue (and of calibrating the response) are likely to coexist messily.

It was by a mixture of pragmatism and happenstance that the Council, rather than wielding force itself, arrived at a system of authorizing other entities—whether states or regional organizations—to use force. Yet this system does make sense. States, for all their faults, have certain necessary prerequisites for the employment of force: these include military decision-making structures and intelligence agencies. And regional bodies may have knowledge of a territory and its languages, and an incentive to act, that those in more distant capitals lack.

Assessing UN Peacekeeping and Authorizations of Force

Any attempt at assessment of the achievements of so many and varied deployments of armed forces—in both peacekeeping and enforcement modes—is fraught with difficulty. There have been many subjects of criticism: the tendency of missions to freeze a conflict but not resolve it; the remoteness of decisionmakers in New York from actual crises; the cumbersome nature of decisionmaking procedures; and the irrelevance of the UN to certain conflicts and crises. Yet some positive achievements should be recognized.

First, both peacekeeping and enforcement operations have sometimes played a significant role in one of their key tasks—helping in the reconstruction of damaged societies. A striking claim along these lines has been made by James Dobbins and Laurel Miller in a study of twenty UN and non-UN interventions:

> Societies emerging from conflict face many obstacles to achieving enduring peace, economic development and political reform. . . . Yet of 20 major peacekeeping or peace-enforcement interventions undertaken since the end of the Cold War, 16 have produced greater peace, 18 saw increases in democratisation (according to Freedom House), 17 saw improvements in government effectiveness (according to the World Bank), 18 experienced economic growth—indeed, generally faster than other countries in their region—and 18 saw improvements in their human development as measured by the UN.[17]

Second, UN-authorized enforcement operations have sent a message that conquering other states by force may provoke an international military response and result in failure. Two of the most egregious attacks by one state on another since 1945—North Korea's invasion of South Korea in June 1950, and Iraq's invasion and occupation of Kuwait in August 1990— were both reversed by UN-authorized and US-led coalitions. The message arising from this may form one part of the explanation for the decline in the incidence of international war.

Third, UN authorization can contribute to the legitimacy and therefore political acceptability of particular uses of force. Indeed, it may increase the willingness of states to use force for an international cause; and it may also increase the chances of securing political and material support from states not directly participating in the use of force. In late November 1990, some months after Iraq had occupied and purportedly annexed Kuwait, the Security Council passed its resolution authorizing the use of force.[18] When, six weeks later, the US Senate voted on whether to support military operations, the resolution passed by just six votes.[19] It is entirely imaginable that it would have failed if there had been no prior Council authorization. In 2003, the lack of explicit Council authorization for the US invasion of Iraq influenced the Turkish parliament in its decision not to grant the United States permission to use Turkey's territory as a staging ground for the opening of a northern front.

Fourth, some uses of force authorized by the Council have contributed to the conclusion of wars. For example, after the hideous massacre of some 8,000 Bosnian Muslims by Serbian forces at Srebrenica in July 1995, the UN and leading NATO members finally took action to end the long-standing siege of Sarajevo, both through the creation of a UN rapid-reaction force, located outside Sarajevo, and by a NATO air campaign against Bosnian Serb targets, Operation Deliberate Force. Of these two actions, the rapid-reaction force was probably the most decisive in ending the siege and then bringing about a ceasefire in mid-October 1995.[20] This was followed, after complex negotiations, by the Dayton Accords of November 20–21, 1995. Curiously, these significant uses of force toward the end of the Bosnian war have scarcely entered into public consciousness in NATO countries. Perhaps this is because, since they were not opposed by any major body of opinion outside Serb areas, there was no memorable controversy about them; and also because they followed the successful Croatian military offensive against the Serb areas of Croatia. Because of this Croatian action, it was hard to judge exactly which events had applied most pressure to the Serb leaders in Bosnia and Belgrade. Yet the lesson of these events has been absorbed nonetheless. As Kofi Annan's memoirs indicate, they marked an important stage in the evolution of thinking at UN headquarters and also in member states.[21] A view emerged that UN passivity in the face of outrages, especially mass killings of civilians, could itself put missions, and indeed the organization itself, at risk. Henceforth, when UN peacekeeping forces were deployed, the old UN dogma that force should not be used to achieve the objectives of a UN peacekeeping operation was called into question. And the NATO-led Implementation Force (IFOR), authorized by the Security Council and deployed in Bosnia in December 1995, had notably broad authority from the UN to use force, and more military credibility than UNPROFOR (UN Protection Force, the peacekeeping force in the former Yugoslavia) had ever had.

Fifth, it is likely that some massacres and forced displacements of populations have been averted. For example, in Libya in 2011, Colonel Muammar Qaddafi's threats and actions against his opponents were extreme. The NATO air operations there probably prevented many killings—particularly in the eastern city of Benghazi, which was a center of opposition to Qaddafi. However, even if it achieved a degree of success, the whole episode constitutes a new chapter in an old story—of the controversial character of many UN-authorized uses of force, and the ambiguity of the eventual outcomes.

Controversies Surrounding UN-Authorized Uses of Force

In earlier centuries, uses of force under international auspices frequently involved controversy. The UN era is no exception. Indeed, it is not only the human and economic costs of military action, but also the disagreements about its conduct and purposes, that help to explain why there has never been a case in which the Security Council has required all states to take part in an action. Theoretically the Council is entitled to make that demand, but prudence has dictated otherwise. All military coalitions are of the willing, or the more-or-less willing. They are never universal. States and their inhabitants have different interests, different perceptions of the world, and different fears. And the more force is used, even if under Council authorization, the more the focus switches to individual states rather than to the UN.

Discussion of five controversies follows. Most if not all of them involve matters that have resulted in considerable loss of life.

Authorized Forces Interpreting the Mandate Broadly

The first and most corrosive criticism of the UN's record is that the country or coalition authorized to use force, even in a perfectly good cause, then proceeds to do so in a manner that goes beyond what were understood to be the initial terms of its mandate. There have been several major controversies of this kind. All have involved the United States and, to a lesser degree, other Western powers. The first was over Korea. In June 1950, following a major North Korean invasion of South Korea, the Council had demanded that the North withdraw its armed forces to the 38th Parallel, and had also authorized the United States to lead a coalition of states "to repel the armed attack and to restore international peace and security in the area."[22] The Council's decision, which was possible only because the Soviet Union had unwisely absented itself from the Council, was from the start the subject of disputes between communist states and the West. Then, during the course of the war, came a further source of acrimony. The US-led forces, after crossing the 38th Parallel, went deep into North Korean territory, and the US government hinted at possible use of atomic weapons. China became deeply involved in support of North Korea. These developments caused strong dissent in the UN and even among US allies. Many states sought to restrain the United States, to some effect. William Stueck, a historian of the Korean War, commenting on the UN role in this process, concluded that "the organization demonstrated a utility of some consequence."[23]

The US involvement in containing Iraq from 1991 onward also involved controversy about whether the original November 1990 Council mandate to use force could be viewed as implying continuing authority over a decade later, and in significantly changed circumstances. At the time of the invasion of Iraq in March 2003, the United States and United Kingdom argued that there was such authority: that because of Iraq's alleged failure to comply with Security Council resolutions, and ceasefire terms concluded at the end of the 1991 Gulf hostilities, they were entitled to invade all of Iraq and to depose Saddam Hussein. The impatience of the United States to do so illustrated a built-in problem of the international security system: the lead state had to carry exceptional burdens, keeping large numbers of troops in the region so as to provide an effective counterweight to Iraq's forces. It was all very well for states not directly involved to counsel patience, but could the United States be expected to keep its forces in the region indefinitely? The rest of the world was deeply skeptical, and with good reason: the United States and its allies were stretching the elastic in their 1990 mandate to the breaking point.

Finally, the Council-authorized and NATO-led military operations in Libya in 2011 led to widespread suspicion that once again Western powers had gone beyond their mandate. The mission had been defined in the authorizing resolution as being "to protect civilians and civilian populated areas under threat of attack," but it quickly assumed the form of attacks on regime installations—in other words, the taking of sides in the ongoing civil war. The Russian and Chinese representatives on the Council, when they joined those abstaining on the resolution (and thus, by not vetoing, ensured that it would pass) should probably have known that the military action would take this form. It was always going to be an air operation, and there is no practical way that air power could have protected Libyan civilians other than by taking sides. Indeed, the whole question of the practical difficulty of protecting civilians is also necessarily raised by that part of the Responsibility to Protect doctrine that allows for the possibility, in extreme circumstances, of external military protection for threatened societies. It is simply not obvious how that purpose is to be implemented. The risk of going beyond a Council mandate would be ever-present.

Other Problems of Mandates

A particular problem associated with UN-controlled operations is the rigidity of their mandates and rules of engagement. For example, the fact that the terms of a peacekeeping mission must be the subject of advance international agreement can seriously reduce its flexibility in fast-changing situations, leading to criticism from within and from outside.

Especially in cases where there is both a UN peacekeeping force in a territory, and provision for certain uses of force (for example, to protect civilians), the resulting arrangements regarding the use of force have sometimes been complex. They have had to be, not least because a widely dispersed UN peacekeeping force in day-to-day contact with the inhabitants may be particularly vulnerable to hostage-taking or reprisals if the UN or UN-authorized powers are simultaneously involved in hostilities in the country. The inevitable outcome is extensive and sometimes acrimonious consultation between the commanders of the peacekeeping force, national capitals, and the Council. In the war in Bosnia and Herzegovina in 1992–1995, such consultations were provided for in some particularly elaborate arrangements for authorization of force. Resolution 836 of June 4, 1993, included this convoluted provision: "Member States, acting nationally or through regional organizations or arrangements, may take, under the authority of the Security Council and subject to close coordination with the Secretary-General and UNPROFOR, all necessary measures, through the use of air power, in and around the safe areas in the Republic of Bosnia and Herzegovina, to support UNPROFOR in the performance of its mandate."

Not surprisingly, the resulting dual-key arrangement between the UN and NATO, which was in fact multi-key, whereby a use of force would in practice require the simultaneous consent of some national governments as well as the two international bodies, was a recipe for frustration. This in turn led to some important developments. In respect of the effective use of force in former Yugoslavia in summer 1995, fewer UN representatives were in the decisionmaking loop than would have been the case just months earlier.

War Crimes, Misconduct, and Unintended Disasters

Occasionally, forces operating in-country with a degree of UN authorization or recognition have engaged in one or another kind of misconduct. There have been serious incidents of violations of the laws of war—for example in Somalia in 1992–1993,[24] and in the occupation phase in Iraq in 2003–2004.[25] There have also been numerous cases of sexual abuse and exploitation by blue helmets: these have led to some disciplinary action by member states, and also to sustained efforts by the UN to prevent and punish such practices.[26]

In Haiti in 2010 a massive outbreak of cholera began, killing over 8,000 people in its first three years. The likely source of the epidemic was eventually traced back to UN peacekeepers from Nepal, one or more of whom may have been symptomless and unwitting carriers of the disease. Among the additional factors contributing to the outbreak was the poor sanitation system at a UN facility, and in the country generally.[27]

In short, the fact that peacekeeping and uses of force take place under UN auspices does not make them immune to the difficulties that have throughout history attended the activities of armed forces acting in distant countries. The Security Council is under an obligation to minimize war crimes, misconduct, and disasters—and it is essential to do so in the interests of the legitimacy and effectiveness of operations.

Is the Council Exceeding Its Authority?

The idea that the Council is going beyond the original conception of its functions has frequently surfaced in debate, especially in the 1990s. The UN was at that time entering new territory by authorizing a strikingly wide range of peacekeeping operations, interventions, and other uses of armed forces, and setting up such innovative bodies as the international criminal tribunals for the former Yugoslavia and Rwanda. Certain specific actions taken under the Council's authority, such as imposing sanctions on lists of individuals and groups involved in terrorism without due process or recourse mechanisms, were questioned on human rights grounds. In addition, there are understandable fears that the enlargement of the areas of

Council responsibility—involvement in intrastate conflicts, attempts to stop states from acquiring weapons of mass destruction, concern with humanitarian crises, or even environmental issues—could have adverse consequences for the powers of the wider membership of the UN as represented in the General Assembly, and indeed for the basic principle of the sovereign equality of states. However, it is hard to sustain the argument that in general the expansion of the Council's range of actions is illegal: the framers of the Charter deliberately accorded to the Council extensive powers to act in a wide variety of situations, not limited to the single case of aggression by one sovereign state against another. The most sensitive issues concern not the lawfulness of the Council's decisions to manage an increased range of activities, but rather its capacity to do so and the wisdom or otherwise of its decisions.

Forces Under UN Command:
Problems of Management and Legitimacy

All international forces, whether for peacekeeping or enforcement, face some familiar problems. Efficient management and strategic coherence are often scarce commodities. For example, in UN peacekeeping operations, all national contingents in reality operate under a dual chain of command, one chain going up to the force commander, and another going to their respective capitals, which generally reserve the right to block specific operations.

Such specific difficulties over the management and use of force are part of a broader picture of the UN having been unprepared for managing a wide range of peacekeeping and coercive operations in the post–Cold War era. That there were problems of supply and of command and control, and a need to strengthen both the staff in New York and headquarters in the field, came to be acknowledged in the Secretariat. Marrack Goulding, who had served as under-secretary-general for peacekeeping from 1986 to 1993, later wrote a book, *Peacemonger,* presenting a vivid picture of the overstretch at the UN in the early 1990s as it sought to cope with several crises simultaneously.[28] In 1993, the former head of UN forces in Sarajevo, Major-General Lewis MacKenzie, made a characteristically colorful complaint about UN management of operations: "Do not get into trouble as a commander in the field after 5 p.m. New York time, or Saturday and Sunday. There is no one to answer the phone."[29] A situation center was created at UN headquarters in the same year, but this was not enough to avert disaster in Africa one year later. The force commander of the UN peacekeeping force in Rwanda, General Roméo Dallaire, was shocked that the UN failed to heed his January 1994 warning of impending mass killings.[30]

Some of the criticisms of the Council's role as a proper authority for managing the possession and use of armed force reflect the awkward fact that powerful states, if they are willing to act on behalf of international order, need some recognized latitude in which to do so. This was a problem in earlier eras, when what was at issue was the rights and duties of "the great powers." It continues in the UN era. To a limited extent the UN Charter and the international order that has evolved since 1945 recognize that certain states have a special degree of latitude. Yet at numerous points— over authorizations to major powers to act on the UN's behalf, the inevitable discretion used in decisions about whether and how to intervene, the maintenance of a nuclear weapons status for some while denying it to others, and the need to involve more powers than the current permanent five in the management of international order—the legitimacy of the present order is continuously in question.

A further challenge to the idea of the Council as legitimizer has arisen repeatedly in the post–Cold War period. In several wars, including in Somalia and Bosnia-Herzegovina in the early 1990s, some parties to the conflicts showed little regard for the UN in general or the forces it had authorized. UN peacekeepers were attacked or kidnapped with alarming frequency. In 1993 alone, over 200 military personnel in UN peacekeeping operations were killed. The confidence that the Council's international legitimacy, and the strength of the powers represented on it, would translate into near-automatic respect, has evaporated.

Four ways of addressing this challenge emerged. One was the adoption, on December 9, 1994, of the Convention on the Safety of United Nations and Associated Personnel. This convention criminalizes attacks on UN personnel and their premises and vehicles, but its protection would not apply to UN forces engaged in combat against organized armed forces—in which case the law of international armed conflict would apply. An optional protocol, adopted in 2005, reflecting concern about a continuing pattern of attacks, enlarged its scope of application. A second way of addressing the vulnerability of UN operations in internal conflicts was to bunker up and hunker down, which tends to limit the possibility of building up relations of trust with the inhabitants of host countries. A third way was to emphasize the importance of building up relations of trust with the inhabitants of areas where they are deployed: in this approach, peacekeeping and other forces need to pay at least as much attention to local sources of legitimacy as they do to that more distant source of legitimacy, the UN.[31] And a fourth way was to attempt to develop a more coherent UN approach to all aspects of the organization and management of force under UN auspices—an approach particularly emphasized in 2000 in the key report of the Panel on UN Peace Operations, chaired by the highly respected Algerian statesman Lakhdar Brahimi.[32] All of these ways of responding to the challenge reflect continuing unease at some of the consequences of the UN being so deeply involved in complex conflicts, often in failing states, where the clarity of the old distinction between peacekeeping and use of force has unavoidably eroded.

The Landscape of Selective Security

The evidence presented here suggests that the UN Security Council's involvement in armed conflicts is always, and necessarily, characterized by selectivity. What are the forms and consequences of this selectivity, and how does it relate to the security landscape of the twenty-first century? Four general issues are touched on briefly here: the forms of selectivity; the complexity of contemporary conflicts; the US role in selective security; and the Council's composition.

Forms of Selectivity

The selectivity regarding the use of force that has been outlined here has several distinct forms: First, selectivity of the Council, and especially of the P5, in deciding which issues to address or not address; and in the framing of a problem and determining which of many possible actions to take. Second, selectivity of all UN member states regarding their willingness to provide military and material resources for Council-mandated operations. Third, selectivity of states involved in a conflict about whether they wish the conflict to be addressed by the Council. Fourth, selectivity of all of these actors in the choice of whether to handle an issue through other organizations, whether regional or global. And fifth, selectivity in the choice of the military means employed by states and coalitions that have been authorized to use force, especially in light of their interests and national military cultures.

When the UN has acted over a particular war or crisis, many of the means employed have been problematic, both because of the difficulty of the issues, and because of the reluctance of states to commit themselves deeply or take great risks. Despite important exceptions, there has been a tendency to prefer methods of remote control (economic sanctions, air exclusion zones, arms embargoes, attempts to broker ceasefires) or limited involvement with the consent of the parties (peacekeeping, observer, and humanitarian activities). Air operations have been particularly prominent, as in the US-led bombing campaign against Iraq in the 1991 Gulf War and the 2011 NATO-led campaign in Libya. This preference for certain types of action over others constitutes another manifestation of selectivity.

There are many explanations for these various forms of selectivity. They include the limitations of the UN's resources and decisionmaking procedures, especially the veto; the continuation of power-political rivalries; and the limited willingness of states, both large and small, to place their military assets at the disposal of the UN. They also include the large number and inherent complexity of conflicts in the postcolonial world.

The Complexity of Contemporary Conflicts

The nature of the problems with which the UN is confronted adds to the case for selectivity. Most contemporary armed conflicts are about the problems of new or reemerging states—problems that in certain respects are more complex than those in international wars, and that have given rise to the need for more robust forms of peacekeeping. In a pioneering study of "the use of force to compel mandate compliance in situations that fall between peacekeeping and full-scale enforcement," Jane Boulden examined UN operations in the Congo (1960–1964), Somalia (1992–1995), and Bosnia (1992–1995). Her conclusion was sobering: "The case studies demonstrate that peace enforcement is not an easy or straightforward undertaking for the United Nations. The complexity of peace enforcement operations creates difficult, sometimes intractable dilemmas at the operational and mandate levels. The situation on the ground is highly changeable. Political and military support from member states is equally changeable. The risks of failure are high."[33]

This observation could apply equally to some recent and ongoing operations of the UN. It points to a worrying fact: if there is an ongoing conflict in which there is no peace to keep, or lassitude in the international community because of the high costs and limited achievements of recent UN-authorized activities, or both, there is bound to be caution, and therefore selectivity, regarding further involvements. Thus it was largely Somalia-induced caution that made the United States and other states particularly reluctant to intervene in Rwanda in 1994 in face of genocide.

The Role of the United States in Selective Security

Historically, the United States has been the country that has most often used its power on the basis of prior UN approval. This has led to criticisms of alleged US domination of the UN. From a US perspective the same pattern is seen in a radically different light: only the United States and its coalition partners are prepared to maintain a military intervention capability, and are willing to put their military resources and their soldiers' lives at risk on behalf of particular causes agreed at the UN, while others criticize from the sidelines; and, what is more, the United States must bear simultaneously the burden not only of acting for the UN, but also of acting independently as a major power and leader of alliances in a world that does not yet have a general system of collective security.

In fact, the United States, along with the NATO alliance in which it is the major stakeholder, is far from being the only state that has been authorized by the Security Council to use force. As noted earlier, Australia, France, Italy, the United Kingdom, ECOWAS, and the African Union are among those that have been authorized to lead particular uses of force. They were chosen by the Council for a variety of reasons, including their capacity and will to provide the necessary intervention forces. The very variety of the different organizations and states that have been authorized to use force reflects a sensible recognition that the United States, which has historically been the main enforcer for the UN as well as having a conflicted relationship with it, is in a state of weariness about its extensive international involvements.

Yet the US role in using force for UN-mandated purposes has undeniably been greater that that of any other state, and raises the question as to whether the US ways of waging war have had a disproportionate effect not only on the military actions of the UN, but also on the whole structure and purpose of UN interventionism. US exceptionalism, notions of manifest destiny, and a belief in spreading democracy to societies without deep understanding of them, have all fed into certain UN-mandated operations and have posed problems in them—never more so than in August 2003 when the headquarters of the UN mission in Baghdad was attacked by insurgents opposed to the US-led invasion of Iraq and all that the US presence stood for.

The US role has also been criticized on the grounds that the United States has taken to exceptional lengths the freedom that the veto confers to each of the P5 to stop any resolution critical of a favored state. There has been much controversy about the repeated US use of the veto to prevent the passage of resolutions critical of Israel. The fact that the Israel-Palestine problem remains unresolved despite having been on the Council agenda for over six decades is regularly upheld as one of the greatest failures of the Council. The fact that Russia has also used its veto power to protect its friends, such as the Syrian government in the civil war from 2011 onward, does nothing to alleviate criticism of the Council system.

Selectivity and the Council's Composition

The fact that the Council must necessarily be selective about which crises to address, and what policies to pursue in them, adds salience to the everdifficult question of the Council's composition. During the Cold War, when the Council was able to act only on a restricted range of issues, its composition was less important than it is today. It is extraordinary that, over threequarters of a century after its creation, the Council still has the same five permanent members. Although enlarging the Council might indeed risk reducing its efficiency, the Council's present composition undoubtedly weakens its legitimacy, and that of the system of selective security.

However, the problem is impossible to solve if an existing permanent member opposes change and is prepared to use the veto on that issue. The permanent member that has the most conspicuous reasons to oppose change is China, for the simple reason that two of the strongest candidates for consideration for permanent member status are India and Japan—two powers with which China has historically had a difficult relationship. In both of these cases, a radical improvement in bilateral relations with China is a precondition for achieving Council reform.

Nor is the veto system likely to be radically changed. It is not plausible that major powers, having remained in the UN for almost seven decades on the basis of a veto power that provides them with important reassurances, will forego those reassurances. The remarkable feature of the UN veto system is how few countries possess this power: the UN Charter provision whereby just five have the veto is actually much less of an obstacle than was the provision in the League of Nations Covenant whereby all members of the League of Nations Council had a de facto veto (because it operated on the basis of consensus). In recent years, there have been some signs that it is no longer automatically accepted that any new permanent members of the UN Security Council would have the veto, but any progress on reform may depend on some significant concession by the veto-wielding states.

As far as the use of force is concerned, by no means all threats and uses of the veto have had negative effects. When the United States and United Kingdom were planning military action over Iraq in 2003, their leaders were furious at the threatened use of the veto by Russia, France, and China, yet in retrospect it is to the credit of the Council that it did not provide support in advance for what turned out to be an operation that was poorly justified and an occupation that was badly planned and executed.

In the absence of major Council reform, the legitimacy of the use of force under UN auspices needs to be ensured in practical and pragmatic ways. There are signs that this is happening. The Council itself, in its decisionmaking processes, has consulted more widely than it did in the Cold War years. Key issues have been discussed with other international organizations, and in other bodies as well as at the UN. A wide range of countries and international organizations has been authorized to use force. And there is a dawning recognition that it is sheer illusion to think that a military or peacekeeping operation can achieve legitimacy purely from above: it also needs to be based on a sound understanding of, and respect for, the society in which it operates, including its history, cultures, and languages.

Combining Selectivity with Legitimacy

As I have sought to show, the process since 1990 whereby the Council has authorized an unprecedented number of uses of force, by a remarkable range of states and regional organizations, has been highly selective, and has also involved a range of problems concerning the legitimacy of UN decisionmaking and operations. It is easy to argue that selectivity has been damaging: that the Council, in deciding where to intervene, has picked the low-hanging fruit; that various kinds of double standards have been involved; that there have been terrible failures; that many serious problems such as Palestine and Syria have received inadequate attention; and that other crises have been handled badly.

Yet overall the process has had beneficial effects: contributing to the saving of lives, assisting the reconstruction of damaged societies, helping to maintain a continuing low incidence of international war, and demonstrating that an international organization can be tough-minded. The Security Council has slowly adapted to address types of conflict very different from those it was set up to tackle, and has learned much from this difficult experience. One of the things it has learned is the necessity for various forms of robust peacekeeping and intervention. Another is the inevitability of selectivity as regards the use of force under its auspices. The Council has at least begun to adjust to a world in which the United States is no longer in quite such a leading position. A complete system of collective security being unattainable in present conditions, it is the Council's job to be selective.

The challenge is to combine selectivity with legitimacy. There is no magic solution. There will always be tension between the Council's global responsibilities and its actual performance, and between the Council's present composition and the changing facts of power in the world. Yet short of solving all of the Council's legitimacy problems, there are means of mitigating some of their damaging consequences: broadening of the Council's consultative processes, as well as its composition, to include a wide range of states and nonstate bodies; continuing the process of cooperation with regional organizations; restraining the threat and use of the veto; explaining better why the Council has acted and not acted in particular situations; and recognizing that any and every UN operation requires local legitimacy (from the forces and populations involved in a conflict area) at least as much as it requires legitimacy from on high (in the form of UN Security Council resolutions).

The UN Security Council frequently finds itself operating in an uncomfortable position, caught between the attractive vision of being at the center of a comprehensive system of collective security and the grim reality of continued power politics that the Security Council can sometimes mitigate but cannot replace. The attractive vision can itself be damaging, because it feeds the very human urge to find some state or other entity to blame for what is in fact a broader failure to achieve a noble goal. A frank recognition not only of the inevitability of selectivity, but also of its multifaceted character, is a necessary basis for constructive international debate about how the Security Council can demonstrate its relevance and legitimacy in the troubled international politics of the twenty-first century.

Notes

1. Adam Roberts and Dominik Zaum, *Selective Security: War and the United Nations Security Council Since 1945,* Adelphi Paper no. 395 (London: International Institute for Strategic Studies, 2008).

370 THE USE OF FORCE

2. These figures are based on a list of cases in "Appendix 7: List of Armed Conflicts and Crises, 1945–2006," in *The United Nations Security Council and War,* edited by Vaughan Lowe, Adam Roberts, Jennifer Welsh, and Dominik Zaum (Oxford: Oxford University Press, 2008). Of the armed conflicts and crises listed, 152 are marked as having no Security Council involvement, and 54 as having "low" or "very low" Council involvement. See also John P. Dunbabin, "The Security Council in the Wings," in the same volume.

3. Tables from Uppsala Conflict Data Program (UCDP), "Armed Conflict by Type, 1946–2013" and "Non-State Fatalities by Year, 1989–2013," both available at http://www.pcr.uu.se/research/ucdp/charts_and_graphs/#type. See also Ralph Sundberg, Kristine Eck, and Joakim Kreutz, "Introducing the UCDP Non-State Conflict Dataset," *Journal of Peace Research* 49, no. 2 (March 2012): 351–362; Lotta Themnér and Peter Wallensteen, "Armed Conflicts, 1946–2013," *Journal of Peace Research* 51, no. 4 (July 2014): 541–554; and Human Security Report Project, *Human Security Report 2012: Sexual Violence, Education, and War—Beyond the Mainstream Narrative* (Vancouver: Human Security Press, 2012), pp. 151–153, 186–189.

4. Lotta Themnér and Peter Wallensteen, "Armed Conflicts, 1946–2012," *Journal of Peace Research* 50, no. 4 (July 2013): 509.

5. Explored in Steven Pinker, *The Better Angels of Our Nature: The Decline of Violence in History and Its Causes* (London: Allen Lane, 2011), pp. 572–573.

6. Points particularly emphasized by Jean-Marie Guéhenno, keynote address, authors' meeting, Greentree Estate, Manhasset, June 13–15, 2013.

7. James Mayall and Ricardo Soares de Oliveira, eds., *The New Protectorates: International Tutelage and the Making of Liberal States* (London: Hurst, 2011).

8. United Nations, *Charter of the United Nations* (San Francisco, June 26, 1945), Articles 42 and 46.

9. Dominik Zaum, "The Security Council, the General Assembly, and War: The Uniting for Peace Resolution," in Lowe et al., *The United Nations Security Council and War,* p. 173.

10. Adam Roberts, "Proposals for UN Standing Forces: A Critical History," in Lowe et al., *The United Nations Security Council and War,* pp. 99–130.

11. The following are just a few examples of the many authorizations to UN peacekeeping operations to use a degree of force, and of mentioning Chapter VII: United Nations Security Council Resolutions 836 (on Bosnia and Herzegovina), S/RES/836 (June 4, 1993); 1272 (on East Timor), S/RES/1272 (October 25, 1999); and 2098 (on the DRC), S/RES/2098 (March 28, 2013).

12. The following are examples of authorizations to non-UN operations; they provide for the operations to use a degree of force, and all mention Chapter VII: United Nations Security Council Resolutions 1031 (December 15, 1995), UN Doc. S/RES/1031 (establishing the NATO-led Implementation Force [IFOR] in the former Yugoslavia); 1101 (March 28, 1997), UN Doc. S/RES/1101 (establishing the Italian-led Multinational Protection Force [MPF] in Albania); and Resolution 1744 (February 20, 2007), UN Doc. S/RES/1744 (establishing the AU Mission in Somalia [AMISOM]).

13. For a list of these twenty-seven cases, with details of authorizing resolutions for all of them, see "Appendix: UN Security Council–Authorised Military Operations, 1950–2007," in Roberts and Zaum, *Selective Security,* pp. 79–83.

14. For example, United Nations Security Council Resolution 2020, S/RES/2020 (November 22, 2011).

15. United Nations Security Council Resolution 1973, S/RES/1973 (March 17, 2011).

16. Adam Roberts, "Refugees and Military Intervention," in *Refugees in International Relations,* edited by Alexander Betts and Gil Loescher (Oxford: Oxford University Press, 2011), p. 220.

17. James Dobbins and Laurel Miller, "Overcoming Obstacles to Peace," *Survival* 55, no. 1 (February–March 2013): 103.

18. United Nations Security Council Resolution 678, S/RES/678 (November 29, 1990).

19. Joint resolution of the US Congress authorizing the use of military force to expel Iraq from Kuwait, January 12, 1991. The vote in the US Senate had been fifty-two to forty-seven.

20. Susan L. Woodward, "The Security Council and the Wars in the Former Yugoslavia," in Lowe et al., *The United Nations Security Council and War,* p. 437.

21. Kofi Annan, with Nader Mousavizadeh, *Interventions: A Life in War and Peace* (New York: Penguin, 2012), pp. 72–73.

22. United Nations Security Council Resolutions 82 (June 25, 1950), UN Doc. S/RES/82; and 83 (June 27, 1950), UN Doc. S/RES/83.

23. William Stueck, "The United Nations, the Security Council, and the Korean War," in Lowe et al., *The United Nations Security Council and War,* p. 279.

24. Commission of Inquiry into the Deployment of Canadian Forces to Somalia, *Dishonored Legacy: Lessons of the Somalia Affair* (Ottawa: Canadian Government Publishing, 1997).

25. In both the United States and the United Kingdom, there have been several official commissions of inquiry into violations of the laws of war that occurred during the occupation of Iraq after the invasion of 2003.

26. A useful account of the problem and the UN's action on it is "Special Measures for Protection from Sexual Exploitation and Sexual Abuse: Report of the Secretary-General," UN doc. A/67/766, February 28, 2013, especially pp. 4–8, http://www.un.org/ga/search/view_doc.asp?symbol=A/67/766.

27. Daniele G. Lantagne, Balakrish Nair, Claudio F. Lanata, and Alejandro Cravioto, "The Cholera Outbreak in Haiti: Where and How Did It Begin?" *Current Topics in Microbiology and Immunology* 379 (2014): 145–164; see "Conclusions."

28. Marrack Goulding, *Peacemonger* (London: John Murray, 2002), pp. 329, 334, 344.

29. Simon Jones, "General MacKenzie Slams UN's Nine-to-Fivers," *The Independent,* January 31, 1993, www.independent.co.uk/news/world/gen-mackenzie-slams-uns-ninetofivers-1481793.html.

30. General Roméo Dallaire, cable to Major-General Maurice Baril, military adviser to the Secretary-General, UN headquarters, January 11, 1994. See also Roméo Dallaire with Brent Beardsley, *Shake Hands with the Devil: The Failure of Humanity in Rwanda* (Toronto: Random House Canada, 2003).

31. Jeni Whalan, *How Peace Operations Work: Power, Legitimacy, and Effectiveness* (Oxford: Oxford University Press, 2013).

32. United Nations General Assembly, *Report of the Panel on United Nations Peace Operations* (Brahimi Report), August 17, 2000. See especially the admirably succinct "Executive Summary," pp. viii–xv, http://unrol.org/doc.aspx?n=brahimi+report+peacekeeping.pdf.

33. Jane Boulden, *Peace Enforcement: The United Nations Experience in Congo, Somalia, and Bosnia* (Westport: Praeger, 2001), p. 129.

18

Robust Peacekeeping and the Limits of Force

Jean-Marie Guéhenno

"ROBUST PEACEKEEPING" REMAINS AN ELUSIVE CONCEPT. AFTER more than half a century of United Nations peace operations, it has proved difficult to adapt a peacekeeping doctrine developed in the 1950s to a strategic context characterized by new types of conflict. Meanwhile, the operational posture of UN peacekeepers has witnessed a major transformation since the early 1990s, as peacekeepers have been deployed in theaters where there was no peace to keep and where they have actually used force to defend themselves, their mandate, and the civilian population. However, the lessons of that experience remain unclear, as United Nations peacekeepers enter uncharted territory in the Democratic Republic of the Congo, where they are mandated to conduct "offensive operations," and in Mali, where they are mandated to fight terrorist and insurgent groups.

In this chapter I trace the evolution of peacekeeping doctrine established by the UN Security Council and Secretariat to evaluate the operational realities of "robust peacekeeping," focusing on the case studies of the DRC, Côte d'Ivoire, and Mali, and to draw policy lessons applicable to the use of force in the context of UN peacekeeping. The chapter is largely based on my own personal experience as the under-secretary-general for peacekeeping from 2000 to 2008, when I was experimenting with new approaches to the role of force in peacekeeping.

The Elusive Quest for Doctrinal Clarity

When the Charter of the United Nations was negotiated in San Francisco, the concept of peacekeeping did not exist, let alone the concept of robust peacekeeping. This is not to suggest that the drafters of the UN Charter ignored the role of military force in the maintenance of peace. On the contrary, they had seen how a lack of decisive action to stop aggressive behavior in international crises had gradually destroyed the authority of the League of Nations and opened the way to World War II.

Determined to create a different system, the countries that had won the war planned to continue their alliance in peacetime: the Military Staff Committee of the chiefs of staff of the five permanent Security Council members provided for in the UN Charter was a reflection of that intent. But this vision was never tested, because the wartime alliance split and the East-West divide became the biggest threat to peace and security. Indeed, the only action taken by the Security Council that follows the spirit, if not the letter, of the Charter may have been the Gulf War in 1990.[1] While the Military Staff Committee was not activated, a coalition of countries led by the United States waged war and repelled the invasion of Kuwait, thus enforcing the agreed international order.

The invention of peacekeeping in the context of the Suez Crisis by UN Secretary-General Dag Hammarskjöld, Canadian foreign minister Lester Pearson, and UN undersecretary for special political affairs Ralph Bunche was a radical departure from the initial vision of the Charter. Despite its name, the first UN Emergency Force (UNEF I)—which was deployed along the Suez Canal in 1956 to supervise the withdrawal of the armed forces of France, Israel, and the United Kingdom from Egyptian territory and, later, to serve as a buffer between the Egyptian and Israeli forces—was never meant to use force, and there was some irony in the fact that two of the permanent members of the Security Council were among the troops withdrawing. The potential enforcers envisaged by the Charter had become part of the problem. The multinational UNEF peacekeeping troops who replaced them lacked the mandate, capacity, and will to conduct any enforcement action. Although they carried guns, their role was a largely symbolic one, intended to provide cover for an orderly withdrawal of British, French, and Israeli troops and act as a political tripwire for the Security Council if it had the will to act.[2]

The Suez crisis thus served to establish three principles governing peacekeeping missions: consent of the parties, impartiality, and use of force only in self-defense. The founders of peacekeeping essentially conceived it as "the projection of the principle of non-violence onto the military plane."[3] Throughout the Cold War, blue helmets continued to refrain from the actual use of force, even when they included armed battalions, as in Cyprus, Lebanon, or the Golan Heights. The first Congo operation of the early 1960s was a major exception, not to be repeated, when the UN force even included Swedish fighter aircraft.[4]

The end of the Cold War and the ensuing enormous expansion of peacekeeping operations, both in scope and in quantity, fundamentally altered the understanding of the use of force in UN operations. Peacekeepers confronted nonstate actors who had little consideration for international law, and were called upon to perform new tasks, such as the protection of humanitarian workers. In this context, a growing number of missions were authorized under Chapter VII of the Charter, which took on a new meaning. Chapter VII provisions were originally intended to override the objections of a member state—especially one that could be the aggressor, like Germany in the 1930s—by allowing the Security Council to decide on the use of force. By the 1990s, Chapter VII became synonymous with "robust use of force" even with consent of the host country, though member states continued to lack consensus on the matter.

The UN Secretariat itself has wavered over the years. In 1992, Secretary-General Boutros Boutros-Ghali recommended in *An Agenda for Peace* the creation of "peace-enforcement units," observing that "there may not be a dividing line between peacemaking and peace-keeping."[5] There were attempts, in Somalia and in Bosnia, to adopt a more robust posture, but they ultimately failed. Somalia is remembered for the precipitous withdrawal of the peacekeeping force after a botched US operation against a Somali warlord, and the tragedy of Srebrenica overshadows the limited accomplishments of the UN in Yugoslavia. After these disasters and the UN's failure to halt the 1994 genocide in Rwanda, Boutros-Ghali reversed his position in his *Supplement to An Agenda for Peace,* released in 1995: "The logic of peace-keeping flows from political and military premises that are quite distinct from those of enforcement; and the dynamics of the latter are incompatible with the political process that peace-keeping is intended to facilitate. To blur the distinction between the two can undermine the viability of the peace-keeping operation and endanger its personnel."[6] In the face of failure, the UN turned an about-face on the use of force.

The next five years saw a precipitous decline of UN peacekeeping until Secretary-General Kofi Annan, who had been in charge of the UN's Department of Peacekeeping Operations (DPKO) during the crises of the early and mid-1990s before ascending to the helm of the organization, saw the need to put peacekeeping on firmer footing.[7] Annan gave the task of elaborating recommendations to an independent panel chaired by Lakhdar Brahimi, a former Algerian foreign minister with a distinguished UN career. While maintaining the "bedrock principles of peacekeeping" established almost half a century before by Hammarskjöld, the Brahimi Report, published in 2000, allowed for an evolution of the doctrine on the use of force. The report noted that consent could be manipulated, that impartiality should not be conflated with moral equivalence, and that UN forces should have the "willingness to accept the risk of casualties on behalf of the mandate."[8]

Although the Brahimi panel stressed that "the United Nations does not wage war,"[9] some states still found cause for concern, notably troop contributors from the Non-Aligned Movement (NAM), the UN's caucus of developing countries, who were concerned that a deviation of the peace-keeping doctrine would increase the level of risk incurred by their troops. These considerations led Secretary-General Annan to reaffirm in his implementation report that peacekeeping troops should always be deployed with the consent of the parties. Annan added: "The Panel's rec-ommendations for clear mandates, 'robust' rules of engagement, and big-ger and better equipped forces . . . are practical measures to achieve deter-rence through strength, with the ultimate purpose of diminishing, not increasing, the likelihood for the need to use force, which should always be seen as a measure of last resort."[10] Annan implicitly excluded the proactive or preemptive use of force. Such nuanced elaborations were, however, of little use to the troops confronting increasingly thorny situa-tions in field operations.

In parallel to these debates, the Security Council further complicated the role of peacekeepers by increasingly including mandates on the protec-tion of civilians. This addition, more than any doctrinal rethinking on the use of force, has driven changes in the posture of peacekeepers. A role for blue helmets in the protection of civilians first appeared in the 1999 resolu-tion authorizing, under Chapter VII, a new mission in Sierra Leone to "take the necessary action to ensure the security and freedom of movement of its personnel and, within its capabilities and areas of deployment, to afford protection to civilians under imminent threat of physical violence."[11] Simi-lar provisions have since been included in the mandates of most peacekeep-ing operations, the UN Mission in Ethiopia and Eritrea (UNMEE), deployed from 2000 to 2008, being an exception. Of the fourteen peace-keeping operations deployed in 2013, nine had a mandate to protect civil-ians, and those that didn't were carryovers from earlier times. And for some of the bigger missions, like the UN Organization Stabilization Mission in the Democratic Republic of the Congo (MONUSCO), the protection of civilians, including in the military dimension through "robust peacekeep-ing," is at the core of the mandate.

Seeking to bring some operational clarity to this debate, the DPKO, in 2008, under my direction, published the Capstone Doctrine on UN peace-keeping. Maintaining adherence to the three fundamental principles of peacekeeping, the Capstone Doctrine differentiated the strategic use of force from its tactical use in new peacekeeping contexts, "often character-ized by the presence of militias, criminal gangs, and other spoilers who may actively seek to undermine the peace process or pose a threat to the civilian population."[12] On the basis of a strategic agreement between the "main parties" to a conflict, against whom force is not to be used, a peace-keeping force with a robust posture would raise the threshold spoilers must cross to have any hope of achieving their goals. Under these assumptions, the tactical use of force is a tool among many others—both carrots and sticks—to shepherd a peace process: it is but one of the levers that can, in a calibrated manner, strengthen the UN's political authority in a conflict situation. As such, force was viewed in the Capstone Doctrine to have no strategic role.

Today, the UN Secretariat tries to find a conclusion to this confusing debate by allowing for the use of force not only in self-defense but also in defense of each operation's mandate, effectively borrowing language from the Brahimi Report and the Capstone Doctrine. Since mandates are determined by the Security Council and can vary considerably, this exception opens the way to all sorts of possibilities for the use of force, most notably when matched with mandates to protect civilians. The debate in effect has shifted from a discussion on the established principles of peacekeeping, which nobody dares challenge, to one on the operational needs of a particular operation.

There is a persistent gap, however, between the debate on robust peace-keeping in the Security Council and the actual practice of robust peace-keeping, because several of the countries that decide on UN mandates are rarely (or, for some, never) engaged in its implementation, which falls mostly on developing countries that are suspicious of the intentions of the Council. In the absence of a shared understanding on the use of force by United Nations troops, the doctrine is thus being gradually defined by the actual practice of peacekeepers as they adjust to new demands and engage in what is known, for lack of a better expression, as "robust peacekeeping" operations.

The Experience of Robust Peacekeeping: Unanswered Questions

This section focuses on three missions that illustrate the operational issues raised by the practice of robust peacekeeping. The mission in the Democratic Republic of the Congo is analyzed in more detail, because it presents a near-complete evolution from traditional peacekeeping to coercive force. The mission in Côte d'Ivoire employed the strategic use of force, raising important questions. And though the mission in Mali had just begun to deploy at the time of writing, the challenges it faces, especially threats by groups employing terror tactics, may be indicative of future situational challenges. Other missions, notably those in Darfur and South Sudan, have also raised overlapping operational issues, but are not discussed here.

The Democratic Republic of the Congo

No mission has tested the concept of robust peacekeeping more than the UN mission in the Democratic Republic of the Congo, deployed in the midst of the Second Congo War, which involved the armies and allied armed groups of nine of Congo's neighbors. Initially deployed in response to the 1999 Lusaka Agreement, the UN Organization Mission in the Democratic Republic of the Congo, known as MONUC after its acronym in French, was tasked with supporting the implementation of a ceasefire among the belligerent groups and several state parties to the conflict. Although MONUC was also tasked from the start to "protect civilians under imminent threat of physical violence,"[13] its force structure was not initially designed for any sort of robust peacekeeping. Conceived essentially as an observer mission, it had slightly more than 5,000 troops for a country nearly the size of Western Europe, and their main task was to ensure the security of the bases from which military observers would monitor the ceasefire lines.

The resolution that established MONUC, while expressing strong support for the Lusaka ceasefire agreement and describing it as the "most viable basis for a resolution of the conflict,"[14] pointedly ignored the agreement's key second component, which requested the Security Council to "mandate the peacekeeping force to track down all armed groups in the DRC."[15] Rwanda, in particular, regularly criticized this omission, expecting MONUC to track down the Rwandan Hutu *génocidaires* who held leadership roles in the 1994 genocide and were since operating in eastern Congo's vast forests. This second, aggressive mandate provision would be included more than a decade later, when MONUC's successor mission, MONUSCO, was enhanced with an "intervention brigade": the UN stumbled into robust peacekeeping in Congo rather than embracing it as part of a strategic vision.

The mission utterly failed its first test to protect civilians when, in Kisangani in 2002, armed groups massacred more than a thousand civilians with no response by the peacekeepers stationed there. The next crisis, in Ituri in 2003, proved to be the first inflection point for a tactical and strategic shift. Under pressure from the international community, Rwanda in 2002 and then Uganda in early 2003 had agreed to withdraw their troops from Congo. Violence spiked in eastern Congo as various groups—some supported by Kinshasa, some by Kigali or Kampala—tried to assert control. The mounting crisis quickly exposed the vacuity of the Security Council's legalistic precautions. When the crisis erupted, MONUC had no troops in Ituri. Though the Security Council had limited its mandate to protect civilians "in the areas of deployment of its armed units,"[16] it was ethically and politically unthinkable not to make every effort to deploy troops where serious violence was occurring. That was the view of the head of MONUC at the time, Namanga Ngongi, and I supported it as under-secretary-general for peacekeeping. It was a risky gamble that would have major strategic implications, but did not need the approval of the Security Council, since it was only a redeployment of troops within Congo. We quickly decided to send the only unit available in MONUC at the time, a Uruguayan guard unit, to Ituri's capital, Bunia.

The mandate also provided that the UN would give protection "within its capacities."[17] That cautious language appears to state the obvious, but it actually ignores the dynamic nature of a crisis: as soon as a handful of Uruguayan troops had deployed, thousands of terrified Congolese civilians converged toward the airstrip where the troops were landing. The peace-keepers were overwhelmed as a spontaneous camp of displaced persons grew, offering an easy target to militias that indiscriminately fired mortar shells at the camp. The UN did not have a reserve capacity to take control of the situation. Civilians, instead of finding a safe haven, were entering a trap that could lead to another Srebrenica.

This perilous situation led to the first intervention of the European Union in Africa, at the request of the UN Secretary-General.[18] The tactical decision to redeploy troops to Ituri district had initiated a new pattern: lacking escalation capacity and, more generally, genuine enforcement capacity, the United Nations would compensate its weakness with the deployment of more robustly equipped forces provided by an external actor or a multinational coalition. In the case of the 2003 crisis, France played the central role in what became Operation Artemis, providing the bulk of some 1,800 troops as well as the command, but the operation was billed as European. As a judicious use of a small force in a small area of operation (Bunia and its immediate surroundings), the operation managed to stabilize the whole district of Ituri. It showed that a well-trained force enjoying solid political backing from at least one permanent member of the Security Council could have a decisive impact through a combination of targeted actions and some intelligent bluffing. When a significantly reinforced MONUC relieved the departing multinational force later that year, it rode on Artemis's success, which had bought some credibility for the United Nations.

That credibility was lost, however, less than a year later in Bukavu, the capital of South Kivu province. In early May 2004, residents of Bukavu found themselves under threat from renegade troops of the Congolese army backed by Rwanda. The mission announced it would stop the rebel advance, and some UN troops took blocking positions north of the city. But owing to differing views within the mission on their actual capacities, and fears that rebels might retaliate against isolated blue helmets deployed elsewhere, the troops were ordered not to take action when they were effectively challenged. The result was disastrous: many civilians were massacred. MONUC was again perceived as an empty force not to be trusted.

The UN responded to the Bukavu crisis by again profoundly reorganizing the mission. The crisis had shown that MONUC's headquarters in Kinshasa, Congo's capital in the country's far west, was too removed to have a good understanding of violence in the east, and that interaction between the mission's civilian and military components was inadequate. In 2005, an eastern-division headquarters was created under the command of a sufficiently senior and autonomous general who reported to the mission's chief through the force commander in Kinshasa. The unusual decision was taken to appoint as division commander Major-General Patrick Cammaert, the Dutch military adviser of the DPKO, who had considerable operational experience. Cammaert, under orders to push UN troops and capacities to their maximum, launched a number of successful operations over the next several months, leading to the disarmament of militias in Ituri and significant security improvements in North and South Kivu. Procedures were adjusted so that civilian logistical support would prioritize military operations, opening the way for a higher operational tempo. Under updated rules of engagement, peacekeepers conducted "cordon and search operations" to collect weapons and dismantle militia camps,[19] the only difference between these and offensive operations being that targeted militias were given some limited warning and an opportunity to voluntarily surrender.

By the end of 2005, MONUC's military posture had been transformed. Seen as a promising example of "robust peacekeeping," the mission remained keenly aware of its limited capacities, leading the UN Secretariat to request, and obtain, the support of a European Union military deployment for the 2006 presidential and parliamentary elections. The European deployment contributed to the relative calm that prevailed during the elections, but it was largely a psychological operation: only a few hundred fighting troops were deployed to Kinshasa, but the political impact of a deployment of European troops was considerable, demonstrating how important a show of force can be if it is well-staged.

The elections, which endorsed President Joseph Kabila as a leader with democratic legitimacy, changed the political context in which the United Nations could engage in robust peacekeeping. At the invitation of the Congolese government, the UN mission was to provide operational support to the Armed Forces of the Democratic Republic of the Congo (FARDC), which were no longer considered a party to the conflict but rather the country's legitimate security force. Over time, the UN's position on possible support evolved from the purely logistical (troop rations, transport for rapid deployment) to, by 2008, jointly planned operations to disarm recalcitrant armed groups.

During my tenure as chief of UN peacekeeping operations until mid-2008, I was myself very reluctant to develop a close operational relationship with the FARDC, which stood accused of previous and ongoing serious abuses, that would go beyond the support to security sector reform. In my view, elections were far from being the end of a reconciliation process in Congo, and a close association with one of the parties, in particular one responsible for significant human rights violations, would make it more difficult for the mission to play a role as mediator and facilitator of a political process. But after a failed offensive by government forces in late 2008, and a credible threat by rebel forces to take the eastern city of Goma, the Security Council mandated the mission to coordinate operations with the FARDC.[20] In view of abuses reportedly committed by some of the FARDC troops involved in combined operations, the Security Council explicitly conditioned support to the FARDC on respect for human rights and international humanitarian law, and requested the Secretary-General "to establish an appropriate mechanism to regularly assess the implementation of this Policy."[21] The joint operations that followed failed to bring about a decisive change, and remained controversial.

After more than three years of UN operational support to the FARDC, both forces were further humiliated when a Rwanda-backed militia briefly occupied Goma in November 2012, in a crisis reminiscent of the Bukavu debacle. This failure became a determining factor in the Security Council's decision to create a Force Intervention Brigade within MONUSCO. "Without creating any precedent or a prejudice to the agreed principles of peacekeeping," the force was composed of 3,000 troops from Malawi, South Africa, and Tanzania and tasked "with the responsibility of neutralizing armed groups."[22]

But precedents cannot be unwished from fact. Both the force's composition and its function demonstrated significant departures from previous peacekeeping practice. The intervention brigade's troops derived their clout not from their impartiality and distance from the conflict, but, quite to the contrary, from the engagement of their home countries. As neighbors and fellow members of the Southern African Development Community (SADC), the contributors to the intervention brigade held direct interests in the resolution of the conflict. Moreover, that the intervention brigade was explicitly mandated to "carry out targeted offensive operations"[23] against armed groups exposed it to new legal risks, yet untested as of this writing. Do members of the intervention brigade still enjoy the special protections provided to peacekeepers by international law? Would it still be a war crime for belligerents to attack blue helmets, as provided for in the 1998 Rome Statute, even when they are themselves engaged in war?[24]

The first months of operations were successful, culminating in the routing of a Rwanda-backed militia, the March 23 Movement (M23), in November 2013. However, this achievement was not the brigade's alone, which has been helped by other factors. First, the United States is now leading the international community in taking a much stronger stance against any foreign interference in Congolese affairs; and second, the Congolese troops have performed in a much better way than in the past, rightly claiming a significant role in the success achieved. Will such progress prove as short-lived as past use of robust force in Congo?

In the end, as "robust" as it claims to be, the intervention brigade has no capacity to stabilize by force the vast expanses of eastern Congo, and strategic victory depends on a Congolese state that has the capacity and the will to protect its own people. In that regard, the most important achievement of the intervention brigade might well be the credibility it has reclaimed for the United Nations in the country. The UN needs that operational credibility to deliver what may be its most strategic contribution: to persuade the leadership of the DRC, with solid backing from the international community, to build effective and trusted institutions.

Côte d'Ivoire

In 2004, following a protracted political crisis splitting Côte d'Ivoire's north and south, the Security Council established the UN Operation in Côte d'Ivoire (UNOCI). Its main focus was to monitor a ceasefire and support a peace agreement that would lead to the reunification of the country and a presidential election. It predictably included in its mandate protection of civilians. In addition, the UN mission enjoyed the backup support of a French contingent deployed on the basis of a bilateral agreement between Paris and Abidjan. Unusually, the mission was given a role to certify the election results, reflecting the Council's frustration with a stalled process. The election, initially due in 2005, was repeatedly postponed until an agreement between the northern rebel forces and President Laurent Gbagbo allowed it to take place in 2010. UNOCI's coercive action in the tumultuous period following the 2010 election provides an interesting example of the strategic use of force in a peacekeeping context.

Amid sporadic violence between government and opposition supporters, the electoral commission named opposition candidate Alassane Ouattara victor of the second round. However, the Constitutional Council, packed with supporters of the incumbent, Laurent Gbagbo, canceled the results in the north (where the opposition controlled polling stations) and declared Gbagbo the winner. UNOCI's chief of mission took the extraordinary step of declaring Ouattara the winner, which was seen by some Security Council members as going beyond certification.

In the worsening political crisis that followed, the Economic Community of West African States (ECOWAS), the African Union, and the UN's General Assembly and Security Council all declared support for Ouattara. For its part, the Security Council issued a resolution urging "all the Ivorian parties and other stakeholders to respect the will of the people and the election of Alassane Dramane Ouattara as President of Côte d'Ivoire," and adopted additional targeted sanctions against Gbagbo and his allies.[25] The Security Council did not clarify how UNOCI should enforce the election results, but did reiterate the authorization to use all necessary means to protect civilians "under imminent threat of physical violence . . . including to prevent the use of heavy weapons against the civilian population."

Ten days later, on April 10, 2011, the French support to the mission was in evidence when missile strikes by French and UN helicopters, allegedly aimed at heavy weapons that could threaten the civilian population, severely damaged the residence of Laurent Gbagbo, who had been holed up in his compound for several weeks, and broke his defense. Troops loyal to Ouattara stormed the building. Gbagbo was arrested under a warrant issued by the International Criminal Court for his role in election-related violence and eventually sent to The Hague. A ten-year crisis had found a provisional conclusion.

Some Security Council members, particularly Russia, criticized this broad interpretation of the protection of civilians mandate as being a dangerous precedent for using the Responsibility to Protect (R2P) norm as a tool for regime change. Criticisms grew when in the same year the NATO intervention in Libya, also authorized by the United Nations with reference to the R2P concept, eventually led to the fall of the Muammar Qaddafi regime.[26] Coercive action by both UN peacekeepers and French troops authorized under a UN mandate exposed UNOCI to criticism that it no longer followed the principle of impartiality, as established at peacekeeping's founding.[27]

Once again, the UN Secretariat and a permanent Council member had initiated the decisive use of force to end a political crisis, without an explicit decision of the Security Council, let alone a deliberation. In contrast to the Ituri crisis, however, France clearly drove policy in Côte d'Ivoire, rather than playing a supporting role for the Secretariat. Furthermore, the explicitly strategic purposes of the actions—to end a protracted stalemate and an almost decade-long crisis—would not have been reachable without the active military leadership of a powerful state. In Côte d'Ivoire, the Security Council was not prepared to give a clear enforcement mandate to a peacekeeping mission, but allowed it to have a creative interpretation of its protection of civilians mandate.

Mali

Mali, a landlocked country whose landscape is dominated by the Sahara desert, sank into crisis in early 2012 when a military coup in the capital, Bamako, was followed by the takeover of the north of the country by a coalition of secessionist groups and Islamic fundamentalists linked with al-Qaeda. As these forces began to move toward Bamako in early 2013, France deployed strike forces to counter the threat of insurgency. On the heels of the French intervention, the Security Council authorized the UN Multidimensional Integrated Stabilization Mission in Mali (MINUSMA), to be supplied with troops by Mali's neighbors in ECOWAS, representing the first time UN peacekeepers were deployed in an environment where the terrorist threat constituted by armed groups with links to al-Qaeda constituted the main security challenge. Terrorism and asymmetric threats are as new to the Security Council today as were intrastate conflicts in the 1990s.

At the time of this writing, the UN mission in Mali has just begun to deploy. It is too early to draw conclusions from the actual operational practice of the mission, but the language of the authorizing resolution, while it includes the now usual sentence on protection of civilians, seems to break new ground. In addition to a very broad stabilization mandate, the Security Council tasked the mission to take "active steps to prevent the return of armed elements" to northern Mali.[28]

As it adopted this rather broad mandate, the Council was probably aware that it was giving the mission a very ambitious role, which might not be backed by adequate means. This may explain why the resolution uses the vague term "active steps" and mandated the mission "to deter threats," a language that ominously echoes the ill-fated Resolution 836 of June 4, 1993, which was meant to enable the UN Protection Force in Bosnia (UNPROFOR) "to deter attacks against the safe areas." At the time, the verb "to deter" was chosen because it diluted an operational task by giving it a political dimension, thus hiding the capacity gap opened by an ambitious but under-resourced mandate. Following the model previously tested in Côte d'Ivoire, the Mali mission may be able to close the gap between its mandate and capacities with the continued support of French troops.[29] In so doing, it may however find itself in the same kind of difficulties that doomed the UN Operation in Somalia (UNOSOM II), when the United States launched an operation without coordinating it with the UN mission. Conversely, if the mission engages in counterterrorism operations, it may undermine its political mediation role as the "terrorist" label may preclude engagement with groups that could otherwise be brought into a political process.

Confronted with the limits of the traditional peacekeeping doctrine and widening capacity gaps in new contexts, the Security Council has tested ad hoc arrangements from Congo to Côte d'Ivoire to Mali. It has not yet been able to agree to jettison the traditional principles of peacekeeping, and it cannot define new ones. The resolution authorizing the mission in Mali, which both reaffirms peacekeeping's founding principles and recognizes the specific needs of each peacekeeping situation, is an awkward attempt to evolve the practice without a doctrinal consensus, and without a clear sense of what the practice should be. The operational experience of the past few years has proved to be as inconclusive as the doctrinal debate in clarifying the concept of robust peacekeeping.

Policy Lessons for the Future

The practice of robust peacekeeping, as carried out by UN missions in the Democratic Republic of the Congo, Côte d'Ivoire, Mali, and elsewhere, has put forward a number of lessons for future peacekeeping policy. Peacekeeping missions have often been given expansive mandates but few resources, leading peacekeepers to compensate for their structural weakness with a judicious use of force and astute politics. The experiences of the three cases discussed in this chapter show that the specific mandates and rules of engagement may have mattered less than the decisions of commanders on the ground, the mission's capacity to escalate, and its ability to draw on backup forces from partnering states, particularly from a powerful permanent member of the Security Council.

Force Posture, Resources, and Command

No discussion of robust peacekeeping can be divorced from an analysis of the force tasked with its implementation. The effectiveness depends on the availability of specific capacities, such as intelligence, transport, and firepower. Reliable intelligence is essential to enable the force to preempt threats and to maximize the psychological impact of operations through good timing and good choice of targets.

Robust operations require sizable and mobile forces, especially when one of the primary goals of robust peacekeeping is the protection of civilians. Lessons from the US experience with counterinsurgency—though markedly different in character from UN missions—suggest that civilian protection from insurgents requires a ratio of troops to population at 20 to 1,000. Obviously, no UN peacekeeping force has ever come close to that ratio. In the DRC, even if only the populations of the two Kivu provinces were to be considered, more than 200,000 troops would be needed.

The lesson to draw from such high figures is not to massively increase the size of peacekeeping operations, which would not be a realistic option in any case, but rather to be aware of the limitations of the use of force so as to use it judiciously. The most successful ones have employed a mobile force—as in Liberia—that adjusts quickly to a fluid situation, backed by careful political calculations. A judicious use of force cannot fully compensate for an excessively small force, but it can multiply the impact of a given operation, by recognizing that the use of force is in large measure part of a strategy designed to convey a political message through a variety of means. The effectiveness of UN contingents, particularly as regards civilian protection, has been shown to be severely weakened when they have insufficient mobility amid daunting logistical challenges, such as those in Darfur, South Sudan, and the areas of the northern DRC affected by the Lord's Resistance Army.

The quality of the troops and the quality of the command at all levels are in that respect of critical importance. Regardless of doctrine and mandate, the single most important factor is the posture of the force and of its commander, because the traditional distinction between the strategic and the tactical level is less pertinent in the fluid situations in which peace-keepers are increasingly engaged. In "wars amongst the people,"[30] percep-tions are a greater part of the balance of power, and perceptions are more often shaped by local incidents than by major battles: a failed engagement can quickly destroy the credibility of a peacekeeping force, while a lim-ited but successful engagement can have oversized repercussions. This means that local commanders have a much greater role, and need to make instant judgments in situations that have a military as well as a political dimension.

The responsibility of senior commanders is different. While they can-not and should not interfere in tactical situations that they cannot properly assess from a distance, they need to impart on their subordinates the proper mind-set: a senior commander who has the courage to push his troops—with the inevitable risks associated with a proactive posture—and the wis-dom to pick his fights, can make a considerable difference. He will need strong backing from his civilian leadership: a head of mission who under-stands how troops can increase political leverage must also be willing to accept risks, and to provide political cover when an operation does not suc-ceed, which will inevitably happen from time to time. There are unfortu-nately situations where that happy combination of military and civilian risk-takers at the top is missing.

Rules of Engagement

Much has been made of the allegedly constraining rules of engagement of the United Nations. Specific rules of engagement—drafted for each peace-keeping operation by the military adviser of the DPKO (who is consulted by the office of legal affairs) and approved by the under-secretary-general for peacekeeping—reflect a specific mandate, and if the mandate provides for offensive operations, as is the case for the intervention brigade in the DRC, these rules will reflect that requirement. It is indeed noticeable, as mentioned earlier, that the United Nations, on several occasions, has been able to conduct robust operations, including by taking preemptive action, without waiting for some militia to burn down a village. Actually, most recent UN mandates, even without explicitly authorizing offensive opera-tions, provide a sufficient legal basis for robust rules of engagement. Expe-rience will tell whether a more explicitly offensive mandate will radically alter the posture of a force, or whether that posture is first and foremost determined by the capacities of the force and its command. In the past, capacities and command have been much more important than rules of engagement.

The Capacity to Escalate and Backup Forces

The capacity of a force to escalate if challenged is a sine qua non of "robustness." In Bunia in 2003, the United Nations did not have that capacity, but fortunately France and the European Union stepped in to fill the void. Since then, a systematic effort has been made to secure in advance reinforcement capacities with interested member states. Discussions took place with key troop contributors from South Asia and Africa, in particular, to explore the possibility to keep forces on call, which would be earmarked for a particular mission, if the need arose to reinforce it in an emergency. The rationale behind the proposal was that important troop contributors would have a particular interest in preventing the failure of a mission in which they were engaged. The proposal eventually failed for budgetary reasons: keeping troops at a high state of readiness entails additional costs, on which no agreement could be found between troop contributors and financial contributors.

In the absence of standing arrangements, the escalation capacity of the United Nations is dependent on backup forces. A well-equipped quick reaction force within the mission is the best solution: it can, with appropriate mobility assets, bring rapid reinforcement in case of need. Some peacekeeping missions[31] have been given such a capacity, but it has often been difficult to recruit the right troops for the force, and the risk is always high that the rapid-reaction force will plug holes in the deployment and compensate for deficiencies, rather than provide real escalation capacity. The alternative solution is to resort to an outside force, as was the case of the EU force in Bunia. The force may then have different rules of engagement, and a distinct chain of command; this duality can strengthen its credibility, but carries the risk of a breakdown of cooperation between the peacekeeping force and the enforcement unit.[32] The offensive operation launched by US forces in Mogadishu against a local warlord was not properly coordinated with the UN peacekeeping force, and the debacle that followed contributed to the precipitous departure of the UN from Somalia. Escalation cannot afford failure, and it must be carefully coordinated in an overall plan.

The Role of Force in Politics and Peace

In the twenty-first century, Carl von Clausewitz's famous edict remains pertinent: "War is not merely an act of policy but a true political instrument, a continuation of political intercourse with the addition of other means."[33] War in itself does not suspend politics. When it authorizes a use of force that falls just short of war-making, the UN cannot escape the two key questions: What are the political goals of "robust peacekeeping"? What is robust peacekeeping meant to achieve in the pursuit of peace?

Acts of war carry certain risks. Because a proactive posture increases the risk of casualties, it is unclear whether the laudable but distant goal of peace is sufficient to motivate troops to take significant risks, which may in some cases present an uncomfortable dilemma for the United Nations: either it relies on troops from countries that have little national interest in the crisis at hand, which protects its impartiality but may affect the motivation of the troops, or it uses troops from countries that have a direct stake in the solution of the crisis. The latter choice was made for the intervention brigade in the DRC, on the assumption that there would be no contradiction between the interests of regional countries and the interests of the affected communities that the UN should stand for.

As one tries to bring clarity to the goals that are being pursued, difficult political questions arise, on which it may not be easy to achieve consensus in the international community. In that respect, the concept of "protection of civilians" has a misleading superficial clarity. At the tactical level, the protection of civilians is an ethical imperative that should be self-evident to any force, but at the strategic level, the answer cannot avoid the fundamental political question of how to achieve a sustainable peace that protects civilians in a lasting way: through negotiation or outright victory?

The distinction mentioned earlier between strategic and tactical threats to a peace process would work if the only judgment required when using force were a military judgment on the capacity of an opposing force to be deterred or cowed into submission. But a political judgment is also required on the wisdom of crushing a force that may be militarily weak but politically significant: as a force engages in coercion tactics, it may lose its capacity to negotiate, which may be fine if it is confident it can crush a spoiler, but dangerous if it does not have the capacity to win decisively and eventually needs to reengage politically.

At a fundamental level, robust use of force aims at tipping the balance of power in favor of a government emerging from a peace process, assuming that the power will not be abused and will contribute to long-term stability. That is the choice that time and again the Security Council has made: after an initial phase of transition concluded by elections, from Liberia to Congo or South Sudan, it has mandated UN peacekeeping forces to prop up weak governments, even if that means not standing up decisively[34] to abuse by government forces, and losing the capacity to be seen as an impartial broker in a peace process to which elections have given only a provisional conclusion. A robust posture may make more visible the double standards of a peacekeeping force.

Recent conflicts have also shown that the very concept of peacemaking may need to evolve, with profound implications for the use of force. Since the end of the Cold War, peacekeeping operations have often been deployed to end civil wars. This important evolution did not initially challenge one essential assumption: consolidating peace might now require going beyond interstate diplomacy, but it was still focused on accommodating conflicting and well-identified centers of power, even if those centers were now within the same state. Rebel movements might have less effective chains of command, but they still had well-identified leaders and it was with them that the negotiation took place and that accommodation was sought.

We may be at the beginning of an evolution of conflict, as profound as the one that separates interstate and intrastate conflicts, as more diffuse threats develop. The change is often conflated with the development of terrorist threats against peacekeeping forces, which pose operational challenges to peacekeeping operations. Since key members of the international community, and in particular the United States, reject as a matter of principle any negotiation with a "terrorist" organization, and enlist the support of the United Nations in an unrelenting war against such groups, the United Nations peacekeepers are now expected to combine a war-fighting posture against them and a more complex peacekeeping posture with other groups. The growing importance given by key member states to counterterrorism is a major challenge to the United Nations peacemaking and peacekeeping roles, as an extensive definition of terrorism increasingly limits the space left for political processes and dangerously broadens the scope of enforcement operations. Meanwhile, the adjustment of peacekeeping forces to asymmetrical threats directly impacts on their peacekeeping role: hunkering down behind blast walls and patrolling in heavily protected convoys isolate the peacekeepers from the population, threatening the continuum that must exist between the military posture and the political posture.

Changing Conflicts, Changing Challenges

The political challenges are even more daunting. The terrorist threat is only one aspect of a deeper transformation of conflict, of which terrorism is but a symptom. The most difficult challenge to peacebuilding is the fragmentation of power in postconflict states, its increasingly elusive character, which makes top-down approaches, whether in negotiation or in combat (through, for instance, the killing of terrorist leaders) less effective. Rebel movements are less and less able or willing to mobilize their followers on the basis of a political program. This leads to ever-shifting alignments and alliances, as groups recruit members not for the program they advocate—they sometimes have none—but for the personal experience they provide, which has been the case with terrorists, gang members, and militias. The line between public and private goals, between criminal and political activities, is increasingly blurred. In this new context, one important political goal of a peace operation is not so much to achieve a sustainable balance between existing centers of power, as to actually facilitate the emergence and consolidation of such centers, and help structure an amorphous and fragmented society.

Under such circumstances, the blunt instrument of force may not be the most adequate in the long term. Those who are seeking the experience of violence will not be deterred, and the systematic targeting of their "leaders," while it weakens the organizational capacity of a movement, may also contribute to further fragmentation, making the pursuit of a negotiated settlement even more elusive.

In the end, the discussion on robust peacekeeping and the use of force leads to a broader discussion on the conditions required for a society to achieve peace and stability. While the experience of Iraq and Afghanistan has generated a healthy humility on what force can achieve, the discussion on "robust peacekeeping"—because the United Nations has historically been a very weak enforcer—has tended to ignore those limitations, looking for a happy medium between the brutality of counterinsurgency and the ineffectiveness of a traditional peacekeeping posture. And indeed, the combined experience of coalition, NATO, and UN operations demonstrates the limits of force as well as the limits of politics. The two need to be combined in varying measures.

It would thus be wrong to assume that UN peacekeeping forces can be the SWAT teams of the world, cleaning up bad neighborhoods. That would assume that there is a preexisting peaceful society waiting to reemerge, once the "spoilers," terrorists, and gangs have been removed. The reality is more complex, because the evolution of our societies is changing the nature of conflict, and conflict transforms the societies it affects. Force, which has created as well as destroyed nations, will continue to be an important component of any sustainable peace. But the peacekeepers who invented a symbolic use of force, in a world in which the symbolic power of norms was the abutment of state power, must now adapt their posture to a world in which the contours of any given society are ill-defined, as the normative structures of states weaken. For the Security Council, which is the ultimate guardian of an international order based on the responsibility of states, this is a new challenge that will test the capacity of international organizations to adapt to a rapidly changing landscape.

Notes

1. See United Nations Security Council Resolution 678 (November 29, 1990), UN Doc. S/RES/678, and subsequent resolutions on Iraq in 1991. Other examples of coercive action authorized by the United Nations do not reflect the original intent of the drafters of the Charter. For example, the Soviet Union was opposed to action related to Korea in 1950, and it boycotted Security Council proceedings, while the 2011 intervention in Libya was not a response to the kind of interstate conflict envisaged by the drafters of the Charter.

JEAN-MARIE GUÉHENNO **391**

2. By 1967, there remained no such will in the Council, and the symbolic nature of the peacekeeping presence was exposed. Secretary-General U Thant had no other option than to withdraw the troops.

3. Brian Urquhart, *A Life in Peace and War* (New York: Norton, 1991), p. 246.

4. Walter Dorn, "The UN's First 'Air Force': Peacekeepers in Combat, Congo, 1960–64," *Journal of Military History* 77 (October 2013): 1399–1425. For a broader account of the UN's involvement in the Congo in 1960–1961, see Brian Urquhart, *Hammarskjöld* (New York: Norton, 1994), pp. 389–456.

5. United Nations Secretary-General, *An Agenda for Peace: Preventive Diplomacy, Peacemaking, and Peace-keeping,* UN Doc. A/47/277-S/24111, June 17, 1992, para. 45.

6. United Nations Secretary-General, *Supplement to* An Agenda for Peace, UN Doc. A/50/60-S/1995/1, January 5, 1995, para. 35.

7. Annan had previously commissioned reports on UN actions in Rwanda and at Srebrenica. The 1999 UN report on the Srebrenica massacre is the most detailed and thoughtful account of a major political and operational failure of the United Nations. See United Nations Secretary-General, *Report of the Secretary-General Pursuant to General Assembly Resolution 53/35: The Fall of Srebrenica,* UN Doc. A/54/549, November 15, 1999.

8. Panel on United Nations Peace Operations, *Report of the Panel on United Nations Peace Operations* (Brahimi Report), UN Doc. A/55/305-S/2000/809, August 21, 2000, paras. 48, 50, 52.

9. Ibid., para. 53.

10. United Nations Secretary-General, *Report of the Secretary-General on the Implementation of the Report of the Panel on United Nations Peace Operations,* UN Doc. A/55/502, October 20, 2000, para. 7(e).

11. United Nations Security Council Resolution 1270, S/RES/1270 (October 22, 1999), para. 14.

12. United Nations Peacekeeping, *United Nations Peacekeeping Operations: Principles and Guidelines* (Capstone Doctrine), March 2008, pp. 34, http://pbpu.unlb.org/pbps/Library/Capstone_Doctrine_ENG.pdf.

13. United Nations Security Council Resolution 1291, S/RES/1291 (February 24, 2000), para. 8.

14. United Nations Security Council Resolution 1279, S/RES/1279 (October 22, 1999), preambular para. 5.

15. United Nations Security Council, "Letter Dated 23 July 1999 from the Permanent Representative of Zambia to the UN Addressed to the President of the Security Council," UN Doc. S/1999/815, July 23, 1999, Annex: Ceasefire Agreement, para.11(a).

16. The provision in place since the 2000 mandate (para. 8) was reiterated in the mandate effective in early 2003. United Nations Security Council Resolution 1417 (June 14, 2002), UN Doc. S/RES/1417, para. 7.

17. United Nations Security Council Resolution 1417, S/RES/1417 (June 14, 2002), op. para. 7.

18. United Nations Security Council Resolution 1484, S/RES/1484 (May 30, 2003).

19. The main legal foundation of robust peacekeeping remained the protection of civilians in imminent danger, but was complemented when, in 2003, the Security Council tasked the mission with a broader stabilization mandate. See United Nations Security Council Resolution 1493 (July 28, 2003), UN Doc. S/RES/1493, para. 27. For the Security Council's explicit authorization of cordon and search

operations, see United Nations Security Council Resolution 1592 (March 30, 2005), UN Doc. S/RES/1592, para. 7.

20. United Nations Security Council Resolution 1856, S/RES/1856 (December 22, 2008), para. 3(g).

21. United Nations Security Council Resolution 1906, S/RES/1906 (December 23, 2009), para.23.

22. United Nations Security Council Resolution 2098, S/RES/2098 (March 28, 2013), para. 9.

23. United Nations Security Council Resolution 2098, S/RES/2098 (March 28, 2013), para. 12(b).

24. See Alice Gadler, "The Protection of Peacekeepers and International Criminal Law: Legal Challenges and Broader Protection," *German Law Journal* 11, no. 6 (2010): 585–608, www.germanlawjournal.com/index.php?pageID=11&artID=1262.

25. United Nations Security Council Resolution 1975, S/RES/1975 (March 30, 2011), paras. 1, 12.

26. The larger impact of such operations with broad mandates on the emerging norm of the Responsibility to Protect or the protection of civilians merits more research of its own and is beyond the scope of this chapter.

27. For discussion on the problem of impartiality in foreign intervention, see Richard K. Betts, "The Delusions of Impartial Intervention," *Foreign Affairs* (November–December 1994).

28. Resolution 2100 of April 25, 2013 (S/RES/2100), under the headline goal of "stabilization of key population centers and support for the reestablishment of State authority throughout the country," mandates the mission, "in support of the transitional authorities of Mali, to stabilize the key population centers, especially in the north of Mali and, in this context, to deter threats and take active steps to prevent the return of armed elements to those areas."

29. The resolution, in its paragraph 18, "authorizes French troops, within the limits of their capacities and areas of deployment, to use all necessary means, from the commencement of the activities of MINUSMA until the end of MINUSMA's mandate as authorized in this resolution, to intervene in support of elements of MINUSMA when under imminent and serious threat upon request of the Secretary-General." United Nations Security Council Resolution 2100, S/RES/2100 (April 25, 2013).

30. The expression was coined by British general Rupert Smith in *The Utility of Force: The Art of War in the Modern World* (New York: Knopf, 2005).

31. The mission in Liberia, for instance.

32. The intervention brigade deployed in eastern DRC should in principle avoid that risk, since it is part of the peacekeeping force and a single chain of command is maintained. But it is likely that the forces it will confront will not distinguish between the intervention force and the other components of the peacekeeping force; on the contrary, it would stand to reason for them to retaliate against the weakest components. Thus a more proactive posture of the intervention brigade will have to be complemented by a higher degree of readiness of the rest of the force, and possibly a change in its posture.

33. Carl von Clausewitz, *On War,* edited and translated by Michael Howard and Peter Paret (Princeton: Princeton University Press, 1989), chap. 1, para. 24.

34. The Security Council has tried to address that problem by establishing a measure of conditionality in the support to government forces in the DRC. See endnote 21.

19

The Security Council and NATO

Herman Schaper

So yes, the instruments of war do have a role to play in preserving the peace. —*President Barack Obama in his Nobel Peace Prize acceptance speech, December 10, 2009*

IN THIS CHAPTER I DISCUSS THE USE OF ARMED FORCE IN THE execution of decisions of the UN Security Council. In particular, I analyze the reasons why the UN—with some rare exceptions—has failed to carry out enforcement operations itself, why it has instead repeatedly turned to NATO to do the job, and why NATO has been willing to do so. I attempt to answer these questions by tracing the evolving relationship between the two organizations since their respective creation, placing particular emphasis on NATO-UN cooperation in the use of military force in the cases of Bosnia, Kosovo, Afghanistan, and Libya.

The UN Charter and the Use of Armed Force

The central aim of the United Nations, according to its Charter, is to "save succeeding generations from the scourge of war," which may require the capacity and willingness to wage war. And indeed, the Charter clearly recognizes this. The first role it gives the organization is a military one: "to take effective collective measures for the prevention and removal of threats to the peace, and for the suppression of acts of aggression or other breaches of the peace."[1]

This was—originally at least—not empty rhetoric: "during the preparatory work on the UN Charter, consensus existed on furnishing the new Organization with the authority to enforce international peace and security by force of arms if necessary."[2] To enable the UN to play this role, an elaborate structure of political and military cooperation was designed. While the Security Council would be in the lead on the political side, and was given unprecedented legal powers, on the military side a standing UN force would be set up. Detailed negotiations followed in 1946 and 1947 on what such a force should look like.[3] All members of the UN were expected to make available to the Security Council armed forces, assistance, and facilities, on its call and in accordance with special agreements. Plans were made to establish "an array of UN army bases, airfields and naval harbors in different parts of the world from Wilhelmshaven and Naples to the Far East."[4] The Charter also set up the Military Staff Committee to advise and assist the Security Council in matters like command and control, military planning, defining military requirements, and deciding on the employment of the military units. The committee would also provide strategic direction to the armed forces placed at the disposal of the Council. All in all, the drafters of the Charter were very serious about the UN's capacity to wage war, so as to fulfill the role the Charter had assigned it.

However, apart from the establishment of the Security Council and the Military Staff Committee, little to nothing came of the arrangements foreseen in Chapter VII of the Charter. The Cold War divisions between the five permanent members of the Council made military cooperation between them impossible. No member state concluded an agreement with the UN to make troops and facilities available to the Security Council, and the Military Staff Committee never developed the capacity to provide the Security Council with sound military advice and support.

The North Atlantic Treaty Organization

The failure of the attempt to develop a global system of collective security around the UN led countries to establish other security arrangements. These took mainly the form of regional collective defense systems. (While both collective security and collective defense arrangements are based on the notion that the security of one is the concern of all, the former are envisioned to be global in scope and commit members to unite against any other member who commits an act of aggression; the latter are alliances that commit their members to help defend any member against an outside aggressor.)

Some perceptive observers had already foreseen this turn toward collective defense during the negotiations on the Charter. Learning that the great powers had reserved for themselves the right to veto Security Council decisions, Dutch foreign minister Eelco van Kleffens concluded that the new international organization would not be able to deliver on its promise of collective security: "Rather this project creates a false sense of security, which I consider to be worse than nothing."[5] His basic argument was that the Soviet Union was for the Western European countries the real postwar security threat, against which, because of the veto, the UN would be unable to provide security.

Other middle-sized countries also tried to limit the reach of the veto, but in vain. This reinforced van Kleffens and other European statesmen in their conviction that the Western European democracies should seek their security in an Atlantic alliance with the United States, and as the Cold War developed this did indeed happen. In 1949, the Washington Treaty was signed, which led to the establishment of NATO.

At the time, a number of observers argued that the treaty was incompatible with, or even undermined, the arrangements for collective security as foreseen by the Charter. The drafters of the treaty were aware of this criticism, and four of its fourteen articles as well as the preamble refer to the UN, while the primary responsibility of the Security Council for the maintenance of international peace and security is explicitly recognized. But in the crucial Article 5 of the treaty, which describes the mutual commitment of the Allies to come to each other's aid in case of an armed attack, it is pointed out that the right of individual or collective self-defense is recognized by Article 51 of the UN Charter. The wording of the Charter is in this respect very strong, as it speaks of the "inherent" right of self-defense, which means that this right is not dependent on a decision of the Security Council.[6]

So, fundamentally, the Atlantic alliance was filling a gap left by the Security Council. Rather than causing the paralysis of the Council, the establishment of NATO was its result. Exactly for that reason, the drafters of the Washington Treaty were very careful not to define NATO as a regional organization under the Charter, in which Article 53 states that "no enforcement action shall be undertaken under regional arrangements or by regional agencies without the authorization of the Security Council." This would have implied that the Soviet Union could veto NATO military action, which would of course defeat the purpose of concluding the alliance.

At the same time, it was recognized that, once the Security Council could function effectively, "NATO would no longer be necessary."[7] Article 12 of the treaty states that after ten years, or any time thereafter, a review of the treaty could take place, having regard for the possible development of universal as well as regional arrangements for the maintenance of international peace and security under the Charter of the UN. Of course, no such review ever took place.

Korea

The North Korean invasion of South Korea in 1950 for a short while changed the debate about the UN and the use of armed force, and its relationship with NATO in this respect. In response to North Korea's act of aggression, the Security Council did what it was supposed to do, adopting a resolution authorizing a large-scale military operation under the UN flag in support of South Korea. This was made possible by a strategic mistake by the Soviet Union, which in protest to an unrelated issue had temporarily withdrawn its representative from the Council. The subsequent military operation was in essence a US operation, fighting under the UN flag: the great majority of troops were American, and their US commander reported to Washington rather than New York. This episode established the template of "the franchise approach," whereby the Security Council "call[s] on willing member states to step in on its behalf."[8] After the end of the Cold War, this approach was used several times, and opened the way for NATO taking on the responsibility for peacekeeping and peace enforcement operations with a Security Council mandate.

For the NATO allies, the Korean War was a confirmation of their worst fears about Moscow's readiness to use military means for its expansionist intentions. It gave a huge impetus to the military cooperation within the alliance through a new integrated military structure and to the rearmament of Western Europe with US military aid.

It also led to a debate on whether NATO could assist the UN militarily in Korea, and in a wider sense could perhaps become "an operating arm of the United Nations serving as its military component whenever circumstances require."[9] Within the UN, Secretary-General Trygve Lie, who had previously denounced the concept of regional defense pacts, and was very cool toward NATO in particular, now conceded that the vision of collective security envisaged in the Charter had not materialized, and that pending its establishment, regional associations, including military ones, did have an important role to play in strengthening the security of UN members.[10] Within NATO, the United States, together with the United Kingdom, were the main drivers behind the debate on NATO taking on such a role: "From mid-1950 until the autumn of 1952, it appeared that some kind of direct institutional relationship between the UN and NATO might be established. . . . In the end, however, nothing happened, and the Korean crisis proved to have no discernible or lasting impact on the remote Cold War relationship between the two institutions."[11] Apart from the strong resistance of the Soviet Union against any such relationship, the European members of the alliance—with the exception of the UK—wanted the alliance to remain firmly focused on Europe, and on the formidable threat to their security and independence that the Soviet Union posed.

Peacekeeping Instead of War-Fighting

While the Cold War made it impossible for the UN to fulfill its Charter responsibility of maintaining international peace and security, a new concept called peacekeeping gave a new military role to the UN. This was first applied in 1948 when a military observer mission, the UN Truce Supervision Organization (UNTSO), was deployed to the Middle East to monitor an armistice agreement between Israel and its Arab neighbors. Its core principles, as developed under the leadership of Secretary-General Dag Hammarskjöld in the 1950s, were consent of the parties, impartiality, and the use of force only in self-defense. In the subsequent decades, peacekeeping came to be seen as the essence of the UN's role in military matters, although it is not mentioned in the Charter. It was, and is, a pragmatic way for involving the military in a supporting role in efforts to solve crises and conflicts by peaceful means. Originally this meant, in most cases, positioning UN troops—provided on a voluntary basis by member states—between opposed armed forces along international borders following a ceasefire. From the 1990s on, peacekeepers were also increasingly deployed in internal conflicts and received broad statebuilding, humanitarian, and civilian protection mandates. But with its explicit exclusion of enforcement action, peacekeeping was in essence also the opposite of the role the Charter assigns to the military: the removal of threats to the peace, and the suppression of acts of aggression, tasks that are difficult to achieve on the basis of consensus of the parties, impartiality, and the use of force only in self-defense.

No Agenda for Peace

The ending of the Cold War in the late 1980s opened the prospect of the UN playing a much larger role in the maintenance of international peace and security. In his report to the Security Council of June 1992, *An Agenda for Peace,* Secretary-General Boutros Boutros-Ghali laid out a very ambitious vision. Against the background of new instabilities and a growing number of local conflicts, and buoyed by the prospect of great power cooperation—a "New World Order," as US president George H. W. Bush called it—the UN would finally have to become serious about its military role as foreseen in the Charter. This meant acquiring the capacity for peace enforcement, "to respond to outright aggression, imminent or actual." While such military action should only be taken when all peaceful means had failed, in his view "the option of taking it is essential to the credibility of the UN as guarantor of international security."[12]

This would require going back to the special agreements foreseen in Article 43, whereby member states undertake to make armed forces, assistance, and facilities available to the Security Council, "not only on an ad hoc basis but on a permanent basis." While Boutros-Ghali admitted that such a new UN army was not likely to become available anytime soon, his fundamental point was that "under the political circumstances that now exist for the first time since the Charter was adopted, the longstanding obstacles to the conclusion of such special agreements should no longer prevail."[13]

Nothing came of these proposals, however, partly because the end of the Cold War did not suddenly create a firm base of shared interests and common values on which to build a system of collective security, partly because the mass killings in Somalia, Rwanda, and Srebrenica drove home the limits of UN peacekeeping. The fundamental reason for these disasters was that, while the world around it was quickly changing, the UN itself had not been willing to redefine the role of the military as it had been developed during Cold War peacekeeping. As Kofi Annan has written, "The Security Council neglected to consciously create or review the possibilities of a distinctive new set of governing principles and structures of UN peacekeeping. . . . The old and creaking Cold War machinery of peacekeeping was being turned to situations for which it was never intended," such as the ones in Somalia, Rwanda, and Bosnia-Herzegovina. "No one was willing to reconfigure the mission to engage in war fighting," which left the UN wholly unprepared to deal with the challenges it faced in these countries.[14]

Boutros-Ghali himself recognized in his 1995 *Supplement to An Agenda for Peace* the failure of his effort to give the UN a role in military enforcement. This was still desirable in the long term, "but it would be folly to attempt to do so at the present time when the Organization is resource-starved and hard pressed to handle the less demanding peacemaking and peace-keeping responsibilities entrusted to it."[15] For enforcement he referred to the precedents of Korea and Iraq, where the Security Council had authorized a group of willing member states to undertake action, and to Bosnia-Herzegovina, mentioning "the unprecedented collaboration" there between the UN and NATO.

NATO Operations Out-of-Area

NATO's involvement in the 1992–1995 war in Bosnia-Herzegovina was a fundamental change in the alliance's security role. Military operations "out-of-area" (meaning outside the territory of alliance members covered by the Washington Treaty) were out of the question for the alliance during the Cold War. In 1964, there had been some discussion, particularly in Washington and London, on a NATO-led instead of a UN-led multinational peacekeeping force in Cyprus, but the idea was dropped because most among the alliance considered that peacekeeping was not NATO's legitimate remit, and the Greek Cypriots opposed it.[16]

The Iraqi invasion of Kuwait in 1990 brought the beginnings of change, however. Although the US-led military response to the invasion took place under the auspices of the UN, with a Security Council mandate, "NATO's de facto involvement was in fact much greater than that of the UN."[17] NATO joint assets and resources were used extensively in support of the buildup in the Gulf. The proposal by the United States to do so was agreed upon in the North Atlantic Council without serious dissent. Mainly for political reasons, in particular relations with the countries of the Middle East, this role of NATO was not publicly highlighted. It did have two long-term effects, however. First, it demonstrated the value of NATO's integrated military structure, with its joint assets and resources, and its procedures and habits of cooperation. Second, it contributed to the beginning of a debate within NATO about its role out-of-area, and its relationship with the UN in this respect. This debate took place as part of a gradual and pragmatic process of change, largely driven by events.

Is NATO a Regional Organization?

In November 1991, NATO received a letter from Boutros-Ghali, asking in general terms what the alliance and its members might be prepared to offer to the UN in support of its security tasks. The UN's new Secretary-General was of the opinion—as he would argue in his *Agenda for Peace*—that regional arrangements and agencies, including "regional organizations for mutual security and defense," could lighten the burden of the Security Council in maintaining international peace and security, by working together with the UN in joint undertakings, in a complementary manner.[18]

The question of whether NATO was a regional organization under Chapter VIII of the Charter was in the 1990s still a hot question, just as it had been when the Washington Treaty was negotiated. "The question of the legal status of NATO under the UN Charter is probably the most debated question concerning NATO in legal literature."[19] Boutros-Ghali was undoubtedly aware of this (he had written his PhD thesis in international law on the relationship between the UN and regional bodies). Describing the alliance as a regional organization under Chapter VIII of the Charter would in NATO's view be "an indirect claim to UN control over the use of force by NATO."[20] So he tried to downplay this question, arguing that "it is not the purpose of the present report to set forth any formal pattern of relationship" between regional organizations and the UN. Without entering into other scenarios in which NATO would use armed force, he limited himself to NATO support of the UN in the maintenance of international peace and security, stressing that in those cases its relationship with the UN, and the Security Council in particular, would have to be governed by Chapter VIII, meaning the Security Council would be in control. For a while this approach made NATO support to the UN's efforts in Bosnia-Herzegovina possible, but as the alliance took on more and more military responsibilities, it increasingly became a bone of contention.

Bosnia and the Failure of the "Double Key"

From the summer of 1992 onward, NATO, on the basis of a series of Security Council resolutions and subsequent decisions by the North Atlantic Council, played an increasingly important military role in the efforts of the international community to end the fighting and establish peace in Bosnia. It did so initially by monitoring compliance with UN sanctions against Serbia and subsequently also with the no-fly zone over Bosnia, followed by the military enforcement of both the sanctions and the no-fly zone "by all necessary means." In June 1993, NATO and the UN agreed that aircraft of NATO countries would provide close air support to UN troops on the ground at the request of the UN. This led, in early 1994, to the first combat operation in the history of the alliance, when NATO fighter jets shot down four Serbian jets near Banja Luka, and later, in August and September 1995, after the mass murders in Srebrenica and the attack on the Sarajevo marketplace, to large-scale bombing of Bosnian-Serb targets. This, together with a successful Croat military campaign on the ground, finally forced the Serbs to agree to negotiations, which, in November 1995, led to the Dayton peace agreement.

Both strategic and humanitarian considerations pushed the Allies down this road of increasing military involvement, together with NATO's capacity through its integrated military structure to execute effectively large-scale multinational military operations. (Because of the refusal of the United States to put troops on the ground, NATO limited itself to air and naval operations.) In doing so, the Allies were very careful, however, to make clear that they would remain masters of their own fate, and that decisions to support the UN in peacekeeping would be "on a case-by-case basis," with NATO making its own judgment, and "in accordance with our own procedures."[21] NATO had no intention to become an executive agency of the UN, as Marrack Goulding, the head of UN peacekeeping, had publicly suggested the year before. Manfred Wörner, NATO's secretary-general, made the point very clear in a speech to the press in 1993: "The Alliance, in the security interests of its own members, is prepared to assist the UN; but it cannot commit itself to supporting globally every peacekeeping operation; especially where the conditions of success are absent, where it believes that the mandate and rules of engagement are inadequate, and where it cannot exercise unity of command."[22]

Unity of Command vs. Dual Key

Unity of command and control gradually became the main area of contention between the two organizations. Both agreed that such unity was essential, but they differed on who would have the last word. A compromise was reached in the arrangement that both organizations had to agree before offensive air operations could be carried out. However, this "dual key" was in military terms a disaster, as it "resulted in differences between the organizations over the threshold for military action and limited the effectiveness of air strikes."[23] Some of the NATO officials directly involved in the difficult discussions with the UN on the dual-key arrangement used more blunt language. The NATO commander responsible for the air strikes is reported to have said: "I hated the double key. I thought it was the worst thing we could have been involved in."[24] NATO's new secretary-general, Willy Claes, reportedly said: "If we cannot set the rules of our military operations, they will have to find other idiots to support peacekeeping."[25]

For the UN the issue was first of all a political and legal one: the primacy of the Security Council in the maintenance of international peace and security. In addition, for the UN "the established principles, procedures and practices of peacekeeping" were still the guidelines for the operations of its peacekeeping force, the UN Protection Force (UNPROFOR). Air strikes were by definition difficult to combine with this, and so a pattern developed of NATO commanders proposing air strikes, and the UN blocking them. For NATO, on the other hand, the issue was first of all one of military effectiveness, and thereby also of the credibility of the alliance. And for the countries with troops on the ground, it became increasingly also an issue of the overall incompetence of the UN in military matters. As French defense minister Francois Léotard said in the General Assembly: "If questions as essential and simple as definition of missions, clarity of command and adequate financing cannot be resolved, the French government will draw a certain number of conclusions from this obtuseness or obscurity coming from the . . . UN."[26] Traditional peacekeeping had poorly prepared the UN for crises like the one in Bosnia. And historian Paul Kennedy rightly notes "the fact that the Military Committee became a casualty of the Cold War meant that the Security Council and the Secretary-General's office were ill-equipped in all sorts of practical ways when later confronted with crises that demanded peacekeeping and peace enforcement measures."[27]

Particularly after the fall of Srebrenica, where NATO aircraft were not allowed by the UN to intervene because of delays and debates within the line of command, and the Serbs subsequently massacred 8,000 Bosnian Muslims, the dual key was on the way out. At an international conference in London, and in subsequent NATO decisions, the procedures for conducting air strikes were simplified, the complications of the dual-key mechanism were reduced, and the targets available for strikes were greatly expanded, as part of the air and ground campaigns that finally brought the war in Bosnia to an end.

NATO Moving Into Peacekeeping

It is difficult to overestimate how much credibility the UN lost in Bosnia as an organization capable of executing military operations in (potentially) difficult circumstances. Certainly among the military in many Western countries, the conclusion was drawn that one could not entrust the UN with the fate of one's soldiers when there was a risk of armed conflict.

The crisis of confidence in UN peacekeeping showed itself also in the steep decline in the number of military personnel employed in UN peace-keeping operations in the second half of the 1990s, from around 76,000 in mid-1993 to around 12,000 in mid-1999. At the same time, NATO moved into the peacekeeping business with its operations in Bosnia (the Imple-mentation Force [IFOR], followed by the Stabilization Force [SFOR]) and three and a half years later in Kosovo (the Kosovo Force [KFOR]). Next to the explicit mentioning of enforcement in IFOR/SFOR's and KFOR's mandates, the main difference between these two NATO-led forces and UN peacekeeping operations were the large numbers of well-trained and well-equipped troops that NATO, which still had much of its Cold War strength intact, could bring to the field under a strong command-and-control structure ready to conduct large-scale and complex multinational military operations.

Russia, which had not agreed to NATO's military interventions in Bosnia and Kosovo, later agreed to the Security Council authorizing NATO-led forces in those two countries, as Serb leader Slobodan Milose-vic had in both cases accepted this under the heavy military pressure brought to bear by NATO. But while Resolution 1031, which authorized the establishment of IFOR in Bosnia-Herzegovina, had only indirectly mentioned NATO by referring to the Dayton peace agreement, Resolution 1244 on Kosovo openly recognized NATO's peacekeeping role, by man-dating an international security presence "with substantial NATO partici-pation . . . under unified command." This was the final goodbye to the dual key. However, the Security Council maintained a certain level of control and accountability of the operations by requiring regular reports. The resolution also stipulated that the international civil and security presences in Kosovo would be established for an initial period of twelve months, but that they would continue unless otherwise decided, meaning that the presence of the NATO troops for a longer period was not a given but that a decision to end their presence would need an explicit vote by the Security Council.

Mass Atrocities and the Necessity
of a Security Council Mandate

Within NATO, the impossibility to get a Security Council mandate for the Kosovo air campaign in the face of Russian opposition had led to long debates in the North Atlantic Council about the campaign's legal base. Most of the Allies, then as now, attached great importance to getting such a mandate for political and legal reasons, as it was not a case of self-defense. However, Russia's position closed this avenue. Doing nothing was also not an option for NATO members in light of Milosevic's past behavior in Bosnia. They could not allow similar atrocities to happen again in Kosovo. After long debates in the North Atlantic Council, all the Allies agreed that there was a sound legal basis for NATO's intervention, although they had different definitions of what that basis was. This was a very pragmatic approach, which serves as a reminder that, to paraphrase von Clausewitz's famous dictum, legal arguments can often be the continuation of politics by other means.

But that did not mean that the issue went away. With NATO's air campaign in Kosovo still under way, it became part of the discussions on the new Strategic Concept of the alliance, adopted at NATO's summit in April 1999. The Strategic Concept, not least upon French insistence, mentioned the primary responsibility of the Security Council for the maintenance of international peace and security and underlined that NATO's role in conflict prevention and crisis management would be "consistent with international law."[28] However, the central question of whether NATO needed a Security Council resolution for the use of force other than in cases of self-defense remained unanswered. That omission made the Strategic Concept and its reference to UN primacy acceptable to the United States.[29]

At the UN, the Kosovo intervention without a Security Council mandate also led to fierce discussions. Only few Council members were actually willing to condemn NATO's intervention. Russia tabled a draft resolution in the Security Council calling NATO's campaign illegal, but could only find two other members who would vote in favor. But among the broader membership, the fundamental question of the international community's responsibilities when confronted with mass atrocities pitted those who emphasized the principle of state sovereignty against those who pointed to a moral imperative to prevent or put an end to mass atrocities and maintained that a blockade in the Security Council could not serve as an excuse for inaction.

Secretary-General Kofi Annan made his position clear in his annual report to the General Assembly on September 20, 1999, which is still worth reading. He agreed that there was a danger that Kosovo might set a dangerous precedent for future interventions in the absence of a clear criterion on who would decide such interventions and under what circumstances they would take place. But at the same time, Annan argued that "the world cannot stand aside when gross and systematic violations are taking place. . . . This developing international norm in favor of intervention to protect civilians from wholesale slaughter . . . will in some quarters be met with distrust, skepticism, even hostility. But it is an evolution that we should welcome."[30]

A number of UN member states did indeed react to Annan's speech with distrust and hostility, and he came under heavy criticism, in particular by the Non-Aligned Movement. But the eloquent manner in which he defined the issues in the debate on humanitarian intervention, and the clear position he took on these issues, triggered the Canadian government to establish in 2001 the International Commission on Intervention and State Sovereignty (ICISS), which succeeded in developing a new approach, based on the concept of the Responsibility to Protect, and bridged the divide between the opposing sides. This concept was subsequently adopted by the UN General Assembly at the World Summit in 2005 and has been invoked several times since, including by the Security Council when it mandated in 2011 military action against Libya.

The UN Is Not a War-Fighting Machine

The debate in the UN on the lessons from Somalia, Rwanda, and Bosnia did not have the same far-reaching consequences. It led first to the appointment of a high-level panel, under the chairmanship of senior UN diplomat Lakhdar Brahimi, to investigate how the UN could conduct peace operations better in the future. The panel presented a comprehensive report, complimenting Secretary-General Kofi Annan on his willingness to undertake highly critical analyses of UN peacekeeping operations, noting: "This degree of self-criticism is rare for any large organization and particularly rare for the United Nations."[31]

The panel's report pointed to serious shortfalls in the way the UN dealt with military matters in such crucial areas as strategic direction, decision-making, rapid deployment, operational planning and support, and the use of modern information technology. The panel made a large number of concrete recommendations to remedy these problems, while emphasizing that it was a question not only of the UN becoming stronger in the military sense, but also of changing "the culture of the organization." It argued that UN forces sent to uphold the peace must have the ability and determination "to confront the lingering forces of war and violence," and that the principle of impartiality should be redefined so that a distinction could be made between victim and aggressor.[32]

The tougher peacekeeping approach proposed by the panel reflected the views of peacekeeping veterans in the Secretariat such as Brian

Urquhart, who felt that the narrow interpretation that was traditionally given to the principle that force should only be used in self-defense "was ridiculously weak."[33] But for many member states, many of the panel's recommendations went too far, and Kofi Annan was immediately put on the defensive. Although the panel had explicitly stated that it recognized that the UN "does not wage war," Annan still felt obliged to explain that the peacekeeping principles remained valid and that the goal was not to turn the UN "into a war fighting machine." On the contrary, implementing the panel's recommendations would make the need to use force less likely: "They are practical measures to achieve deterrence through strength, with the ultimate purpose of diminishing, not increasing the likelihood for the need to use force."[34] (For a detailed discussion on what came to be known as robust peacekeeping, see Chapter 18).

Afghanistan

In practice, the rejection by many UN members of some of the most important recommendations in the Brahimi Report meant that the precedent of the 1991 Gulf War became the default mode. In cases where the Security Council saw the need for large-scale military operations, it turned not to the UN but to coalitions of the able and willing "to take all necessary measures." And NATO became the preferred option for such a coalition. A first example was the case of Afghanistan. After the successful US campaign against the Taliban, the Security Council authorized the establishment of the International Security Assistance Force (ISAF) to assist the Afghan interim authority with establishing security. Member states were asked to provide contributions of personnel and equipment to ISAF, and states participating in the force were authorized to take all necessary measures in order to fulfill its mandate. The UN made very clear right from the beginning that taking on a security role in Afghanistan was beyond its capacity, and thus command over ISAF rotated among successive troop-contributing countries.

However, the feeling quickly took hold that a less ad hoc approach was necessary, and in August 2003 NATO took over command. The role of the Security Council in this was limited and basically boiled down to expanding ISAF's mandate to the regions outside Kabul, without specifying who should hold the command, as this was a matter for the countries concerned, the Afghan authorities, and NATO to decide.

It soon became clear that Afghanistan would be a much tougher nut to crack for NATO than Bosnia and Kosovo. The military, drawing on insights from earlier counterinsurgency campaigns, became convinced that for the Afghanistan operation to be successful, the support of the civilian population was essential, which would require progress in all three of the interlinked domains of security, reconstruction, and governance.[35] This insight, together with the constraints imposed on other actors by the difficult security situation in many provinces, led ISAF to take on a role in the nonmilitary fields of reconstruction and governance in the form of so-called provincial reconstruction teams consisting of military officers, diplomats, and relevant experts.

The discussion is still continuing on the effectiveness and desirability of the contribution NATO made to reconstruction and governance in Afghanistan.[36] In some provinces NATO and the reconstruction teams played a welcome and useful role. In other places this was less the case. Former ISAF commander General Stanley McChrystal, for instance, after his retirement, criticized the force for "a frighteningly simplistic view" of the situation in Afghanistan and a lack of local knowledge.[37]

But for its relationship with the UN, NATO experience in Afghanistan had some positive effects. First, NATO's involvement in reconstruction and governance sensitized it to the difficulties the UN faces in peacekeeping and statebuilding. Second, it gave a strong impetus to the practical cooperation between the UN and NATO. On September 23, 2008, the two secretaries-general, Ban Ki-moon of the UN and Jaap de Hoop Scheffer of NATO, signed a joint declaration on UN-NATO secretariat cooperation, establishing a framework of consultation including regular exchanges and dialogue on political and operational issues.

Libya

The crisis in Libya in 2011 is the most recent example of NATO waging war out-of-area with a Security Council mandate. As the crisis worsened in early 2011, military action quickly became the preferred course of action. With the UN lacking the will and the capacity to conduct a major military operation, it soon became clear in the Security Council that NATO would become the executing agency, although the alliance was not explicitly mentioned in the mandating resolution, which used the generic wording: "Member States . . . acting nationally or through regional organizations and arrangements."

NATO's mandate developed step-by-step in a more or less synchronized process of decisionmaking in the Security Council and the North Atlantic Council, with the former authorizing military action, followed by decisions in the latter on the military implementation of the mandate. Planning focused first on humanitarian assistance and the arms embargo, the two areas mentioned in Resolution 1970, which was adopted unanimously on February 26, 2011. On the basis of military response options provided by NATO's Military Strategic Command, guidelines were drafted, which were approved by the defense ministers at their meeting on March 10. Resolution 1973, adopted by the Security Council on March 17 with five abstentions, subsequently gave states and regional organizations the mandate to enforce the arms embargo. It also included the mandate to impose a no-fly zone. This was expected and the North Atlantic Council had already agreed planning guidelines on the matter. Somewhat unexpectedly, the resolution also included a protection of civilians mandate, and repeatedly used the term "by all necessary means," indicating authorization of military enforcement. The North Atlantic Council decided on March 27 to take on the responsibility also for this new and most difficult element in the mandate, after the alliance's decisionmaking process on the arms embargo and the no-fly zone was concluded. Subsequently, on March 31, the alliance took sole command and control of the international military effort in Libya.

In its preparation for this operation, NATO used a ninety-day planning format, with the extension of the mission beyond this period requiring a new decision by the North Atlantic Council. Synchronization of the two processes, in New York and Brussels, mainly took place via NATO members sitting on the Security Council, in particular the so-called P3: the United States, France, and the United Kingdom. In addition, officials of the secretariats of NATO and of the UN were in regular contact. This was generally seen as very useful, to keep the headquarters of each apprised of the developments in the other organization, but also to keep NATO members not present in the Security Council apprised.

Resolution 1973 requested "Member States concerned"—that is, NATO members—to coordinate closely with the UN Secretary-General and to report to the Security Council on the implementation of the resolution. NATO's secretary-general sent monthly—short and not particularly newsworthy—reports to his counterpart at the UN. On the arms embargo, NATO sent separate and more frequent reports. In addition, NATO's assistant secretary-general for operations sent a weekly update to New York. NATO's liaison office there played a critical role by ensuring regular interaction among representatives of UN member states as well as relevant UN agencies and departments.

In an exchange of letters after the end of the crisis in Libya, the two secretaries-general agreed that the early cooperation and consultation between their two organizations had ensured coherence and effectiveness in the discharge of the mandates entrusted to them. Unlike during the Bosnia crisis, there was now a clear division of labor between them, and potential areas of discord, such as untangling the UN's humanitarian efforts and NATO's military activities, had been handled well. An experienced civilian adviser at NATO's military headquarters in Mons, Belgium, was appointed the sole point of contact, and he played a crucial role in bridging the gulf and building trust between the military and the humanitarians.

At the UN, however, as Muammar Qaddafi held out longer than had been generally expected, a debate ensued over whether or not NATO had moved beyond the mandate given by the Security Council. Some members of the Council, arguing that NATO had gone further than what they thought was decided, became fiercely critical of the intervention. This is disputed by other members of the Council, who maintain that the implications of the mandate had been thoroughly discussed. And on December 14, 2011, Secretary-General Ban Ki-moon stated that NATO's military operation had been conducted strictly within the limits of Resolution 1973.[38]

What this debate did make clear is that the process of decisionmaking in the Security Council on such an important matter as mandating aerial bombardments against a country that had not attacked another country, but had attacked its own population, was not as strongly based on sound military advice as one would expect, even allowing for the time pressure under which the Council was operating with Qaddafi's forces approaching the gates of Benghazi. This somewhat nonchalant approach to important military issues also applies to many UN-led missions, whose mandates are often broad and lack specificity, leaving implementation to a large degree to the commander in the field. The criticism of the Brahimi Report on the UN's shortcomings in strategic direction and decisionmaking remain as valid as they were in 2000.

What can be done to remedy this fundamental weakness in the UN's role in military matters? One recurrent proposal is to enhance the role of the Military Staff Committee.[39] Another, perhaps complementary option is to strengthen the DPKO, which has a staff of only a few hundred, an astoundingly low number given that at no time since 2008 has the UN had fewer than 90,000 troops and police deployed in the field. A third option is to involve NATO in the military advice given to the Council in the mandate formulation process. While surely controversial in some quarters, such a supporting role of NATO's military staff could prevent later divisive debates on how NATO has implemented the mandate. And it would also support the further development of practical cooperation between the two organizations, to the benefit of both.

Practical Cooperation Between the UN and NATO

UN and NATO officials have for some time now explored ways to strengthen practical cooperation between the two organizations. The UN is interested because of the growing number of mandates for robust peacekeeping operations that—notwithstanding the UN's insistence that they remain based on the traditional peacekeeping principles—confront the UN with challenges on which NATO has considerable expertise. NATO is interested because it can learn from the UN's expertise in peacekeeping, and also because a more capable UN would mean less asked of NATO.

Practical cooperation between the UN and NATO is a sensitive issue for a large number of countries from the global South, but also for Russia. The two secretaries-general therefore took care in their joint declaration of September 23, 2008, to define their cooperation as being between the two secretariats, and not between the two organizations. While this cooperation is not revolutionary, its implementation is still considered useful by both sides, having led to regular staff-to-staff talks and exchanges on lessons learned in relevant areas, and participation of UN staff in courses at NATO schools. The overall approach is to work on the basis of progressive, pragmatic goals, which, if politics permit, could lead to important improvements in the capacities of the two organizations, and those of the UN in particular, to manage crises that threaten or undermine international peace and security.

Conclusion

As both the UN and NATO have taken on new military roles not foreseen by their respective founders—peacekeeping in the case of the UN, out-of-area crisis management operations in the case of NATO—the relationship between the two organizations has moved gradually from complete separation, through a phase of confrontation, and toward complementarity and even cooperation.[40] The question of whether NATO is a regional arrangement under Chapter VIII has become moot, as NATO has extended its military presence as far away as Afghanistan, with a mandate from the Security Council.

Two general divisions of labor present themselves. First, when a Security Council resolution mandates enforcement that requires robust offensive operations with the possibility of actual war-fighting, the UN turns to coalitions of the able and the willing, with NATO often in the lead, although others—individual countries or regional organizations—are not excluded. Second, if both organizations are present on the ground in (post)conflict countries, the UN is in the lead on the civilian side and NATO on the military side, with NATO sometimes making a limited nonmilitary contribution in specific areas where the alliance has expertise.

Even with such a division of labor, however, the UN needs to focus more on its significant military shortcomings, given the immense numbers of troops and police it has deployed in conflict zones. While high-quality commanders in the field can sometimes compensate for these shortcomings,[41] many of the weaknesses identified by the Brahimi Report remain to be addressed. Here, cooperation with NATO could lead to improvements in areas such as force generation, force preparation, troop certification, training and exercises, and operational planning, improvements that would be of particular importance in light of the mandate that the Security Council, under pressure from African countries, gave in March 2013 to MONUSCO, the UN peacekeeping operation in the DRC. This mandate, as defined in Resolution 2098, includes carrying out "offensive operations . . . to neutralize" armed groups "posing a threat to state authority and civilian security." References to "offensive operations" or "neutralizing opponents" were once taboo in UN peacekeeping jargon. But at the same time, the resolution underlines that this is "on an exceptional basis and without creating a precedent or any prejudice to the agreed principles of peacekeeping." So it is too early to say whether or not Resolution 2098 has set a precedent. If it has not, and the Security Council continues to use the classical template of peacekeeping in situations where a more robust operation is needed, it cannot be excluded that the African Union will gradually replace the UN as the lead organization in military operations in Africa, just as NATO (and now also the European Union) has done in Europe.

NATO on its side should resist the temptation to expand the existing and useful units for civil-military cooperation into an independent NATO capacity for reconstruction, development, and governance, as this would duplicate or compete with the work done by civilian actors. And it should invest in building support among UN member states for UN-NATO military cooperation. After all, many of the countries who have hesitations about such cooperation, or oppose it outright, participate themselves in NATO's expanding partnership network.

Through such military cooperation, the UN can strengthen its position as a credible agency for more robust peacekeeping operations, while NATO, without giving up its role in the collective defense of the Allies, can over time see its integrated military structure develop into something like an international military public good, supporting the Security Council in the exercise of its primary responsibility for the maintenance of international peace and security.

Notes

1. United Nations, *Charter of the United Nations* (San Francisco, June 26, 1945), Article 1(1).
2. Bruno Simma, Daniel-Erasmus Khan, Georg Nolte, and Andreas Paulus, eds., *The Charter of the United Nations: A Commentary* (Oxford: Oxford University Press, 2012), p. 1332.
3. Alex J. Bellamy, Paul Williams, and Stuart Griffin, *Understanding Peacekeeping* (Cambridge: Polity, 2004), p. 148.
4. Paul Kennedy, *The Parliament of Men: The United Nations and the Quest for World Government* (London: Allen Lane, 2006), p. 38.
5. Quoted in Herman Schaper, "Nederlands Veiligheidsbeleid, 1945–1950," *Low Countries Historical Review* 96, no. 2 (1981): 280.

6. On limitations to the inherent right of self-defense, see Simma et al., *The Charter of the United Nations,* pp. 1403–1406.

7. Marten Zwanenburg, "NATO, Its Member States, and the Security Council," in *The Security Council and the Use of Force: Theory and Reality—A Need for Change?* edited by Niels Blokker and Nico Schrijver (Leiden: Martinus Nijhoff, 2005), p. 191.

8. Simma et al., *The Charter of the United Nations,* pp. 36–37.

9. Inis J. Claude Jr., *Swords into Plowshares: The Problems and Progress of International Organization* (New York: Random, 1971), p. 116.

10. Martin A. Smith, *On Rocky Foundations: NATO, the UN, and Peace Operations in the Post–Cold War Era,* Peace Research Report no. 37 (Bradford: University of Bradford, Department of Peace Studies, 1996), p. 3.

11. Ibid., p. 4.

12. United Nations Secretary-General, *An Agenda for Peace: Preventive Diplomacy, Peacemaking, and Peace-keeping,* UN Doc. A/47/277-S/24111, June 17, 1992, para. 43.

13. Ibid.

14. Kofi Annan with Nader Mousavizadeh, *Interventions: A Life in War and Peace* (New York: Penguin, 2012), pp. 36, 63.

15. United Nations Secretary-General, *Supplement to* An Agenda for Peace, UN Doc. A/50/60-S/1995/1, January 5, 1995, para. 77.

16. Smith, *On Rocky Foundations,* p. 7.

17. Ibid., p. 12.

18. United Nations Secretary-General, *An Agenda for Peace,* para. 61.

19. Zwanenburg, "NATO," pp. 194–195.

20. Ibid., p. 200.

21. North Atlantic Treaty Organization (NATO), "Final Communiqué of the Ministerial Meeting of the North Atlantic Council," June 1, 1992.

22. Manfred Wörner, speech to the International Press Institute, Venice, May 10, 1993.

23. US Department of State, Bureau of Public Affairs, "95/11/01 Fact Sheet: Bosnia—NATO Involvement in the Balkan Crisis," November 1995, http://dosfan.lib.uic.edu/ERC/bureaus/eur/releases/951101BosniaNATO.html.

24. Quoted in Zwanenburg, "NATO," p. 201.

25. Quoted in Smith, *On Rocky Foundations,* p. 34.

26. Ibid., p. 30.

27. Kennedy, *The Parliament of Men,* p. 55.

28. NATO, *The Alliance's Strategic Concept,* April 24, 1999, www.nato.int/cps/en/natolive/official_texts_27433.htm.

29. Zwanenburg, "NATO," p. 202.

30. United Nations Meetings Coverage and Press Releases, "Secretary-General Presents His Annual Report to the General Assembly," SG/SM/7136, GA/9596, September 20, 1999, www.un.org/News/Press/docs/1999/19990920.sgsm7136.html.

31. See "Letter Dated 17 August 2000 from the Chairman of the Panel on United Nations Peace Operations to the Secretary-General," in United Nations Secretary-General, "Identical Letters Dated 21 August 2000 to the President of the General Assembly and the President of the Security Council," A/55/305–S/2000/809, August 21, 2000.

32. United Nations General Assembly and Security Council, *Report of the Panel on United Nations Peace Operations* (Brahimi Report), A/55/305-S/2000/809, August 21, 2000, pp. viii, ix.

33. Niels Blokker, "On Recent Practice," in Blokker and Schrivjer, *The Security Council and the Use of Force,* p. 18.

34. United Nations Secretary-General, "Report to the Security Council on the Implementation of the Report of the Panel on UN Peace Operations," S/2000/1081, October 20, 2000, para. 7c, 7h.

35. See, for instance, Rupert Smith, *The Utility of Force: The Art of War in the Modern World* (New York: Knopf, 2005).

36. For a critical analysis of the provincial reconstruction teams, see, for instance, Michael F. Harsch, *NATO and the UN: Partnership with Potential?* (Berlin: SWP, January 2012), pp. 12–16.

37. Harsch, *NATO and the UN,* p. 15.

38. United Nations Meetings Coverage and Press Releases, "Press Conference by Secretary-General Ban Ki-moon at United Nations Headquarters," UN Doc. SG/SM/14021, December 14, 2011, www.un.org/press/en/2011/sgsm14021.doc.htm.

39. Most recently, Portugal made this suggestion during the thematic debate it organized in 2012 on the working methods of the Security Council.

40. An important earlier analysis of the evolving relationship between the UN and NATO, published a decade ago, can be found in Michael Pugh and Waheguru Pal Singh Sidhu, eds., *The United Nations and Regional Security: Europe and Beyond* (Boulder, CO: Lynne Rienner, 2003).

41. One such example is Major-General Patrick Cammaert, who performed stellarly as commander of MONUC's Eastern Division in the DRC in 2005–2007.

20

The Role of Sanctions

Sue Eckert

INTERNATIONAL SANCTIONS ARE AMONG THE VITAL AND INDIS-
pensable tools available to the United Nations Security Council in addressing threats to international peace and security. From human rights violations in Darfur, to Iranian and North Korean efforts to acquire nuclear
capabilities, to the protection of civilians in Libya, the Security Council
imposes targeted sanctions with growing frequency and for an increasing
range of purposes. The reluctance of many countries to support the use of
military force accentuates the essential space that sanctions occupy—a middle ground between "war and words."[1] Indeed, sanctions have become *the*
instrument of choice in responding to contemporary international security
challenges.

The past quarter century has witnessed a significant transformation in
the use of UN targeted sanctions. Instead of comprehensive economic
embargoes such as the one employed against Iraq in the early 1990s, with
resulting injurious humanitarian consequences, the Security Council deliberately shifted to "targeted" or "smart" sanctions as a means of focusing
measures on the decisionmakers and their principal supporters responsible
for violations of international norms. All UN sanctions since 1994 have
been targeted in some manner.

As global threats have evolved, innovation in the design and application of UN sanctions has ensued. From the original focus on cross-border
attacks, civil wars, and terrorism, the rationale for sanctions has expanded
to encompass preventing new forms of human rights violations such as sexual and gender-based violence and recruitment of child soldiers, thwarting
the development of unconventional arms and their delivery systems, coun-

413

tering financing of conflict through exploitation of natural resources or criminal activities, and forcing the restoration of democratically elected governments.

At the same time, the range of international organizations, instruments, and initiatives dealing with many of these threats has multiplied. The growing frequency with which other crisis management tools are employed alongside UN sanctions—mediation, peacekeeping, referrals to international judicial processes, as well as the imposition of sanctions by entities other than the UN, including regional groups as well as individual countries—raises issues of coordination and complementarity.

With UN sanctions targeting specific goods or services, individuals and entities, new issues have arisen over time—the need to ensure that UN sanctions are reconciled with the rule of law, particularly respect for due process and human rights; the focus on nonstate actors; new expert mechanisms to monitor implementation; and greater reliance on the private sector to implement sanctions, requiring new partnerships and strategies to ensure effectiveness. These institutional dynamics reflect the need for the Security Council, the Secretariat and UN agencies, member states, and related international actors to adapt continually to the intricacies of new threats to international peace and security.

In this chapter I explore the evolution of UN sanctions; explain the objectives, types, and actors involved therein; and discuss institutional innovations and trends as well as ongoing challenges limiting the efficacy of multilateral sanctions. I conclude with broad suggestions of measures to strengthen management and implementation of UN sanctions to be more effective instruments of international conflict resolution.

Objectives and Types of UN Sanctions

Sanctions provide the international community a potentially potent instrument to address threats to international peace and security.[2] Under Chapter VII of the UN Charter, Article 41 authorizes the Security Council to adopt coercive nonmilitary measures, short of the use of force, to deal with "any threat to the peace, breach of the peace, or act of aggression."[3] Every member state is obliged to implement such measures at the national level. Although some countries willingly enact sanctions on a unilateral basis, for many other countries Chapter VII mandates provide the only legal basis upon which to impose sanctions.

The specific goals of UN sanctions have expanded over time as the Security Council has encountered a broader array of threats to international peace and security. Originally crafted to confront cross-border aggression and civil wars, sanctions now address security threats of terrorism and the proliferation of weapons of mass destruction (WMD), as well as promote human rights and protect civilians by aiming to neutralize spoilers in conflict and peacekeeping contexts. The Security Council has also employed targeted sanctions in nontraditional ways, for instance against perpetrators of sexual and gender-based violence against civilians in conflict zones, and has signaled its intention to sanction recruiters of child soldiers, suspected pirates, and groups using natural resources, including wildlife products, to finance conflict.[4] Today the UN utilizes sanctions to address six general categories of threats to international peace and security: armed conflict (including support for peace negotiations and peace enforcement), terrorism, WMD proliferation, illegal change of government, governance of resources, and protection of civilians.[5]

To address these challenges, the international community generally employs sanctions to achieve three strategic purposes: to *coerce targets* into changing policies or behavior (the most widely perceived goal of sanctions); to *constrain targets* in their ability to conduct proscribed activities; and to *signal support* for an international norm or *stigmatize targets.*[6] Such purposes are not mutually exclusive, and most sanctions have multiple objectives. For example, nonproliferation sanctions against Iran and North Korea attempt to change regimes' behavior and to stigmatize their violations of nonproliferation norms, but primarily focus on constraining access to goods, technology, and finance that could assist WMD programs. All UN sanctions address threats to international peace and security and involve signaling or stigmatizing in some manner. Notwithstanding the multiple purposes of sanctions, however, much of the popular discourse surrounding sanctions remains fixated on the coercive aspect, often to the exclusion of the other purposes. Public discourse commonly focuses on whether sanctions "work" in forcing a change of behavior, failing to understand and appreciate the important constraining and signaling functions of UN sanctions.

Sanctions are targeted in a variety of ways—against individuals, corporate entities (e.g., firms, political parties, or other nonstate actors such as UNITA, al-Qaeda, and the Taliban), sectors of an economy (e.g., aviation or arms, financial, or commodities such as oil or timber); or specific regions of a country (as in Darfur in western Sudan). Targeted sanctions attempt to deny targets the means to wage conflict or otherwise threaten international peace and security, while minimizing the impact on innocent civilians and the population as a whole.[7] Specifically, targeted measures include asset freezes, travel or visa restrictions, aviation bans, arms embargoes, and restrictions on commodities such as diamonds, timber, oil, charcoal, and luxury goods. The most frequently utilized sanctions include arms embargoes, and financial and travel measures.

For the past two decades, the Security Council has utilized sanctions with increased frequency. Table 20.1 provides an overview of all targeted

Table 20.1 Security Council Sanctions, 1990–2015

	Comprehensive	Arms	Financial	Travel	Aviation	Oil	Diamonds	Timber	Other	Panel of Experts	Security Council Resolutions[a]
Iraq (1990–)	[√]	√	√[b]								661 (1990), 1483/1518 (2003), 1546 (2004)
[Former Republic of Yugoslavia] (1991–1996)	[√]	[√]	[√]	[√]	[√]						713 (1991), 757 (1992), 820 (1993), 942 (1994)
Somalia/Eritrea (1992–)		√	√	√					√[c]	√	733 (1992), 1407 (2002), 1772 (2007) 1844 (2008), 1907 (2009), 2023 (2011), 2036 (2012), 2093 (2013), 2142 (2014)
[Libya I] (1992–2003)		[√]	[√]		[√]				[√][d]		748 (1992), 883 (1993), 1970/1973/2009/2016 (2011), 2095 (2013), 2146 (2014)
Libya II (2011–)		√	√	√		√				√	
Liberia (1992–)		√	√	√			[√]	[√]		√	788 (1992), 1343 (2001), 1478/1521 (2003), 1532 (2004), 1753 (2006), 1903 (2009)
[Haiti] (1993–1994)	[√]	[√]	[√]	[√]	[√]	[√]					841 (1993), 873 (1993), 917 (1994)

	Comprehensive	Arms	Financial	Travel	Aviation	Oil	Diamonds	Timber	Other	Panel of Experts	Security Council Resolutions[a]
[Angola (UNITA)] (1993–2002)		[√]	[√]	[√]		[√]	[√]		[√]c	[√]	864 (1993), 1127 (1997), 1173 (1998)
[Rwanda] (1994–2008)		[√]								[√]f	918 (1994), 997/1011 (1995), 1823 (2008)
[Sudan I] (1996–2001) Sudan II (2004–)		√	√	[√] √	[√]				[√]g	√	1054 (1996), 1070 (1996), 1556 (2004), 1591 (2005), 1672 (2006), 1945 (2010)
[Sierra Leone] (1997–2010)		[√]	√	[√]		[√]	[√]			[√]	1132 (1997), 1171 (1998), 1306 (2000), 1940 (2010)
al-Qaeda/Taliban[b] (1999–)		√	√	√	[√]					√	1267 (1999), 1333 (2000), 1393 (2002), 1526 (2004), 1617 (2005), 1735 (2006), 1822 (2008), 1904 (2009), 1988/1989 (2011), 2082/2083 (2012), 2199 (2015)
[Eritrea/Ethiopia] (2000–2001)		[√]									1298 (2000)
Democratic Republic of the Congo (2003–)		√	√	√	√					√	1493 (2003), 1596 (2005), 1807/1857 (2008), 1952 (2010)
Côte d'Ivoire (2004–)		√	√	√			√			√	1572 (2004), 1584/1643 (2005), 1893 (2009), 1975/1980 (2011)

continues

Table 20.1 continued

	Comprehensive	Arms	Financial	Travel	Aviation	Oil	Diamonds	Timber	Panel of Experts	Other	Security Council Resolutions[a]
Lebanon/Syria[i] (2005–)			√	√					√		1636 (2005), 1701 (2006)
North Korea (2006–)		√	√	√					√	√[j]	1718 (2006), 1874 (2009), 2087/2094 (2013)
Iran (2006–)		√	√	√					√		1737 (2006), 1747 (2007), 1803, (2008), 1929 (2010)
Guinea-Bissau (2012–)				√							2048 (2012)
Central African Republic (2013–)		√	√	√					√		2127 (2013), 2134 (2014)
Yemen (2014–)		√	√	√					√		2140 (2014), 2216 (2015)
South Sudan (2015–)			√	√					√		2206 (2015)

Notes: Brackets [ ] indicate UN sanctions that have been terminated.

a. Includes resolutions imposing sanctions only (subsequent resolutions extending but not imposing new measures are not included). As of May 2015.

b. Frozen assets to be transferred to Iraqi development fund.

c. Charcoal exports and imports.

d. Oil-related equipment.

e. Sanctions against UNITA included diplomatic measures (closing of offices); a ban on the supply of aircraft, spare parts, and servicing; prohibition on equipment for mining and mining services; and a transportation ban on motorized vehicles, watercraft, and ground- or water-borne services to areas in Angola.

f. Commission of inquiry to collect information on the arms embargo (first expert panel–type mechanism).

g. Diplomatic restrictions including reduction in the number and level of staff at Sudanese missions.

h. S/RES/1988 (June 17, 2011) separated the Taliban from al-Qaeda and established a new Taliban sanctions regime.

i. S/RES/1636 (October 31, 2005) authorized measures against individuals designated by the international independent investigation commission or the government of Lebanon suspected of involvement in the February 14, 2005, terrorist bombing in Beirut, Lebanon, that killed former Lebanese prime minister Rafik Hariri and twenty-two others. No individuals have ever been designated.

j. Luxury goods.

sanctions imposed by the United Nations from 1990 to 2015. As of May 2015, the UN maintained sixteen sanctions regimes—thirteen country-based regimes (Somalia/Eritrea, Iraq, Liberia, the Democratic Republic of the Congo, Côte d'Ivoire, Sudan, North Korea, Iran, Libya, Guinea-Bissau, the Central African Republic, Yemen, and South Sudan), as well as sanctions against al-Qaeda and globally affiliated groups, the Taliban, and individuals suspected of involvement in the February 14, 2005, bombing in Beirut that killed then–Lebanese prime minister Rafik Hariri. While UN Security Council Resolution 1636 authorized sanctions against any individuals involved in the 2005 assassination of Lebanese prime minister Rafik Hariri, no designations have been made. Prior to the most recent South Sudan sanctions, the fifteen sanctions regimes were supported by sixty-five experts working on twelve monitoring teams, groups, and panels, at a price tag of about $32 million a year.[8]

The Evolution of UN Sanctions

After the end of the Cold War, the United Nations began imposing sanctions more frequently, leading the 1990s to be characterized as the "sanctions decade"[9] (see Figure 20.1). Previously, the UN had imposed sanctions only twice—against Rhodesia in 1966 and South Africa in 1977. From 1992 to 1999, UN targeted sanctions focused primarily on intrastate armed conflict, with all sanctions other than those imposed on Libya and Sudan (for terrorism) and Haiti (restoration of the democratically elected leader) seeking to prevent conflict, promote peace and reconciliation processes, or protect human rights in African conflicts (Somalia, Liberia, Angola, Rwanda, Sudan, and Sierra Leone). Following the 1998 bombings of US embassies in East Africa, Resolution 1267 imposed sanctions on the Taliban and al-Qaeda and associated groups in an effort to thwart international terrorism.

The terrorist attacks of September 11, 2001, represented a turning point in UN sanctions. The creation of the Counter-Terrorism Committee (CTC) pursuant to Resolution 1373, while not technically a sanctions committee, placed new emphasis on stemming the financing of terrorism, including through adoption of domestic legislation, national implementation measures, and reporting to the CTC. Innovative measures such as the 1267 Monitoring Team gradually became the standard that other sanctions committees emulated. Even while sanctions from 2001 to 2005 primarily addressed armed conflict in African countries (the DRC, Côte d'Ivoire, Sudan, and Eritrea), in 2006 Council sanctions shifted to focus on nonproliferation. Modeled on the 1267 counterterrorism measures, nonproliferation sanctions attempted to constrain Iran's and North Korea's nuclear capabilities by limiting their access to relevant goods, technology, and financing. At the same time, the Security Council continued to adapt sanctions to focus on perpetrators of

Figure 20.1 UN Sanctions Timeline, 1990–2015

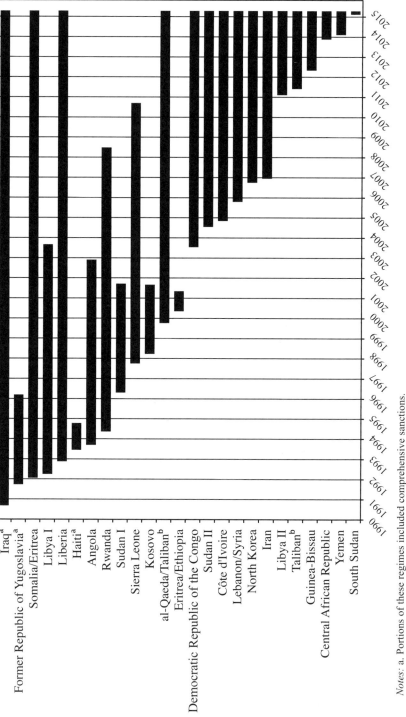

Notes: a. Portions of these regimes included comprehensive sanctions.
b. The combined sanctions regime for al-Qaeda and the Taliban was split into two distinct regimes in 2011.

sexual and gender-based violence against civilians and dealers of minerals funding conflict in African countries. The Security Council also moved to sanction actors disrupting peace agreements and peacekeeping missions, those involved in unconstitutional changes of government (Côte d'Ivoire, Sierra Leone, and Guinea-Bissau), as well as those recruiting child soldiers.

The year 2011 marked what, at the time, was hoped to be a new phase in the evolution of UN sanctions. In March, the Council adopted measures against the regime of former Ivorian president Laurent Gbagbo to quell violence and pressure it to accept the results of the November 2010 elections. In February and March, Security Council Resolutions 1970 and 1973 imposed sanctions against the Muammar Qaddafi regime, alongside a no-fly zone to protect civilians facing imminent danger in Benghazi, in effect operationalizing the principle of the Responsibility to Protect (R2P). The authorization of the use of force and subsequent NATO military action soon led to differences among Council members, with Russia, China and others accusing NATO of overreaching its mandate to pursue "regime change." Subsequently, both China and Russia vetoed multiple draft resolutions to address violence in Syria, frequently citing the Libyan experience as the basis for opposition, portending greater difficulty in adopting sanctions for the purpose of R2P or protection of civilians in the future.

While more than three-fifths (ten of sixteen) of the current UN sanctions regimes remain focused on armed conflict and peacebuilding objectives in African countries, sanctions focused on the threat of terrorism (al-Qaeda and the Taliban) and the threat of nuclear proliferation (Iran and North Korea) receive a disproportionate share of the Security Council's attention and resources.[10] In part, this reflects greater consensus among the permanent Council members on "hard" security issues in which core national interests coincide.

Primary Sanctions Actors and Organizations

As with most other Council business, the five permanent members of the Council (China, France, Russia, the United Kingdom, and the United States) typically dominate the negotiations concerning sanctions, with the P3 (France, the United Kingdom, and the United States) responsible for drafting most resolutions. Routinely, when new sanctions are imposed, the resolution creates a sanctions committee composed of the fifteen Council members to oversee the measures. Chairs of sanctions committees are usually selected from the elected ten nonpermanent members of the Security Council (E10). In general, sanctions committees meet at the expert level but are chaired by an ambassador.

Operating on the basis of consensus, sanctions committees receive information from member states, designate individuals and entities subject to sanctions (unless included in the resolution), consider exemption requests for basic expenses, and monitor implementation. Meetings are informal and held in closed session; websites provide what public information is available related to the regimes, generally including member states' reports on national implementation, resolutions, reports of expert panels, and press releases.

The E10 representatives chairing the sanctions committees largely set the tone and agenda for committee activities. Indeed, the effectiveness of committees directly relates to the leadership, level of involvement, and support of the ambassador and his or her country. For elected members of the Council from smaller states who chair two or more committees (including the CTC and the so-called 1540 Committee), the burden can be quite heavy, often with little to no advance preparation.

Within the UN Secretariat, the sanctions branch of the Security Council's Affairs Division assigns each committee a staff secretary to provide administrative support and guidance. While the frequency of meetings varies according to the workload, most committees meet on a regular (weekly or biweekly) basis. Daily operations of the sanctions committee—preparing agendas, considering exemption requests, reviewing national reports, issuing notifications of committee decisions, responding to questions, updating the committee website, and providing support to expert panels—are the responsibility of the sanctions committee secretary. Over time, the workload of sanctions committees has grown significantly, while the number of professionals has declined. As a result, committee secretaries are often overburdened, without adequate training to advise committee chairs and support expert panels. Proactive policy development, information-sharing, and coordination with other UN bodies, and briefing of new Council members, have been lacking in recent years.

One of the most significant developments in recent years concerns the widespread use of panels of experts—small independent investigative teams to monitor implementation of sanctions. Authorized by resolution and appointed by the Secretary-General, these panels assist committees in assessing compliance with UN sanctions. They have been instrumental in calling attention to sanctions violations, as well as providing the international community with information and analysis regarding targets' evasion strategies and suggestions to enhance the effectiveness of measures. While the quality and impact of panel reports vary, they remain a crucial mechanism for the Security Council to monitor sanctions implementation.

In addition to the sanctions committees, panels of experts, and Secretariat staff, other parts of the UN and international organizations and mechanisms play increasingly important roles in sanctions-related issues. Countries subject to sanctions often host peacekeeping operations, field-based political missions, and UN special envoys. The Office of the UN High Commissioner for Human Rights, and the UN Office for the Coordinator of

Humanitarian Affairs, the Human Rights Council, and other entities whose remits involve international human rights and humanitarian law, as well as functional agencies such as the Office for Disarmament Affairs, the International Atomic Energy Agency, and specialized dual-use nonproliferation arrangements (e.g., Wassenaar Arrangement, Nuclear Suppliers Group, Missile Technology Control Regime), have responsibilities related to sanctions implementation. Thus, the range of international actors, organizations, and instruments dealing with threats to international peace and security has multiplied. The growing frequency with which other crisis resolution instruments are employed—mediation, referrals to international judicial processes, as well as regional and unilateral sanctions—raises issues of coordination and complementarity.

Ultimately, it is the 193 members of the United Nations who are responsible for implementing sanctions. Article 25 of the UN Charter requires all members to comply with, and implement decisions of, the Security Council; as such, sanctions are mandatory and legally binding on member states. Many countries utilize general legal authorities (analogous to the United Nations Participation Act in the United States or the United Nations Act in the United Kingdom) to transpose sanctions into national measures, while others require specific legislative or executive action. In many countries, significant gaps exist in both legal authority and administrative mechanisms to give full force to UN sanctions.

Innovations and Trends

With more than two decades of experience in targeted sanctions, the Security Council and its sanctions committees have proven remarkably adept in refining these measures. Significant institutional learning—based in part on external reform initiatives by Groups of Friends such as the Interlaken (financial), Bonn-Berlin (arms and travel bans), and Stockholm (implementation) processes—together with greater emphasis on the importance of implementation and enforcement of sanctions measures, have resulted in innovations in designing and implementing UN sanctions.[11] Today, UN resolutions and committees overseeing sanctions utilize more systematic procedures, common guidelines and definitions, standardized humanitarian exemptions, and panels of experts to monitor sanctions compliance, making the application of UN sanctions more consistent. These innovations represent important enhancements in the working methods of the Security Council and development of the sanctions tool.

Panels of Experts

Utilization and acceptance of panels of experts in assisting committees in monitoring sanctions implementation represent one of the most remarkable innovations in this realm. Some panels have garnered controversy, as their reports name countries or entities violating sanctions. The 1999 Angola panel of experts and monitoring mechanism under the leadership of Canadian ambassador Robert Fowler pioneered the "naming and shaming" of sanctions busters (including neighboring heads of state); Fowler also established expert panels as independent expert bodies sensitive to geographical balance. Subsequent committees increasingly utilized such panels, to the point that they are routinely established with the adoption of most sanctions regimes (all committees since 2006 with the exception of Guinea-Bissau). Detailed reports concerning violations and developments in the sanctioned countries by recognized arms, finance, natural resources, and regional experts generally form the basis of respected credible analysis and fact-based recommendations.

Until recently, most decisions regarding appointments to panels of experts were made by the UN Secretariat on the basis of expertise. However, the North Korea and Iran sanctions regimes departed from prior practice, with P5 members proposing their own national experts rather than allowing the Secretary-General to appoint the panel members from the compiled roster of independent professionals. This perceived politicization of expert appointments, combined with recent criticism regarding the inconsistency of evidentiary standards, has the potential to damage the credibility of expert panels. Increased scrutiny of panel initiatives, for example a 2010 report disclosing the presence of Chinese arms in Darfur, has resulted in attempts by some member states to impede the release and publication of panel reports and to exert influence over the bodies through blocking renewal of individual experts. For panels to continue to provide much-needed impartial analysis of sanctions compliance, they need to be free of political considerations to the greatest extent possible and independent in their recommendations and assessment. Otherwise, the essential innovation of expert panels in monitoring UN sanctions implementation will be impaired.

Regional Sanctions

The past several decades have witnessed an increase in sanctions applied by regional organizations, especially in Europe and Africa.[12] In 73 percent of the episodes analyzed by the Targeted Sanctions Consortium, other regional sanctions by the European Union (EU), the African Union (AU), or the Economic Community of West African States preceded initial imposition of UN sanctions. This suggests that states subject to sanctions are increasingly targeted by a combination of UN and regional measures. The EU employs sanctions, as part of its common foreign and security policy, frequently to promote human rights and support for democratic rule. Whereas the UN applies sanctions to address a range of objectives constituting threats to international peace and security, the AU utilizes sanctions for the single purpose of targeting unconstitutional changes of government with a suspension of membership.

The interplay among UN sanctions and other coordinated unilateral and regional sanctions represents another trend of multilayered sanctions. In the cases of Iran and North Korea, UN sanctions constitute a baseline or minimum threshold, while the United States, the European Union, and others supplement these sanctions with more extensive measures at the national and regional levels. UN sanctions against Iran, thus, became a "floor" or foundation upon which the United States, the EU, Australia, Canada, Japan, Norway, South Korea, and others adopted even more stringent measures, some of which had been rejected during UN negotiations. Western countries welcome this development as enhancing the effectiveness of UN sanctions, in part by using the UN to establish the legal basis and legitimacy for coordinated multilateral action. As might be expected, Russia and China do not share this view and regard UN sanctions as the "ceiling" reflecting international consensus. Using Security Council sanctions to legitimize additional measures is viewed as distorting the carefully negotiated balance within the Council. The long-term implications of this trend remain to be seen and may be unsustainable; some observers fear that future consensus on UN sanctions among the P5 will suffer.

Proliferation of Sanctions Actors and Mechanisms

The range of actors and mechanisms associated with sanctions has multiplied over the past two decades. Peacekeeping missions, mediation and other diplomatic efforts, humanitarian assistance, special envoys, and the work of specialized agencies are among the policy instruments regularly employed in conjunction with sanctions to address evolving threats to international peace and security.

In addition to other entities mandated by the Security Council, such as peacekeeping and political missions, and functional international organizations and entities (dealing with nonproliferation, arms control, and disarmament mechanisms, such as the IAEA; human rights and humanitarian law protection, such as the High Commissioner for Human Rights; international judicial processes, such as the International Criminal Court; mediation efforts, such as UN envoys; financially and commodity-focused entities such as the Financial Action Task Force, and the Kimberley Process regarding diamonds), civil society organizations, including the private sector and NGOs, are increasingly performing sanctions-related roles.

Responsibility for implementation of travel, aviation, and arms embargoes rests primarily with national governments, but financial measures—among the most widely deployed UN sanctions—require action by financial institutions. While government agencies issue regulations, only a bank or financial institution can actually freeze assets. With financial measures as well as commodity restrictions, the private sector has a critical role to play in implementing UN sanctions. With corporate entities required to investigate their supply chain to preclude the purchase of conflict resources, greater systematic cooperation with the private sector on sanctions issues is necessary.

NGOs supporting corporate social responsibility guidelines and codes of conduct to promote peace and security in conflict zones have actively engaged on sanctions. Advocacy groups such as Global Witness and Human Rights First, concerned about natural resource–financed conflict, corruption, and human rights abuses, have issued reports publicizing exploitation of timber, diamonds, and oil resources and calling for individuals and corporations trading in conflict areas to be subject to sanctions. Due diligence guidelines, first promoted by the 2009 report of the Sudan panel of experts and supported by human rights groups, were formally operationalized in Resolution 1952, requiring consideration of due diligence in designations of targets. NGOs play an increasingly important role as advocates for sanctions and sources of information concerning sanctions violations.

National and regional courts are among the more recent entrants into the sanctions realm. Legal challenges to member states' implementation of Security Council measures under Resolution 1267 (al-Qaeda and the Taliban) have raised serious questions and pose challenges to the future viability of UN sanctions. Courts have found fault with the procedures used to designate individuals and entities subject to counterterrorism sanctions, as well as with the adequacy of UN measures for challenging such designations.[13]

The Complexity of Targeted Sanctions

Targeted sanctions are more complicated to design and implement than comprehensive economic measures, in part due to the expansion of actors and instruments. Greater technical expertise is required to freeze assets, enforce travel sanctions, implement arms embargoes, and calibrate sanctions. The 2011 Libyan experience demonstrated this increased complexity of targeted sanctions. With reported Libyan assets in excess of $160 billion frozen pursuant to Council Resolutions 1970 and 1973, an unprecedented array of resources and activities were caught under the financial measures—overnight, Libyan students in the United States and Canada found their bank accounts frozen, and telecommunications providers in neighboring countries teetered on the verge of bankruptcy. Given the sheer volume of assets frozen (including those of the Libyan central bank and the country's national oil corporation), the sanctions committee and national governments faced an unprecedented workload of requests for exemptions and information. The process to release $1.5 billion in US-held Libyan assets for humanitarian purposes proved quite difficult, and required extensive negotiations for extraordinary exemptions. The experience underscored the need for further procedural refinements to implement financial measures and relax sanctions in a flexible manner, so measures can be appropriately calibrated.

The Libyan sanctions also provided an indication of the effect of certain sectoral sanctions. Less targeted financial measures against a central bank or economic sector such as petroleum, for example, affect a greater portion of the population as a whole. Broadening financial sanctions beyond individuals or limited commodities can have the effect of making sanctions more comprehensive.[14] While UN sanctions (with the exception of those on Libya) remain relatively targeted (the UN has not imposed broad sectoral sanctions since the 1998 oil sanctions on Sierra Leone), coordinated EU regional, US, and other unilateral sanctions against Iran, targeting oil and financial sectors, have had significant consequences on the Iranian economy. The distinction between targeted UN measures and other multilayered sanctions is often not understood, with sanctions writ large cast in negative terms due to humanitarian consequences.

Nonstate Actors

Given that the UN is an intergovernmental body established to manage interstate conflict, the increasing frequency with which the Security Council targets nonstate actors with sanctions is a relatively new and remarkable phenomenon. Sanctions against the Angolan rebel group UNITA in 1993 led the way and were followed by targeted measures against the Revolutionary United Front (RUF) in Sierra Leone in 1997 and al-Qaeda and the Taliban in 1999. Designations of rebel groups and their leaders have increased significantly in recent years, including al-Shabaab in Somalia, the M23 and the Lord's Resistance Army (LRA) in the DRC, the Democratic Forces for the Liberation of Rwanda (FDLR), the Sudan Liberation Army (SLA), and the Islamic State in Iraq and the Levant (ISIL). At the same time, the move from state-centric sanctions to sanctions targeted against individuals and nonstate actors has generated new challenges and issues, particularly regarding the rights and standing of parties that might be wrongly listed and want to appeal their designations ("due process challenges"). As a result, the Security Council has had to adjust its practice of dealing exclusively with states.

Institutional learning by the Security Council over the past two decades in implementing UN sanctions reflects undeniable progress. Challenges persist, however, that continue to hamper more effective utilization of the sanctions instrument to limit conflict and build peace.

Challenges to Effective Sanctions

As the international community increasingly relies on United Nations sanctions, problems regarding implementation have become more pronounced.

Insufficient political will, weak implementation, inadequate monitoring and enforcement, legal challenges, and misperceptions and a lack of under-standing constitute the primary obstacles to more effective UN sanctions.

Insufficient Political Will

Just as the UN is inherently a political entity, sanctions are essentially polit-ical instruments that can be neither separated from the politics of the Secu-rity Council, nor considered in isolation. Conflicting perspectives among the P5 regarding the objectives and utility of sanctions often result in a lack of unity of purpose and political will. China and Russia resent the P3's ten-dency to use sanctions as punitive rather than as bargaining instruments, and are predisposed against them. With a strong aversion to coercive diplomacy and anything that suggests interference in internal affairs, the two countries consistently contend that sanctions are ineffective and succeed only in isolat-ing targets, limiting diplomatic leverage, and increasing risks of instability.

Competing political and economic interests often lead to political horse-trading,[15] and compromises mask differing objectives, resulting in diluted or unclear language in Council resolutions. Vague terms requiring states to "exercise extreme vigilance" or prohibit "luxury goods," without agreed definitions or guidelines, allow for inconsistent interpretations and often result in confusion down the road as member states struggle with national implementation. Operating procedures within sanctions commit-tees requiring consensus (defined as unanimity among all fifteen Council members) allow any country to block enhancing measures, with little or no explanation or consequence.[16]

Until the high-level review of UN sanctions in 2014–2015, there had been little systematic focus on, or attention to, sanctions implementation by senior Secretariat officials and the Security Council.[17] From 2000 to 2006, the Security Council Informal Working Group on General Issues of Sanc-tions provided a regular forum for members to explore crosscutting issues and to develop general recommendations to improve the effectiveness of UN sanctions. Thematic meetings allowed testimony and interaction with outside experts and interest groups, resulting in the development of best practices with respect to UN sanctions. The December 2006 final report of the working group contained important recommendations, many of which have become standard operating procedures within committees.[18] Subse-quently, however, discussion of crosscutting sanctions implementation issues and recommendations to integrate sanctions into broader UN peace and security objectives has been irregular.

Weak Implementation and Capacity

Once sanctions are adopted by the Security Council, practical problems regarding implementation, both at the member-state level and the UN level, abound. While the UN Secretariat shares responsibility to support and monitor implementation of UN sanctions, responsibility falls primarily to member states.

Many countries, however, lack basic legal authority and executive bodies to translate UN sanctions into domestic law and regulations, which is fundamental to give full force to sanctions. The ability to freeze assets without prior judicial action, exercise appropriate border and visa controls, and enforce restrictions on exports of arms and dual-use goods and technology is often limited or nonexistent. In many cases, failure to implement sanctions boils down to simple lack of capacity at the domestic level. There are no systematic methods of UN attention, resources, and training to support national sanctions capacity, aside from the focus of the CTC and 1540 Committee on counterterrorism and nonproliferation mandates.

Within the UN Secretariat, misperceptions regarding the purposes of sanctions, as well as tensions with other UN missions over seemingly incompatible mandates, prevail. The result is a fragmented approach to sanctions and conflict resolution, and a lack of Secretariat capacity and resources to support sanctions implementation.[19] No central body within the Security Council or Secretariat exists to integrate and coordinate sanctions policies with overall UN objectives. The result is an ad hoc system of individual sanctions committees with little coordination with other UN missions and little cross-regime learning. A "silo" approach to the role of sanctions in peacekeeping and mediation persists, notwithstanding increasing overlap between these various approaches to conflict resolution.[20] Such a fragmented approach fails to integrate sanctions within an overall strategy for a country or region, thereby undermining the effectiveness of sanctions and other UN peace and security objectives.

Organizational and resource challenges within the UN loom large. The sanctions branch, located within the Department of Political Affairs of the UN Secretariat, is overextended and lacks adequate staff and resources. Previous studies universally endorse the need for greater Secretariat capacity to support the work of the Security Council, sanctions committees, and panels of experts. Beyond inadequate resources, however, leadership and vision in the Secretariat have been wanting; especially when the Security Council is divided, the Secretariat fears taking the initiative on sanctions issues, and is often perceived as passive in addressing challenges. While the Secretariat has a limited role in political decisions to impose sanctions, much more can and should be done to promote implementation once sanctions are adopted.

Inadequate Monitoring and Enforcement

After expending significant political capital to reach agreement to impose sanctions, member states often falter in their attention to monitoring and compliance. Policymakers tend to view sanctions implementation as "technical" and accord it low priority. Outside the work of panels of experts, there is little tracking of sanctions implementation or other means for committees to monitor national compliance efforts. Committees rely on reports by member states, which reached a peak a few years after the CTC innovated reporting procedures and interaction with states; however, there is widespread reporting fatigue, and reporting remains spotty for sanctions regimes not focused on counterterrorism and nonproliferation. As is prevalent with other UN mandates, there is no enforcement mechanism or body to address sanctions violations.

Monitoring of violations and sanctions evasions largely depends on the capabilities of independent panels of experts to assess sanctions compliance. Panel reports identifying actors who violate sanctions provide important public information that "names and shames" sanctions busters and countries facilitating noncompliance.[21] Unfortunately, however, violations reported by the expert panels, as well as recommendations for improving sanctions implementation, often go unaddressed. When no consequences result, targets come to regard the threat of coercion as empty, which further erodes the credibility of sanctions. No systematic follow-up for alleged violations, or procedures to hold the sanctions committee accountable for recommendations of expert panels, exist.

Moreover, the predominant focus of P5 members on counterterrorism and nonproliferation issues results in disproportionate attention and resources flowing to related sanctions. Those regimes addressing armed conflict, especially in Africa, represent the majority of current sanctions, yet receive little sustained attention and far fewer resources. There is neither a comparable level of analysis and strategic assessment (by states or the academic community), nor a systematic approach to sanctions designations. There are, of course, distinct challenges posed by African regimes—including inconsistent cooperation with peacekeeping operations and the failure to devote adequate attention to human rights, conflict prevention, and peace enforcement sanctions. These factors translate into weaker enforcement than for counterterrorism and nonproliferation sanctions.[22]

Legal Challenges

Because of the significant expansion of the 1267 list of individuals associated with al-Qaeda in the aftermath of the 9/11 attacks, legal challenges in national and regional courts represent substantial risk to the legitimacy of targeted sanctions. Several member states have found themselves in the difficult position of contravening either rulings of their own domestic courts and decisions of their own legislative bodies, on the one hand, or their obligations to implement binding Chapter VII decisions of the Security Council. The successful appeal by Yassin Kadi in the European Court of Justice in 2013 potentially has profound implications for sanctions designations and could result in selective implementation of UN measures.[23]

In response, the Security Council has reformed its delisting procedures, albeit reluctantly, through the creation of an ombudsperson to whom 1267-sanctioned individuals may appeal their designation. Notwithstanding the importance of procedural reforms to afford more due process, it is unlikely that such measures will sufficiently address the concerns of the courts. Failure to make the sanctions process more transparent, accessible, and subject to greater review threatens to undermine the credibility and effectiveness of UN sanctions generally.

Misperceptions and Lack of Understanding

Notwithstanding the move to targeted measures and significant procedural innovations, public perception remains largely skeptical of sanctions. The Fourth Freedom Forum noted that "misperceptions about how sanctions work, poor coordination, and inadequate information sharing among Member States and within the [UN] organization" hamper effectiveness.[24] Many UN conflict resolution actors view sanctions as politically toxic complications for their mandates, and shy away from association, contributing to a lack of coherence and effective implementation of UN peace and security policies.

More broadly, public understanding of the purpose and effects of sanctions is extremely limited. Concern for the consequences of comprehensive economic sanctions persists, despite the fact that the last time the Security Council imposed comprehensive measures was in 1994. All UN sanctions since have been targeted. Policy and scholarly debates remain fixated on whether they "work" in forcing a change of behavior, failing to recognize the important constraining and signaling functions of UN sanctions. Perceptions that "sanctions don't work" contribute to a profound cynicism regarding the utility and efficacy of UN sanctions.

Notwithstanding progress, innovations, and institutional learning over the past two decades by the Security Council, Secretariat, and member states, further improvement of UN sanctions remains an important and necessary objective for the promise of effective sanctions to be realized.

Measures to Strengthen UN Sanctions

P5 interests will continue to diverge, limiting the potential for agreement on new sanctions regimes, especially those concerning core national interests. Nevertheless, more can and should be done to prioritize and strengthen the implementation of United Nations sanctions. Even in the absence of new sanctions, there are concrete actions that Security Council members, the Secretary-General, and the Secretariat can undertake to overcome current challenges and make UN sanctions more effective. The 2015 *Compendium of the High-Level Review of UN Sanctions* contains a detailed discussion of these issues and related recommendations.

Establish Mechanisms for Coordinated UN Sanctions Policy and Oversight

With deliberation of sanctions issues limited to individual committees, there is little consideration of implementation challenges, definitional concerns, and enforcement issues across the sixteen sanctions regimes. Greater coherence and support from senior UN officials is needed; the Security Council Informal Working Group on General Issues of Sanctions provides a precedent for regular exploration of crosscutting issues and the development of general recommendations to improve the effectiveness of UN sanctions.[25] As recommended by the high-level review of UN sanctions, the Security Council should establish new mechanisms to coordinate and guide sanctions policy and implementation.[26] Such high-level focus would positively affirm the vital role sanctions play in promoting international peace and security, and signal that the Security Council is elevating the effectiveness of sanctions to a higher priority. Proactive leadership and a unified sanctions policy are crucial to provide the necessary coherence among the various UN actors, in the interest of more effective sanctions implementation.

Improve Implementation and Capacity

Notwithstanding practical limitations on the adoption of new sanctions, as witnessed in the case of Syria, the Security Council should vigorously implement and enforce existing UN sanctions—not just those related to nonproliferation and counterterrorism. Selective implementation weakens sanctions overall; greater focus on conflict-related sanctions is important for sustained credibility of the sanctions instrument. The Security Council should build capacity among member states and the Secretariat to provide essential support to sanctions committees and panels of experts.

Because many states simply do not have the capacity to monitor transactions within their borders, the UN should promote initiatives to develop model legislation for imposing sanctions, training of national officials on sanctions lists, border controls, financial restrictions and export controls, and new procedures to inspect and interdict proscribed goods. While there has been greater recognition of the need for capacity assistance, capacity-building initiatives comparable to those for counterterrorism and nonproliferation are still lacking. The high-level review recommended that new measures and resources should be undertaken for sanctions assistance more generally, including cooperation with regional organizations, which could play an important role in strengthening and coordinating efforts to implement asset freezes, travel bans, and arms embargoes. In particular, the African Union has expressed interest in such assistance previously and represents an ideal opportunity to develop new approaches to capacity-building training and services.

Enhance Sanctions Monitoring and Enforcement

More vigorous monitoring and enforcement of UN sanctions, as well as specific consequences for noncompliance, would strengthen their credibility. Measures should include better utilizing expert panels and systematic implementation of their recommendations, addressing noncompliance, reviving enforcement assistance, and strengthening cooperation with the private sector.

For expert panels to continue to provide much-needed analysis of sanctions implementation, they must be as free of political considerations as possible. Panel reports should be public, as effective monitoring depends on the ability to publicly name and shame. Allegations of noncompliance must be routinely reported and addressed. Chronic, substantiated, but unaddressed assertions of noncompliance should be made public. Panel recommendations, however, are only effective if they are adopted, and a standard system to track and monitor their implementation should be developed. When the Security Council determines that a country is deliberately violating Council sanctions, consequences should result. The Security Council should develop a menu of secondary sanctions against UN members found to violate sanctions.[27]

As well, member states should revive enforcement assistance, particularly initiatives similar to the sanctions assistance missions (SAMs) deployed in the early 1990s to monitor implementation of sanctions against the former republic of Yugoslavia.[28] Rigorous and routine monitoring and enforcement of sanctions should be expanded beyond border controls to enforcement of travel bans, financial sanctions, and arms embargoes.

Strengthen Cooperation with Civil Society

Civil society, including both the private sector and NGOs, is a critical partner in implementing UN sanctions. The Security Council and member states should engage the private sector in a systematic discussion of sanctions.

The UN Secretariat should develop a sustained dialogue with private companies as legitimate partners in multilateral sanctions—enlisting them to advise on, participate in the monitoring of, and even help to enforce sanctions. To this end, the Global Compact initiative and the Organization for Economic Cooperation and Development's (OECD) Guidelines for Multinational Corporations are useful foundations on which to build. As part of a follow-up to the "Guiding Principles on Business and Human Rights: Implementing the United Nations 'Protect, Respect, and Remedy'

Framework"—an initiative led by UN special representative for business and human rights John Ruggie and endorsed unanimously by the General Assembly in June 2010—the UN Secretary-General should initiate a focused discussion with relevant groups (especially financial institutions, resource-related corporations, and NGOs) on UN sanctions. Existing capacities aimed at terrorists and proliferators should be applied to enforcement of arms embargo violators and enablers of atrocities.[29]

For the private sector to be a true partner in strengthening sanctions, new methods of information-sharing among governments and industry are also needed. The UK's system of clearing financial industry representatives to receive restricted government information regarding bad actors financing conflict, terrorism, or proliferation provides a model to be emulated and developed further.

Develop Better Analysis and Understanding of UN Sanctions

Finally, the UN and member states should promote better understanding and analysis of conditions under which more effective sanctions are likely to result. It is important to raise the quality of public discourse about sanctions. Effective implementation of sanctions is made more difficult by the lack of accurate information and basic misperceptions about the impacts and effectiveness of UN targeted sanctions. Informing the broader public debate with empirically based information and engaging relevant stakeholders will help in addressing pervasive misperceptions about UN sanctions and provide a basis for more informed engagement and education of various publics at multiple levels.

Part of such an initiative is a sound analytical understanding of the optimal conditions under which sanctions are most effective. Data from the Targeted Sanctions Consortium, an international research consortium of more than fifty scholars and policy practitioners worldwide conducting an analysis of the impacts and effectiveness of UN targeted sanctions, should be explored, further developed, and refined. Based on research results through 2014, we know that UN sanctions have multiple and simultaneous purposes of coercion, constraint, and signaling. While the public and even the Council continue to disproportionately focus on the coercive purpose of sanctions (60 percent of sanctions are coercive), such measures are effective only 10 percent of the time. In contrast, as shown in Table 20.2, UN targeted sanctions are more effective in constraining (28 percent effectiveness) or signaling (27 percent) a target than in coercing a change of behavior. Clear understanding of the purposes for which sanctions are more likely to work, and more realistic expectations as to what sanctions can reasonably achieve, will likely increase the overall effectiveness of the UN sanctions instrument.

Table 20.2 Distribution of Sanctions Effectiveness (percentages)

	Effective	Mixed	Ineffective
Coerce	10	27	63
Constrain	28	22	50
Signal	27	44	29

Source: Graduate Institute of International and Development Studies and Watson Institute for International Studies, "The Effectiveness of United Nations Targeted Sanctions: Findings from the Targeted Sanctions Consortium (TSC)," November 2013, p. 21, http://graduateinstitute.ch/files/live/sites/iheid/files/sites/internationalgovernance/shared/Effectiveness%20of%20UN%20Targeted%20Sanctions%20-%206.Nov.2013%20.pdf.

Conclusion

Notwithstanding the mixed record of effectiveness of UN sanctions, the fact remains that sanctions are one of the few tools of the international community to promote international peace and security, short of the use of force. Sanctions will continue as an essential component of the UN Security Council's response to international threats. Concerted attention, leadership, and action by the Security Council and like-minded states to strengthen the implementation and enforcement of sanctions, as well to enhance the capacity of member states to carry out their obligations, are necessary to make UN sanctions an even more potent and indispensable tool of collective security.

Notes

The views expressed in this chapter are those of the author alone, but are based on two research and policy initiatives of the Watson Institute for International Studies with other collaborators: First, the data and methodology concerning effectiveness of UN sanctions reflects the research of the Targeted Sanctions Consortium (TSC), codirected by Thomas Biersteker, The Graduate Institute in Geneva, and the author. Commenced in 2009, the TSC is an international research consortium of more than fifty scholars and policy practitioners worldwide conducting analysis of the impacts and effectiveness of UN targeted sanctions. The TSC assembled two new databases—one qualitative and one quantitative—on the full universe of UN targeted sanctions regimes over the past twenty-five years, introducing new conceptual and methodological innovations and applying them to the new data. See *The Effectiveness of UN Targeted Sanctions: Findings from the Targeted Sanctions Consortium,* released November 2013, at http://graduateinstitute.ch/files/live/sites/iheid/files/sites/internationalgovernance/shared/Effectiveness%20of%20UN%20Targeted%20Sanctions%20-%206.Nov.2013%20.pdf. The first scholarly publication discussing results of the TSC research is the volume, *Targeted Sanctions: The Impacts and Effectiveness of UN Action,* edited by Thomas J. Biersteker, Sue E. Eckert, and Marcos Tourinho (Cambridge: Cambridge University Press, 2015). The second cooperative endeavor, *The High-Level Review of UN Sanctions,* commenced May 2014 through June 2015, supported by the governments of Australia, Finland, Germany, Greece, and Sweden to examine ways to enhance the implementation of UN sanctions. It was organized by Rico Carisch and Loraine Rickard-Martin of Compliance and Capacity Skills International, and the author. Final results and recommendations from the year-long review are published in *Compendium of the High-Level Review of UN Sanctions,* available at http://www.HLR-unsanctions.org/. The author expresses sincere appreciation to these colleagues for the experiences and interactions from which she has benefited greatly.

1. United Nations High-Level Panel on Threats, Challenges, and Change, *A More Secure World: Our Shared Responsibility,* UN Doc. A/59/565, December 2, 2004, para. 178, https://www1.umn.edu.humanrts/instree/report.pdf.

2. Other instruments under the UN Charter include preventive diplomacy, peacemaking, peacekeeping and peace enforcement, peacebuilding, and disarmament.

3. While Article 41 of the Charter does not specifically refer to the term "sanctions," it contains a list of measures that can be taken that do not involve the use of force, including "complete or partial interruption of economic relations." Measures involving the use of force are addressed in Article 42 of the Charter.

4. United Nations Security Council, "Statement by the President of the Security Council," UN Doc. S/PRST/2010/10, June 16, 2010, expressing the Council's readiness to adopt targeted and graduated measures against persistent perpetrators, encouraging greater exchanges between sanctions committees and the working group on children and armed conflict and recommending that the special representative of the Secretary-General for children and armed conflict share relevant information with sanctions expert groups. In Resolutions 1820 (June 19, 2009), UN Doc. S/RES/1820, and 1888 (September 30, 2009), UN Doc. S/RES/1888, the Security Council also affirmed its intention to use targeted sanctions against parties who commit rape and other forms of sexual violence against women and girls in situations of armed conflict (such designations were made for the first time in 2009). In 2010, the Somalia sanctions committee proposed targeting two individuals suspected of organizing piracy and thereby threatening the peace, security, and stability of Somalia; Michael Peel, "UK Blocks UN Move to End Pirate Funding," *Financial Times,* August 8, 2010.

5. Principal objectives of sanctions referred to here reflect the general categories adopted by the Targeted Sanctions Consortium to differentiate the political objectives that UN sanctions seek to achieve. Following are the categories and percentages of sanction episodes as determined by the consortium: armed conflict (cease hostilities, negotiate or enforce peace agreement, support peacebuilding), 60 percent; counterterrorism, 15 percent; nonproliferation, 10 percent; and support democracy (restoration of an elected government), 10 percent. The remaining 5 percent includes protection of civilians under the Responsibility to Protect, support of judicial processes, and more effective governance of natural resources. While respect and support for human rights is a frequently cited rationale for UN sanctions, human rights is rarely a primary objective of sanctions.

6. The characterization of three primary purposes of sanctions is based on the Security Council's methodology as it adapted the typology of Francesco Giumelli in *Coercing, Constraining, and Signalling: Explaining and Understanding International Sanctions After the End of the Cold War* (Colchester: European Consortium for Political Research Press, 2011).

7. The humanitarian costs of sanctions became a particularly controversial issue in the aftermath of the Iraq War, in which allegations of child mortality and suffering of the Iraqi population due to UN sanctions were widespread.

8. Deputy Secretary-General Jan Eliasson, remarks on May 28, 2014, High-Level Review of UN Sanctions, New York, http://webtv.un.org/watch/briefing-on-high-level-review-of-united-nations-sanctions/3593626070001.

9. David Cortright and George A. Lopez, *The Sanctions Decade: Assessing UN Strategies in the 1990s* (Boulder, CO: Lynne Rienner, 2000).

10. Funding by specific sanctions committees was not available, but a 2010 study of UN expert panels contains information indicative of the imbalance. Funding for UN expert panels for all African sanctions regimes totaled $6.8 million in 2010–2011, while funding for the terrorism and WMD sanctions-related committees (including the nonsanction 1373 and 1540 Committees) totaled $19.7 million (the latter amount does not include funding for the Iran expert panel, which was established at the end of 2010). See Alix Boucher, *UN Panels of Experts and UN Peace Operations: Exploiting Synergies for Peacebuilding* (Washington, DC: Stimson Center, September 2010), www.stimson.org/books-reports/un-panels-of-experts-and-un-peace-operations.

11. Sponsored by the Swiss, German, and Swedish governments respectively. The Interlaken, Bonn-Berlin, and Stockholm processes provided practical guidelines for improving the design, implementation, enforcement, and monitoring of targeted sanctions at both the UN level and the national level. The common approach in each of these initiatives is the focus on "technical" issues regarding targeted sanctions implementation, rather than the policy or "political will" question surrounding UN sanctions.

12. See Andrea Charron and Clara Portela, "The Relationship Between United Nations Sanctions and Regional Sanctions Regimes," in *Targeted Sanctions: The Impacts and Effectiveness of UN Action,* edited by Thomas J. Biersteker, Sue E. Eckert, and Marcos Tourinho (Cambridge: Cambridge University Press, 2015).

13. For discussion of the legal challenges to UN sanctions, see Chapters 13, 14, 15, and 37 in this volume.

14. See Graduate Institute of International and Development Studies and Watson Institute for International Studies, "Effectiveness of United Nations Targeted Sanctions: Findings from the Targeted Sanctions Consortium (TSC)," November 2013, p. 17, http://graduateinstitute.ch/files/live/sites/iheid/files/sites/internationalgovernance/shared/Effectiveness%20of%20UN%20Targeted%20Sanctions%20-%206.Nov.2013%20.pdf.

15. See WikiLeak document published June 19, 2010, discussing the complex negotiations to get China and Russia to back tough UN sanctions against Iran, in which Saudi Arabia reportedly assured China of a guaranteed oil supply in return for Chinese pressure on Iran not to develop nuclear weapons. Available in *New York Times,* November 28, 2010, www.nytimes.com/interactive/2010/11/28/world/20101128-cables-viewer.html#report/iran-10RIYADH123.

16. In 2010, China impeded the initiatives of several sanctions committees threatening to block the renewal of the Sudan expert panel, objecting to publication of the panel's report, and placing a hold on the reappointment of an individual expert responsible for reports of Chinese arms being smuggled into Darfur.

17. Previous Secretaries-General addressed sanctions as part of broader reform initiatives. Boutros Boutros-Ghali suggested the establishment of a mechanism to monitor the application of sanctions, measure their effects so as to fine-tune them, and assess the potential impact of sanctions before their imposition, as part of his 1992/1995 *Agenda for Peace: Preventative Diplomacy, Peacemaking, and Peacekeeping* (UN Doc. A/47/277-S/24111, June 17, 1992, and UN Doc. A/50/60-

S/1995/1, January 3, 1995), and in a nonpaper on the human rights aspects of sanctions (UN Doc. S/1995/300, April 13, 1995). Kofi Annan addressed sanctions as part of his reform report "In Larger Freedom," A/59/2005, March 21, 2005, and in the 2005 World Summit outcome document (UN Doc. A/RES/60/1, October 24, 2005), which emphasized that the Security Council should "improve its monitoring of the implementation and effects of sanctions." While no overarching policy statements or initiatives have been undertaken by Ban Ki-moon, he has stated that "sanctions have enormous potential to contribute to the maintenance of international peace and security when used not as an end in themselves, but in support of a holistic conflict resolution approach that includes prevention, mediation, peacekeeping and peace-building"; Ban Ki-moon, "Speech to the Symposium on Enhancing the Implementation of Security Council Sanctions," New York, April 30, 2007, www.un .org/apps/news/infocus/sgspeeches/print_full.asp?statID=81.

18. United Nations Security Council, "Report of the Security Council Informal Working Group on General Issues of Sanctions," UN Doc. S/2006/997, December 22, 2006, www.securitycouncilreport.org/atf/cf/%7B65BFCF9B-6D27-4E9C-8CD3 -CF6E4FF96FF9%7D/WG%20Sanctions%20S2006997.pdf.

19. See David Cortright, George Lopez, and Linda Gerber-Stellingwerf, "Integrating UN Sanctions for Peace and Security," Fourth Freedom Forum, October 2010.

20. See James Cockayne's discussion of organized crime and piracy in Chapter 15 of this volume.

21. Allegations of noncompliance revealed in expert panel reports have resulted in some member states trying to prevent public release of reports. See "China Seeks to Block U.N. Report on Darfur, Diplomats Say," *International New York Times,* October 19, 2010, www.nytimes.com/2010/10/20/world/asia/20sudan.html?scp =9&sq=Sudan%20sanctions&st=cse.

22. Of the approximately $20 million allocated annually for expert panels, nearly three-quarters of the resources were devoted to the three nonproliferation and counterterrorism missions, while only $6 million supported sanctions monitoring in Africa as of 2010. See Boucher, *UN Panels of Experts.*

23. See Sue E. Eckert and Thomas J. Biersteker, "Due Process and Targeted Sanctions: An Update of the Watson Report," December 2012, www.watsoninsti tute.org/pub/Watson%20Report%20Update%2012_12.pdf.

24. See Cortright, Lopez, and Gerber-Stellingwerf, "Integrating UN Sanctions for Peace and Security."

25. The December 2006 final report of the working group contained important recommendations, many of which have become standard operating procedures within committees. See United Nations Security Council, "Report of the Informal Working Group on General Issues of Sanctions," UN Doc. S/2006/997, December 22, 2006.

26. See *Compendium of the High-Level Review of UN Sanctions,* http:// www.hlr-unsanctions.org/ for recommendations, including the creation of a Sanctions Technical Committee. See also Enrico Carisch and Loraine Rickard-Martin, "Proposal for a United Nations Sanctions Implementation Task Force (SITF)," Compliance and Capacity International, October 1, 2010, www.comcapint.com /sanctions-reform.html#sanctions-task-force. The SITF is modeled on the Counter-Terrorism Implementation Task Force (CTITF), which provides policy guidance for the UN's multifaceted programs against violent extremism.

27. While secondary sanctions engender controversy, the Security Council has in fact imposed such measures in the cases of Liberia and Somalia/Eritrea, and the Targeted Sanctions Consortium has found secondary sanctions to be highly effective.

28. For a discussion of SAMs created to monitor Yugoslav sanctions in the early 1990s, see David Cortright and George A. Lopez, *The Sanctions Decade: Assessing UN Strategies in the 1990s* (Boulder, CO: Lynne Rienner, 2000); Peter Wallensteen and Carina Staibano, eds., *International Sanctions: Between Words and Wars in the Global System* (Abingdon: Taylor and Francis, 2005). SAMs have been recognized as among the most sophisticated mechanism for enforcing UN sanctions.

29. See Rico Carisch, "Repositioning Security Council Targeted Economic and Financial Sanctions," Compliance and Capacity International, August 23, 2010, www.comcapint.com/due-diligence.html#economic-sanctions.

Part 4

Evolving Institutional Factors

21

Relations with the UN Secretary-General

Simon Chesterman

THE ROLE OF THE UN SECRETARY-GENERAL IS ONLY PARTIALLY
sketched out in the legal architecture of the Charter. Heading one of the
principal organs of the UN, he or she occupies a unique space in the
increasingly global political system; comparisons to a "secular pope" are
suggestive of the lofty expectations invested in the office. Yet lack of political and financial resources has meant that incumbents have always had to
maintain an uneasy balance between wide support among the membership
of the organization and deference to the interests of the most powerful and
wealthy.

That tension is played out most prominently in the Secretary-General's
relationship with the Security Council. The relationship is linked to the
greatest potential power of the office: the ability, under Article 99 of the
Charter, to bring to the attention of the Council "any matter which in his
opinion may threaten the maintenance of international peace and security."
How this relationship has been managed has been a defining factor for
every Secretary-General's legacy. Within that context, the most difficult
balancing act has been managing relations with the five permanent members of the Council—especially when they have been divided.

In this chapter I first consider the relationship between the Secretary-
General and the Security Council in general, and then examine the functions of the office linked to the Security Council in particular. These functions will be examined in two parts: tasks formally assigned to the
Secretary-General, and the exercise of his or her independent political
authority. It is in the latter area that the tensions with the Council and the
P5 are most prominently on display.

Those tensions reflect fundamental divisions as to the role of the Secretary-General. The Charter defines the position as being "chief administrative officer" of the organization. As we will see, powerful states such as the United States, Russia, and China see this as the proper role for him or her to play—sometimes described as being more "secretary" than "general." Yet there is a large constituency of other states and civil society actors that would embrace a significantly larger role for the Secretary-General as the world's diplomat, representing not just the UN as an organization but the hopes and aspirations for which it stands. An example is the key influence that past Secretaries-General have had in advancing norms that seek to transcend the self-interest of states, such as the Responsibility to Protect doctrine and the Millennium Development Goals. I therefore also address this aspect of the Secretary-General as a norm entrepreneur.

It quickly becomes apparent that the Charter offers an incomplete answer to the relationship between the Secretary-General and the Council. Legally, this can be understood if the Charter is interpreted as a "living tree," more like a constitution than a traditional treaty.[1] But to understand how that relationship has developed over time requires an examination of the personalities—as well as the political contexts—that have shaped it. Following is a list of the Secretaries-General of the United Nations since its inception:

- Trygve Lie (Norway), 1946–1952
- Dag Hammarskjöld (Sweden), 1953–1961
- U Thant (Burma), 1961–1971
- Kurt Waldheim (Austria), 1972–1981
- Javier Pérez de Cuéllar (Peru), 1982–1991
- Boutros Boutros-Ghali (Egypt), 1992–1996
- Kofi Annan (Ghana), 1997–2006
- Ban Ki-moon (Republic of Korea), 2007–

The Role of the Secretary-General

Speaking at Oxford in 1961, Dag Hammarskjöld famously described the problematic position of the international civil servant. Earlier in the year, Soviet chairman Nikita Khrushchev had reportedly dismissed the very idea of such an individual: "While there are neutral countries, there are no neutral men." Walter Lippmann, who had interviewed Khrushchev on this subject in 1961, interpreted the Soviet position as being that the "political celibacy" called for in the ideal British civil servant was, in international affairs, a fiction.[2] Hammarskjöld, in articulating his vision of precisely such an individual, archly suggested that it was possible to be politically celibate without being politically a virgin.[3]

The political fate of the Secretary-General is bound to the Council even before he or she assumes office. Though the Secretary-General is technically appointed by the General Assembly, in which each member state has one vote, the Assembly acts only on the basis of a recommendation from the Security Council. Throughout the history of the UN, the Security Council has only ever recommended one candidate, and the General Assembly has always accepted that candidate. In practice, then, the permanent five members of the Council have the decisive role in determining the Secretary-General.

There are numerous examples of the ways in which individual members of the P5 have influenced the selection. Most commonly, this has been through the use of the veto. Trygve Lie offended the Soviet Union in 1950 and continued in office only through a resolution of the General Assembly.[4] Kurt Waldheim was denied a third term in 1981 only after sixteen Chinese vetoes. Boutros Boutros-Ghali's reappointment was vetoed by the United States in 1996.[5] Indirectly, this has established a lowest-common-denominator aspect to the selection process, whereby any candidate must ensure that he or she is not opposed by any of the P5. It is less clear what positive attributes the members of the P5 would seek. Formal statements about the office tend to be platitudinous, but an outspoken candidate with grand ambitions for an activist UN would be unlikely to gain the support of all the P5. Nationality is also important. There is, for example, an informal understanding that none of the P5 will put up their own nationals for the office—though key under-secretary-general positions are distributed among them. Drawing on the past few appointments, a basic guide might be that candidates for Secretary-General should come from countries that are friendly with the United States, but not so friendly as to worry China and Russia. Historically, it was also desirable that candidates should speak passable French.

This is not to say that the Secretary-General cannot be independent. But if he or she were, it would not be by design. The two individuals typically regarded as the best and most independent officeholders are Dag Hammarskjöld and Kofi Annan. Both came into office with low expectations: Hammarskjöld was a little-known Swedish cabinet minister; Annan was seen as "America's man" to succeed the uncontrollable Boutros-Ghali. Once in office, however, they each significantly expanded the role and prestige of the office.

A key determinant of the success of a Secretary-General, then, is how he or she manages the relationship with the Council. This is made difficult when the Council is divided. When the Council supports an action, the Secretary-General may face operational and tactical challenges of implementation; in some cases, this may extend to unrealistic mandates and inadequate resources. But when there is a split among the P5—typically involving the different positions of the United States, Russia, and China—the Secretary-General may face a strategic choice: aligning him- or herself with one side might infuriate the other, perhaps poisoning a relationship and undermining future possibilities for cooperation. In most such cases, the Secretary-General has tended to hedge: either avoiding adopting a position that is at odds with one of the P5, or at least not doing so publicly.

Assigned Tasks

The functions of the Secretary-General in relation to the Security Council can be loosely divided into those entrusted to him or her by the Council, and those exercisable independently of the Council. The former fall under Article 98 of the Charter, which provides that the Secretary-General "shall [i.e., must] perform such . . . functions as are entrusted to him"; the latter fall under Article 99, which enables him or her to "bring to the attention of the Security Council any matter which in his opinion may threaten the maintenance of international peace and security."

The tasks assigned to the Secretary-General (and the UN Secretariat, which the Secretary-General heads) have grown significantly over time. The most common category of tasks is administrative, supporting the activities of the UN and its organs. In the case of the Council this includes running meetings themselves but also providing materials as requested. This typically involves the writing of reports on specified operations or topics. Often this may be little more than an update on UN activities, but the Secretary-General has also been asked to engage in sensitive fact-finding activities—for example, into the 2005 assassination of former Lebanese prime minister Rafik Hariri.[6] In some cases, the Secretary-General may be asked to provide strategic options to the Council. In the course of the 1994 Rwandan genocide, for example, Boutros-Ghali provided the Council with three options concerning the 2,500-strong UN peacekeeping force on the ground: a massive reinforcement of troops, reduction to a token 270 who would attempt to negotiate a ceasefire, or complete withdrawal.[7] Resolution 912 (1994) merely stated that the Council would "adjust the mandate" of the peacekeeping force "as set out in paragraphs 15 to 18 of the Secretary-General's report"[8]—allowing the Council to reduce the number of peacekeepers on the ground during the genocide without having to say so in words.

Second, the Secretary-General also carries out important military functions. Hammarskjöld, for example, exercised a significant measure of control over the first major such operation in the Congo from 1960 until his death in 1961, though peacekeeping from the Congo operation until the end of the Cold War tended not to see comparable levels of hostilities. Boutros-Ghali insisted on a "dual-key" system in Bosnia, in which both NATO commanders and the UN had to agree before individual air strikes could be authorized. Unhappiness with this approach was cited by the United States as one of the main reasons for opposing his reappointment as Secretary-General.[9] In practice, the Secretary-General exercises more of a coordinating than a commanding function with respect to national contingents, even when they wear blue helmets.[10]

A third important area has been the Secretary-General's role in managing sanctions regimes. Concerns about the humanitarian consequences of comprehensive economic sanctions, in particular those imposed on Iraq beginning in 1990, led to efforts to make them "smarter" by targeting sectors of the economy or specific individuals more likely to influence policies—or at least confining sanctions to ensure that those who bore the brunt of their consequences were also those perceived as most responsible for the situation that led to their imposition. The Secretariat now supports various committees and panels of experts in overseeing and monitoring these regimes, though the experience of the oil-for-food program—a massive program intended to alleviate humanitarian suffering caused by sanctions on Iraq—has highlighted the limits of what the UN can and should take on in terms of operational responsibilities.[11] In rare cases, the Council has delegated to the Secretary-General the power to commence the implementation of sanctions. Following the overthrow of democratically elected president Jean-Bertrand Aristide of Haiti in October 1991, the Council decided that a suite of economic sanctions would come into force at a designated time "unless the Secretary-General . . . has reported to the Council that . . . the imposition of such measures is not warranted."[12] The same resolution provided that if, at a later date, the Secretary-General reported to the Council that the coup leaders had failed to comply in good faith with their undertakings, then sanctions would come into force immediately.[13]

Finally, the Council has also given specific political functions to the Secretary-General. These include, most prominently, good offices and mediation functions, and may overlap with the role implied by Article 99, discussed later. Specific political functions might also include the UN's evolving role in elections, ranging from directly overseeing the elections in Namibia (1989–1990), in Cambodia (1992–1993), and on the long-postponed Western Sahara referendum (1991–), to the more technical support that tends to be offered today, as in Nepal (2008) and South Sudan (2011 referendum). More recent innovations in the area of specific political functions would include the temporary administration of Kosovo (1999–2008) and Timor-Leste (1999–2002).[14] Broad but vague responsibilities were also given to the Secretary-General in Afghanistan (2002) and Iraq (2003).

Occasional arguments have been made that the Secretary-General should be able to say no to the Council if given an impossible mandate.[15] Nevertheless, the only basis on which entrusted functions have been essentially abandoned is in the face of insuperable security concerns, such as those confronted in Somalia in 1993–1995[16] and Iraq after 2003.[17]

Political Role

Explicit Invocation of Article 99

Article 99 most clearly articulates the political role that the Secretary-General is expected to play, though the provision is rarely invoked explicitly. In Kofi Annan's ten years as Secretary-General, for example, he never saw the necessity to invoke this provision of the Charter directly—even as he came to be seen as one of the more politically assertive to fill the office.[18] Such reticence runs counter to the views of many academic and policy experts, who routinely call for greater use of Article 99.[19] Yet this in turn rests on the assumption that the Council's failure to act in a given situation is due either to lack of information that the Secretary-General can provide, or to the absence of political will that he or she can muster. Neither assumption withstands much scrutiny. The Secretary-General's powers of information-gathering and analysis are vastly inferior to those of the major powers, at least in places where the UN has no peace mission deployed on the ground; efforts to develop an independent analytical capacity have consistently been rebuffed.[20] And though it might be possible for the Secretary-General to attempt to embarrass states into acting, the long-term costs of such an approach have been judged by most incumbents to outweigh any short-term benefits—a calculation most recently, and controversially, on display with respect to Sri Lanka.[21]

From the early days of the UN, it was understood that Article 99 created important and sensitive powers.[22] Indeed, there are only two occasions in which it was explicitly used to put a matter onto the agenda of the Security Council primarily at the initiative of the Secretary-General.

The first was Dag Hammarskjöld's actions in response to the 1960 Congo crisis. In July 1960, he received cables from the president and prime minister of the Republic of Congo requesting the urgent dispatch of UN military assistance. Hammarskjöld could have merely forwarded the cables to the Council as he had done regarding a previous crisis in Laos, or he could have privately consulted with members and allowed them to decide on the appropriate response.[23] Instead, in a letter dated July 13, 1960, he wrote to the president of the Security Council that he wished "to bring to the attention of the Security Council a matter which, in my opinion, may threaten the maintenance of international peace and security."[24]

The second overt invocation of the Article 99 powers occurred in November 1979 in connection with the Iranian occupation of the US embassy in Tehran. Following a request from the United States, the president of the Security Council had issued a statement urging the release of hostages.[25] Iran then sent a letter to the Secretary-General outlining various grievances against the United States. As in the case of the Congo, Kurt Waldheim did not merely forward the communications but took the initiative himself to write to the president of the Council, briefly outlining the situation. "In my opinion," he concluded, "the present crisis poses a serious threat to international peace and security. Accordingly, in the exercise of my responsibility under the Charter of the United Nations, I ask that the Security Council be convened urgently in an effort to seek a peaceful solution of the problem in conformity with the principles of justice and international law."[26] The Council duly met and, among other things, asked the Secretary-General to offer his good offices in the implementation of the resolutions subsequently adopted.

Implicit Exercise of Article 99

Though the list of occasions in which Article 99 has been invoked explicitly is short, there are many occasions in which the Secretary-General's actions in relation to the Council have been exercised under its implicit authority.

At the outbreak of the Korean War in 1950, Trygve Lie received cables warning him that the situation "may endanger the maintenance of peace and security" and suggesting that he bring the matter "to [the] notice of the Security Council."[27] Though Lie himself stated that this was the first use of Article 99,[28] it was the United States that requested a meeting of the Council.

In addition to the Congo crisis, mentioned earlier, Hammarskjöld referred to his powers under Article 99 on a number of other occasions— without expressly invoking them. On other occasions Hammarskjöld made clear that he had not relied on Article 99. In 1959, for example, the government of Laos wrote to him requesting UN support in response to alleged Vietnamese attacks. Hammarskjöld duly called for an urgent meeting of the Council but said during the meeting that his request was not based on Article 99.[29] In responding to French military action against Tunisia in 1961, Hammarskjöld adopted an extremely broad interpretation of Article 99. After returning from a trip to Tunisia, he stated that his acceptance of the invitation was part of the functions of his office. Given the provisions of Article 99, "it is obvious that the duties following from this Article cannot be fulfilled unless the Secretary-General, in case of need, is in a position to form a personal opinion about the relevant facts of the situation which may represent such a threat."[30]

For U Thant, the controversies created by his predecessors and criticism by the Soviet Union in particular made him more conservative in his use of the political powers of the office. One innovation was the appointment of a special representative for Cambodia and Thailand in 1966. Neither country had called upon the Council for assistance, but both had been consulted and agreed to share the costs of the special representative. The Soviet Union objected, arguing that all decisions—including such appointments—should be taken by the Council itself, though it was accepted by others that the decision fell within the broad scope of Article 99, as U Thant had consulted with the parties and obtained their consent, as well as informed the Council. Without making reference to Article 99, U Thant also extended his good offices to the Bahrain question and reported to the Council in 1971 on the deteriorating situation in East Pakistan (now Bangladesh), including efforts at peacemaking "under the broad terms of Article 99."[31]

Kurt Waldheim expressly invoked Article 99 once, in respect of the Tehran hostage situation. But he also expanded the good offices role of the Secretary-General significantly. On the Cyprus question in particular he submitted reports to the Council and embarked upon trips to Cyprus, Greece, and Turkey on his own initiative.

Javier Pérez de Cuéllar, in his first annual report to the General Assembly, suggested that the Security Council often became involved in crisis situations too late: "It may well be that the Secretary-General should play a more forthright role in bringing potentially dangerous situations to the attention of the Council within the general framework of Article 99 of the Charter. My predecessors have done this on a number of occasions, but I wonder if the time has not come for a more systematic approach."[32]

This does not appear to have been intended to suggest a broadening of the authority conferred on the Secretary-General; rather, it was to create a larger and more systematic capacity for investigations into matters that might properly be brought to the attention of the Council. On this basis, Pérez de Cuéllar used his good offices, traveled to conflict zones, and designated personal representatives.

He later extended his own role in mediation and observation in the maintenance of international peace. In 1987, he encouraged members of the Council to promote a settlement to the ongoing Iran-Iraq War; Resolution 598 (1987) in turn requested that his office observe a ceasefire and gave him a broad mandate to "examine, in consultation with Iran and Iraq and with other States of the region, measures to enhance the security and stability of the region." Two years later, he relied similarly on his implicit Article 99 powers in relation to the situation in Lebanon.

Boutros Boutros-Ghali's *Agenda for Peace*—a landmark document adopted at the height of optimism for the UN after the thawing of the Cold War—highlighted the possible links between Article 99 and fact-finding.[33] The General Assembly resolution that welcomed the report went further, encouraging the Secretary-General to "continue, in accordance with Article 99 of the Charter of the United Nations, to bring to the attention of the Security Council, at his discretion, any matter which in his opinion may threaten the maintenance of international peace and security, *together with his recommendations thereon.*"[34]

Nevertheless, the more congenial political climate of the post–Cold War period meant that Boutros-Ghali and his successors needed to rely even less frequently on Article 99 than had their predecessors. As the Council met more frequently and political barriers to putting items on the agenda tended to decline, the need for the Secretary-General to use his initiative was reduced. In addition, the far greater number of interactions—including a monthly lunch between the Secretary-General and members of the Council—meant that there were more opportunities to raise matters informally. Two occasions on which Boutros-Ghali implicitly relied on Article 99 were his proposal to send a fact-finding mission to the Bakassi Peninsula between Cameroon and Nigeria, and his dispatching of a good offices mission to assist the government of Zaire in assessing the deteriorating situation in South Kivu province.

Kofi Annan explicitly denied ever invoking Article 99 as such.[35] Nevertheless, he relied on the ability to justify independent action on a number of occasions; it is also arguable that he used it as the foundation for more general normative developments. Unlike previous Secretaries-General, the most prominent situations in which Annan exercised an independent political role concerned situations already on the agenda of the Council. For this reason, they were clearly not direct invocations of Article 99, though they did relate to the perceived role of the Secretary-General in supporting the Council in maintaining international peace and security. In 1998, when tensions arose over Iraq's weapons inspection program, he persuaded members of the Council to authorize a trip to Baghdad so that he could negotiate directly with Saddam Hussein.[36] The memorandum of understanding that emerged temporarily defused the situation and won Annan considerable praise, but began to unravel quickly when the Iraqi government violated its terms. Similar efforts to achieve compromise in difficult circumstances with the halfhearted support of a divided Council saw Annan deeply involved in Kosovo and Cyprus, neither of which reached a satisfactory or stable outcome during his tenure.

Ban Ki-moon's first seven years in office did not see any explicit invocation of Article 99. He exercised modest degrees of political discretion through the extension of his good offices with respect to the ongoing Cyprus negotiations, Guinea, Madagascar, the Maldives, Malawi, Myanmar, Kyrgyzstan, the dispute over the name of the former Yugoslav Republic of Macedonia, and the Venezuela-Guyana border dispute. He also established inquiries into the 2009 assassination of former prime minister of Pakistan Benazir Bhutto, alleged violations of international humanitarian law in the final stages of Sri Lanka's civil war, and Israel's 2010 commando raid on a flotilla of boats carrying aid to Gaza.

On rare occasions, the Council has encouraged the Secretary-General to exercise his Article 99 powers. In Resolutions 1366 (2001) and 1625 (2005) the Council "encouraged" the Secretary-General to convey to the Council his assessment of potential threats to international peace and security. Resolution 1379 (2001) specifically requested that he highlight situations in which children are being recruited or used in conflicts that are on the Council's agenda or which may be brought to its attention under Article 99.

Nevertheless, such statements have not generally been supported by resources to ensure that the Secretary-General's "opinion" is an informed one. Indeed, there has long been considerable resistance to the Secretariat developing a significant analytical capacity independent of the member states. It is debatable how much impact this has had on the role of the United Nations in international peace and security, however. When a matter is not on the Council's agenda, or when the Council declines to act decisively, it is not generally because the member states are unaware of the situation.

Norm Entrepreneur

An extension of the political functions of the Secretary-General is his or her role as a "norm entrepreneur." Linked to the constructivist turn in international relations theory, this concept describes the role in shaping norms—understood broadly here as collective expectations for the proper behavior of actors with a given identity. Norm entrepreneurs are "actors with a cause" who generate support for that cause with the aim of having it crystallized as an accepted standard of behavior.[37] This is clearly broader than the Secretary-General's relationship with the Council, but a key area in which he has played these roles is the realm of peace and security, where the Council jealously guards its "primary responsibility" guaranteed under the Charter.

The most prominent example of such entrepreneurship is Hammarskjöld's mischievous argument that "peacekeeping"—a term that does not appear in the UN Charter—could be found in "Chapter VI½." This followed Hammarskjöld's earlier assertion that the Secretary-General must be allowed a free hand in implementing a mandate given to him by the Council or the General Assembly. That formulation came to be known as the "Peking formula" after a situation in which Hammarskjöld negotiated the release of seventeen US airmen from Communist Chinese custody in 1955.[38]

On some occasions, UN Secretaries-General have spoken out explicitly in support of the lawfulness of particular actions, as when Boutros Boutros-Ghali declared that a 1993 strike against Iraq "conforms to the resolutions of the Security Council and conforms to the Charter of the United Nations,"[39] or when Ban Ki-moon stated that controversial military action in Libya was "strictly within" the bounds of Resolution 1973 (2011).[40] More rarely—and controversially—Secretaries-General have spoken out on the unlawfulness of a particular act, as when Kofi Annan declared the 2003 invasion of Iraq "illegal." Predictably, this led to apoplexy on the part of the United States and complicated the remainder of Annan's tenure.[41]

Perhaps of more lasting significance was Annan's championing of the doctrine of Responsibility to Protect. Following a speech to the General Assembly after the Kosovo intervention in 1999, Annan had been excoriated for his apparent tolerance of so-called humanitarian intervention. By framing the debate not as a license for humanitarian intervention but as an effort to prevent situations from spiraling out of control, R2P offered a more palatable version that focused on preventing future Rwandas rather than authorizing future Kosovos. This led to concern on the part of many states that it might open the door to intervention by major powers; for some members of the P5, by contrast, the concern was that such a doctrine might limit their discretion in determining whether and how to respond to a given crisis.[42]

Annan's successor, Ban Ki-moon, also embraced the language of Responsibility to Protect. But although early warning was routinely highlighted as a key aspect of effective implementation, Article 99 was not directly mentioned in either the report or the General Assembly resolutions on the topic. A rare exception was in a meeting convened by the Security Council's Ad Hoc Working Group on Conflict Prevention and Resolution in Africa. At this meeting, the Secretary-General's special adviser, Edward Luck, suggested that Article 99 might encompass the responsibility to protect, with the Secretary-General bringing relevant matters to the attention of the Security Council under its auspices.[43] There does not appear to have been any follow-up, and, for all the reasons cited earlier, there is no reason to expect that the Secretary-General will be bringing matters to the attention of the Security Council of which they would prefer not to be reminded.

Conclusion

The role of the Secretary-General has always been defined by politics. For the first decades of the United Nations, Cold War rivalry paralyzed the institution but created space for entrepreneurship in the office, as demonstrated by Hammarskjöld. After the Cold War ended, there was a need to manage expectations about the office and its independence from the Council, a story told in Boutros-Ghali's rise and fall, while Kofi Annan sought to lay a more solid foundation for the office even as East-West rivalries were replaced by North-South rivalries. These newer tensions operated primarily outside the Council, but they impacted on the budget of the organization in particular.[44]

Interestingly, however, the personalities of the individual Secretaries-General have also played a key role in the evolution of the office. It is striking that the two most highly regarded Secretaries-General—Hammarskjöld and Annan—were chosen precisely because they were expected to be less troublesome to the P5 than had been their predecessors—Lie and Boutros-Ghali. Success or failure thus depended on the political context, personal chemistry, and doubtless no small measure of luck. Little wonder that the first Secretary-General famously welcomed his successor to New York's Idlewild Airport with the words: "You are about to enter the most impossible job on this earth."[45]

Notes

This chapter draws on material discussed at greater length in Simon Chesterman, "Article 99," in *The Charter of the United Nations: A Commentary,* edited by Bruno Simma, Daniel-Erasmus Khan, Georg Nolte, and Andreas Paulus (Oxford: Oxford University Press, 2012).

1. See Thomas M. Franck, "Is the UN Charter a Constitution?" in *Verhandeln für den Frieden: Negotiating for Peace—Liber Amicorum Tono Eitel,* edited by Jochen Abr Frowein, Klaus Scharioth, Ingo Winkelman, and Rüdiger Wolfrum (Berlin: Springer, 2003).

2. Walter Lippmann, "Interview with Chairman Nikita Khrushchev," *New York Herald Tribune,* April 17, 1961.

3. Dag Hammarskjöld, "The International Civil Servant in Law and in Fact" (congregation lecture delivered at Oxford University, May 30, 1961), in *Servant of Peace: A Selection of the Speeches and Statements of Dag Hammarskjöld, Secretary-General of the United Nations, 1953–1961,* edited by Wilder Foote (New York: Harper and Row, 1962), p. 335.

4. Brian Urquhart, "The Evolution of the Secretary-General," in *Secretary or General? The UN Secretary-General in World Politics,* edited by Simon Chesterman (Cambridge: Cambridge University Press, 2007), p. 18.

5. Adekeye Adebajo, "Pope, Pharaoh, or Prophet? The Secretary-General After the Cold War," in Chesterman, *Secretary or General?* p. 144.

6. United Nations Security Council, "Statement by the President of the Security Council," UN Doc. S/PRST/2005/4, February 15, 2005.

7. United Nations Security Council, *Special Report of the Secretary-General on the United Nations Assistance Mission for Rwanda,* UN Doc. S/1994/470, April 20, 1994.

8. United Nations Security Council Resolution 912, S/RES/912 (April 21, 1994), para. 7(c).

9. Edward C. Luck, "The Secretary-General in a Unipolar World," in Chesterman, *Secretary or General?* p. 218.

10. Edward Newman, *The UN Secretary-General from the Cold War to the New Era: A Global Peace and Security Mandate* (New York: Palgrave Macmillan, 1998), p. 33; Trevor Findlay, *The Use of Force in UN Peace Operations* (Oxford: Stockholm International Peace Research Institute and Oxford University Press, 2002), p. 10.

11. Independent Inquiry into the Oil-for-Food Programme, *The Management of the United Nations Oil-for-Food Programme: Volume 1—The Report of the Committee* (New York: September 7, 2005).

12. United Nations Security Council Resolution 841, S/RES/841 (June 16, 1993), para. 3.

13. Ibid., para. 4.

14. See, generally, Simon Chesterman, *You, the People: The United Nations, Transitional Administration, and State-Building* (Oxford: Oxford University Press, 2004).

15. See, for example, United Nations General Assembly and Security Council, *Report of the Panel on United Nations Peace Operations* (Brahimi Report), UN Doc. A/55/305-S/2000/809, August 21, 2000, para. 64(d); Simon Chesterman and Thomas M. Franck, "Resolving the Contradictions of the Office," in Chesterman, *Secretary or General?* p. 239.

16. United Nations Security Council, *Report of the Secretary-General,* UN Doc. S/1994/1068, September 17, 1994, paras. 17–21.

17. United Nations Security Council, *Report of the Secretary-General,* UN Doc. S/2003/1149, December 5, 2003, paras. 17–47.

18. Kofi A. Annan, foreword to Chesterman, *Secretary or General?*

19. See, for example, United Nations, *Report of the Secretary-General's Internal Review Panel on United Nations Action in Sri Lanka* (New York, November 2012), www.un.org/News/dh/infocus/Sri_Lanka/The_Internal_Review_Panel_report_on_Sri_Lanka.pdf, 34.

20. Simon Chesterman, "Shared Secrets: Intelligence and Collective Security," 2006, www.lowyinstitute.org/files/pubfiles/Chesterman%2C_Shared_secrets.pdf.

21. United Nations Secretary-General's Internal Review Panel, *Report of the Secretary-General's Internal Review Panel on United Nations Action in Sri Lanka* (New York, November 2012), www.un.org/News/dh/infocus/Sri_Lanka/The_Internal_Review_Panel_report_on_Sri_Lanka.pdf.

22. United Nations, *Report of the Preparatory Commission of the United Nations (1945),* chap. 8, sec. 2, para. 16, reprinted in Chesterman, *Secretary or General?* p. 243.

23. Leon Gordenker, *The UN Secretary-General and the Maintenance of Peace* (New York: Columbia University Press, 1967), p. 140.

24. United Nations Security Council, "Letter Dated 13 July 1960 from the Secretary-General Addressed to the President of the Security Council," UN Doc. S/4381, July 13, 1960.

25. United Nations Security Council, "Statement by the President of the Security Council," UN Doc. S/13616, November 9, 1979.

26. United Nations Security Council, "Letter Dated 25 November 1979 from the Secretary-General Addressed to the President of the Security Council," UN Doc. S/13646, November 25, 1979.

27. United Nations Security Council, "Cablegram Dated June 25, 1950 from the United Nations Commission on Korea to the Secretary-General Concerning Aggression upon the Republic of Korea," UN Doc. S/1496, June 25, 1950.

28. Trygve Lie, *In the Cause of Peace: Seven Years with the United Nations* (New York: Palgrave Macmillan, 1954), p. 371.

29. United Nations, *Repertory of Practice of United Nations Organs,* vol. 4, supp. 3 (New York, 1955), p. 162.

30. Ibid., p. 161.

31. United Nations, *Report of the Secretary-General,* UN Doc. S/10410, December 3, 1971.

32. United Nations, *Annual Report of the Secretary-General on the Work of the Organization,* UN Doc. A/37/1, 1982.

33. United Nations Secretary-General, *An Agenda for Peace: Preventive Diplo-*

macy, Peacemaking, and Peacekeeping (Report of the Secretary-General Pursuant to the Statement Adopted by the Summit Meeting of the Security Council on January 31, 1992), UN Doc. A/47/277-S/24111, June 17, 1992, para. 25(a).

34. United Nations General Assembly Resolution 47/120, A/RES/47/120 (February 10, 1993), pt. 2, para. 4 (emphasis added).

35. Annan, foreword to Chesterman, *Secretary or General?* p. xi.

36. James Traub, *The Best Intentions: Kofi Annan and the UN in the Era of American Power* (New York: Farrar, Straus, and Giroux, 2006), pp. 75–85.

37. Ian Johnstone, "The Secretary-General as Norm Entrepreneur," in Chesterman, *Secretary or General?* pp. 125–126.

38. James Cockayne and David M. Malone, "Relations with the Security Council," in Chesterman, *Secretary or General?* p. 72.

39. Quoted in British Foreign and Commonwealth Office, "Letter from the Foreign Secretary to the Chairman of the Select Committee on Foreign Affairs: Iraq— Legal Basis for the Use of Force" (London, March 17, 2003), para. 7, www .publications.parliament.uk/pa/cm200203/cmselect/cmfaff/405/3030407.htm.

40. United Nations Secretary-General Ban Ki-moon, "Press Conference at UN Headquarters," UN Doc. SG/SM/14021, December 14, 2011, www.un.org/News /Press/docs/2011/sgsm14021.doc.htm. See also Fredrik A. Holst and Martin D. Fink, "A Legal View on NATO's Campaign in Libya," in *The NATO Intervention in Libya: Lessons Learned from the Campaign,* edited by Kjell Engelbrekt, Marcus Mohlin, and Charlotte Wagnsson (New York: Routledge, 2014), p. 89.

41. "Iraq War Illegal, Says Annan," *BBC News,* September 16, 2004, http:// news.bbc.co.uk/2/hi/3661134.stm. See also Cockayne and Malone, "Relations with the Council," p. 82.

42. See, generally, Gareth Evans, *The Responsibility to Protect: Ending Mass Atrocity Crimes Once and for All* (Washington, DC: Brookings Institution, 2008).

43. United Nations Security Council, "Letter Dated 30 December 2008 from the Permanent Representative of South Africa to the United Nations Addressed to the President of the Security Council," UN Doc. S/2008/836, December 31, 2008, p. 13.

44. Adebajo, "Pope, Pharaoh, or Prophet?"

45. United Nations Meetings Coverage and Press Releases, "Dag Hammarskjöld's Speech to the Staff," UN Doc. SG/299, New York, May 1, 1953.

22

Special Representatives of the Secretary-General

Connie Peck

SPECIAL REPRESENTATIVES OF THE SECRETARY-GENERAL (SRSGs) have been a regular feature of UN practice since the early days of the organization, when it quickly became clear that the Secretary-General could not possibly carry out assignments in the field without the assistance of trusted envoys.[1] The practice continued throughout the decades, but accelerated with the end of the Cold War due to the increased demands for UN involvement in crises around the world. As the Security Council took on responsibility for a range of different types of peace operations, SRSGs were appointed in increasing numbers to head and implement these operations. In this chapter I argue that SRSGs have become a major instrument for carrying out the Council's work in the area of peace and security, and that a close relationship between SRSGs and the Council is required to enhance the success of peace operations.

The Relationship Between SRSGs and the Security Council

When the Security Council authorizes a new peace operation, the Secretary-General typically appoints a special representative to head the mission, following consultation with the Department of Political Affairs (DPA) and the Department of Peacekeeping Operations (DPKO), and in some cases with the relevant parties and member states. While the Secretariat tries to preserve the prerogative of the Secretary-General to appoint his own representatives, member states have sometimes been known to lobby intensely on behalf of preferred candidates (often their own nationals). As well, the parties may add to the complexity of the situation when they strongly resist

457

a candidate (or a nationality). SRSGs can come from inside or outside the UN system. Many have worked in the foreign service or parliaments of their country, and a number have served as permanent representatives to the United Nations (in some cases also serving on the Security Council, giving these individuals a unique perspective on both roles). A number have also worked in the UN system, and some have had experience in regional organizations or nongovernmental organizations.[2]

The nature of the relationship between SRSGs and the Council depends on the type of mission and whether it has been mandated by the Council. Peacekeeping, political, and peacebuilding missions are usually mandated by the Security Council. Some good offices missions, however, do not have a formal Council mandate and are instead based on letters of understanding between the parties and the Secretary-General, or between the Secretary-General and the Council, or based on a framework agreement negotiated with the parties. The DPA is currently responsible for overseeing special political, peacebuilding, and good offices missions, and the DPKO is responsible for the oversight of all peacekeeping operations.[3] The intensity of reporting and contact also vary, depending on the degree of the crisis and the geostrategic importance of the situation to Council members, especially to the five permanent members.

A mission is mandated through a Security Council resolution that sets out the operation's mandate and size (in terms of the authorized number of military troops and police) and details the tasks the mission will be responsible for performing. If the mission is a new one, the mandate may be based on recommendations of a technical assessment or planning mission that has been sent by the Secretary-General to the field to determine what is required (although the Council does not always follow those recommendations to the letter, and on occasion exerts pressure on the Secretariat to adjust its recommendations to the Council's preferences, especially with respect to troop size). The overall budget and resources are then subject to approval by the General Assembly, as discussed later. Mandates are provided for a given period specified by the Council (these vary depending on the urgency and complexity of the situation; the standard for nonurgent situations tends to be six months). The Secretary-General is responsible for reporting to the Council on the progress of each peace operation and for making recommendations for action when deemed necessary. SRSGs report to the Secretary-General through the under-secretary-general for political affairs or the under-secretary-general for peacekeeping operations, depending on which department is in the lead. Reports of the Secretary-General are regularly submitted to the Council (based on a schedule determined by the Council) and prepared by SRSGs and their staff in the field, working in close cooperation with the relevant lead department at headquarters.

Following consideration of a report of the Secretary-General and discussion with the Secretary-General and relevant staff (including the SRSG),
the Council reconsiders the mandate for possible renewal and amendment.
The Council can alter the mandate at any time (including modification of
the objectives of the mission or its authorized strength of military troops or
police) in response to developments on the ground. One of the major challenges for the Security Council is therefore to provide and maintain an
appropriate mandate and adequate human resources for each mission. To
ensure that these are indeed in accordance with the needs on the ground,
SRSGs (through the Secretary-General and the Secretariat) need to work
closely with the Council to keep it thoroughly briefed, to offer a clear
analysis of each situation, and to provide cogently argued recommendations
when Council action is required.

In addition to furnishing the mandate, the Council provides overall
direction with regard to the situations with which it must handle, through
resolutions that instruct the Secretary-General (and by implication the SRSG
and the mission). These also provide direction to the conflicting parties and
to other member states as to how they should interact with the parties. As
well, the Council may comment on the actions of regional and subregional
organizations. Thus there is an ongoing interplay between the Security
Council, which provides overall direction for the mission from New York
(after feedback from the field), and the SRSG, who is responsible for the
day-to-day decisionmaking on the ground and who in turn keeps the Council
informed regarding the challenges encountered, the mission's response, and
new mission needs. Mediating this interaction are the Secretary-General and
the Secretariat, who provide operational guidance to the SRSG and who
report to the Council on the progress and problems of the mission.

Moreover, as will be discussed in more detail later, an effective relationship between the SRSG and the Security Council also provides synergy
in terms of the UN's ability to leverage the parties to constructively engage
in the peace process. SRSGs often find it helpful to use the political weight
of the Council to enhance their own authority and influence.

The Unique Role of SRSGs in Peace Operations

Upon arrival in the mission area, an SRSG becomes the head of mission and
has authority over all its components, as well as all aspects of its management and functioning. To accomplish the mission's objectives, the special
representative is required to engage in constant negotiation with a wide range
of actors. In conjunction with his or her senior management team, the SRSG
is responsible for developing a clear analysis of the situation and further
elaborating the mission's objectives and strategy. He or she also faces the

challenge of harmonizing different mission cultures and components (e.g., military, police, civil affairs, electoral, human rights, administration) into a well-functioning team. The SRSG must also provide leadership and be able to communicate effectively with the diverse international and local staff, as well as with the rotating national contingents of peacekeepers and police, to keep them working toward the same objectives and to maintain morale. SRSGs must also create good working relationships with staff at headquarters, who monitor and support their work in order to keep the Secretary-General, the Security Council, and the membership as a whole informed.

Crucial to the work of SRSGs is the development of a solid working relationship with the conflicting parties, as well as with those who surround and influence the decisionmaking process. Bringing them to a unity of purpose is not an easy task, and SRSGs must constantly engage in persuasion, problem solving, and the skillful use of leverage to find ways around the many obstacles that constantly present themselves. Building a relationship with a broad base of civil society, especially those who support the peace process, as well as with the local population, can also help to keep the process on track and the population on one's side.

Moreover, SRSGs need to negotiate solid working relationships with UN specialized agencies, funds, and programs in order to overcome the inherent institutional rivalries and create an atmosphere in which the UN can truly work as a family—with coordinated objectives and approaches. Indeed, many UN peace operations are now structurally integrated, facilitating strategic planning and coordination between the mission and the country team of specialized agencies under the overall direction of the SRSG.

SRSGs must also develop a close relationship with regional and subregional organizations and regional leaders active in the mission area, to foster a coordinated approach. Among the host of other actors that SRSGs have to work with are nongovernmental organizations, which are often pursuing their own objectives and funding, but whose energy and flexibility, if harnessed appropriately, can add synergy to particular mission goals. In addition, SRSGs have to develop effective relationships with the media in order to raise international awareness and communicate with the local population about the mission's objectives and methods.

Further, SRSGs must be able to work closely with interested member states, developing the necessary relationships with ambassadors on the ground, with permanent missions in New York, and within relevant ministries in key capitals, to engender political support, to mobilize leverage, and to make a significant impact on the mission area. Finally, they must be able to develop a supportive relationship with the Security Council in order to keep the Council informed and actively engaged, as well as to ensure that the mission's mandate and human resources remain appropriate to the evolving situation on the ground.

To bring such difficult missions to a successful outcome, SRSGs require excellent political, negotiation, leadership, and management skills. SRSGs also mention the need for a superabundance of optimism, persistence, and patience. The 2000 UN Panel on Peace Operations,[4] in its so-called Brahimi Report, named after the panel's chairman, noted: "Effective, dynamic leadership can make the difference between a cohesive mission with high morale and effectiveness despite adverse circumstances and one that struggles to maintain any of those attributes. That is, the tenor of an entire mission can be heavily influenced by the character and ability of those who lead it."[5]

The tasks required for an SRSG managing a transitional authority in which the UN temporarily takes over the function of a government (e.g., in Cambodia, East Timor, and Kosovo) are even more challenging. SRSGs in these types of missions are given wide-ranging executive authority, which must be exercised to establish order, but which must also be carefully balanced with the need to build local capacity for governance, to create local ownership for key decisions, and to devolve institutional power to local authorities as quickly as possible.[6]

It should be noted, however, that not all SRSGs are appointed to head a peace operation. Three subregional offices have been established in recent years, headed by special representatives, with a focus on preventive diplomacy in their respective regions. The first of these was the UN Office for West Africa (UNOWA). Subsequently the UN Regional Center for Preventive Diplomacy for Central Asia (UNRCCA) was created, followed by the UN Regional Office for Central Africa (UNOCA).[7] More recently, the Secretary-General has deployed a special representative to the African Union. A few SRSGs involved in good offices missions are nonresident in the country in which they are working and come and go as required. A number of other special representatives have been chosen to work on specific thematic issues, such as the special representative for children and armed conflict, the special representative on sexual violence in conflict, and the special adviser on the prevention of genocide. These SRSGs are assigned to raise awareness of major problems, to develop relevant policy, and to work with member states and the UN system to ensure that the problems receive appropriate attention and action.

Working Together to Provide Appropriate Mandates and Adequate Resources

To carry out the objectives of peace operations in such complex situations requires a strategic approach at all levels of the UN system. As Ellen Løj, former SRSG for Liberia, notes: "It is a triangle—the mission, Headquarters and the Security Council. It's important to get it right in all three."[8]

Lack of a sharply defined strategic approach at any of these levels can affect the outcome of a mission. Such an approach begins with the mission mandate and the resources allocated to achieve it.

SRSGs stress that Security Council mandates should be clear, with achievable, well-defined end goals; should fit the experience in the field; and should provide adequate human resources. Several SRSGs also complain about "one size fits all" mandates. "Mandates need to be tailored to the mission," stresses Løj. "We can't copy the Congo in Liberia. We have to have a fresh look at each situation. It is especially important to have a more focused mandate when resources are scarce."[9] As some SRSGs point out, UN headquarters must also tailor its planning to the needs on the ground rather than engaging in "template planning."

Another issue is the tendency for the mandate to expand over time. As more and more problems arise in the mission area, the Security Council often adds new tasks to the mission's mandate without a comparable increment in resources, resulting in the mission becoming overburdened with responsibilities that it cannot adequately fulfill. Roger Meece, former SRSG for MONUSCO, notes that "what happens is that there's a problem or an issue and Council members say, 'OK, we've got this big peacekeeping mission, let's ask them to deal with it.' I always say to the Council, 'Please identify mandated tasks that are not unreasonable and that do not exceed our resources and capacity.'"[10]

Preferable to incremental "mandate creep" is a more strategic approach, whereby, as the situation changes, the Council reevaluates the strategic aims of the mission and adjusts the mandate accordingly. As noted during a retreat the Security Council held in 2010 in Istanbul: "Mandate design is just the beginning of the process. Mandates need to be continually reassessed against developments on the ground. This requires continual engagement by the Council, matched by strong analytical capacity within the Secretariat. Mandate reviews should be seen as moments to assess and address shortcomings in strategy and capacity. Prioritization and sequencing are essential in implementing mandates."[11]

Elsewhere it has been suggested that since the originating mandate is often ill-suited to address the situation on the ground, it should be considered "provisional" and be subject to frequent review and alterations as required.[12]

As several SRSGs stress, there is often a disconnect between what members of the Security Council are requesting a mission to do and what financial resources are being allocated by the Advisory Committee on Administrative and Budgetary Questions (ACABQ), which is a subcommittee of the General Assembly's Fifth Committee (dealing with administrative and budgetary issues). In some cases, the delegates on the ACABQ are from the same member states as those that sit on the Security Council, but their decisions about funding for a mission's civilian tasks may fall short of what is required by the Council mandate, posing, in some cases, a real problem for the mission and the SRSG. As Meece comments: "There is a tendency to have a lack of synchronization between what the Council wants done and identifies as tasks and what the ACABQ or the Fifth Committee are willing to do in terms of allocating resources to it. So, all peacekeeping missions face the question of 'OK, we're supposed to do X, Y and Z, but we are not being given the money or the necessary resources to do it.'"[13] Indeed, the Council, in its discussions at the Istanbul retreat, agreed "that the Council should do a better job of matching ends and means . . . [and] should work more closely with the Fifth Committee of the General Assembly to ensure more appropriate resourcing for Council mandated missions."[14]

Another major issue is the different procedures for funding special political missions and peacekeeping missions. Peacekeeping missions have a separate funding mechanism that provides flexibility and allocation of funds as required, whereas political missions are still reliant on the biennial UN regular budget, which is not well suited to their needs. In a report by the Secretary-General to the General Assembly on review of arrangements for the funding and backstopping of special political missions,[15] the Secretary-General notes that political missions have grown exponentially in the past two decades in terms of "number, size and operational scope," and that the current funding arrangements for these and their backstopping are totally inadequate. The current approach significantly impedes the timely deployment and startup of political missions and, thus, the UN's ability to offer a rapid response. It also presents problems when the situation on the ground requires the expansion of a mission and adversely affects the transition from a peacekeeping mission to a political mission with a potential risk to mandate implementation.

With the tripling of mandated tasks of these missions since 1995,[16] there are also major problems with the backstopping of special political missions, which typically require considerable assistance from headquarters in planning and direction, especially for smaller missions that do not have support structures. A number of options for correcting this situation are offered by the report, which at the time of this writing have not yet been acted upon by the General Assembly. In response to this inaction, Ian Martin, former special representative in East Timor, Nepal, and Libya, states: "Member states [principally the P5] are utterly irresponsible in the way they are refusing to move special political missions out of the regular budget and onto a separate assessment which is the only reasonable thing to do."[17] Regarding Nepal, he explains:

> Build-up of the mission was hampered by the limited pre-commitment authority available to special political missions, and by the classic hurdles of recruitment and procurement procedures. . . . The handicap of being a special

> political mission, funded from the regular budget, rather than a peacekeeping
> mission funded by separate assessment, went beyond the limitation on pre-
> commitment authority. . . . The downward pressures on staffing and funding
> to be provided from the regular budget are inevitably acute.[18]

Agreement on mandates and resources is not, however, always easy to
achieve. The fifteen governments represented on the Council (as well as
those represented on the ACABQ) each have their own individual geopolitical and domestic interests, and the compromises necessary to reach consensus can sometimes result in decisions that do not match the needs on the
ground.

Another problem is that the highly complex nature of the many situations upon which the Council must authoritatively pronounce itself creates
a real challenge for Council members in terms of possessing sufficient
familiarity with each situation. Indeed, in recent years the Council has been
charged with oversight of approximately thirty missions per year.[19] It is
vital, therefore, that the Secretary-General, the departments, and the SRSGs
view themselves not as passive recipients of mandates, but rather as key
actors who can, through their careful analysis and well-argued recommendations, assist the Council in the formulation of appropriate mandates.
Indeed, the Council's Ad Hoc Working Group on Conflict Prevention and
Resolution in Africa[20] notes: "The special representative is often the Council's primary source of information on a conflict or postconflict situation
and it is through the special representatives that many of the Council's decisions are implemented."[21] Thus, two of the central recommendations of the
UN Panel on Peace Operations remain as valid today as they were when the
Brahimi Report was issued in 2000:

> The Secretariat must tell the Security Council what it needs to know, not
> what it wants to hear when recommending force and other resource levels
> for new missions and it must set those levels according to realistic scenarios
> that take into account likely challenges to implementation. Security Council
> mandates, in turn, should reflect the clarity that peacekeeping operations re-
> quire for unity of effort when they deploy into potentially dangerous situa-
> tions. . . . [And] the Secretariat must not apply best-case planning assump-
> tions to situations where the local actors have historically exhibited
> worst-case behaviour.[22]

In his book describing his experience as head of the UN mission in
East Timor, Martin notes that the lack of contingency planning for the
worst-case scenario became particularly critical when widespread violence
broke out in 1999 after the announcement of the result of the independence
referendum, eventually leading to the evacuation of the mission, the local
staff, and the internally displaced persons sheltered in the UN compound.
He proposed that worst-case planning *must* be instituted as a matter of gen-

eral practice and that the Council should take this into consideration in its own planning.[23]

While the Council has yet to fully internalize this insight, the opportunity to do this is provided by the regularly scheduled formal reports of the Secretary-General to the Security Council for each mission. These are entered into the Council's public record and then considered in either open (public) consultations or in informal (private) consultations or both, which involve briefings by the SRSG or senior Secretariat staff. Typically, these regular reports cover events in the mission area and actions of the mission during the previous reporting period.

SRSGs are typically enthusiastic about appearing in person before the Council. They report that the opportunity to brief the Council and to answer questions enables them to highlight issues of importance and to go into much more depth on key topics. SRSGs and Secretariat staff also note that oral briefings ensure that discussions are more candid and allow issues that cannot be published in a public document to be raised and discussed. As Jan Kubiš, special representative of the Secretary-General for Afghanistan, points out: "I try to amplify certain points, certain messages, sometimes going beyond what is in the report. Of course, the members of the Council have their own concerns and I listen very carefully and try to understand what they are and, if I don't understand, I ask. So, it is an interaction."[24] Martin argues for honesty and candor: "If the SRSG gives the Council too rosy a picture, then it is suddenly surprised when everything goes pear-shaped. There is no reason why an SRSG should not be frank about the political problems in the country, because the success or failure of missions ultimately depends on the parties."[25] Many SRSGs also find it helpful to call on ambassadors represented on the Security Council bilaterally before Council meetings, in order to brief them on a one-to-one basis about difficult or complex issues.

Good offices and preventive diplomacy missions do not always submit formal reports to the Council, although in some cases the SRSG may still brief the Council, usually in informal consultations. As Miroslav Jenča, former SRSG for the UNRCCA, explains: "Preventive diplomacy is an activity that requires a lot of quiet efforts, a lot of discreet talks and Central Asian countries don't want to be under the spotlight of the Security Council."[26]

But briefings to the Council can also have useful benefits on the ground. As Jenča continues: "I always meet the Permanent Representatives of the five Central Asian countries; I discuss with them what I have said and what the discussion was about and what were the key issues raised by the Security Council members."[27] Regarding Libya, Martin notes:

> One of the useful things about the briefings was that we circulated them, and they were quite closely followed by the people in the interim government.

They were a way of conveying messages, but also of getting a positive response from the Libyans as to the objectivity of the picture that we were giving to the Council. Then, of course, it also enhances the way they listen to you, if they know that you are the principal conveyor of the picture to the international community. It's a good excuse if you want to have more than a routine meeting with the Prime Minister, to say, "I want to see you before I go to New York to make sure I get the messages right." Conversely, you can do the same when you come back.[28]

In addition to scheduled reports, when situations are developing rapidly the Council may ask for special briefings, either in person or by video teleconferencing.

An interesting precedent was established by Martin when he published in Nepal (with permission from headquarters) his briefings to the Council in a book titled *Nepal's Peace Process at the United Nations*. The purpose was "to give a history of how the peace process unfolded."[29] Subsequently, SRSG Karin Landgren, Martin's successor in Nepal, did the same in a second volume. This is an example that other SRSGs may wish to follow, as it assists in preserving the institutional memory of both UN operations and in-country historical events.

Another innovation that has improved member states' understanding of the situation on the ground is visits by the Security Council to peace operations in the field. Terms of reference are usually drawn up for the Council visits, and following those visits a report is issued, setting out its activities, findings, and recommendations. These visits can be used instrumentally by the Council or the peace operation when facing a need for stronger involvement by the international community in response to a blocked peace process. Such visits allow Council members to see the situation firsthand and to have face-to-face meetings with key actors on the ground; they also give Council members a much clearer picture of the issues and problems, as well as the different personalities and perspectives. SRSGs report that such Council visits are highly useful in providing support to the mission and in bringing the Council's influence to bear on those who are obstructing the process. As noted by the International Peace Institute's research project on understanding compliance with UN Security Council resolutions:

> Security Council members have traveled to the DRC ten times [between 2000 and 2010], meeting a broad range of representatives of the government, rebel groups, members of parliament and political parties, civil society, the media, the UN peacekeeping force, and the field officers of international financial institutions. All of this suggests that the Security Council . . . developed new ways of communicating confidentially with leaders of warring factions.[30]

SRSG Augustine Mahiga relates how a Security Council visit in 2010 had a major impact on his efforts to establish a more inclusive peace process in Somalia, when the visiting Security Council ambassadors gave clear direction to the parties that they should all meet together under the facilitation of the SRSG: "This was the beginning of a close working relationship with the Council which really made a big difference."[31] Such Council visits, however, need to be carefully timed and coordinated with the peace operation on the ground if they are to be useful. Martin, for example, advised against a Council visit to Libya because the Libyans did not want to feel that they were "under Council scrutiny and because of divisions in the Council."[32]

In the Democratic Republic of the Congo (DRC), a visit from a delegation of the General Assembly's Fifth Committee was also exceedingly useful. Meece explains: "These are people who don't necessarily know the specifics of a peacekeeping mission, especially one as large as MONUSCO. But helping to give them an idea was very useful in terms of our budget submissions."[33]

Another way that SRSGs can affect decisionmaking on the Council is by working closely with ambassadors in the field whose countries are represented on the Council. Many SRSGs establish regular meetings with a core group of key ambassadors to share information, brainstorm solutions to problems, and engage in joint strategizing, so that relevant member states feel more engaged, accept responsibility, and transmit similar recommendations back to their capitals. Even when these core groups are not formalized, SRSGs stress that a close relationship with member-state representatives on the ground gives them much greater authority and leverage in working with the parties, as well as providing useful ideas and much-needed support for their work. A number of SRSGs call their groups the "P5 Plus" or similar names.

Former SRSG Aldo Ajello called his group of ambassadors in Mozambique his "mini Security Council." As he explains: "What I was doing was simple. When I briefed them each week, I was basically dictating the reports they would write to their capitals—which had two good results. First, I knew they were sending the right information. Second, I knew they were all sending the same information at the same time. So, all the capitals were reacting in the same way."[34]

SRSGs also can attempt to influence policy through visits to key capitals to discuss issues directly with policymakers there. Some SRSGs indicate that they do this particularly when they believe that a member state is badly informed or has strong vested interests that blind it to the realities of the situation.

Factors to Consider in Mission Mandating and Resourcing

One factor that the Council should take into account in determining the authorized troop and police size of missions is the difficulty of the conflict environment. Stephen Stedman, Donald Rothchild, and Elizabeth Cousens, based on their research into the success of implementation of peace agreements, strongly urge that if missions are to be undertaken in difficult conflict environments, they *must* be given adequate resources to succeed.[35] The authors commissioned studies of implementation following a peace agreement in sixteen cases of civil war to determine the extent to which a number of factors affected implementation. Their findings suggest that four variables were most determinant. The three that were likely to make implementation more difficult were the presence of spoilers, the presence of lootable natural resources, and the presence of a neighboring state hostile to the peace agreement. The factor most likely to predict implementation success was the presence of major power interest. Stedman and colleagues argue that if sufficient resources cannot be provided, the UN should not become involved at all, since failed interventions can dramatically exacerbate the costs of war in terms of human lives, as we saw in Rwanda and Angola.

Another factor concerns peace agreements themselves. As Jean Arnault, one of the few SRSGs to have been involved in both the negotiation of a peace agreement and its subsequent implementation (in Guatemala), argues: "The first thing you learn by combining the two experiences is that the implementation process is as viable as the peace agreement on which it is based."[36] Several SRSGs maintain that in deciding whether or not to authorize a mission, it is incumbent on the Security Council to consider whether the agreement on which the mission will be based is appropriate and will be able to withstand the test of implementation. From my interviews with SRSGs, a number of factors emerged as essential ingredients. SRSGs maintain that the peace agreements most likely to be successfully implemented are those that contain sufficient detail and specificity; resolve the most crucial issues, including how power will be shared or divided; are acceptable to a majority of constituents; meet international standards; provide clear guidelines about implementation priorities; contain realistic implementation timetables; give a lead role to the UN in implementation; and set forth an effective implementation mechanism for resolving disputes. SRSGs recommend that the Council should examine peace agreements more carefully before agreeing to implement them, especially agreements that have not been negotiated with significant UN involvement. Of course, no peace agreement is going to be perfect, so even when peace agreements do not meet all of these criteria, there may be cases when it will still be important for the UN to become involved, as was the case, for instance, in Nepal.

Working Together to Maximize Leverage

Another area where SRSGs and the Council can create synergy is in the coordinated use of leverage. Different stages of the peace process are likely to bring to the fore different kinds of leverage. The main sources of leverage at the peacemaking stage are likely to be the personal suasion of the SRSG and the Secretary-General, as well as progress in the negotiation process itself. Public and international opinion can also play a pivotal role, and one of the major ways in which an SRSG can enhance his or her own leverage is by working to ensure that the P5 (and other Council members) are aligned in supporting the SRSG's approach, objectives, and ultimately the outcome of the process. SRSGs can also overtly use the Council's authority by making it clear to the parties that the Security Council stands behind them and supports their efforts and that they speak on behalf of the Council. In their interviews, SRSGs report being keenly aware of the need to maximize the use of influence from the international community. As one SRSG states: "It was because people were aware that I had the total support of the international community that they accepted my authority. If you think you have power because you represent the United Nations Secretariat, you'll find that this is not sufficient. People must feel that you have someone backing you. For that, the international community was my best asset."[37] Another comments: "To coordinate and spearhead international action, I had to identify countries on whose shoulders I could stand."[38] As SRSG Lisa Buttenheim notes with regard to Cyprus: "Although Council members do not always read the reports, the parties *do* read them, and the reports, therefore, provide useful leverage, since the parties want to be considered in a good light and do not like to be criticized."[39]

James Cockayne, Christoph Mikulaschek, and Chris Perry argue that almost half of the Council's demands addressed at parties to an internal conflict "take the form of an iterative process designed to reinforce the bargaining under way between civil war parties and to support the implementations of agreements they conclude."[40] They state that the Council's leverage in such situations derives from four factors:

> First, the reiteration of existing commitments in a Security Council resolution raises the reputational costs of deviating from those commitments, because of the public, high-profile nature of such a reiteration and the political—if not legal—force such a reiteration places on compliance. . . . Second, the Security Council's seal of approval on a peace agreement might also send a positive signal to providers of external political, military and financial assistance to peace processes, opening the door to greater benefits from compliance. Often, the Council attaches an appeal for external support for peace processes to a resolution calling on civil-war parties to live up to their commitments. . . . Third, the highly visible endorsement of the settlement terms of a peace agreement through a Security Council resolution may give potential spoilers additional incentives to participate in the agreement. . . . Actors who are sitting on the sidelines of a peace process may fear being left behind by the "departing" train. . . . Fourth, a Security Council resolution reiterating prior commitments

of the parties may sometimes reduce the domestic political costs incurred by them in the course of implementing hard compromises.[41]

In addition to setting benchmarks for expected behaviors in its resolutions, the Council can also employ a range of other instruments to exert influence, including letters from the president of the Council to the parties, presidential statements, changes in the mandate, Council visits to the mission area, and even requests for representatives of the parties to address the Council in person. These, in turn, affect the national and international image of the parties and have positive and negative consequences regarding various kinds of bilateral and multilateral assistance. As well, the Council has at its disposal a range of punitive measures (should they be deemed necessary) that can be applied under Chapter VII of the UN Charter.

Another factor is the expanding involvement of the international community, where UN agencies, other multilateral and bilateral actors, as well as nongovernmental organizations become involved in humanitarian, development, or reconstruction aid. Promises of relief and reconstruction can provide a powerful set of positive incentives. It should be noted, however, that failure to deliver pledged aid can seriously undermine this useful source of leverage.

The mere presence of a peacekeeping mission can, in itself, offer multiple sources of influence—the supervision, monitoring, and reporting functions of the peacekeeping troops (whether unarmed, lightly armed, or heavily armed), military observers, civilian police, human rights monitors, civil or political affairs officers, and electoral monitors. Their actions exert a range of implicit and explicit positive and negative influences on the leaders, their constituents, and the population at large.

During the peacebuilding phase, the amount of potential leverage often diminishes as Council involvement lessens, the mission is downsized, and the international community's presence dwindles. The conclusion one might draw is that the amount of leverage is greatest during the peacekeeping phase, but as Michael Doyle points out, there is a paradox in peacekeeping situations that gives the parties considerable counterleverage over the UN and the SRSG:

> The spirit of the agreement is never more exalted than at the moment of the signing of the peace treaty; the authority of the United Nations is never greater. . . . Although the United Nations has put some of its diplomatic prestige on the line, it as yet has no investment in material resources. The United Nations, in short, holds most of the cards. But as soon as the United Nations begins its investment of money, personnel and operational prestige, then the bargaining relationship alters its balance. The larger the UN investment . . . the greater the independent UN interest in success is, the greater the influence of the parties becomes. Since the parties control an essential element in the success of the mandate, their bargaining power rapidly rises.[42]

This paradox suggests that SRSGs and the Security Council need to consider carefully who is leveraging whom, as well as how and why.

SRSGs also call for a more sophisticated use of leverage than blunt carrots and sticks to compel compliance. A number of SRSGs argue that the key to effective leverage is understanding parties' motivations and working from there to provide incentives that are tailored to their interests. They contend that involving the parties as partners in the mutual process of agreeing on objectives and exploring incentives is the best way to give them a greater sense of ownership and responsibility. Many SRSGs stress that this is why inclusiveness of all the major protagonists as partners—whether at peace talks or as part of an implementation commission—is so important. Even when it does not seem possible for SRSGs to work with certain parties (e.g., when they have excluded themselves from the process or are "proscribed" by terrorist-designation lists), a good understanding of their motivations is certain to assist with a more effective use of incentives. The bottom line, they suggest, is that the better one understands the motivation of the parties, the more likely one is to be able to influence the process. Thus, in considering the overt use of leverage, the Council would be well advised to consult with SRSGs about what they think could be effective.

Several SRSGs propose a greater use of positive incentives. Former special adviser Jan Egeland asserts:

> When we consider using leverage, what tends to happen is that the stick becomes bigger than the carrot or the stick comes before the carrot. But we need to realize that threats backfire more often than they create progress. The most effective leverage is usually moral pressure over time or positive incentives such as recognition, invitations and assistance. This works better than negative sanctions and we need to make more use of this approach.[43]

Another SRSG suggests that "there are two main carrots, one is economic support and the other is legitimacy."[44] Research in conflict resolution also supports this conclusion. As Melanie Greenberg, John Barton, and Margaret McGuiness argue in their study of twelve conflict resolution efforts: "Positive pressures where the parties are offered a promising future seem more likely to be effective than negative pressures."[45]

But Council practice suggests that sticks are still used more than carrots. Cockayne and colleagues state: "The frequency with which the Security Council imposed sanctions against civil-war parties suggests that one of its preferred strategies to obtain leverage over [such] parties was to impose sanctions and then use their removal as an incentive for [them] to meet Security Council demands to end the fighting and reach a sustainable settlement."[46]

"Reactance" is a well-studied psychological phenomenon that typically occurs when the party trying to achieve influence does not fully take into account all the factors that affect the motivation of those they are trying to influence. In such cases, the blunt use of leverage may be seen by a party for what it is—an attempt to "manipulate" it to act in a certain manner against what it perceives to be its own interests. The party may react against the attempt to influence its behavior and refuse to comply in order to preserve its freedom of choice and control over a situation. When internal approval from followers is crucial to a leader, not being seen by one's constituents to be caving to external pressure may be more important to a leader than avoiding punitive sanctions—even when they are severe. In such situations, the use of sticks can backfire badly—not only failing to bring about the desired result, but even causing the obstinate party to become more entrenched in its resistance to influence. SRSGs also caution that sticks—as well as carrots—that are not delivered as promised, erode the credibility of both the Council and the SRSG.

Conclusion

The relationship between an SRSG and the Security Council resembles that between a CEO and a company's board of directors. Although the board may have the power to give direction to its senior staff, a wise board will realize that it does not usually have the detailed information to micromanage each situation and that the best way to proceed is to work closely to support those who are working on a day-to-day basis to carry out the broad objectives of the organization that have been set by the board.

By working closely with the members of the Council, the Secretary-General and his SRSGs are more likely to obtain the support they need to get the job done. This involves close collaboration with representatives of member states who are on the Council, on the ground, and in key capitals. In all cases, clear analysis and well-argued recommendations stand the best chance of being heeded. Direct reporting by the SRSG to the Council is to be encouraged, as are visits by Council members to the mission area so that they can see the situation firsthand. Since the situations into which SRSGs and missions are deployed are extraordinarily complex, a strategic partnership is crucial for meeting the many challenges that arise.

Notes

Many of the observations in this chapter derive from the UN Institute for Training and Research's "Program for Briefing and Debriefing Special and Personal Representatives and Envoys of the Secretary-General," which involved in-depth interviews that I conducted with current and past SRSGs, the preparation of a book and set of DVDs for new SRSGs based on a distillation of the major issues raised in these interviews, as well as a regular seminar for SRSGs and senior headquarters staff. The objective has been to preserve and pass on the valuable lessons and experience of SRSGs and to ensure that these are used to refine and enhance UN practice.

1. Representatives of the Secretary-General have various titles: special representative, personal representative, representative, envoy, special adviser, and the like. The terms *special representative* and *SRSG* will be used in this chapter to refer to all of these.

2. Based on my interviews conducted for my book *On Being a Special Representative of the Secretary-General* (Geneva: UNITAR, 2006), and also on a prepublication copy of Manual Fröhlich, "Leadership for Peace: The Special Representatives of the Secretary-General," in *Peace Operations as Political and Managerial Challenges,* edited by Till Blume, Julian Junk, Francesco Mancini, and Wolfgang Seibel (Boulder, CO: Lynne Rienner, forthcoming).

3. The only exception has been the UN Assistance Mission in Afghanistan (UNAMA), which is a special political mission and has been under the supervision of the DPKO since early 2015.

4. The report was compiled by a distinguished group of panelists who undertook a thorough review of UN peace and security activities and offered a set of concrete and practical recommendations, many of which are still applicable. See United Nations General Assembly and Security Council, *Report of the Panel on United Nations Peace Operations* (Brahimi Report), UN Doc. A/55/305-S/2000/809, August 21, 2000.

5. United Nations General Assembly and Security Council, *Report of the Panel on United Nations Peace Operations,* p. 16.

6. Sebastian von Einsiedel, "You, the People: Transitional Administration, State-Building, and the United Nations," International Peace Academy Conference Report, New York, October 2002.

7. The mandate of these three offices does not derive from a Security Council resolution but is laid down in an exchange of letters between the Secretary-General and the Security Council, indicating Council endorsement. The heads of these missions brief the Council on a semiannual basis.

8. Interview with Ellen Margrethe Løj, Switzerland, 2013.

9. Ibid.

10. Interview with Roger Meece, Switzerland, 2013.

11. Adam Smith and Vanessa Wyeth, "Meeting Notes: Security Council Istanbul Retreat—At the Crossroads of Peacemaking, Peacekeeping, and Peacebuilding" (New York: International Peace Academy, September 30, 2010), p. 3.

12. Center on International Cooperation, "Towards More Inclusive Mandate-Making, More Effective Mandate Implementation," background paper for the thematic series *Building More Effective UN Peace Operations* (New York, November 2009), p. 1.

13. Meece interview.

14. Smith and Wyeth, "Meeting Notes: Security Council Istanbul Retreat," p. 4.

15. United Nations General Assembly, *Report of the Secretary-General to the General Assembly on Review of Arrangements for Funding and Backstopping Special Political Missions,* UN Doc. A/66/340, October 12, 2011.

16. Ibid.

17. Interview with Ian Martin, by Skype, 2013.

18. Ian Martin, *All Peace Operations Are Political: A Case for Designer Missions and the Next UN Reform* (New York: Center on International Cooperation, 2010), pp. 11–12.

19. Alexandra Novosseloff and Richard Gowan, *Security Council Working Methods and UN Peace Operations: The Case of Chad and the Central African*

Republic, 2006–2010 (New York: Center on International Cooperation, April 2012).

20. The ad hoc Working Group on Conflict Prevention and Resolution in Africa was established by the Security Council in 2002 to monitor the implementation of recommendations in presidential statement 2 of January 31, 2002, S/PRST/2002/2, and has been active ever since.

21. United Nations Security Council, "Recommendations of the Ad Hoc Working Group on Conflict Prevention and Resolution in Africa on Enhancing the Effectiveness of the Representatives and Special Representatives of the Secretary-General in Africa, Agreed as of 9 December 2002," UN Doc. S/2002/1352, December 12, 2002, p. 3.

22. United Nations General Assembly and Security Council, *Report of the Panel on United Nations Peace Operations,* p. x.

23. Ian Martin, *Self-Determination in East Timor: The United Nations, the Ballot, and International Intervention* (Boulder, CO: Lynne Rienner, 2001), pp. 126–127.

24. Interview with Jan Kubiš, Switzerland, 2013.

25. Martin interview.

26. Interview with Miroslav Jenča, Switzerland 2013.

27. Ibid.

28. Martin interview.

29. Ibid.

30. James Cockayne, Christoph Mikulaschek, and Chris Perry, *The United Nations Security Council and Civil War: First Insights from a New Dataset* (New York: International Peace Institute, September 2010), p. 14.

31. Interview with Augustine Mahiga, Switzerland, 2013.

32. Martin interview.

33. Meece interview.

34. Interview with Aldo Ajello, Belgium, November 2000.

35. Stephen John Stedman, Donald Rothchild, and Elizabeth M. Cousens, *Ending Civil Wars: The Implementation of Peace Agreements* (Boulder, CO: Lynne Rienner, 2002).

36. Interview with Jean Arnault, Switzerland, November 2001.

37. Interview with Samuel Nana-Sinkam, Switzerland, 2002.

38. Interview with Francis Okelo, Zimbabwe, 2000.

39. Interview with Lisa Buttenheim, Switzerland, 2013.

40. Cockayne, Mikulaschek, and Perry, *The United Nations Security Council and Civil War,* p. 31.

41. Ibid., pp. 33–34.

42. Michael W. Doyle, "War-Making and Peace-Making: The United Nations' Post–Cold War Record," in *Turbulent Peace: The Challenges of Managing International Conflict,* edited by Chester A. Crocker, Fen Osler Hampson, and Pamela Aall (Washington, DC: US Institute of Peace, 2001), p. 542.

43. Interview with Jan Egeland, Norway, 2000.

44. Interview with Jean Arnault, Switzerland, 2001.

45. Melanie Greenberg, John H. Barton, and Margaret E. McGuiness, *Words over War: Mediation and Arbitration to Prevent Deadly Conflict* (Boston: Rowman and Littlefield, 2000), p. 366.

46. Cockayne, Mikulaschek, and Perry, *The United Nations Security Council and Civil War,* p. 39.

23

Collaborating with Regional Organizations

Bruno Stagno Ugarte

WITH VERY FEW EXCEPTIONS, THE CHARTER OF THE UNITED
Nations is a self-contained treaty that prescribes principles and purposes for
the member states of the UN and enumerates the various powers and functions regulating its six principal organs. One of the exceptions is Chapter
VIII, which addresses the potential interaction of the Security Council with
one of the few categories of non-UN entities mentioned in the Charter, what
Chapter VIII calls regional arrangements or agencies, more commonly
known nowadays as regional and subregional organizations.[1] In this chapter
I review the struggle for primacy that initially characterized the relationship
between regional and subregional organizations and the Council, which has
yielded to the promise of complementarity largely due to there being "so
much peace to keep."[2]

First, I lay out the contradictions built into Chapter VIII and the negotiating history behind them. Next I deal with the interpretation and application of Chapter VIII during the Cold War (1946–1989) and under the so-
called New World Order from 1990 to the present, concentrating on some
of the most important precedents established by the Council in its interpretation and application of Chapter VIII and related articles of the UN Charter. Finally, beyond reviewing relevant trends in the interaction of the
Council with regional and subregional organizations, I posit some challenges and opportunities for increased cooperation between them.

The Internal Contradictions of Chapter VIII
In a mere three articles (52–54), Chapter VIII ambiguously and superfi-
cially defines what at first appears to be the primary nature (Article 52[1–

475

3]) but is then specified to be the complementary and subsidiary nature (Articles 52[4] and 53) of regional and subregional organizations vis-à-vis the Council. Whereas Article 52(2) provides for primary resort to regional organizations in instructing member states to "make every effort to achieve pacific settlement of local disputes through such regional arrangements or by such regional agencies *before* referring them to the Security Council" (emphasis added), Article 52(4) succinctly but clearly states that Article 52 "in no way impairs" direct recourse to the Security Council, and Article 53 makes clear that "no enforcement action shall be taken under regional arrangements or by regional agencies without the authorization of the Security Council."

The primacy apparently accorded by Article 52(2) to regional organizations to discharge disputes, with the Council acting on a basis of complementarity, seems also to be supported by Articles 52(1) and 52(3). These respectively prescribe that "nothing in the present Charter precludes the existence of regional arrangements or agencies for dealing with such matters relating to the maintenance of international peace and security as are appropriate for regional action, provided that . . . their activities are consistent with the Purposes and Principles of the United Nations"; and that "the Security Council shall encourage the development of pacific settlement of local disputes through such regional arrangements or by such regional agencies." Article 33 additionally stipulates that "parties to any dispute . . . shall, *first of all*, seek a solution by negotiation, enquiry, mediation, conciliation, arbitration, judicial settlement, resort to regional agencies or arrangements, or other peaceful means of their own choice" (emphasis added).

Looking at the UN Charter in its entirety, however, it becomes clear that the Security Council has primacy vis-à-vis the regional organizations with which it is interlocked based on the principle of subsidiarity. Alongside Articles 52(4) and 53, Articles 34 and 35, on the other hand, respectively prescribe that the Security Council "may investigate any dispute, or any situation which might lead to international friction or give rise to a dispute"; and that any state "may bring any dispute, or any situation . . . to the attention of the Security Council." Article 36 additionally confers on the Security Council the authority to, "at any stage of a dispute . . . , recommend appropriate procedures or methods of adjustment." Along with Article 24, they individually and collectively assign a pride of place to the Security Council as the body having "primary responsibility" for the maintenance of international peace and security. However, whereas Article 24 establishes this primacy within the UN—in relation with the other principal organs with the exceptions provided for in Articles 11 and 12 as regards the General Assembly—in Articles 34, 35, 36, and 52(4) and 53 this primacy transcends the UN to likewise encompass regional and subregional organizations under Chapter VIII. Additionally, Article 51 provides for an exclusively temporal primacy to regional and subregional organizations in stating that "nothing in the present Charter shall impair the inherent right of individual or collective self-defense if an armed attack occurs against a member of the United Nations, *until* the Security Council has taken the measures necessary to maintain international peace and security" (emphasis added). Article 51 furthermore establishes that the measures taken in the exercise of the right of self-defense "shall be immediately reported to the Security Council and shall not in any way affect the authority or responsibility of the Security Council under the present Charter to take at any time such action as it deems necessary to maintain or restore international peace and security." Finally, Article 103 confirms the complementary and subsidiary, not primary, nature of regional and subregional organizations vis-à-vis the Council in stating that in the event of a conflict between obligations under the UN Charter and any other international agreement, "obligations under the present Charter shall prevail."[3]

Beyond the prescriptions of the Charter, the negotiating and drafting history of Chapter VIII at the 1945 San Francisco Conference, at which the United Nations was founded, provides additional evidence of the subsidiary status of regional organizations. Before the San Francisco Conference opened on April 25, several states of the Western Hemisphere had convened in Mexico City and adopted the Act of Chapultepec on March 8, one of the precursor treaties to the formation of the Organization of American States (OAS). These states, composing twenty-one of the fifty-one founding member states of the UN, were keen on having the UN Charter acknowledge a role for regional organizations and provide for direct recourse to the precursors of the OAS in lieu of the Security Council, which they feared as a source of "political infiltration from abroad."[4] Despite being one of the signatories of the Act of Chapultepec, the United States was not of a single frame of mind at San Francisco, as key advisers within its delegation viewed regional organizations as "spheres of influence" or "balance of power" enclaves that threatened to undermine the promise and scope of the United Nations.[5] Other (future) permanent members were not as willing to allow recourse to regional arrangements beyond their reach, which they also perceived as instruments of the United States and its Monroe Doctrine.[6] In the end, however, as the Soviet Union was likewise interested in exempting its own areas of occupation—what would become in 1955 the Warsaw Treaty Organization—from the Security Council, a compromise was possible. However, the ambiguous language of Chapter VIII provided for an imperfect solution, with Article 52(2) most clearly expressing the position of the future member states of the OAS, and Articles 52(4) and 53 that of their detractors. As with most compromise language, the devil remained in the details, allowing for contradictory interpretations and applications of the prescriptions contained in Chapter VIII.

Since the entry into force of the UN Charter, the tension and contradiction between Article 52(2) on the one hand, and Articles 52(4) and 53 on the other, have unsurprisingly cast a long shadow on the interaction of the Security Council with regional and subregional organizations. Ironically, the inclusion of Chapter VIII in the UN Charter actually encouraged the emergence of regional organizations.[7] Initially, the ambiguities of the compromise reached at San Francisco affected only the League of Arab States (LAS) and the precursors of the OAS, but as other regional and subregional organizations came into being, their own interaction with the Security Council was likewise affected.

The Preeminence of Article 52(2) and Regional Organizations During the Cold War

With some exceptions, throughout most of the Cold War, regional organizations interpreted Article 52(2) literally, mostly refusing to defer to the Security Council for the primary responsibility for the maintenance of international peace and security. This is not surprising, as the OAS, to begin with, as well as other regional organizations, were either established, or perceived—rightfully or wrongfully—by the Soviet Union and its allies, as instruments of the United States and its policy of containment of the communist threat.[8]

The United States, in turning to regional organizations it politically and financially dominated, and forcefully advocating for an expansive interpretation of Article 52(2) and its preeminence over Articles 52(4) and 53, sought, with the support of its allies, to avoid Soviet interference in the Council on issues it considered falling within its own area of influence.

Interestingly, however, the first regional organization to run into trouble due to differing interpretations of Chapter VIII was the LAS, certainly not a product or instrument of Western diplomacy. On May 21, 1948, at what would also be the first Council meeting to debate the appropriate role of regional organizations, Syria contended that the enforcement action undertaken by some LAS states in Palestine was in conformity with Article 52(1), as Palestine was an associate member of the LAS. Moreover, Syria argued that the LAS had to assume responsibility for the restoration of order in Palestine, as "neither the Security Council, nor the United Nations as a whole—nor any other power—could stop the atrocities which were going on, or subdue the insurrection. . . . But those members of the United Nations entering into such regional arrangements are obliged to interfere on behalf of the United Nations."[9] Notwithstanding these arguments, the Council adopted Resolution 49 (1948), the draft for which was presented by the United States, which called on all parties to cease hostile military action, with Syria, the Soviet Socialist Republic of Ukraine, and the Soviet Union abstaining.[10]

Operating a volte-face with respect to its position toward the enforcement action of the LAS in Palestine, by 1954 the United States and its allies dealt a first blow to Articles 52(4) and 53. On June 20, the left-wing government of Guatemala, facing an invasion by a CIA-sponsored mercenary army, informed the Council of the "outright aggression" it had suffered from Honduras and Nicaragua and its "unchallengeable right" to appeal to the Security Council.[11] In response, both Honduras and Nicaragua asked that the matter "be referred to the appropriate organization, where it can be heard and where we can defend ourselves."[12] The United States argued that "the effort to by-pass the OAS was, in substance, a violation of Article 52.2."[13] Staunchly anticommunist US allies Brazil and Colombia echoed similar positions, pointing to the "traditional way to settle disputes among American republics"[14] and claiming that Articles 33 and 52(2) imposed on all member states "the duty to apply first to the regional organization, which is of necessity the court of first appeal."[15] Disregarding the legal arguments presented by Guatemala—that it was not referring a dispute but appealing to the Council following an act of aggression and that by reason of Article 103 any conflicting obligations to the OAS were overridden—Brazil and Colombia cosponsored a draft resolution to refer the complaint to the OAS.[16] The draft was vetoed by the Soviet Union, which argued it was contrary to Articles 24 and 52(4) of the Charter.

The alleged "repeated threats [and] harassments" of the United States toward communist Cuba[17] provided the next opportunity for a debate on the interpretation of Chapter VIII and concurrent consideration of the same situation. At the Council meeting held on July 18, 1960, Cuba argued that the right to access the Security Council could not be questioned, as regional organizations "can never signify one recourse less but rather one recourse more,"[18] whereas Argentina called on all Council members to "agree on the practical proposition that, since the regional organization has already taken cognizance of the matter, it is desirable to await the results of its action."[19] Ecuador added that not doing so "would place member states of a regional organization in a position of *capitis diminutio* in the United Nations."[20] Argentina and Ecuador then jointly presented a draft text, adopted as Resolution 144 (1960), adjourning consideration of the question pending the receipt of a report from the OAS.[21]

The next important debate focused on whether notification of regional decisions and actions was sufficient to comply with Article 53, or whether authorization from the Council was necessary. Following the imposition of diplomatic sanctions by the OAS against the authoritarian Rafael Trujillo regime in the Dominican Republic for its complicity in an assassination attempt against President Rómulo Betancourt of Venezuela, a fierce critic of nondemocratic rulers in the hemisphere, the Soviet Union asked that the situation be discussed in the Security Council on September 8, 1960, leading to two different draft resolutions being tabled. Whereas the Soviet Union tabled a draft "guided by Article 53" that approved of the decisions taken by the OAS,[22] Argentina, Ecuador, and the United States sought to avoid a precedent for Security Council authorization in presenting a draft, later adopted as Resolution 156 (1960), that made no reference to Chapter VIII and merely took note of the report already submitted by the OAS on the matter.[23]

The imposition of sanctions by and suspension from the OAS of Cuba provided a first precedent for the interpretation of Chapter VIII in regard to sanctions and Article 41 of the Charter. The United Kingdom spoke for several Council members in stating that "it was not necessary or appropriate for this Council either to approve or to disapprove—or indeed pronounce at all upon—resolutions or actions of the kind taken at that time by the OAS."[24] By a vote,[25] the Security Council on February 27, 1962, declined to invite Cuba and pursue the matter any further, although Egypt called the Council's attention to the annual report of the Secretary-General, which stated "the importance of regional arrangements in the maintenance of international security is fully recognized in the Charter and the appropriate use of such arrangements is encouraged. But in those cases where resort to such arrangements is chosen in the first instance, that choice should not be permitted to cast any doubt on the ultimate responsibility of the United Nations. Similarly, a policy giving full scope to the proper role of regional agencies can and should at the same time fully preserve the right of a member state to a hearing under the Charter."[26]

The debate on the suspension of and sanctions against Cuba also provided a first precedent for the interaction between Chapter VIII and Article 36 on referral of questions to the International Court of Justice, and Article 40 on provisional measures. Chile opposed both requests by Cuba on the grounds that the Council should limit itself to taking note of the decisions of the OAS to the extent that they were in conformity with Article 53. Otherwise the Council would be setting a disturbing precedent "for the inference of the Security Council, where the five Great Powers have the right of veto, in the affairs of the regional organizations which are entitled to establish themselves by agreement and to impose obligations upon their members, in order to advance regional interests on the principles which determine the attitude of such regional agencies." A draft resolution presented by Cuba was defeated.

On May 3, 1965, following the deployment of 4,200 US troops to the Dominican Republic, driven by fears of a communist victory in the civil war ravaging the country, the Council was split three ways. Uruguay, representing one camp, presented a draft resolution highlighting that Security

Council authorization was necessary as per Articles 52(4) and 34 and 35, and was "even more appropriate when the situation appeared prima facie to contravene international law, in particular Article[s] 2.4 and 2.7 of the Charter." The Soviet Union, representing a second camp, tabled its own draft resolution condemning what it termed a "gross violation" of the Charter and demanding the immediate withdrawal of the United States (representing the third camp) from the Dominican Republic.[27]

With Cold War dynamics having undermined the primacy of the Security Council vis-à-vis regional organizations, it is not surprising that the Council did not substantively consider Chapter VIII issues for a number of years.[28] Others likewise turned to liberal interpretations of Article 53 and previous precedent to operate via regional organizations without proper Council authorization, as best demonstrated by the LAS in Lebanon (1976–1983) and the Organization of African Unity (OAU) in Chad (1981).[29] Potentially the most serious confrontation, however, arose from the Falklands War in 1982, when the United Kingdom sought to give primacy to the Security Council, whereas Argentina and its regional allies sought to find recourse in the OAS. After the Security Council adopted Resolution 502 (1982), calling the military action by Argentina an "invasion" and demanding "an immediate withdrawal" from the Falkland Islands (Islas Malvinas),[30] Argentina turned to the OAS, which urged in a resolution that the United Kingdom "cease the hostilities it is carrying on within the security region . . . of the Inter-American Treaty of Reciprocal Assistance, and also to refrain from any act that may affect inter-American peace and security."[31] Different points of view emerged within the OAS, however, regarding the adequacy and primacy of the regional organ, effectively weakening any potential challenges to the Security Council thereafter.[32]

The Decline of Article 52(2) and the Primacy of the Security Council

The end of the Cold War gradually opened new possibilities and opportunities for Council interaction with regional organizations. As a result, in 1990 the Council expressed "its full support" for the good offices pursued jointly by the UN and the OAU regarding Western Sahara,[33] and "appreciation" for the efforts of the Association of Southeast Asian Nations (ASEAN) regarding Cambodia.[34] In 1991, the Council expressed similar support for the collective efforts undertaken by the European Community (EC) and the Conference for Security and Cooperation in Europe (CSCE) in Yugoslavia, inviting the Secretary-General to offer assistance to the ongoing efforts.[35] The Council also commended the efforts by the Economic Community of West African States (ECOWAS) to restore peace in Liberia and called on the parties to the conflict to "cooperate fully" with ECOWAS in this regard.[36]

482 COLLABORATING WITH REGIONAL ORGANIZATIONS

The two main salvos that respectively laid the political and intellectual foundation for increased Chapter VIII interactions were the first-ever summit meeting of the Security Council, on January 31, 1992, and its direct byproduct, the Secretary-General's *An Agenda for Peace* report, issued later that year, which included, as requested, recommendations regarding "the contribution to be made by regional organizations in accordance with Chapter VIII of the UN Charter in helping the work of the Council."[37]

Faulting the Cold War for impairing the proper functioning of Chapter VIII, and recognizing that some regional actions had worked against resolving disputes in the manner foreseen in the Charter, the *Agenda for Peace* pragmatically emphasized that "regional action, as a matter of decentralization, delegation and cooperation with UN efforts could not only lighten the burden of the Council, but also contribute to a deeper sense of participation, consensus and democratization in international affairs."[38] Acting on the report, the Secretary-General also initiated periodic meetings with the heads of regional organizations as of 1994,[39] anticipating by a decade the first such meetings organized by the Security Council. In the course of 1992, the Council adopted no less than eighteen resolutions mentioning one or more regional organizations by name, sixteen of which explicitly referenced Chapter VIII.

Moreover, in quick succession after the *Agenda for Peace,* the Security Council adopted a number of precedent-setting resolutions under Chapters VII and VIII. Resolution 787 (1992), on the Federal Republic of Yugoslavia, provided the first sanctions enforcement authorization for regional organizations while emphasizing that they would be doing so "under the authority of the Security Council."[40] Resolution 816 (1993) first authorized military action by regional organizations, to enforce a no-fly zone over Bosnia and Herzegovina, albeit restating that they would be operating "under the authority of the Security Council."[41] Resolution 866 (1993) established the UN Observer Mission in Liberia (UNOMIL) in what the Council acknowledged was "the first peace-keeping mission undertaken by the United Nations in cooperation with a peace-keeping mission already set up by another organization, in this case ECOWAS."[42]

In these and a number of other decisions, the Council clearly asserted its primacy while allowing for pragmatic divisions of labor with regional organizations. However, despite the expectations within some regional organizations that working in tandem with the UN would engender enhanced financial and logistical support, starting with UNOMIL—and running through the more recent AU Mission in Somalia (AMISOM) or the African-led International Support Mission to Mali (AFISMA)—these expectations have proven to be largely misplaced. Tellingly, the potentially mismatched expectations[43] had been foretold by the 1995 *Supplement to An Agenda for Peace* in its noting "that the political, operational and financial aspects of the arrangement [with regional organizations] give rise to questions of some delicacy." The Security Council, moreover, started to authorize an unprecedented number of UN peacekeeping missions—fifteen between 1991 and 1993 alone, compared to eighteen between 1946 and 1990—deploying 69,961 uniformed personnel by December 31, 1993, up from only 10,304 just three years earlier. This increase in deployment obviously demanded more financial and operational resources, leaving the UN with little capacity to financially or operationally support operations by third parties.

This newfound confidence in UN peacekeeping came under fire with the failure of both the UN Assistance Mission in Rwanda (UNAMIR) in 1994 and the ill-named UN Protection Force (UNPROFOR) in Bosnia and Herzegovina in 1995 to protect civilians. It was also undermined by the low threshold for casualties most poignantly evidenced by the second UN Operation in Somalia (UNOSOM II) following the killing of eighteen US troops on October 3–4, 1993, and the death of ten Belgian UN peacekeepers in Rwanda on April 7, 1994, both incidents precipitating the effective implosion of the associated UN operations. The overly ambitious plans contained in the *Agenda for Peace* for robust UN peacekeeping were soon replaced by more prudent provisions in the 1995 *Supplement to the Agenda for Peace.* By December 31, 1995, the Council had already scaled back peacekeeping (and particularly peace enforcement), with only 31,031 uniformed personnel deployed, which fell to 24,919 a year later and 14,879 a year thereafter. As a result, the Council was ever more ready to defer to regional organizations to keep the peace, referencing by name different regional or subregional organizations in twenty-four resolutions in 1996, albeit not once explicitly mentioning Chapter VIII. As its capacity to keep the peace dwindled, the Security Council turned to outsourcing or subcontracting operations to willing partners, including regional and subregional organizations.

Toward the end of 1999, as the Council started to overcome the sobering effects of Somalia, Srebrenica, and Rwanda, and facing new challenges in Kosovo, East Timor, and elsewhere, authorizing 37,733 uniformed personnel by December 31, 2000, and 47,108 a year thereafter, it sought to once again impose its primacy. However, times had changed, and some regional organizations, now fully appraised of the limitations of the Council, were more aggressively advocating for regional solutions to regional problems. By then, ECOWAS, originally conceived to address economic issues, had already tackled political and operational issues following its peacekeeping deployments in Liberia and Sierra Leone. However, it was the AU that truly led the charge, with the establishment on July 9, 2002, of its own Peace and Security Council (PSC) "to ensure that Africa, through the AU, plays a central role in bringing about peace, security and stability on the Continent."[44]

In response, the Security Council changed tactics. On March 3, 2003, the 1373 Counter-Terrorism Committee, one of the subsidiary bodies of the Security Council, held the first-ever Council-related meeting with regional organizations, albeit in a closed format and within the limited thematic confines of counterterrorism. However, on April 11, 2003, at the initiative of then Council member Mexico, the Council held an open meeting with six regional organizations in attendance titled "The Security Council and Regional Organizations: Facing New Challenges to International Peace and Security."[45] At a follow-up open meeting held on July 20, 2004, the Council adopted for the first time a presidential statement exclusively dealing with its cooperation with regional organizations in general.[46]

In the meantime, some regional and subregional organizations had overextended themselves, lacking the financial or operational resources to keep the peace. As a result, the UN took over from ECOWAS in Liberia (2003) and Côte d'Ivoire (2004), as it had already done in Sierra Leone (2000), as well as from the AU in Burundi (2004). Soon thereafter, the report by the High-Level Panel on Threats, Challenges, and Change, *A More Secure World;*[47] the Secretary-General's response thereto, *In Larger Freedom;*[48] and the outcome document of the 2005 World Summit,[49] all advocated for improved interaction and coordination between the Security Council and regional organizations. Responding to these calls, on October 17, 2005, the Council adopted Resolution 1631, its first on cooperation with regional and subregional organizations. Although not ready to characterize them as strategic partners as recommended by the high-level panel and others, but ever ready to pragmatically consider them as available partners of lesser standing, the Council even took the dramatic step of authorizing the UN-AU Hybrid Operation in Darfur (UNAMID), the first of its kind, in Resolution 1769 (2007) to replace the largely ineffectual AU Mission in Sudan (AMIS). Moreover, arguably in response to the calls by the AU for "African solutions to African problems," and partly out of recognition of the high number of African situations on the agenda of the Council, by 2007 Council members agreed to meet with the members of the AU's Peace and Security Council on an annual basis.

By 2008, the Security Council took another unprecedented step, adopting Resolution 1809, in which it recognized "the need to enhance the predictability, sustainability and flexibility of financing regional organizations when they undertake peacekeeping under a United Nations mandate."[50] Following up on this theme in regard to peacekeeping in Africa, a joint AU-UN panel chaired by Romano Prodi presented a number of recommendations to address the "growing anomalous and undesirable trend in which organizations lacking the necessary capabilities have been left to bear the brunt in terms of providing the international community's initial response, while others more capable have not engaged."[51]

In recent years, the Security Council has devolved to regional organizations like never before, effectively responding to regional requests or buying
into institutional or operational arrangements or political settlements proposed by the latter while formally asserting its primacy. In Libya, it explicitly used the LAS request for intervention there to justify the adoption of
Resolutions 1970 (2011) and 1973 (2011). The Council was likewise surprisingly responsive to the Gulf Cooperation Council's (GCC) mediation and
implementation plan on Yemen in Resolution 2014 (2011), notwithstanding
its serious defects on the accountability front due to its acknowledgment of
an amnesty for former president Ali Abdullah Saleh. With regard to the AU,
the Council unreservedly supported the AU High-Level Implementation
Panel's road map on Sudan–South Sudan in Resolution 2046 (2012).

However, the inroads registered by some regional organizations are not
necessarily sustainable into the future or transferable to other partners, but
rather are entirely time- and case-specific. The AU offers the best example,
as it is the regional organization that has developed the most institutionalized relationship with the Council yet still suffers from its inconsistency
and selectivity. Whereas the Council sidelined the AU in Libya, thwarting
its attempt at mediation through the adoption of Resolution 1973, it has
largely deferred to the AU on Sudan and South Sudan. Whereas it at first
delayed action on Mali, calling on the AU and ECOWAS to deploy
AFISMA, it then abruptly changed course and established a UN peacekeeping mission without properly coordinating with its previous partners, provoking a stern rebuke from the AU.[52] While disregarding the AU on Mali,
the Council almost simultaneously deferred to the AU and the Southern
African Development Community (SADC) in authorizing, on an exceptional basis, an intervention brigade to operate within the UN peacekeeping
mission in the Democratic Republic of the Congo, despite its decision
upending long-established principles for UN peacekeeping.

In 2013, Council members had a first-ever informal exchange of views
with the members of the EU's Political and Security Committee, while
postponing the scheduled annual exchange with the AU's Peace and Security Council, which continues to be the sole regional organ or organization
with which Council members meet regularly. Aware of the lacunae that continue to pervade its cooperation with regional organizations more generally,
the Security Council, at the initiative of Argentina, organized a high-level
debate on the issue on August 5, 2013, the first to consider the issue since
it was last generically debated in 2010. Unfortunately, the debate failed to
take the issue further, and the presidential statement adopted at the meeting
merely restated previously agreed language. As such, as of the time of writing, the Council has yet to prove that it is ready to meaningfully engage
with regional and subregional organizations on a more consistent and permanent manner.

Conclusion

In its interaction with regional and subregional organizations, the Security Council can opt for hybrid, parallel, or sequential peace settlement efforts or peacekeeping deployments, circumscribe the relationship to logistical and financial support, or simply keep these potential partners at bay. There is therefore no single relationship, no "one size fits all" model, yet it seems that the time has come for the Council to move from ad hoc responses to more structured partnerships with its most frequent regional and subregional partners. Whether these partnerships are premised on strategic or pragmatic foundations is somewhat beside the point, as long as they are acceptable and workable. Unfortunately, the Council is not yet prepared to buy into an "interlocking system" that would require predictable and reliable responses, first and foremost for political reasons, as well as for financial reasons. Some Council members still see added benefits to a case-by-case approach that allows them to weigh the merits, benefits, and costs of each situation.

Not all regional or subregional organizations are alike. In fact, some refuse to be recognized as Chapter VIII arrangements (NATO),[53] some always have some constituent members on the Security Council, and some have even undergone important philosophical and related political change internally, as has the LAS in its positions on Libya and Syria in recent years. In addition, especially in Africa, most of the subregional organizations were originally established to advance economic integration, yet several have since tackled peace and security issues.[54] Moreover, whereas some regional organizations have developed some early-warning, mediating, or peacekeeping capacities, save for the EU and NATO, they are generally unable to provide the financial and operational support required to countenance prolonged or expanded commitments even within their home turf. As the gap between their promise and performance is wide, the Council, in calling on regional organizations, especially since the 2007 financial downturn, has been cautious to avoid having to provide adequate "backstopping" or altogether "rehatting" the deployments as UN peacekeeping operations.

Adding to differences in capabilities, opportunities, and priorities, the Council can at times shop around for the regional organization(s) that best fits its own interests to the detriment of the interest of others. At the same time, the Council also runs the risk of having to maintain adequate relations, or siding with one or more regional or subregional organizations working at cross-purposes with the Council or with each other. The differences between ECOWAS and the Community of Portuguese Speaking Countries (CPLP) in Guinea-Bissau, or the AU and LAS in Libya, are recent examples. What is indisputable, however, is that following the end of the Cold War, the Security Council basically changed from burden-shedding to burden-sharing with regional and subregional organizations. Moreover, as the ambit of peace and security has expanded since the end of the Cold War to include a host of nontraditional situations,[55] the "new" peace to keep will probably require further burden-sharing into the future.

As already mentioned, Boutros-Ghali stated that "regional action . . . could not only lighten the burden of the Council but also contribute to a deeper sense of participation, consensus and democratization in international affairs." Although these words seem reasonable to many, dynamics that shift the onus of power away from the Security Council will be viewed with skepticism by the permanent members. The more the Council is incapable of keeping peace and security, the more unlikely it will be, at least in the short term, to agree to any standing arrangements that could be perceived as an acknowledgment of its own shortcomings and failings. In doing so, it clearly runs the risk of compounding the very gap between its promise and performance, calling further into question its efficacy and legitimacy. Yet despite these risks, as so well-captured by Thucydides, "the strong do what they can and the weak suffer what they must." In the foreseeable future, the Council will likely maintain the pretense that in cooperating with regional and subregional organizations, it does so by choice, as is the prerogative of the strong, and not by necessity.

Notes

1. The UN Charter also makes reference to "specialized agencies," which it defines in Article 57(1) as "established by intergovernmental agreement and having wide international responsibilities, as defined in their basic instruments, in economic, social, cultural, educational, health, and related fields." However, the Charter also prescribes, in Article 57(2), that these specialized agencies, unlike regional and subregional organizations, "shall be brought into relationship with the United Nations." Article 63, in turn, clearly stipulates that the Economic and Social Council "may enter into agreements with any of the agencies referred to in Article 57, defining the terms on which the agency concerned shall be brought into relationship with the United Nations [and] co-ordinate the activities of the specialized agencies through consultation with and recommendations to such agencies." Beyond the specialized agencies, the UN Charter makes reference to other non-UN entities, including nonmember states, enemy states, and non-self-governing territories. See United Nations, *Charter of the United Nations* (San Francisco, June 26, 1945).

2. Kennedy Graham and Tânia Felício, *Regional Security and Global Governance: A Study of Interaction Between Regional Agencies and the UN Security Council with a Proposal for a Regional-Global Security Mechanism* (Brussels: Brussels University Press VUB, 2006), p. 33.

3. Bruno Simma, Daniel-Erasmus Khan, Georg Nolte, and Andreas Paulus, eds., *The Charter of the United Nations: A Commentary* (Oxford: Oxford University Press, 2012), pp. 583–628, 788–895.

4. Stephen C. Schlesinger, *Act of Creation: The Founding of the United Nations* (Boulder, CO: Westview, 2003), p. 175.

5. Ibid., p. 176.

6. The Covenant of the League of Nations tellingly stipulated in Article 21 that "nothing . . . shall be deemed to affect the validity of international engagements, such as treaties of arbitration or regional understandings like the Monroe Doctrine, for securing the maintenance of peace." See League of Nations, *Covenant of the League of Nations* (April 28, 1919). See also Simma et al., *The Charter of the United Nations,* p. 813.

7. John Lewis Gaddis, *Strategies of Containment: A Critical Appraisal of Postwar American National Security Policy* (Oxford: Oxford University Press, 1982), pp. 152–154.

8. Defined as such following the publication of George Kennan, "The Sources of Soviet Conduct," *Foreign Affairs* 25, no. 4 (July 1947): 566–582.

9. United Nations Security Council, "Provisional Verbatim Record of the 299th and 300th Meetings," UN Doc. S/PV.299, May 21, 1948, pp. 14–15.

10. United Nations Security Council Resolution 49, S/RES/49 (May 22, 1948).

11. United Nations Security Council, "Cablegram Dated 19 June 1954 from the Minister of Foreign Affairs of Guatemala Addressed to the President of the Security Council," UN Doc. S/3232, June 19, 1954.

12. United Nations Security Council, "Provisional Verbatim Record of the 675th Meeting," UN Doc. S/PV.675, June 20, 1954, p. 13.

13. United Nations Security Council, "Provisional Verbatim Record of the 676th Meeting," UN Doc. S/PV.676, June 25, 1954, p. 30.

14. Ibid., pp. 14–15.

15. Ibid., p. 16.

16. United Nations Security Council, "Letter Dated 19 June 1954 from the Minister of Foreign Affairs of Guatemala Addressed to the President of the Security Council," UN Doc. S/3236, June 20, 1954.

17. United Nations Security Council, "Letter Dated 11 July 1960 from the Minister for Foreign Affairs of Cuba to the President of the Security Council," UN Doc. S/4378, July 11, 1960.

18. United Nations Security Council, "Provisional Verbatim Record of the 874th Meeting," UN Doc. S/PV.874, July 18, 1960, p. 2.

19. Ibid., p. 35.

20. Ibid., p. 39.

21. United Nations Security Council, "Argentina and Ecuador: Joint Draft Resolution," UN Doc. S/4392, July 18, 1960, adopted as Security Council Resolution 144, S/RES/144 (July 19, 1960). Adopted by a vote of nine for, none against, and two abstentions, by Poland and the Soviet Union.

22. United Nations Security Council, "Union of Soviet Socialist Republics: Draft Resolution," UN Doc. S/4481, September 7, 1960; United Nations Security Council, "Union of Soviet Socialist Republics: Revised Draft Resolution," UN Doc S/4481/Rev.1, September 8, 1960.

23. United Nations Security Council, "Resolution Adopted by the Security Council at Its 895th Meeting on 9 September 1960," UN Doc. S/4491, September 9, 1960, adopted as Security Council Resolution 156, S/RES/156 (September 9, 1960), with Poland and the Soviet Union abstaining.

24. United Nations Security Council, "Provisional Verbatim Record of the 991st Meeting," UN Doc. S/PV.991, February 27, 1962, p. 2.

25. Ibid., pp. 23, 28. Chile, China, France, Ireland, the United Kingdom, the United States, and Venezuela abstained, whereas Ghana, Romania, the Soviet Union, and the United Arab Republic (Egypt) voted in favor.

26. United Nations Security Council, "Provisional Verbatim Record of the 991st Meeting," pp. 12–13.

27. United Nations Security Council, "Union of Soviet Socialist Republics: Draft Resolution," UN Doc. S/6328, May 4, 1965.

28. Following its May 4, 1965, meeting on the situation in the Dominican Republic, the Council met only on Haiti (1427th meeting, on May 27, 1968).

29. Although the Security Council did not authorize the OAU peacekeeping force in Chad, in Resolution 504 it asked the Secretary-General to establish a fund to finance the peacekeeping force through voluntary contributions. Security Council Resolution 504, S/RES/504 (April 30, 1982).

30. United Nations Security Council Resolution 502, S/RES/502 (April 3, 1982).

31. United Nations Security Council, "Letter Dated 28 April 1982 from the President of the Twentieth Meeting of Consultation of Ministers of Foreign Affairs of the Organization of American States Addressed to the President of the Security Council," UN Doc. S/15008, April 28, 1982.

32. Domingo E. Acevedo, "The Right of Members of the Organization of American States to Refer Their 'Local' Disputes Directly to the United Nations Security Council," *American University International Law Review* 4, no. 1 (1989): 25–66.

33. United Nations Security Council Resolution 658, S/RES/658 (June 27, 1990).

34. United Nations Security Council Resolution 668, S/RES/668 (September 20, 1990).

35. United Nations Security Council Resolution 713, S/RES/713 (September 25, 1991).

36. United Nations Security Council, "Note by the President of the Security Council," UN Doc. S/22133, January 22, 1991.

37. United Nations Security Council, "Note by the President of the Security Council," UN Doc. S/23500, January 31, 1992. Statement issued following the summit-level meeting.

38. United Nations Secretary-General, *An Agenda for Peace: Preventive Diplomacy, Peacemaking, and Peacekeeping,* UN Doc. A/47/277-S/24111, June 17, 1992, p. 64.

39. The seven high-level meetings were held on August 1, 1994; February 15, 1996; July 28–29, 1998; February 6–7, 2001; July 29–30, 2003; July 25–26, 2005; and September 22, 2006. Whereas ten regional organizations attended the 1994 meeting, twenty participated in the 2005 meeting. See Security Council Report, "Update Report no. 3: The United Nations and Regional Organizations," March 23, 2007, www.securitycouncilreport.org/update-report/lookup-c-glKWLeMTIsG-b-207 1503.php?print=true.

40. United Nations Security Council Resolution 787, S/RES/787 (November 16, 1992), p. 12.

41. United Nations Security Council Resolution 816, S/RES/816 (March 31, 1993), p. 4.

42. United Nations Security Council Resolution 866, S/RES/866 (September 22, 1993). See also Herbert Howe, "Lessons of Liberia: ECOMOG and Regional Peacekeeping," *International Security* 21, no. 3 (Winter 1996–1997): 145–176.

43. Shepard Forman and Andrew Greene, "Collaborating with Regional Organizations," in *The UN Security Council: From the Cold War to the 21st Century,* edited by David M. Malone (Boulder, CO: Lynne Rienner, 2004), p. 297.

44. *Protocol Relating to the Establishment of the Peace and Security Council of the African Union,* First Ordinary Session of the Assembly of the AU, July 9, 2002.

45. United Nations Security Council, "Provisional Verbatim Record of the 4739th Meeting," UN Doc. S/PV/4739, April 11, 2003.

46. United Nations Security Council, "Statement by the President of the Security Council," UN Doc. S/PRST/2004/27, July 20, 2004.

47. United Nations High-Level Panel on Threats, Challenges, and Change, *A More Secure World: Our Shared Responsibility,* UN Doc. A/59/565, December 2, 2004.

48. United Nations Secretary-General, *In Larger Freedom: Towards Security, Development, and Human Rights for All,* UN Doc. A/59/2005, March 23, 2005.

49. United Nations General Assembly Resolution 60/1, A/RES/60/1 (October 24, 2005).

50. United Nations Security Council Resolution 1809, S/RES/1809 (April 16, 2008)\.

51. United Nations General Assembly and United Nations Security Council, *Report of the African Union–United Nations Panel on Modalities for Support to African Union Peacekeeping Operations,* UN Doc. A/63/666-S/2008/813, December 31, 2008.

52. African Union Peace and Security, "Communiqué of the 371st Meeting on the Situation in Mali," April 25, 2013, www.peaceau.org/en/article/communique-of -the-371st-psc-meeting-on-the-situation-in-mali.

53. The chapter mentions NATO only in passing, as Chapter 19 specifically deals with it.

54. Adekeye Adebajo, *UN Peacekeeping in Africa: From the Suez Crisis to the Sudan Conflicts* (Boulder, CO: Lynne Rienner, 2011), p. xiii.

55. David M. Malone, "The Security Council in the Post–Cold War Era: A Study in the Creative Interpretation of the UN Charter," *New York University Journal of International Law and Politics* 35, no. 2 (Winter 2003): 489.

24

Groups of Friends

Teresa Whitfield

INFORMAL GROUPS OF STATES KNOWN AS GROUPS OF FRIENDS have made important contributions to the work of the Security Council. Over the years, a range of activities extending from their direct involvement in peacemaking and crisis management to regular cooperation among Friends at the working level, have brought both substantive and procedural benefits to the work of the Council. Friends have also enhanced the legitimacy of Council action by privileging the engagement of nonmembers on issues in which they might have particular interest or expertise. However, positive impacts have not been uniform. Divisions within Groups of Friends have at times replicated the divide in the conflict concerned. Meanwhile even effective groups have been criticized by other members as contributing to the Council's lack of transparency and excluding others from the decisionmaking process.

I begin this chapter with a brief review of the history and evolution of Groups of Friends, and then address significant changes in the presence and influence of Groups of Friends in the work of the Council during the past decade. These can crudely be characterized by the continuing engagement of a few "old" Groups of Friends; the proliferation of "new" Groups of Friends and Contact Groups outside the Council for reasons that reflect evolving patterns of economic and political influence, an ever more crowded field of peacemaking actors, and deep divisions within the Council, especially since the cleavages that opened up as a consequence of the NATO intervention in Libya in 2011; and the significant role played by Friends of thematic issues in encouraging the Council's engagement with crosscutting questions, sometimes in the face of resistance from individual Council members.

A Brief History

As conflict resolution activity surged at the end of the Cold War, mediators and others developed a wide array of new arrangements. Prominent among them were informal mini-coalitions of states or intergovernmental organizations that provide support for resolving conflicts and implementing peace agreements, an innovation often referred to as Groups of Friends. Some of these groups have driven the work of the Security Council and supported the efforts of a UN Secretary-General or his representatives. Many more have not. Their formation reflected a number of different factors: the Security Council's limited membership; the optimism prevalent at the Cold War's end; the rise in peacemaking and the development of human rights norms—including the Responsibility to Protect—that followed in its wake; and the perceived benefits of a coordinated multilateral approach to issues that threaten international peace and security.

The first Group of Friends, of the Secretary-General, was formed in 1990 to support negotiations between the government of El Salvador and insurgents in the Farabundo Martí National Liberation Front (FMLN) mediated by the United Nations. Consisting of Colombia, Mexico, Spain, and Venezuela, it drew on earlier efforts to promote peace in Central America by the Contadora group of countries. As an example of collective support to UN peacemaking, it also echoed the Contact Groups that contributed to the peace processes in both Namibia and Cambodia. The Friends developed a relationship of "solidarity, even complicity" with the group's architect, the Secretary-General's personal representative, Alvaro de Soto.[1] He engaged regularly with their representatives in New York, San Salvador, and their capital cities, while the Friends, acting individually and collectively, offered encouragement, leverage, and concrete assistance to the parties. During implementation of the peace agreements signed in 1992, the Friends—now joined by the United States—also successfully managed the issue of El Salvador in the Security Council and General Assembly.

Success bred imitation. Between 1992 and 1995, Friends of the Secretary-General or individual peace processes were formed in Haiti, Georgia, Guatemala, Tajikistan, and Western Sahara, even as, outside the Security Council, policies toward the former Yugoslavia were driven by a Contact Group formed of the most interested external actors. The Groups of Friends were composed of a mix of permanent members of the Security Council and other states, and in general derived from Friends' direct diplomatic engagement in a particular issue and stated support of a UN lead. The Friends of the Guatemala Peace Process (Norway and the United States, in addition to the El Salvador configuration) were closely engaged with the negotiations that concluded in early 1996. In 1993, the four Friends of the Secretary-General for Haiti—Canada, France, the United States, and Venezuela—played a central role in persuading the Security Council to overcome its reluctance to engage in Haiti's internal affairs and restore the exiled president, Jean-Bertrand Aristide, to power—the opening chapter in the Council's long engagement in that country.

Elsewhere, the pronounced interests of the Friends contributed to a mixed trajectory. Conflicts were "managed" in the Security Council by the Friends, but several did not advance toward resolution. Negotiations within the Friends of Georgia between France, Germany, the United Kingdom, and the United States—the "Western Friends"—and Russia mirrored the conflict divide between Georgia and Abkhazia (and prefigured a similar split within the Balkans Contact Group between Russia and the western states of the "Quint" over Kosovo). A bottom-line support of the position of Morocco within the Friends of Western Sahara—especially pronounced in the case of France (other long-term members of this group include Russia, Spain, the United Kingdom, and the United States)—impeded forward progress toward the UN's stated goal of self-determination for the people of Western Sahara.

Efforts by the Secretary-General to corral or control the formation and behavior of Friends were not successful. In 1995, in his *Supplement to An Agenda for Peace,* Boutros Boutros-Ghali assumed a slightly hectoring tone in attempting to delineate "who is responsible for what": "The Secretary-General has the mandate from the relevant inter-governmental body and must remain in the lead. The members of the 'Friends' group have agreed to support the Secretary-General at his request. If they take initiatives not requested by the Secretary-General, there is a risk of duplication or overlapping of efforts, which can be exploited by recalcitrant parties."[2] But the UN's credibility was deeply battered by its travails in the Balkans and Rwanda, and the positive impetus that had characterized the immediate post–Cold War moment had already dissipated. Groups of Friends proliferated in an inherently disorganized fashion. The domination of those groups active within the Council met with increased resistance from elected members, who resented the imposition of draft resolutions on which they were given no opportunity to provide input. In February 1999 this led to the issue of a Council presidential note that acknowledged that contributions of Friends and of "other such mechanisms" were welcome, but that tartly observed that "the drafting of resolutions and statements by the President of the Council should be carried out in a manner that will allow adequate participation of all members of the Council."[3]

Due regard to this warning was evident in the conduct of the Core Group on East Timor formed later in that year, in some respects the last of the formal groups with origins analogous to the Friends of the Secretary-General for El Salvador. The group was composed of Australia, Japan, New Zealand, the United Kingdom, and the United States—permanent members of the Security Council and interested regional actors well placed to provide UN officials with the diplomatic and practical assistance required to hold a popular consultation on East Timor's future in August 1999. Core Group members, led by Australia, greatly facilitated the Security Council's prompt response to the postballot crisis that developed, and assumed a leading role in guiding action in the Security Council in the years that followed. Under the coordination of the United Kingdom, the group took pains to draft and coordinate texts for Council members with sufficient time for their proper consideration.

After a slump in activity in the late 1990s, the launch of large peace operations in both Kosovo and East Timor in 1999 opened a new period of activism within the Security Council. It was marked by both changes in the nature of conflicts addressed by the international community and the emergence of regional organizations, individual states, nongovernmental actors, and prominent individuals as active peacemakers. A natural shift away from peace processes in which the UN Secretary-General had a clear lead limited the creation of Groups of Friends of the Secretary-General (in the case of Cyprus, Secretary-General Kofi Annan referred positively to the support provided him by unspecified Friends;[4] a Group of Friends of the Secretary-General for Myanmar was established in late 2007, but never developed into an operational mechanism). In their stead, a wide variety of Groups of Friends, Contact Groups, Core Groups, and other such mechanisms mushroomed from four in 1990 to more than thirty by 2009, a more than sevenfold increase.[5]

Old Friends

In the new century, the role played by country-specific Friends in the work of the Security Council gradually shifted, as individual states asserted themselves on particular files and as divisions within the five permanent members assumed an increasingly significant influence. With the exception of Haiti—where the UN's departure in 2001 led to the demise of the old Friends of the Secretary-General for Haiti, the UN's return in 2004 after the outbreak of violence and abrupt removal of Aristide, and the formation of a new and distinct Group of Friends of Haiti—no new group of country-specific Friends assumed a prominent role within the Security Council. This fact did not diminish the influence wielded by the existing Friends, but it did suggest that the use of Friends would remain limited to situations of secondary importance to the permanent members on which the Council was able to act with a broad degree of consensus.

One group, the Friends of Georgia, fell victim to the implosion of a peace process whose structural faults had been evident for many years. The descent into a brief armed conflict between Georgia and Russia—the latter still nominally a "Friend" of Georgia—in August 2008, highlighted the hypocrisy of the internationally mediated settlement of the conflict advocated by the Friends and the Security Council even as their national allegiances undermined it. Secretariat officials struggled against the inherent bias of a process that was from the beginning restricted by the Security Council's commitment to upholding the territorial integrity of Georgia. They had tried to maintain impartiality between the two parties in negotiations, but as genuine friends of Georgia and the Abkhaz, respectively, the Western members of the Friends and Russia were unable to do the same. Protracted negotiations—especially of a document known as the Boden Paper (named for Dieter Boden, the SRSG from 1999 to 2002) that addressed the political status of Abkhazia—sought to find a proxy resolution of the conflict within the Friends, but were not successful. By 2008, the actions of both the Friends and the Security Council had strengthened both sides' expectations of the imposition of a settlement in their favor.

Like the Friends of Georgia, the Friends of Western Sahara retained a tight grip on Security Council management of the file, effectively coordinating the drafting of resolutions and other texts, but also dramatically failing to contribute to concrete advances. A core problem was that in neither the Georgia-Abkhazia nor the Western Sahara conflict did the situation on the ground—in both cases one of a ceasefire, refugees, and political acrimony between the parties—threaten the economic or security interests of members of the Group of Friends. In the case of Western Sahara, the Friends were divided on the central issue of self-determination of the Saharawi people, but driven, to varying degrees, by realpolitik. Bilateral relations with Morocco, of greater importance as counterterrorism became a priority after 2001, ensured strong support for Morocco's insistence that the question of Western Sahara could be resolved only in accordance with its sovereignty and territorial integrity—even as the entire UN process (in stark contrast to that which addressed the Georgian-Abkhaz conflict) was predicated on the basis that this sovereignty was contested.

The failings of the Friends, and with them the Council, were particular evident on the issue of human rights. Persistent reports and allegations of human rights violations in both Western Sahara and the Saharawi refugee camps near Tindouf in Algeria led to increasing demands for a human rights component to be included within the UN Mission for the Referendum in Western Sahara (MINURSO). Although this suggestion would have been unremarkable in another context, it prompted vehement opposition from Morocco, and was thus routinely opposed by France and not pushed with any conviction by other members of the Friends. This changed in April 2013 when, to the surprise of many watchers of Western Sahara, the United States presented the Friends with a draft resolution that would have provided MINURSO with a mandate to monitor and gather information on human rights violations. News of this draft was reported by a US-based human rights organization.[6] Morocco quickly mobilized against it, issuing credible threats that it would withdraw its cooperation from MINURSO and thus effectively bring the UN presence in Western Sahara to an end. The other Friends did little to support what was seen as a unilateral initiative, and the United States quickly capitulated. Security Council Resolution 2099, approved on April 25, 2013, followed earlier resolutions in mentioning human rights only in its preamble.

The Core Group on East Timor—or Timor-Leste, as the UN began referring to it after the country's independence in 2002—and the Friends of Haiti, formed in 2004, both had a more productive trajectory, despite the vicissitudes in each country's progression toward the consolidation of a stable peace. The Core Group gradually expanded to include Brazil, France, Malaysia, Portugal, and South Africa, in addition to its original five members. It provided sustained support to the transition in Timor-Leste, albeit one marked by a series of differences within the Core Group and with the Secretariat over the scale of the UN presence required. Some members of the Core Group—with Australia and the United States foremost among them—favored a more rapid drawdown than the Secretariat, at least from early 2003, believed was warranted. Differences again emerged in 2005; however, they were overtaken by the eruption of violence in mid-2006. The Core Group supported the Secretary-General's recommendations for a robust presence to assist Timor-Leste in overcoming the failings in its security sector and preparing for elections in 2007, and would provide effective accompaniment and oversight of the UN Integrated Mission in Timor-Leste (UNMIT) until its conclusion in 2012.

The UN's return to Haiti in 2004 was shaped by the long engagement in the country of the Organization of American States (OAS) and the direct involvement of Latin American states. During the years of UN absence, the OAS had maintained a small special mission in Haiti, which had been supported by a Group of Friends of the Secretary-General of the OAS formed on the initiative of Canada. As Haiti descended into crisis in early 2004, the United States and France reconstituted the UN's Friends of Haiti, deciding that its composition "was and is the United States, France, Canada and the Latin Americans on the Security Council" (Brazil and Chile at the time).[7] The Friends ensured that the Security Council did nothing until Aristide had left the country, but then proposed the immediate deployment of a multinational force. The UN Stabilization Mission in Haiti (MINUSTAH), established later in 2004, was supported in Port-au-Prince by a Core Group composed of a mix of states, the OAS, the Caribbean Community (CARICOM), and the international financial organizations, while the Friends of Haiti continued to drive decisionmaking in the Security Council. In marked contrast to earlier UN missions in Haiti, this time around it was not the United States, France, and Canada that were the troop contributors, but Latin American countries including Chile, Argentina, Uruguay, Peru, and Ecuador, operating under Brazil's lead.

Membership of the Friends, while consistently including Argentina, Brazil, and Chile, was monitored by Canada, the group's coordinator, and reflected both the presence of Latin American states on the Council and their contribution to MINUSTAH. (An unwritten rule that kept Panama, a Council member from 2007 to 2008, out of the Friends as a noncontributor to MINUSTAH, was relaxed to allow Mexico, Colombia, and Costa Rica to join the Friends during their Council membership; Uruguay, a substantial troop contributor, but not a Council member, petitioned for three years before being allowed to join the Friends.) The composition of the Friends contributed to a tight correlation between the political and other concerns of the largest troop contributors to MINUSTAH and discussions in the Security Council. As one Latin American member of the Friends explained in 2013, an inner group of Latin states coordinated positions prior to consultation with Canada, France, and the United States.[8] As in Timor-Leste, differences developed both within the Friends and between the Friends and other members of the Council over issues such as the pace of scaling up or down the presence of MINUSTAH. After Haiti's devastating earthquake in 2010, Mexico and Brazil pushed strongly for the mandate to be updated and the UN police presence enhanced. During 2012, as the Council began to wonder about the longer-term perspective for the UN presence in Haiti, the Friends pushed back against pressures for what many of them saw as precipitous reductions in the UN presence. However, such differences were over the means rather than the ends of international involvement in Haiti; no one disputed that the quality of their debate was greatly assisted by the involvement of the Friends.

New Friends

A key contribution of Groups of Friends—evident for both Timor-Leste and Haiti—was the possibility they offered for engagement in the work of the Security Council by interested and knowledgeable states other than the Council's members. This benefit was recognized in a document summarizing discussions on Security Council working methods that was circulated as the annex to a Council presidential note in July 2006. Members of the Security Council, it was observed, would continue to consult with the broader UN membership and interested states, "including countries directly involved or specifically affected, neighboring States and countries with particular contributions to make, as well as with regional organizations and Groups of Friends, when drafting, *inter alia,* resolutions, presidential statements and press statements, as appropriate."[9]

The observation reflected a decrease in tension within the Security Council regarding the role played by different Groups of Friends, but also their diminishing profile, as individual states, especially permanent members, asserted themselves as penholders of draft resolutions and other Security Council texts. By 2013, as Security Council Report noted, "in most, but not all cases," penholders were permanent members.[10] At the same time, on issues of the highest concern to the major powers—most notably with regard to the Middle East—diplomacy was conducted by ad hoc coalitions outside the Security Council: the Quartet on the Middle East Peace Process of the European Union, the United States and Russia, and the five permanent members plus Germany (the P5+1) on Iran. These formations were more closely related to the Contact Group on the former Yugoslavia than to Groups of Friends; their heavyweight composition ensured little direct interaction with the Security Council, even as the processes with which they were engaged had obvious influence on the Council's responsibilities.

Meanwhile on issues of secondary international importance, Groups of Friends had become one among a number of actors and configurations engaging with members of the Security Council. The diffusion of power and influence—most obviously attributable to the burgeoning economic and political strength of the BRICS powers of Brazil, Russia, India, China, and South Africa, but also the rise of states such as Indonesia, Mexico, Nigeria, and Turkey—and the increased involvement in crisis response and peacemaking by regional and subregional organizations, individual states, and nongovernmental actors, shaped a new international environment. This complicated the creation of Groups of Friends in the form of small and exclusive groups of states, but encouraged both the proliferation and the diversity of other mechanisms.

A number of groups directly supporting peacemaking or the implementation of an agreement (such as the Committee in Support of the Transition [CIAT] in the Democratic Republic of the Congo, or the Contact Group in Sudan) were located in the field and did not engage in the procedural business of the Security Council. International Contact Groups, including that formed in the early 2000s to address Liberia and the Mano River Union, the group on Somalia established in 2006, or that on Guinea-Conakry established in 2009, similarly did not interact directly with the Council, even when—as in these cases—their efforts aligned with and reinforced its goals. Like the Friends of Yemen, formed in 2010 to support that country's political transition, these groups provided a venue for the coordination of international attention and assistance in which individual states, regional organizations, and international financial institutions could all participate as appropriate.

Other groups engaged on issues that were never likely to be addressed by the Security Council either because they supported peacemaking for which no Council involvement was required, or as a consequence of sensitivities to national sovereignty. As in the case of the earlier groups, the existence of a group offered no guarantee of positive results, or even a collaborative process. The Friends of Pakistan, established in 2008, contributed little other than a forum for discussion. The International Contact Group on Madagascar, created in 2009 to address the crisis precipitated by the coup in Antananarivo, notably failed to reconcile the divergent approaches to restoring constitutional order pursued by the African Union, the Southern African Development Community, and the UN. The International Contact Group established to support the peace process in the Southern Philippines, on the other hand, used its innovative membership of states and nongovernmental organizations to provide hands-on support to the government of the Philippines and the Moro Islamic Liberation Front (MILF) and the Malaysian facilitator as they worked toward a framework peace accord agreed in October 2012 and the final peace agreement reached in January 2014.

Despite the mixed path of many groups, the practical experience of cooperation within and around the Security Council in situations that did not touch upon the major powers' core strategic interests reinforced the use of some kind of collective diplomatic mechanism even in those—like the conflicts in Libya and Syria that developed from 2011—that did. In both of these cases, divisions within the Security Council, as well as debate over the relative responsibilities of the UN and regional organizations in legitimizing crisis response, made the formation of Council-specific Groups of Friends impossible. On the contrary, the polemics surrounding, in the first instance, Security Council action on Libya, and in the second instance its inaction on Syria, contributed to the creation of group structures—a Contact Group and then a large Group of Friends of Libya, and a Group of Friends and then an Action Group on Syria—outside the Council. In different ways, both tested and vindicated the utility of multilateral crisis diplomacy and the resilience of the Security Council.[11]

The divisions in the Security Council over the interpretation by Western powers—with the critical backing of the Arab League—of Resolution 1973's authorization of "all necessary measures" to protect civilians as the pursuit of regime change, invalidated the Security Council as the locus for discussion of international policies toward the Libyan war. The focus passed instead to a Contact Group that emerged from the London Conference, held in late March 2011 as the NATO air campaign took hold. The group was conceived as a mechanism to give political guidance to the NATO action and thus initially reinforced tensions around the Libyan intervention. The AU remained outside the group for some months, while the West's exclusion of the BRICS countries (all of which were members of the Security Council in 2011) increased the disconnect between NATO's use of force and the search for a political solution favored by the AU and non-Western states. In mid-July the Contact Group formally recognized the Transitional National Council (TNC) as the legitimate representative of the

Libyan people more than a month before the opposition forces entered Tripoli. In the following period, disagreements within the international community dissipated, although not without leaving their scars, notably on attitudes toward the possibility of international intervention in Syria. A broad-based Friends of Libya forum, cochaired by the interim government of Libya and the United Nations, was established in September 2011 to coordinate international assistance as discussion of Libya's transition returned to the Security Council.

The large Group of Friends of Syria, formed in early 2012 on the initiative of the United States, had a particular problem of nomenclature. It was variously referred to as the "Friends of Democratic Syria" and the "Friends of the Syrian People" in an effort to dodge the obvious point that the group was anything but friendly toward the Syria of Bashar al-Assad. However, it could do nothing to overcome Russia's and China's refusal to join it on the grounds that it was committed to providing support to the opposition and regime change. It was with a nod to the group's limitations, as well as the incapacity of the Security Council to take action on Syria, that in mid-2012 Kofi Annan, the joint special envoy of the United Nations and the Arab League, created a high-level "Action Group" consisting of the secretaries-general of the UN and Arab League, the foreign ministers of the permanent members of the Security Council, Turkey, Iraq, Kuwait, Qatar, and the EU high representative for foreign and security policy.

The Action Group met in Geneva and on June 30, 2012, reached agreement on a six-point plan that would lead to elections via a transitional government and thus end the violence. This Geneva communiqué appeared a significant achievement for multilateral diplomacy. However, inaction—not action—soon set in, as forward movement was stymied by disagreements over a role for Assad in any future government. The following year brought a tragic escalation of violence in Syria and failure of all diplomatic efforts to address it. In May 2013 an apparent breakthrough in bilateral talks between Russia and the United States raised hopes of a return to a diplomatic process in Geneva. Once more, this was to be led by the Action Group. However, in the slow process toward the opening of new talks, the number of interested states swelled far beyond the members of the original Action Group. When the process known as "Geneva II" eventually convened in Montreux, Switzerland, in January 2014, more than forty states were present. But two rounds of talks produced no tangible results, and the Syrian conflict continued.

Thematic Friends

Thematic groups of some kind had been active at least since the late 1990s (one of the most durable was the Group of Friends of Conflict Prevention).

They are formed to address the contextual concerns of member states (Morocco hosted the first meeting of a Group of Friends on Counter-Terrorism in March 2015) and serve as issue-specific discussion groups and at times advocacy groups within the broader framework of the General Assembly. However, most had little or no impact on the work of the Security Council, even when, as in the case of the Group of Friends of the Responsibility to Protect, or the Friends of Mediation, formed in 2010, they addressed issues that could be considered to be core Council responsibilities.

Quite different in their functional role were the Groups of Friends that developed around the thematic issues that the Security Council addressed with increasing seriousness in the years following its adoption of its first presidential statement on children and armed conflict in June 1998. This was followed in 1999 by its first resolution on the subject, Resolution 1261, and also Resolution 1265, on the protection of civilians; and in 2000 by the groundbreaking Resolution 1325, on women, peace, and security. To different extents, the fact that the Council adopted these resolutions at all—in the face of considerable skepticism of some permanent members regarding the desirability of the Council's attention to thematic issues, and concern among some G-77 states regarding the imposition of a liberal Western agenda they believed these resolutions represented—could be attributed to the advocacy of coalitions of interested member states and nongovernmental actors. In the following years, the former would coalesce into Groups of Friends of each of the thematic issues. As such, they came to fulfill a role as forums of advocacy and expertise, able to exert direct influence upon Council action, while providing a useful interface between the preoccupations of Council members and other states.

Council attention to these three thematic issues advanced at different paces. It was susceptible to tension regarding the reach of thematic concerns—essentially whether they were applicable only to the country-specific issues already on the agenda of the Security Council or had universal application—but in each case continued to reflect the partnership between Council members and the advocacy community outside it, including the Friends. One factor that contributed to the efficacy of these three groups was that the issues themselves were priorities in the national policy of the groups' coordinators—Canada in the case of children and armed conflict and women, peace, and security, and Norway and then Switzerland in that of protection of civilians. (In this respect the groups differed from the less active Friends of Security Sector Reform and the Friends of Rule of Law, convened by Slovakia and Austria respectively.) Under their leadership, the groups moved forward, pushing for attention to crosscutting issues of children and armed conflict, gender, and protection of civilians in country-specific mandates, but also for concrete action to further the Security Council's stated goals in these areas.

The Group of Friends of Women, Peace, and Security developed naturally out of the long campaign for the adoption of Resolution 1325 pursued by women's advocates within the UN system, interested member states, and a network of women's and human rights NGOs, many of which were gathered into the NGO Working Group for Women, Peace, and Security (NGOWG). Soon after the resolution's adoption, the states coalesced into a Group of Friends under the coordination of Canada. Although anchored in the states that had most actively promoted the women, peace, and security agenda—Bangladesh, Namibia, the Netherlands, the Nordic countries, and the United Kingdom, in addition to Canada—the group grew to a total of forty-five states by 2013, comprising the P3 (United States, France, and the UK) and a cross-regional mix of other states.

For many years, however, progress in implementation of the broad sweep of provisions contained in Resolution 1325 proved elusive. There was much discussion around the introduction of national action plans and the representation of women, but little concrete "unpacking" of Resolution 1325. This changed in 2008 when, after a big push from the UN Development Fund for Women (UNIFEM), the Friends, and the NGOWG, the Council moved to narrow down the discussion to sexual violence in armed conflict and approved Resolution 1820, quickly followed by the Council's creation, in Resolution 1888, of a dedicated special representative on sexual violence in conflict. During 2013 a similar coalition pushed hard for return of attention to the participation of women in peace processes, in an effort that culminated in the Council's adoption that October of the far-reaching Resolution 2122.

The Friends of Children and Armed Conflict had a somewhat different origin, and a trajectory marked by the relative speed with which the Security Council created structures to implement its mandated activities—a monitoring and reporting mechanism and a Security Council working group were both established in 2005 by Resolution 1612, following the active lobbying by the Group of Friends formed earlier that year. The Friends had grown out of an earlier group of donors that had been created to provide support (and a degree of informal oversight) to the first special representative for children and armed conflict, Olara Otunnu. Canada took steps to broaden the group's membership (to thirty-eight by 2013) to include an appropriate regional mix. By 2013 the group still did not include permanent members of the Security Council; nor had the Friends quite overcome the perception by some in the South, especially African states, that the group pursued an agenda on children and armed conflict that was inherently biased against them. This Group of Friends also differed in important functional respects from the Friends of Women, Peace and Security. It was both less open to the nongovernmental advocacy community, and closely engaged with the Security Council working group. During 2011, for example, the Friends provided close support to Germany, president of the working group at the time, in its successful effort to introduce attacks on schools and hospitals as a new trigger for listing parties in the annexes of reports by the Secretary-General.

Much smaller than either of these groups was the fifteen-member Friends of the Protection of Civilians, which first met informally under the chairmanship of Norway—with the active support of Canada—and later came to be chaired by Switzerland. With a primarily European membership—Australia, Brazil, and Uruguay being the only exceptions—the Friends worked closely with the UN's Office for the Coordination of Humanitarian Affairs (OCHA). The group's role, however, was somewhat limited by its narrowly defined membership, by the establishment of an informal expert group on protection of civilians within the Council in early 2009, and by the concern on the part of the P5—the UK was the penholder on the file—that the protection agenda should not get out of hand. Sensitivities were increased by the legacy of the controversy over the protection mandate in Libya during 2011, and implementation of the normative agenda flagged. It was, nevertheless, established practice to hold two open Council debates a year on the protection of civilians as a thematic issue, even as an increasing number of UN peace operations included protection within their mandates (nine by December 2013).[12] During 2013, the challenge this represented was increased by the crises in Syria, the Central African Republic, and South Sudan, prompting new attention to the need to invigorate the role of the Friends, including, perhaps, by its expansion.

Beyond their structural differences, the thematic Groups of Friends shared a number of working practices. They held regular meetings convened by the coordinator, prepared joint statements for open debates of the Security Council, and delivered messages to permanent representatives at key moments of negotiations. They also represented important allies for the Secretariat officials charged with the implementation of Security Council resolutions, sometimes in the face of considerable political opposition. During 2011 and 2012, in the context of a particularly difficult environment within the Council, the Friends helped provide "pushback" to a number of states, including Azerbaijan, Colombia, India, Pakistan, and Russia, which were increasingly sensitive to the possibility that thematic issues may be subject to "mandate creep."[13]

Conclusion

The evolution of the roles played by Groups of Friends in the past three decades suggests that, moving forward, the contribution of Friends to the country-specific work of the Council may remain relatively modest, while the role to be played by related diplomatic mechanisms for crisis management and to support peace consolidation—outside the Security Council but also engaging closely with it—is potentially very significant. Beyond these two points, the thematic Friends that have come to the fore in recent years are at the frontline of an area of Security Council work of particularly interesting normative evolution.

Together these developments illustrate both the extent to which the idea of ad hoc coalitions of states and other actors has become normalized as a necessary corollary to the outmoded composition of the Security Council, and their utility for the future. Crisis- or issue-specific formations of states have evolved far from the original models of the Contact Group on Namibia or the Friends of the Secretary-General pioneered in El Salvador. Messy and imperfect as many of them might appear, they have nevertheless emerged as a necessary and important element within the international security architecture. Members of such groups do not necessarily have to share a strategic vision or goals, although forward movement will depend on their being "like-minded enough" to pursue a peaceful outcome over continuing violence. At moments of profound difference, informal but focused mechanisms offer their members the possibility of exploring some minimum degree of common ground, and maintaining communication even when the particular dynamics of the Security Council render this untenable. As such, the groups offer an important complementarity to the Security Council, while leaving open the possibility that it is to the Security Council they will return when the path ahead is clearer.

Notes

This chapter draws on my book *Friends Indeed? The United Nations, Groups of Friends, and the Resolution of Conflict* (Washington, DC: US Institute of Peace, 2007), as well as on subsequent research.

1. Alvaro de Soto, "Ending Violent Conflict in El Salvador," in *Herding Cats: Multiparty Mediation in a Complex World,* edited by Chester A. Crocker, Fen Osler Hampson, and Pamela Aall (Washington, DC: US Institute of Peace, 1999), p. 368.

2. United Nations Secretary-General, *Supplement to* An Agenda for Peace, UN Doc. A/50/60-S/1995/1, January 3, 1995, paras. 83–84.

3. United Nations Security Council, "Note by the President of the Security Council," UN Doc. S/1999/165, February 17, 1999.

4. United Nations Security Council, *Report of the Secretary-General on His Mission of Good Offices in Cyprus,* UN Doc. S/2003/398, April 1, 2003, para. 149.

5. Teresa Whitfield, *Working with Groups of Friends,* Peacemaker's Toolkit Series (Washington, DC: US Institute of Peace, 2010), pp. 27–32, tab. 1, "Major Groups of Friends and Related Mechanisms, 1990–2009."

6. Robert F. Kennedy Center for Justice and Human Rights, "U.S. Announces Ground-Breaking Draft Resolution for Human Rights," April 12, 2013, www.defenseforumfoundation.org/western-sahara/148-u-s-announces-groundbreaking-draft-resolution-for-human-rights.html. See also Security Council Report, "Western Sahara Mission Mandate Renewal," *What's in Blue,* April 24, 2013, www.whatsinblue.org /2013/04/western-sahara-mission-mandate-renewal.php.

7. Interview, New York, September 2004, cited in Whitfield, *Friends Indeed?* p. 126.

8. Interview, New York, May 2013.

9. United Nations Security Council, "Note by the President of the Security Council," UN Doc. S/2006/507, July 19, 2006.

10. Security Council Report, "Subsidiary Chairs and Pen Holders for 2013," February 2013 Monthly Forecast, January 31, 2013, www.securitycouncilreport.org /monthly-forecast/2013-02/subsidiary_chairs_and_pen_holders_for_2013.php.

11. This discussion draws on Richard Gowan and Emily O'Brien, *The Use of Force, Crisis Diplomacy, and the Responsibilities of States* (New York: Center on International Cooperation, May 2012), especially the "Reflection Paper," pp. 3–9.

12. Security Council Report, "Protection of Civilians in Armed Conflict," in *Cross-Cutting Report: Protection of Civilians in Armed Conflict* (New York, 2013), pp. 36–38, www.securitycouncilreport.org/cross-cutting-report/protection-of-civilians -in-armed-conflict.php.

13. On these issues, see the sections on "Council Dynamics" in Security Council Report's *Cross-Cutting Report: On Children and Armed Conflict* (New York, 2012), p. 30, and *Cross-Cutting Report: Women, Peace, and Security—Sexual Violence in Conflict and Sanctions* (New York, 2013), p. 30.

25

International Courts and Tribunals

Eran Sthoeger

BY THE TIME THE COLD WAR CAME TO A CLOSE, FEW COULD
have predicted the central normative and institutional role of international
criminal courts and tribunals both in international relations and within the
international legal system. And even fewer would have foreseen the important role the Security Council would play in advancing international criminal justice, by establishing ad hoc tribunals and referring cases to a permanent international criminal court.[1]

When the Security Council established the International Criminal Tribunal for the Former Yugoslavia (ICTY) in 1993, the first international tribunal since the Nuremberg and Tokyo tribunals following World War II,
and, the following year, the International Criminal Tribunal for Rwanda
(ICTR), much criticism arose. At the time, some took the view that by
establishing a criminal court, the Council had exceeded its powers under
Article 41 of the UN Charter to take measures not involving the use of
armed force,[2] a view that seems obsolete today. More important, the tribunals were seen as a poor substitute for the Council's failure to prevent or
effectively stop the atrocities in the former Yugoslavia and Rwanda. The
latter criticism is entirely justified, as the ICTY did not contribute to the
end of hostilities or the accompanying atrocities in the former Yugoslavia,
and the ICTR was established after the genocide in Rwanda had ended. Yet
the establishment of the criminal tribunals has proved one of the most
groundbreaking steps taken by the Council, highlighting the relevance of
criminal justice and individual accountability to the maintenance of international peace and security. As will be seen, both tribunals have been fairly
successful in holding accountable those responsible for war crimes, crimes
against humanity, and genocide.

The Council continued to partake in the creation of judicial institutions: in Resolution 1315 (2000), the Council requested the Secretary-General to negotiate an agreement with Sierra Leone on the establishment of a Special Court for Sierra Leone (SCSL) to try those bearing the greatest responsibility for crimes against humanity and war crimes committed in the country. In Resolution 1757 (2007), the Council established the Special Tribunal for Lebanon (STL). Since the entry into force of the Rome Statute of the International Criminal Court (ICC) in 2002, the Council has twice acted in accordance with its powers under Article 13 of the statute and referred the situations in Darfur (Resolution 1593 in 2005) and in Libya (Resolution 1970 in 2011) to the ICC.

In this chapter I focus on the dynamics and relationship between the Council and the international courts that possess institutional ties to it. As will be seen, these relations touch upon common tensions. One is the enduring question of peace versus justice. Another is the tensions that rise from political institutional backing of judicial processes, meant to be free of political consideration. These tensions are all the more visible when a political body creates a judicial institution in order to advance the former's agenda. A final tension is the inevitable temporal disparity between fast-moving political developments and their solution, and the much slower pace of judicial institutions.

The International Court of Justice

Certain elements of the Council's responsibility that touch upon international justice predate the Council's interest in international criminal institutions. While the UN Charter accorded the Security Council primary responsibility for the maintenance of international peace and security, it also envisioned certain interaction between the Council and the principal judicial organ of the UN, the International Court of Justice (ICJ).[3] The UN Charter envisioned a symbiotic relationship between the Security Council and the "World Court." Under Chapter VI, the Council, when recommending a specific method of dispute settlement, is supposed to bear in mind that legal disputes should generally be referred to the ICJ.[4] The only example of the Council recommending two parties to settle their dispute before the Court was on April 9, 1947,[5] when it recommended that Albania and the UK immediately refer their dispute in relation to the Corfu Channel incident.

The Council is also to assist in the enforcement of judgments of the ICJ, in cases of noncompliance brought before it by one of the parties, though it has yet to make use of this power to date.[6] On October 17, 1986, Nicaragua sent the president of the Council a letter invoking Article 94 regarding US noncompliance with the ICJ's judgment in the *Military and*

Paramilitary Activities case.[7] A draft resolution calling for "full and immediate compliance" with the judgment was vetoed by the United States,[8] demonstrating the futility of the procedure in the case of judgments against any of the five permanent Council members.

Finally, Article 96 authorizes the Council to request that the ICJ give an advisory opinion on any legal question. The Council has requested one such opinion to date, in 1970 on the legal consequences of the South African presence in Namibia.[9]

The Council and the General Assembly elect the judges of the ICJ in a procedure that requires the two organs to reach agreement independently of each other. Though not required by the Court's statute, in practice the P5 all have judges on the Court. As the Council has not made much use of the provisions of the Charter enumerated earlier, the relations between the ICJ and the Council revolve on the most part around the election of judges.

International Criminal Tribunals

Among the most innovative measures ever taken by the Security Council was the establishment of the ICTY and ICTR in 1993 and 1994 respectively. Two decades later, with the tribunals winding down their activities, debates over their successes and failures will inevitably follow, as will questions of their effectiveness and their legacy.

If one considers the prosecution of high-level individuals, who bear the greatest responsibility for the perpetration of mass atrocities, as an indicator of effectiveness, both tribunals have a respectable track record. As of January 1, 2014, the ICTY had concluded proceedings against 136 individuals, with trials of twenty-five indictees still ongoing. Over time, all of those against whom arrest warrants were issued were brought before the tribunal, including high-profile individuals such as the former president of Serbia, Slobodan Milosevic (who died of a heart attack while detained in The Hague); and the political leader of the Republica Srpska, Radovan Karadzic, and its chief military officer, Ratko Mladic (both on trial at the time of this writing). As of December 2014, the ICTR had completed cases against all ninety-three indicted individuals, one of which (against six individuals) was pending appeal. Nine indicted individuals were still at large.[10]

Establishment of the Tribunals

As news of the horrendous acts taking place in the former Yugoslavia spread, and with mounting pressure to intervene, the Council's first step was to call on the Secretary-General to establish a commission of experts to investigate accounts of violations of international humanitarian law and fundamental human rights. Upon the commission's recommendation and based on a report of the Secretary-General, the Council established the

ICTY on May 25, 1993, in Resolution 827, with its statute set out in the Secretary-General's report. The driving force behind the swift move to establish the ICTY was the United States, amid criticism of the international community's inability to bring the conflict and the atrocities to an end.

With war in the Balkans still raging, violence against Tutsis erupted in Rwanda on April 6, 1994, when President Juvénal Habyarimana's plane was shot down. Hundreds of thousands had been slaughtered by Hutus by the time the Tutsi-led Rwandan Patriotic Front (RPF) seized Kigali on July 4. Subsequent retaliations against Hutus by Tutsis forced the former to flee the country in mass numbers. As in the former Yugoslavia, the Council was unable to stop the atrocities as they happened, and may have even made things worse by downscaling the UN presence on the ground despite the Secretary-General's observation that "this situation could only be changed by the immediate and massive reinforcement of UNAMIR [UN Assistance Mission for Rwanda] and a change in its mandate so that it would be equipped and authorized to coerce the opposing forces into a ceasefire, and to attempt to restore law and order and put an end to the killings."[11]

In a pattern that resembled the establishment of the ICTY, a commission was set up, which recommended the establishment of an international tribunal, to make up for inaction on the preventive side. The RPF itself requested the Council to establish a criminal tribunal, but only with jurisdiction over acts committed in the course of the genocide and not for the retaliatory violence that followed. On November 8, 1994, the Council adopted Resolution 955, establishing the ICTR to adjudicate crimes committed in Rwanda and against Rwandan nationals in 1994 (i.e., including events that occurred in the aftermath of the genocide). Rwanda, at the time an elected member of the Council, voted against the resolution, objecting to the exclusion from jurisdiction of events prior to 1994,[12] the absence of the death penalty, and the tribunal's seat outside of the country. While temporal jurisdiction of the ICTR potentially covers acts both before and after the genocide proper, the prosecution has refrained from indicting members of the Rwandan Defense Forces, for which it has been heavily criticized by NGOs.

Relationship Between the Security Council and the Ad Hoc Tribunals

The statutes of the ICTY and ICTR covered war crimes, crimes against humanity, and genocide. Both tribunals were bestowed with considerable powers: they were to have primacy over national courts, with concurrent jurisdiction over the crimes in question. States themselves were obligated to cooperate with the tribunals, potentially opening the door for Council enforcement measures in case of failure of states to produce indictees or evidence. The tribunal's statutes also gave the Council oversight on the quality of judges, who are elected by the General Assembly from a list submitted to it by the Council.

Not long after the establishment of the ICTY, the Council realized the difficulties that could arise in relation to an international criminal tribunal, and the tension between professional-judicial considerations and political ones. One of the first points of contention was the appointment of the prosecutor. Apparently the pool of candidates with the requisite experience as criminal prosecutors willing to accept the position was fairly small. The Council's appointment of Ramón Escovar-Salom of Venezuela remained a dead letter (he preferred to take a domestic ministerial position), and thus the first prosecutor to accept the position was appointed on July 8, 1994 (Resolution 936), more than a year after the establishment of the ICTY. The fact that the position of the prosecutor was first shared between the two tribunals created further difficulties. While such a cost-effective decision may have been justified at the very beginning, it proved problematic as the workload of the tribunals intensified. The negative effects were felt in particular in the ICTR, as prosecutors were based in The Hague and spent little time in Arusha. Voices in Africa were also critical of the fact that Rwandans would be answerable to a non-African prosecutor. It was not until August 2003 that the Council finally created two separate prosecutor positions, appointing Hassan Bubacar Jallow of Gambia as ICTR prosecutor.

The tribunals themselves were slow to get off the ground. Few cases were initiated at first, only against "low-level" culprits, and there was general lack of cooperation in the execution of arrest warrants. In the Balkans, where conflict was ongoing, there was an additional fear that warrants against "high-profile" individuals would undermine political processes to end the conflict. Starting in 1997, however, NATO forces became increasingly active in executing arrest warrants, coming to the conclusion that it was the continued presence of indicted individuals on the ground that was preventing the stabilization of the former Yugoslavia.

The Council was reluctant to use its powers or even forceful language to follow up on warrants or take serious action against noncooperating states, their Chapter VII obligations notwithstanding. It wasn't that allegations of noncooperation were not frequently laid at the Council's doorstep. For example, the ICTY president sent the Council three letters in the fall of 1998 informing the Council that the Federal Republic of Yugoslavia refused to issue visas for investigators to enter Kosovo or to apprehend fugitives within its territory. The president tried to convince Council members that noncompliance of the former Republic of Yugoslavia with the tribunal was "an affront to the Security Council and to all law-abiding nations," arguing that it was the Council's responsibility "to bring noncooperating States into compliance" and to "provide the support necessary to enable the Tribunal to discharge its mandate."[13] The Council, in response, reiterated the obligation of states to assist the tribunal and demanded that the former Republic of Yugoslavia comply with the arrest warrants, in Resolution 1207 of November 17, 1998. Over the next few years the Council was informed time and again of noncompliance of the former Republic of Yugoslavia with the ICTY and Resolution 1207, but did not pursue the matter any further.

The work of the ICTR commenced just as slowly, amid tensions between Rwanda and the tribunal that were brought to the attention of the Council, including complaints of Rwandan noncooperation with proceedings against RPF members. Complaints were also lodged against other states suspected of harboring fugitives. For example, on June 18, 2010, both the ICTR president and the ICTR prosecutor informed the Council of Kenya's lack of cooperation with the office of the prosecutor regarding fugitives allegedly in its territory.[14] As with the ICTY, the Council took a rather passive approach and did not make use of its powers to ensure cooperation with the ICTR.

Costs and Completion Strategy

Though independent judicial bodies, the tribunals are subsidiary organs of the Council, and over the years the Council has been called upon to attend to issues such as amending their statutes. A Council working group on international criminal tribunals was formed in June 2000 to discuss a specific issue relating to the ICTY statute, and later became a venue for private Council discussions regarding the tribunals. A difference in the intensity was noticed when the Council, weary of the costs of the tribunals and their protracted existence, initiated a completion strategy for their work in 2002. The Council since has been receiving biannual reports on the implementation of the strategy.

An important step of the completion strategy was the establishment, in 2010, of the International Residual Mechanism for Criminal Tribunals, with one "branch" for each of the two tribunals and a roster of judges to adjudicate as needed.[15] The mechanism is to perform the functions of the tribunals. In the short term, these include securing the arrest, transfer, and prosecution of the nine remaining fugitives still wanted for trial by the ICTR, and attending to the expected appeals in several cases. More permanent responsibilities include the maintenance of archives, protection of witnesses, and supervision of sentences.

When the tribunals were established, Council members probably did not anticipate that their operation would continue into a third decade. But political concerns change much faster than extended trials and appeals. With the Council no longer preoccupied with conflict in Rwanda or the Balkans, it became more and more concerned with the financial burden imposed by the tribunals than with their successful conclusion. Although the Council could have helped increase the effectiveness of the tribunals, it learned that it had little influence over their timetables. It thus had no choice but to extend judges' terms upon the requests of the tribunals, albeit with the occasional threat to refrain from doing so, and despite frustration over the dragging out of cases. And on occasion, politics further complicated the dynamics. For example, during a debate on the tribunals on December 5, 2012,[16] Russia expressed its dismay with the acquittal and release of two Croatian generals by the ICTY's appeals chamber. Russia, often vocal against what it perceives as an unjustified ICTY focus on Serbian perpetrators, tied this political criticism to its consideration of a pending request from the ICTY for an extension of judges' terms attached to a notification from the tribunal that it would not be able to end its proceedings by 2014. Russia commented on the appeal decision that "such actions of the ICTY only generate mutual distrust among peoples across the former Yugoslavia. In that situation, a legitimate question arises: how to deal with the ongoing requests of the ICTY for indefinite extensions of the terms of its judges?" While the relationship between the content of the ICTY's judgments and its extended existence is highly questionable, the Council's role in authorizing the latter allowed Russia to express its dismay over the former. Later that month Russia postponed an adoption of a resolution to extend the judges' terms, insisting on an independent analysis of the "legal and administrative activities of the ICTY." Resolution 2081, adopted on December 17, 2012, requested the ICTY itself to produce a comprehensive plan on the completion strategy, but extended the judges' terms. Russia abstained in the vote.

The Special Tribunal for Lebanon

Establishment of the Tribunal

The only other tribunal of an international character established by the Security Council is the Special Tribunal for Lebanon. On February 14, 2005, a large explosion in downtown Beirut killed twenty-three people, including former Lebanese prime minister Rafik Hariri, and injured many others. National and international condemnation of the bombing soon followed.

The Council had already called for the withdrawal of all foreign forces from Lebanon in Resolution 1559 of September 2004, and the assassination presented a political opportunity for Western powers to exert pressure on Syria, the suspected culprit. Led by France, with its historical ties to Lebanon, the Council imposed a sanctions regime (which remains dormant) and set up the International Independent Investigative Commission (IIIC), which eventually led to the establishment of the STL, all of which was widely seen as part of a broader political effort to strengthen pro-Western Lebanese factions and undermine Syrian influence in the country.

Despite the fact that the UN and the Lebanese government had signed an agreement to establish a tribunal, internal political difficulties made it impossible to secure its ratification, eventually leading the Council to bring its provisions into effect through the force of Resolution 1757 of May 30, 2007. The need to resort to Chapter VII to substitute for the failed Lebanese ratification of an international treaty served as an indication of the fraught political environment in which the STL would have to operate.

The statute of the STL is unique in several respects. First, it allows for trial *in absentia*.[17] Second, at the insistence of Russia in particular, jurisdiction is limited to the applicable provisions of the Lebanese criminal code, rather than the much more broadly defined "crimes against humanity" under international criminal law.[18] Third, it is a mixed tribunal composed of both Lebanese and international judges.[19] Fourth, the STL is financed from voluntary contributions (51 percent) and by Lebanon itself (49 percent), as opposed to assessed contributions.[20]

By the time the trial commenced, in January 2014, against four individuals *in absentia* (with their whereabouts unknown), in the context of heightened sectarian tensions and the destabilizing impact of the crisis in Syria, "the court ha[d] become something of a political football, used by each side to highlight the perceived wrongs being committed against it."[21]

Relationship Between the Security Council and the STL

The Council, having established the STL, did not express its interest in following up on its operations, though to be fair it has not been called to do so by the STL or Lebanon. Resolution 1757 requested the Secretary-General to report to it periodically, but this was understood as an obligation to report on his work to facilitate the establishment of the tribunal and not on the work of the tribunal itself. Also, the Council could have substantively reviewed the work of the tribunal under Resolution 1757 when its mandate was to expire after three years. Yet it chose to view the matter as a procedural obligation and the STL mandate was renewed by an exchange of letters with the Secretary-General instead.

As of January 2014, the Council has only once held informal consultations related to the STL, with respect to a minor attack on STL investigators in Beirut in October 2010. A major factor in the Council's general passivity is the concern that any intervention from the Council may play into the hands of those in Lebanon who perceive the STL as a political tool of the West and particular Gulf states to undermine Hezbollah and pro-Syrian forces. There is a fear that Council action may affect, as a result, the general cooperation of the Lebanese authorities with the STL, despite Hezbollah's presence in the cabinet. The STL itself has refrained from calling on the Council to use its powers to assist it, for the very same reasons. And thus far, it seems that the operations of the tribunal have not been a catalyst of instability but rather another aspect of the overall sectarian internal conflict.

The International Criminal Court

While the ICC was established by treaty and not by the Council, its statute reserves a unique role for the Council, raising interesting questions about the relationship between peace and justice. To date, the Council has referred two cases to the ICC and twice applied Article 16, though not in a manner foreseen by the statute. The relationship between the Council and the ICC continues to develop.[22]

Establishment of the Court

The idea of a permanent international criminal court first came about after the horrendous events of World War II, and criticism of the Nuremberg and Tokyo tribunals as reflecting "victor's justice," when the General Assembly asked the International Law Commission to consider the desirability and possibility of establishing such a body. The Assembly essentially abandoned the issue as a result of the Cold War dynamics, but the establishment of the ICTY and ICTR revived the idea of creating a permanent international criminal court. The Rome Statute was adopted on July 17, 1998, and came into force on July 1, 2002, with jurisdiction over war crimes, crimes against humanity, genocide, and the crime of aggression (though the latter crime was to be defined at a later time). As of January 1, 2014, 122 states were parties to the statute, not including three of the P5: China, Russia, and the United States.[23]

The Security Council's Role Under the Rome Statute

During the negotiations, the role of the Council in relation to the ICC was a major dividing issue. While the P5 (and the United States in particular) were interested in securing an exclusive right for the Council to trigger the jurisdiction of the Court, other states (in particular from the nonaligned caucus) wanted to exclude any role for the Council.[24] (To date, India lists the Council's competencies under the Rome Statute as a key reason for not joining the treaty.)

If the Council and the ICC were to interact and work together, a balance would need to be struck between the Council's political role, with primary responsibility for international peace and security, and the function of the ICC as an independent judicial body not subject to political influence. The Rome Statute, along with the rules of procedure and evidence and the relationship agreement between the ICC and the UN, try to reflect that balance.

The main role of the Council under Article 13(b) of the Rome Statute is the power to refer situations to the ICC, potentially expanding the jurisdiction of the Court over crimes committed in the territory of nonparty states to the Rome Statute and their nationals. The article requires the Council to refer a "situation," thus excluding the Council's ability to refer a specific act committed by just one party of the conflict. After a referral, the ICC prosecutor and the Court itself retain their discretion: the prosecutor may decide not to proceed with the investigation, but must inform the Council, which may choose to challenge this decision before the Court. The Court, for its part, is to inform the Council of noncooperation of states with investigations initiated by a Council referral. The balance struck in the Rome Statute may also allow for the prosecutor to account for political considerations: he or she can weigh if "there are . . . substantial reasons to believe that an investigation would not serve the interests of justice."[25]

Perhaps the most controversial of the Council's roles with respect to the ICC is its power under Article 16 of the Rome Statute to defer an investigation or prosecution for a renewable period of twelve months through a Chapter VII resolution. Much like the case of referral, the article also attempts to balance judicial independence with peace and security considerations (and, potentially, great power interests).

Unlike the other crimes enumerated in the Rome Statute, the definition of the crime of aggression was left to be decided at a later date. After years of preparatory work, in June 2010 the Assembly of State Parties to the Rome Statute adopted Resolution RC/Res.6 for ratification by states, defining the crime of aggression for the purposes of the statute. Perhaps the most contentious and politically sensitive issue in the negotiations was the Council's role. This should not come as a surprise, as determining that an act of aggression was committed is at the core of the Council's functions—such a determination is envisioned in Article 39 and can lead to enforcement action under Chapter VII. The P5 argued that the determination of an act of aggression was the exclusive competence of the Council. Jurisdiction over this crime should therefore be dependent on a prior determination of the Council. Other states argued that this solution would create an inequity between the P5 and other parties and allow the P5 to politically control and interfere with the judicial process. The compromise solution gave the Council an elevated yet purely procedural role with respect to the crime, while maintaining the independence of the prosecutor and the Court.[26] Thus it was agreed that the Court may exercise jurisdiction over the crime without a Council referral, and that, vice versa, a prior determination of the Council that an act of aggression has occurred should not prejudice the findings of the Court, even in the case of a Council referral. In case there is basis to investigate, the prosecutor is to first ascertain whether the Council has determined that an act of aggression was committed and inform the

Secretary-General of his or her investigation. If the Council has not made such a determination within six months, the prosecutor may proceed with the investigation after obtaining the Court's approval. One final concession to convince the P5 to agree to the compromise was that only in the case of a Council referral may the Court exercise its jurisdiction for aggression over states, including nonstate parties and state parties to the ICC, that have not accepted the amendment defining the crime of aggression. The amendment will enter into force when seven-eighths of the parties to the statute have ratified it, but no earlier than 2017.[27]

The Relationship Between the Security Council and the ICC

The relationship between the Council and the ICC was tense at first. Under strong US pressure and amid vocal criticism from a number of states and the NGO community, the Council, shortly after the Rome Statute entered into force, adopted Resolution 1422 (2002), subsequently renewed in Resolution 1487 (2003), providing immunity for twelve months to nationals of nonstate parties to the Rome Statute participating in Council-mandated peacekeeping operations, referring to Article 16 as its legal basis. It granted the same immunity to peacekeepers in Liberia in 2003 as well (Resolution 1497). To get its way, the United States even vetoed a draft resolution extending the UN mission in Bosnia.[28] Many criticized this approach as seemingly at odds with Article 16, which was not meant to be used as a blanket immunity for certain nationals in a given situation.[29]

Despite this controversy, it was not long before the Council would make its first use of its powers to refer situations to the Court under Article 13(b). The first referral was reminiscent of an all-too-familiar situation, where the Council was unsuccessful in stopping the ongoing onslaught on civilians in Darfur. Faced with reports of atrocities committed against civilians in Darfur by the Sudanese government and allied Janjaweed militia, the Council was reluctant to take action that could negatively affect prospective political agreement to the other ongoing conflict in the war-torn country, between Sudan and southern Sudan. It did, however, request the Secretary-General to establish a commission of inquiry that recommended a Council referral of the situation in Darfur to the ICC, a recommendation with which the Council obliged on March 31, 2005, by a vote of eleven in favor (with Algeria, Brazil, China, and the United States abstaining).[30] The resolution obligated parties in Darfur to cooperate with the Court and the prosecutor, yet only "urged"—not obligated—other states to do the same. As with the "immunity" resolutions mentioned previously, the referral contained provisions excluding non-Sudanese peacekeeping personnel from a state not party to the Rome Statute from the jurisdiction of the ICC. It established a regular reporting schedule for the ICC prosecutor to the Council and resolved—disregarding provisions to the contrary in the Rome

Statute—that the ICC, not the UN, would incur the costs stemming from the referral. These concessions were essential to secure the abstaining votes, particularly of the United States, that was adamantly opposed to the ICC at the time (see Chapter 30).

As of January 1, 2014, the prosecutor had issued six arrest warrants, of which four were still in effect with the individuals concerned at large. These included President Omar al-Bashir and two sitting ministers.

Sudan made clear its refusal to cooperate with the ICC from the very beginning. In 2009, when the prosecutor presented an application for the arrest of President Bashir, the AU and the Arab League took the position that the Council should defer the prosecution of Bashir from the ICC under Article 16.[31] The Council did not adhere to these requests, but was far from unequivocal. For example, in one resolution it noted the concerns of some Council members on the potential destabilizing consequences of the implementation of the arrest warrant, and took note of their intention to consider the matter further.[32] The United States abstained, fearing that the resolution was sending the wrong message to Sudan. The ambivalent message from the Council seemed to imply that it might consider a deferral if certain conditions were met. More ambivalence was displayed when the Council was not able to agree on including ICC cooperation in its terms of reference for its mission to Sudan in June 2008. Instead, there was a general reference to implementing Council resolutions and respect for the rule of law and due process, and the issue was, unsurprisingly, a central point of contention when Council members raised the issue with Sudanese officials during the mission itself.[33]

Perhaps of greater concern is that the Council, on the whole, has not taken any serious measures to apply pressure on states that have refused to cooperate with the ICC and its own Chapter VII resolution on referral. For example, the Council remained silent when ICC indictees were appointed to prominent positions in Sudan, such as the governor of South Kordofan and the minister of defense. The Council also refrained from taking action against several states that hosted President Bashir, some of which are ICC members. The Council's inaction did not change despite being forewarned by the prosecutor that Sudan would interpret the Council's passiveness as a weakening of international resolve. The prosecutor also voiced his opinion that the indictment of Sudanese officials by the ICC should serve as an example of the dire consequences of impunity as these officials continued to commit heinous crimes against their population.[34] Steps like strong condemnation or concrete steps such as targeted sanctions imposed on ICC indictees were not taken, though the situation in Darfur remained grave. With the Council rarely voicing itself firmly on Sudanese and other states' noncooperation, its passiveness is perceived by many observers as a de facto deferral of the Bashir case from the ICC.[35]

The Council has referred one more situation to the ICC. In quick actions demonstrating much resolve, and at the request of the Libyan permanent mission in New York, the Council, with reference to the Responsibility to Protect doctrine and as part of a broader resolution that also imposed travel and financial sanctions as well as an arms embargo, unanimously referred the situation in Libya to the ICC on February 26, 2011, just days after the outbreak of widespread violence and systematic attacks against civilians by the Muammar Qaddafi regime were reported. The resolution contained clauses on the terms of ICC jurisdiction similar to those for the Darfur referral. Four months later, on June 27, the Court issued three arrest warrants, against Muammar Qaddafi, his son Saif al-Islam Qaddafi, and former intelligence chief Abdullah al-Senussi. The Council's decisiveness against the Qaddafi regime stood in contrast to its passive stance toward the tensions between post-Qaddafi Libya and the ICC. It did not take action on the new Libyan government's refusal to cooperate with the ICC in accordance with its Chapter VII resolution and hand over Saif Qaddafi and Senussi. Both were in Libyan custody for more than six months before Libya filed an inadmissibility application before the ICC under Article 19, challenging the jurisdiction of the Court on the basis of complementarity (i.e., that this was not a situation where the home country was unwilling or unable to conduct its own fair criminal proceedings). While the application in the case of Senussi was entertained,[36] the Court refused to relent on its jurisdiction over Saif Qaddafi.[37] If Libya does not cooperate with the Court on this case, the Council will be expected once again to ensure that its resolutions are upheld. After expressing its concern over the detention of ICC defense counsel staff by militia members in Zintan,[38] the Council stood back from the crisis, which was resolved between the Court and Libya with their release three weeks later.

While the referrals in the cases of Sudan and Libya form the core of the Council's relationship with the ICC, the relationship between the two has evolved beyond referrals. It has become more common for Council resolutions to include references to cooperation with the ICC. For example, one of the tasks of the UN Organization Mission in the Democratic Republic of the Congo (MONUC) is to assist the country in bringing perpetrators of war crimes and crimes against humanity to justice, including through cooperation with the ICC.[39] While the mission has provided the prosecutor with information regarding several indictees, it was also criticized for failing to act on the arrest of Bosco Ntganda, who was eventually found and extradited to the ICC by Rwanda. In another resolution, the Council encouraged Côte d'Ivoire to continue its cooperation with the Court.[40]

In terms of concrete action, the Council enabled the transfer of former president Laurent Gbagbo to stand trial in The Hague when its Côte d'Ivoire sanctions committee lifted the travel ban against him for that purpose.

At the same time, recent references to the ICC and their particular language have become highly contentious when negotiating Council decisions,[41] even those on issues that have contained such references in the past. In addition, there has been a reluctance to establish a forum for interaction with the ICC prosecutor on issues that go beyond regular biannual reporting on the two deferrals. And of course, while two issues have been referred to the ICC, several issues on the Council's agenda could be thought to merit such a referral.[42]

From March to April 2011, Council members held two informal meetings in which they heard Kenya's request for the Council to defer the ICC's prosecution against it under Article 16. The Council decided not to act upon the request, as Kenya essentially raised issues of complementarity that should be argued before the Court itself. The issue came back to the Council in 2013, and gained traction after the terrorist attacks in Nairobi on September 21, 2013, and in light of the imminent commencement of the trials against the now reelected President Uhuru Kenyatta and Prime Minister William Ruto. The AU and Kenya were now of the firm position that proceedings against Kenya's incumbent heads of state and government may adversely affect peace and security in the country and the region, a position also entertained by several Council members. These particular events added to the growing feelings of hostility and resentment of African countries toward the ICC, for what they feel is a deliberate focus of the Court—a Western creation in their opinion—on Africa and its leaders, while other situations are ignored.

The AU and the vast majority of its members decided that it was time to put the issue to the test and, after several informal meetings, tabled a draft resolution on a deferral of the proceedings against the two Kenyan officials. The resolution did not gather the nine necessary votes for a resolution to pass, with Azerbaijan, China, Morocco, Pakistan, Russia, Rwanda, and Togo (seven in total) voting in favor, and Argentina, Australia, France, Guatemala, Luxembourg, South Korea, the United Kingdom, and the United States (eight in total) abstaining. The decision by the eight to abstain may be seen as an attempt to appease the African countries by refraining from voting "against" them, though the result remains the same. This may not have been the last time the Council deals with the Kenyan deferral issue.

Finally, some Council members have tried to find other ways to enhance cooperation with the ICC, in light of the current state of affairs as discussed earlier. Guatemala initiated the first open debate in the Council that focused on strengthening cooperation with the ICC and the role of the ICC in assisting the Council to carry out its mandate.[43] States took the opportunity to criticize Council practice on referrals, in particular with respect to financing, exemption clauses, and lack of follow-up, and to recommend improvements such as considering sanctions against ICC indictees or creating new or using existing forums to further discuss the relationship and consider communications from the Court such as notifications on non-cooperation. Guatemala later proposed to use the informal working group on tribunals as such a forum, but several Council members are of the view that this would go beyond the agreed mandate of the working group.[44] Efforts to hold informal discussions with the prosecutor on ICC-related issues (such as noncompliance of states with ICC arrest warrants) in the working group thus far have been met with objections from China, Russia, and others.

Conclusion

It is hard to ignore the Security Council's contribution to both the institutional and the normative development of international criminal law. The establishment of an ad hoc tribunal or a referral to the ICC may still be a rare choice, but it has become a plausible option that the Council may consider in a given situation. The Council's interaction with the ICC may increase when the Court's jurisdiction over the crime of aggression comes into force, as early as 2017.

Many consider the tribunals to be a success story. Many perpetrators, some of "high profile," were held accountable, a fact that may have worked (and may work in the future) as a deterrent for other prospective criminals. The tribunals were able to bring a sense of justice and closure to affected communities, allowing them to reconcile and move forward, give a voice to victims, and leave a tangible historical account of the events. From the legal perspective, the tribunals' jurisprudence elevated and developed international criminal law (as was recognized by the Council itself)[45] and were a catalyst for renewed interest in international adjudication of grave crimes, reflected by the establishment of the ICC and the substance of the crimes enumerated in its statute. On the other hand, at the time the idea of the tribunals was conceived, Council members did not give much thought to their costs, to what extent the Council would need to enforce cooperation with them, the length of their operation, and a completion strategy. The Council was further criticized for establishing ad hoc tribunals for crimes in a particular state or region while ignoring grave crimes elsewhere.

The ICC was supposed to answer these concerns. It was to allow the Council to refer situations to an already-existing body that could act as a constant deterrent to perpetrators, surpassing tough negotiations over the establishment of an ad hoc tribunal and the attached costs. Both ICC referrals are a positive sign that the Council can and will use its referral powers to promote individual accountability in its efforts to maintain international peace and security. Moreover, the fact that the Libya referral was unanimous demonstrates the degree to which the relevance of individual accountability to the Council's work has now been accepted, even by non-ICC members China, the United States, and Russia.

Yet concerns about the political influence of the Council on the ICC persist. While it is not surprising that the Council would refer situations on its own terms, the restrictions and conditions contained therein cast doubt on the Council's commitment to a successful ICC process and may eventually undermine the legitimacy of the Court itself, let alone the legitimacy of the Council's referral itself, and lead pro-ICC states to rethink their position on the merits of referrals. First, the conformity with due process of granting immunity to nationals of one state in a given situation, while the nationals of another state in the same situation fall under the ICC's jurisdiction, is highly questionable. Such practice also promises that the nonparties among the P5 will enjoy immunity for their citizens in cases of Council referrals. These provisions taint the perception of the ICC as an independent judicial institution by limiting the discretion of the prosecutor for obvious political considerations.[46] In fact, these provisions could end up being a point of confrontation between the Council and the Court in a future case. Furthermore, the ICC statute anticipates that the UN will cover the costs of Council referrals.[47] By denying UN funding for the costs of referrals, the Council has provided the ICC jurisdiction sans the tools to implement it. Some ICC members have voiced their opinion that the Council should refrain from this practice in the future.

Moreover, as with the tribunals, criticism over selective justice at the ICC continues. The two Council referrals to the ICC contrast with the non-referral in other cases, raising allegations of double standards. In particular, the vast majority of AU members are of the position that the ICC is biased in exclusively targeting Africa and its leaders (indeed, all situations in which the Court has opened investigations are on that continent, and warrants have been issued against two heads of state). Second, the lack of follow-up on state cooperation with the tribunals or with the Council's resolutions referring a situation to the ICC, let alone the Council's reluctance to obligate all states to cooperate with the Court, cast serious doubt on the Council's resolve and commitment to back its rhetoric on accountability and cooperation with action. In the case of Darfur, for example, the Council's unwillingness to follow up on the implementation of ICC warrants has amounted to a de facto deferral of the Darfur situation thus far. Additionally, it is highly questionable whether the Council will be willing to take necessary steps, if called upon, to assist the Special Tribunal for Lebanon. On the other hand, the hesitancy of the Council to use its deferral powers may show that Council members understand that only in rare occasions does justice actually interfere with the pursuit of peace and security.

As the ICC referrals raise issues similar to those of the ad hoc tribunals, and considering that the ICC has yet to prove itself and is being criticized by some as a slow body overly focused on Africa, it is too soon to dismiss the appeal of ad hoc or hybrid tribunals in the future. But whatever the forum, the Council's involvement ensures some degree of political consideration, as it is a political body entrusted with the responsibility to promote peace and security. To a certain degree, this is the trade-off for using the Council to increase the number of situations that fall under the jurisdiction of the ICC. The drafters of the Rome Statute did in fact understand that in some cases, the political considerations override the interest of justice, hence the Council's role in the statute including deferral.

The Council has only given serious attention to issues of accountability in the past two decades or so, and rarely does the Council take the time—and some may argue it lacks the luxury of time—to holistically reflect on principle issues. Such is the equilibrium of peace versus justice, which the Council has perhaps only begun to consider, through its growing practice. With that in mind, the Council's practice thus far demonstrates a lack of internalization that judicial processes are lengthy and require a consistent commitment. Their very nature, necessitating meticulous consideration of numerous facts and questions of law, means that they may outlast any short-term political solutions necessary to prevent or address conflicts as they unfold. Indeed, judicial proceedings will usually continue even when the politics have changed, a fact that may give the Council second thoughts in the future. However, the international community will be best served if the Council uses its past experience to bridge the gaps between peace and justice and the dissonance between lengthy judicial proceeding and faster political solutions, by proper backing of judicial procedures and ensuring cooperation of all states and parties with its resolutions.

Notes

1. For an overview and analysis of the Security Council's attitude, treatment, and contribution to the promotion of individual accountability, see Security Council Report, "The Security Council and Accountability," in *Cross-Cutting Report: The Rule of Law—The Security Council and Accountability* (New York, 2013), www.securitycouncilreport.org/cross-cutting-report/the-rule-of-law-the-security -council-and-accountability.php.

2. The Federal Republic of Yugoslavia challenged the possibility of a Security Council subsidiary body acting independently of political considerations. Mexico and Cuba, for example, questioned the legal authority in the Charter for the establishment of an international criminal tribunal by the Council; see Philippe Kirsch, John T. Holmes, and Mara Johnson, "International Tribunals and Courts," in *The UN Security Council: From the Cold War to the 21st Century,* edited by David M. Malone (Boulder, CO: Lynne Rienner, 2004), p. 284. These issues were also raised as legal arguments and rejected by the tribunal's appellate chamber in *Prosecutor v. Dusko Tadic a/k/a "Dule," Decision on the Defence Motion for Interlocutory Appeal on Jurisdiction,* October 2, 1995, www.icty.org/x/cases/tadic/acdec/en/51002.htm.

3. It is also noteworthy that international courts that are not directly linked to the Council may affect its practice and thus develop a relationship with it. For example, the European Court of Justice's jurisprudence on due process rights of individuals subject to Council-mandated sanctions has, among other things, been a catalyst for Council reforms in the listing and delisting procedures.

4. United Nations, *Charter of the United Nations* (San Francisco, June 26, 1945), Article 36(3).

5. United Nations Security Council Resolution 22, S/RES/22 (April 9, 1947).

6. United Nations, *Charter of the United Nations,* Article 94.

7. United Nations Security Council, "Letter Dated 17 October 1986 from the Permanent Representative of Nicaragua to the United Nations Addressed to the President of the Security Council," UN Doc. S/18415, October 20, 1986.

8. United Nations Security Council, "Congo, Ghana, Madagascar, Trinidad and Tobago, and United Arab Emirates: Draft Resolution," UN Doc. S/18428, October 28, 1986.

9. United Nations Security Council Resolution 284, S/RES/284 (July 29, 1970).

10. For more on the jurisprudence of the tribunals, see Vladimir Tochilovski, *The Law and Jurisprudence of the International Criminal Tribunals and Courts* (Cambridge: Intersentia, 2014). For a completed caseload see the report on the completion strategy of the International Criminal Tribunal for Rwanda of May 5, 2014, which is contained in United Nations Security Council, "Letter Dated 15 May 2014 from the President of the International Criminal Tribunal for Rwanda Addressed to the President of the Security Council," S/2014/343, May 15, 2014.

11. United Nations Security Council, *Special Report of the Secretary-General on the United Nations Assistance Mission for Rwanda,* UN Doc S/1994/470, April 20, 1994.

12. Violence and tensions between the Hutus and Tutsis in Rwanda predates the 1994 genocide, with significant outbreaks of violence between the two communities during the "Hutu Revolution" of 1959–1961 and during the civil war of 1990–1994, just prior to the genocide.

13. See the following letters to the president of the Security Council: "Letter Dated 8 September 1998 from the President of the International Tribunal for the Prosecution of Persons Responsible for Serious Violations of International Humanitarian Law Committed in the Territory of the Former Yugoslavia Since 1991," UN Doc. S/1998/839, September 8, 1998; "Letter Dated 22 October 1998 from the President of the International Tribunal for the Prosecution of Persons Responsible for Serious Violations of International Humanitarian Law Committed in the Territory of the Former Yugoslavia Since 1991," UN Doc. S/1998/990, October 23, 1998; "Letter Dated 6 November 1998 from the President of the International Tribunal for the Prosecution of Persons Responsible for Serious Violations of International Humanitarian Law Committed in the Territory of the Former Yugoslavia," UN Doc. S/1998/1040, November 6, 1998.

14. United Nations Security Council, "Provisional Verbatim Record of the 6342nd Meeting," UN Doc. S.PV/6342, June 18, 2010.

15. United Nations Security Council Resolution 1966, S/RES/1966 (December 22, 2010).

16. United Nations Security Council, "Provisional Verbatim Record of the 6880th Meeting," UN Doc. S/PV.6880, December 5, 2012.

17. *Statute of the Special Tribunal for Lebanon* (May 30, 2007), Article 2.

18. Ibid., Article 22.

19. Ibid., Article 8.

20. Ibid., Article 5.

21. Somini Sengupta, "Mideast Strife Turns Trial on Beirut Assassination into Another Fault Line," *International New York Times,* January 14, 2014.

22. For more on the place of the ICC vis-à-vis the international system, including the Security Council, see David Bosco, *Rough Justice: The International Criminal Court in a World of Power Politics* (New York: Oxford University Press, 2014).

23. For more on the ICC itself, see William A. Schabas, *An Introduction to the International Criminal Court* (Cambridge: Cambridge University Press, 2011).

24. For more on this, see Kirsch, Holmes, and Johnson, "International Tribunals and Courts," p. 281.

25. *Rome Statute* (July 17, 1998), Article 53.1(c).

26. For more, see Claus Kreβ and Leonie von Holtzendorff, "The Kampala Compromise on the Crime of Aggression," *Journal of International Criminal Justice* 8, no. 5 (2010): 1179–1217.

27. For more on the definition of the crime of aggression under the ICC's Rome Statute, see Carrie McDougall, *The Crime of Aggression Under the Rome Statute of the International Criminal Court* (New York: Cambridge University Press, 2013).

28. United Nations Security Council, "Bulgaria, France, Germany, Ireland, Italy, Norway, Russian Federation, and United Kingdom of Great Britain and Northern Ireland: Draft Resolution," UN Doc. S/2002/712, June 30, 2002.

29. Neha Jain, "A Separate Law for Peacekeepers: The Clash Between the Security Council and the International Criminal Court," *European Journal of International Law* 16, no. 2 (2005): 239–254.

30. United Nations Security Council Resolution 1593, S/RES/1593 (March 31, 2005).

31. See the following letters to the president of the Security Council, "Letter Dated 16 March 2009 from the Permanent Observer of the League of Arab States to the United Nations," UN Doc. S/2009/148, March 18, 2009; "Letter Dated 6 March 2009 from the Chargé d'Affaires a.i. of the Permanent Mission of the Libyan Arab Jamahiriya to the United Nations," UN Doc. S/2009/144, March 6, 2009.

32. United Nations Security Council Resolution 1828, S/RES/1828 (July 31, 2008).

33. United Nations Security Council, "Report of the Security Council Mission to Djibouti (on Somalia), the Sudan, Chad, the Democratic Republic of the Congo, and Côte d'Ivoire, 31 May to 10 June 2008," UN Doc. S/2008/460, July 15, 2008.

34. United Nations Security Council, "Provisional Verbatim Record of the 6548th Meeting," UN Doc. S/PV.6548, June 8, 2011.

35. One notable exception being the statement by the president of the Security Council on June 16, 2008, UN Doc. S/PRST/2008/21.

36. International Criminal Court, *Decision on the Admissibility of the Case Against Abdullah al-Senussi,* October 11, 2013.

37. International Criminal Court, *Prosecutor v. Gaddafi, Decision on the Request for Suspensive Effect and Related Issues,* July 18, 2013.

38. United Nations Meetings Coverage and Press Releases, "Security Council Press Statement on International Criminal Court Staff Detained in Libya," UN Doc. SC/10674, June 15, 2012.

39. United Nations Security Council Resolution 2098, S/RES/2098 (March 28, 2013).

40. United Nations Security Council Resolution 2062, S/RES/2062 (July 26, 2012).

41. See, for example, in the case of Côte d'Ivoire, Security Council Report, "UN Operation in Côte d'Ivoire Mandate Renewal," *What's in Blue,* July 29, 2013, www.whatsinblue.org/2013/07/un-operation-in-cote-divoire-mandate-renewal.php.

42. For example, on January 14, 2013, Switzerland submitted a letter to the Council, cosigned by fifty-six other member states, requesting that it refer the situation in the Syrian Arab Republic as of March 2011 to the ICC (UN Doc. S/2013/19). An early version of draft resolution S/2012/77 ("Bahrain, Colombia, Egypt, France, Germany, Jordan, Kuwait, Libya, Morocco, Oman, Portugal, Qatar, Saudi Arabia, Togo, Tunisia, Turkey, United Arab Emirates, United Kingdom of Great Britain and Northern Ireland, and United States of America: Draft Resolution," February 4, 2012) that was eventually vetoed contained a reference to the ICC, but only in the preamble.

43. United Nations Security Council, "Provisional Verbatim Record of the 6849th Meeting," UN Doc. S.PV/6849(Res. 1), October 17, 2012.

44. Costa Rica, Jordan, and Liechtenstein submitted a formal request to this effect to the Council (UN Doc. S/2012/860, November 20, 2012).

45. United Nations Meetings Coverage and Press Releases, "Security Council Press Statement on the Contribution of Courts and Tribunals in the Fight Against Impunity," UN Doc. SC/10700, July 5, 2012.

46. See Jennifer Trahan, "The Relationship Between the International Criminal Court and the U.N. Security Council: Parameters and Best Practices," *Criminal Law Forum* 24, no. 4 (December 2013): 417–473.

47. *Rome Statute,* Article 115(b).

Part 5

Key Country Cases

26

The Arab-Israeli Conflict

Markus E. Bouillon

ONE OF THE FIRST UNITED NATIONS MEDIATORS CALLED THE
Middle East "the sort of problem for which no really satisfactory solution is
possible."[1] Indeed, for seven decades, the "situation in the Middle East,"
particularly the "Palestinian question," to use the Security Council's own
terminology for the interlocking issues related to the Arab-Israeli conflict,
has presented the Council with one of the most vexing problems on its
agenda: "No issue has been on the agenda of the Council as long as that of
the Middle East; nor has any issue generated as many resolutions . . . or as
many vetoes."[2] As a result, the region has shaped the United Nations in
many ways.

Brian Urquhart noted that "the UN's actual role in critical situations
was, to a considerable extent, pioneered in Palestine."[3] Bruce Jones, more
recently, enumerated the instances in which "the Arab-Israeli theatre has
been a laboratory for UN innovation: the first subsidiary organ (UNSCOP),
the first specialized agency (UNRWA), the first mediator (Count Folke
Bernadotte), the first observer mission (UNTSO), the first peacekeeping
mission (UNEF), the first integrated mission (UNSCO),[4] and the first
instance of investigatory challenge to a member state," the UN International Independent Investigation Commission (UNIIIC) in Lebanon.[5]

But while the Security Council has been deeply and often innovatively
(as far as institutional mechanisms are concerned) involved in the Middle
East, it has rarely been able to set defining parameters. In fact, the Council
has often struggled to uphold its own norms in the region. In consequence,
"the UN's performance in the Arab-Israeli theatre, and in the broader Middle East, has long shaped public perception of the body"; and at the same

time, peacekeeping has been "a key element in whatever peace the people of the region have enjoyed."[6] And one has to acknowledge that "when the UN's intergovernmental debates became vociferously partisan, the organization lost much of its credibility, although it unquestionably provided a useful safety valve for dangerous passions and resentments, and kept vital issues—Palestinian rights, the status of Jerusalem—alive."[7]

In this chapter I explore the Council's involvement in and on the Middle East in more detail. The picture that emerges is profoundly mixed. While the Council has addressed acute crises and ensured a degree of stability through the instruments at its disposal, it has all too often been unable to play a leading, decisive, or norm-setting role. Divisions within the Council, particularly between the United States and the rest of the Council, have run deep. All too often, the Security Council has remained mired in discussions over issues that, albeit important, are but facets of the bigger conflict, rendering it less and less likely (or possible) that the Council could contribute decisively to settling the Arab-Israeli conflict.

Acute Crisis Management and Peacekeeping: From 1947 Until the End of the Cold War

For the first several decades of its engagement in the Middle East, the Security Council "did not succeed in preventing conflict, though it often contributed to the process of bringing hostilities to an end."[8] It also set out important principles for peacemaking, before it became increasingly "irrelevant to events on the ground."[9]

The Council's involvement began shortly after the General Assembly recommended the partition of mandatory Palestine in November 1947.[10] As soon as Israel declared independence in May 1948 and five Arab states invaded it, the Council appointed its first-ever mediator, Count Folke Bernadotte, who began to engage in shuttle diplomacy between the parties. Bernadotte engineered the Security Council's first truce resolution (Resolution 50 of May 29, 1948) and the subsequent establishment of the first United Nations observer mission, the UN Truce Supervision Organization (UNTSO).[11] Following Bernadotte's assassination by a Jewish terrorist group in September 1948, Ralph Bunche assumed charge of UN efforts to end the conflict, obtaining Council resolutions that called, once again, for a ceasefire (Resolution 59 of October 19, 1948) and then for "permanent armistice" arrangements between Israel and each of its Arab neighbors (Resolution 62 of November 16, 1948). By March 1949, Bunche had successfully negotiated a series of bilateral armistice agreements, which were endorsed by the Security Council. Shortly thereafter, the Council voted to admit Israel as a member of the United Nations (Resolution 69 of March 4, 1949).

This early experience exhibits several important characteristics of how the Council would continue to address conflict not only in the Middle East, but also globally. First, the Council relied to a large extent on the active engagement of a representative of the Secretary-General (in later parlance, a special envoy), who worked closely with key Council members. Second, the Council refrained from direct (military) intervention, instead resorting to cautious diplomacy, not least against the background of diverging interests among its members.[12]

The next major crisis in the region established further patterns of typical Council action. In the context of the Suez crisis of 1956, the Soviet Union first vetoed a draft resolution proposed by Britain and France, which in turn vetoed two successive drafts calling for a ceasefire and the withdrawal of their forces. As would happen on other occasions in the face of Council deadlock, it was the General Assembly that convened in an emergency session and called for a ceasefire, the withdrawal of all foreign forces, and the establishment of what would become the first United Nations peacekeeping mission, the UN Emergency Force (UNEF I).[13] Peacekeeping to preserve fragile ceasefires, in the absence of a consensus on how to resolve the underlying issues, would henceforth become the primary manifestation of Council involvement in the Middle East.[14]

The next war erupted when, in a climate of growing tension, Egypt demanded the withdrawal of UNEF from the Sinai Peninsula in 1967. The acute crisis prompted lengthy debate in the Council as well as several, initially unsuccessful, attempts to address the renewed conflict.[15] But Cold War dynamics and great power divisions meant that the Council was incapable of taking early action, and the Council was more successful in addressing the aftermath of the war and shaping the political process ahead than in preventing or halting the conflict on the ground.

Resolution 242, perhaps the "most famous resolution in the Security Council's history,"[16] was thus adopted several months *after* the Six-Day War, on November 22, 1967. Presented as a compromise by the United Kingdom, the resolution was "ambiguous on important points and vague enough to command general approval."[17] It asserted the inadmissibility of acquisition of territory by force and stipulated that Israel should return "territories" occupied in the conflict. Crucially, the resolution's English version refers ambivalently to "territories" without the definite article, thus leaving open whether Israel would be required to withdraw from *all* territory occupied in the course of the war. Although its British drafters have made it clear that the definite article was dropped deliberately, the French version of the resolution at the very least *can* be read as including it (*"retrait des forces armées israéliennes des territoires occupés au cours du récent conflit"*) and is often cited to support a broader interpretation.

Despite this never conclusively resolved ambiguity, Security Council Resolution 242 established the fundamental principle of "land for peace," creating a link between Israel's relinquishing of occupied territory and recognition and negotiations to settle the conflict. In doing so, the Security Council laid down perhaps the most enduring principle of the search for peace in the Middle East, even if it did not manage to contribute much to achieving its implementation in practice in subsequent decades. The renewed mission of a UN mediator, Gunnar Jarring, came to naught and was abandoned by 1971.[18]

The pattern of unheeded ceasefire calls during conflict and the shaping of the aftermath of crisis continued with the next war, in October 1973. Direct US-Soviet negotiations during the latter stages of the conflict— "facilitated" by a threat of unilateral Soviet intervention—laid the ground for the adoption of Security Council Resolution 338, which restated and codified Resolution 242 and called for negotiations to establish a "just and durable peace in the Middle East," another formula that has since become indelible from the dictionary of Middle East peacemaking. Much like before, the Council established a static peacekeeping force, UNEF II, to create a buffer along the Egypt-Israel ceasefire line.[19] A similar arrangement was agreed with some delay in 1974 along the Israel-Syria line, resulting in the deployment, to this day, of the UN Disengagement Observer Force (UNDOF).[20]

When Israel invaded Lebanon in 1978, a similar buffer force was created in south Lebanon in the form of the UN Interim Force in Lebanon (UNIFIL), through the adoptions of Security Council Resolutions 425 and 426, despite serious misgivings in the UN Secretariat over the absence of actual truce conditions.[21] Both UNDOF and UNIFIL would continue to play an important role for several decades, although the latter found itself overrun and sidelined during Israel's renewed invasion of Lebanon in 1982 and the Israel-Lebanon war of 2006. Both missions also came under growing pressure amid rising tensions and violence in the context of the Arab Spring. UNDOF, in particular, was weakened. Initially, several troop-contributing countries withdrew their contingents in late 2012 and early 2013 when the civil war in Syria threatened to affect the mission. In the course of 2014, Syrian rebels took control of large parts of UNDOF's mission area and at one stage held sizable contingents of Filipino and Fiji peacekeepers hostage, drawing into question whether the mission would be able to remain *in situ* altogether.

For decades, however, static peacekeepers and military observers brought about considerable stability and predictability along the fault-lines of the Middle East. This was also the case in the Egyptian Sinai following the conclusion of the Camp David Accords in 1978, which led to the deployment of the (non-UN) Multilateral Forces and Observers in Sinai

(MFO Sinai). However, the blocking of a UN peacekeeping force by the Arab states marked a low point for the Council.[22] Nonetheless, the fact that the Council chose to maintain its peacekeeping and observer missions over many years "testifies both to the unfinished business before them and to their continued utility in the eyes of the Security Council and most of the actors in the region."[23]

Yet it is equally important to record the shortcomings of these missions as well as the limits of the Council's ability to "manage" conflict. Prior to 2006, as a research paper by Security Council Report noted: "None of the decisions to deploy a new peace operation in the Middle East had the united support of the five permanent members of the Security Council. . . . None of the missions has had an explicit Chapter VII mandate. The deployments have always followed, never preceded, the outbreak of large-scale hostilities [and] peacekeeping in the area has been more successful at helping prevent inter-state conflict than at curbing the use of violence by nonstate actors."[24]

In addition, with the exception of Resolutions 242 and 338, which defined fundamental parameters of peace, the Security Council rarely sought to resolve the underlying issues. Indeed, perhaps the most noteworthy aspect of the Geneva peace conference, convened under UN auspices after the October 1973 war, was that it was endorsed by the Security Council in Resolution 344 of December 15, 1973, with ten votes in favor and four abstentions—the latter of which came from permanent members France, the UK, the United States, and the Soviet Union (China did not vote).[25]

As Cold War dynamics impeded Council action, there were many debates, "innumerable resolutions, and almost as many vetoes, but little result."[26] In consequence, the Security Council, and the United Nations at large, became all but marginal in the Middle East until well after the end of the Cold War. In fact, the UN remained sidelined in the two most significant breakthroughs in the region during the immediate post–Cold War era, the 1991 Madrid peace conference—in which Israel agreed to participate only on condition that the United Nations would not—and the 1993 Oslo Accords, which provided for mutual recognition between Israel and the Palestine Liberation Organization (PLO) and autonomous Palestinian self-rule in the West Bank and Gaza Strip.[27]

Serial Crises and the Delegation of Norm-Setting: Into the Twenty-First Century

The end of the Cold War ushered in a period of unprecedented activism and expansion of the Council's agenda. But although the United Nations gained, for the first time, a role on the ground with Secretary-General Boutros

Boutros-Ghali's appointment of one of the architects of the Oslo process, Terje Rød-Larsen, as his special coordinator in the occupied territories in 1994, the Security Council did not assume a bigger role. Indeed, Rød-Larsen operated on the basis of his personal networks and under a General Assembly mandate, rather than the aegis of the Security Council.

This did not change when the al-Aqsa intifada erupted in September 2000. Indeed, the Security Council soon yielded any policymaking and norm-setting function to a new mechanism, the Quartet, which was not directly linked to it. Established in April 2002, the Quartet grouped together the political power of the United States and Russia, the financial clout of the European Union, and the international legitimacy represented by the United Nations—albeit in the person of the Secretary-General, rather than the Security Council.[28] The Council, by contrast, became more and more of a talk-shop on the region, unable to take decisive action. As bilateral ties between the United States and Israel grew closer as well, the Council faced deepening divisions and successive US vetoes against resolutions it considered biased against Israel, a trend that would continue under Presidents George W. Bush and Barack Obama. From 1991 to 2012, the United States cast fourteen vetoes, all but one of them on the Middle East (there were a total of twenty-seven vetoes during that period). In each instance, and in a rare break of the unity between the United States, France, and the United Kingdom, the United States found itself isolated, with all other Council members supporting the proposed draft resolution. Seven of these vetoes came during the years of the intifada, between 2001 and 2004, alone.[29]

But the Council was not entirely inactive with respect to the Middle East during those years. On October 7, 2000, the United States enabled, by refraining from a veto, the adoption of Resolution 1322, which condemned Israel's excessive use of force and called for an international commission of inquiry into the violence of the intifada.[30] Subsequently, in the context of the September 11, 2001, attacks and the growing focus of the Council on terrorism, a number of resolutions—three in the course of 2002 alone—and statements were adopted, which for the first time, and then regularly as standard practice, condemned terrorist actions against Israeli citizens (albeit balanced by cautioning against or criticizing Israel's use of force in Palestinian areas).[31] The peak of the intifada, with Israel's reoccupation of the West Bank following a wave of Palestinian attacks against Israeli targets, also prompted the adoption of US-sponsored Council Resolution 1397 (2002), which still stands as the Council's most significant pronouncement on the Arab-Israeli conflict since Resolution 242 by, for the first time, envisioning clearly the *outcome* of peace negotiations: "a region where two states, Israel and Palestine, live side by side within secure and recognized borders."[32]

Yet the Council's dedication of a growing amount of time to the Middle East reflected deterioration, rather than progress. In practical terms, the Security Council became essentially a venting mechanism. Indeed, the worse the situation became, the more the Council talked—and the less it acted. Starting in February 2002, it began to receive "periodic" (soon monthly) briefings from the Secretariat on the situation on the ground, initially in the private setting of informal consultations, later complemented by quarterly open debates, which allowed the wider membership to air its views as well.[33]

Policy was instead defined by the Quartet. It was the Quartet that presented the so-called road map in 2003, which set out parallel actions that Israelis and Palestinians would need to take to achieve the eventual peaceful coexistence of two states, the goal defined in Resolution 1397. The Quartet would also oversee and endorse the process leading to Israel's unilateral withdrawal from the Gaza Strip in August 2005, which was considered an important step toward peace and the creation of a Palestinian state.[34] Finally, the Quartet defined the international community's stance vis-à-vis the Palestinian Authority in the wake of legislative elections in January 2006 won by Hamas.[35]

In all these instances, the Security Council had no role other than to legitimate Quartet positions. On November 19, 2003, the Council adopted Resolution 1515, endorsing the road map. In September and November 2005, the Council issued presidential statements mirroring the Quartet's positions on Israel's "disengagement" from Gaza and the subsequent agreement on movement and access, largely negotiated by Quartet special envoy James Wolfensohn.[36] And on February 3, 2006, the Council endorsed the Quartet's January 30 "principles" limiting international donor assistance and diplomatic contact with the Hamas-led Palestinian Authority.[37] The Quartet was far from uncontroversial: Alvaro de Soto, Rød-Larsen's successor as special coordinator for the Middle East peace process, would depart his post in May 2007, criticizing it—in an internal document that was leaked to the press—as a mere tool to endorse biased US policy.[38] And the efforts of several elected Council members to at least obtain a briefing from Quartet representative Tony Blair in the years after he succeeded Wolfensohn in August 2007 would also remain unsuccessful.

In subsequent years, there was even less action from the Council. Despite significant developments on the ground—the widening split between the Fatah-dominated West Bank and the Hamas-run Gaza Strip, escalating rocket fire from Gaza and Israeli air-strikes and incursions, as well as the abduction of Israeli soldier Gilad Shalit in June 2006—there was only one Council presidential statement on the Israeli-Palestinian conflict in 2006 and two Council press statements in 2007.[39] Indeed, the Council found itself incapable of responding to an unusually candid, impromptu

Middle East report submitted by departing Secretary-General Kofi Annan in December 2006, which exhorted member states to "match their professions of concern with a concerted effort to empower the United Nations to make a strategic difference."[40] In November 2007, the United States tabled a resolution to endorse the first major international peace meeting in more than a decade, the Annapolis Conference, but withdrew it the following day. Israel, long dismissive of the United Nations as inherently biased and preferring to work bilaterally with the United States, had rejected even a US-sponsored welcoming statement or resolution out of fear that this would "multilateralize" the process.[41]

More than a year later, and only with a strong push from the United States and the Quartet, the Security Council adopted Resolution 1850 of December 16, 2008, its first on the Middle East in nearly five years. The resolution finally declared the Council's commitment to the Annapolis process. It was followed by a presidential statement in May 2009, which— as the Council's last overall pronouncement on the Arab-Israeli conflict for at least the next four years—noted the "urgency of reaching comprehensive peace in the Middle East" as well as the need for "vigorous diplomatic action" to realize the two-state solution. Both had little impact.[42]

While the Council found it increasingly difficult to address the overall parameters of the Israeli-Palestinian conflict, repeated crises, particularly related to Gaza, did capture its attention. But a rare May 2004 resolution calling on Israel to halt house demolitions in the southern Gaza Strip aside,[43] the Council took action only when Israel launched a major military offensive against Gaza on December 27, 2008. Security Council Resolution 1860 of January 8, 2009, the last resolution on the Israeli-Palestinian conflict until the time of writing, called for an immediate and durable ceasefire, leading to the full withdrawal of Israeli forces, and defined key parameters for humanitarian access and the movement of people and goods in and out of Gaza. Still, on the ground, it was an effort led by Egypt, with French and US support, which ended Israel's Operation Cast Lead (indeed, the United States abstained on the vote, arguing that the Egyptian efforts required more time), while in New York, it took a special mission by Arab League secretary-general Amr Moussa and eight Arab foreign ministers for the Security Council to act at all.

A subsequent Human Rights Council–mandated investigation into the twenty-eight-day conflict, led by South African judge Richard Goldstone, called on the Security Council to pronounce itself on the Gaza war.[44] Yet despite repeated consideration of the so-called Goldstone Report and a renewed Human Rights Council resolution in March 2011, which recommended that the Security Council refer the situation in the occupied Palestinian territory to the International Criminal Court, the Council could not agree on any action. The same held true for a report of a board of inquiry set up by the UN Secretary-General to investigate the damage to UN facilities and loss of life during the Gaza war, which was forwarded to the Council in May 2009.

In May 2010, following the death of nine people in an Israeli military operation aboard a Turkish humanitarian flotilla headed to Gaza, the Council adopted a presidential statement expressing deep regret at the loss of life and injuries and calling for a "prompt, impartial, credible and transparent investigation."[45] However, the subsequent investigation was driven by Israel and Turkey themselves, and the Council did not consider the matter further after the report of Secretary-General Ban Ki-moon's investigation panel was made public on September 2, 2011.

Further episodes in and around Gaza in November 2012 and in the summer of 2014—when Israel and Hamas fought out a vicious fifty-day war—followed the pattern of deep division and Council inability to act early and decisively. In November 2012, renewed Israeli military action prompted the Council to meet in emergency consultations. However, first, the United States blocked a Council press statement condemning the violence, before Russia circulated a draft resolution, suggesting it would call for a vote if the press statement could not be adopted. Achievement of an Egyptian-brokered ceasefire on November 21 preempted a visible Council split and likely US veto. The Council instead adopted a different press statement, welcoming the ceasefire and calling on the international community to contribute to improving the living conditions of the people in the Gaza Strip.[46]

When in the summer of 2014 the bodies of three Israeli teenagers who had been abducted and murdered in the West Bank were discovered on June 30, and a Palestinian youth was subsequently abducted and killed in Jerusalem on July 2, the Council issued press statements condemning the incidents. However, as intensifying rocket fire soon after led to Israel's Operation Protective Edge, which would last for seven weeks and far exceed all previous conflicts in Gaza, leaving more than 2,100 Palestinians and 73 Israelis dead, the Council played no major role in managing the conflict. A brief press statement was issued on July 12, in which the members of the Security Council expressed "serious concern regarding the crisis related to Gaza and the protection and welfare of civilians on both sides."[47]

However, it was only two weeks later and after intense efforts by US secretary of state John Kerry, Secretary-General Ban Ki-moon, as well as Egypt, Turkey, and Qatar, that the Council could agree on a presidential statement expressing "strong support" for calls (by others) for an immediate and unconditional humanitarian ceasefire.[48] The United States, Egypt, and other actors remained the main players brokering a series of unsuccessful ceasefires before an enduring cessation of hostilities was finally agreed on August 26. The widespread recognition in the international community that the situation in Gaza had become untenable and that the fundamental concerns of both sides—Israel's insistence that Hamas needed to be disarmed, Hamas's emphasis that the blockade of Gaza had to be broken—would need to be addressed did translate into a draft resolution backed by several Council members. Yet, lengthy discussions over the exact language and parameters of a resolution meant that it was never adopted, and the Council remained essentially mute on what stands as the most serious conflict in Gaza to date—and on all critical underlying issues, such as Israel's blockade against Gaza, Hamas's militancy and rearming, the deep split among Palestinians, as well as the need to revive a further-reaching political process between Israelis and Palestinians.

In many ways, by this point, the deep schism in the Council, particularly between the United States and the rest of the Council, had long made meaningful action all but impossible, and the Council was unable even to uphold its own norms and values. Despite the immense growth of Israeli settlements in the West Bank since the Oslo years—the Council had declared that settlements had "no legal validity and constitute a serious obstruction to achieving a comprehensive, just and lasting peace" in a series of resolutions in 1979 and 1980—the Security Council had never taken much action.[49] The strong focus of the Obama administration on settlements from 2009 onward, however, prompted the Council to consider the issue. Yet a draft resolution on settlements, submitted by Lebanon with a total of 122 cosponsors in January 2011, led to the first instance that the Obama administration resorted to a veto and the first US veto overall since 2006. The United States had sought to avert a vote, proposing instead a Council presidential statement along the lines of the resolution, stronger Quartet language on 1967 borders, and endorsement of a Russian-backed proposal for a Security Council mission to the occupied Palestinian territory—all in vain. The US veto underlined how difficult Council action had become at this stage, even on issues where clear precedents appeared to exist. It also reflected the strong domestic pressure within the United States that made it impossible for the Obama administration to sanction a resolution that, by all accounts, it agreed with.

Twice more during this period, in December 2011 and in December 2012, the United States found itself isolated and exposed in public, when members of the Council—including all its European representatives—made strong statements to the press denouncing Israeli settlement activity.[50] On both occasions, Council members embarked on this course of action because it was clear that the United States would block any collective pronouncement.

The Council was equally split and unable to respond coherently when the Palestinian Authority applied for United Nations membership in September 2011. Whereas the Council had unanimously welcomed South

Sudan's membership application only months earlier, its standing committee overseeing admission of new members reported that it was unable to
reach the required unanimous recommendation on Palestine's application
by November 2011. A year later, the General Assembly would vote to confer nonmember observer state status on Palestine with the votes of nine
Council members, five abstentions from Council members, and one against,
from the United States.

Hope emerged briefly during 2013 that the long-standing deadlock in
the peace process would be broken, as US secretary of state John Kerry's
intense diplomatic efforts led to a resumption of negotiations before they
ultimately failed in April 2014. Throughout, however, these efforts
remained driven by the United States and saw the involvement of neither
the Quartet (which issued a statement welcoming the renewed talks) nor the
Security Council. As so often, momentum on the peace process reinforced
bilateral, rather than multilateral, engagement—a tendency that was also on
display during the 2014 war in Gaza when all serious efforts to broker a
ceasefire were bilateral or, if they did involve multiple parties, excluded the
formal mechanics of the Security Council.

Overall, in recent years, the Council has thus found it increasingly difficult to focus on the "big picture" of the Arab-Israeli conflict. Divided over
acute crises and subdimensions of the conflict, the Council has been unable
to act or—as the most recent discussions over Israeli settlement policy
illustrate—even restate language that had been agreed in earlier years. The
polarization has grown deeper as the 2000s have unfolded, limiting the
prospects for an eventual, more decisive engagement by the Council. This
has harmed the reputation and image of the Council and of the United
Nations at large, particularly when compared to instances elsewhere in the
region where the Council acted—and acted decisively.

Growing Regional Focus and
Micromanagement of Lebanese Affairs

The first decade of the twenty-first century saw the Security Council
increasingly involved in the wider region, particularly in Lebanon, where it
created a dense framework of norms and parameters through a large number of resolutions and presidential statements. It deployed not only the
UN's third largest peacekeeping operation—with the highest density of
troops by far—in Lebanon, but also an unparalleled number of senior UN
officials and envoys.[51]

The Council's deep involvement began in 1999 when Ehud Barak
became Israeli prime minister on the back of a campaign pledge to withdraw Israel's troops from south Lebanon and sought Security Council certification that the withdrawal satisfied the requirements of Resolution 425. In

an unprecedented operational engagement, a UN team worked closely with the Council to first identify the route of the so-called blue line, then to confirm Israel's withdrawal behind that line, in compliance with the resolution. The Council endorsed both in presidential statements in the course of 2000.[52]

On September 2, 2004, prompted by the crude effort of a Syrian-backed Lebanese government to prolong then-president Emile Lahoud's term in office, the Council adopted Resolution 1559. The resolution called not only for a free and fair electoral process, but also for the withdrawal of all remaining foreign (i.e., Syrian) forces and the disbanding and disarming of all Lebanese and non-Lebanese militias (i.e., the Syrian-supported Hezbollah and Palestinian groups). Although approved with only the minimum nine votes in favor and with six abstentions, the resolution marked the beginning of unprecedented Council involvement in Lebanese affairs (Terje Rød-Larsen would serve as special envoy for the implementation of Resolution 1559 from January 2005 through the time of writing) and represented a watershed. First, it was the cause through which France and the United States reconciled after their deep split in the Council over the Iraq War in 2003.[53] Second, the intense engagement of the Council in pursuit of Resolution 1559 as well as the subsequent "road map" for its implementation, Resolution 1680 of May 17, 2006, yielded undeniable results.

By April 2005, Syria had ended its three-decade military presence in Lebanon. A national dialogue agreed on the disarmament of Palestinian militias (even if no concrete action followed) and began debating Hezbollah's arms. In August 2008, Lebanon and Syria established diplomatic relations for the first time in their history.

At the same time, Resolution 1559 contributed to deepening existing sectarian and political divisions in Lebanon.[54] In the context of a highly charged political climate, on February 14, 2005, former prime minister Rafik Hariri was killed by a car bomb.[55] The next day—and invoking previous resolutions on international terrorism—the Council called on the Lebanese government to "bring to justice the perpetrators, organizers and sponsors of this heinous terrorist act."[56] On April 7, 2005, the Council adopted Resolution 1595, creating UNIIIC, which was mandated to gather evidence and assist the Lebanese authorities in their investigation of the assassination.

In the following months, the Council utilized the two-pronged set of Resolutions 1559 and 1595 to exert intense pressure on Syria and its Lebanese allies. By August 2005, Detlev Mehlis, the first head of UNIIIC, had four powerful, previously nearly untouchable Lebanese generals arrested in conjunction with the Hariri assassination. An advance version of his first report to the Security Council in October 2005, circulated in electronic format, inadvertently displayed tracked changes showing that an earlier version of the draft had explicitly suggested the involvement of senior Lebanese and Syrian figures, including President Bashar al-Assad's brother and brother-in-law.[57] Mehlis also obtained Security Council backing for his request to interview senior Syrian officials in the form of Resolution 1636 of October 31, 2005. Shortly afterward, the Council first acknowledged a request from the Lebanese government to establish a tribunal of "international character," then requested the Secretary-General to negotiate the necessary agreement on the establishment of such a tribunal.[58] While UNIIIC took on a much lower profile once Mehlis was replaced by Serge Brammertz in January 2006, its work continued, and the probe's mandate was extended repeatedly until it was eventually absorbed into the Special Tribunal for Lebanon (STL) as of March 1, 2009.[59]

Lebanese politics remained in turmoil. A number of prominent Lebanese politicians and public figures were targeted in a series of assassinations and assassination attempts that began in October 2004 and would continue until January 2008, when the top Lebanese official working with UNIIIC on the Hariri assassination was killed. The Security Council condemned these incidents and widened the investigation to include some of them, although few concrete leads emerged. Amid deep polarization, two Lebanese governments would fall over issues immediately linked to the investigation and the STL. In November 2006, pro-Syrian Shiite ministers resigned from prime minister Fouad Siniora's government, questioning its constitutionality. In this context, the Security Council responded to Siniora's request to establish the STL by adopting a Chapter VII resolution.

Resolution 1757 of May 30, 2007, passed with five abstentions, including from China and Russia as well as the Arab representative on the Council, Qatar, further fueled the divisions in Lebanon. Prolonged protests in downtown Beirut would escalate in May 2008 into the most serious episode of internecine violence since the end of the civil war before a national unity government was negotiated under Qatari sponsorship, a new president was agreed, and elections were held in 2009. The cabinet formed after these elections, headed by Saad Hariri (Rafik's son), would fall in January 2011 as speculation peaked that a widely anticipated STL indictment would accuse Hezbollah, not Syria, of having assassinated Rafik Hariri.

The STL would remain controversial, even if the issuing of arrest warrants against four Hezbollah members following an indictment by STL prosecutor Daniel Bellemare—who had succeeded Serge Brammertz as head of UNIIIC in November 2007—did not trigger widely feared protests or violence. In November 2011, Hezbollah prioritized the maintenance of the new government it was backing over its own earlier insistence that Lebanon cease all cooperation with the STL and enabled Prime Minister Najib Miqati to comply with Lebanon's funding obligations for it. The long-delayed trial started in January 2014, but against the background of the tumultuous events in Syria—whose repercussions triggered Miqati's resignation in March 2013—the STL had become largely irrelevant to politics in Lebanon. Instead, the intensifying Syrian civil war became the decisive determinant of political dynamics in Lebanon, prompting growing instability and creating a prolonged vacuum when factions could not agree on a new president after Michel Sleiman's term ended in May 2014. Although the Security Council adopted presidential statements appealing to the Lebanese to maintain national unity and elect a new president, a newly created "International Support Group" for Lebanon soon usurped the Council's role.[60]

Nevertheless, the Council's two-pronged engagement in Lebanon in the years after 2004 was instructive. First, the Council issued far-reaching and binding parameters on how Lebanon was to deal with major—and domestically highly divisive—issues. This contrasts with the Council's inability to set similar defining norms on the Israeli-Palestinian conflict, reflecting relative unity on Lebanon and deep divisions between Council members—particularly between the United States and the other members—on Israeli-Palestinian issues. Second, following its mixed experience with legal investigation and the establishment of a subsequent tribunal, the Council has refrained from repeating the experiment, at least to date. Third, the political turmoil that accompanied and followed the Hariri assassination and the establishment of the Special Tribunal for Lebanon highlights the inherent tension between justice and stability in the Council's engagement. In the case of Lebanon, the Council appeared to value principles of justice more highly than stability, although the abstentions in the vote on the establishment of the STL in 2007 underline that the Council was far from united. Yet the Council's actions in Lebanon differ significantly from its inability to be similarly principled—for example, on settlements—in the Israeli-Palestinian arena, where the United States, in particular, is under strong domestic pressure to protect Israeli interests.

But the Security Council was not focused just on the situation inside Lebanon during this period. The drawing of the blue line separating Lebanon and Israel had not brought the stability the Council had hoped for in 2000. The so-called Shebaa Farms, a small hamlet of farms claimed by Lebanon but determined (by the Secretariat, with subsequent Council endorsement) to be part of Israeli-occupied Syria, had grown into the purported justification for Hezbollah to maintain its arms and continue its attacks against Israel. The first such instance, in October 2000, left three Israeli soldiers dead, whose bodies were not returned until January 2003, but did not trigger wider conflict. The next major instance, on July 12, 2006, when Hezbollah fighters crossed the blue line to ambush an Israeli patrol, killing three soldiers and abducting two others, sparked war. Thirty-four days of conflict would leave 1,200 Lebanese and 140 Israelis dead and vital infrastructure destroyed, particularly in Lebanon. The Security Council, however, could not act for several weeks.

Indeed, its first reaction to the fighting was a presidential statement on July 27, 2006, to express "shock" and "distress" at the killing of four United Nations observers when Israeli aircraft struck their outpost.[61] Although most Council members favored calling for an immediate and unconditional ceasefire, some contended that it would be better to wait to allow Israel to defeat Hezbollah. Talks by a UN delegation dispatched to Lebanon and Israel laid the foundations for an eventual ceasefire resolution, but it took several weeks until agreement was reached. Resolution 1701, cosponsored by France and the United States, was adopted on August 11, 2006. Two days later, a ceasefire took hold.[62]

Resolution 1701 marked the first time that the Council agreed unanimously on the mandate of an essentially new peacekeeping mission in the region. Israel lobbied hard for the deployment of a NATO-led force to replace UNIFIL, but instead, UNIFIL was expanded sixfold, to the authorized troop strength of 15,000, and its mandate was reinforced significantly. UNIFIL would henceforth assist the Lebanese government—which agreed to deploy 15,000 troops in south Lebanon as well—to establish an area "free of armed personnel, assets and weapons other than those of the Lebanese government." European troop contributors, particularly France, Italy, and Spain, provided the force's backbone. In return, these troop contributors insisted on unprecedented operational control, prompting the establishment of a separate "military strategic cell" in New York, which comprised personnel from the troop-contributing countries and was designed to reinforce the chain of command between the troops on the ground and New York headquarters. In addition, a maritime task force was created to support the Lebanese navy in patrolling territorial waters.[63]

In the following years, Resolution 1701 and the reinforced UNIFIL would enable the longest period of relative stability between Israel and Lebanon in more than three decades. However, the new UNIFIL continued to come under criticism. Israel wanted the force to be more proactive in searching for arms, which it alleged continued to be smuggled into south Lebanon after 2006, allowing Hezbollah to rebuild a significant arsenal of missiles and rockets. Israel also maintained its intrusive regime of aerial surveillance of Lebanese territory, prompting bitter Lebanese complaints. UNIFIL itself pointed out that it could not exceed its mandate under Resolution 1701, which tasked it with only *supporting* the Lebanese armed forces. UNIFIL troops also walked a fine line between taking an assertive stance on the one hand, and compromising their own security on the other. An attack against a Spanish-Colombian contingent in 2007 killed six soldiers; subsequent attacks were also committed against French and Italian troops in May and July 2011. The attacks—never conclusively investigated—underlined UNIFIL's precarious position and ultimately precipitated significant reductions by European troop contributors. By the end of 2011, Indonesia was the largest troop contributor, and UNIFIL had settled into a mode of operations reminiscent of the pre-2006 period.

The reinforced UNIFIL had been intended to "buy time, not substitute, for progress on the political track both within Lebanon and also between Lebanon and its neighbours."[64] But there was no progress toward the disarmament of Hezbollah or the clarification of Lebanon's international boundaries, including in the disputed Shebaa Farms area. The northern half of the village of Ghajar, which had been divided by the blue line in 2000, remained under Israeli occupation after 2006, despite the fact that neither side actually disputed its status as belonging to Lebanon.

Resolution 1701 was successful in outlining the principles and elements for a "permanent ceasefire and a long-term solution" between Israel and Lebanon. But it did not achieve either in practice. In addition, Resolutions 1559 and 1701, despite the considerable overlap between them, continued to coexist alongside each other, with reporting cycles that led to the Council hearing briefings on almost identical issues within weeks of each other twice a year. Although some Council members suggested merging the two mandates, their coexistence, and the density of parallel processes and resolutions on Lebanon, also enabled the Council to maintain a degree of unity, precisely because the plurality of mandates and issues allowed each Council member to choose their respective areas of emphasis.

Nonetheless, the Council's unprecedented activism in and around the Lebanese arena during the 2000s contrasted starkly with its inability to shape events, establish broader frameworks, or uphold norms on the Israeli-Palestinian front where the deepening divisions in the Council, particularly between the United States and the other Council members, made action impossible. As a result, of this imbalance, the Council increasingly distanced itself from its erstwhile aspiration to address the Arab-Israeli conflict in its regional totality. This trend grew more and more pronounced following the onset of the Arab Spring in 2011, when the acute crisis in Syria as well as its reverberations in Lebanon and Jordan absorbed most of the Council's attention, while Middle East peace remained a domain of bilateral, US-led efforts.

Conclusion

The Middle East is one of the Security Council's longest-standing and most labor-intensive agenda items. Yet over the decades, the Council has found it difficult to play a leading role in addressing the Arab-Israeli conflict, defining decisive parameters, and contributing to resolve major crises conclusively. Instead, the Council became increasingly focused on acute crisis management issues that are but facets or subdimensions of the overall Arab-Israeli conflict, as well as with the definition and implementation of temporary and stopgap measures, including its primary tool, peacekeeping.

That said, the Council has defined—if not proactively, then through its endorsement, at least—the key parameters of what an eventual Arab-Israeli peace settlement would look like. It has also contributed over the decades to maintaining considerable stability along the borders separating Israel from the Arab world, notably by deploying peacekeeping operations.

For many years, the Council consciously approached the different dimensions of the Arab-Israeli conflict as parts of a wider issue that needed to be addressed holistically. Since the early to middle 2000s, this effort to maintain a broad regional perspective has been hollowed out, particularly as a result of the Council's deep engagement on Lebanon under Resolutions 1559, 1701, and 1595 and the subsequent Special Tribunal for Lebanon. This trend has accelerated significantly since the onset of the Arab Spring, with Council discussions dedicated to the situation in Syria, for example, in a way that has been disconnected entirely from the Arab-Israeli conflict. In this regard, the Council's increasing focus on country-specific situations and its decreasing consideration of the Arab-Israeli conflict in its regional totality, of course, reflects a wider reality shaping the Middle East itself: to a considerable extent, the importance ascribed to the Arab-Israeli conflict has receded, and domestic developments within the countries in the region have begun to take precedence and priority.

The Council's engagement in and on the Middle East over the past seven decades has also been a struggle with the specific nature of the Arab-Israeli conflict as an almost singularly high-profile conflict that evokes strong sentiments around the world. Divisions that have deepened over the past decade reflect that the conflict is relevant or closely related to important national security and domestic interests of key permanent Council members. Burgeoning bilateral ties between the United States and Israel have made it increasingly difficult for the former to support meaningful Council pronouncements on the Arab-Israeli or Israeli-Palestinian conflict. As a result, Council action has become an ever more distant prospect.

The United States remains indispensable to settling the conflict but has, because of domestic political constraints, found it difficult to use the Council as a policy-defining mechanism, or even an arena for constructive debate. It played a key role in the establishment of the Quartet as a mechanism intended to convey the legitimacy of the United Nations, but the Quartet encountered criticism precisely because it did not encompass the same legitimating breadth of views as the Council.

It would be in the interest of the Council—collectively, as well as in terms of its individual members—to seek to overcome the debilitating divisions that have characterized it in recent years. As a result of the inability of

Council members to use the instruments at their disposal more effectively, arguably the Council and the UN as a whole have been weakened. Public perception of the United Nations has often been susceptible to the Security Council's failures in and on the Middle East—especially if one includes Iraq and Syria. The Council's role as the primary guardian of international peace and security has, against a reality of deadlock and its own inability to act, often been usurped by other mechanisms, such as the Quartet, the General Assembly, or at times an enterprising Secretary-General or special envoy.

It might therefore be useful for the Council to try to refocus on the bigger picture, on broad parameters. Instead of being drawn into addressing acute crises, it could, in fact, leave the "day-to-day" management of crises to others—whether special envoys or the Quartet. In doing so, it would retain the role of ultimate arbiter and norm-setter. Given the difficulties and sensitivities related to the Middle East—and the deep polarization within the Council—a focus instead on broad, strategic, general parameters might indeed facilitate constructive engagement.

The Council has also suffered from a deep mismatch of expectations and political realities. To satisfy public expectations, the Council devotes much time to the Middle East—but it fails to meet those expectations precisely because it talks too much and does too little. Ostensible dedication of time to the issue must be better matched with concrete outcomes and actions.

At the time of writing, the Middle East was in the process of undergoing the most far-reaching changes since the end of the mandate period. This will inevitably alter not only political constellations and dynamics across the region, but also the Council's perspective and ability to address conflict in the Middle East. That said, if the Council cannot find a constructive role to play while the region transforms, it may find itself without any role or relevancy to speak of. The Middle East will undoubtedly remain one of the most vexing problems on its agenda.

Notes

The views expressed in this chapter are solely my own and not those of the United Nations.

1. Ralph Bunche, quoted in Brian Urquhart, *Ralph Bunche: An American Life* (New York: Norton, 1993), p. 150.

2. Bruce Jones, "The Middle East Peace Process," in *The UN Security Council: From the Cold War to the 21st Century,* edited by David M. Malone (Boulder, CO: Lynne Rienner, 2004), p. 400.

3. Brian Urquhart, "The United Nations in the Middle East: A Fifty-Year Retrospective," *Middle East Journal* 49, no. 4 (Autumn 1995): 1.

4. In integrated missions, all United Nations operations in a country fall under a single management structure, overseen by the special representative of the Secretary-General.

5. Bruce Jones, "The Security Council and the Arab-Israeli Wars: Responsibility Without Power," in *The United Nations Security Council and War: The Evolution of Thought and Practice Since 1945,* edited by Vaughan Lowe, Adam Roberts, Jennifer Welsh, and Dominik Zaum (Oxford: Oxford University Press, 2008), p. 322.

6. Ibid., p. 299.

7. Urquhart, "The United Nations in the Middle East," p. 6.

8. Jones, "The Security Council and the Arab-Israeli Wars," pp. 299–300.

9. Ibid.

10. Security Council Report, *Special Research Report, No. 4: The Middle East 1947–2007: Sixty Years of Security Council Engagement on the Israel/Palestine Question,* December 17, 2007, p. 10, www.securitycouncilreport.org/special-research-report/lookup-c-glKWLeMTIsG-b-3748287.php.

11. UNTSO's mandate of monitoring the 1948 truce was superseded by realities in subsequent years, but the mission continues to exist, now primarily lending support to two other regional peacekeeping operations, the UN Interim Force in Lebanon (UNIFIL) and the UN Disengagement Observer Force (UNDOF) through the Observer Group Lebanon (OGL) and Observer Group Golan (OGG).

12. Jones, "The Security Council and the Arab-Israeli Wars," pp. 303–304.

13. Urquhart, "The United Nations in the Middle East," p. 3; Security Council Report, *Special Research Report,* p. 13.

14. William Roger Louis and Roger Owen, *Suez 1956: The Crisis and Its Consequences* (New York: Oxford University Press, 1989).

15. The Council did unanimously adopt four resolutions calling for a ceasefire during June 1967 (Resolutions 233, 234, 235, and 236, adopted June 6, 7, 9, and 11 respectively), but the parties simply ignored them.

16. Jones, "The Security Council and the Arab-Israeli Wars," p. 308.

17. Urquhart, "The United Nations in the Middle East," p. 4.

18. Jones, "The Security Council and the Arab-Israeli Wars," pp. 308–309.

19. United Nations Security Council Resolution 340, S/RES/340 (October 25, 1973).

20. United Nations Security Council Resolution 350, S/RES/350 (May 31, 1974).

21. Urquhart, "The United Nations in the Middle East," p. 5.

22. Jones, "The Middle East Peace Process," p. 394.

23. Security Council Report, *Special Research Report,* p. 24.

24. Ibid.

25. Jones, "The Security Council and the Arab-Israeli Wars," p. 311.

26. Ibid., p. 313.

27. Jones, "The Middle East Peace Process," p. 395.

28. Kofi Annan with Nader Mousavizadeh, *Interventions: A Life in War and Peace* (New York: Penguin, 2012), chap. 7.

29. Sahar Okhovat, *The United Nations Security Council: Its Veto Power and Its Reform,* Working Paper no. 15/1 (Sydney: Center for Peace and Conflict Studies, 2012). See also UN overviews of Security Council meetings and outcomes for 2011 and 2012, from the Dag Hammarskjöld Library Research Guides, http://research.un.org/en/docs/sc/quick/meetings/2011 and http://research.un.org/en/docs/sc/quick/meetings/2012 respectively.

30. Jones, "The Middle East Peace Process," p. 397; Jones, "The Security Council and the Arab-Israeli Wars," p. 317. The Sharm el-Sheikh Fact-Finding Committee, led by former US senator George Mitchell, submitted its report—commonly

known as the Mitchell Report—in April 2001. It was an important reference point, but quickly receded into the background due to the continuing escalation of violence on the ground. The report is available at http://eeas.europa.eu/mepp/docs /mitchell_report_2001_en.pdf.

31. See, for example, United Nations Security Council Resolutions 1402, S/RES/1402 (March 30, 2002); 1435, S/RES/1435 (September 24, 2002); and 1450, S/RES/1450 (December 13, 2002).

32. Jones, "The Middle East Peace Process," pp. 398–399; Jones, "The Security Council and the Arab-Israeli Wars," pp. 318–319.

33. Security Council Report, *Special Research Report,* p. 10.

34. United Nations Secretary-General and Department of Public Information, "Transcript of Press Conference on Middle East, by Secretary-General Kofi Annan, Quartet Foreign Ministers, at United Nations Headquarters, September 20, 2005," UN Doc. SG/SM 10115, September 20, 2005.

35. United Nations Secretary-General and Department of Public Information, "Statement by Middle East Quartet," UN Doc. SG/2104-PAL2042, January 30, 2006.

36. United Nations Security Council, "Statement by the President of the Security Council," UN Doc. S/PRST/2005/44, September 23, 2005; and "Statement by the President of the Security Council," UN Doc. S/PRST/2005/57, November 30, 2005.

37. United Nations Security Council, "Statement by the President of the Security Council," UN Doc. S/PRST/2006/6, February 3, 2006.

38. De Soto's confidential report, of May 2007, was leaked to and published by *The Guardian,* http://image.guardian.co.uk/sysfiles/Guardian/documents/2007/06/12 /DeSotoReport.pdf.

39. Security Council Report, "Special Research Report," p. 2.

40. United Nations Security Council, *Report of the Secretary-General on the Middle East,* UN Doc. S/2006/956, December 11, 2006.

41. Security Council Report, "Special Research Report," pp. 3–4.

42. United Nations Security Council, "Statement by the President of the Security Council," UN Doc. S/PRST/2009/14, May 11, 2009.

43. United Nations Security Council Resolution 1544, S/RES/1544 (May 19, 2004).

44. United Nations General Assembly, *Report of the United Nations Fact-Finding Mission on the Gaza Conflict* (Goldstone Report), UN Doc. A/HRC/12/48, September 25, 2009.

45. United Nations Security Council, "Statement by the President of the Security Council," UN Doc. S/PRST/2010/9, June 1, 2010.

46. Security Council Report, "Israel/Palestine: January 2013 Monthly Forecast," December 21, 2012, www.securitycouncilreport.org/monthly-forecast/2013-01 /israelpalestine_1.php.

47. United Nations Meetings Coverage and Press Releases, "Security Council Press Statement on Middle East," UN Doc. SC/11472, July 12, 2014.

48. United Nations Security Council, "Statement by the President of the Security Council," UN Doc. S/PRST/2014/13, July 28, 2014.

49. United Nations Security Council Resolution 446, S/RES/446 (March 22, 1979), followed by Resolutions 452, S/RES/452 (July 20, 1979); 468, S/RES/468 (May 8, 1980); 469, S/RES/469 (May 20, 1980); 476, S/RES/476 (June 30, 1980); 478, S/RES/478 (August 20, 1980); and 484, S/RES/484 (December 19, 1980). See Security Council Report, "Special Research Report," p. 18.

50. Michelle Nichols, "Israeli Settlements Leave U.S. Odd Man Out at U.N. Security Council," *Reuters,* December 19, 2012, www.reuters.com/article/2012 /12/19/us-palestinians-israel-usa-un-idUSBRE8BI1KF20121219.

51. Markus E. Bouillon, "Zwischen den Stühlen: Von der schwierigen Rolle der Vereinten Nationen im Nahen Osten," *Vereinte Nationen* 55, no. 6 (2007): 221–227.

52. United Nations Security Council, *Report of the Secretary-General on the Implementation of Security Council Resolutions 425 (1978) and 426 (1978),* May 22, 2000, UN Doc. S/2000/460; United Nations Security Council, *Report of the Secretary-General on the Implementation of Security Council Resolutions 425 (1978) and 426 (1978),* June 16, 2000, UN Doc. S/2000/590; United Nations Security Council, "Statement by the President of the Security Council," UN Doc. S/PRST/2000/18, May 23, 2000; United Nations Security Council, "Statement by the President of the Security Council," UN Doc. S/PRST/2000/21, June 18, 2000.

53. David M. Malone, *The International Struggle over Iraq: Politics in the UN Security Council, 1980–2005* (Oxford: Oxford University Press, 2006).

54. Reinoud Leenders, *How UN Pressure on Hizballah Impedes Lebanese Reform* (Washington, DC: Middle East Research and Information Project, 2006).

55. Nicholas Blanford, *Killing Mr. Lebanon: The Assassination of Rafik Hariri and Its Impact on the Middle East* (London: Tauris, 2006); Michael Young, *The Ghosts of Martyr Square: An Eye-Witness Account of Lebanon's Life Struggle* (New York: Simon and Schuster, 2010).

56. United Nations Security Council, "Statement by the President of the Security Council," UN Doc. S/PRST/2005/4, February 15, 2005.

57. United Nations Security Council, "Letter Dated 20 October 2005 from the Secretary-General Addressed to the President of the Security Council," UN Doc. S/2005/662, October 20, 2005. The marked-up advance version is available at www.washingtonpost.com/wp-srv/world/syria/mehlis.report.doc.

58. United Nations Security Council Resolutions 1644, S/RES/1644 (December 15, 2005); and 1664, S/RES/1664 (March 29, 2006).

59. United Nations Security Council Resolutions 1686, S/RES/1686 (June 15, 2006); 1748, S/RES/1748 (March 27, 2007); 1815, S/RES/1815 (June 2, 2008); and 1852, S/RES/1852 (December 17, 2008).

60. United Nations Security Council, "Statement by the President of the Security Council," UN Doc. S/PRST/2013/9, July 10, 2013; and "Statement by the President of the Security Council," UN Doc. S/PRST/2014/10, May 29, 2014.

61. United Nations Security Council, "Statement by the President of the Security Council," UN Doc. S/PRST/2006/34, July 27, 2006.

62. Amos Harel and Avi Issacharof, *34 Days: Israel, Hezbollah, and the War in Lebanon* (New York: Palgrave Macmillan, 2008).

63. Security Council Report, "Special Research Report," p. 27.

64. United Nations Security Council, *Report of the Secretary-General on the Middle East,* UN Doc. S/2006/956, December 11, 2006, para. 32.

27

Iraq

David M. Malone and Poorvi Chitalkar

IRAQ HAS OCCUPIED A PLACE ON THE UN SECURITY COUNCIL'S
agenda for over three decades. In fact, the different phases of the Security
Council's engagement with Iraq provide a useful lens through which to
study the evolution of the Council since the end of the Cold War. It began
with tentative decisionmaking during the Iran-Iraq War in 1980, but shifted
to a more proactive stance as the Cold War started to thaw. In 1987, the
Council adopted a settlement plan, which Iraq and Iran accepted in 1988,
bringing active hostilities to an end. These developments foreshadowed
growing cooperation among the permanent five members of the Council in
the post–Cold War era.

When Iraq invaded Kuwait in 1990, the Council responded by imposing mandatory sanctions against Iraq and later that year authorizing a US-
led military intervention (which was carried out in early 1991), the deployment of weapons inspectors, and the creation of a complex sanctions
regime to encourage compliance with the disarmament obligations the
Council had imposed. Later, the Council created an even more complex
humanitarian program to mitigate the deleterious effects of those sanctions.
In the next round of events, in 2002–2003, the Council played the role of an
ultimately unsuccessful political broker and finally that of a marginal
peacebuilder after 2003.

In this chapter we first retrace the Council's engagement with Iraq from
1980 onward, and then explore in greater detail Security Council decisionmaking on Iraq from 2002 to 2013. The Council's engagement with Iraq
since 1980 has not only reflected wider patterns of international relations but
also defined them. Further, some of the lessons from its involvement with

551

Iraq have changed the Council's approach to promoting international security in many ways. Those lessons and others are discussed in our conclusions.

Tracing History

Iran and Iraq

The Iranian revolution in 1979, during which the Western-backed Shah of Iran was ousted and Ayatollah Ruhollah Khomeini established a new theocratic regime, proved to be the impetus for the decade-long Iran-Iraq War, which would claim hundreds of thousands of lives. Seeking to capitalize on the upheavals in Iran, Iraq attacked Iran, unprovoked. Among the P5, opinion overwhelmingly favored Iraq. The United States had been jolted by the loss of a key ally in the region, the Shah of Iran, and pained by a long-lasting hostage crisis in Tehran affecting staff of the US embassy there. The Soviet Union had faced criticism from Iran over its 1979 invasion of Afghanistan. Iraq had been a longtime trading partner of both the Soviet Union and France. The United Kingdom and China remained more neutral, the latter supplying arms to both sides in the course of the conflict.[1]

Constrained by the Cold War standoff among the P5, the Security Council failed to take any strong action. It adopted Resolution 479, calling upon Iran and Iraq to cease hostilities and settle their dispute through negotiations, but conspicuously failed to condemn the Iraqi aggression. The Council thus alienated a justly aggrieved Iran for many years, as a result of which Iran boycotted the Security Council.[2] This also emboldened Saddam Hussein, with fateful consequences for many years.

In the absence of convincing action by the Council, UN Secretary-General Kurt Waldheim offered his good offices to facilitate discussions, but to no avail. In 1980, Secretary-General Javier Pérez de Cuéllar appointed a former Swedish prime minister, Olof Palme, to help nudge Iran and Iraq toward a compromise. Finally, in 1987, Pérez de Cuéllar's efforts, coupled with a shifting dynamic within the P5 due to Mikhail Gorbachev's rise to power in the Soviet Union, led to the adoption of Resolution 598, which imposed a cease-fire (accepted by the two parties only after a further year of hostilities) to be monitored by the UN Iran-Iraq Military Observer Group (UNIIMOG)—a classic Cold War peacekeeping operation leveraging the political capital of neutrality to provide a buffer between warring parties.[3] The withdrawal of forces to internationally recognized borders was complete by 1990.

Iraq and Kuwait

The Iran-Iraq War is estimated to have cost Iraq over $450 billion.[4] Taking advantage of this war and Iraq's financial ruin, Kuwait began to press for concessions in its border disputes with Iraq. It exceeded its Organization of

Petroleum Exporting Countries (OPEC) oil production quota, flooding the market and depressing prices for Iraq's oil, which plummeted from $20 to $14 a barrel between January and June 1990. At a time when Saddam Hussein needed to deliver reward to his country, the demands of Kuwait risked further humiliating him in the eyes of Iraqi people as well as the Arab world.

Perhaps driven by these considerations, Iraq invaded Kuwait on August 2, 1990. Now demonstrating dynamics starkly different from those of the Cold War period, the Security Council, within a matter of hours of the invasion, condemned it, mobilized to declare a breach of the peace (under the terms of the UN Charter's Chapter VII), and demanded a complete withdrawal.[5] Four days later, Resolution 661 imposed comprehensive sanctions on both Iraq and occupied Kuwait, and established the 661 Committee to implement the same. This swift action signaled a fundamental shift in the UN's capacity to act, promising a new decisiveness and effectiveness in the post–Cold War era.[6] US secretary of state James Baker stated: "That August night, a half-century after it began in mutual suspicion and ideological fervour, the cold war breathed its last."[7] Resolution 661's sweeping sanctions regime, requiring careful monitoring and humanitarian management, represented a bold shift in the Council's approach to international peace and security. With it, the Council initiated a move beyond its hitherto preferred politico-military mode as mediator and peacekeeper between warring parties, to a more legal-regulatory approach seeking to enforce compliance with its demands, an evolution in Council disposition greatly amplified in Resolution 687 some months later.[8] This new approach would play out in the Council's engagement in Iraq over the next two decades.

When sanctions did not achieve the desired results, the Security Council moved to authorizing the use of force, driven by determined and highly effective US diplomacy managed by President George H. W. Bush, Secretary of State James Baker, and their UN ambassador, Thomas Pickering. In November 1990, Resolution 678 called on member states "to use all necessary means to uphold and implement Resolution 660 . . . and restore international peace and security in that region," unless Iraq were to comply with earlier resolutions by January 15, 1991.[9] When Iraq failed to comply, a military offensive, Operation Desert Storm, was unleashed by a US-led coalition importantly including leading Arab states such as Egypt and Syria. A powerful air campaign of overwhelming firepower and organization was followed by a ground war that, within a hundred hours, routed Iraqi forces, liberating Kuwait and driving Iraqi forces well into their own country before stopping. Bush later wrote that the decision not to move on to Baghdad was taken on the grounds that the Security Council had not authorized an advance on Iraq's capital, and also because it might provoke a disintegration of Iraq were its government to fall apart.[10] As Simon Chesterman and Sebastian von Einsiedel have written:

Resolution 678 provided the template for most of the enforcement actions taken through the 1990s: it was dependent on the willingness of certain states to undertake (and fund) a military operation; it conferred a broad discretion on those states to determine when and how the enumerated goals might be achieved; it limited Council involvement to a vague request to "keep the Security Council regularly informed"; and, most importantly, it failed to provide an endpoint for the mandate.[11]

Humanitarian response. Soon after Operation Desert Storm ended, insurgencies and humanitarian crises erupted in Iraq. Shiite militias rose up in rebellion in southern Iraq, and Kurdish rebels mounted an offensive in the north.[12] Although President Bush had called upon the Iraqi people to "take matters into their own hands and force Saddam Hussein to step aside,"[13] the United States would not intervene in the south and did so only belatedly in the north. The Security Council passed Resolution 688, condemning Iraqi repression and casting the refugee flows as a threat to international peace and security. Meanwhile, close to 2 million Kurdish civilians fled for their lives. Under strong media pressure, the United States led a coalition effort, Operation Provide Comfort, acting unilaterally without explicit Council authorization to address a humanitarian crisis. This effort relied on Resolution 688 and on international humanitarian law for justification, and was quietly accepted by Russia and China. Coalition forces, including the UK and France, imposed no-fly zones in both the north and the south. The UN Secretariat meanwhile devised an innovative stopgap arrangement stationing UN guards in northern Iraq, which permitted the return of thousands of Kurdish refugees and the safe delivery of a large international assistance program carried out by several UN agencies.

Resolution 688 signaled a significant shift in the Security Council, with human rights and broader humanitarian issues becoming prominent in the Council's decisionmaking. The resolution represented the first instance in which the Council explicitly stated that internal repression can lead to a threat against international peace and security. However, addressing human rights issues, which were hitherto seen as internal matters of states, remained controversial, and several countries, including India and China, voiced their reservations clearly.[14] Nevertheless, since then, the Council has increasingly invoked human rights in its decisions and addressed them in its mandates, although its practice has remained inconsistent across the range of crises it has addressed since 1991 (see Chapter 13).

Finally, the UN Iraq-Kuwait Observer Mission (UNIKOM) was established by Resolution 689 in April 1991. Once again, signaling a new a post–Cold War vigor, the Council empowered UNIKOM with duties under a Chapter VII mandate, implying coercive powers if necessary.

All of these developments to a degree provided grist for President Bush's vision of a "New World Order" as outlined in a speech to a joint session of Congress on September 11, 1990, prompted by the Iraqi invasion of Kuwait.[15]

Sanctions and weapons inspections. While international attempts to address some of Iraq's humanitarian needs were being made, Iraq's military capacity remained worrying, particularly after coalition forces uncovered the previously unknown extent of Iraq's weapons programs. Resolution 687, widely known as the "mother of all resolutions," required, among a range of other exacting provisions, the elimination of Iraqi weapons of mass destruction and missiles with a range of over 150 kilometers. In order to implement the disarmament of Iraq through weapons inspection and destruction, Resolution 687 put in place an unprecedented and complex regulatory machinery. The Council aimed to compel Iraq's compliance and cooperation through the continued imposition of wide-ranging sanctions. Together with an ambitious humanitarian program established a few years later, the overall result, seriously underestimated at the time, was one of regulatory and administrative overload for the UN.

The UN Special Commission (UNSCOM) was established in Resolution 687 to monitor the destruction or removal of Iraq's chemical and biological weapons. The International Atomic Energy Agency (IAEA) was charged with similar responsibility with respect to Iraq's nuclear capability. Iraq's compliance with UNSCOM was reluctant, at best. Over time, the climate of controversy and brinkmanship fostered by Saddam Hussein around the weapons inspectors undermined faith in the inspections approach, with Washington pressing for a confrontation between UNSCOM and Saddam Hussein in 1998. Following P5 divisions over the usefulness of the "inspections plus sanctions" approach, the United States and United Kingdom once again acted unilaterally to bomb Baghdad (Operation Desert Fox) for not allowing UNSCOM access to disputed sites. By December 1999 (with Resolution 1284), UNSCOM was disbanded amid acrimony over evidence of a degree of UNSCOM collusion with the CIA.[16] As Seymour Hersh succinctly put it, "The result of the American hijacking of the UN's intelligence activities was that Saddam Hussein survived but UNSCOM did not."[17]

Although the stated aim of UNSCOM was Iraq's disarmament, it soon became apparent that for the United States the goal was different. Secretary of State Madeleine Albright confirmed this in 1997, saying: "We do not agree with the nations that argue that sanctions should be lifted. Our view . . . is that Iraq must prove its peaceful intentions. . . . Is it possible to conceive of such a government under Saddam Hussein? The evidence is overwhelmingly that Saddam Hussein's intentions will never be peaceful. Clearly, a change in Iraq's government could lead to a change in US policy."[18] Washington's stance gave Saddam Hussein little incentive to cooperate with UNSCOM.

Even prior to this, the sanctions proved critically ill-suited to induce compliance with the UN's wider demands articulated in Resolution 687, as the Saddam Hussein regime itself suffered little from the effects of sanctions. Worse still, the sanctions created the potential for a lucrative black market largely controlled by and benefiting those in power in Baghdad while the Iraqi population suffered "near-apocalyptic" humanitarian consequences.[19] Although the exact numbers vary, by some estimates 500,000 Iraqi children under the age of five died as a result of the sanctions, and child mortality rates more than doubled between 1991 and 1999.[20] Some even compared the sanctions regime itself to a weapon of mass destruction.

By 1995, the sanctions were becoming unpopular well beyond Iraq and led to a division within the P5, with France and Russia, in particular, pressing to end them, for humanitarian and perhaps also commercial reasons. The devastating impact and overall ineffectiveness of the sanctions regime in Iraq, which mostly remained in place until 2003 due to disagreement and lack of unanimity among the P5 over ending it (although some measures lingered thereafter), created widespread negative perceptions globally of sanctions, one of the few coercive instruments at the Council's disposal. While, as a result, the design and application of sanctions has been refined, the overall impact on the UN's reputation of their use in Iraq was and remains singularly negative.

The vast humanitarian oil-for-food program was created in 1995 under Resolution 986 to respond to the perverse outcomes of these sanctions. Under the program, Baghdad was allowed to sell oil, with the export revenues devoted to purchasing humanitarian supplies under the controlling eye of the UN. A few years later, Baghdad was allowed to take over the distribution of goods within the country and choose who would buy Iraqi oil, greatly expanding the opportunities for corruption.[21] Over its lifetime, the oil-for-food program handled $64 billion worth of Iraqi revenue and served as the main source of sustenance for over 60 percent of Iraq's population. Meanwhile, Iraq continued to channel oil illegally to Jordan, Turkey, and Syria (with some of the P5 actively looking the other way), while billions of dollars were stolen by Iraqi and other intermediaries in the form of kickbacks. Frustratingly for UN staff, everything about the oil-for-food program, not unlike the Security Council itself, was inherently political. The selection of oil-sale overseers, the bank to hold the revenues in escrow, and the firms to provide the supplies were all negotiated among member states in the Council, particularly the P5.[22]

Thus, the strategy of containment based on "inspections plus sanctions," buttressed by the occasional unilateral use of force, ultimately sundered P5 unity. Crumbling international support for this approach on the one hand, and the relentless pursuit of this approach by the United States and United Kingdom on the other, ultimately undermined the credibility and legitimacy of the related (and for some, wider) Council decisions for many other member states.[23] Its standing, greatly elevated in 1990 and 1991, never fully recovered.

As a result of its learning from the Iraq experience, the Security Council now imposes time limits as common practice in sanctions regimes. This has not only altered the power dynamics within the Council, but also forced it, at regular intervals, at least in theory, to assess the effectiveness of its measures in relation to other UN objectives such as the protection of human rights. Further, there has been an impetus to craft "smart sanctions"—those that target perpetrators and avoid adverse impact on civilian populations.

A legal-regulatory approach. The evolution of the Security Council's role on Iraq points to one significant shift—from a mainly politico-military approach to international peace and security to a greater reliance on a legal-regulatory approach. In its legal-regulatory approach, the Council establishes detailed rules governing the behavior of states or other entities and devolves power to implement and monitor those rules to administrative delegates.

UNSCOM, the sanctions regime, and the oil-for-food program are examples of this legal-regulatory approach, and each provides examples of the Council's failures of oversight. Yet the Council is not likely to abandon this approach. Given the nature of contemporary threats that are diffuse, global, and often propagated through nonstate actors, collaborative, proactive, and complex solutions, for which the politico-military approach is insufficient, are required.

Just as agencies in the domestic national spheres are bound by principles of administrative law in regulatory decisionmaking, so should be institutions of global governance, like the Security Council, when they act in legal-regulatory capacities.[24] In adopting this perspective, the Council would be not only upholding the rule of law, but also enhancing its own legitimacy and credibility. The Council's effectiveness ultimately rests on UN member states recognizing its authority—and a Council seen to be accountable and responsible has a better chance at that.[25]

There are important lessons from Iraq for the Council's effectiveness in this legal-regulatory approach. First, regulatory agencies need clear mandates. Resolutions must be precise, specifying what rules the delegated agent is to implement, the powers available to it in implementing them, and the process by which they should be enforced. The Iraq sanctions regime was the biggest, most complex, and longest-lasting ever implemented by the UN. Yet whether its goal was disarmament, regime change, or achievement of broader regional stability in the Middle East was not clear, and the P5 disagreed among themselves on this key point. The duration of the sanctions regime was also not specified, and the "reverse veto" dynamic, requiring P5 unanimity for change, turned it into an indefinite one, long after support for it had evaporated internationally.

Second, member states as well as regulatory agents must be accountable. UNSCOM is an excellent example of an ambitious regulatory attempt by a Security Council encumbered with muddled lines of accountability. The chairs of UNSCOM were appointed by the Secretary-General, but were to report to the Council. The triangular relationship became highly problematic when UNSCOM head Richard Butler and Secretary-General Kofi Annan differed on issues of substance. When claims arose that the United States was using UNSCOM for its own intelligence purposes, there was no clarity on whom UNSCOM was answerable to. Similarly, the Volcker inquiry report found "egregious lapses" in the management of oil-for-food program both by the UN Secretariat and by member states, also noting that neither the Security Council nor the Secretariat was in clear command, producing evasion of personal responsibility at all levels.[26]

Third, agents must be independent and adequately resourced so as to maintain their capacity to perform effectively. For example, regarding sanctions, the 661 Committee, which consisted of Council members, was required to oversee extremely lengthy and complex contracts under Resolution 661. However, with some exceptions, members did not have the expertise or the resources to perform this task. The Secretariat also was apparently somewhat adrift. No wonder problems set in.

The UN and Iraq, 2001–2003

By 2001 the Security Council was stuck in an impasse over Iraq recalling the Cold War. Any adjustments to strategies earlier agreed without an endpoint were prevented by the "reverse veto." The terrorist attacks of September 11, 2001, only strengthened Washington's resolve. The risk of proliferation of weapons of mass destruction to terrorists became a driving preoccupation for the United States, as did determination to get rid of Saddam Hussein once and for all.

President George W. Bush's "National Security Strategy" of 2002 advocated preemptive use of force, and made clear that the United States would not hesitate to act alone.[27] This largely new doctrine suggested that the nation was free to use force against any foe it perceived as a potential threat to its security, at any time of its choosing, and with any means at its disposal. In the words of legal scholar Thomas M. Franck, this "stood the UN Charter on its head."[28]

It is now clear that a decision to go to war against Iraq was taken within the Bush administration by the late spring of 2002.[29] Nonetheless, under pressure from some of its traditional allies (mainly the UK), the United States adopted the "UN route." But President Bush delivered an ultimatum to the UN: if the Security Council would not back the US demand for forceful disarmament of Iraq and regime change, the Council would be sidelined and, in effect, deemed irrelevant.

Seeking a "middle ground" between unarmed inspections and military intervention, the Security Council adopted Resolution 1441 in November 2002. It decided that Iraq had been in "material breach" of its disarmament obligations and gave it one final opportunity to comply, failing which it would face serious consequences. It required Iraq to allow inspections of the UN Monitoring, Verification, and Inspection Commission (UNMOVIC), which was created by the Council in 1999 to replace UNSCOM, to operate freely, as well as to provide a complete disclosure of Iraq's WMD activities. However, Resolution 1441 suffered from creative ambiguity—it was unclear what would constitute a failure by Iraq to comply, what would happen in the event of the failure, and most important, who was to decide. Mainly, it left unanswered the question of whether "failure" by Iraq would automatically permit states to enforce the resolution, or whether a second resolution would be necessary for that purpose.

Following the resolution, UNMOVIC deployed to Iraq under Hans Blix, an energetic leader. In January 2003, Blix told the Council that Iraq had not accepted the disarmament demanded of it, but that UNMOVIC was doubtful of Iraq's possession of biological and chemical weapons. Mohammad El Baradei of the IAEA told the Council that Iraq was not in the process of reconstituting its nuclear program. Further, both UNMOVIC and the IAEA pointed to Western intelligence failures in Iraq. Sharp divisions within the P5 flared up, with France threatening to veto any attempt to go to war, supported by Germany, Russia, and China. In a final attempt along the "UN route," the United States, Britain, and Spain introduced a draft resolution stating that Iraq had failed to take the "final opportunity" afforded by Resolution 1441. If passed, this resolution would have provided a rationale for the use of force. However, the deadlock within the P5 persisted, and on March 19, 2003, the invasion of Iraq by a US-led coalition began, absent Security Council authorization. (The United Kingdom and United States had withdrawn their draft resolution not because of a veto, but because they had been unable to secure the nine positive votes among Council members required for its adoption.)

A number of the episodes of sharp diplomatic confrontation over a six-month period in 2002–2003, particularly in February 2003, involving foreign ministers and ambassadors, unfolded before the eyes of the world, broadcast by television all over the globe. The UN Security Council chamber and its surroundings offered nonstop drama, becoming a crucible for world politics as it had been before only during the Cuban missile crisis of 1962 and in the run-up to Operation Desert Storm in 1990–1991. Counterintuitively, the decision by Washington and London to attack Iraq without a

UN mandate proved highly negative for the UN in world public opinion. The Council was written off—in the United States for failing to confront the threat of weapons of mass destruction, and around the world for its failure to prevent the invasion of Iraq.

In this sidelining of the UN, the United States signaled a new approach. It would look to the UN as one potential source of legitimacy and support—one coalition among many—but if the UN could not contribute to the achievement of its foreign policy goals, the United States would act without its support. The sidelining of the UN by the United States prompted widespread criticism not only of the United States but also the UN. Many argued that there had been a twin failure on the part of the UN: failure to contain Iraq and the failure to contain the United States. Further, the UN's failure was seen as a sign of an international system that was insufficiently responsive to the needs of the day and didn't mirror the evolving realities of world power. James Traub describes the Catch-22 situation that the Security Council found itself in: "Containing the Bush administration has meant finding a middle ground between rubber stamping American policy—and thus making the Council superfluous—and blocking American policy, and thus, provoking America to unilateral action, which of course would make the Council irrelevant."[30]

However, the sidelining of the UN did not come without its costs for the United States, both financial and reputational. When the United States acted unilaterally without explicit authorization from the UN, it showed disregard for the principles (and benefits) of collective decisionmaking. Soon after its intervention in Iraq, the United States began to realize that it needed far more resources and troops than previously anticipated.[31] Embarrassingly, the claims of WMD that justified its decision to go to war have since been proven unfounded. International skepticism of US intelligence-based assertions was bound to be greater in the future, as witnessed in reactions to US allegations against Iran's nuclear program in recent years (however much these have often been buttressed by IAEA reports).[32]

The Occupation of Iraq and Beyond, 2003–2013

With the coalition-led invasion under way, both the coalition powers and other UN member states were left to decide what its future role there could be. While the establishment of a new UN political office in Iraq to support the transition process now risked retrospectively lending legitimacy to the coalition's purposes and methods, its absence would represent an abdication of its essential peacebuilding role. Striking a balance, once the major coalition military campaign to occupy and subdue the country was over, the Security Council on May 22, 2003, adopted Resolution 1483, which recognized the United States and United Kingdom as occupying powers, which was followed by the appointment of a special representative of the Secretary-General (SRSG) to Iraq, Sergio Vieira de Mello. Secretary-General Kofi Annan envisaged a broad multidisciplinary assistance operation, to be carried out by the new UN Assistance Mission in Iraq (UNAMI), including constitutional, legal, and judicial reform; police training; demobilization and reintegration of former military forces; public administration; and economic reconstruction. However, on the ground, the United States resisted any significant role for the SRSG.

On August 19, 2003, the UN suffered the largest loss of its civilian employees to date. A truck-bomb detonated outside UNAMI headquarters in Baghdad, killing Vieira de Mello and twenty-one others. The terrorist attack shocked the UN community and cooled its ardor to play a leading role in Iraq, but also carried implications for its approach to peace operations elsewhere thereafter. Any notion of the UN and its staff somehow rising above conflict and enjoying a degree of immunity from attack due to its humanitarian mission vanished.

Soon after securing Baghdad, the slow and rocky task of nation (re)building began for the coalition. A Coalition Provisional Authority, headed by US administrator Paul Bremer, was established, and together with the SRSG it was tasked with appointing an interim Iraqi administration. The appointed Iraqi Governing Council (IGC) served as a provisional government for Iraq, and on November 15, 2003, the provisional coalition authority and the IGC entered into an agreement on the political process, involving several steps: a transitional national assembly would prepare a constitution; an interim government would be formed by June 2004; and national elections for a post-transition government would be held by December 2005. However, finding support for this arrangement, particularly among the Shiites and the Kurds, proved challenging.

Recognizing the difficulty of the task, the United States called upon the UN to play a role in gaining acceptance for the plan. Lakhdar Brahimi, the UN's most respected mediator, and the architect of the Taif Agreement, which ended the Lebanese civil war, working with the provisional coalition authority and the Iraqis as a UN special envoy, was able to engineer an acceptable interim government until elections could be held and, importantly, injected much-needed legitimacy into the political process. Nevertheless, at his mission's end in May 2004, he expressed some frustration over the difficulty of working with the provisional coalition authority, characterizing Bremer as "dictator of Iraq" in a parting shot.[33] British officials working within the provisional coalition authority and in London expressed similar reservations, more privately.

On March 8, 2004, a "transitional administrative law" was signed to serve as a constitutional framework until elections allowed for drafting a new constitution.[34] At the same time, the IGC was replaced by a transitional government that would prepare for elections. On June 28, 2004, sovereignty was restored to the Iraqis, and a transitional government headed by Iyad Allawi took over.

Throughout this period, the security situation remained tenuous. The provisional coalition authority disbanded the Iraqi military and oversaw de-Baathification of the security forces. In the resulting security vacuum, the coalition was unable to meet the most basic security needs of Iraq's citizens. Further, the effect of a disenfranchised Sunni community was underestimated. An energetic insurgency that destabilized an already fragile Iraq with an intense cycle of conflict ensued (also involving elements of the al-Qaeda terrorist movement).[35] A decade later, domestic security is still seriously impaired by patterns of sectarian and insurgent violence, with murderous crescendos of bombings punctuating political life in ways often difficult to decode from outside the country.

The humanitarian costs of the decade of war continue to burden Iraq. About 5 million Iraqis have been displaced from their homes since 2003. While hundreds of thousands fled to Jordan and Syria, nearly 3 million are displaced within Iraq.[36] While estimates vary, in all likelihood some 100,000 civilians lost their lives during these years.[37] Minority ethnic and religious groups, including the Bahais, Christians, Shabaks, and others, have been and continue to be particularly vulnerable in the face of insecurity.[38]

UNAMI

Since 2003, the UN's role in Iraq has been that of a peacebuilder. UNAMI was established by Resolution 1500 in 2003, with its role greatly expanded in 2007. Its mandate included supporting political dialogue and national reconciliation, assisting in electoral processes, facilitating regional dialogue between Iraq and its neighbors, and promoting the protection of human rights and judicial and legal reform.[39] Between 2003 and 2005, UNAMI remained seriously handicapped by the bombing of its headquarters and the lack of political space to play a meaningful role. Ben Rowswell, senior program manager of the National Democratic Institute in Erbil and then Canada's diplomatic resident representative in Baghdad from 2003 to 2005, recalls: "After de Mello's death the UN played important technical roles such as with the surprisingly successful organization of three national polls in 2005, but exercised little significant political influence."[40] Jeremy Greenstock, the UK's senior representative in the provisional coalition authority, in 2003 noted: "The main stumbling blocks for greater UN involvement were a), of course, big power disagreement but also b) the Iraqi people's distaste for the UN after sanctions."[41]

However, UNAMI played an important role in the process of drafting and adopting a constitution in 2005 as well as with elections in 2009 and

2010. In 2006 the International Compact with Iraq was entered into—an agreement between the Iraqi government and the United Nations, with the support of the World Bank, aimed at normalizing the security environment, reconciling the political environment, and revitalizing the economy.[42]

Current signals from the ground are hardly encouraging, except per-haps for developments in the Kurdish provinces. There is widespread recognition that at times, on politically sensitive issues such as the status of Kirkuk, UNAMI has made real contributions. That said, like much else in Iraq, Kirkuk's status remains unresolved. UNAMI represents one of the UN's largest political deployments, along with its cousin UNAMA in Afghanistan (which equally wrestles with unpromising local circum-stances). As of March 2015, UNAMI included 241 troops (responsible for protecting UN buildings and staff), 326 international civilian staff, and 460 national civilian staff, with a projected budget that year of $137.2 million.[43]

Depressingly, despite hard and at times bold and effective work by UN staff, no meaningful reconciliation has been achieved. The Kurdish territo-ries continue their transition toward complete autonomy, the economy is still hamstrung, and violence remains endemic. Iraq's public life stumbles from crisis to crisis, UN and other international efforts notwithstanding.[44]

Joost Hilterman, who has contributed so much to the excellent analyti-cal work on Iraq of the International Crisis Group concludes: "On balance, within Iraq, the UN has made the best of a bad hand, lying low when it was most vulnerable to US manipulation, then playing to its strength on issues that the US was willing to hand over, such as disputed territories. Now, with US troops gone and the situation deteriorating partly as a result of developments in neighbouring Syria, the UN could play a more prominent role but would probably achieve less due to local dynamics."[45]

Conclusion

The Iraq experience demonstrates that the Security Council is tremendously vulnerable to the ebb and flow of international politics, especially the rela-tionship among the P5 at any given time. P5 members alienate each other at considerable risk, as happened during the 1990s and again between 2000 and 2003 regarding Iraq. When the Iran-Iraq War broke out, Cold War divi-sions prevented an effective Council response. By contrast, freed from the Cold War stasis, the Council acted swiftly and effectively in addressing Iraq's aggression against Kuwait. Indeed, this success triggered in the Council a short-lived era of euphoria, during which, between 1991 and 1993, it passed 209 resolutions and authorized fifteen peacekeeping and observer missions. But that euphoria soon gave way to bitter experience in the Balkans, Somalia, and Rwanda, while P5 divisions over Iraq grew only more pronounced. As a result, P5 relationships frequently curdled.

Although their capitals continued to be disposed to and capable of cooperation on most Security Council files, their disagreements over sensitive ones, most recently Syria, are much harsher in nature and tone than should be the case, exhibiting little taste and capacity for compromise.

The Iraq case after 1990 points to real limitations of the Security Council's ability to oversee the implementation of its decisions impartially and effectively (for example, with active collusion of leading Council members, the awarding of contracts under the oil-for-food program was highly politicized, with benefits "carved up" between member states). These have been addressed to some extent through the professional staffs of several of the Council's committees, but the instinct in P5 capitals to advance national objectives, including commercial ones, through Council decisions, remains strong. Administrative probity lost out to diplomatic realpolitik in the Council on Iraq. But most of the blame of the Volcker Report fell on the Secretary-General and others in the Secretariat.

The 2003 invasion also holds important lessons for postconflict reconstruction and statebuilding. In the case of Operation Iraqi Freedom, the insufficient number of boots on the ground to secure key locations, coupled with a lack of postwar planning, resulted in widespread looting and collapse of basic services like electricity, medical, and local security. Observing the multiple failures by the invading coalition, Larry Diamond articulated important lessons for postconflict reconstruction: preparing for a major commitment, committing enough troops with the proper rules of engagement to secure the postwar order, mobilizing international legitimacy and cooperation, as well as generating legitimacy and trust within the postconflict country. Perhaps most important, he advised, are humility and respect, since the act of seizing the sovereignty of a nation is a particularly bold and assertive one.[46] These recommendations apply to the Security Council in planning UN operations just as much as to Washington in planning US interventions. Similarly, cautioning against the underestimation of the fallouts of interventions, Phebe Marr warns: "If you cannot garner adequate resources and public opinion at home and abroad to rebuild a nation, don't start."[47]

Even for the most powerful nation in the world, the quality and quantity of member states it keeps as company in its international ventures matter. In 1990 the US administration, working closely with P5 capitals, Arab governments, and many others, patiently built the consensus necessary for the formidable military and political coalition, with significant regional participation, to which Operation Desert Storm gave expression under an expansive but nevertheless well-defined Council mandate. It stopped well short of toppling the government and taking over the country. The result was, overall, a very good one for coalition members and for the UN. In 1999, facing a Russian veto threat, NATO acted without Council authorization in launching air strikes against Serb forces in Kosovo (and eventually in Serbia), but enjoyed significant support in the Muslim world and beyond, while Moscow's attempt to have the Council condemn NATO could garner only three of the Council's fifteen votes. But in 2003, the United States and United Kingdom led a narrowly gauged coalition involving no active Arab participation (although several Gulf countries did provide quiet support). Washington and London overestimated their own capacity to govern a country of which they knew all too little, and failed in all but the narrow objective of overthrowing Saddam Hussein, at huge cost to Iraq, the region, and themselves. The very lack of broadly based (particularly regional) company in this venture should have served as a warning flare that sailing would not be easy and that the venture was highly risky. A Security Council mandate in and of itself, because of the legitimacy it confers, tends to produce company.

Deliberately vague resolutions seeking to bridge deep differences can be dangerous. The lack of clarity about what amounted to "material breach" of Resolutions 687 and 1441, about "serious consequences" threatened by Resolution 1441, as well as about who would enforce those provisions, and what powers were available to actors, made it tempting for the United States (if not the United Kingdom) to undertake unilateral military action relying on implied authorization as justification. Short-term diplomatic cleverness in the form of sleight of hand in capitals and within the Council carries great risk. Meaning of mandates needs to be clear and widely shared, at the very least among the P5.

The Security Council engaged in a flight forward on Iraq as of 1991, imposing ever sterner restrictions and conditions on the country, hoping against the evidence that these would compel cooperation with its objectives. The humanitarian costs of the strategy caused France to defect from the critical P3 consensus, which the United Kingdom and United States, in their agitation, hardly seemed to notice. And they hardly seemed to notice that international public opinion had abandoned them. This speaks to the isolation of chanceries that can convince themselves of almost anything. Reflecting on a failure to secure Council approval for the invasion of Iraq in 2003 might productively have prompted second thoughts. The United States and United Kingdom largely lost the 2003 Iraq War, after briefly winning it. In public opinion, the Security Council lost a great deal of legitimacy for failing to prevent the war (and it would have been compromised even further had it endorsed the war under US pressure). There were thus no winners from this fiasco.

And perhaps the central lesson in this sorry saga is that there is nothing inevitable about a new cold war among the P5 members unless there is greater sensitivity to each other's concerns and ability and willingness to craft compromises that are operationally viable. On Iraq's legacy within the

Council, Lord Mark Malloch Brown, former administrator of the UNDP
and UN deputy secretary-general, and later a minister in the UK government of Gordon Brown, sums up aptly if gloomily:

> The Security Council is inhabited by the Ghost of Iraq. Crisis after crisis
> seems to re-open the distrust sowed by that conflict. The West is branded as
> having manipulated intervention into a means of projecting its power and in-
> fluence under a UN banner. The opposition, notably Russia and China, is por-
> trayed as having turned its back on the Responsibility to Protect and human
> rights more generally. The result is a broken-backed unreformed Council no
> longer representative of the distribution of global power, let alone the Charter
> Principles, but only of the world's basest fears and suspicions.[48]

Notes

This chapter draws on David M. Malone, *The International Struggle over Iraq: Politics in the UN Security Council, 1980–2005* (Oxford: Oxford University Press,
2006), and on the scholarship and ideas of James Cockayne, who has written extensively on the Security Council's involvement in Iraq.

1. Ramesh Thakur and Waheguru Pal Singh Sidhu, eds., *The Iraq Crisis and
World Order: Structural, Institutional, and Normative Challenges* (Tokyo: United
Nations University Press, 2006).

2. Javier Pérez de Cuéllar, *Pilgrimage for Peace: A Secretary-General's Memoir* (New York: St. Martin's, 1997), p. 132.

3. David M. Malone and James Cockayne , "Lines in the Sand: The UN in Iraq,
1980–2001," in Thakur and Sidhu, *The Iraq Crisis and World Order,* p. 5.

4. Kamran Mofid, *Economic Consequences of the Gulf War* (London: Routledge, 1990), p. 133.

5. United Nations Security Council Resolution 660, S/RES/660 (August 2,
1990).

6. Malone and Cockayne, "Lines in the Sand," p. 7.

7. James A. Baker, *The Politics of Diplomacy: Revolution, War, and Peace,
1989–1992* (New York: Putnam's Sons, 1995), p. 16.

8. Malone, *The International Struggle over Iraq;* James Cockayne and David
Malone, "The UN Security Council: 10 Lessons from Iraq on Regulation and
Accountability," *Journal of International Law and International Relations* 2, no. 2
(Fall 2006): 1–24.

9. United Nations Security Council Resolution 678, S/RES/678 (November 29,
1990).

10. George H. W. Bush and Brent Scowcroft, *A World Transformed* (New York:
Knopf, 1998), p. 303.

11. Simon Chesterman and Sebastian von Einsiedel, "Dual Containment: The
United States, Iraq, and the U.N. Security Council," in *September 11, 2001: A Turn-
ing Point in International and Domestic Law,* edited by Paul Eden and Thérèse
O'Donnell (Ardsley, NY: Transnational, 2005).

12. Malone and Cockayne, "Lines in the Sand," p. 9.

13. George H. W. Bush, "Remarks to the American Association for Advancement of Science," Washington, DC, February 15, 1991, www.presidency.ucsb.edu
/mediaplay.php?id=19306&admin=41.

14. Joanna Weschler, "Human Rights," in *The UN Security Council: From the Cold War to the 21st Century,* edited by David M. Malone (Boulder, CO: Lynne Rienner, 2004), p. 58.

15. George H. W. Bush, "Address Before a Joint Session of the Congress on the Persian Gulf Crisis and the Federal Budget Deficit," Washington, DC, September 11, 1990, http://en.wikisource.org/wiki/Toward_a_New_World_Order.

16. David M. Malone, "Iraq: No Easy Response to 'The Greatest Threat,'" *American Journal of International Law* 95, no. 1 (January 2001): 239.

17. Seymour M. Hersh, "Saddam's Best Friend," *The New Yorker,* April 5, 1999, p. 32.

18. Madeleine K. Albright, "Preserving Principle and Safeguarding Stability: United States Policy Toward Iraq," *Foreign Policy Bulletin* 8 (March 1997): 109–112.

19. United Nations Security Council, *Annex: Report to the Secretary-General on Humanitarian Needs in Kuwait and Iraq in the Immediate Post-Crisis Environment by a Mission to the Area Led by Mr Martti Ahtisaari, Under-Secretary-General for Administration and Management, Dated 20 March 1991,* UN Doc. S/22366, March 20, 1991, para. 8.

20. Joy Gordon, *The Invisible War: The United States and the Iraq Sanctions* (Cambridge: Harvard University Press, 2010); Mohamed M. Ali and Iqbal H. Shah, "Sanctions and Childhood Mortality in Iraq," *The Lancet* 355, no. 9218 (May 2000): 1851–1857, relying on UNICEF, *The State of the World's Children 1997* (New York, 1997).

21. James Traub, "The Security Council's Role: Off Target," *The New Republic* 232, no. 6 (February 21, 2005): 14.

22. Ibid., p. 16.

23. Malone, "Iraq: No Easy Response," p. 240.

24. See, generally, the New York University School of Law's "Global Administrative Law Research Project," http://iilj.org/GAL; Benedict Kingsbury, Nico Krisch, and Richard Stewart, *The Emergence of Global Administrative Law,* Working Paper no. 2004/1 (New York: Institute for International Law and Justice, 2004).

25. Simon Chesterman, *The Security Council and the Rule of Law: The Role of the Security Council in Strengthening a Rules Based International System* (Vienna: Federal Ministry of European and International Affairs and Institute for International Law and Justice, 2008).

26. Paul A. Volcker, Richard J. Goldstone, and Mark Pieth, *Manipulation of the Oil-for-Food Programme by the Iraqi Regime* (Volcker Report) (New York: Independent Inquiry Committee into the United Nations Oil-for-Food Programme, 2005).

27. Office of the President of the United States, *The National Security Strategy of the United States of America* (Washington, DC: White House, September 17, 2002).

28. Thomas M. Franck, "What Happens Now? The UN After Iraq," *American Journal of International Law* 97, no. 3 (July 2003): 619.

29. Walter Pincus and Dana Priest, "Some Iraq Analysts Felt Pressure from Cheney Visits," *Washington Post,* June 5, 2003. See also Nicholas Lehman, "How It Came to War: When Did Bush Decide That He Had to Fight Saddam?" *The New Yorker,* March 31, 2003, p. 36.

30. James Traub, "Who Needs the Security Council?" *New York Times,* November 17, 2002, www.nytimes.com/2002/11/17/magazine/17UNITED.html.

31. US Department of Defense, Office of the Assistant Secretary of Defense (Public Affairs), "On Iraq: Testimony As Delivered by Deputy Secretary of Defense Paul Wolfowitz, Director, Office of Management and Budget, Joshua Bolten, and Acting Chief of Staff, US Army, Gen. Keane, Tuesday, July 29, 2003," July 29, 2003, www.defense.gov/speeches/speech.aspx?speechid=494.

32. Kenneth M. Pollack, "Spies, Lies, and Weapons: What Went Wrong," *The Atlantic*, January/February 2004, p. 92, www.theatlantic.com/magazine/archive /2004/01/spies-lies-and-weapons-what-went-wrong/302878.

33. Tom Lasseter, "Brahimi: Bremer the 'Dictator of Iraq' in Shaping Iraqi Government," *Knight Ridder Newspapers,* June 2, 2004.

34. US General Accounting Office, "Iraq's Transitional Law," May 25, 2004, www.gao.gov/assets/100/92639.html.

35. Freedom House, "Iraq," in *Freedom in the World 2013,* https://freedom house.org/report/freedom-world/2013/iraq#.VMA7jS5cBKo.

36. Ibid.

37. For one serious estimate slightly larger than this, see figures from the Iraq Body Count database "Documented Civilian Deaths from Violence," www.iraq bodycount.org/database.

38. Human Rights Watch, "Iraq: At a Crossroads," February 2011, p. 65, www.hrw.org/sites/default/files/reports/iraq0211W.pdf; Bill Bowring, "Minority Rights in Post-War Iraq: An Impending Catastrophe," *International Journal of Contemporary Iraqi Studies* 5, no. 3 (2011): 332.

39. United Nations Security Council Resolution 1770, S/RES/1770 (August 10, 2007).

40. Correspondence with the authors, September 7, 2013.

41. Correspondence with the authors, August 29, 2013.

42. United Nations Meetings Coverage and Press Releases, "United Nations, Iraq Jointly Announce Launch of Five-Year International Compact Aimed at Achieving National Vision of United, Federal, Democratic Country," UN Doc. IK/552, July 27, 2006, www.un.org/News/Press/docs/2006/ik552.doc.htm.

43. United Nations, "Factsheet: United Nations Political and Peacebuilding Missions," March 31, 2015, www.un.org/en/peacekeeping/documents/ppbm.pdf. For budget figures, see United Nations General Assembly, "Report of the Secretary-General: Estimates in Respect of Special Political Missions, Good Offices and Other Political Initiatives Authorized by the General Assembly and/or the Security Council," A/69/363, October 17, 2014.

44. Regular reports to the Council document the dire conditions in the country. The most recent, at the time of writing, dated July 11, 2013, is *Third Report of the Secretary-General Pursuant to Paragraph 6 of Resolution 2061 (2012),* UN Doc. S/2013/408. Also see the Iraq archive of the research NGO Security Council Report, www.securitycouncilreport.org/un-documents/iraq; and assessments by New York University's Center on International Cooperation documenting both UN peace missions in Center on International Cooperation and Alischa Kugel, Richard Gowan, Bruce Jones, and Megan Gleason-Roberts, *Annual Review of Global Peace Operations 2013* (Boulder, CO: Lynne Rienner, 2013).

45. Correspondence with the authors, August 29, 2013.

46. Larry Diamond, "Building Democracy After Conflict: Lessons from Iraq," *Journal of Democracy* 16, no. 1 (January 2005): 20.

47. Phebe Marr, "Occupational Hazards: Washington's Record in Iraq," *Foreign Affairs* 84, no. 4 (July–August 2005): 186.

48. Correspondence with the authors, August 30, 2013.

28

The Balkans

Mats Berdal

THE BREAKUP OF THE SOCIALIST FEDERAL REPUBLIC OF YUGO-
slavia and the humanitarian consequences and regional repercussions it
spawned were prominent, at times even dominant, items on the Security
Council agenda for much of the early post–Cold War period. There were
good reasons for this. The violent dissolution of a founding member of the
United Nations, occurring at a time when the geopolitical certainties of the
Cold War were fast eroding, presented the international community with a
series of profound challenges and, as became clear soon enough, deeply divisive issues. These ranged from the evolving meaning of self-determination
and how best to protect minorities when borders change and new states are
created, to the use and utility of military force in response to large-scale
humanitarian emergencies and gross violations of human rights.

Examining the international response to these challenges must of
necessity touch on the long-term and proximate origins of the wars of
Yugoslav succession. A detailed discussion of those origins, however, is
beyond the scope of this chapter.[1] Instead, my main concern here is with the
decisions and actions of the Security Council: its functioning as a decisionmaking body, the factors that impaired its effectiveness, and the controversies to which its performance in the Balkans gave rise. It is through the
prism of the Council's handling of the Yugoslav crisis and wars that I will
explore these larger issues.

To this end, the chapter proceeds in three parts. The first explores the
initial stages of the Council's involvement in the Yugoslav crisis from early
1991 through to the establishment of a UN peacekeeping force in Croatia in
February 1992. The Council's direct engagement during this period was ini-

tially limited, though it grew in importance as the crisis deepened, violence spread, and the confused and ineffectual peacemaking efforts of the European Community (EC) made little substantive headway.

The second and principal part of the chapter focuses on the war in Bosnia and Herzegovina (hereafter Bosnia)—that is, the phase of the conflict in which the Council was most deeply and controversially engaged. The discussion here is framed around two key sets of questions: What were the driving factors behind Council decisionmaking and how did the cumulative impact of its decisions influence the nature of the UN's activities on the ground? And why did the central issue of the use of military force prove so divisive within the Council?

The final and concluding section considers the period following the Dayton peace accords in 1995. It examines the escalating crisis in Kosovo in 1998 and 1999, which culminated in NATO's bombing campaign against the Federal Republic of Yugoslavia in March and April 1999. That campaign was designed, in part, to halt the excesses of Milosevic's violent crackdown against the province's Albanian population, but was initiated, controversially, without explicit Security Council authorization for the use of force. This fact provides the basis for a final set of reflections on the legacy and long-term significance of the Council's involvement in the Balkans between 1991 and 1999.

The Security Council and the Disintegration of Yugoslavia, 1991–1992

"A Detached Bystander"

The results of the multiparty elections held on the republican level throughout Yugoslavia in 1990 brought home a discomforting truth. While democracy is a laudable ideal, the process of democratization can be divisive and conflict-generating, especially so in economically weak and ethnically fragmented societies where the nerve of local nationalisms has been prodded by ruthless, unscrupulous, and self-serving politicians. As Warren Zimmerman, the last ambassador of the United States to Yugoslavia, would later reflect: with the elections of 1990 "the age of naked nationalism had begun."[2] Even so, there was nothing preordained about Yugoslavia's descent into war and violence. The ethnic heterogeneity of the federation and its constituent republics and provinces did, however, make the system of constitutional checks and balances bequeathed by Josip Broz Tito acutely vulnerable to virulent ethnonationalism of the kind unleashed by Slobodan Milosevic of Serbia and Franjo Tudjman, elected president of Croatia, in 1990. Among the republics, the ethnic mix was most pronounced in Bosnia, where, according to the 1991 census, 43.5 percent of the population considered themselves "Muslims by nationality," 31.2 percent Bosnian Serbs, and 17.4

percent Bosnian Croats. Croatia also had a significant Serbian minority population geographically concentrated in the Krajina region and in Western and Eastern Slavonia.[3] It was in these two republics that the unleashing of nationalism would prove most catastrophic in its consequences, and where the fighting that accompanied Yugoslavia's breakup would prove most destructive.

For all the warning signs, as tensions rose and relations among the republics worsened in the first half of 1991, the Security Council maintained its distance to events, passing its first resolution on the Yugoslav crisis only in late September. In the words of David Hannay: "as Yugoslavia slid towards disintegration and tipped over into civil war the UN remained a detached bystander."[4]

There were several reasons for this. To start, the federal government, even though its authority and legitimacy were fast seeping away, resisted bringing the Yugoslav crisis to the UN, insisting it was a matter of domestic concern. This was a view that found particular resonance with nonaligned countries, wary of the precedent-setting effect of involving the UN in a matter they deemed to fall "essentially within the domestic jurisdiction" of a member state.[5] Moreover, for much of the first half of 1991, the Council was primarily focused on the war in Iraq and its messy aftermath, while two of its permanent members, the Soviet Union and China, were preoccupied by domestic turmoil and political challenges. Above all, however, the Council's comparative aloofness stemmed from the fact that the European Community had taken the lead in international efforts to find a diplomatic solution to the developing crisis and, initially at least, did not wish to pass the baton on to the UN. The presumption that the EC would lead the search for a solution, with the UN in a supporting role, remained in place throughout the second half of 1991.

War and Growing Council Involvement

On June 25, 1991, Croatia and Slovenia proclaimed their independence from Yugoslavia. Within days, fighting and violent clashes erupted, though the attempt by the Federal Yugoslav Army (JNA) to halt Slovenia's secession was halfhearted and "Slovenia's war of independence" lasted barely ten days. Croatia's determination to secede, however, provoked a far more violent response, with the JNA lending both direct and indirect support to the Serb paramilitary forces fighting for their self-proclaimed "Republic of the Serbian Krajina." The war in Croatia during the latter half of 1991 saw large-scale civilian suffering and atrocities, widespread physical destruction, and a rapidly growing refugee crisis.

It was against this backdrop of mounting violence and civil war that the UN Security Council, at the formal initiative of Belgium, France, and the UK, first met to discuss the breakup of Yugoslavia. Security Council Resolution 713, adopted under Chapter VII and passed unanimously on September 25, 1991, is best remembered for having imposed a "general and complete" arms embargo on Yugoslavia. The wisdom of that decision would later, once the conflict had spread to Bosnia, become a subject of intense controversy among key Council members, as the United States, against the wishes of the UK, France, and Russia, began supporting calls for a partial lifting of the embargo as it applied to the Bosnian government. More immediately, however, Resolution 713 invited the UN Secretary-General to "offer his assistance" to those promoting peace efforts, specifically to the EC, whose Conference on Yugoslavia, chaired by Peter Carrington, had convened in The Hague for the first time earlier that month. To Secretary-General Javier Pérez de Cuéllar, anxious to avoid competition with the EC over management of the crisis, the main emphasis of the resolution was to signal the "Council's support for the efforts of the Community to restore peace and dialogue in Yugoslavia."[6] There was no discussion, at this stage, of deploying a UN force to Yugoslavia.

The difficulty, it soon emerged, was that Resolution 713 did little either to reduce the fighting or to strengthen the negotiating hand of the EC. As one EC-brokered ceasefire after another collapsed and The Hague conference made no progress toward an overall settlement, an increased UN role was sought, first to assist diplomatic efforts to negotiate a settlement, then through humanitarian assistance (under the auspices of the UN High Commissioner for Refugees), and eventually in a peacekeeping capacity. The first step was the appointment by Pérez de Cuéllar of a personal envoy to Yugoslavia, Cyrus Vance, who, together with Carrington, would work to bring an end to the fighting and reach a wider political settlement and, thus, hopefully, prevent the violence from spreading further. There was, however, a further and complicating aspect to the EC's efforts to deal with the Yugoslav crisis in the autumn of 1991.

As the federation broke up into its constituent parts following Slovenia and Croatia's declarations of independence, it soon became clear that a profound division existed within the EC regarding the diplomatic approach to the escalating crisis. The point at issue centered on the question of whether early recognition should be extended by the EC to Slovenia and Croatia as independent states, or whether recognition should await agreement of an overall political settlement that, crucially, would have to include "adequate guarantees for human rights and rights of national or ethnic groups."[7] The former view was strongly favored by Germany, whose foreign minister, Hans-Dietrich Genscher, began to push for recognition soon after Slovenia and Croatia's declarations of independence. The United Kingdom, France, the United States, and Cyrus Vance all opposed early and selective recognition, as, initially, did the EC as a whole and Bosnia's president, Alija Izetbegovic, who feared the potentially destabilizing consequences of such a decision for his own republic.[8] The bone of contention was not, in other words, whether or not the old Yugoslavia could be held together indefinitely by withholding recognition, as, plainly, by the autumn of 1991, Yugoslavia was in a state of dissolution. Opposition to premature and selective recognition stemmed instead from the fear that it would, in the words of Pérez de Cuéllar, "widen the present conflict and fuel an explosive situation especially in Bosnia-Herzegovina and Macedonia."[9]

At a deeper level, of course, the controversy surrounding the recognition of former republics was not simply about crisis management and diplomatic timing. Beneath it lurked more fundamental issues for the international community raised by the violent collapse of Yugoslavia. Not only did the unraveling of Yugoslavia point to possible tensions between widely accepted values and principles of international society, but differences were also emerging about how some of those very principles, enshrined in the UN Charter as well as the Helsinki Final Act of 1975, to which Yugoslavia was a signatory, should be interpreted or reinterpreted in light of the developing crisis itself. How should one reconcile the sanctity of the principle that borders cannot be changed by the use of force, with demands for "equal rights and self-determination of peoples"? How exactly should those rights be understood in the context of a multiethnic federal structure in a state of dissolution? In particular, how could one ensure that the rights of minorities would be adequately protected and their "legitimate aspirations" satisfied? What emerged, unsurprisingly, from the Council's early discussions on Yugoslavia, insofar as these questions were systematically broached at all, were a series of unresolved tensions, underlying disagreements, and question-begging statements rather than clear answers.[10]

In the end, the issue of recognition itself, or rather its timing, was quickly settled. On December 16, 1991, EC leaders reversed their earlier stance and lined up behind the German position, agreeing to extend recognition to all those republics wishing it by mid-January 1992, "subject to the normal standards of international practice and the *political realities* in each case."[11]

By the time the EC recognition of Croatia and Slovenia came into effect (Germany had recognized Croatia on December 23, 1991), preparations were under way for a UN peacekeeping force to be deployed to Croatia, where the frontlines were beginning to stabilize following a period of intense and bloody fighting. Agreement on the principle of a UN force to monitor a viable ceasefire had already been reached some two months earlier in discussions between Milosevic, Tudjman, and Defense Minister Veljko Kadijevic. It had been made conditional, however, at the strong insistence of the Secretary-General and Cyrus Vance, who brokered the agreement, on the existence and continued observance of an effective ceasefire, a condition that was unanimously endorsed by the Council.[12] The proposed deployment would be based on the established principles of peacekeeping—consent, impartiality, and minimum use of force except in self-defense—and would form an "ink blot" pattern where fighting had been intense and tensions remained high. The ceasefire proved difficult to establish and the Council resisted authorizing a deployment of UN troops until the conditions laid down had been met. By the time a more durable ceasefire was reached between Croatian authorities and the JNA in early January 1992, the fighting on the ground had reached a stalemate that left a quarter of the republic under control of Serbian paramilitary forces supported by the JNA. On February 21, the Council finally authorized the establishment of a UN Protection Force (UNPROFOR) in and around Serbian-controlled "protected areas" in the Krajina region, as well as Western and Eastern Slavonia.[13] According to the mandate, the UN would help demilitarize the UN-protected areas, control access to them, and monitor the JNA's withdrawal from Croatia along with that of other irregular forces. It would also be "an interim arrangement to create the conditions for peace and security required for the negotiation of an overall settlement of the Yugoslav crisis."[14] In essence, the UN deployment, which got under way in March 1992, froze the situation on the ground, as it would remain, to the growing frustration of Croatian authorities, until the spring of 1995, when all but Eastern Slavonia was overrun in two Croat military offensives.

However much one allows for the complexity of the issues presented by the disintegration of old Yugoslavia, the EC's handling of the Yugoslav crisis in 1991 proved a deeply unimpressive and inauspicious start to its stated ambition of forging an effective external policy following the end of the Cold War. Indeed, as Lawrence Freedman observed of its efforts, "at times [it] seemed bent more on crisis aggravation than management: first, by failing to acknowledge the strength of ethnic feeling; and, second, by making the creation of an independent Bosnian state almost unavoidable but doing little to guarantee its integrity."[15] The EC's manifest failure to manage the crisis was one reason why the Council gradually came to assume a more central role in international efforts to mitigate, contain, and resolve the conflict. With the conflict about to enter a more violent and catastrophic phase, the Yugoslav crisis was set to remain firmly on the Council's agenda for the next four years. Even so, the Council, but also the Secretariat, was initially wary of becoming more deeply involved, especially if this meant authorizing a peacekeeping operation in the absence of a viable ceasefire and a credible political process.

The War in Bosnia, 1992–1995

May 1995: A Vignette

In May 1995, as Bosnia was rapidly returning to a state of all-out war, the commander of UN forces for the whole of the former Yugoslavia, General Bernard Janvier, was preparing to leave his headquarters in Zagreb for New

York. The Council was awaiting a report from Secretary-General Boutros Boutros-Ghali on the state of the UN's mission, and Janvier was scheduled to brief its members. On the eve of his trip he received an assessment from his commander in Sarajevo, General Rupert Smith, on the immediate challenges facing UN forces in Bosnia. Noting how matters had deteriorated since the collapse of the fragile ceasefire negotiated by former president Jimmy Carter in late 1994, and convinced that "both sides intend to fight to a solution," Smith carefully spelled out three possible options for the UN force: muddle on, a "stronger military response," or withdrawal. The first and last of these were not, he assumed, realistic options. As for the second, he candidly identified, as he had on previous occasions, the implications it carried for the Security Council. He wrote that it would have to "answer the fundamental question of whether the UN should enforce and escalate for aims other than self-defence."[16] It would take two more months and many more deaths before key Council members, as well as troop-contributing countries, were prepared seriously to confront Smith's question.

Smith's letter to Janvier in May 1995 points to a basic political reality of the period between 1992 and the summer of 1995 that does much to explain why the Bosnian war came to represent such a sorry chapter in the Council's history. Throughout this period, key Council members proved unable to forge a common *strategic* purpose that went beyond a limited set of objectives on which they could all agree. The tireless pursuit of more easily agreed goals—including the provision of humanitarian relief and other efforts to mitigate and contain the conflict—should not be dismissed as insignificant or wasted.[17] They did not, however, provide strategic direction for a large-scale military force that was plainly configured for peacekeeping of a traditional kind but that was operating in an environment where, for much of the time, there was no peace to keep. Operationally, the absence of such direction and the reactive nature of Council decisionmaking had the effect of generating ever more conflicting demands on UN forces in the field, nearly to the point, when Janvier set off to brief the Council in May 1995, of paralysis.

The Limits of Involvement: The Security Council and Bosnia, March 1992–July 1995

The war in Bosnia began in late March 1992. Unwilling to accept the prospect of minority status within an independent Bosnia, Bosnian Serbs had boycotted a referendum on independence held in late February, following the EC's earlier recognition of Croatia and Slovenia. The war intensified dramatically after the formal recognition of Bosnia by the EC on April 6, 1992. Over the course of the next three months, a murderous onslaught by Bosnian Serb forces, aided and abetted by the JNA following their withdrawal from Croatia, triggered an immediate and massive humanitarian emergency. Writing to Boutros-Ghali in mid-April, the UN's high commissioner for refugees, Sadako Ogata, spoke of "a human drama of enormous proportions," with the number of people fleeing their homes having "to be revised upwards by the hour."[18] The offensive, designed to "ethnically cleanse" territory of non-Serb populations, resulted in Bosnian Serb forces securing control of more than 60 percent of the territory of the newly recognized republic. That figure remained fairly constant until the summer of 1995. The Security Council, having received an assessment of the situation on the ground following a UN fact-finding mission in early May headed by Marrack Goulding (in charge of UN peacekeeping at the time), initially decided against the deployment of a peacekeeping force to the country, accepting the argument that "in its present phase" the conflict was not "susceptible to the UN peacekeeping treatment."[19]

Not long after this assessment had been received, Croatia, Slovenia, and Bosnia were all, following the formal recommendation of the Council, admitted as new members of the UN by the General Assembly. An immediate technical consequence of this was to make military involvement in Bosnia by Serbia and Croatia into acts of international aggression in defiance of the Charter. It was against this background that the Council, in Resolution 757, adopted on May 30, 1992, imposed comprehensive economic sanctions on Serbia and Montenegro while demanding "swift action to end all interference and respect the territorial integrity of Bosnia and Herzegovina."[20]

As the full extent of the conflict in Bosnia and its humanitarian consequences became ever more apparent in the summer of 1992, pressures on the Council to act and for the UN to become more directly involved intensified, notwithstanding the findings of Goulding's mission. Thus, on September 14, 1992, the Council, adopting Resolution 776, formally authorized the enlargement and geographic expansion of the UN Protection Force to support the efforts of the UNHCR to deliver humanitarian relief throughout Bosnia on the basis of "normal" peacekeeping principles. By late autumn 1992, the UN's overall objectives for the former Yugoslavia on which Council members were able to agree, and which would continue to define the common ground for Council action until summer 1995, had crystallized. These were threefold: first, relieving as far as possible the human suffering caused by the wars, initially by operating the Sarajevo airport and by protecting UNHCR convoys; second, containing the conflict to the territories of the former Yugoslavia and limiting, to the extent possible within an existing peacekeeping mandate, the intensity of fighting; and third, facilitating the efforts of the warring parties themselves to reach a political settlement. In the course of the mission, the mandate evolved and new tasks were added onto existing ones, yet the deployment of UN troops remained geared toward the achievement of these three basic purposes.

The limited and reactive nature of these goals reflected disagreements among member states about the origins and the nature of the conflict, disagreements that had been evident during the war in Croatia the previous year and that became more acute as the conflict wore on. As the war continued, an increasing number of UN member states, notably the United States, Germany, and several prominent members of the nonaligned caucus, questioned the wisdom and the viability of the initial assumptions on which UN involvement had been based. And yet, until the summer of 1995 and after the fall of Srebrenica, the Council and other troop-contributing countries displayed little or no willingness to move toward taking enforcement action. Nor did the United States or Germany suggest they might provide troops for such action themselves. In short, UNPROFOR remained a "peacekeeping" mission—lightly equipped, widely dispersed, and vulnerable—in the midst of an ongoing war. The result was an ever-widening list of Council resolutions and presidential statements aimed at addressing specific contingencies arising in the field and adopted under Chapter VII of the Charter, with a view not to enforce or impose a solution but to demonstrate resolve. As the war dragged on, conflicting pressures on UNPROFOR— urged to take more forceful action, though without changing the peacekeeping basis of its mandate—only intensified.

One Council resolution adopted under Chapter VII before the events of the summer of 1995 that would eventually prove to have important long-term consequences was the establishment in May 1993 of the International Criminal Tribunal for the Former Yugoslavia (ICTY). At the time, the establishment of an ad hoc tribunal in the midst of an ongoing war was greeted, not unjustifiably, with cynicism in many quarters as yet another attempt to "demonstrate resolve" in the continuing absence of a credible political strategy among Council members for dealing with the conflict. As of late 2013, 161 persons had in fact been indicted by the ICTY, while its creation had also provided an important background development to the subsequent establishment of the permanent International Criminal Court (ICC), which came into force in 2002. None of this, it should be added, has removed controversy surrounding the ICTY's performance and lasting contribution to building peace in the region.[21]

Consequences of Council Action: US-European Tensions and the "Safe-Area" Regime

The establishment of the "safe-area" regime in Bosnia in May and June 1993 provides the clearest example of how tensions within the Council and among member states ushered in decisions that were ultimately to have catastrophic consequences on the ground. In the spring and summer of 1993, against the backdrop of a major Bosnian Serb offensive in eastern Bosnia, the Council passed a series of resolutions conferring safe-area status on the towns of Sarajevo, Tuzla, Zepa, Gorazde, Bihac, and Srebrenica.[22] The critical resolution—Resolution 836, passed under Chapter VII of the Charter—extended the mandate of UNPROFOR to enable it "to deter attacks against the safe areas" and decided that member states, "acting nationally or through regional organisations or arrangements, may take, under the authority of the Security Council . . . all necessary measures, through the use of air power, in and around the safe areas in the Republic of Bosnia and Herzegovina, to support UNPROFOR in the performance of its mandate."[23] The tough wording notwithstanding, to the sponsors of the resolution, France and Britain, 836 did not signify any commitment actually to "protect" or "defend" the designated areas.[24] Although the establishment of the safe areas was intended to address an increasingly desperate situation on the ground, London and Paris were also responding to other pressures. In particular, the creation of safe areas served to forestall growing pressure from the new US administration for the adoption of a "lift and strike" policy—that is, for a partial lifting of the arms embargo as it applied to the Bosnian government, combined with air strikes against Bosnian Serb targets throughout Bosnia.[25] Pressures for more forceful action against the Bosnian Serbs did not, however, come only from the United States. The nonaligned caucus, represented by Venezuela and Pakistan, which were then on the Council, also played a key role in the actions and decisions that led to the creation of the safe-area regime (in the end, though, both countries chose to abstain on Resolution 836).[26]

The implementation of the safe-area concept soon ran into major difficulties as, initially, few countries offered to make *additional* troops available to meet even the "light minimum option" of 7,600 troops that had been agreed by the Council.[27] In late October 1993—more than four months after the adoption of Resolution 836—General Jean Cot, the UN force commander at the time, informed New York that "until arrival of Dutchbat [the promised Dutch battalion] in January 1994, I have no force to put into the three eastern enclaves," and that in the meantime Gorazde was only monitored by one team of UN military observers.[28]

But just as serious in the long run were the continuing tensions among key Council members about the appropriate policy toward Bosnia and, resulting from these tensions, the failure to align activities on the ground with diplomatic efforts, such as they were, aimed at reaching an overall political settlement. At the time of its adoption, Resolution 836 was justified in the only way that it could be justified: a short-term initiative to stabilize a precarious humanitarian situation and to buy time for diplomatic efforts to bear fruit. The sponsors of the resolution were not blind to what Boutros Boutros-Ghali would later refer to as the "inherent deficiencies of the safe-area regime"; yet they still hoped in May and June 1993 that a political breakthrough toward a settlement would prevent these deficiencies from becoming too acute. Ambassador Jean-Bernard Mérimée, explaining

France's sponsorship of the resolution, made it clear that "the designation and protection of the safe areas [was] not an end in itself, but only a temporary measure: a step towards a just and lasting political solution."[29] Yet this is precisely where progress continued to prove most elusive.

Given that UNPROFOR was already overstretched and unable to meet the expectations of the Sarajevo government, the continuation of the war meant that the disjunction between Security Council decisions and UNPROFOR activities on the ground only widened further. After the collapse of the European Union's action plan in late 1993, the third peace plan to be presented to the parties, more than sixteen months were to pass before all three parties to the Bosnian conflict would again be present at negotiations. As a result, the safe-area regime "was left without any political underpinning."[30] At the same time, the number of agreements, partial ceasefires, military exclusion zones, and ultimatums that UNPROFOR was given the task of supervising and monitoring—issued not just by the Security Council but now also by NATO—continued to grow. By early 1995 the remarkable list of agreements whose implementation the UN was committed to support included the Sarajevo Airport Agreement of June 1992, the Srebrenica Agreement of April 1993, the Srebrenica and Zepa Agreements of May 1993, the Mount Igman Demilitarized Zone Agreement of August 1993, the Sarajevo Airport Agreement of February 1994, the agreement on the use of civilian traffic across the Sarajevo airport of March 1994, the Gorazde Agreement of April 1994, and the Anti-Sniping Agreement of August 1994.[31] In addition to this came the commitments arising out of the ceasefire in 1994 between the Bosnian Croat and government forces in central Bosnia. And all the while, as the UNHCR's special envoy for the former Yugoslavia in 1993–1994, Nicholas Morris, would later observe, the humanitarian operation "itself increasingly became a factor in the political considerations of the parties to the conflict and of the international community."[32]

The deepening of tensions between the Americans, on the one hand, and European troop contributors, above all France and Britain, on the other, provides the key to understanding dynamics of Council decisionmaking following the creation of the safe-area regime. Bill Clinton had as presidential candidate promised tough military action against Bosnian Serbs and initially encouraged the view that he would deliver on his promise. In reality, the incoming administration was deeply divided over Bosnia policy, with its foreign policy team, in Madeleine Albright's own words, engaging in "numerous rambling and inconclusive meetings about the crisis . . . without achieving consensus" during the early months of 1993.[33] The failure to make political and diplomatic progress in the wake of Resolution 836, followed soon afterward by humiliating setbacks in Somalia and Haiti, contributed to what Ambassador Albright pointedly told a congressional committee was "a period of recalibrating our expectations."[34] The result of this process did not, however, have the effect of dampening tensions with the Europeans over Bosnia policy. Indeed, in many ways it had the very opposite effect. On the one hand, foreign policy setbacks made the Clinton administration far more sensitive to domestic and specifically congressional criticism of its Bosnia policy and thus more susceptible to domestic political pressure for "action" to be taken. On the other hand, events in Somalia in particular only reinforced a determination *not* to become involved militarily. The result was a pattern of being "in" politically and "out" militarily, which the Europeans, above all Britain, France, and to a lesser degree Russia, resented. In their view, the US attitude acted as an obstacle to end the war, because it provided a powerful disincentive for the parties to stop fighting. As long as none of the external powers were prepared to impose a solution by force of arms, while at the same time continuing to differ profoundly on the way forward, the warring parties would persist in seeking to obtain a decisive political or military advantage. In the second half of 1994, mounting evidence of covert US support for the Bosnian-Croat federation in violation of the arms embargo only added further to the transatlantic tensions. The effect of these tensions, not just on Council decisionmaking but also on other efforts to bring the war to an end—notably those of the International Conference on the Former Yugoslavia (ICFY) and from April 1994 onward the Contact Group for Bosnia—were profound. As David Hannay acknowledged not long after leaving New York, the fact that a "more robust and less vulnerable policy" was not adopted in Bosnia before the summer of 1995 "was more due to the tensions between those member states with troops on the ground and those like the US without, than it was to any disembodied entity thought of as 'the UN' pursuing a policy of excessive caution."[35]

Russian and Chinese Security Council Priorities

From early 1993 onward, then, policy differences and simmering tensions between the United States on the one hand and Britain and France on the other provided the most significant fault-line within the Council.[36] This is not, of course, to suggest that London and Paris always saw eye to eye on the conflict and its management through the UN. Nor does it mean that Russia and China, the other two permanent members of the Council, had no views or interests of their own that they sought to advance within the Council chamber. It is a striking feature of both Russian and Chinese policy toward Bosnia, however, that it was driven primarily by considerations extraneous to the conflict itself. Put more bluntly, Russian diplomatic actions and Chinese voting behavior reflected concerns *other* than the effect that their policies might have had on the course of the conflict and the UN's involvement in it.

In the case of Russia, the critical backdrop to an understanding of its policies was the recent dissolution of the Soviet Union and Moscow's loss of empire. Although the dissolution itself was blissfully peaceful, the loss of superpower status was traumatic and induced within the Russian foreign policy elite an acute concern about its status as a great power alongside other Council members. Although many—including the Bosnian government in Sarajevo and influential members of the US Congress—saw in Moscow's Balkan policies the influence of supposedly deeply felt and long-standing pan-Slav sentiments, there is little evidence indicating that such sentiments shaped policy in any decisive fashion. The communist-nationalist opposition and its media outlets were often vocal in expressing support for their "Serbian brothers," but President Boris Yeltsin and Foreign Minister Andrey Kozyrev's chief priority remained the perceived need to assert Russia's credentials as major power and constructive partner of the West on the international stage.[37] To this end, diplomatic initiatives (such as the effort in the spring of 1993 to save the faltering Vance-Owen plan, and Vitaly Churkin's intensive shuttle diplomacy in 1994) were geared, above all, toward strengthening Russia's international standing and avoiding diplomatic marginalization. If meeting those key objectives required that relations with Russia's "Bosnian Serb brothers" be severed, then Moscow had few qualms about doing so, as indeed events in 1994 and 1995 were to show. Insofar as Russia developed distinctive views on the *substantive* issues raised by UNPROFOR's mission in Bosnia, they tended to echo the positions of Britain and France. Still, Moscow was not deeply wedded to any particular policy or initiative and remained principally concerned with proving that it was "the diplomatic successor to the USSR not just in name but also in might and importance."[38]

Unlike Russia, China did not launch any diplomatic initiatives of its own in relation to the Bosnian conflict, and its attitudes more generally must be viewed against the backdrop of the Chinese Communist Party's continuing efforts to reassert its legitimacy and deal with domestic challenges following its violent crackdown on the democracy movement in Tiananmen Square in 1989. Its voting behavior in the Security Council in relation to the Yugoslav crisis was primarily designed, through abstentions rather than vetoes, to register Chinese disquiet with the UN's growing involvement in the internal affairs of member states and, in particular, with what appeared to be an increased readiness to invoke Chapter VII with respect to humanitarian emergencies. China's anxieties about this trend led it to abstain on a large number of Chapter VII resolutions relating to Bosnia.[39] These included, among other things, resolutions authorizing the delivery of humanitarian assistance to parts of the country and the further expansion of UNPROFOR's mandate; the decision to impose a ban on military flights over Bosnia; and the Council's demand in May 1995 for the release of UN personnel held hostage by the Bosnian Serb army. China's chief priority, then, was not to influence the course of the conflict or the UN's handling of it. It was instead to express its disapproval of what it saw as the erosion, encouraged and supported by Western countries, of key Charter principles—above all, that of nonintervention in the internal affairs of member states. In doing so, China claimed to be defending the views and interests of developing countries and the nonaligned movement, though as we have seen, what many of these countries wanted was *more* and not less intervention in Bosnia.

The Resort to Chapter VII and the Question of the Use of Force

At the heart of the disagreements over the Council's handling of the war in Bosnia was the question of the use of force. Since the end of UNPROFOR's mission in 1995, several public inquiries—including one by the UN Secretariat itself as well as others ordered by national governments—into the circumstances surrounding the fall of the Srebrenica enclave in July 1995, have kept the debate on the use of force alive.[40] In essence it is a debate that has centered around one key question: Should UNPROFOR have taken *enforcement* action much earlier on in the conflict in order to impose a settlement on recalcitrant parties?

The view that UNPROFOR "failed" to take such action when in fact there was nothing to prevent it from doing so is based on a combination of two arguments: first, that UNPROFOR did not act on Chapter VII resolutions that explicitly allowed for "all necessary measures" to be used; and second, that the manner in which the parties were finally brought to the negotiating table (emphasizing, in particular, the role played by NATO's extensive use of airpower in August and September 1995) shows that a more forceful approach had always been an option. Though flawed in important respects, both arguments merit closer attention, as they highlight key aspects of the Security Council's approach to the war in Bosnia.

Throughout the Cold War, determining "the existence of any threat to the peace, breach of the peace or act of aggression" was not something on which the Security Council, for obvious reasons, could easily agree. Between 1945 and 1989, the Council adopted only twenty-one resolutions that cited Chapter VII, or used its wording.[41] By contrast, between 1990 and 1999 the Council passed 174 Chapter VII resolutions.[42] A disproportionate number of these were adopted in relation to the conflict in the former Yugoslavia and, in particular, the war in Bosnia. As indicated elsewhere in this book, the increased resort to Chapter VII in the 1990s is suggestive of a greater willingness on the part of the "international community" to treat intrastate or internal conflict as matters of legitimate international concern and, in extreme cases, to take enforcement action in response to massive violations of human rights. The use of Chapter VII during the war in Bosnia, however, also points to another, more instrumental reason for its frequent application, one that had little to do with any emerging consensus among member states around a broader and more permissive interpretation of threats to international peace and security. The fact is that by invoking Chapter VII the Council was often just as concerned with conveying the impression of resolve as it was with taking meaningful action on the ground. As the story of Resolution 836 illustrates only too clearly, using Chapter VII language did not mean that the Council was prepared to abandon UNPROFOR's limited core objectives. The circumstances surrounding the adoption of other hard-hitting resolutions, including those designed to meet concerns about security for UNPROFOR personnel and the restrictions placed on their freedom of movement by the warring parties, tell the same story.[43] The Council simply had no intention of jettisoning "peacekeeping" principles in favor of enforcement. This is also clear from the fact that troop contributors to UNPROFOR remained not only wary but also extremely reluctant to expose their troops to risks, a reality reflected in the restrictions and caveats imposed by governments on the employment of their troops, as well as in their continuing interference in the UN chain of command.[44]

It might still be argued, as indeed it was by critics of the UN operation at the time, that resolutions allowing for "all necessary measures" did nonetheless provide UN forces with the appropriate mandate for taking coercive action and that, thus, there was nothing preventing them from doing so. The difficulty with this argument is that although it is true that the Council passed new and "tougher" resolutions authorizing the use of force, it expressly did not annul its earlier resolutions. Given the scale and importance of the UN's humanitarian activities in-theater—activities on which the Council could in fact agree and to which its members remained firmly committed—this was not merely a technical or legal obstacle. By reaffirming all previous resolutions, UNPROFOR was left with the "challenge of reconciling its authority to use force with its obligation to perform all the other tasks mandated by the Security Council—tasks which required the cooperation of, and deployment among, all parties to conflict."[45]

The Use of Force in 1995:
From Peacekeeping to Enforcement
The NATO-led military campaign against Bosnian Serb forces, involving the extensive use of airpower and artillery over a two-week period in late August and early September 1995, played an important role in bringing about the conditions that allowed for the establishment of a permanent ceasefire and for an overall settlement to the conflict in Bosnia. The campaign and the events surrounding it, however, have given rise to many

myths, encouraged in part by the self-serving and less-than-accurate accounts provided by some of the actors involved at the time.[46] Perhaps the most persistent myth has been that it was coercive airpower *alone* that forced the Bosnian Serbs to the negotiating table and that the failure to use airpower in this fashion earlier in the conflict had needlessly prolonged the war. Reality, as is so often the case, was more complex. The significance of Operation Deliberate Force—the name given to the military operation against the Bosnian Serb army in 1995—can be assessed only in conjunction with several other developments that, in the summer and early autumn of 1995, *combined* to create conditions that until then had not existed for the effective application of military force.

The first of these was the weakening of the military position of the Bosnian Serbs and the loss of their ability to hold vulnerable UN forces for ransom. Reaching this stage, however, involved a process that began well before Operation Deliberate Force. Specifically, the spectacular success of Croat military offensives, first in Sector West in Croatia in May 1995, and later in the Krajina region in August, had dramatically altered the strategic predicament of the Bosnian Serbs. The Croat offensives, supported and strongly encouraged by the United States and resulting in a massive displacement of Croatian Serbs, were one of the preconditions for the effective use of force by NATO and the UN in September. So was the withdrawal of UNPROFOR troops from exposed and indefensible positions in Bosnian Serb–controlled territory, a process that started in June with the removal of UN peacekeepers from the weapons collection points around Sarajevo and Gorazde and completed with the stealthy withdrawal of British troops from Gorazde on the eve of Operation Deliberate Force in late August. In the meantime, the other two eastern enclaves of Srebrenica and Zepa had, at a terrible cost in human lives, fallen to Bosnian Serbian forces. The removal of troops from vulnerable and isolated locations, a policy actively pursued by General Rupert Smith after the "hostage crisis" in late May 1995 when more than 300 UN peacekeepers had been taken hostage following two air strikes against Bosnian Serb ammunition bunkers near Sarajevo (with some of the hostages chained as "human shields" to fixed installations by the Bosnian Serbs), significantly reduced the scope for politically paralyzing action on the part of the Bosnian Serb leadership in the event of renewed crisis.

In yet another development, British and French forces deployed a rapid-reaction force to Bosnia in June and July, providing for the very first time mortar and artillery support on Mount Igman near Sarajevo. Placed under direct command of General Rupert Smith in Sarajevo, this gave UN forces a capability that had hitherto been lacking and one that was used with devastating effect in August and September 1995.

A final though crucial factor in preparing the ground for a more forceful military action was the agreement, reached only after the disaster of

Srebrenica in July 1995, to simplify command-and-control arrangements for the use of NATO airpower in support of UN forces. Significantly, the agreement, enshrined in a memorandum of understanding between the Commander in Chief, Allied Forces Southern Europe (CINCSOUTH), and the UN force commander, held that the conditions triggering "graduated air operations" would now be "determined by the common judgement of NATO and UN military commanders."[47] Specifically, this meant that the authority to authorize NATO air operations in support of UNPROFOR was delegated, on July 26, 1995, from the Secretary-General (represented by the SRSG based in Zagreb, Yasushi Akashi, who until then had held the UN "key" that needed to be turned for air strikes to be launched) to the military force commander, who in turn was authorized to delegate further to the tactical commander on the ground. Pressure for this change came above all from US administration officials who had long been unhappy with the "dual-key" arrangement. Mindful of Russian resistance to any "wide scale air operation"[48] in Bosnia—as Russian representatives made very clear during the international meeting on former Yugoslavia held in London soon after the fall of Srebrenica in July 1995—the United States leaned strongly on Boutros Boutros-Ghali "to use administrative measures to take away Akashi's key without going back to the Security Council for a formal resolution."[49]

Taken together, the combined effect of these developments was to prepare the ground for the second option outlined by General Smith in his letter to Janvier in May: a deliberate transition from peacekeeping to peace *enforcement* action, or more precisely, war-fighting. Thus the necessary steps, which until then had been consistently rejected by the Security Council and troop-contributing countries, were finally taken.

It is important to stress that this move to enforcement and the enabling steps that made it possible did not come about as a result of any carefully considered and deliberate strategy agreed upon by Council members. At the time, it was not at all clear, for example, whether the rapid-reaction force was designed to cover the withdrawal of UN troops from Bosnia or whether it was intended to give UN forces a war-fighting capability. Certainly, the British government was anxious not to raise expectations about the effect of its reinforcements and continued to stress the need for "local consent" and adherence to "peacekeeping principles." When European Union and NATO ministers and their chiefs of staff met in Paris on June 3, 1995, during the hostage crisis, they also reaffirmed that UNPROFOR's "mission was not to enforce a solution by military force, but to operate in support of the peace process, to ensure essential humanitarian aid to the civilian population and to monitor [a] ceasefire concluded between belligerents."[50] The problem was that, by this time, these objectives had simply ceased to have much meaning on the ground.

The stark reality of the situation was more honestly spelled out by Rupert Smith in a note, prepared a few days after the meeting of EU and NATO ministers, for SRSG Akashi and other senior UNPROFOR officials. Reviewing various reinforcement plans for UNPROFOR then being discussed, he concluded: "we face a simple but difficult choice between being prepared to fight and escalate or not. Attempts at finding a middle ground are doomed to disappointment and possibly disaster when standing in the middle of someone else's war."[51]

In an effort to break the stalemate and avert possible "disaster," General Smith and his staff in Sarajevo had, in the late winter and early spring of 1995, worked on and developed a detailed plan for the forceful replenishment by air of the besieged enclaves in eastern Bosnia. Anticipating, soon after his arrival in the country, that the situation in the eastern enclaves—especially in Srebrenica and Zepa—was likely to deteriorate in the coming months, General Smith authorized planning to proceed for a helicopter resupply operation. The purpose of the plan, finalized in late April and greeted with skepticism by UN officials in Zagreb and New York, was expressly "to seek to face down [Bosnian Serb military commander] General Mladic, by carrying out a notified helicopter resupply with armed escorts and NATO air support with the clear intention of reacting violently to any interference."[52] In other words, the plan was designed to confront the Bosnian Serb army and, as such, could be undertaken, as Smith fully recognized and told his superiors, only if troop-contributing countries were prepared not only to risk the loss of aircraft but also to escalate for aims other than self-defense. Enthusiasm for the concept in the capitals and among the major troop-contributing countries, when they were first sounded out in April, was decidedly mixed. Crucially, key Security Council members, notably the UK, were unsupportive. In the end, the plan was overtaken by events on the ground, and in the aftermath of the hostage crisis it was effectively shelved. "Muddling on" remained, for a few more fateful weeks, the preferred option.

When the Bosnian Serb mortar attack in Sarajevo that triggered Operation Deliberate Force occurred on August 28, 1995, the force commander for UN peace forces in the whole of Yugoslavia was General Janvier. Given that Janvier had earned the reputation as "a serial rejecter of almost any request for the use of air power,"[53] his absence from the theater proved critical to the unfolding course of events. It meant that the UN air-strike "key" devolved to General Rupert Smith, who, as Harland notes, "took the decision to turn [it] alone."[54] Indeed, in this, as in decisions taken earlier in the year, Rupert Smith emerges as a "central figure" in the events that saw the abandonment of peacekeeping in favor of peace enforcement, a fact that makes his absence from Holbrooke's account all the more striking.[55]

Aftermath: From Dayton to Kosovo

The peace accord for Bosnia, reached in Dayton and formally signed in Paris in December 1995, largely froze realities on the ground at war's end, establishing two separate entities—the Federation and the Bosnian Serb Republic—that would now have to coexist within the country's internationally recognized borders. Earlier and ultimately abortive peace plans, notably the Vance-Owen plan of 1993, would in fact have done more to preserve the multiethnic character of prewar Bosnia. Still, agreement did mean an end to the fighting, itself a major achievement. It also unlocked reconstruction aid and, crucially, triggered the deployment of a 60,000-strong NATO-led multinational force (SFOR)—robust and well equipped in a way that UNPROFOR had never been—to monitor and enforce the ceasefire.[56]

By the time the conflict had come to an end, the UN-protected area of Eastern Slavonia in Croatia was still under the control of the self-styled Serbian Republic of Krajina. In November 1995, agreement was reached between the Croatian government and weakened and isolated local Serbian authorities on the peaceful incorporation of Eastern Slavonia into Croatia. On January 15, 1996, the Security Council duly authorized the establishment of the UN Transitional Administration of Eastern Slavonia, Baranja, and Western Sirmium (UNTAES) to oversee the process of incorporation.[57] Over the next two years, the mission oversaw the transfer of control to Croatia and was held out, at the time and since, as a unique "success" story, in sharp contrast to the experience of UN forces elsewhere in the Balkans. While the incorporation was indeed peaceful, both its success and the comparison to the UN's performance in neighboring Bosnia need to be qualified in two important respects. First, and in marked contrast to Bosnia, UNTAES benefited from the fact that the mission's political end-state was never in doubt: Croatia was asserting full sovereignty within an agreed period over a piece of territory temporarily occupied by the Krajina Serbs. Second, while the transition itself was peaceful, the real test of success is arguably whether the multiethnic character of the province was preserved or, indeed, whether Croatian authorities made much of an attempt to preserve that character.[58] The answer to this is largely negative: the majority of the Croatian Serbs, indigenous to the region or refugees from elsewhere, voted with their feet and chose to leave Eastern Slavonia.

Kosovo—the province of Serbia where Milosevic had first exploited the grievances of the local Serb community in order to consolidate his own powerbase and thus set in motion the events that would lead to the violent collapse of Yugoslavia—was not discussed at Dayton. Its exclusion from the talks left the majority Kosovo Albanian population deeply concerned about their future within Milosevic's rump Yugoslavia, even though at this stage "no one but the Albanians themselves disputed that Kosovo was an integral part of Serbia."[59] It also had the effect of undermining the policy of nonviolent resistance that had been pursued by Ibrahim Rugova's Democratic League of Kosovo since 1989, while strengthening the hand of those inside Kosovo, notably the Kosovo Liberation Army (KLA), who championed armed struggle and independence and were now portraying Dayton as a "selling out" of the Kosovar Albanians by the international community.

From 1996 onward, the KLA stepped up attacks, using terrorist tactics, against Serbian targets and security forces in Kosovo, as well as against Albanian "collaborators." In February 1998, Milosevic responded by ordering his security forces to crack down on the KLA, intensifying its operations in the province and, true to form, employing indiscriminate and brutal force. Responding to these developments, the Security Council, on March 31, 1998, and acting under Chapter VII, condemned "the use of excessive force by Serbian police forces against civilians and peaceful demonstrators in Kosovo, as well as all acts of terrorism by the Kosovo Liberation Army."[60] The resolution called on the parties to find a peaceful solution to their differences, and to do so without violating the territorial and legal integrity of Yugoslavia. Predictably, the resolution did nothing to arrest the momentum toward further violence, and by the end of the year an estimated 230,000 people had been displaced, while the conflict was increasingly assuming the character of an "all-out civil war."[61]

As far as achieving a peaceful resolution was concerned, the reality was that the deteriorating situation in Kosovo from 1997 onward presented the Council with, if anything, an even greater challenge than that faced in Bosnia. On the one hand, Council members were all agreed, as was plainly and unambiguously stated in Resolution 1160 of March 1998, that a "solution of the Kosovo problem should be based on the territorial integrity of the Federal Republic of Yugoslavia."[62] To this end, they called on the parties to agree on an "enhanced status for Kosovo which would include a substantially greater degree of autonomy and meaningful self-administration."[63] There was at this stage agreement among Council members that the case of Kosovo differed from that of other former Yugoslav republics that now enjoyed full independence, even though it was far from clear what "enhanced status" and "meaningful self-administration" might entail in practice.[64] On the other hand, it was perfectly clear that the KLA, politically in the ascendance, would accept nothing short of independence, while Milosevic's villainous record and ruthless support for "ethnic cleansing" in Bosnia made it well-nigh impossible to see how a "meaningful dialogue on political status issues" could be entered into, let alone how an agreement on greater autonomy and "meaningful self-administration" could ever be achieved.[65]

It is beyond the scope of this chapter to trace the diplomatic developments from Resolution 1160 to the start of NATO's air campaign against
Yugoslavia on March 24, 1999, in part because much of the diplomatic
action occurred outside the Council chamber.[66] What is clear is that the shift
away from what was initially "a seemingly even-handed approach"[67] toward
placing responsibility for the crisis squarely on Milosevic was powerfully
shaped by the experience and memory of the Council's handling of the war
in Bosnia, not only Milosevic's sinister role in it but, equally, the Council's
inability to develop a credible policy toward it and thus, ultimately, to prevent the horrors of Srebrenica. As Adam Roberts perceptively observed not
long after NATO's "humanitarian war" in Kosovo:

> The main underlying explanation for the willingness of NATO's 19 member
> states to take action over Kosovo is not their interpretations of particular
> events, such as the failure of the negotiations over the province at Rambouil-
> let and Paris in February and March 1999. Nor was it a shared vision as to
> what the future of the province should be. Rather, the NATO states were
> united by a sense of shame that, in the first four years of atrocious wars in the
> former Yugoslavia, they had failed, individually and collectively, to devise
> coherent policies and to engage in decisive actions.[68]

This sense of shame also helps to explain why the decision to go to
war was taken, controversially, without securing an explicit authorization
from the Security Council for the use of force. Recognizing that Russia
and China would veto such a resolution, NATO based its decision instead
on the view—articulated and circulated to other NATO countries by the
UK government in advance of the operation—that military action by
NATO would still be "lawful on the grounds of overwhelming humanitarian necessity."[69]

Following NATO's military campaign in June 1999, the Security Council agreed to establish a large-scale interim "international civil and security
presence" in the province.[70] Disagreement among Council members over
the recognition of Kosovo, which has persisted since the province declared
its independence in February 2008, means that the UN Mission in Kosovo
(UNMIK) remains in place, though its size and functions have been significantly scaled down. UNMIK's presence and the extensive executive powers it initially enjoyed have not resolved the underlying question of
Kosovo's status, and the tensions between the majority Kosovar Albanians
and the shrinking non-Albanian population (predominantly Serbs but also
Roma) continue to run deep, evidenced by the de facto partition between
the Serb-populated northern municipalities and the rest of Kosovo since
1999.[71] While more than 100 out of the UN's 193 member states had recognized Kosovo by mid-2013, this still leaves a significant minority, ensuring
that the international community remains divided on the question of recog-

nition, its precedent-setting effects, and the wider lesson to draw from the UN's engagement in the conflict.

Conclusion

As the conflict within Yugoslavia deepened and the prospects for violence grew in early 1991, optimism about the UN's post–Cold War role in the field of peace and security, paradoxically, was reaching its peak. That optimism rested crucially on the belief that the Security Council, no longer at the mercy of East-West rivalry, would finally be able to assume the role originally envisaged for it. To many, the Council's response to Iraq's invasion of Kuwait in August 1990 only strengthened that conviction. That case, however, was unique: one state had annexed another; it could hardly be more clear-cut. Yugoslavia and the case of Bosnia in particular—and on this the Council was initially agreed—was very different.

The Council's handling of the wars of Yugoslav succession did much to shatter the optimism that had characterized early debates about the likely impact of the end of the Cold War for the UN's peace and security role. In particular, it brought home that civil wars—or, more precisely in the case of the former Yugoslavia, conflicts that could not easily be categorized as either internal or international in nature—posed unique challenges and raised issues for the Council on which consensus for action will always be difficult to obtain. In a broader sense, therefore, the war in Bosnia undermined the belief, surprisingly widespread in the early 1990s, that the end of the Cold War also signaled the end of conflicts of interest and value among member states of the UN.

At the same time and in a longer-term historical perspective, it is clear that the Council's performance in the Balkans, together with its still more shameful response to the genocide in Rwanda in 1994, has helped to reinforce a wider normative shift in international relations. As Kofi Annan put it shortly before stepping down as Secretary-General: "Respect for national sovereignty can no longer be used as a shield by governments intent on massacring their own people, or as an excuse for the rest of us to do nothing when such heinous crimes are committed."[72] As the fraught debate over the implementation of the Responsibility to Protect doctrine following the NATO-led campaign against Libya in 2011 has clearly demonstrated, divisions still run deep among member states about how best to protect human rights and, in particular, what role, if any, the use of force can play in advancing humanitarian objectives. What is now much less controversial—and for this to have become generally accepted, the Balkans experience played a key role—is the view that massive violations of human rights, involving mass atrocity crimes or the prospect thereof, cannot be treated merely as a matter of domestic concern but are a legitimate concern for the international community as a whole, and therefore also for the Security Council.

Notes

1. For an excellent overview of different, partly competing approaches to the origins and course of Yugoslavia's disintegration, see Jasna Dragović-Soso, "Why Did Yugoslavia Disintegrate? An Overview of Contending Explanations," in *State Collapse in South-Eastern Europe: New Perspectives on Yugoslavia's Disintegration,* edited by Lenard J. Cohen and Jasna Dragović-Soso (West Lafayette, IN: Purdue University Press, 2008).

2. Warren Zimmermann, *The Origins of a Catastrophe* (New York: Times Books, 1996), p. 70.

3. Serbs constituted some 12 percent of the population in the constituent republic of Croatia in 1991.

4. David Hannay, *New World Disorder* (London: Tauris, 2008), p. 59. For a thoughtful assessment of US policy toward Yugoslavia in 1990 and 1991 that downplays (though does not entirely reject) charges of ignorance, inattention, and incompetence on the part of the administration in favor of a greater appreciation of the sheer complexity of the policy challenges presented by the evolving crisis, see Paul Shoup, "The Disintegration of Yugoslavia and Western Foreign Policy in the 1980s," in Cohen and Dragović-Soso, *State Collapse in South-Eastern Europe,* especially pp. 339–346.

5. The position of the Non-Aligned Movement (NAM) regarding intervention would later change in favor of more direct involvement in Bosnia, but this was after Croatia, Slovenia, and Bosnia had all been accepted as new member states of the UN (in May 1992), at which point, so it was argued, the issue was no longer one of internal conflict but of international aggression across recognized borders.

6. Javier Pérez de Cuéllar, *Pilgrimage for Peace* (London: Palgrave Macmillan, 1997), p. 477.

7. European Community, *Declaration on the Suspension of the Trade and Cooperation Agreement with Yugoslavia* (Rome, November 8, 1991).

8. Zimmermann, *The Origins of a Catastrophe,* p. 173.

9. Pérez de Cuéllar, *Pilgrimage for Peace,* p. 490.

10. United Nations Repertoire of the Practice of the Security Council, "Items Relating to the Situation in the Former Yugoslavia," www.un.org/en/sc/repertoire/studies/europe.shtml.

11. Danilo Türk, "Recognition of States," annex 1, "Guidelines on the Recognition of New States in Eastern Europe and in the Soviet Union," and annex 2, "Declaration on Yugoslavia" (Extraordinary EPC Ministerial Meeting, Brussels, December 16, 1991), *European Journal of International Law* 4, no. 1 (1993): 72–73 (emphasis added). On the legal and political issues raised by the recognition of Yugoslavia's constituent republics, a clear contemporary perspective is provided in Roland Rich, "Recognition of States: The Collapse of Yugoslavia and the Soviet Union," *European Journal of International Law* 4, no. 1 (1993): 36–65.

12. United Nations Security Council Resolution 721, S/RES/721 (November 27, 1992). See also Marrack Goulding, *Peacemonger* (London: Murray, 2002), p. 296.

13. UNPROFOR was later extended to Bosnia and Macedonia and enlarged. In March 1995, UNPROFOR was restructured and replaced with three separate though linked operations under the umbrella of UN Peace Forces (UNPF). UNPROFOR in

Croatia was renamed the UN Confidence Restoration Operation in Croatia (UNCRO), the UN force in Macedonia was renamed the UN Preventive Deployment Force (UNPREDEP), and the force in Bosnia continued to go by the name of UNPROFOR. For details, see Resolutions 981, S/RES/981; 982, S/RES/982; and 983, S/RES/983 (March 31, 1995). In the discussion that follows, unless otherwise stated, UNPROFOR refers to the UN operation in Bosnia.

14. United Nations Security Council Resolution 743, S/RES/743 (February 21, 1992).

15. Lawrence Freedman, "International Security: Changing Targets," *Foreign Policy* 110 (Spring 1998): 59.

16. General Smith to Janvier (UNPF), "The Future Mandate of UNPROFOR," May 21, 1995, UN document.

17. According to the UNPF's own end-of-mission report, the UNHCR delivered over 853,000 metric tons of aid by road convoys to the whole of the former Yugoslavia, while a further 159,000 tons were airlifted to Sarajevo. At the war's end in 1995, UNHCR beneficiaries in Bosnia numbered 2.7 million. United Nations Peace Forces, "Force Commander's End of Mission Report" (Zagreb, January 31, 1996).

18. UN High Commissioner for Refugees Sadako Ogata, "Letter to UN Secretary-General Boutros Boutros-Ghali," internal UN Document, New York, April 16, 1992. The prewar population of Bosnia was 4.3 million. By the end of the war in 1995, some 1.3 million of these had become internally displaced persons (IDPs), while another 900,000 had become refugees.

19. United Nations Security Council, *Further Report of the Secretary-General Pursuant to Security Council Resolution 749 (1992),* UN Doc. S/23900, May 12, 1992; United Nations Security Council Resolution 752 (May 15, 1992), UN Doc S/RES/752. See also Goulding, *Peacemonger,* pp. 311–315.

20. United Nations Security Council Resolution 757, S/RES/757 (May 30, 1992).

21. For a hard-hitting critique, see David Harland, "Selective Justice for the Balkans," *International New York Times,* December 7, 2012.

22. See United Nations Security Council Resolutions 819, S/RES/819 (April 16, 1993); 824, S/RES/824 (May 6, 1993); and 836, S/RES/836 (June 4, 1993).

23. United Nations Security Council Resolution 836, S/RES/836 (June 4, 1993), paras. 5, 9.

24. UN Department of Peace-Keeping Operations to Stoltenberg, "Subject: Implementation of Security Council SCR 836 (1993)," June 7, 1993, UN document.

25. Madeleine Albright, *Madam Secretary: A Memoir* (New York: Pan Books, 2003), p. 180.

26. For some NAM members, traditionally staunch defenders of sovereignty and nonintervention, the stance taken toward the conflict was influenced by sympathy with the Muslim victims of the war. As noted, however, greater involvement was also justified, once Bosnia had been formally accepted as a UN member state, as a defense against external aggression.

27. Iran offered 10,000 troops or "a complete mechanized division," an offer that was politely turned down.

28. General Jean Cot (FC) to Kofi Annan, October 24, 1993, UN document.

29. Ibid., p. 287.

30. David Hannay, *New World Disorder: The UN After the Cold War—An Insider's View* (London: Tauris, 2008), p. 126.

31. "Agreement on Complete *Cessation of Hostilities,*" UN Doc. S/1995/8, December 31, 1994, para. 6, available at http://peacemaker.un.org/bosniacomplete-cessation94.

32. Nicholas Morris, "Humanitarian Intervention in the Balkans," in *Humanitarian Intervention and International Relations,* edited by Jennifer M. Welsh (Oxford: Oxford University Press, 2004), p. 99.

33. Albright, *Madam Secretary,* p. 180.

34. US Department of State, "Statement of Ambassador M. Albright," House of Representatives, 103rd Congress, May 17, 1994, p. 8.

35. David Hannay, "The UN's Role in Bosnia Assessed," *Oxford International Review* 7, no. 2 (1996): 9.

36. An indication of those tensions can be found in the reference that David Hannay makes to reflections he himself made shortly after leaving New York in 1995, when he bluntly noted that "infirmity of purpose is endemic in this administration." Hannay, *New World Disorder,* p. 196.

37. Christina von Siemens, "Russia's Policy Towards the War in Bosnia-Herzegovina (1992–1995)," M.Phil. dissertation, University of Oxford, April 2001, p. 54.

38. Ibid., p. 33.

39. Sally Morphet, "China as a Permanent Member of the Security Council: October 1971–December 1999," *Security Dialogue* 31, no. 2 (June 2000): 154.

40. United Nations General Assembly, *Report of the Secretary-General Pursuant to General Assembly Resolution 53/35: The Fall of Srebrenica,* UN Doc. A/54/549, November 15, 1999. On July 11, 1995, the "safe area" of Srebrenica was overrun by Bosnian Serb forces. In the days that followed, more than 8,000 Bosniaks were massacred by their Bosnian Serb captors.

41. See Chapter 2 in this volume.

42. Morphet, "China as a Permanent Member," p. 154.

43. See United Nations Security Council Resolutions 807 (February 19, 1993), UN Doc. S/RES/807; and 847 (June 30, 1993), UN Doc. S/RES/847.

44. United Nations Under-Secretary-General for Peacekeeping, "Talking Points for UNPROFOR Troop Contributing Meeting," UN document, New York, October 1, 1993.

45. Shashi Tharoor, "Should UN Peacekeeping Go 'Back to Basics'?" *Survival* 37, no. 4 (Winter 1995–1996): 59.

46. One of these is Richard Holbrooke's *To End a War* (New York: Random, 1998). Holbrooke's account, as David Harland has noted in an unpublished review of the book, "plays fast and loose with the known record," a fact that has not prevented the book from continuing to be widely cited. David Harland, *"To End a War* by Richard Holbrooke: Draft Comment," unpublished and undated review essay. I am grateful to David Harland for permission to cite his review essay.

47. United Nations Peace Forces, "Force Commander's End of Mission Report."

48. "Note for File," London Conference, UNHCR, July 1995, UN document.

49. Tim Ripley, *Operation Deliberate Force: The UN and NATO Campaign in Bosnia, 1995* (Lancaster: Lancaster University Center for Defense and International Security Studies, 1999), p. 160. See also Linda Nordin, "The NATO Air Strikes over Bosnia-Herzegovina," MA dissertation, University of Stockholm, February 1998, p. 49.

50. United Nations Peace Forces, "Force Commander's End of Mission Report," Annex D, p. 6.

51. Rupert Smith to Yasushi Akashi, "UNPROFOR Reinforcements," Bosnia-Herzegovina Command, June 6, 1995, UN document.

52. Bosnia-Herzegovina Command, "Bosnia-Herzegovina Command Situation Report," April 5, 1995; General Bernard Janvier to Kofi Annan, "Subject: Air Supply

of Eastern Enclaves," April 18, 1995; author interviews with former UNPROFOR staff, 1997, 1998, and 2012.

53. Hannay, *New World Disorder,* p. 191.

54. Harland, "Draft Comment," p. 2. As Harland makes clear, Holbrooke played no role in the decision.

55. Ibid.

56. United Nations Security Council Resolution 1031, S/RES/1031 (December 15, 1995).

57. United Nations Security Council Resolution 1023, S/RES/1023 (November 22, 1995).

58. Derek Boothby, "Application of Leverage in Eastern Slavonia," in *Leveraging for Success in Peace Operations,* edited by Jean Krasno, Bradd Hayes, and Donald Daniel (Westport: Praeger, 2003), p. 136.

59. Tim Judah, *Kosovo: War and Revenge* (New Haven: Yale University Press, 2000), p. 124.

60. United Nations Security Council Resolution 1160, S/RES/1160 (March 31, 1998).

61. United Nations Security Council, *Report of Secretary-General Prepared Pursuant to Resolutions 1160 (1998), 1199 (1998), and 1203 (1998) of the Security Council,* UN Doc. S/1999/99, January 30, 1999, para. 35; United Nations Security Council Resolution 1199, S/RES/1199 (September 23, 1998).

62. United Nations Security Council Resolution 1160, S/RES/1160 (March 31, 1998), para. 5.

63. Ibid.

64. Resolution 1160 was adopted with fourteen votes in favor and only one abstention (China).

65. United Nations Security Council Resolution 1160 (March 31, 1998), para. 5.

66. See Spyros Economides, "Kosovo," in *United Nations Interventionism, 1991–2004,* edited by Mats Berdal and Spyros Economides (Cambridge: Cambridge University Press, 2007).

67. Ibid., p. 223.

68. Adam Roberts, "NATO's 'Humanitarian War' over Kosovo," *Survival* 41, no. 3 (Autumn 1999): 104.

69. For the range of views and the international debate unleashed by the decision, see Albrecht Schnabel and Ramesh Thakur, eds., *Kosovo and the Challenge of Humanitarian Intervention* (Tokyo: United Nations University Press, 2000). See also United Kingdom House of Commons, Foreign Affairs Committee, "Minutes of Evidence and Appendices," session 1999–2000, 4th report, Kosovo, vol. 2 (London: Stationery Office, May 2000).

70. United Nations Security Council Resolution 1244 (June 10, 1999), UN Doc. S/RES/1244.

71. An agreement on "normalization of relations" between the Serbian and Kosovo governments concluded in April 2013 appears only partially to have overcome the state of de facto partition. See "Kosovo Votes Amid Violence and Ethnic Serb Boycott Fear," *BBC News,* November 3, 2013, www.bbc.co.uk/news/world -europe-24798397.

72. Kofi Annan, "Farewell Speech," Truman Presidential Library, Independence, MO, December 11, 2006.

29

Somalia

John L. Hirsch

THE CASE OF SOMALIA IS OF PARTICULAR IMPORTANCE FOR THE
United Nations, having been on the Security Council's agenda for more
than two decades.[1] The purpose of this chapter is to link the role of the
Council to the changing fortunes of Somalia in this lengthy timeframe.
When the Security Council in December 1992 authorized the US-led
Unifed Task Force (UNITAF) to create secure corridors for the delivery of
humanitarian assistance to people in the south, Somalis initially welcomed
an active international role. When seven months later the Security Council
was perceived as imposing an arbitrary outcome (i.e., seeking the arrest of
warlord Mohamed Farah Aidid), the tide of Somali public opinion turned
against the peacekeepers. The withdrawal of UN peacekeepers in 1995 and
the subsequent diminution of the Council's role were followed by a decade
of unsuccessful efforts by United Nations officials and regional leaders to
restore a functioning central government. It was only with the reengagement of the United States and hence the Security Council in responding to
the threats posed by al-Shabaab and maritime piracy starting in 2006 that
Somalia began to emerge from the crisis created by the long collapse of its
state institutions. Continued engagement of the Security Council will be an
important determinant to its future.

Security Council engagement in Somalia has covered a broad range of
responsibilities, from managing three successive peacekeeping operations
in the 1990s, to developing and managing long-term sanctions regimes and
arms embargoes, to ongoing logistical and financial support for the African
Union Mission in Somalia (AMISOM). Somalia provided the earliest
example of humanitarian intervention with the deployment from 1992 to

1995 of over 20,000 troops from a wide range of Western and developing countries. The collapse of UN peacekeeping efforts in Somalia after the death of eighteen US soldiers in October 1993 (widely known as Black Hawk Down) contributed to the fateful Council decisions against active engagement to stop the Rwandan genocide in April 1994. Notwithstanding these major setbacks, the United Nations remained involved in Somalia over the following decade through maintenance of an arms embargo and provision of humanitarian assistance to millions of displaced citizens. From 2000 to 2007, regional leaders convened conferences in Djibouti, Ethiopia, and Kenya. They established a series of weak transitional governments, all of which ended in failure, unable to win popular support or restore a national governing structure. In the same timeframe, Islamic radicalism and maritime piracy became issues of major international concern, spurring renewed Council engagement.

Since 2012 the Security Council has made a renewed commitment to Somalia's political and economic reconstruction.[2] With the United Kingdom, the former colonial power in the north, as the "penholder" of its resolutions, the Security Council has been working with the new Somali government to rebuild its state institutions while supporting development initiatives to give the Somali people a more secure and economically viable future. Against this broad backdrop, consideration of the Somalia case can provide insights into the Council's continually evolving role, its achievements as well as its failures, and the importance of agreement among the permanent members of the Security Council on medium- and long-term strategies for sustained reconstruction and development. Over more than two decades, the Council has moved from dealing with the harsh consequences of state collapse to assisting Somalia, heretofore regarded as irreparably damaged, to regain its standing as a viable albeit fragile nation.

International Engagement, 1991–1995

Somalia, 1960–1991

For centuries before the colonial era, Somalia was a pastoral and nomadic society whose clan structure had functioned cohesively in a harsh and difficult terrain. The division of Somalia into British, Italian, and French colonies in the 1880s (the latter subsequently became Djibouti) has had a lasting impact on the country's history. On July 1, 1960, an independent and unified Somali Republic was declared, formally uniting the country. The nine years of civilian government, from 1960 to 1969, were notable primarily for the plethora of competing political parties and dispersal of patronage on the basis of clan and personal relationships. When Somali president Abdirashid Ali Shermake was assassinated by a bodyguard in October 1969, the stage was set for a military coup.

Major-General Mohamed Siad Barre and his Marehan group (a subclan of the Darods) took power, ushering in twenty-one years of military dictatorship under a putative socialist political structure. Cold War politics played a major role in these two decades. After Barre's request for arms was rebuffed by the Richard Nixon administration, he turned to Moscow and Somalia became a Soviet client state. When Ethiopian emperor Haile Selassie was assassinated by junior army officers in 1974, and a power struggle ensued among the Ethiopian military council, Siad Barre regarded this as an opportunity to regain the contested Ogaden lands in eastern Ethiopia. It proved to be a fatal mistake. The Soviets, having first sought to mediate the conflict, decided to throw their support behind the new Marxist leadership in Ethiopia, a much larger and strategically more important country, and overnight withdrew their military advisers and equipment from Mogadishu. In the 1977–1978 war, Ethiopian forces, with military support from the Soviet Union and Cuba, quickly inflicted a major defeat on Somalia. These events coincided with the fall of the Shah in Iran in January 1979 and the Soviet invasion of Afghanistan in December 1979. The Carter Doctrine, declaring the Persian Gulf an area of vital strategic importance, led the United States in the early 1980s to enter into an economic and military assistance program with Somalia, providing the United States with access to the airfield and port facilities in Berbera to support the overflights of US reconnaissance aircraft in the Persian Gulf.

Siad Barre's rule politicized the traditional clan system. Government policies favored economic development and resources for his Marehan followers in the south while marginalizing the Isaaqs in the north. In the late 1980s, Barre's rule became more brutal and repressive as rival political and clan groups mobilized from Ethiopia and Libya. The civil war started in 1988 as the Somali National Movement, led by Mohamed Farah Aidid, with considerable popular support in the north, launched a major offensive. Siad's forces counterattacked, with a "widespread, systematic and extremely violent assault" including aerial bombardment and brutal massacres of women and children in Hargeisa and Burao.[3] An estimated 300,000 Isaaqs became refugees in Ethiopia. Over the following two years the insurgency closed in on Mogadishu. In January 1991, Siad Barre was forced to flee from Aidid's advancing forces, which had captured his arsenal as they entered Mogadishu. Siad Barre and his remaining supporters sought to return to the capital a few months later, adopting the scorched earth policy that engulfed southern Somalia from mid-1991.

Enter the United Nations

The civil war turned much of southern Somalia into a zone of crisis. As famine spread throughout the region, UN Secretary-General Boutros Boutros-Ghali castigated the Western powers for caring more about victims of war in the Balkans than in Africa.[4] UN envoys James Jonah and

Mohamed Sahnoun tried to persuade the Somali warlords to desist from fighting each other. In April 1992 the Security Council authorized the establishment of the first UN Operation in Somalia (UNOSOM I), consisting of 50 unarmed observers supported by 500 Pakistani troops to facilitate an immediate nationwide cessation of hostilities among rival factions and observance of a ceasefire.[5] The Council, however, misjudged the security situation. The UN troop deployments were slow, and the Pakistanis lacked even the minimal capacity to act, unable as they were to respond to the shelling or go beyond the airport, much less carry out the Council's goals.

US human rights groups and members of Congress appealed to President George H. W. Bush to act. On the advice of the chairman of the Joint Chiefs, Colin Powell, the president offered the UN Secretary-General US leadership of an interim multinational force acting under Chapter VII of the UN Charter to relieve the famine crisis until a regular UN peacekeeping operation could act. The Unified Task Force (UNITAF), with 13,000 troops led by US Marine lieutenant-general Robert Johnston, with the participation of US, European, African, and Asian contingents, was requested "to use all necessary means to establish as soon as possible a secure environment for humanitarian relief operations" in the south.[6] The presence of these forces from December 1992 to May 1993, and a strengthened diplomatic effort by US ambassador Robert Oakley, quickly led the warlords to stand down, alleviated the worst of the humanitarian crisis, and opened the way to the reestablishment of local governance in much of the south. In the north, Somaliland had declared independence on May 18, 1991; for the following years it has stood apart. Albeit unrecognized by either the African Union or the United Nations, Somaliland has since become a model of peaceful development. Puntland followed suit in May 1997, announcing its own autonomous administration but without asserting independence.

When President Bill Clinton entered office in January 1993, Somalia seemed on its way to recovery, protected by international (largely Western) UN-authorized forces. The US ambassador to the UN, Madeleine Albright, told the Security Council of the new international commitment to Somalia. "Assertive multilateralism" was the new watchword of the administration.[7] While the Security Council planned to govern Somalia until it could manage itself, the warlords resumed fighting.[8] When Ambassador Oakley met with General Mohamed Farah Aidid, by then chairman of the United Somali Congress, in the fall of 1992, he was assured that Somalis appreciated international support for relieving the famine crisis. In reality, Aidid quickly understood that the US-led forces and the subsequent UN peacekeeping operation threatened to thwart his aspiration to assume command of the Somali state.

UNOSOM II was established in March 1993 to succeed UNITAF with an authorized troop strength of 28,000.[9] The United States offered to provide an offshore quick-reaction force to demonstrate its continued support.

UNOSOM II's mandate was to establish a secure environment in Somalia, to promote disarmament and reconciliation, and to lay the groundwork for a new national government. The mission was authorized to take action against any faction threatening the ceasefire or a resumption of violence. The Somali warlords, however, saw the weakness of the new force without full-scale US participation. Moreover, the new SRSG, US admiral Jonathan Howe, and the new force commander, Turkish lieutenant-general Cevik Bir, had never been in Somalia before. They misunderstood the broader security situation and Somali culture. When they decided to close down Aidid's radio station, which was broadcasting anti-UN diatribes, the denouement came quickly. The murder of twenty-four Pakistani peacekeepers by Aidid's militia in early June was followed by a Security Council bounty for information leading to his capture.[10] Two unsuccessful efforts by US Delta forces to capture and bring Aidid to justice brought more Somali fatalities and fueled popular anger. By the summer, the UN mission, which had started as a humanitarian relief effort, had gone to war with the Somali warlord and his clan supporters.

Clinton's Change of Heart: Exit the United States

Admiral Howe prevailed on Joint Chiefs chairman Powell to dispatch a small compartmentalized force of US Army soldiers (Delta and Ranger forces) not under UN command to capture Aidid. When eighteen US soldiers (and hundreds of Somalis) were killed in a night-long firefight to capture two of Aidid's top lieutenants in Mogadishu's crowded city center on October 3–4, 1993, "assertive multilateralism" died with them. The administration, under attack by Republican leaders in the Senate and House, withdrew its support for the UN mission, although it extended its presence to spring 1995 and helped organize its logistical departure. As former US ambassador to Somalia Peter Bridges famously wrote: "Operation Restore Hope did not live up to its name. The Somali debacle and Clinton's change of heart left the United States and the international community as a whole no closer than they had been to devising effective ways to restore peace to countries that, like Somalia, had blown apart."[11]

The regional impact was even stronger. On April 6, 1994, six months after Black Hawk Down, the presidents of Rwanda and Burundi died in a plane crash over Kigali, the signal for the start of the Rwandan genocide. The response of the United States was to withdraw its support for the UN Assistance Mission for Rwanda (UNAMIR), opening the way over the next six weeks for the murder of 800,000 Rwandans by Hutu extremists.[12] Years later, Clinton apologized to President Paul Kagame for the US decision to disengage and the administration's opposition to any kind of meaningful UN role to stop the genocide.[13] While never stated, Clinton's advisers were more concerned about the 1996 election and did not want to be charged with the deaths of any more US military personnel in battles in Africa.

Boutros-Ghali's harsh assessment was correct: Somalia, and indeed Africa, were not important for US foreign policy.

The UN Security Council and Somalia, 1995–2007

After the withdrawal of UNOSOM II, the Security Council did not set up a major new peacekeeping operation in Africa or elsewhere for the next four years. The new approach of the United States to peacekeeping, as established in Presidential Decision Directive 25, set a high bar for further US participation or even support. The directive required agreement on a clear strategy in advance, commitments of other financial and troop contributors, an estimate of anticipated costs and how they would be shared, and an exit strategy with a clear timetable. While these requirements seemed reasonable, the intent of the United States was to stand down from UN peacekeeping. The Security Council's next major peacekeeping operations came only in 1999, in Sierra Leone, the DRC, Ethiopia/Eritrea, and East Timor.

For Somalia, the Security Council assumed two roles: adoption of hortatory resolutions and presidential statements encouraging regional efforts by the Intergovernmental Authority on Development (IGAD), the League of Arab States, and the Organization of the Islamic Conference to restart the peace process; and monitoring implementation of the arms embargo established in 1992, including appointment of a panel of experts to make recommendations on strengthening its enforcement. The UNDP and OCHA continued to provide humanitarian and other aid. The Secretary-General and his successive special representatives at the helm of the UN Political Office for Somalia (UNPOS), based in Nairobi, sought unsuccessfully to develop a viable peace process with the regional and Somali leaders to restore the Somali state.[14] The Council periodically considered authorizing a new UN peace operation, but the circumstances were never deemed appropriate.

As UN special representative Augustine Mahiga put it in 2011, the international community had effectively abandoned Somalia to its fate.[15] The Council's role was significantly diminished. The arms embargo did little to stop arms from entering the country across its porous borders. While Somalia went without a functioning government, a checkered pattern emerged. Where local government had been established in parts of the south, there was relative calm; in Mogadishu, where the key hubs of the port and airport were located, violence was both random and pervasive. Somalis, Arabs, Russians, and various soldiers of fortune sold weapons, provided security services to the few remaining NGOs and visiting journalists, and exacted fees by controlling access to Mogadishu's airstrips and seaport. The private sector also flourished while remittances from relatives abroad kept most Somalis afloat.

International conferences in Djibouti, Ethiopia, and Kenya convened from 2002 to 2005 by IGAD, a regional body of seven East African states, were presented in the Security Council as new opportunities for peace. As BBC correspondent Mary Harper has noted, these conferences actually served two quite different purposes: first they allowed Western governments to assuage their guilt at having abandoned Somalia by seeming to be doing something useful, and second they enabled the warlords to live in comfort and safety at international hotels for protracted periods of time without coming to any firm commitments on rebuilding Somalia's future. Moreover, the discussion at these conferences was directed to reestablishing a central government. This inevitably alienated the leaderships in Puntland and Somaliland, already embittered and suspicious from years of repression under Siad Barre.[16]

A series of so-called transitional governments were agreed upon with the political support of the UN and the African Union; these were actually ghost (or virtual) governments.[17] The transitional national government, led by Abdikassim Salad Hassan from 2002 to 2004 and based in Nairobi, was rife with corruption and disinterested in promoting reconciliation. The first transitional federal government, led by Adbullahi Yusuf from 2004 to 2008, was also located initially in Nairobi (for over two years) then in Jowhar followed by Baidoa. Ethiopian forces entered Baidoa in July 2006 to bolster security for the transitional federal government and prevent a total takeover by the Union of Islamic Courts (UIC), a coalition of local Islamic groups. Ethiopia's intervention created considerable consternation among many Somalis wary of Ethiopia's long-term aspirations. In December 2006, Somali and Ethiopian forces captured Mogadishu and enabled the transitional federal government to return to the capital; two years later an agreement was reached for Ethiopian troops to withdraw in January 2009 and be replaced by African Union forces. Sharif Sheikh Ahmed, who succeeded Abdullahi Yusuf as president, the same month was virtually a prisoner of the security situation, unable to move even a few blocks without AMISOM troops accompanying him. It became the task of the African Union to begin to change the situation.[18]

The Radicalization of Islam, Al-Shabaab, and International Reengagement, 2007–2013

Somalia under Siad Barre, notwithstanding its clan divisions and other shortcomings, was a remarkably tolerant society. Women worked in professional occupations and marketplaces, owned businesses, wore mostly traditional dress, and moved about freely on their own; the schools provided free secular education for boys and girls; and the university, staffed by Somali and foreign professors mostly from Italy, was quite Western in its orientation. All this changed from my first tour in Somalia as deputy chief of mission at the US embassy in the mid-1980s to my return to Mogadishu with the US-led UNITAF in late 1992. Under Wahhabi and other religious influences from the Arabian Peninsula, the secular education system had disappeared and been replaced by religious schools focused on Islamic education; women and girls wore the hijab, and boys and girls went to separate schools.

This was part of a broader transformation. In 1975, Siad Barre had crushed religious opposition and expression, executing ten clerics and imprisoning others who challenged the state's secular approach and more permissive family legislation. With Siad Barre's fall "a bewildering array of Islamic associations suddenly emerged. . . . Their common denominator was the desire for an 'authentic' form of Islamic governance in Somalia."[19] The rise of al-Shabaab followed al-Qaeda's growing role in Pakistan and Afghanistan and the attack on the World Trade Center and the Pentagon in September 2001. Al-Shabaab also benefited from the spread of mobile phone networks as means of communication and mobilization.

Al-Shabaab followed its predecessor al-Itihaad in espousing the idea that religion and politics could not be separated in seeking to fill the void left by the collapse of central government.[20] In some communities in southern Somalia, al-Shabaab had brought order and discipline to an otherwise ungoverned space. It also brought prohibitions on the use of qaat and other narcotics, required the veiling of women, and carried out amputations and other severe punishments allowed under sharia law.

From 2001 to 2005, Islamic courts in local communities gradually coalesced into the Union of Islamic Courts (UIC), which to the surprise of many observers defeated a coalition of warlords indirectly backed by the West. For six months in 2006, life in Mogadishu, which had completely deteriorated for over a decade into a battleground, significantly improved: "Road blocks were removed. The main Mogadishu airport and seaport were reopened and rehabilitated for the first time in a decade. Squatters were made to vacate government buildings, illegal land grabs were halted, and special courts were opened to deal with the myriad claims for the restitution of property."[21] Many Somalis returned from abroad, new markets opened, and evening life returned. The Security Council urged the transitional federal government and the Union of Islamic Courts to enter into "an inclusive political process."[22]

Notwithstanding these achievements, the UIC soon split into moderate and radical factions. The UIC alienated many Somalis by its increasing inclination toward harsh sharia punishments and arbitrary financial penalties against the use of qaat, prohibiting the watching of soccer, and barring other traditional practices. Moreover, after the UIC declared jihad on Ethiopia in October 2006, the United States and Ethiopia identified the UIC as a terrorist organization, conflating the political battle among Somali clans for control of the country with a global war on terror, hereafter focused on al-Shabaab.[23] Ethiopian air attacks on Mogadishu's air and sea port on Christmas Day 2006, abetted by US drone strikes in the south, were too much for the UIC, which a week later quit Mogadishu and on January 1, 2007, abandoned its last urban stronghold Kismayo. The moderate leadership went to Eritrea while al-Shabaab fled south.[24] These attacks defeated the UIC but did not end radical Islamism in Somalia. Instead they led to strong anti-American and anti-Ethiopian sentiment among the Somali population, and further strengthened the appeal of al-Shabaab, which controlled much of southern and central Somalia, including most of Mogadishu, from 2007 to 2011.

The New Partnership: The AU and the UN Security Council

As early as 2005, IGAD was authorized by the African Union's Peace and Security Council (PSC) to establish a peace support mission in Somalia (IGASOM), but it never deployed. By January 2007, Somalia's security situation was precarious. Al-Shabaab was in control in most of the south. The transitional federal government held only a few streets in Mogadishu, and was clearly incapable of providing security for the Somali population. On January 19, 2007, the Peace and Security Council authorized the deployment of AMISOM to provide protection for the (recently reinstated) transitional federal institutions. The AU outlined an ambitious set of peace support objectives and projected deployment of nine infantry battalions as well as maritime and air components for an initial six-month period. This set the stage for the active reentry of the Security Council into Somalia. On January 20, 2007, the day after the PSC decision, the Security Council endorsed the deployment of AMISOM and mandated the force, among other matters, to protect transitional federal institutions, and provide security for key infrastructure as well as for humanitarian assistance and repatriation of refugees.[25]

The PSC, cognizant of the AU's material and financial limitations, also "urge[d] the United Nations Security Council to consider authorizing a United Nations operation in Somalia that would take over from AMISOM at the expiration of its six month mandate."[26] The AU was led to believe that a UN peacekeeping operation was under active consideration in the Security Council. This, as it turned out, was not the case.

Since then, the African Union's focus has been primarily on improving security in Somalia, while the Security Council has been concerned mainly with containing the international repercussions of the Somali crisis, preventing al-Shabaab from extending its terrorism beyond Somalia's borders, and responding to the new challenge of maritime piracy as a clear threat to international shipping.[27] This has had the advantage of keeping the Security

Council engaged on Somalia, but also the disadvantage of hindering the ability of the Somali leadership and elites to sort out their own destiny. At the time of writing, AMISOM, with the support of the Security Council, is still responsible for ensuring and expanding security for the government and the population.

AMISOM and the UN Security Council: Against All Odds

Somalia has been the major test case of the Security Council's evolving relationship with the African Union. The AU's Constitutive Act, committing it to act in cases of war crimes, crimes against humanity, and genocide (Article 4H), created a new situation for the Security Council. Whereas UN peacekeeping has been traditionally predicated on the idea that there is already a peace to keep, the African Union was prepared to deploy peacekeepers even where a peace agreement was not yet at hand. The Security Council has been compelled to consider and authorize new strategies for UN peacekeeping in Africa. The first test case came in Darfur, where a hybrid UN-AU peacekeeping mission, UNAMID, was deployed in December 2007, with mixed results. The dual-hat setup, with a UN political representative and an African Union military commander, has proven difficult to implement.

AMISOM was established in very difficult political and economic circumstances, immediately on the heels of Ethiopia's defeat of the UIC forces and the establishment of the transitional federal government in Mogadishu. Most outside observers believed AMISOM had little prospect of achieving its mandate; some even questioned its moral and political legitimacy.[28] Even though approved by the AU's Peace and Security Council and endorsed by the UN Security Council,[29] for many Somalis AMISOM was seen as "a tool of Western interests," given the immediately preceding Ethiopian-US campaign against the UIC. Moreover, AMISOM was perceived as supporting "a weak, divided and (in the view of many Somalis) illegitimate transitional government" that could barely control a few streets around Villa Somalia.[30] Many Somalis viewed the transitional federal government as a dysfunctional, warlord-dominated government beholden to Ethiopia rather than committed to the best interests of the Somali people.[31]

At the operational level, the AU took a big risk in establishing AMISOM. It lacked sufficient troop commitments as well as the financial resources and logistics to deploy even the initial 8,000-strong authorized force. Until December 2007, only Uganda agreed to supply troops, reflecting the deep skepticism of a number of African leaders as to AMISOM's prospects. In reality there was no alternative—as member states soon found out. Over the next two years the Security Council periodically considered various options to replace AMISOM. The George W. Bush administration wanted the Council to approve a new UN peacekeeping mission. Only the United States and the Netherlands, however, were prepared to commit funds, and no country was prepared to send troops. This perhaps reflected the skepticism of Council members regarding the prospects for an international force to stabilize Somalia. When the Barack Obama administration came into office in January 2009, the idea of a UN peacekeeping force was quietly dropped.

Since its initial deployment, AMISOM forces, mainly from Uganda and Burundi, have significantly improved security in Somalia. After three years of intense fighting and the al-Shabaab bombings in Kampala in July 2010 (on the eve of the World Cup soccer finals), AMISOM units finally succeeded in pushing al-Shabaab out of Mogadishu in late 2011, and subsequently out of the southern port city of Kismayo in late 2012. Kenyan troops operated independently in southern Somalia from October 2011 to stop infiltration of al-Shabaab and to protect Kenya's border-joining AMISOM in mid-2012. Al-Shabaab's surprise attack on the Westgate Mall on September 21, 2013, and the attack on the University of Garissa on April 2, 2015, however, underscored the vulnerability of the border as well as the organizational and logistical strength of al-Shabaab functioning within the large Somali refugee community in and around Nairobi.

AMISOM is continuing to provide the key security functions for the Somali government while retraining of the Somali army and police slowly proceeds. This has come at a great price in manpower. AMISOM forces have taken heavy troop losses; while AMISOM does not provide official casualty counts, estimates range from 2,000 to 3,000 troops, numbers that would be unacceptable for any UN peacekeeping operation.[32]

AMISOM and the UN Security Council: Multiple Challenges

Maintaining AMISOM has involved multiple challenges for the African Union and the Security Council, requiring a new degree of consultation and cooperation. The UN recognized that the international community would need to provide the financial resources and support package to sustain AMISOM operations. In April 2008, at the recommendation of the Secretary-General, the Security Council established a high-level panel, named after its chairman, former Italian prime minister Romano Prodi, to consider options for supporting AU peace operations. The Council, however, has been reluctant to accept the panel's main recommendation: an open-ended commitment to provide a reliable and consistent funding stream from assessed contributions.[33] The P5 insist on approving the concept of operations and maintaining effective oversight on an annual basis.[34] Since the establishment of the UN Support Office for AMISOM (UNSOA) in 2009, the Security Council has provided a logistical support package through assessed contributions at an estimated annual cost of $485 million. The EU has been playing an important financial role, footing the gap the UN was unable to cover by paying allowances for AMISOM troops of several hundred million euros annually.[35]

Another important issue is the operational relationship between the AU's Peace and Security Council and the UN Security Council. Annual meetings of the two bodies are held alternately in New York and Addis Ababa. An unresolved issue remains the status of these deliberations, which the UN insists are between "some members of the Council" and the PSC. This has rankled the AU which wants these meetings to be accepted as consultations between equals, whereas the Security Council regards them as between a principal and a subordinate body. Since 2011, the UN has significantly expanded staffing of its liaison office in Addis Ababa, now headed by Under-Secretary-General Haile Menkerios, a distinguished UN diplomat formerly in charge of UN-AU peace negotiations for Darfur. UN-AU relations will continue to be tested as the Somalia operation proceeds.

Security Council Sanctions

The Security Council first established a sanctions regime in April 1992, under Resolution 751, to oversee "the general and complete arms embargo" established under Resolution 733 three months earlier.[36] The overall goal was to stop more arms from entering Somalia and to prevent the continuation of fighting among rival Somali factions. Since then the sanctions regime has been repeatedly renewed and supervised by a sanctions committee under rotating membership. A series of Security Council resolutions have clarified its objectives and concerns, applying asset freezes and travel bans to individuals believed to have violated the arms embargo. Exemptions allowed limited arms to the transitional governments and the current federal government of Somalia.[37] In 2010, sanctions were extended to include Eritrea after credible evidence emerged that the government was serving as an active conduit for weapons to enter Somalia. Somali charcoal exports also have been sanctioned in view of evidence suggesting these were another source of funding for al-Shabaab. In July 2013, the Security Council again extended the mandate of the Somalia and Eritrea monitoring group to November 2014.[38] Overall, the sanctions, in place for more than two decades, have had only minimal impact on the situation on the ground. Somalia was already awash with arms from the Cold War era; Aidid's militia, for instance, seized the entire government arsenal when it entered Mogadishu in January 1991. Porous borders and the long-unmonitored coastline have made it relatively easy for al-Shabaab and others to bring weapons into Somalia. Moreover, the UN has virtually no enforcement capacity. An open arms market continues to flourish in Mogadishu only a few kilometers from UN offices as well as elsewhere.

Targeted financial sanctions aimed at al-Shabaab, on the other hand, have been more effective in significantly disrupting its funding stream. Disruption of the informal hawala money-transfer system and court proceedings against Somalis around the world have further contributed to reducing al-Shabaab's operational effectiveness.[39] At the behest of the Somali government and with the support of the United States, the Security Council on March 6, 2013, lifted the sanctions partially, allowing importation of limited-caliber weapons and ammunition with specific reporting requirements.[40]

A New Beginning

Toward a Post-Transition Government

The 2004 transitional federal government was conceived as an interim step toward a more broadly acceptable government. The UN, the AU, and the major donors recognized that the transitional federal government had neither the powers nor the capacity to govern. Its authority barely extended beyond Mogadishu, while al-Shabaab continued to control much of the south. In the north, Somaliland and Puntland remained separate and refused to cooperate with the transitional federal government. At a meeting in Nairobi in August 2009, US secretary of state Hillary Clinton promised US funding for training and equipment for the Somali defense force, but in reality this had little impact. Most US funding was committed to supporting AMISOM. Four years into its existence, the transitional federal government was plagued by corruption, political infighting, and incompetence, and had virtually no credibility.[41]

International pressure was needed to move to a new government. The Security Council came to Nairobi in May 2011 to lend direct support to the UN push to end the transition. The Kampala Accord, negotiated by UN special representative Augustine Mahiga and Ugandan president Yoweri Museveni that summer, set forth a road map with a deadline of August 2012 for the selection of a new parliament, the drafting of a new constitution, and the election of a new president. The road map was adopted by the Somali stakeholders in September 2011 and given further international support at the London Conference in February 2012, where the leaders of the transitional federal government, with presidents from Puntland and Somaliland in attendance, committed themselves to completing the transition on schedule.[42] At this conference, Secretary-General Ban Ki-moon asked British prime minister David Cameron to take the lead in bolstering political and financial support for AMISOM in the Security Council and the European Union.[43]

As AMISOM pushed al-Shabaab out of Mogadishu and pursued it in the south, the UN and Western governments intensified pressure on the Somali leaders to act. In the summer of 2012, SRSG Mahiga officially announced the end of the transition. The newly appointed Somali parliament of 275 elders elected a well-known civil society leader, Hassan Sheikh Mohamud, as president of the new federal government of Somalia. These steps did not bring an end to Somalia's many difficulties, nor did they change the realities of daily life for most Somalis. The election, however, marked the victory of civil society groups who had remained in the country throughout the past two decades over the corrupt transitional government and the mafia surrounding it.[44] It remains to be seen which of these groups will prevail in the months and years ahead.

The Security Council and the African Union in 2013: New Mandates and Strategies

By spring 2013, President Mohamud had staked out a new position, asserting his government's determination to exercise its sovereign powers and insisting that the roles of the UN and AMISOM be determined in accordance with its priorities and active participation.[45] The government was no longer to be seen as the helpless victim requiring life support, but as an active force in the determination of the country's future. "We are the Somali government and we determine the type of assistance we want, and where and when we want it."[46] Mohamud pressed for the transfer of the UN political office from Nairobi to Mogadishu, which took place in April 2013.

For its part, the Security Council recognized that this was a moment of both challenge and opportunity. Al-Shabaab still constituted a threat to the establishment of government authority in the south and elsewhere. The "liberated areas" had yet to receive government services. President Mohamud's key priority was security sector reform. The Security Council had already supported an enlarged AMISOM, increasing its authorized strength from 12,000 to 17,731 in 2013; with the addition of Ethiopian forces as of February 2014, AMISOM troop strength was 22,126.[47]

In 2013, UN Secretary-General Ban Ki-moon recommended that the Council create a new UN assistance mission that would deliver political and peacebuilding support with a presence across Somalia alongside AMISOM. SRSG Nicholas Kay, who arrived in June 2013, has focused on supporting the political process, including the drafting of a new constitution and improving the rule of law as well as restructuring the Somali security sector. As of April 2013, the new UN Assistance Mission in Somalia (UNSOM), the successor to UNPOS, was established in Mogadishu and located inside the AMISOM security perimeter at the airport. The UNDP and other UN offices have remained outside.

As of early 2014, the future of the joint AU-UN political arrangement and of AMISOM itself remained to be decided. Within the UN Secretariat, a possible new UN peacekeeping operation to replace AMISOM is under consideration; the Security Council has yet to place this on its agenda. There is recognition within the Council that AMISOM cannot remain indefinitely, but also considerable reluctance to reinsert a UN peacekeeping force after the experience of the 1990s.

What Future for Somalia?

By spring 2014, security remained a major challenge; al-Shabaab retained the capacity to launch attacks and targeted assassinations in Somalia and the region. The June 2013 attack on the UN offices in Mogadishu adjacent to the airport killed a number of security guards and civilians and nearly breached the main security perimeter. There followed the audacious onslaught on the Westgate Mall in Nairobi on September 21 that left at least sixty-eight civilians dead, and the failed attempt by US Navy Seals on October 7 to capture a key al-Shabaab leader in Baraawe, an al-Shabaab stronghold south of Mogadishu. All these events underscored the durability of al-Shabaab's capabilities and support structure.

The cohesion and staying power of President Mohamud's government is being severely tested. Opposition forces contend that an Islamist force (New Blood) supported by Qatar is pressing President Mohamud to accommodate religious tendencies, while paying lip service to the principles of the secular state. The drafting of a new federal constitution and other long-term issues are on hold, strengthening the supporters of the status quo. Competition and internal rivalries among government ministers have created confusion as to the government's main aspirations and agenda, presaging further disagreements along clan and regional lines.[48]

Beyond these security, political, and financial challenges, the underlying question remains the future of the Somali state. Will it be a centralized state with power remaining in the hands of the elites based in Mogadishu, or a decentralized federal structure in which power is shared with the regions? This will be the core of future power struggles between the government and leaders in other regions. A more stable Somalia will require a significant sharing of power with the regions. Successive transitional federal governments were dominated by the same parochial interests that had marginalized the Isaaqs in the north for more than thirty years. The leaders of Somaliland and Puntland have set up their own administrations, even though unrecognized by the international community for more than two decades. Somaliland has been a significant success, avoiding the conflict in the south while maintaining good relations with its neighbors in Djibouti,

Ethiopia, and the Arabian Peninsula. The inclusion of Puntland and possibly, in the long term, Somaliland in a united Somalia will only happen if there is agreement on a decentralized power-sharing structure. Not everyone in Mogadishu is in agreement on this goal. The competition between these competing visions of Somalia will determine the country's future.

Conclusion

It would be foolhardy to try to predict what will happen in Somalia over the next years. Its leaders and elites can choose the path of reconciliation and reconstruction, or continue the deleterious conflict and power struggle of the past two decades. The Security Council and the African Union have played important roles in shaping Somalia's destiny to date. When the Council was engaged in the early 1990s, it offered hope that a peaceful path could be followed. In the twelve years from 1995 to 2007, Somalia descended into near anarchy while the Security Council distanced itself, preoccupied with other conflicts in the Middle East and Africa. Since then, with the new focus on the continuing threat posed by the rise of al-Shabaab, the Security Council has reengaged. Through the new UNSOM presence and its continuing financial and logistical support for AMISOM, the Security Council has again given Somalia a new lease of life. The 2012 election and its aftermath have created a new opportunity. It is to be hoped that the Security Council will stay actively engaged even as other issues—Mali, the Democratic Republic of the Congo, the Central African Republic—crowd in for attention. The United Nations and the African Union have formed a new partnership to assist Somalia to move from being a failed state to an example of postconflict recovery. But in the end, only the Somali people can determine their destiny.

Notes

1. Somalia was first placed on the UN Security Council agenda with the adoption of Resolution 733, S/RES/1992 (January 23, 1992).

2. See United Nations Security Council, "Statement by the President of the Security Council," UN Doc. S/PRST/2012/4, March 5, 2012.

3. See John L. Hirsch and Robert B. Oakley, *Somalia and Operation Restore Hope: Reflections on Peacemaking and Peacekeeping* (Washington, DC: US Institute of Peace, 1995), pp. 3–16; Ioan Lewis and James Mayall, "Somalia," in *United Nations Interventionism, 1991–2004,* edited by Mats Berdal and Spyros Economides (Cambridge: Cambridge University Press, 2006).

4. Secretary-General Boutros Boutros-Ghali has no recall of remarks widely attributed to him about the Council's attention to a "rich man's war" in Bosnia while ignoring a "poor man's war in Somalia." He has acknowledged, however, his concern that the Security Council had given excessive attention to the wars in Bosnia and Kosovo and had disregarded Somalia before finally establishing an under-resourced UN peacekeeping force (UNOSOM I) in April 1992. See his interview

with Stanley Meisler, "UN Chief Fears Bosnia Could Be a Quagmire: Balkans: Boutros-Ghali Warns That Dispatching Peacekeepers on Mission Impossible Could Harm Organization's Credibility," *Los Angeles Times,* August 10, 1992.

5. United Nations Security Council Resolution 751, S/RES/751 (April 24, 1992).

6. United Nations Security Council Resolution 794, S/RES/794 (December 3, 1992); UNITAF at its peak reached 37,000 troops.

7. In speaking to the Security Council, Ambassador Madeleine Albright described Resolution 814 as "an unprecedented enterprise aimed at nothing less than the restoration of an entire country." US-UN Press Release no. 37-93, March 26, 1993.

8. United Nations Security Council Resolution 814, S/RES/814 (March 26, 1993).

9. Ibid.

10. United Nations Security Council Resolution 837, S/RES/837 (June 6, 1993).

11. Peter Bridges, *Safirka: An American Envoy* (Kent, OH: Kent State University Press, 2000), p. 208.

12. Samantha Powers, "Rwanda: Mostly in a Listening Mode," in *A Problem from Hell: America and the Age of Genocide* (New York: Harper Perennial, 2002).

13. President Bill Clinton's speech at Kigali Airport, Rwanda, March 26, 1998.

14. After 1995, UN special representatives for Somalia were David Stephen (UK), 1997–2002; Winston Tubman (Liberia), 2002–2005; Francis Lonsey Fall (Senegal), 2005–2007; Ahmedou Ould Abdullah (Mauritania), 2007–2010; Augustine Mahiga (Tanzania), 2010–2013; and Nicholas Kay (United Kingdom), appointed April 2013. UNPOS, from 2009 onward, operated on the basis of a Security Council mandate.

15. International Peace Institute, "Stabilizing Somalia: Featuring Augustine Mahiga," IPI Special Representatives of the Secretary-General Series Policy Forum, New York, September 20, 2011.

16. Mary Harper, *Getting Somalia Wrong* (London: Zed, 2012), pp. 64–65.

17. See Security Council Report, "Working Together for Peace and Security in Africa: The Security Council and the AU Peace and Security Council," Special Research Report no. 2, May 10, 2011, pp. 20–22.

18. See the *CIA World Factbook,* Somalia section, for more information on the various transitional governments and the political agreements that led to the transitional federal government's return to Mogadishu; www.cia.gov/library/publications /the-world-factbook/geos/so.html.

19. Harper, *Getting Somalia Wrong,* p. 77.

20. For a detailed analysis of al-Shabaab and the currents that sustain it, see Stig Jarle Hansen, *Al-Shabaab in Somalia: The History and Ideology of a Militant Islamist Group, 2005–2012* (Oxford: Oxford University Press, 2013).

21. Cedric Barnes and Harun Hassan, *The Rise and Fall of Mogadishu's Islamic Courts* (London: Chatham House, 2007), quoted in Harper, *Getting Somalia Wrong,* p. 81.

22. See United Nations Security Council Resolution 1725, S/RES/1725 (December 6, 2006).

23. Harper, *Getting Somalia Wrong,* pp. 81–85.

24. Ibid.; author discussion with Augustine Mahiga, October 18, 2013.

25. United Nations Security Council Resolution 1744, S/RES/1744 (January 20, 2007).

26. See AU Peace and Security Council, "Communiqué of the 69th Meeting of the Peace and Security Council," AU Doc. PSC/PR/COMM (LXIX), January 19, 2007.

27. For a detailed discussion of the international response to maritime piracy, see James Cockayne's discussion of organized crime and piracy in Chapter 15 of this volume.

28. For a further account of the AMISOM situation in 2007, see Paul Williams, "Into the Mogadishu Maelstrom: The African Union Mission in Somalia," *International Peacekeeping* 16, no. 14 (October 2009): 514–530.

29. United Nations Security Council Resolution 1744, S/RES/1744 (January 20, 2007).

30. Williams, "Into the Mogadishu Maelstrom."

31. See Ken Menkhaus, *Somalia: A Country in Peril, a Policy Nightmare,* Strategy Paper no. 1 (Washington, DC: Enough Project, September 2008), pp. 7, 10.

32. United Nations deputy secretary-general Jan Eliasson: "You would be shocked to learn that maybe it is up to 3,000 AMISOM soldiers that have been killed during these years that AMISOM has been there." United Nations Meetings Coverage and Press Releases, "Press Conference by Deputy Secretary-General Jan Eliasson at United Nations Headquarters," UN Doc. DSG/SM/668, May 9, 2013, www.un.org/News/Press/docs/2013/dsgsm668.doc.htm. Some analysts believe that these numbers are very inflated. Author interview with Paul Williams, June 20, 2014.

33. United Nations General Assembly and Security Council, *Report of the African Union–United Nations Panel on Modalities for Support to African Union Peacekeeping Operations,* UN Doc. A/63/666-S/2008/813, December 31, 2008.

34. The United States is the leading provider of financing, airlift, and predeployment training for AMISOM. Assessed contributions are delivered through UNSOA to AMISOM. In addition, the European Union, through its Peace Support Fund, voluntarily contributes an estimated $200 million a year for allowances and other requirements. See Adam C. Smith, "United States of America," in *Providing Peacekeepers,* edited by Alex J. Bellamy and Paul Williams (Oxford: Oxford University Press, 2013).

35. Interview with Neil McKillip, UK Mission to the UN, March 4, 2014.

36. United Nations Security Council Resolutions 733, S/RES/733 (January 23, 1992); and 751, S/RES/751 (April 24, 1992).

37. Major Security Council decisions on sanctions include: "Prohibition on the Financing of Arms Acquisitions as well as the Direct or Indirect Sale or Supply of Technical Advice or Military Training to Combatants" (Resolution 1425, S/RES/1425, July 22, 2002); "Partial Lifting of the Embargo to Enable IGAD and the AU to Deploy a Regional Intervention Force to Protect the TFG" (Resolution 1725, S/RES/1725, December 6, 2006); "Authorization of Weapons and Military Equipment for the TFG by Limiting the Embargo to Non-State Actors" (Resolution 1744, S/RES/1744, February 21, 2007); "Application of Sanctions Including Travel Bans and Asset Freezes on Individuals and Entities Responsible for Recruiting Child Soldiers or Targeting Civilians Including Women and Children in Situations of Armed Conflict" (Resolution 1844, S/RES/1844, November 20, 2008); "Extension of Sanctions to Eritrea in Response to Reports That It Had Violated the Above Mentioned Embargoes" (Resolution 1907, S/RES/1907, December 23, 2009); "Partial Lifting of the Embargo to Allow Certain Arms to Be Provided to Help Strengthen the Army and Police" (Resolution 2093, S/RES/2093, March 6, 2013).

38. United Nations Security Council Resolution 2111, S/RES/2111 (July 23, 2013).

39. See Matt Freear and Cedric de Coning, "Lessons from the African Union Mission for Somalia (AMISOM) for Peace Operations in Mali," *Stability: International Journal of Security and Development* 2, no. 2 (June 12, 2013): 1–11.

40. The partial lifting of the embargo was renewed for a further eight months by Security Council Resolution 2142 (March 5, 2014), UN Doc. S/RES/ 2142.

41. Remarks by Secretary Clinton and President Sheikh Sharif, August 6, 2009, www.state.gov/secretary/20092013clinton/rm/2009a/08/126956.htm. For a characterization of the outgoing transitional federal government, see Ken Menkhaus, "The Somali Spring," *Foreign Policy,* September 24, 2012.

42. "London Conference Backs Somalia Terror Fight," *BBC News,* February 23, 2012, www.bbc.co.uk/news/uk-politics-17131208.

43. McKillip interview.

44. Menkhaus, "The Somali Spring."

45. The federal government of Somalia's six-pillar strategy is focused on stability, economic recovery, peacebuilding, service delivery, international relations, and unity. Paul D. Williams, *AMISOM in Transition: The Future of the African Union Mission in Somalia* (Nairobi: Rift Valley Institute and Nairobi Forum, February 13, 2013).

46. Williams, *AMISOM in Transition,* p. 1.

47. United Nations Security Council Resolution 2036, S/RES/2036 (February 22, 2012); AMISOM reached this force level, including 360 police, in December 2012. Resolution 2073, S/RES/2073 (November 7, 2012), added an additional 50 civilian personnel. In 2014, Ethiopia's national defense force provided 4,395 uniformed personnel. See http://amisom-au.org/2014/01/ethiopian-troops-formally -join-amisom-peacekeepers-in-somalia.

48. See Mulkahir M. Muhamud, "Nairobi Attack Puts Pressure on Somali Leader to Shape Up or Ship Out," *Africa: News and Analysis—The East African,* October 10, 2013, http://africajournalismtheworld.com/2013/10/10/somalias -government-under-pressure-ater-kenya-mall-attack; author discussion with former special representative of the Secretary-General Augustine Mahiga, New York, October 10, 2013.

30

Sudan

Heiko Nitzschke

WHILE SUDAN HAS BEEN PLAGUED BY INTERNAL CONFLICTS FOR much of its post-independence history, these conflicts made it on the agenda of the Security Council only after the end of the Cold War.[1] Initially, the Council focused on Khartoum's entanglement with international terrorism. Only in the new millennium did it address war and peace in Sudan by overseeing completion of the 2005 north-south peace deal, responding to the bloodshed in Darfur, and shepherding the peaceful separation of what are now Sudan and South Sudan, followed by efforts to avert a new war between Khartoum and Juba and prevent ethnic strife in the south.

Over the years, the Council employed a range of measures at its disposal, breaking, at times, new ground in international law and peacekeeping. These included two sanctions regimes, several trips by the Council to the region, various peacekeeping operations, including the first mission jointly conducted with the African Union (AU), and the first-ever referral by the Council of a conflict situation to the International Criminal Court. Many of these measures were related to the Darfur conflict, which enjoyed a degree of international attention rare to African conflicts. In fact, for many observers, the Darfur conflict had become synonymous for Council action—or rather inaction—vis-à-vis Sudan.

By distinguishing between five phases of Council engagement with Sudan during the past twenty years, I seek to provide a more differentiated picture. By also taking into account dynamics on the ground and the role of regional organizations, media, and advocacy, it will become clear that not only did the Council's attention oscillate substantially between the north-south and the Darfur dimension, but cooperation and confrontation in the

Council also varied considerably on both files, given the respective interests of the Council members, particularly of the permanent five. These dynamics also reflect the central shortcoming in the Council's Sudan engagement over the years, namely the lack of a common and strategic approach. While Council members invested heavily in the shared goal of peace and stability, these efforts were ultimately limited by diverging interests and shifting priorities. Consequently, the Council was often at war with itself, rather than using its political clout and tools at its disposal in a way required to effectively influence developments on the ground.

Isolating a Rogue State

When the Republic of the Sudan gained independence on January 1, 1956, the country had already started to suffer from what was to become one of the longest and deadliest civil wars in Africa. The conflict was rooted in the systematic socioeconomic marginalization of the south, a pattern institutionalized under colonial rule and maintained by the various post-independence regimes in Khartoum. Elite rule by the center also came at the expense of other peoples in the periphery, especially in eastern Sudan and the Darfur region. Grievances in the south were further exacerbated by the imposition of sharia on the southerners, the majority of whom adhered to Christian or other beliefs.[2] Fighting escalated in the mid-1980s, when the main rebel group, the Sudan People's Liberation Movement/Army (SPLM/A) under the leadership of John Garang, took the battle to Kordofan and Blue Nile, strategically important regions that straddled the north-south border, and Khartoum responded with indiscriminate aerial bombardments, ground assaults by the army and militias, and the denial of humanitarian access.[3]

Yet like many other conflicts, the Sudanese civil war did not make it on the agenda of the Security Council during the Cold War. Even during the 1990s, the Council followed the situation largely from the sidelines. The violent implosion of the Balkans and brutal civil wars in West Africa dominated international attention, and the peacekeeping debacles in Somalia and Rwanda left little appetite in Western capitals for further involvement in African conflicts. Inconceivable today, the UN in 1989 launched Operation Lifeline Sudan, a massive UN-coordinated humanitarian operation to deliver aid across frontlines, without a formal Council endorsement. Attempts by the Bill Clinton administration in 1994 to have the Council condemn Khartoum's bombing raids in the south were stymied by China, which was reluctant to allow meddling in the internal affairs of a member state and eager to protect its nascent commercial ties with Khartoum.[4] In an informal meeting held at the Swedish UN mission in 1998, Oxfam, Save the Children, Care International, and Doctors Without Borders lobbied Council members to urgently engage on a peace process, but to no avail.[5]

The Council did, however, act at that time on Khartoum's entanglement with international terrorism. This was largely driven by US efforts to isolate the Islamist regime of President Omar al-Bashir and his influential ideologue-in-chief, Hassan al-Turabi.[6] In an effort to turn Sudan into an Islamist state and the new center for the global Islamic ummah, the regime in Khartoum had come to host a veritable "who's who" of global radicals and terrorist organizations, including Osama bin Laden and his nascent al-Qaeda network.[7] When several Sudanese were implicated in the 1993 World Trade Center bombing, Washington took the far-reaching step of declaring Sudan a state sponsor of terrorism and imposed bilateral trade and financial sanctions on Khartoum. Following the involvement of Sudanese intelligence officials and Egyptian radicals based in Khartoum in the 1995 failed assassination attempt of Egyptian president Hosni Mubarak in Addis Ababa, Washington's UN ambassador Madeleine Albright called for broad UN sanctions against Khartoum.[8]

The conditions seemed promising: Egypt had in January 1996 become a nonpermanent member of the Security Council, and Ethiopian prime minister Meles Zenawi requested the Council "to adopt a resolution commensurate with the crime."[9] But Albright's push for sanctions met with strong resistance from China, Russia, and France in the Council at a time when the humanitarian fallout from the comprehensive Iraq embargo had discredited sanctions as a policy tool. Even Cairo pushed back on comprehensive sanctions, fearing that a weapons embargo against Khartoum would favor the southern rebels with potential risks for Egypt's steady supply of Nile water, Cairo's primary strategic interest in Sudan. Cairo had also come under pressure from fellow Arab states that were critical of the UN sanctions imposed at that time against Iraq and Libya.[10] Against this background, the Council, in January 1996, only reiterated a demand earlier made by the Organization of African Unity that Sudan extradite the alleged attackers to Ethiopia (Resolution 1044). When Khartoum ignored the call, the divided Council in April could only impose mild diplomatic sanctions, including travel restrictions on regime members (Resolution 1054). Moscow and Beijing abstained in the vote, starting a pattern that was repeated in subsequent Sudan sanctions resolutions. With the P5 divided and no sanctions committee established due to Chinese and Russian opposition, implementation of the UN sanctions by member states was limited, and their effect was little more than a nuisance for Khartoum. A subsequent Council decision, in August, to impose a flight ban on Sudanese aircraft (Resolution 1070) never came into force, because Russia, China, France, and other Council members demanded that the UN Secretariat first assess the potential humanitarian consequences of the ban. When this first-ever humanitarian pre-assessment report was presented to an already skeptical Council membership, the flight ban was off the table.[11]

A frustrated Washington stepped up action outside of the Council to isolate Khartoum by propping up the southern rebels and Sudan's neighbors.[12] The US-Sudanese relationship reached a nadir in the wake of the 1998 al-Qaeda bombings of the US embassies in Tanzania and Kenya when US cruise missiles destroyed the al-Shifa pharmaceutical factory in Khartoum for its alleged production of nerve gas precursor chemicals, a claim subsequently proven to rest on questionable intelligence.[13] Washington claimed that its Operation Infinite Reach, primarily aimed at al-Qaeda training camps in Afghanistan, was covered under the self-defense Article 51 of the UN Charter.[14] Supported by African and Arab Council members, Khartoum responded by requesting a UN fact-finding mission. But the United States blocked any formal Council follow-up, claiming to have sorted things out bilaterally with Khartoum.

In the meantime, the regime in Khartoum had taken some calculated steps to shed its pariah status, albeit without changing its Islamist course or easing its brutal reign. With a costly war to finance against the south, the bilateral US sanctions and their knock-on effects on Western trade and investment had taken their toll on the Sudanese economy, creating tensions also between moderates and hardliners in the regime. Responding also to key US demands, Khartoum clamped down on Sudan-based radicals and in 1996 expelled bin Laden, who then set up his base in Afghanistan. When President Bashir in 1999 stripped his former mentor Turabi of his official positions and embarked on a charm offensive with Cairo and Addis Ababa, his former foes backed Khartoum's request in June 2000 to have the UN sanctions lifted. Yet Washington repeatedly delayed Council action by referring to a pending internal assessment of Khartoum's antiterrorism cooperation. US-Sudanese relations suffered a new blow in the last months of the Clinton administration when Washington blocked Sudan's election to the Security Council for 2000–2001. A temporary détente set in under the new George W. Bush administration when Washington concluded that Khartoum had largely cooperated on the antiterror file and a Sudan peace deal became a priority for Bush's Africa policy. Ironically, only a week after the terrorist attacks of September 11, 2001, the Security Council lifted the Sudan sanctions, with only the US abstaining (Resolution 1372). Yet Sudan's flirtation with terrorism would also influence future international peacemaking efforts. For Khartoum, the quest to shed bilateral US sanctions, together with its classification by the United States as a state sponsor of terrorism, became a major bone of contention with Washington. Subsequent US administrations meanwhile had to square security interests of the intelligence community, which was eager to cooperate with Khartoum on broader political and humanitarian goals. It was also during the 1990s that a growing anti-Khartoum constituency emerged in Congress and among advocacy groups calling for US action against the regime's Islamic radicalism and its use of slavery and jihad against the Christians in the south.[15]

Making Peace, Containing Darfur

The new millennium also rang in a new phase in the Council's engagement with Sudan, as mediation efforts by Sudan's neighbors in the Intergovernmental Authority on Development (IGAD) on a north-south peace deal progressed. The civil war almost made it formally onto the Council agenda in 2000, when Canada, a nonpermanent Council member at the time and embarrassed by the alleged complicity of Canadian oil company Talisman in Khartoum's scorched earth campaign, proposed that the Council publicly endorse the IGAD mediation efforts.[16] But Ottawa had to drop the idea when IGAD, pressured also by Khartoum, warned that this "might have a negative impact on the peace process," and even Washington opposed the move because China had threatened to bring up again in this context the controversial al-Shifa bombing.[17] In August of 2000, the Council could only agree on the weakest of its public pronouncements, "elements for a statement to the press," voicing concern over aerial bombings in the vicinity of UN aid operations. Two years later, however, with IGAD peace talks making headway under able Kenyan mediation and with strong support from the Sudan Troika (the United States, the United Kingdom, and Norway), the Council issued its first-ever press statement on the civil war, endorsing a breakthrough agreement reached between Khartoum and the SPLM/A on the parameters for a future peace deal.[18]

But just when the north-south conflict was winding down, the long-simmering Darfur conflict erupted into open rebellion in early 2003. Khartoum had a long history of marginalizing "non-Arabs" in Darfur, and inter-communal tensions there had been exacerbated in the 1980s amid desertification and famine. When Khartoum allowed Libyan strongman Muammar Qaddafi to use Darfur as a staging ground to overthrow the regime in neighboring Chad, his fighters, recruited from the Sahel region, brought not only sophisticated weapons but also Arab supremacist ideology to Darfur, where it fell on fertile ground. Catering to the growing Arab constituency in Darfur, Khartoum stepped up land and local governance reforms to further disenfranchise non-Arab communities. Military suppression increased following the Bashir-Turabi split in 1999, when many of Turabi's followers, "African" Islamists from Darfur, now deprived of political representation in Khartoum, returned to Darfur and reverted to armed opposition. Their self-defense groups were crushed by the Sudanese army with the help of locally recruited Arab militias. While "historically and anthropologically bogus,"[19] the "Arab versus African" dichotomy became a narrative accepted by both the perpetrators and the victims of violence. It would also find traction with international policymakers and advocacy groups familiar with this dichotomy from the north-south war.

The timing of the Darfur rebellion was no coincidence, as the rebels feared being excluded from the future political dispensation of Sudan, subject to the exclusive negotiations between Khartoum and the SPLM/A. Juba halfheartedly invited the Darfur rebels to participate in the peace talks, but only under the SPLM/A umbrella. Khartoum meanwhile refused IGAD attempts to include Darfur in the negotiations with the south. It instead unleashed government-armed and -financed militias and thugs, soon universally known as Janjaweed, against the "African" population. Indiscriminate aerial bombardments and ground assaults by the Sudanese army often preceded these attacks.[20]

Despite gruesome reports from NGOs and UN humanitarian personnel of widespread violence and displacement, the Security Council throughout 2003 ignored Darfur.[21] Capitals were busy at that time dealing with post-9/11 Afghanistan and the diplomatic fallout from the US intervention in Iraq. Regarding Sudan, their priority was to conclude a north-south peace deal first. The international community pursued a sequenced approach, arguing that a peace deal reached first between Khartoum and Juba would also help address Darfuri grievances through the Sudan-wide sociopolitical reforms foreseen therein.[22] This resonated well with China and Russia, which considered the Darfur conflict an internal matter of a sovereign state, a principled policy position certainly also informed by their substantial oil and arms deals signed with Khartoum. The United States and United Kingdom, too, had no interest in antagonizing the regime in Khartoum, for fear of jeopardizing its buy-in for the peace deal with the south and losing a valuable counterterrorism partner.[23] The Bush administration thus bet on silent diplomacy, warning Khartoum that the promised normalization in relations following a peace deal would not be forthcoming if fighting in Darfur continued.[24] Khartoum cleverly played on these fears by threatening to pull out of the north-south peace talks when international pressure over Darfur became too high.[25]

It was only when the large-scale violence in Darfur could no longer be ignored that Council members in 2004 reacted. Numerous church organizations, student activists, and advocacy groups had begun to pressure Washington and other capitals to take action, and Darfur soon was portrayed as a test case for the then-nascent principle of Responsibility to Protect.[26] In view of the ten-year commemoration of the Rwandan genocide that year, Darfur featured prominently in the media and newspaper op-eds, and UN Secretary-General Kofi Annan became a prominent advocate for tough Council action.[27] When nonpermanent member Germany used its Council presidency in April 2004 to invite UN emergency coordinator Jan Egeland to brief exclusively on Darfur, the Council finally broke its silence by publicly expressing "deep concern about the massive humanitarian crisis."[28]

But sudden international attention on Darfur also proved to be a double-edged sword. What Deborah Murphy observed of US media coverage at that time was largely true also for policy responses, including by the Security Council: "In general, Darfur was removed from the Sudanese context and was instead incorporated into the history of genocide."[29] The conflict was thus addressed mainly as a humanitarian and accountability issue, not a political one.[30] Accordingly, Washington in July 2004 initiated the Council's first Darfur resolution, calling for accountability for the crimes committed, demanding that Khartoum disarm the Janjaweed militias, and imposing an arms embargo against them and the Darfur rebels (Resolution 1556). In September, the United States significantly upped the ante when Secretary of State Colin Powell testified before Congress that Khartoum had pursued "genocide" in Darfur, and a US-sponsored Security Council resolution broadened the arms embargo and authorized a UN commission of inquiry to investigate the Darfur crimes (Resolution 1564). China wielded its veto threat to block sanctions against the Sudanese oil industry and to limit the arms embargo to Darfur (rather than all of Sudan), thus allowing for continued arms deliveries to Khartoum. Still, Beijing abstained on both resolutions, joined on the latter by Russia, Algeria, and Pakistan.

While the Council focused on sanctions and accountability, the newly established African Union had stepped into the peacemaking void with mediation efforts and the deployment of an observer mission to monitor AU-brokered yet largely ineffective ceasefires.[31] Showing little appetite for more direct engagement, Western capitals instead strengthened the AU Mission in Sudan (AMIS) with personnel, funding, and logistical support, including from NATO and the European Union. The Security Council duly endorsed this "African ownership" and authorized UN support to AMIS, while the AU considered Darfur a test case for its emerging peace and security structures.[32]

With a token AU presence on the ground and the band-aid of largely ineffective sanctions imposed against the Janjaweed, the Council could again concentrate on the north-south peace process, with Washington's UN ambassador and former US Sudan envoy John Danforth as the driving force. Contrary to Darfur, cooperation among Council members was largely forthcoming. For Beijing, Khartoum's sovereignty was not at stake, since the regime had principally agreed not only on a possible future secession of the south but also an active UN role in Sudan, including a future observer mission.[33] At Danforth's initiative, the Council held a rare away session in Nairobi in November 2004 to nudge the parties to finally conclude the long-awaited peace deal (Resolution 1574).[34] Concerted efforts culminated in the signing of the Comprehensive Peace

Agreement (CPA) between the government in Khartoum and the SPLM/A on January 9, 2005, that foresaw a complete restructuring of Sudan's political, security, and economic architecture within a six-year interim period. The key provision of the agreement, undoubtedly, was that the South Sudanese could decide in 2011 whether to remain in a united Sudan or become an independent state.

All Eyes on Darfur

The ink was not yet dry on the CPA when the Council's focus shifted almost exclusively to Darfur. This was driven also by star-powered advocacy campaigns of unprecedented magnitude, which received further impetus with the Darfur inquiry commission's January 2005 recommendation that the Council refer the situation to the International Criminal Court.[35]

Meanwhile, the flaw of the "sequencing approach" soon became apparent. Not only did Khartoum and the SPLM/A, now forming a joint government, show little interest in sharing the spoils of peace with the Darfur rebels, but also, with Khartoum ramping up its military campaign in Darfur, the Council soon found itself in the paradoxical situation of pledging support to Khartoum and Juba on implementing the north-south peace deal "while trying to play hardball over Darfur with the same Khartoum interlocutors."[36] The effect this had on the Council's peacemaking efforts had already become palpable by the end of March 2005, when diverging views in the Council resulted in the adoption of three separate Sudan resolutions.[37] While the Council unanimously authorized the UN Peacekeeping Mission in Sudan (UNMIS) to monitor and support CPA implementation (Resolution 1590), disagreements persisted over the course of action in Darfur. China, Russia, and Algeria first watered down and then abstained on a US-sponsored resolution that banned offensive military flights over Darfur and established a Sudan sanctions committee and panel of experts to help monitor the sanctions (Resolution 1591). Divisions of different sorts had emerged over the question of accountability for the Darfur crimes. When Washington lobbied with African members of the Security Council for a special Darfur court based in Tanzania, in an attempt to prevent the Council from referring the Darfur conflict to the ICC, France and the UK secured support from eleven Council members for a referral resolution. Even Russia was on board, having signed but not ratified the ICC's Rome Statute in September 2000. Wary of the political costs of vetoing the French draft, Washington ultimately abstained, but not without having obtained immunity for US peacekeepers from ICC jurisdiction (Resolution 1593). China, Algeria, and Brazil also abstained, with the former two claiming that the referral would undermine prospects for a political solution, and the latter in protest of the US exemptions.[38]

The first-ever ICC referral by the Council was heralded as a historic step for the advancement of international criminal justice, not least because of Washington's tacit approval.[39] While China's decision not to veto the referral came as a shock for Khartoum, it also reflected Beijing's pragmatic approach to Sudan. With a US veto becoming unlikely and no prospect for a joint veto with Russia, the political costs of a lone Chinese veto in the face of the atrocities committed by Khartoum were presumably deemed too high. That the ICC would eventually issue an arrest warrant against President Bashir was probably not contemplated in Beijing and Moscow, which no doubt would have otherwise voted differently.

On the ground in Darfur, meanwhile, the sanctions imposed by the Council and the ICC referral had little tangible effect. Weapons continued to flow into Darfur, and aerial bombardments by the Sudanese air force continued as the flight ban over Darfur lacked a monitoring and enforcement mechanism. As violence and displacement continued unabated, Western capitals changed course. With the international spotlight firmly on Darfur, and amid increasing donor fatigue with AMIS, the goal now became to replace the overwhelmed and under-resourced African force with UN peacekeepers.

Throughout 2006 and 2007, the push for "rehatting" AMIS dominated the international debate on Sudan. At the same time, it would also expose the limits of the Council, hampered by internal rifts and faced with a recalcitrant regime in Khartoum.[40] With President Bashir categorically rejecting UN troops in Darfur and the AU reticent to be sidelined, Washington's firebrand UN ambassador John Bolton encountered strong pushback from Beijing and Moscow.

While not opposed to a UN Darfur mission per se, both China and Russia were unwilling to impose it on Khartoum, citing the Charter principle of noninterference and the peacekeeping principle of host-country consent. Even France initially balked at the prospects of yet another large UN mission in Sudan, fearing a depletion of scarce peacekeeping capacities that Paris preferred to see deployed to francophone Africa instead.[41]

Faced with this resistance, the United States first wrestled a general commitment from the AU to an eventual UN takeover. After Khartoum signaled that it may agree to UN troops once a Darfur peace deal was signed, the focus then turned to reviving the somnolent AU-mediated peace talks.[42] Meant also to pressure Khartoum and the rebels to come to the negotiation table, the United States, in April 2006, pushed through travel restrictions and an asset freeze against two mid-level regime officials, one Janjaweed leader and one rebel commander (Resolution 1672). This largely symbolic step was accompanied by concerted international efforts to cajole Khartoum and the various rebel groups to finally conclude the Darfur peace agreement. Though Khartoum and smaller rebel factions eventually signed the deal, the major rebel groups refused. The agreement was thus effectively dead on arrival.[43]

Back in New York, the United States and United Kingdom nevertheless called for the UNMIS operation, strengthened with a robust force to protect the civilian population, to be expanded into Darfur. But China and Russia were adamant: no Sudanese consent, no UN mission. When Bolton forced a vote on a Chapter VII resolution in August that merely "invited" the consent of Khartoum for UN peacekeepers in Darfur, they and Qatar abstained (Resolution 1706). President Bashir defiantly rejected the decision, knowing well that he could hold the divided Council at bay. With Khartoum stonewalling on UN peacekeepers, international saber-rattling increased as advocacy organizations, think tanks, and officials demanded more sanctions, the establishment of a no-fly zone, or even military intervention to force Khartoum to accept UN peacekeepers.[44] But Khartoum called the bluff, certain that its friends on the Council would shield it from such coercive measures. And with the United States and its allies overstretched in Afghanistan and Iraq, and weary of entanglement in yet another Muslim conflict theater, unilateral military action was hardly a possibility.

With no agreement in sight, outgoing Secretary-General Annan in November 2006 proposed to instead deploy a joint UN-AU operation in Darfur in the hope that this would provide a face-saving alternative for Khartoum and the AU. Unexpected support came from China, whose Sudan policy had come under strong international public scrutiny, culminating in international campaigns to boycott the 2008 "Genocide Olympics" in Beijing. More important, however, the spillover of the Darfur conflict into neighboring Chad and Sudan's Kordofan region threatened China's substantial oil interests there. Containing the Darfur conflict thus became of vital interest for Beijing, and a de facto UN takeover of the fledgling African mission was seen as the best option to achieve this goal.[45] Thanks largely to Chinese efforts, Khartoum finally relented and the Council, in July 2007, unanimously authorized the UN-AU Hybrid Operation in Darfur (UNAMID) to take over from AMIS on January 1, 2008 (Resolution 1769). UNAMID was to become the largest and most expensive UN-run peacekeeping mission at that time, and its joint AU-UN command structures made it a peacekeeping novelty. Resolution 1769 also replaced Bolton's ill-fated Resolution 1706, which one observer subsequently ranked among "the 10 worst UN Security Council resolutions ever."[46]

While international efforts were focused on getting UN boots on the ground, follow-up on the Darfur peace agreement had taken a back seat. Rebel groups proliferated and banditry was rampant. Veteran UN diplomat Jan Eliasson had been appointed in November 2006 to team up with AU mediator Salim Ahmad Salim to reinvigorate the peace process, but their efforts had soon stalled given Khartoum's continuing military campaign and the refusal by the rebels to join the talks.[47] Amid growing tensions between Chad and Sudan and increasing cross-border refugee flows and rebel movements, France pushed for, and ultimately attained, the deployment of a UN peacekeeping presence in Chad and the Central African Republic.[48]

With all eyes on Darfur, the Council largely neglected the north-south process, despite warning signs of significant slippage in CPA implementation.[49] The peace deal had already sustained a heavy blow in July 2005 when the untimely death of SPLM/A leader Garang also put to rest his vision of a united yet reformed Sudan, and independence became the tacit goal for the new SPLM/A leadership rather than a fallback option. In the first of many future crises, Juba in 2007 temporarily left the joint government in protest over Khartoum's foot-dragging on CPA implementation, particularly its back-tracking on the border delineation of the oil-rich Abyei area, where the CPA stipulated that a separate referendum in 2011 would be held to determine whether Abyei would remain in the north or become part of the south.[50] Yet overall, the Council maintained its low-key approach on north-south dynamics. This negligence would later backfire.

Safeguarding the Referendum

With UNAMID finally in charge of keeping a peace that existed only on paper, the Council in early 2008 focused on getting the mission up and running. Initially heralded as a new model for UN-AU cooperation, its operational limitations soon surfaced.[51] Problems abounded, ranging from coordination issues with the AU, to enormous logistical challenges in a hostile terrain with next to no infrastructure. Even more problematic was the systematic obstruction by Khartoum, which refused to accept crucial non-African mission personnel, created massive backlogs on visa and customs clearances, and curtailed the mission's movements on the ground. UNAMID meanwhile was reluctant to implement its robust mandate to protect civilians, causing increasing resentment among the Darfuri population amid allegations of partiality toward Khartoum. With UNAMID gradually following in the footsteps of its hapless predecessor mission, calls grew louder to revive the comatose Darfur peace deal, and the former foreign minister of Burkina Faso, Djibril Bassolé, was eventually appointed as joint UN-AU chief mediator for Darfur. He soon shared the file with Qatar, which had stepped onto the scene with its own peace initiative, unlimited petrodollars, and all-inclusive conference facilities in Doha.

But with Council discussions largely consumed by the technicalities of outstanding visas and a lack of helicopters for UNAMID, and the Doha process going nowhere, an international Darfur-fatigue soon set in. Capitals had also shifted their attention back to the north-south process.

National elections were to be held and the 2011 referendum on southern self-determination was already casting its shadow. UN Secretary-General Ban Ki-moon warned in April 2008 that "the crisis in Darfur has diverted attention from the strategic road map offered by the Comprehensive Peace Agreement process."[52] And when heavy clashes between the SPLA and the army erupted in the contested Abyei area in May that year, even the Darfur advocacy groups found a new calling, warning of a looming war between Khartoum and Juba.

But just when the international community began belatedly to focus on the CPA again, the dynamics were further complicated. In July 2008, ICC chief prosecutor Luis Moreno-Ocampo announced that he would seek an arrest warrant against President Bashir for crimes committed in Darfur. On the ground, the Darfur rebels were jubilant, while Khartoum, as expected, was furious. The SPLM/A meanwhile hedged its bets. Human rights activists and ICC proponents worldwide celebrated the announcement, while criticism came from some legal scholars and Sudan experts, who not only complained about the style and tactics of Moreno-Ocampo, but also warned that the announcement would derail the fragile north-south and Darfur peace processes.[53] The ensuing "peace versus justice" debate was further incensed when the ICC issued an arrest warrant against Bashir on March 4, 2009, creating a dilemma for the international community. While Bashir was rightly vilified for his responsibility for the Darfur crimes, his commitment to the CPA, not least in the face of regime hardliners eager to renounce the deal, was deemed necessary for the 2011 referendum to take place.[54]

Not surprisingly, the international community was struggling with this challenge. The AU and Arab League demanded that the Council defer the ICC proceeding, in line with Article 16 of the Rome Statute. The cause was initially championed in the Council by nonpermanent member Libya and supported by South Africa, Uganda, and Burkina Faso, all three of which were parties to the Rome Statute.[55] China and Russia supported the call but made little effort in the Council to help it succeed against Western opposition. Fearing a breakdown of the CPA, some European capitals quietly contemplated a deferral. Ironically, it was Washington that publicly rejected this option. In a far-reaching move, the AU stepped up its political role and tasked former South African president Thabo Mbeki to provide a road map for peace and accountability in Darfur, followed by a comprehensive mandate to mediate between Khartoum and Juba to resolve outstanding CPA issues.

With the dust slowly settling over the Bashir arrest warrant, attention focused on the national elections held in April 2010 with the logistical support of UNMIS. While initially meant to bring democratic reform to the country, the elections effectively consolidated the respective dominance of the regime in Khartoum and the SPLM in the south. But what mattered to the international community was that another crucial step had been taken toward the January 9, 2011, referendum. With only a few months left until that date, Khartoum and Juba were oscillating between threats of renewed war and vows of brotherly cooperation. Amid a spike in intercommunal violence and fighting between the SPLA and renegade militias in the south, the international community slowly woke to the challenges awaiting in the future independent state, with some warning of a "failed state" being born in 2011.[56] But for now, the international focus was on safeguarding the referendum, and the Council ambassadors traveled to Sudan again in October 2010 to underscore that the referendum date was sacrosanct. This was also the key message of a high-level Security Council meeting in November, at which US secretary of state Hillary Clinton repeated President Barack Obama's offer that Khartoum would be taken off the US terrorism blacklist should it accept the outcome of the referendum.[57]

Averting New Wars

The January 9, 2011, referendum was a resounding vote for separation, and Khartoum was quick in accepting the outcome. As the independence date of July 9 was fast approaching, it became clear that many of the key CPA provisions would not be implemented by then. With mediation efforts by Mbeki on a post-independence road map in full force, the Council focused in early 2011 on the future peacekeeping presence in Sudan. The UNMIS mission, set up to monitor and support the CPA during the interim period, was due to end, and there was agreement that a follow-up mission would be established in the independent south as requested by Juba. But questions remained over what would follow UNMIS in the volatile Abyei area, where the referendum had been postponed ad infinitum, as well as in the hotspot states of Southern Kordofan and Blue Nile, where the population had fought alongside the SPLM/A during the war but was not granted the option in the CPA to join the south. Secretary-General Ban Ki-moon asked the Council to extend UNMIS beyond July 9 to maintain a presence until growing tensions were resolved.[58] But Khartoum was reluctant to keep UN peacekeepers in the north, a position echoed in the Council by China and Russia. Juba meanwhile wanted its "own" mission in place for independence, a demand strongly supported by Washington's UN ambassador Susan Rice.

Discussions in New York were overtaken by events on the ground in May 2011, when the Sudanese army, reacting to an SPLA attack, seized Abyei in an ostensible attempt to create facts on the ground. Incidentally, the Council ambassadors were just en route to Sudan and had to cancel their visit of Abyei. Khartoum showed how much it appreciated the Council's hands-on crisis management by canceling previously agreed high-level meetings with the visitors from New York. With Khartoum and Juba beating the drums of war, Ethiopian prime minister Zenawi offered his troops as a temporary buffer force to monitor a Mbeki-brokered disengagement deal, provided the UN would foot the bill. Khartoum was reluctant to accept yet another UN mission in Sudan, and relented only when a narrow mandate and solely Ethiopian composition of the mission were agreed to in a deal brokered by Mbeki and Zenawi. Some Council members noted that a UN mission staffed essentially by one nationality, especially from a neighboring state, would contradict long-standing peacekeeping doctrine. The UK and France in particular balked at the curtailment of Council prerogatives in determining the mandate of the mission. But for Khartoum, this was a take-it-or-leave-it deal. And with both the United States and China pushing hard, the UN Interim Security Force for Abyei (UNISFA) was unanimously authorized on June 27 (Resolution 1990).[59]

But more trouble was to come. Though Abyei was contained, fighting had broken out between the local SPLA and the army in Southern Kordofan, and similar tensions had increased in Blue Nile. Council members belatedly called for a continued UN presence there, but the window of opportunity for united Council pressure to sway Khartoum had closed by then. Khartoum demanded that UNMIS leave Sudan on July 9, ostensibly to have a free hand in dealing with the unrest. The Council had to follow suit, as maintaining UN peacekeepers on the ground against Khartoum's will was not a feasible option. But with independence of the south around the corner, international attention lay elsewhere. On July 8 the Council unanimously adopted Resolution 1996, authorizing the deployment of the UN Mission in South Sudan (UNMISS). The next day, the Republic of South Sudan declared itself an independent state. A few days later, it became the 193rd UN member state.[60]

But the celebratory mood did not last long. Fighting intensified in Southern Kordofan and clashes broke out between the local SPLM/A (now called the SPLM/A North) and the army in Blue Nile. The SPLM/A North in both states teamed up with the Darfur rebels and other opposition groups to form the Sudan Revolutionary Front, calling for the overthrow of the Bashir regime in Khartoum. This evoked strong reactions from Russia and China at a time when Council dynamics had already suffered from the controversial NATO operation in Libya and the deadlock over the civil war in Syria. In a reversal of roles, Russia led the charge in defending Khartoum's sovereignty, while China, which by then had also established strong economic ties with Juba, took a back seat to safeguard its stakes in the north and south.[61] Already under pressure from regime hardliners over his "loss" of the south, President Bashir meanwhile launched a military campaign against the Sudan Revolutionary Front, including occasional air strikes of southern territory, and accused Juba of supporting its erstwhile comrades.

Despite serious fighting and mass displacement on the ground, the Council became deadlocked, with US ambassador Rice at loggerheads with her Russian counterpart. Rice insisted that the Council demand Khartoum to allow humanitarian access and condemn indiscriminate aerial bombings by Khartoum, including of South Sudan territory. Ambassador Vitaly Churkin meanwhile called for a denunciation of the Sudan Revolutionary Front's regime-change agenda, and Juba's support for the rebels.[62] Divisions were only briefly overcome in April 2012, when the SPLA seized Heglig, the most important remaining oilfield for Khartoum. With Khartoum mobilizing for war, Council members demanded that the SPLA immediately withdraw its forces, and Juba, having alienated even its supporters in the Council, eventually relented.[63]

But the Council was soon again deadlocked, unable for months to agree even on nonbinding press statements. The resulting leadership void was readily filled by AU mediator Mbeki, who, with the help of the UN Secretary-General's envoy to Sudan/South Sudan, Haile Menkerios, brokered agreement after agreement between Khartoum and Juba to defuse the tensions. These also helped the divided Council to overcome its stalemate by endorsing, at times near-verbatim, the AU-mediated deals. This was the case most notably in May 2012 with the unanimously adopted Resolution 2046, which mirrored a detailed road map on north-south cooperation endorsed earlier by the AU, and threatened both sides with sanctions in case of noncompliance. The AU's call for a Chapter VII Council resolution, together with the threat of sanctions, made it difficult for Russia and China—traditional proponents of the regional conflict solution mechanism—to reject the draft. Resolution 2046, along with biweekly Council follow-up meetings, was applauded as a serious attempt by the Council to engage in conflict prevention.[64] But Khartoum and Juba soon called the bluff. With both parties missing deadline after deadline, and even Mbeki snubbing the Council with only rare appearances at the horseshoe table in New York, the Council's interest soon started to fade. Not only were Council members content to leave containment of the crisis in the hands of the AU, but also the bloodshed in Syria had monopolized international attention, and the little interest left for Africa was focused on developments in Mali and, more recently, the Central African Republic.

The situation in the contested Abyei area had become marked by a similar standstill. Calls by the United States and United Kingdom to finally bring the outstanding Abyei referendum in line with the CPA provisions were stymied by Russia and China, which claimed that Khartoum had to consent. Interestingly, this found traction also with such diverse nonpermanent Council members as Pakistan, Morocco, Azerbaijan, and Argentina, each with little direct interest in Sudan but wary of referenda for domestic reasons. With no mutually acceptable political solution in sight, Abyei showed all signs of becoming "Africa's Kashmir," with the Council and the UNISFA peacekeepers probably in it for the long haul.

For South Sudan, the honeymoon period came to a bitter end, as its fighters-turned-politicians struggled to uphold their promises of democracy and good governance, and the young country became marred by political infighting and ethnic strife.[65] Relations with the Security Council became increasingly strained when even its traditional supporters would no longer shield the new government from Council scrutiny. Having learned a lesson or two from its northern neighbor in how to keep the UN at bay, Juba responded to criticism with threats against the mission and the expulsion of UN staff.[66] In a nightmare-come-true development, longstanding leadership rivalries erupted into heavy intra-SPLA clashes in December 2013, quickly eroding into wider interethnic violence.[67] Foregoing its traditional Christmas slumber, the Council called for an end to the violence and on December 24, 2013, strengthened UNMISS's capacities to protect itself and the tens of thousands of South Sudanese who sought refuge from the violence (Resolution 2132). Led once more by IGAD, the international community meanwhile sought to broker a political deal to stop the young country from sliding deeper into a fratricidal civil war. As the world commemorated the twentieth anniversary of the Rwandan genocide in April 2014, it was not Darfur but ethnic killings in South Sudan that stirred international attention, accompanied by calls from some Council members for UN sanctions and an ICC referral. A year later, with IGAD mediation efforts frustrated by foot-dragging on all sides, the Council unanimously imposed a sanctions regime against spoilers of the peace process (Resolution 2206).

The Darfur conflict had meanwhile become routine Council business, in stark contrast to its prominence of earlier years. Even AU mediator Mbeki showed little interest in his Darfur mandate, delegating the task to the UNAMID leadership instead, which had also taken over the UN-AU mediation file following Bassolé's resignation in 2011. Traditional divisions in the Council persisted, with Russia, China, and the African and Arab members supporting Khartoum and the AU in their call to move the peace talks from Doha to Darfur, while Western Council members were reluctant to give up Doha as the only real game in town. Regular briefings by the ICC prosecutor and the chairs of the sanctions committee had over the years become all but ritualistic nonevents, as Khartoum's violations of the sanctions and noncooperation with the ICC remained without consequences mainly due to Chinese opposition to meaningful Council follow-up action.[68] With the UN peacekeeping budget reaching a record high and an acute demand for UN peacekeepers for other African crises, the Council in July

2013 ordered a substantive review of the UNAMID operation (Resolution 2113). Although the Council in August 2014 mandated a streamlined UNAMID to focus its efforts on protecting civilians, the regime in Khartoum demanded that the mission be shut down. Meanwhile, more than ten years since the outbreak of the conflict, and amid continuing violence and displacement, peace in Darfur remained elusive.

Conclusion

A snapshot view of the Council's work-plan a decade after the 2005 Comprehensive Peace Agreement is informative. The Council's meetings on Sudan are structured along no less than six different agenda items, covering Darfur and UNAMID; Abyei and UNISFA; southern Sudan and UNMISS; Sudan–South Sudan relations; the Darfur sanctions; as well as briefings by the ICC chief prosecutor. While mainly due to internal procedures, this also reflects the fragmented nature in which the Council has come to deal with war and peace in Sudan.

With perfect hindsight it is of course easy to criticize the lack of a more strategic, "whole of Sudan" strategy, and the effect this may have had on the Council's ability to influence developments on the ground.[69] As highlighted in this chapter, a different approach would have required a fundamental change in mind-set not only on the side of the international community, but also of the parties on the ground.[70] And to be fair, one can hardly expect the Council to devise strategic policies when these are lacking in key capitals. And herein lies the crux of the matter.

The P5 and E10

Not surprisingly, the Council's Sudan agenda was driven by the five veto powers, with the United States as first among equals. All professed the need for peace and stability in Sudan. But given their diverging interests, perspectives and prescriptions differed considerably as to how this could be achieved. For Washington, Cold War–era geopolitical and economic interests in Sudan became largely superseded in the 1990s by concerns with terrorism. With its subsequent focus also on regional stability and humanitarian and human rights issues, Washington had to balance competing internal intelligence with diplomatic interests. All US administrations meanwhile grappled with the right policy mix vis-à-vis Khartoum. While the promise of the lifting of bilateral sanctions served as a "carrot," the Security Council came to be used mainly as a "stick," in reaction also to strong pressure from advocacy groups and Congress particularly over the Darfur violence. Locked in this logic, US-Sudanese relations have remained in a Catch-22 situation. Washington on several occasions promised Khartoum a normalization of relations, but did not—or could not—deliver. Khartoum meanwhile felt betrayed and reacted accordingly, making it even more difficult for Washington to convince Congress and the domestic public that a détente was warranted.[71] By contrast, Washington was a staunch supporter of the south, with independence the preferred end-state for many US policymakers.[72] This special relationship became strained, however, with an increasingly assertive Juba challenging international stewardship and looking eastward for unconditional aid, trade, and weapons, and the postindependence violence in the south threatening to erase Washington's significant investments in peace and development.[73]

During the 1990s, the UK and France in particular took a more accommodating stance vis-à-vis Khartoum. Since then, the UK has usually acted in tandem with the United States in the Council and beyond on Sudan, and both eventually came to share the "penholdership" of Council resolutions (the United States on the north-south file, Abyei, and South Sudan, the United Kingdom on Darfur). An important exception was the ICC referral in 2005, when London teamed up with Paris instead. For France, Sudan was of secondary importance for its Africa policy. While Darfur certainly mattered for Paris, this was the case also because of the conflict's spillover into francophone Chad and the Central African Republic, Paris's historical *chasse gardée*.[74]

Washington's main opponent in the Council was undoubtedly Beijing, which masked its substantial economic interests in Sudan behind principled foreign policy positions of noninterference and state sovereignty. Lacking a critical home audience, Beijing could afford to pay only lip service to human rights, while effectively shielding Khartoum from Western pressure. Within these parameters, however, China's Sudan policy was more nuanced than often assumed, in a reflection, maybe, of its increasingly active role on the world stage.[75] Beijing was largely cooperative on the north-south file, for which stability between the two neighbors was important in safeguarding China's growing economic interests both north and south of the border. In Darfur, by contrast, the Western push for sanctions and accountability also touched on Beijing's key foreign policy principles. China thus wielded its veto threat to water down resolutions and subsequently ensured that the already weakened measures taken by the Council remained largely toothless.[76] On the political and peacekeeping front, Beijing became more active, as noninterference became more difficult to maintain amid the international spotlight shone on Beijing, and the unraveling of the Darfur peace deal threatening Chinese oil interests in the region.[77] Given similar economic and policy interests in Sudan, Moscow usually sided with China in the Council. In the wake of Russia's "post-Libya assertiveness," Moscow even took over Beijing's role as Washington's main opponent in defense of noninterference and Khartoum's sovereignty.

Divisions also existed between the nonpermanent Council members, reflecting also the social geography of Sudan—a country straddling the Muslim-Christian and Arab-African divides in Africa. Khartoum could safely bank on the support from Arab and Muslim Council members, most notably Pakistan, Algeria, Qatar, and Libya. "Western" delegations and those from sub-Saharan Africa by contrast generally took a hard line against Khartoum over Darfur and sided with Juba on the north-south file.[78] African delegations faced a dilemma, however, when AU positions diverged from the Western script, most notably on the ICC arrest warrant against President Bashir.

Peacemaking

Against this background, it comes as no surprise that the Council's peacemaking record in Sudan was mixed at best. Its clout seemed strongest when interests among its members were broadly aligned. This was generally the case related to the north-south file, for which the conclusion of the CPA and the shepherding of the peaceful independence of the south was indeed no small feat. Yet the key was probably that neither Khartoum nor Juba were willing to revert to full-scale war. This also contrasted with peacemaking efforts in Darfur as well as Southern Kordofan and Blue Nile, where the Council remained divided and the conflict parties bet on victory on the ground rather than at the negotiating table. But peacemaking efforts were also hampered by shifting priorities in capitals. The focus on ending the north-south civil war first resulted in a "comprehensive" peace agreement that was far from comprehensive, at least in the eyes of the Darfuris.[79] That Darfur subsequently monopolized international attention was understandable given the moral imperative felt by advocacy organizations and some P5 capitals to stop the killing.[80] But references to the Responsibility to Protect and calls for sanctions and criminal accountability soon rang hollow, given that the Council was unwilling and unable to ensure their enforcement. They also crowded out calls for a political solution to what was ultimately a political problem. Furthermore, the vacillating by the Council between the north-south file and the Darfur file was of course ill-suited to the sustained engagement that peacemaking required, beyond the mere signing of a peace deal or the authorization of a peacekeeping mission. Most critically, it allowed the conflict parties to "kick the can down the road" and thus implementation of much-celebrated peace agreements and road maps remained limited at best. This also planted the seeds for future conflicts not only over Abyei, Southern Kordofan, and Blue Nile, but also within North and South Sudan, where both Khartoum and Juba pursue regime stability rather than the inclusive governance required to address the long-standing grievances of the respective populations.[81]

Limits to Council Effectiveness

Whether more pressure or more persuasion would have changed the behavior of the conflict parties in Sudan is a pertinent, albeit largely theoretical, question. As highlighted in this chapter, deep divisions in the Council ensured that more pressure was not a real option, and that those measures ultimately adopted had only limited effect. The Council's reaction to the Darfur conflict serves as an example. Enforcement action by individual member states, in particular action authorized by the Council, was not a credible threat, despite much saber-rattling from the Western camp and pressure exerted by advocacy groups. The sanctions, the lowest common denominator short of coercive measures, were effectively rendered toothless by China and Russia. But even a united Council would have had its limits, faced with a ruthless yet extremely shrewd regime in Khartoum and an increasingly difficult leadership in Juba. In fact, Sudan repeatedly highlighted the Council's impotence in the face of missing or fluctuating "host-nation consent."[82] The most glaring case was of course Khartoum's rejection of UN peacekeepers in Darfur as authorized in Resolution 1706, as well as the subsequent systematic obstruction of UNAMID's day-to-day operations. Similarly, the Council was ultimately powerless in the face of Khartoum's demand that UNMIS leave the north following the southern referendum, the conditions that Khartoum set for a UN peacekeeping presence in Abyei, as well as Juba's increasingly hostile stance vis-à-vis UNMISS. The withdrawal of peacekeepers was not an option despite all harassment, and neither was a deployment against the will of Khartoum and Juba. As a result, and reflecting a general dilemma of consent-based peacekeeping, Council action tended not to reflect what was operationally sound, but politically doable.

Peacekeeping

These limitations were even more pertinent given the priority that the Council had afforded peacekeeping in Sudan. Since 2003, the AU and UN deployed six different missions, and about a third of all UN peacekeepers were deployed there since 2008 at the cost of about a third of the UN peacekeeping budget.[83] But the peacekeeping record was also mixed.[84] The "stovepiping" by the international community of the different conflicts, a result also of Khartoum's successful divide-and-rule policy, led to the peculiar and unprecedented situation of two major UN peace operations being deployed in parallel in the same country (UNMIS, UNAMID). This was followed by three UN missions in an intricately linked conflict theater (UNAMID, UNISFA, UNMISS). Apart from operational limitations, peacekeeping in Sudan also faced a fundamental problem encountered elsewhere: the oft-cited truism that peacekeeping needs a peace to keep was not adequately heeded. This was the case particularly in Darfur, where the deployment of peacekeepers amid massive public pressure to stop the bloodshed was of course a more tangible and visible output for the Council than political investment in a drawn-out peace process. And to be fair, doing nothing or waiting for a negotiated end to the conflict was not a real option, and the peacekeepers helped save lives, at least where they were deployed. But the focus on getting UN boots on the ground also created expectations among the international public and in Darfur that UNAMID could not or would not meet. Paired with Khartoum's continued military campaigns and systematic obstruction of the mission, the result was not only a credibility crisis for UNAMID but also a wider systemic crisis for UN peacekeeping.[85] Similar dynamics played out elsewhere. The deployment of UNMIS followed the north-south peace deal, but peacekeeping largely became a substitute for Council investment in the political reform process. The mission's authorized capacities were meanwhile insufficient to effectively implement its mandated task of protecting civilians. While UNISFA had proven effective in containing the security situation in Abyei, a political settlement of the status of the contested region remained elusive. More recently, the ethnic clashes in South Sudan, sparked by political infighting, forced the Council back to the drawing board as to what role UNMISS could and should assume in the future.

Regional Organizations

Last, the Council's interplay with regional organizations, namely IGAD and the AU, was key for peacemaking and peacekeeping in Sudan.[86] For the P5, eager to safeguard the Council's primary responsibility for international peace and security, this was a double-edged sword. Commitment to "African solutions to African problems" was convenient when the AU deployed peacekeeping personnel and brokered deals between the conflict parties while the Council was unwilling or unable to do so. In an interesting dynamic, the post-secession mediation efforts by the AU helped the Council overcome its paralysis, albeit at the cost of practically rubber-stamping what the parties had agreed to with Mbeki's help and what the AU had previously endorsed. Problems also arose for the P3, when the AU invoked African solidarity to shield Khartoum from Western "neocolonialism," a call deftly exploited by Khartoum to its own advantage. In a pick-and-choose approach not limited to the Sudan context, the Council thus endorsed African regional views only selectively. Most famously, it did not endorse the AU's request to defer the Bashir arrest warrant. This also strained relations with the AU, and culminated in calls made by some African leaders in 2013 at the fiftieth AU summit—attended also by none other than President Bashir—to "unsign" the Rome Statute. How to resolve this crisis for the ICC will require much political finesse, including by the Security Council.

Notes

The views expressed in this chapter are mine alone and do not represent the views of the German Foreign Office. I wish to thank Alex de Waal, Wibke Hansen, Colum Lynch, Stefan Roessel, Paul Romita, James Traub, UN colleagues familiar with the file, and the editors for their valuable comments. I benefited tremendously from three excellent studies: Hugo Slim, "Dithering over Darfur? A Preliminary Review of the International Response," *International Affairs* 80, no. 5 (2004): 811–833; Marijan Zumbulev, "Irresolution: The UN Security Council on Darfur," in *Failed and Failing States: The Challenges to African Reconstruction,* edited by Muna Ndulo and Margaret Gricco (Newcastle upon Tyne: Cambridge Scholars, 2010); and James Traub, *Unwilling and Unable: The Failed Response to the Atrocities in Darfur* (New York: Global Centre for the Responsibility to Protect, 2010), as well as from the analysis and information provided by Security Council Report.

1. Before that, Sudan was subject to formal Security Council consultations in 1956, when the Council recommended to the General Assembly that Sudan become a UN member state (Resolution 112 [February 6, 1956], UN Doc. S/RES/112), and in February 1958, when Khartoum requested a meeting of the Council on the border dispute with Egypt related to the Hayaib triangle.

2. For a more comprehensive history of the Sudanese civil war, see Francis M. Deng, *War of Visions: Conflict of Identities in the Sudan* (Washington, DC: Brookings Institution, 1995); Jok Madut Jok, *Sudan: Race, Religion, and Violence* (Oxford: Oneworld, 2007); Douglas H. Johnson, *The Root Causes of Sudan's Civil Wars: Peace or Truce?* (Rochester, NY: Currey, 2011).

3. Arop Madut Arop, *Sudan's Painful Road to Peace: A Full Story of the Founding and Development of SPLM/SPLA* (Charleston, SC: BookSurge, 2006); International Crisis Group, *God, Oil, and Country: Changing the Logic of War in Sudan,* Africa Report no. 39 (Brussels, January 2002), www.crisisgroup.org/~/media/Files/africa/horn-of-africa/sudan/God%20Oil%20and%20Country%20Changing%20the%20Logic%20of%20War%20in%20Sudan.

4. Steven Greenhouse, "U.S. Asks U.N. to Condemn Sudan," *International New York Times,* February 26, 1994, www.nytimes.com/1994/02/26/world/us-asks-un-to-condemn-sudan-on-bombings.html.

5. Paul Lewis, "Aid Groups Press U.N. for New Effort to End Sudan's Civil War," *New York Times*, November 1, 1998.

6. Don Petterson, *Inside Sudan: Political Islam, Conflict, and Catastrophe* (Boulder, CO: Westview, 2003).

7. Millard Burr and Robert O. Collins, *Revolutionary Sudan: Hasan al-Turabi and the Islamist State, 1989–2000* (Leiden: Brill, 2003); Alex de Waal and Abdel A. H. Salam, "Islamism, State Power, and Jihad in Sudan," in *Islamism and Its Enemies in the Horn of Africa,* edited by Alex de Waal (London: Hurst, 2004); Lorenzo Vidino, "The Arrival of Islamic Fundamentalism in Sudan," *Al Nakhla: The Fletcher School Online Journal for Issues Related to Southwest Asia and Islamic Civilization* (Fall 2006): 1–14; Douglas Farah, *The Role of Sudan in Islamist Terrorism: A Case Study* (Alexandria, VA: International Assessment and Strategy Center, 2007).

8. Tim Niblock, *"Pariah States" and Sanctions in the Middle East: Iraq, Libya, Sudan* (Boulder, CO: Lynne Rienner, 2001).

9. United Nations Security Council, "Letter Dated 9 January 1996 from the Permanent Representative of Ethiopia to the United Nations Addressed to the President of the Security Council," UN Doc. S/1996/10, January 9, 1996. In addition to the formal Council meetings on the incident, several "Arria formula" meetings were

held in 1995–1996, including with the OAU, Ethiopia, and Sudan. See Security Council Report, "Arria-Formula Meetings," February 2014 Monthly Forecast, January 31, 2014, www.securitycouncilreport.org/monthly-forecast/2014-02/arria-for mula_meetings.php.

10. Jaleh Dashti-Gibson and Richard W. Conroy, "Taming Terrorism: Sanctions Against Libya, Sudan, and Afghanistan," in *The Sanctions Decade: Assessing UN Strategies in the 1990s,* edited by David Cortright, George A. Lopez, Richard W. Convoy, Jaleh Dashti-Gibson, and Julia Wagler (Boulder, CO: Lynne Rienner, 2000); Robert Waller, "Sudanese Security: Rogue State in Crisis," *Jane's Intelligence Review* (July 1996): 311–315. While Egypt and Ethiopia pushed the terrorism agenda in the Council, they were reluctant to see the Council engage also on the political file. Both were long-standing public defenders of state sovereignty and noninterference, and both were militarily engaged at that time against the regime in Khartoum: Cairo in the disputed Hayaib triangle, Addis Ababa with troops in the south in support of the SPLA. I thank Alex de Waal for pointing this out to me.

11. Niblock, *"Pariah States" and Sanctions,* p. 208.

12. In a well-noted show of support for the anti-Bashir coalition, Albright, by then US secretary of state, met with SLPM/A chairman Garang and other Sudanese opposition leaders in Uganda in December 1997. James C. McKinley Jr., "Albright, in Uganda, Steps Up Attack on Sudan's War on Terror," *International New York Times,* December 11, 1997, www.nytimes.com/1997/12/11/world/albright-in-uganda -steps-up-attack-on-sudan-s-war-of-terror.html.

13. Tim Weiner and James Risen, "Decision to Strike Factory in Sudan Based on Surmise Inferred from Evidence," *International New York Times,* September 21, 1998, www.nytimes.com/1998/09/21/world/decision-to-strike-factory-in-sudan -based-on-surmise-inferred-from-evidence.html; Seymour M. Hersh, "The Missiles of August," *The New Yorker,* October 12, 1998, www.newyorker.com/magazine /1998/10/12/the-missiles-of-august.

14. United Nations Security Council, "Letter Dated 20 August 1998 from the Permanent Representative of the United States of America to the United Nations Addressed to the President of the Security Council," UN Doc. S/1998/780, August 20, 1998.

15. Walid Phares, "The Sudanese Battle for American Opinion," *Middle East Quarterly* 5, no. 1 (March 1998): 19–31.

16. Stephen J. Kobrin, "Oil and Politics: Talisman Energy and Sudan," *International Law and Politics* 36 (2004): 425–456. Clinton's Sudan envoy, Melissa Wells, suggested already in 1994 that Washington should push for a Security Council presidential statement that supported the IGAD mediation efforts, but "fearing an imposed settlement, Khartoum was opposed to any Security Council involvement in the peace process, however tangential. . . . [A]nd with help from friends, the Sudanese easily forestalled a Security Council statement." Petterson, *Inside Sudan,* p. 163.

17. United Nations Security Council, "Letter Dated 5 April 2000 from the Permanent Representative of Djibouti to the United Nations Addressed to the President of the Security Council," UN Doc. S/2000/288, April 5, 2000. Human Rights Watch, *Sudan, Oil, and Human Rights* (Washington, DC, 2003), p. 550.

18. United Nations, "Press Statement on Sudan by Security Council President," press release SC/7466, July 25, 2002. For an insider account of the IGAD peace talks, see Hilde F. Johnson, *Waging Peace in Sudan: The Inside Story of the Negotiations That Ended Africa's Longest Civil War* (Brighton: Sussex Academic, 2011).

19. Alex de Waal, "Tragedy in Darfur," *Boston Review,* October 5, 2004, www.bostonreview.net/de-waal-tragedy-in-darfur. For more comprehensive analy-

ses of the Darfur conflict, see Alex de Waal, ed., *War in Darfur and the Search for Peace* (Cambridge: Harvard University Press, 2007); Gérard Prunier, *Darfur: The Ambiguous Genocide* (Ithaca: Cornell University Press, 2007).

20. Alex de Waal, "Counter-Insurgency on the Cheap," *London Review of Books* 26, no. 15 (2004): 25–27. According to Hugo Slim, "Key members of the Sudanese government elite feared that a Darfur insurgency—with support from their reviled enemy Hassan Turabi—had the potential to become the vanguard for a widespread northern movement for regime change that could easily unravel their regime." Slim, "Dithering over Darfur," p. 822.

21. Slim, "Dithering over Darfur"; Oliver Ulich, "The UN Security Council's Response to Darfur: A Humanitarian Perspective," *Humanitarian Exchange Magazine* no. 30 (London: Humanitarian Practice Network, 2005).

22. Slim, "Dithering over Darfur," p. 822; International Crisis Group, *Darfur Deadline: A New International Action Plan,* Africa Report no. 83 (Brussels, 2004), pp. 17–20; Zumbulev, "Irresolution," p. 164.

23. Richard Cockett, *Sudan: Darfur and the Failure of an African State* (New Haven: Yale University Press, 2010), p. 195.

24. Cheryl O. Igiri and Princeton N. Lyman, *Giving Meaning to 'Never Again': Seeking an Effective Response to the Crisis in Darfur and Beyond,* Special Report no. 5 (Washington, DC: Council on Foreign Relations, 2004), pp. 10–11, www.cfr .org/sudan/giving-meaning-never-again/p7402; Andrew S. Natsios, *Sudan, South Sudan, and Darfur: What Everyone Needs to Know* (Oxford: Oxford University Press, 2012), p. 158.

25. International Crisis Group, *Sudan's Dual Crises: Refocusing on IGAD,* Africa Briefing no. 5 (Brussels, 2004), p. 3.

26. Rebecca Hamilton, *Fighting for Darfur: Public Action and the Struggle to Stop Genocide* (New York: Palgrave Macmillan, 2011). For a critical assessment of the role of the Darfur advocacy, see Mahmood Mamdani, *Saviors and Survivors: Darfur, Politics, and the War on Terror* (New York: Pantheon, 2009).

27. See, for example, the articles of two future UN ambassadors, Susan Rice (2009 to 2013) and Samantha Power (since 2013): Samantha Power, "Remember Rwanda, but Take Action in Sudan," *International New York Times,* April 6, 2004, www.nytimes.com/2004/04/06/opinion/remember-rwanda-but-take-action-in -sudan.html; Gayle E. Smith and Susan E. Rice, "The Darfur Catastrophe," *Washington Post,* May 30, 2004, www.washingtonpost.com/wp-dyn/articles/A64717 -2004May28.html. For an insider account of Annan's lobbying on Darfur, see James Traub, *The Best Intentions: Kofi Annan and the UN in the Era of American Power* (New York: Farrar, Straus, and Giroux, 2006).

28. United Nations, "Press Statement on Darfur, Sudan, by Security Council President," press release, SC/8050, April 2, 2004. For his own account of the Darfur crises, see Jan Egeland, *A Billion Lives: An Eyewitness Report from the Frontlines of Humanity* (New York: Simon and Schuster, 2008). In May 2004, Germany also organized an "Arria formula" meeting of the Council members with Doctors Without Borders, the International Crisis Group, Human Rights Watch, and the deputy permanent representative of Sudan.

29. Deborah Murphy, "Narrating Darfur: Darfur in the U.S. Press, March–September 2004," in de Waal, *War in Darfur*, p. 320.

30. Traub, *Unwilling and Unable;* Alex Bellamy and Paul D. Williams, "The UN Security Council and the Question of Humanitarian Intervention in Darfur," *Journal of Military Ethics* 5, no. 2 (2006): 144–160; Nick Grono, "Darfur: The International Community's Failure to Protect," *African Affairs* 105, no. 421 (2006): 621–631.

31. Seth Appiah-Mensah, "AU's Critical Assignment in Darfur: Challenges and Constraints," *African Security Review* 14, no. 2 (2005): 7–21.

32. Cristina Badescu and Linnea Bergholm, "The African Union," in *The International Politics of Mass Atrocities: The Case of Darfur,* edited by David Black and Paul D. Williams (London: Routledge, 2010).

33. In June 2004, the Council unanimously authorized the UN Advance Mission in Sudan (UNAMIS) to prepare for the eventual establishment of a comprehensive peacekeeping mission (Resolution 1547 [June 11, 2004], UN Doc. S/RES/1547).

34. The Council had previously met formally outside of its New York headquarters only in Addis Ababa in February 1972 (under Sudan's Council presidency), in March 1973 in Panama City, and in May 1990 in Geneva. See Sydney D. Bailey and Sam Daws, *The Procedure of the UN Security Council* (Oxford: Clarendon, 1998), pp. 40–43.

35. International Commission of Inquiry on Darfur, *Report of the International Commission of Inquiry on Darfur to the United Nations Secretary-General Pursuant to Security Council Resolution 1564 of 18 September 2004,* Geneva, January 25, 2005, www.un.org/news/dh/sudan/com_inq_darfur.pdf; Colin Thomas-Jensen and Julia Spiegel, "Activism and Darfur: Slowly Driving Policy Change," *Fordham International Law Journal* 31, no. 4 (2007): 843–858.

36. Zumbulev, "Irresolution," p. 165.

37. The United States had initially circulated one long draft resolution covering the establishment of a UN peacekeeping mission, the imposition of sanctions, and the accountability aspect. But when controversial Council discussions dragged on for weeks, given diverging views over the latter two elements, the United States decided to split its draft text into three separate resolutions to allow for the least-contentious peacekeeping mission to finally be authorized. As Hamilton states: "The long-term effect was to solidify what had already been the instinct of the Security Council members—to put the issues related to the CPA and those related to Darfur in separate silos"; Hamilton, *Fighting for Darfur,* p. 63.

38. Robert Cryer, "Sudan, Resolution 1593, and International Criminal Justice," *Leiden Journal of International Law* 19 (2006): 195–222.

39. Corrina Heyder, "The U.N. Security Council's Referral of the Crimes in Darfur to the International Criminal Court in Light of U.S. Opposition to the Court: Implications for the International Criminal Court's Functions and Status," *Berkeley Journal of International Law* 24, no. 2 (2006): 650–671.

40. Michael G. MacKinnon, "The United Nations Security Council," in *The International Politics of Mass Atrocities: The Case of Darfur,* edited by David R. Black and Paul D. Williams (London: Routledge, 2010), pp. 90–93; Zumbulev, "Irresolution," pp. 169–171.

41. For his own account of Council dynamics on Darfur, see John Bolton, *Surrender Is Not an Option: Defending America at the United Nations and Abroad* (New York: Threshold, 2007).

42. Julie Flint, *Rhetoric and Reality: The Failure to Resolve the Darfur Conflict,* Working Paper no. 19 (Geneva: Small Arms Survey, 2010), p. 48.

43. For insider accounts of the negotiations leading to the Darfur peace agreement, see Alex de Waal, "I Will Not Sign," *London Review of Books* 28, no. 23 (2006): 17–20; Laurie Nathan, "The Making and Unmaking of the Darfur Peace Agreement," in de Waal, *War in Darfur.*

44. See, for example, Anthony Lake, Donald M. Payne, and Susan E. Rice, "We Saved Europeans; Why Not Africans?" *Washington Post,* October 2, 2006, www.washingtonpost.com/wp-dyn/content/article/2006/10/01/AR2006100100871.html.

45. Jonathan Holslag, "China's Diplomatic Manoeuvring on the Question of

Darfur," *Journal of Contemporary China* 17, no. 54 (2008): 71–84; Chin-Hao Huang, "U.S.-China Relations and Darfur," *Fordham International Law Journal* 31, no. 4 (2007): 827–842.

46. Colum Lynch, "The 10 Worst U.N. Security Council Resolutions Ever," *Foreign Policy,* May 21, 2010.

47. Flint, *Rhetoric and Reality.*

48. In 2008 the Council authorized an EU military operation deployed in parallel to a UN police mission, followed by a UN peacekeeping force in the Central African Republic and Chad (MINURCAT) in 2009–2010. See Alexandra Novosseloff and Richard Gowan, *Security Council Working Methods and UN Peace Operations: The Case of Chad and the Central African Republic, 2006–2010* (New York: Center on International Cooperation, 2012).

49. International Crisis Group, *Sudan's Comprehensive Peace Agreement: The Long Road Ahead,* Africa Report no. 106 (Brussels, 2006), p. i.

50. On the relevance of Abyei for war and peace in Sudan, see Douglas H. Johnson, "Why Abyei Matters: The Breaking Point of Sudan's Comprehensive Peace Agreement?" *African Affairs* 107, no. 426 (2008): 1–19.

51. Festus Aboagye, *The Hybrid Operation in Darfur: A Critical Review of the Concept of the Mechanism,* ISS Paper no. 149 (Pretoria: Institute for Security Studies, August 2007); Appiah-Mensah, "AU's Critical Assignment in Darfur"; Adekeye Adebajo, *UN Peacekeeping in Africa: From the Suez Crisis to the Sudan Conflicts* (Boulder, CO: Lynne Rienner, 2011), pp. 211–216.

52. United Nations Security Council, *Report of the Secretary-General on the Sudan,* UN Doc. S/2008/267, April 22, 2008. See also Andrew S. Natsios, "Beyond Darfur: Sudan's Slide Toward Civil War," *Foreign Affairs* 87, no. 3 (May–June 2008): 77–93.

53. Julie Flint and Alex de Waal, "Case Closed: A Prosecutor Without Borders," *World Affairs* 171, no. 4 (Spring 2009): 23–38; Natsios, *Sudan, South Sudan, and Darfur,* p. 169.

54. See, for example, Julie Flint and Alex de Waal, "To Put Justice Before Peace Spells Disaster for Sudan," *The Guardian,* March 5, 2009, www.theguardian.com /commentisfree/2009/mar/06/sudan-war-crimes; Natsios, *Sudan, South Sudan, and Darfur,* pp. 160–161.

55. Charles C. Jalloh, Dapo Akande, and Max du Plessis, "Assessing the African Union Concerns About Article 16 of the Rome Statute of the International Criminal Court," *African Journal of Legal Studies* 4 (2011): 23; Noha Bakr and Essam Abdel Shafi, *Arab Official Positions Towards President al Bashir's Indictment* (Madrid: FRIDE, March 2010).

56. "Promise and Peril in Sudan," *The Economist,* June 13, 2009, www.econo mist.com/node/13849342; "Are They Heading for a Crash?" *The Economist,* September 23, 2010, www.economist.com/node/17103885; International Crisis Group, *Jonglei's Tribal Conflicts: Countering Insecurity in South Sudan,* Africa Report no. 154 (Brussels, 2009).

57. United Nations Security Council, "Provisional Verbatim Record of the 6425th Meeting," UN Doc. S/PV.6425, November 16, 2010.

58. United Nations Security Council, *Special Report of the Secretary-General on the Sudan,* UN Doc. S/2011/314, May 17, 2011.

59. As de Waal reminded me, Khartoum was weary of a repetition of the events in 2004–2005, when it had expected that a small UN observer mission with a restricted mandate would be deployed following the CPA, but the Council eventually authorized a large, multidimensional peacekeeping mission (UNMIS). US secretary

of state Clinton was in Khartoum when the Abyei agreement was being finalized and assured Khartoum's negotiator that the United States would abide by its provisions.

60. Upon recommendation by the Security Council (Resolution 1999 [July 13, 2011], UN Doc. S/RES/1999), the Republic of South Sudan became the 193rd UN member state on July 14, 2011 (General Assembly Resolution 65/308, UN Doc. A/RES/65/308).

61. Daniel Large and Luke Patey, *Caught in the Middle: China and India in Sudan's Transition,* Working Paper no. 36 (Copenhagen: Danish Institute for International Studies, 2010).

62. International Crisis Group, *Sudan's Spreading Conflict (I): War in South Kordofan,* Africa Report no. 198 (Brussels, 2013).

63. United Nations Security Council, "Statement by the President of the Security Council," UN Doc. S/PRST/2012/12, April 12, 2012.

64. Colum Lynch, "UN SC to Sudan: We'll Sanction You, You, and You," *Foreign Policy,* May 2, 2012

65. Jok Madut Jok, "State, Law, and Insecurity in South Sudan," *Fletcher Forum of World Affairs* 37, no. 2 (2013): 69–80.

66. Josh Kron and Nicholas Kulish, "For South Sudan and the U.N., a Relationship of Growing Distrust," *International New York Times,* July 20, 2013, www.nytimes.com/2013/07/21/world/africa/for-south-sudan-and-the-un-a-relationship-of-growing-distrust.html?pagewanted=all&_r=0.

67. Peter Martell and Adrian Blomfield, "Sudan Referendum: Birth of a Failed State?" *The Telegraph,* January 9, 2011, www.telegraph.co.uk/news/worldnews/africaandindianocean/sudan/8248001/Sudan-Referendum-birth-of-a-failed-state.html.

68. Claudio Gramizzi and Jérôme Tubiana, *Forgotten Darfur: Old Tactics and New Players,* Small Arms Survey Report no. 28 (Geneva: Graduate Institute of International and Development Studies, 2012). The Council only once, in a 2008 presidential statement, criticized Khartoum's noncooperation with the ICC, when nonpermanent member Costa Rica outmaneuvered China and other Council members who opposed the statement by threatening to put an eponymous resolution to a vote instead. With Costa Rica having secured the required nine votes in favor, China would have had to veto the draft. Hamilton, *Fighting for Darfur,* pp. 150–151.

69. Cockett, *Sudan,* p. 195; Zumbulev, "Irresolution."

70. Alex de Waal, "Sudan's Choices: Scenarios Beyond the CPA," *Sudan: No Easy Ways Ahead,* edited by Heinrich Böll Foundation (Berlin: Heinrich Böll Stiftung, 2010), pp. 11–13.

71. According to then–US ambassador to Sudan Don Petterson, this conundrum existed already in the 1990s, when "one problem we faced was that the Sudanese gave us no lasting opportunity to do anything positive toward them to demonstrate that we were not locked into unremitting hostility regardless of circumstances. . . . And so we had a catch-22 situation: Washington would stint on praise unless the Sudanese made major changes, and the Sudanese wanted more up-front praise from Washington before they would consider going in the direction Washington was stipulating"; Petterson, *Inside Sudan,* pp. 109–110. Subsequently, these dynamics played out in 2005, following the Comprehensive Peace Agreement (because of Khartoum's action in Darfur); in 2006, after the Darfur peace agreement (because of Khartoum's refusal to accept UN peacekeepers); and in 2011, after Khartoum's acceptance of the independence of the south (because of its military operations in Southern Kordofan and Blue Nile); Natsios, *Sudan, South Sudan, and Darfur,* pp. 168–169.

72. Rebecca Hamilton, "The Wonks Who Sold Washington on South Sudan," *Reuters,* July 11, 2012, www.reuters.com/article/2012/07/11/us-south-sudan-mid wives-idUSBRE86A0GC20120711.

73. Colum Lynch, "How the U.S. Triumph in South Sudan Came Undone," *Foreign Policy,* December 24, 2013, http://foreignpolicy.com/2013/12/24/how-the-u-s -triumph-in-south-sudan-came-undone/.

74. For UK and French policy on Darfur in particular, see the chapters by Paul Williams, "The United Kingdom," and by Bruno Charbonneau, "France," in *The International Politics of Mass Atrocities: The Case of Darfur,* edited by David R. Black and Paul D. Williams (London: Routledge, 2010), pp. 195–212 and 213–231, respectively.

75. Stephanie Kleine-Ahlbrandt and Andrew Small, "China's New Dictatorship Diplomacy: Is Beijing Parting with Pariahs?" *Foreign Affairs* 87, no. 1 (January– February 2008): 38–56.

76. Joel Wuthnow, *Chinese Diplomacy and the UN Security Council: Beyond the Veto* (New York: Routledge, 2013).

77. Victor D. Cha, "Beijing's Olympic-Sized Catch-22," *Washington Quarterly* 31, no. 3 (Summer 2008): 105–123; Daniel Large, "China's Sudan Engagement: Changing Northern and Southern Political Trajectories in Peace and War," *China Quarterly* 199 (September 2009): 610–626.

78. MacKinnon, *The United Nations Security Council,* p. 89; Annette Weber, *Bridging the Gap Between Narrative and Practice: The Role of the Arab League in Darfur* (Madrid: FRIDE, February 2010), p. 14.

79. Khartoum also concluded a separate peace agreement with the rebels in eastern Sudan in 2006. This agreement ended the rebellion, but the underlying causes of the conflict and the grievances of the population remained.

80. Bellamy and Williams, "The UN Security Council"; Grono, "Darfur."

81. Marina Ottaway and Mai el-Sadany, *Sudan: From Conflict to Conflict* (Washington, DC: Carnegie Endowment for International Peace, May 2012), http://carnegieendowment.org/files/sudan_conflict.pdf.

82. Ian Johnstone, "Managing Consent in Contemporary Peacekeeping Operations," *International Peacekeeping* 18, no. 2 (April 2011): 168–182.

83. These were AMIS (2003–2008) and UNAMID (since 2008) in Darfur; UNAMIS (2004–2005) and UNMIS (2005–2011) in Sudan; UNISFA in Abyei (since 2011); and UNMISS in South Sudan (since 2011). My calculation, based on information provided by UN's Department of Peacekeeping Operations, www.un .org/en/peacekeeping/resources/statistics/factsheet_archive.shtml.

84. See Jaïr van der Lijn, *To Paint the Nile Blue: Factors for Success and Failure of UNMIS and UNAMID* (The Hague: Clingendael Institute, 2008); Adebajo, *UN Peacekeeping in Africa.*

85. Richard Gowan, "The Strategic Context: Peacekeeping in Crisis, 2006– 2008," *International Peacekeeping* 15, no. 4 (August 2008): 454.

86. See Traub, *Unwilling and Unable,* p. 25.

31

Afghanistan

Francesc Vendrell

BY THE TIME I WAS APPOINTED AS THE SECRETARY-GENERAL'S personal representative and head of the UN Special Mission to Afghanistan (UNSMA) in January 2000, the Afghan conflict was in its twenty-second year. The Taliban's Islamic Emirate was in control of approximately 90 percent of the country, while the Islamic State of Afghanistan (ISA) was holding areas to the northeast of Kabul up to the Tajik border as well as some "pockets" mainly in the central highlands of the country. Because the United Nations had not recognized the Islamic Emirate, and the ISA retained Afghanistan's seat in the United Nations, it had been decided that I, together with some of UNSMA's staff, should be based in Islamabad, from where I would shuttle frequently between Kabul and Kandahar (where the core Taliban leadership was based) on the one hand, and on the other, Faisalabad, where the ISA's president Burhanuddin Rabbani resided, and Dushanbe, where I would meet with Ahmad Shah Massoud, the commander of the Northern Alliance military forces, who also held the titular positions of vice president and minister of defense of the ISA. UNSMA maintained nonetheless its office in Kabul and opened, shortly after my arrival, six civil affairs offices in five provincial centers under Taliban control and one in the ISA-controlled province of Badakhshan.

Origins of the Conflict

The Afghan conflict had been brewing since the late 1960s. At the University of Kabul, political confrontation became increasingly acute between Marxist students gathered around the People's Democratic Party of

Afghanistan (PDPA) and those who adhered to, or were influenced by, the Islamist ideology of Egypt's Muslim Brotherhood. The coup d'état of July 1973 against King Zahir Shah (1933–1973) by his cousin Daoud Khan enjoyed the support of the former as well as of army officers, many trained in the Soviet Union, and led to intensified persecution of Islamists. Five years later, in April 1978, a group of PDPA army officers and civilians overthrew and killed Daoud. The PDPA, however, lacked popular support, and its hasty land and social reforms had alienated many Afghans, particularly those in the rural areas. It was also riven by a long-standing internal division between the rival political factions of the more hard-line Khalkis and the more pragmatic Parchamis. An increasingly beleaguered regime turned to Moscow for support, including the dispatch of a military force, which the Soviet leadership, after much hesitation, agreed to.[1] Soviet forces crossed the Afghan border on December 26, 1979. The conflict had been internationalized and would become an important front in the Cold War with the US decision to support the Islamic mujahidin insurgency.

The United Nations and Afghanistan, 1980–1995

When the Security Council convened in early January 1980, the Soviet Union not unexpectedly vetoed a resolution that would have called for the withdrawal of its forces from Afghanistan. Two days later, however, the Security Council, in a procedural vote (i.e., one in which permanent members have no veto right) of twelve for, two against, and one abstention, adopted Resolution 462, invoking the "Uniting for Peace" resolution and referring the matter to the General Assembly.[2]

Convened in an emergency special session, the Assembly in turn adopted a resolution that, without naming the Soviet Union or its Warsaw Pact allies, "strongly deplored the recent armed intervention in Afghanistan" and called for the "immediate, unconditional and total withdrawal of the foreign troops" from the country.[3] Months later, the Assembly expressed the hope that the Secretary-General would continue his efforts in the search for a solution, "including the appointment of a special representative with a view to promoting a political solution" in Afghanistan.[4] Although the Soviet Union voted against this and subsequent resolutions calling for its withdrawal, it did, however, accept the Secretary-General's offer of good offices. Little progress was achieved in the period 1981–1985, when the Soviet Union and the Afghan government hoped to achieve a military victory over the mujahidin. With the arrival of Mikhail Gorbachev to power, the Soviet Union replaced Afghan president Babrak Karmal with Mohammad Najibullah, a more competent and astute personality, and opted for a political solution that would permit the withdrawal of Soviet forces. The Secretary-General's personal representative intensified his efforts, which led to the signature on April 14, 1988, of the Geneva Accords between Afghanistan and Pakistan, with the Soviet Union and the United States serving as guarantors, thus enabling the Soviet Union and its allies to begin their military withdrawal, which was completed in February 1989. The mujahidin, who were not a party to the accords and refused to abide by their terms, continued their military campaign against the Najibullah government, which, following the Soviet Union's collapse, they defeated by the spring of 1992.[5]

Interestingly, while the texts of the Geneva Accords were communicated to the Security Council by the Secretary-General,[6] the Council continued to ignore the conflict in Afghanistan, limiting itself six months later to "taking note" of the accords when supporting the temporary dispatch of military officers to assist in the UN Mission of Good Offices in Afghanistan and Pakistan (UNGOMAP),[7] an operation set up by the Secretary-General and approved by the General Assembly to assist in ensuring the implementation of the Geneva Accords and in this context to investigate and report possible violations.[8] And it was the Secretary-General, supported by annual General Assembly resolutions, who continued to play the lead role in efforts to find a solution to the Afghan civil war, which, after Najibullah's fall, mutated into an even more deadly conflict, this time among the various mujahidin factions, leading to the deaths of tens of thousands of people, the destruction of the city of Kabul, the atomization of power, generalized anarchy, and gross human rights violations, some of whose more notorious perpetrators would reemerge in powerful positions after the terrorist attacks of September 11, 2001.

It was against the background of these excesses that a group of young Pashtun mujahidin largely educated in Pakistani Deobandi madrasahs rose up. Calling themselves the Taliban,[9] they quickly took over Kandahar in 1994, acclaiming Mullah Mohammed Omar as "Emir el-Momeenin" (Commander of the Faithful) and establishing a rigorous Islamic regime that harked back to the days of the Prophet.[10] Two years later, they had reached the doors of the capital.

The Taliban, 1996–2001

It was only then, in the fall of 1996, that the Council took up the Afghanistan issue and, in a presidential statement, deplored the armed hostilities, expressed concern about terrorism, drug trafficking, and arms transfers, called for noninterference in Afghanistan's internal affairs, and supported the efforts of the UN Special Mission to Afghanistan (UNSMA)[11] to bring about a peaceful resolution to the conflict.[12] Following the Taliban's capture of Kabul, the Security Council adopted its first-ever resolution on Afghanistan—which elaborated on its previous presidential statements,[13] called for an immediate cessation of all armed hostilities, denounced discrimination against women and girls and other human rights and international humanitarian law violations, and expressed support for the Secretary-General and UNSMA—declaring itself convinced that the United Nations should continue to play "the central role" in efforts to achieve a peaceful resolution of the conflict.[14]

In the following twenty-two months, the Council discussed the situation in Afghanistan in the course of informal consultations, and adopted a series of presidential statements increasingly critical of the Taliban.[15] It was only in late August 1998, following the terrorist bombings of the US embassies in Nairobi and Dar-es-Salaam and the Taliban's capture of the Iranian consulate in Mazar-i-Sharif and the killing of several of its diplomats, that the Council passed a new resolution calling upon all states to prohibit their military personnel from planning or participating in military operations in Afghanistan and to immediately end the supply of arms and ammunition to all parties to the conflict, while also demanding that "all Afghan factions" refrain from harboring and training terrorists in the areas under their control.[16]

These calls having gone unheard, the Council went further three months later, singling out the Taliban for refusing to conclude a ceasefire and enter into a political dialogue with the opposition, and demanding the conclusion of a ceasefire and resumption of negotiations, while for the first time calling attention to the ethnic nature of the conflict. The Council also welcomed the initiative of the Secretary-General's special envoy in establishing the Six Plus Two group (discussed later) and the adoption of its Points of Common Understanding; supported the establishment within UNSMA of a civil affairs unit with the primary objective of monitoring the situation, promoting respect for human rights, and deterring massive and systematic violations of humanitarian law; and demanded the Taliban cease providing sanctuary and training for international terrorists and their organizations, backed by threat of sanctions to ensure implementation of the Council's resolutions.[17]

During the period 1996–2001, the Secretary-General periodically provided the Security Council with detailed information about the situation in Afghanistan and the diplomatic activities of UNSMA and of his special envoy, or later his personal representative, without, on the whole, eliciting much of a substantive response. It was left to the General Assembly to adopt yearly resolutions welcoming or, more frequently deploring, political, military, and diplomatic developments as well as violations of human rights and international humanitarian law.

However, the persistent refusal of the Taliban to hand over Osama bin Laden, for reasons that combined a shared ideology with a commitment to traditional Pashtun hospitality precepts, led the Council to invoke Chapter

VII of the UN Charter, imposing in late 1999 a series of sanctions on the Taliban, including denial of landing rights to aircraft owned by, or operated on behalf of, the Taliban and a freeze of their funds and other financial resources.[18]

It was in these circumstances that, following the resignation of the previous special envoy, I was designated as full-time personal representative as well as head of UNSMA.[19] I was conscious that previous efforts to convene direct talks between the Taliban and the United Front, the Northern Alliance's official name, had given rise to expectations that were dashed when those talks either failed to materialize or were quickly followed by the violation of the undertakings arrived at, as is often the case with unmonitored ceasefires. I therefore opted for pendular talks with the more modest objective of persuading the two fighting sides to enter into a framework agreement, committing themselves to resolving their conflict by political means.

In the belief that the future of Afghanistan should not be left entirely in the hands of the two fighting sides, I also decided to be in regular touch with noncombatant groups based abroad and, in particular, involve once again the former king of Afghanistan, with whom contact had been suspended in 1997, and who, in April 1999, had launched from Rome an initiative for the convening of an Emergency Loya Jirga.[20]

As my predecessors had pointed out, a prerequisite to reach a peaceful end to the Afghan conflict was the cessation of arms supplies and other forms of interference by neighboring and other countries. With that reasoning in mind, a group that became known as the Six Plus Two had been set up in 1997, consisting of the six countries with which Afghanistan shared a common border together with the Russian Federation and the United States, the two countries with greatest actual or potential interest and influence in the region. Unfortunately, it had become apparent two years later that the Six Plus Two mechanism was outlasting its usefulness, particularly after its members' failure to comply with their commitments under the Tashkent Declaration.[21] So, while the Six Plus Two continued to meet approximately twice a year, I thought it best to privilege instead bilateral meetings with its members where more candid exchanges could be held. I also found it useful to develop other mechanisms, including a group of eight member states, most of which had been members of the Group of 21, which, created in early 1997, had become moribund because at such large and heterogeneous gatherings a frank and honest discussion is hard to achieve. This new group, akin to a Group of Friends of the Secretary-General, but that called itself the Luncheon Group,[22] because its members met regularly for a meal in Islamabad, consisted of countries whose national interests were less directly involved in the fate of Afghanistan but because of their homogeneity proved to be a useful sounding board for ideas and initiatives that my

UNSMA colleagues and I put to them. Virtually all the governments involved would take over important military and peacebuilding roles in the post-Taliban period.

Another diplomatic avenue explored was the convening of the Geneva Initiative, consisting of Germany, Iran, and Italy, three countries associated with Afghan nonfighting groups together with the United States, which had expressed interest in participating. It was to become a useful venue, after the 9/11 events, for talks between Iran and the United States centered on how best the United States could assist the United Front on the ground as well as on the future political dispensation in Afghanistan. These strictly confidential talks, which facilitated the success of the Bonn Conference in December 2001, ended in the wake of President George W. Bush's 2002 State of the Union address when he lumped Iran into an "axis of evil" together with Iraq and North Korea.

Prior to this, my attempts to persuade the two Afghan warring parties to enter into a framework agreement had had a measure of success when, following my meeting with Mullah Mohammed Omar, both the Taliban and the United Front on November 2, 2000, sent identical letters agreeing to enter into a process of dialogue without preconditions, through direct or indirect talks, under United Nations auspices, to bring to an end the Afghan conflict by political means, with the commitment not to abandon the process unilaterally until all issues in an agenda to be agreed upon had been satisfactorily concluded.[23] While the chances of success looked somewhat slim, our hope was that as the dialogue progressed, differences that we believed existed between moderate and hard-line Taliban members might come to the fore.

When I communicated the agreement to the Security Council in informal consultations, the Council's reaction was, not unexpectedly, skeptical, given the Taliban's unwillingness to either surrender or expel Osama bin Laden from their territory, a key demand of the international community without whose compliance, as I was repeatedly telling the Taliban leadership, their international isolation would continue to deepen. The attack by al-Qaeda against the USS *Cole* off the coast of Yemen in October 2000 occurred at about the same time, ensuring that international terrorism would dominate the discussion in the Security Council. And so it was that shortly thereafter, the Council, while verbally supporting the personal representative's efforts to advance the peace process, expanded the sanctions against the Taliban, imposing, among other things, an arms and flight embargo, travel restrictions on the Taliban senior officials, as well as the immediate closure of "all Taliban offices" in the territory of UN member states (Resolution 1333).[24] The Taliban had been recognized as Afghanistan's legitimate government by only three countries.[25] By early 2000, its only embassy was in Islamabad. Unfortunately, the resolution's wording suggested that even unofficial Taliban offices should be closed, although providing that "in the case of Taliban missions to international organizations, the host state may, as it deems necessary, consult the organizations concerned" on its implementation.

It was thus not entirely surprising that, when I met again with the Taliban in January 2001 its foreign minister informed me that the imposition of new sanctions against the Taliban confirmed their view that the United Nations was not impartial, and thus that the Taliban could no longer accept the Secretary-General's good offices. My somewhat theological explanation that the Secretary-General and the UN's intergovernmental bodies were separate organs was always unlikely to cut much ice, although the Taliban agreed to continue to receive me, while warning that the expulsion of their representative to the United Nations in New York would result in the closure of UNSMA's office in Kabul.

The months between June and December 2000 had seemed to suggest a relative softening of the Taliban line, for their acceptance of the framework agreement on November 2 had been preceded by a decree by Mullah Omar banning the cultivation of poppy, an issue of major international concern since Afghanistan was, and remains, the largest world opium producer. It will remain a matter of debate whether the decree, which was widely implemented, was a genuine effort by the Taliban to win some degree of international acceptance and receive substantial crop-substitution assistance, or whether it reflected a temporary glut in the world heroin market.

However, this relative accommodating line was replaced in the months preceding September 2001 with a more radical approach, exemplified by the decree for the destruction of the Bamyan Buddhas and other pre-Islamic artifacts,[26] a new school curriculum emphasizing Islamic and Arab-language subjects, a ban on Internet use, and further restrictions on women. This harsher approach might be variously attributed to the new sanctions, to the international community's perceived delay to provide crop-substitution assistance, to the Taliban's increased reliance on funding from Islamic institutions and individuals, or to the growing ascendancy of the cosmopolitan, wealthy Osama bin Laden over the parochial Mullah Omar. UNSMA's five civil affairs offices were finally forced to close in mid-May 2001, with its premises in Kabul relocated by late June, while their complete closure seemed likely after the US Justice Department, ignoring the UN Secretariat's views to the contrary, ordered in June the expulsion from its territory of the unofficial Taliban representative to the United Nations.

Confronted with this impasse, the Secretary-General asserted that sanctions could not be a substitute for a comprehensive policy based on clear objectives with a coherent strategy to achieve them.[27] This remark elicited no response from the Council, which in late July 2001 remained solely focused on the monitoring and implementation of sanctions.[28] In mid-

August, the Secretary-General, pointing to the deteriorating situation, urged the Council once again to adopt a comprehensive approach and a coherent strategy to the settlement of the Afghan conflict.[29] The need for the Council to do just that would become even more pressing after the terrorist attacks of September 11, 2001.

The 9/11 Terrorist Attacks and the Fall of the Taliban, September–December 2001

The Council's immediate reaction to the terrorist attacks was to convene an urgent session and recognize the individual and collective right to self-defense in accordance with the Charter, though leaving it to the United States to decide how to respond to the attack.[30] The Council did not tackle the future of Afghanistan until considerably later but in late September decided on a series of measures to confront international terrorism[31] while implicitly accepting, as Adam Roberts argues, the George W. Bush administration's proposition that a state could take action against another state if the latter failed to stop terrorist attacks launched from its territory.[32]

In the meantime, conscious that a window of opportunity had suddenly opened, that the United States would intervene militarily in Afghanistan, and that the rapid fall of the Taliban regime was inevitable, my UNSMA colleagues and I moved quickly to accelerate the existing contacts between the United Front and the former king's supporters to reach agreement on the shape of a new political dispensation. I urged UN headquarters to convene an urgent meeting of the two Afghan sides to reach agreement on an interim authority that would occupy Afghanistan's seat in the United Nations and request the dispatch of an international military force to those areas that would be vacated by the Taliban. Our reasoning was that, unless this were speedily done, and given the understandable reluctance of the United States to send land forces and its consequent reliance on those from the United Front, it was likely that the old United Front warlords and commanders, who were as deeply disliked by the majority of Afghans as the Taliban was, would seize control of most of the country and present the international community with a fait accompli. Other than an instruction not to meet again with the Taliban, no response was forthcoming from New York until I was informed in early October to report to a newly appointed special representative, whose deputy I had apparently become. The new SRSG did not share my sense of urgency and took his time to formulate his ideas on how to proceed.

While the US air campaign began on October 6, 2001, a series of informal consultations were held in the first half of October in the Security Council, where a variety of options were canvassed on the future UN role in Afghanistan, but in the end Council members left it to the Secretary-

General and the SRSG to formulate their ideas on the subject. As the latter ended his consultations with the governments of Pakistan and Iran and with a variety of Afghans living in those countries, news of the fall of Mazar-i-Sharif to the United Front came through on November 6, followed in rapid succession by news of the fall of Herat, Kunduz, and Kabul.

It was under those circumstances that the Council held a further series of consultations to discuss both written and oral reports from the Secretary-General and his special representative,[33] and it was only in the wake of the fall of Kabul that the Council adopted its first resolution on Afghanistan since 9/11.[34]

In it the Council, after recognizing, none too early, the urgency of the security and political situation in Afghanistan, welcomed the SRSG's intention to convene an "urgent meeting" of the United Front and "various Afghan processes"[35] at an "appropriate location," and somewhat enigmatically "encourage[d] Member States to support efforts to ensure the safety and security of areas of Afghanistan no longer under Taliban control, and in particular to ensure respect for Kabul as the capital for all the Afghan people." This was the authorization the UK required to promptly send a small contingent of forces to Kabul.

The Bonn Conference was not a peace conference but an emergency meeting between the United Front and the ex-king's delegation and two smaller groups to formulate a road map that would lead, within an optimistic target of two and a half years, to the establishment of Afghan political institutions, elections, and the full normalization of the country. There was no question of inviting the Taliban, who were still struggling to hold Kandahar and who, in the mind of the United States and most other member states, deserved to be consigned to the rubbish bin of history.

Unfortunately, as some of us had feared, there were facts on the ground that had to be taken into account by the time the conference was held in late November 2001. The United Front was in control of approximately three-fourths of Afghanistan and, being still the internationally recognized government, felt free to install both in the capital and in the provinces many of the very persons whose abusiveness and rapaciousness had brought ruin to Afghanistan a few years earlier. Not only did this ensure that the largely non-Pashtun United Front would leave Bonn with the lion's share of positions in the new interim authority, but it also meant that the Pashtuns, the largest ethnic group in the country, would feel largely disenfranchised under the new dispensation, while corruption, bad governance, and impunity would reign untrammeled across the country.

In Bonn the participants had requested the early deployment of a UN-mandated force to Kabul and then, as appropriate, to other urban centers and areas in Afghanistan.[36] In turn, the Council promptly authorized the dispatch of a multinational assistance force (ISAF) to assist the interim authority in the maintenance of security in Kabul and its surrounding areas, though underlining that "the responsibility for providing law and order throughout the country" laid "with the Afghans themselves," a mantra that would be repeated in subsequent years when it was evident that the Afghans were hardly in a position to do so unless reliance was placed on the United Front militias, which, more often than not, were a source of insecurity and intimidation to the population.[37] It would be almost two years before the United States, which had dispatched its own forces under Operation Enduring Freedom[38] and did not wish to see a parallel military force deployed on the same locale, accepted, in the midst of its military involvement in Iraq, ISAF's geographical expansion, which was authorized by the Council in Resolution 1510 (2003). By then, the initial European willingness to commit forces to Afghanistan had begun to wane and the operation, now under NATO command, was hobbled by a series of "caveats" reflecting the various interpretations its members gave to ISAF's Chapter VII mandate, which for some included peace enforcement, while for others it was limited to peacekeeping or simply assistance in peacebuilding.

The Transition, 2002–2014

The handing of the military and security aspects of the Afghan operation to a multinational force and to the United States through Operation Enduring Freedom for an indefinite period of time, coupled with the Council's agreement to the Secretariat's recommendation that its reconfigured UN Assistance Mission in Afghanistan (UNAMA) should have a light footprint, inevitably resulted in a weakened role for the UN in the formulation of overall policy toward Afghanistan. Henceforth the leadership would be assumed by the United States with the largely unquestioned support of its NATO allies. The Council's repeated calls for ISAF to consult closely with successive SRSGs were largely ignored, while the direction of ISAF, despite frequent discussions in the NATO council, and of Operation Enduring Freedom, was essentially handled by the military command on the ground, in contrast with classic UN peacekeeping operations where the military chief is subordinate to whomever is the civilian head of the mission.

US policy toward Afghanistan—it would never amount to a coherent strategy—oscillated over the years. Focused at the beginning on the elimination of al-Qaeda and "the remnants of the Taliban" to the virtual exclusion of nationbuilding, it had, by mid-2002, become subordinated to the planning and execution of the invasion of Iraq. Although Operation Enduring Freedom and indeed ISAF had enforcement powers, neither chose to invoke them, to ensure that the disarmament, demobilization, and reintegration process or its follow-up, the disbandment of illegal armed groups, would be anything other than symbolic, thus depriving the government of

Hamid Karzai[39] a monopoly on the means of violence. Indeed, the United States, having told the Afghan president that its forces would not intervene were his government to face a security threat in trying to bring the warlords to heel, continued for several years to provide financial means to them. Thus a foreign military intervention that had been initially broadly welcomed by the Afghan public was replaced by growing cynicism about its underlying intentions, facilitating the reemergence by late 2005 of the Taliban, whose leaders had found refuge in Pakistan, as an insurgent force.

The warlords' retention of many of the levers of power, never questioned by the Council, even if alluded to in the Secretary-General's reports, had a deleterious impact on institution-building and other peacebuilding programs. The proceedings and conclusions of the Emergency Loya Jirga, convened in mid-2002 in Kabul, which thanks to UNAMA's efforts had achieved a more representative composition than previous or future ones, were disrupted by the uninvited and intimidating presence of jihadist warlords and their refusal to abide by its rules of procedure. Thus the former king, whose forty-year reign was widely remembered as Afghanistan's golden age, was consigned to the role of "father of the nation" rather than head of state as a large majority in the Emergency Loya Jirga appeared to favor. Likewise, President Karzai's selection of the members of the unelected Constitutional Commission was heavily influenced by jihadist leaders, as were to a lesser degree the proceedings at the Constitutional Loya Jirga in 2004. An "Islamic republic" with an overcentralized presidential system was adopted to universal international acclaim. Afghanistan's national army never really shed its Northern Alliance origins, and southern Pashtuns have remained under-represented in its officer corps while unaccountable foreign and Afghan private security companies have proliferated. The reform of the police was hampered by the retention of, or interference by, jihadist commanders and, since 2010, by ISAF's sponsoring of new militias under the guise of "Afghan local police." New political parties with a reformist or pluralistic outlook never elicited Western support, while the old jihadist parties, linked to warlords and never short of money, continued to prevail.

As the United States became bogged down in Iraq, it became politically expedient to present Afghanistan as a victory, something that senior military and diplomatic officials, frequently rotating with little opportunity to become familiar with Afghanistan, were ready to supply in their reports.[40] Even the Afghan presidential elections were moved forward one year ahead of those for the parliament, to enable the US president to present Afghanistan to voters in the November 2004 elections as a democratic success.

A mid-2004 US policy review led, after thirty months of neglect, to a deeper US military and civilian engagement. The number of forces was increased and the United States became more heavily involved in rebuilding Afghan institutions, the army and the police in particular, with poppy eradication becoming a priority.

With the establishment of the Afghan parliament in late 2005, the road map agreed in Bonn was formally concluded. However, it was evident that the international community's assistance was still required in building up security and rule of law institutions, as well as in economic reconstruction and development. Thus, at a conference convened in London in January 2006, a compact was signed between the eighty-one international participants and the Afghan government committing both sides to a partnership and a new road map, to be implemented within five years, with detailed goals, benchmarks, and timelines covering issues ranging from security to rule of law, human rights, governance, disbandment of illegal armed groups, and counternarcotics.[41] The Afghanistan Compact was endorsed by the Security Council, calling on the Afghan government and members of the international community to implement it in full, while reaffirming the central and impartial role of the United Nations in Afghanistan.[42]

A joint coordination and monitoring board was established under the chairmanship of the Afghan government and UNAMA. With more than twenty-five members, the joint board proved too large to be effective. It focused excessively on formalistic compliance with benchmarks, rather than on their practical impact on the ground, as its foreign members were often unwilling to challenge the optimistic reports presented by the Afghan government. In particular, international donors proved unwilling or unable to link their assistance to Afghan performance. Regrettably, the Afghanistan Compact failed to achieve most of its goals.

It was inevitable that a new policy review would be undertaken under the newly elected US administration of President Barack Obama. Heavily influenced by the Pentagon,[43] it deemphasized counternarcotics and nation-building, adopting a counterinsurgency policy instead that in reality became an antiterrorist one, since the military surge failed to be matched by other components essential to win the support of the population, such as improved governance, and major steps to combat corruption and impunity. It was only in early 2011 that the State Department expressed willingness to open a dialogue with the Taliban, although it would remain unclear for the following two years whether this was embraced by other departments of the US government.

For its part, the Security Council's resolutions since mid-2002 have largely mirrored whatever approach the United States is currently pursuing, taking note of successive developments in Afghanistan, periodically renewing UNAMA's and ISAF's mandates, and supporting UNAMA's role in assisting in the implementation of the Bonn Agreement and the London Compact.

Since the conclusion of the Bonn process, the Council's role has been further constrained by the existence of an Afghan government that, notwithstanding its dependence on international assistance, has increasingly insisted on the recognition of its sovereignty, demanding that the constant reference to an "Afghan-led process" become a reality rather than a convenient slogan. Thus the Council in 2012, when renewing UNAMA's mandate, limited the SRSG's good offices to providing "support" if "requested by the Afghan Government in the Afghan-led process of peace and reconciliation," and accepted that any UN role in support of future Afghan electoral processes should be at that government's request.[44] In doing so, the Council was responding to a curt letter from the Afghan government reflecting its growing tensions with UNAMA, particularly over the controversial 2009 presidential and 2010 parliamentary elections.

One area in which the Council retains a key role is the sanctions regime. As the search for a political solution to the Afghan conflict, including opening talks with the Taliban, became unavoidable, the Council, under pressure from the Afghan government, the United States, and its Western allies, overcame Russian objections and in June 2011 placed the Taliban on a separate sanctions list from the "comprehensive list" it had shared with al-Qaeda since 1999, making it easier to remove individuals from it.

Recently the Security Council has fallen into the habit of adopting, in parallel with the General Assembly, ever more lengthy resolutions reflecting the favorite concerns of its members on a range of issues including counternarcotics, human rights, gender equality, governance and anticorruption measures, law and justice, adherence to humanitarian law, and refugees and displaced persons. More a Christmas tree of pious hopes and admonitions, they have mostly failed to change behavior or practices on the ground, all the more so since the resolutions have rarely been followed up by corresponding diplomatic demarches in Kabul. Sadly, the impact of resolutions such as one adopted in March 2013, with its thirty-seven preambular and forty-nine operative paragraphs, is likely to be in reverse proportion to their length.[45]

Conclusion

In the more than three decades since the onset of the Afghan conflict, the Security Council has more often than not played a secondary role in the country. Between 1979 and 1996 it left the initiative to the Secretary-General and to the General Assembly. This was unsurprising during the Cold War, though it is harder to understand why the Council did not take up the issue after the 1988 Geneva Accords or when, after the victory of the mujahidin in 1992, Afghanistan was plunged into another civil war with the covert participation of its neighbors. While it should not be the Security

Council's role to micromanage the Secretary-General's good offices, the latter would have benefited from more explicit support from the former during the years 1992–2001. It was only with the advance of the Taliban and its capture of Kabul that the Council mobilized itself to condemn and subsequently impose sanctions on the movement, but without seeking to adopt, as the Secretary-General suggested, an overarching political strategy to deal with the prevailing situation.

While the desire of Council members to punish the Taliban for harboring bin Laden and al-Qaeda was understandable, the timing of Resolution 1333 (2000) was bound to have negative repercussions on the Secretary-General's good offices. A resolution that would have welcomed instead the commitment of the two fighting sides to the framework agreement negotiated by the personal representative, and offering on the one hand a number of carrots if the peace process advanced while threatening further sanctions on the other if it stalled, might have had greater effectiveness than their actual imposition. As it was, sanctions against a pariah regime, already isolated from the rest of the world, had little chance of modifying its behavior, and but for the events of 9/11, the Taliban might well have become a fixture of the landscape in years to come.[46] In addition, closer Council consultation with the Secretariat might have led to a modification in the resolution's wording to prevent the closure of the Taliban's New York office and avoid the retaliation to which UNSMA became exposed.

In the wake of 9/11 the Council legitimized the US intervention in Afghanistan and relied on the Secretariat's advice, which tallied with US preferences, on the diplomatic steps required to deal with the resulting power vacuum in Afghanistan and on the role and shape (the "light footprint") assigned to the United Nations, in contrast to its heavier footprint in situations such as Cambodia, Kosovo, or East Timor. The Council failed to take full advantage of the window of opportunity that had opened, taking its cue from the United States and its allies, something perhaps inevitable given that three permanent members and often three nonpermanent ones participated in the NATO operation.

With Afghanistan being of secondary importance to the Council's African and Latin American members, it would have been left to China and particularly to Russia to seek to modify the Council's line, something that would have severely damaged their ties with the West when they too benefited from the "war against terror," while the subsequent establishment of the Shanghai Cooperation Organization gave them a new instrument to manage their interests in Central Asia. Still, one wishes, as have some Afghan analysts,[47] that the Council would have found the courage to at least attempt to express concern at the treatment and detention without trial of suspected Taliban and other alleged terrorists in Bagram and other US detention centers, calling on all sides to respect international humanitarian norms rather than supinely recognizing "the robust efforts of ISAF and other international forces to minimise the risks of civilian casualties," despite evidence that this was not always necessarily the case.[48]

With the United States and Western governments having concluded, much as the Soviet Union had in 1986, that no military solution to the Afghan conflict is achievable, a political settlement is urgently required, beginning with the development of a consensus within the Afghan political elite on possible concessions and implicit red lines in any talks with the Taliban. A structure and agenda for the negotiations need also to be agreed with the insurgency, while continuing, in parallel, close discussions with Pakistan as well as Iran, India, the United States, and other concerned governments on the kind of settlement that might be acceptable to them.

As of mid-2015, none of these elements were actually in place, though the establishment of a National Unity government in late 2014 following the disputed presidential elections may facilitate the achievement of such an internal Afghan consensus. It is hard to believe that such a complex network of negotiations can be successfully concluded without the involvement of a third-party facilitator, which the UN would be best suited for.[49] Although so far, none of the main parties have formally made such a request, the Security Council could consider, before the situation becomes intractable, asking the Secretary-General to sound out the Afghans, their neighbors, and other concerned parties on how the UN might assist in reaching a comprehensive settlement. With the departure of most Western military forces, this might enable the United Nations to be better placed to play the "central international role" in Afghanistan.

Notes

1. See Rodric Braithwaite, *Afgantsy: The Russians in Afghanistan, 1979–1989* (London: Profile Books, 2011), pt. 1.

2. The "Uniting for Peace" resolution (A/RES/377A), adopted by the General Assembly on November 3, 1950, after the outbreak of the Korean War, and which was last invoked by the Security Council in 1983, has fallen into disuse with the end of the Cold War and the increased influence of the United States seeking to shelter Israel from UN condemnation. See Dominik Zaum, "The Security Council, the General Assembly, and War: The Uniting for Peace Resolution," in *The UN Security Council and War: The Evolution of Thought and Practice Since 1945*, edited by Vaughan Lowe, Adam Roberts, Jennifer Welsh, and Dominik Zaum (Oxford: Oxford University Press, 2008).

3. United Nations General Assembly Resolution ES-6/2 (January 14, 1980), UN Doc. A/RES/ES-6/2.

4. United Nations General Assembly Resolution 35/37 (November 20, 1980), UN Doc. A/RES/35/37.

5. See Martin Ewans, *Afghanistan: A Short History of Its People and Politics* (London: Curzon, 2001).

6. United Nations Security Council, "Letter Dated 14 April 1988 from the Secretary-General Addressed to the President of the Security Council," UN Doc. S/19834; and "Letter Dated 22 April 1988 from the Secretary-General Addressed to the President of the Security Council," UN Doc. S/19835; and "Letter Dated 25 April 1988 from the President of the Security Council Addressed to the Secretary-General," UN Doc. S/19836, April 26, 1988.

7. United Nations Security Council Resolution 622 (October 31, 1988), UN Doc. S/RES/622.

8. United Nations General Assembly Resolution 43/20 (November 3, 1988), UN Doc. A/RES/43/20.

9. Taliban is the Pashto word for "students."

10. Ahmed Rashid, *Taliban: The Power of Militant Islam in Afghanistan and Beyond* (London: Tauris, 2000), chap. 1

11. UNSMA, which replaced UNGOMAP in 1993, was established under General Assembly Resolution 48/208 (December 21, 1993), UN Doc. A/RES/48/208.

12. United Nations Security Council, "Statement by the President of the Security Council," UN Doc. S/PRST/1996/6, February 15, 1996.

13. United Nations Security Council, "Statement by the President of the Security Council," UN Doc. S/PRST/1996/6, February 15, 1996; and "Statement by the President of the Security Council," UN Doc. S/PRST/1996/40, September 30, 1996.

14. United Nations Security Council Resolution 1076, S/RES/1076 (October 22, 1996).

15. United Nations Security Council, "Statement by the President of the Security Council," UN Doc. S/PRST/1997/20, April 16, 1997, pp. 35, 55; and "Statement by the President of the Security Council," UN Doc. S/PRST/1998/9, April 6, 1998, pp. 22, 27.

16. United Nations Security Council Resolution 1193, S/RES/1193 (August 28, 1998).

17. United Nations Security Council Resolution 1214, S/RES/1214 (December 8, 1998).

18. United Nations Security Council Resolution 1267, S/RES/1267 (October 15, 1999).

19. The position of full-time personal representative of the Secretary-General and head of the special mission had been held by separate officials since 1992.

20. A traditional Afghan grand assembly of notables.

21. Under its terms, the eight countries had promised not to provide military support to the Afghan sides and not to allow the use of their territory for such purposes; United Nations General Assembly and Security Council, *Tashkent Declaration on Fundamental Principles for a Peaceful Settlement of the Conflict in Afghanistan,* UN Doc. A/54/174-S/1999/812, July 22, 1999. At the same time, the Taliban and the United Front agreed to a ceasefire and to enter into direct talks. The Taliban launched a major offensive one week later.

22. Its members were France, the United Kingdom, Germany, Italy, Japan, Norway, and Sweden. In other conflicts, they might have been referred to as a "Group of Friends of the Secretary-General," but in deference to the "Six Plus Two" were not so called.

23. United Nations General Assembly and Security Council, *Report of the Secretary-General: The Situation in Afghanistan and Its Implications for International Peace and Security,* UN Doc. A/55/633-S/2000/1106, November 20, 2000.

24. United Nations Security Council Resolution 1333, S/RES/1333 (December 19, 2000).

25. Pakistan, Saudi Arabia, and the United Arab Emirates.

26. Both the Secretary-General in person and I pleaded in vain with the Taliban foreign minister to halt implementation of the decree until at least a group of international Islamic scholars could have the opportunity of discussing the matter with their Afghan counterparts.

27. United Nations General Assembly and Security Council, *Report of the Secretary-General: The Situation in Afghanistan and Its Implications for International Peace and Security,* UN Doc. A/55/907-S/2001/384, April 19, 2001.

28. United Nations Security Council Resolution 1363, S/RES/1363 (July 30, 2001).

29. United Nations General Assembly and Security Council, *Report of the Secretary-General: The Situation in Afghanistan and Its Implications for International Peace and security,* UN Doc. A/55/1028-S/2001/789, August 17, 2001.

30. United Nations Security Council Resolution 1368, S/RES/1368 (September 12, 2001).

31. United Nations Security Council Resolution 1373, S/RES/1373 (September 28, 2001).

32. Adam Roberts, "Afghanistan and International Security," in *The War in Afghanistan: A Legal Analysis,* edited by Michael N. Schmitt (Washington, DC: Naval College and Government Printing Office, 2009).

33. See United Nations Security Council, "Provisional Verbatim Record of the 4414th Meeting," UN Doc. S/PV.4414, November 13, 2001.

34. United Nations Security Council Resolution 1378, S/RES/1378 (November 14, 2001). Previous resolutions since 9/11 had been under agenda item "threats to international peace and security caused by terrorist acts."

35. A rather infelicitous description of the nonfighting groups with which I had been in contact, including one, the Peshawar group, that, though sympathetic to the ex-king, was invited separately to the Bonn Conference.

36. The Bonn Agreement is contained in the annex to United Nations Security Council, "Agreement on Provisional Arrangements in Afghanistan Pending the Re-establishment of Permanent Government Institutions," UN Doc. S/2001/1154, December 5, 2001.

37. United Nations Security Council Resolution 1386, S/RES/1386 (December 20, 2001).

38. Operation Enduring Freedom was deployed under Article 51 of the United Nations Charter (June 26, 1945).

39. Karzai was selected by the December 2001 Bonn Conference as chairman of the interim administration, was appointed interim president by the 2002 Loya Jirga, and was elected president of Afghanistan in the country's 2004 elections.

40. With some notable exceptions, such as those of the EU mission forwarded to member states in 2002–2008.

41. The text of the compact is available at www.nato.int/isaf/docu/epub/pdf /afghanistan_compact.pdf.

42. United Nations Security Council Resolution 1659, S/RES/1659 (February 15, 2006).

43. See Bob Woodward, *Obama's Wars* (New York: Simon and Schuster, 2010).

44. United Nations Security Council Resolution 2041, S/RES/2041 (March 22, 2012), though similar formulations began to appear in other Council resolutions going back to 2008 (e.g., Resolution 1806, S/RES/1806, March 20, 2008).

45. United Nations Security Council Resolution 2096, S/RES/2096 (March 19, 2013); General Assembly Resolution 67/16, A/RES/67/16 (December 13, 2012). GA resolution 67/16 contains 110 operative paragraphs.

46. Ahmad Shah Massoud was assassinated on September 9, 2001, and for

forty-eight hours it looked as if with his death the Taliban would be able to take over the areas not yet under its control.

47. Gilles Dorronsoro, "The Security Council and Afghanistan," in Lowe et al. *The UN Security Council and War.*

48. See United Nations Security Council Resolutions 1776, S/RES/1776 (September 19, 2007); and 1806, S/RES/1806 (March 20, 2008).

49. Lakhdar Brahimi and Thomas R. Pickering, *Afghanistan: Negotiating Peace—The Report of the Century Foundation International Task Force on Afghanistan in Its Regional and Multilateral Dimensions* (New York: Century Foundation, 2011).

32

The Democratic Republic of the Congo

Tatiana Carayannis

THE UNITED NATIONS SECURITY COUNCIL CAME OF AGE IN THE
Congo. Barely an adolescent, the United Nations was first introduced to the
Congo in July 1960, when UN Secretary-General Dag Hammarskjöld
invoked Article 99 of the UN Charter for the first time in the organization's
history and the Security Council responded by authorizing the UN Operation in the Congo (ONUC). That was the UN's largest and most expensive
peace operation until the UN Security Council authorized its second peace
operation in the Congo, MONUC, nearly four decades later. One can identify three broad legacies of the UN that still haunt the wars in the Congo
today, as well as efforts to resolve them: the legacy of suspicion of the UN
in the region as an instrument of imperialism and domination; the legacy of
the affirmation of Congolese unity and territorial integrity; and the legacy
of robust peacekeeping and peace enforcement, which had and continues to
have mixed results in the Congo.[1] It would thus not be an exaggeration to
say that the Congo has been the de facto laboratory for the UN Security
Council's response to complex conflicts, especially since the end of the
Cold War.

In the post–Cold War era, 45 percent of Security Council meetings
have focused on Africa,[2] and 50 percent of Security Council resolutions
have dealt with conflict issues in Africa.[3] The past two decades of Security
Council activity in Africa, and in particular its engagement in the Congo
and the Great Lakes since 1994, show some distinct post–Cold War trends
in how the Council deals with conflict: greater cooperation and interaction
with regional actors; authorization of increasingly robust mandates with
increasing focus on protection of civilians; and innovation in UN responses

mostly through "ad hocery" and in reaction to events on the ground. The Council's experience with the Congo, as with its Great Lakes neighbor Burundi, has also shown us that consent for peace operations still matters.

Finally, a trend that has sounded alarms in many capitals is the authorization of ad hoc so-called coalitions of the willing, or groups of states that sometimes bypass the Council, as with the Balkans, and sometimes act on behalf of the Council, as in the Congo, but not with blue helmets. The Congo has thus far seen three such missions—the French-led Operation Turquoise during the Rwandan genocide in 1994; the EU-hatted International Emergency Force in Ituri in 2003, code-named Artemis; and most recently, in 2013, the Force Intervention Brigade (FIB), a Council-mandated regional force embedded within the UN Organization Stabilization Mission in the Democratic Republic of the Congo (MONUSCO). A fourth and earlier multinational force was authorized by the Council in 1996, but never deployed. The operational tensions and contradictions raised between the Council's multiple mandates and between multiple missions have been acutely felt in the Congo.

Background to the Conflict

Over the past decade and a half, the Congo has witnessed an extraordinary number of attempts by regional and international actors to resolve the largest conflict that Africa has seen since independence.[4] The conflict persists, however, at an enormous cost. The most that these attempts have achieved are several partially respected ceasefire agreements. They have failed to end the violence or to reestablish central government authority throughout the DRC.

The conflict in the Congo is best understood as three interlocking wars. While the Congo's wars trace their roots to the Rwandan genocide of 1994, the first war began in September 1996 as an invasion by a coalition of neighboring states of what was then Zaire, and resulted in the replacement of President Mobutu Sese Seko with Laurent Kabila in May 1997. The second war broke out in August 1998 when a similar configuration of neighboring states, some of which had been Kabila's patrons in the first war, broke with him and attempted a similar ouster, but without their earlier success. It ended with the signing of the Lusaka ceasefire agreement in July 1999 by the Kabila government and the two rebel groups fighting it (the Movement for the Liberation of the Congo [MLC] and the Rally for Congolese Democracy [RCD]), the result of a stalemate in the war and considerable external pressure.

In both the first and second wars, neighboring states established local proxy movements in an attempt to put a local stamp on their activities. However, the bulk of Kabila's Alliance of Democratic Forces for the Liberation of Congo (AFDL) fighters in the first war were foreign (mostly Rwandan), while in the second war this was less so. During the second war, the MLC rebel group fighting Kabila consisted largely of Congolese trained by Ugandan officers, while the Rwandan-backed rebel group, the RCD, was largely integrated with Rwandan troops and commanders.

When the Lusaka ceasefire agreement was signed, three rival Congolese rebel groups—the MLC and the RCD (at the time split between two factions, RCD-Goma and RCD–Kisangani/Movement for Liberation [RCD-K/ML])—controlled two-thirds of the DRC's territory.[5] Laurent Kabila's government in Kinshasa, which had itself come to power by force two years earlier, controlled the remaining third. The withdrawal of most foreign troops shortly thereafter created a power vacuum in rebel-held territories, and a third "war" began behind UN-monitored ceasefire lines in northeastern Congo. This war was fought between ever smaller groups—foreign and domestic—that have since become significant actors in the illicit activities in that region. In June 2003, following a national dialogue and a series of regional agreements, the DRC swore in a government of national unity consisting of leaders representing almost every local actor in the wars. This transition culminated in a UN-supported national election in 2006 that narrowly elected Joseph Kabila president after two hotly contested rounds of voting.

Though the Security Council has passed a total of forty-six resolutions on the DRC since the outbreak of the first war in 1996, over 90 percent of them (forty-two) have been passed since the start of the third war and the authorization of the UN peace operation in the DRC (first MONUC then MONUSCO) in 1999. The first Congo war saw only two Council resolutions when the war broke out in 1996 and one in February 1997, just weeks before the anti-Mobutu alliance took the capital. Surprisingly, the Council was mostly silent during the second war, which broke out on August 2, 1998, passing just one resolution, in April 1999. Once the Lusaka ceasefire agreement was signed in the summer of 1999, Council Resolution 1258 in August 1999 authorized the deployment of military observers to the Congo, the precursor to MONUC.

Operation Turquoise

The first event to transform an impoverished yet relatively nonviolent Congolese society into an arena of conflict and war was the genocide of the Rwandan Tutsis in 1994 and the ensuing Operation Turquoise. For several years, the Rwandan Hutu-dominated government, led by President Juvénal Habyarimana, and the Rwandan Patriotic Front (RPF), a Tutsi-led rebel group, had been embroiled in a civil war. The genocide, which began in early April 1994 and lasted for approximately three months, saw Hutu leaders mobilize almost the entire Hutu population in the organized mass murder of up to a million Tutsis and "moderate" Hutus.[6]

The loss of ten Belgian peacekeepers in early April 1994 and the deteriorating security situation in Rwanda prompted the UN, at the urging of the Belgian government, to withdraw most of its UN Assistance Mission for Rwanda (UNAMIR) forces two weeks into the genocide.[7] France offered to lead a humanitarian mission to the region until the United Nations could mobilize support for a new operation with a mandate appropriate to the new situation on the ground. On June 22, 1994, UN Security Council Resolution 929 authorized a temporary French mission "for humanitarian purposes in Rwanda until UNAMIR is brought up to the necessary strength."[8] Its mandate was to use "all necessary means" to ensure the humanitarian objectives spelled out earlier that month in Council Resolution 925 on UNAMIR,[9] though the resolution stressed "the strictly humanitarian character of this operation which shall be conducted in an impartial and neutral fashion."[10]

The first of the 2,500 heavily armed French troops of Operation Turquoise began arriving in Goma, in eastern Congo, across the Congo-Rwanda border, the following day. Although the Security Council authorized a multinational force under French command and control, it was de facto an exclusively French military intervention.[11] This was problematic, as the Rwandan Hutu-dominated government had received political and financial support as well as military training from the French since 1990. The arrival of French troops in the last weeks of the genocide, while the Habyarimana government was under heavy attack by the RPF, was seen by Rwandan government leaders as an intervention in their favor, while the RPF saw it as an attempt to shore up the weakening *génocidaire* government.

Operation Turquoise established a so-called safe humanitarian zone in southern Rwanda, to which many Hutu leaders, Rwandan military, and civilians retreated. But the operation had three principal effects that were contrary to its mandate of protection and neutrality. First, it jeopardized the lives of retreating UNAMIR troops who were under the command of Canadian general Roméo Dallaire, as the perceived anti-Tutsi bias of the French (but UN-mandated) operation led the RPF to retaliate against the United Nations by attacking the remaining UNAMIR troops left largely helpless with little heavy artillery and no communication with Operation Turquoise commanders.[12] Second, it failed to stop the bulk of the massacres of civilians that were still occurring. And third, the operation did not disarm the Hutu militias, known as the Interahamwe, nor the defeated Rwandan Armed Forces (FAR) units.[13] Instead, it allowed them and their political leaders, along with masses of Rwandan Hutu civilians, to escape across the border into the Congo. This mix of so-called ex-FAR/Interahamwe and Rwandan civilians established refugee camps just across the border that were supported by the UNHCR and used by the ex-FAR/Interahamwe as bases from which to regroup. These effects resulted in the profound destabilization of eastern Congo.

The First Congo War

The conflict in the Congo has involved at least nine African states and a number of proxy movements with varying degrees of local mobilization and support. As mentioned, the first war began in September 1996 as an invasion by a coalition of neighboring states of what was then Zaire, and succeeded in replacing Mobutu with Kabila as president in May 1997. This coalition of states—Rwanda, Uganda, Angola, Eritrea, and to a lesser extent others, and led principally by Rwanda and Uganda—coalesced around a common interest: that of ending Mobutu's support to armed groups in the region, which had been a perennial thorn in the side of Mobutu's neighbors.

The Mobutu regime tried to convince the world that the Congo was facing a foreign invasion, but to little avail. Neither the United Nations nor the Organization of African Unity condemned the invading forces, an indication of a general feeling in key capitals that Mobutu had to go. The notion that what was happening was largely a revolution against the Mobutu regime gained wide currency in the Western press, which from the start of the war referred to it as a civil war or rebellion. Mobutu failed to obtain any serious military support from abroad. The forces that did the bulk of the fighting for the Mobutu regime were the ex-FAR/Interahamwe, Serbian mercenaries, and UNITA rebel forces from Angola.[14] By the end of 1996, Mobutu's army was being routed and was in full retreat, though looting, raping, and killing Congolese civilians along the way.

Calls for a Multinational Force

In early November 1996, with pressure mounting for international action, the Bill Clinton administration began probing the Canadian government for possible interest in leading a mission to the Congo, suggesting that the United States would be willing to support a Canadian-led, but not a blue-helmet, intervention.[15] Once Canada and the United States reached a minimum agreement over US participation in the mission, Security Council Resolution 1080, adopted on November 15, 1996, authorized a Canadian-led "temporary multinational force to facilitate the immediate return of humanitarian organizations and the effective delivery by civilian relief organizations of humanitarian aid to alleviate the immediate suffering of displaced persons, refugees and civilians at risk in eastern Zaire, and to facilitate the voluntary, orderly repatriation of refugees by the United Nations High Commissioner for Refugees as well as the voluntary return of displaced persons." As part of the resolution, the Security Council noted that these efforts were also requested by regional leaders at the Nairobi summit of November 5, 1996, and that the Security Council intended "to respond positively on an urgent basis to those requests." The multinational force was not authorized, however, to disarm the ex-FAR/Interahamwe[16] in the Congo. Neither Canada nor the United States wanted to assume responsibility for disarming combatants who were not likely to give up their weapons voluntarily.[17]

At the Security Council discussions on the resolution, the representative of the Zairian government, Lukabu Khabouji N'Zaji, expressed dismay at what he saw to be the Security Council's unresponsiveness to a foreign act of aggression perpetrated against his state by the invading forces of Rwanda and Uganda. He complained about a Security Council double standard in the application of international law, and noted that since the Council had responded forcefully to Iraq's invasion of Kuwait in August 1990, he could not understand "the Council's reluctance to defend Zaire against a similar aggression."[18] Canada announced that already twenty countries had committed over 10,000 troops for the mission; and Madeleine Albright reminded the Council of the "shock and horror" of the genocide in Rwanda two years earlier, adding that the international community was now prepared to assist "those most in need."[19]

Despite the many pronouncements in favor of the mission and mounting pressure from the region, the authorized Canadian-led multinational force was never deployed. By the time the resolution was adopted, the situation on the ground had changed dramatically. As soon as the attacks on the refugee camps started in September 1996, hundreds of thousands of Hutu civilians began marching back across the border into Rwanda.[20] It did not take much for the United States, already reluctant to intervene, to seize upon these events as reason enough for not deploying the multinational force.[21] Two resolutions, 1078 and 1080, adopted within days of each other less than eight weeks into the first war, were the only Security Council actions in 1996 that dealt with the conflict in the Congo. The emphasis of both resolutions was the humanitarian needs of the Hutu "refugee" population; neither addressed the presence of foreign troops in the Congo.

On February 18, 1997, five months into the anti-Mobutu military campaign and three months before Mobutu relinquished power, the Security Council adopted a five-point peace plan for eastern Zaire. The plan called for the immediate cessation of hostilities; withdrawal of all external forces, including mercenaries; respect for the sovereignty and territorial integrity of Zaire and other states of the Great Lakes region; protection of all refugees and facilitation of humanitarian assistance; and peaceful settlement of the conflict through dialogue, elections, and the convening of an international conference.[22] Although this resolution recognized, for the first time, the presence of foreign forces in the Congo and called for their withdrawal, the Security Council stopped short of identifying any one force as the aggressor. An internationally recognized government, albeit an unpopular one, was claiming invasion, yet the United Nations and the OAU were united in not responding substantively to a clear violation of international law and the UN Charter. The general sentiment seemed to be that a handful of states in the region were doing everyone a favor by assuming the responsibility of ridding Africa of one of its more embarrassing and enduring dictators who had, over several years, hosted insurgency movements aiming to overthrow the governments of its neighbors.

International action during the first war took the form of weak declaratory UN resolutions, and intense international and regional diplomatic efforts to negotiate Mobutu's exit. Ambassador Mohamed Sahnoun of Algeria was appointed in January 1997 as joint UN-OAU special representative for the Great Lakes region, and South African president Nelson Mandela emerged as the principal mediator in the first war. The first meeting between Mobutu's government and the rebels took place in Cape Town on February 20, 1997, and was brokered largely by the United States and South Africa. Despite the presence of high-level envoys from the United States (George Moose, assistant secretary of state for African affairs, and Susan Rice, President Clinton's then special assistant on Africa) and South Africa (Aziz Pahad, deputy foreign minister), the talks collapsed and subsequent talks failed to reach agreement. On May 17, 1997, after a failed last-minute effort by Mandela and Sahnoun to produce agreement for another round of talks, and facing certain military defeat, Mobutu left the Congo for the last time, and the anti-Mobutu alliance marched into Kinshasa unopposed. This ended the first war.

The Second Congo War and the
Origins of the UN Mission in the DRC

The second war broke out in August 1998 when a similar configuration of neighboring states, some of which had been Kabila's patrons in the first war, broke with him and attempted a similar ousting. By early 1999, the war had acquired an even greater complexity, as there were now three rebel groups operating in the Congo, collectively controlling over half the country. The UN was largely prevented from taking a more active role in resolving the conflict, due to the reluctance of the major powers, especially the United States, to intervene in such a large-scale and complex regional conflict before a peace agreement had been reached. This inaction created space for a number of local initiatives. Between the outbreak of the war in August 1998 and the signing of the Lusaka peace agreement in July 1999, there were twenty-three failed SADC- or OAU-sponsored meetings at the ministerial or presidential level aimed at brokering an end to the war, as well as numerous other unsuccessful efforts by individual leaders in the region.

The second Congo war ended with the signing of the Lusaka ceasefire agreement in July 1999,[23] the result of a stalemate in the war and considerable external pressure, though largely a region-led process. Despite the agreement, violence among armed groups continued behind the ceasefire lines until the establishment of a government of national unity in 2003, in what some observers refer to as the third war.[24]

The Lusaka agreement called for the immediate cessation of hostilities within twenty-four hours of its signing. By "hostile action," it meant not only military attacks and reinforcements, but all hostile propaganda as well—an important emphasis in a region where hate speech has incited violence with devastating consequences. Furthermore, the agreement called for disarming foreign militia groups in the Congo, withdrawal of all foreign forces from the country, and exchange of hostages and prisoners of war. It also called for the establishment of a joint military commission composed of representatives of the belligerents, each armed with veto power. The commission was to be headed by a neutral chair appointed by the OAU, and charged with ensuring, alongside UN and OAU observers, compliance with the ceasefire until the deployment of a UN peacekeeping force mandated to ensure implementation of the agreement. The signatories of the agreement asked that this mission have both a peacekeeping and a peace enforcement mandate, and explicitly asked the Security Council to authorize coercive force, if necessary, to achieve its objectives of disarming the various armed groups.

Most significant, the agreement also provided for an all-inclusive process, the Inter-Congolese Dialogue, to produce a new political order for the Congo. The former president of Botswana, Ketumile Masire, was appointed to facilitate that process in December 1999. A key provision was that all domestic parties to the dispute, whether armed or not, were to participate in this dialogue as equals. The inclusion of the nonviolent political opposition and of civil society groups was a positive element, and in sharp contrast to the previous exclusion of these groups from earlier mediation efforts in the DRC.

There were encouraging signs for substantive UN involvement in Central Africa coming out of the Security Council in late 1998 and early 1999. UN Security Council statements soon after the second Congo war broke out commended the region's diplomatic efforts for a peaceful settlement, and called for the withdrawal of all foreign forces in the Congo.[25] The Security Council's presidential statement of December 11, 1998, said that the body was prepared to consider, in light of efforts toward peaceful resolution of the conflict, the active involvement of the United Nations in coordination with the OAU.[26] There were other signs that could have been interpreted as a greater willingness of the UN to help enforce peace agreements negotiated by the region. Security Council Resolution 1208, on the plight of refugees in African conflicts, adopted a month earlier, called on African states to develop procedures to separate refugees from "other persons who do not qualify for international protection afforded refugees or otherwise do not require international protection," and urged African states to "seek international assistance, as appropriate," to do this. Resolution 1234, adopted on April 9, 1999, supported SADC's regional mediation efforts by name, and, for the first time since the second war began, made a clear distinction between invited and uninvited forces in the Congo. This was in contrast to the Lusaka agreement, which made no such distinction.

The Security Council rejected the signatories' calls for a peacekeeping mission with an enforcement mandate. Once the agreement was signed in Lusaka, UN Security Council Resolution 1258, on August 6, 1999, welcomed the agreement and authorized the deployment of ninety military liaison officers to the headquarters of the belligerents for three months to assist the joint military commission in the peace process, and to determine when there might be sufficient security guarantees to deploy a larger UN force. In defending this preliminary action against critics who argued it was insufficient, a UN spokesperson noted that, although small in number, "these [military liaison officers] will contribute to confidence-building among the parties and represent the vanguard of further UN involvement."[27] The Congolese mission at the UN pushed hard for this resolution, and even embarked on a successful campaign to lobby African members of the Security Council and other nonpermanent members through the Non-Aligned Movement caucus. The Congo viewed a UN intervention as being very much in its interest, both because Kinshasa recognized that it would not easily defeat the Rwandan military, but also because it would address Rwandan security concerns and thus help eliminate the principal justification for that country's presence in the Congo.[28]

Once this small team was deployed, the Security Council adopted Resolution 1279 on November 30, 1999, authorizing the UN Organization Mission in the Democratic Republic of the Congo (MONUC), which would be constituted by the earlier deployment of military liaison personnel and increased by an additional 500 military observers.[29] Its mandate largely mirrored that of the earlier deployment. The deployment of MONUC was to occur in three phases, conditional on the security situation on the ground. The first phase, the deployment of military liaison officers to the headquarters of all the signatories to the agreement to help coordination, had already been launched under Resolution 1258. The deployment of military observers inside the Congo, authorized by Resolution 1279 to monitor compliance with the peace agreement, constituted the second phase.

In January 2000, the warring parties met in New York under the auspices of the UN Security Council during "Africa Month"—an initiative of US ambassador Richard Holbrooke, who held the Security Council presidency during that month.[30] This was a public relations victory for Kabila. The Security Council accorded him all of the trimmings reserved for a head of state, while the rebel leaders or their representatives sat in the gallery. On February 24, 2000, the Security Council adopted Resolution 1291, extending MONUC's mandate for another six months and expanding the force to over 5,500 military personnel, including 500 observers and appropriate civilian staff. The resolution gave the mission the authority, under Chapter VII of the UN Charter, "to take the necessary action . . . to protect United Nations personnel . . . and protect civilians under imminent threat of physical violence." Kabila, demonstrating his long-standing suspicion of Westerners, supported the resolution only on the condition that the UN force would be composed solely by troops from the global South, preferably from Africa, and reserved the right to reject or approve any of the contributions. The size of the force authorized was criticized again as being far too small to effectively monitor a peace agreement with multiple belligerents in a country with little infrastructure.

Eventually, agreement was reached on the condition that the authorized force would constitute only a second phase, with a larger force deployed in a subsequent phase.[31] Frequent ceasefire violations and Kinshasa's continued refusal to allow the UN unfettered access made deployment of the second phase difficult, and the monitoring of the disengagement of forces nearly impossible. Because of these difficulties, the OAU deployed thirty "neutral verification teams" inside the Congo beginning in November 1999, for a year, to help monitor the ceasefire, pending the deployment of MONUC observers. President Kabila assured a delegation of Security Council ambassadors, who, led by Ambassador Holbrooke, were visiting the Congo from May 4 to May 8, 2000, that Kinshasa would fully cooperate with MONUC, though he criticized the United Nations for "failing to condemn the presence of uninvited troops" in the Congo.[32] Disagreements over where to co-locate the joint military commission and MONUC, and the MLC's refusal to withdraw its forces as demanded by the second phase, further delayed deployment.[33]

The growing rift between Uganda and Rwanda that had been foreshadowed in the earlier RCD leadership split and worsened as these former allies increasingly competed for influence and control of resources in eastern Congo, came to a head on June 5, 2000, in Kisangani. A fight between Ugandan and Rwandan troops resulted in thousands of civilian casualties and neither inspired confidence at the UN that there would soon be any peace to keep, nor favored calls for a more robust UN force in the Congo. A strongly worded resolution adopted by the Security Council on June 16 expressed "outrage" at the fighting, called for the immediate demilitarization of Kisangani and the withdrawal of foreign troops from the country, and, for the first time, directly accused Uganda and Rwanda of violating "the sovereignty and territorial integrity of the Democratic Republic of the Congo," asking them to "pay reparations for the loss of life and the property damage they have inflicted on the civilian population in Kisangani."[34] Laurent Kabila's assassination on January 16, 2001, removed some of the obstacles to further MONUC deployment, as his twenty-nine-year-old son and successor, Joseph Kabila, soon consented to the full deployment of UN forces. On February 22, 2001, the Security Council demanded in Resolution 1341 that "Ugandan and Rwandan forces and all other foreign forces withdraw" from the Congo, and asked that a timetable for that withdrawal be prepared within the next three months.

On April 26, 2001, six International Committee of the Red Cross workers were killed by armed groups near Bunia, leading the Security Council president at that time, UK ambassador Jeremy Greenstock, to note that the incident "made us not just worry about the safety of humanitarian and other UN international workers, but also for the peace process in the Congo."[35] It was in this climate that the Security Council, this time led by French ambassador Jean-David Levitte, visited the Central African region in midMay 2001 to assess efforts to implement the peace plan. On the day the Security Council was due to arrive in Kinshasa, Kabila repealed Decree 194, imposed by his father to restrict political party activity. This high-level delegation determined that "the ceasefire is holding and the parties to the conflict, with one exception, have disengaged their forces in accordance with the agreement they have signed."[36] The Security Council took the opportunity of MONUC's imminent receipt of two fast patrol boats to announce that the peace operation was reopening the vast Congolese river network. What the delegation failed to mention was that there was a third war emerging in eastern Congo.

On the basis of MONUC's report, the Security Council decided that disengagement was nearly complete, and on June 15, 2001, adopted Resolution 1355, authorizing preparations for the deployment of the third phase, including plans for the voluntary disarmament, demobilization, repatriation, reintegration, and resettlement of all armed groups in the Congo. A joint communiqué, signed by all the parties at the conclusion of the Security Council's visit, assigned to the UN the role of "impartial arbiter" in this process,[37] with responsibility for coordinating all aspects of this process, including screening of *génocidaires* and war criminals and turning them over to the international tribunal investigating the Rwandan genocide.[38] The role of the UN and the OAU, therefore, would be one of coordination, verification, and monitoring. But much of this was conditional on the voluntary compliance of the armed groups, a process that remained a failure.

The Third Congo War and
Continued Violence in Eastern DRC

After the signing of the Lusaka agreement, there was relatively little violence or combat along the ceasefire lines between Kinshasa-controlled and rebel-controlled regions. Violence and the accompanying humanitarian disaster were largely limited to the struggle between the Mai Mai (loose groupings of self-defense groups that emerged in the Kivus to fight the presence of anyone perceived as foreign), the Democratic Forces for the Liberation of Rwanda (FDLR), and Burundi's Forces for the Defense of Democracy (FDD), all fighting against Rwanda and the RCD. A bilateral agreement signed between Kinshasa and Kigali in Pretoria on July 30, 2002, resulted in the complete withdrawal of Rwandan forces in return for Kinshasa's promise to dismantle the Hutu militias and hand them over to Rwanda. A similar ceasefire agreement with Kampala in Luanda on September 6, 2002, resulted in the withdrawal of Ugandan forces. While the withdrawal of foreign troops paved the way for the formation of a government of national unity and for the first national elections, in 2006, it also created a power vacuum in the east, and a significant increase in violent, anarchic conflict between ever smaller groups that no major actor effectively controlled.

This power vacuum was particularly acute in Ituri, where the Ugandan and Rwandan occupation had created rival proxy groups along ethnic lines. The withdrawal of Ugandan troops in the spring of 2003 precipitated a deadly spate of factional fighting between ethnic-based militias controlled by the Hendu and Lendu ethnic groups, causing thousands of civilians to flee the violence in the town of Bunia and seek refuge around the MONUC compound, which housed 700 Uruguayan peacekeepers, who proved unable to stop the violence. With tensions and public outcry mounting at MONUC's inability to respond effectively, calls for a multinational force would be more successful in 2003 than they were in 1996. In May 2003, the UN Security Council authorized the deployment of an EU-led Interim Emergency Multinational Force (IEMF) named Operation Artemis, to Ituri. Authorized under a Chapter VII mandate, Artemis was to deploy as an interim force for three months to stabilize the region and give MONUC time to be reinforced. Artemis successfully managed to stabilize Ituri in a short period of time.

In June 2003, following a national dialogue and a series of regional agreements, the DRC swore in a government of national unity consisting of leaders representing almost every local actor in the wars. This transition culminated in a UN-supported national presidential election in 2006 that Joseph Kabila narrowly won. The relatively successfully concluded election of 2006—the most expensive in the UN's history—led the Council to see this as an opportunity for exit, with the United States and United Kingdom in particular pushing for drawdown. The Council subsequently disengaged politically and diplomatically from the DRC, while placing ever greater emphasis on protection. The new government's crackdown on the opposition and growing authoritarian tendencies cloaked in the rhetoric of sovereignty, coupled with Congo donor fatigue, led to increasingly deteriorating security conditions, particularly in eastern DRC. A poorly run and largely fraudulent second national election in 2011, with tepid international support, precipitated a crisis of legitimacy that was used by Rwanda and its proxies to further destabilize the country. Thus, despite two national elections since the transition, violence persists to this day. The majority of the UN's assets in the DRC have been deployed in eastern Congo, where the bulk of the ongoing violence remains concentrated, as new alliances of convenience continue to compete for control over land, people, and lucrative mining interests.

The Council's sanctions regime was strengthened during this period (since 2000), particularly in an effort to limit the trade in conflict resources. Since 2004, it has been supported by a group of experts on the DRC with a Council mandate to assess violations of the arms embargo by tracing the funding of armed groups through illicit (and sometimes licit) networks involved in the exploitation of natural resources. One of the few nimble instruments the UN has that can cross borders where peacekeeping missions cannot, the group of experts repeatedly exposed the involvement in illegal resource exploitation of many Western companies in the Great Lakes region and became a model for much of what the Council did in this field in the following years in the DRC and elsewhere.[39]

The CNDP, the M23, and the Intervention Brigade

Beginning in 2009, rebels of the formerly Rwandan-backed National Congress for the Defense of the People (CNDP) who had been integrated into the national army as part of a Kinshasa-Kigali peace deal came to dominate local economies in North Kivu. Their integration into the army solidified and legitimized the CNDP's control over the southern areas of North Kivu province. These former CNDP contingents refused to deploy outside of North Kivu, and maintained a parallel chain of command that continued to control economic networks tied to Rwanda and based on illicit mineral extraction.

In April 2012, elements of the Congolese Armed Forces (FARDC) in the Kivu provinces, consisting mostly of former members of the CNDP, mutinied from the national army, and in May 2012 named themselves the March 23 Movement (M23). The UN's group of experts on the DRC, in its report of November 15, 2012, documented evidence of Rwandan and to a lesser extent Ugandan logistical, financial, and recruitment support for these rebels, highlighting the total breakdown of the earlier rapprochement between the DRC and Rwanda.[40] The Council placed several M23 leaders on the UN's sanctions list. While the report of the group of experts, and the experts themselves, were loudly denounced by Kigali, Western donors, including the United States and United Kingdom, temporarily suspended aid to Rwanda in reaction to its support of the M23 rebellion. In light of Rwanda's election to a nonpermanent seat in the Security Council for the 2013–2014 term, the UN sanctions committee overseeing the independent group of experts extended the latter's mandate in December 2012 for an additional fourteen months, to ensure that Rwanda, which continued to be adamantly opposed to the group, would have only a delayed opportunity to block the expert group and its investigations.

On November 20, 2012, M23 rebel forces occupied the city of Goma, the most strategic city in the east, meeting limited resistance from the FARDC and the UN mission, which on July 1, 2010, had been renamed MONUSCO. The inability of the world's largest peacekeeping mission, MONUSCO, to stop Goma from falling to a foreign-backed rebellion marked a major and embarrassing failure of UN peacekeeping in the DRC. With confidence in the UN in the region at an all-time low, on July 15, 2012, the African Union announced that it was "prepared to contribute to the establishment of a regional force to put an end to the activities of armed groups" in the DRC. The International Conference on the Great Lakes Region (ICGLR), while initially a welcome expression of regional interest to end the violence, raised financing and logistical support issues. While Tanzania and South Africa had offered troops, it became quickly clear that the ICGLR had no operational capacity to field such a force. On March 28, 2013, amid frustration with MONUSCO's failure to halt the M23 advance, the Council adopted Resolution 2098, authorizing the Force Intervention Brigade (FIB) to operate within MONUSCO with a mandate to engage in offensive operations to neutralize armed groups. The FIB was authorized despite concerns among many about the modalities of how this so-called neutral combat force would relate to the existing presence of some 19,000 UN troops already on the ground. Would this be a UN-regional hybrid force, a regional force supported by the UN, or a troop enhancement of the existing UN operation?

Amid discussions about military action, the escalation of violence in Goma underscored the urgency for a revived, sustained political process in the region. A high-level UN meeting on the eastern DRC convened by UN Secretary-General Ban Ki-moon in New York on September 27, 2012, on the margins of the UN General Assembly suggested that the deployment of a high-level effort could provide the impetus to launch a political process to end the violence. After repeated criticism that efforts to end the violence in DRC had deeply neglected politics in favor of military solutions with mixed results, the Council in the same resolution authorizing the intervention brigade authorized the appointment of a high-level UN special envoy to lead a comprehensive political process to bring peace to the Great Lakes region. Mary Robinson was appointed to that position on March 18, 2013.

The M23 insurrection was eventually defeated in November 2013, the result of joint FARDC-FIB military operations and international pressure on Rwanda to halt its support to the group. The signing of the Nairobi Declarations on December 12, 2013, may have temporarily put an end to the M23 rebellion, but many challenges remain, including the disposition of M23 combatants, the majority of whom are in camps in Rwanda and Uganda, and reports that the remaining M23 leadership continue to recruit in Rwanda.[41] Moreover, the jury is still out on whether FIB operations will be as effective against other remaining armed groups, like the FDLR, that are much more embedded in Congolese society than was the M23.

Conclusion

The Security Council in the past two decades has been largely reactive to the situation in the Great Lakes region, and the DRC in particular, often finding itself having to play catch-up. By the time resolutions are adopted, the context on the ground has shifted. The intense engagement during the 2003–2006 transition was followed by a gradual disengagement, in particular after the 2006 elections, but then again by crisis after the botched 2011 elections. This reactiveness has been reflected in Council mandates.

This is particularly evident in the Council's growing trend toward authorizing robust peacekeeping mandates. A study conducted by the Stimson Center for the UN Department of Peacekeeping Operations in 2009 revealed several gaps in capacity, knowledge, and training regarding the protection of civilians.[42] While the Council was authorizing strong civilian protection mandates, there was little operational guidance and, as a result, little consensus on what was meant by civilian protection in the context of peacekeeping.

This ad hocery also exposed the operational tensions in the mission's multiple and sometimes competing mandates. Another growing trend alongside the trend toward greater peace enforcement is the automatic addition of civilian protection mandates alongside robust peacekeeping. In 2008, following some targeted and reprisal killings by the CNDP of an estimated 150 villagers in the village of Kiwanja, Council Resolution 1856 mandated MONUC to attach the highest priority to the protection of civilians and tasked the mission with coordinating operations with the Congolese army. The resulting joint MONUC-FARDC military operations yielded mixed results, with some operations called "catastrophic" for civilians by international human rights observers.[43] In contrast to Council intent, robust military action undermined civilian protection and led to growing pressure to either condition support to the FARDC in joint operations or cease operations altogether.

Another and related observation is that consent still matters, which makes the implementation of political mandates all that more difficult. Key members of the Council have consistently faced the dilemma between supporting key actors in the region and condemning human rights violations, and have often remained silent in the face of exactions against civilians—both to protect regional allies (as in the case of the United States and Rwanda) but also to avoid alienating the Kinshasa authorities, who over the years have repeatedly threatened the expulsion of the UN mission.

A further observation from the Congo wars is that, while the post–Cold War trend in the Council has been increased reliance on regional actors to intervene in their own regions, "backyard operations" have their limits. When an entire region is deeply divided by war, the Council cannot effectively enforce the peace by relying on regional actors, even when such an approach has been successful in reaching a negotiated settlement. In other words, combatants cannot enforce the peace against themselves. They can participate in peacemaking, and ultimately must do so, but if there is to be peace enforcement, forces from outside the region will have to do it. Those forces must have a Council mandate. The FIB is an example. Though the region faced logistical and financial constraints in fielding an intervention force, those constraints could have been addressed by international actors while keeping the force under a regional (ICGLR or AU) mandate.

But despite the limits of regional actors, given deep regional divisions, they can (and did) initiate and successfully negotiate agreements to end conflicts in which large and important groups of that region were themselves participants in the conflict. Still, the lessons from the Congo also suggest that the more regionally based the conflict is in terms of state actors involved, the more difficult the task of mediation becomes without external partners—partly due to capacity constraints but mostly due to the need for external guarantors and credible, punitive threats for noncooperation. In the Great Lakes, the problem has not been negotiating agreements but ensuring their implementation once they have been signed.

Finally, if we can draw one overarching conclusion from Council action in the Great Lakes region, it is the growing disconnect between the international conflict response toolkit and the complexity of violence on the ground—a disconnect that is not limited to the Great Lakes, as trends in the changing nature of organized violence globally attest.

Notes

This chapter draws on my earlier publications, primarily Tatiana Carayannis, "The Democratic Republic of the Congo, 1996–2012," in *Responding to Conflict in*

Africa: The United Nations and Regional Organizations, edited by Jane Boulden (New York: Palgrave Macmillan, 2013).

1. Tatiana Carayannis, *Pioneers of Peacekeeping: ONUC, 1960–1964* (Boulder, CO: Lynne Rienner, forthcoming).

2. A low of 29 percent in 1990 and a high of 56 percent in 2011. See Boulden, *Responding to Conflict in Africa.*

3. With a low of 0.5 percent in 1990 and 1991 to a high of 66 percent in 2011. See Boulden, *Responding to Conflict in Africa.*

4. Much of this background is drawn from Tatiana Carayannis and Herbert F. Weiss, "The Democratic Republic of the Congo, 1996–2002," in Jane Boulden, *Dealing with Conflict in Africa: The United Nations and Regional Organizations* (Basingstoke, UK: Palgrave, 2003); and Tatiana Carayannis, *The Challenge of Building Sustainable Peace in the DRC* (Geneva: Centre for Humanitarian Dialogue, 2009).

5. The RCD quickly split into two movements as a result of internal disagreements: the RCD-ML (Movement for Liberation), backed by Uganda, and the RCD-Goma, backed by Rwanda. The MLC, another anti-Kabila armed group in the second war, was established with Ugandan support in northern Equateur province some months after the founding of the RCD. The MLC was a way for Uganda to hedge its bets against the faltering RCD-ML.

6. For details regarding the failure of international interventions in Rwanda, see Gérard Prunier, *The Rwanda Crisis: History of a Genocide* (New York: Columbia University Press, 1995); Linda Melvern, *A People Betrayed: The Role of the West in Rwanda's Genocide* (New York: Zed, 2000); J. Matthew Vaccaro, "The Politics of Genocide: Peacekeeping and Disaster Relief in Rwanda," in *UN Peacekeeping, American Policy, and the Uncivil Wars of the 1990s,* edited by William J. Durch (New York: St. Martin's, 1996); Philip Gourevitch, *We Wish to Inform You That Tomorrow We Will Be Killed with Our Families: Stories from Rwanda* (New York: Farrar, Straus, and Giroux, 1998); Scott Peterson, *Me Against My Brother: At War in Somalia, Sudan, and Rwanda* (New York: Routledge, 2000); Bruce D. Jones, *Peacemaking in Rwanda: The Dynamics of Failure* (Boulder, CO: Lynne Rienner, 2001); United Nations Security Council, *UN Report of the Independent Inquiry into the Actions of the United Nation During the 1994 Genocide in Rwanda,* UN Doc. S/1999/1257, December 16, 1999, http://daccess-dds-ny.un.org/doc/UNDOC/GEN /N99/395/47/IMG/N9939547.pdf?OpenElement.

7. UNAMIR forces were mandated to help implement a ceasefire agreement and transitional arrangements. On April 21, 1994, the Security Council voted to reduce its UNAMIR forces by 90 percent, to 270 troops. France voted in favor of the withdrawal.

8. Six weeks earlier, on May 6, Security Council Resolution 918 (May 17, 1994; UN Doc. S/RES/918) authorized UNAMIR II, a redeployment of 5,500 UN troops with a Chapter VII humanitarian mandate, and imposed an arms embargo on Rwanda. However, delays in contributions meant that UNAMIR II was not deployed until August, three months later, just as Operation Turquoise was withdrawing its forces.

9. Security Council Resolution 925 (UN Doc. S/RES/925) was adopted on June 8, 1994, to extend UNAMIR's mandate for another six months, until December 9, 1994. UNAMIR's mandate required it to protect internally displaced persons, refugees, and civilians by establishing "secure humanitarian areas," and to "provide security and support for the distribution of relief supplies and humanitarian relief operations."

10. Security Council Resolution 929 (UN Doc. S/RES/929) was adopted on June 22, 1994.

11. Within days, in what was a quid pro quo for each power, the Security Council authorized similar operations for the United States in Haiti and for Russia in Georgia.

12. Romeo A. Dallaire, "The End of Innocence: Rwanda 1994," in *Hard Choices: Moral Dilemmas in Humanitarian Intervention,* edited by Jonathan Moore (Lanham: Rowman and Littlefield, 1998).

13. Once out of power, known as "the ex-FAR."

14. Throughout the Cold War, UNITA received Western support largely through Mobutu, which also allowed them to maintain a rear base across the border from Angola, on Zairian soil.

15. For an account of the process that led to the decision to authorize the Canadian operation, including the debates within the Canadian government and between Canada and the United States, see John B. Hay, "Conditions of Influence: An Exploratory Study of the Canadian Government's Effect on U.S. Policy in the Case of Intervention in Eastern Zaire," unpublished MA thesis, Carleton University, Ottawa, May 1998. See also James Appathurai and Ralph Lyshysyn, "Lessons Learned from the Zaire Mission," *Canadian Foreign Policy* 5, no. 2 (Winter 1998): 93–105.

16. Now the FDLR, although nearly two decades after the Rwanda genocide the FDLR looks very different from the earlier ex-FAR/Interahamwe, as only a few of the FDLR's commanders are hardcore *génocidaires.* Many in the FDLR rank and file were too young to have been involved in the 1994 genocide.

17. Although Rwanda eventually went along with the proposed intervention, it objected to any efforts to repatriate Hutu refugees that were not authorized to disarm them first. Humanitarian NGOs were also insisting upon disarmament as a necessary condition for humanitarian relief efforts.

18. United Nations Meetings Coverage and Press Releases, "Security Council Authorizes Establishment, for Humanitarian Purposes, of Temporary Multinational Force in Eastern Zaire," UN Doc. SC/6291, November 15, 1996.

19. Ibid.

20. Those Rwandan Hutus who remained in the Congo were probably largely made up of ex-FAR/Interahamwe, their families, and some ordinary civilians who either had been forced, or volunteered, to withdraw westward to escape the advancing forces of the anti-Mobutu alliance.

21. The mission was abandoned despite arguments by the UNHCR and humanitarian relief organizations questioning the numbers of refugees actually returning to Rwanda. "Newsletter," *Info-Zaire,* November 26, 1996.

22. United Nations Security Council Resolution 1097, S/RES/1097 (February 18, 1997).

23. The MLC and the RCD signed in August, as a leadership quarrel within the RCD had held up its signing since neither faction's leaders could agree on who should sign for the movement. Eventually, that disagreement was overcome by having all fifty founding members of the RCD become signatories.

24. Tatiana Carayannis, "The Complex Wars of the Congo: Towards a New Analytic Approach," *Journal of Asian and African Studies* 38, nos. 2–3 (2003): 232–255.

25. See United Nations Security Council, "Statement by the President of the Security Council," UN Doc. S/PRST/1998/26, August 31, 1998; and "Statement by the President of the Security Council," UN Doc. S/PRST/1998/36, December 11, 1998.

26. United Nations Security Council, "Statement by the President of the Security Council," UN Doc. S/PRST/1998/36, December 11, 1998.

27. United Nations Integrated Regional Information Network, "DRC: UN Military Officers Prepare for Deployment," September 9, 1999, www.irinnews.org /report/8972/drc-un-military-officers-prepare-for-deployment.

28. Interview with André Kapanga, Congolese ambassador to the UN under Laurent Kabila, April 4, 2002.

29. South Africa's Institute for Security Studies has correctly noted that MONUC is "arguably the most complicated and ambitious post–Cold War experiment in the creation of peace from chaos with fairly modest resources." Jakkie Cilliers and Mark Malan, *Peacekeeping in the DRC: MONUC and the Road to Peace*, Monograph no. 66 (Pretoria: Institute for Security Studies, October 2001), executive summary, p. 3. Given the size of the country and the number of different combatants, domestic and foreign, one could well amend "fairly modest" to "inadequate"— in terms of both mission mandate and mission size.

30. During this "Africa Month," the Security Council also discussed the problem of the AIDS pandemic in Africa, an unprecedented step that moved the Council closer to a broader conceptualization of security. In an equally unusual development, Holbrooke invited Vice President Al Gore to address the Council on the issue of AIDS.

31. Interview with André Kapanga, March 14, 2002.

32. United Nations Security Council, "Security Council Mission Visit to the Democratic Republic of the Congo, 4–8 May 2000," UN Doc. S/2000/416, May 11, 2000.

33. MLC leader Jean-Pierre Bemba, fearing a power vacuum in Equateur province, insisted that he would not withdraw unless the UN deployed a force large enough to guarantee the security of over 100,000 people in villages that MLC forces had "liberated." Said Bemba: "I think this UN and the international community only cares about my army withdrawing, but do not care if the black Congolese are massacred by the Interahamwe and government forces." Quoted in "DRC: MLC Still Hanging onto Two Positions," United Nations Integrated Regional Information Network, May 2, 2001, http://www.irinnews.org/report/20888/drc-mlc-still-hanging -onto-two-positions. The reason he mentions the Interahamwe—usually associated with the conflict in the Kivus—is that Kabila had deployed Hutu battalions in the Congolese Armed Forces to the Equateur front, where they were considered by the MLC as being Kinshasa's best soldiers. These Rwandan Hutu soldiers were mobilized by the Kabila regime, largely from UNHCR camps, in both the Congo and Congo-Brazzaville shortly after the second Congo war started.

34. United Nations Security Council Resolution 1304, S/RES/1304 (June 16, 2000). The Security Council also asked the Secretary-General "to submit an assessment of the damage as a basis for such reparations."

35. "DRC: Annan, Security Council Deplore ICRC Murders," United Nations Integrated Regional Information Network, April 30, 2001, http://www.irinnews.org /report/20854/drc-annan-security-council-deplore-icrc-murders.

36. The exception was Bemba's Congolese Liberation Front, the now defunct and short-lived Yoweri Museveni–initiated alliance between the MLC and the RCD-ML in North Kivu. United Nations Security Council, *Report of the Security Council Mission to the Great Lakes Region, 15–26 May 2001*, Addendum, UN Doc. S/2001/521/Add.1, Annex I, para. 4.

37. Ibid., Annex III, para. 11.

38. This process would be facilitated by a radio and print media information

campaign undertaken by "the UN, the OAU and the signatories" (paragraph 16) on the incentive packages for disarmament.

39. One point of controversy is that while some of the reports named and shamed such companies, others did not, under pressure of powerful Council members wishing to protect companies based in their countries and other actors implicated in those networks. In recent years, expert groups have also come under fire for their methodology.

40. United Nations Security Council, "Letter Dated 12 November 2012 from the Chair of the Security Council Committee Established Pursuant to Resolution 1533 (2004) Concerning the Democratic Republic of the Congo Addressed to the President of the Security Council," S/2012/843, 15 November 2012.

41. "Consolidating the Peace: Closing the M23 Chapter," paper prepared for the DRC Affinity Group (New York: Social Science Research Council, December 2014).

42. Victoria K. Holt and Glyn Taylor with Max Kelly, *Protecting Civilians in the Context of Peacekeeping* (Washington, DC: Stimson Center, 2009), www.stimson .org/books-reports/protecting-civilians-in-the-context-of-un-peacekeeping-operations.

43. Philip Alston, special rapporteur for human rights, on MONUC's Kimia II operations, which resulted in an estimated 1.7 million IDPs in the Kivus, and thousands killed. "UN Rights Official Denounces Drive Against Rebels in Congo," *Washington Post,* October 16, 2009, www.washingtonpost.com/wp-dyn/content /article/2009/10/15/AR2009101503635.html.

33

Côte d'Ivoire

Arthur Boutellis and Alexandra Novosseloff

THE INVOLVEMENT OF THE SECURITY COUNCIL IN CÔTE D'IVOIRE over a decade of mostly low-intensity conflict since the civil war erupted in 2002, and up until the 2011 post-election crisis, has been governed by several considerations and contradictions. First, one permanent member (France, the former colonial power) continuously pushed for the UN to get involved, while other permanent members with different priorities (the United States and the United Kingdom) were more reluctant. The phased UN involvement was also shaped by the growing—and sometimes contradictory or competing—role of subregional and regional organizations (the Economic Community of West African States [ECOWAS] and the African Union). Last, UN involvement was affected by doubts of parts of the UN Secretariat over the adequacy of the UN peacekeeping tool when dealing with limited host-government consent, but ultimately encouraged by robust action in defense of its mandate to protect civilians.

The Ivorian crisis has attracted significant attention from the international community, and over the years the Security Council has used almost all the tools at its disposal, including diplomatic engagement through support to regional mediations, the establishment of a field-based political mission (the UN Mission in Côte d'Ivoire [MINUCI]), the deployment and mandating of "impartial forces" (the UN Operation in Côte d'Ivoire [UNOCI] peacekeeping mission, and France's parallel Operation Licorne force), the imposition of an arms embargo and targeted sanctions against spoilers, the threat of international prosecutions by the International Criminal Court, as well as the establishment of a commission of inquiry into human rights abuses. The Council has also innovated by entrusting the UN

681

with a unique and controversial "election certification mandate," by endorsing the forced removal of Laurent Gbagbo under cover of a protection of civilians mandate, interpretation of which was influenced by the Responsibility to Protect (R2P) principle, and by authorizing inter-mission cooperation with the UN Mission in Liberia (UNMIL).

The main challenge for the Security Council in Côte d'Ivoire, however, has been to effectively enforce its resolutions with relatively little leverage over the host government and a defiant President Gbagbo, despite the presence of UN peacekeepers and French troops on the ground. In this sense, the Ivorian case puts into question the authority and credibility of the Security Council, but also its legitimacy when it is perceived that one of its permanent members, France, has used the body to "multilateralize" its own foreign policy. But the collective failure by the international community to move forward the political process also highlights the importance of a coherent and coordinated international effort by subregional, regional, and international actors for the Security Council to support. Ultimately, the Security Council ended the 2011 post-electoral crisis by endorsing the forceful diplomatic and military action by France as a last resort and with the tacit agreement of its subregional and regional partners. The Security Council has since refocused the mandate of its UN mission on the ground on supporting the new government, while looking for an exit strategy at a time when new crises in neighboring Mali and the Central African Republic call for attention (and resources).

The Subregion and France Lead; the Council Supports

The decade-long Ivorian crisis can be traced back to the failed military coup attempt of September 2002 against President Laurent Gbagbo by junior officers, which led to a de facto partition of the country and insurgent groups coalescing under the Forces Nouvelles, led by Guillaume Soro, gaining control of the northern 60 percent of the country. Neighboring countries, with a significant diaspora presence in Côte d'Ivoire, were the first to attempt to resolve the crisis by creating a Contact Group to lead mediation efforts under the banner of the Economic Community of West African States. ECOWAS also started planning for the deployment of a subregional peacekeeping force in December 2002.

Meanwhile, France, the former colonial power, had deployed a military operation, Licorne, days after the attempted coup, at the request of the Ivorian president. This effectively froze the conflict by creating a buffer zone between rebel-held north and the government-controlled south. Seeking Security Council support for its efforts, France started pushing for the body to get involved, after securing support from the United Kingdom and United States. And while the first official statement by the Council on the

Ivorian crisis expressed its strong support for ECOWAS mediation, it also commended France for the efforts it had made to contain fighting pending the planned deployment of an ECOWAS force, the capacities of which many doubted.[1]

France would soon also take a leadership role in the political process with the tacit agreement of a divided ECOWAS. Peace talks organized outside Paris led to the signing on January 24, 2003, of the Linas-Marcoussis comprehensive peace agreement, which established a transitional power-sharing government until the holding of presidential elections, initially scheduled for 2005. The Security Council subsequently authorized, in Resolution 1464 on February 4, 2003, the deployment under Chapter VII of the ECOWAS Mission in Côte d'Ivoire (ECOMICI), supported by France's Operation Licorne, to monitor the ceasefire and support the implementation of security aspects of the Linas-Marcoussis Agreement. After the signing of a complete ceasefire by the Ivorian armed forces and the Forces Nouvelles rebels throughout the entire territory, the Council decided in Resolution 1479, on May 13, 2003, on the addition of a small UN political presence (MINUCI) supported by a team of military liaison officers, to monitor implementation of the French-brokered agreement. Albert Tévoédjrè from Benin was appointed special representative of the Secretary-General and head of MINUCI, and chair of the Linas-Marcoussis Agreement monitoring committee.

The progressive shift in conflict resolution responsibilities from ECOWAS to France and on to the UN had started. In the face of costly military deployment and support to the ECOWAS force, and increasing anti-French mobilization by pro-Gbagbo partisans who opposed the Linas-Marcoussis Agreement, France started pushing for greater burden-sharing and the "multilateralization" of its involvement in Côte d'Ivoire through the world body. As France started to encourage a move toward a full-fledged UN peacekeeping operation, it initially faced some resistance from other Council members, including the budget-wary United States, which foresaw a more limited role for the UN in the crisis. Some of the African nonpermanent members of the Council were also concerned about the respect for host-government consent and continued to favor a regional approach.

The Council nevertheless renewed the mandate of ECOWAS and French forces for six months in August 2003,[2] and extended MINUCI until February 4, 2004.[3] It was only after the Council visited Côte d'Ivoire in July 2003, and an ECOWAS delegation traveled to New York in November to ask the Security Council to consider transforming the ECOWAS force into a UN peacekeeping force, that the French proposal would be seriously considered. This was "a clear recognition by the regional organization of its incapacity to sustain a fully-fledged and autonomous peacekeeping force in a large country such as Côte d'Ivoire where the proliferation of armed militias and re-arming of both governmental and rebel forces were not pointing to a quick resolution of the conflict."[4]

Rolling Out a UN Peacekeeping Mission and Parallel French Force

The Security Council unanimously decided on the establishment of a United Nations peacekeeping operation in Côte d'Ivoire, UNOCI, in April 2004, for an initial period of twelve months and with an initial maximum strength of 6,240 troops. This decision would make the UN the uncontested leading organization on the ground, taking over from ECOWAS troops and MINUCI, with a mandate to monitor the implementation of the comprehensive ceasefire agreement of May 3, 2003, and movements of armed groups; assist with disarmament, demobilization, reintegration, repatriation, and resettlement; protect civilians; support humanitarian assistance; and support the implementation of the peace process in cooperation with ECOWAS, including by preparing for "the conduct of free, fair and transparent electoral processes linked to the implementation of the Linas-Marcoussis Agreement, in particular the presidential election."[5]

The Council decided at the same time that France's Operation Licorne forces present in Côte d'Ivoire would be authorized to use all necessary means in order to support UNOCI in ensuring security in general and to intervene against belligerent actions if required. The two operations were thereafter referred to as "impartial forces." This original arrangement for an independent parallel force under a national flag and command but authorized by the Council was made possible by France's readiness to keep its troops on the ground to protect its nationals living in the country, and justified by the fact that the situation on the ground had not been fully stabilized.[6] Such a parallel security umbrella provided by French forces to a UN mission would later be reproduced in Mali following the January 2013 French military intervention Serval[7] and in the Central African Republic in December 2013 with Operation Sangaris under Resolution 2127.

Following a brief period of hope that the government of national reconciliation that came out of the Linas-Marcoussis Agreement could initiate the progressive reunification of the country, the political climate started to worsen, leading Forces Nouvelles leader Soro to suspend his group's participation in the government in February. The repression of an opposition demonstration by security forces on March 25, 2004, and a subsequent report by the UN high commissioner for human rights on the killing of at least 120 civilians during these events, led the Security Council to request the Secretary-General to establish an international commission of inquiry "in order to investigate all human rights violations committed in Côte d'Ivoire since September 19, 2002, and determine responsibility."[8] But this

2004 inquiry report would be kept secret up until the 2011 electoral crisis, due to "some domestic and international concerns at the time that its findings would derail peace negotiations."[9]

Tensions continued to rise despite the Accra III Agreement, of July 30, 2004, reaffirming the Linas-Marcoussis Agreement, and reached a new peak when Forces Nouvelles rebels did not meet the government-imposed deadline for disarming. On November 4, the Gbagbo-loyal armed forces of Côte d'Ivoire took the offensive and launched air strikes against Forces Nouvelles rebel positions in Bouaké and the northern town of Korhogo. Meanwhile in Abidjan, armed forces expelled Prime Minister Seydou Diarra of the national reconciliation government from his offices, and pro-Gbagbo youth groups, the Jeunes Patriotes, surrounded the Golf Hotel, where several Forces Nouvelles ministers were residing. Following the attacks, Soro declared Linas-Marcoussis and Accra III "null and void."

On November 6, 2004, one of the air strikes hit the French forces in Bouaké, killing nine French soldiers and one US citizen. France responded with a counter-raid rendering inoperable all planes and military helicopters used by the Ivorian armed forces. This marked an initial peak of the tensions between Gbagbo and France, which had started in September 2002 when France hesitated to intervene to halt the rebel advance on Abidjan at the request of the Ivorian government, based on the defense agreements. The French raid led to clashes between French forces and pro-Gbagbo troops and youth groups. Those incidents were followed by massive anti-French protests in Côte d'Ivoire, prompting an evacuation of foreign nationals and the temporary closing of several diplomatic missions.

Although the French military retaliation was criticized by some and presented by Gbagbo as evidence that the conflict was primarily a battle for the independence vis-à-vis its former colonial power, Security Council members expressed their unambiguous solidarity with France's Operation Licorne forces and condemned the violation of the ceasefire by government forces. Little by little, France had been able to forge a consensus on Côte d'Ivoire in the Council behind the peacekeeping operation, and to build a shared analysis of the crisis.

Arms Embargo and Sanctions, but Limited Compliance

The deterioration of the situation triggered a new set of more robust responses from the Security Council. While condemning the government's air strikes as "flagrant violations of the ceasefire agreement," the Council also imposed an arms embargo on the country, and created a regime of targeted sanctions (travel bans and asset freezes) against individuals who "block the implementation of the Linas-Marcoussis and Accra III Agreements, [and] any other person determined as responsible for serious violations of human rights and international humanitarian law in Côte d'Ivoire." Following the vote on Resolution 1572 of November 2004, China, France, and Angola took the floor to "deplore the impasse in the situation owing to the refusal by all the Ivorian parties to honor their own commitments."[10]

When the Council renewed the mandate of UNOCI in early 2005, it included the monitoring of the arms embargo in coordination with a group of experts it had created earlier to gather and analyze information on the implementation of the embargo.[11] It reported that despite the arms embargo, northern and southern Ivorian parties had begun to rearm and reequip themselves.[12] The Council also intended to keep its focus on the country by recommending two consecutive increases in the strength of the mission's military and police components, by a total of 1,875 troops and 1,200 civilian police personnel, respectively.[13]

But these sanctions and the increased attention of the Council constantly renewing and adapting the mandate of the mission on the ground did not have the desired impact on the so-called spoilers, nor did they really improve the precarious security situation in a context where the socioeconomic conditions of the broader population, particularly in the northern part of the country, continued to worsen. Meanwhile, there were continued "human rights abuses both in the south and in the north, with little or no effort being made to curtail the widespread culture of impunity."[14]

Furthermore, the impact of this intense and multifaceted Council activity (including a second visit to the country in June 2004) did not result in greater compliance by the parties.[15] Some UNOCI officials at the time attributed this to the fact that these decisions were not accompanied by necessary pressure on the parties to comply, and "expressed frustration at the wide gap between the numerous statements against impunity emanating from Council resolutions and presidential declarations and [the Council's] reluctance to take concrete action against the perpetrators of human rights violations and the political actors who encouraged them."[16]

Election Certification

The inability of the Council to shape the behavior of Ivorian authorities through successive resolutions opened the way for the return of the African Union, taking over from the failed ECOWAS and French political attempts to resolve the crisis, with South African president Thabo Mbeki as an emergency mediator. Under his auspices, the Ivorian parties signed a new agreement, in Pretoria in April 2005, calling upon the UN to play an enhanced role in the organization of the upcoming general elections.

Against this background, the Security Council therefore requested the designation by the Secretary-General of a high representative for the elections, autonomous from UNOCI (even if electoral advisers were deployed under the umbrella of the UN mission), who would assist the work of the independent electoral commission and of the constitutional council.[17] The high representative's technical mandate was "to verify all stages of the electoral process" and "to provide all the necessary guarantees for the holding of open, free, fair and transparent presidential and legislative elections within the time limits laid down in the Constitution of the Republic of Côte d'Ivoire" (by October 2005), with "all necessary advice and guidance" to "prevent and resolve any difficulty which may jeopardize the holding of" this electoral process. In short, Côte d'Ivoire "needed UN assistance and an election certification mechanism as a remedy to the total lack of confidence between the Ivorian parties."[18]

Antonio Monteiro of Portugal was appointed as high representative for the elections in July 2005, and replaced by Gérard Stoudmann of Switzerland in April 2006. Initially, this certification role was not supported by all Council members, but once established the Security Council counted on this mandate to give credibility to the electoral process and make Ivorian authorities accountable. Russia and China opposed a more intrusive role of the Council in Ivorian internal affairs that would have implied, for example, the designation of ministers.

When the constitutional term of President Gbagbo expired on October 30, 2005, no elections could yet be organized, mainly due to the delays in the establishment of the reconstituted independent electoral commission, the lack of agreement over a voter registry, and the volatility of the security situation. Therefore the Security Council, acting on a proposal from ECOWAS and a decision of the AU's Peace and Security Council, adopted Resolution 1633 to support the establishment of a ministerial-level international working group and a mediation group (cochaired by the SRSG) mandated "to draw up a road map . . . in consultation with all Ivorian parties, with a view to hold free, fair, open and transparent elections as soon as possible" (no later than October 31, 2006). But elections kept getting postponed, as President Gbagbo had little political interest in holding them, which led to rising tensions between the stakeholders of the Ivorian crisis and the international working group on the one hand, and President Gbagbo on the other, and to a new deterioration of the security situation.[19]

The Security Council nonetheless maintained pressure by giving greater powers to the prime minister and reinforcing the mandate of the high representative for the elections, in an attempt to curtail President Gbagbo's influence. In November 2006, in Resolution 1721, the high representative, "in full support of and in consultation with the Prime Minister," became the "sole authority authorized to arbitrate any problems or disputes related to the electoral process" and to "certify that all stages of the electoral process, including the process of identification of the population, the establishment of a register of voters and the issuance of voters' cards, [and to] provide all the necessary guarantees for the holding of open, free, fair and transparent presidential and legislative elections."

Defied by Gbagbo, the Council
Endorses the Ouagadougou Process

President Gbagbo, however, rejected this new resolution and instead proposed a direct dialogue with the Forces Nouvelles, under the exclusive facilitation of his former regional adversary, the president of neighboring Burkina Faso, Blaise Compaoré. This nationally owned political process led to the adoption of a new peace agreement—the eighth since 2002—the Ouagadougou peace agreement, signed on March 4, 2007. Guillaume Soro became prime minister under President Gbagbo.

Left with little choice, the Security Council endorsed the peace agreement in Resolution 1765 in July 2007.[20] This led to the abolition of the high representative for the elections, whose mandate was transferred to the SRSG after long debates with President Gbagbo, who considered that the role of the United Nations in the electoral process should be limited to observation and technical advice.[21] But the Security Council refused to relinquish the certification role of the UN. The Ouagadougou peace agreement immediately followed by Burkina Faso's 2008–2009 Security Council membership—with Burkina Faso de facto playing the role of co-penholder with France—nonetheless contributed to further marginalizing the Council in the Ivorian crisis and tempered its readiness to pressure President Gbagbo into the holding of elections.

As time passed, the continuous postponement of the presidential elections appeared unsustainable, even for Gbagbo. UNOCI had already completed the voter identification and registration operation by November 2009. In August 2010, Prime Minister Soro suddenly announced that the presidential elections would be held on October 31 (first round) and November 28 (second round), based on a proposal by the independent electoral commission. On September 9, a presidential decree authorized the issuance of national identity cards to the 5.7 million Ivorian on the final voter list, which was later certified by the SRSG.[22]

Gbagbo accepted the calendar, seemingly convinced by opinion polls that he would win. But his projections would turn out to be wrong: Gbagbo won the first round, but lost in the second due to an alliance between former president Aimé Henri Konan Bédié (who placed third in the first round)[23] and Alassane Ouattara.[24] The UN's certification role would bind all stakeholders to the election's result. The certification mandate was considered as "an additional safeguard to guarantee the credibility of the elections," through both the electoral process and the results of the poll: "candidates may ignore the conclusions of an observation mission, but it is more difficult to do so with a UN-led certification process."[25]

Divided over Management of the Post-Electoral Crisis

On December 2, 2010, the electoral commission announced Ouattara as the winner of the second round of the presidential elections, with 54.1 percent of the vote compared to Gbagbo's 45.9 percent. SRSG Choi Young-jin initially hesitated to make a pronouncement on the elections, fearing that direct involvement at an early stage would forfeit UNOCI impartiality and leverage, as well as jeopardize the safety of UN personnel. However, under significant diplomatic pressure particularly from France, the United States, and the United Kingdom during a closed meeting of the Council, the SRSG soon confirmed Ouattara as the winner of the presidential elections.[26]

The same day, the Security Council issued a press statement welcoming the announcement of the provisional results by the Ivorian electoral commission. But the president of the constitutional council—a largely pro-Gbagbo body—declared this announcement "to be null and void," and the following day declared what it claimed to be the final results of the presidential elections: Gbagbo 51.4 percent and Ouattara 48.5 percent. ECOWAS as well as the African Union, European Union, the International Organisation of La Francophonie, and the Carter Center had also declared Ouattara the winner of the elections. Nevertheless, on December 4, Gbagbo took an oath of office before the constitutional council in Abidjan, while Ouattara took his in writing from the Golf Hotel.

In the following month, none of the diplomatic and mediation efforts undertaken by African countries and organizations were able to overcome this impasse.[27] The stalemate was therefore complete: "Gbagbo [still] had power without legitimacy, while Ouattara had legitimacy without power."[28] What followed was a struggle between two sides mobilizing their support in the Security Council and in the subregional and regional organizations in the context of a constant worsening of the security situation in Abidjan. UNOCI forces were caught in the middle, trying to keep an untenable impartiality, since the mission's certification role and the decisions of the Council led it to protect the elected president and his government in the Golf Hotel.

Between December 2010 and April 2011, the Security Council was divided on the outcome of the election. The "legalists" (France, the United Kingdom, the United States, and Germany) wanted to stick to the letter of previous Council's resolutions and to the certification role of the SRSG. The "sovereignists" (Russia, South Africa, China, Brazil, and India) were not comfortable with what they considered an inappropriate pressuring of the SRSG by the P3 and an interference of the Council in Ivorian internal affairs, even more so after the intervention in Libya, and what could represent a "precedent" for international law.[29] Among the sovereignists, South Africa and Russia were the most vocal, but were never able to form a group strong enough for Russia to wield the veto, and managed only to delay the vote of some resolutions. In the end, the legalists prevailed over the sovereignists and all five Council resolutions of this period were adopted with a unanimous vote.

African nonpermanent members South Africa, Nigeria, and Gabon were also divided. On the one side, Nigeria, presiding over ECOWAS, led an unambiguously anti-Gbagbo front, and briefly contemplated a subregional military intervention together with Burkina Faso and Senegal. On the other side, South Africa, more favorable to the incumbent president, reengaged in the Ivorian crisis—and even deployed a navy ship off the coast of Côte d'Ivoire—in an attempt to assert its continental leadership and counter its Nigerian rival for a permanent Security Council seat.[30] The nomination of an AU high-level panel for the resolution of the crisis in Côte d'Ivoire was partly designed to reconcile these diverging African views. Instead, the successive AU representatives' visits to Abidjan did not convince the incumbent Gbagbo to leave power and contributed to sidelining ECOWAS in the process, leading to an official protestation by ECOWAS on February 22, 2011.[31]

These divisions between ECOWAS and the AU may have played in favor of the Council reasserting its role in the Ivorian crisis. On December 20, 2010, Resolution 1962 had "[urged] all the Ivorian parties and stakeholders to respect the will of the people and the outcome of the election in view of ECOWAS and the African Union's recognition of Ouattara as President-elect of Côte d'Ivoire." The legalists also prevailed in taking more coercive steps to weaken Gbagbo's regime. In addition to suspension from both the AU and ECOWAS, individual travel bans and asset freezes were implemented by the United States and European Union, and an embargo on cocoa and coffee exports was declared. These measures were in addition to existing UN sanctions that remained in effect,[32] but had a limited impact due to the ability of Gbagbo to secure other revenues from taxing the Abidjan port, nationalization of the cocoa and coffee industries, as well as funding that was made available from friendly African countries. The Council also threatened to refer Gbagbo to the International Criminal Court.[33]

In March 2011, the Human Rights Council decided "to dispatch an independent international commission of inquiry to investigate the facts and circumstances surrounding the allegations of serious abuses and violations of human rights committed in Côte d'Ivoire following the presidential elections" (with a death toll estimated to be at least 3,000). Its report was released in June 2011.[34] Interestingly, by then the Security Council had still not published the above-mentioned 2004 inquiry report on crimes committed between 2002 and 2004.

The Council was also able to strengthen the peacekeeping operation on the ground through the mechanism of intermission cooperation, authorizing temporary redeployments of troops and attack helicopters from UNMIL (Liberia) to UNOCI, and by again authorizing an increase in the authorized strength of military personnel by 2,000.[35]

Authorizing the "Impartial" Use of Force

Although the combined effect of sanctions, including the freezing of assets by the United States, European Union, and the ECOWAS central bank, progressively limited Gbagbo's ability to pay his security forces and civil servants, it did not prove decisive.[36] The security situation worsened, as government forces largely remained loyal to Gbagbo and started targeting civilians in Abidjan and other parts of the country. UNOCI headquarters and patrols were also targeted, with no unity among UNOCI leadership and troop-contributing countries on how to respond to these attacks by pro-Gbagbo forces. The "African voice" in the Security Council was split, with South Africa favoring a diplomatic solution to the crisis through the AU, and Nigeria initially seeming open to ECOWAS military action but unable to gather other countries of the region into a coalition that would intervene in Côte d'Ivoire, while itself preparing to hold its own presidential elections in April 2011.

The March 24, 2011, ECOWAS statement calling on the Security Council to reinforce the mandate of UNOCI to allow it to use all necessary means to protect people and to facilitate the immediate transfer of power to Alassane Ouattara confirmed that the subregion was not ready to intervene militarily, but also that it no longer believed in the AU's ability to resolve the crisis through political means, thus putting the responsibility squarely back on the Council to act.[37] In the Council, Russia and South Africa also joined the consensus.

Meanwhile, Ouattara issued a decree on March 17, 2011, creating the Republican Forces of Côte d'Ivoire (FRCI) to symbolically unify Forces Nouvelles ex-rebels and those members of the national armed forces who would side with Ouattara. These pro-Ouattara forces launched a military offensive on Yamoussoukro on March 28, committing violations against civilians along the way, and reaching Abidjan three days later, where they would be stopped. On April 9, Gbagbo-loyal forces managed to launch a counterattack on the Golf Hotel with mortars and heavy machine guns, which was successfully repelled.[38]

At that time, the Council had already strengthened the sanctions against Gbagbo's supporters and had authorized UNOCI "while impartially implementing its mandate, to use all necessary means . . . to prevent the use of heavy weapons against the civilian population."[39] As such, the UN peace-keepers protecting the Golf Hotel were not acting against Gbagbo's forces—and India, Brazil, and South Africa in particular were still not comfortable with UN forces "taking sides"—but preventively to protect civilians.[40]

On April 3, UN Secretary-General Ban Ki-moon wrote to French president Nicolas Sarkozy to request that French forces participate in strikes on sites of forces loyal to Gbagbo.[41] On April 4, he informed the Security Council that he had "instructed the Mission to take the necessary measures to prevent the use of heavy weapons against the civilian population, with the support of the French forces pursuant to paragraph 17 of Security Council resolution 1962."[42]

These provisions were used by UNOCI, in coordination with Operation Licorne, when "two UN MI24 helicopters [Ukrainian attack helicopters redeployed from UNMIL] swooped down along with French Puma and Gazelle attack helicopters target[ing] Gbagbo strongholds used to store heavy artillery and munitions" in areas around the presidential palace and residence, and several military camps.[43] It was politically important for both the French government and President Ouattara that the French intervention be perceived as being as legitimate as possible.

This use of force by UN peacekeepers and French troops was framed by the UN Secretariat and the Council alike in terms of self-defense (including the defense of the mandate) and the protection of civilians mandate of the mission, but the interpretation of this mandate was also influenced by the institutionalization of the R2P principle at the UN since 2005. Although the use of force in the Ivorian context was not as controversial as the multistate coalition military intervention in Libya—which had started on March 19 following Resolution 1973—Russia in particular argued that the use of UN helicopters exceeded the protection of civilians mandate set out in Resolution 1975.[44] Such military action would certainly not have been possible if not for the coinciding of ECOWAS, the African Union, France, and the United States in recognizing Ouattara as the de jure president, and also the presence of French troops on the ground in support of the UN mission.

On April 11, Gbagbo, his wife, and members of his family, staff, and cabinet were apprehended by the FRCI in the presidential residence. Gbagbo was then flown to The Hague to face international prosecution, thereby becoming the first former head of state to be taken into custody by the International Criminal Court. In a rare instance of the Security Council cooperating with the ICC, on November 29, 2011, the Côte d'Ivoire sanctions committee (a 1572 Committee) lifted the travel ban on former president Gbagbo to enable his transfer to The Hague.[45]

As stated by the Secretary-General, "The apprehension of former President Gbagbo closed a painful chapter in the history of Côte d'Ivoire."[46] It also inaugurated a new era for the UN presence in the country. But a decade after the beginning of UN involvement in the country, priorities remained much the same: economic recovery; reform of the security sector; disarmament, demobilization, and reintegration of an estimated 65,000 combatants; securing Abidjan and stabilizing the west and border areas; and national reconciliation. Most sanctions were lifted soon after President Ouattara was installed, and Resolution 2112 of July 30, 2013, changed the mandate of UNOCI to support the new government and empower the national authorities, while the forces of both the UN operation and France's Operation Licorne were downsized. However, in April 2015 the Security Council extended for another year a modified arms embargo on Côte d'Ivoire, as well as the targeted travel and financial sanctions on individuals deemed to threaten reconciliation in the country.

President Ouattara clearly saw an interest in peacekeeping troops remaining for some time to contribute to the stabilization efforts, particularly as he faced a series of attacks during the summer of 2012 targeting the FRCI. However, the nonmilitary role of the UN mission has been limited by his presidency's focus on economic recovery over political reconciliation.[47] In June 2014, the Security Council reduced UNOCI's military component by 1,700, to a strength of 5,437 by June 30, 2015, and the police component from 1,555 to 1,500, and extended its authorization of the deployment of French forces supporting UNOCI for one year. It was also contemplating a further downsizing of the UN mission, transitioning it to a peacebuilding office—following a similar path to those in Sierra Leone, Timor Leste, and Burundi—and possibly terminating it after the October 2015 presidential elections, in which Ouattara is expected to run again.

Conclusion

The case of Côte d'Ivoire illustrates the complexity for the Security Council of dealing with a country that is on the brink of civil war while needing to operate with the limited consent of a host government—and sometimes even defiance in the face of what is perceived as UN interference. This relationship was rendered all the more complex by the fact that the penholder and leading member of the Security Council on Côte d'Ivoire, France, was also the former colonial power, had deployed troops on the ground in parallel to the UN operation, and was perceived to have used the Council to "multilateralize" its own foreign policy at the risk of jeopardizing the authority and legitimacy of the world body, both of which are increasingly questioned on the African continent.

This limited consent of the host government, and limited ability of the Security Council to get the parties to comply with its many decisions, left the UN peacekeeping mission, UNOCI, and its successive leadership in a difficult situation. "Even if UNOCI was able to ensure overall stability in Côte d'Ivoire despite the recurrent phases of violence, it had no grip over the political actors of the crisis who instrumentalized the UN resolutions to their own ends."[48] In this political game, SRSGs often became scapegoats, caught between the need to obtain a minimum level of cooperation from host authorities for the UN mission to operate on the ground, and the necessity to implement difficult decisions by the Security Council, including the election certification mandate.

This unique election certification role initially generated controversy because the result of the elections led to a full-fledged crisis in which both parties resorted to force. However, certification allowed for early warning at different points in the process leading to the elections, and contributed to unifying a divided international community (ECOWAS, AU, EU, and the UN) around the election results, even though Council members themselves remained divided between legalists and sovereignists, some of whom may not have fully envisaged the implications of such a certification. Ultimately, it is unlikely that a host country, the UN Secretariat, or the Security Council will support such an election certification role again in the near future.

The Ivorian case also raises the issue of the use of force in defense of a protection of civilians mandate influenced by the R2P principle, in this case made possible by the presence (and availability) of French troops on the ground backed up by a politically robust Security Council. The joint UN-French military intervention following Resolution 1975 did not create as big and lasting a controversy as the simultaneous Libyan intervention, for a number of reasons. First, the use of force in Côte d'Ivoire was tactically limited in scale and framed as a direct response to Gbagbo using heavy weapons against civilians. Second, Ouattara being the legal president-elect, the removal of Gbagbo did not qualify as "regime change." Last but not least, the military intervention was swift and decisive, with limited collateral damage. This "successful" use of force in which UN peacekeepers were involved has likely contributed to increasing the willingness of Council members (but not of troop-contributing countries) to authorize the use of military force for protection purposes, even though they may continue to differ over the practical interpretation of such mandates and the need for peacekeepers to remain impartial and not take sides.

The decade-long Ivorian crisis more generally illustrates the importance of the unity of action among the Security Council, the UN Secretariat, and peacekeeping operations on the ground, especially in times of crisis. It also illustrates the importance of a coherent and coordinated international effort by subregional, regional, and international actors for the Security Council to support. While African continental rivalries between South Africa and Nigeria may have delayed the resolution of the final crisis, divisions between the AU and the subregional organization ECOWAS (repeated in following years in the Mali and Central African Republic cases) may have nonetheless played in favor of the Council reasserting its role in the Ivorian crisis and ultimately creating some level of unity behind its decision to forcefully remove Gbagbo. The four months it took for the Council to reach such a consensus, however, resulted in the deaths of 3,000 people. Ultimately, this outcome was the result of the collective failure to move forward the political process and to address the fundamental causes of the conflict throughout the decade-long crisis and prior to the holding of presidential elections, a failure that has left profound and enduring political, economic, and social scars.

Notes

1. United Nations Security Council, "Statement by the President of the Security Council," UN Doc. S/PRST/2002/42, December 20, 2002.

2. United Nations Security Council Resolution 1498, S/RES/1498 (August 4, 2003).

3. United Nations Security Council Resolution 1514, S/RES/1514 (November 13, 2003).

4. Fabienne Hara and Gilles Yabi, "Côte d'Ivoire, 2002–2011," in *Responding to Conflict in Africa: The United Nations and Regional Organizations,* edited by Jane Boulden (New York: Palgrave Macmillan, 2013), p. 145.

5. United Nations Security Council Resolution 1528, S/RES/1528 (February 27, 2004).

6. Under Resolution 1484 (S/RES/1484, May 30, 2003), the Council had already authorized a parallel force the year before in the Democratic Republic of the Congo, but the French-led Operation Artemis, an EU Interim Emergency Multinational Force (IEMF), was different in nature in that it was a short-term (three-month) force designed to restore security in the Ituri province while a larger UN force was being deployed.

7. United Nations Security Council Resolution 2100, S/RES/2100 (April 25, 2013).

8. United Nations Security Council, "Statement by the President of the Security Council," UN Doc. S/PRST/2004/17, May 25, 2004.

9. See Human Rights Watch, "Côte d'Ivoire: Act Swiftly on UN Inquiry," June 15, 2011, www.hrw.org/news/2011/06/15/cote-d-ivoire-act-swiftly-un-inquiry.

10. United Nations Security Council, "Statement by the President of the Security Council," UN Doc. S/PV.5078, November 15, 2004.

11. United Nations Security Council Resolution 1584, S/RES/1584 (February 1, 2005).

12. See United Nations Security Council, *Final Report of the Group of Experts Submitted in Accordance with Paragraph 11 of Security Council Resolution 1842 (2008),* UN Doc. S/2009/521, October 9, 2009.

13. United Nations Security Council Resolutions 1609, S/RES/1609 (June 24, 2005); and 1682, S/RES/1682 (June 2, 2006).

14. United Nations Security Council, *Fourth Progress Report of the Secretary-General on the United Nations Operation in Côte d'Ivoire,* UN Doc. S/2005/186, March 18, 2005, para. 80.

15. For an analysis of the various UNSC resolutions throughout the peace process and their implementation, see Gilles Yabi, "Côte d'Ivoire," in *Security Council Resolutions Under Chapter VII: Design, Implementation, and Accountabilities—The Cases of Afghanistan, Côte d'Ivoire, Kosovo, and Sierra Leone,* edited by Blanca Antonini (Madrid: FRIDE, 2009).

16. Yabi, "Côte d'Ivoire," p. 98.

17. United Nations Security Council Resolution 1603, S/RES/1603 (June 3, 2005).

18. Yabi, "Côte d'Ivoire," p. 104.

19. According to the Secretary-General, "The rampant insecurity in Abidjan is linked to the possibility of violent street demonstrations and mob violence, organized crime, extortion and racketeering activities. . . . In the western part of the country, widespread incidents of targeted ethnic killings, perpetrated mainly by militia groups, continued to be reported." United Nations Security Council, *Seventh Progress Report of the Secretary-General on the United Nations Operation in Côte d'Ivoire,* UN Doc. S/2006/2, January 3, 2006.

20. For the Secretary-General, "the agreement will be judged by the political will of the parties to implement it. The agreement also carries special significance, because it was drawn up by the Ivorian leaders themselves, which places on them a special responsibility to implement it in full." United Nations Security Council, *Twelfth Progress Report of the Secretary-General on the United Nations Operation in Côte d'Ivoire,* UN Doc. S/2007/133, March 8, 2007, para. 59.

21. See all the elements of that debate and of the negotiations between the Ivorian and UN authorities in United Nations Security Council, *Thirteenth Progress Report of the Secretary-General on the United Nations Operation in Côte d'Ivoire,* UN Doc. S/2007/275, May 14, 2007, paras. 31–33.

22. See United Nations Security Council, *Progress Report of the Secretary-General on the United Nations Operation in Côte d'Ivoire,* UN Doc. S/2010/537, October 18, 2010, paras. 2–21.

23. Bédié, formerly president of the country's national assembly, became president of Côte d'Ivoire after the death of Félix Houphouët-Boigny in 1993, and remained in office until 1999, when he was deposed by the military coup of General Guei. As a member of the constitutional council, Bédié ran in the 2010 presidential elections, winning 25.2 percent of the vote in the first round.

24. An economist by profession, Ouattara worked for the International Monetary Fund and the Central Bank of West African States. He was the prime minister of Côte d'Ivoire from November 1990 to December 1993 under President Houphouët-Boigny. Ouattara became the president of the Rally of the Republicans (RDR), an Ivorian political party, in 1999.

25. Lori-Anne Théroux-Bénoni, *Lessons for UN Electoral Certification from the 2010 Disputed Presidential Poll in Côte d'Ivoire,* Policy Brief no. 1 (Waterloo: Centre for International Governance Innovation, June 2012), p. 3.

26. The UNOCI certification cell reviewed the voter tally sheets and calculated that Ouattara would have still won with a majority of votes even with the most favorable view on the complaints made by pro-Gbagbo supporters, particularly with respect to unsigned tally sheets. See Hara and Yabi, "Responding to the Conflict in Côte d'Ivoire."

27. See United Nations Security Council, *Twenty-Seventh Progress Report of the Secretary-General on the United Nations Operation in Côte d'Ivoire,* UN Doc. S/2011/211, March 30, 2011, paras. 25–38.

28. Adekeye Adebajo, *UN Peacekeeping in Africa: From the Suez Crisis to the Sudan Conflicts* (Boulder, CO: Lynne Rienner, 2011), p. 159.

29. "Moscou et Pékin Contraignent l'ONU à Ajourner un Texte sur la Côte d'Ivoire," *Le Monde,* January 15, 2011; Security Council Report, "Update Report no. 2: Côte d'Ivoire," December 7, 2010, www.securitycouncilreport.org/update -report/lookup-c-glKWLeMTIsG-b-6433491.php.

30. For a detailed account of the roles played by Angola, South Africa, and ECOWAS member countries in the current Ivorian crisis, refer to International Crisis Group, *Côte d'Ivoire: Faut-il se Résoudre à la Guerre?* Africa Report no. 171 (Brussels, 2011), p. 12.

31. CEDEAO ECOWAS, "The Absence of the ECOWAS Delegation on the African Union High-Level Panel Mission to Côte d'Ivoire," press release, February 21, 2011.

32. See the following press releases of the Council of the European Union: "Côte d'Ivoire: Council Adopts Visa Ban List," December 22, 2010; "Côte d'Ivoire: Council Extends Visa Ban List," December 31, 2010; and "Côte d'Ivoire: Council Adopts Assets Freeze and Designates Additional Persons and Entities Subject to Restrictive Measures," January 14, 2011. See also United Nations Security Council Resolutions 1572, S/RES/1572 (November 15, 2004); 1643, S/RES/1643 (December 15, 2005); and 1946, S/RES/1946 (October 15, 2010).

33. Even though Côte d'Ivoire is not party to the Rome Statute, the situation in Côte d'Ivoire has been under preliminary examination by the ICC Office of the Prosecutor since the receipt on October 1, 2003, of a declaration from the government of Côte d'Ivoire, dated April 18, 2003, by which it accepted the exercise of jurisdiction by the Court in accordance with Article 12(3) of the Rome Statute. See ICC, "Situation in the Republic of Côte d'Ivoire," June 23, 2011, http://www.icc -cpi.int/iccdocs/doc/doc1097345.pdf. Then, Security Council Resolution 1975 recalled: "*Considering* that the attacks currently taking place in Côte d'Ivoire against the civilian population could amount to crimes against humanity and that perpetrators of such crimes must be held accountable under international law and noting that the International Criminal Court may decide on its jurisdiction over the situation in Côte d'Ivoire on the basis of article 12, paragraph 3 of the Rome Statute" S/RES/1975 (March 30, 2011) (original emphasis).

34. United Nations General Assembly, Human Rights Council, *Report of the Independent, International Commission of Inquiry on Côte d'Ivoire,* UN Doc. A/HRC/17/48, June 6, 2011: "The commission concludes that during the period under consideration, many serious violations of human rights and international humanitarian law were perpetrated by different parties: some might amount to crimes against humanity and war crimes. They were perpetrated by the defence and security forces and their allies (militias and mercenaries) and later, during their counteroffensive and once they had taken control of the country, by the Forces Républicaines de Côte d'Ivoire (FRCI). The many victims in the west, the southwest and Abidjan are paying a heavy penalty."

35. United Nations Security Council Resolutions 1951, S/RES/1951 (November 24, 2010); 1962, S/RES/1962 (December 20, 2010); and 1967, S/RES/1967 (January 19, 2011).

36. Arthur Boutellis, *The Security Sector in Côte d'Ivoire: A Source of Conflict and a Key to Peace* (New York: International Peace Institute, May 2011).

37. CEDEAO ECOWAS, "The Absence of the ECOWAS Delegation."

38. United Nations Security Council, *Twenty-Eighth report of the Secretary-General on the United Nations Operation in Côte d'Ivoire,* UN Doc. S/2011/387, June 24, 2011, para. 6.

39. United Nations Security Council Resolution 1975, S/RES/1975 (March 30, 2011). The draft resolution had been presented jointly by France and Nigeria.

40. United Nations Security Council, "Provisional Verbatim Record of the 6508th Meeting," UN Doc. S/PV.6508, March 30, 2011. For India, "United Nations peacekeepers . . . cannot be made instruments of regime change. Accordingly, UNOCI should not become a party to the Ivorian political stalemate." For China, "peacekeeping operations should strictly abide by the principle of neutrality."

41. "Anatomy of an Intervention: Why France Joined the U.N. Action in Abidjan," *Time Magazine,* April 6, 2011.

42. United Nations Security Council, "Letter Dated 4 April from the Secretary-General Addressed to the President of the Security Council," UN Doc. S/2011/221, April 5, 2011.

43. Ibid.

44. Alex J. Bellamy and Paul D. Williams, "The New Politics of Protection? Côte d'Ivoire, Libya, and the Responsibility to Protect," *International Affairs* 87, no. 4 (2011): 825–850.

45. Security Council Report, "Chronology of Events: Côte d'Ivoire," www .securitycouncilreport.org/chronology/cote-divoire.php.

46. United Nations Security Council, *Twenty-Eighth Report of the Secretary-General on the United Nations Operation in Côte d'Ivoire,* para. 78.

47. Arthur Boutellis, "Côte d'Ivoire's Ouattara Puts Economic Recovery Ahead of Political Reconciliation," *World Politics Review,* March 19, 2013.

48. Alexandra Novosseloff, "United Nations Operation in Côte d'Ivoire (UNOCI)," in *Oxford Handbook on UN Peacekeeping Operations,* edited by Joachim A. Koops, Thierry Tardy, Norrie MacQueen, and Paul D. Williams (Oxford: Oxford University Press, 2015).

34

Libya

Alex J. Bellamy and Paul D. Williams

ON MARCH 19, 2011, MILITARY FORCES FROM FRANCE, CANADA, the United Kingdom, and the United States struck the air defenses and soldiers of Muammar Qaddafi's regime in Libya. These countries led a wider coalition of states with the stated aim of enforcing the objectives set out by Security Council Resolution 1973, principally the enforcement of a no-fly zone over Libya, imposition of an arms embargo, and the protection of civilians. On March 31, NATO assumed full control of military operations under what was now called Operation Unified Protector. Not all NATO members participated—Poland and Germany were notably absent—but several others, including Sweden, Jordan, Qatar, and the United Arab Emirates, joined the alliance.[1] NATO-led operations prevented the fall of the rebel stronghold of Benghazi and a widely anticipated massacre, and after a period in which the frontline moved backward and forward with alarming rapidity the conflict settled into a period of stalemate. NATO and its allies continued to use force against Libyan targets, including command-and-control facilities, and on August 19 forces loyal to the rebel National Transitional Council (NTC) stormed Tripoli and the city was taken in the space of a week. Fighting continued around government strongholds until October, when the town of Sirte fell to rebel forces and Qaddafi himself was captured and executed.

The UN Security Council's response to the Libyan crisis in 2011 was significant for a number of reasons. Most notably, Resolution 1973 (March 17, 2011) was the Council's first to mandate the use of military force against the de jure authorities of a UN member state for the purpose of human protection. Although the Council had come close in the past—in

Somalia (1992) and Rwanda (1994)—it had never before crossed the line. It was also, as Tom Malinowski, Washington, D.C., director of Human Rights Watch, wrote, "the most rapid multinational military response to an impending human rights crisis in history."[2]

Even prior to the use of force, the Council's willingness to quickly apply a raft of measures short of military force to coerce the Libyan authorities into changing course was remarkable. Resolution 1970 (February 26, 2011) imposed targeted financial sanctions and an arms embargo, referred the situation to the International Criminal Court, mandated diplomacy, and demanded a peaceful resolution. In doing so, the Council utilized almost the whole of its "preventive toolkit."[3]

Finally, because the Council referred to the Responsibility to Protect (R2P) principle in four of its resolutions on Libya—1970 (2011), 1973 (2011), 2016 (2011), 2040 (2012)—its response to the situation there has unsurprisingly been characterized as a key test of this principle. For some of the principle's most prominent supporters, such as Gareth Evans, Resolutions 1970 and 1973 represented "a textbook example of how R2P is supposed to work in the face of a rapidly unfolding mass atrocity situation."[4]

However, controversy surrounded the implementation of Resolution 1973, stemming from the widely held view that the actions of NATO and its allies exceeded the terms of the resolution. Key in this regard were the coalition's pursuit of regime change despite the absence of a specific mandate to that effect; the supply of arms to rebel groups potentially in contravention of the Council's arms embargo; NATO's unwillingness to countenance a negotiated settlement; NATO's decision to continue using force after the fall of Tripoli; and its contribution to Qaddafi's untimely demise. These concerns prompted criticism from some Council members, including two permanent members (China and Russia) and several significant emerging powers, who sat on the Council at the time, notably Brazil, India, and South Africa. These concerns also reawakened the lingering suspicions of states that were worried about R2P's potential to legitimize forcible "regime change and gave rise to the Brazilian concept of 'responsibility while protecting' (RWP)." Some commentators have also argued that the Council's inability to reach a consensus on Syria was effectively "collateral damage" from Libya.[5]

In this chapter we explain why the Council adopted its unprecedented approach and offer an initial sketch of the longer-term effects of Resolution 1973 and its implementation. First, we summarize the Council's response to the Libyan crisis in early 2011. Second, we explain how the Council authorized this unprecedented use of military force against the will of the de jure authorities in Libya. And third, we analyze the implementation of Resolution 1973 and its wider effects.

Getting to Resolution 1973

Resolution 1973 has its origins in the political upheavals associated with the protests across the Arab world that spread in 2011 from Tunisia to Egypt and beyond. In Libya the protests, which started on February 17, 2011, quickly turned violent, partly because of the regime's crackdown and partly because an armed opposition group was quickly established under the interim National Transitional Council. The NTC coalesced around a mixture of Libyan diplomats who publicly denounced the Qaddafi regime from their posts abroad and switched their allegiance, segments of the armed forces who had also defected, and leaders of the opposition within Libya, particularly those in Benghazi. While the NTC enjoyed rapid successes in mid-February 2011, declaring that its forces had taken control of most of the major cities, in late February and early March Qaddafi's forces tipped the balance back in their own favor and by mid-March were threatening to crush the rebellion's eastern epicenter in Benghazi.

The first sign that the international response would be unusual came on February 22, when the League of Arab States—which now, crucially, included post-revolution authorities from Egypt and Tunisia—suspended Libya's participation. On February 23, the African Union's Peace and Security Council, of which Libya was a member, condemned "the indiscriminate and excessive use of force and lethal weapons against peaceful protestors" in Libya.[6] Two days later, on February 25, the UN Human Rights Council established a commission of inquiry to investigate the situation and urged the General Assembly to suspend Libya from the Human Rights Council—which it duly did on March 1.

On February 26, the Security Council voted unanimously to pass Resolution 1970. Among other things, this condemned "the widespread and systematic attacks" against civilians, which the Council suspected "may amount to crimes against humanity"; welcomed the earlier criticisms of the Libyan government's actions by the Arab League, the AU, and the Organization of the Islamic Conference (OIC); and underlined the Libyan government's responsibility to protect its population. Acting under Chapter VII of the UN Charter, the Council demanded an immediate end to the violence, urged Qaddafi's government to ensure safe passage for humanitarian and medical supplies, referred the situation in Libya since February 15 to the prosecutor of the International Criminal Court,[7] established an arms embargo on the country, imposed travel bans on sixteen individuals of the Libyan regime, froze the assets of six members of the ruling regime; established a sanctions committee to monitor the implementation of these measures, and called upon UN member states to make available humanitarian and related assistance for Libya.

Resolution 1973 was agreed after a week of frantic diplomacy. It started on March 7, when the Gulf Cooperation Council (GCC) called on "the UN Security Council [to] take all necessary measures to protect civilians, including enforcing a no-fly zone over Libya" and condemned "crimes committed against civilians, the use of heavy arms and the recruitment of mercenaries" by the Libyan regime.[8] That same day, the Libyan mission to the UN in New York—many of whose members had by now defected from Qaddafi's regime—urged UN member states to recognize the NTC as Libya's legitimate authority. At this stage, UN Secretary-General Ban Ki-moon appointed former Jordanian foreign minister Abdelilah al-Khatib as his special envoy to Libya, and UN Security Council members held informal consultations about possible further measures against Libya, including the option of a no-fly zone.[9]

On March 8, the OIC echoed the GCC position by calling for a no-fly zone over Libya, while excluding foreign military operations on the ground.[10] On March 10, the GCC claimed that Qaddafi's regime had lost all legitimacy and urged the Arab League to initiate contact with the NTC. That same day, France, Italy, and EU high representative for foreign affairs Catherine Ashton also opened dialogue with the NTC.

In Addis Ababa, however, the AU's Peace and Security Council was rather less generous to the NTC. Although it called the situation in Libya "a serious threat to peace and security," the AU condemned "the indiscriminate use of force and lethal weapons . . . and the transformation of pacific demonstrations into an armed rebellion."[11] It went on to emphasize its "strong commitment to the respect of the unity and territorial integrity of Libya, as well as its rejection of any foreign military intervention, whatever its form."[12]

On the diplomatic front, Qaddafi's regime rejected the demands set out in Security Council Resolution 1970 and refused to permit humanitarian aid convoys into besieged towns such as Misrata and Ajdabiya. Secretary-General Ban personally contacted the Libyan leader and in a forty-minute conversation tried—but failed—to persuade Qaddafi to comply with the Council's demands. Thus, while the search for a diplomatic solution through the UN special envoy and the AU high-level committee enjoyed widespread support, many governments, commentators, and UN officials alike were coming to the view that diplomacy alone would not prevent a massacre should Benghazi fall.

It was the March 12 declaration by the Arab League, however, that proved the game-changer. Among other things, the League called for the UN Security Council to impose a no-fly zone and establish safe havens.[13] In the transatlantic region, Britain and France led the call for a tougher international response. Britain and France joined with Lebanon to propose a draft resolution authorizing the imposition of a no-fly zone. The draft was, however, viewed skeptically by several states, including Germany and Russia, the latter of whose foreign minister, Sergei Lavrov, declared that military intervention would be "unacceptable"—though he clarified that Russia would "closely study" any such proposals.[14] The Barack Obama administration was also, at best, uncommitted. Lacking instructions from Washington, on March 15 the US permanent representative to the UN, Susan Rice, reportedly told her French counterpart that "you're not going to drag us into your shitty war."[15] Without a change of heart in the White House and Kremlin, the prospect of military action appeared very slim. That change of heart came later that very same day.

Inside the Obama administration, the Arab League statement and impending rebel defeat in Benghazi strengthened the interventionists' hand.[16] A few hours after Rice's rebuke to the French on March 15, senior officials held two "extremely contentious" meetings that resulted in President Obama accepting the case for intervention argued by Secretary of State Hillary Clinton and senior National Security Council staffer Samantha Power over the more cautious position expressed by Defense Secretary Robert Gates and National Security Adviser Tom Donilon.[17] Clinton and Power argued that Qaddafi's forces were close to seizing Benghazi and that a massacre was likely. Advised that the no-fly zone proposed by the French, British, and Lebanese would not prevent Benghazi's fall, the US president demanded and was presented with the option of a broader mandate to use force to protect civilians, which Obama instructed Rice to pursue in the Council. US diplomats then modified the language of the proposed resolution and brought significant diplomatic pressure to bear on wavering Council members.[18] Russia was apparently the first target of intense US telephone diplomacy, its acquiescence being necessary to set up the vote in the Security Council; South Africa's support was reportedly courted until the vote itself.[19]

It was in this context that Security Council members debated whether to authorize the use of force to establish a no-fly zone and protect civilians.[20] One of the central arguments made in the Council, and outside, was that the situation in Libya was both an ongoing threat to international peace and security and a humanitarian crisis that was likely to become significantly worse without urgent and decisive action. From this perspective, Qaddafi's description of the protesters as "cockroaches," his promise to "cleanse Libya house by house," and his threat to attack Benghazi and show its residents "no mercy," provided evidence of the regime's intent to commit mass atrocities.

Within an unusually "heavyweight" Security Council, including Brazil, Germany, India, and South Africa as nonpermanent members, there were a number of sticking points. The rationales offered by the skeptics were in part principled. China, for instance, deferred to its long-established "Five

Principles of Peaceful Coexistence" foreign policy, which include the nonuse of force, and Brazil was intuitively cautious about US intentions.[21] China, Russia, and India also raised procedural and pragmatic questions that were left unanswered in Resolution 1973: How would the no-fly zone be enforced? What assets would be used? What rules of engagement would the coalition adopt? And crucially, what might the end game entail? The Russian delegation also complained about the new provisions providing a wider mandate to use force to protect civilians, which had been added to the original text proposed by France, the UK, and Lebanon, that went beyond the no-fly zone requested by the Arab League. India also questioned the timing of the decision to use force before the UN special envoy had delivered his report to the Council. Brazil questioned whether the use of military force by external actors would change the homegrown nature of the rebellion and thereby inhibit long-term conflict resolution. With a highly skeptical domestic audience, South Africa was also deeply concerned about the use of force.

The skeptics were left with little diplomatic room for maneuver, however, since the Council had accepted the legitimacy of international engagement by unanimously adopting Resolution 1970, and was confronted with advice from the UN Secretariat and elsewhere that mass atrocities were imminent. Hence when Russia circulated a draft resolution calling for political dialogue, this secured little support, in part because it seemed dangerously out-of-step with the rapidly evolving situation on the ground and in part because of the momentum that had built up around the revised draft circulated by France, Britain, and Lebanon.[22]

The vote on March 17 saw Resolution 1973 pass with ten votes in favor (Bosnia and Herzegovina, Colombia, France, Gabon, Lebanon, Portugal, Nigeria, South Africa, the United Kingdom, and the United States), zero votes against, and five abstentions (Brazil, China, Germany, India, and Russia). The Council, in its eight-page resolution, defined the situation in Libya as a threat to international peace and security and, acting under Chapter VII of the UN Charter, demanded, among other things, an immediate ceasefire and intensified efforts to find a political solution to the crisis. The Council authorized the use of "all necessary measures . . . to protect civilians and civilian populated areas under threat of attack . . . while excluding a foreign occupation force of any form on any part of Libyan territory." It also established "a ban on all flights in the airspace of the Libyan Arab Jamahiriya in order to help protect civilians," except those flights necessary to enforce the no-fly zone and those flights "whose sole purpose is humanitarian," and also refined the arms embargo and asset freeze detailed in Resolution 1970 by creating a panel of experts to review implementation.

Explaining Resolution 1973

Although the decision to authorize the use of military force to protect civilians in Libya was driven, in large part, by factors specific to the case (and thus not likely to be often repeated), it was made possible by a deeper and more long-term transformation in the Council's attitude toward civilian protection. Until the late 1990s and early 2000s, human protection was not widely regarded as a core function of the Security Council, but global expectations about the UN's role in civilian protection have grown to such an extent that it is now commonly thought that the UN's legitimacy is determined by its performance in this area.[23]

Starting late, the Council moved rapidly to embrace civilian protection. This coincided with the adoption of the R2P principle by the General Assembly in 2005, and the Security Council's reaffirmation of this principle in Resolutions 1674 (2006) and 1894 (2009), and its application in relation to situations in Africa's Great Lakes region (Resolution 1653 [2006]), Darfur (Resolution 1706 [2006]), Libya (Resolutions 1970 and 1973 [2011]), Côte d'Ivoire (Resolution 1975 [2011]), South Sudan (Resolution 1996 [2011]), Yemen (Resolution 2014 [2011]), and Mali (Resolutions 2085 [2012] and 2100 [2013]). From hesitant beginnings in Sierra Leone and the DRC, the Council has gradually moved civilian protection to the center of UN peacekeeping, granting protection mandates to a majority of its peacekeeping operations. These mandates were established under Chapter VII of the Charter and permit the use of "all necessary measures" to protect civilians, albeit with some caveats. This trend accelerated markedly in early 2011. Since then, the Council has authorized the use of military force to protect populations in Côte d'Ivoire, mandated a UN mission to assist the government of Mali (MINUSMA) to protect the population from Tuareg/Islamist militias, and established an intervention brigade authorized to use force against militias as part of the UN stabilization mission in the DRC (MONUSCO).

This represents a profound transformation in the Council's underlying attitude toward civilian protection. Of the major protection crises of the past decade, only Sri Lanka (2009) did not make it onto the Council's formal agenda, though the Council did receive informal briefings. However, most of these mandates placed geographical, material, and political limits on the use of military force for civilian protection purposes. Key among them is that UN peacekeepers and its humanitarian and development agencies are charged with *assisting* host states to protect populations and operating with their consent.

Thus, while the transformation of the Council's attitude toward civilian protection is significant, this did not mean it was a foregone conclusion that the Council would cross the Rubicon over Libya by authorizing force for protection purposes against the regime's wishes. The fragile consensus on Resolution 1973 was made possible by at least four additional factors that were specific to the Libyan case.

First, the situation on the ground presented the Council with an unusually clear threat of atrocity crimes facing Benghazi, an absence of plausible alternatives to the use of force, and a seemingly credible military option. Together, these factors created a degree of "normative capture" in which Council members that had committed themselves to R2P (in 2005, and in subsequent Council resolutions), but that were generally skeptical of military intervention, could not find plausible arguments to legitimize opposition to Resolution 1973 and therefore decided to abstain instead. One of the reasons why Russia abstained on Resolution 1973 was that it did not want to be held responsible for blocking intervention if massacres were then perpetrated.[24]

Not since Rwanda's 1994 genocide has a regime so clearly signaled its intent to commit crimes against humanity. As noted earlier, with direct echoes of Rwanda, Qaddafi told the world that "officers have been deployed in all tribes and regions so that they can purify all decisions from these cockroaches," and that "any Libyan who takes arms against Libya will be executed." It is far more usual for regimes bent on mass atrocities to try to hide their intentions. With the rebel stronghold of Benghazi set to fall to a regime with an appalling human rights record and a long history of using force to repress its citizens, with that regime openly pronouncing its determination to execute its opponents, and with Qaddafi unwilling to respond positively to diplomatic entreaties, Council members who were opposed to, or cautious about, the use of force were unable to offer a compelling alternative strategy for protecting vulnerable populations.

The apparent lack of viable options was evident in the statements of several Council members who abstained on Resolution 1973. Brazil, for example, noted that its abstention "should in no way be interpreted as condoning the behaviour of the Libyan authorities or as disregard for the need to protect civilians and respect their rights." However, its representative remained unconvinced "that the use of force as provided for in paragraph 4 of the resolution will lead to the realization of our common objective—the immediate end to violence and the protection of civilians." Russia also claimed that it was a "consistent and firm" advocate of the "basic principle" of protecting civilians and stressed that it "did not prevent the adoption of this resolution." However, it judged that "the quickest way to ensure robust security for the civilian population and the long-term stabilization of the situation in Libya is an immediate ceasefire." Finally, China emphasized that it supported "the Security Council's adoption of appropriate and necessary action to stabilize the situation in Libya as soon as possible and to halt acts of violence against civilians," but that it was "always against the use of force in international relations."[25] Each of these statements exhibited wariness about the use of force, but these countries concluded that, on balance, this was better registered via an abstention than a negative vote.

The second factor was that the timeframe for decisionmaking was extremely short. At the time violence broke out in February 2011, none of the world's various risk-assessment frameworks had viewed Libya as posing any sort of threat of mass atrocities. Neither was an armed conflict widely anticipated. For example, CrisisWatch, the early-warning arm of the International Crisis Group, did not even mention Libya in its February report and did not issue a "conflict risk alert" until after armed conflict had actually erupted. The rapidity of rebel gains and subsequent losses, which left the stronghold of Benghazi vulnerable to Qaddafi's forces and their promised retribution, left little time to try either the new round of mediation proposed by Russia or the more graduated response preferred by some UN officials.[26] Decisionmaking was so rapid that the United States went from opposing a no-fly zone to advocating a wider mandate to use force within the space of thirty-six hours, and in more or less the same timeframe Russia went from declaring that it would not contemplate a no-fly zone to acquiescing in this much wider authorization to use force. Germany's decision to abstain—the first time ever the country voted alongside Russia and China against its three Western allies in the Council—was the result of a combination of domestic politics, fear of being drawn into a protracted military intervention, and Berlin's difficulty to keep pace with Washington's volte-face.[27]

The Council's first resolution on Libya, Resolution 1970, bundled together a variety of punitive, coercive, and diplomatic measures when slower-moving events might have facilitated a more graduated approach to coercive inducement. At the time Resolution 1973 was presented to the Council, the fall of Benghazi was said to be days, if not hours, away. Among other things, this short window of opportunity limited the search for alternatives to the use of force and prevented the entrenchment of postures and positions. In the immediate run-up to Resolution 1973, the main diplomatic alternative was the African Union's "road map" to peace, which was being pushed by a high-level committee including the presidents of Mauritania, Congo, Mali, South Africa, and Uganda.[28]

The third reason Libya was exceptional was the role played by regional organizations. Qaddafi's regime had few reliable friends in the region, and it was the calls for a no-fly zone by the Arab League, OIC, and GCC that proved to be the diplomatic game-changer. Without the backing of these organizations, it is unlikely that the United States would have thrown its weight behind the use of force and very likely that China and Russia would have vetoed any draft resolution (such as the original text on the no-fly zone by France, the UK, and Lebanon) that countenanced force. Among the reasons for the adoption of these positions were Qaddafi's unpopularity, the influence of the pro-US Gulf Cooperation Council, and the fact that many key Arab League members were not present when it voted on the no-fly zone. These factors were probably just as important as any feelings of humanitarian solidarity generated in part by the interrelated nature of the Arab Spring uprising in early 2011.[29]

One curiosity of the Libya case was that the Security Council preferred the views of the Arab League, GCC, and OIC over those of the African Union, of which Libya was also a member. To the extent that the AU was able to find a common position on the situation, it was more reticent about the use of force and more concerned from the outset about the potential for regime change.[30] This was in part because Libya was one of the organization's principal donors and in part because Article 30 of the AU's Constitutive Act prohibits those that come to power through unconstitutional means from participating in the work of the African Union. Originally intended to deter coups, this principle also condemns foreign-imposed regime change. Had China and Russia paid more attention to the AU's position on Libya, they may have found grounds for justifying a veto of Resolution 1973. As a result, future Council members may be more likely to go "forum-shopping" to find regional arrangements whose position reflects, and hence legitimizes, their own.

Fourth, with a few exceptions, the Qaddafi regime was isolated and devoid of friends, including among the permanent members of the Security Council. Few if any states thus had an interest in protecting the Libyan regime. Even those African states that were more sympathetic to Qaddafi did not come to his aid.[31] Indeed, most African states were happy to see Qaddafi gone, not least because of his long history of interfering in the affairs of neighboring states and backing armed groups in a variety of theaters, including Liberia, Sierra Leone, Sudan, and Mali.[32] Although a major financial contributor to the AU, Qaddafi's proclivity to use force to undermine other African leaders and his often condescending approach to fellow heads of state left the regime with few friends. Likewise, Libya had few close allies in the Middle East: Qaddafi had personally offended many leaders at one point or another, and his erratic policies on Palestine and attempts to assert his primacy among leaders had alienated many countries in the region. Nor did Qaddafi enjoy close ties with Russia or China. Although Russia had significant trade relations with Libya, its political and economic ties with Europe were significant too, and two of its main Western partners, France and Italy, were among those countries most committed to the use of force against Libya.[33] Other analysts suggest that US diplomacy was helped by Bill Clinton's policy "reset" on Russia, which had at least persuaded the Kremlin not to go out of its way to stymie US objectives when Russia's own interests were not involved.[34] Without strong interests in the conflict, China's default position was to acquiesce to the wishes of the relevant regional arrangement, the League of Arab States.

Overall, therefore, while broader transformations in the Security Council's relationship with civilian protection facilitated the intervention in Libya, factors specific to the case at hand played the crucial role in driving decisionmaking. Most notably, the clarity of the threat, the rapidity of the decisionmaking timelines, the support of (some) regional arrangements, and the extremely low international standing of the Qaddafi regime resulted in a situation where Council members skeptical about the use of force could not plausibly contest the threat assessment, lacked alternative policy routes, and risked the opprobrium of key regional players if they decided to support a regime they had no particular interest in supporting. In that context, the Council took a series of decisions that broke new ground and surprised many.

The Aftermath and Consequences of Resolution 1973

Resolution 1973 was a landmark moment in the Council's history, but differences of interpretation and recriminations over its implementation came to the fore almost immediately. After the enforcement campaign began, it was South African president Jacob Zuma who was among its most vocal critics. While the intervention was under way, South Africa told the Security Council that "international actors and external organizations . . . should . . . comply with the provisions of the United Nations Charter, fully respect the will, sovereignty and territorial integrity of the country concerned, and refrain from advancing political agendas that go beyond the protection of civilian mandates, including regime change."[35] Although South Africa was a member of the AU's Peace and Security Council, which had earlier rejected the use of force, Pretoria's representative in New York voted in support of Resolution 1973. South Africa's decision about which way to vote was apparently taken at the highest level and at the last possible moment, with its permanent representative to the UN arriving late to the Council meeting because he was receiving last-minute instructions. Moreover, Zuma's vote of support for Resolution 1973 was apparently cast after his foreign ministry had warned him that the words "all necessary measures" were open to flexible interpretation and might offer a pretext for regime change.[36] It was probably for this reason that South Africa's statement in support of Resolution 1973 also noted its rejection of "any foreign occupation or unilateral military intervention under the pretext of protecting civilians."[37] Zuma's subsequent criticisms of the enforcement campaign seemed to revolve largely around his concerns that the coalition had overstepped the terms of its mandate, its lack of support for the AU's "road map," and because of vocal criticism of the bombing campaign made by a number of influential domestic groups within South Africa.

In addition to South Africa, the other BRICS countries (Brazil, Russia, India, and China) expressed similar views. China argued that "there must be no attempt at regime change or involvement in civil war by any party under the guise of protecting civilians."[38] Brazil concurred, noting that "the protection of civilians is a humanitarian imperative. It is a distinct concept that must not be confused or conflated with threats to international peace and security, as described in the Charter, or with the responsibility to protect. We must avoid excessively broad interpretations of the protection of civilians, which could . . . create the perception that it is being used as a smokescreen for intervention or regime change."[39]

The evidence that NATO adopted a policy of using Resolution 1973 to deliberately engineer regime change in Libya is less than clear, and certainly there is no evidence that this was specifically identified as a mission goal prior to the resolution's adoption. The now infamous letter by Barack Obama, David Cameron, and Sarkozy that purportedly identified regime change as the primary military objective came not at the beginning of military operations, but more than a month into the campaign, on April 15, 2011.[40] This suggests that rather than being the initial strategic impulse, regime change was adopted late and hesitantly, only once it became clear that Qaddafi would not honor the ceasefire commitment and withdraw unilaterally. Second, contrary to much of the commentary, the letter did not actually identify regime change as a mission goal. Indeed, it specifically noted that civilian protection, not regime change, was the primary objective. The leaders did write that "it is impossible to imagine a future for Libya with Gaddafi in power," noting that "the International Criminal Court is rightly investigating the crimes committed against civilians and the grievous violations of international law" and that "it is unthinkable that someone who has tried to massacre his own people can play a part in their future government." But these statements carefully avoided claiming regime change as an objective and did not rule out the possibility of a negotiated settlement with the regime sans Qaddafi. Three weeks later, Russia joined the other members of the G8 in calling for Qaddafi to stand aside.

The jury also remains out on whether NATO and its allies exceeded the substantive elements of Resolution 1973 or failed to perform the procedural tasks therein. While a strong case can be made that NATO and its allies overstepped the tactical and operational spirit of Resolution 1973 by conducting such activities as bombing retreating Libyan forces, targeting security forces in areas that supported Qaddafi, continuing with military operations after the fall of Tripoli, and providing material assistance (intelligence, arms, training, etc.) to the rebels, it is less clear that these activities were all done with the explicit goal of regime change. In the judgment of UN Secretary-General Ban Ki-moon, for example, NATO complied with its mandate: "Security Council resolution 1973, I believe, was strictly enforced within the limit, within the mandate. . . . This military operation done by the NATO forces was strictly within [Resolution] 1973. . . . I believe this is what we have seen, and there should be no misunderstanding on that."[41]

Whatever the relative merits of the critiques of how Resolution 1973 was implemented, the debates themselves have sparked renewed thinking about the problem of "abuse" with respect to humanitarian intervention and the Security Council's working practices. This has crystallized around the concept of "responsibility while protecting" (RWP), meant as a corollary to R2P, which contains a number of proposals for the reform of Council working practices in relation to the use of force. The concept was first proposed by Brazilian president Dilma Rousseff at the September 2011 plenary of the UN General Assembly. Toward the end of 2011, the Brazilian permanent mission to the UN circulated a note outlining the concept in more detail and later, in February 2012, cohosted an informal dialogue. Although there was some initial skepticism among some Western states that saw the RWP concept as an attempt to derail implementation of R2P, the initiative was welcomed by many others, including by the Secretary-General in his 2012 report on R2P, as a constructive contribution to debates about how to implement these most controversial aspects of R2P.[42]

In light of the previous discussion, there are three particularly important elements of the RWP concept. First, it includes a call for agreement on informal decisionmaking criteria for the use of force. The Brazilian paper called for the Council to consider a set of criteria when deciding whether to use force. Based on the criteria identified by the International Commission on Intervention and State Sovereignty, which first coined the term "R2P" in 2001, these included principles of last resort (all peaceful means should be exhausted before the Council employs force), proportionality and balance of consequences (any use of force must produce less violence than it is trying to prevent), and right authority (interestingly, Brazil's concept note included a provision for the General Assembly to authorize force in extreme situations, something that obviously goes beyond both the UN Charter and the 2005 agreement on R2P).[43]

Second, Brazil argued in its RWP concept note that the "use of force must be preceded by comprehensive and judicious analysis of the possible consequences of military action on a case-by-case basis." While this is obviously sensible to some extent, concerns have been expressed about the demand that the analysis be "judicious," because this could be used to delay Council action indefinitely. Information and assessment is a necessary component of decisionmaking, but building a "judicious" assessment might take months, if not years.

Third, RWP includes a call for the establishment of an accountability mechanism to oversee the Council's work. The Brazilian letter specifically calls for enhanced procedures to "monitor and assess the manner in which resolutions are interpreted and implemented" to ensure "responsibility while protecting" and for the Council to ensure "the accountability of those to whom authority is granted to resort to force." These are important considerations if the Council is to continue to play an active role in the protection of civilian populations from atrocity crimes. Security Council resolutions generally do contain reporting requirements, as did Resolution 1973, but there is concern that these requirements are not sufficiently complied with. Brazil's calls for strengthened procedures to allow the Security Council to hold states that act on its mandate accountable flow directly from the Libya experience. However, there are several problems with this line of politics. First, the UN Charter gives the Security Council wide flexibility in terms of the actions it can take in pursuit of its primary responsibility for international peace and security and deliberately makes the Council self-regulating. As other chapters in this volume attest, this has allowed the Council to be innovative when it has needed to be, and has helped the Council find consensus when that has proven difficult. New mechanisms might require a change to the Charter, which could have unintended negative consequences. Second, the Council's responsibility covers international peace and security and not just R2P cases. It would make no practical sense to have one set of rules for some Chapter VII resolutions and another set for others. Third, the UN has had some bad previous experience with excessive political interference in military matters. The trials and tribulations of the United Nations Protection Force (UNPROFOR) in Bosnia are a testament to what can happen when the Security Council tries to micromanage military operations. Fourth, excessive political requirements might inhibit states from enforcing Council mandates, weakening the Council's credibility and legitimacy.

Conclusion

With Resolution 1973, the Security Council entered uncharted territory by adding further conditionality to the sovereign prerogatives of modern states. It remains to be seen whether future historians will view the Libyan intervention of 2011 as a crucial turning point in Council practice, or an outlier facilitated by the idiosyncrasies of Qaddafi's regime at a time of unparalleled turbulence in the Arab world. But in the nearer term, debates will continue about the way in which Resolution 1973 was implemented. Whatever the relative merits of the competing sides in this debate, two points are abundantly clear. First, although the Council has crossed the Rubicon by authorizing force against a UN member state for protection purposes, the whole question of using force against states remains highly controversial, and the questions that NATO and its allies exceeded their mandate have only further inflamed those controversies. This reinforces our assessment that Libya sets a precedent that is unlikely to be followed often by the Council, if ever. Second, in the longer run, if the Security Council is to continue to move in the direction of arguing, in line with R2P, that sovereignty is conditional on conduct such that states that commit certain crimes might be exposed to collective enforcement action, as in the Libyan case, it will need to address its own "accountability deficit" if it is to avoid a crisis of legitimacy.[44] RWP emerged directly from concerns such as this and suggests the sorts of issues that the Council will need to address if it is to stay in the civilian protection business and safeguard its own legitimacy in an era in which the distribution of global power is shifting away from the liberal West.

Notes

1. Ben Barry, "Libya's Lessons," *Survival* 53, no. 5 (2011): 6.
2. Cited in Ryan Lizza, "The Consequentialist," *The New Yorker,* May 2, 2011, www.newyorker.com/magazine/2011/05/02/the-consequentialist.
3. Ruben Reike, "Libya and the Responsibility to Protect: Lessons for the Prevention of Mass Atrocities," *St. Antony's International Review* 8, no. 1 (2012): 122–149.
4. Gareth Evans, "Responding to Mass Atrocity Crimes: The Responsibility to Protect After Libya and Syria," public lecture, Central European University, Budapest, October 24, 2012.
5. This phrase is attributed to Jean-Marie Guéhenno. See Mark Leon Goldberg, "How Libya's Success Became Syria's Failure," *UN Dispatch,* January 19, 2012.
6. African Union, "Communiqué of the Peace and Security Council (Libya)," AU Doc. PSC/PR/COMM(CCLXI), February 23, 2011. This communiqué came despite the attempts by the Libyan ambassador in Addis Ababa to change the Council's mind. Alex de Waal, "African Roles in the Libyan Conflict of 2011," *International Affairs* 89, no. 2 (2013): 369–370.
7. On March 3, the ICC prosecutor, Luis Moreno-Ocampo, said his office was investigating crimes against humanity that may have been committed by Qaddafi's regime.
8. Wissam Keyrouz, "Gulf States Back Libya No-Fly Zone," *Daily Telegraph,* March 7 2011, www.dailytelegraph.com.au/gulf-states-back-libya-no-fly-zone/story-e6freuyi-1226017478548?nk=245759727ec24ee608a2ac6b2d4183ef.
9. Security Council Report, "Update Report no. 1: Libya," March 14, 2011, www.securitycouncilreport.org/update-report/lookup-c-glKWLeMTIsG-b-6621881.php.
10. Organization of the Islamic Conference, "Final Communiqué Issued by the Emergency Meeting of the Committee of Permanent Representatives to the Organization of the Islamic Conference on the Alarming Developments in Libyan Jamahiriya," March 8, 2011, www.lcil.cam.ac.uk/sites/default/files/LCIL/documents/arabspring/libya/Libya_16_Final_Communique_Committee_of_Permanent_Representatives%20.pdf.

11. This was in line with the AU's general commitment to condemn all efforts to engage in "unconstitutional forms of government" on the continent.

12. African Union, "Communiqué of the 265th Meeting of the Peace and Security Council," AU Doc. PSC/PR/COMM.2(CCLXV), March 10, 2011.

13. Council of the League of Arab States, Resolution 7360 (March 12, 2011), paras. 1–2.

14. "Libya Uprising: Thursday 10 March," *The Guardian,* March 10, 2011, www.theguardian.com/world/blog/2011/mar/10/libya-uprising-gaddafi-live.

15. Colum Lynch, "The Libya Debate: How Fair Is Obama's New Claim That the US Led from the Front?" *Foreign Policy,* October 23, 2013.

16. On the significance of both, see Lizza, "The Consequentialist." The article quotes Clinton saying that Arab League support for action in Libya was crucial.

17. Josh Rogin, "How Obama Turned on a Dime Toward War," *Foreign Policy,* March 18, 2011, http://thecable.foreignpolicy.com/posts/2011/03/18/how_obama _turned_on_a_dime_toward_war.

18. Lizza, "The Consequentialist."

19. See Bruce D. Jones, "Libya and the Responsibilities of Power," *Survival* 53, no. 3 (2011): 54.

20. See United Nations Security Council, "Provisional Verbatim Record of the 6498th Meeting," UN Doc. S/PV.6498, March 17, 2011.

21. On Brazil, see Jones, "Libya and the Responsibilities of Power," p. 54.

22. Lebanon was acting as the representative of the Arab League.

23. A central argument of Siobhan Wills in *Protecting Civilians: The Obligations of Peacekeepers* (Oxford: Oxford University Press, 2009).

24. Dmitry Gorenberg, "Russia's Conflicts in Libya," *Atlantic Sentinel,* March 31, 2011.

25. All quotes are from United Nations Security Council, "Provisional Verbatim Record of the 6498th Meeting."

26. These views were aired to us by officials from two separate UN departments in New York.

27. We are grateful to the editors for this point. A more common explanation of the German vote was that it was a product of domestic politics, especially the coming election in Baden-Wurttemberg. See Jones, "Libya and the Responsibilities of Power," p. 55.

28. For details, see de Waal, "African Roles in the Libyan Conflict."

29. On the interconnections that justify the use of the singular in the phrase "*the* Arab uprising," see Marc Lynch, *The Arab Uprising: The Unfinished Revolutions of the New Middle East* (New York: PublicAffairs, 2012).

30. See de Waal, "African Roles in the Libyan Conflict."

31. Ibid., p. 373.

32. Sudan even dispatched an infantry battalion and a tank company to fight against Qaddafi's forces around the town of Kufra. See de Waal, "African Roles in the Libyan Conflict," p. 377.

33. Gorenberg, "Russia's Conflicts in Libya."

34. Hannah van Hoose, "Understanding the Russian Response to the Intervention in Libya," April 12, 2011, www.americanprogress.org/issues/security/news /2011/04/12/9529/understanding-the-russian-response-to-the-intervention-in-libya.

35. United Nations Security Council, "Provisional Verbatim Record of the 6531st Meeting," UN Doc. S/PV.6531, May 10, 2011.

36. de Waal, "African Roles in the Libyan Conflict," p. 368.

37. United Nations Security Council, "Provisional Verbatim Record of the 6498th Meeting," p. 10.

38. United Nations Security Council, "Provisional Verbatim Record of the 6531st Meeting."

39. Ibid.

40. Barack Obama, David Cameron, and Nicolas Sarkozy, "The Bombing Continues Until Gaddafi Goes," *The Times,* April 15, 2011, www.thetimes.co.uk/tto /opinion/columnists/article2986866.ece.

41. Louis Charbonneau, "UN Chief Defends NATO from Critics of Libya War," *Reuters,* December 14, 2011, www.reuters.com/article/2011/12/14/libya-nato-un -idAFN1E7BD0DP20111214.

42. United Nations General Assembly and Security Council, *Responsibility to Protect: Timely and Decisive Response—Report of the Secretary-General,* UN Doc. A/66/844-S/2012/578, July 25, 2012, para. 50.

43. See International Commission on Intervention and State Sovereignty, *The Responsibility to Protect* (Ottawa: International Development Research Centre, 2001).

44. Amitai Etzioni, *Security First: For a Muscular, Moral Foreign Policy* (New Haven: Yale University Press, 2007), p. 207.

35

Syria

Salman Shaikh and Amanda Roberts

THE SYRIAN CRISIS HAS POSED ONE OF THE GREATEST CHAL-
lenges to the Security Council in its recent history, thwarting the Council's
ability to fulfill its mandate to mitigate, prevent, and respond to threats to
international peace and security. Inspired by other Arab uprisings in
Tunisia, Libya, and Egypt, protests against the regime of Syrian president
Bashar al-Assad began on January 26, 2011. Escalating protests were met
with violent repression from state security forces less than two months
later, on March 18. The use of force against civilians provoked still further
demonstrations, as protests that began with demands for greater freedom
and political and economic reforms quickly transformed into calls for the
downfall of the Assad regime.

For longtime observers of Syria, the fact that a largely peaceful protest
movement would be met with exceptional force by the Assad regime,
backed up by entrenched political, social, and economic elites, was not surprising. Syrians who opposed the Hafez al-Assad regime had not forgotten
the Hama massacre of thousands of civilians in 1982. What has frustrated so
many, though, has been the inability of the international community to protect Syria's civilians during the conflict, which by spring 2015 had entered
its fifth year, despite the widely touted domestic and international Responsibility to Protect. In particular, the inability of the Security Council to effectively unite to promote the protection of civilians has exasperated and
angered ordinary Syrians as well as regional and international advocates of
action. It has frustrated the UN's highest officials, including Secretary-
General Ban Ki-Moon and the two subsequent UN–Arab League joint special envoys for Syria, Kofi Annan and Lakhdar Brahimi, each of whom has

717

repeatedly implored the Council to unite and take decisive action. It has raised questions about the relevance and influence of the Council and the UN itself, especially among Arab publics and leaderships.

In the first eighteen months of the conflict there was a concerted effort by many Council members to adopt meaningful resolutions to stop the violence, with consequences for noncompliance. It was in the period from spring 2011 to the summer of 2012 when three draft resolutions were jointly vetoed by China and Russia and a short-lived UN observer mission was withdrawn almost as quickly as it was deployed. Following the third veto and the withdrawal of the UN observer mission, the Council has dithered between trying to overcome the paralysis in order to satisfy the impulse "to do something" based on its responsibilities, and doing nothing at all because the competing Russian and US interests trump any course of action in the Council.

As peaceful protests have turned into a vicious war between the Assad regime and an armed opposition resulting in a major humanitarian crisis with regional repercussions, the Council has largely been a bystander, unable to impact the situation on the ground. It is grappling with what is so far the worst humanitarian catastrophe of the twenty-first century, made worse by "siege and starvation" tactics that have severely limited humanitarian access to vulnerable civilian populations; the use of chemical and other weapons that indiscriminately target civilians; and metastasizing al-Qaeda–inspired extremism and sectarianism within Syria and its neighbors that has led to the de facto merger of the battlefields in Iraq and Syria through the rise of the jihadist Islamic State of Iraq and ash-Sham (ISIS).

Most telling, the Council has watched helplessly as Syria has become the epicenter of the region's greatest proxy conflict, one that pits the Gulf Cooperation Council states, particularly Saudi Arabia and Qatar, against Iran and its regional partners—Hezbollah in Lebanon and the Shiite-led government in Iraq. These states have backed opposing sides in the Syria conflict, transforming it into the main venue for a struggle over the region's balance of power. Further entrenching the proxy conflict are Russia and the United States. While Russia has provided consistent political and military support to the Assad regime, the United States has wavered in its support to the opposition, resisting becoming too heavily embroiled in the conflict as it draws down from its involvement in Afghanistan and Iraq. The tentative US approach to Syria has been more recently demonstrated following the surprise expansion of ISIS into northwestern Iraq in early June 2014 and eastern Iraq and central Syria in May 2015. US air strikes against ISIS targets in Iraq began on August 8. These strikes were extended to Syria several weeks later on September 22, 2014, and remain tightly targeted on ISIS. The scale of US-led strikes in Syria is smaller than in Iraq and, unlike the strikes in Iraq, the Syria strikes have been carried out in active cooperation with Jordan and the Gulf Cooperation Council states. There was some hope that the thaw in diplomatic relations between the United States and Iran—following the November 24, 2013, agreement between the five permanent members of the Security Council plus Germany (P5+1) with Iran regarding its nuclear program—might ease regional tensions around the Syrian conflict. However, it seems to have had the opposite effect. The measured calculation of the P5+1 and Iran to keep the nuclear and Syrian issues distinct has raised fears of the Gulf and other regional states that the West is only interested in containing Iran's nuclear capabilities, not in pressuring Iran to prove its peaceful intentions and operate as a constructive actor in the region, particularly in Syria. As talks on the Iranian nuclear issue are set to conclude in July 2015, it remains an open question whether a rapprochement between Washington and Tehran will create momentum for a political solution in Syria or further aggravate regional rivalries between Saudi Arabia and Iran.

The Syrian conflict was always going to be a difficult challenge for the international community to handle. It comes at a time of increasingly complex great power relations in a fragmenting world. The perception of US retrenchment in the wider Middle East, Russia's ambitions to reestablish its great power status, the strengthening of a Sino-Russian alliance opposed to Western influence, as well as the growing role of nonaligned actors such as India and Brazil, have been notable features of a new multipolar world and changing international order. It is this dynamic that has also contributed to an absence of clear leadership in responding to the Syrian crisis, including within the Security Council.

A fairly common explanation for the Council's inability to respond to the Syrian crisis is the fallout from the polarizing Libya intervention authorized in March 2011 under Resolution 1973. If the UN-sanctioned action in Libya represented a high-water mark for a muscular Council mandate to protect civilians, any attempt to do so in the case of Syria faced a challenge from a powerful coalition of veto-wielding powers (China and Russia) and elected members (initially Brazil, India, and South Africa) who strongly criticized the pursuit of regime change in the name of protecting civilians. It would be fair to argue that Brazil, India, and South Africa's abstentions on the Syria vote in October 2011 were significantly influenced by the perception that the NATO-led intervention in Libya had gone beyond its protection mandate, instead directly aiding the opposition and enabling the overthrow of Muammar Qaddafi.

The ensuing controversy over postconflict Libya was therefore a convenient and compelling public argument for Russia to use, but by no means was it the sole or even dominant factor in Russia's ongoing defense of the Assad regime in the Security Council, nor in China's consistent backing of the Russian veto. Still, the Libyan case has continued to impact Syria-related discussions within the Council over the implementation and enforcement of various agreements. Nowhere was this more damaging than when the Council failed to agree on a Chapter VII resolution in support of the June 2012 Geneva communiqué, an agreement among P5 foreign ministers and regional representatives facilitated by the first UN–Arab League joint special envoy, Kofi Annan, that offered a blueprint for the government and opposition to agree to a political solution to the conflict. Did that moment, in particular, constitute a missed opportunity—a fork in the road—for a united Council effort to impact the conflict and mitigate its disastrous effects since? Had the P5 effectively supported the communiqué's blueprint, the Syrian conflict may have claimed the lives of only 19,000 civilians and fighters,[1] leaving Syria and the international community to resettle and rehabilitate some 98,000 registered refugees.[2] However, as of March 2015 the conflict had left a conservative estimate of 220,000 dead, nearly half of the country's population displaced, and almost 4 million registered Syrian refugees, and 7.6 million internally displaced.

Syria Raised in the Security Council

From the start, the UN Security Council has dealt with Syria under a catchall agenda item that has existed since 1960: "the situation in the Middle East." It held its first public debate on the situation in Syria on April 27, 2011, the day after Security Council members received a briefing on the unfolding crisis in Syria by the head of the UN's Department of Political Affairs at the time, B. Lynn Pascoe. The Council was particularly interested in reports that the Syrian army had initiated a major military operation following mass demonstrations in Dera'a, with media reports of mass graves and 1,100 dead.

The divisive dynamics among the P5 seemed to have already crystallized at the outset of the Council's treatment of the Syrian crisis. As early as June 2011, supporters of Council action on Syria—such as the so-called P3 (France, the United Kingdom, and the United States) and elected Council members Germany and Portugal—had the necessary nine votes for a draft resolution condemning the Syrian government's violent response to the crisis. However, China and Russia emphasized the internal nature of the situation, while elected members Brazil, India, Lebanon, and South Africa were also wary of Council action. The draft text was never voted on.

In August 2011, the UK—with support from France, the United States, Germany, and Portugal—circulated a draft resolution calling for an asset freeze and a travel ban on President Assad and other senior regime officials, and an arms embargo on Syria. However, Russia, China, Brazil, India, and South Africa, having the Libya intervention fresh in mind, argued that dialogue, not sanctions, should be pursued, and that the principles of state sov-

ereignty and nonintervention should be respected. To address these concerns, the draft was watered down in subsequent negotiations, and provisions on sanctions as well as references to accountability and human rights
violations were replaced by language underlining the need for a peaceful
resolution of the crisis. The draft condemned Syria's excessive use of force
and expressed the Council's intention to consider further nonmilitary measures in the case of noncompliance, but the immediate threat of sanctions
was removed.[3] Despite these concessions, when the draft resolution was put
to a vote on October 4, 2011, China and Russia cast a joint veto and four
Council members abstained (Brazil, India, Lebanon, and South Africa).

In retrospect, questions have been raised about whether it was wise to
push for a vote in such a divisive atmosphere and whether it would have
been better to put forward a text devoid of blame on any particular side,
while still affirming the responsibility of all parties to protect civilians.
However, such a text at that stage of the conflict would have been blatantly
disingenuous. As early as August 2011, Navi Pillay, UN high commissioner
for human rights, had briefed the Council members that war crimes were
being committed by the Syrian government and recommended a referral of
the situation to the International Criminal Court. Supporters of the draft resolution held firm that at a bare minimum it should reflect as accurately as
possible the situation on the ground. In their view, the fact that the draft had
no real teeth was concession enough.

Different Year, Same Divisions

The Second Veto

The Security Council's paralysis opened the way for a new initiative
emerging from the Arab region. On February 1, 2012, newly elected Council member Morocco formally submitted a new draft supporting the Arab
League's recent proposal for a gradual political transition process in Damascus.[4] The Western Council members welcomed this initiative, hoping that
an Arab-led call for Council action would exert pressure on Russia, China,
and the nonaligned elected members to follow suit. However, the fact that
the Arab League had suspended Syria's membership in November 2011 and
that a majority of its members were siding with the opposition forces ultimately meant it was unable to play the role of bridge-builder between the
opposing camps in the Council. Nor was it influential or persuasive enough
for China and Russia to break with its noninterventionist and sovereignty-
focused approach.

The key issues dividing the Council on this draft resolution continued
to be language threatening sanctions as well as the call for a political transition. Further, the reference to the Arab League proposal left Russia and

China along with elected Council members Azerbaijan, India, Pakistan, and South Africa concerned that this could be perceived as a call for regime change and a repeat of the Libya situation. While the draft resolution made no mention of the use of force, Russia insisted that the text would need to explicitly rule out military intervention.

The draft that was tabled for a vote on February 4 supported the Arab League proposal but did not include any details regarding how a political transition might take place.[5] Additionally, the text explicitly stated that nothing in the resolution authorized measures under Article 42 of the UN Charter, removing the threat of the use of force. The possibility of considering further measures (i.e., sanctions) remained.

The final draft of the resolution substantively addressed all of the concerns raised during the negotiations and included eight cosponsors who were Council members, in addition to eleven other UN member states comprising Turkey and ten Arab states. By the evening of February 3, it seemed that a compromise had been reached and that all fifteen Security Council members, including Russia, would be able to adopt a resolution addressing the Syrian crisis the next day.

However, on the morning of the vote, Moscow reversed direction and sent instructions to vote the resolution down, taking Council members, in particular the P3, by surprise. Beijing followed suit, leading to the second joint veto on Syria. However, this was the first instance of the Chinese and Russian position being isolated, as all other Security Council members voted in favor of the draft.

The General Assembly and Syria

As the crisis escalated and the Council's impotence became evident, the General Assembly became a sort of pressure valve to circumvent the impasse in the Council, particularly for Arab states, led chiefly by Saudi Arabia and Qatar, which were increasingly exasperated by Council inaction and the use of the veto. Behind the scenes, the P3 and likeminded Council members Germany and Portugal were driving the effort to transfer the struggle over Syria into the General Assembly, where more political traction, if not decisive action, could be gained in comparison to the Council.

After the first veto in October 2011, the General Assembly adopted a resolution on December 19 condemning violence in Syria.[6] On February 16, 2012, it adopted a resolution nearly identical to the text vetoed in the Security Council on February 4, condemning the violence in Syria, endorsing the Arab League proposal for a gradual political transition, and establishing the mandate of a special envoy for Syria.[7] In August 2012, again, following the third joint veto on Syria in July 2012 (discussed later), the General

Assembly deplored the Security Council's failure to act in a rare moment of censure and called for a political transition in Syria.[8] In May 2013, it condemned the Syrian government's indiscriminate violence against civilian populations.[9] Seven months later, the General Assembly called for peace talks, condemned human rights violations in Syria, and urged the Security Council to take measures to end violations in Syria and take action to facilitate humanitarian access.[10] An effort by Arab states to have the General Assembly invoke the "Uniting for Peace" formula—whereby the General Assembly should take action when the P5 are deadlocked—was successfully discouraged by the P3.

Special Envoy Kofi Annan, UNSMIS, and the Third Veto

The most lasting contribution of the General Assembly to address the Syrian crisis was the creation, on February 16, 2012, of the mandate for a special envoy after the second veto in the Council.[11] Former UN Secretary-General Kofi Annan was appointed shortly thereafter to the position. During the short period of Annan's mediation efforts, the Council acted with a degree of unanimity, as demonstrated on March 21 when the Council adopted a presidential statement supporting Annan's six-point plan.[12] This called for an inclusive political process, cessation of all violence, humanitarian access, release of those arbitrarily detained, access for journalists, and the right to peaceful demonstrations. On April 5, the Council issued another presidential statement calling on the Syrian government to cease violence by April 10, and the opposition to do likewise within forty-eight hours thereafter.[13]

Subsequently, in Resolution 2042 on April 14, the Council authorized the deployment of an advance team of thirty unarmed military observers to report on the implementation of the cessation of armed violence by all parties. On April 21, the Council adopted Resolution 2043, establishing the UN Supervision Mission in Syria (UNSMIS) for ninety days and calling for the urgent implementation of Annan's six-point plan. The mission, under the command of Major General Robert Mood of Norway, was authorized at a strength of up to 300 military observers.

Russia, in particular, was supportive of the mission, as opposition forces were still on the upswing at the time and Moscow saw the deployment of observers as a chance to freeze the conflict for a while and buy Damascus time and breathing space. However, less than two months later, Major General Mood decided to suspend UNSMIS activities on June 16, 2012, due to the deliberate targeting of the mission with heavy weapons and other security concerns. From that point, the relatively unified approach of Council members began to dissolve, as it appeared UNSMIS would not have the desired impact on the ground. P5 foreign ministers met in Geneva—along with Annan and regional representatives—and this action group on Syria issued a communiqué (the aforementioned Geneva communiqué) on June 30 calling for all parties to recommit to the six-point plan, mapping out steps for a Syrian-led political process that would lead to a mutually agreed transition. Yet predictable differences quickly emerged as to what this political transition would involve and whether it was contingent on Assad's removal from power; this division was the fundamental obstacle to progress in the Geneva talks.

On July 11, the UK circulated a draft resolution under Chapter VII. The text endorsed the June 30, 2012, Geneva communiqué, renewed UNSMIS for forty-five days, and threatened to sanction the Syrian government if it did not cease its attacks against civilians within ten days.[14] During negotiations, Russia had apparently proposed that a Chapter VII resolution would only be appropriate if it applied to both the Syrian government and armed opposition groups. The P3 were open to the proposal, which seemed to take Russia by surprise, but in the end there was no compromise. According to one Western P5 ambassador, if there was ever a fork in the road leading to greater Council cohesion and purpose, this was the opportunity. However, the inability of the Council to give the resolution heft and agree on Chapter VII provisions, as Annan had indicated would be required to make tangible progress, led to a predictable breakdown. Rather than contribute to a political solution, the Council's inability to agree on this point highlighted two main issues plaguing the Geneva process and the Council's work on Syria more generally: how to move from the Geneva communiqué's principles to its actual implementation, and how to enforce its compliance.

On the morning of July 19, 2012, Russia along with China vetoed this draft. In the afternoon of that same day, a new draft resolution extending UNSMIS—whose mandate was to end the next day, July 20—was tabled for a vote. The draft did not have any Chapter VII provisions and renewed UNSMIS for a final period of thirty days, linking any further renewal of the mission to the cessation of the use of heavy weapons—though the resolution did not specifically call on the Syrian regime to do so; rather it de facto applied to the Syrian authorities only, as they were the only ones using such weapons at the time. It seems Russia was prepared to veto this draft as well, but Russia refrained from doing so after China indicated it was willing to go along with the draft given that Chapter VII language and explicit demands on the Syrian government had been removed. In the end, the Council unanimously adopted Resolution 2059, tersely renewing UNSMIS for a final thirty days.

By the autumn of 2012, exhaustion had set in after nearly a year and a half of stalemate in the Council, interrupted by the short-lived unity on the deployment of Special Envoy Annan and UNSMIS. The ten elected Council members (E10) were trapped among a P5 power struggle with very little room to influence outcomes beyond aligning positions on either side of the P5 divide.

Frustrated by little traction gained by the six-point plan and the seeming inability of major international players such as Russia and the United States to agree on an approach, Annan announced his resignation on August 2, 2012. Lakhdar Brahimi of Algeria was appointed joint special representative for Syria two weeks later. Brahimi consistently kept expectations of what could be achieved rather low. Realizing that the Council was hopelessly deadlocked, he distanced himself from the body and instead focused on behind-the-scenes diplomacy with the United States, Russia, and key regional players.

Yet, to the growing frustration of Arab states, the Syrian opposition, as well as the UK and France, it took Brahimi eight months to get any traction with Moscow and Washington, and it was not until May 2013 that Russia and the United States announced they would bring the Syrian government and opposition to the negotiating table, effectively sidelining the Council on the Syrian political track. Council members avoided any contentious discussions of further Geneva talks so as to not upset the process, despite the significant delays in convening the talks. Meanwhile, Brahimi spent a large part of 2013 trying to create consensus on the implementation of the Geneva communiqué between the parties and trying to enlist the backing of the two main sponsors of the process, Russia and the United States. This did lead to a much-delayed round of direct talks between the Syrian government and opposition, dubbed "Geneva II," in January and February 2014.

When it seemed that no progress was being made in the second round of talks, Brahimi met with Russia and the United States on February 13, 2014, in an attempt to bring fresh momentum to the process. However, the meeting was acrimonious, with Russian foreign minister Sergey Lavrov criticizing the United States for using the talks to achieve "regime change," and his US counterpart, John Kerry, accusing Russia of backtracking on previous commitments on a transitional government.

On March 13, 2014, Brahimi reported to Council members that the process had so far failed, due to the Syrian government's unwillingness to accept the proposals to negotiate the formation of a transitional governing body. Brahimi said he would not call for a third round of talks if there were no constructive ideas to break the stalemate. Furthermore, he stressed the incompatibility of the government's plans to hold presidential elections, possibly as early as May or June, with the Geneva process. In the regime's view, elections would render the process moot—in particular the requirement to form a transitional governing body. Finally, Brahimi conveyed to Council members that if a date for elections were set, this would mean the end of the Geneva process.

Chemical Weapons, Terrorism, and a Change in Council Dynamics

On August 21, 2013, the Syrian government carried out a chemical weapons attack that reportedly killed approximately 1,300 civilians in eastern Ghouta, outside Damascus. The attack was carried out the same day a UN team, sent by the Secretary-General, arrived in Syria to investigate the alleged use of chemical weapons in a number of incidents earlier in 2013. The Secretary-General instructed the team to investigate the August 21 attack immediately. On September 16, the Secretary-General shared the results of the investigation, which confirmed the use of chemical weapons. While the team was not mandated to attribute blame for the attacks, the report provided detailed information on delivery systems pointing to government culpability.

As early as August 2012, US president Barack Obama had said his "red line" on Syria was the use of chemical weapons. Compelled to uphold the credibility of the red line, the US administration prepared for air strikes but ran into trouble when the UK Parliament rejected Prime Minister David Cameron's motion to join the United States in its military endeavor, leaving France as Washington's only ally. Meanwhile, the US Congress, too, seemed unwilling to grant President Obama the authority to use force, leaving him with the unappealing prospect of waging war with little domestic and international support. Syrian civil society actors recall that the threat of US military action had the effect of grounding Assad's air force for ten days following the Ghouta attack—the last time they recalled any significant period of time passing without incessant aerial bombardment by the government.

Russia skillfully seized the opportunity this situation provided, proposing on September 9, 2013, that Syrian chemical weapon stocks be put under international control. This proposal offered a face-saving measure for Obama to back away from an unplanned military intervention. In a matter of days, Russia and the United States bilaterally agreed to a framework for the elimination of such weapons by the end of June 2014—an unprecedented pace for the removal and destruction of such an arsenal.

The P5 briefly consulted on the agreement and the E10 had no choice but to swallow the deal, enshrining it in Resolution 2118 on September 27, which required the verification and destruction of Syria's chemical weapons and also called for the convening of the Geneva II peace talks and endorsed the establishment of a transitional governing body in Syria with full executive powers.

The fact that the Assad regime complied with such demands and that by late June 2014 the last of Syria's declared chemical weapon stocks had been removed from the country showed that the Council was indeed able to take effective action when there was agreement between Washington and

Moscow. Yet, ironically, Russia emerged as the winner from this episode, achieving three major objectives in one fell swoop. First, it was able to avert the use of force and remove any credible threat of US use of force in the foreseeable future. Second, by doing so, it was able to recast itself from the main obstacle to Council action to a leadership position in the Council, having engineered the Council's only robust action on Syria since the conflict erupted. And third, the chemical weapons agreement re-legitimized Assad as a partner whose cooperation was needed to implement security commitments important to the international community. Indeed, the agreement actually bought the regime enough time to hold in June 2014 what most considered sham elections in the midst of a violent civil war that bestowed upon Assad an alleged democratic mandate and—in the regime's view—rendered the Geneva process moot. Assad's gradual and relative re-legitimization was reinforced by another, longer-term development, the spread and growth of al-Qaeda–inspired extremist groups in Syria. The alleged imperative of the fight against terrorism had been used by the Syrian regime since the beginning of the crisis as justification for its military tactics against civilians, despite the near absence of this phenomenon in the first year of the crisis. Many Council members had criticized the fact that Russia shielded Syria from international pressure and, from the earliest days of the crisis, echoed the regime's propaganda on terrorism. Yet, with escalating violence and lawlessness in Syria, foreign fighters and Islamic extremists were drawn into the conflict, eventually making the terrorist threat in Syria a reality. By early 2012, the proliferation of armed extremist groups was a concern shared by all Council members, as demonstrated by the increasing reference to terrorism in Council press statements and presidential statements and resolutions. Russia, however, was alone in reducing the security challenge in Syria to a terrorist threat and using it to justify regime brutality that was, in its eyes, beyond criticism. The P3 in particular had held to the view that the real threat was the Assad regime.

The threat of ISIS in Syria became particularly prevalent in late 2013, and by mid-2014 the proliferation of ISIS fighters from Syria into Iraq and its expanding control of territory, strategic infrastructure, military hardware, and natural resources shifted the P3's calculations toward viewing ISIS as another primary threat on par with the Assad regime. The potential transnational reach of ISIS brought the P3 closer to the Russian position on terrorism in Syria. On July 28 the Council adopted a presidential statement prohibiting illicit oil trade as a source of revenue for terrorists,[15] on August 15 it adopted Resolution 2170, condemning the recruitment of foreign fighters by ISIS, on September 24 it adopted Resolution 2178, imposing obligations on UN member states to respond to the threat of foreign terrorist fighters, and on February 12, 2015, it adopted Resolution 2199, addressing illicit funding of ISIS and al-Nusra Front via oil exports, traffic of cultural heritage, ransom payments, and external donations. It seems that the counterterrorism aspect of the conflict, because it was easier to garner consensus for in the Council, overwhelmingly overshadowed any serious thinking about how to revive the stalled political track.

The Battle over Humanitarian Access
and Failed Efforts to Ensure Accountability

Meanwhile, the situation on the ground had dramatically deteriorated, in particular since the chemical weapons agreement was inked, with significant increases in the death toll, refugee flows, numbers of internally displaced persons, as well as numbers of people trapped in besieged areas, leading to a humanitarian crisis of unprecedented proportions. Throughout 2013, delivery of humanitarian goods had become increasingly difficult, particularly because of the Assad government's use of aid as a war tactic and its efforts to deny aid to areas outside its control.

Yet the Council, led by nonpermanent members Australia, Luxembourg, and Jordan, was unable, until February 2014, to agree on a resolution (2139) addressing the humanitarian crisis, demanding that all parties, in particular Syrian authorities, allow humanitarian access across conflict lines, in besieged areas, and across borders, and expressing its intent to take further steps in case of noncompliance. It also included important references to aerial bombardment and demanded that all parties immediately cease indiscriminate use of weapons, including the use of barrel bombs, which the regime has increasingly used since late 2013. And, while the reference to the use of barrel bombs in Resolution 2139 is not a specific demand on the government, its meaning is easily inferred because only the government has aerial capacity. Once again, the Western camp had to make significant compromises to secure Russian approval, including on references to Syria's failure to implement a presidential statement the Council had adopted in October 2013 on humanitarian access, possible sanctions in case of noncompliance, cross-border access and access to besieged areas, aerial bombardment, accountability, and counterterrorism. The key issue for Syria, and for Russia, was that Syria's sovereignty should not be impacted by Resolution 2139, and in fact the resolution stopped short of authorizing cross-border aid operations in the absence of the Syrian government's consent.

The Council's efforts to address the humanitarian crisis did not result in any significant material improvements on the ground. As detailed in UN humanitarian chief Valerie Amos's first follow-up report to Resolution 2139, on March 28, the Syrian government continued its use of aid as a war tactic, flouting of the Council's demands for humanitarian access.[16] This and subsequent reports spurred discussion among Council members about what the next steps should be to compel meaningful compliance with Resolution 2139.

However, so long as there was some hope for the Geneva II peace talks, the United States, as well as many other Council members including Russia, eschewed any genesis of credible discussions on follow-up action to Resolution 2139, and also avoided any strong pursuit of the accountability track in the Council. But the collapse of peace talks and Brahimi's resignation in May, followed by the announcement of presidential elections in Syria for June 3, rendered the political track dead and contributed to the shift in the US position to support further action on the humanitarian track as well as an ICC referral, leaving just one question remaining, that of timing.

The P3 decided to move forward on the accountability track first. Two factors were at play. First, in the absence of a credible political solution on the horizon, France initiated a strategy to bring accountability to the fore of Council action. France argued that after more than three years of mass atrocities in Syria, the situation should be referred to the International Criminal Court. Second, and more cynically, some Council members anticipated that an ICC referral would be vetoed, which might make it more difficult for Russia and China to veto any follow-up resolution on humanitarian access.

As early as August 2011, Navi Pillay, UN high commissioner for human rights at the time, had urged the Security Council to consider referring the situation in Syria to the ICC. In January 2013, Switzerland sent a letter to the Security Council requesting the same. The letter was cosigned by fifty-six other member states, including seven Security Council members from the 2014 constellation: Australia, Chile, France, Lithuania, Luxembourg, the Republic of Korea, and the UK.[17] Pillay briefed Council members on Syria on April 8, 2014, reporting massive evidence that war crimes and crimes against humanity had been committed. Even though Pillay indicated that the Syrian government was responsible for most violations and that her office could identify the perpetrators in the case of an ICC referral, the Council, which at the time included eleven members that were also parties to the ICC's Rome Statute, had only been able to muster a meek general call for those responsible for international crimes to be brought to justice. While Russia's opposition to an ICC referral was well known, the United States too continued to remain reluctant, apparently out of concern that such a referral would place Israel under ICC jurisdiction, given that Israel occupies the Syrian Golan. Negotiations on the resolution in April and May 2014 culminated in a text drafted to make the ICC referral as palatable as possible to both the United States and Russia. For Russia, the text was carefully neutral on the issue of assigning blame and specified that all violations should be investigated. For the United States, carve-outs to jurisdiction were provided that would exclude nationals of nonstate parties to the Rome Statute as well as excluding Israel from any possible jurisdiction by defining the conflict as beginning in March 2011 between Syrian authorities, pro-government militias, and nonstate armed groups. The changes were sufficient to ensure US support, but Russia publicly stated that the initiative was poorly timed and would serve only to exacerbate existing divisions. Russia and China cast their fourth joint veto on May 22, blocking the referral of Syria to the ICC.[18]

Five days later, on May 27, Australia, Jordan, and Luxembourg began an arduous six weeks of negotiations on a resolution that would have a pragmatic, operational, and positive effect on the humanitarian situation on the ground in Syria. The draft resolution, under Chapter VII, permitted the UN to carry out cross-border and cross-line aid operations in the absence of state consent, and included the threat to impose sanctions.

Russia and China, clearly uncomfortable with the prospect of casting a fifth veto on Syria so soon after the ICC veto, genuinely engaged in negotiations while firmly flagging their objection to a Chapter VII resolution challenging state sovereignty and objecting to any threat of sanctions. Both references were dropped early in the negotiations, but another serious hurdle emerged that took weeks of haggling to resolve.

Russia had managed to get Syria to agree to UN aid operations traversing four border crossings outside government control. However, Syria insisted that such aid would need to be redistributed under the government's authority. Such a demand undermined the fundamental intent of enabling aid to reach those in need via the most direct route. In addition, given that the Assad regime used the distribution of humanitarian aid as a tactic of war, it was impossible to agree to a text that could potentially bolster this tool in Syria's war strategy.

By late June, Australia, Jordan, Luxembourg, and the P3 informed Russia that their flexibility on this issue was exhausted, as it violated their guiding principle of devising a formula in New York that would have a positive impact on the ground in Syria. A final suggestion was put forward in early July that the UN would notify the Syrian authorities of the contents of the humanitarian convoys, creating a notification system that would offer transparency with no corresponding requirement for the regime's approval.

Russia's position on cross-border humanitarian access shifted during the drawn-out negotiations. At the outset Russia insisted that all of Syria's conditions be met, although this was incompatible with the spirit and intent of Resolution 2139 and the resolution under negotiation. By July 2, Russia finally signaled its comfort with such aid deliveries and the UN notification system. Such comfort may have been helped by the fact that China was more supportive and constructive during these negotiations than it was in the lead-up to the four vetoed resolutions. During negotiations, China indicated it was satisfied now that Chapter VII language had been removed, leaving Russia isolated. On July 14, Resolution 2165 was unanimously adopted. The authorization for cross-border access was renewed until January 2016, when the Council adopted Resolution 2191 on December 17, 2014.

Evolving Security Council Dynamics

P5 dynamics have been fairly consistent in the Council since the beginning of the Syrian crisis, with the main shifts happening among the elected members, who have increasingly aligned their positions with the P3, further isolating the Chinese and Russian position. The shift among elected members can be attributed to three factors: the escalation of violence in the conflict itself and its alarming humanitarian consequences, which rendered moot the debate over whether the situation was a threat to international peace and security; temporal and comparative distance from the Libya situation; and finally the rotation of five of the ten elected members every year, with new members necessarily filtering their positions on Syria through a different constellation of foreign policy objectives and alignments.

The Permanent Five

Russia consistently protected the Assad regime from any significant Security Council criticism and consequence, initially arguing that Council action on Syria would constitute interference in a domestic matter. Its motivations were multifold and based on long and established interests in Syria. These included preserving its security and arms-trading agreements and keeping its largely symbolic naval base in Tartous on the eastern Mediterranean coast. However, Russian-Syrian relations go beyond these interests to deeper strategic concerns such as Russia maintaining its last significant sphere of influence in the region, containing Islamist extremism (a concern that is amplified by the significant presence of foreign fighters in ISIS, al-Nusra front, and other Syrian al-Qaeda affiliates), and ensuring the safety of Syria's Christian community. Specifically with regard to its support for Assad, Russia maintained an "uber-realist" perspective, saying that it was not wedded to keeping him in place but giving him strong support as it increasingly looked that he was not leaving anytime soon.

As the crisis escalated, so did the effects on both the security and political sectors in Iraq and Lebanon, though Jordan and Turkey were significantly affected as well. The clear spillover of the Syrian crisis to neighboring countries, as well as the growing refugee crisis, made Russia's initial argument, that the Syrian crisis did not pose a threat to international peace and security, untenable. Moscow then quickly shifted to a threefold argument in the Security Council: rejecting regime change by external force, denying any legitimacy to the opposition, and amplifying the threat of terrorism.

From the earliest days of the Security Council's consideration of the Syrian crisis, Russia insisted that all sides of the conflict be portrayed with absolute parity and symmetry, in terms of both fighting efficacy and human suffering. As early as April 2011, Russia expressed concern for the "suffering among demonstrators, law enforcement and the army." This component of Russia's position carried through to later discussions of Syria in the Council, with various proposed texts repeatedly being blocked or criticized by Russia as "one-sided, politicized and not practical"—in many ways a mirror of the US treatment of the Israel/Palestine issue in the Council. Russia consistently refused to acknowledge the Syrian government's responsibility to protect civilians as a paramount obligation, even when the reciprocal requirement of armed rebel groups to observe international human rights and humanitarian law was similarly highlighted.

Meanwhile, China, as with many other issues on the Council agenda that do not directly affect its national interests, was tepid in its treatment of Syria in the Council, offering, in its public statements, little more than a reiteration of well-established principles about the need for dialogue. However, China's less-than-robust engagement with Syria did not deter Beijing from exercising its veto power alongside Moscow on four occasions from 2011 to 2014. (See Table 35.1 for an overview of Syria-related votes in the Security Council.) China has used the veto only eleven times since the founding of the UN, the fewest of any of the other P5 members. However, six have been cast in tandem with Russia since 2007: on Myanmar (January 2007), Zimbabwe (July 2008), and Syria (October 2011, February and July 2012, and May 2014). China's rare use of the veto is in keeping with its quiet profile on the Council, where Beijing rarely comes out strongly on any issue except on those of critical national concern—such as North Korea, Myanmar, Sudan/South Sudan, and issues related to Taiwan. Given China's discomfort in exercising its veto on high-profile issues, its consistent backing of Russia's position is all the more difficult to explain and could be interpreted as a tactical quid pro quo in the Security Council—a way to bank on reciprocal support from Russia when needed in the future.

The US position on Syria in the Security Council, from the outset, was consistently characterized by strong condemnation of the regime in its public statements, together with simultaneous caution about whether and when to throw its weight behind efforts of its like-minded partners among the P5—France and the UK—for concrete Council outcomes. When it did choose to engage, the pace and seriousness of Council activity around Syria intensified—as demonstrated by the deployment of UNSMIS, the chemical weapons agreement, the resolutions on humanitarian access, as well as the lead-up to the four vetoed resolutions.

A component of the US calculation since the beginning of the Syrian crisis was its impact on Israel's security. This played itself out in New York, with the United States restraining a too-vociferous use of the Security Council to respond to the crisis. This restraint was initially governed by concerns regarding Iran's regional influence, Hezbollah's military reach, and statements by Syrian authorities that without security in Syria there would be no stability in Israel. Even before the Syrian crisis, the United States had been focused on Syria in the Council's work, in particular by keeping a spotlight on the conduit Syria provided for a flow of weapons from Iran to Hezbollah in Lebanon and the deleterious impact of this on Israel's security.

The cautious US approach in the Security Council was a reflection of President Obama's reluctance to become drawn into yet another military confrontation in the wider Middle East just as US forces were drawing down in Iraq and Afghanistan. The United States was consistently concerned about the risks the Syrian crisis posed to security in the region, particularly Israel, yet ironically it was precisely those risks that initially led it to be cautious about Council action. The bulk of Syria's and Hezbollah's threats to Israel have proven to be rhetorical. As the Syrian conflict escalated, its impact on Israel's security continued to be one of many factors flavoring the US approach in the Security Council, but not with the primacy of place it had in 2011.

The escalation of the conflict to a zero-sum war between the Assad regime and an armed opposition, fueled by a proxy war for regional influence between Iran and Saudi Arabia, gave Syria all the trappings of an international fault-line. US support for the opposition did not match Russia's robust support for the regime. After late 2011, this necessitated that the United States broaden its calculations on Syria beyond its concerns over Israel's security.

By August 2011, President Obama had explicitly called for Assad's ouster, a position that was at least partly driven by the US desire to remove Iran's key ally in the region in order to contain Iran's regional influence and reach. However, Washington's strong anti-Assad rhetoric was not matched by action, and it wavered in providing consistent support to the Syrian opposition and failed to act with any strategic leadership with its allies in the region—particularly the Gulf states.

The United States also shied away from military action when Syria crossed the chemical weapons "red line" in August 2013, instead accepting the proposal put forth by adept Russian diplomatic maneuvering. By coming out so early in the conflict with a demand for Assad's ouster without any substantial investment in the opposition, the United States arguably contributed greatly to the stalemate. By the time Geneva talks were held in January and February 2014, the United States had limited political capital, having already bartered away its credible threat of the use of force, to change the Syrian regime's calculations about its ability to remain in power.

Table 35.1 Security Council Votes Taken on Syria Draft Resolutions

Date of Vote	Document	Contents	Outcome of Vote
October 4, 2011	S/2011/612	Condemned use of force by Syrian authorities; expressed intent to consider further options, including measures under Article 41	*Not adopted* (9–2–4) Veto: China, Russia Abstention: Brazil, India, Lebanon, South Africa
February 4, 2012	S/2012/77	Supported Arab League's January 22 decision to facilitate Syrian-led political transition	*Not adopted* (13–2–0) Veto: China, Russia
April 14, 2012	S/RES/2042	Authorized deployment of thirty military observers to Syria	*Adopted* (15–0–0)
April 21, 2012	S/RES/2043	Established UNSMIS for ninety days	*Adopted* (15–0–0)
July 19, 2012	S/2012/538	Stipulated that Syrian authorities cease troop movements—and use of heavy weapons—in population centers; stipulated that Article 41 measures would be imposed in case of noncompliance	*Not adopted* (11–2–2) Veto: China, Russia Abstention: Pakistan, South Africa
July 20, 2012	S/RES/2059	Extended UNSMIS for a final thirty days	*Adopted* (15–0–0)
September 27, 2013	S/RES/2118	Required verification and destruction of Syria's chemical weapons stockpiles; called for convening of Geneva II peace talks; endorsed establishment of transitional governing body in Syria with full executive powers	*Adopted* (15–0–0)
February 22, 2014	S/RES/2139	Demanded that all parties, in particular Syrian authorities, allow humanitarian access across conflict lines, in besieged areas, and across borders; expressed intent to take further steps in case of noncompliance	*Adopted* (15–0–0)

Date of Vote	Document	Contents	Outcome of Vote
May 22, 2014	S/2014/348	Referred Syria to the ICC	*Not adopted* (13–2–0) Veto: China, Russia
July 14, 2014	S/RES/2165	Authorized cross-border and cross-line access for UN and its partners to deliver humanitarian aid in Syria without state consent; established monitoring mechanism for 180 days	*Adopted* (15–0–0)
August 15, 2014	S/RES/2170	Condemned recruitment by ISIS and al-Nusra of foreign fighters; listed six individuals affiliated with those groups under 1267/1989 al-Qaeda sanctions regime	*Adopted* (15–0–0)
September 24, 2014	S/RES/2178	Imposed obligations on member states to respond to the threat of foreign terrorist fighters	*Adopted* (15–0–0)
December 17, 2014	S/RES/2191	Renewed authorization for cross-border humanitarian access until January 10, 2016	*Adopted* (15–0–0)
February 12, 2015	S/RES/2199	Addressed ISIS and al-Nusra's illicit funding via oil exports, traffic of cultural heritage, ransom payments, and external donations	*Adopted* (15–0–0)
March 6, 2015	S/RES/2209	Condemned the use of toxic chemicals, such as chlorine, without attributing blame; stressed that those responsible should be held accountable; recalled resolution 2118; supported the February 4, 2015, decision of the OPCW	*Adopted* (14–0–1) Abstention: Venezuela

After the surprise takeover of Mosul in Iraq by ISIS in early June 2014, President Obama asked Congress for $500 million to train and equip Syrian rebel forces to push ISIS back in Syria. By summer 2015, such train and equip programs had begun in very limited numbers in Jordan and Turkey with a great deal of uncertainty about whether the United States would provide air support to rebels trained to counter ISIS in Syria. Separately, the United States accelerated its supply of arms and ammunition to a small number of vetted opposition groups in northern Syria. These efforts perhaps came too late to staunch the proliferation of ISIS and did little to help opposition forces counter the Assad regime.

France and the UK were more proactive on the Syrian file and often led on the issue, simultaneously admonishing Russia to uphold its responsibilities on the UN Security Council and prodding the United States toward action. The activism of France and the UK has often—and rightly—been attributed to the fact that the two countries, no longer qualifying as great powers, need to work all the harder to justify their permanent seats on the Council. Indeed, Council initiatives on Syria have invariably begun with France and the UK, along with like-minded elected Western and Arab Council members, pushing for strong Council outcomes, only to encounter a cautious United States and an adamantly resistant Russia.

The UK has been particularly practiced at keeping consistent pressure on Russia and the United States to make the Council a relevant voice on the Syrian crisis. In many ways, alongside the obvious overriding foreign policy objectives, the UK was able to play this role, because its mission to the UN had more autonomy to negotiate outcomes in tandem with directions from London, though not as a top-down exercise. The UK led on drafting and negotiating three of the four vetoed resolutions. Without the UK leadership in the early days of the Syrian crisis, it is likely that neither the Russian nor the US position would have been significantly challenged in the Security Council.

The Elected Ten

Over the course of the past decade, the P5 have increasingly consolidated their hold over almost all of the issues on the Security Council's agenda. When the P5 are fundamentally divided, as in the case of Syria, one might think this would open up possibilities for the E10 to shape developments. Yet this has only been the case very recently, and only to a limited degree. In 2013, Australia and Luxembourg were able to take the lead in the humanitarian track on Syria, with Jordan joining them in 2014. These three elected Council members, in the face of not inconsiderable P5 pressure to relinquish the lead they had carved out, drafted and facilitated the negotiations leading up to the adoption of Resolutions 2139, 2165, and 2191 on the humanitarian situation. However, this role by E10 members has been the exception. By and large the E10, in their various groupings, have been able to do little more than shore up the opposing positions of the P5 on the Syria file over the course of the conflict.

In 2011, Lebanon was reluctant to pronounce itself too boldly on the Syria file, owing to its close links with Syria. For example, on August 3, 2011, the Council adopted its first presidential statement condemning the widespread violations of human rights and the use of force against civilians by the Syrian authorities.[19] Following its adoption, Lebanon used a rare procedural move disassociating itself from the statement. Morocco, taking over the Council's "Arab seat" from Lebanon in early 2012, faced no such constraints and spearheaded in the Council the Arab League's January 2012 proposal for a Syrian-led political transition. Beyond that, Morocco showed little initiative, however.

Saudi Arabia was elected by the General Assembly to replace Morocco for the 2014–2015 term, only for the kingdom to announce on October 18, 2013—shortly after US air strikes on Syria had been averted by the chemical weapons agreement—that it would not accept its seat on the Security Council, signaling a rupture with the US approach toward Syria and a lack of confidence in the Security Council to deal with the crisis. On December 6, the General Assembly held an extraordinary session to elect Jordan to the seat vacated by Saudi Arabia.

As of June 2015, Jordan had served eighteen months of its two-year term, and had actively engaged with Australia and Luxembourg in leading negotiations on Resolutions 2139, 2165 and 2191 on the humanitarian situation. It was no small feat that these three elected Council members proactively carved out a lead for themselves by drafting and negotiating important Council outcomes, given the P3's tendency to claim the lead on these issues for themselves. Jordan has also used its seat on the Council to draw attention to the impact of the humanitarian crisis in Syria on neighboring countries, of which it is one.

Important Security Council alliances emerged in 2011 and 2012. Germany and Portugal were both elected to the Council and, along with permanent members France and the UK, formed what was known as the EU4 bloc. The EU4 were consistently supportive of Security Council outcomes that had strong civilian protection, human rights, and accountability components, and also advocated consequences for noncompliance. Another group active in 2011 consisted of India, Brazil, and South Africa (IBSA), which carried their well-established cooperation in the context of the IBSA Dialogue Forum into the Security Council, advocating for a more cautious approach to the Syrian crisis. While the IBSA view was not fully aligned with the Russian and Chinese positions, there was significant overlap in placing a premium on dialogue to resolve the crisis and a great deal of wariness about the intent behind urging political transition and threatening coercive measures.

Conclusion

Despite episodic instances of cooperation among the P5 on issues such as chemical weapons and humanitarian access, the Security Council was never able to seriously tackle the central issue of the Syrian conflict—a political solution. With the Council locked in continued stalemate, the Assad regime unlikely to ever consent to its own replacement even as it loses more terri- tory, and the opposition relying increasingly on efforts to increase its mili- tary and political leverage, the Syrian crisis is poised to enter an even more deadly phase.

With the Council apparently unable to adopt meaningful action—and ensure its implementation—the UN's potential impact is limited to the mediation efforts of its special envoy (a position held since September 2014 by Staffan de Mistura, after Brahimi's resignation). The newest special envoy has attempted and failed to negotiate a freeze of hostilities in Aleppo and has facilitated low-level consultations among the parties in Geneva. Absent a clearer international consensus on a leadership transition in Syria and strong backing from the Council to implement and, if necessary, enforce certain measures to support such a transition, these efforts are unlikely to yield groundbreaking results. Most Council members are com- placent and view de Mistura's efforts as little more than a place holder until there is a major shift on the part of the United States or Russia to tilt the balance toward a political solution.

There is no serious discussion among Council members about acting on the veiled threat in Resolutions 2118, 2139, 2165, 2191, and 2209 to impose sanctions on Syria for its noncompliance with Council demands. In fact, the massive effort that went into agreeing on Resolution 2165 on cross-border humanitarian access has shifted down into monitoring mode. Similarly on the chemical weapons track, in March 2015, the Council con- demned the use of toxic chemicals such as chlorine (Resolution 2209), but subsequently failed to take further steps in response to allegations that the government continued to employ these weapons. In the early summer of 2015, efforts by the United States to establish an accountability mechanism that would attribute blame for the use of chemical weapons were opposed by Russia, for which the introduction of Chapter VII provisions remained a red line. Meanwhile, the Council was also unable to take up allegations that Syria had not fully declared its stocks of VX and Sarin nerve gases.

By early 2015, crises in Iraq, Libya, and Yemen had drawn attention away from Syria, and Council members seemed generally despondent over how to have any meaningful role in ceasing the civil war in Syria. At this time, activity by the Council was limited to counterterrorism efforts, and the emergence of ISIS as a wider regional threat seemed likely to exacerbate that trend. Despite its own hard-won resolutions deploring the dire Syrian humanitarian situation and calls for the protection of civilians, the Council has done nothing to enforce compliance, despite its demands for opening up sieges of population areas and halting the use of barrel bombs, toxic gasses, and chemical weapons. Realpolitik and competing national interests have proven more important than Syrian lives. The Secretary-General has reminded the Council that the Syrian conflict cannot also be reduced to the problem of combatting violent extremism, terrorism, and foreign fighters, and that all concerned should not lose sight that the best way to stop such extremism is a political solution. For the Council and its reputation, the stakes remain high. Continued paralysis on Syria—and its relegation to being a bit player in addressing the spread of the ISIS insurgency to Iraq—will reinforce the widespread perception of the UN's growing marginalization in world affairs. Aspirants for permanent membership in the Council have pointed to the Council's inability to meaningfully respond to the Syrian crisis as an indication for urgent reform. Yet the argument that a more representative Council would have been more effective remains unconvincing. The French-led and Syria-inspired initiative launched in October 2013 by Foreign Minister Laurent Fabius to rein in the P5's use of the veto when considering situations of mass crimes seems like a more appropriate solution, although it is unlikely to gain much traction among the other P5 members.

Notes

This chapter is informed by a large number of interviews conducted since 2011. The permanent representatives of Australia, China, France, Jordan, Luxembourg, and the United Kingdom as well as a representative of Human Rights Watch were interviewed specifically for the purposes of this chapter in February 2014. However, much of the research is also based on our interviews conducted over the course of 2011–2015 with diplomats to the UN from Argentina, Australia, Chile, China, Egypt, France, Germany, Guatemala, India, Israel, Jordan, Lebanon, Lithuania, Luxembourg, Malaysia, Morocco, New Zealand, Norway, Pakistan, Palestine, Portugal, the Russian Federation, South Africa, Spain, the United Kingdom, and the United States. Interviews over the same period of time were regularly conducted with UN Secretariat staff from the Department of Political Affairs and the Department of Peacekeeping Operations and civil society organizations such as Human Rights Watch, Oxfam, Crisis Group, and Crisis Action as well as civil society actors in Syria. The research is also based on extensive interviews and meetings with officials and leaders in the Gulf and Middle East region, as well as representatives of the Syrian opposition and Syrian figures not aligned to any particular grouping.

1. "Syrian Death Toll Tops 19,000, Say Activists," *The Guardian,* July 22, 2012, www.theguardian.com/world/2012/jul/22/syria-death-toll-tops-19000.

2. United Nations Refugee Agency, http://data.unhcr.org/syrianrefugees/regional.php.

3. United Nations Security Council Draft Resolution, UN Doc. S/2011/612, October 4, 2011.

4. United Nations Security Council Draft Resolution, UN Doc. S/2012/77, February 4, 2012.

5. Ibid.

6. United Nations General Assembly Resolution 66/176, A/RES/66/176 (December 19, 2011).

7. United Nations General Assembly Resolution 66/253A, A/RES/66/253A (February 16, 2012).

8. United Nations General Assembly Resolution 66/253B, A/RES/66/253B (August 3, 2012).

9. United Nations General Assembly Resolution 67/262, A/RES/67/262 (May 15, 2013). This resolution was not as clearly related to blockages in the Security Council, but it was nevertheless highly contentious due to the perception that language in the original draft was setting the stage to recognize the Syrian opposition as the legitimate representative of Syria at the UN, a step many member states were unwilling to take. (The Syrian opposition had some assumed privileges at the Arab League in March 2013.) Finally, the language was changed to welcome the establishment of the National Coalition for Syrian Revolutionary and Opposition Forces as an interlocutor needed for a political transition. The resolution passed with the least number of votes (107) of any of the General Assembly resolutions addressing the Syrian crisis.

10. United Nations General Assembly Resolution 68/182, A/RES/68/182 (December 18, 2013).

11. United Nations General Assembly Resolution 66/253A (February 16, 2012).

12. United Nations Security Council, "Statement by the President of the Security Council," UN Doc. S/PRST/2012/6, March 21, 2012.

13. United Nations Security Council, "Statement by the President of the Security Council," UN Doc. S/PRST/2012/10, April 5, 2012.

14. United Nations Security Council Draft Resolution, UN Doc. S/2012/538, July 19, 2012.

15. United Nations Security Council, "Statement by the President of the Security Council," UN Doc. S/PRST/2014/14, July 28, 2014.

16. United Nations Security Council, *Report of the Secretary-General on the Implementation of Security Council Resolution 2139 (2014),* UN Doc. S/2014/208, March 24, 2014.

17. United Nations General Assembly and Security Council, "Letter Dated 14 January 2013 from the Chargé d'Affaires a.i. of the Permanent Mission of Switzerland to the United Nations Addressed to the Secretary-General," UN Doc. A/67/694-S/2013/19, January 16, 2013.

18. United Nations Security Council, Draft Resolution, UN Doc. S/2014/348, May 22, 2014; and United Nations Security Council, "Provisional Verbatim Record of the 7180th Meeting," UN Doc. S/PV.7180, May 22, 2014.

19. United Nations Security Council, "Statement by the President of the Security Council," UN Doc. S/PRST/2011/16, August 3, 2011.

Commentary:
The Council's Failure on Syria

Raghida Dergham

THE STARKEST CONTEMPORARY FAILURE OF THE SECURITY COUN-
cil is Syria. With 140,000 dead, 5 million displaced, and 2 million refugees
three years after the first protesters were inspired by the Jasmine and
Tahreer Square revolutions in Tunisia and Egypt, Syria is a continuing
humanitarian catastrophe. Its escalating civil war has a huge destabilizing
impact on an already fragile region fraught with challenges.

The "coalition of defiance" mounted from within the Security Council
by the BRICS bloc—Brazil, Russia, India, China, and South Africa—in
2011 as a result of the NATO "mandate creep" in Libya, as well as an acute
disinterest by the United States in the crisis and its shifting "red lines" for
intervention, forestalled early engagement by the Council on Syria. Later
on, the joint vetoes on three draft resolutions in 2011 and 2012 by Russia
and China paralyzed the Council.

Shaming became partly an excuse and partly a pretext for the United
States, whose policy was not to get dragged into the Syria quagmire. Russia
manipulated the isolationist tendencies of the Obama administration—attributed to US fatigue with the wars in Iraq and Afghanistan—to its advantage
in Syria and in the bilateral relationship with the United States. Moscow
understood exactly where Washington was and decided to bet on weakness.
Syria became the launching pad for Moscow to teach the West a lesson—to
never again dismiss Russia as a major world power—in an effort to regain
the international influence once wielded by the former Soviet Union. Russia
remembered too well that the Soviet Union fell in Afghanistan at the hands
of jihadists supported by the United States and Arab countries. Beyond
deciding it was time for payback, Moscow also had vital economic and

strategic interests, such as preventing a Qatari gas pipeline through Syria to Europe and maintaining its military base in Tartus.

Russian foreign minister Sergei Lavrov referred to the United States as "the old lady" and told a Syrian national whom he met at the time that this was "Moscow's war in Syria," pledging that "terrorists will never ever" return to Chechnya or anywhere else in Russia or the five Central Asian Islamic republics.

China joined ranks with Russia after seeing the decline of US interest and engagement in the Middle East and reasoning that its economic interests—not withstanding its huge bilateral trade with Saudi Arabia—were better guaranteed by the winners in Syria: Russia and Iran. Beijing opted for a strategic alliance with Moscow and found comfort in following its lead on Syria in the Security Council. Moreover, both China and Russia feared that the Arab revolts might inspire their Muslim minorities.

The League of Arab States never put to the Security Council a demarche similar to the one it did for Libya bluntly requesting military intervention. But the Arab League took a major initiative outside the Security Council in November 2011 that resembled to a large degree the Gulf Cooperation Council–brokered transitional agreement in Yemen. It called for a halt to the Syrian regime's crackdown on protesters, for President Bashar al-Assad to delegate power to his vice president, and for elections to be held under a "national unity government." Under pressure, Damascus allowed Arab observers into the country in response to the Arab League proposal, but the League suspended its mission because of the worsening violence in the country. In an unprecedented move, the Arab League voted to suspend Syria as a member, accusing it of failing to implement an Arab peace plan. Nineteen Arab countries imposed economic sanctions against the Syrian regime.

Former UN Secretary-General Kofi Annan was appointed as a UN–Arab League joint envoy. His six-point plan echoed elements of the Arab peace plan as he tried to rally the Security Council behind him. After months of ill-tempered disagreement, a UN-backed Action Group on Syria met in Geneva in June 2012, issuing a communiqué on June 30 that found consensus among Western countries as well as Russia and its allies. The communiqué called for a "sustained cessation" of violence and the establishment of a transitional government that "could include members of the present government and the opposition, and other groups."

Then–US secretary of state Hillary Clinton was confident she had won Russia to the side of the argument that Assad could not be part of a transition. She was in for a surprise. Russia dug in its heels, utterly rejecting the interpretation that Assad would have to leave power, either at the start or the end of the political transition agreed to in Geneva. The war of interpretations over the Geneva communiqué and the "Assad knot" would contribute to further hindering action in the Security Council.

Led by Saudi Arabia and Qatar, the UN General Assembly tried to fill the vacuum created by the Security Council, but never went the distance to convene under "Uniting for Peace," which would have given its resolutions weight similar to those of the Security Council. One General Assembly resolution demanded that Assad step down while the UN appointed veteran Algerian diplomat Lakhdar Brahimi as the new UN–Arab League representative for Syria after Annan resigned.

Annan had approached the solution of the Syrian crisis primarily through the prism of a necessary agreement among the five permanent members of the Security Council. Brahimi reckoned that the route to a solution was above all in a US-Russian understanding, angering some permanent members who felt slighted by his focus on the United States and Russia.

The failure of the Security Council to comprehensively address Syria contributed in no small measure to al-Qaeda and similar groups filling the vacuum, with Sunni fundamentalist militants multiplying in the third year of the conflict. Syria became the magnet for neojihadists from all over the world and the epicenter for the war on terror, led this time by Russian president Vladimir Putin, who was replicating what former US president George W. Bush did in Iraq a few years earlier: waging a war on terror in the faraway Arab lands of Iraq and Syria to keep terrorism away from US and Russian cities.

The moderate Syrian opposition, represented by the Free Syria Army and the Syrian National Coalition, was set to pay the price for the neojihadists who hoped to hijack the Syrian revolution with no small help from the Assad regime itself. The US designation of the al-Nusra front as a terrorist organization in December 2012, even though it was one of the most effective forces fighting Assad, proved to be a move that had far-reaching consequences on the military balance of power in Syria. The Security Council blacklisted al-Nusra as a front group for al-Qaeda in Iraq on May 31, 2013. Yet it took no action against Hezbollah (also listed by the United States as a terrorist organization), despite its military support of the Syrian government with arms provided by Iran. The Council also turned a blind eye to Iran's military role in Syria despite the fact that Syria is in violation of Resolution 1737. An unusual de facto alliance among Russia, the United States, Iran, and Israel against the neojihadists was manifesting itself in Syria.

Ghouta, site of a massive chemical attack seemingly perpetrated by the Assad regime, would go down in history as the town that sparked an outraged President Barack Obama to go all the way to the brink before he blinked. It would become the game-changer not only in Syria's political and chemical weapons landscape but also in US-Russian relations. This in turn would impact a historic change in Iran's relations with the United States and consequently to a new chapter in the P5+1 nuclear negotiations with Iran.

In the Security Council, the United Kingdom distributed its draft resolution calling for limited military measures against Syria in response to the use of chemical weapons. But action never took place on this draft, as something stunning happened on August 29, 2013: Prime Minister David Cameron was defeated in the House of Commons on a carefully worded motion in support of an air strike on Syria. No British prime minister had been so defeated on a foreign policy motion for centuries. The development demonstrated the extent to which UK decisionmakers had come to distrust a military venture with the United States after the fiasco by former prime minister Tony Blair in joining US president George W. Bush in the Iraq War.

It also demonstrated the UK public's growing disengagement with the Middle East, as the majority looked at the Syrian war through the prism of Arabs fighting Arabs. Similarly, public opinion in the United States was determined this would not become a US war. The majority saw Syria's war of attrition as a collective quagmire for al-Qaeda, Hezbollah, and the Assad regime, as well as potentially Iran's Vietnam. Both publics, in the United States and the United Kingdom, looked away from the atrocities and consequently could no longer claim the higher moral ground.

An axis of Russia, China, Iran, the Assad regime, and Hezbollah was wagering on Obama's weakness, on the American public's distaste for another military intervention in the Middle East, as well as on isolationist sentiments in Western parliaments. What happened in the UK House of Commons proved them right. At first, it seemed as though this axis had triumphed over the United States, or even over the North Atlantic alliance in the form of NATO, which appeared fragmented, divided, scattered, and frightened. This impression quickly dissipated when the Obama administration metamorphosed from a group of doves into a group of hawks, and headed to the US Congress with overwhelming confidence that Congress would authorize military action.

But the "upset" in the House of Commons contributed to Obama's sudden backing down from military action, which came as a shock to several capitals—including Paris, where socialist president François Hollande had resolved to replace the United Kingdom with the United States in the alliance on Syria. On August 31, President Obama found his own exit, having locked himself into a countdown to a military strike that looked imminent, announcing that he would first seek authorization from Congress.

President Obama headed to the September 5, 2013, Group of 20 summit in Saint Petersburg intent on embarrassing others so as to reverse the impression that this predicament was his own. But all of this was to take a different turn in Saint Petersburg when Presidents Obama and Putin met cordially and their foreign ministers engaged heavily to create what would become a major shift in the Syrian conflict. Obama's red lines were erased: Assad would become a needed interlocutor in the new arrangement.

On September 13, a deal was struck in what became the "framework" agreement, which offered President Obama the chance to step away from his red lines and from his threat to use military force on Damascus while still securing the destruction of Syria's chemical weapon stockpiles. On the same day, at UN headquarters, Secretary-General Ban Ki-moon said that Assad has "committed many crimes against humanity" while adding: "I'm sure that there will be the process of accountability when everything is over."

The "surprise" Russian proposal turned out to be a well-negotiated process between the United States and Russia. Russia, on its part, secured an astounding diplomatic and political victory in the UN while continuing to supply the Assad regime with military assistance. Russia confined the chemical issue to a bilateral framework with Washington and navigated the political track in Geneva II away from the "Assad knot."

The confirmed use of chemical weapons in August 2013 partially ended the deadlock within the Security Council and forged a consensus on Resolution 2118, under which Syria's chemical arsenal would be destroyed by June 2014. However, the architects of the consensus, Russia and the United States, arrived at bilateral understandings and then proceeded to seek the Council's rubber stamp. Moreover, through Resolution 2118, Assad turned from outcast into a necessary partner in the process of implementing the US-Russian framework of understanding on Syria's chemical weapons.

Another consensus emerged in that there was seen to be no military solution in Syria, only a political solution. Convening the Geneva II talks would put Syria in a political transition process. Immunity for Assad would be the unspoken part of the process, at least until presidential elections in Syria in June 2014. This date coincided, rather curiously, with several timelines and agendas including the completion of the destruction of Syria's chemical arsenal, as well as the target date for a transitional agreement in the nuclear negotiations between the P5+1 and Iran, whose military role inside Syria—directly and through its Shiite ally Hezbollah—was decisive for the survival of Assad.

Ban Ki-moon invited Iran to the launch of the Geneva II conference in Montreux on January 22, 2014, but was immediately forced to retract the invitation when Tehran could not accept the Geneva I communiqué as the terms of reference for Geneva II. Acceptance would have been inconsistent with Iran's policy of adhering to the Assad regime and the holding of the presidential elections as a means of preventing the materialization of a transitional governing body in Syria.

Representatives of Assad at Geneva II went to the talks to impose their agenda of "fighting terrorism" in an effort to torpedo the agenda as stated by the UN: a mutual agreement between the government and the opposition on a transitional governing body with full executive authority. Russia and Iran backed Damascus in its macabre attempt to reduce the Syrian tragedy to a "war against terror" and torpedoed the Geneva process and the transitional governing body by extending their support for elections that would surely secure another seven-year term for Assad, with the opposition's constituency either internally displaced or in refugee camps abroad. Without a major shift in US and Russian policies, Geneva II was doomed to be only and simply a process of lip service without results. Geneva II came to an end accompanied by an atrocious escalation of violence on the ground by both the regime and its extremist opponents, whether by dropping "barrel bombs" from planes or by despicable war crimes and crimes against humanity committed by both sides.

The United States seemed unwilling to sway away from its policy of disassociation with the Syrian conflict, which was becoming a quagmire for all involved as they sunk deeper into the illusion of their false victory. Equally as important is that Obama was not eager to compete with Putin in leading the war on Islamic extremists or the fight against terrorism. It was fine, in fact welcomed, that Russia and Putin would be on the frontlines of this war, sparing the United States the cost entailed on multiple levels. Regardless of any pragmatic calculation, inherent in both policies was an amoral and unethical use of Syria and the innocent Syrians, particularly by two major powers on the Security Council.

Washington and Moscow fell further apart due to the crisis in Ukraine in March 2014. Putin was more hardened on Syria as a result of his clash with Western powers on Crimea and Ukraine. He would not allow a Russian retreat of any kind in Syria—strategic or within the context of his war on Islamic extremism. Syria was poised to go down in history as a testimony to the utter bankruptcy of the Security Council, as this body, entrusted with safeguarding international peace and security, became an accomplice to atrocities and impunity.

The UN projected that the number of Syrian refugees would nearly double in 2014 to exceed 4 million. Another 9.3 million people will need aid inside Syria. Millions will remain displaced from their homes. Neighboring countries, particularly Lebanon, Iraq, and Jordan have been pulled into the sphere of Syria's disaster. They entered the eye of the storm with all intended and unintended consequences. The unofficial death-toll estimate by the beginning of 2014 exceeded 140,000. But no one could predict the full magnitude of the tragedy as the conflict continued. The United Nations officially has stopped counting the dead.

Part 6

The Security Council and International Order

36

The Security Council and Peacekeeping

Richard Gowan

ON AUGUST 5, 2006, FRANCE AND THE UNITED STATES TABLED A draft Security Council resolution signaling that the UN Interim Force in Lebanon (UNIFIL) faced closure after nearly thirty years of service.[1] The mission's future had been in doubt since Israeli forces entered Lebanon in an effort to suppress Hezbollah just less than a month earlier. Four UN observers had been killed by Israeli fire, and Secretary-General Kofi Annan had laid out options including the partial or total withdrawal of the peacekeepers. US policymakers had floated the idea of deploying Turkish and Egyptian troops, while Israel had mooted a NATO force. The Franco-American text called upon UNIFIL to monitor an initial ceasefire, but also promised "to authorize in a further resolution under Chapter VII of the Charter the deployment of a UN-mandated international force to support the Lebanese armed forces and government in providing a secure environment and contribute to the implementation of a permanent ceasefire and a long-term solution." All sides understood that this force would be far more robust than UNIFIL, which numbered fewer than 4,000 troops, and that its goal would be to keep Hezbollah down.

In the days that followed, the proposal unraveled. The Lebanese government, under pressure from Hezbollah, signaled that it would not accept the multinational force. Instead, it insisted that UNIFIL remain in place and continue to operate under Chapter VI of the UN Charter as a consent-based mission rather than an enforcement action. On August 11, the Security Council passed Resolution 1701, authorizing the expansion of UNIFIL to 15,000 personnel. While the new text directed the mission to respond firmly to any challenges it faced, it avoided any explicit reference to Chap-

749

ter VII. European governments rushed troops to southern Lebanon. The episode appeared to highlight both the enduring importance of the Security Council and the flexibility of UN peacekeeping as a crisis management tool.

Yet it arguably also highlighted the limitations of both peacekeeping and the Council. The initial Franco-American draft indicated that the two permanent members of the Council with the greatest interests in Lebanon did *not* believe a blue helmet mission was a sufficient response to the war. This reflected the views not only of hawks in the US administration of President George W. Bush, but also of French military leaders. But the combined weight of these two powers was not enough to sway the government of Lebanon, an already weak state that had been further destabilized by the Israeli assault. Beirut, rather than the permanent members of the Security Council, shaped the political parameters for reinforcing UNIFIL.

Indeed, this episode exposed precisely how difficult it is for even the strongest members of the Council to set the direction for peace operations to their satisfaction. I argue here that this has been a recurring feature of Council diplomacy in the early twenty-first century. This may seem counterintuitive, as peacekeeping has emerged as one of the Council's premiere crisis management tools in this period. Blue helmet operations went through a "boom and bust" cycle after the Cold War, successfully supporting the implementation of peace agreements from Namibia and Mozambique to Central America and Cambodia, in the late 1980s and early 1990s, before going dreadfully awry in Somalia, Rwanda, and the former Yugoslavia in the mid-1990s.[2] After 1999, when the Council mandated the UN missions in Kosovo and Timor-Leste, peacekeeping appeared to enter a prolonged new boom phase. The number of uniformed peacekeepers worldwide, having dipped as low as 12,000 in the late 1990s, now broke all previous records, hovering near 100,000 from 2010 on.[3] While these soldiers and police have been scattered, from Haiti to the Middle East, the large majority have been deployed in Africa, sustaining long-term and large-scale missions in cases including Liberia, the Democratic Republic of the Congo, and Sudan. Although missions inevitably suffer individual setbacks, the overall resurgence in UN deployments has defied widespread predictions of peacekeeping's demise in the 1990s.

The story of this resurgence also appears to highlight the Council's ability to shape the internal affairs of states by means including the use of force. Rather than trust in consent-based missions, the Council has increasingly referred to Chapter VII of the UN Charter in authorizing enforcement action when launching new operations, at a minimum directing peacekeepers to use force to protect civilians where possible.[4] Many of the Council's mandates, especially those relating to long-running missions, have become both increasingly detailed and ambitious. When the Council approved a phased buildup of peacekeepers in the DRC in 2000, the elements of the relevant resolution covering the mission's activities ran to 400 words, with only a small section referring to the protection of civilians falling under Chapter VII.[5] By 2008, the equivalent text was over a thousand words in length, was entirely under Chapter VII, and included a sweeping injunction that the operation should "contribute to the promotion of good governance and respect for the principle of accountability."[6]

Even critics of the Security Council argue that its utilization of peace operations is evidence of its power, or more accurately the power of the five permanent members that oversee Council affairs. Michael Pugh, placing UN peacekeeping in the context of debates about US hegemony, argued in 2004 that Washington and its allies in the Council had achieved "dominance" through means including "use of the Security Council veto, the design of mandates and the withholding of funds and support."[7] Mats Berdal also attributes the rapid growth of peacekeeping after 1999 to "the strategic calculations of the P5 and, depending on the mission, key troop contributors."[8] There have been many analyses from the ideological left and global South emphasizing the neoimperialist characteristics of UN operations, including the fact that most peacekeepers now come from former African and Asian colonies. "The institutions of UN peacekeeping," Philip Cunliffe argues, "allow states in the global North to displace the political risks and military commitments of international security onto poorer and weaker states in the global South. In so doing, wealthy and powerful states reduce the global costs of hegemony."[9]

I argue in this chapter that neither the Security Council nor the West dominate peacekeeping as decisively as such critiques suggest. I begin by setting out an alternative narrative of the evolution of peacekeeping that highlights how the Council has often had to react to, rather than shape, events, and go on to show how Council members not only have to compromise among themselves over UN operations, but also have to make concessions to other actors including UN officials, troop contributors, and regional players such as the European Union and African Union, which both cooperate and compete with the UN in crisis management. I also highlight that the countries that "host" UN operations have shown both the ability and the will to disrupt peacekeepers' efforts and even expel missions in defiance of a surprisingly passive Security Council. Lebanon's refusal of the Franco-American plan to replace UNIFIL was, we shall see, actually a fairly mild instance of such resistance to the Council.

I conclude the chapter by looking at the tools available to Council members to assert authority over missions, and find them wanting. Whether making mandates, releasing statements on individual missions, or discussing overall peacekeeping strategies, the Council often fails to find the right formula to elicit action on the ground. Although I offer a variety of proposals for strengthening the Council's grip on operations, there is no guarantee that any option can break the cycle of haphazard crisis responses, contingent decisions, and unintended consequences that has shaped peace-keeping thus far.

The Return of Peacekeeping: One Damn Thing After Another?

Peacekeeping's future was uncertain at the end of the 1990s and there was little reason to think that a new boom in UN operations beckoned. The Security Council was haunted by its failures earlier in the decade. The P3, the three Western permanent members of the Council, had experimented with working militarily through the UN, but the US debacle in Somalia and the French and British travails in the former Yugoslavia left the trio deeply skeptical toward blue helmet missions. Two trends appeared to be reshaping international crisis management. The first was an increasing reliance on regional organizations, ranging from NATO and the OSCE to ECOWAS, to run operations. The second was a shift from peacekeeping to peace enforce-ment by some of these actors, observable both in NATO's Balkan missions and in Africa. As David Malone and Karin Wermester noted in 2000, the Security Council "alternately both worried about and supported in qualified terms enforcement activities" in Sierra Leone and Liberia, where ECOWAS forces were trying to rein in widespread violence.[10]

Peacekeeping's Uncertain Recovery, 1999–2005

Three non-UN peace enforcement operations paved the way for a new era of UN operations. The first of these was NATO's intervention in Kosovo, which set the stage for the deployment of UN police and civilian personnel to manage the former Yugoslav territory in June 1999. The second was the Australian-led deployment to Timor-Leste that September, which again cre-ated the need for a longer-term peacekeeping presence that the Security Council mandated UN personnel to fill. Finally, the ECOWAS-backed force in Sierra Leone (ECOMOG) was in need of assistance as a new democratic government in Nigeria, which provided the bulk of the force, was keen to bring its soldiers home. While the Security Council responded to all three of these cases by mandating UN operations, this did not necessarily signify a rebirth of large-scale blue helmet military missions. The transitional administration in Kosovo (UNMIK) had immense executive responsibilities but operated under the protection of NATO forces and alongside significant OSCE and EU presences. The parallel transitional administration in Timor-Leste (UNTAET) had a significant military component, but while it did have to use force to handle residual militia groups, the mission soon focused on economic and political issues as it prepared the territory for independence. The decisive test for the new generation of UN operations was to come in West Africa instead.

In Sierra Leone, the Security Council stumbled into a major military peacekeeping operation through a series of errors and crises. As John Hirsch noted in the previous edition of this volume, the Council took up a proposal from the Secretariat for a 6,000-strong force of troops from developing countries that apparently reflected what UN officials "thought the traffic from the [P5] would bear."[11] This force (UNAMSIL) was meant to work alongside ECOMOG on disarming former combatants and preparing for elections. Although the Council directed the mission to protect civilians within its capabilities, there was a presumption that it would not face major threats. However, ECOMOG's sudden withdrawal precipitated an outburst of violence in which hundreds of peacekeepers were taken hostage. While a British intervention helped restore order, the Council increased UNAMSIL to an eventual peak of 17,000 troops and gave it an expansive mandate to ensure longer-term stability.

The Council encountered frictions that foreshadowed recurrent problems for later peacekeeping operations. The poor coordination with ECOMOG highlighted the difficulties of aligning the UN's plans with those of regional and subregional organizations. Council members had urged ECOMOG to maintain security in Sierra Leone's capital, Freetown, but Nigeria was angered by the UN's refusal to pay for the force. There was discontent within UNAMSIL too. Jordan, unhappy with the expansion of UNAMSIL's mandate and critical of NATO countries' refusal to participate in the mission, withdrew its troops from Sierra Leone in late 2000. India also pulled out its contingent, although this reflected tensions between its commander and African units. A Security Council mission in October 2000 observed that "different contingents had different perceptions of the mandate and tasks of UNAMSIL."[12]

The Council diplomats visiting Sierra Leone thus glimpsed the difficulties inherent in turning diplomatic agreements into operational directives. It was proving equally difficult to provide effective oversight of the new operations' civilian tasks, especially in governing Kosovo and Timor-Leste. Richard Caplan observes that in these cases the Council proved "concerned chiefly with establishing broad strategic direction and not with the more particular aspects of administration."[13] The Council has also been accused of pushing for an early and rapid downsizing of the UN administration in Timor-Leste for budgetary reasons, skimping on capacity building, and leaving the country poorly prepared for independence (ironically ensuring that the UN had to maintain peacekeepers there until 2012). Having revitalized UN operations, the Council was finding it difficult to stay on top of them all.

At the same time, it was unintentionally sowing the seeds for an even larger and more controversial operation in the DRC. It initially deployed a small observer mission to the Congo at the end of 1999, and this expanded gradually to a force of 4,300 personnel (MONUC) by late 2002. This remained a very limited mission considering the sheer scale and level of violence in the DRC, and a major crisis in the Ituri region in the east of the country in mid-2003 precipitated a series of events reminiscent of those that shaped UNAMSIL. Another Western force (this time a largely French EU-flagged mission) was deployed to restore order, and the Security Council boosted MONUC to 10,000 personnel, including a special brigade to maintain stability in Ituri. MONUC would face further crises—including major attacks by militia forces in 2004 and 2008 that threatened to overwhelm the mission—and the Council responded by expanding the force repeatedly until it surpassed 20,000 troops and police officers yet still struggled to keep order.

The MONUC and UNAMSIL stories highlight a basic fact about the resurgence of peacekeeping after 1999: though the Council's initial preference in both cases was for relatively limited missions, events on the ground forced it to expand its ambitions. Once committed to a country, Council members found it extremely difficult to back out—perhaps reflecting the lessons learned during the 1990s, when their predecessors had been too quick to withdraw troops in cases such as Angola and Rwanda. But the new dynamic in favor of increasing peacekeeping commitments in the face of a crisis soon began to raise questions about the overall burden on UN operations, with recurrent talk about the risk of overstretch.

This did not stop the Council from proceeding to mandate a series of new UN missions, including those in Liberia (2003); Burundi, Côte d'Ivoire, and Haiti (2004); and South Sudan (2005). P3 members used UN forces to take pressure off their own militaries, which were simultaneously heavily engaged in Afghanistan and Iraq. Thus the United States and France jointly deployed a multinational force to Haiti, but quickly handed operations over to the UN, while France wanted blue helmets to back up its own military presence (Operation Licorne) in Côte d'Ivoire. More positively, the Council appeared willing to make more serious initial investments in the operations it mandated in 2003–2005 than it had in Sierra Leone and the DRC. In the Liberian case, with the United States driving the process, the Council suggested that it had learned the lesson of Sierra Leone by mandating an initial force of over 14,000 personnel. Its decision to send 6,700 troops and 1,600 police to Haiti also indicated a willingness to anticipate and counter potential violence, although this sparked debates among troop contributors about the definition of "robust" peacekeeping.[14]

Darfur and Council Divisions, 2006–2011

If Council members seemed to be progressing toward a collective under-standing of peacekeeping in this period, the impression did not last. From 2006 to 2008, fissures emerged among both the P5 and the P3 over a series of crises, the most divisive of which was in the Darfur region of Sudan. While the conflict in Darfur began in 2003 and claimed hundreds of thou-sands of lives in the years that followed (see Chapter 30), it initially seemed beyond the reach of UN peacekeeping. While US and British officials were concerned by the crisis, the situation in southern Sudan was a higher prior-ity. China wished to protect its allies in the Sudanese government from Western interference in Darfur, while France wanted the stability of Chad and the Central African Republic, two former colonies neighboring Darfur, to receive greater attention. These competing interests hampered Council debates until late 2005, and a weak African Union mission (AMIS) was left to handle the situation. By 2006, international outrage over the continued violence in Darfur and signs that AMIS was failing pushed the Council to discuss alternatives. A Council mission led by the British and French ambassadors visited Darfur and Chad that June, while AU and UN officials discussed bringing AMIS under UN control.

As Alexandra Novosseloff and I have noted, differences among the P3 complicated these processes, and it is worth pausing to review the transac-tional nature of their efforts to find a common position: "The United States and United Kingdom prepared a draft resolution that first simply asked the Secretary-General 'to report to the Council on the protection of civilians in . . . camps in Chad.' A second draft mentioned the possibility that the UN operation in Darfur could monitor crossborder activities. It also mentioned the possible establishment of a UN multidimensional presence in Chad and, if necessary, the Central African Republic. A third draft included all three possibilities. The changes from the first draft reflected French pressure to include serious proposals for stabilizing Chad and the Central African Republic rather than treating them as secondary to the Darfur situation."[15]

This brief narrative illustrate how the Council's "strategies" result from diplomatic bargaining rather than rational planning processes. In this case the bargaining was in vain. While the P3 finally agreed on a text (Resolu-tion 1706) that authorized a UN operation in Darfur accompanied by sup-porting activities (although not a complete operation) in Chad, China and Russia abstained, signaling to Sudan that it need not comply. Khartoum duly refused to let the UN replace AMIS. A further round of diplomatic haggling resulted in a final compromise in 2007 on the creation of an UN-AU "hybrid" mission in Darfur (UNAMID), while France orchestrated the deployment of parallel EU and UN missions to Chad and the Central African Republic. The net results of these efforts were disappointing. Khar-toum managed to undercut the deployment and operations of UNAMID in

2008 through tactics discussed later, crippling the mission. The EU deployment to Chad, also in 2008, went smoothly enough, but the Europeans left after one year, and the Chadian government treated the UN operation (MINURCAT) with contempt, expelling it in 2010.

Darfur and Chad thus undermined any hopes that the Council might be evolving into a cohesive strategy-making body for peacekeeping operations. The year 2008 was a damaging one for P5 and P3 cooperation on peacekeeping more generally. Kosovo's unilateral declaration of independence early in the year sparked fierce debates between the P3—which insisted that an EU mission should replace the UN administration—and Russia and China. It took most of the year to agree a compromise by which a rump UN mission stayed on in Kosovo, while the EU took over policing and justice duties. P5 relations worsened after Russia's invasion of Georgia in August 2008, which precipitated the closure of the long-standing UN mission there. But the P5 split on different lines at the end of the year over Somalia, where, as in Sudan, an existing AU peace operation was in trouble. The George W. Bush administration, in its final months, pushed for a UN mission in Somalia with support from African states. China backed this position out of deference to its African allies. Britain, France, and Russia were unconvinced that a UN mission could succeed, and fought fiercely against the proposal. The incoming Barack Obama administration shared their doubts, and the Council agreed to fund the AU mission and provide it UN logistical support rather than fully replace it.[16]

These converging disputes raised doubts about both the future of UN peacekeeping and the Council's capacity to manage it. The fact that MONUC had been through one of its periodic crises in late 2008, moving Secretary-General Ban Ki-moon to plead unsuccessfully for help from the EU, did not help matters.[17] In January 2009, Britain and France circulated a nonpaper addressing the military ineffectiveness of UN missions, but a more serious shadow loomed over peacekeeping: the global financial crisis.[18] The peacekeeping budget was now over $7 billion, and the economic situation set clear limits to what the UN could do. From 2009 to the start of 2012, the Council mandated only two new missions: one for newly independent South Sudan (UNMISS) and the other in the disputed Abyei region on the new inter-Sudanese border. While cooperation between China and the United States over the Sudans had improved since the nadir of the Darfur debates, other peacekeeping crises continued to roil the Council. In late 2010, the P3 and Russia fought a public battle over Côte d'Ivoire as Moscow tried to protect President Laurent Gbagbo after he lost long-delayed national elections (see Chapter 33). Russia only backed down once supporters of Gbagbo's opponent, Alassane Ouattara, were on the verge of military victory, acquiescing to the use of force by French and UN units to limit the chaos.

Approaching a New Generation of Crises, 2012–2013

The Council continued to stumble through further crises in 2012 and 2013, although there was some new willingness to fund fresh missions and boost existing operations. The P3, Russia, and China attempted to shelve their differences over Syria by deploying the short-lived UN supervision mission there in the second quarter of 2012 (see Chapter 35). This failed, but the Council also struggled to keep abreast of new crises in Mali and the DRC. In the former case, the Council, led by France, tried to avoid deploying UN forces after secessionists and Islamists seized the north of the country in early 2012. There were lengthy discussions of cheaper options, including an ECOWAS deployment to strengthen the Malian army. The Council finally agreed on a version of this plan in December 2012, whereupon rebel advances in January 2013 compelled France to intervene directly. Recalling Côte d'Ivoire and Haiti, Paris called for a UN mission to reinforce it in Mali. This force, initially made up of weak African units, began operations in mid-2013 and soon faced attacks by Islamist groups.

Meanwhile the P3 and African states were crafting plans for a new Force Intervention Brigade (FIB) to bolster the mission in the DRC (renamed MONUSCO) after it had failed to block rebel forces from seizing the important city of Goma in November 2012. It is striking that in many ways the creation of the FIB followed the same pattern seen in the reinforcement of UNAMSIL and MONUC in 2000 and 2003. Once again, the Council found itself outpaced by events and grasping for a response. Although it directed the FIB to "neutralize" militia opponents, giving an impression of strength, this was a last-ditch effort to regain some initiative (see Chapter 18 for a more in-depth discussion of the FIB and robust peacekeeping). The degree of pressure on the Council rose further at the very end of 2013 due to deteriorating crises in the Central African Republic and South Sudan. The Council's management of peacekeeping operations looked to be as flawed and reactive as it was in 1999.

The Council and the Wider Peacekeeping Universe

While the Security Council has struggled to keep up with the multiple peacekeeping challenges on its agenda, the P3 also struggled to overcome political and operational obstacles to the implementation of their mandates. To understand the limits on their actions more fully, it is necessary to analyze the Council's relations with the wider universe of actors involved in peacekeeping, ranging from troop contributors to regional organizations. Before turning to these external actors, we must ask whether the nonpermanent members of the Council have much influence over peace operations.

Nonpermanent Council Members

Many of the states that run for election to the Council refer to peacekeeping in their campaigns, even if they are not major troop contributors. In 2012, for example, Australia and Finland both held public events in New York on the topic, while competing with Luxembourg for two Council seats representing the Western European and Others Group (WEOG).[19] The Finns also sent a new contingent to UNIFIL to show their commitment. It is not clear whether this was a winning theme. While Australia won handily, the Finns lost badly. An analysis of the latter's campaign suggested that peacekeeping might have been too "broad" a topic to excite other states.[20] Once on the Council, nonpermanent members sometimes take a greater role in blue helmet missions. In 2000, for example, the Netherlands deployed troops to help launch the UN's mission in Ethiopia and Eritrea (UNMEE) and convened a public debate on the operation in order to publicize this. Existing major troop contributors, such as India and Pakistan, have also organized thematic debates on peacekeeping and vied to chair the Council's Working Group on Peacekeeping Operations (which Japan, as a major financial contributor, has also prioritized). All this activity should not be mistaken for influence.

The P3 have in fact increased their grip on peacekeeping negotiations within the Council since the early 2000s. From the start of this period, it was understood that each of the P3 had "lead" status vis-à-vis particular missions: Britain oversaw Sierra Leone, France handled Côte d'Ivoire, and so on. Many nonpermanent members have been quite happy with this arrangement, not least because they often lack the diplomatic resources to cover all the countries on the Council's agenda. The P3 have taken steps to institutionalize their leadership roles. Whereas mission mandates were often agreed in consultation with Groups of Friends in the 1990s, the P3 have pushed for greater direct control. This has translated into the informal but generally accepted "penholder" system, through which P3 members take the lead on drafting mandates on the situations and missions that concern them. As Security Council Report, a nonprofit group in New York monitoring the Council, notes, the P3 tend to agree on a draft resolution, share it with China and Russia, and only then pass it on to nonpermanent members: "The elected members are often discouraged from making amendments because this might disturb the sometimes painstakingly achieved consensus among the P5."[21] While nonpermanent members act as penholders on thematic issues such as women and peace and security, only a very few have done so vis-à-vis peace operations. Germany and Australia, during their tenure on the Council, have both led on Afghanistan, and South Africa briefly handled Timor-Leste (hardly the situation of greatest strategic relevance to Pretoria) in 2011–2012, but for the most part the P3's role remains uncontested.

Troop Contributors

If the P5 dominate inside the Council, do they face serious challengers outside it? The most obvious potential challengers are the countries that provide the troops and police necessary for UN missions to function at all. Troop contributors including Jordan and India balked at the Council's expansion of UNAMSIL's mandate in 2000, and diplomats working in the Council in that era expected similar crises to disrupt future missions. The likelihood of friction has been raised by the fact that the P5 have contributed relatively few troops to UN missions since 1999 (with the exception of China, which has gained positive publicity through small but growing deployments), while calling on developing nations to fill the gap. By 2012, 37 percent of UN troops came from Africa, 43 percent from Asia, and 9 percent from Latin America.[22] These commitments should give non-Western troop contributors leverage over the Council.

Council members have engaged sporadically with the problems of partnership with troop and police contributors. In 2001, attempting to resolve the tensions revealed in Sierra Leone, the Council passed Resolution 1353, outlining formats for consultations with contributors to specific missions. These soon became known as "ritualistic meetings and sterile briefings," and efforts to improve them (ensuring that they are held well in advance of Council votes on relevant resolutions, for example) have achieved little.[23] P3 diplomats grouse that many troop contributors' representatives seem unwilling to engage on substance.

There are examples of individual troop contributors asserting greater influence. In 2004, Argentina, Brazil, and Chile agreed to send troops to Haiti on the condition that the mission should prioritize peacebuilding rather than peace enforcement, for fear of drawing comparisons with Iraq.[24] The United States and France had hoped for a more robust mandate but compromised—although once on the ground, Latin American officers actually argued for a tougher approach to stabilize Port-au-Prince. In the more recent debates over Mali and the DRC, African governments have also been increasingly active in discussing strategic options: the proposal for the FIB deployment in the eastern Congo was initially championed by Tanzania and South Africa, and both deployed battalions within the new brigade.[25] But this initiative also highlighted other troop contributors' lack of leverage. India, Pakistan, and Uruguay (all significant troop contributors in the Congo) opposed the FIB, complaining that it contravened the principles of peacekeeping and would put their personnel at risk. The P3 made rhetorical concessions to these concerns, promising that the FIB would not create a precedent, but these promises carried little weight.

Non-Western troop contributors have used the General Assembly's Special Committee on Peacekeeping Operations (the C34) as one platform for these arguments, virtually paralyzing it. Western and non-Western states also repeatedly clash over the details of peacekeeping missions' budgets in the General Assembly's Fifth Committee. As Mats Berdal and Hannah Davies have argued, the "essentially intergovernmental and inevitably headquarters-focused" budgeting process can undermine peacekeeping missions' efforts by denying them timely access to resources and personnel.[26] Troop contributors have complicated mission strategies more directly by placing caveats on the use of their personnel and effectively setting up a shadow chain of command for their contingents, with contingent leaders taking orders from their capitals rather than from UN mission leaders. In some cases, the quality of soldiers and police made available to the UN has been so low that mission leaders have simply been unable to implement their mandates. While reliably objective public surveys of UN contingents are rare, one survey of formed (armed) police units in 2008 identified widespread problems "ranging from poor sanitary and living conditions, to inadequate and inappropriate equipment, to dysfunctional command arrangements, and to a lack of fire-arms proficiency and crowd control skills."[27] Such flaws are a frequent source of exasperation to the P3. French president Nicolas Sarkozy captured these frustrations during the 2008 Congo crisis when he suggested that only 800 of the thousands of soldiers in MONUC were "doing their job."[28]

UN Officials

Troop contributors have therefore often challenged the Security Council's leadership of UN operations, but they have only infrequently set out compelling peacekeeping strategies of their own. By contrast, the UN Secretariat has consolidated its position as an essential tool for the Council in managing multiple operations. As Hylke Dijkstra has argued, one of the striking features of the post-1999 resurgence in peacekeeping has been UN members' willingness to delegate increasing responsibilities to the Department of Peacekeeping Operations (DPKO).[29] During the "boom and bust" period of peace operations in the 1990s, the DPKO had remained small, buttressed by gratis personnel seconded from primarily Western governments. As peacekeeping gathered pace again, the department was woefully understaffed to handle the flood of new tasks set before it, with fewer than a hundred personnel in 1999. The 2000 Brahimi Report on UN operations identified this as a major challenge, persuading the General Assembly to launch a major expansion of the department. By 2011, the DPKO and the Department of Field Support, the latter hived off from the DPKO in 2007 to concentrate on logistics and administrative issues, numbered 800 staff.[30]

The expansion of the DPKO still left it far short of the headquarters capacity enjoyed by NATO. But this was accompanied by a deliberate effort to strengthen its analytical and strategic capabilities under the auspices of Kofi Annan and the under-secretary-general for peacekeeping operations, Jean-Marie Guéhenno.[31] This process covered issues such as the protection of civilians (a priority for UN officials still traumatized by Srebrenica and Rwanda), the need for "integrated missions" bringing together UN funds and agencies alongside peacekeepers, and the importance of civilian policing in blue helmet operations. In some cases, thinking about the UN's strategies emerged through a dialectical process between the Council and Secretariat. Ian Johnstone has shown, for example, that work within the DPKO and other UN departments on protection of civilians stimulated the Council to hold a series of debates and pass resolutions on the topic—as well as to routinely integrate protection tasks into individual mission mandates.[32]

Nonetheless, the Secretariat's collective thinking on peacekeeping can also create problems for Council members. DPKO officials have, for example, frequently defended the principle that peacekeepers should not deploy where "there is no peace to keep," to the irritation of the P3. UN officials briefed particularly hard against deploying to Darfur and Chad on this basis in 2005–2006. The Security Council can usually overcome such opposition, not least by leaning on the Secretary-General. Kofi Annan, facing pressure from the United States, advocated for a mission in Darfur in 2006 despite his advisers' doubts. Annan did recommend against deploying to Chad at the end of his term, but his successor, Ban Ki-moon, reversed this position and also prioritized Darfur. Ban has generally been perceived as more skeptical of peacekeeping than his predecessor, and made a point of strengthening the UN's Department of Political Affairs (DPA) as an institutional counterbalance to the DPKO.[33] But while the Security Council has authorized the DPA to deploy a growing number of civilian special political missions to trouble-spots such as Nepal, Libya, and Somalia as an alternative to peacekeeping, these are still dwarfed in terms of size and expense by military and police-heavy blue helmet operations.

Council members and New York–based UN officials also have to contend with the behavior of civilian peacekeeping staff in the field and especially the special representatives of the secretary-general tasked with overseeing the majority of peace operations. The Council gives mission leaders considerable leeway to interpret their mandates. Many have shown considerable independence. The first SRSG in Sudan, Jan Pronk, lobbied for international action in Darfur via a blog that eventually led to his expulsion from the country. Other SRSGs take a much softer approach, trying to balance the Security Council's demands with complex local political realities. Victor Angelo, the first SRSG in Chad, accused his counterparts in New York of believing in "the old time mode of having a mission that had very little to do with the host government," whereas he felt close political coordination was necessary.[34] Other mission leaders come to resent the Council. Robert Mood, the Norwegian general in charge of the UN brief's supervision mission in Syria (UNSMIS) in 2012, recalls that he "observed up close how Western politics is about national interests, international rivalry, and the constituency at home rather than about the moral responsibility to effectively protect innocent civilians in harm's way."[35]

John Karlsrud makes a strong case for emphasizing the "bottom-up" influence of SRSGs, who often simply do not have the time for prolonged discourses with the Security Council over fast-moving crises.[36] The Council's response to the crisis in Côte d'Ivoire in 2010–2011 was complicated by Russian opposition to forceful action. South Africa, which joined the Council as a temporary member in 2011, shared Russia's position. Once Russia finally backed down, it fell to the SRSG in Abidjan, Choi Young-jin, to decide on specific military tactics. He eventually sent attack helicopters into action alongside French forces. "There was no time for the Security Council to convene to discuss the potential risks of the action," Karlsrud points out, so "the SRSG proceeded to authorize the attack without Council intervention."[37] Even in a period in which real-time communication with SRSGs is easy enough (the Council now holds videoconferences with missions), the Council's immediate control of events is limited.

This is equally true where institutional politics are concerned. While Kofi Annan and the DPKO lobbied for "integrated missions" to bring together the UN's strengths on the ground, many UN agencies actively and passively resist integration at every opportunity. As Arthur Boutellis notes, "All of the actors involved in integrated planning approaches have their own goals and visions, which may carry equal legitimacy but are not always aligned with the Security Council mandate that an SRSG has to implement."[38] In cases such as the eastern DRC, humanitarian actors in particular fear that being associated with heavily armed peacekeepers will undermine their perceived impartiality. Frustrated by the UN's incoherence and lack of clear progress toward implementing exit strategies, the Council has pushed peace operations to define benchmarks for success on issues like civilian protection and the rule of law, a practice that was launched in Sierra Leone and became increasingly commonplace from 2009 onward.[39] But these benchmarks, typically drafted by missions and at most tweaked by Council members, actually increase the "bottom-up" influence of SRSGs and other field-based staff, as they allow these officials to elaborate or subtly expand on their mandated tasks.

Regional Organizations

The Council's direction of missions is further complicated by the need to parlay with regional and subregional organizations. Entities ranging from NATO to ECOWAS appeared to be eclipsing the UN in peace operations in the 1990s. These actors have remained significant players despite the rise of UN operations. ECOWAS and African Union forces paved the way for the UN's wave of deployments in Liberia, Côte d'Ivoire, and Burundi in

2003–2004, for example. Suspicions remained after Sierra Leone, and the African organizations demanded assurances about the timing and credibility of the UN's deployments.[40] Although cooperation between the AU and UN continued and deepened in Darfur and Somalia in the years that followed, tensions remained, especially as many African officials were offended by the Council's and UN Secretariat's failure to deploy a UN force to Somalia or to agree to pay for regional operations through the UN budget, an issue flagged in Sierra Leone. Serious frictions also emerged between the EU, NATO, and the UN over Chad and Kosovo in 2007 and 2008.

Nonetheless, there has been progress in institutionalizing the UN's relations with these partners, including the agreement of numerous memoranda of understanding and establishment of UN offices in both Addis Ababa and Brussels. However, much of this cooperation was initially driven by the different organizations' secretariats rather than by the Security Council and the regional organizations' intergovernmental organs. While the Security Council and the African Union's Peace and Security Council have met annually since 2007, their interactions have been complicated by questions of protocol, precedence, and language. This relationship has matured since 2011 with more substantive consultations on individual crises, although the Libyan conflict in 2012 briefly upset relations again. Meanwhile, the Security Council and the EU's Political and Security Committee began regular informal consultations in 2013. Such dialogues may reflect a gradual recognition of the diminution of the UN's status in an era of increasingly institutionalized regional activities. When dealing with specific crises, however, such formal mechanisms are of little use and individual states and officials tend to drive serious decisionmaking.

This can be seen in two cases referred to frequently here. During planning for the parallel EU and UN missions to Chad, for example, France drove diplomacy in both New York and Brussels while also bargaining bilaterally with the Chadian authorities. This created a high degree of suspicion in both the Security Council and Brussels, but a more transparent EU-UN dialogue would have been unwieldy.[41] Similarly, South Africa responded to the Ivorian crisis in 2010–2011 not only by supporting Russia's opposition to robust action in the Council but also through trying to manage AU efforts to find a political solution (see Chapter 33). Nigeria, also in the Security Council at the time and in favor of tougher action, responded through multiple diplomatic channels, including the AU and ECOWAS. The Security Council's decisions on future peace operations may well be similarly entangled in other organizations' politics.

Host States: The Greatest Challengers of All?

By now it should be clear that neither the P5 nor the P3 enjoy easy dominance over peace operations, because of a multiplicity of countervailing forces: uncooperative or underequipped troop contributors, independent-minded UN officials, and increasingly autonomous regional "partners." A fuller survey would also bring in actors including international nongovern-mental organizations such as Human Rights Watch and the International Crisis Group, which persistently lobby ambassadors in New York and UN officials in missions. Civil society activists played a major role in creating pressure for the deployment of UNAMID, for example, without fully artic-ulating or perhaps understanding the obstacles to a successful peace opera-tion in Darfur.[42] But as the Darfur case showed, the greatest challengers to the Security Council's "dominance" of peacekeeping are the states that host peacekeepers themselves.

Complicating the image of peacekeeping as latter-day imperialism, host states have repeatedly found ways to disrupt UN forces. This some-times involves placing tactical limitations on UN operations—the Sudanese government has blocked night flights by UNAMID for example—or politi-cally targeting specific troop contributors. Sudan exploited a phrase in UNAMID's mandate, stating that the mission should have an "African char-acter," to block advanced non-African countries from deploying to Darfur, forcing the mission to rely on a very weak contingent. Other governments have used subtler methods, such as orchestrating peace talks so as to cut out UN officials and denying visas to UN officials or humanitarian workers in order to disrupt international aid and keep the UN off balance.

Bolder host countries have gone further. The Burundian government eased the UN mission off its territory in 2007 after the SRSG appeared to support opposition politicians. Eritrea, unhappy with the performance of UNMEE, first insisted that all Western personnel leave the mission, and eventually evicted UNMEE altogether in 2008, just as Chad would insist that peacekeeping cease on its territory in 2010. Sudan refused to let any UN personnel patrol its side of the border with South Sudan after the latter gained independence, allowing Khartoum to launch a vicious campaign against rebels remaining in the area. The Congolese government has threat-ened to do the same on a number of occasions, gaining concessions by frightening the P3 with the prospect of renewed chaos across central Africa. In cases including Darfur, pro-government militias have repeatedly harassed UN forces. This sort of intimidation reached bloody peaks in Côte d'Ivoire in 2010, where forces loyal to Laurent Gbagbo disarmed peace-keepers, blocked their patrols, and burned their vehicles; and in South Sudan in 2013, where groups loyal to the government and its foes besieged UN camps and targeted civilians sheltering with the peacekeepers.[43]

As noted at the outset of this chapter, Lebanon's refusal of a Chapter VII mission on its territory pales in comparison with some of these displays of resistance to the Council. But while there is general acknowledgment that UN operations face a problem of "withering consent," there is no consensus on how to respond.[44] Efforts to intimidate peacekeepers drive wedges between troop contributors, UN officials, and the Security Council. The Council has rarely found ways to respond to such opposition effectively. It eventually acquiesced to the withdrawal of peacekeepers from Burundi, Ethiopia and Eritrea, and Chad. In the latter case, it attempted to build trust with Chadian officials through informal dialogues in New York, but these smoothed rather than reversed the process. In the DRC, the Council attempted to restore its relations with the government by reconfiguring MONUC as a "stabilization" force with a clearer mandate to support the Congolese authorities. In the case of Darfur, it has accepted the need to keep UNAMID in place for humanitarian reasons in the face of evidence of its political and military failures. The result has been a mission that, in the words of Colum Lynch, has been "bullied by government security forces and rebels, stymied by American and Western neglect, and left without the weapons necessary to fight in a region where more peacekeepers have been killed than in any other U.N. mission in the world."[45]

The Council's Limited Tools

The Council's difficulties in dealing with such fragile states as Lebanon and Chad can be indicative of divisions among the P5 or P3. Sudan's position vis-à-vis the UN is still strengthened by its close relations to China. The Council might have dealt better with Chad if the United States and United Kingdom had not questioned the value of maintaining the mission there. Although China and Russia played a limited public role over Lebanon in 2006, they signaled that they would not accept any resolution that directly contradicted Beirut's wishes. Yet it is also not clear whether the Council has the diplomatic tools to resolve many of the challenges it faces, especially given the strains in its relations with troop contributors and other actors.

The Council's collective tools for directing peacekeeping missions fall into three categories: its mandates, the political signals that it can send through presidential statements and other means, and the use of coercive measures including sanctions and accountability mechanisms in support of peace operations. None of these are as strong as they first appear. Critics of the Council object to its frequent resort to Chapter VII mandates and the increasing complexity of its resolutions, as noted earlier. But both of these factors may be overrated. While it is true that the Council has made frequent use of Chapter VII with regard to peacekeeping, this is not quite as decisive at it first appears. The Council was initially cautious with its use of Chapter VII in the early 2000s, only applying it to specific parts of the original mandates for UNAMSIL and MONUC.[46] It changed course after the crises that rocked these missions. Between 2003 and 2005, the Council mandated a number of missions (including those in Burundi, Côte d'Ivoire, and Liberia) entirely on the basis of Chapter VII, in line with the more strategic approach noted earlier. But it avoided doing so when ordering troops to Sudan in 2005 and Darfur in 2007, fearing clashes with Khartoum, and yielded to Lebanese concerns on the issue in 2006. It is not clear that Chapter VII strikes much fear into the Council's opponents anyway: this certainly did not guarantee respect for the UN operations in Burundi, Côte d'Ivoire, or Chad.

The increasing length and complexity of Council mandates may also be a sign of the Council's limitations. Council members often add new clauses to existing mandates in response to immediate crises, as well as incorporating standard language on issues such as the protection of women and children. The amount of verbiage in a resolution can signal a lack of clear vision for a mission. As noted, MONUC's mandate grew increasingly bloated after 2000. After it was shaken by crisis in 2008, the Council for the first time clarified its order of priorities for the mission.[47] When it was reconfigured as MONUSCO in 2010, the Council cut out various secondary tasks that had built up over the years, and in 2013 it directed the mission to offer options for further narrowing its focus.[48] P3 members have pushed for regular comprehensive reviews of mission mandates. Rather than treat the legal basis and contents of resolutions for peacekeeping operations as evidence of the Council's inherent authority, it may make more sense to view them as part of the P3 and P5's efforts to keep an extremely unruly system in check.

While mere words may not have much impact, tools such as sanctions and referrals to the International Criminal Court may have greater effect. A 2012 study of the UN's targeted sanctions regimes finds that nearly two-thirds of these efforts have overlapped with UN or non-UN peacekeeping forces.[49] The Council has mandated a number of UN operations, including those in the DRC and West Africa, to monitor sanctions regimes in conjunction with the UN's independent panels of experts; although, as Alix Boucher has observed, this relationship has sometimes been rocky.[50] The Council has tried to incentivize local political actors by promising to relax sanctions if they cooperate with peacekeepers on issues such as security sector reform and elections, while launching new targeted sanctions to try to halt peacekeeping crises like that in Côte d'Ivoire. Similarly, the Council can use the threat of the ICC in parallel with peace operations, but the results are uncertain. While the Council referred the situation in Darfur to the ICC in 2005 before serious discussions on peacekeeping options began, its decision to do so made it harder to persuade Khartoum to accept a UN mission (see Chapter 30). Although the ICC has been involved in other cases where peacekeepers are deployed—notably the DRC and Côte d'Ivoire—this has been on the basis of the host country's adherence to the ICC's Rome Statute. The tensions inherent in the use of sanctions and international justice (see Chapters 20 and 25 respectively) mean that they cannot be consistently exploited to assist beleaguered peacekeepers.

Council members of course have other tools available to reinforce UN missions, ranging from bilateral diplomacy to direct military interventions such as the British mission in Sierra Leone and France's deployments (sometimes under the cloak of EU missions) in former colonies such as Chad and Mali. But these tools are not consistently reliable. Britain and France were not willing to send troops to the DRC in 2008, while neither US nor Chinese diplomacy could avert the collapse of South Sudan. All too often, the Council's only real policy option in response to a crisis involving a peacekeeping operation is to send more troops (although these reinforcements can take months to arrive) and try to inspire them with some firm language in a new resolution. This often just signals a pause before a new round of crises and reactions.

Conclusion

There are four interconnected points to take from this narrative. First, the resurgence of peacekeeping after 1999 has been driven by events rather than any grand design, and the P3 and P5 have often stumbled into launching and expanding missions rather than making rational, strategic decisions. Second, the P5 have arrogated even greater power within the Council than they held before as they try to keep a grip on these proliferating operations. Third, this level of P5 power within the Council is offset by a struggle to manage the panoply of other actors involved in making any military or civilian intervention work. Fourth, the Council's tools for guiding those other actors are often notably ineffectual. These points add up to a picture of a Council that is far weaker than its critics sometimes claim it is.

Is there any way to overcome these dilemmas? Western diplomats sometimes muse about further strengthening the UN's headquarters-level command and control, probably on the model of NATO. But this would be both expensive—not least for the P3—and disturb the troop contributors, whose personnel would come under greater scrutiny. The DPKO and independently minded SRSGs would not necessarily welcome such a change to their business model. Critics of the Council often argue that the Western powers could get a better grasp of events in missions if they deployed more of their own forces in blue helmets, overturning the post-1999 division of labor between North and South. In private, P3 diplomats concede this point and France has been willing to keep a central role in UNIFIL on this logic. But memories of Bosnia and Somalia still linger. Moreover, the presence of thousands of British and French troops under UN command in the former Yugoslavia resulted in dysfunctional diplomacy in the Council (see Chapter 28). Western troops are not a panacea for the UN.

Finally, troop contributors argue that Council decisionmaking on peace operations should be opened up, through either formal reform of the bodies' membership or new consultation mechanisms. As we have seen, efforts to start strategic conversations with troop contributors in New York have never been promising. The Council's dialogues with regional organizations may offer a better route for serious discussions of future crises, at least in Africa. But perhaps all these reform proposals miss a basic point: the Council will always be a crisis management institution, whatever its exact composition and working methods. By definition, crisis management is a disorderly and imperfect political business that can be improved at the margins but not made into a science. The Council will never truly escape its constraints.

Notes

1. This discussion of UNIFIL follows Richard Gowan and Alexandra Novosseloff, "Le Renforcement de la Force Intérimaire des Nations Unies au Liban: Etude des Processus Décisionnels au Sommet," *Annuaire Français de Relations Internationales* 11 (2010): 245–267.

2. See David M. Malone and Karin Wermester, "Boom and Bust? The Changing Nature of UN Peacekeeping," *International Peacekeeping* 7, no. 4 (2000): 37–54.

3. At the time of writing, recent mandates for the missions in Mali, South Sudan, and the Central African Republic appear likely to push the overall number of peacekeepers well above 100,000 for some time.

4. Security Council Report, "Security Council Action Under Chapter VII: Myths and Realities," Special Research Report no. 1, June 23, 2008, p. 24.

5. See United Nations Security Council Resolution 1291, S/RES/1291 (February 24, 2000).

6. United Nations Security Council Resolution 1856, S/RES/1856 (December 22, 2008), para. 4(f).

7. Michael Pugh, "Peacekeeping and Critical Theory," *International Peacekeeping* 11, no. 1 (2004): 45.

8. Mats Berdal, "The Security Council and Peacekeeping," in *The United Nations Security Council and War: The Evolution of Thought and Practice Since 1945,* edited by Vaughan Lowe, Adam Roberts, Jennifer Welsh, and Dominik Zaum (Oxford: Oxford University Press, 2008), p. 202.

9. Philip Cunliffe, *Legions of Peace: UN Peacekeepers from the Global South* (London: Hurst, 2013), p. 2.

10. Malone and Wermester, "Boom and Bust?" p. 47.

11. John L. Hirsch, "Sierra Leone," in *The UN Security Council: From the Cold War to the 21st Century,* edited by David M. Malone (Boulder, CO: Lynne Rienner, 2004), p. 527.

12. United Nations Security Council, *Report of the Security Council Mission to Sierra Leone,* UN Doc. S/2000/992, October 16, 2000, para. 9.

13. Richard Caplan, "The Security Council and the Administration of War-Torn and Contested Territories," in Lowe et al., *The United Nations Security Council and War,* p. 573.

14. See Chapter 18 in this volume. For an earlier reckoning with "robustness," see Ian Johnstone, "Dilemmas of Robust Peace Operations," in *Annual Review of Global Peace Operations 2006* (Boulder, CO: Lynne Rienner, 2006).

15. Alexandra Novosseloff and Richard Gowan, *Security Council Working Methods and UN Peace Operations: The Case of Chad and the Central African Republic, 2006–2010* (New York: Center on International Cooperation, 2012), p. 9.

16. See United Nations Security Council Resolution 1863, S/RES/1863 (January 16, 2009).

17. Richard Gowan, "From Rapid Reaction to Delayed Inaction? Congo, the UN, and the EU," *International Peacekeeping* 18, no. 5 (2011): 593–611.

18. Thierry Tardy, "France," in Alex J. Bellamy and Paul D. Williams, *Providing Peacekeepers: The Politics, Challenges, and Future of United Nations Peacekeeping Contributions* (Oxford: Oxford University Press, 2013), p. 134.

19. John Langmore, "Australia's Campaign for Security Council Membership," *Australian Journal of Political Science* 48, no. 1 (2013): 101–111.

20. François Carrel-Billard, *Taking Stock, Moving Forward: Report on the 2012 Elections to the Security Council* (New York: International Peace Institute, 2013), p. 17, www.ipinst.org/publication/policy-papers/detail/392-taking-stock-moving-forward-report-on-the-2012-elections-to-the-un-security-council.html.

21. Security Council Report, "In Hindsight: Penholders," September 2013 Monthly Forecast, August 29, 2013, www.securitycouncilreport.org/monthly-forecast/2013-09/in_hindsight_penholders.php.

22. Center on International Cooperation and Alischa Kugel, Richard Gowan, Bruce Jones, and Megan Gleason-Roberts, eds., *Annual Review of Global Peace Operations 2013* (Boulder, CO: Lynne Rienner, 2013).

23. Security Council Report, "Update Report no. 4: Peacekeeping: Relationship with TCCs/PCCs," June 24, 2009, p. 7, www.securitycouncilreport.org/update-report/lookup-c-glKWLeMTIsG-b-5273681.php?print=true.

24. Amélie Gauthier and Sarah John de Sousa, *Brazil in Haiti: Debate over the Peacekeeping Mission* (Madrid: FRIDE, 2006), pp. 1–2.

25. Patrick Cammaert and Fiona Blyth, *The UN Intervention Brigade in the Democratic Republic of the Congo* (New York: International Peace Institute, 2013), pp. 5–6, www.ipinst.org/publication/policy-papers/detail/403-the-un-intervention-brigade-in-the-democratic-republic-of-the-congo-.html.

26. Mats Berdal and Hannah Davies, "The United Nations and International Statebuilding After the Cold War," in *Political Economy of Statebuilding: Power After Peace,* edited by Dominik Zaum and Mats Berdal (Abingdon: Routledge, 2013), p. 126.

27. Annika Hansen, *Policing the Peace: The Rise of United Nations Formed Police Units* (Berlin: ZIF, 2011), p. 3.

28. Quoted in Gowan, "From Rapid Reaction to Delayed Inaction?" p. 601.

29. Hylke Dijkstra, "Efficiency Versus Sovereignty: Delegation to the UN Secretariat in Peacekeeping," *International Peacekeeping* 19, no. 5 (2012): 581–596.

30. Center on International Cooperation and Megan Gleason, ed., *Annual Review of Global Peace Operations 2012* (Boulder, CO: Lynne Rienner, 2012).

31. The best account of this process is Thorsten Benner, Stephan Mergenthaler, and Philipp Rotmann, *The New World of UN Peace Operations: Learning to Build Peace?* (Oxford: Oxford University Press, 2011).

32. Ian Johnstone, *The Power of Deliberation: International Law, Politics, and Organizations* (Oxford: Oxford University Press, 2011), pp. 136–159.

33. See Richard Gowan, "'Less Bound to the Desk': Ban Ki-moon, the UN, and Preventive Diplomacy," *Global Governance* 18, no. 4 (2012): 387–404.

34. Giulia Piccolino and John Karlsrud, "Withering Consent, but Mutual

Dependency: UN Peace Operations and African Assertiveness," *Conflict, Security & Development* 11, no. 4 (2011): 461.

35. Robert Mood, "My Experiences as the Head of the UN Mission in Syria," January 21, 2014, http://carnegieendowment.org/syriaincrisis/?fa=54238.

36. John Karlsrud, "Special Representatives of the Secretary-General as Norm Arbitrators? Understanding Bottom-Up Authority in UN Peacekeeping," *Global Governance* 19, no. 4 (2013): 525–544.

37. Ibid., p. 530.

38. Arthur Boutellis, *Driving the System Apart? A Study of United Nations Integration and Integrated Strategic Planning* (New York: International Peace Institute, 2013), p. 12, www.ipinst.org/publication/policy-papers/detail/407-driving-the-system-apart-a-study-of-united-nations-integration-and-integrated-strategic-planning.html.

39. Nathaniel Olin, *Measuring Peacekeeping: A Review of the Security Council's Benchmarking Process for Peacekeeping Missions* (New York: Conflict Prevention and Peace Forum, 2013), p. 2.

40. On the difficulties of ECOWAS-UN cooperation in this period, see United Nations Department of Peacekeeping Operations, *Re-Hatting ECOWAS Forces as UN Peacekeepers: Lessons Learned* (New York: UN Peacekeeping Best Practices, 2005).

41. Novosseloff and Gowan, *Security Council Working Methods,* pp. 22–23.

42. See Rebecca Hamilton, *Fighting for Darfur: Public Action and the Struggle to Stop Genocide* (New York: Palgrave Macmillan, 2011).

43. Colum Lynch, "Laurent Gbagbo's Guide to Crippling a UN Peacekeeping Mission," *Foreign Policy,* April 1, 2011.

44. A phenomenon well-captured in Piccolino and Karlsrud, "Withering Consent, but Mutual Dependency," pp. 462–464.

45. Colum Lynch, "They Just Stood Watching," *Foreign Policy,* April 7, 2014.

46. See Security Council Report, "Security Council Action Under Chapter VII," pp. 23–25.

47. United Nations Security Council Resolution 1856, S/RES/1856 (December 22, 2008).

48. United Nations Security Council Resolution 2147, S/RES/2147 (March 28, 2014), paras. 8–10.

49. Thomas J. Biersteker, Sue E. Eckhert, and Marcos Tourinho, *Designing United Nations Targeted Sanctions: Evaluating Impacts and Effectiveness of UN Targeted Sanctions* (Geneva: Graduate Institute of International and Development Studies, August 2012), p. 13.

50. Alix J. Boucher, *UN Panels of Experts and UN Peace Operations: Exploiting Synergies for Peacebuilding* (Washington, DC: Stimson Center, September 2010).

37

The Security Council and International Law

Ian Johnstone

THE UN SECURITY COUNCIL IS AN IMPORTANT BODY IN THE decentralized international legal system precisely because the system is decentralized. There is no global legislature to make law, no global supreme court to provide authoritative interpretations of the law, and no global executive body to implement and enforce the law. Yet in exercising its responsibility, the Security Council has performed aspects of all three functions. This is what makes the Council such a powerful institution, but this also explains why questions about accountability and legitimacy are so pervasive. What empowers the Security Council to make law? What kind of law does it make? What law applies to it? What law does it apply? How does it interpret and enforce the law? Are there any constraints on how it acts? These questions about the nature and impact of law, moreover, are situated in a political context where relations of powers, definitions of security, and calculations of interest are highly fluid.

In this chapter I seek to work through this conceptual thicket in two parts. The first considers the legal powers of the Security Council and how it has exercised those powers, starting from a conception of law as both constraining and enabling. International law is not merely a set of injunctions and prohibitions, but also a structure that defines and empowers actors. After looking at the relevant language of the UN Charter, I consider the expansive manner in which the Council has acted as lawmaker, as a quasi-judicial body, and as enforcer of international law. Examples of each function illustrate the extent to which the Council has pushed the limits of its competence beyond the crisis management role it was originally conceived to perform.

The second part considers whether there are any constraints on the Council and, if so, how meaningful they are in practice. In examining both legal checks and political constraints, I claim that the Council has not acted *ultra vires* (beyond its legal authority) but this highly concentrated form of power does raise questions about accountability. While the Council is subject to more checks and balances than meets the eye, in order to perform those multiple functions effectively it must remain attentive to legitimacy concerns. I conclude by highlighting one of those concerns, namely the consistency dilemma: while treating like cases alike is a fundamental principle of justice, it is politically unrealistic to expect the Council to act with perfect consistency. From that perspective, an important function of international law is as an advocacy and diplomatic tool to generate more consistency in political bodies like the Security Council.

Charter-Based Powers and Council Practice

Viewing international law as only a set of prescriptions and proscriptions (do this and don't do that) misses the point that some rules are enabling. John Searle draws a distinction between regulative and constitutive rules, which he explains as follows:

> Some rules regulate antecedently existing forms of behavior. For example, the rules of polite table behavior regulate eating, but eating exists independently of those rules. Some rules, on the other hand, do not merely regulate but create or define new forms of behavior: the rules of chess, for example, do not merely regulate an antecedently existing activity called playing chess; they, as it were, create the possibility of or define that activity. The activity of playing chess is constituted by action in accordance with these rules. Chess has no existence apart from these rules.[1]

Arguably, elements of Article 2 of the UN Charter are constitutive norms of the international system. States are what they are and the international system is what it is because of the fundamental principles of sovereign equality, territorial integrity, and nonintervention in internal affairs (plus a few other rules, like *pacta sunt servanda,* meaning "agreements must be kept").

A related idea is that some rules constrain and others empower. Thus, for example, the UN Charter constrains states by prohibiting the use of force except in self-defense and empowers the Council by authorizing it to override that prohibition in certain circumstances. In the remainder of this first section, I review the empowering provisions of the UN Charter and then examine how those powers have been exercised in practice. In the next section I review Charter provisions that purport to constrain the Council and consider whether and how they are meaningful in practice.

Charter-Based Powers

The UN Charter endows the Security Council with certain powers its members would not otherwise have. The most important is the power to make law that binds all members of the organization (Article 25). Moreover, law made by the Security Council supersedes obligations that states may have under any other international agreement (Article 103).[2] These two features of the Charter give it a constitution-like character.[3] This means the Charter should be and has been interpreted as a "living tree," broadly, in light of changing circumstances. This approach to Charter interpretation is consistent with the implied powers doctrine, affirmed by the International Court of Justice in the 1949 reparations case, which holds that an international organization has those powers "conferred upon it by necessary implication as being essential to the performance of its duties."[4] The combination of a constitution-like reading of the Charter and implied powers doctrine is necessary if the Council is to remain relevant in an evolving global order and effective in managing new threats and crises. Yet the implications are far-reaching and worrying to those who fear a hegemonic Security Council creating law and imposing it on the world.

The second most important power the Charter grants the Security Council is to authorize military force in circumstances that would otherwise be illegal. Enforcement action based on Article 42 is one of the two explicit exceptions to the prohibition against the use of force embodied in Article 2(4). Thus, from the point of view of the five permanent Council members (P5), the Charter both *prohibits* them from using force unilaterally other than in self-defense (Article 51) and *enables* them to authorize states to use force in circumstances beyond self-defense. As an institution, the Council empowers the P5 to take coercive action that they deem to be necessary for the maintenance of peace and security. Again, this extraordinary grant of authority was thought to be necessary to avert another world war, and remains a supremely important mechanism for the management of international and internal security crises. How and how well the authority has been exercised is a major fault-line of debate on the power of the Council.

Other provisions in the UN Charter empower the Security Council to act in a manner that impacts the legal order. The Council may request advisory opinions of the International Court of Justice (ICJ) (Article 96). It can investigate disputes (Article 34) and recommend judicial settlement (Article 36). It can impose sanctions for the purpose of maintaining peace and security, and to enforce its own decisions (Article 41). It can create subsidiary organs to oversee the sanctions regimes (Article 29). It also has various powers that have never been exercised, such as the power to formulate a system for the regulation of armaments (Article 26), the power to enter into special agreements with states to provide military assets for enforcement action (Article 43), and the power to enforce ICJ decisions in contentious cases (Article 94).

Security Council Practice

More important than the words of the Charter is how those words have been interpreted in practice. That practice has been extraordinary, far beyond what the founders of the UN intended or perhaps even imagined. The Council was set up as an executive body whose principal function would be crisis management, not lawmaking, adjudication, or even, strictly speaking, enforcement of the law. Yet in exercising its responsibilities for the maintenance of international peace and security, the Council has done all three: based on an expansive interpretation of its own role, it has acted as legislature, court, and enforcer. I review each of these functions in turn here, highlighting the cases that have drawn most scrutiny because they provide the best lens for understanding the scope and limits of the Council.

The Security Council as legislature. Article 25 ("the Members of the UN agree to accept and carry out the decisions of the Security Council") empowers the Security Council to make binding law for those at whom its decisions are directed. This lawmaking power does not fit neatly into the sources of law set out in Article 38 of the ICJ statute: treaties, custom, general principles, and, as subsidiary means of determining the law, judicial opinions and the opinions of "the most highly qualified publicists." Of course, the Council's mandate flows from a treaty—the UN Charter—and so every state that joins the UN accepts it. Nevertheless, this is an extraordinary form of supranational power: in order to ensure "prompt and effective action" (Article 24), the P5 plus four elected Council members (nine affirmative votes are necessary for any resolution to take effect) can impose binding obligations on 193 countries.

Council decisions may be directed against one state, like Resolution 660 (1990), which demanded that Iraq withdraw from Kuwait; or against all states, like sanctions resolutions (for example Resolution 661 of 1990, which required UN members to sever economic relations with Iraq). Resolution 660 did not include provisions to enforce its demands, but it was binding on Iraq nevertheless. Resolution 661 was an enforcement resolution, designed to compel Iraq to comply with Resolution 660. Security Council resolutions may also bind nonstate parties to conflicts, like UNITA in Angola or the RUF in Sierra Leone.

While most Security Council resolutions seek to end a conflict or resolve a particular crisis, some go further. An example is Resolution 687 (1991), on Iraq's weapons of mass destruction, the so-called Gulf War ceasefire resolution. Its purpose was not simply to reverse the consequences of Iraq's invasion of Kuwait, but also to try to control its *future* behavior.

The obligations went beyond any required by a WMD treaty, and they were of unlimited duration. Iraq was required to accept the long-term monitoring of its nuclear, chemical, biological, and ballistic missile programs, without any indication of when—if ever—that might end.

Resolutions 660, 661, and 687 were all adopted under Chapter VII of the UN Charter and all clearly imposed binding obligations within the meaning of Article 25. Can resolutions not adopted under Chapter VII impose binding obligations as well? The ICJ addressed this question in its advisory opinion on Southwest Africa (Namibia today). In 1970, the Security Council adopted Resolution 276, which declared the continued presence of the South African authorities in Southwest Africa to be illegal, and "call[ed] upon all states to refrain from any dealings with South Africa that were inconsistent with that declaration" (paragraph 5). Though the resolution was not adopted under Chapter VII, the ICJ judged the Council's action to be a binding decision under Article 25. Despite this unequivocal statement of the Court that *decisions* adopted under Chapter VI are binding, there is a widespread misperception among scholars and UN diplomats that only Chapter VII resolutions constitute hard law. The weight of international legal opinion, record of negotiations in San Francisco, and long-standing practice suggest otherwise, but this continues to be a source of controversy.[5]

Of course, the Council need not make a "decision" under either Chapters VI or VII: it can make recommendations, appeals, requests, or other nonbinding statements. Determining whether a particular measure is a decision is not always easy. In Resolution 276 it used the operative words "calls upon," not "decides," "demands," or "requires," and yet the ICJ held the resolution to be binding. On the other hand, many resolutions since then have used the words "calls upon" yet are clearly not meant to impose a binding obligation.[6] Back in 1970, the ICJ offered this not very helpful advice: "In view of the nature of the powers under Article 25, the question whether they have been in fact exercised, is to be determined in each case, having regard to the terms of the resolution to be interpreted, the discussions leading to it, the Charter provisions invoked and, in general all circumstances that might assist in determining the legal consequences of the resolution of the Security Council."[7]

That standard did not help former UN Secretary-General Boutros Boutros-Ghali—a scholar of international law himself—when he stated early in his term that Security Council Resolution 242 was not binding.[8] That resolution stipulates that lasting peace in the Middle East "should include the application of the following principle . . . withdrawal of Israel armed forces from territories occupied in the recent conflict." Boutros-Ghali's interpretation that it was not binding led to howls of outrage in the Arab world. He later backtracked, calling it binding but not an enforcement decision.

In addition to making binding decisions that seek to constrain state and nonstate actors, the Council also empowers its subsidiary organs and other entities to make law. For example, it has established peace operations with full governing powers. The most dramatic examples are the transitional administrations in Kosovo and East Timor, given the power "to exercise all legislative and executive authority."[9] The Council has approved similar though less comprehensive governing powers for other peace operations, like the UN transitional administrations in Cambodia and Eastern Slavonia, the Governance and Economic Management Assistance Program (GEMAP) in Liberia, and the Office of the High Representative in Bosnia.[10]

In establishing the international criminal tribunals for Yugoslavia and Rwanda, the Security Council created law. Under Chapter VII of the UN Charter, it legislated these tribunals into existence and approved statutes originally drafted by the International Law Commission. It also empowered the tribunals to elaborate and give content to the corpus of international criminal law through their jurisprudence. The Council did not create the International Criminal Court, but it can refer cases to it, giving the Court jurisdiction over situations that it would not otherwise have—which could be seen as a form of lawmaking. The ICC's Rome Statute, while a treaty and therefore formally binding only on its parties, opens up a new channel for the Council to exercise its supranational powers.

The Security Council took its lawmaking function a step further when it enacted quasi-legislative resolutions in the aftermath of the events of September 11, 2001. The first of these was Resolution 1373, adopted on September 28, 2001. By a unanimous vote, under Chapter VII of the UN Charter, the Council *decided* among other things that all states shall "prevent and suppress the financing of terrorist acts," "freeze financial assets of persons who commit terrorists acts," and "deny safe haven to those who finance, plan, or support terrorist acts." This looks like a sanctions resolution, in that it imposes obligations on every state in the world. But it is not related to a particular incident, nor does it seek to enforce a decision against a particular state. Rather, it imposes general obligations on all states in a broad issue area for an indefinite period. This is qualitatively different from the Council's normal crisis management role. In adopting Resolution 1373, the Council acted less like an executive body issuing directives and more like a legislature. The Council did it again in April 2004, when it adopted Resolution 1540, which requires all states to adopt laws and take other measures designed to prevent weapons of mass destruction from falling in to the hands of terrorists. Then, after a lengthy hiatus, the Council adopted a third quasi-legislative resolution in 2014 on the "recruiting, organizing, transporting or equipping" of foreign terrorist fighters (Resolution 2178, September 24, 2014).

Does the Council have the competence to legislate in that way? Article 2(7) prohibits the UN from interfering in domestic matters, except when it is engaging in "enforcement measures" under Chapter VII. Are Resolutions 1373 and 1540 enforcement measures? If not, does "legislating" run afoul of Article 2(7)? The legal response is twofold: these are Chapter VII resolutions designed to compel action, and therefore constitute "enforcement" within the meaning of Article 2(7); and even if not, they address matters that are clearly of international rather than purely domestic concern, namely terrorism and WMD proliferation. That the resolutions are *intra vires* (within the legal authority of the Council) does not necessarily mean it is wise for the Council to legislate in this way. Elsewhere, I have considered some of the reasons why this may be unwise:[11]

- The Council legislating circumvents the normal treaty-making process. The signing and ratification of treaties is the principal mechanism by which states consent to be bound by an international legal rule. Bypassing this process usurps the power of states to decide for themselves what laws to be bound by.
- The Council is not well-equipped to balance interests and weigh long-term policy implications in the way legislatures are. Consider Resolution 1540. It fills gaps in the nonproliferation regimes, but could throw off the "grand bargain" embodied in the Nuclear Non-Proliferation Treaty, which requires disarmament by the nuclear weapon states (who happen to be the P5) as well as nonproliferation.
- There is the obvious question of whether a "nonrepresentative" political institution like the Security Council will act in the interests of its most powerful members rather than all states. Some scholars describe Resolution 1373 as "international hegemonic law in action," and worry about the United States using its overwhelming influence in the Council to rewrite international law.[12]

While the concern about hegemony is real, I would argue that it is appropriate for the Security Council to legislate from time to time. It should fill gaps in the law when urgent action is required, precisely because normal lawmaking processes are too slow. Moreover, Resolutions 1373 and 1540 have a preventive element, namely to forestall future acts of terrorism—surely something that should be encouraged. As for legitimacy concerns, as I discuss later, these are less acute than meets the eye.

The Security Council as a court. In addition to these quasi-legislative acts, the Security Council has also acted like a court. It has done this in two ways: by determining legal liability, and by interpreting the law.

With respect to the first way, the most straightforward kind of legal determination the Council can make is the finding that a country has violated international rules on the use of force, like when Iraq invaded Kuwait. Less straightforward, the Council found in Resolution 1368 that the 9/11 attacks on the World Trade Center and Pentagon were armed attacks within the meaning of Article 51, justifying a military response in self-defense. The finding was in the preamble of the resolution because self-defense does not require Security Council authorization and so there was no need—nor a desire on the part of the United States—to seek that authorization in order to be able to act in Afghanistan. In that sense, the finding could be regarded as an interpretation of Article 51 by the Council, the legal weight of which depends on the degree of support it received from other states.[13] More controversial are findings of violations of non-Charter law. An early post–Cold War example is the imposition of liability on Iraq for all losses caused by its invasion of Kuwait (Resolution 687). It is highly unusual for the Security Council to make legal findings in this way, as it is not equipped to weigh evidence and legal arguments the way courts do. More controversial still was the decision to demarcate the Iraq-Kuwait border based on the Agreed Minutes of 1964 (a treaty-like instrument struck between the UK and Iraq in the decolonization era). The act of demarcation was presented as a technical exercise: the border had already been delimited, and all that the boundary-demarcation commission created by the Council would do was to draw the line on a map and erect pillars on the ground. Nevertheless, the decision to treat the Agreed Minutes as authoritative was a quasi-judicial ruling. Moreover, the maritime boundary was demarcated based on general legal principles—clearly not a purely technical exercise.

The Security Council has also made determinations that international human rights, humanitarian, or criminal law has been violated. Thus in Resolution 2098, on the conflict in the eastern Democratic Republic of the Congo, the Council expressed concern about the "serious violations of international humanitarian law and abuses of human rights by the M23 and other armed groups" (preambular paragraph 9). In Resolution 1970, on Libya, the Council deplored the gross violations of human rights, which it said "may amount to crimes against humanity"—and then referred the matter to the ICC.

Perhaps surprisingly, determinations that security treaties have been violated are more rare. Thus, for example, the Security Council has never formally declared Iran to be in violation of the Nuclear Non-Proliferation Treaty (NPT). However, it has done so implicitly—by declaring it to be in violation of its IAEA safeguards agreement, adherence to which is a requirement of Article III of the NPT.

A more common way for the Council to act like a court is by—explicitly or implicitly—interpreting the law. Indeed, the Council is often required to interpret the UN Charter itself. It does so in three ways: explicitly in particular cases, explicitly or implicitly through statements on thematic issues, and implicitly through operational activities.

First, the Security Council decides what constitutes a "threat to the peace" within the meaning of Article 39—the threshold for action under Chapter VII. In the post–Cold War era, it has been expanding the definition of that concept. It has been used on numerous occasions to authorize military action in internal conflicts (starting with Bosnia in the early 1990s), to secure the delivery of humanitarian relief (Somalia in 1992), to restore a democratically elected president (Haiti in 1994), and to protect civilians (Sierra Leone in 1999 and in many other places in the 2000s). Second, the Council engages in Charter interpretation through thematic meetings on issues like nonproliferation, the protection of civilians, postconflict peacebuilding, and the role of women in peace processes. At the end of these meetings the Council typically—though not always—adopts a presidential statement. These statements may be interpretations of what constitutes a "threat to the peace" within the meaning of Article 39 of the UN Charter. Thus the Council implicitly described genocide, war crimes, crimes against humanity, and ethnic cleansing as threats to the peace by reaffirming the "responsibility to protect" language from the General Assembly's outcome document of the 2005 world summit (Resolution 1674 of 2006). On a number of occasions the Council has declared organized crime to be a threat to international peace and security.[14] These normative declarations do not purport to impose compulsory obligations, but they may later be invoked by a member of the Council in calling for action—or resisting calls for action—when a particular case implicating the norm arises.

Third, the Council engages in implicit interpretations of the law through its operational activities. As Oscar Schachter put it in 1997, "Unlike judicial interpretation, UN interpretation does not usually have an adjudicative character. The task faced by most UN bodies is practical and instrumental. . . . Problems are analyzed, proposed solutions negotiated, decisions reached. Interpretation is implicit in the measures adopted."[15] Consider, for example, consent-based multidimensional peacekeeping. As noted earlier, Article 2(7) prohibits UN intervention in domestic matters, except in enforcement measures under Chapter VII. Purely Chapter VI–based peacekeeping does not fall within the exception, yet many of the UN's functions impinge on internal affairs—from human rights monitoring and rule of law work to institution building. The same could be said about the UN's electoral assistance and democracy promotion activities. Though these activities are undertaken with the consent of host governments and therefore not a direct infringement on sovereignty, one can nevertheless imagine some member states refusing to finance them on the grounds that they violate Article 2(7). The response must be the one given by Judge Rosalyn Higgins (before she was an ICJ judge): some historically "domestic matters" are now treated as matters of international concern.[16] That evolution has occurred in part as a result of the Council's practices and acquiescence to those practices by the vast majority of member states.

In addition to interpreting the Charter itself, the Security Council sometimes empowers other actors to engage in legal interpretation. The request to the ICJ to give an advisory opinion in the case of Southwest Africa is an example.[17] The Council has also created bodies that have the power to interpret the law or make legal determinations. The International Criminal Tribunal for the Former Yugoslavia (ICTY) and the International Criminal Tribunal for Rwanda (ICTR) interpret their own statutes and other aspects of international criminal law, like the Genocide Convention. The Council created a compensation commission to dole out awards for loss suffered as a result of Iraq's invasion of Kuwait. It created a boundary commission to decide on the border between Ethiopia and Eritrea. It has set up commissions of inquiry and other investigative bodies to engage in investigations, which necessarily must draw conclusions of law—even if those conclusions are not formally binding.[18] And of course there are many UN entities, like the Secretary-General and Human Rights Council, that, in reporting to the Council, influence how the law is interpreted, even if they have not been asked to engage in legal interpretation.[19]

The Council's most consequential quasi-judicial acts are the so-called sanctions regimes. In these, either the Council itself or a committee it has formed identifies individuals who are subject to asset freezes and other forms of sanctions. The most controversial of these is the 1267 sanctions regime (established through Resolution 1267), which required states to freeze the assets of al-Qaeda, the Taliban, and their associates. The regime operated on the basis of a "list" compiled by the sanctions committee, based on submissions by member states. While there was much sympathy for the Council taking a preventive approach to terrorism, and while there still is wide support for targeted as opposed to comprehensive sanctions, these listing regimes have been a source of controversy. Indeed, one of the main objections raised by the European Court of Justice and others is precisely that the Council was making quasi-judicial decisions that resulted in severe penalties without providing those placed on the list with any procedural rights.

The Security Council as enforcer. The Security Council does not enforce international law per se, but in carrying out its responsibility to maintain international peace and security it often engages in a form of law enforcement. This is obviously true with respect to the prohibition against the use of force specified in Article 2(4). If a state threatens or uses force in violation of the UN Charter, the Security Council can respond under Chapter

VII. Thus when North Korea invaded the South in 1950, it called it an act of aggression and authorized a military response.

While clear cases of Council-authorized military enforcement action are rare, implied authorizations are not. The United States, the United Kingdom, and France interpreted Resolution 688 (1991) as authorizing Operation Provide Comfort in northern Iraq and no-fly zones in the north and south. Some NATO countries claimed that the intervention in Kosovo in 1999 was implicitly authorized by earlier Council resolutions. The main legal debate over intervention in Iraq in 2003 was whether a combined reading of Resolutions 678, 687, and 1441 constituted authorization to use force. These cases have been considered elsewhere.[20]

A more recent case is France's intervention in Mali in early 2013. Resolution 2085 "*urges* Member States, regional and international organizations to provide coordinated support to AFISMA, including . . . any necessary assistance in efforts to reduce the threat posed by terrorist organizations, including AQIM, MUJWA and associated extremist groups in accordance with paragraph 9(b), in close coordination with AFISMA and the Malian authorities."[21]

France claimed that this, plus the invitation of the government of Mali, gave it the legal authority it needed to intervene. Yet the authorization is at best implicit, and the value of the invitation is at least questionable—given that the insurgent groups had effective control over substantial portions of Mali. Moreover, the legitimacy of the Malian government was in question, given that it had come to power through a coup in March 2012, which had been condemned by the Council.[22] Leaving aside the merits of France's claim, the larger point is that the Security Council often relies on constructive ambiguity in its resolutions. The politics behind this are simple and not without merit: an imprecise resolution is often better than no resolution at all. Consider Resolution 1701, on southern Lebanon. It authorized an expansion of the UN peacekeeping operation there (UNIFIL) in the aftermath of the 2006 war between Israel and Hezbollah. The mandate is entirely under Chapter VI, yet includes Chapter VII–style language, including the right to take "all necessary action . . . to ensure that its area of operations is not utilized for hostile activities of any kind . . . and to protect civilians under imminent threat of physical violence," as well as the decision to impose an arms embargo on forces other than those of the Lebanese government. The reason for the odd formulation is that the government of Lebanon and some Council members did not want the resolution to be under Chapter VII, yet others felt that the volatile environment required a robust presence. The compromise lacked elegance, but it was better than the alternative—a continuation of UNIFIL's old mandate in a completely different political and security environment.

What other law does the Security Council enforce? All of the WMD treaties designate the Council as the ultimate enforcement agency. Action has been rare, but the sanctions on North Korea and Iran qualify.[23] Cases of Council-mandated humanitarian intervention could be characterized as de facto enforcement of human rights, humanitarian, and international criminal law. Consider Libya: Resolutions 1970 and 1973 both invoked the "responsibility to protect." As noted earlier, this principle had been endorsed by the General Assembly in 2005 in the following terms: every state has the responsibility to protect its citizens from the four mass atrocity crimes; if it fails, the international community may step in and "take collective action, in a timely and decisive manner, through the Security Council, in accordance with the UN Charter, including Chapter VII, on a case by case basis." That does not create new law because the General Assembly cannot make binding decisions. Moreover, the responsibility imposed on states vis-à-vis their own citizens already existed in international human rights and international humanitarian law. What this statement from the outcome document of the 2005 World Summit represents is an affirmation of the right of the Council to do what it had been doing for years, albeit selectively, and an attempt to mobilize support for enforcement of existing international law on those four crimes.

Some economic sanctions are also designed to enforce international law. When the Council imposes sanctions on states, it often does so in order to compel compliance with its own demands—for example the WMD obligations imposed on Iraq in the aftermath of the Gulf War. By Resolution 2087, in response to North Korea's nuclear test in December 2012, the Security Council imposed new sanctions to enforce earlier resolutions demanding that it not conduct any more tests.[24] On at least two occasions it has imposed secondary sanctions, namely the sanctions on Liberia for failing to comply with the diamond sanctions imposed on the RUF in Sierra Leone in 2000, and the sanctions on Eritrea for flouting the arms embargo on Somalia in 2009.

Thus sanctions can have the character of all three functions: lawmaking (because they impose binding obligations), interpretation of the law (sanctions on Iran are an implicit interpretation of Article III of the NPT), and law enforcement (the Iraq, North Korea, and Liberia sanctions). This shows that the line between them is blurry. Enforcement can constitute implicit interpretation of the law; interpretation can harden or even create new law. It also highlights the fact that the Security Council's impact on international law is not straightforward or entirely transparent. The organ is not bound by its own precedents, but its actions can have precedential effects by impacting the political dynamics in the future—making it easier to engage in similar action and harder to resist.

Accountability

That the Security Council has pushed the limits of its competence is clear. Add to this the fact that it does not always speak clearly about what it is doing and concerns about accountability naturally arise. What gives it the authority to act as legislature, court, and enforcer? Are there any checks and balances to ensure the Council exercises that authority responsibly?

Questions about accountability are important because the functions the organ is performing are important. A hyperactive Council may be worrisome, but so too is the opposite: a Council that is inert, as it was during much of the Cold War. Would that not simply invite powerful states to bypass the Council, acting unilaterally or in ad hoc coalitions? Efforts to tie the Council down to a narrow interpretation of its own role could do more harm to global order than condoning the proactive approach it has demonstrated in fits and starts since the end of the Cold War.

Moreover, the Council is not entirely unaccountable and free of any checks and balances. Some of the constraints are legal, others are political; most are a mix of the two. Concerns about the accountability of the Council come down to questions about how powerful those constraints are.

Charter Constraints

Article 24(1) of the UN Charter specifies that the Council has primary responsibility "for the maintenance of international peace and security"— implying it does not have responsibility in other areas. Thus, for example, if a member of the Security Council wants it to act on human rights, it must make the case that the action is for the purpose of maintaining international peace and security. Indeed, the Council's definition of a threat to peace has been expanding ever since the end of the Cold War. It stated as far back as 1992 that it could include economic, social, and other sources of instability.[25] In early 2000, it held a meeting on HIV/AIDS, implying that AIDS could be a security concern. It met on climate change in early 2007 and again in 2011. It has discussed organized crime on multiple occasions since 2009. The Council has not taken coercive action to counter environmental or economic threats, but it has done so to protect human rights— making the defenders of state sovereignty nervous about the scope of matters that fall within the Council's competence. It broke new ground in September 2014 by adopting Resolution 2177, declaring the Ebola crisis in West Africa a threat to international peace and security and paving the way for the Secretary-General to dispatch a coordinating mission, the United Nations Mission for Ebola Emergency Response (UNMEER), which bore some of the hallmarks of a peacekeeping mission.

Assuming the Council gets over the Article 24(1) hurdle and nine members including the P5 agree that a situation constitutes a threat to international peace and security, are there limits on what the Council can do to address that threat? As a matter of common sense, one would suppose there are. Surely the Council cannot authorize the torture of suspected terrorists (though it has authorized the freezing of their assets), or the physical separation of ethnic groups in order to end a civil war (though it has endorsed political arrangements that have had the effect of reinforcing ethnic divisions). Fortunately, these commonsense judgments have a basis in Article 24(2) of the UN Charter: "in discharging these duties, the Security Council shall act in accordance with the Purposes and Principles of the United Nations." Those purposes and principles are enumerated in the preamble and Articles 1 and 2. They may also be gleaned from elsewhere, for example Article 51 on self-defense and Article 55 on human rights.

Yet as the examples here illustrate, the line between permissible and impermissible action is not self-evident. In theory, Article 24(2) provides some guidance on where to draw the line, but the purposes and principles are expressed at a high level of generality and often point in opposite directions. State sovereignty is an important principle, but so is the promotion of human rights. Territorial integrity is fundamental, but so is self-determination. An important question then is who decides how to balance these competing principles. Who decides where the line is between acts that are within the Council's competence and those that are beyond its legal authority? At the San Francisco Conference of 1945, in founding the UN, it was decided that "each United Nations organ interprets such parts of the Charter as are applicable to its functions."[26] The Security Council may ask the ICJ to give an advisory opinion on the limits of its competence, as it did in the case of Southwest Africa, but otherwise each organ decides for itself what it can and cannot do. Does this suggest that the Council operates free of all practical constraint, despite Article 24?

Indirect Judicial Review

No court has a formal power of judicial review over the Security Council. In the Lockerbie and Bosnia genocide cases, some of the judges hinted that the ICJ should assume a power of judicial review as the US Supreme Court did in *Marbury v. Madison*. Tom Franck has argued that the ICJ did engage in judicial review in the Lockerbie case, not by striking down a Council resolution but in effect by declaring it to be within the Council's legal authority.[27] Yet, however carefully one reads between the lines in those cases, it is clear that the ICJ is a long way from claiming a right to overturn Council decisions.

Returning to a question asked earlier, this does not mean Article 24(2) is meaningless. The International Court of Justice, the European Court of Justice (ECJ), and many national courts have engaged in indirect judicial review. José Alvarez wrote after the Lockerbie and Bosnia genocide cases that the ICJ had engaged and would continue to engage in an "expressive mode of review"—a sort of ongoing dialogue with the Council.[28] The opinions of some of the judges could be read as warnings, "*cueing* the Council to internalize the limits suggested, and to impose restraints on itself that would prevent violations of the law."[29]

Moreover, the ICJ is not the only institution capable of commenting on Council action. The International Criminal Tribunal for the Former Yugoslavia did it, by deciding in one of its first rulings that the Security Council's powers, "*while not unlimited*," encompassed the creation of a judicial tribunal under Article 41 of the Charter.[30] The Secretary-General has commented on the propriety of Council action on a number of occasions, for example the resolutions that in effect exempted peacekeepers from the jurisdiction of the ICC.[31] When the Human Rights Council established a commission of inquiry on Libya to look into possible violations of humanitarian law during the NATO air campaign, that was an indirect check on the Council, since that campaign was authorized by it.[32]

Most dramatically, the ECJ engaged in indirect judicial review of the 1267 sanctions regime in the *Kadi* case. When an individual and a foundation complained to the European Court of First Instance that the listing regime deprived them of fundamental rights, the Court ruled that it could not engage in judicial review of Council decisions in light of Article 103 of the UN Charter, but could check "indirectly the lawfulness of the resolutions of the Security Council in question with regard to *jus cogens*." Surprisingly, the Court of First Instance concluded that the Council's actions did not violate any of those norms. On appeal, the European Court of Justice ruled that it did not have the power to review Council decisions, not even their compatibility with *jus cogens* norms, but could review the compatibility of the EU regulations enacted to implement the resolution with the fundamental human rights embodied in the EU's legal order. The ECJ concluded that the EU had violated those rights and gave the Council of Ministers three months to remedy the defect.

The European Commission did so by adopting a new regulation that required the EU to provide individuals with reasons for their being listed and to give them an opportunity to respond. These were applied to Kadi, whose placement on the list was promptly reaffirmed by the EU. He then went back to the European Union General Court (the new name of the Court of First Instance) with the same complaints about due process as before. The Court ruled that the summary of reasons was not good enough; the applicant's rights of defense were infringed; and the lack of any independent review of listing decisions was problematic. In October 2012, Kadi was finally delisted, first by the UN, then by the EU.

Meanwhile, the Security Council made significant adjustments to the listing regime in Resolutions 1822 (2008), 1904 (2009), and 1989 (2011)—

for example by creating an ombudsperson to serve as a conduit for complaints from those who believe they were falsely listed. Thus the Council has gone a long way toward accommodating criticisms of the 1267 regime. Most of its members would never say this was in direct response to the ECJ's judgment (and similar judgments by other courts), but arguably it was in indirect response. Just like the ECJ engaged in indirect judicial review, the Council engaged in indirect compliance with the ECJ decision.

Political Checks

As the ten-year saga of Kadi shows, indirect judicial review of the Council is not an efficient mode of accountability—although the prospect of court challenges may deter the Council from overstepping in the future. Of more consequence are political checks. To begin with, the P5 are a check on each other. Given who the P5 are, the veto power provides considerable assurance that the Council is not going to casually stomp on the rights of small states and individuals. Counterterrorism and counterproliferation are two areas in which the P5 share a lot of common ground, but even in those areas, agreement among them has not been easy to achieve.

New working methods pushed by the group of small countries (the so-called S5, comprising Costa Rica, Jordan, Liechtenstein, Singapore, and Switzerland) and others have had a similar effect.[33] Greater transparency, publicity, and consultation are accountability mechanisms. Elsewhere, I have described the Security Council as a four-tier, deliberative setting, composed of the P5, the E10, the rest of the UN membership, and a constellation of engaged nonstate actors.[34] While the P5 hold the lion's share of material, voting, and discursive power, the felt need to engage with these other actors imposes a considerable constraint on the Council. It can adopt binding resolutions, but there is only so much coercive power it can bring to bear to ensure those resolutions are implemented. Noncooperation by some or all states and relevant nonstate actors can render sanctions regimes ineffective, quasi-legislative resolutions scraps of paper, and peace operations useless. The imperative of effectiveness is a powerful check on an overreaching Council.

For example, the Secretary-General and other high UN officials, like the special rapporteur on human rights and counterterrorism, added their voices to the chorus that critiqued the 1267 sanctions regime.[35] The OAU collectively refused to implement the sanctions on Libya in the early 1990s, claiming they were illegitimate.[36] The AU has called for the ICC charges against President Omar al-Bashir of Sudan to be dropped, defying Security Council resolutions that require all states to cooperate with ICC investigations. Moreover, several AU states have invited Bashir to visit in defiance of the arrest warrant.

These accountability mechanisms, though weak, suggest that the fears of a hegemonic Security Council are exaggerated. This is not to say that the legitimacy concerns raised by a Council making, interpreting, and enforcing the law are not real, especially for a Council whose composition is outdated. But the imperative of effectiveness can be a powerful check. If it is not attentive to these concerns, the world will be left with an unpalatable choice: an active Council whose edicts are systematically ignored, or a quiescent one that is systematically bypassed.

The Consistency Dilemma

No discussion of accountability and legitimacy—or the impact of international law for that matter—is complete without considering the problem of selective application. Consistency may seem a simplistic pursuit, but it is also a fundamental principle of justice: like cases ought to be treated alike. The problem is that in the realm of international politics, perfect consistency is not possible: power matters and inequalities in power inevitably result in inconsistency. It is always possible to find examples of double standards and hypocrisy in international affairs. It would be naive to expect otherwise. Moreover, the desire for consistency cannot be allowed to trump all else. The Security Council did nothing to stop the genocide in Rwanda in 1994. Does this mean that, for the sake of consistency, it should not stop genocide anywhere?[37]

That being said, we should not simply resign ourselves to hypocrisy and double standards. Part of the reason that norms and laws emerge is to generate more consistency: they are general standards that can be used to pressure decisionmakers to treat like cases alike. Consider the norm of Responsibility to Protect (R2P). A cynical view is that it is simply an excuse the powerful states use to intervene for ulterior motives; a less cynical view is that, while the risk of abuse is real, norms can mitigate the problem of selectivity. R2P cannot compel or prevent action, and it certainly cannot guarantee consistency. But as an advocacy tool, it can make Council-authorized intervention a little more likely when justified, and a little less likely when not.

Conclusion

What this analysis suggests is how deeply law and politics are intertwined in the Security Council. The legal checks and political constraints described here are two sides of the same coin. The Council is not formally bound by indirect judicial review, nor do its members feel legally obliged to act on the basis of that review, but an authoritative opinion from a credible court impacts the political dynamics in and around the Council. When members of the UN deliberate on what the Council should or should not do to address a particular crisis, legal considerations matter. This is even truer when states calculate whether to join in an enforcement action. Being able to claim solid legal grounds for the action makes it easier for those who want to participate to join, and harder for those who disapprove to resist; conversely, the lack of a clear legal basis has the opposite effect, making it harder for those who might want to participate to do so. The interventions in Iraq, Côte d'Ivoire, and Libya—and debates on intervention in Syria— are illustrative. It would be foolish to suggest that international law trumps power in these situations, but it is also wrong to suggest that legal considerations are irrelevant.

Notes

1. John R. Searle, "How to Derive 'Ought' From 'Is,'" *Philosophical Review* 73, no. 1 (January 1964): 55.

2. Article 103 reads: "In the event of a conflict between the obligations of the Members of the United Nations under the present Charter and their obligations under any other international agreement, their obligations under the present Charter shall prevail." There has been debate about whether Charter obligations supersede customary law and *jus cogens* (peremptory) norms, but there is no doubt that they trump treaty law. On the debates, see Judge Oda in the *Lockerbie* case: International Court of Justice, *Questions of Interpretation and Application of the 1971 Montreal Convention Arising from the Aerial Incident at Lockerbie (Libyan Arab Jamahiriya v. United States of America), Summary of the Judgment 27 February 1998, Annex 98/5bis, Dissenting Opinion of Judge Oda,* February 27, 1998; and European Court of First Instance in the *Kadi* case: European Court of First Instance Second Chamber, Extended Composition, *Yassin Abdullah Kadi vs. Council of the European Union and the Commission of the European Communities,* T-315/01, September 21, 2005.

3. Other features that give the Charter that character are its perpetuity (there is no withdrawal clause) and the difficulty of amending it (Article 108). Simon Chesterman, Thomas M. Franck, and David M. Malone, *Law and Practice of the United Nations: Documents and Commentary* (Oxford: Oxford University Press, 2008). On the UN Charter as constitution, see also Michael W. Doyle, "The UN Charter: A Global Constitution?" in *Ruling the World? Constitutionalism, International Law, and Global Governance,* edited by Jeffrey L. Dunoff and Joel P. Trachtmann (New York: Columbia University Press, 2009); Bardo Fassbender, "Rediscovering a Forgotten Constitution: Notes on the Place of the UN Charter in the International Legal Order," in Dunoff and Trachtmann, *Ruling the World?*

4. International Court of Justice, "Reparation for Injuries Suffered in the Service of the United Nations," Advisory Opinion, April 11, 1949. On the doctrine of implied powers, see also European Court of Justice, *Commission v. Germany,* Judgment C-518/07, March 9, 2010.

5. See Security Council Report, "Security Council Action Under Chapter VII: Myths and Realities," Special Research Report no. 1, June 23, 2008, pp. 5–9. See also "Article 25," in *The Charter of the United Nations: A Commentary,* 3rd ed., edited by Bruno Simma, Damiel-Erasmus Khan, Georg Nolte, and Andreas Paulas (Oxford: Oxford University Press, 2012).

6. Contrast paragraphs 11–13 of Security Council Resolution 1874, S/RES/1874 (June 12, 2009), which uses the words "calls upon," with paragraphs 8–11 of Security Council Resolution 2094, S/RES/2094 (March 7, 2013), which uses the word "decides." Both resolutions are on North Korea.

7. International Court of Justice, "Legal Consequences for States of the Continued Presence of South Africa in Namibia (South West Africa) Notwithstanding Security Council Resolution 276 (1970)," Advisory Opinion, June 21, 1971.

8. See Boutros Boutros-Ghali, *Unvanquished: A US-UN Saga* (New York: Random, 1999), p. 182. On differences of opinion among member states on this issue, see Security Council Report, "Security Council Action Under Chapter VII," p. 5.

9. United Nations Security Council Resolutions 1244 (June 10, 1999), UN Doc. S/RES/1244; and 1272 (October 25, 1999), UN Doc. S/RES/1272.

10. See Simon Chesterman, "Virtual Trusteeship," in *The UN Security Council: From the Cold War to the 21st Century,* edited by David M. Malone (Boulder, CO: Lynne Rienner, 2004). See also Simon Chesterman, *You, the People: The United Nations, Transitional Administration, and Statebuilding* (Oxford: Oxford University Press, 2005); Richard Caplan, *International Governance of War Torn Territories: Rule and Reconstruction.* (New York: Oxford University Press, 2005); Roland Paris, *At War's End: Building Peace After Civil Conflict* (Cambridge: Cambridge University Press, 2004).

11. Ian Johnstone, "Legislation and Adjudication in the UN Security Council: Bringing Down the Deliberative Deficit," *American Journal of International Law* 102, no. 2 (2008): 275–308. See also Stefan Talmon, "The Security Council as World Legislature," *American Journal of International Law* 99 (2005): 175–193.

12. Detlev F. Vagts, "Hegemonic International Law," *American Journal of International Law* 95, no. 4 (2001): 843–848; Jose E. Alvarez, "Hegemonic International Law Revisited," *American Journal of International Law* 97, no. 4 (2003): 873–888; Nico Krisch, "The Rise and Fall of Collective Security: Terrorism, US Hegemony, and the Plight of the Security Council," in *Terrorism as a Challenge for National and International Law: Security Versus Liberty?* edited by Christian Walter, Silja Vöneky, Volker Röben, and Frank Schorkopf (Berlin: Springer, 2004).

13. See Ian Johnstone, *The Power of Deliberation: International Law, Politics, and Organizations* (New York: Oxford University Press, 2011), pp. 83–86.

14. United Nations Security Council, "Presidential Statements," S/PRST/2010/4, February 24, 2010; and S/PRST/2012/2, February 21, 2012.

15. Oscar Schachter, "The UN Legal Order: An Overview," in *The United Nations and International Law,* edited by Christopher C. Joyner (Cambridge: Cambridge University Press, 1997), p. 9.

16. Rosalyn Higgins, *Problems and Process: International Law and How We Use It* (Oxford: Oxford University Press, 1994).

17. United Nations Security Council Resolution 284 (July 29, 1970), UN Doc. S/RES/284.

18. For example, International Commission of Inquiry on Darfur, *Report of the International Commission of Inquiry on Darfur to the United Nations Secretary-General Pursuant to Security Council Resolution 1564 of 18 September 2004* (Geneva, January 25, 2005). For a full list of the commissions and investigative bodies established by the Council, see United Nations Repertoire of the Practice of the Security Council, "Commissions and Investigative Bodies," www.un.org/en/sc/repertoire/subsidiary_organs/commissions_and_investigations.shtml.

19. I thank my research assistant Bret McEvoy for this observation.

20. These cases have been discussed at length elsewhere. See Simon Chesterman, *Just War or Just Peace? Humanitarian Intervention and International Law* (Oxford: Oxford University Press, 2001); Christine Gray, *International Law and the Use of Force* (New York: Oxford University Press, 2008); Ian Johnstone, "When the Security Council Is Divided: Imprecise Authorizations, Implied Mandates, and the

Failure to Act," in *Oxford Handbook on the Law on the Use of Force,* edited by Marc Weller (Oxford: Oxford University Press, 2015).

21. United Nations Security Council Resolution 2085, S/RES/2085 (December 20, 2012), para. 14 (original emphasis).

22. Whether the "legitimacy" of the governmental entity—as opposed to effective control of the territory and population—is a valid criterion for determining the legality of intervention by invitation is a contested question. See Gray, *International Law and the Use of Force,* chap. 3.

23. On North Korea, see United Nations Security Council Resolutions 1718 (October 14, 2006), UN Doc. S/RES/1718; 1874 (June 12, 2009), UN Doc. S/RES/1874; 2087 (January 22, 2013), UN Doc. S/RES/2087; and 2094 (March 7, 2013), UN Doc. S/RES/2094. On Iran, see United Nations Security Council Resolutions 1737 (December 27, 2006), UN Doc. S/RES/1737; 1747 (March 24, 2007), UN Doc. S/RES/1747; 1803 (March 3, 2008), UN Doc S/RES/1803; and 1929 (June 9, 2010), UN Doc. S/RES/1929.

24. United Nations Security Council Resolutions 1718 (October 14, 2006), UN Doc. S/RES/1718; and 1874 (June 12, 2009), UN Doc. S/RES/1874.

25. United Nations Security Council, "Provisional Verbatim Record of the 3046th Meeting" (presidential statement "The Responsibility of the Security Council in the Maintenance of International Peace and Security"), UN Doc. S/PV.3046, January 31, 1992.

26. United Nations, *Report of Rapporteur of Committee IV/2 Technical Committee 2 (Legal Problems) of Commission IV (Judicial Organization),* United Nations Conference on International Organization, San Francisco, June 12, 1945, pp. 879–880.

27. Thomas M. Franck, "The Powers of Appreciation: Who Is the Ultimate Guardian of UN Legality?" *American Journal of International Law* 86, no. 3 (July 1992): 519–523. The ICTY did the same in *Tadic* when its first defendant claimed that the tribunal did not have a right to exist since the Security Council did not have the power to create it. See International Criminal Tribunal for the Former Yugoslavia, Appeals Chamber, *Prosecutor v. Dusko Tadic (Appeal Judgement),* IT-94-1-A, Bosnia and Herzegovina/Serbia, July 15, 1999, paras. 28–48, www.ref world.org/docid/40277f504.html.

28. Jose E. Alvarez, "Judging the Security Council," *American Journal of International Law* 90, no. 1 (1996): 28.

29. Ibid., p. 30 (emphasis added).

30. International Criminal Tribunal for the Former Yugoslavia, Appeals Chamber, *Prosecutor v. Dusko Tadic.*

31. Statement of the Secretary-General on the Adoption of Security Council Resolution 1487 (2003), United Nations Press Release SC/7789, June 12, 2003, p. 6, available at http://www.un.org/press/en/2003/sc7789.doc.htm.

32. I thank Sebastian von Einsiedel for this perceptive observation.

33. United Nations General Assembly, "Costa Rica, Jordan, Liechtenstein, Singapore, and Switzerland: Draft Resolution," UN Doc. A/60/L.49, March 17, 2006; United Nations Security Council, "Letter Dated 20 June 2008 from the Permanent Representative of Switzerland to the United Nations Addressed to the President of the Security Council," UN Doc. S/2008/418, June 24, 2008; United Nations General Assembly, "Costa Rica, Jordan, Liechtenstein, Singapore, and Switzerland: Revised Draft Resolution," UN Doc. A/66/L.42/Rev.2., May 15, 2012.

34. Johnstone, *The Power of Deliberation.*

35. The Secretary-General's implicit critique is contained in a letter that his legal counsel, Nicolas Michel, read into the record at a public meeting of the Security Council. United Nations Security Council, "Provisional Verbatim Record of the 5474th Meeting," UN Doc. S/PV.5474, June 22, 2006, pp. 7–8. The special rapporteur's assessment is contained in a statement he made to the press on June 29, 2011.

36. Analyzed at length in Ian Hurd, *After Anarchy: Legitimacy and Power in the United Nations Security Council* (Princeton: Princeton University Press, 2007).

37. See Nicholas D. Kristof, "Is It Better to Save No One?" *International New York Times,* April 2, 2011, www.nytimes.com/2011/04/03/opinion/03kristof.html?_r=0.

38

The Security Council and the Changing Distribution of Power

Bruce Jones

THE COMMON LORE OF THE HISTORY OF THE UN SECURITY COUN-
cil is quickly told. After a brief flurry of activity in the years immediately
after it was formed, Cold War rivalry between the United States and the
Soviet Union froze the Council into stasis and inaction, the veto from the
superpower rivals blocking any prospects for unified action. Then, the end
of the Cold War unfroze the body, allowing for expansion of the Council
into a wide range of conflict management activities, which continue to this
day, making the body a critical pillar of overall international governance of
conflict and recovery therefrom.

This brief history begs the question: If we witness a return to great
power tensions, will we also return to a point of great power blockage in
the Security Council, and a consequent retrenchment of the UN's ability to
engage in conflict management and humanitarian actions? This is the essential question for this chapter.

The common history glosses over two important issues. First, during
the Cold War, as many of the chapters in this volume have illustrated, the
Council was actually used more than is often understood. There was, of
course, the Korean War (formally a UN-mandated operation), and then the
large, complex peacekeeping operation deployed in the Congo in 1960—
replete with an air force and a cadre of teachers. This is sometimes referenced in discussions of the evolution of the UN, often lauded. (Its admirers
never seem to be concerned by the fact that the operation left behind in
Congo one of the most kleptocratic and dysfunctional governments in contemporary history, perhaps an early illustration of the point that ending
wars is easier than political reconstruction.) More salient for our purposes

were a series of moments, around Arab-Israeli wars, when the Council was used by the United States and the Soviets to avoid having wars between their proxies spiral into direct clashes between the superpowers. Many of the major tools that the Council would wield to effect in the post–Cold War period—special envoys, mediators, observer missions, peacekeeping operations, political missions, humanitarian agencies—were born on the borders between Israel and its Arab neighbors.[1] The second point is that the attention given to the post–Cold War expansion of the UN, and to concepts like the Responsibility to Protect (R2P) and humanitarian intervention, have occluded a quite different evolution. While the UN has developed an ever larger and more complex role in crisis management, we have seen a parallel evolution: the forging of a series of instruments or tools or bodies for dealing with other aspects of international security, primarily outside the Council, not within it. Thus, while the Council, in the context of recessive great power tensions, has become the central body in the international system to deal with crises (and far more important than regional organizations), it has not assumed the same prominence in the management of international security as a whole. During a period when great power tensions and other forms of international security threat were recessive, the crisis management role of the UN was prominent; as geopolitical tensions mount, this role of the UN may continue, but will have less relative weight.

To situate the Security Council in the changing distribution and dynamics of power, we first need to clarify what those dynamics are. For some time now, we have been mesmerized by the rapid rise of the so-called BRIC bloc of countries (Brazil, Russia, India, and China)—so much so that we have barely begun to notice an important slowing of that trend and important new strengths in the US economy (especially in energy and manufacturing). There is one scenario where China overtakes the United States as the largest economy in the world by 2020—but equally credible estimates push that timeline closer to 2030 or beyond; and whenever this event occurs, China will still be a developing economy and less powerful than the United States by several metrics.[2] Until then, and quite probably beyond, the United States will remain in a category of one in the international system in terms of its military, intelligence, and diplomatic capability—and this is without making reference to its allies, who still constitute three-quarters of the world's top economic and military nations.

Indeed, the phrase "rising powers" obscures more than it clarifies. In economic terms, China, India, and Brazil have already risen to the status of top economic powers, and they will continue to grow, albeit probably more slowly than in the past decade.[3] China is now also the number two military spender in the world, although there remains a huge gulf between Chinese and US military spending and capacity;[4] and India and Brazil are still second-tier players in global military terms. Other countries often counted among the "rise of the rest"—countries like Turkey, Indonesia, Mexico, South Africa—are third-tier military players, and have found that even in so-called soft power and diplomacy, there are sharp limits to their current influence (as is true for India, Brazil, and even China).

Still, quite evidently, these countries are changing the face of international politics. China's economic rise, even if now likely to slow, has already been sufficient to thrust it onto the global stage and stoke its sense of confidence. India and Brazil are important new diplomatic and economic players (and India is investing in its armed services, especially its navy, which currently rivals China's in the Indian Ocean).[5] China's recent assertiveness has reinvigorated neglected alliance relationships in Asia, and may yet pull Japan out of its decade-and-a-half-long "lost decade."[6] Russia is managing to rise and slump all at the same time—its economy has rebounded from its post-Soviet collapse, but to nowhere near its Soviet-era heights, and it suffers from serious internal political dysfunction, including a return to more authoritarian patterns. Still, it can pose serious challenges, as the Ukraine crisis illustrates. And across all of this, the United States–China relationship is being forged anew—with what balance between rivalry and cooperation yet to be seen.

We are also entering a period of great power tensions and competition, including in Asia, replete with risks of clashes (most likely limited clashes) among the Asian powers—that is, China, India, Japan, and the Koreas. But of these, only China has a permanent seat on the Security Council. Thus it is unclear how or whether tensions in Asia would constrain the UN's role. A serious deterioration in relations between the United States and China (which would most likely come as a result of security tensions in Asia) could see a return to great power tensions blocking Council action; but so far, the two powers seem able to spar in Asia and cooperate globally, and there are good reasons for that, grounded in a deep convergence of interests that is likely to endure.[7] But of course, to take the flip side of the argument: precisely because its membership is limited, it is hard to see how the Council could play a useful role in the management of great power tensions in Asia (though there are some very modest steps it could take to contribute, even now).

Similarly, the crisis in Ukraine has meant deadlock in the Council, but has not spilled out into Africa or the broader Middle East. Still, it is blocking action on Ukraine itself, much as tensions between Russia and the West were a major stumbling block to Security Council action in Bosnia and even more so in Kosovo. Furthermore, the Ukraine crisis could divert what has until now been an essential source of energy, diplomatic weight, and money for the UN—that is, European political attention. Absent sustained political and financial engagement from countries like the United Kingdom, France, the Netherlands, and the Scandinavian countries, the UN would have had a far less energetic evolution, and far less flexible income, than it has had in the post–Cold War era. If those countries feel compelled to divert their energies to more traditional defense issues and to the security of the European theater, the UN may feel the effects of that shift.

So far, though, the evidence suggests that the places where great power competition will affect the Security Council are limited, and there is no evidence yet of spillover into the wider crisis management role. It is true, of course, that Russia is in an increasingly assertive mode, and where its interests clash with those of the West it can—and as Syria and Ukraine demonstrate, will—use its veto in the Council to frustrate Western policy. But this is more continuity than change—Russia was just as active in blocking Western policy in the Council on Kosovo as it has been on Syria, and just as willing to sign off on peacekeeping and other crisis management operations in Mali, the DRC, Sudan, and Somalia as it was in the late 1990s in West Africa, Central Africa, and elsewhere.

Will all of this reshape the dynamics of decisionmaking in the UN? The Security Council is first and foremost a body designed to manage great power relations, and justly so. It is easy to forget what it meant for the broader agenda of international and human security for the powers to be deeply divided among themselves, as they were during the Cold War—to say nothing of the interwar period or the bloody conflicts it punctuated. How much of the new agenda—of rapid response to conflict, of protection of civilians, of postconflict stabilization and reconstruction—will erode as we move away from an era of dominance? What are the early signs?

Crisis Management:
The Still-Central Role of the Security Council

Let's start with crisis management. Over the past quarter century, the UN Security Council has emerged as the central actor in the international crisis management system. Many have noted that regional organizations play a role, and they do;[8] but in terms of sheer quantity of peacekeepers, not only does no individual regional organization even come close to the UN, but all regional organizations taken together deploy a fraction of the peacekeepers that the UN does—and even then, mostly in combination with the UN.[9] There are, however, important regional variations here. The bulk of current wars and crises are in two regions, Africa and the Middle East, which face very different sets of challenges and evoke very different patterns of great power interest.[10] In both, the Security Council remains deeply engaged, and in both there are more themes that unify than divide the powers, for now. Europe and Latin America mostly reside in that comfortable zone where most countries are too rich for Security Council intervention, but not yet much troubled by great power entanglement; only at the very margins of these continents is the Council present in any operational ways. (There is a looming question about whether Central America can alone deal adequately with the challenge of organized crime or whether it needs some outside help; but even if so, I anticipate that such help will come through less intrusive bodies.)[11]

Africa has been the host to the majority of Security Council operations in the post–Cold War era.[12] But the realities of Africa are changing. A steady and continuous decline in the number and levels of war on the continent[13] (a result that the Security Council can take some credit for)[14] is producing new realities, which can be described in terms of three factors. First, there is economic opportunity—it is a point more neglected than realized, but Africa now rivals China in terms of the number of middle-class consumers, albeit spread across several countries.[15] Second, there is energy— wherever war recedes, international investors are finding oil and gas reserves, as well as other minerals (and land, for food imports). And third, it is emerging powers that are doing a lot of the finding. Western powers remain major players on the continent, but emerging powers are critical to frontier markets and resource development—whether in gas development off the coast of Mozambique (Brazil), or oil exploration off the coast of Somaliland (Turkey).

And then there is Asia. On the margins of that continent, in Timor-Leste, the Council has been operationally engaged, just as it has on the margins of Europe (Kosovo, Bosnia). And great power politics have pulled the Council into one of the central security crises the region confronts—deft diplomacy between the United States and China, notably at the level of the permanent representatives in New York, which has put the Council more firmly into the inner circle of crisis prevention and management in North Korea. But it would be a far overreach to say that the Security Council is central to the changing security politics of Asia—which we will return to later.

Afghanistan is a partial exception. The UN was neither a central player during the post-9/11 counterterrorism, nationbuilding, and statebuilding operations in Afghanistan, nor irrelevant—in the realm of political negotiations and elections, the UN played important (if often flawed) roles.[16] And it is well within the realm of possibility that we will see a growing role for the Security Council in the period following the drawdown of the US security presence there. There are important issues here that unite the powers: forestalling a major resurgence of the Taliban, stabilizing Afghanistan for resource development, preventing subregional turmoil, and preventing a further deterioration in Pakistan. But whether a larger role for the Security Council in Afghanistan proves the "transnational threats unite the powers" thesis or the "garbage can theory" of the UN (when a problem is too hard or too messy, throw it at the UN) remains to be seen.

There are not only regional variations. A scan of recent UN actions reveals different types of crises in play, and they draw on different politics of the powers and the relations between them.

Categories of Crises

First, there are crises that are largely about internal security, and threaten the integrity of the state or territory in question. Civil wars and separatist/irredentist wars, especially in Africa—where until now the stakes have been fairly low from a great powers perspective—unite the Council more than they divide. There is after all a strong attachment among the great powers to state integrity. This is true of the rising powers most of all, but even the United States has a strong residual bias toward keeping states intact. Of course, there are mixed motivations here—the United States, the United Kingdom, and France in particular are often motivated in part by humanitarian concerns. But the humanitarian impulse is in constant tension with an impulse toward strengthening the institution of the state—in particular after 9/11 concentrated the mind of the powers on the threat posed by substate actors. No surprise, really, that threats to state sovereignty or integrity should continue to unite the powers and that the Security Council has been able to sustain large-scale engagement in civil-war management through the post–Cold War period. I see no signs of that role abating, though the number of engagements or of troop levels may decline—because of success, not failure.

It is striking that this willingness to act together extends to the question of protection of civilians—an issue that less obviously unifies the powers. Perhaps if the shift toward protection of civilians mandates had been tried in the present day, when the confidence and influence of China, India, and Russia are greater than at the onset of this century, we might not have seen the progress we have. It might have eroded—after all, Russia has thrown sand into the gears on protection mandates in Sudan, among other things, though not to the point of ultimately impeding reasonably strong resolutions and rules of engagement.[17] Still, China and Russia have both backed innumerable resolutions and operations that put the protection of civilians front and center, and have even allowed the Council to pursue an agenda one would have expected to be more divisive among the P5, such as the establishment of democratic institutions, elections, and the building of institutions for the rule of law.[18] Virtually every time that China votes for a resolution, especially a resolution under Chapter VII that emphasizes these issues, it notes that it is doing so on an exceptional basis, one that sets no precedents—and it has made this "no precedents" argument while voting in favor of missions almost sixty times now since the end of the Cold War (see Chapter 4).

Then there are crises that are exploited or aggravated by international terrorist groups. It might not have been evident that the UN would end up engaged in operations that have a counterterrorist dimension, given contemporary political limitations on UN force generation, and enduring limitations on UN force management. But what is not surprising is that these operations—in Somalia, Mali, Lebanon—unify the Security Council. There are divides, of course, within the West, especially between the United States and Europe, over matters of international legal due process in the listing and delisting of sanctioned individuals. But these do not drive differences of policy about whether or not to act in specific crises. And more important in terms of understanding the future trajectory, among the set of nonallied powers, terrorism is a strong unifying factor. The United States, Russia, China, and India all perceive an important threat from Islamic radicalism, both in the form of al-Qaeda and its affiliates, and for Russia, China, and India in the form of regional or domestic Islamist groups. Anybody looking to measure how far the Council will go on this should take a close read of its resolutions on Mali—particularly striking are the passages where the Council calls on Mali's rebel groups (not, normally, the kind of groups the body would address itself except from the perspective of demandeur) to break from al-Qaeda in the Maghreb.[19] To see China and Russia voting alongside the West, and China agreeing to contribute troops to a UN operation deployed alongside a Western intervention force, is a reminder just how far we have come from the old patterns of proxy warfare in the so-called third world of that era. But not all crises unify, of course. The ones that divide are the ones that bring to the fore the revolutionary tendencies of one of the powers—that is, the United States.

R2P and Regime Change

The question is often posed: Will the rising powers agree to operate largely within the terms and rules of the established order, limiting their challenge to gaining more space and more weight *within* the order?[20] Or will they try to overturn some of the cardinal principles of that order? My own view is that while it is too early to tell for sure (and much will be shaped by the West's reaction to the current, limited challenge), the balance of evidence suggests that most of the rising powers, most of the time, will seek to challenge within the order. But there are important exceptions. On security arrangements in Asia there is a more concerted effort to reorder relationships. And in Europe, Russia's moves in Ukraine constitute a major violation of two of the cardinal principles of international order—sovereign inviolability and nonuse of force. Of course, the only formal effort to rewrite the rules of sovereignty—a gradually building effort from the earliest days of the post–Cold War moment in northern Iraq, through to the Responsibility to Protect operation in Libya—has been driven by the West. And the effort overlaps with the one area where the United States, not the rising powers, inclines to being a revolutionary and not a status quo power: its desire to foster a steady shift toward democratic rule, including episodically through forceful regime change.

Here, two crises draw the attention of commentary and politics alike, and are often conflated: in Syria and Libya. The two are seen as common, tied together by the blurry boundaries between the humanitarian impulse behind the Responsibility to Protect and the question of forceful regime change. But the two crises are in fact very different.

Libya started more clearly in the humanitarian category, and at that stage generated a surprising degree of unity within the Security Council—including all of the BRIC countries, which happened to sit in the body when the Libya crisis broke, voting for a resolution that had three elements that were potentially divisive: referral of Libyan authorities to the International Criminal Court; imposition of sanctions; and most important, invocation of the concept of Responsibility to Protect.[21] Even when it came to the question of using force to tackle the Libyan army, through the R2P lens, there was more support than blockage: the BRIC countries plus Germany abstained, but Russia and China, in particular, made clear that their abstentions were meant to facilitate action, rather than to register dissent. Of course, when the United States shifted the balance of its policy from halting Muammar Qaddafi's advance on Benghazi in the east, to overthrowing the Qaddafi regime in western Libya, the concerns of the emerging powers rose.

In the wake of the Libyan episode, there has been a lot of discussion about the way in which the move to regime change in Libya has doomed the R2P concept, including in Syria.[22] I doubt this. First, it is worth noticing that while heavy NATO action was already under way in Libya—at a time when the emerging powers had already begun to argue that NATO had gone beyond the remit provided by the authorizing resolution—there was a second R2P vote: in Côte d'Ivoire. There, a democratic election was being held hostage by the electoral loser, and renewed conflict was imminent. France offered to deploy a military intervention. The issue was debated in the Council, and an R2P authorization was granted—with a vote of fifteen in favor and zero against.[23]

And there is very little evidence to suggest that Russian and Chinese opposition to intervention in Syria has anything to do with Libya. Russia is typically suspicious of any intervention (other than its own). Russian opposition to the West's position in Syria had two strategic logics that were not linked to Libya. First, Syria was one of Russia's few remaining allies in the world, and the site of its only base outside former Soviet territory. Second, Russia had a serious—and I would argue genuine—concern that the fallout from chaos in Syria would be the metastasis of a new strand of Islamic radicalism, made all the more worrying by strong links to Islamic radicals in Chechnya.[24] The United States offered no compelling counter to this argument. Bottom line: even absent an R2P intervention in Libya, Russia would hardly have simply waved the West on into intervention in Syria. As for China: it was basically following the Russian line, and with some discomfort, given the depth of its oil relationship with the Gulf. (And worth noting: it's not as if the West were looking to get waved in; despite a steady and consistent chorus of calls by Western and Arab voices for military intervention, there have to date been no takers in the West.)

More to the point, the core impulse for potential Western action in Syria is not primarily humanitarian, though there is an important humanitarian component. The core of the Western perspective of the crisis in Syria is a blend of wanting to back what the West perceives as democratic forces arrayed against the Bashar al-Assad government, as part of the wider Arab Spring, and a strategic concern about the balance of power in the region, the link to the Iran crisis, and the relationship with Russia.[25] In other words, whereas Western action in Libya was primarily a humanitarian impulse with a dose of interest in regime change, Syria is largely a strategic concern with a dose of humanitarian interest. That may change over time as death tolls mount, but the emphasis on regime change shapes the debate in the UN Security Council about Syria.

It is no surprise that regime-change questions divide the Council, and will continue to do so. But if we ask about the relevance of the Security Council in today's evolving geopolitics, we have to bear in mind that these questions affect a very small subset of Council actions. By my count, the Council has authorized offensive military action against the consent of the state in question only eight times through its entire nearly seventy-year existence.[26] Far more frequent has been action to defend states against disintegration or to quell internal war, supported by the targeted country. And to that we now add efforts to defend states against terrorist or other transnational threats. All these forms of crisis management unify more than they divide the powers, and so far I see no genuine evidence that the shift in power balances in the international system is set to erode Security Council action in this sphere.

Threats Beyond Crises: Evolution Beyond the UN

The picture looks somewhat different, though, if we widen our gaze beyond crises, toward the broader set of threats and concerns dealt with by the international security architecture. Here we see some surprising political developments. I would sum them up this way: the Republican administration of President George W. Bush expanded the remit and authority of the Security Council, and the Democratic administration of President Barack Obama shifted the emphasis to new tools outside the UN.

Of course, this is too bold a statement. After all, one of the significant multilateral innovations of the Bush administration was the proliferation security initiative, a voluntary, multinational mechanism, developed outside the UN, designed to amplify and coordinate countries' efforts at interdiction on the high seas against the proliferation of nuclear materials. This was met with substantial diplomatic concern about why it had not been pursued within the UN.[27] At the same time, though, the Bush administration pursued two other initiatives, both of which were also met with controversy, for the opposite reason: pushing the authority of the UN too far. These were two Council resolutions, 1373 and 1540, that substantially expanded the remit of the Security Council, under Chapter VII, to engage member states on their responsibilities, and their domestic legal framework, for dealing with terrorism and proliferation. Because of the rhetoric of its first term, and more importantly because of the decision to mount a war in Iraq in the absence of Council authorization, the Bush administration earned a reputation for anti-multilateralism. But this obscures the fact that when President Bush took office, there were 20,000 UN peacekeepers deployed overseas; when he left, the number had risen to 100,000.[28] Important political roles on the Middle East and Afghanistan were added at the same time. This did not happen despite US policy or against US reluctance, but with US support, insistence, and sometimes direct leadership. Rarely has there been a government where the first term, often hostile to the UN, was so different from the second, or where the rhetoric was so different from the reality of its actions (after the Iraq debate, that is).

The Obama administration inherited these outcomes. Among the consequences was serious overstretch in the Council, which by 2009 was straining to stay on top of about twenty peacekeeping operations (depending on the year), several of them in strategically significant contexts. In an earlier era, ambassadors in the Council would develop substantial expertise on individual files, and could engage the Secretariat in in-depth conversations about their mandate, management, and guidance. Those days are largely gone, as ambassadors now flit back and forth across a wide range of mission contexts. And because Iran, the Middle East, North Korea, and cases involving terrorism are also on the Council's agenda, much of the political attention and Council ambassadors' time drive to those contexts. The Obama administration also confronted the fact that steps taken to expand the remit of the Council on terrorism and proliferation had run up against hard limits of effectiveness.

The result is that the more important innovations by the Obama administration on international security architecture have been taken outside of the UN. There are two, and they are similar. First was the establishment of the Nuclear Safety Summit, convened by President Obama as part of his Prague disarmament agenda, and designed as a onetime effort to bolster leaders' engagement on tightening up the security of nuclear supplies. Both the success of the summit and the character of its membership—forty-seven countries, including all of the significant G-20+ powers, from every region and income level and walk of life—led to a continuation of the summit process, and it has already emerged as a significant new international, multinational mechanism. A similar mechanism was brought to life in the counterterrorism field, the Global Counter-Terrorism Forum. Conceived as a tool for capacity building, lesson learning, and strategy sharing among countries with interests in counterterrorism, it was deliberately established outside the UN framework to avoid falling victim to the organization's politics and bureaucracy.

I do not ascribe either administration's actions primarily to ideology—after all, it would be hard to find a more pro-UN team than that which led foreign policy in the Obama administration's first term, and that team brought major, strategic files to the UN, to good effect. But there are institutional factors that both the Democratic and Republican administrations encounter, about the limit of the Security Council's bandwidth (causing evolution outside the UN), and the absence of other good options for crisis management (causing expansion inside). Still, we might have envisaged a deepening of the UN's part in the infrastructure for terrorism and proliferation, but this is not the direction things are going.

This gets blurred when it comes to crises that involve the proliferation of nuclear weapons. Here, two impulses converge. The P5 have overlapping (not identical) interests in avoiding a situation in which either of the current potential contenders—Iran and North Korea—actually end up with a nuclear weapon. The P5 have similarly overlapping interests in ensuring that these two countries' search for a nuclear capacity does not become a cause of major regional instability, although they may differ in their precise calculations about risks and timelines. The Security Council has been important to the steady accumulation of sanctions and other measures in Iran; the sanctions that have had most effect on the Iranian economy have been direct US sanctions, to be sure, but these operated under, and gained legitimacy through, the overall umbrella of the UN Security Council.[29] It is notable, too, that China worked with the United States to generate a new Council resolution before implementing new, direct Chinese sanctions and other forms of pressure on North Korea—moves that produced a substantial convergence of US-Chinese approaches to North Korea. Both cases defy worst-case predictions about great power divisions and a breakdown in negotiations in the Council.

We see similar mixed patterns of institutional developments inside and outside the purview of the Security Council when it comes to an issue of growing importance, namely maritime security. There we see a number of innovations. The most salutary, in my view, was the way in which the

Council initiated, authorized, encouraged, and enabled multinational counter-piracy and protection of trade operations off the Somali coast, from 2008 onward. The UN has played critical roles here, not only through the Security Council, but also through special advisers to the Secretary-General who have opened up legal space and helped facilitate necessary capacity building. Since that time, though, most of the innovation on maritime security has been outside the UN—whether in the Arctic, in informal arrangements on counter-piracy, in the G8, and in other ways.[30] And that is especially true in the East and South China seas.

Which brings us to a further, less salutary, issue. The most worrying long-term dynamic in great power security relations is the steady upward spiral of nationalist sentiment reinforcing territorial claims stoking preexisting strategic tension, all building into an arms race among Asia's several powers—and already a series of near-crises between Japan and China in the East and South China seas. All of which results in the emerging reality that the most important challenge to international peace and security is one in which the Security Council is not present, and arguably not relevant.

Great Power Security and the Asia Challenge

It is an oft-cited claim that when one power rises and another falls, war results.[31] History is actually more complex than that, and besides, the United States is not a falling power. History also tells us that in situations of power transition, war between the second- and third-tier powers is as common as between the top powers[32]—a lesson Chinese, Japanese, and Korean nationalists would be wise to heed. The risk of limited military clashes, perhaps worse, is mounting. For now at least, the Security Council remains far removed from this key security dynamic.

Part of the reason is who sits in the Council. Of the Asian powers, only China is a permanent member. The lessons of the Cold War tell us that the Council is likely to act when several conditions are met: the major powers implicated in a given crisis are present in the Council; and either their interests converge, or they see a need to avoid an acute crisis and use the UN as an instrument to help them avoid that outcome. The fact that neither Japan nor India hold permanent seats in the Council reduces the likelihood of this scenario in Asia.

Are there parts of the Asia challenge where the Council could, in principle, help slow the upward spiral of tensions? Let's first acknowledge that the most important issues—China's strategic perspective and economic/resource claims in the East and South China seas, and the sustained naval role of the United States in the Pacific and in these same seas—are ones that fall squarely into the realm of bilateral relations and perhaps bilateral arms control regimes. But there are other issues.

I would focus on the issue of crisis incidents—playing to the Council's comparative advantages. For example, in 2010 a Korean naval ship was sunk, reportedly by North Korean mines or torpedoes. In the wake of this, Korea created an ad hoc, multinational investigation team, to bolster its case that it had been the victim of a North Korean attack. Sweden, Australia, and the United States joined Korea's investigation.[33] Unsurprisingly, China rejected its findings: the United States, two close allies, and one Scandinavian does not a neutral body make.[34] Might it have added value if, at the time, there had been a standing investigation mechanism, established by the Council (where China would ensure that the membership of the investigation mechanism included countries it trusted), on which an aggrieved country could draw?

Still, even if the Council finds some ways to develop tools that are useful to crisis mitigation and de-escalation in the Asian security game, it will be modest at best. It is this contrast between a rapidly deepening security dilemma in Asia and the seeming absence of the Council from these dynamics that makes it seem like the UN's relevance is drifting. In this regard, the joint United States–China resolution on North Korea is a very significant counterpoint to this story line, but it remains to be seen how far that exception can or will extend. It is certainly an important point to build on.

Of course, it is conceivable—albeit not likely—that the Council could prove useful in Asia during a genuine crisis in the way that it was in the Middle East during the Cold War. Imagine if Japan and China end up engaged in a limited military clash over the Senkaku/Diaoyu islands; say one side shoots down a military aircraft of the other, which retaliates in kind. The United States would immediately be involved in crisis diplomacy, trying to stop the situation from escalating. This would take the form of US diplomatic pressure on both sides, forceful statements from the US president, travel to the region by a top cabinet figure, and pre-emptive military moves. If successful, there would be a need for a stand-down mechanism. This could be accomplished through trilateral talks—but it might be that there would be a temptation to reach for the Security Council to have it spell out the terms of disengagement. The United States and China would be in direct negotiations then, with the United States representing Japan—but also keeping Japan at a slight distance from the negotiations, which would have its advantages. But of course, it is possible that the Chinese would insist on avoiding the Council because of their desire to avoid "internationalizing" any dispute to which they are a party.

All of this then brings us to the final political theme: the question of whether or not the Council is misaligned with the contemporary distribution of power in the international system, and whether or not this matters.

Council Membership and the Distribution of Power

The question of membership reform of the Security Council is often debated through the lens of adapting the Council to the new realities of power. In point of fact, the Council is closer to the current military distribution than this logic suggests. Indeed, under normal historical circumstances, we would now be grappling with a very thorny question, about whether China, which has not been a major international military player in the past five decades, should now be given a permanent seat and veto in the Council—and that might prove to be a very hard and divisive challenge, especially in US congressional terms. But we are not grappling with that challenge: the actions of the framers of the UN Charter mean that this most important rising power already has a permanent seat with a veto attached. In this important sense the current Council is more aligned with contemporary power realities than the need-for-reform narrative suggests.

Moreover, none of the main aspirants for permanent seats—Japan, Germany, Brazil, and India—are currently major global military players. Brazil's global military role is negligible, and even its regional role is modest. India has a sizable army, but wields it primarily for national self-defense—yes, Indian troops make an outsized contribution to UN peacekeeping operations, but that is not the metric of global military power. Japan has a larger and more effective army—and navy—than is commonly assumed, but continues to interpret its constitution as forcing it to avoid even the most modest contributions to international security.[35] Germany actually has the most military power of the four, measured in terms of spending and modern military equipment, but its claim to a permanent seat is the most complicated of the four because it is situated within the EU, which notionally aspires to a common foreign policy and is already over-represented on the Council anyway. A related point: in real military terms, France and Britain are in fact substantial players. Thus, again, the need for adapting the Council's permanent membership to current power realities may be less pressing than often suggested.

And yet, much of what the Council does falls into the domain of diplomacy, not military might; and ultimately I am sympathetic to former US secretary of state Hillary Clinton's claim that we are in the first moment in history when countries can become major global players without being major global military powers.[36] Seen through that lens, and taking into consideration where likely growth will take us, it does seem that there is a case for new actors to come into the Council. This is especially true for Asia, where many of the contemporary security tensions will play out, and where some of the key players are not permanent members of the Council.

The most obvious case is for India, with its 1.2 billion population, its rapidly growing navy, and its strategic role in Asia. India utterly lacks the diplomatic and intelligence infrastructure to handle a permanent seat on the

Council,[37] but that could be an issue where the cart would simply have to lead the horse. Then there is a compelling, though less automatic, case for a series of countries that either are rising economically, or have major diplomatic roles, or both, and can make targeted military contributions; among this list are Brazil, Turkey, Germany, Japan, Korea, and Australia. None of the African claimants to an enhanced role have anything like comparable influence, but political realities suggest that if a reform is to happen, Africa will gain more than global power realities would suggest; and of course, on the African continent, where the Council's role has been prominent, both South Africa and Nigeria are important players. (It is worth pointing out that the total deadlock around African representation has proved the hardest nut to crack in reform pre-negotiations.)

There are important cross-alliance dynamics here. Let me put this more bluntly: successive summits of the BRIC countries make a point of stressing in their joint summit communiqués that they share a fundamental interest in reform of the global governance architecture, including on Council reform. But in reality they don't. As pre-negotiations at the UN and bilateral talks have continued over time, it has become more and more apparent to Brazil and India that the biggest obstacles to change lies not in Washington but in Beijing and Moscow—and this has started to become a serious irritant in the relationships among the BRIC countries (there are far more important divisions among the BRICs, of course).[38]

This is not to say that Washington is in any great rush to see reform to the membership of the Council; it is not. Washington's view on Council reform has been through an evolution.[39] The Bush administration started with a negative view on the issue, but substantial collaboration with China, Russia, and India on counterterrorism and Islamic extremism issues resulted in a softening of its position by the time the administration was winding down. The Obama administration entered office with mixed views: some officials were positively inclined; others recalled the traumas of an earlier reform initiative during the Clinton administration and wanted nothing to do with the file.[40] And then the Brazil/Turkey gambit on Iran, clashes with Brazil and India over Libya, and tensions between the United States and Brazil/India in the first phase of the Syria debates reinforced two views: that the United States stood to lose, in tactical terms, if there was an expansion; and that neither Brasilia nor Delhi were ready for prime time. As the Libya episode recedes, there is something of a reconsideration: Washington has noticed, for example, that the Indian government was lambasted by its domestic press and opposition for its "against it, for it, can't decide" stance on Syria, and its lack of intelligence and information during Libya.[41] That is salutary, because it reinforces the argument that seats at the top table drive more disciplined policymaking, because this exposes the government in question to a series of domestic and international pressures.

Still, I do not anticipate that the United States will decide, anytime soon, to lead the charge on reform.

So does this matter? I think it does, though perhaps less than proponents for reform tend to suggest. It matters in terms of the ability to marshal military power to tackle problems, for two reasons. The emerging powers, if and when they are willing at all to contribute to multinational efforts, are likely to be more willing to do so when actions are taken within a UN framework than outside. That is important, because while coalitions of the willing will remain a tool at the disposal of the West, we will be in bad shape in the evolving international order if we see too frequent use of them—it will deepen concerns on the part of countries like India and Brazil that there is no place for them in the international security order, and this will erode relations with the West and solidify relations within the BRIC countries, and that is not an outcome conducive to stable international relations. Second, Council reform will often matter to US allies too: one of the little-understood legacies of the 2003 Iraq War was to reinforce the political consensus in several European capitals that their armed services should only fight, including in NATO out-of-area operations, with Council authorization. That is an important shift in international politics, although one that may reverse itself. Then, the question of reform becomes relevant in terms of where some of the countries with diplomatic capacity—Turkey, Brazil, Indonesia, Australia—choose to wield it. The ability to forge multinational diplomatic coalitions will increase if there is a successful Council reform.

But I stress: a *successful* reform. The more I watch Council interactions on top-tier issues, the more I am sympathetic to those who want to see reform happen, but at a cautious rate. A reform movement that ends up producing more deadlock or more division in the Council will help neither on the substance of the UN's agenda, nor on broader international politics.

There are interim steps that can be taken. There are two that are worth briefly touching on. One is that the Council's role on Iran, which already brings in Germany, through the P5+1 framework, could be further broadened to bring in two critically important players, Turkey and India. Turkey would like this role; India will resist this—it has influence in Iran, but wants to avoid paying the price for using it to shape the nuclear file. But it could be made clear to India that it cannot seriously sustain a campaign for a permanent Council seat while refusing to join multilateral diplomacy on this critical case. An initiative of this type would begin to forge the kinds of sustained diplomatic coordination between capitals that are the necessary condition for successful reform.

The second would be for the United States to create a side-forum, for consultation with non-NATO allies and partners. This would include India, Japan, Brazil, Turkey, Korea, Australia, and some of the Middle East and Gulf allies. Such a setup would provide all of those activist middle powers with a desire for a greater role in a forum in which to share intelligence and ideas prior to Council action. This will not satisfy the reform aspirations of the rising powers. But given that reform is likely to be blocked for some time, though not primarily by the United States, there might be an interest in seeing informal mechanisms fill part of the space for coordination and relationship building among the wider set of actors that could contribute diplomatically and otherwise to the Council's agenda.

Indeed, the aspirant powers may come to regret their decision not to pursue more aggressively the option that was dangled in front of them in 2005, of long-term interim seats on the Council (see Chapters 9 and 10). That option, presented by Kofi Annan in his *In Larger Freedom* report, had the support of China, and could have passed muster in Washington.[42] There was opposition, to be sure, but it was not nearly as fulsome as the opposition to new permanent seats. Had India, Brazil, Japan, and Germany organized a successful effort to rally for that option, there's a good chance that it would have succeeded—and all of those actors would now be looking back on a nearly decade-long tenure on the Council, with the serious prospect of having their long-term seats rolled into a permanent or semipermanent arrangement.

And the issue matters, to conclude, with reference to the rising tensions in Asia. But here it is a double-edged sword. On the one hand, membership reform that brought India and Japan into the Council might increase the odds that the Council could serve as an instrument for crisis management and the de-escalation of tensions between the powers in Asia, at a time when such mechanisms are sorely lacking. On the other hand, it would also carry a much higher risk that tensions between the powers would infect the broader workings of the Council, and lead to a curtailment of its continuing role on crisis management and the protection of civilians.

Conclusion

It may well prove to be that we already have seen the high-water mark of Council action in the late 2000s—with about twenty peacekeeping operations under way, several of them in strategically significant cases; with an important role on proliferation crises in Iran and North Korea; with political missions and political roles in crises high on the US agenda, like Afghanistan and Iraq; and with a direct role in shaping the contours of international criminal courts and other tools of postconflict justice. It is possible that great power tensions in Asia and the rapid erosion of relations between Russia and the West will thoroughly poison Council dynamics, though the evidence still suggests that the impact of these will be limited unless there is a genuine and sustained deterioration in United States–China relations that take us toward a new Cold War—a scenario I believe unlikely but cannot discount altogether.

In short: I see few issues in the dynamics of the current redistribution of power at the international level that look set to dramatically alter the current course of Council actions. There is a strong case for all the major powers to continue to use the UN to mitigate and contain many forms of crisis. There is no particular evidence to suggest, in the other direction, that the changing distribution of power will lead to stronger roles for the Council, either in managing great power tensions or in other areas of international security like terrorism or proliferation, let alone newer challenges like cybersecurity. The realm of maritime security and energy security may offer spaces for Council innovation, but innovations are just as likely outside the UN.

The UN has often proved useful even when most analysts have written it off—witness Syria, where the UN was thrust onto center stage after the August 2013 chemical weapons attack, when most had dismissed any prospect for United States–Russia cooperation on any aspect of crisis management in that desperate war. And adherents of "global governance" schools of thought routinely overstate the UN's centrality to great power decisionmaking. If we look hard at the evolving dynamics of great power relations, and how they might impact the Council, the most likely scenario ahead has the following components. We will thus likely see: first, serious tensions between the great powers, with the Council largely sidelined in direct contests and possibly in proxy wars between them; second, restrained competition and continuing cooperation on crisis management, increasingly through the Security Council; third, continued evolution of the international security architecture outside the Council—with some informal linkages between the UN and non-UN architecture; and finally, despite the important change in the distribution of power, limited if any change to the formal composition of the Council, unless there is a major change in US and Chinese thinking. That said, there is the possibility, and certainly the desirability, of some evolution of patterns of genuine consultation and engagement through semiformal structures, perhaps even some modest innovations that could allow the UN to contribute to lowering the risk of great power tensions spilling into conflict or erosion of the broader international order.

Notes

1. Bruce Jones, "The Security Council in Arab-Israeli Wars," in *The United Nations Security Council and War: The Evolution of Thought and Practice Since 1945,* edited by Vaughan Lowe, Adam Roberts, Jennifer Welsh, and Dominik Zaum (Oxford: Oxford University Press, 2008).

2. The National Intelligence Council estimates that China's economy will surpass that of the United States a few years before 2030; National Intelligence Council, *Global Trends 2030: Alternative Worlds* (Washington, DC, 2012), www.dni.gov /files/documents/GlobalTrends_2030.pdf. For examples of predictions that delay

that shift until after 2030, see Karen Ward, *The World in 2050: From the Top 30 to the Top 100* (London: HSBC Global Research, 2012), www.us.hsbc.com/1/PA_1 _083Q9FJ08A002FBP5S00000000/content/usshared/Premier/Promotions/2012/Jan /pdf/The_World_in_2050.pdf; Uri Dadush and Bennett Stancil, *The World Order in 2050* (Washington, DC: Carnegie Endowment for International Peace, 2010).

3. Ruchir Sharma, *Breakout Nations: In Pursuit of the Next Economic Miracles* (New York: Norton, 2012); Ruchir Sharma, "The New Breakout Nations," *Foreign Policy,* November 26, 2012.

4. James Steinberg and Michael E. O'Hanlon, *Strategic Reassurance and Resolve: U.S.-China Relations in the Twenty-First Century* (Princeton: Princeton University Press, 2014).

5. For more on the Sino-Indian naval rivalry, see C. Raja Mohan, *Samudra Manthan: Sino-Indian Rivalry in the Indo-Pacific* (Washington, DC: Carnegie Endowment for International Peace, 2012).

6. Bruce Einhorn, "Japan's Abe Looks for Asian Allies to Say No to China," *Bloomberg Businessweek,* November 18, 2013, www.businessweek.com/articles /2013-11-18/japans-abe-looks-for-asian-allies-to-say-no-to-china.

7. An argument I make at greater length, and with more evidence arrayed, in *Still Ours to Lead: The United States, Rising Powers, and the Tensions Between Rivalry and Restraint* (Washington, DC: Brookings Institution, 2014).

8. Suyash Paliwal, "The Primacy of Regional Organizations in International Peacekeeping: The African Example," *Virginia Journal of International Law* 51, no. 1 (2010): 185–230; Peter Arthur, "ECOWAS and Regional Peacekeeping Integration in West Africa: Lessons for the Future," *Africa Today* 57, no. 2 (2010): 2–24.

9. Center on International Cooperation and Alischa Kugel, Richard Gowan, Bruce Jones, and Megan Gleason-Roberts, eds., *Annual Review of Global Peace Operations 2012* (Boulder, CO: Lynne Rienner, 2012).

10. For a review of conflict locations, see Lotta Themnér and Peter Wallensteen, "Armed Conflict, 1946–2013," *Journal of Peace Research* 51, no. 4 (2014): 541–554.

11. For a discussion of organized crime in Central America and the involvement of the international community, see Michael Shifter, *Countering Criminal Violence in Central America,* Special Report no. 64 (New York: Council on Foreign Relations, 2012).

12. Michael Gilligan and Stephen J. Stedman, "Where Do the Peacekeepers Go?" *International Studies Review* 5, no. 4 (2003): 37–54. See also Center on International Cooperation and Alischa Kugel, Richard Gowan, Bruce Jones, and Megan Gleason-Roberts, eds., *Annual Review of Global Peace Operations 2013* (Boulder CO: Lynne Rienner, 2013).

13. Human Security Report Project, *Human Security Report 2009/2010: The Causes of Peace and the Shrinking Costs of War* (New York: Oxford University Press, 2011).

14. Virginia Page Fortna, *Does Peacekeeping Work? Shaping Belligerents' Choices After Civil War* (Princeton: Princeton University Press, 2008).

15. Peter Wonacott, "A New Class of Consumers Grows in Africa: Market on Par with China's and India's," *Wall Street Journal,* May 2, 2011.

16. Barnett R. Rubin, *Afghanistan in the Post–Cold War Era* (Oxford: Oxford University Press, 2013).

17. Richard Gowan, "Floating Down the River of History: Ban Ki-moon and Peacekeeping, 2007–2011," *Global Governance* 17, no. 4 (2011): 399–416.

18. Christoph Mikulaschek, *From Paper to Peace? Compliance with UN Secu-*

rity Council Resolutions in Civil War (Princeton: Princeton University, Department of Politics, March 2013).

19. United Nations Security Council, "Statement by the President of the Security Council," UN Doc. S/PRST/2012/9, April 4, 2012.

20. John Ikenberry, *After Victory: Institutions, Strategic Restraint, and the Rebuilding of Order After Major Wars* (Princeton: Princeton University Press, 2001).

21. Alex J. Bellamy, *Responsibility to Protect* (Malden, MA: Polity, 2009).

22. For example, see Mohammed Nuruzzaman, "The 'Responsibility to Protect' Doctrine: Revived in Libya, Buried in Syria," *Insight Turkey* 15, no. 2 (Spring 2013): 57–66; David Bosco, "Did Libya Kill R2P? Not Likely," *Foreign Policy,* July 15, 2011; "Responsibility to Protect: The Lessons of Libya," *The Economist,* May 19, 2011; David Rieff, "R2P, R.I.P.," *New York Times,* November 7, 2011.

23. United Nations Security Council Resolution 1975, S/RES/1975 (March 30, 2011). See also International Crisis Group, *Côte d'Ivoire: Defusing Tensions,* Africa Report no. 193 (Brussels, 2012).

24. See Fiona Hill, "The Real Reason Putin Supports Assad: Mistaking Syria for Chechnya," *Foreign Affairs,* March 25, 2013.

25. The content of US policy in Syria is of course hotly debated. See Max Fisher interview with Michael Doran, "Syria's Plan to Give Up Its Chemical Weapons Could Make Things Worse, Not Better," *Washington Post,* September 10, 2013; Daniel L. Byman, Michael Doran, Salman Shaikh, and Jeremy Shapiro, "Syria Crisis and Military Action: What Should Be Done, Why, and How," *UpFront,* August 27, 2013, www.brookings.edu/blogs/up-front/posts/2013/08/27-syria-crisis-military -action; Suzanne Maloney, "The Iran Fallacy," *Foreign Affairs,* September 11, 2013.

26. In Korea, Iraq, Somalia, Haiti, Bosnia, Eastern Slavonia, Libya, and Côte d'Ivoire.

27. For example, see Mark Valencia, "Policy Forum 08-043: Put the Proliferation Security Initiative Under the UN," May 29, 2008, http://nautilus.org/napsnet /napsnet-policy-forum/put-the-proliferation-security-initiative-under-the-un.

28. United Nations Department of Peacekeeping Operations, "Peacekeeping Fact Sheet," www.un.org/en/peacekeeping/resources/statistics/factsheet.shtml.

29. Suzanne Maloney, "Six Myths About Iran Sanctions," *Markaz,* January 13, 2014, www.brookings.edu/blogs/iran-at-saban/posts/2014/01/7-iran-sanctions-nuclear -deal-myths.

30. Australian Strategic Policy Institute, *Calming Troubled Waters: Global and Regional Strategies for Countering Piracy,* Special Report no. 47 (Barton: Australian Strategic Policy Institute, 2012), www.aspi.org.au/publications/special -report-issue-47-calming-troubled-waters-global-and-regional-strategies-for -countering-piracy/SR47_Piracy.pdf.

31. The pinnacle of this argument can be seen in Paul Kennedy's *The Rise and Fall of the Great Powers* (New York: Random, 1987).

32. Richard Lebow and Benjamin Valentino, "Lost in Transition: A Critical Analysis of Power Transition Theory," *International Relations* 23, no. 9 (2009): 389–410.

33. For more on the investigation, see United Nations Security Council, "Letter Dated 4 June 2010 from the Permanent Representative of the Republic of Korea to the United Nations Addressed to the President of the Security Council," UN Doc. S/2010/281, June 4, 2010.

34. For example, see Yoichi Shimatsu, "Did an American Mine Sink South Korean Ship?" *New America Media,* May 27, 2010, http://newamericamedia.org /2010/05/did-an-american-mine-sink-the-south-korean-ship.php.

35. For example, during the South Sudan crisis in early 2014, Japan decided that its planes could not be used to move UN peacekeepers that were in harm's way.

36. Hillary R. Clinton, "Economic Statecraft," remarks at the Economic Club of New York, October 14, 2011.

37. On India's weak foreign policy infrastructure, see Tanvi Madan, "What in the World Is India Able to Do? India's State Capacity for Multilateralism," in Waheguru Pal Singh Sidhu, Pratap Bhanu Mehta, and Bruce Jones, *Shaping the Emerging World: India and the Multilateral Order* (Washington, DC: Brookings Institution, 2013), www.brookings.edu/~/media/research/files/papers/2014/07/indias%20state%20capacity%20for%20multilateralism/indias%20state%20capacity%20for%20multilateralism%20madan.pdf.

38. Author interviews, Brasilia, July 2012, and Delhi, November 2013.

39. Kara C. McDonald and Stewart M. Patrick, *UN Security Council Enlargement and U.S. Interests,* Special Report no. 59 (New York: Council on Foreign Relations, 2010).

40. Author interviews, Washington, DC, 2009.

41. For examples of domestic criticism of Indian policy on Syria, see P. R. Kumaraswamy, *Silence on Syria Is No Option* (New Delhi: Institute for Defense Studies and Analysis, 2012), www.idsa.in/idsacomments/SilenceonSyriaisnooption_PRKumaraswamy_210212; and Seema Mustafa, "India's Silence on Syria Will Antagonise Its Friends," *Rediff News,* September 5, 2013, www.rediff.com/news/column/indias-silence-on-syria-will-antagonise-its-friends/20130905.htm.

42. United Nations Secretary-General, *In Larger Freedom: Towards Development, Security, and Human Rights for All,* UN Doc. A/59/2005, March 21, 2005. When the idea of long-term interim seats was proposed in the precursor document, *A More Secure World,* China was enthusiastic about the proposal, to the point of briefing it actively in capitals and New York. Negotiations with Washington at the time suggested that the United States could support the proposal, under conditions spelled out by the United States, as Undersecretary for State Nicolas Burns stated in a summer 2005 speech. United Nations High-Level Panel on Threats, Challenges, and Change, *A More Secure World: Our Shared Responsibility* (New York, December 2004); R. Nicholas Burns, "On United Nations Reform," testimony as prepared before the Senate Foreign Relations Committee, Washington, DC, July 21, 2005.

39

The Security Council in a Fragmenting World

Jeremy Greenstock

IN THIS CHAPTER I LOOK AT THE CONSEQUENCES FOR THE UNITED Nations, and particularly for the Security Council, of geopolitical change since 1990. I trace the origins of the current state of global politics and then analyze the factors underpinning and complicating the work of the present-day Security Council. As the UK's permanent representative on the Council between 1998 and 2003, and as a close observer of the international scene since then, I aim to describe the strengths and weaknesses of today's instruments for maintaining international peace and security and to warn of possible trouble if we do not capitalize on the former and remedy the latter.

A more open and equal world, whose political structures are tending to fragment under the pressure of subjective national and local preferences, is an increasingly hard one for the Security Council to manage in the field of international peace and security if it sticks with its traditional methods. Why is this happening and what are the implications?

Understanding and anticipating the polarizing trend in geopolitics could be the key to containing its damaging potential for global stability. If greater freedom among both nations and individuals is not accompanied by greater responsibility for ensuring order, in particular from those who derive benefit from an open global environment, we must expect increasingly severe difficulties in solving problems at the global or regional level. In other words, freedom does not come free.

The Origins of Trouble

The opening years of the twenty-first century have not gone well for global governance. The momentum toward international cooperation and the containment of conflict generated by the peaceful resolution of the Cold War and concomitant regeneration of the UN Security Council became, from the mid-1990s onward, dissipated in the reassertion of national priorities and narrow identities. The greater freedom of choice for nations and for individuals that has blossomed since the end of the Cold War, and the equality and sovereign independence that now characterize the relationships between nation states, have distributed global power more widely and made the international stage more complex. Multipolarity marks a welcome trend toward a more open and meritocratic world, but keeping international order becomes a sharper challenge if the principles established under the UN to give an ordered shape to human interactions lose their universal appeal and if the institutions are widely regarded as unrepresentative of the current distribution of power.

The evolution of the modern geopolitical structure started with the end of colonialism. World War II, following so soon after World War I, had illuminated the failure of powerful states, constituting a small minority of the world's population, to keep peace responsibly among them in the interests of all, though World War II's victors sought to redress that by focusing on the need to eradicate interstate conflict and to promote a structure of law, rights, and sovereign equality. From the beginning, the United Nations built its legitimacy and its utility on the need, in certain respects the obligation, for the stronger and richer states to contribute to peace, development, and human rights as the pillars of a better and fairer world. This new set of values spelled the end of any justification for one people to rule another without their agreement, and advanced the moral primacy, as well as the general benefit, of the concept of self-determination.

The United States led this campaign. US distaste for colonialism contributed as much to the advance of freedom as did US hostility to communism. The European colonial powers, weakened both materially and morally by the two world wars, could not defend their subjugation of peoples in other continents. Neither could the Soviet Union in its own imperial territory. The prolongation of the Cold War well beyond the period of rapid decolonization in the 1950s and 1960s may have delayed the full effects of global political liberalization, but the full force of the change was felt from the early 1990s onward. It is surprising to look back and observe how many people missed the real geopolitical implications of that surge of freedom, which lay not so much in the victory of the superpower that championed liberty as in the emergence of a large number of independent and capable states whose potential had been released to follow their own path.

The Postwar Institutions

That rapid conversion of a big power–dominated world into a multiplicity of sovereign states had two notable effects: it concentrated the attention of governments on their own domestic imperatives, including self-preservation; and it widened the gap between different national cultures and experiences. Greater freedom narrows horizons. The inherent rationality of globally shared interests—easily recognized in such fields as conflict prevention, trade liberalization, sustainable development, and disease control—has been offset by a growing polarization in culture, religion, identity, and therefore politics. Human society has the tribal instinct as its default setting. The freer and more secure we feel, the more we can indulge in the comfort of living and sharing with those we see as most closely identified with us. Paradoxically, the converse is also true: communities under pressure of conflict or poverty rely closely on the few people they really trust. This focus on identity can take effect as strongly at the subnational as at the national level, depending on how coherent the national society proves to be. Larger societies of different identities are held together by history, fear, temporary self-interest, or repression. They tend not to last long with the comfortable exercise of free will. No wonder, then, that a burgeoning collection of sovereign and group interests stimulates a growing variety of styles of interaction and behavior.

The international institutions were set up to handle those diversities. But the empirical record shows that the effectiveness of institutions, and especially international institutions, fades with time, because they do not reform themselves as fast as the political environment changes. The longer the institutions survive, even in an extended period of international peace, the more they struggle to maintain impact. This is because the compromises on which they were founded no longer carry the same relevance and weight in evolving political circumstances as they did when they started; and because attempts at partial reform fail too easily when different stakeholders have different subjective priorities for what needs reforming first. The old foundations of consensus get washed away.

This does not mean that the institutions cease to be useful. Certain parts of them continue to serve a purpose while others slide into disuse. The UN Trusteeship Council stopped meeting when the business of decolonization was largely done, while the Security Council and the Economic and Social Council have expanded their agendas. The UN family of organizations, whether they come under the Secretary-General or are run by the UN funds, agencies, or programs, remains for the most part engaged and productive.

At the political level, however, where intergovernmental activities are played out among a constantly increasing and assertive membership, the trend toward a widening spectrum of incompatible national preferences is a marked one.

The UN in Operation

From the start, the United Nations as an instrument of global cooperation had to find compromises to accommodate diverging national priorities. That was the origin both of the Security Council veto for the most powerful states and of Article 2(7) of the Charter, which protects sovereign independence except when international peace and security are threatened. Those compromises could be accepted and sustained when the memory of the scourge of war was fresh, when the number of member states was relatively low, and when the leadership of the richer and more powerful countries was too pronounced to resist. The collective approach gathered momentum and paid dividends. The West, under strong US influence, distinguished itself for turning the tide against dictatorship and imperialism, including—up to a point—its own. But its example was neither compelling nor altruistic enough to steer the choices of other peoples who did not identify with it, once they were free to make those choices. Freedom was seen not so much as a gift as a restored right.

As the membership of the UN now approaches the 200 mark, the capacity of a free and equal system to administrate itself has grown markedly weaker as the spectrum of subjective national preferences widens. The largely dysfunctional workings of the UN's General Assembly reflect this. Nevertheless, international business has to be done. The habit of debate is well ingrained—a vital legacy of the UN experience however long it now lasts. It is increasingly becoming the norm for groups of states to develop informal channels of coordination or negotiation when the institutional ones appear not to serve the purpose. The groups multiply: G2, G3, G5, G7, G8, G-20, G-77 (and several others), and more will follow. The Contact Group is another well-known format. It was regularly used during the Cold War, especially on the Western side, and played a particularly useful part in the establishment of new relationships in Europe after 1990. At the UN, Groups of Friends often form among countries closely concerned with a specific issue. The P5+1 mechanism (composed of the five permanent Council members and Germany) now carries the main burden of negotiations on the Iranian nuclear issue. As the difficulties facing global trade arrangements grow, regional and subregional ones take over. We can expect an increasing role for small-group activity as this century progresses, and as rivalries between collections of like-minded states resist treatment in larger forums.

The changing nature of these formats, alongside the different characteristics of the regional groups, provides flexibility to ride with the times. The Ottawa process on landmines and the Oslo negotiations on the Middle East peace process, for example, have been (largely) positive examples. The problem with such variable geometry is that its pragmatic approach diminishes the transparent impact of the norms and principles established by the institutions. We are watching the major highways of international communication break up into a thousand smaller tracks. Some are beneficial, some less so; but the overall effect is to lower the chances of acceptable global governance.

Other factors have added to the weight of national and subnational groupings. The voice of the people has grown in volume and influence because a better-informed and better-connected world creates stronger resentments and broader possibilities for action when inequalities become obvious or demands for a better life are denied. Governments, not only in democratic but also in authoritarian states, find it more necessary to respond to domestic than to international pressures. A more open and equal world allows cultural differences and memories of past injustices to be played out in politics with a stronger sense of moral rightness. Tribal identities, in a literal or metaphorical form, are reasserting themselves. If one group of states tries to maintain that the global good trumps the national one, its capacity to persuade other groups can be blunted by association with past excesses or mistakes, or by appearing to represent one distinctive regional or ideological culture. There are now too many impulses in international affairs to reject a reasonable intellectual proposition in the global interest on narrow national or emotional grounds.

The Effect on the Security Council

This is the geopolitical context for the operation of the modern Security Council. Some things, of course, have not changed. The intergovernmental activities of the UN are the responsibility of the member states, not of the Secretary-General or the UN as an organization. Solutions to problems of international peace and security depend on understandings between governments, or on a simultaneous realization in relevant capitals that the achievable good of a joint remedy wins over the vulnerable best of a national preference. Where the national interests of the bigger powers are not affected, as for example in many African conflict situations, Security Council business proceeds with reasonable efficiency. Where they are, however, objectivity recedes. It has been a particular problem that more advanced countries have been reluctant to devote human or material resources to remedy conflict in the developing world, as the stories of Rwanda, Somalia, Syria, and Sudan, for instance, indicate. Where deeper political differences persist, as over Palestine, Cyprus, or Kashmir, the collective mechanisms of the UN are left stranded by intergovernmental stalemate.

If a capital takes a decision not to make concessions on its preferred outcome, because important domestic principles or interests are at stake, then it has to be prepared to pay the costs of an unresolved problem. These can come in the form of a wider regional disturbance, or of higher material destruction from a larger conflict; of damaged reputations if injustice is widely perceived, or of lower capacity in the global system to address other issues such as terrorism, climate change, or nuclear proliferation. Miscalculations are frequently made of the relative value and costs of embracing or resisting compromise, with the national and short-term route most commonly preferred to the multilateral one, but often delivering a poorer result over time than was assumed at the moment of decision.

Before illustrating and drawing lessons on these Council dynamics from particular instances such as Kosovo (1999), Afghanistan (2001), Iraq (2003), Libya (2011), and Syria (2012–2013), it might first be helpful to describe briefly the way in which the Security Council works on the inside, because it is often misunderstood or criticized.

The UN in its political clothes is a forum, with each member state wearing its national label in negotiation or debate and each representative acting on instructions from the national capital. At UN headquarters, member states interact in both formal and informal ways, transparently or confidentially. In addition, capitals often communicate away from New York, bilaterally or in self-selected groups, to find ways through the undergrowth. Sometimes permanent representatives in New York act a little beyond their capital's instructions, to explore an alternate route when their preferred national route looks to be leading to a dead end. This combination of informal activities, especially if handled resourcefully by skilled professionals, can open up paths out of trouble that seem inaccessible when incompatible preferred routes are examined in the glare of publicity.

Particular Security Council members may also have regional loyalties or affiliations on certain subjects, necessitating parallel consultations or negotiations in well-honed regional or like-minded groups—the European Union and the Arab League States are good examples—while Security Council business is proceeding. In this way, a good deal of preparation of both substance and attitudes is carried out before the issue even reaches informal discussion in the Security Council's back room. This variable structure of diplomatic activity helps to promote positive approaches to problem solving. The atmosphere in New York is normally—that is, outside periods of high tension such as the lead-up to the Iraq invasion in 2003—more likely to generate constructive compromises than is the atmosphere in capitals, because the global benefits of give-and-take are built into the UN's life. Permanent representatives, especially the more experienced and resourceful ones, are also more inclined in the multilateral context to place a higher value on a collective solution, even if their national instructions imply a lower one, and they use their personal relationships and creativeness to shape one.

One other important factor is worth mentioning: the impact of multilateral responsibility on the foreign minister or head of government in the capital. I noticed on several occasions that my political bosses were ready in the domestic arena to explain a failure to achieve their preferred route by arguing that the solution that had just been reached benefited a wider group of countries, or that it was right for the UN to impose collective obligations from time to time. For the UK, keeping the EU together or the United States on board might be one such "good"; but as often as not, it was the advantages for the developing world and the longer term that gave the explanation value. It is surprising how often such arguments resonate with parliaments and the public, and not just in democratically governed states.

In these ways the UN, just by existing as a forum and a mechanism, and through its record of norm-setting and problem solving, generates a wider momentum for collective approaches than any previous institution has ever managed. Nevertheless, the compelling pressures of the domestic agenda, often fed by historical, cultural, or issue-based subjectivity, can prove too powerful. Governments can as readily appeal to national as to collective sentiment to resist compromise. The current trend in geopolitics suggests things will not grow any easier in the period ahead.

Some Recent History

The standoff in the Council on Kosovo in the first half of 1999 is a good illustration of the UN's continuing centrality as a de facto arbiter of legitimacy. British prime minister Tony Blair had just made his notable speech in Chicago, appealing for humanitarian intervention to be added to the toolbox of collective instruments, when NATO decided, under British and then US pressure on behalf of the ethnic Albanians in Kosovo, to take military action from the air against Serbia without Security Council authorization, because President Slobodan Milosevic was manifestly beyond moral persuasion. The Russians, whose relationship with the Serbs was close and sensitive, were doubly incensed at this "unilateral" decision because it followed so soon after the brief but unauthorized US attack on Iraq in December 1998. After some apparent argument between Moscow and its mission in New York, Permanent Representative Sergey Lavrov proposed a condemnatory resolution in harsh terms in an open session of the Council. It was defeated by twelve votes to three, and served the NATO allies as a kind of retrospective justification of their action, which was never severely criticized at the UN thereafter.

The atmosphere in the Council at that point was explosive. Yet in June 1999, when NATO was struggling to bring Milosevic to order through its bombing campaign, it was a Russian diplomatic intervention, led by former prime minister Viktor Chernomyrdin and supported by the experienced Finnish president Martti Ahtisaari, that finally persuaded the Serbian president to back down. Only a Russian wish to see the international structure preserved from ad hoc decisionmaking by powers outside the Council could have convinced Milosevic that this was his better choice. The episode, which the Russians saw as unrequited by the West, increased the subsequent bitterness over the Iraq invasion in 2003.

For it was Iraq above all that tested multilateral cohesion, in the new context of 9/11. The response at the UN to al-Qaeda's attack on the United States in September 2001 went through a remarkable sequence of stages. The horror at wanton destruction from a clear blue sky, starting in the UN's own city and encompassing the possibility that the UN building was itself a target, was widespread and genuine. Resolutions sympathetic to the United States were adopted in the Security Council and General Assembly with a minimum of preparation or consultation, one of which, drafted by the quick-footed French, helped to legitimize the subsequent attack by the United States on the Taliban government of Afghanistan. Within three weeks of 9/11, an extraordinary draft resolution was presented by the United States and adopted with barely a murmur of dissent by a unanimous Council, even though it broke precedent by setting mandatory tasks for all member states to legislate on combating terrorist activity (undefined) and any kind of support for it (Security Council Resolution 1373). The consensus that al-Qaeda had crossed an unforgivable line was so strong that minds started wondering whether the UN was entering a new era of international cooperation on security issues.

UN member states waited for the United States to capitalize on this unexpected rebirth of multilateralism and apply it to other global problems. Six months later, the cooperative mood had dissipated. The impression grew among member states that the United States saw support for its stance as based on right rather than on the attractions of collective action, as justification for the unilateral use of force rather than as evidence of the effectiveness of consensus. There was no particular moment when the penny of realism dropped with the majority of UN members. It was just that US rhetoric, diplomatic body language, and decisionmaking fell back into uncompromising channels that seemed to most observers to place the national projection of force too high up the priority list.

The invasion of Iraq then sealed the regressive trend. The United States lost its audience on two counts: first, in relating its policy choices on Iraq, which included regime change, and an exaggerated claim that Saddam Hussein had a hand in 9/11, as though it could count on greater domestic and international support for that line of argument; and second, in rejecting—beyond a few moments of lip service—the need for a clear UN basis for the legitimacy of its military action. Many UN representatives cast their minds back to the assertion of Senator Jesse Helms, when invited to address the Security Council by Ambassador Richard Holbrooke in January 2000, that the ultimate arbiter of the legitimacy of international action by the United

States was the voice of the American people. The subsequent arrival of the neoconservatives under George W. Bush took that argument to a new level of aggressiveness.

As a result, the main opponents of the use of force in the Security Council, Russia and France, decided to place their antagonism to unilateral action by the United States (which France had promoted and the Security Council had endorsed in respect of Afghanistan in 2001) above their wish to see Saddam Hussein compelled to respect UN resolutions. Yet when the efforts of collective diplomacy lay in shards on the floor, even while the US-led coalition was approaching the outskirts of Baghdad in late March 2003, the instinct to pick up the pieces brought the five permanent members together at Secretary-General Kofi Annan's instigation to restart a conversation about the role of the UN in Iraq. That scratchy beginning eventually led to Resolution 1483 in late May 2003, which provided not a post facto justification of the invasion—certainly not, with the Russians on full watch—but at least a legal basis for the UN to play a part on the ground thereafter (a "vital role" was the phrase that President Bush was persuaded by the British to mouth) in the construction of a new Iraq. The UN's involvement was to prove limited and tragic (twenty-two staff members including the Baghdad head of mission, Sergio Vieira de Mello, lost their lives in a terrorist attack in August 2003), but the importance of preserving the usefulness of the world's only global institution inspired this immediate if partial effort.

I shall not go into detail on the more recent sagas of Libya and Syria, except to point out why, in my view, Moscow went along with Resolution 1973 on Libya in March 2011 and then resolutely refused to do anything similar on Syria in 2012. Against their natural instincts, the Russians recognized that a destructive civil war was developing in Libya, that the Arab League had declared against the Muammar Qaddafi regime and that Moscow had only a moderate stake in Qaddafi's survival. They could accept UN authorization of an air campaign, though not of a ground intervention. Perhaps there was also a flicker of a thought that the West might get itself stuck in yet another Middle East swamp. Fortunately for NATO, the air campaign achieved its aim without dragging the organization in deeper—though the longer-term consequences for the Libyan people have so far proved very discouraging.

On Syria, by contrast, Russian historical and military involvement had been far deeper and Arab opinion was divided. In addition, Moscow had reached the end of its tether on the authorization of the use of force inside a state's domestic territory, which it (and China) had always wanted to constrain in case precedents accumulated that might bear on interests closer to home. The result was a series of vetoes—cast jointly with China—at some cost to Russia's image in supporting a brutally repressive regime, but with grudging acceptance in the international community that Moscow's under-lining of the downsides of intervention had a point. Throughout these episodes, both the Western powers (for all their growling over "red lines" regarding chemical weapons) and Russia (with China as a passive second) never set aside the importance and the concrete advantage of seeking the UN's legitimization of their action, even though each party diluted its approach with a strong dose of national perception.

The True Quality of the Security Council

It has always been the case that the Security Council falls short on issues that divide member states most sharply. The formation of Israel in 1948 and the Korean War in 1950–1951 were the earliest examples with global impact. In fact, neither issue has yet reached the point of settlement sixty or more years on, because conflicting claims on a single territory provoke the strongest political emotions, and because usually the big powers take sides. As the instances of failure on hard issues (Palestine, Kashmir, Sri Lanka, Cyprus, the former Yugoslavia, Darfur, Iraq, Afghanistan, Libya, Syria) pile up over the decades, criticism of the Council accumulates.

But this does not mean that its usefulness is actually declining. Since the end of the Cold War, the Council has adopted more than 1,500 resolu-tions, over twice as many as before 1990. The P5 have exercised their veto on only 27 substantive occasions, compared to 193 times in the previous four and a half decades. The first instinct among competing powers nowa-days is to debate the problem, publicly or privately. That in itself is an exer-cise in responsibility instilled by the UN. And a greater respect for the choices people make in a free environment has gradually developed, to the point where, more often than not, legitimacy is seen to rest with the local people of a territory rather than with those who can project power onto it. A world in which persuasion has become as potent a force as military capabil-ity must surely be a safer one.

The workings and procedures of the Security Council bear this out. As the fifteen members, with the Secretariat always present, settle down to debate a new issue, the room where informal consultations are conducted is filled with an expectation that international law and the norms of peaceful coexistence will apply. Permanent representatives who argue on a basis of strong national subjectivity can, if they are not too blinkered, sense the shadow of moral disapproval cast by their colleagues. What a pity that the most senior decisionmakers in capitals so seldom undergo that experience. Frequent exposure to the arena of collective judgment based on statutory international obligations changes the nature of political responsibility. The way the world works, alas, is that distant capitals have the final say.

The power of important capitals makes itself felt especially in the case of claims to independence by subject peoples. The concept of self-determination remains a highly subjective one despite the strength of its universal appeal. Much of the developing world benefited from it from the 1950s onward, but people in, for example, Kashmir, Tibet, Chechnya, Palestine, Northern Cyprus, and Kurdistan have been disappointed, as others may be in the coming decades. They will keep hoping for the chance that former parts of the Soviet Union and Yugoslavia, Timor-Leste, and South Sudan were given, and that Scotland, Northern Ireland, Catalonia, and Texas can freely debate in their democratic environments.

Sometimes the Security Council has determined such situations as matters of international peace and security, sometimes not. In respect of the cases mentioned earlier, India, China, Russia, Israel (plus the United States), and Turkey have been influential enough to fend off Council discussion, action, or implementation when they did not see it as appropriate for their sovereign preferences. Serbia, Indonesia, and Sudan have not.

On the other hand, the P5 have on occasion been able to compromise on situations, such as Georgia, North Korea, and Iran, that have great national significance to one or more of them. China did not stop Darfur's referral to the International Criminal Court in 2005, although Sudan was among its top five oil suppliers at the time. Even after the controversy over the way force was used in Libya, the Council was able to adopt unanimously robust resolutions on Mali and the Democratic Republic of the Congo. Both of these texts are indicative of the evolution of Security Council resolutions in assigning a broader role to UN peacekeeping missions, adopting a more proactive approach to civilian protection, and containing references to war crimes, crimes against humanity, and the ICC.

Power and Responsibility

So, hard power has not altogether gone to sleep. Size and strength do matter. The little guy is not yet equal to the big one—by what universally agreed criterion could he be, in the constant pushing and shoving of the human race? Yet below the category of cases that are "too difficult," look at the remarkable achievement of the United Nations over two-thirds of a century, whether through direct action or through the forming of mechanisms and habits, in deterring or shortening interstate war (Israel/Palestine since 1973, the Congo, Cyprus, Yugoslavia, Ethiopia/Eritrea, Georgia) and constraining great power arguments from descending into violence (above all during the Cold War). Count the number of times where the work of the Security Council on Africa, or Central America, or Southeast Asia, or the more troubled parts of Europe, has averted the worst outcomes, introduced peacekeepers, organized postconflict reconstruction, or underwritten settlements. Note in particular, as the history of the new millennium lengthens its stride, how the United Nations, for all the impression it gives of an aging machine, represents the primacy of justice and decent governance at the global level in a way that no ideology, culture, or political system can.

The nation-state will not give up its political appeal within the foreseeable future because that is the power-base of political leaderships. The link between freedom of choice and sense of identity will sustain it for a good while longer, even under the pressure of the need for collective compromises on issues such as climate change, finance for development, peacekeeping resources, and open trading systems. But responsibility has a meaning at both the national and the international level. Within a state, communities of a different ethnic or cultural identity have to be allowed an equal place under the law even if they are a minority. Among nations, similar compromises are essential, not least because they are fast becoming a matter of pragmatic self-interest. When the point comes where catastrophic war must be avoided, or disastrous impoverishment remedied, or lethal natural disasters recovered from, most states understand that they cannot deal with large-scale problems such as these on their own. Yet they seem too easily seem to get caught up with shorter-term challenges that leaderships see as essential to their claim to power; and they either cannot or will not find the resources or the mentality to confront the strategic issues. Climate change is the classic area where arguments over blame, cost, and the next election appear to overwhelm the search for long-term solutions.

The trends in current international relations are so strongly weighted toward the local and the short-term that the costs of the sacrifices required for collective remedies are constantly rising. In previous eras, the result of the failure to compromise was always war. Not only is large-scale war unthinkable now that the power of weapons is so massive, but the habits and methods of avoiding interstate war have been refined, through the existence of the UN, to a point unprecedented in human history. We cannot preserve freedoms at the global level unless we capitalize responsibly on those partial achievements. The UN and its Security Council, founded on the experience of world war in the first half of the twentieth century, are still there to provide the arguments and the mechanisms for peaceful compromise. If national capitals now fail to make maximum use of them, succeeding generations will suffer the consequences, and then have to pick up the pieces all over again.

40

Conclusion:
The Security Council and
a World in Crisis

Sebastian von Einsiedel, David M. Malone,
and Bruno Stagno Ugarte

AS THE UNITED NATIONS REACHES ITS SEVENTIETH ANNIVER-
sary, a severe proliferation of serious international security failures is challenging the UN Security Council's ability to address them effectively.
Crises in Libya, Syria, and Ukraine have precipitated a worrisome erosion
of great power relations that has complicated the Security Council's decisionmaking across a number of trouble spots and issue areas. Its inability to
devise consensus responses to the escalating civil war in Syria has been
particularly troubling, resulting in the regional spillover into Iraq and the
emergence of the Islamic State as a new threat to peace in the region and
beyond. Meanwhile, the UN's often underequipped blue helmets have
struggled to carry out ambitious mandates while facing severe challenges in
the Central African Republic, Mali, South Sudan, and elsewhere. In a number of regions, the growth in international drug trafficking and related violence undermines democratic governance and the rule of law. The spread of
violent Islamist extremism is a growing concern around the world. The
mass outbreak of Ebola in 2014 has threatened to stall and even reverse
over a decade of UN peacebuilding progress in West Africa. And around the
world, the numbers of civil wars and battle deaths are again on the
upswing, after over a decade of decline.[1] Some observers go as far as to
conclude that "a breakdown in world order is occurring."[2]

While this seems to us a premature assessment, it is undeniable that the
Security Council finds itself in real difficulty, not unlike in 2004, when this
volume's forerunner, *The UN Security Council: From the Cold War to the
21st Century*, was published. Back then, the 2003 US-led invasion of Iraq
absent Security Council authorization had triggered widespread concerns

that the drive of the United States toward unilateralism would lead it to turn its back on the United Nations.[3] The volume concluded that "in the post–Cold War world the key issue for the Council is whether it can engage the United States, modulate its exercise of power, and restrain its impulses. . . . For the United States, the key issue on the Council is the extent to which it can serve as an instrument for the promotion of U.S. interests."[4]

Since then, the shift in power and policies of the five permanent members, as well as the complex relations among them, have significantly altered the dynamics of the body, giving rise to a new set of concerns. Today, the greatest threat to the relevance of the Security Council is the possibility of a standoff between the newly assertive Russia and China and a United States that, after its spectacular misadventures in Iraq and its discomfiting experiences in Afghanistan, is seen as increasingly unwilling to shoulder more international burdens than absolutely necessary. Compounding the sense of growing irrelevance is the fact that the UN's operational activities in peacemaking and peacekeeping are nowadays largely confined to Africa and the Middle East. This feeds the perception that the UN has become a niche actor specializing in countries gasping for life support. Finally, the UN faces growing skepticism regarding its ability to develop operational responses to new security challenges that arise out of the empowerment of nefarious nonstate actors, whether in the form of organized crime, terrorist groups, or nuclear proliferation networks.

And yet the overall picture may not be as bleak as some pessimists suggest. Bad news always crowds out the good, overshadowing the UN's several meaningful successes in stopping war, building peace, and developing global norms. Indeed, this book provides a nuanced assessment of the Council's record over the past decade or two. It attests to the Council's ability to adapt and innovate in the face of new challenges, explains why even the most powerful countries continue to find it useful to work through the Council, and suggests that the Council will likely remain relevant beyond the current tension in great power relations.

Interests and Powers

Changing Power, Policies, and Perceptions of the P5

With the P5 deadlocked over Syria and Ukraine, there was a growing fear in 2014 that the Security Council might soon find itself sidelined by a newly emerging cold war. This is somewhat ironic given that the election of President Barack Obama in the United States in 2008 had promised to restore a central place for the Security Council in world diplomacy. Obama was ideologically inclined toward multilateralism and determined to improve the standing of the United States in the world. He also pursued a "reset" of fraught relations with Russia and courted China, not least to enlist the support of both countries in strengthening Council-based coercive diplomacy vis-à-vis Iran. Along the way, he made important concessions to Moscow on missile defense in Europe and de-emphasized democracy and human rights in the relationship with Beijing. Leading a nation that was exhausted after two costly wars in Afghanistan and Iraq, he was more preoccupied with extracting the United States from military commitments than starting new ones. Initially, the Obama administration's approach paved the way for remarkable Council action, strengthening sanctions on Iran and North Korea over their nuclear programs and authorizing the use of force for civilian protection in Côte d'Ivoire and Libya.

However, the honeymoon was not meant to last. The upheavals of the Arab Spring ultimately proved divisive for the P5, who started to fall out over NATO's alleged overreach in implementing the 2011 Council mandate for intervention in Libya (Resolution 1973). The dividing line was between the P3—the United States, France, and the United Kingdom—on the one hand, and Russia and China on the other. The relations between the two camps deteriorated further over the question of how to respond to the escalating civil war in Syria, which was seen by both Moscow and the P3 through the lens of their competing interests in the wider region. China, meanwhile, seems to have stuck with Russia more out of tactical considerations, rather than due to Syria-specific interests. Subsequently, Russia's stealth invasion and subsequent annexation of the Crimea Peninsula in the spring of 2014 led to a serious breakdown of East-West relations inside and outside the Council, exemplified by Moscow's expulsion from the circles of G8 summitry.

However, Libya, Syria, and Ukraine are more the symptoms than the causes of a divide that was some time in the making. Rising tensions in the Security Council have been a reflection of the growing power and assertiveness of Beijing and a newly muscular Moscow. China's dramatic economic rise—having become by 2010 the world's second largest economy and by 2013 the largest importer of oil—has affected its approach to a number of situations on the Council's agenda. This is a significant change from the 1990s, when China was mainly preoccupied with using the Council to enforce its policy of nonrecognition of Taiwan. Meanwhile, as detailed by Dmitri Trenin in Chapter 5, Vladimir Putin, since his return to the presidency in 2012, has increasingly perceived Moscow's interests as diverging from those of the West, which he casts as deliberately seeking to obstruct Russia's reemergence as a great power. Beyond the UN, however, Russia's relative economic decline and its antagonistic relations with the West since 2014 make it increasingly reliant on China for sale of its natural resources, at a time when China's economic potential and ability to invest in the former Soviet republics of Central Asia far outstrips that of Russia.

Thus, for all the noise made by Russia compared to China's preference for a relatively low profile within the Council, the relationship is an increasingly uneven one, favoring China.

Reinforcing the P5 divide in the Council is the fact that China and Russia have been increasingly working in tandem in the body. Having improved their relations since solving their remaining territorial disputes in the early 2000s, they share a common approach to the Council, one that is guided by the strong attachment of both countries to the principles of state sovereignty and nonintervention—notions that seem to apply considerably less when it comes to Moscow's relations with the former republics of the Soviet Union, such as Georgia and Ukraine. Their shared and much-invoked goal of "multipolarity" suggests that they see the Council in part as a convenient forum to constrain and "soft-balance" US power, as well as to underpin their own claims to great power status.

Deepening Russian-Chinese cooperation in the Security Council is most starkly illustrated by the fact that they cast six joint vetoes between 2007 and 2014: one on Myanmar (2007), one on Zimbabwe (2008), and four on Syria (2011–2014) (see Figure 40.1). This compares to just one joint veto in the preceding thirty-six years since the People's Republic of China replaced the Republic of China at the United Nations in 1971. Whether the relationship between Moscow and Beijing represents a significant new alliance beyond the UN—complemented also in the heterogeneous BRICS partnership with Brazil, India, and South Africa—or simply a relationship of convenience for Security Council purposes, is, as of now, hard to assess. Unlike the United States, whose sixteen vetoes in the Council from 1990 to 2014 were all cast alone, with fourteen of them pertaining to the Israeli-Palestinian conflict, China still appears reluctant to use its veto in isolation. Joining forces in the Council with Russia can be convenient for Beijing. Tellingly, however, China did not join Russia's vetoes on draft resolutions addressing the Georgian crisis in 2008 and the Ukraine crisis in 2014, given its own preoccupations with countering separatist tendencies at home.

However, the body is still a long way from descending into Cold War–level paralysis. Despite P5 relations reaching another low point in 2014, the Council has continued to show encouraging signs of vitality. In 2014, notwithstanding the two vetoes cast that year, the Council adopted sixty-three resolutions, sixty of which unanimously, including the thirty-eight resolutions under Chapter VII of the UN Charter.[5] This confirms two remarkable trends of the post–Cold War era: first, a trend toward consensus decisionmaking in the Council, with at least 90 percent of resolutions since 2001 adopted by consensus;[6] and second, a trend toward the ever greater resort to Chapter VII of the UN Charter, with the share of such resolutions rising from 25 percent in 2000 to above 60 percent since 2010 (see Chapter 2).

Figure 40.1 Number of Vetoes in the Security Council, 1987–2014

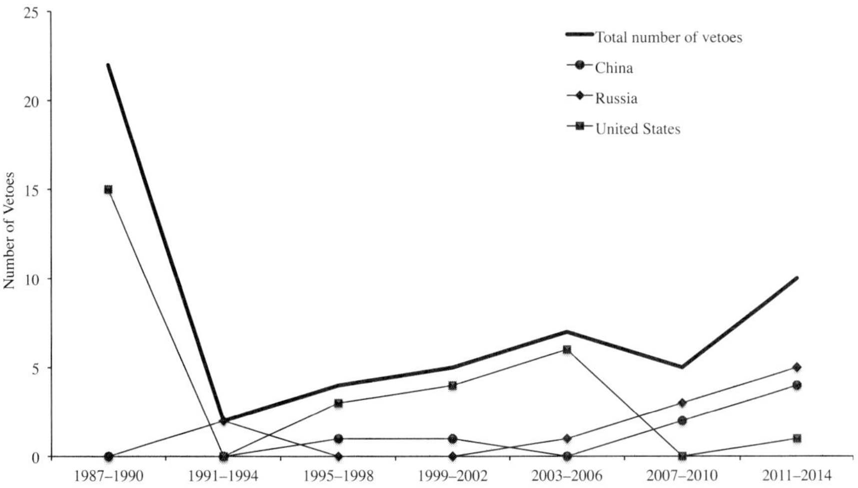

Source: Security Council Veto List, available at http://research.un.org/en/docs/sc/quick.

This reflects the P5's continued recognition that the Council can serve their interests where these converge—and they still do converge on a number of situations and issues. Chief among them is counterterrorism, which, even though mostly driven by the United States, has united the Council behind some highly consequential decisions, most recently in September 2014 when it adopted a far-reaching Chapter VII resolution aimed at preventing the flow of "foreign fighters" to terrorist groups in Syria and elsewhere. Noticeably, only mild protests were proffered by Russia and China when the United States, with neither a request from the Syrian government, a credible self-defense claim, nor an authorizing Council mandate, initiated air strikes against the terrorist group Islamic State in Syria that same month. There is also general convergence among the P5 on peacekeeping, the UN's flagship activity. China, in particular, has significantly increased its contribution to UN peacekeeping since the early 2000s, as part of a broader effort to be recognized as a responsible stakeholder in the multilateral system.

Furthermore, when the United States shows a determination to lead, as it did in spearheading a Chapter VII resolution on Ebola in the fall of 2014, there is still a general willingness in the Council to rally behind the US banner. Indeed, even today, with US initiatives increasingly challenged by others, Washington's instincts and impulses continue to drive the Council more than any other single factor.[7] Yet, as Stephen Stedman noted in Chapter 3, a foreign policy culture prizing freedom of action, domestic policy constraints, and the absence of a memory of multilateral muscle in the foreign policy bureaucracy will often work counter to any US administration's impetus to make the Council more central to US foreign policy. David Bosco, in Chapter 3.1, points out that the power of the veto has, on the one hand, led the United States to safeguard the Council's nominal preeminence in the multilateral system while, on the other, encouraging a highly selective approach in practice in terms of when to engage the Council and when to work around it.

However, as detailed in Chapter 6 by Thierry Tardy and Dominik Zaum, the most significant signs of life in the Council in recent years have come from the two permanent members whose legitimacy in the club of veto holders is most often questioned: France and—to a lesser degree—the UK. Keenly aware of their deteriorating claim to permanency, and often acting in concert, they tend to work hardest to justify their presence in the Council and are widely considered to punch well above their weight—even more so as the United States is seen as being in retreat. The UK, for example, played a key role on the Libya intervention and continues to conduct business in the Council with an air of authority only rarely challenged by others. The profile of France in the Council is particularly striking, especially with respect to Africa. There, Paris has led a number of recent military interventions in trouble spots, paving the way for the subsequent arrival or reinforcement of UN peacekeepers, as in Côte d'Ivoire, the Central African Republic, and Mali. While France's actions, like those of every other country, tend to be largely driven by its own interests (in this case stability in its former colonial dependencies), its recent multilaterally supported interventions differ significantly from the unilateral ones it carried out in the 1990s and before. Meanwhile, none of the other Council members' interests are sufficiently engaged as to trigger opposition to France's initiatives in Africa, which have also mostly met with favor in the African Union. Indeed, French leadership on African security challenges within the Council is widely welcomed.

Overall, as Jeremy Greenstock highlights in Chapter 39, by having provided for decades a framework for continuous consultation, the Council has instilled in the great powers the habit and instinct to debate international problems and seek constructive solutions. Through the Council the three major military powers of our era (the United States, China, and Russia) are in constant contact with each other, exchanging views and messages. Moreover, the Council has in the past repeatedly proven its value by offering a venue in which the great powers can find common ground even after highly divisive episodes like those in Kosovo (1999), Iraq (2003), and Libya (2011). And, conveniently, agreements reached elsewhere can be multilateralized by the Council, as was the case with Resolution 1244 of June 1999 bringing to an end the most active phase of the Kosovo crisis, and with the 2013 US-Russian deal on Syria's chemical weapons.

The P5, E10, and Broader Council Dynamics

Over the years, successive waves of elected Council members (the E10) have attested to their frustration with how little influence they wield in the Council in the face of the overbearing dominance of the P5. Indeed, the P5 benefit not only from the power of the veto (with the mere threat of a veto often enough to suppress any unwelcome initiatives by elected members), but also from the often underestimated advantage of institutional memory and mastery of the Council's procedures. Delegates from powerful elected members, such as Germany or India, are particularly taken aback by P5 collusion and find their resulting second-class status doubly grating. That being said, Germany's close ties with France and, to a lesser degree, the UK during its Council membership in 2011–2012 helped Berlin to be more "in the loop" than other E10 members.

The power differential between the P5 and the E10 determines Council dynamics to a large degree. Because of the need to reach a consensus among the P5 "vetocracy" for any decision to be taken by the Council, the permanent members tend to negotiate draft resolutions first among themselves, before submitting them to the full Council for discussion. And before a draft is negotiated by all of the P5, it has generally been discussed by the P3, from where nearly all Council initiatives originate. Only after the P3 reach at least broad agreement among themselves can they begin the generally more difficult process of enlisting Russian and Chinese support. Indeed, among the more surprising aspects of Council dynamics for outsiders tends to be the near absence of any attempt by Russia or China to proactively shape the Council's agenda. Only rarely are P3 drafts met by a counterdraft of Russian confection, as in the case of Syria, on which Moscow was unusually active in tabling its own texts. Chinese draft resolutions, meanwhile, are virtually unheard of. Fashioning themselves as the guardians of state sovereignty and noninterference, Russia and China instead adopt a wait-and-see approach as the most promising strategy to ensure that Western-driven interventionism does not infringe upon their interests, knowing that, ultimately, they can always block a decision, by a veto or its threat, that they view as inimical to their interests. It is thus only on rare occasions that deals are pre-cooked outside the P3. Notable examples include the 2013 chemical weapons resolution on Syria, which was the result of a bilateral agreement reached between the foreign ministers of Russia and the United States; and resolutions on North Korea, which are usually negotiated directly between the United States and China.

Once the P5 agree to submit a draft resolution for consultation to the wider Council, it tends to represent delicate compromises, with little room for any further changes by any of the E10 when the text is circulated to them. Indeed, it is not unheard of for draft resolutions to be shared with the E10 for the first time just hours before they are put to a vote. With increasing frequency, draft resolutions also seem to be "strategically leaked" beforehand by those in the know, usually to gain the upper hand in the fierce media battles waged around controversial Council files in the age of the Internet, blogs, and Twitter.

A noteworthy trend that has cemented the P3's grip on the Council agenda in recent years is the so-called penholder system, which emerged in the late 2000s. Around that time, the P5 began to claim a monopoly of the pen when drafting Council resolutions detailing peacekeeping mandates, sanctions regimes, or other Council actions, with only rare attempts to wrestle this power away from them. As of March 2015, the P5 served as penholders for thirty out of the thirty-seven country- or region-specific files on the Council's agenda.

Yet the P5 tend to reject the often heard criticism that they prevent and suppress engagement by elected members in the Council and instead criticize elected members for lacking initiative. On occasion, that criticism is warranted, as some nonpermanent members see getting elected to the Council as the centerpiece of their UN diplomacy, only to have little of substance to contribute once they get there, redoubling the condescension that the P5 rain down on their temporary cousins.

So what role, then, does this leave for the E10? While any combination of seven nonpermanent members would constitute a blocking minority in the Council, they have only rarely managed to turn that fact into leverage over the P5. Elected members can also achieve influence by withholding consent in sufficiently large numbers, as they did on December 30, 2014, in abstaining on a resolution that held out the prospect of Palestinian statehood within a set timeframe. Together with the United States and Australia, which voted against the resolution, the abstainers, four of them from the E10, denied the resolution's supporters the nine positive votes they would have needed to give the no vote by the United States the effect of a veto.[8] However, there has not been a single instance in which the E10 made use of their collective "sixth" veto in response to draft resolutions that had the support of all permanent Council members. Potential openings occur for the E10 to take initiatives when the P5 find themselves divided on an issue. However, in those situations the E10 tend to either take sides to shore up the opposing camps of the P5 divide, as was the case with respect to the standoff over Syria from 2011 to 2013, or stay neutral, as was the case in the Iraq debate of 2002 to 2003, when nonpermanent members feared getting chewed up in the quarrel between great powers.

However, over the years, a significant number of elected members have played larger-than-life roles on the Council, leaving lasting imprints on its agenda. Sometimes, they manage to do so on country-specific files, such as Australia, Luxembourg, and Jordan in 2014, when they introduced new momentum into the deadlocked Council discussions on Syria with an initiative—closely coordinated with the P3—on humanitarian access to the conflict zones. The most significant change that active elected members have brought to the Council, however, is their pushing of thematic issues that have come to occupy large parts of its work. It was the Council's nonpermanent members who made issues such as children and armed conflict; women, peace, and security; sexual and gender-based violence; civilian protection; climate change; and the role of regional organizations fixtures on the Council agenda.

Another area in which nonpermanent members can make significant contributions to Council business is in their role as chairs of Council committees overseeing individual sanctions regimes. Indeed, all chairs of these committees are nowadays drawn from the ranks of the E10, although it is largely the P5 who decide which incoming elected member should chair which sanctions committee. There is some grumbling among E10 ambassadors that the tedious burden of running the day-to-day work of these committees draws their attention away from the key crises of the day, further reinforcing P5 domination. However, the quality of a committee's chairmanship can make a huge difference in the vitality and effectiveness of sanctions.

While the member states are those ultimately taking decisions, the Council has an additional de facto permanent member that plays an important role in shaping the body's dynamics: the UN Secretariat. Indeed, all Council meetings are attended and serviced by staff of the Security Council Affairs Division of the Department of Political Affairs. Many Council meetings feature briefings by the Secretary-General or his special representatives, as well as senior Secretariat staff, most often the heads of the Departments of Political Affairs or Peacekeeping, but increasingly, to the chagrin of China and Russia, briefings by the high commissioner for human rights. And often, information or recommendations contained in such briefings, as well as the written reports prepared by the Secretariat in the name of the Secretary-General, play an important role in shaping the Council's decisions. It is partly because of this central role of the Secretariat that the P3 place great pressure on the Secretary-General to ensure that the three main "peace and security departments" are headed by nationals of their respective countries.[9] Nevertheless, the Secretariat has often been reluctant to resist the elaboration of clearly under-resourced mandates it will find impossible to implement fully. This was the case with the excessively optimistic (or arrogantly negligent) ones on safe areas in Bosnia-Herzegovina in 1993–1995 or, with less dramatic consequences, the hopelessly understaffed UN Supervision Mission in Syria (UNSMIS), which was supposed to oversee a ceasefire in Syria that never had much chance of holding. Already the famous 2000 Brahimi Report on the reform of UN peacekeeping demanded clearer articulation of Secretariat resistance, if necessary publicly, to bad ideas being forced on it by Council members. It is easy to see why the Secretariat all too often quails: the Secretary-General's relevance to global diplomacy hinges in large part on his access to P5 members. Successive Secretaries-General have been desperate, sometimes too desperate, to retain good relations with all of the P5 to the extent humanly possible, and sometimes to the exclusion of more admirable objectives.

Working Methods

Despite pressure since the early 1990s from member states not serving on the Council for the body to become more transparent, there are persistent complaints about its autocratic and opaque proceedings. These complaints result not only from collusion among the P5, eager to maintain their privileged position, but also from the fact that much of the Council's business continues to be conducted in informal consultations, or "informals," closed to all non-Council members and most Secretariat staff and leaving no formal record (although some delegations, to the great annoyance of some P5 members, have made it a habit to "live-tweet" impressions from those informals). Nonmembers are thus often in the dark and must continue to scramble for information, feeding off scraps in antechambers, a thoroughly humiliating experience. Many regional groups as well as the European Union have thus established the practice—frowned upon by the non-European states among the P5—of their respective representatives in the Council debriefing the eager crowd of delegation experts and interns waiting patiently in front of the Council chamber. In particular, countries contributing troops to UN peacekeeping operations have long argued that if the Council expects them to provide national assets in support of Council decisions, greater consultation is required.

A number of innovations have been introduced over the years aimed at allowing participation of non-Council members in Council matters. These include Arria-formula briefings (under which individuals with relevant information, such as NGO representatives, share with Council members real-time information from the field); putting Security Council missions to conflict countries on the agenda, which allows Council members to engage in discussions with stakeholders on the ground; open thematic debates, which allow non-Council members to deliver statements on crosscutting issues; wrap-up sessions, which provides an opportunity for Council members—under the watchful eye of non-Council members—to reflect on the body's performance during the past month, with the rest of the membership allowed to follow the debate; and informal interactive dialogues, which allow for situations of concern that are too politically sensitive for formal meetings.

While these innovations attest to a certain creativity, Christian Wenaweser notes in Chapter 9 that "these tools have remained underutilized and applied inconsistently." Often, it depends on the readiness of the monthly Council presidency whether these formats feature on the Council's monthly program of work, and, specifically in the case of wrap-up sessions, on how useful and informative they are. Indeed, the most important contribution to improving the Council's transparency may have been brought to the Council from the outside with the establishment of the research NGO Security Council Report, which provides real-time information and contextual commentary on ongoing Council business. Often, useful information is also provided by some of the New York–based journalists and bloggers who specialize in Council affairs and are cultivated by the press secretaries of the larger UN delegations.

Is this lack of transparency a necessary sacrifice on the altar of Council efficiency? It has sometimes been argued that the fact that the Council pursues much of its business away from the glare of the public eye has allowed it to engage in the type of frank exchanges that are necessary to hammer out common solutions to difficult problems. Unfortunately, this seems to be the exception rather than the rule. Indeed, incoming ambassadors are often taken aback by the scripted and formal nature of much of the Council's interaction—even when dubbed "informal." Even when it meets for its annual two-day retreats, which should be an opportunity for the Council to step back and reflect self-critically on its role in key areas of current concern, most ambassadors simply read written statements that have been cleared by their respective capitals. When controversies erupt in the Council chamber, chances are they are over procedure, not substance (although issues of substance are often clouded in procedure).

In the remainder of this chapter, we analyze how these Council dynamics play out in the various substantive areas of the Council's work by looking at its performance in relation to crisis and conflict management, regional organizations, human rights, sanctions, and emerging threats. We end with some thoughts on Council reform efforts and the body's legitimacy.

Crisis and Conflict Management

Even though the Council was created primarily to respond to interstate rather than intrastate conflict, it has proven adept and innovative in adapting its powers under the UN Charter to civil war contexts by engaging in norm-setting, mediation, and investigation; by establishing tribunals, sanctions, and peace operations; and by authorizing the use of force. Along the way, the Council has emerged as the central actor in the international crisis management system addressing the intrastate conflicts that now occupy the vast majority of the Council's agenda. In the decade from 2003 to 2012, roughly 79 percent of its resolutions fell into this category.[10] This section seeks to shed some light on why, when, how, and where the Council intervenes in civil wars (or not).

While the Council's sustained engagement in civil wars has been primarily driven by the P3, it has generally been supported by Russia and China, albeit more passively. The Council's motivations in mandating interventions in civil wars vary from case to case. But one constant motivation has been that civil wars rarely remain strictly internal for long. They can draw in neighboring countries, as in the case of the Democratic Republic of the Congo, and they can also spill over into the wider region either through refugee flows or armed groups operating across borders. Thomas Weiss rightly notes in Chapter 11 that in these situations, "the humanitarian 'impulse'" is a key motivating factor for the P3's leadership in this area. However, as Bruce Jones argues in Chapter 38, what united all of the P5 around the Council's interventionism was their shared attachment to the integrity of the state, which is all too often under threat in civil wars, and the emergence of terrorism as a major factor in conflict settings like Afghanistan, Lebanon, Mali, and Somalia.

While early post–Cold War interventions were spread across multiple continents, with major operations in Central America, the Balkans, Southeast Asia, and Africa, the Council's activities have since converged on Africa and, to a lesser degree, the Middle East. This is partly the result of demand factors, most importantly the fact that most of today's civil wars take place in these two regions. African countries are also—at least for now—more willing to accept UN interventions than those in Asia and Latin America, which display a strong attachment to the principle of nonintervention. At the same time, the new geographical distribution of Council interventions is a function of supply factors, given that the P5 can most easily agree on collective action in Africa, which does not fall into the exclusive zone of influence of any P5 member or any other major power. France alone has displayed willingness to drive Council action to address crises there with significant numbers of its own troops. Although France has been supported by its P5 partners, all with varying interests in Africa, none of them have frequently or recently volunteered to deploy significant national military contingents of their own, except to fight terrorism and piracy, the latter mainly off the shores of Africa.

A number of authors in this volume have pointed out that the UN's, and in particular the Council's, increased activism in conflict management following the end of the Cold War played an important role in bringing down the number of armed conflicts by 40 percent in the decade from 1992 to 2002.[11] Indeed, taking advantage of the more cooperative environment created by the end of the Cold War, the Council provided a useful venue for the superpowers by facilitating their disengagement from Cold War–fueled proxy conflicts in Namibia, El Salvador, Nicaragua, Guatemala, Mozam-bique, and Cambodia. But in a way, these were easy cases, as these con-flicts were "ripe for resolution," both locally and in terms of the larger geopolitical context, given that they took place in relatively small territories where a few thousand peacekeepers could tip the balance toward resolution. Where these factors were present in subsequent Council-mandated opera-tions—as in Eastern Slavonia, East Timor, Sierra Leone, or Liberia—the UN was able to replicate its early post–Cold War successes.

In contrast to these success stories, the Council has struggled to bring lasting stability to a number of conflict situations on its agenda since the turn of the millennium, with many of them experiencing recurring crises. Part of the explanation for this may be that the nature of conflicts is chang-ing in ways that make them more intractable and less conducive to political settlements.[12] One factor at play is the growing ease (due to globalization) with which parties to a conflict can tap into illicit markets—whether con-sisting of arms, oil, drugs, cocoa, timber, or minerals. This reduces both the barriers to entry for disaffected actors into the market of organized vio-lence, as well as the incentives for conflicting parties to conclude peace agreements.[13] A second element is the significant rise of internationalized civil wars, that is, internal conflicts in which other states intervene militar-ily on one or both sides. Indeed, research shows that when external inter-ventions in domestic conflicts do not lead to a rapid military victory, they are likely to make internal conflicts deadlier and longer.[14] A third factor is the growing presence of violent Islamist extremist groups in conflict set-tings where the UN operates, as their maximalist goals are often difficult to meet through political negotiation. Together with other factors, in particular the instability generated by the Arab Spring, this may go a long way in explaining why the number of major civil wars has almost tripled in recent years, from four in 2007 to eleven in 2014 with a near-tripling of battle-related deaths along the way.[15]

Of course, the increase of civil wars is not necessarily an indicator of the Security Council's failure, as one could well argue that absent any Council action the number of violent conflicts and their death tolls would be considerably higher in places like Côte d'Ivoire, the DRC, and South Sudan.

Yet the fact that nine of the eleven major civil wars of 2014 are on the Security Council's agenda (Afghanistan, the DRC, Central African Repub-lic, Iraq, Libya, Somalia, South Sudan, Syria, and Ukraine) obscures the important observation by Adam Roberts in Chapter 17 that the Council-centered system of collective security is more aptly described as "selective security." The selective security system is one in which it is not objective criteria that determine whether, or how meaningfully, the Council will get involved in a conflict, but rather the interplay of interest-based calculations of Council members, their allies, countries potentially contributing troops to peacekeeping operations, and often the conflict states themselves. And as Peter Wallensteen and Patrik Johannsson point out in Chapter 2, the Security Council has failed to adopt *any* resolution on ten of the twenty-five most deadly conflicts of the post–Cold War era, as "major power interests in combination with sovereignty concerns have often trumped the impulse for international action based on concerns over humanitarian plight or the threat of regional diffusion of conflict."

The Council's selectivity—due to P5 politics and interests, sovereignty barriers, or reluctance by key players to deploy the necessary resources for adequate action—will become clearer as we look in greater detail at the Council's performance in its responses to humanitarian crises, conflict prevention, and peacekeeping.

The Humanitarian Impulse and the Responsibility to Protect

Concern over humanitarian distress—amplified by concerns over the destabilizing effects of refugees on host countries—remains a key driver of Council action. Given the Council's original design as an organ that would primarily address international conflict, it is remarkable that today much of global public opinion judges its effectiveness in terms of its ability to prevent genocide and other mass atrocities within state boundaries. The UN's failures in the early 1990s to avert mass killings in Angola, Bosnia, and Rwanda, despite having missions on the ground, constituted the ultimate failures in atrocity prevention, generating much introspection at the UN and beyond on how to avoid such disasters in the future. The Council's inability to act in response to ethnic cleansing in Kosovo in 1999 triggered renewed controversies around the "right to intervene," leading to a reframing of the concept, by an independent international commission, into the Responsibility to Protect (R2P), which simultaneously reinforces and qualifies the notion of sovereignty. Under R2P, the responsibility to protect populations lies with states themselves, but their failure to fulfill this responsibility shifts the onus onto the international community. At the 2005 World Summit, UN member states unanimously adopted the concept, while adding that only the Security Council, acting on a "case-by-case basis," would have the authority to invoke it in practice.

Yet in much of the global South, as well as in Beijing and Moscow, suspicion of the concept as a smokescreen for Western interventionism has remained strong. And the World Summit's emphasis on "case-by-case" consideration of each situation foreshadowed the selective nature of its application. Weiss notes in Chapter 11 that only "when humanitarian and strategic interests coincide" does a window of opportunity open for the humanitarian impulse to gain traction in the Security Council. Indeed, the

Council's painful dithering in the face of unfolding mass killings in Darfur (where China's efforts to shield the regime in Khartoum from overly coercive measures were reinforced by the unwillingness of the P3 to invest the resources required to mount an effective intervention) illustrated this reality early on. A few years later, when the Sri Lankan government's final military campaign against the Liberation Tigers of Tamil Eelam (LTTE) resulted in an estimated 40,000 civilian deaths, the Council failed to hold a single formal meeting on the situation due to opposition from Russia, China, and the Asian nonpermanent members on the Council.[16]

However, this does not mean that R2P turned out to be a mere paper tiger. As Weiss points out, since the early 2000s, UN peacekeeping operations were routinely equipped with civilian protection mandates. The Council and UN Secretariat have also shown an increasing willingness to muster robust yet risky responses to crises in the DRC in 2003 and 2012, in Côte d'Ivoire in 2010, and in Mali in 2013. And after crisis broke out in South Sudan in late 2013, the UN mission there saved countless lives by sheltering tens of thousands of civilians under threat. As Arthur Boutellis and Alexandra Novosseloff detail in Chapter 33, the R2P norm was very much behind the Council's mandating of the use of force to remove the Gbagbo regime in Côte d'Ivoire, which had refused to accept its electoral defeat a few months earlier. Where protective Council action was swift and robust, it usually resulted from a confluence of factors, which tended to consist of an acute crisis in which large-scale loss of life was imminent, there was an absence of any major power objecting to UN action, and there was a willingness of at least one major power to take the lead in the international response.

The biggest controversy around R2P—and challenge to the norm itself—has undoubtedly arisen from the 2011 NATO campaign in Libya. As Alex Bellamy and Paul Williams recount in Chapter 34, when the Council authorized an intervention against the Qaddafi regime in Libya in March 2011 in the name of R2P, it was the first time the Council had ever mandated the use of force against the de jure government of a UN member state for the purpose of protecting civilians. (In its history, the Council has authorized offensive military action against the consent of seven sitting governments, but never before for the protection of civilians.)[17] While noting that broader transformations in the Security Council's view of civilian protection facilitated the intervention in Libya, Bellamy and Williams argue that the intervention would not have been possible without a number of factors specific to the Libyan case, which suggests that such interventions will remain extremely rare.

However, NATO's interpretation of the Libya mandate to cover not only the enforcement of a no-fly zone—but also the bombing of retreating Libyan forces, the targeting of regime installations, the continuation of military operations after the fall of Tripoli, and provision of material assistance to the rebels—has resulted in serious controversy. This was aggravated by the circumstances of Qaddafi's death, when his convoy was hunted down and attacked by NATO aircraft and a Libyan mob on the ground summarily executed him. Russia and China, as well as their fellow BRICS members who happened to be sitting on the Council at the time (Brazil, India, and South Africa), and many other countries, accused NATO of having overstepped its mandate by pursuing regime change under the cover of R2P.

Authors in this volume have offered nuanced views on whether and to what degree NATO was in compliance with its mandate. In Chapter 34, Bellamy and Williams acknowledge that NATO and its allies may have "overstepped the tactical and operational spirit of Resolution 1973," but they argue that it was "less clear that these activities were all done with the explicit goal of regime change." In Chapter 17, Adam Roberts posits that in light of the limited effectiveness of air power in ensuring civilian protection, Russia and China "should probably have known that the military action would take this form." And in Chapter 19, Herman Schaper points out that the implications of the mandate had been thoroughly discussed by the Council. Given the tendency of Secretaries-General not to take sides when the P5 are divided, it is noteworthy that Ban Ki-moon chose to weigh in on this dispute with his assessment that NATO had stayed well within the limits of its mandate. Ultimately, the biggest indictment of NATO's Libya intervention relates not to whether it stayed within the Council mandate, but to the civil war it triggered in the country, casting severe doubts over the effectiveness of militarily engineered regime change as a tool to protect civilians.

There is also a wide spectrum of views among authors in this volume on whether and to what degree divisions over Libya account for the Council's paralysis over Syria. In Chapter 5, Trenin argues that the Libyan experience, in combination with arguments advanced by the United States in the run-up to the 2003 Iraq invasion, fed deep suspicions in Moscow, leading it to veto resolutions with any language that might later be construed to justify military action against the Assad regime, on the basis of noncompliance with past Council demands. In Chapter 35, Salman Shaikh and Amanda Roberts argue that the controversy over Libya helped Russia and China rally support among some nonpermanent Council members for their intransigent stance, which was ultimately motivated by factors other than the Libya precedent. Meanwhile, in Chapter 38, Bruce Jones contends that "there is very little evidence to suggest that Russian and Chinese opposition to intervention in Syria has anything to do with Libya," arguing instead that Russia's position on Syria was motivated by the desire to protect its last remaining ally in the Middle East, as well as genuine concern that destabilizing the Assad regime might lead to metastasizing Islamic radicalism.

While Russia condemning the Council to inaction may have turned that latter concern into a self-fulfilling prophecy, the truth may be a combination of these factors, together with the possibility that leaders in Russia, China, and elsewhere were genuinely offended by NATO's direct involvement in precipitating Qaddafi's end.

But even absent the vetoes of Russia and China, Council action over Syria may have fallen short of what would have been needed to decisively affect the course of events on the ground. In Chapter 35.1, Raghida Dergham points to the acute reluctance of the United States to involve itself militarily in the confrontation, not least reflected in its shifting "red lines" for intervention. And the discrepancy between the stated goal of the United States for regime change in Syria (which fed Russian and Chinese suspicion, complicating the forging of a consensus in the Council), and the limited means it was willing to deploy to this end, was actively unhelpful.

Part of the reluctance of the United States and others to forcefully intervene in Syria goes back to Colin Powell's famous warning with respect to Iraq, adapted from the Pottery Barn stores, that if "you break it, you own it," as well as the experiences in Kosovo, Afghanistan, Iraq, and Libya, which have proved the difficulty of establishing new order after forceful regime change. It is thus likely that the issue of regime change may confront the Council less rather than more often in the coming years, although there remain real and potential regimes around the world that, in unpredictable circumstances, the P5 likely could agree on removing if the military and other risks involved were to be acceptably small.

Despite all of the disagreements in the Council over the Responsibility to Protect and regime change in Libya and Syria, Council members have shown over the years a remarkable ability to compartmentalize their differences, dealing productively on one issue while arguing bitterly over another. As Jones notes in Chapter 38, crisis management interventions continue to unify the Council more than they divide it, especially as these interventions increasingly assume the form of defending states against terrorism or other transnational threats.

Conflict Prevention

Unfortunately, general P5 unity around crisis response rarely translates into a willingness to address an emerging conflict before it erupts into widespread bloodshed. Despite the UN Charter's emphasis on early action and the preventive role of the Security Council,[18] the Council's record on conflict prevention remains poor. Indeed, absent a major crisis to mobilize collective action, the Council tends to stand back. The enduring prevalence of sovereignty concerns, P5 interests (with Russia and China viewing the concept of conflict prevention with particular suspicion), and the tendency of countries in conflict or experiencing unrest to resist their inclusion on the

Council's agenda out of concern of being stigmatized as "conflict-prone" or fear of possible coercive measures, have prevented the Council from meeting the post–Cold War expectation that it would progressively move from reaction to early action.[19]

The Council's reactive nature and tendency to become involved in conflict situations late has been a standing criticism of the body since the end of the Cold War, and recommendations on how to address this problem invariably center on Article 99 of the UN Charter, which gives the Secretary-General the authority to "bring to the attention of the Security Council any matter which in his opinion may threaten the maintenance of international peace and security." Yet as Simon Chesterman notes in Chapter 21, the insistence of the United States, Russia, and China to have exclusive control over the Council agenda goes a long way in explaining why Article 99 has been explicitly invoked only twice in the Council's history, although there have been a handful of implicit references to it over the years.

As Christian Wenaweser and Joanna Weschler note in Chapters 9 and 13 respectively, even modest attempts to improve the Council's ability to anticipate crises face an uphill battle. One striking example was the "horizon-scanning" briefings introduced by the UK in 2010, in which the head of the UN Secretariat's Department of Political Affairs is invited to discuss with the Council, in closed session, emerging situations of concern that were not formally on the Council agenda. The briefings, which could be described as "Article 99 light," proved a difficult exercise from the outset, not least because the Council insisted on knowing in advance which topics would be raised. Affected countries, once they got wind that they might be a subject of Council discussions, would often fiercely lobby the Secretariat to ensure they would remain unmentioned. And Russia, China, and particularly the United States were hostile to these briefings, out of concern that they could be used by others to raise issues that are sensitive for them. Their efforts to end the briefings were temporarily successful, although in late 2013 the practice was reactivated in a modified and weakened format (i.e., below ambassadorial-level participation and no longer taking place in Security Council premises).

Peacekeeping

As Adam Roberts points out in Chapter 17, peacekeeping "has become a symbol of the UN itself." Close to sixty years since it mandated its first peacekeeping operation, this form of international action has remained the Council's most visible and most discussed conflict management tool. However, the dynamics of "selective security" are at play in this area as well.

During the 1990s, peacekeeping went through a boom-and-bust cycle, with the overall number of peacekeepers (troops, police, and military observers) dropping to just above 12,000 by June 1999. That same year, however, the Council embarked on a prolonged surge period deploying major new operations in Kosovo, East Timor, Sierra Leone, and the DRC (see Figure 40.2). In the following fourteen years, the Council mandated fourteen further peacekeeping operations, bringing the overall number of deployed troops to around 100,000 by the fall of 2009, the level around which peacekeeping forces has since remained.

This resurgence in peacekeeping reflects the enduring utility of this tool to the P5, who see it as a cost-effective and politically expedient means of providing stability in situations where few vital national interests are at stake, while spreading the costs and risks of response. Yet as Richard Gowan points out in Chapter 36, this resurgence was not driven by a grand strategy devised by the P5, but rather represents a series of reactive responses to unforeseen crises, which in some cases (as in Sierra Leone and the DRC) needed to be reinforced dramatically after the initial deployment proved inadequate.

Gowan also illustrates how peacekeeping mandates are often not the result of rational planning processes but of diplomatic bargaining among the P5, with the P3 not always presenting a united front. Indeed, France and the UK—and to a lesser degree the United States—have tended to push the Council to direct attention and resources to the countries in whose stability they individually are most interested. Meanwhile, as the authors in this volume have described with respect to Lebanon, the DRC, and Sudan (Darfur),

Figure 40.2 Overall Number of UN Peacekeepers, 1990–2014

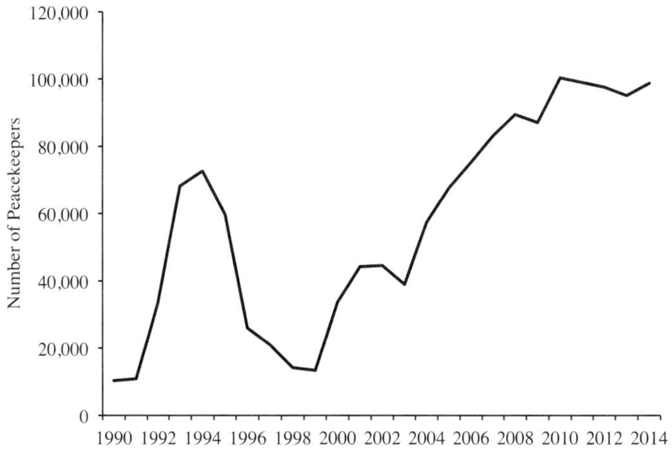

Source: United Nations, http://www.un.org/en/peacekeeping/resources/statistics/contributors.shtml.
Note: Includes peacekeeping troops, police, and military observers.

reluctant host countries have often been able to successfully resist the P3's preferred peacekeeping mandate and configuration.

The growth in peacekeeping has led to rising concerns of UN over-stretch, not unlike that faced by the organization in the early 1990s. As Council ambassadors and their sometimes modestly scaled staffs in New York are forced to split their time and attention among a growing array of issues, they are less able fully to focus on any one of them. There are also nagging doubts among governments, in the media, and among experienced UN officials about the UN Secretariat's ability to provide adequate management and oversight of over 100,000 deployed troops. Raising and maintaining necessary troops and getting them on the ground quickly have also become a constant headache for the organization, forcing the UN to make compromises in quality in order to attempt to meet the quantitative desiderata of the Council on the one hand, while fully taking into account local conditions in the field on the other.

The onset of the global financial crisis in 2008 and the subsequent economic slowdown have compounded the growing sense, particularly among the P3, that the peacekeeping budget would need to be contained. By the late 2000s, they started exerting increasing pressure on the UN Secretariat to wind or close down missions.[20]

Meanwhile, so-called special political missions (civilian field-based operations, which have no uniformed personnel and are significantly smaller than peacekeeping missions) were increasingly seen by Council members, and promoted by the Secretary-General, as more cost-effective alternatives to peacekeeping missions. Some of these political missions proved effective in supporting peace processes (e.g., UNMIN in Nepal from 2007 to 2011), facilitating political transitions (e.g., Yemen, through the efforts of the Secretary-General's special adviser from 2011 to 2012, although progress has been subsequently reversed), advancing longer-term peacebuilding (e.g., UNIPSIL in Sierra Leone from 2008 to 2014), or serving as platforms for preventive diplomacy (e.g., the UN's regional office in West Africa with respect to Guinea and Niger following coups). However, they soon started to be deployed to situations that, in hindsight, may have warranted significant peacekeeping or multinational stabilization missions, such as Libya, Mali, and the Central African Republic (before just such a stabilization force was deployed). Indeed, the footprint of political missions proved to be too light at times.

And erupting crises in these and other countries gave peacekeeping a new lease on life and reinforced the sense that growing robustness and an increasing focus on protection of civilians were necessary. It was against this backdrop that Ban Ki-moon, who had "entered office with both an ambivalent attitude toward the effectiveness of peacekeeping" and "wanted to shift his organization's focus away from military peace operations to crisis diplomacy,"[21] became more focused on peacekeeping as he entered his second term, culminating in his initiation of a major review of peace operations in the summer of 2014.

Indeed, such a review seemed timely in light of significant developments in peacekeeping since its last major review in 2000 by the so-called "Brahimi Panel." Among the most striking of these has been the changing geography of peacekeeping. As of July 2014, nine of the UN's sixteen peacekeeping missions and 79 percent of its blue helmets were deployed in Africa. By contrast, two decades earlier, over 50 percent of peacekeepers were deployed in Europe, where the upheavals in the Balkans consumed much of the Council's attention (see Figure 40.3).

As Herman Schaper, Mats Berdal, and John Hirsch point out in Chapters 19, 28, and 29 respectively, it was the UN's unhappy experience with the use of force in Somalia and the former Yugoslavia that led Western countries to withdraw from UN peacekeeping, reserving their troop deployments for NATO-led operations in Bosnia, Kosovo, and Afghanistan. In turn, NATO's travails in Afghanistan sensitized its member states to the difficulties the UN faces in carrying out stabilization operations in other difficult countries, especially considering the UN's cost-effectiveness relative to NATO's high-tech and sometimes gold-plated failures.

The changing profile of blue helmets, with 80 percent of peacekeepers now coming from Africa or Asia while the P5 are near absent,[22] creates

Figure 40.3 Total Number of UN Peacekeepers by Region Deployed, 1991–2014

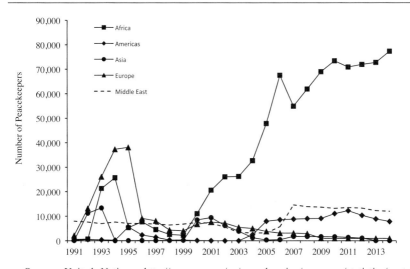

Source: United Nations, http://www.un.org/en/peacekeeping/resources/statistics/contri butors.shtml

challenges for the Council, not least in equity and burden-sharing terms, with a common complaint being that the West pays for peacekeeping with its wallet while the global South pays for it with its blood. This chasm between the Council and its agents on the ground has found expression in increasing instances of peacekeepers refusing to carry out the Council's orders, in particular in relation to the rise in robust peacekeeping discussed later. As Zhu Wenqi and Leng Zinyu point out in Chapter 4, one important exception to this trend has been China, whose growing engagement in peacekeeping over the past two decades is a reflection of both its desire to be seen as a responsible stakeholder in the international system, as well as, doubtless, its growing economic stake in Africa and the resultant need for stability there.

Starting in the early 1990s, the trend toward greater multidimensional-ity of missions has continued and mandates have grown ever broader. Along the way, mission models have also grown more diverse in terms of mandates, posture, configuration, and cooperation arrangements with regional organizations.[23] In particular, the growth of police components in peace operations is remarkable.

In addition to security functions, blue helmets are now regularly tasked with supporting security sector reform and good governance; carrying out electoral assistance; promoting human rights; helping with the disarma-ment, demobilization, and reintegration of combatants; delivering humani-tarian assistance; and promoting national dialogue and reconciliation.[24] While the broadening of mandates reflects a deepened sensitivity in the Council toward the multifaceted nature of the root causes of conflict and the need for comprehensive political and socioeconomic approaches toward peacebuilding, it has also proved distracting and created a growing gap between mission tasks and what realistically could be achieved. Connie Peck points out in Chapter 22 that, faced with such "Christmas tree" man-dates, heads of UN missions have increasingly complained about the lack of focus and prioritization by the Council. Moreover, the Council's growing ambition does not seem to have resulted in greater peacebuilding success on the ground. Consequently, a process of rethinking seems to have set in, with the P3 in particular now insisting that the protection of civilians must be the number one priority of the blue helmets.[25]

Another remarkable trend in the Council's decisionmaking has been a marked increase in its willingness to have peacekeepers use force in the pursuit of their mandates, discussed in detail by Jean-Marie Guéhenno in Chapter 18. While peacekeeping doctrine, to this day, remains nominally based on its three bedrock principles of impartiality, consent of the host country, and limitation of the use of force to self-defense, there has been a growing gap between doctrine and practice, as peacekeeping mandates since the late 1990s have increasingly contained elements of peace enforcement.[26] Most strikingly, a 3,000-strong Force Intervention Brigade was established inside the long-standing peacekeeping operation in the DRC (MONUSCO) "to carry out targeted offensive operations" against armed groups. And in Côte d'Ivoire, the UN went as far as to use force not only at the tactical level against spoilers but at the strategic level against a de facto government.

This trend toward robust peacekeeping has been driven by a number of interconnected factors, including the legacies of Srebrenica and Rwanda, which led to the routine inclusion of protection of civilians provisions in peacekeeping mandates; the lessons from Sierra Leone in 2000 that peacekeepers, in order to succeed, need to have both the mandate and the resources to repel spoilers who have a vested interest in seeing a peace process fail;[27] and the Council's tendency to increasingly deploy peacekeepers into situations where there is no peace to keep.[28] UN peacekeeping doctrine has evolved along the way, with self-defense being reinterpreted as "defense of mandate."

The move toward more robust peacekeeping elicits a great deal of unease among a number of member states and parts of the UN Secretariat, for several reasons. First, the traumatic Somalia experience in the early 1990s had reaffirmed the lesson initially drawn following the UN's Congo mission in the 1960s that the UN should stay clear of enforcement operations. Second, the major non-African troop-contributing countries—all members of the Non-Aligned Movement and much attached to the nonintervention principle—remain deeply suspicious of robust peacekeeping and resent the prospect of seeing their soldiers placed in the line of fire in the pursuit of Council mandates that they have little input in formulating.[29] This partly explains the finding of a 2014 report by the UN Secretariat's Office of Internal Oversight Services that "force is almost never used to protect civilians under attack." Third, robust peacekeeping by definition requires soldiers willing to die for the cause, naturally drawing neighboring countries with a stake in the conflict, with the risk of undermining the UN's impartiality or regionalizing civil wars.[30] Fourth, the UN's limited ability to deploy the necessary troop numbers to provide effective civilian protection or establish a credible deterrent against rebel forces in some of its larger host countries risks inviting spoilers to call the UN's bluff, with terrible consequences—as happened in Srebrenica over two decades ago. Finally, enforcement action by UN peacekeepers such as the Force Intervention Brigade has significant legal implications, because—as the UN's Legal Counsel warned Council ambassadors, to their apparent surprise, at a Council retreat in 2013—it makes them a party to the conflict, thus potentially depriving them of the special protections they normally enjoy under international humanitarian law.

Nevertheless, is it possible that the Force Intervention Brigade may become a model for future peacekeeping? On the one hand, it did play a role in defeating the March 23 Movement (M23), alongside increased international pressure on Rwanda to halt its support to the group, thus helping at least temporarily to stabilize a deteriorating situation in eastern DRC, and to restore the UN mission's credibility. On the other hand, as noted by Tatiana Carayannis in Chapter 32, in the DRC the UN has gone through repeated cycles in which crises are met with bouts of Council resolve, only to be succeeded by new crises after periods of Council inattention. Enforcement action can serve as a shock-dispenser and shock-absorber. But it cannot create a new political order by itself. Indeed, reliance on the use of force often detracts from the importance of nurturing the political processes that are ultimately required to resolve deep-seated political problems. As Napoleon said, one "may do anything with bayonets except sit on them."

This may partly explain why political solutions prove highly elusive in places, like the DRC, Somalia, Haiti, Iraq, Darfur, Afghanistan, and the Central African Republic, in which the UN has been engaged for a decade or more. This poses great challenges, as the UN's ability to influence the course of events in countries in which it has deployed long-term missions tends to diminish over time, as the leverage of these missions over the conflict parties dissipates and as the support they tend initially to enjoy among the host country populations erodes. It has been pointed out that, while transitional governments in the immediate postconflict phase tend to need a UN presence for security and other assistance, this dependence declines as these governments establish control or gain legitimacy through elections, making them less willing to tolerate the involvement or interference of a UN peacekeeping or political presence.[31] It is partly this dynamic that explains why long-running UN missions are finding themselves increasingly challenged by their host countries, which in recent years have called for their premature withdrawal (Ethiopia/Eritrea, Chad, Sudan, Burundi), pushed for their downsizing (DRC), seriously obstructed their operations (Sudan), or evicted heads of UN missions (Sudan, Burundi, Sierra Leone). This worrisome trend is also a reflection of the declining respect and authority for the Security Council in Africa, discussed in the next section.

Meanwhile, efforts to improve the Council's ability to advance longer-term peacebuilding once peacekeepers have left have had only limited success. At the 2005 World Summit, the General Assembly and the Security Council jointly established the Peacebuilding Commission, a new intergovernmental body tasked with devising long-term and integrated peacebuilding strategies for countries transitioning from war to peace, with a special focus on reconstruction and institution-building efforts.[32] The creation of the commission was a response to a high rate of relapse of conflict countries into violence, and also reflected a recognition of the Security Council's inability to remain focused on specific situations over an extended period of time while dealing with multiple crises. Still, the Peacebuilding Commission has not yet been able to live up to expectations, consequently suffering potentially irreversible damage to its reputation, at least partly because the P5 were uninterested in working through an oversized body that was not established as the Council's exclusive subsidiary organ. This institutional quagmire was generated by a not untypical negotiating fix among member states generally suspicious of the Council's tendency toward mandate creep.

Regional Organizations

Among the most important shifts in the Council's efforts to address civil wars are the deepening ties with regional organizations, recognized by at least some of the P5 as "the biggest strategic issue facing the Council today."[33] As Bruno Stagno Ugarte points out in Chapter 23, throughout much of the Cold War, regional organizations were locked in an intermittent struggle for primacy with the UN that gave way to tentative cooperative arrangements in the early 1990s (particularly in Bosnia and Liberia). Reliance on regional organizations grew from the mid-1990s onward, as the UN scaled down its own involvement in peacekeeping following the Rwanda and Somalia disasters. When UN peacekeeping revived in the early 2000s, Stagno Ugarte notes, regional and subregional organizations, especially those in Africa, had gained confidence and were "aggressively advocating for regional solutions to regional problems." In particular, the AU's Peace and Security Council, created in 2002, was increasingly demanding to be treated as the UN Security Council's equal partner.

Despite their rhetoric to the contrary, the P5 view this newfound assertiveness of the AU with alarm, perhaps fearing it will prove contagious with other regional organizations, and continue to insist on the UN Security Council's primacy. Playing in the Security Council's favor is the fact that regional organizations themselves are painfully aware that they continue to lack the financial and operational resources to realize their ambitions, fully and unassisted, as is the case with the AU—the operationally and institutionally most mature regional organization other than the European Union. Indeed, most African nonpermanent members on the Security Council wind up voting for Council solutions to African problems, rather than insisting on AU-led initiatives.

At the same time, the UN, like the AU, became increasingly overstretched as its peacekeeping engagements rose after 2000. In situations where the Council, and in particular the P3, was unwilling or unable to take the lead in responding to a crisis, it was all too happy to defer to the AU, fueling the notion of African self-reliance. As a result, the Council lost significant ground to African regional and subregional organizations in the area of conflict management.[34] This development was underpinned by the fact that African countries with powerful militaries were willing to deploy their troops to places where there was no peace to keep. Indeed, as John Hirsch details in Chapter 29, the AU fielded a Council-mandated peace-keeping operation in Somalia, which has suffered casualty figures that no UN operation would be willing to sustain. This has fueled AU demands that such missions be financed by the UN, which continue to be rejected by the P5. In Darfur, as Heiko Nitzschke shows in Chapter 20, joining forces with the AU in the creation of the first-ever hybrid UN-AU peacekeeping opera-tion (UNAMID) was necessary for the Council to overcome the Sudanese government's opposition to the deployment of blue helmets. Yet the mis-sion's operational limitations and political difficulties have so far prevented that model from being transferred to other settings. Nitzschke also argues that the Council, when faced with an acute crisis or divisions within the P5, had to rely on the AU to negotiate key agreements on the north/south issue in Sudan, reducing it to the role of "rubber stamping" outcomes that were reached without its involvement.

Adding to the leverage of regional organizations is the fact that they can confer much valued legitimacy on Council action. In particular, this was the case for the Arab League during the Arab Spring, with the P5 find-ing themselves competing for the blessing or cover of the League to legit-imize their preferred approach to given situations (as in Syria) or even make their assent a sine qua non for action (as in Libya). In these contexts, the Council occasionally benefits from political competition and disagree-ment among regional and subregional organizations themselves, allowing it to "forum-shop"—to pick and choose which organization to partner with. This is precisely what happened with respect to Libya and Côte d'Ivoire when the Council used the political cover of the Arab League and ECOWAS, respectively, for forceful action, in both cases pitting the League against the AU and creating deep resentments and frustration especially with South Africa, then a Council member and the self-declared African voice in the Council (which Nigeria, obviously, saw otherwise). Despite these disagreements, the "mutual dependence"[35] of both organizations—the realization that neither of them alone is able to cope with the multitude of peace and security crises on the continent—has forced them to set aside political disagreements in some cases (such as Libya) in favor of coopera-tion in others (such as Mali).

Human Rights, Accountability, and the Role of Civil Society

Throughout the Cold War, the superpower conflict, along with absolute notions of sovereignty, ensured that human rights issues would be kept outside the Security Council chamber. In the 1990s, however, human rights began creeping onto the Security Council's agenda along with the realization that civil strife was not amenable to negotiated solutions as long as human rights continued to be massively violated. In the context of Iraq in 1991, the Council acknowledged for the first time that human rights violations, by causing refugee flows, could amount to a threat to international peace and security, and in a number of other settings the Council began to deploy human rights monitors, including in El Salvador, Guatemala, and Haiti.[36] However, lingering Chinese sensitivities, in particular, long prevented the Council from developing a systematic approach to human rights in its work. (The same applies to democracy promotion, addressed by Francesco Mancini in Chapter 12. Chinese sensitivities were often outweighed, however, by the pragmatic need to promote elections as part of an exit strategy for peace operations, which explains why, between 1999 to 2013, 85 percent of them featured mandates calling for ensuring or promoting elections and democracy.)

It was the mass atrocities in Rwanda and Srebrenica that led to a more serious integration of human rights as a central element of the Council's conflict resolution efforts—although it took a few years before these lessons were fully reflected in Council decisionmaking. Toward the late 1990s, almost all new peacekeeping missions were equipped with a human rights component and, starting in 1999, also with a protection of civilians mandate, and discussions started within and beyond the UN that laid the conceptual basis for R2P, examined earlier.

Among the direct results of these incidents was the creation of the position of UN high commissioner for human rights in 1994. Although the first incumbent proved lackluster in this role, many of his successors, from Mary Robinson to Louise Arbour and Navanethem Pillay, adopted a more assertive approach to their responsibilities, not least in their dealings with the Council. However, direct interaction between the high commissioner and the Council remained controversial for many years, and successive high commissioners were only sporadically asked to address the body. As Joanna Weschler notes in Chapter 13, this began to change in 2009 when, largely thanks to Austrian efforts, the high commissioner began to receive regular invitations to brief the Council, including on country-specific situations. It is not clear that the later creation of the posts of special adviser on the prevention of genocide and special adviser on R2P added much to the work of the high commissioner, although they may have reinforced the Council's and the larger UN membership's focus on the worst human rights abuses.

Another key factor in making human rights a mainstay of the Council's agenda was its increasing interaction with nongovernmental organizations, which both grew significantly and evolved in nature during the 1990s. The role of NGOs as major partners for the UN in humanitarian operations, as well as the mediagenic nature of some NGO activity, encouraged the Council to display greater openness to NGO views and more generously recognize NGO achievements. One of the most practical early innovations in this respect was the so-called Arria formula, introduced in 1992 by Venezuela's ambassador to the Council, Diego Arria. Under this arrangement, the Council continues intermittently to meet with civil society representatives or other individuals with relevant expertise or information to receive briefings outside the Council chamber, which often address the human rights or humanitarian situations in conflict countries. In 2014, the Council received seven Arria briefings.

However, today, NGO influence over Council deliberations goes far deeper than just occasional appearances in Arria-formula meetings. In particular, elected members of the Council have come to rely heavily on NGOs such as the International Crisis Group, Human Rights Watch, Crisis Action, Enough, and Oxfam for information and analysis from conflict zones, ensuring that NGO concerns occasionally are reflected in Council mandates. Also, some of these NGOs, along with Security Council Report, increasingly act as a repository of institutional memory about certain files and peace missions, thus helping the E10 to balance the P5's home-court advantage. Meanwhile, one relatively new UN-focused NGO, Independent Diplomat, acts as a specialist multilateral diplomacy consultant to very small countries, or entities wishing to achieve statehood or self-determination, such as the government of Somaliland, particularly for Council-related activities.

In partnership with nonpermanent Council members, NGOs have also been instrumental in raising the profile of a number of thematic human rights issues that have become central features of the Council agenda. These include the agenda items on the protection of civilians, established by Resolution 1265 (1999); women, peace, and security, established by Resolution 1325 (2000); and children and armed conflict, established by Resolution 1539 (2004). As Teresa Whitfield points out in Chapter 24, the mechanisms established under these agenda items are remarkable in light of the strong initial skepticism of the P5 and many members of the Non-Aligned Movement who were suspicious of the imposition of a liberal Western agenda that they believed was contained in these resolutions. Whitfield also explains how these agenda items were kept alive and further developed by groups of countries that coalesced around these three thematic agenda items and served as important coordination and advocacy mechanisms, often working closely alongside relevant Secretariat departments and NGO communities.

Of the three thematic human rights issues, children and armed conflict is the most procedurally advanced, with a well-established Security Council subsidiary working group since 2005 and an explicit Article 99 mandate for the Secretary-General to report on situations of concern not otherwise on the Council agenda. Protection of civilians, albeit the oldest thematic issue, has only an informal working group that has yet to capitalize on the benefits of informality (China does not participate at the working-group level). All three thematic issues, however, have generated country-specific improvements, with action plans against recruitment of child soldiers or military use of schools being potent examples, and have been, despite ongoing pushback within the Council, substantively reflected in country-specific resolutions.

Along with human rights, the issue of accountability for war crimes and mass atrocities became increasingly prominent in the Council during the 1990s, an issue covered by Eran Sthoeger in Chapter 25. The most striking manifestations of this trend was the Security Council's creation of the International Criminal Tribunal for the Former Yugoslavia (ICTY) and the International Criminal Tribunal for Rwanda (ICTR) in 1993 and 1994 respectively. This intensified calls for a more universal International Criminal Court (ICC), which was eventually established through a statute signed at a diplomatic conference in Rome in 1998.

The Rome Statute, which entered into force in July 2002, gave the ICC jurisdiction over genocide, crimes against humanity, war crimes, and the crime of aggression,[37] and accorded the Security Council the authority to refer cases to the Court and to suspend investigations or prosecutions for a period of up to twelve months (known as deferral). The latter was particularly controversial at the time of the negotiations, but the P5 made it a non-negotiable precondition for agreeing to the statute.

Even though three of the P5 (China, Russia, and the United States) have yet to become parties to the Rome Statute, the Council has so far used its right to refer cases to the ICC in two instances. Although the referral of the Darfur situation in 2005,[38] and the later issuance of an arrest warrant for Sudanese president Omar al-Bashir, led to considerable backlash in Africa, the Council used those powers again in 2011 in the case of Libya.[39] (A 2014 draft resolution that would have referred the Syrian case to the ICC was vetoed by Russia and China.) Both referrals were possible only because Washington's intense efforts to undermine the Court in the early years of its existence eventually gave way to a more pragmatic approach, perhaps in realization that it could be helpfully instrumentalized in the pursuit of US foreign policy goals. However, the Council has refused to follow up on its referrals with any kind of support to the Court, whether diplomatically or financially.[40] Most disappointingly, Beijing's decision to host a visit by President Bashir in June 2011 signaled that it had little interest in the credibility of the Court or its arrest warrants. Growing hostility to the ICC in Africa, due to cases against the leaders of Sudan, Kenya, and Libya, is particularly worrying, given that African countries had been the strongest group of supporters of the Court's creation.

Requests from the AU for the Council to exercise its deferral powers with respect to the indictments of Bashir as well as Kenyan president Uhuru Kenyatta and his deputy William Ruto were rejected by the Council, to the great annoyance of African leaders, who have increasingly denounced the ICC, along with the Council, as merely another tool through which Western powers impose standards on Africa that they would not accept themselves.[41] As if preemptively to underline this point, the Council, in 2002 and 2003, and again in 2011, used its deferral powers under intense US pressure to provide immunity to nationals of nonstate parties to the Rome Statute participating in Council-mandated peacekeeping operations, illustrating the limits of P5 interest in accountability. Partly because of the sensitivities and controversies surrounding ICC referrals, the Council has continued to consider establishment of specialized ad hoc tribunals to try international crimes even after creation of the ICC, as evidenced by the Council's involvement in (or promotion of) the creation of hybrid courts in Sierra Leone, Lebanon, and the Central African Republic.

Sanctions

Among UN scholars, the 1990s are often referred to as the "sanctions decade," in allusion to the title of an influential book on UN sanctions published in 2000.[42] However, this much-quoted reference obscures the fact, covered by Sue Eckert in Chapter 20, that the Security Council has since continued to use an ever greater variety of sanctions for an ever greater variety of goals. Indeed, a total of fifteen sanctions regimes were in place as of December 2014, eleven of which were established after January 1, 2000. Part of the reason why the sanctions tool is used with such frequency is the fact that it is one of the few coercive tools at the Council's disposal and is more palatable than the use of force. Another is that sanctions are initially cheap for those who impose them, with costs assumed to be borne mostly by the governments of targeted states and their enablers.

Over the years, the Council has displayed a remarkable degree of learning and adaptation in its application of sanctions. Most noticeable is the Council's abandonment of broad trade embargoes after their humanitarian impact became clear in Iraq, Haiti, and Yugoslavia during the early 1990s. The controversy around the Iraq sanctions in particular "has colored in a negative way more positive changes that have occurred in sanctions, especially since the mid-1990s."[43]

Indeed, all sanctions regimes the Council has imposed since 1994 have been of a targeted nature, in terms of either the individuals, entities, industries, or goods against which they were applied. Over the years, the Council has also become more inventive in devising different types of sanctions, imposing travel bans or financial and arms embargoes against certain individuals, groups, or entities; flight bans against a country's aircraft; diplomatic sanctions against government representatives; or embargoes on commodities coming from a certain region. Most of these sanctions regimes have been imposed for one of the following four objectives: ending civil wars (as in Liberia, Sierra Leone, the DRC, Côte d'Ivoire, and Sudan/Darfur); countering terrorism (as in Sudan and Libya, and for individuals or entities associated with al-Qaeda); preventing or reversing nuclear proliferation (Iran and North Korea); or promoting human rights, including restoration of constitutional order and civilian protection (as in Haiti, Côte d'Ivoire, Guinea-Bissau, and Libya).

The move toward targeted sanctions required greater sophistication in their design, and thus a number of international research and dialogue processes were launched to identify best practices in relevant areas: the Interlaken process on financial sanctions, sponsored by Switzerland in 1998–1999; the Bonn-Berlin process, sponsored by Germany in 1999–2001; and the Stockholm process on strengthening the implementation of targeted sanctions, sponsored by Sweden in 2002–2003. In response to these processes, the Council established a subsidiary working group on sanctions, discontinued in 2006, which helped it improve its use of targeted sanctions. However, much of this effort to strengthen the effectiveness of sanctions remains a work in progress, as it requires a high degree of coordination among member states, UN entities, and a wide array of other international agencies ensuring international cooperation on matters such as police, civil aviation, transport, nuclear arms, conventional arms, and dual-use goods. It also increasingly implies heavier reliance on the private sector as an implementing partner of sanctions, for instance the diamond industry for the Kimberley Process Certification Scheme to identify "conflict diamonds," or the banking industry for Council-backed anti–money laundering measures in the counterterrorism context.

Targeted sanctions also required improvements in monitoring mechanisms, leading to the establishment of independent panels of experts, the first of which was set up in 1995 to address the conflict in eastern Zaire. A few years later, Canada provided creative and energetic leadership to the Council's Angola sanctions committee in 1999–2000, sponsoring a panel of experts which broke new ground in engaging for the first time in "naming and shaming" third countries as "sanctions-busters." Such panels of experts are now generally established along with a sanctions committee of the Council as part of any new sanctions regime.[44] While panels of experts have significantly improved sanctions monitoring, they have repeatedly become the object of criticism and controversy over the years, including with respect to the evidentiary standards they have applied, the inconsistency in evidence-gathering methodology across panels, and the politicization of some panels, in particular those dealing with nonproliferation issues, which the P5 are keen to keep under their direct control. Meanwhile, China has reacted with particular sensitivity when panels of experts unearth evidence of Chinese armaments in regions under arms embargoes, such as Darfur, Côte d'Ivoire, the DRC, or Somalia.[45]

Sanctions may have become more targeted over the years, but they certainly have not become less controversial. Indeed, Russia and China, along with their fellow BRICS members, tend to view sanctions with much skepticism, especially when they are imposed against sitting governments. (By contrast, they tend readily to support sanctions measures against nonstate actors and rebel groups.) Indeed, Moscow's and China's vetoes of proposed sanctions against Myanmar and Zimbabwe in 2007 and 2008 (arguing, with some justification, that neither situation had a link to international peace and security), and of a draft resolution threatening sanctions against Syria in 2011, indicate that this pushback may be becoming more assertive. Similarly, China's aversion to sanctions, combined with its economic interests, has led it to invest considerable effort in watering down sanction measures imposed against North Korea, Iran, and Sudan.

It is largely this skeptical view that Russia, China, and other sovereignty-conscious countries harbor against sanctions that has led to a move away from punitive sanctions against sitting government representatives, and toward sanctions that are "protective" of the state and political transition processes. The latest case is Yemen, where the Council, in 2014, imposed sanctions against spoilers of the delicate, and since aborted, transition led by then-President Hadi. Indeed, of the sanctions regimes currently in place, only those imposed against Eritrea, Iran, and North Korea are framed as sanctions exclusively against state authorities. As one senior Council diplomat working on sanctions put it, "All recent sanctions resolutions envisage the states as willing partners."[46] Given the nature of many states in which sanctions are imposed, this approach may appear overly optimistic at times.

Of course, an important question is whether UN sanctions actually work. In 2004, David Cortright and George Lopez estimated that about half of the Security Council sanctions regimes of the 1990s were partially effective. In Libya, Sudan, and Yugoslavia (up to 1995), sanctions provided bargaining leverage that helped to produce negotiated agreements; in Cambodia, Angola, and Sierra Leone, sanctions combined with military pressure to weaken and isolate rebel groups; in Iraq and Liberia, sanctions contributed to the isolation and containment of the targeted regimes. However, in Liberia (until 2001), Rwanda and Yugoslavia (after 1998), and Ethiopia, Eritrea, and Afghanistan, sanctions had little or no impact.[47] Where sanctions did not work, it was often because they were used as a substitute for strategic action and without consensus about their purpose. In Chapter 31 of this volume, Francesc Vendrell illustrates this with respect to Afghanistan, where the reinforcement of sanctions against the Taliban in 2000 undercut the UN's mediation efforts with the regime without offering anything in terms of a political strategy to replace it.

Another factor in the relative ineffectiveness of UN sanctions regimes is the fact that they do not receive the necessary institutional support and willingness to enforce them. Here the onus is particularly on active engagement by the chairs of sanctions committees, who are almost exclusively drawn from the elected members of the Security Council and who have all too often viewed their chairmanship as a nuisance. But ultimately, the effectiveness of sanctions is primarily a function of the readiness of relevant powers to place resources and political weight behind their implementation, a readiness that has all too often been in short supply. An intergovernmental high-level review of sanctions launched in 2014 by a number of governments together with two think tanks was expected to infuse a new dynamic into sanctions implementation, but seems to have become a victim of deteriorating P5 relations in the wake of the 2014 Crimea crisis.[48]

New Issues on the Council Agenda:
Terrorism, WMD, Organized Crime, and Pandemics

One remarkable trend in the Council since the turn of the millennium is its increasing attention to transnational threats, particularly terrorism, proliferation of weapons of mass destruction, transnational organized crime, and pandemics. Overall, the P5 display a remarkable degree of unity on these issues, with most resolutions on terrorism and weapons of mass destruction being adopted under Chapter VII. This reflects a convergence of interests among the P5 on these issues as well as a deepening concern among the wider membership around the growing threat emanating from transnationally operating nonstate actors. At the same time, the Council's legislative approach to these issues has generated a considerable backlash among much of the membership about Council overreach. Meanwhile, the faith of the P3 in the UN's ability to effectively organize collective action against these threats has waned in recent years, which led the Obama administration to complement the UN architecture with important new counterterrorism and nonproliferation initiatives outside the UN framework.

Terrorism

The Council was much more active in addressing terrorism prior to the attacks of September 11, 2001, than is commonly realized. In the 1990s, the Council imposed sanctions against Libya over its noncooperation with the investigation of two airline bombing incidents; against Sudan for harboring those responsible for the assassination attempt on Egyptian president Mubarak; and against the Taliban regime for harboring the al-Qaeda leadership. (The Libya and Sudan sanctions regimes have been credited in playing a significant role in ending the sponsorship of terrorist groups by both countries.)

However, the real game-changer for the Council on terrorism was the events of September 11. The attacks led to the proclamation of a global "war on terror" by the United States as its new grand strategy, which it prioritized in both its bilateral and multilateral engagements. The attacks of September 11 highlighted the increasingly transnational nature of the threat, making the Security Council a natural venue to lead the charge. Resolution 1368, adopted on September 12, 2001, established an important precedent by invoking—for the first time—the right of self-defense under Article 51 against terrorist attacks, providing an international seal of legal approval to the subsequent US invasion of Afghanistan. The Council also extended what had originally been a set of sanctions (asset freezes, arms embargoes, and travel bans) solely focused on Afghanistan, to all parts of the globe, vastly expanding the list of individuals and entities associated with al-Qaeda or the Taliban against whom the sanctions would be applied (the so-called 1267 sanctions regime).

Less than three weeks later, the Council adopted Resolution 1373, one of the most groundbreaking resolutions in the body's history. It imposed legally binding obligations on all UN member states to, among other things, enhance legislation, strengthen border controls, coordinate executive machinery, and increase international cooperation in combating terrorism. The Council also established, and later expanded and institutionalized, a support structure to monitor member-state implementation of Resolution 1373.

As Edward Luck noted in his chapter in the 2004 edition of this volume, the "rapidity, unanimity, and decisiveness" with which the Council responded to the 9/11 attacks were "without precedent."[49] And the new counterterrorism architecture established by the Council was a remarkable development for an organization whose membership had been deeply divided on the question of the legitimacy of nonstate violence, in light of the fact that many liberation movements had at one point or another been labeled "terrorist" by former colonial powers. However, as Eric Rosand and Sebastian von Einsiedel have written: "While the UN's pre-9/11 effort was ambivalent, the new focus on al-Qaeda allowed UN members to unite to condemn a specific terrorist group and thus enable the US to move terrorism near the top of the UN's agenda."[50]

As detailed by Peter Romaniuk in Chapter 14, the Council's counterterrorism effort soon attracted growing criticism from a number of quarters, which began to erode its legitimacy and effectiveness. First, the legislative nature of Resolution 1373, which created far-reaching and binding obligations on all member states without their prior agreement elicited much resentment. Second, the George W. Bush administration's invasion of Iraq under the banner of his global war on terror delegitimized Washington's counterterrorism endeavor in the eyes of many member states. Third, the resistance of the Council to include human rights issues relevant to terrorism in its decisions led to some outrage among the NGO community and beyond. Even more concerning, the complete disregard of due process in the 1267 sanctions listing procedures, which did not offer any recourse or review mechanism for individuals who argued they were wrongfully sanctioned, came under increasing criticism and were eventually deemed by the European Court of Justice to have violated fundamental human rights. In response the Council reluctantly established, in 2009, an ombudsperson to review requests for delisting of sanctioned individuals.[51] Meanwhile, the effectiveness of the sanctions themselves remained limited in terms of constraining the access to arms and funds by terrorists and preventing their ability to travel.

With the legitimacy of the UN's Council-centered counterterrorism effort increasingly questioned, the Secretary-General in 2005 tabled a blueprint for a global counterterrorism strategy that was meant to loosen the Council's exclusive grip on the issue and place greater emphasis on addressing root causes and respect for human rights. At the same time, he established an interagency counterterrorism task force to ensure that the wide array of UN agencies would bring their combined strength to bear in the implementation of the strategy. The following year, the General Assembly followed suit, unanimously endorsing a modified version of the Secretary-General's strategy, which helped transform a previously acrimonious UN discussion on counterterrorism into a comparatively constructive one. However, it is debatable whether either the strategy or the task force produced much in terms of concrete achievements on the ground, other than generating a cottage industry of meetings and expert workshops in New York and elsewhere.

As the decade drew to a close, the United States had become increasingly disillusioned with what could be achieved in the fight against terrorism within a UN setting, whether based in the Council, the Secretariat, or the General Assembly. It had even lost faith in its own creation, the Council's Counter-Terrorism Committee, which was unable to name and shame countries believed to be hostile or unresponsive to Resolution 1373 and had become a largely process-oriented body that failed to deliver quality analysis on country needs and priorities or serve as an effective clearinghouse for technical assistance requests.

It was against this background that the United States, under President Obama, in 2011 created the Global Counter-Terrorism Forum, an "action-oriented" platform outside the UN framework to foster effective multilateral cooperation in counterterrorism. While the United States thus moved the locus of much of the action outside the UN, it continued to value the Council's norm-setting role in counterterrorism. Thus, in September 2014, at a time of deep concern about thousands of foreign nationals from over eighty countries having joined extremist Islamist groups in Syria and Iraq, the United States spearheaded the adoption of a Council resolution that obliged all member states to prevent, criminalize, and prosecute international travel by their citizens to join terrorist groups. Adopted at a summit-level meeting of the Security Council that was chaired by President Obama himself (only the second instance ever that a US president has chaired a Council session), the "foreign fighters" resolution may well prove to have a mobilizing effect on member states. At the same time, it will be difficult to implement and monitor, and its breadth and vagueness raise serious human rights concerns about the potential for abuse by repressive states against separatist or opposition forces branded as "terrorist."[52]

While the Council thus remains an important forum for the P5 to set norms (no matter how flawed they may be) and mobilize the wider membership around them, operationally the UN's main contribution in counterterrorism likely lies in its conflict resolution and peacekeeping efforts in conflict countries in which terrorist groups take advantage of the widespread instability, such as Mali or Somalia. Vice versa, there has been a recurrent complaint that the UN's counterterrorism regime has undermined the UN's conflict resolution and humanitarian roles, including by imposing sanctions on (and thus de facto outlawing) groups such as the Taliban, thus complicating efforts to enter into peace negotiations with them.

Weapons of Mass Destruction

Similar to counterterrorism, there has also been increasing convergence of P5 interests around the proliferation of weapons of mass destruction, which has, since the mid-2000s, led to far-reaching Council resolutions, addressed in Chapter 16 by Waheguru Pal Singh Sidhu. This is all the more remarkable in light of the Council's deep divide a few years earlier over the question of how to pursue Iraq's disarmament. Imposed by the Council in 1990 and 1991 after Iraq's invasion of Kuwait and Kuwait's subsequent liberation by a US-led coalition, the inspections and sanctions regimes had come under increased criticism in the middle to late 1990s by Russia, China, and France, which questioned the regimes' utility and legitimacy in light of the inspection regime's infiltration by the CIA and the sanctions regime's nefarious humanitarian consequences. The controversy around unilateral air strikes in 1998 by the United States and the United Kingdom to compel Iraqi compliance with Council demands presaged the even more contentious disagreements over the US-UK invasion of Iraq in 2003 in the face of strong Russian, Chinese, and French opposition, as detailed by David Malone and Poorvi Chitalkar in Chapter 27.[53]

Bygone disagreements over Iraq notwithstanding, the P5 are united in their desire to see no expansion of the small club of nuclear weapon states and to achieve a diplomatic solution to the North Korean and Iranian nuclear crises. Indeed, in 2006 the Council imposed sanctions against both North Korea and Iran, the former of which had carried out its first nuclear test that year after leaving the Non-Proliferation Treaty in 2003, and the latter of which is suspected of harboring nuclear weapon ambitions after having failed to disclose the extent of its nuclear program.

However, in the following years, US efforts to strengthen sanctions in response to continued Iranian and North Korean defiance of Council demands ran up against the skeptical attitudes of China and Russia, both of which tended to advocate for a less confrontational and less forceful approach. Partly, this reticence may have been motivated by important political and economic ties that Moscow, and even more so Beijing, maintain with Pyongyang and Tehran. More important, though, it reflected their general aversion to any Chapter VII measures, which was reinforced by the still fresh memories of the George W. Bush administration's attempt to justify the 2003 Iraq invasion with reference to Baghdad's alleged noncompliance with previous disarmament demands made under Chapter VII. And the subsequent failure of the United States to find any WMD in Iraq later fueled suspicions of US allegations against Iran.

Nevertheless, from 2009 onward, the Council gained new momentum on these issues, progressively adding new layers of sanctions against both Iran and North Korea. This reflected growing concern from all of the P5 about the failure to make headway in resolving the twin nuclear crises, fueled in the case of North Korea by its decision to carry out further nuclear tests in 2009 and 2013 and leading in both cases to reinforced sanctions. With respect to Iran, the Council's newfound resolve was also the result of intense US diplomacy under President Obama (energetically implemented at the UN by his envoy Ambassador Susan Rice), who made nuclear nonproliferation, and in particular enlisting Russian and Chinese support for Council-based coercive diplomacy vis-à-vis Tehran, one of the top priorities of his first term. That effort yielded important results when the Council in 2010 imposed a new round of sanctions on Iran. It is well possible that the impact of those sanctions tipped the balance in Iran's 2013 presidential election in favor of moderate candidate Hassan Rouhani, who seemed to offer the best hope for his country to overcome the nuclear dispute with the Council.

Even before the cases of Iran and North Korea ended up on its agenda, the Council, in 2004, embarked on an ambitious effort to keep weapons of mass destruction out of terrorist hands. That year, after the discovery of the clandestine nuclear proliferation network operated by Pakistani nuclear scientist A. Q. Khan, the Council unanimously adopted the far-reaching landmark Resolution 1540, which requires all UN member states to take legislative and regulatory steps to prevent terrorists and other nonstate actors from getting their hands on weapons of mass destruction and their means of delivery.

Resolution 1540 was modeled after, and bore many similarities to, the Council's counterterror effort under Resolution 1373. Like Resolution 1373, it was legislative in nature (causing renewed unease among the member states about Council overreach), and led to the creation of a committee and monitoring mechanism that could help states with implementation of the resolution's onerous obligations. And as in the case of the 1373 regime, the Obama administration eventually concluded that while Resolution 1540 provided a useful normative framework, it was operationally too slow, bureaucratic, and tedious, leading the US government to establish a new initiative outside the UN framework, namely the Nuclear Security Summit process, meant to enhance international cooperation to prevent nuclear trafficking and terrorism.

Organized Crime, Drug Trafficking, and Piracy

Transnational organized crime, including drug trafficking, is a more recent addition to the agenda of the Security Council, and its treatment by the body exhibits a much lower degree of P5 consensus than in the fields of terrorism or weapons of mass destruction. Nevertheless, in the early 2000s the issue started increasingly to appear in the Council's country-specific discussions and peacekeeping mandates, reflecting the growing realization that organized crime was a destabilizing factor in many of the postconflict situations in which the Council was engaged. The United States and Russia emphasized the role of drug trafficking in funding terrorist groups in Afghanistan, while France (along with African nonpermanent members of the Council) played an important role in directing the Council's attention to the Europe-bound cocaine flows through West Africa, which also threaten to reverse peacebuilding progress in the region.

It was also these concerns that led the Council, after 2009, to address transnational organized crime and drug trafficking as a thematic issue, delinked from any particular country, region, or conflict. Between 2009 and 2013, the Council thus adopted a number of presidential statements calling on the UN to pay increasing attention to the issue in its reporting to the Council as well as in its conflict prevention and peacebuilding strategies. The fact that these calls were never enshrined in a Council resolution reflected the suspicions of the more sovereignty-conscious member states inside and outside the Council that it might once again start legislating on behalf of member states. These suspicions reached a boiling point when the United States, in 2012, introduced into the Council the issue of illicit cross-border trafficking, which led China and the Non-Aligned Movement to rebuke the United States for its attempt to have the Council encroach on both state sovereignty and the mandate of UN organs competent to deal with crime and justice matters.

Still, these concerns have not prevented the Council from developing innovative approaches to dealing with organized crime and trafficking in specific countries that, as James Cockayne points out in Chapter 15, draw "increasingly on domestic criminal justice discourse and techniques," including engaging in direct law enforcement. Depending on the setting, this could take the form of fact-finding (through panels of experts monitoring commodity sanctions), use of force by blue helmets against criminal groups (for instance MINUSTAH in the slums of Port-au-Prince), or the imposition of punitive sanctions against government officials suspected in drug trafficking (as in 2012 with respect to Guinea-Bissau).

In no area of organized crime was Council action as robust as in its response to piracy off the coast of Somalia, where the Council, in 2008, authorized states and regional organizations to use all necessary means "within the territorial waters of Somalia" to repress acts of piracy. Since then, the Council has authorized measures to be taken onshore in Somalia, while also encouraging regional capacity building to ensure maritime and land-based security, prosecution, transfer, and imprisonment of suspected and convicted pirates, and reiterating the need for targeting the financial and arms dealings of pirate gangs. Cockayne explains that the Council's unparalleled resolve on this issue is due to, among other things, the strong international consensus around the illegitimacy of piracy, the fact that acts on the high seas are not protected by sovereignty barriers, and the economic cost that piracy inflicts not only on the P5 but also on important NAM members, such as India.

Infectious Diseases

On rare occasions the Council has also addressed infectious diseases as a potential threat to international peace and security. In 2000, AIDS was strongly promoted in the Council as a critical security threat in Africa by the US permanent representative, the late Richard Holbrooke. Indeed, this saga reached its kinetic apogee when US vice president Al Gore, while pursuing his candidacy for the US presidency, chaired a Council meeting in January 2000 pressing for more international action on the disease. In light of complaints from many delegations questioning the link to international security and the Council's competence on this issue, the resolution that the Council eventually adopted, in July 2000, was anchored around "concern at the potential damaging impact of HIV/AIDS on the health of international peacekeeping personnel."[54] However, the operational effect of the resolution remained limited.[55]

While the Council occasionally returned to the AIDS issue without adding much in terms of a response mechanism, many member states remained apprehensive of any effort to further broaden the Council's purview in this area.[56] Indeed, in November 2011, when the Portuguese Council presidency organized a thematic debate around the issue of "emerging security threats" including pandemics, organized crime, and climate change, a number of Council members, including Brazil and India, refused to address the issues of pandemics and climate change in substantive terms, instead using their interventions to criticize the Council for even considering these issues in the first place.[57]

In light of these sensitivities, it is all the more remarkable that the Council, in September 2014, held an emergency meeting on the Ebola epidemic, in which it adopted a Chapter VII resolution declaring Ebola a threat to international peace and security.[58] The fact that this resolution attracted the highest number of cosponsors in the Council's history (134) was both a reflection of the seriousness with which the crisis was viewed by much of the world and a testament to the focused, high-intensity leadership of the United States, which had championed the resolution, the adoption of which coincided with a visit to the UN (and to the Security Council) by President Obama. Unlike the 2000 AIDS resolution, the Council's Ebola resolution was accompanied by an outburst of international activism, including the deployment of 3,000 US troops to the affected region to help with efforts to contain the spread of the disease as well as the establishment, by the Secretary-General, of the UN's first medical mission, the UN Mission for Ebola and Emergency Response (UNMEER).[59]

Reform

Security Council reform remains a live issue at the UN, and at regular intervals generates much excitement and attention as it moves to the forefront of the agenda—only to recede again to the backburner after failure to achieve progress.[60] The need and pressures for reform are real, and if anything the Security Council's failure in Syria has only added to these pressures, but inertia and P5 preferences have conspired against them.[61]

Most people—at least in the wider public—tend to equate Council reform with efforts to expand the Council's membership, in particular the number of its permanent seats. This is also the reform topic that has absorbed the most attention in New York and in capitals around the world. The central argument raised is that the composition of the P5, the victorious powers of World War II, no longer reflects today's distribution of power.

Some of the authors in this volume remind us that the composition of today's P5 is not quite as anachronistic as is sometimes suggested. Both the Charter and the Council's original conception indicate that permanent membership should be a reflection of a country's ability (and willingness) to maintain international peace and security. As of 2014, the existing P5 account for over 56 percent of the world's total defense spending, and the P3 are the world's top three actors in terms of capability and readiness to project military power globally. Yet as Bruce Jones concedes in Chapter 38, "much of what the Council does falls into the domain of diplomacy, not military might," so economic weight and political power have become relevant factors.

This is the case made by the so-called G4 grouping of aspirants for new permanent seats, Brazil, Germany, India, and Japan, all of which are among the world's top ten economic powers but each of which exhibits important limitations in its willingness or ability to deploy military power for UN enforcement action. The G4 tabled a reform blueprint in 2005 that also foresaw two permanent seats for Africa. The initiative, while attracting significant support among the wider membership, was aborted shortly thereafter, in part because the AU—unlike the G4—insisted on full veto rights for any new permanent members. As well, China at the time signaled strong opposition to close neighbor Japan's aspirations, thereby also scotching those of India, another neighbor with which China entertains significant boundary differences. While the G4 continue to lobby for their proposal, most members and observers of the UN are not holding their breath for fast-moving developments.

While the G4 proposal represents a balanced effort (other than refraining from insisting on the veto right, the effort included sensitive recommendations for the reform of working methods), it faces formidable political hurdles. First and foremost among them is the fact that the United States, China, and Russia (which on this issue have blocking power)[62] remain highly skeptical of adding new permanent members. Their combined lobbying power has arguably increased in recent years in light of China's growing influence in Africa. US opposition is strongly motivated by concerns over Council effectiveness (as expressed by Luck in this volume) and the increased difficulties it would face in enlisting the support of an expanded Council behind any of its endeavors. This concern only grew in light of strongly anti-interventionist positions displayed by India, Brazil, and South Africa (and to a lesser degree Germany) during Council debates on Libya and Syria.

A second major hurdle to reform is the fact that a number of powers that are regionally influential but that do not have a credible claim to occupy any newly created permanent seats (such as Italy, Spain, Pakistan, Mexico, Argentina, South Korea, Indonesia, and Turkey) oppose expansion of permanent membership, which they believe would result in a relative downgrading of their own status. Many of these states—along with others among the wider membership—object in principle to the very idea of permanent membership and feel that the granting of permanent privileges in 1945 was a historical mistake that should not be repeated. They thus tend to support reform models that would create a new category of longer-term seats, occupancy of which could rotate among each region's key powers.

Two authors in this volume propose very different reform models, which they suggest could attract sufficient support to overcome the reform logjam. Kishore Mahbubani, in Chapter 8, advocates for the expansion of the number of permanent members with veto rights as well as the creation of a new category of semipermanent seats, while Edward Luck, in Chapter 10, suggests that the most promising way forward would lie in increasing the number of nonpermanent seats, extending their term to three years and making them reelectable.

Meanwhile, in Chapter 9, Christian Wenaweser reminds us that a significant majority of member states, those that are too small to aspire to either a permanent or a longer-term seat and that are only rarely elected as nonpermanent members, have little to gain from reform of the Council's composition. Yet these states are often affected by Council decisions (e.g., as contributors of troops for peacekeeping operations or addressees of far-reaching "legislative" resolutions mentioned earlier). These states therefore tend to see an urgent need for reform of the Council's working methods and in particular measures to constrain the veto and increase the Council's transparency and to facilitate participation of non-Council members in the body's deliberations. The most significant such effort in recent years was the widely popular yet ultimately unsuccessful S5 initiative (referring to the "Small Five" countries leading it: Costa Rica, Jordan, Liechtenstein, Singapore, and Switzerland). The unqualified defeat of this brave "Lilliputian uprising"[63] by the P5, recounted in detail by Wenaweser, offers a telling case study of both the enduring influence of the P5 over large parts of the UN membership and the UN Secretariat, as well as their unity of purpose—even in times of rising great power tensions—when it comes to efforts to infringe on the exclusive control of the P5 over the Council's rules of procedure.

Legitimacy

The question of reform is often linked to the question of the Council's legitimacy, and the argument is often made that the former is necessary to maintain the latter. However, authors in this volume reflect a wide variety of views of the sources of the Council's legitimacy, partly accounting for differences in opinion on what perceived shortcomings reform should address. Legitimacy has been variously understood to be a function of the Council's representativeness, decisionmaking processes, respect for the rule of law, consistency, and performance in civilian protection.

Kishore Mahbubani, in Chapter 8, gives voice to the argument most often heard around the UN that the Council's legitimacy is most endangered by the fact that its composition is no longer perceived to be representative of today's world. Yet, while representativeness matters in terms of how the Council is perceived among the wider membership, an enlarged Council is unlikely to gain in legitimacy if representativeness comes at the cost of its ability to act decisively in the face of crisis.

Others, including Colin Keating and Christian Wenaweser, in Chapters 7 and 9 respectively, argue that it is the Council's secretive decisionmaking and P5 collusion that eat away at the Council's legitimacy. This resonates with Ian Hurd's study on the source of the Council's legitimacy, locating it in the Council's deliberative process in which the weaker feel their views have been adequately heard and considered.[64] In theory, Luck may be right that the Council gains much of its legitimacy from the fact that the majority of its members are nonpermanent ones who are elected by a two-thirds majority of the General Assembly. Yet if they are consistently marginalized in Council decisionmaking, the Council's image and credibility suffer.

In terms of legitimacy, a particular concern is the fact that the Council has repeatedly violated due process, human rights norms, and international law. Wenaweser cites the example of Resolution 1422 (2002), providing immunity to nationals of nonstate parties to the Rome Statute participating in Council-mandated peacekeeping operations in a manner widely considered to violate both the Rome Statute and the UN Charter. Equally if not more worrisome was the Council's disregard, mentioned earlier, of due process norms in the process of adding individuals to terrorism sanctions lists without giving them any legal recourse.

The Council's decisions are currently reviewed mainly by the media, scholars, and, over time, history. But unless it works harder to craft better decisions and to make a better case for them publicly, it could find itself facing more systematic judicial review, reluctant as the International Court of Justice has been to wade into these murky waters. Council dysfunction and mistakes create openings for other entrepreneurial international actors (like the European Court of Justice recently). Any Council delusions of unlimited power, especially in the service of weak arguments and questionable decisions, will create their own comeuppance.

Another standard complaint about the Council that is said to erode its legitimacy is the lack of consistency in its decisionmaking. And indeed, its biased treatment of different conflicts and its occasional displays of double standards are understandably grating to many member states. In particular, the more than a dozen US vetoes since the end of the Cold War blocking Council resolutions critical of Israel have been a bone of contention for many member states. While greater consistency is certainly desirable (and laws and norms, as Johnstone points out, work toward that end), authors in this volume have tended to agree that to expect the Council, as a political rather than a principled body, to act with perfect consistency, would be naive.

That said, one specific form of inconsistency is particularly damaging for the Council's legitimacy, namely its failure to respond to the worst mass atrocities. As Alex Bellamy and Paul Williams note in Chapter 34, "Global expectations about the UN's role in civilian protection have grown to such an extent that it is now commonly thought that the UN's legitimacy is determined by its performance in this area." Relative to this view, nothing has damaged the Council's legitimacy more than its inability to take appropriate action when genocide or mass atrocities were unfolding in Srebrenica, Rwanda, Kosovo, Darfur, Sri Lanka, and Syria. A French proposal, tabled in 2013, for the P5 to adopt a voluntary code of conduct to renounce the use of the veto in R2P situations where no vital interests are at stake, seems admirable, but it is highly unlikely to ever be supported by the United States, China, or Russia.[65]

Why does legitimacy matter? The perception that the Council's decisions are legitimate ensures that member states respect and implement them. Failure to implement and respect Council resolutions in itself has a delegitimizing effect on the body. As Hurd has pointed out elsewhere, this tends to be of great concern to the P5, who "rely on [the Council's] legitimacy to reduce their reliance on coercion to manage the international system." When their strategies and decisions ultimately fail to gain the respect of key member states—as when the Organization of African Unity, the AU's predecessor, decided to ignore UN sanctions against Libya in the 1990s—the P5 have often shown a willingness to readjust their strategies, as their "desire to defend the Council's legitimacy ultimately trumped their initial policy preferences."[66]

However, in other instances, some of the P5, individually or jointly with one or two others, have been willing to incur severe damage to Council legitimacy in pursuit of their policy preferences. How the P5 strike a balance between pursuing their own interests and preserving the Council's legitimacy will, to a large degree, determine the UN's relevance in peace and security in years to come.

Frozen Files

We have not written much or at all here about the Arab-Israeli conflicts, Kashmir, Cyprus, the Korean peninsula, and several other situations that are or have been on the Council's agenda and that, while at times showing some promise of resolution or alternatively flaring up every now or then, are essentially "frozen." The reason is that few in the Council, particularly among the P5, believe that these situations are, in fact, ripe for resolution and thus that new Council measures and decisions (rather than routine renewals of peacekeeping operations) are likely to be effective (even assuming they were desirable).

Notably, while acquiescing in sanctions and occasionally betraying impatience with Pyongyang, China has not been willing to consider more drastic measures. The same is true of the United States vis-à-vis Israel. As Markus Bouillon points out in Chapter 26 on the Arab-Israeli conflict, deep divisions on the ground are mirrored by divisions in the Council between the United States and the rest, limiting the Council to the role of shock absorber and preventing it from contributing to the conflict's decisive settlement. Meanwhile, Pakistan's frequent attempts to internationalize its dispute with India over Kashmir find few takers in the Council. Indeed, China, sometimes described as Pakistan's "all-weather friend" and in some respects a close ally, has acted prudently, indeed responsibly, in the face of Pakistani adventurism at Kargil in 1999 and after evidence emerged of the Pakistani origins of the Mumbai terrorist attackers in 2008.

Envoi

The UN's credibility is under ever greater strain as new threats to global health, to our ecosystem, and in other spheres beyond the security preoccupations at the heart of the Council's mandate meet a shrinking purse of those countries that have overwhelmingly funded UN activities since 1945. The slow-moving global financial and economic crisis since 2008, sparked in the West, has taken a heavy toll on the ability and willingness of those countries to take on additional international burdens, while emerging powers have not yet fully stepped up to help meet these challenges.

Indeed, whether and how the "status quo" powers can recognize and accept a different balance of power holds the answer to whether the post–World War II framework of multilateral institutions centered on the UN, but also including the International Monetary Fund (IMF), the World Bank, and the International Trade Organization, can continue as central actors in international relations. Breakthroughs on new approaches to governance, key in rebalancing such institutions, are more likely to be achieved at the IMF and World Bank first, but then the onus will be on the P5 to allow change within the Council as well. Are they up to it?

It is on this conundrum, as well as improved decisionmaking drawing on greater consensus within the Security Council on key challenges, that the continued relevance of the forum appears to hinge.

Notes

The authors would like to thank Louise Bosetti, Rahul Chandran, James Cockayne, John de Boer, Chantal Doran, Alexandra Ivanovic, Heiko Nitzschke, and Anthony Yazaki for helpful comments on this chapter.

1. Sebastian von Einsiedel et al., *Major Recent Trends in Violent Conflict* (Tokyo: United Nations University Center for Policy Research, February 2015). http://cpr.unu.edu/the-un-security-council-in-an-age-of-great-power-rivalry.html.

2. Robert Kagan, "Superpowers Don't Get to Retire: What Our Tired Country Still Owes the World," *New Republic,* May 26, 2014, www.newrepublic.com /article/117859/allure-normalcy-what-america-still-owes-world.

3. See the concluding chapter in David M. Malone, *The International Struggle over Iraq: Politics in the UN Security Council, 1980–2005* (Oxford: Oxford University Press, 2006).

4. David M. Malone, "Conclusion," in *The UN Security Council: From the Cold War to the 21st Century,* edited by David M. Malone (Boulder, CO: Lynne Rienner, 2004), p. 617.

5. United Nations Department of Political Affairs, "Highlights of Security Council Practice 2014," Security Council Affairs Division, New York, January 2015, http://www.un.org/en/sc/inc/pages/pdf/highlights/2014.pdf.

6. Security Council Report, "Non-Consensus Decision-Making in the Security Council: An Abridged History," January 2014, www.securitycouncilreport.org/atf /cf/%7B65BFCF9B-6D27-4E9C-8CD3-CF6E4FF96FF9%7D/January _2014_Insert .pdf.

7. Bruce Jones, *Still Ours to Lead: America, Rising Powers, and the Tension Between Rivalry and Restraint* (Washington, DC: Brookings Institution, 2014).

8. See United Nations Meetings Coverage and Press Releases, "Resolution in Security Council to Impose 12-Month Deadline on Negotiated Solution to Israeli-Palestinian Conflict Unable to Secure Nine Votes Needed for Adoption," UN Doc. SC/11722, December 30, 2014.

9. Since the late 2000s, the Department of Political Affairs has been headed by a US national, the Department for Peacekeeping Operations by a French national, and the Office for the Coordination of Humanitarian Affairs by a British national.

10. Peter Wallensteen and Patrik Johannsson shared with the coeditors the raw data underpinning Figure 2.5 in their chapter. The raw data covering the years 2003–2012 show 404 resolutions on intrastate conflicts over control of government, plus 93 on intrastate conflicts over territory, adding up to a total of 497 resolutions on civil wars, which constitutes 79 percent of the total of 630 resolutions adopted during the period.

11. United Nations High-Level Panel on Threats, Challenges, and Change, *A More Secure World: Our Shared Responsibility* (New York, December 2004); Human Security Report Project, *Human Security Report 2013: The Decline in Global Violence: Evidence, Explanation, and Contestation* (Vancouver: Human Security Press, 2013); Page Fortna, *Does Peacekeeping Work? Shaping Belligerents' Choice After Civil War* (Princeton: Princeton University Press, 2008); James Dobbins and Laurel Miller, "Overcoming Obstacles to Peace," *Survival* 55, no. 1 (February 2013): 103–120; Michael Doyle and Nicholas Sambanis, *Making War and Building Peace* (Princeton: Princeton University Press, 2006).

12. von Einsiedel et al., *Major Recent Trends in Violent Conflict.*

13. James Fearon, "Why Do Some Civil Wars Last So Much Longer Than Others?" *Journal of Peace Research* 41, no. 3 (May 2004): 275–301. See also Karen Ballentine and Heiko Nitzschke, eds., *Profiting from Peace: Managing the Resource Dimensions of Civil War* (Boulder, CO: Lynne Rienner, 2005); von Einsiedel et al., *Major Recent Trends in Violent Conflict.*

14. Human Security Report Project, *Human Security Report 2013: The Decline in Global Violence—Evidence, Explanation and Contestation* (Vancouver: Human

Security Press, 2014), p. 90; David E. Cunningham, "Blocking Resolution: How External States Can Prolong Civil Wars," *Journal of Peace Research* 47, no. 2 (2010): 115–127.

15. von Einsiedel et al., *Major Recent Trends in Violent Conflict;* Lotta Themner and Peter Wallensteen, "Armed Conflicts, 1946–2013," *Journal of Peace Research* 51, no. 4 (July 2014): 541–554.

16. United Nations Secretary-General's Internal Review Panel, *Report of the Secretary-General's Internal Review Panel on United Nations Action in Sri Lanka,* November 2012, www.un.org/News/dh/infocus/Sri_Lanka/The_Internal_Review _Panel_report_on_Sri_Lanka.pdf. See also Security Council Report, "Update Report no. 5: Sri Lanka," April 21, 2009, www.securitycouncilreport.org/update -report/lookup-c-glKWLeMTIsG-b-5113231.php.

17. In Korea (1950), Iraq (1990), Somalia (1992), Haiti (1993), Bosnia (1995), Eastern Slavonia (1997), and Côte d'Ivoire (2011).

18. Edward C. Luck, *UN Security Council: Practice and Promise* (London: Routledge, 2006), pp. 21–23.

19. See Elizabeth Cousens, "Conflict Prevention," in Malone, *The UN Security Council,* p. 105.

20. The UK, for instance, started pushing the Council around that time to ask missions to develop benchmarks measuring peacebuilding progress in host countries as a tool to argue for withdrawal.

21. Richard Gowan, "Floating Down the River of History: Ban Ki-moon and Peacekeeping, 2007–2011," *Global Governance* 17, no. 4 (October–December 2011): 400.

22. While in 1994 there were nine NATO members among the top twenty troop-contributing countries, that number had shrunk to zero in 2014, by which time nineteen of the top twenty troop-contributing countries were Asian or African (with four of the top five being South Asian). By implication, the P5, too, have turned their backs on peacekeeping. While in December 1994 France, the United Kingdom, Russia, and the United States were all among the top twenty-five troop contributors, twenty years later none of them ranked among the top forty.

23. The UK, for instance, counts seven distinct models, but member states and experts have their own count. See Security Council, "Provisional Verbatim Record of 7196th Meeting," S/PV.719 6, June 11, 2014, p. 12.

24. According to a 2010 internal analysis of the UN Department of Peacekeeping Operations, these tasks were given to at least nine of the seventeen peacekeeping operations deployed at the time. UN Department of Peacekeeping Operations, unpublished paper.

25. The French permanent representative to the UN, Ambassador Gérard Arraud, insisted at a Council debate on peacekeeping in June 2014 that "peacekeepers' operational priority must always be the protection of civilians."

26. According to an internal and unpublished DPKO analysis, the mandates of UNTAET, MONUC, UNMIL, UNOCI, MINUSTAH, UNAMID, MONUSCO, UNISFA, and UNMISS all featured more enforcement elements than any but four UN peacekeeping missions established between 1945 and 1999 (ONUC, UNPROFOR, UNTAC, UNOSOM II).

27. United Nations General Assembly and Security Council, *Report of the Panel on United Nations Peace Operations* (Brahimi Report), UN Doc. A/55/305-S/2000/809, August 21, 2000; United Nations High-Level Panel on Threats, Challenges, and Change, *A More Secure World.*

28. By mid-2014, two-thirds of peacekeeping personnel were deployed in five

theaters of operation that experienced significant levels of active violence: Darfur, South Sudan, Mali, the Central African Republic, and the Democratic Republic of the Congo. See Secretary-General Ban Ki-moon's speech to the UN Security Council in United Nations Security Council, "Provisional Verbatim Record of the 7196th Meeting," p. 2.

29. At a thematic Council debate in June 2014 on UN peacekeeping, the member states who took the floor to voice their concern over the trend toward robust peacekeeping, and the mandate of the Force Intervention Brigade in particular, included India, Pakistan, China, Guatemala, Thailand, the Philippines, Peru, Uruguay, and Indonesia. See United Nations Security Council, "Provisional Verbatim Record of the 7196th Meeting."

30. For instance, at a thematic Council debate on peacekeeping in June 2014, the Chilean ambassador suggested that "should the use of force be authorized, we believe that neighboring countries and countries of the subregion should not undertake the tasks that involve the use of force." See United Nations Security Council, "Provisional Verbatim Record of the 7196th Meeting."

31. Ian Johnstone, "Managing Consent in Contemporary Peacekeeping Operations," *International Peacekeeping* 18, no. 2 (April 2011): 168–182.

32. United Nations Security Council Resolution 1645 (December 20, 2005), UN Doc. S/RES/1645.

33. Address by UK ambassador Lyall Grant at authors' meeting for this volume at Greentree Estate, New York, June 14, 2013.

34. Fabienne Hara, "Preventive Diplomacy in Africa: Adapting to New Realities," in *Preventive Diplomacy: Regions in Focus,* edited by Francesco Mancini (New York: International Peace Institute, December 2011), pp. 4–14, www.ipinst .org/media/pdf/publications/ipi_epub_preventive_diplomacy.pdf.

35. Arthur Boutellis and Paul Williams, *Peace Operations, the African Union, and the United Nations: Toward More Effective Partnerships* (New York: International Peace Institute, 2013).

36. The rapid and largely improvised deployment of human rights observers in Haiti in 1993, in fact a joint OAS-UN operation, was eventually subsumed into a Security Council strategy. But its dispatch was initially engineered largely through the consent of both the legitimate government (in exile) and the military junta that had displaced it, and cobbled together from disparate sources and financial resources, demonstrating that multilateral organizations can be both nimble and creative with the right leadership, member-state support, and incentives. See David M. Malone, *Decision-Making in the UN Security Council: The Case of Haiti* (Oxford: Clarendon, 1998), pp. 79–80.

37. The exercise of jurisdiction over the crime of aggression, which was only defined at a review conference of the state parties to the Rome Statute in Kampala, May 31–June 11, 2010, is subject to a further vote by the General Assembly after January 1, 2017.

38. United Nations Security Council Resolution 1593, S/RES/1593 (March 31, 2005).

39. United Nations Security Council Resolution 1970, S/RES/1970 (February 26, 2011).

40. Till Papenfuss, "The Relationship Between the ICC and the Security Council: Challenges and Opportunities," meeting note of roundtable discussion hosted by the International Peace Institute and the Permanent Mission of Liechtenstein to the UN, November 8, 2012 (New York: March 2013), http://www.ipinst.org/2013/03/the -relationship-between-the-icc-and-the-security-council-challenges-and-opportunities.

41. United Nations Security Council, "Provisional Verbatim Record of the 7060th Meeting," UN Doc. S/PV.7060, November 15, 2013.

42. David Cortright and George A. Lopez, *The Sanctions Decade: Assessing UN Strategies in the 1990s* (Boulder, CO: Lynne Rienner, 2000).

43. Alexandra dos Reis Stefanopoulos and George Lopez, "Getting Smarter About Sanctions: Has Security Council Learning Occurred in Targeted Sanctions, 1993–2013?" paper presented at the annual convention of the International Studies Association, April 2012.

44. However, as of November 2014, the following four sanctions regimes did not have a dedicated committee: Iraq, Lebanon, Yemen, and Guinea-Bissau.

45. Colum Lynch, "China's Arms Exports Flooding Sub-Saharan Africa," *Washington Post,* August 25, 2012, www.washingtonpost.com/world/national-security /chinas-arms-exports-flooding-sub-saharan-africa/2012/08/25/16267b68-e7f1-11e1 -936a-b801f1abab19_story.html.

46. Interview with Sebastian von Einsiedel, New York, September 20, 2014.

47. David Cortright and George A. Lopez, "Reforming Sanctions," in Malone, *The UN Security Council.*

48. The high-level review was initiated by the governments of Australia, Finland, Germany, Greece, and Sweden, in partnership with the Watson Institute of Brown University and Compliance and Capacity International. See www.hlr-un sanctions.org.

49. Edward C. Luck, "Tackling Terrorism," in Malone, *The UN Security Council,* p. 85.

50. Eric Rosand and Sebastian von Einsiedel, "9/11, the War on Terror, and the Evolution of Multilateral Institutions," in *Cooperation for Peace and Security,* edited by Bruce Jones, Shepard Forman, and Richard Gowan (Cambridge: Cambridge University Press, 2010), p. 145.

51. See Juliane Kokott and Christoph Sobotta, "The *Kadi* Case: Constitutional Core Values and International Law—Finding the Balance?" *European Journal of International Law* 23, no. 4 (2012): 1015–1024.

52. Colum Lynch and Elias Groll, "Obama's Foreign Fighters Campaign Is a Gift to the World's Police States," *Foreign Policy,* September 30, 2014.

53. For greater depth and detail, see Malone, *The International Struggle over Iraq.*

54. United Nations Security Council Resolution 1308, S/RES/1308 (July 17, 2000).

55. Nonconventional security issues first reared their head in the Council in the late 1980s when the UK, represented by Crispin Tickell, a keen environmentalist, argued that the Council should concern itself with ecological threats. This was coolly received by other delegations, not least those of the G-77 and the Non-Aligned Movement, which considered environmental protection as squarely within the ambit of the Economic and Social Council and of the General Assembly.

56. Security Council Report, "In Hindsight: The Security Council and Health Crises," October 2014 Monthly Forecast, September 30, 2014, www.security councilreport.org/monthly-forecast/2014-10/in_hindsight_the_security_council _and_health_crises.php.

57. United Nations Security Council, "Provisional Verbatim Record of the 6668th Meeting," UN Doc. S/PV.6668, November 23, 2011.

58. United Nations Security Council Resolution 2177, S/RES/2177 (September 18, 2014).

59. United Nations General Assembly and Security Council, "Identical Letters

Dated 17 September 2014 from the Secretary-General Addressed to the President of the General Assembly and the President of the Security Council," UN Doc. A/69/380-S/2014/679, September 18, 2014.

60. Jonas von Freiesleben, "Reform of the Security Council," in *Managing Change at the United Nations* (New York: Center for UN Reform Education, 2008).

61. Richard Gowan and Nora Gordon, *Pathways to Security Council Reform* (New York: Center on International Cooperation, 2014).

62. According to Article 108 of the UN Charter, for any amendments to become effective, they have to garner a two-thirds majority vote in the General Assembly, and be "ratified in accordance with their respective constitutional processes" by two-thirds of UN members, "including all the permanent members of the Security Council."

63. Colum Lynch, "Rise of the Lilliputians," *Foreign Policy,* May 10, 2012.

64. Ian Hurd, *After Anarchy: Legitimacy and Power in the United Nations Security Council* (Princeton: Princeton University Press, 2007).

65. Laurent Fabius, "A Call for Self-Restraint at the U.N.," *New York Times,* October 4, 2013, www.nytimes.com/2013/10/04/opinion/a-call-for-self-restraint-at -the-un.html?_r=0.

66. Hurd, *After Anarchy,* p. 178.

Appendixes

Appendix 1 Security Council–Mandated UN Peacekeeping Operations and Observer Missions, 1945–2014

Name (original mandating Security Council Resolutions)	Location	Time	Mandate	Maximum Number of Deployed Troops / Military Observers / Civilian Police / Civilian Staff (national and international)[a]	Chapter VII?
1945–1987					
UNTSO (Resolution 50)	Middle East	Since June 1948	Assist UN mediator and Truce Commission in supervising observance of the truce in Palestine. Since, UNTSO has performed various tasks entrusted to it by the Security Council, including supervision of the General Armistice Agreements of 1949 and observation of the ceasefire in the Suez Canal area and the Golan Heights following the Arab-Israeli War of June 1967. At present, UNTSO assists and cooperates with UNDOF on the Golan Heights in the Israel-Syria sector, and with UNIFIL in the Israel-Lebanon sector. UNTSO is also present in the Egypt-Israel sector in the Sinai.	— / 562 / — / 236	
UNMOGIP (Resolutions 47, 91)	India/Pakistan	Since January 1949	Supervise ceasefire between India and Pakistan in the state of Jammu and Kashmir.	— / 102 / — / 94	
UNOGIL (Resolution 128)	Lebanon-Syria border areas	June–December 1958	Ensure no illegal infiltration of personnel or supply of arms or other matériel across Lebanese borders.	— / 591 / — / —	
ONUC (Resolutions 143, 169)	Republic of Congo (now Democratic Republic of the Congo)	July 1960–June 1964	Ensure withdrawal of Belgian forces, assist the government in maintaining law and order, and provide technical assistance. The function of ONUC was subsequently modified to include maintaining the territorial integrity and political independence of the Congo, preventing the occurrence of civil war, and securing removal of all foreign military, paramilitary, and advisory personnel not under the UN command, and removal of all mercenaries.	19,828 / — / — / —	Yes[b]
UNYOM (Resolution 179)	Yemen	July 1963–September 1964	Observe and certify implementation of disengagement agreement between Saudi Arabia and the United Arab Republic.	— / 1,895 / — / 48	

878

continues

Operation	Location	Dates	Mandate	Numbers
UNFICYP (Resolution 186)	Cyprus	Since March 1964	Originally established to prevent recurrence of fighting between the Greek Cypriot and Turkish Cypriot communities and contribute maintenance and restoration of law and order and a return to normal conditions. Following the hostilities of 1974, the Security Council adopted a number of resolutions expanding the mandate of UNFICYP to include supervising a de facto ceasefire that came into effect on August 16, 1974, and maintaining a buffer zone between the lines of the Cyprus national guard and of the Turkish and Turkish Cypriot forces.	6,411 / 12 / 175 / 366
DOMREP (Resolution 203)	Dominican Republic	May 1965–October 1966	Observe the situation and report on breaches of ceasefire between the two de facto authorities in the Dominican Republic.	—/ 2 / — / small number of support staff
UNIPOM (Resolution 211)	Along India-Pakistan border between Kashmir and Arabian Sea	September 1965–March 1966	Supervise ceasefire along the India-Pakistan border except in the state of Jammu and Kashmir, where UNMOGIP operated, and supervise withdrawal of all armed personnel to their positions as held before August 5, 1965.	—/ 96 / — / 60
UNEF II[c] (Resolution 340)	Suez Canal sector and later Sinai Peninsula	October 1973–July 1979	Supervise ceasefire between Egyptian and Israeli forces and, following the conclusion of the agreements of January 18, 1974, and September 4, 1975, supervise redeployment of Egyptian and Israeli forces and control the buffer zones established under those agreements.	6,973/ —/ — / —
UNDOF (Resolution 350)	Syrian Golan Heights	Since June 1974	Maintain ceasefire between Israel and Syria, supervise disengagement of Israeli and Syrian forces, and supervise areas of separation and limitation, as provided in the disengagement agreement.	1,450 / — / — / 160
UNIFIL (Resolutions 425, 426)	Lebanon	Since March 1978	Confirm withdrawal of Israeli forces from southern Lebanon, restore international peace and security, and assist the government of Lebanon in ensuring the return of its effective authority in the area. Resolution 1701 (2006) expanded the mandate to include monitoring of cessation of hostilities, assistance to Lebanese Armed Forces (LAF) in their southern deployment as Israeli forces withdraw, extended assistance for humanitarian access and voluntary return of displaced people, and assisted government of Lebanon in securing its borders and other entry points.	13,264 / — / — / 1,021

Appendix 1 continued

Name (original mandating Security Council Resolutions)	Location	Time	Mandate	Maximum Number of Deployed Troops / Military Observers / Civilian Police / Civilian Staff (national and international)[a]	Chapter VII?
1987					
UNGOMAP (Resolution 622)	Afghanistan/ Pakistan	May 1988–March 1990	Assist in ensuring implementation of the settlement agreements related to Afghanistan and in this context monitor (1) noninterference and nonintervention by the parties in each other's affairs, (2) withdrawal of Soviet troops from Afghanistan, and (3) voluntary return of refugees.	— / 50 / — / small civilian auxiliary staff	
UNIIMOG (Resolution 619)	Iran/Iraq	August 1988– February 1991	Verify, confirm, and supervise ceasefire and withdrawal of all forces to the internationally recognized boundaries, pending a comprehensive settlement.	— / 400 / — / 236	
UNAVEM I (Resolution 626)	Angola	December 1988–May 1991	Verify withdrawal of Cuban troops.	— / 70 / — / 37	
1989					
UNTAG (Resolution 632)	Namibia	April 1989–March 1990	Assist the SRSG to ensure the early independence of Namibia through free and fair elections under the supervision and control of the UN.	4,493 / — / 1,500 / 2,000 (plus 1,695 electoral observers during election)	
ONUCA (Resolution 644)	Central America	November 1989– January 1992	Verify compliance by the governments of Costa Rica, El Salvador, Guatemala, Honduras, and Nicaragua with ceasing aid to irregular forces and insurrectionist movements in the region, and not allowing their territory to be used for attacks on other states.	800 / 260 / — / 184	
1991					
UNIKOM (Resolutions 689, 806)	Iraq/Kuwait	April 1991–October 2003	Monitor demilitarized zone along boundary between Iraq and Kuwait and the Khawr 'Abd Allah waterway, deter violations of the boundary, and observe any hostile action mounted from the	933 / 300 / — / 229	Yes

Operation (Resolution)	Location	Dates	Mandate	Numbers
MINURSO (Resolution 690)	Western Sahara	Since April 1991	territory of one state against the other. In February 1993 the mandate was extended to include the capacity to take physical action to prevent violations of the demilitarized zone and of the newly demarcated boundary between Iraq and Kuwait. In accordance with the settlement proposals as accepted on August 30, 1988, by Morocco and the Frente Polisario, the mandate provided for a transitional period during which the SRSG would have sole and exclusive responsibility over all matters related to a referendum in which the people of Western Sahara would choose between independence and integration with Morocco. MINURSO has been mandated to monitor the ceasefire, verify the reduction of Moroccan troops in the territory, monitor the confinement of Moroccan and Frente Polisario troops to designated locations, take steps with the parties to ensure the release of all Western Saharan political prisoners or detainees, oversee the exchange of prisoners of war (ICRC), implement the repatriation program (UNHCR), identify and register qualified voters, organize and ensure a free and fair referendum, and proclaim the results.	242 / 240 / 98 / 267
UNAVEM II (Resolution 696)	Angola	June 1991–February 1995	Verify peace agreement by UNITA and the government of Angola, monitor ceasefire and the Angolan police, and observe and verify elections.	11 / 210 / 126 / 242 (plus 400 electoral observers)
ONUSAL (Resolutions 693, 729)	El Salvador	July 1991–April 1995	Verify implementation of all agreements between the government of El Salvador and the FMLN. The agreements involved a ceasefire and related measures, reform and reduction of the armed forces, creation of a new police force, and reform of the judicial and electoral systems, human rights, land tenure, and other economic and social issues.	— / 368 / 315 / 101 (plus 900 local observers during election)
UNAMIC (Resolution 717)	Cambodia	October 1991–March 1992	Assist the four Cambodian parties to maintain their ceasefire during the period prior to the establishment and deployment of UNTAC, and initiate mine-awareness training of civilian populations. Later the mandate was enlarged to include a major training program for Cambodians in mine detection and mine clearance in regard to repatriation routes, reception centers, and resettlement areas.	1,090 / — / — / 184[d]

Appendix 1 continued

Name (original mandating Security Council Resolutions)	Location	Time	Mandate	Maximum Number of Deployed Troops / Military Observers / Civilian Police / Civilian Staff (national and international)[a]	Chapter VII?
1992					
UNPROFOR (Resolutions 743, 776, 795, 982)	Former Yugoslavia	February 1992–March 1995	Initially established in Croatia to ensure demilitarization of designated areas. The mandate was later extended to Bosnia and Herzegovina to support the delivery of humanitarian relief and to monitor no-fly zones and safe areas. Subsequently the mandate was again extended to the former Yugoslav Republic of Macedonia for preventive monitoring in border areas.	38,332 / 693 / 803 / 4,632	Yes
UNTAC (Resolution 745)	Cambodia	March 1992–September 1993	Ensure implementation of the Paris Accords, including human rights monitoring, organization of elections, maintenance of law and order, repatriation and resettlement of refugees and internally displaced persons, and rehabilitation of Cambodian infrastructure.	15,991 / — / 3,600 / 1,580 plus approx.7,000 local staff assisting during election	
UNOSOM I (Resolution 751)	Somalia	April 1992–March 1993	Monitor ceasefire in Mogadishu and escort deliveries of humanitarian supplies to distribution centers in the city. The mission's mandate and strength were later enlarged to enable it to protect humanitarian convoys and distribution centers throughout Somalia. It later worked with UNITAF in the effort to establish a safe environment for the delivery of humanitarian assistance.	893 / 54 / — / 79	
ONUMOZ (Resolutions 797, 898)	Mozambique	December 1992–December 1994	Help implement the general peace agreement, monitor ceasefire and withdrawal of foreign troops and provide security in transport corridors, provide technical assistance, and monitor the entire electoral process.	6,576 / 204 / 1,087 / 861 (plus approx. 900 electoral observers during election)	
1993					
UNOSOM II (Resolution 814)	Somalia	March 1993–March 1995	Establish throughout Somalia a secure environment for humanitarian assistance. To that end, UNOSOM II was to complete, through disarmament and reconciliation, the task	25,747 / — / 41 / 499	Yes

begun by UNITAF for the restoration of peace, stability, and law and order.

Mission	Location	Dates	Mandate	Numbers
UNOMUR (Resolution 846)	Rwanda/Uganda	June 1993–September 1994	Monitor border between Uganda and Rwanda and verify that no military assistance was provided across it.	— / 81 / 60 / 22
UNOMIG (Resolutions 849, 858)	Georgia	August 1993–June 2009	Verify compliance with ceasefire agreement between the government of Georgia and the Abkhaz authorities in Georgia. UNOMIG's mandate was expanded following the signing by the parties of the 1994 agreement on a ceasefire and separation of forces.	— / 134 / 16 / 313
UNOMIL (Resolution 866)	Liberia	September 1993–September 1997	Exercise good offices in support of ECOWAS efforts to implement the peace agreement, investigate alleged ceasefire violations, assist in demobilization of combatants, support humanitarian assistance, and investigate human rights violations.	65 / 368 / — / 667
UNMIH (Resolution 867)	Haiti	September 1993–June 1996	Help implement provisions of the Governor's Island Agreement of July 3, 1993. The mandate was later revised to assist the democratic government to sustain a stable environment, professionalize the armed forces and create a separate police force, and establish an environment conducive to free and fair elections.	6,000 / 18 / 850 / 619
UNAMIR (Resolution 872)	Rwanda	October 1993–March 1996	Originally established to help implement the peace agreement signed by the Rwandese parties at Arusha on August 4, 1993. UNAMIR's mandate and strength were adjusted on a number of occasions in the face of the tragic events of the genocide and the changing situation in the country.	5,740 / 309 / 120 / 320
UNASOG (Resolution 915)	Aouzou Strip, Republic of Chad	May–June 1994	Verify withdrawal of Libyan administration and forces from the Aouzou Strip in accordance with the ICJ decision.	— / 9 / — / 6
UNMOT (Resolutions 968, 1138)	Tajikistan	December 1994–May 2000	Monitor ceasefire agreement between the government of Tajikistan and the United Tajik Opposition. Following the signing by the parties of the 1997 general peace agreement, UNMOT's mandate was expanded to help monitor its implementation.	— / 81 / 2 / 170
1995				
UNAVEM III (Resolution 976)	Angola	February 1995–June 1997	Assist the government of Angola and UNITA in restoring peace and achieving national reconciliation on the basis of the 1991 peace accords and the 1994 Lusaka Protocol.	6,709 / 349 / 296 / 679

continues

Name (original mandating Security Council Resolutions)	Location	Time	Mandate	Maximum Number of Deployed Troops / Military Observers / Civilian Police / Civilian Staff (national and international)[a]	Chapter VII?
UNCRO (Resolution 981)	Croatia	March 1995–January 1996	Replacing UNPROFOR in Croatia, UNCRO's task was to perform the functions envisaged in the ceasefire agreement of March 29, 1994; facilitate implementation of the economic agreement of December 2, 1994; monitor the crossing of military equipment and personnel over specified international borders; facilitate humanitarian assistance to Bosnia and Herzegovina through the territory of Croatia; and monitor the demilitarization of the Prevlaka Peninsula.	3,294 / 290 / 168 / —	Yes
UNPREDEP (Resolution 983)	Former Yugoslav Republic of Macedonia	March 1995–February 1999	Monitor and report any developments in the border areas that could undermine confidence and stability in the former Yugoslav Republic of Macedonia and threaten its territory.	1,120 / 35 / 26 / 203	
UNMIBH (Resolution 1035)	Bosnia and Herzegovina	December 1995–December 2002	Exercise a wide range of functions related to law enforcement activities and police reform in Bosnia and Herzegovina, and coordinate other UN activities in the country related to humanitarian relief and refugees, demining, human rights, elections, and economic reconstruction.	5 / 5 / 2,057 / 1,569	
1996					
UNTAES (Resolution 1037)	Eastern Slavonia, Croatia	January 1996–January 1998	Supervise and facilitate demilitarization, monitor return of refugees, contribute to the maintenance of peace and security, establish a temporary police force, undertake tasks related to civil administration and public services, and organize elections.	4,791 / 100 / 453 / 1,231	Yes
UNMOP (Resolution 1038)	Prevlaka Peninsula, southern border between Croatia and Federal Republic of Yugoslavia	January 1996–December 2002	Taking over from UNCRO, UNMOP had the task to monitor demilitarization of the Prevlaka Peninsula.	— / 28 / — / 9[d]	

continues

Mission (Resolution)	Country	Dates	Mandate	Numbers
UNSMIH (Resolution 1063)	Haiti	July 1996–July 1997	Assist the government of Haiti in professionalization of the police and maintenance of a secure and stable environment.	1,287 / — / 267 / 275[d]
1997				
MINUGUA (Resolution 1094)	Guatemala	January 1997–May 1997	Verify agreement on the definitive ceasefire between the government of Guatemala and the Guatemalan National Revolutionary Unity (URNG) party, signed in Oslo on December 4, 1996. Verification functions included observation of a formal cessation of hostilities, separation of forces, and demobilization of URNG combatants.	— / 132 / 51 / 277
MONUA (Resolution 1118)	Angola	June 1997–February 1999	Assist Angolan parties in consolidating peace and national reconciliation, enhancing confidence building, and creating an environment conducive to long-term stability, democratic development, and rehabilitation of the country.	4,433 / 302 / 361 / —
UNTMIH (Resolution 1123)	Haiti	August 1997–December 1997	Support and contribute to professionalization of Haiti's national police force.	1,175[e] / — / 242 / —
MIPONUH (Resolution 1141)	Haiti	December 1997–March 2000	Assist government of Haiti in professionalization of the national police force.	— / — / 284 / 195[d]
1998				
UNPSG (Resolution 1145)	Croatia	January 1998–October 1998	Taking over from UNTAES, UNPSG's mandate was to continue monitoring the performance of the Croatian police in the Danube region, particularly with respect to the return of displaced persons, for a single nine-month period.	— / — / 177 / 208[d]
MINURCA (Resolution 1159)	Central African Republic	April 1998–February 2000	Assist with maintaining and enhancing security and stability in Bangui and vicinity, disarmament, capacity building of national police, and electoral assistance.	1,347 / — / 22 / 225[d]
UNOMSIL (Resolution 1181)	Sierra Leone	July 1998–October 1999	Monitor military and security situation in Sierra Leone, as well as disarmament and demobilization of former combatants, and assist in monitoring respect for international humanitarian law.	15 / 192 / 5 / 173[d]

Appendix 1 continued

Name (original mandating Security Council Resolutions)	Location	Time	Mandate	Maximum Number of Deployed Troops / Military Observers / Civilian Police / Civilian Staff (national and international)[a]	Chapter VII?
1999					
UNMIK (Resolution 1244)	Kosovo	Since June 1999	Perform civilian administration functions, maintain law and order, promote human rights, and ensure safe return of refugees and displaced persons. UNMIK's mandate has been altered to monitoring and supporting local institutions and supporting security, stability, and human rights.	37 / 40 / 4,519 / 4,575	Yes
UNAMSIL (Resolutions 1270, 1289)	Sierra Leone	October 1999– December 2005	Originally established to cooperate with the government of Sierra Leone and the other parties to the Lomé Agreement in implementation of the agreement, and to assist the government of Sierra Leone in implementing the DDR program. In 2000 the mandate was revised to include providing security at key locations and government buildings; facilitating the free flow of people, goods, and humanitarian assistance along specified thoroughfares; providing security at all sites of the DDR program; coordinating with and assisting the Sierra Leone law enforcement authorities in the discharge of their responsibilities; and guarding and destroying collected armaments.	17,105 / 269 / 130 / 893	Yes
UNTAET (Resolution 1272)	East Timor	October 1999–May 2002	Administer the territory, exercise legislative and executive authority, and support capacity building for self-government during the transition period toward independence, for which the people of East Timor voted on August 30, 1999.	8,950 / 200 / 1,640 / 2,668	Yes
MONUC (Resolution 1279)	Congo	November 1999– June 2010	Monitor implementation of ceasefire agreement, investigate violations of the agreement, work with the parties to obtain the release of all prisoners of war and military captives, supervise and verify disengagement and redeployment of the parties' forces, monitor compliance with the provision of the ceasefire	18,646 / 705 / 1,216 / 3,769	Yes

agreement on the supply of war-related matériel to the field, facilitate humanitarian assistance and human rights monitoring, with particular attention to vulnerable groups, and demining.

Mission	Location	Dates	Mandate	Strength	
2000					
UNMEE (Resolutions 1312, 1430)	Ethiopia/Eritrea	July 2000–July 2008	Maintain liaison with the parties and establish a mechanism for verifying the June 2000 ceasefire between Eritrea and Ethiopia. The mandate was later extended to include deployment within UNMEE of up to 4,300 military personnel to monitor the cessation of hostilities and to help ensure the observance of security commitments.	4,013 / 219 / — / 508	
2002					
UNMISET (Resolution 1410)	East Timor	May 2002–May 2005	Provide assistance to core administrative structures critical to the viability and political stability of East Timor, provide interim law enforcement and public security to assist in the development of a new law enforcement agency in East Timor, and contribute to maintenance of the external and internal security.	4,665 / 111 / 771 / 1,321	Yes
2003					
MINUCI (Resolution 1479)	Côte d'Ivoire	May 2003–April 2004	Facilitate the implementation by the Ivorian parties of the Linas-Marcoussis Agreement.	— / 75 / — / 99	Yes
UNMIL (Resolution 1509)	Liberia	Since September 2003	Support implementation of ceasefire agreement and the peace process, support humanitarian and human rights activities, and assist in national security reform, including training of national police and formation of a new and restructured military.	14,824 / 250 / 1,454 / 2,151	Yes
2004					
UNOCI (Resolution 1528)	Côte d'Ivoire	Since April 2004	Monitor ceasefire agreement and prevent movement of combatants and arms across shared borders with Liberia and Sierra Leone, assist the interim government of national reconciliation, and facilitate provision of humanitarian assistance.	9,419 / 199 / 1,370 / 1,204	Yes
MINUSTAH (Resolution 1542)	Haiti	Since June 2004	Ensure a secure and stable environment to enable the peace process to be carried forward, assist the government's efforts in national	8,743 / — / 3,534 / 1,991	Yes

continues

Appendix 1 continued

Name (original mandating Security Council Resolutions)	Location	Time	Mandate	Maximum Number of Deployed Troops / Military Observers / Civilian Police / Civilian Staff (national and international)[a]	Chapter VII?
			security reform, assist with the restoration and maintenance of rule of law, and support humanitarian and human rights activities. Resolution 1892 tasked MINUSTAH with supporting the Haitian political process and providing logistical and security assistance for anticipated elections. Resolution 1908 increased overall force levels to support recovery, reconstruction, and stability efforts following the 2010 earthquake.		
ONUB (Resolution 1545)	Burundi	June 2004–December 2006	Ensure respect of ceasefire agreement, promote reestablishment of confidence between the Burundian forces through a comprehensive program, and assist in successful completion of the electoral process.	5,378 / 182 / 89 / 785	Yes
2005					
UNMIS (Resolution 1590)	Sudan	March 2005–July 2011	Support implementation of the Comprehensive Peace Agreement; perform certain functions relating to humanitarian assistance, protection, and promotion of human rights; and support AMIS.	9,390 / 577 / 693 / 3,835	Yes
2006					
UNMIT (Resolution 1704)	Timor-Leste	August 2006– December 2012	Support government of Timor-Leste in postconflict peacebuilding, including capacity building, support and training of the East Timorese national police, and organization and holding of presidential and parliamentary elections in 2007.	— / 35 / 1,517 / 1,292	
2007					
MINURCAT (Resolution 1778)	Central African Republic/Chad	September 2007– December 2010	Provide security and protect civilians by advising the Chadian police and liaising with parties, and monitor and promote human rights and rule of law.	3,531 / 24 / 264 / 1,028	Yes

Mission	Location	Date	Mandate	Strength	POC
UNAMID (Resolutions 1769, 2113)	Sudan (Darfur)	Since July 2007	Established by a decision of the AU's Peace and Security Council and by Resolution 1769, UNAMID is mandated to contribute to restoration of a secure environment, protect the civilian population, facilitate humanitarian assistance, monitor implementation of related ceasefire agreements, and promote rule of law and human rights. Resolution 2113 emphasized UNAMID's Chapter VII mandate to deliver core tasks to protect civilians.	17,767 / 330 / 5,182 / 4,054	Yes
2010					
MONUSCO (Resolutions 1925, 2098)	Democratic Republic of the Congo	Since July 2010	Use all means necessary to protect civilians, humanitarian personnel, and human rights defenders under imminent threat of physical violence; and support the government of the DRC in its stabilization and peace consolidation efforts. In March 2013 with Resolution 2098, the UN Security Council created a specialized intervention brigade for the DRC operating within MONUSCO with the responsibility of neutralizing armed groups.	19,558 / 526 / 1,380 / 3,969	Yes
2011					
UNISFA (Resolution 1990)	Abyei	Since June 2011	Monitor and verify redeployment of any Sudanese and South Sudanese armed forces from the Abyei area, provide demining assistance, facilitate delivery of humanitarian aid, strengthen capacity of the Abyei police, and provide security for oil infrastructure in the Abyei area. In 2011 the mandate was broadened to include assistance in normalizing the South Sudan–Sudan border process.	3,955 / 140 / 24 / 193	Yes
UNMISS (Resolutions 1996, 2155)	South Sudan	Since July 2011	Support peace consolidation in order to foster longer-term statebuilding and economic development, support the South Sudanese government in conflict prevention, protect civilians, provide security, establish rule of law, and strengthen the security and justice sectors. Resolution 2155 authorized UNMISS to use all necessary means to protect civilians, monitor and investigate human rights abuses and violations, create conditions for the delivery of humanitarian assistance, and support the implementation of the Cessation of Hostilities agreement.	10,483 / 178 / 1,015 / 2,213	Yes

continues

Appendix 1 continued

Name (original mandating Security Council Resolutions)	Location	Time	Mandate	Maximum Number of Deployed Troops / Military Observers / Civilian Police / Civilian Staff (national and international)[a]	Chapter VII?
2012					
UNSMIS (Resolution 2043)	Syria	April–August 2012	Monitor cessation of armed violence in all forms by all parties, and monitor and support implementation of the joint Arab League–UN special envoy's six-point plan to end the conflict in Syria.	— / 150 / — / —	
2013					
MINUSMA (Resolution 2100)	Mali	Since April 2013	Support the political process and carry out a number of security-related stabilization tasks, protect civilians, monitor human rights, create conditions for the provision of humanitarian assistance and the return of displaced persons, and prepare for elections.	8,831 / — / 1,052 / 1,065	Yes
2014					
MINUSCA (Resolution 2149)	Central African Republic	Since April 2014	Protect civilians, support the transition process, facilitate humanitarian assistance, promote and protect human rights, support justice and rule of law, and oversee the disarmament, demobilization, reintegration, and repatriation processes.	8,305 / 131 / 1,466 / 392	Yes

Sources: For mandates, UN Department of Peacekeeping Operations website, www.un.org/depts/dpko. For maximum numbers of deployed troops, military observers, civilian police, and civilian staff (including international and national civilian staff), SIPRI Yearbook (Oxford: Oxford University Press, 1994–2014).

Notes: Current as of December 2014.

a. These numbers refer only to actual deployed personnel at the moment of maximum strength and do not indicate the strength of the international presence as authorized in the respective Security Council resolutions.

b. Resolution 169 does not explicitly refer to Chapter VII but uses the phrase "authorizes the Secretary-General to take vigorous action, including the use of the requisite measure of force."

c. UNEF II's predecessor force, UNEF I, was mandated by the General Assembly under its 1956 "Uniting for Peace" resolution.

d. Where no actual figures were available for international and national civilian staff, authorized numbers from respective Security Council resolutions have been used as an indication of approved staffing levels.

e. Of the 1,175 military personnel, 1,125 were provided on the basis of voluntary funding.

Appendix 2   Security Council–Mandated UN Political Missions, 1989–2014

Name (original mandating resolution or Council document)	Location	Time	Mandate	Maximum Number of Deployed Troops / Military Observers / Civilian Police / Civilian Staff (national and international)ª	Chapter VII?
1993					
UNOB (S/26757)	Burundi	November 1993–May 2004	Provide good offices and facilitate restoration of constitutional rule following a coup d'état in October 1993; initiatives aimed at promoting peace and reconciliation between the parties to the conflict. In 2004, UNOB was replaced by a UN peacekeeping operation, ONUB.	– / – / – / 12	
1995					
UNPOS (Presidential Statement 1995/15)	Somalia	April 1995–June 2013	Assist the Secretary-General in advancing the cause of peace and reconciliation through contacts with Somali leaders, civic organizations, and the states and organizations concerned.	2 / – / 2 / 82	
MINUSAL (Resolution 991)	El Salvador	May 1995–May 1996	Small team to verify implementation of Chapultepec Accord.	– / – / 8 / 11	
1997					
UNOL (S/1998/1080, Presidential statement 2002/36)	Liberia	November 1997–September 2003	Succeeding the UN peacekeeping operation UNOMIL, UNOL was to promote reconciliation and strengthening of democratic institutions, provide support for local human rights initiatives, provide political support for efforts to mobilize international resources and assistance for national recovery and reconstruction, and coordinate UN peacebuilding efforts. The mandate was expanded in 2002 to include electoral assistance and promotion of human rights. In 2003, UNOL's functions were transferred to UN peacekeeping operation UNMIL.	– / – / – / 15	

continues

Appendix 2 continued

Name (original mandating resolution or Council document)	Location	Time	Mandate	Maximum Number of Deployed Troops / Military Observers / Civilian Police / Civilian Staff (national and international)[a]	Chapter VII?
1998					
UNPOB (S/1998/506-S/1998/507)	Bougainville	August 1998– December 2003	Established following ceasefire and signing of the Lincoln Agreement in January 1998 between the government of Papua New Guinea and the Bougainville parties to the conflict. UNPOB was mandated to monitor implementation of the Lincoln and Arawa Agreements, including activities of the Peace Monitoring Group, in relation to its mandate.	2 / — / — / 3	
1999					
UNOGBIS (Resolution 1233)	Guinea-Bissau	March 1999– December 2009	Facilitate the general election in Guinea-Bissau and assist in implementation of the Abuja Agreement of August 26, 1998. Following the ouster of the president of Guinea-Bissau on May 7, 1999, UNOGBIS was adjusted to assist in national reconciliation efforts, create a stable environment to allow free elections, and promote confidence-building measures.	2 / — / 1/ 23	
UNSCO (S/1999/983)	Israel/Palestine	Since September 1999	UNSCO was initially established under a General Assembly mandate in June 1994 following the signing of the Oslo Accord, to strengthen UN interagency cooperation to respond to the needs of the Palestinian people, mobilizing financial, technical, economic, and other assistance. In 1999, UNSCO's mandate was enhanced by the Security Council charging the mission with providing good offices and boosting UN development assistance in support of the peace process.	— / — / — / 61	
UNOA (Resolution 1268)	Angola	October 1999– March 2003	Liaise with political, military, police, and other civilian authorities, with a view to exploring effective measures for restoring peace, assisting the Angolan people in the area with capacity building, providing humanitarian aid, and promoting human rights.	— / — / — / 30	

UNAMET (Resolution 1246)	East Timor	August 1999– October 1999	Organize and conduct a ballot in order to ascertain whether the East Timorese people accepted the proposed constitutional framework providing for special autonomy for East Timor within the unitary Republic of Indonesia, or rejected the proposed special autonomy for East Timor.	50 / — / 280 / 174
2000				
BONUCA (S/2000/24, Presidential Statement 2000/5)	Central African Republic	February 2000– December 2009	Taking over from UN peacekeeping operation MINURCA, BONUCA was to support the government of the Central African Republic's efforts to consolidate peace and national reconciliation, strengthen democratic institutions, facilitate mobilization of international political support and resources for national reconstruction and economic recovery, and promote human rights.	5 / — / 6 / 79
UNTOP (S/2000/518- S/2000/519)	Tajikistan	June 2000–July 2007	In order to consolidate peace and promote democracy in Tajikistan, UNTOP was mandated to provide the political framework and leadership for postconflict peacebuilding activities of the UN system in the country, and mobilize international support for the implementation of targeted programs aimed at strengthening rule of law, demobilization, voluntary arms collection, and employment creation for former irregular fighters.	— / — / 1 / 17
2001				
UNOWA (S/2001/1128- S/2001/1129)	West Africa	Since November 2001	Initially mandated to better address the cross-border impact of conflict in West Africa and harmonize UN activities in the subregion. UNOWA's mandate was later expanded to include monitoring of political developments in West Africa, carrying out good offices roles, enhancing subregional capacities for conflict prevention and mediation, enhancing subregional capacities to address cross-border and cross-cutting threats to peace and security, and promoting good governance and respect for the rule of law and human rights.	3 / — / — / 46

continues

Appendix 2 continued

Name (original mandating resolution or Council document)	Location	Time	Mandate	Maximum Number of Deployed Troops / Military Observers / Civilian Police / Civilian Staff (national and international)[a]	Chapter VII?
2002					
UNAMA (Resolution 1401)	Afghanistan	Since March 2002	Initially set up to support the Afghan transition process, promote national reconciliation, fulfill tasks and responsibilities entrusted to the UN in the Bonn Agreement, and manage all UN humanitarian relief, recovery, and reconstruction activities in Afghanistan, UNAMA's mandate was later refocused on leading and coordinating international civilian efforts to assist the country, supporting the organization of future elections, providing good offices to support the Afghan-led and owned peace and reconciliation process, and supporting and strengthening the capacity of human rights.	15 / — / 4 / 2,087	
UNMA (Resolution 1433)	Angola	August 2002–April 2003	Assist the parties in concluding the Lusaka Protocol and assist the government of Angola in the areas of human rights, economic recovery, and development.	— / 8 / — / 134	
2003					
MINUCI (Resolution 1479)	Côte d'Ivoire	May 2003–April 2004	Facilitate implementation of the Linas-Marcoussis Agreement following the cessation of the Ivorian civil war. In April 2004, MINUCI was replaced by UN peacekeeping operation UNOCI.	— / 75 / — / 54	Yes
UNAMI (Resolution 1500)	Iraq	Since August 2003	Support and assist the government in advancing their inclusive political dialogue and national reconciliation, including promote developing processes for holding elections and referenda and resolving internal boundaries disputes, facilitate regional dialogue on border security, energy, and refugees, support and facilitate the coordination and delivery of humanitarian assistance, and the protection of human rights and strengthening the rule of law.	13 / 294[b] / 5 / 900	Yes

2004

UNOMB (S/2003/1199)	Bougainville	January 2004–June 2005	Finish residual tasks of UNPOB and support efforts of the parties in the transitional period leading to the elections, as well as assess whether the level of security in Bougainville was conducive to the holding of elections.	—/—/—/2
UNAMIS (Resolution 1547)	Sudan (Darfur)	June 2004–March 2005	Prepare the international monitoring foreseen in the September 25, 2003, Naivasha Agreement on Security Arrangements, to facilitate contacts with the parties concerned and to prepare for the introduction of a peace support operation following signing of the Comprehensive Peace Agreement.	—/24/6/164

2005

UNOTIL (Resolution 1599)	Timor-Leste	May 2005–August 2006	Support capacity development of state institutions, including the national police and border-patrol unit, and provide human rights training.	15/—/—/56/439

2006

UNIOSIL (Resolution 1620)	Sierra Leone	January 2006–September 2008	Assist in capacity building of state institutions, democratization, good governance, rule of law, human rights promotion, strengthening of security sector, and preparation for elections in 2007.	—/14/21/274

2007

UNMIN (Resolution 1740)	Nepal	January 2007–January 2011	Monitor and assist in implementing the management of arms and armed personnel of the Seven Party Alliance–led government and the Communist Party of Nepal (Maoist) in line with the provisions of the November 2006 Comprehensive Peace Agreement, assist in monitoring ceasefire arrangements, and support electoral processes.	—/152/—/450
BINUB (Resolution 1719)	Burundi	January 2007–December 2010	Assist the Burundian government in peace consolidation and democratic governance, DDR and security sector reform, promotion and protection of human rights and ending impunity, and coordinating donors and UN agencies.	—/8/12/333

continues

Appendix 2 continued

Name (original mandating resolution or Council document)	Location	Time	Mandate	Maximum Number of Deployed Troops / Military Observers / Civilian Police / Civilian Staff (national and international)[a]	Chapter VII?
2008					
UNSCOL (S/2007/85-S/2007/86)	Lebanon	Since February 2007	Authorized through an exchange of letters between the Secretary-General and the president of the Security Council to represent the Secretary-General politically and coordinate the work of the UN in the country following the July 2006 war. The office of the special coordinator replaced the personal representative of the Secretary-General for Lebanon and predecessors that had been in Lebanon since 2000.	– / – / – / 80	
UNRCCA (S/2007/279-S/2007/280)	Central Asia	Since September 2007	Authorized through an exchange of letters between the Secretary-General and the president of the Security Council at the initiative of the governments of the five Central Asian countries. While initiating this proposal, the governments took into consideration the multiple threats facing Central Asia, including international terrorism and extremism, drug trafficking, organized crime, and environmental degradation.	– / – / – / 25	
UNIPSIL (Resolution 1829)	Sierra Leone	August 2008–March 2014	Mandated as a follow-on operation to UNIOSIL, UNIPSIL was mandated to provide political support to national and local peacebuilding efforts; and to monitor and protect human rights, democratic institutions, and rule of law.	– / 5 / 6 / 59	
2009					
BINUCA (Presidential Statement 2009/5)	Central African Republic	April 2009–April 2014	Succeeding BONUCA, it was mandated to ensure the coherence of peacebuilding support activities by the various UN entities present in the Central African Republic. In April 2014, BINUCA was incorporated into MINUSCA, the newly established peacekeeping mission in the country.	5 / – / 6 / 143	

2010

UNIOGBIS (Resolution 1876)	Guinea-Bissau	Since January 2010	Support an inclusive political dialogue and national reconciliation process, provide advice and support in implementing the national security sector reform and rule of law strategies, support the coordination of international assistance, support the strengthening of democratic institutions, build capacity of state organs, provide advice regarding establishment of effective and efficient law enforcement and criminal justice systems, assist with the promotion and protection of human rights, provide advice to combat drug trafficking and organized crime, and work with the Peacebuilding Commission in support of the country's peacebuilding priorities.	2 / — / 15 / 109

2011

UNSMIL (Resolution 2009)	Libya	Since September 2011	Support the Libyan government to ensure a transition to promote rule of law and protect human rights, restore public security, control unsecured arms and counter their proliferation, and build governance capacity as part of a coordinated international effort.	— / — / 7 / 224
BNUB (Resolution 1959)	Burundi	January 2011– December 2014	Support the government in strengthening the independence, capacities, and legal frameworks of key national institutions, in particular the judiciary and parliament; protect dialogue between national actors; promote impunity; and fight human rights.	1 / — / 1 / 108
UNOCA (S/2009/697-S/2010/457)	Central Africa	Since January 2011	A regionally focused political office with a mandate to help prevent conflict and consolidate peace in Central Africa. UNOCA supports preventative diplomacy and mediation in situations of tensions or potential conflict. It also works closely with UN entities on the ground, governments, and regional and subregional organizations to address cross-border challenges, including arms trafficking, organized crime, and the presence of armed groups such as the Lord's Resistance Army.	1 / — / — / 24

Appendix 2 continued

Name (original mandating resolution or Council document)	Location	Time	Mandate	Maximum Number of Deployed Troops / Military Observers / Civilian Police / Civilian Staff (national and international)[a]	Chapter VII?
2013					
UNSOM (Resolution 2102)	Somalia	Since May 2013	Provide policy advice to the federal government and AMISOM on peacebuilding and statebuilding in the areas of governance, security sector reform, and rule of law (including disengagement of combatants); development of a federal system (including preparations for elections in 2016); and coordination of international donor support. UNSOM also helps to build the federal government's capacity to promote respect for human rights and women's empowerment, promote child protection, prevent conflict-related sexual and gender-based violence, and strengthen justice institutions.	7 / — / 14 / 124	
OPCW- UN Joint Mission (Resolution 2118)	Syria	September 2013– September 2014	Oversee timely elimination of the Syrian chemical weapons program.	— / — / — / 23	
2014					
UNMEER (S/2014/679)	West African states affected by Ebola crisis	September 2014	Lead operational response and provide strategic direction to activities of the UN system and other implementing partners to ensure a rapid and effective response to the Ebola crisis, provide needed field-level support to the governments and peoples of West Africa, and assist member states and regional and subregional organizations in delivering their bilateral and multilateral assistance in a coordinated and coherent manner on the ground.	— / — / — / 278	

Sources: UN Security Council, Security Council Resolutions, http://www.un.org/en/sc/documents/resolutions/; UN Department of Political Affairs, http://www.un.org/wcm/content/site/undpa/main/about/field_operations; United Nations Department of Public Information, "Annual Fact Sheets on United Nations Political and Peacebuilding Missions, 2000–2015"; *SIPRI Yearbook* (Oxford: Oxford University Press, 1994–2013); Center on International Cooperation, *Annual Review of Global Peace Operations* (Boulder: Lynne Rienner, 2006–2013).

Notes: a. These numbers refer only to actual deployed personnel at the moment of maximum strength and do not indicate the strength of the international presence as authorized in the respective Security Council resolutions.

b. This figure does not refer to military observers but to troops deployed for staff protection.

Appendix 3 Non-UN Peace or Enforcement Operations Mandated by the Security Council, 1945–2014

Name (original mandating resolution)	Location	Time (Security Council authorization)	Mandate	Maximum Number of Deployed Troops / Military Observers / Civilian Police[a]	Chapter VII?
1950					
United Nations Command (Resolutions 83, 84)	South Korea	June–July 1950	Recommended all member states under the unified command of the United States to provide assistance to Republic of Korea to repel armed attack from North Korea.	932,964 / — / —	Yes
1990					
Gulf War Coalition (Resolution 678)	Iraq	November 1990– February 1991	Authorized a coalition of member states (eventually led by the United States) to evict Iraqi forces from Kuwait and restore international peace and security in the area.	580,000 / — / —	Yes
1992					
United Task Force (UNITAF) (Resolutions 794, 837)	Somalia	December 1992–May 1993	Authorized a coalition of member states (eventually led by the United States) to establish a secure environment for humanitarian relief operations in Somalia.	37,000 / — / —	Yes
1994					
Operation Turquoise (Resolution 929)	Rwanda	June–August 1994	Authorized the governments of France and Senegal to contribute, in an impartial way, to security and protection of displaced persons, refugees, and civilians at risk in Rwanda.	3,060 / — / —	Yes
Multinational Force (MDNF) / Operation Uphold Democracy (Resolution 940)	Haiti	July 1994–March 1995	Authorized member states to form a multinational force under unified command (eventually led by the United States) and remove the de facto regime and create a secure environment for restoration of the legitimate government of Haiti; restore and preserve civil order; and prepare to pass responsibility for military operations in Haiti to UNMIH.	7,412 / — / 717	Yes

continues

Appendix 3 continued

Name (original mandating resolution)	Location	Time (Security Council authorization)	Mandate	Maximum Number of Deployed Troops / Military Observers / Civilian Police[a]	Chapter VII?
1995					
Implementation Force (IFOR) (Resolution 1031)	Bosnia and Herzegovina	December 1995– December 1996	Authorized a multinational force (eventually led by NATO) to oversee implementation of military aspects of Dayton peace agreement: bring about and maintain end to hostilities; separate armed forces of Bosnia's two newly created entities, the Federation of Bosnia and Herzegovina and the Republika Srpska; transfer territory between the two entities according to the peace agreement; and move the parties' forces and heavy weapons into approved storage sites.[b]	60,000 / — / —	Yes
1996					
Stabilization Force (SFOR) (Resolution 1088)	Bosnia and Herzegovina	December 1996– December 2004	Authorized a multinational force (eventually led by NATO) to take over from IFOR and deter hostilities and stabilize the peace, contribute to a secure environment by providing a continued military presence in the area of responsibility, target and coordinate SFOR support to key areas including primary civil implementation organizations, and progress toward lasting consolidation of peace.[c]	36,300 / — / —	Yes
1997					
MISAB (Resolution 1125)	Central African Republic	August 1997– April 1998	Approved the continued conduct by member states participating in the inter-African force, MISAB (established in January 1997 by Gabon, Burkina Faso, Chad, and Mali) to restore peace and security by monitoring implementation of the Bangui Agreements and conducting operations to disarm former rebels, militia, and all other unlawfully armed individuals.[d]	6,294 / — / —	Yes
Multinational Protection Force (MPF) (Resolution 1101)	Albania	March–August 1997	Authorized a multinational force (eventually led by Italy) to ensure safe delivery and distribution of humanitarian aid, take control of the Adriatic ports from which refugees and other would-be immigrants were leaving for Italy, and stabilize the internal situation so as to allow elections to take place in June 1997.[e]		Yes

1998

Operation	Location	Dates	Description	
Extraction Force (XFOR) (Resolution 1203)	Kosovo	October 1998–June 1999	Endorsed the OSCE's intention to enter into arrangements with other organizations (with NATO eventually taking on this task) to extract OSCE verifiers or other designated persons from Kosovo should all other measures be unsuccessful and at OSCE request.	2,300 / — / — Yes

1999

Kosovo Force (KFOR) (Resolution 1244)	Kosovo	Since June 1999	Authorized a multinational force (eventually led by NATO) to establish and maintain secure environment in Kosovo, including public safety and order to monitor, verify, and when necessary enforce compliance with the agreements that ended the conflict; and provide assistance to UNMIK.[f]	42,700 / — / — Yes
International Force for East Timor (INTERFET) (Resolution 1264)	East Timor	September 1999–February 2000	Authorized a multinational force (eventually led by Australia) to restore peace and security to East Timor, protect and support UNAMET, and facilitate humanitarian assistance operations.	11,285 / — / — Yes

2001

Task Force Fox (TFF) (Resolution 1371)	Former Yugoslav Republic of Macedonia	September 2001–December 2002	Supported the establishment of a multinational security force (eventually led by NATO) as a follow-on force to NATO Task Force Harvest, which operated without UN mandate. Task Force Fox was to contribute to the protection of international monitors who would oversee the peace plan in the former Yugoslav Republic of Macedonia.	965 / — / — Yes
International Security Assistance Force (ISAF) (Resolution 1386)	Afghanistan	December 2001–December 2014	Authorized a coalition of member states (led by the United States) to assist the Afghan transitional authority in maintaining security within the ISAF area of responsibility so that the transitional authority, as well as UN personnel, could operate in a secure environment enabling the transitional authority to build up security structures in Afghanistan in accordance with the Bonn Agreement and the Military Technical Agreement.[g]	4,600 / — / — Yes

continues

Appendix 3 continued

Name (original mandating resolution)	Location	Time (Security Council authorization)	Mandate	Maximum Number of Deployed Troops / Military Observers / Civilian Police[a]	Chapter VII?
2003					
International Emergency Force in Ituri (Operation Artemis) (Resolution 1484)	Ituri/ Democratic Republic of the Congo	May– September 2003	Authorized an interim emergency multinational force (eventually led by the European Union) to assist the MONUC contingent already in Bunia, stabilize the security situation, improve the humanitarian situation, protect Bunia Airport and internally displaced persons, and contribute to protection of the civilian population and UN and humanitarian personnel.	1,400 / — / —	Yes
Multinational Force (MNF) (Resolutions 1511, 1546)	Iraq	October 2003– December 2011	Authorized a multinational force led by the United States to contribute to the maintenance of security and stability in Iraq including preventing and deterring terrorism; contribute to the security of UNAMI, the Governing Council of Iraq, and other institutions of the Iraqi interim administration, and key humanitarian and economic infrastructure.	183,000 / — / 1,051	Yes
2004					
AMIS (Resolution 1556)	Sudan (Darfur)	July 2004– December 2007	Endorsed the African Union protection force initially established by the Agreement with the Sudanese Parties on the Modalities for the Establishment of the Ceasefire Commission and the Deployment of Observers in the Darfur, on May 28, 2004. AMIS's mandate was expanded pursuant to a decision adopted at the seventeenth meeting of the AU's Peace and Security Council. AMIS was further mandated to monitor the N'Djamena ceasefire agreements, assist in confidence building between the parties, and contribute to a secure environment in Darfur.	790 / 356 / 7	Yes
EUFOR ALTHEA (Resolution 1551)	Bosnia and Herzegovina	Since July 2004	Welcomed the European Union's intention to launch an EU-led mission to continue from NATO's SFOR due for completion in December 2004. EUFOR ALTHEA was mandated to maintain a	7,000 / — / —	Yes

secure environment for implementation of the 1995 Dayton Agreement, assist in strengthening local capacity, and support Bosnia and Herzegovina's progress toward EU integration.

Mission (Resolution)	Country	Dates	Personnel	
NTM-I (Resolution 1546)	Iraq	June 2004–December 2011	65 / — / —	Yes
2006				
EUFOR R.D Congo (Resolution 1671)	Democratic Republic of the Congo	April 2006– November 2006	2,275 / — / —	Yes
ISF (Resolution 1690)	Timor-Leste	June 2006– November 2012	930 / — / —	Yes
2007				
AMISOM (Resolution 1744)	Somalia	Since February 2007	1,792 / — / —	Yes
EUFOR Tchad/RCA (Resolution 1778)	Central African Republic, Chad	September 2007– March 2009	3,420 / — / —	Yes
2012				
AFISMA (Resolution 2085)	Mali	December 2012– July 2013	1,400 / — / —	Yes

Descriptions:

NTM-I: As part of the authorization for the MNF to assist in the building of the capability of Iraqi security forces, the NATO Training Mission in Iraq was established in July 2004 as a distinct mission under the political control of the North Atlantic Council, to assist in the development of Iraqi security forces' training structures and institutions.

EUFOR R.D Congo: Authorized the temporary deployment of a European Union force (EUFOR R.D Congo) to support MONUC during the election process in the DRC.

ISF: Supported the coalition of member states (led by Australia), initially deployed at the request of the government of Timor-Leste, to assist in stabilizing the security environment.

AMISOM: Authorized the establishment of an African Union mission to support the dialogue and reconciliation process by supporting the transitional federal institutions, facilitating the provision of humanitarian assistance, and contributing to the overall security situation.

EUFOR Tchad/RCA: Authorized a European Union operation to support MINURCAT, contribute to the protection of civilians and UN personnel, and facilitate humanitarian aid efforts.

AFISMA: Authorized an African force (eventually jointly led by ECOWAS) to provide coordinated and coherent support to the ongoing political and security processes. In July 2013, AFISMA transformed into MINUSMA, a UN peacekeeping operation.

continues

Appendix 3 continued

Name (original mandating resolution)	Location	Time (Security Council authorization)	Mandate	Maximum Number of Deployed Troops / Military Observers / Civilian Police[a]	Chapter VII?
2013					
MISCA (Resolution 2127)	Central African Republic	December 2013– September 2014	Authorized an African-led force (eventually led by the African Union) to protect civilians, stabilize the country and restore state authority, and create conditions conducive to the provision of humanitarian assistance. In September 2014, MISCA's functions were transferred to the new UN peacekeeping mission in the Central African Republic, MINUSCA.	5,400 / — / —	Yes
Operation Sangaris (Resolution 2127)	Central African Republic	Since December 2013	Authorized French forces to take all necessary measures to support MISCA in the discharge of its mandate.	2,000[h] / — / —	Yes
2014					
EUFOR RCA (Resolution 2134)	Central African Republic	Since January 2014	Authorized a European Union operation to provide temporary support in achieving a safe and secure environment in the Bangui area, with a view to handing over to African partners; contribute to international efforts to protect the populations most at risk, creating the conditions for providing humanitarian aid.	3,420 / — / —	Yes

Sources: UN Security Council, Security Council Resolutions, http://www.un.org/en/sc/documents/resolutions/; *SIPRI Yearbook* (Oxford: Oxford University Press, 1994–2013).

Notes: a. These numbers refer only to actual deployed personnel at the moment of maximum strength and do not indicate the strength of the international presence as authorized in the respective Security Council resolutions.

b. See North Atlantic Treaty Organization, www.nato.int/docu/facts/2000/role-bih.htm.

c. See SFOR homepage at www.nato.int/sfor/organisation/mission.htm.

d. See Relief Web, http://reliefweb.int/w/rwb.nsf/0/ad813ef76087cd74852565fd0069c4f3?OpenDocument.

e. See WEU Assembly, www.assembly-weu.org/en/documents/sessions_ordinaires/reports/1650.html.

f. See KFOR homepage at www.nato.int/kfor/kfor/about.htm.

g. See ISAF homepage at www.isafkabul.org.

h. As of February 28, 2014.

Security Council Resolution or Presidential Statement	Date	Mandate
Southern Rhodesia		
Resolution 232	December 16, 1966	Imposed sanctions on Southern Rhodesian export commodities as well as an oil and arms embargo.
Resolution 253	May 29, 1968	Established a Security Council sanctions committee.
Resolution 460	December 21, 1979	Lifted all sanctions against Southern Rhodesia.
South Africa		
Resolution 418	November 4, 1977	Imposed an arms and nuclear weapons embargo.
Resolution 421	December 9, 1977	Established a Security Council sanctions committee.
Resolution 919	May 25, 1994	Terminated the arms embargo and other restrictions imposed on South Africa.
Iraq		
Resolution 661	August 6, 1990	Imposed comprehensive, sanctions; established a Security Council sanctions committee; banned all trade; imposed oil and arms embargoes; suspended international flights; froze Iraqi government financial assets and prohibited financial transactions.
Resolution 687	April 3, 1991	Established a set of eight specific conditions for the lifting of sanctions.
Resolution 706	August 15, 1991	Authorized oil-for-food program; permitted sale of up to $1.6 billion in Iraqi oil over six-month period; directed those proceeds be deposited into UN escrow account to finance humanitarian imports and war reparations [Iraq rejected this resolution].
Resolution 712	September 19, 1991	Established basic structure for oil-for-food program implementation.
Resolution 778	October 2, 1992	Called upon member states to transfer to the UN escrow account Iraqi oil funds generated prior to the Gulf crisis.
Resolution 986	April 14, 1995	Established new formula for oil-for-food program; permitted sale of up to $1 billion in Iraqi oil every three months; gave Baghdad primary responsibility for distribution of humanitarian goods [came into force December 1996].
Resolution 1111	June 4, 1997	Extended oil-for-food program [Baghdad withheld distribution plans and oil sales].

continues

Appendix 4 continued

Security Council Resolution or Presidential Statement	Date	Mandate
Resolution 1153	February 20, 1998	Extended oil-for-food program again; raised oil sales to $5.25 billion every six months; permitted revenues to finance urgent development needs.
Resolution 1284	December 17, 1999	Declared Security Council's intention to suspend sanctions for renewable 120-day periods if Iraq cooperated with UNMOVIC and IAEA weapons inspectors.
Resolution 1409	May 14, 2002	Adopted a revised "Goods Review List" of military-related goods or commodities, which was to enter into effect on May 30, 2002. From that date onward, states were authorized to sell or supply any commodities not included on the list, while the Security Council would regularly conduct thorough reviews of the list.
Resolution 1472	March 28, 2003	Made technical and temporary adjustments to the oil-for-food program on an interim and exceptional basis, to ensure implementation of approved contracts concluded by the government of Iraq for the relief of the Iraqi people. The resolution also authorized a general arms embargo and targeted asset freeze.
Resolution 1483	May 22, 2003	Ended all sanctions except those related to the sale or supply to Iraq of arms and related matériel; requested the Secretary-General to terminate the oil-for-food program after a period of six months.
Resolution 1518	November 24, 2003	Created a new Security Council sanctions committee as the successor body to the Security Council Committee established pursuant to Resolution 661 (1990) concerning Iraq and Kuwait. The committee was established to continue to identify senior officials of the former Iraqi regime and their immediate family members, including entities owned or controlled by them or by persons acting on their behalf, who are subject to an assets freeze, and update the list of those already identified by the previous sanctions committee.
Resolution 1546	June 8, 2004	Endorsed the formation of the interim Iraqi government and set out exemptions to the sanctions regime.
Former Yugoslavia		
Resolution 713	September 25, 1991	Imposed an arms embargo on Yugoslavia.
Resolution 724	December 15, 1991	Established a Security Council sanctions committee.
Resolution 757	May 30, 1992	Banned all international trade with Yugoslavia; prohibited air travel; blocked

Resolution 787	November 15, 1992	financial transactions; banned sports and cultural exchanges; suspended scientific and technical cooperation; allowed transshipment of goods through Yugoslavia; exempted humanitarian goods.
Resolution 820	April 17, 1993	Prohibited transshipment of strategic goods through Yugoslavia; halted all maritime shipping on Danube River.
		Froze Yugoslav government financial assets; prohibited the transit through any country of vessels owned by or registered in Yugoslavia; further limited the transshipment of goods through Yugoslavia.
Resolution 942	September 23, 1994	Extended full range of sanctions to Bosnian-Serb–controlled territory.
Resolution 943	September 23, 1994	Eased some restrictions on Serbia; suspended sanctions on air and ferry service between Montenegro and Italy; suspended ban on sporting and cultural events.
Resolution 1160	March 31, 1998	Imposed arms embargo on Yugoslavia; established new Security Council sanctions committee to monitor membership compliance.

Somalia and Eritrea

Resolution 733	January 23, 1992	Imposed arms embargo.
Resolution 751	April 24, 1992	Established a Security Council sanctions committee.
Resolution 954	November 4, 1994	Requested the Somalia sanctions committee to fulfill its mandate (due to poor monitoring).
Resolution 1356	June 19, 2001	Exempted nonlethal military equipment from the arms embargo.
Resolution 1407	May 3, 2002	Requested the Secretary-General to establish a team of experts that could provide the Council's Somalia sanctions committee with an action plan to improve enforcement of the arms embargo.
Resolution 1425	July 22, 2002	Established a panel of experts on Somalia.
Resolution 1474	April 8, 2003	Reestablished the panel of experts.
Resolution 1519	December 16, 2003	Established a monitoring group on Somalia, which replaced the panel of experts.
Resolution 1766	July 23, 2007	Extended the mandate of the monitoring group.
Resolution 1844	November 20, 2008	Expanded the Somalia sanctions regime and imposed targeted sanctions on individuals, including a targeted arms embargo, travel ban, and asset freeze.
Resolution 1907	December 23, 2009	Imposed a two-way arms embargo on Eritrea and targeted sanctions on individuals, including a targeted arms embargo, travel ban, and asset freeze; expanded mandate of the monitoring group to include Eritrea.
Resolution 2002	July 29, 2011	Added the following to the designation criteria: obstructing humanitarian assistance, recruitment and use of children in armed conflicts, and targeting of civilians, including women and children.

continues

Appendix 4 continued

Security Council Resolution or Presidential Statement	Date	Mandate
Resolution 2036	February 22, 2012	Imposed a ban on direct or indirect import of charcoal from Somalia, whether or not such charcoal originated in Somalia.
Resolution 2093	March 6, 2013	Partially lifted the arms embargo on Somalia for a period of twelve months.
Resolution 2111	July 24, 2013	Consolidated the exemptions to the arms embargo on Somalia and Eritrea; lifted arms embargo for deliveries of weapons or military equipment or the provision of advice, assistance, or training intended solely for the development of the federal government's security forces.
Libya I		
Resolution 748	March 31, 1992	Imposed aviation sanctions; banned the supply of weapons; required reductions in personnel at Libyan diplomatic/consular missions abroad; restricted travel of Libyan nationals suspected of terrorist activity; established a Security Council sanctions committee.
Resolution 883	November 11, 1993	Froze Libyan government assets abroad; tightened aviation sanctions; banned import of some oil-transporting equipment.
Resolution 1192	August 27, 1998	Decided that sanctions shall be suspended immediately if the Secretary-General reported to the Council that the two Lockerbie accused had arrived in the Netherlands for trial.
Presidential Statement 1999/10	April 8, 1999	Noted that the conditions for suspending the wide range of aerial, arms, and diplomatic measures against Libya had been fulfilled.
Libya II		
Resolution 1970	February 26, 2011	Established a Security Council sanctions committee; imposed an arms embargo and targeted sanctions, including a travel ban and asset freeze; referred the situation in Libya to the International Criminal Court.
Resolution 1973	March 17, 2011	Authorized all necessary measures to protect civilians in Libya and enforce the arms embargo; imposed a no-fly zone; imposed a ban on flights; strengthened the sanctions regime; established a panel of experts.
Resolution 2009	September 16, 2011	Modified the arms embargo; partially lifted the asset freeze; lifted the ban on flights.

Resolution 2016	October 27, 2011	Lifted the no-fly zone and the provision for all necessary measures for the protection of civilians.
Resolution 2017	October 31, 2011	Requested the sanctions committee to assess arms proliferation from Libya to the region and to submit a report to the Security Council.
Resolution 2040	March 12, 2012	Amended the arms embargo and extended and modified the mandate of the panel of experts.
Resolution 2095	March 14, 2013	Further eased the arms embargo and renewed the mandate of the panel of experts.
Resolution 2146	March 19, 2014	Imposed measures for one year on vessels designated by the committee in relation to attempts to illicitly export crude oil from Libya.
Resolution 2174	August 27, 2014	Reinforced arms embargo and expanded criteria for the designation of individuals or entities as subject to the travel ban and assets freeze.

Cambodia

Resolution 766	July 21, 1992	Specified that international financial assistance for reconstruction would go only to factions supporting the Paris Accords.
Resolution 783	October 13, 1992	Demanded compliance with the Paris Accords (again); confirmed that elections would proceed regardless of obstruction by the Party of Democratic Kampuchea (PDK).
Resolution 792	November 30, 1992	Imposed sanctions on PDK-controlled areas of Cambodia; imposed an oil embargo; supported a moratorium on log exports, previously adopted by Cambodia's Supreme National Council, to go into effect January 1, 1993; urged the Supreme National Council to embargo the export of minerals and gems.

Liberia

Resolution 788	November 19, 1992	Imposed limited arms embargo (exempted ECOMOG forces).
Resolution 985	April 13, 1995	Established a Security Council sanctions committee.
Resolution 1071	August 30, 1996	Welcomed proposed ECOWAS punitive measures (including travel and voting restrictions) but did not threaten additional UN sanctions.
Resolution 1343	March 7, 2001	Reimposed the arms embargo; imposed additional sanctions, including a ban on trade in rough diamonds and a travel ban against senior members of the government of Liberia or their spouses, as well as of any other individuals providing financial and military support to armed rebel groups in countries neighboring Liberia.
Resolution 1478	May 6, 2003	Extended the existing sanctions measures until May 7, 2004; decided that all states shall take the necessary measures to prevent, for a period of ten months, the import into their territories of all round logs and timber products originating in Liberia.

continues

Appendix 4 continued

Security Council Resolution or Presidential Statement	Date	Mandate
Resolution 1521	December 22, 2003	Established a Security Council sanctions committee; imposed revised prohibitions on arms, diamonds, and travel of designated individuals; imposed a timber ban; established a panel of experts.
Resolution 1532	March 12, 2004	Imposed an asset freeze on Charles Taylor, Jewell Howard Taylor, Charles Taylor Jr., and other individuals designated by the sanctions committee.
Resolution 1683	June 13, 2006	Clarified which sanctions would not apply to Special Security Services for training or against those members of the police and security forces approved by the committee.
Resolution 1689	June 20, 2006	Ceased the timber sanctions.
Resolution 1753	April 27, 2007	Ceased the diamond sanctions.
Resolution 1903	December 17, 2009	Terminated the general arms embargo with regard to the government of Liberia; imposed a targeted arms embargo on nongovernmental entities and individuals.
Resolution 2079	December 12, 2012	Renewed the arms embargo and travel ban; extended the mandate of the panel of experts.
Haiti		
Resolution 841	June 16, 1993	Imposed a fuel and arms embargo; established a Security Council sanctions committee.
Resolution 873	October 13, 1993	Reimposed the fuel and arms embargo.
Resolution 875	October 16, 1993	Called on member states to enforce the fuel and arms embargo with a naval blockade.
Resolution 917	May 6, 1994	Imposed comprehensive sanctions; imposed a flight ban; froze assets of the military junta and of its supporters and families.
Resolution 944	September 29, 1994	Moved to terminate sanctions upon Aristide's return to power.
Angola		
Resolution 864	September 15, 1993	Imposed an arms embargo on UNITA; imposed a petroleum embargo except through ports of entry designated by the Angolan government; established a Security Council sanctions committee.
Resolution 1127	August 28, 1997	Imposed sanctions banning travel of senior UNITA officials and prohibiting flights

Resolution	Date	Description
Resolution 1173	June 12, 1998	to and from UNITA-held territory; demanded closing of UNITA diplomatic offices; held that sanctions would come into effect on September 30, 1997, unless UNITA would comply with its disarmament efforts. Froze UNITA financial assets; banned all financial transactions with UNITA; imposed an embargo on diamond imports not certified by the Angolan government; banned any form of travel to UNITA-controlled territory.
Resolutions 1202, 1203	October 15, 1998	Requested the Secretary-General to submit recommendations regarding means for improving implementation of the measures imposed on UNITA.
Resolution 1237	May 7, 1999	Established a panels of expert to undertake studies to trace violations in arms trafficking, oil supplies, and the diamond trade, as well as the movement of UNITA funds.
Resolution 1295	April 18, 2000	Established a monitoring mechanism for a period of six months in order to collect information concerning violations of the Security Council's previous sanctions resolutions against UNITA.
Resolution 1412	May 17, 2002	Suspended the travel ban on senior UNITA officials for a period of ninety days, with the Security Council to decide before the end of that period whether to extend the suspension.

Rwanda

Resolution 918 Resolution 997	May 17, 1994 June 9, 1995	Imposed an arms embargo; established a Security Council sanctions committee. Specified that the arms embargo applied to groups in other countries operating against Rwanda.
Resolution 1011	August 16, 1995	Suspended the arms embargo on the Rwandan government; maintained the sanctions on the rebel Hutu groups in eastern Zaire.
Resolution 1013	September 6, 1995	Established the UN International Commission of Inquiry (UNICOI) to investigate and report violations of the arms embargo.

Sudan

Resolution	Date	Description
Resolution 1054	April 26, 1996	Imposed diplomatic sanctions; called on member states to reduce the number and level of their staff at Sudanese diplomatic missions and consular posts in their respective countries and restrict the movement within their territories of those who remained; restricted entry into member states' territory of Sudanese government officials and military personnel; required international institutions and regional organizations to refrain from convening any conferences in Sudan.

continues

Appendix 4 continued

Security Council Resolution or Presidential Statement	Date	Mandate
Resolution 1070	August 16, 1996	Imposed travel sanctions requiring all states to deny Sudanese aircraft permission to take off from, land in, or overfly their territories; called for a separate Security Council decision within ninety days to determine a date for entry into force [aviation ban never went into effect].
Resolution 1372	September 28, 2001	Lifted the sanctions detailed in Resolution 1054.
Resolution 1556	July 30, 2004	Imposed an arms embargo on nonstate actors in Darfur.
Resolution 1591	March 29, 2005	Widened the arms embargo and imposed targeted measures including a travel ban and asset freeze; established a Security Council sanctions committee.
Resolution 1593	March 31, 2005	Referred the situation in Darfur to the International Criminal Court.
Resolution 1672	April 25, 2006	Listed four individuals to the Sudan 1591 sanctions committee.
Resolution 2091	February 14, 2013	Extended the mandate of the panel of experts.
Resolution 2138	February 13, 2014	Extended the mandate of the panel of experts
Sierra Leone		
Resolution 1132	October 8, 1997	Imposed an oil embargo and an arms embargo; imposed travel sanctions on members of the Armed Forces Revolutionary Council (AFRC) junta and their families; conditioned the lifting of sanctions on the junta relinquishing power; established a Security Council sanctions committee.
Resolution 1156	March 16, 1998	Lifted the oil embargo.
Resolution 1171	June 5, 1998	Confirmed removal of sanctions on the government; reimposed the arms embargo and travel ban on the Revolutionary United Front (RUF) and members of the former military junta.
Resolution 1306	July 5, 2000	Imposed a diamond embargo and requested the government of Sierra Leone to establish an effective certificate-of-origin regime for trade in diamonds.
Afghanistan, Taliban, and al-Qaeda		
Resolution 1267	October 15, 1999	Established a Security Council sanctions committee; imposed aviation and financial sanctions against the Taliban regime.
Resolution 1333	December 19, 2000	Imposed an arms embargo on territory of Afghanistan under Taliban control; imposed financial sanctions against Osama bin Laden and individuals and entities

Resolution	Date	Description
Resolution 1363	July 30, 2001	associated with him as designated by the committee. Requested the committee to maintain an updated list of the individuals and entities designated as being associated with Osama bin Laden and al-Qaeda organization. Requested the Secretary-General to establish within thirty days a monitoring group to monitor implementation of the sanctions.
Resolution 1388 / Resolution 1390	January 15, 2002 / January 16, 2002	Terminated the sanctions measures that applied to Ariana Afghan Airlines. Maintained all sanctions measures in Resolution 1267 except the flight embargo for a period of twelve months.
Resolution 1455	January 17, 2003	Renewed sanctions; declared the Security Council's intention to improve those measures within the next twelve months; requested the monitoring group for the sanctions to report on further improvements.
Resolution 1526	January 30, 2004	Improved the implementation of measures from previous resolutions, strengthened the mandate of the committee, and established for a period of eighteen months an Analytical Support and Sanctions Monitoring Team.
Resolution 1617	July 29, 2005	Continued sanctions against al-Qaeda, the Taliban, Osama bin Laden, and associated individuals and groups; defined the meaning of "associated with"; and extended the mandate of the monitoring team.
Resolution 1822	June 30, 2008	Extended the mandate of the monitoring team, directing the committee to provide access on its website of releasable reasons for listing of individuals or entities, and directed the committee to conduct a review of all names on the consolidated list.
Resolution 1904	December 17, 2009	Introduced measures to streamline the listing process of names on the consolidated list; established the office of the ombudsperson, to be appointed by the Secretary-General, for an initial period of eighteen months to assist the committee in its consideration of delisting requests. Extended the mandate of the monitoring team.
Resolution 1988	June 17, 2011	Created a new sanctions regime directed at individuals, entities, and other groups associated with the Taliban. Those previously listed under the consolidated list as Taliban and individuals, groups, undertakings, or entities associated with the Taliban were transferred to this new sanctions list. A new sanctions committee was established and the existing monitoring team was to support this new sanctions committee as well as the existing committee under Resolution 1267.
Resolution 1989	June 17, 2011	Modified the 1267 sanctions regime to only apply to designated individuals, other groups, entities, and undertakings associated with al-Qaeda; expanded the mandate of the ombudsperson to make recommendations to the committee; and extended the monitoring team's mandate.

continues

Appendix 4 continued

Security Council Resolution or Presidential Statement	Date	Mandate
Resolution 2082	December 17, 2012	Extended the sanctions measures and extended the monitoring team mandate.
Resolution 2083	December 17, 2012	Refined the separated sanctions regimes on al-Qaeda and the Taliban, detailed the criteria for designation of individuals or entities associated with al-Qaeda and subject to sanctions, and extended the mandate of the office of the ombudsperson.
Resolution 2060	June 17, 2014	Extended the sanctions measures against individuals and entities associated with the Taliban and extended the mandate of the monitoring team.
Resolution 2161	June 17, 2014	Extended the sanctions measures against individuals and entities associated with al-Qaeda and extended the mandate of the office of the ombudsperson and the mandate for the monitoring team.
Ethiopia and Eritrea		
Resolution 1298	May 17, 2000	Imposed an arms embargo against Eritrea and Ethiopia; established a committee consisting of all the members of the Security Council.
Presidential Statement 2001/14	May 15, 2001	Noted that the sanctions would expire on May 16, 2001.
Resolution 1907	December 23, 2009	Imposed a two-way arms embargo, as well as targeted sanctions on individuals and entities.
Resolution 2023	December 6, 2011	Expanded the restrictive measures regarding Eritrea in the areas of "diaspora taxes," the mining sector, and financial services.
Democratic Republic of the Congo		
Resolution 1493	July 28, 2003	Imposed an arms embargo on all foreign and Congolese armed groups and militias operating in the territory of North and South Kivu and Ituri, and on DRC groups not party to the Global and All-Inclusive Agreement.
Resolution 1533	March 12, 2004	Established a Security Council sanctions committee and group of experts.
Resolution 1596	April 18, 2005	Amended and expanded the arms embargo and imposed targeted measures including a travel ban and asset freeze.
Resolution 1649	December 21, 2005	Expanded the arms embargo and the financial and travel sanctions to include political and military leaders of foreign armed groups operating in the DRC and leaders receiving support from outside the DRC.
Resolution 1698	July 31, 2006	Expanded the sanctions imposed under Resolution 1596 to include political and military leaders recruiting or using children in armed conflict in violation of

applicable international law, and individuals committing serious violations of international law involving the targeting of children in situations of armed conflict, including killing and maiming, sexual violence, abduction, and forced displacement.

Resolution 1768	July 31, 2007	Extended arms, transport, financial, and travel sanctions, and mandate of group of experts.
Resolution 1771	August 10, 2007	Extended arms, transport, financial, and travel sanctions, and mandate of group of experts.
Resolution 1799	February 15, 2008	Extended arms, transport, financial, and travel sanctions, and mandate of group of experts.
Resolution 1807	March 31, 2008	Terminated the general arms embargo with regard to the government of the DRC; imposed a targeted arms embargo on nongovernmental entities and individuals.
Resolution 1952	November 29, 2010	Extended arms, transport, financial, and travel sanctions, and mandate of group of experts.
Resolution 2078	November 28, 2012	Amended and expanded the targeted arms embargo, travel ban, and asset freeze; renewed the sanctions regime.
Resolution 2136	January 30, 2014	Extended arms, transport, financial, and travel sanctions, and mandate of group of experts.

Côte d'Ivoire

Resolution 1572	November 15, 2004	Established a Security Council sanctions committee; imposed a general arms embargo and targeted measures including a travel ban and asset freeze.
Resolution 1584	February 1, 2005	Established a group of experts.
Resolution 1643	December 15, 2005	Added sanctions on diamond exports to the measures imposed on Côte d'Ivoire.
Resolution 1975	March 20, 2011	Imposed targeted measures on former president Laurent Gbagbo and four members of his inner circle.
Resolution 2045	April 26, 2012	Modified the general arms embargo.
Resolution 2101	April 25, 2013	Renewed the sanctions regime and extended the mandate of the group of experts.
Resolution 2153	April 29, 2014	Renewed the arms embargo, travel ban, and assets freeze measures.

Lebanon

Resolution 1595	April 7, 2005	Established the International Independent Investigation Commission.
Resolution 1636	October 31, 2005	Established a Security Council sanctions committee; imposed a travel ban and asset freeze for individuals designated by the International Independent Investigation Commission or the government of Lebanon as suspected of involvement in the February 14, 2005, terrorist bombing in Beirut.

continues

Appendix 4 continued

Security Council Resolution or Presidential Statement	Date	Mandate
Resolution 1757	May 30, 2007	Set out guidelines for the establishment of the Special Tribunal for Lebanon.
Resolution 1852	December 16, 2008	Extended the mandate of the International Independent Investigation Commission until February 28, 2009.
Democratic People's Republic of Korea		
Resolution 1695	July 15, 2006	Imposed nonproliferation sanctions to prevent the transfer of missile and missile-related items, materials, goods, and technology to North Korea's missile or WMD programs, as well as to prevent the procurement of such items and technology from North Korea.
Resolution 1718	October 14, 2006	Established a Security Council sanctions committee; imposed a general arms embargo; imposed an embargo on nuclear weapons, ballistic missiles, and other WMD programs; imposed a ban on the export of luxury goods; imposed targeted measures including a travel ban and asset freeze.
Resolution 1874	June 12, 2009	Imposed additional measures including an expansion of the embargo on arms and related material and technology, as well as financial measures including a ban on financial transactions, technical training, advice, services, or assistance related to such arms and matériel; established the panel of experts.
Resolution 2087	January 22, 2013	Condemned the December 12, 2012, nuclear test by North Korea and added individuals and entities to the list of sanction targets.
Resolution 2094	March 7, 2013	Imposed additional sanctions against North Korea in response to a February 12, 2013, nuclear test; extended the mandate of the panel of experts.
Resolution 2141	March 5, 2014	Extended the mandate of the panel of experts.
Islamic Republic of Iran		
Resolution 1696	July 31, 2006	Demanded the suspension of all enrichment-related and reprocessing activities, including research and development.
Resolution 1737	December 23, 2006	Established a Security Council sanctions committee; imposed a ban on trade with Iran of certain nuclear proliferation–sensitive items; imposed an asset freeze on individuals and entities involved in proliferation-sensitive activities.

Resolution 1747	March 24, 2007	Imposed a general arms embargo and ban on financial services believed to contribute to proliferation-sensitive nuclear activities or development of nuclear weapon delivery systems.
Resolution 1803	March 3, 2008	Added a travel ban to the sanctions regime against Iran.
Resolution 1929	June 9, 2010	Modified the arms embargo, travel ban, asset freeze, nuclear proliferation ban, and provision of financial services ban; established a panel of experts; imposed a ban on the provision of bunkering services of vessels believed to be carrying prohibited items.
Resolution 2049	June 7, 2012	Extended the mandate of the panel of experts.
Resolution 2105	June 5, 2013	Extended the mandate of the panel of experts.
Resolution 2159	June 9, 2014	Extended the mandate of the panel of experts
Guinea-Bissau		
Resolution 2048	May 18, 2012	Imposed a travel ban on coup leaders; established a Security Council sanctions committee.
Central African Republic		
Resolution 2127	December 5, 2013	Imposed an arms embargo; established a Security Council sanctions committee.
Resolution 2134	January 28, 2014	Imposed a travel ban on individuals and assets freeze on individuals or entities designated by the committee.
Yemen		
Resolution 2140	February 26, 2014	Established a Security Council sanctions committee; imposed an asset freeze and travel ban against those threatening the peace, security, or stability of Yemen.

Sources: David Cortright and George Lopez, *The Sanctions Decade* (Boulder, CO: Lynne Rienner, 2000); United Nations sanctions homepage, http://www.un.org/sc/committees/index.shtml; www.securitycouncilreport.org/sanctions.

Appendix 5 Vetoes Cast in the UN Security Council, 1989–2014

Date	Draft Resolution	Meeting Record	Agenda Item	Permanent Members Casting Negative Vote
January 11, 1989	S/20378	S/PV.2841	Letters dated January 4, 1989, from Libya and Bahrain to the president of the Security Council	France, United Kingdom, United States
February 17, 1989	S/20463	S/PV.2850	Situation in the occupied Arab territories	United States
June 9, 1989	S/20677	S/PV.2867	Situation in the occupied Arab territories	United States
November 7, 1989	S/20945/Rev.1	S/PV.2889	Situation in the occupied Arab territories	United States
December 23, 1989	S/21048	S/PV.2902	Situation in Panama	France, United Kingdom, United States
January 17, 1990	S/21084	S/PV.2905	Letter dated January 3, 1990, from Nicaragua to the president of the Security Council	United States
May 31, 1990	S/21326	S/PV.2926	Situation in the occupied Arab territories	United States
May 11, 1993	S/25693	S/PV.3211	Situation in Cyprus	Russia
December 2, 1994	S/1994/1358	S/PV.3475	Situation in the Republic of Bosnia and Herzegovina	Russia
May 17, 1995	S/1995/394	S/PV.3538	Situation in the occupied Arab territories	United States
January 10, 1997	S/1997/18	S/PV.3730	Efforts toward peace in Central America	China
March 7, 1997	S/1997/199	S/PV.3747	Situation in the occupied Arab territories	United States
March 21, 1997	S/1997/241	S/PV.3756	Situation in the occupied Arab territories	United States
February 25, 1999	S/1999/201	S/PV.3982	Situation in the former Yugoslav Republic of Macedonia	China
March 27–28, 2001	S/2001/270	S/PV.4305	Middle East situation, including the Palestine question	United States
December 14–15, 2001	S/2001/1199	S/PV.4438	Middle East situation, including the Palestine question	United States
June 30, 2002	S/2002/712	S/PV.4563	Situation in Bosnia and Herzegovina	United States
December 20, 2002	S/2002/1385	S/PV.4681	Middle East situation, including the Palestine question	United States

Date	Document	Topic	Veto
September 16, 2003	S/2003/891	Middle East situation, including the Palestine question	United States
October 14, 2003	S/2003/980	Middle East situation, including the Palestine question	United States
March 25, 2004	S/2004/240	Middle East situation, including the Palestine question	United States
April 21, 2004	S/2004/313	Cyprus	Russia
October 5, 2004	S/2004/783	Middle East situation, including the Palestine question	United States
July 13, 2006	S/2006/508	Middle East situation, including the Palestine question	United States
November 11, 2006	S/2006/878	Middle East situation, including the Palestine question	United States
January 12, 2007	S/2007/14	Myanmar	China, Russia
July 11, 2008	S/2008/447	Peace and security in Africa (Zimbabwe)	China, Russia
June 15, 2009	S/2009/310	Georgia	Russia
February 18, 2011	S/2011/24	Middle East situation, including the Palestine question	United States
October 4, 2011	S/2011/612	Middle East: Syria	China, Russia
February 4, 2012	S/2012/77	Middle East: Syria	China, Russia
July 19, 2012	S/2012/538	Middle East: Syria	China, Russia
March 15, 2014	S/2014/189	Ukraine	Russia
May 22, 2014	S/2014/348	Middle East: Syria	China, Russia

Source: United Nations, "Security Council: Veto List," http://www.un.org/depts/dhl/resguide/scact_veto_en.shtml.

Acronyms

ACABQ	Advisory Committee on Administrative and Budgetary Questions
ACT	Accountability, Coherence, and Transparency Group (UN)
AFDL	Alliance of Democratic Forces for the Liberation of Congo
AFISMA	African-led International Support Mission to Mali
AFRC	Armed Forces Revolutionary Council (Sierra Leone)
AMIS	AU Mission in Sudan
AMISOM	AU Mission in Somalia
APEC	Asia Pacific Economic Cooperation
ASEAN	Association of Southeast Asian Nations
AU	African Union
BINUB	UN Integrated Office in Burundi
BINUCA	UN Integrated Peacebuilding Office in the Central African Republic
BNUB	UN Office in Burundi
BONUCA	UN Peacebuilding Support Office in the Central African Republic
BRIC	Brazil, Russia, India, China
BRICS	Brazil, Russia, India, China, South Africa
CAR	Central African Republic
CARICOM	Caribbean Community
CGPCS	Contact Group on Piracy off the Coast of Somalia
CIA	Central Intelligence Agency (United States)
CIAT	Committee in Support of the Transition (DRC)
CICIG	International Commission Against Impunity in Guatemala
CINCSOUTH	Commander in Chief, Allied Forces Southern Europe
CIRT	Committee for the International Repression of Terrorism (Council of the League of Nations)
CNDP	National Congress for the Defense of the People (DRC)
CPA	Comprehensive Peace Agreement (Sudan)
CPLP	Community of Portuguese Speaking Countries
CSCE	Conference for Security and Cooperation in Europe
CSTO	Collective Security Treaty Organization
CTBT	Comprehensive Test Ban Treaty
CTC	Counter-Terrorism Committee (UN)

CTED	Counter-Terrorism Committee Executive Directorate (UN)
CTITF	Counter-Terrorism Implementation Task Force (UN)
CVE	countering violent extremism
DDR	disarmament, demobilization, and reintegration
DHA	Department of Humanitarian Affairs (UN)
DOMREP	Mission of the Representative of the Secretary-General in the Dominican Republic
DPA	Department of Political Affairs (UN)
DPKO	Department of Peacekeeping Operations (UN)
DPRK	Democratic People's Republic of Korea
DRC	Democratic Republic of the Congo
E10	elected ten members of the UN Security Council
EC	European Community
ECJ	European Court of Justice
ECOMICI	ECOWAS Mission in Côte d'Ivoire
ECOMIL	ECOWAS Mission in Liberia
ECOMOG	ECOWAS Ceasefire Monitoring Group
ECOSOC	Economic and Social Council (UN)
ECOWAS	Economic Community of West African States
EIDHR	European Instrument for Democracy and Human Rights
EU	European Union
EU3	European Union Three (France, Germany, United Kingdom)
EU4	European Union Four (France, Germany, Italy, United Kingdom)
EUFOR	European Union Force
FAR	Rwandan Armed Forces
FARDC	Armed Forces of the Democratic Republic of the Congo
FATF	Financial Action Task Force
FCO	Foreign and Commonwealth Office (UK)
FDD	Forces for Democracy and Development (Burundi)
FDLR	Democratic Forces for the Liberation of Rwanda
FIB	Force Intervention Brigade (UN)
FMLN	Farabundo Martí National Liberation Front (El Salvador)
FRCI	Republican Forces of Côte d'Ivoire
G2	Group of Two (China, United States)
G4	Group of Four (Brazil, Germany, India, Japan)
G5	Group of Five (Brazil, China, India, Mexico, South Africa)
G7	Group of Seven (Canada, France, Germany, Italy, Japan, United Kingdom, and United States)
G8	Group of Eight (G7 plus Russia)
G-20	Group of 20 major economies
G-77	Group of 77 developing countries
GCC	Gulf Cooperation Council
GCTF	Global Counter-Terrorism Forum
GDP	gross domestic product
GEMAP	Governance and Economic Management Assistance Program
HRC	Human Rights Council (UN)
IAEA	International Atomic Energy Agency
IBSA	India, Brazil, and South Africa
ICAO	International Civil Aviation Organization
ICC	International Criminal Court

ICCPR	International Covenant on Civil and Political Rights
ICFY	International Conference on the Former Yugoslavia
ICGLR	International Conference on the Great Lakes Region
ICISS	International Commission on Intervention and State Sovereignty
ICJ	International Court of Justice
ICRC	International Committee of the Red Cross
ICTR	International Criminal Tribunal for Rwanda
ICTY	International Criminal Tribunal for the Former Yugoslavia
IDP	internally displaced person
IEMF	International Emergency Multinational Force
IFOR	Implementation Force
IGAD	Intergovernmental Authority on Development
IGASOM	IGAD Peace Support Mission to Somalia
IGC	Iraqi Governing Council
IMF	International Monetary Fund
INTERFET	International Force for East Timor
Interpol	International Criminal Police Organization
IPI	International Peace Institute
ISA	Islamic State of Afghanistan
ISAF	International Security Assistance Force
ISF	International Stabilization Force
ISIS	Islamic State of Iraq and Syria or Islamic State of Iraq and ash-Sham
IWG	Informal Working Group on Documentation and Other Procedural Questions (UN)
JNA	Federal Yugoslav Army
KFOR	Kosovo Force
KLA	Kosovo Liberation Army
LAS	League of Arab States
LRA	Lord's Resistance Army
LTTE	Liberation Tigers of Tamil Eelam (Sri Lanka)
M23	March 23 Movement (DRC)
MDNF	Multinational Force
MFO Sinai	Multinational Forces and Observers in Sinai
MICECI	ECOWAS Mission in Côte d'Ivoire
MILF	Moro Islamic Liberation Front
MINT	Mexico, Indonesia, Nigeria, Turkey
MINUCI	UN Mission in Côte d'Ivoire
MINUGUA	UN Mission in Guatemala
MINURCA	UN Verification Mission in the Central African Republic
MINURCAT	UN Mission in the Central African Republic and Chad
MINURSO	UN Mission for the Referendum in Western Sahara
MINUSAL	UN Mission in El Salvador
MINUSCA	UN Multidimensional Integrated Stabilization Mission in the Central African Republic
MINUSMA	UN Multidimensional Integrated Stabilization Mission in Mali
MINUSTAH	UN Stabilization Mission in Haiti
MIPONUH	UN Civilian Police Mission in Haiti
MISAB	Inter-African Mission to Monitor the Implementation of the Bangui Agreements
MISCA	International Support Mission to the Central African Republic

MLC	Movement for the Liberation of the Congo
MONUA	UN Observer Mission in Angola
MONUC	UN Organization Mission in the Democratic Republic of the Congo
MONUSCO	UN Organization Stabilization Mission in the Democratic Republic of the Congo
MPF	Multinational Protection Force (for Albania)
NAM	Non-Aligned Movement
NATO	North Atlantic Treaty Organization
NGO	nongovernmental organization
NGOWG	NGO Working Group for Women, Peace and Security (UN)
NPT	Nuclear Non-Proliferation Treaty
NSC	National Security Council (United States)
NSG	Nuclear Suppliers Group
NTC	National Transitional Council (Libya)
NTIM-I	NATO Training Implementation Mission in Iraq
OAS	Organization of American States
OAU	Organization of African Unity
OCHA	Office for the Coordination of Humanitarian Affairs (UN)
OECD	Organization for Economic Cooperation and Development
OGG	Observer Group Golan
OGL	Observer Group Lebanon
OHCHR	Office for the High Commissioner of Human Rights
OIC	Organization of the Islamic Conference (until 2011; Organization of Islamic Cooperation since then)
ONUB	UN Operation in Burundi
ONUC	UN Operation in the Congo
ONUCA	UN Observer Group in Central America
ONUMOZ	UN Operation in Mozambique
ONUSAL	UN Observer Mission in El Salvador
OPCW	Organisation for the Prohibition of Chemical Weapons
OPEC	Organization of Petroleum Exporting Countries
OSCE	Organization for Security and Cooperation in Europe
P3	permanent three Western members of the UN Security Council (France, United Kingdom, United States)
P5	permanent five members of the UN Security Council (China, France, Russia, United Kingdom, United States)
P5+1	P5 plus Germany
PBC	Peacebuilding Commission (UN)
PDPA	People's Democratic Party of Afghanistan
PDK	Party of Democratic Kampuchea (Cambodia)
PFLP	Popular Front for the Liberation of Palestine
PLA	People's Liberation Army (China)
PLO	Palestine Liberation Organization
PPP	purchasing power parity
PRC	People's Republic of China
PSC	Peace and Security Council (AU)
R2P	Responsibility to Protect
RCD	Rally for Congolese Democracy
RCD-K/ML	Rally for Congolese Democracy–Kisangani/ Movement for Liberation

RDR	Rally of the Republicans (Côte d'Ivoire)
ROC	Republic of China
RPF	Rwandan Patriotic Front
RUF	Revolutionary United Front (Sierra Leone)
RWP	responsibility while protecting
S5	Small Five (Costa Rica, Jordan, Liechtenstein, Singapore, Switzerland)
SADC	Southern African Development Community
SAM	sanctions assistance mission
SCO	Shanghai Cooperation Organization
SCSL	Special Court for Sierra Leone
SFOR	Stabilization Force (NATO)
SIPRI	Stockholm International Peace Research Institute
SITF	Sanctions Implementation Task Force (UN)
SLA	Sudan Liberation Army
SPLA	Sudan People's Liberation Army
SPLM	Sudan People's Liberation Movement
SRSG	special representative of the Secretary-General
STL	Special Tribunal for Lebanon
TFF	Task Force Fox
TNC	Transitional National Council (Libya)
UIC	Union of Islamic Courts
UNAEC	UN Atomic Energy Commission
UNAMA	UN Assistance Mission in Afghanistan
UNAMET	UN Mission in East Timor
UNAMI	UN Assistance Mission in Iraq
UNAMIC	UN Advance Mission in Cambodia
UNAMID	UN-AU Hybrid Operation in Darfur
UNAMIR	UN Assistance Mission for Rwanda
UNAMIS	UN Advance Mission in Sudan
UNAMSIL	UN Assistance Mission in Sierra Leone
UNASOG	UN Aouzou Strip Observer Group
UNAVEM	UN Angola Verification Mission
UNCCA	UN Commission for Conventional Armaments
UNCCT	UN Counter-Terrorism Centre
UNCRO	UN Confidence Restoration Operation (in Croatia)
UNDEF	UN Democracy Fund
UNDOF	UN Disengagement Observer Force
UNDP	UN Development Programme
UNEF	UN Emergency Force
UNESCO	UN Educational, Scientific, and Cultural Organization
UNFICYP	UN Peacekeeping Force in Cyprus
UNGOMAP	UN Good Offices Mission in Afghanistan and Pakistan
UNHCR	UN High Commissioner for Refugees
UNICEF	UN Children's Fund
UNICOI	UN International Commission of Inquiry
UNIFEM	UN Development Fund for Women (now UN Women)
UNIFIL	UN Interim Force in Lebanon
UNIIIC	UN International Independent Investigation Commission
UNIIMOG	UN Iran-Iraq Military Observer Group
UNIKOM	UN Iraq-Kuwait Observation Mission

UNIOGBIS	UN Integrated Peace-Building Office in Guinea-Bissau
UNIOSIL	UN Integrated Office in Sierra Leone
UNIPOM	UN India-Pakistan Observer Mission
UNIPSIL	UN Integrated Peacebuilding Office in Sierra Leone
UNISFA	UN Interim Security Force for Abyei
UNITA	National Union for the Total Independence of Angola
UNITAF	Unified Task Force
UNITAR	UN Institute for Training and Research
UNMEE	UN Mission in Ethiopia and Eritrea
UNMEER	UN Mission for Ebola and Emergency Response
UNMIBH	UN Mission in Bosnia and Herzegovina
UNMIH	UN Mission in Haiti
UNMIK	UN Mission in Kosovo
UNMIL	UN Mission in Liberia
UNMIN	UN Mission in Nepal
UNMIS	UN Mission in Sudan
UNMISET	UN Mission of Support in East Timor
UNMISS	UN Mission in South Sudan
UNMIT	UN Integrated Mission in Timor-Leste
UNMOGIP	UN Military Observer Group in India and Pakistan
UNMOP	UN Mission of Observers in Prevlaka
UNMOT	UN Mission of Observers in Tajikistan
UNMOVIC	UN Monitoring, Verification, and Inspection Commission
UNOA	UN Office in Angola
UNOB	UN Operation in Burundi
UNOCA	UN Regional Office for Central Africa
UNOCI	UN Operation in Côte d'Ivoire
UNODC	UN Office on Drugs and Crime
UNOGBIS	UN Peace-Building Support Office in Guinea-Bissau
UNOGIL	UN Observation Group in Lebanon
UNOL	UN Peacebuilding Support Office in Liberia
UNOMB	UN Observer Mission in Bougainville
UNOMIG	UN Observer Mission in Georgia
UNOMIL	UN Observer Mission in Liberia
UNOMSIL	UN Observer Mission in Sierra Leone
UNOMUR	UN Observer Mission in Uganda-Rwanda
UNOSOM	UN Operation in Somalia
UNOTIL	UN Office in East Timor
UNOWA	UN Office for West Africa
UNPF	UN Peace Forces
UNPOB	UN Political Office in Bougainville
UNPOS	UN Political Office for Somalia
UNPREDEP	UN Preventive Deployment Force (in Macedonia)
UNPROFOR	UN Protection Force
UNPSG	UN Police Support Group
UNRCCA	UN Regional Center for Preventive Diplomacy for Central Asia
UNRWA	UN Relief and Works Agency
UNSCO	Office of the UN Special Coordinator for the Middle East Peace Process
UNSCOL	Office of the UN Special Coordinator for Lebanon
UNSCOM	UN Special Commission

UNSCOP	UN Special Committee on Palestine
UNSMA	UN Special Mission to Afghanistan
UNSMIH	UN Support Mission in Haiti
UNSMIL	UN Support Mission in Libya
UNSMIS	UN Supervision Mission in Syria
UNSOA	UN Support Office for AMISOM
UNSOM	UN Assistance Mission in Mogadishu
UNTAC	UN Transitional Authority in Cambodia
UNTAES	UN Transitional Administration for Eastern Slavonia, Baranja, and Western Sirmium
UNTAET	UN Transitional Administration in East Timor
UNTAG	UN Transition Assistance Group
UNTMIH	UN Transition Mission in Haiti
UNTOP	UN Tajikistan Office of Peace-Building
UNTSO	UN Truce Supervision Organization
UNU	United Nations University
UNYOM	UN Yemen Observation Mission
URNG	Guatemalan National Revolutionary Unity
USAID	US Agency for International Development
WEOG	Western European and Others Group
WMD	weapons of mass destruction
XFOR	Extraction Force (NATO)

Bibliography

United Nations Documents

Independent Inquiry Committee into the United Nations Oil-for-Food Programme (Paul A. Volcker, Richard J. Goldstone, and Mark Pieth). *The Management of the United Nations Oil-for-Food Programme.* New York, 2005.

———— (Paul A. Volcker, Richard J. Goldstone, and Mark Pieth). *Manipulation of the Oil-for-Food Programme by the Iraqi Regime.* (Volcker Report). New York, 2005.

Panel of Experts on Accountability in Sri Lanka. *Report of the Secretary-General's Internal Review Panel on United Nations Action in Sri Lanka.* New York: United Nations, November 2012.

United Nations. *Repertory of Practice of United Nations Organs.* New York, 1955.

————. *Report of the International Commission of Inquiry on Darfur to the United Nations Secretary-General, Pursuant to Security Council Resolution 1564 of 18 September 2004.* Geneva, 2005.

————. "Verbatim Minutes of the Fourth Meeting of Commission III, 20 June 1945." *United Nations Conference on International Organization (UNCIO), Selected Documents.* Washington, DC: US Government Printing Office, 1946.

United Nations Department of Peacekeeping Operations. *Re-Hatting ECOWAS Forces as UN Peacekeepers: Lessons Learned.* New York: UN Peacekeeping Best Practices, 2005.

————. *United Nations Peacekeeping Operations: Principles and Guidelines.* New York: Department of Peacekeeping Operations and Department of Field Support, 2008.

United Nations Department of Political Affairs. *2012 Annual Report.* New York, 2013.

United Nations General Assembly. *Enhancing the Accountability, Transparency, and Effectiveness of the Security Council.* UN Doc. A/66/L.42/Rev.2, May 15, 2012.

————. *A More Secure World: Our Shared Responsibility—Report of the High-Level Panel on Threats, Challenges, and Change.* UN Doc. A/59/565, December 2, 2004.

————. *Report of the Open-Ended Working Group on the Question of Equitable Representation on and Increase in the Membership of the Security Council and Other Matters Related to the Security Council.* UN Doc. A/51/47, 1997.

————. *Report of the Secretary-General: Estimates in Respect of Special Political*

Missions, Good Offices and Other Political Initiatives Authorized by the General Assembly and/or the Security Council. UN Doc. A/69/363, October 17, 2014.

———. *Report of the Secretary-General on the Work of the Organization.* UN Doc. A/37/1, 1982.

———. *Report of the Secretary-General on the Work of the Organization.* UN Doc. A/54/PV.4, 1999.

———. *Report of the Secretary-General Pursuant to General Assembly Resolution 53/35: The Fall of Srebrenica.* UN Doc. A/54/549, November 15, 1999.

———. *Report of the Secretary-General to the General Assembly: Implementation of General Assembly Resolutions 55/235 and 55/236.* UN Doc. A/67/224/Add.1, December 27, 2012.

———. *Report of the United Nations Fact-Finding Mission on the Gaza Conflict.* UN Doc. A/HRC/12/48, September 25, 2009.

United Nations General Assembly and Security Council. *Report of the African Union–United Nations Panel on Modalities for Support to African Union Peacekeeping Operations.* UN Doc. A/63/666-S/2008/813, December 31, 2008.

———. *Report of the Panel on United Nations Peace Operations.* UN Doc. A/55/305-S/200/809, August 21, 2000.

———. *Report of the Policy Working Group on the United Nations and Terrorism.* UN Doc. A/57/273-S/2002/875, August 6, 2002.

United Nations Office on Drugs and Crime. *Drug Trafficking as a Security Threat in West Africa.* Vienna, 2008.

———. *Estimating Illicit Financial Flows Resulting from Drug Trafficking and Other Transnational Organized Crimes.* Vienna, 2011.

United Nations Secretary-General. *An Agenda for Democratization.* UN Doc. A/51/761, December 20, 1996.

———. *An Agenda for Peace: Preventive Diplomacy, Peacemaking, and Peacekeeping (Report of the Secretary-General Pursuant to the Statement Adopted by the Summit Meeting of the Security Council on 31 January 1992).* UN Doc. A/47/277-S/24111, June 17, 1992.

———. *Fourth Progress Report of the Secretary-General on the United Nations Operation in Côte d'Ivoire.* UN Doc. S/2005/186, March 18, 2005.

———. *Implementing the Responsibility to Protect: Report of the Secretary-General.* UN Doc. A/63/677, January 12, 2009.

———. *In Larger Freedom: Towards Development, Security, and Human Rights for All—Report of the Secretary-General.* UN Doc. A/59/2005, March 21, 2005.

———. *Overall Policy Matters Pertaining to Special Political Missions, Report of the Secretary-General.* UN Doc. A/68/223, July 29, 2013.

———. *Report of the Secretary-General (on the situation along the borders of East Pakistan and elsewhere in the sub-continent).* UN Doc. S/10410, December 3, 1971.

———. *Report by the Secretary-General Concerning the Situation in Somalia.* UN Doc. S/1994/1068, September 17, 1994.

———. *Report of the Secretary-General on His Mission of Good Offices in Cyprus.* UN Doc. S/2003/398, April 1, 2003.

———. *Report of the Secretary-General on Illicit Cross-Border Trafficking and Movement.* UN Doc. S/2012/777, October 19, 2012.

———. *Report of the Secretary-General on Possible Options to Further the Aim of Prosecuting and Imprisoning Persons Responsible for Acts of Piracy and Armed Robbery at Sea off the Coast of Somalia.* UN Doc. S/2010/394, July 26, 2010.

———. *Report of the Secretary-General on Specialized Anti-Piracy Courts in Somalia and Other States in the Region.* UN Doc. S/2012/50, January 20, 2012.

———. *Report of the Secretary-General on the Implementation of the Report of the Panel on United Nations Peace Operations.* UN Doc. A/55/502, October 20, 2000.

———. *Report of the Secretary-General on the Middle East.* UN Doc. S/2006/956, December 11, 2006.

———. *Report of the Secretary-General on the Modalities for the Establishment of Specialized Somali Anti-Piracy Courts.* UN Doc. S/2011/360, June 15, 2011.

———. *Report of the Secretary-General on the Situation in Mali.* UN Doc. S/2013/189, March 26, 2013.

———. *Report of the Secretary-General on the Situation in the Sahel Region.* UN Doc. S/2013/354, June 14, 2013.

———. *Report of the Secretary-General on the Sudan.* UN Doc. S/2008/267, April 22, 2008.

———. *Responsibility to Protect: Timely and Decisive Response—Report of the UN Secretary-General.* UN Doc. A/66/874-S/2012/578, July 25, 2012.

———. *Special Measures for Protection from Sexual Exploitation and Sexual Abuse: Report of the Secretary-General.* UN Doc. A/67/766, February 28, 2013.

———. *Special Report of the Secretary-General on the Sudan.* UN Doc. S/2011/314, May 17, 2011.

———. *Special Report of the Secretary-General on the United Nations Assistance Mission for Rwanda.* UN Doc. S/1994/470, April 20, 1994.

———. *Supplement to* An Agenda for Peace: *Position Paper of the Secretary-General on the Occasion of the Fiftieth Anniversary of the United Nations.* UN Doc. A/50/60-S/1995/1, January 25, 1995.

———. *Support by the United Nations System of the Efforts of Governments to Promote and Consolidate New or Restored Democracies: Report of the Secretary-General.* UN Doc. A/52/513, October 21, 1997.

———. *Twenty-Eighth Report of the Secretary-General on the United Nations Operation in Côte d'Ivoire.* UN Doc. S/2011/387, June 24, 2011.

———. *Uniting Against Terrorism: Recommendations for a Global Counter-Terrorism Strategy—Report of the Secretary-General.* UN Doc. A/60/825, April 27, 2006.

United Nations Security Council. *Annex to the Letter Dated 24 January 2011 from the Secretary-General to the President of the Security Council: Report of the Special Adviser to the Secretary-General on Legal Issues Related to Piracy off the Coast of Somalia.* UN Doc. S/2011/30, January 25, 2011.

———. *Final Report of the Group of Experts Submitted in Accordance with Paragraph 11 of Security Council Resolution 1842 (2008).* UN Doc. S/2009/521, October 9, 2009.

———. *Further Report of the Secretary-General Pursuant to Security Council Resolution 749 (1992).* UN Doc. S/23900, May 12, 1992.

———. *Recommendations of the Ad Hoc Working Group on Conflict Prevention and Resolution in Africa on Enhancing the Effectiveness of the Representatives and Special Representatives of the Secretary-General in Africa, Agreed as of 9 December 2002.* UN Doc. S/2002/1352, December 12, 2002.

———. *Report of the Assessment Mission on the Impact of the Libyan Crisis on the Sahel Region.* UN Doc. S/2012/42, January 18, 2012.

———. *Report of the Independent Inquiry into the Actions of the United Nation During the 1994 Genocide in Rwanda.* UN Doc. S/1999/1257, December 16, 1999.

———. *Report of the Informal Working Group on General Issues of Sanctions.* UN Doc. S/2006/997, December 22, 2006.

———. *Report of the Secretary-General Prepared Pursuant to Resolutions 1160 (1998), 1199 (1998), and 1203 (1998) of the Security Council.* UN Doc. S/1999/99, January 30, 1999.

———. *Report of the Secretary-General Pursuant to Paragraph 24 of Resolution 1483 (2003) and Paragraph 12 of Resolution 1511 (2003).* UN Doc. S/2003/1149, December 5, 2003.

———. *Report of the Secretary-General Pursuant to Security Council Resolution 1070 (1996).* UN Doc. S/1996/940, November 14, 1996.

———. *Report of the Secretary-General Pursuant to Security Council Resolution 2020 (2011).* UN Doc. S/2012/783, October 22, 2012.

———. *Report of the Security Council Mission to Sierra Leone.* UN Doc. S/2000/992, October 16, 2000.

———. *Report of the Security Council Mission to the Great Lakes Region, 15–26 May 2001.* UN Doc. S/2011/521/Add.1, May 30, 2001.

———. *Report of the United Nations Assessment Mission on Piracy in the Gulf of Guinea (7 to 24 November 2011).* UN Doc. S/2012/45, January 19, 2012.

———. *Report to the Secretary-General on Humanitarian Needs in Kuwait and Iraq in the Immediate Post-Crisis Environment by a Mission to the Area Led by Martti Ahtisaari, Under-Secretary-General for Administration and Management, Dated 20th March 1991.* UN Doc. S/22366, March 20, 1991.

———. *Second Report of the Analytical Support and Sanctions Implementation Monitoring Team Submitted Pursuant to Resolution 1988 (2011) Concerning the Taliban and Other Associated Individuals and Entities.* UN Doc. S/2012/971, December 31, 2012.

———. *Security Council Mission Visit to the Democratic Republic of the Congo, 4–8 May 2000.* UN Doc. S/2000/416, May 11, 2000.

Other Sources

Aboagye, Festus. *The Hybrid Operation in Darfur: A Critical Review of the Concept of the Mechanism.* ISS Paper no. 149. Pretoria: Institute for Security Studies, August 2007.

Acevedo, Domingo E. "The Right of Members of the Organization of American States to Refer Their 'Local' Disputes Directly to the United Nations Security Council." *American University International Law Review* 4, no. 1 (1989): 25–66.

Adebajo, Adekeye. *UN Peacekeeping in Africa: From the Suez Crisis to the Sudan Conflicts.* Boulder, CO: Lynne Rienner, 2011.

Ahrnens, Anette. *A Quest for Legitimacy: Debating UN Security Council Rules on Terrorism and Non-Proliferation.* Lund: Lund University, Department of Political Science, 2007.

Albright, Madeleine. *Madam Secretary: A Memoir.* New York: Miramax, 2003.

———. "Preserving Principle and Safeguarding Stability: United States Policy Toward Iraq." Address by the US secretary of state. *Foreign Policy Bulletin* 8 (1997): 109–112.

Alger, Chadwick F., Gene M. Lyons, and John E. Trent, eds. *The United Nations System: The Policies of Member States.* Tokyo: United Nations University Press, 1995.

Ali, Mohamed M., and Iqbal H. Shah. "Sanctions and Childhood Mortality in Iraq." *The Lancet* 355, no. 9218 (2000): 1851–1857.

Alvarez, Jose E. "Hegemonic International Law Revisited." *American Journal of International Law* 97, no. 4 (2003): 873–888.

———. "Judging the Security Council." *American Journal of International Law* 90, no. 1 (1996): 1–39.

American Presidency Project. *Public Papers of the Presidents of the United States: George Bush.* 4 vols. Washington, DC: US Government Printing Office, 1990–1993.

Andersen, Louise Riis, and Peter Emil Engedal. *Blue Helmets and Grey Zones: Do UN Multidimensional Peace Operations Work?* Copenhagen: Danish Institute for International Studies, 2013.

Andersson, Andreas. "Democracies and UN Peacekeeping Operations, 1990–1996." *International Peacekeeping* 7, no. 2 (Summer 2000): 1–22.

Annan, Kofi A. *The Question of Intervention: Statements by the Secretary-General of the United Nations.* New York: United Nations, 1999.

Annan, Kofi, with Nader Mousavizadeh. *Interventions: A Life in War and Peace.* New York: Penguin, 2012.

Antonini, Blanca, ed. *Security Council Resolutions Under Chapter VII: Design, Implementation, and Accountabilities—The Cases of Afghanistan, Côte d'Ivoire, Kosovo, and Sierra Leone.* Madrid: FRIDE, 2009.

Appathurai, James, and Ralph Lyshysyn. "Lessons Learned from the Zaire Mission." *Canadian Foreign Policy* 5, no. 2 (Winter 1998): 93–105.

Appiah-Mensah, Seth. "AU's Critical Assignment in Darfur: Challenges and Constraints" *African Security Review* 14, no. 2 (2005): 7–21.

Australian Strategic Policy Institute. *Calming Troubled Waters: Global and Regional Strategies for Countering Piracy.* Special Report no. 47. Barton, 2012.

Axworthy, Lloyd. "Human Security and Global Governance: Putting People First." *Global Governance* 7, no. 1 (2001): 19–23.

Baer, George W. *Test Case: Italy, Ethiopia, and the League of Nations.* Stanford: Hoover Institution, 1976.

Bailey, Sydney D. *The UN Security Council and Human Rights.* New York: St. Martin's, 1994.

———. "The UN Security Council and Terrorism." *International Relations* 11, no. 6 (1993): 537–538.

Bailey, Sydney D., and Sam Daws. *The Procedure of the UN Security Council.* 3rd ed. Oxford: Clarendon, 1998.

Baker, James A. *The Politics of Diplomacy: Revolution, War, and Peace, 1989–1992.* New York: Putnam's Sons, 1995.

Bakr, Noha, and Essam Abdel Shafi. *Arab Official Positions Towards President al Bashir's Indictment.* Madrid: FRIDE, March 2010.

Barnes, Cedric, and Harun Hassan. *The Rise and Fall of Mogadishu's Islamic Courts.* London: Chatham, 2007.

Barnett, Michael. "The UN Security Council: Indifference and Genocide in Rwanda." *Cultural Anthropology* 12, no. 4 (1997): 551–578.

Barry, Ben. "Libya's Lessons." *Survival* 53, no. 5 (2011): 5–14.

Bellamy, Alex J. *Responsibility to Protect: The Global Effort to End Mass Atrocities.* Cambridge: Polity, 2009.

Bellamy, Alex J., and Paul D. Williams. "The New Politics of Protection? Côte d'Ivoire, Libya, and the Responsibility to Protect." *International Affairs* 87, no. 4 (2011): 825–850.

———. *Providing Peacekeepers. The Politics, Challenges, and Future of UN Peacekeeping Contributions.* Oxford: Oxford University Press, 2013.

———. "The UN Security Council and the Question of Humanitarian Intervention in Darfur." *Journal of Military Ethics* 5, no. 2 (2006): 144–160.

Bellamy, Alex J., Paul Williams, and Stuart Griffin. *Understanding Peacekeeping.* Cambridge: Polity, 2004.

Benner, Thorsten, Stephan Mergenthaler, and Philipp Rotmann. *The New World of UN Peace Operations: Learning to Build Peace?* Oxford: Oxford University Press, 2011.

Bennett, Andrew, Joseph Lepgold, and Danny Unger. "Burden-Sharing in the Persian Gulf War." *International Organization* 48, no. 1 (Winter 1994): 39–75.

Berdal, Mats. "The UN Security Council: Ineffective but Indispensable." *Survival* 45, no. 2 (2003): 7–30.

Berdal, Mats, and Spyros Economides, eds. *United Nations Interventionism, 1991–2004.* Cambridge: Cambridge University Press, 2007.

Bettati, Mario. *Le Droit d'Ingérence.* Paris: Odile Jacob, 1996.

Bettati, Mario, and Bernard Kouchner. *Le Devoir d'Ingérence.* Paris: Denoël, 1987.

Betts, Alexander, and Gil Loescher, eds. *Refugees in International Relations.* Oxford: Oxford University Press, 2011.

Betts, Richard K. "The Delusions of Impartial Intervention." *Foreign Affairs* 73, no. 6 (1994): 20–33.

Biersteker, Thomas J., Sue E. Eckhert, and Marcos Tourinho. *Targeted Sanctions: The Impacts and Effectiveness of UN Action.* Cambridge: Cambridge University Press, 2015.

Bjurner, Anders, and Peter Wallensteen, eds. *Regional Organizations in Peacemaking: Challengers to the UN?* London: Routledge, 2014.

Black, David R., and Paul D. Williams, eds. *The International Politics of Mass Atrocities: The Case of Darfur.* London: Routledge, 2010.

Blanford, Nicholas. *Killing Mr. Lebanon: The Assassination of Rafik Hariri and Its Impact on the Middle East.* London: Tauris, 2006.

Blix, Hans. *Disarming Iraq.* New York: Pantheon, 2004.

Blokker, Niels, and Nico Schrijvers, eds. *The Security Council and the Use of Force.* Leiden: Martinus Nijhoff, 2005.

Bolton, John. *Surrender Is Not an Option: Defending America at the United Nations and Abroad.* New York: Threshold, 2007.

Bosco, David L. *Five to Rule Them All: The UN Security Council and the Making of the Modern World.* New York: Oxford University Press, 2009.

———. *Rough Justice: The International Criminal Court in a World of Power Politics.* New York: Oxford University Press, 2014.

Boucher, Alix J. *UN Panels of Experts and UN Peace Operations: Exploiting Synergies for Peacebuilding.* Washington, DC: Stimson Center, September 2010.

Bouillon, Markus E. "Zwischen den Stühlen: Von der schwierigen Rolle der Vereinten Nationen im Nahen Osten" [All Over the Place: On the Difficult Role of the United Nations in the Middle East]. *Vereinte Nationen: Zeitschrift für die Vereinten Nationen und ihre Sonderorganisationen* [German Review on the United Nations] 55, no. 6 (2007): 221–227.

Boulden, Jane, ed. *Dealing with Conflict in Africa: The United Nations and Regional Organizations.* New York: Palgrave Macmillan, 2003.

———. *Peace Enforcement: The United Nations Experience in Congo, Somalia, and Bosnia.* Westport: Praeger, 2001.

———, ed. *Responding to Conflict in Africa: The United Nations and Regional Organizations.* New York: Palgrave Macmillan, 2013.

Boulden, Jane, and Thomas G. Weiss, eds. *Terrorism and the UN: Before and After September 11.* Bloomington: Indiana University Press, 2004.

Bourloyannis, Christine. "The Security Council of the United Nations and the Implementation of International Humanitarian Law." *Denver Journal of International Law and Policy* 20, no. 2 (Winter 1992): 335–356.

Boutellis, Arthur. *Driving the System Apart? A Study of United Nations Integration and Integrated Strategic Planning.* New York: International Peace Institute, 2013.

———. *The Security Sector in Côte d'Ivoire: A Source of Conflict and a Key to Peace.* New York: International Peace Institute, May 2011.

Boutellis, Arthur, and Paul D. Williams. *Peace Operations, the African Union, and the United Nations: Toward More Effective Partnerships.* New York: International Peace Institute, 2013.

Boutros-Ghali, Boutros. *Unvanquished: A US-UN Saga.* New York: Random, 1999.

Bowden, Mark. *Black Hawk Down: A Story of Modern War.* New York: Atlantic Monthly, 1999.

Bowring, Bill. "Minority Rights in Post-War Iraq: An Impending Catastrophe." *International Journal of Contemporary Iraqi Studies* 5, no. 3 (2011): 319–335.

Boyd, Andrew. *Fifteen Men on a Powder Keg.* London: Methuen, 1971.

Brahimi, Lakhdar, and Thomas R. Pickering. *Afghanistan: Negotiating Peace—The Report of the Century Foundation International Task Force on Afghanistan in Its Regional and Multilateral Dimensions.* New York: Century Foundation, 2011.

Braithwaite, Rodric. *Afgantsy: The Russians in Afghanistan, 1979–1989.* London: Profile, 2011.

Bridges, Peter. *Safirka: An American Envoy.* Kent, OH: Kent State University Press, 2000.

Brown, Michael, Sean Lynn-Jones, and Steven Miller, eds. *Debating the Democratic Peace.* Cambridge: MIT Press, 2001.

Bueno de Mesquita, Bruce, and George W. Downs. "Intervention and Democracy." *International Organization* 60, no. 3 (Summer 2006): 627–650.

Bull, Hedley. *The Anarchical Society: A Study of Order in World Politics.* 3rd ed. New York: Columbia University Press, 2002.

Burr, Millard, and Robert O. Collins. *Revolutionary Sudan: Hasan al-Turabi and the Islamist State, 1989–2000.* Leiden: Brill, 2003.

Bush, George H. W., and Brent Scowcroft. *A World Transformed.* New York: Knopf, 1998.

Call, Charles T., and Susan E. Cook. "On Democratization and Peacebuilding." *Global Governance* 9, no. 2 (April–June 2003): 233–246.

Cammaert, Patrick, and Fiona Blyth. *The UN Intervention Brigade in the Democratic Republic of Congo.* New York: International Peace Institute, 2013.

Caplan, Richard. *International Governance of War Torn Territories: Rule and Reconstruction.* New York: Oxford University Press, 2005.

Carayannis, Tatiana. *The Challenge of Building Sustainable Peace in the DRC.* Geneva: Centre for Humanitarian Dialogue, 2009.

———. "The Complex Wars of the Congo: Towards a New Analytic Approach." *Journal of Asian and African Studies* 38, nos. 2–3 (2003): 232–255.

———. *Pioneers of Peacekeeping: ONUC, 1960–1964.* Boulder, CO: Lynne Rienner, forthcoming.

Carothers, Thomas. *U.S. Democracy Promotion During and After Bush.* Washington, DC: Carnegie Endowment for International Peace, 2007.

Carrel-Billard, François. *Taking Stock, Moving Forward: Report on the 2012 Elections to the Security Council.* New York: International Peace Institute, 2013.

Center for UN Reform Education, ed. *Managing Change at the United Nations.* New York, 2008.

Center on International Cooperation. *Annual Review of Global Peace Operations 2006.* Boulder, CO: Lynne Rienner, 2006.

———. *Annual Review of Global Peace Operations 2010.* Boulder, CO: Lynne Rienner, 2010.

———. *Towards More Inclusive Mandate-Making, More Effective Mandate Implementation.* Summary of thematic series panel discussion. New York: Center on International Cooperation, 2009.

Center on International Cooperation, and Megan Gleason, ed. *Annual Review of Global Peace Operations 2012.* Boulder, CO: Lynne Rienner, 2012.

Center on International Cooperation, and Alischa Kugel, Richard Gowan, Bruce Jones, and Megan Gleason-Roberts, eds. *Annual Review of Global Peace Operations 2013.* Boulder CO: Lynne Rienner, 2013.

Cha, Victor D. "Beijing's Olympic-Sized Catch-22." *Washington Quarterly* 31, no. 3 (2008): 105–123.

Chesterman, Simon. "Blue Helmet Blues." *Security Dialogue* 34, no. 3 (September 2003): 369–379.

———. *Just War or Just Peace? Humanitarian Intervention and International Law.* Oxford: Oxford University Press, 2001.

———, ed. *Secretary or General? The UN Secretary-General in World Politics.* Cambridge: Cambridge University Press, 2007.

———. *The Security Council and the Rule of Law: The Role of the Security Council in Strengthening a Rules Based International System.* Vienna: Federal Ministry of European and International Affairs and Institute for International Law and Justice, 2008.

———. *Shared Secrets: Intelligence and Collective Security.* Sydney: Lowy Institute for International Policy, 2006.

———. *You, the People: The United Nations, Transitional Administration, and Statebuilding.* Oxford: Oxford University Press, 2005.

Chesterman, Simon, Thomas M. Franck, and David M. Malone. *Law and Practice of the United Nations: Documents and Commentary.* Oxford: Oxford University Press, 2008.

Chowdhury Fink, Naureen. "Preventing Terrorism and Conflict in Libya: An Innovative Role for the United Nations?" *CTC Sentinel* 5, no. 2 (2012): 16–20.

Cilliers, Jakkie, and Mark Malan. *Peacekeeping in the DRC: MONUC and the Road to Peace.* Monograph no. 66. Halfway House: Institute for Security Studies, October 2001.

Clary, Christopher. "Dr. Khan's Nuclear Walmart." *Disarmament Diplomacy* 76 (March–April 2004): 35.

Claude, Inis L., Jr. *Swords into Plowshares: The Problems and Progress of International Organization.* 4th ed. New York: Random, 1971.

Clausewitz, Carl von. *On War.* Edited and translated by Michael Howard and Peter Paret. Princeton: Princeton University Press, 1989.

Cockayne, James. "Chasing Shadows: Developing a Strategic Approach to Organized Crime in Post-Conflict Situations." *RUSI Journal* 158, no. 2 (April–May 2013): 10–24.

———. "The Futility of Force? Strategic Lessons for Dealing with Unconventional Armed Groups from the UN's War on Haiti's Gangs." *Journal of Strategic Studies* 37, no. 5 (2014): 736–769.

———. *Transnational Threats: The Criminalization of West Africa and the Sahel.* New York: Center on Global Counterterrorism Cooperation, 2011.

Cockayne, James, and Adam Lupel, eds. *Peace Operations and Organised Crime: Enemies or Allies?* London: Routledge, 2011.

Cockayne, James, and David Malone. "The UN Security Council: 10 Lessons from Iraq on Regulation and Accountability." *Journal of International Law and International Relations* 2, no. 2 (Fall 2006): 1–24.

Cockayne, James, Christoph Mikulaschek, and Chris Perry. *The United Nations Security Council and Civil War: First Insights from a New Dataset.* New York: International Peace Institute, 2010.

Cockayne, James, Alistair Millar, David Cortright, and Peter Romaniuk. *Reshaping United Nations Counterterrorism Efforts: Blue-Sky Thinking for Global Counterterrorism Cooperation 10 Years After 9/11.* New York: Center on Global Counterterrorism Cooperation, 2012.

Cockayne, James, Alistair Millar, and Jason Ipe. *An Opportunity for Renewal: Revitalizing the United Nations Counterterrorism Program—An Independent Strategic Assessment.* New York: Center on Global Counterterrorism Cooperation, 2010.

Cockayne, James, and Phil Williams. *The Invisible Tide: Towards a Strategy to Deal with Drug Trafficking Through West Africa.* New York: International Peace Institute, October 2009.

Cockett, Richard. *Sudan: Darfur and the Failure of an African State.* New Haven: Yale University Press, 2010.

Cohen, Jared. *One Hundred Days of Silence: America and the Rwanda Genocide.* Lanham: Rowman and Littlefield, 2007.

Cohen, Lenard J., and Jasna Dragović-Soso, eds. *State Collapse in South-Eastern Europe: New Perspectives on Yugoslavia's Disintegration.* West Lafayette, IN: Purdue University Press, 2008.

Coleman, Isobel, and Terra Lawson-Remer, eds. *Pathways to Freedom: Political and Economic Lessons from Democracy Transitions.* New York: Council on Foreign Relations, 2013.

Collier, Paul. *Wars, Guns, and Votes: Democracy in Dangerous Places.* New York: HarperCollins, 2009.

Commission of Inquiry into the Deployment of Canadian Forces to Somalia. *Dishonoured Legacy: The Lessons of the Somalia Affair.* Ottawa: Canadian Government Publishing, 1997.

Commission on Global Governance. *Our Global Neighbourhood.* Oxford: Oxford University Press, 1995.

Cooper, Andrew, Jorge Heine, and Ramesh Thakur, eds. *The Oxford Handbook of Modern Diplomacy.* Oxford: Oxford University Press, 2013.

Cortright, David, and George A. Lopez, eds. *The Sanctions Decade: Assessing UN Strategies in the 1990s.* Boulder, CO: Lynne Rienner, 2000.

Cortright, David, George A. Lopez, and Linda Gerber-Stellingwerf, with Eliot Fackler and Joshua Weaver. *Integrating UN Sanctions for Peace and Security.* Goshen, IN: Sanctions and Security Research Program, 2010.

Crawford, Adam, ed. *International and Comparative Criminal Justice and Urban Governance: Convergence and Divergence in Global, National, and Local Settings.* Cambridge: Cambridge University Press, 2011.

Crenshaw, Martha. *Terrorism and International Cooperation.* Institute for East-West Security Studies, Occasional Paper no. 11. Boulder, CO: Westview, 1989.

Crocker, Chester A., and Fen Osler Hampson, with Pamela Aall, eds. *Herding Cats: Multiparty Mediation in a Complex World.* Washington, DC: US Institute of Peace, 1999.

———. *Managing Global Chaos: Sources of and Responses to International Conflict.* Washington, DC: US Institute of Peace, 1996.

———. *Turbulent Peace: The Challenges of Managing International Conflict.* Washington, DC: US Institute of Peace, 2001.

Croissant, Aurel. "The Perils and Promises of Democratization Through UN Transitional Authority: Lessons from Cambodia and East Timor." *Democratization* 15, no. 3 (2008): 649–668.

Cronin, Bruce, and Ian Hurd, eds. *The UN Security Council and the Politics of International Authority.* London: Routledge, 2008.

Cryer, Robert. "Sudan, Resolution 1593, and International Criminal Justice." *Leiden Journal of International Law* 19 (2006): 195–222.

Cunliffe, Philip. *Legions of Peace: UN Peacekeepers from the Global South.* London: Hurst, 2013.

Dadush, Uri, and Bennett Stancil. *The World Order in 2050.* Washington, DC: Carnegie Endowment for International Peace, 2010.

Dallaire, Roméo, with Brent Beardsley. *Shake Hands with the Devil: The Failure of Humanity in Rwanda.* Toronto: Random House Canada, 2003.

de Bont, Saoirse. *Prosecuting Pirates and Upholding Human Rights Law: Taking Perspective.* Broomfield, CO: One Earth Future Foundation, 2010.

de la Sablière, Jean-Marc. *Dans les Coulisses du Monde.* Paris: Laffont, 2013.

de Waal, Alex. "African Roles in the Libyan Conflict of 2011." *International Affairs* 89, no. 2 (2013): 369–370.

———. "Counter-Insurgency on the Cheap." *London Review of Books* 26, no. 15 (2004): 25–27.

———. "I Will Not Sign." *London Review of Books* 28, no. 23 (2006): 17–20.

———, ed. *Islamism and Its Enemies in the Horn of Africa.* Addis Ababa: Shama, 2004.

———, ed. *War in Darfur and the Search for Peace.* Cambridge: Harvard University Press, 2007.

de Wet, Erika. *The Chapter VII Powers of the United Nations Security Council.* Portland: Hart, 2004.

Deng, Francis M. *War of Visions: Conflict of Identities in the Sudan.* Washington, DC: Brookings Institution Press, 1995.

Deng, Francis M., et al. *Sovereignty as Responsibility: Conflict Management in Africa.* Washington, DC: Brookings Institution Press, 1996.

Deudney, Daniel, and Hanns W. Maull. "How Britain and France Could Reform the UN Security Council." *Survival* 53, no. 5 (2011): 107–128.

Diamond, Larry. "Building Democracy After Conflict: Lessons from Iraq." *Journal of Democracy* 16, no. 1 (January 2005): 9–23.

Dijkstra, Hylke. "Efficiency Versus Sovereignty: Delegation to the UN Secretariat in Peacekeeping." *International Peacekeeping* 19, no. 5 (2012): 581–596.

Dobbins, James, and Laurel Miller. "Overcoming Obstacles to Peace." *Survival* 55, no. 1 (February–March 2013): 103–119.

Dorn, Walter. "The UN's First 'Air Force': Peacekeepers in Combat, Congo 1960–64." *Journal of Military History* 77 (October 2013): 1399–1425.

Doyle, Michael. *Liberal Peace.* New York: Routledge, 2012.

Doyle, Michael W., Ian Johnstone, and Robert C. Orr, eds. *Keeping the Peace: Multidimensional UN Operations in Cambodia and El Salvador.* Cambridge: Cambridge University Press, 1997.

Doyle, Michael W., and Nicholas Sambanis. *Making War and Building Peace: United Nations Peace Operations.* Princeton: Princeton University Press, 2006.

Dunoff, Jeffrey L., and Joel P. Trachtman, eds. *Ruling the World: Constitutionalism, International Law, and Global Governance.* New York: Cambridge University Press, 2009.

Durch, William J., ed. *The UN, Peacekeeping, American Policy, and the Uncivil Wars of the 1990s.* New York: St. Martin's, 1996.

Economy, Elizabeth, and Michael Oksenberg, eds. *China Joins the World: Progress and Prospects.* New York: Council on Foreign Relations, 1999.

Eden, Paul, and Thérèse O'Donnell, eds. *September 11, 2001: A Turning Point in International and Domestic Law.* Ardsley: Transnational, 2005.

Edgren-Schori, Maud, Débora García-Orrico, Pierre Schori, Shahrbanou Tadj-bakhsh, and Gilles Yabi, eds. *Security Council Resolutions Under Chapter VII: Design, Implementation, and Accountabilities.* Madrid: FRIDE, 2009.

Egeland, Jan. *A Billion Lives: An Eyewitness Report from the Frontlines of Humanity.* New York: Simon and Schuster, 2008.

Engelbrekt, Kjell, Marcus Mohlin, and Charlotte Wagnsson, eds. *The NATO Intervention in Libya: Lessons Learned from the Campaign.* New York: Routledge, 2014.

Etzioni, Amitai. *Security First: For a Muscular, Moral Foreign Policy.* New Haven: Yale University Press, 2007.

Evans, Gareth. *Co-operating for Peace: The Global Agenda for the 1990s and Beyond.* St. Leonard's, Australia: Allen and Unwin, 1993.

———. *The Responsibility to Protect: Ending Mass Atrocity Crimes Once and For All.* Washington, DC: Brookings Institution Press, 2008.

Ewans, Martin. *Afghanistan: A Short History of Its People and Politics.* London: Curzon, 2001.

Farah, Douglas. *The Role of Sudan in Islamist Terrorism: A Case Study.* Alexandria, VA: International Assessment and Strategy Center, 2007.

Fearon, James. "Why Do Some Civil Wars Last So Much Longer Than Others?" *Journal of Peace Research* 41, no. 3 (May 2004): 275–301.

Findlay, Trevor. *The Use of Force in UN Peace Operations.* Oxford: Stockholm International Peace Research Institute and Oxford University Press, 2002.

Flint, Julie. *Rhetoric and Reality: The Failure to Resolve the Darfur Conflict.* Working Paper no. 19. Geneva: Small Arms Survey, 2010.

Foot, Rosemary. "The United Nations, Counterterrorism and Human Rights: Institutional Adaptation and Embedded Ideas." *Human Rights Quarterly* 29, no. 2 (2007): 489–514.

Foote, Wilder, ed. *Servant of Peace: A Selection of the Speeches and Statements of Dag Hammarskjöld, Secretary-General of the United Nations, 1953–1961.* New York: Harper and Row, 1962.

Forsythe, David P. *The UN Security Council and Human Rights.* Berlin: Friedrich Ebert Stiftung, 2012.

Fortna, Virginia Page. *Does Peacekeeping Work? Shaping Belligerents' Choices After Civil War.* Princeton: Princeton University Press, 2008.

Fox, Gregory H. "International Law and the Entitlement to Democracy After War." *Global Governance* 9, no. 2 (2003): 179–197.

Fox, Gregory H., and Brad R. Roth. "Democracy and International Law." *Review of International Studies* 27, no. 3 (2001): 327–352.

Franck, Thomas M. "The 'Powers of Appreciation': Who Is the Ultimate Guardian of UN Legality?" *American Journal of International Law* 86, no. 3 (July 1992): 519–523.

———. *Recourse to Force: State Action Against Threats and Armed Attacks.* Cambridge: Cambridge University Press, 2002.

———. "What Happens Now? The UN After Iraq." *American Journal of International Law* 97, no. 3 (July 2003): 607–620.

Franck, Thomas M., and Edward Weisband. *Word Politics: Verbal Strategy Among the Superpowers.* New York: Oxford University Press, 1971.

Freear, Matt, and Cedric de Coning. "Lessons from the African Union Mission for Somalia (AMISOM) for Peace Operations in Mali." *Stability: International Journal of Security and Development* 2, no. 2 (2013): 1–11.

Freedman, Lawrence. "International Security: Changing Targets." *Foreign Policy* 110 (Spring 1998): 48–63.

Freedom House. *Freedom in the World: Democratic Breakthroughs in the Balance.* New York, 2013.

Frowein, Jochen Abr, Klaus Scharioth, Ingo Winkelman, and Rüdiger Wolfrum, eds. *Verhandeln für den Frieden: Negotiating for Peace—Liber Amicorum Tono Eitel.* Berlin: Springer, 2003.

Frye, Alton, ed. *Humanitarian Intervention: Crafting a Workable Doctrine.* New York: Council on Foreign Relations, 2000.

Fukuyama, Francis. *Democracy's Century: A Survey of Global Political Change in the 20th Century.* New York: Freedom House, 2000.

Fullilove, Michael. "China and the United Nations: The Stakeholder Spectrum." *Washington Quarterly* 43, no. 3 (Summer 2011): 63–85.

Gaddis, John Lewis. *Strategies of Containment: A Critical Appraisal of Postwar American National Security Policy.* Oxford: Oxford University Press, 1982.

Gadler, Alice. "The Protection of Peacekeepers and International Criminal Law: Legal Challenges and Broader Protection." *German Law Journal* 11, no. 6 (2010): 585–608.

Gaer, Felice D., and Christen L. Broecker. *The United Nations High Commissioner for Human Rights: Conscience for the World.* Leiden: Martinus Nijhoff, 2014.

Gauthier, Amélie, and Sarah John de Sousa. *Brazil in Haiti: Debate over the Peacekeeping Mission.* Madrid: FRIDE, 2006.

Gehring, Thomas, and Thomas Dörfler. "Division of Labor and Rule-Based Decisionmaking Within the UN Security Council." *Global Governance* 19, no. 4 (2013): 567–587.

Geneva Declaration on Armed Violence and Development. *Global Burden of Armed Violence 2011: Lethal Encounters.* Geneva, 2011.

Genser, Jared, and Bruno Stagno Ugarte, eds. *The United Nations Security Council in the Age of Human Rights.* Cambridge: Cambridge University Press, 2014.

Gharekan, Chinmaya. *The Horseshoe Table: An Inside View of the UN Security Council.* Delhi: Pearson Longman, 2006.

Gill, Bates, and Chin-Hao Huang. *China's Expanding Role in Peacekeeping: Prospects and Policy Implications.* Policy Paper no. 25. Stockholm: Stockholm International Peace Research Institute, November 2009.

Gilligan, Michael, and Stephen J. Stedman. "Where Do the Peacekeepers Go?" *International Studies Review* 5, no. 4 (2003): 37–54.

Gilmore, Bill. *Dirty Money: The Evolution of International Measures to Counter Money Laundering and the Financing of Terrorism.* 4th ed. Strasbourg: Council of Europe Publishing, 2011.

Giumelli, Francesco. *Coercing, Constraining, and Signalling: Explaining and Understanding International Sanctions After the End of the Cold War.* Colchester: European Consortium for Political Research, 2011.

Global Issues Research Group. *Table of Vetoed Draft Resolutions in the United Nations Security Council, 1946–2002.* Research and Analytical Papers. London: Foreign and Commonwealth Office, 2003.

Goldblat, Jozef. *Nuclear Non-Proliferation: A Guide to the Debate.* Stockholm: Stockholm International Peace Research Institute, 1985.

Goldschmidt, Pierre. "Safeguard Noncompliance: A Challenge for the IAEA and the UN Security Council." *Arms Control Today* 40, no. 1 (January–February 2010): 22–28.

Goldstone, Richard J., and Adam Smith. *International Judicial Institutions.* London: Routledge, 2009.

Gordenker, Leon. *The UN Secretary-General and the Maintenance of Peace.* New York: Columbia University Press, 1967.

Gordon, Joy. *The Invisible War: The United States and the Iraq Sanctions.* Cambridge: Harvard University Press, 2010.

Goulding, Marrack. *Peacemonger.* London: John Murray, 2002.

Gourevitch, Philip. *We Wish to Inform You That Tomorrow We Will Be Killed with Our Families: Stories from Rwanda.* New York: Farrar, Straus, and Giroux, 1998.

Gowan, Richard. *Five Paradoxes of Peace Operations.* Berlin: ZIF, 2011.

———. "Floating Down the River of History: Ban Ki-moon and Peacekeeping, 2007–2011." *Global Governance* 17, no. 4 (2011): 399–416.

———. "From Rapid Reaction to Delayed Inaction? Congo, the UN, and the EU." *International Peacekeeping* 18, no. 5 (2011): 593–611.

———. "'Less Bound to the Desk': Ban Ki-moon, the UN, and Preventive Diplomacy." *Global Governance: A Review of Multilateralism and International Organizations* 18, no. 4 (2012): 387–404.

———. "The Strategic Context: Peacekeeping in Crisis, 2006–2008." *International Peacekeeping* 15, no. 4 (August 2008): 453–469.

Gowan, Richard, and Nora Gordon. *Pathways to Security Council Reform.* New York: Center on International Cooperation, 2014.

Gowan, Richard, and Alexandra Novosseloff. "Le Renforcement de la Force Intérimaire des Nations Unies au Liban: Etude des Processus Décisionnels au Sommet." *Annuaire Français de Relations Internationales* 11 (2010): 245–267.

Gowan, Richard, and Emily O'Brien. *The Use of force, Crisis Diplomacy, and the Responsibilities of States.* New York: Center on International Cooperation, May 2012.

Graham, Kennedy, and Tânia Felício. *Regional Security and Global Governance: A Study of Interaction Between Regional Agencies and the UN Security Council with a Proposal for a Regional-Global Security Mechanism.* Brussels: VUB Press and Brussels University Press, 2006.

Gramizzi, Claudio, and Jérôme Tubiana. *Forgotten Darfur: Old Tactics and New Players.* Small Arms Survey Report no. 28. Geneva: Graduate Institute of International and Development Studies, 2012.

Gray, Christine. *International Law and the Use of Force.* 3rd ed. New York: Oxford University Press, 2008.

Greenberg, Melanie, John H. Barton, and Margaret E. McGuiness, eds. *Words over War: Mediation and Arbitration to Prevent Deadly Conflict.* Lanham: Rowman and Littlefield, 2000.

Greenstein, Fred I., and Nelson W. Polsby, eds. *Handbook of Political Science.* Vol. 7, *Strategies of Inquiry.* Reading, MA: Addison-Wesley, 1975.

Greenwood, Christopher. *Humanitarian Intervention: Law and Policy.* Oxford: Oxford University Press, 2001.

Grono, Nick. "Darfur: The International Community's Failure to Protect." *African Affairs* 105, no. 421 (2006): 621–631.

Hamilton, Rebecca. *Fighting for Darfur: Public Action and the Struggle to Stop Genocide.* New York: Palgrave Macmillan, 2011.

Hannay, David. *New World Disorder: The UN After the Cold War—An Insider's View.* London: Tauris, 2008.

———. "The UN's Role in Bosnia Assessed." *Oxford International Review* 7, no. 2 (1996): 4–12.

Hansen, Annika. *Policing the Peace: The Rise of United Nations Formed Police Units.* Berlin: ZIF, 2011.

Hansen, Stig Jarle. *Al-Shabaab in Somalia: The History and Ideology of a Militant Islamist Group, 2005–2012.* Oxford: Oxford University Press, 2013.

Harel, Amos, and Avi Issacharoff. *34 Days: Israel, Hezbollah, and the War in Lebanon.* New York: Palgrave Macmillan, 2008.

Harper, Mary. *Getting Somalia Wrong.* London: Zed, 2012.

Harsch, Michael F. *NATO and the UN: Partnership with Potential?* Berlin: SWP, January 2012.

Hay, John B. "Conditions of Influence: An Exploratory Study of the Canadian Government's Effect on U.S. Policy in the Case of Intervention in Eastern Zaire." Unpublished MA thesis, Carleton University, Ottawa, May 1998.

Hegre, Håvard, Tanja Ellingsen, Scott Gates, and Nils Petter Gleditsch. "Toward a Democratic Civil Peace? Democracy, Political Change, and Civil War, 1816–1992." *American Political Science Review* 95, no. 1 (March 2001): 16–33.

Hehir, Aidan. "The Permanence of Inconsistency: Libya, the Security Council, and the Responsibility to Protect." *International Security* 38, no. 1 (2013): 137–159.

———. *The Responsibility to Protect: Rhetoric, Reality, and the Future of Humanitarian Intervention.* Houndmills: Palgrave Macmillan, 2012.

Heinrich Böll Foundation, ed. *Sudan: No Easy Ways Ahead.* Berlin: Heinrich Böll Stiftung, 2010.

Helman, Gerald B., and Steven R. Ratner. "Saving Failed States." *Foreign Policy* 89 (Winter 1992): 3–20.

Heyder, Corrina. "The U.N. Security Council's Referral of the Crimes in Darfur to the International Criminal Court in Light of U.S. Opposition to the Court: Implications for the International Criminal Court's Functions and Status." *Berkeley Journal of International Law* 24, no. 2 (2006): 650–671.

Higgins, Rosalyn. *Problems and Process: International Law and How We Use It.* Oxford: Oxford University Press, 1994.

Hilderbrand, Robert C. *Dumbarton Oaks: The Origins of the United Nations and the Search for Postwar Security.* Chapel Hill: University of North Carolina Press, 1990.

Hirsch John L., and Robert B. Oakley. *Somalia and Operation Restore Hope: Reflections on Peacemaking and Peacekeeping.* Washington, DC: US Institute of Peace, 1995.

Hmoud, Mahmoud. "Negotiating the Draft Comprehensive Convention on International Terrorism." *Journal of International Criminal Justice* 4, no. 5 (2006): 1031–1043.

Holbrooke, Richard. *To End a War.* New York: Random House, 1998.

Holslag, Jonathan. "China's Diplomatic Manoeuvring on the Question of Darfur." *Journal of Contemporary China* 17, no. 54 (2008): 71–84.

Holt, Victoria K., and Glyn Taylor, with Max Kelly. *Protecting Civilians in the Context of Peacekeeping.* Washington, DC: Stimson Center, 2009.

Holzgrefe, Jeff F., and Robert O. Keohane. *Humanitarian Intervention: Ethical, Legal, and Political Dilemmas.* Cambridge: Cambridge University Press, 2003.

Hoopes, Townsend, and Douglas Brinkley. *FDR and the Creation of the U.N.* New Haven: Yale University Press, 1997.

Huang, Chin-Hao. "U.S.-China Relations and Darfur." *Fordham International Law Journal* 31, no. 4 (2007): 827–842.

Hudson, Andrew, and Alexandra W. Taylor. "The International Commission Against Impunity in Guatemala: A New Model for International Criminal Justice Mechanisms." *Journal of International Criminal Justice* 8, no. 1 (2010): 53–74.

Human Rights Watch. *Human Rights Watch World Report 2004: War in Iraq—Not a Humanitarian Intervention.* New York, 2004.

———. *Iraq: At a Crossroads—Human Rights in Iraq Eight Years After the US-Led Invasion.* New York, 2010.

———. *Sudan, Oil, and Human Rights.* Washington, DC, 2003.

Human Security Centre. *Human Security Report 2005: War and Peace in the 21st Century.* New York: Oxford University Press, 2005.

Human Security Report Project. *Human Security Report 2009/2010: The Causes of Peace and the Shrinking Costs of War.* Vancouver: Human Security Press, 2010.

———. *Human Security Report 2012: Sexual Violence, Education, and War— Beyond the Mainstream Narrative.* Vancouver: Human Security Press, 2012.

Hume, Cameron. *The United Nations, Iran, and Iraq: How Peacemaking Changed.* Bloomington: University of Indiana Press, 1994.

Huntington, Samuel. *The Third Wave: Democratization in the Late Twentieth Century.* Norman: University of Oklahoma Press, 1993.

Hurd, Ian. *After Anarchy: Legitimacy and Power in the United Nations Security Council.* Princeton: Princeton University Press, 2007.

Igiri, Cheryl O., and Princeton N. Lyman. *Giving Meaning to "Never Again": Seeking an Effective Response to the Crisis in Darfur and Beyond.* Special Report no. 5. Washington, DC: Council on Foreign Relations, 2004.

Ignatieff, Michael. "Intervention and State Failure." *Dissent* (Winter 2002): 115–123.

Ikenberry, John. *After Victory: Institutions, Strategic Restraint, and the Rebuilding of Order After Major Wars.* Princeton: Princeton University Press, 2001.

Independent International Commission on Kosovo. *The Kosovo Report: Conflict, International Response, Lessons Learned.* New York: Oxford University Press, 2000.

Inoguchi, Takashi, Edward Newman, and John Keane, eds. *The Changing Nature of Democracy.* Tokyo: United Nations University Press, 1995.

International Commission on Intervention and State Sovereignty. *The Responsibility to Protect.* Ottawa: International Development Research Centre, 2001.

International Crisis Group. *China's Myanmar Dilemma.* Asia Report no. 177. Brussels, 2009.

———. *Côte d'Ivoire: Defusing Tensions.* Africa Report no. 193. Brussels, 2012.

———. *Côte d'Ivoire: Faut-il se Résoudre à la Guerre?* Africa Report no. 171. Brussels, 2011.

———. *Darfur Deadline: A New International Action Plan.* Africa Report no. 83. Brussels, 2004.

———. *God, Oil, and Country: Changing the Logic of War in Sudan.* Africa Report no. 39. Brussels, 2002.

———. *Jonglei's Tribal Conflicts: Countering Insecurity in South Sudan.* Africa Report no. 154. Brussels, 2009.

———. *Sudan's Comprehensive Peace Agreement: The Long Road Ahead.* Africa Report no. 106. Brussels, 2006.

————. *Sudan's Dual Crises: Refocusing on IGAD*. Africa Briefing no. 5. Brussels, 2004.

————. *Sudan's Spreading Conflict (I): War in South Kordofan*. Africa Report no. 198. Brussels, 2013.

International IDEA. *Constitution Building After Conflict: External Support to a Sovereign Process*. Stockholm, 2011.

International Maritime Bureau and Oceans Beyond Piracy. *The Human Cost of Somali Piracy, 2011*. Broomfield, CO, 2012.

Jain, Neha. "A Separate Law for Peacekeepers: The Clash Between the Security Council and the International Criminal Court." *European Journal of International Law* 6, no. 2 (2005): 239–254.

Jalloh, Charles C., Dapo Akande, and Max du Plessis. "Assessing the African Union Concerns About Article 16 of the Rome Statute of the International Criminal Court." *African Journal of Legal Studies* 4 (2011): 5–50.

Jarstad, Anna K., and Timothy D. Sisk, eds. *From War to Democracy: Dilemmas of Peacebuilding*. New York: Cambridge University Press, 2008.

Johansson, Patrik. "The Humdrum Use of Ultimate Authority: Defining and Analysing Chapter VII Resolutions." *Nordic Journal of International Law* 78, no. 3 (2009): 309–342.

Johnson, Douglas H. *The Root Causes of Sudan's Civil Wars: Peace or Truce?* Rev. ed. Rochester, NY: Currey, 2011.

————. "Why Abyei Matters: The Breaking Point of Sudan's Comprehensive Peace Agreement?" *African Affairs* 107, no. 426 (2008): 1–19.

Johnson, Hilde F. *Waging Peace in Sudan: The Inside Story of the Negotiations That Ended Africa's Longest Civil War*. Brighton: Sussex Academic, 2011.

Johnstone, Ian. "Legislation and Adjudication in the UN Security Council: Bringing Down the Deliberative Deficit." *American Journal of International Law* 102, no. 2 (2008): 275–308.

————. "Managing Consent in Contemporary Peacekeeping Operations." *International Peacekeeping* 18, no. 2 (April 2011): 168–182.

————. *The Power of Deliberation: International Law, Politics, and Organizations*. Oxford: Oxford University Press, 2011.

Jok, Jok Madut. "State, Law, and Insecurity in South Sudan." *Fletcher Forum of World Affairs* 37, no. 2 (2013): 69–80.

————. *Sudan: Race, Religion, and Violence*. Oxford: Oneworld, 2007.

Jones, Bruce D. "Libya and the Responsibilities of Power." *Survival* 53, no. 3 (2011): 51–60.

————. *Peacemaking in Rwanda: The Dynamics of Failure*. Boulder, CO: Lynne Rienner, 2001.

————. *Still Ours to Lead: The United States, Rising Powers, and the Tensions Between Rivalry and Restraint*. Washington, DC: Brookings Institution Press, 2014.

Jones, Bruce D., Shepard Forman, and Richard Gowan, eds. *Cooperating for Peace and Security: Evolving Institutions and Arrangements in a Context of Changing U.S. Security Policy*. New York: Cambridge University Press, 2010.

Jones, Bruce, and Andrew Hart. "Keeping Middle East Peace?" *International Peacekeeping* 15, no. 1 (2008): 102–117.

Joyner, Christopher C., ed. *The United Nations and International Law*. Cambridge: Cambridge University Press, 1997.

Judah, Tim. *Kosovo: War and Revenge*. New Haven: Yale University Press, 2000.

Karlsrud, John. "Special Representatives of the Secretary-General as Norm Arbitrators? Understanding Bottom-Up Authority in UN Peacekeeping." *Global Governance* 19, no. 4 (2013): 525–544.

Kemp, Walter, Mark Shaw, and Arthur Boutellis. *The Elephant in the Room: How Can Peace Operations Deal with Organized Crime?* New York: International Peace Institute, June 2013.

Kennan, George. "The Sources of Soviet Conduct." *Foreign Affairs* 25, no. 4 (July 1947): 566–582.

Kennedy, Paul. *The Parliament of Men: The United Nations and the Quest for World Government.* London: Allen Lane, 2006.

———. *The Rise and Fall of the Great Powers.* New York: Random House, 1987.

Keohane, Robert O. "The Globalization of Informal Violence, Theories of World Politics, and 'The Liberalism of Fear.'" *Dialog-IO* 1, no. 1 (2002): 29–43.

———. "Twenty Years of Institutional Liberalism." *International Relations* 26, no. 2 (June 2012): 125–138.

Kim, Samuel S., ed. *China and the World: Chinese Foreign Policy Faces the New Millennium.* Boulder, CO: Westview, 1998.

Kingsbury, Benedict, Nico Krisch, and Richard Stewart. *The Emergence of Global Administrative Law.* Working Paper no. 2004/1. New York: Institute for International Law and Justice, 2004.

Klein, P. W., and G. N. van der Plaat, eds. *Herrijzend Nederland.* Den Haag: Martinus Nijhoff, 1981.

Kleine-Ahlbrandt, Stephanie, and Andrew Small. "China's New Dictatorship Diplomacy: Is Beijing Parting with Pariahs?" *Foreign Affairs* 87, no. 1 (January–February 2008): 38–56.

Kobrin, Stephen J. "Oil and Politics: Talisman Energy and Sudan." *International Law and Politics* 36 (2004): 425–456.

Kohut, Andrew, and Bruce Stokes. *America Against the World.* New York: Times Books, 2006.

Kontorovich, Eugene. "'A Guantanamo on the Sea': The Difficulties of Prosecuting Pirates and Terrorists." *California Law Review* 98 (2010): 243–276.

Koops, Joachim A., Thierry Tardy, Norrie MacQueen, and Paul D. Williams, eds. *The Oxford Handbook on United Nations Peacekeeping Operations.* Oxford: Oxford University Press, 2015.

Krasner, Stephen D. *Sovereignty: Organized Hypocrisy.* Princeton: Princeton University Press, 1999.

Krasno, Jean E. ed. *United Nations: Confronting the Challenges of a Global Society.* Boulder, CO: Lynne Rienner, 2004.

Krasno, Jean E., Bradd Hayes, and Donald Daniel, eds. *Leveraging for Success in Peace Operations.* Westport: Praeger, 2003.

Kreβ, Claus, and Leonie von Holtzendorff. "The Kampala Compromise on the Crime of Aggression." *Journal of International Criminal Justice* 8, no. 5 (2010): 1179–1217.

Kugel, Alischa. *No Helmets, Just Suits: Political Missions as an Instrument of the UN Security Council for Civilian Conflict Management.* Berlin: Friedrich Ebert Stiftung, 2011.

Kumar, Krishna, ed. *Post-Conflict Elections, Democratization, and International Assistance.* Boulder, CO: Lynne Rienner, 1998.

Lagon, Mark. *Promoting Democracy: The Whys and Hows for the United States and the International Community.* New York: Council on Foreign Relations, 2011.

Langmore, John. "Australia's Campaign for Security Council Membership." *Australian Journal of Political Science* 48, no. 1 (2013): 101–111.

Lantagne, Daniele, G. Balakrish Nair, Claudio F. Lanata, and Alejandro Cravioto. "The Cholera Outbreak in Haiti: Where and How Did It Begin?" *Current Topics in Microbiology and Immunology* 379 (2014): 145–164.

Large, Daniel. "China's Sudan Engagement: Changing Northern and Southern Political Trajectories in Peace and War." *China Quarterly* 199 (September 2009): 610–626.

Large, Daniel, and Luke Patey. *Caught in the Middle: China and India in Sudan's Transition.* Working Paper no. 36. Copenhagen: Danish Institute for International Studies, 2010.

Larkin, Bruce D. *Designing Denuclearization: An Interpretive Encyclopedia.* New Brunswick, NJ: Transaction, 2008.

Lebow, Richard, and Benjamin Valentino. "Lost in Transition: A Critical Analysis of Power Transition Theory." *International Relations* 23, no. 9 (2009): 389–410.

Leenders, Reinoud. *How UN Pressure on Hizballah Impedes Lebanese Reform.* Washington, DC: Middle East Research and Information Project, 2006.

Lehman, Volker. *Reforming the Working Methods of the UN Security Council: The Next Act.* New York: Friedrich Ebert Stiftung, 2013.

Liberman, Peter. "Israel and the South African Bomb." *Nonproliferation Review* 11, no. 2 (Summer 2004): 1–35.

Lie, Trygve. *In the Cause of Peace: Seven Years with the United Nations.* New York: Macmillan, 1954.

Lin, Justin Yifu. *Demystifying the Chinese Economy.* New York: Cambridge University Press, 2012.

Lombardo, Caroline E. "The Making of an Agenda for Democratization." *Chicago Journal of International Law* 2, no. 1 (2001): 253–266.

Louis, William Roger, ed. *Still More Adventures with Britannia: Personalities, Politics, and Culture in Britain.* London: Tauris, 2003.

Lowe, Vaughan, Adam Roberts, Jennifer Welsh, and Dominik Zaum, eds. *The United Nations Security Council and War: The Evolution of Thought and Practice Since 1945.* Oxford: Oxford University Press, 2008.

Luck, Edward C. *Reforming the United Nations: Lessons from a History in Progress.* Occasional Paper no. 1. New Haven: Academic Council on the United Nations System, 2003.

———. *UN Security Council: Practice and Promise.* London: Routledge, 2006.

Lupel, Adam, and Ernesto Verdeja, eds. *Responding to Genocide: The Politics of International Action.* Boulder, CO: Lynne Rienner, 2013.

Lyon, Peter. "The Rise and Fall and Possible Revival of International Trusteeship." *Journal of Commonwealth and Comparative Politics* 31, no. 1 (1993): 96–110.

MacFarlane, S. Neil. *Intervention in Contemporary World Politics.* Adelphi Paper no. 350. Oxford: Oxford University Press, 2002.

Madut-Arop, Arop. *Sudan's Painful Road to Peace: A Full Story of the Founding and Development of SPLM/SPLA.* Charleston, SC: BookSurge, 2006.

Mahbubani, Kishore. *The Great Convergence: Asia, the West, and the Logic of One World.* New York: PublicAffairs, 2013.

Malone, David M. "Goodbye UNSCOM: A Sorry Tale in US-UN Relations." *Security Dialogue* 30, no. 4 (1999): 393–411.

———. *The International Struggle over Iraq: Politics in the UN Security Council, 1980–2005.* Oxford: Oxford University Press, 2006.

———. "Iraq: No Easy Response to 'The Greatest Threat.'" *American Journal of International Law* 95, no. 1 (January 2001): 235–245.

———. "The Security Council in the Post–Cold War Era: A Study in the Creative Interpretation of the UN Charter." *New York University Journal of International Law and Politics* 35, no. 2 (Winter 2003): 487–517.

———, ed. *The UN Security Council: From the Cold War to the 21st Century.* Boulder, CO: Lynne Rienner, 2004.

Malone, David M., and James Cockayne. "The UNSC: 10 Lessons from Iraq on Regulation and Accountability." *Journal of International Law and International Relations* 2, no. 2 (Fall 2006): 1–24.

Malone, David M., and Karin Wermester. "Boom and Bust? The Changing Nature of UN Peacekeeping." *International Peacekeeping* 7, no. 4 (2000): 37–54.

Mamdani, Mahmood. *Saviors and Survivors: Darfur, Politics, and the War on Terror.* New York: Pantheon, 2009.

Mancini, Francesco, ed. *Preventive Diplomacy: Regions in Focus.* New York: International Peace Institute, 2011.

Mani, Rama, and Thomas G. Weiss, eds. *The Responsibility to Protect: Cultural Perspectives in the Global South.* London: Routledge, 2011.

Mansfield, Edward D., and Jack Snyder. *Electing to Fight: Why Emerging Democracies Go to War.* Cambridge: MIT Press, 2007.

Månsson, K. "A Communicative Act: Integrating Human Rights in UN Peace Operations—Dialogues from Kosovo and Congo." PhD thesis, National University of Ireland, Galway, 2008.

Marr, Phebe. "Occupational Hazards: Washington's Record in Iraq." *Foreign Affairs* 84, no. 4 (July–August 2005): 180–186.

Marston, Geoffrey. "Early Attempts to Suppress Terrorism: The Terrorism and International Criminal Court Conventions of 1937." *British Yearbook of International Law* 73, no. 1 (2002): 293–313.

Marten, Kimberly Zisk. *Enforcing the Peace: Learning from the Imperial Past.* New York: Columbia University Press, 2004.

Martin, Ian. *All Peace Operations Are Political: A Case for Designer Missions and the Next UN Reform.* Thematic essays. New York: Center on International Cooperation, 2010.

———. *Self-Determination in East Timor: The United Nations, the Ballot, and International Intervention.* Boulder, CO: Lynne Rienner, 2001.

Masiza, Zondi. "A Chronology of South Africa's Nuclear Program." *Nonproliferation Review* 1, no. 1 (Fall 1993): 35–55.

Matheson, Michael J. *Council Unbound: The Growth of UN Decision Making on Conflict and Postconflict Issues After the Cold War.* Washington, DC: US Institute of Peace, 2006.

———. "United Nations Governance of Postconflict Societies." *American Journal of International Law* 95, no. 1 (January 2001): 76–85.

Mayall, James, and Ricardo Soares de Oliveira, eds. *The New Protectorates: International Tutelage and the Making of Liberal States.* London: Hurst, 2011.

Mazower, Mark. *Governing the World: The History of an Idea.* New York: Penguin, 2012.

———. *No Enchanted Palace: The End of Empire and the Ideological Origins of the United Nations.* Princeton: Princeton University Press, 2009.

McDonald, Kara C., and Stewart Patrick. *UN Security Council Enlargement and US Interests.* Council Special Report no. 59. New York: Council on Foreign Relations, 2010.

McDougall, Carrie. *The Crime of Aggression Under the Rome Statute of the International Criminal Court.* New York: Cambridge University Press, 2013.

Melvern, Linda. *A People Betrayed: The Role of the West in Rwanda's Genocide.* New York: Zed, 2000.

Menkhaus, Ken. *Somalia: A Country in Peril, a Policy Nightmare.* Strategy Paper no. 1. Washington, DC: Enough Project, September 2008.

Millar, Alistair, and Eric Rosand. *Allied Against Terrorism: What's Needed to Strengthen the Worldwide Commitment.* New York: Century Foundation, 2006.

Mofid, Kamran. *Economic Consequences of the Gulf War.* London: Routledge, 1990.

Mohan, C. Raja. *Samudra Manthan: Sino-Indian Rivalry in the Indo-Pacific.* Washington, DC: Carnegie Endowment for International Peace, 2012.

Moore, Jonathan, ed. *Hard Choices: Moral Dilemmas in Humanitarian Intervention.* Lanham: Rowman and Littlefield, 1998.

Morphet, Sally. "China as a Permanent Member of the Security Council: October 1971–December 1999." *Security Dialogue* 31, no. 2 (June 2000): 151–166.

Murithi, Tim. "The African Union's Foray into Peacekeeping: Lessons from the Hybrid Mission in Darfur." *Journal of Peace, Conflict, and Development* 14 (July 2009): 1–19.

National Intelligence Council. *Global Trends 2030: Alternative Worlds.* Washington, DC, 2012.

Natsios, Andrew S. "Beyond Darfur: Sudan's Slide Toward Civil War." *Foreign Affairs* 87, no. 3 (May–June 2008): 77–93.

———. *Sudan, South Sudan, and Darfur: What Everyone Needs to Know.* Oxford: Oxford University Press, 2012.

Ndulo, Muna, and Margaret Grieco, eds. *Failed and Failing States: The Challenges to African Reconstruction.* Newcastle: Cambridge Scholars, 2010.

Nealin Parker, J., ed. *Robust Peacekeeping: The Politics of Force.* New York: Center on International Cooperation, 2009.

Newman, Edward. *The UN Secretary-General from the Cold War to the New Era: A Global Peace and Security Mandate.* New York: Palgrave Macmillan, 1998.

Newman, Edward, and Roland Rich, eds. *The UN Role in Promoting Democracy.* New York: United Nations University Press, 2004.

Niblock, Tim. *"Pariah States" and Sanctions in the Middle East: Iraq, Libya, Sudan.* Boulder, CO: Lynne Rienner, 2001.

Nordin, Linda. "The NATO Air Strikes over Bosnia-Herzegovina." MA dissertation, University of Stockholm, February 1998.

North Atlantic Treaty Organization. *The Alliance's Strategic Concept.* Washington, DC, April 24, 1999.

Novosseloff, Alexandra, and Richard Gowan. *Security Council Working Methods and UN Peace Operations: The Case of Chad and the Central African Republic, 2006–2010.* New York: Center on International Cooperation, 2012.

Nuruzzaman, Mohammed. "The 'Responsibility to Protect' Doctrine: Revived in Libya, Buried in Syria." *Insight Turkey* 15, no. 2 (Spring 2013): 57–66.

O'Brien, Emily, and Andrew Sinclair. *The Libyan War: A Diplomatic History, February–August 2011.* New York: Center on International Cooperation, 2011.

Oceans Beyond Piracy. *The Economic Costs of Piracy 2011.* Broomfield, CO: Oceans Beyond Piracy, 2012.

Okhovat, Sahar. *The United Nations Security Council: Its Veto Power and Its Reform.* Working Paper no. 15/1. Sydney: CPACS, University of Sydney, 2012.

Olin, Nathaniel. *Measuring Peacekeeping: A Review of the Security Council's Benchmarking Process for Peacekeeping Missions.* New York: Conflict Prevention and Peace Forum, 2013.

Ombudsperson Institution in Kosovo. *Second Annual Report 2001–2002.* Prishtina, 2002.

Orford, Anne. *International Authority and the Responsibility to Protect.* Cambridge: Cambridge University Press, 2011.

Organization for Economic Cooperation and Development. "Development Cooperation 2000 Report: Efforts and Policies of the Members of the Development Assistance Committee." Paris: OECD Publishing, 2001.

Ottaway, Marina. "Promoting Democracy After Conflict: The Difficult Choices." *International Studies Perspectives* 4, no. 3 (2003): 314–322.

Ottaway, Marina, and Mai el-Sadany. *Sudan: From Conflict to Conflict.* Washington, DC: Carnegie Endowment for International Peace, May 2012.

Paliwal, Suyash. "The Primacy of Regional Organizations in International Peacekeeping: The African Example." *Virginia Journal of International Law* 51, no. 1 (2010): 185–230.

Pape, Robert. "When Duty Calls: A Pragmatic Standard of Humanitarian Intervention." *International Security* 37, no. 1 (2012): 41–80.

Paris, Roland. *At War's End: Building Peace After Civil Conflict.* Cambridge: Cambridge University Press, 2004.

Patil, Anjali V. *The UN Veto in World Affairs, 1946–1990: A Complete Record and Case Histories of the Security Council's Veto.* Sarasota: UNIFO, 1992.

Pattison, James. *Humanitarian Intervention and the Responsibility to Protect: Who Should Intervene?* Oxford: Oxford University Press, 2010.

Pérez de Cuéllar, Javier. *Pilgrimage for Peace: A Secretary-General's Memoir.* New York: St. Martin's, 1997.

Peterson, Scott. *Me Against My Brother: At War in Somalia, Sudan, and Rwanda.* New York: Routledge, 2000.

Petterson, Don. *Inside Sudan: Political Islam, Conflict, and Catastrophe.* Boulder, CO: Westview, 2003.

Phares, Walid. "The Sudanese Battle for American Opinion." *Middle East Quarterly* 5, no. 1 (March 1998): 19–31.

Piccolino, Giulia, and John Karlsrud. "Withering Consent, but Mutual Dependency: UN Peace Operations and African Assertiveness." *Conflict, Security & Development* 11, no. 4 (2011): 447–471.

Pickering, Jeffrey, and Mark Peceny. "Forging Democracy at Gunpoint." *International Studies Quarterly* 50, no. 3 (September 2006): 539–560.

Pinker, Steven. *The Better Angels of Our Nature: The Decline of Violence in History and Its Causes.* London: Allen Lane, 2011.

Plachta, Michael. "The Lockerbie Case: The Role of the Security Council in Enforcing the Principle *Aut Dedere Aut Judicare.*" *European Journal of International Law* 12 (2001): 125–140.

Polman, Linda. *The Crisis Caravan: What's Wrong with Humanitarian Aid?* New York: Holt, 2010.

Power, Samantha. *A Problem from Hell: America and the Age of Genocide.* New York: Harper Perennial, 2002.

Prunier, Gérard. *Darfur: The Ambiguous Genocide.* Ithaca: Cornell University Press, 2007.

———. *The Rwanda Crisis: History of a Genocide.* New York: Columbia University Press, 1995.

Pugh, Michael. "Peacekeeping and Critical Theory." *International peacekeeping* 11, no. 1 (2004): 39–58.

Pugh, Michael, and Waheguru Pal Singh Sidhu, eds. *The United Nations and Regional Security: Europe and Beyond.* Boulder, CO: Lynne Rienner, 2003.

Rajaee, Farhang, ed. *The Iran-Iraq War: The Politics of Aggression.* Gainesville: University Press of Florida, 1993.

Ramsbotham, Oliver, and Tom Woodhouse. *Encyclopedia of International Peacekeeping Operations.* Santa Barbara, CA: ABC-CLIO, 1999.

Rashid, Ahmed. *Taliban: The Power of Militant Islam in Afghanistan and Beyond.* London: Tauris, 2000.

Reike, Ruben. "Libya and the Responsibility to Protect: Lessons for the Prevention of Mass Atrocities." *St. Antony's International Review* 8, no. 1 (2012): 122–149.

Reinalda, Bob, ed. *Routledge Handbook of International Organization.* London: Routledge, 2013.

Rich, Roland. "Bringing Democracy into International Law." *Journal of Democracy* 12, no. 3 (July 2001): 20–34.

———. "Recognition of States: The Collapse of Yugoslavia and the Soviet Union." *European Journal of International Law* 4 (1993): 36–65.

Ripley, Tim. *Operation Deliberate Force: The UN and NATO Campaign in Bosnia, 1995.* Lancaster: Lancaster University Center for Defense and International Security Studies, 1999.

Roberts, Adam. "NATO's 'Humanitarian War' over Kosovo." *Survival* 41, no. 3 (Autumn 1999): 102–123.

———. "The Role of Humanitarian Issues in International Politics in the 1990s." *International Review of the Red Cross* 81, no. 833 (March 1999): 19–44.

Roberts, Adam, and Benedict Kingsbury, eds. *United Nations, Divided World: The UN's Roles in International Relations.* Oxford: Clarendon, 1993.

Roberts, Adam, and Dominik Zaum. *Selective Security: War and the United Nations Security Council Since 1945.* Adelphi Paper no. 395. London: International Institute for Strategic Studies, 2008.

Romaniuk, Peter. *Multilateral Counterterrorism: The Global Politics of Cooperation and Contestation.* New York: Routledge, 2010.

Rotberg, Robert I. "Failed States in a World of Terror." *Foreign Affairs* 81, no. 4 (2002): 127–140.

Rubin, Barnett R. *Afghanistan in the Post–Cold War Era.* Oxford: Oxford University Press, 2013.

Rummel, R. J. *Power Kills: Democracy as Method of Nonviolence.* New Brunswick, NJ: Transaction, 1997.

Russell, Ruth B. *A History of the United Nations Charter: The Role of the United States, 1940–1945.* Washington, DC: Brookings Institution Press, 1958.

Russett, Bruce, ed. *The Once and Future Security Council.* New York: St. Martin's, 1997.

Saul, Ben. "The Legal Response of the League of Nations to Terrorism." *Journal of International Criminal Justice* 4, no. 1 (2006): 78–102.

Schabas, William A. *An Introduction to the International Criminal Court.* Cambridge: Cambridge University Press, 2011.

Scheffer, David. *All the Missing Souls: A Personal History of the War Crimes Tribunals.* Princeton: Princeton University Press 2012.

Schlesinger, Stephen C. *Act of Creation: The Founding of the United Nations.* Boulder, CO: Westview, 2003.

Schmitt, Michael M., ed. *The War in Afghanistan: A Legal Analysis.* Washington, DC: US Government Printing Office, 2009.

Schnabel, Albrecht, and Ramesh Thakur, eds. *Kosovo and the Challenge of Humanitarian Intervention.* Tokyo: United Nations University Press, 2000.

Schott, Jared. "Chapter VII as Exception: Security Council Action and the Regulative Ideal of Emergency." *Northwestern Journal of International Human Rights* 6, no. 1 (2007): 24–80.

Searle, John R. "How to Derive 'Ought' from 'Is.'" *Philosophical Review* 73, no. 1 (January 1964): 43–54.

Security Council Report. "Chairs of Subsidiary Bodies and Pen Holders for 2013." Monthly Forecast. New York, February 2013.

———. "Chairs of Subsidiary Bodies and Penholders for 2014." Monthly Forecast. New York, February 2014.

———. "Cross-Cutting Report: Children and Armed Conflict." New York, 2012.

———. "Cross-Cutting Report: Protection of Civilians in Armed Conflict." New York, 2013.

———. "Cross-Cutting Report: The Rule of Law—The Security Council and Accountability." New York, 2013.

———. "Cross-Cutting Report: The Security Council's Role in Disarmament and Arms Control—Nuclear Weapons, Non-Proliferation, and Other Weapons of Mass Destruction." New York, 2009.

———. "Cross-Cutting Report: Women, Peace, and Security—Sexual Violence in Conflict and Sanctions." New York, 2013.

———. "In Hindsight: Appointment of Chairs of Subsidiary Bodies." Monthly Forecast. New York, December 2013.

———. "In Hindsight: Penholders." Monthly Forecast. New York, September 2013.

———. "In Hindsight: The Veto." Monthly Forecast. New York, November 2013.

———. "Israel/Palestine." Monthly Forecast. New York, January 2012.

———. "Non-Consensus Decision-Making in the Security Council: An Abridged History." Monthly Forecast. New York, January 2014.

———. "Security Council Statistics in 2012." Monthly Forecast. New York, February 2013.

———. "Special Research Report: Security Council Working Methods—A Tale of Two Councils?" New York, 2014.

———. "Special Research Report no. 1: Security Council Action Under Chapter VII—Myths and Realities." New York, 2008.

———. "Special Research Report no. 1: Security Council Working Methods—A Work in Progress?" New York, 2010.

———. "Special Research Report no. 2: Security Council Transparency Legitimacy and Effectiveness." New York, 2007.

———. "Special Research Report no. 2: Working Together for Peace and Security in Africa—The Security Council and the AU Peace and Security Council, 2011." New York, 2011.

———. "Special Research Report no. 3: Security Council Transparency, Legitimacy, and Effectiveness—Efforts to Reform Council Working Methods, 1993–2007." New York, 2007.

———. "Special Research Report no. 4: The Middle East, 1947–2007—Sixty Years of Security Council Engagement on the Israel/Palestine Question." New York, 2007.

———. "Update Report no. 1: Drug Trafficking as a Threat to International Security." New York, 2009.

———. "Update Report no. 1: Libya." New York, 2011.

————. "Update Report no. 2: Côte d'Ivoire." New York, 2010.

————. "Update Report no. 3: The Resurgence of Coups d'État in Africa." New York, 2009.

————. "Update Report no. 3: The United Nations and Regional Organizations." New York, 2007.

————. "Update Report no. 4: Peacekeeping—Relationship with TCCs/PCCs." New York, 2009.

————. "Update Report no. 5: Sri Lanka." New York, 2009.

————. "Western Sahara Mission Mandate Renewal." *What's in Blue.* New York, 2013.

Serrano, Mónica, and Thomas G. Weiss. *The International Politics of Human Rights: Rallying to the R2P Cause?* London: Routledge, 2014.

Shambaugh, David. *China Goes Global: The Partial Power.* Oxford: Oxford University Press, 2013.

————, ed. *Tangled Titans: The United States and China.* Lanham: Rowman and Littlefield, 2013.

Shapiro, Ian, and Joseph Lampert, eds. *Charter of the United Nations.* New Haven: Yale University Press, 2014.

Sharma, Ruchir. *Breakout Nations: In Pursuit of the Next Economic Miracles.* New York: Norton, 2012.

Sidhu, Waheguru Pal Singh, Pratap Bhanu Mehta, and Bruce Jones, eds. *Shaping the Emerging World: India and the Multilateral Order.* Washington, DC: Brookings Institution Press, 2013.

Sievers, Loraine, and Sam Daws. *The Procedure of the Security Council.* 4th ed. Oxford: Oxford University Press, 2014.

Simma, Bruno, Daniel-Erasmus Khan, Georg Nolte, and Andreas Paulus, eds. *The Charter of the United Nations: A Commentary.* 3rd ed. Oxford: Oxford University Press, 2012.

Slater, Robert, Barry Schutz, and Steven Dorr, eds. *Global Transformation in the Third World.* Boulder, CO: Lynne Rienner, 1993.

Slaughter, Anne-Marie. "Luncheon Address: Rogue Regimes and the Individualization of International Law." *New England Law Review* 36, no. 4 (2002): 816–824.

Slim, Hugo. "Dithering over Darfur? A Preliminary Review of the International Response." *International Affairs* 80, no. 5 (2004): 811–833.

Smith, Martin A. *On Rocky Foundations: NATO, the UN, and Peace Operations in the Post–Cold War Era.* Peace Research Report no. 37. Bradford: University of Bradford, Department of Peace Studies, 1996.

Smith, Rupert. *The Utility of Force: The Art of War in the Modern World.* London: Allen Lane, 2005.

Snyder, Jack. *From Voting to Violence.* New York: Norton, 2000.

Sripati, Vijayashri. "UN Constitutional Assistance Projects in Comprehensive Peace Missions: An Inventory, 1989–2011." *International Peacekeeping* 19, no. 1 (February 2012): 93–113.

Standing, André. *Transnational Organized Crime and the Palermo Convention: A Reality Check.* New York: International Peace Institute, 2011.

Stedman, Stephen John, Donald Rothchild, and Elizabeth M. Cousens, eds. *Ending Civil Wars: The Implementation of Peace Agreements.* Boulder, CO: Lynne Rienner, 2002.

Steinberg, James, and Michael E. O'Hanlon. *Strategic Reassurance and Resolve: U.S.-China Relations in the Twenty-First Century.* Princeton: Princeton University Press, 2014.

Stiles, Kendall W. "The Power of Procedures and the Procedures of the Powerful: Anti-Terror Law in the United Nations." *Journal of Peace Research* 43, no. 1 (2006): 37–54.

Szasz, Paul C. "The Security Council Starts Legislating." *American Journal of International Law* 96, no. 4 (2002): 901–905.

Talmon, Stefan. "The Security Council as World Legislature." *American Journal of International Law* 99 (2005): 175–193.

Thakur, Ramesh. *The United Nations, Peace, and Security: From Collective Security to the Responsibility to Protect.* Cambridge: Cambridge University Press, 2006.

Thakur, Ramesh, and Waheguru Pal Singh Sidhu, eds. *The Iraq Crisis and World Order: Structural, Institutional, and Normative Challenges.* Tokyo: United Nations University Press, 2006.

Tharoor, Shashi. "Should UN Peacekeeping Go 'Back to Basics'?" *Survival* 37, no. 4 (Winter 1995–1996): 52–64.

Themnér, Lotta, and Peter Wallensteen. "Armed Conflicts, 1946–2012." *Journal of Peace Research* 50, no. 4 (July 2013): 509–521.

———. "Armed Conflicts, 1946–2013." *Journal of Peace Research* 51, no. 4 (July 2014): 541–554.

Théroux-Bénoni, Lori-Anne. *Lessons for UN Electoral Certification from the 2010 Disputed Presidential Poll in Côte d'Ivoire.* Policy Brief no. 1. Waterloo: Centre for International Governance Innovation, June 2012.

Thomas-Jensen, Colin, and Julia Spiegel. "Activism and Darfur: Slowly Driving Policy Change." *Fordham International Law Journal* 31, no. 4 (2007): 843–858.

Tieh, Susan. "China in the UN: United with Other Nations?" *Stanford Journal of East Asian Affairs* 4, no. 1 (2004): 19–28.

Tochilovski, Vladimir. *The Law and Jurisprudence of the International Criminal Tribunals and Courts.* Cambridge: Intersentia, 2014.

Trahan, Jennifer. "The Relationship Between the International Criminal Court and the U.N. Security Council: Parameters and Best Practices." *Criminal Law Forum* 24, no. 4 (December 2013): 417–473.

Traub, James. *The Best Intentions: Kofi Annan and the UN in the Era of American Power.* New York: Farrar, Straus, and Giroux, 2006.

———. "The Security Council's Role: Off Target." *The New Republic* 232, no. 6 (February 21, 2005): 14–17.

———. *Unwilling and Unable: The Failed Response to the Atrocities in Darfur.* New York: Global Centre for the Responsibility to Protect, 2010.

Treves, Tullio. "Piracy, Law of the Sea, and Use of Force: Developments off the Coast of Somalia." *European Journal of International Law* 20, no. 2 (2009): 399–414.

Tubilewicz, Czeslaw. *Taiwan and Post-Communist Europe: Shopping for Allies.* London: Routledge, 2007.

Ulich, Oliver. "The UN Security Council's Response to Darfur: A Humanitarian Perspective." *Humanitarian Exchange Magazine* no. 30. London: Humanitarian Practice Network, 2005.

United States Congressional Research Service. *Piracy off the Horn of Africa.* R40528. Washington, DC, 2011.

Urquhart, Brian. *Hammarskjöld.* New York: Norton, 1994.

———. *A Life in Peace and War.* New York: Norton, 1991.

———. *Ralph Bunche: An American Life.* New York: Norton, 1993.

———. "The United Nations in the Middle East: A Fifty-Year Retrospective." *Middle East Journal* 49, no. 4 (Autumn 1995): 572–581.

Vagts, Detlev F. "Hegemonic International Law." *American Journal of International Law* 95, no. 4 (2001): 843–848.

van Baarda, Th. A. "The Involvement of the Security Council in Maintaining International Law." *Netherlands Quarterly of Human Rights* 12, no. 1 (1994): 137–152.

van der Lijn, Jaïr. *To Paint the Nile Blue: Factors for Success and Failure of UNMIS and UNAMID.* The Hague: Clingendael Institute, 2008.

Venter, A. J. "How Saddam Almost Built His Bomb." *Middle East Policy* 6, no. 3 (February 1999): 45–61.

Vidino, Lorenzo. "The Arrival of Islamic Fundamentalism in Sudan." *Al Nakhlah: The Fletcher School Online Journal for Issues Related to Southwest Asia and Islamic Civilization* (Fall 2006): 1–14.

Voeten, Erik. "The Political Origins of the UN Security Council's Ability to Legitimize the Use of Force." *International Organization* 59, no. 3 (2005): 527–557.

von Einsiedel, Sebastian. "You, the People: Transitional Administration, State-Building, and the United Nations," International Peace Academy Conference Report. New York: International Peace Academy, 2002.

von Einsiedel, Sebastian et al. *Major Recent Trends in Violent Conflict.* Tokyo: United Nations University Center for Policy Research, 2015.

von Siemens, Christina. "Russia's Policy Towards the War in Bosnia-Herzegovina (1992–1995)." MPhil dissertation, University of Oxford, April 2001.

Wako, Amos. *The Carter Camp Massacre: Results of an Investigation by the Panel of Inquiry Appointed by the Secretary-General into the Massacre Near Harbel, Liberia, on the Night of 5–6 June 1993.* New York: United Nations, September 1993.

Wallensteen, Peter. *Peace Research: Theory and Practice.* London: Routledge, 2011.

———. *Understanding Conflict Resolution.* 3rd ed. London: Sage, 2012.

Wallensteen, Peter, and Helena Grusell. "Targeting the Right Targets? The UN Use of Individual Sanctions." *Global Governance* 18, no. 2 (2012): 207–305.

Wallensteen, Peter, and Carina Staibano, eds. *International Sanctions: Between Words and Wars in the Global System.* Abingdon: Taylor and Francis, 2005.

Walter, Christian, Silja Vöneky, Volker Röben, and Frank Schorkopf, eds. *Terrorism as a Challenge for National and International Law: Security Versus Liberty?* Berlin: Springer-Verlag, 2004.

Walzer, Michael. "The Argument About Humanitarian Intervention." *Dissent* (Winter 2002): 29–37.

Ward, Curtis A. "Building Capacity to Combat International Terrorism: The Role of the United Nations Security Council." *Journal of Conflict Security Law* 8, no. 2 (2003): 289–305.

Ward, Karen. *The World in 2050: From the Top 30 to the Top 100.* London: HSBC Global Research, 2012.

Weber, Annette. *Bridging the Gap Between Narrative and Practice: The Role of the Arab League in Darfur.* Madrid: FRIDE, February 2010.

Weiss, Thomas G., ed. *Beyond UN Subcontracting: Task-Sharing with Regional Security Arrangements and Service-Providing NGOs.* London: Macmillan, 1998.

———. *Humanitarian Intervention: Ideas in Action.* 2nd ed. Cambridge: Polity, 2012.

———. "Humanitarian Intervention and US Policy." In *Great Decisions 2012.* New York: Foreign Policy Association, October 2012.

———. "Humanitarian Shell Games: Whither UN Reform?" *Security Dialogue* 29, no. 1 (March 1998): 9–24.

———. *Military-Civilian Interactions: Humanitarian Crises and the Responsibility to Protect.* 2nd ed. Oxford: Rowman and Littlefield, 2005.

———. "Moving Beyond North-South Theatre." *Third World Quarterly* 30, no. 2 (2009): 271–284.

Weiss, Thomas G., and Sam Daws, eds. *The Oxford Handbook on the United Nations.* New York: Oxford University Press, 2007.

Weiss, Thomas G., and Don Hubert. *The Responsibility to Protect: Research, Bibliography, and Background.* Ottawa: International Development Research Centre, 2001.

Weller, Marc, ed. *Oxford Handbook on the Law on the Use of Force.* Oxford, UK: Oxford University Press, 2015.

Welsh, Jennifer M., ed. *Humanitarian Intervention and International Relations.* Oxford: Oxford University Press, 2003.

Whalan, Jeni. *How Peace Operations Work: Power, Legitimacy, and Effectiveness.* Oxford: Oxford University Press, 2013.

Wheeler, Nicholas J., and Tim Dunne. "Good International Citizenship: A Third Way for British Foreign Policy." *International Affairs* 74, no. 4 (1998): 847–870.

Whitfield, Teresa. *Friends Indeed? The United Nations, Groups of Friends, and the Resolution of Conflict.* Washington, DC: US Institute of Peace, 2007.

———. *Working with Groups of Friends.* Peacemaker's Toolkit Series. Washington, DC: US Institute of Peace, 2010.

Williams, Michael C. *Civil-Military Relations and Peacekeeping.* London: Oxford University Press, 1998.

Williams, Paul D. "Into the Mogadishu Maelstrom: The African Union Mission in Somalia." *International Peacekeeping* 16, no. 14 (October 2009): 514–530.

———, ed. *Security Studies: An Introduction.* 2nd ed. London: Routledge, 2012.

Wills, Siobhan. *Protecting Civilians: The Obligations of Peacekeepers.* Oxford: Oxford University Press, 2009.

Wing, Christine, and Fiona Simpson. *Detect, Dismantle, and Disarm: IAEA Verification, 1992–2005.* Washington, DC: US Institute of Peace, 2013.

Woodward, Bob. *Obama's Wars.* New York: Simon and Schuster, 2010.

World Bank. *World Development Report 2011: Conflict, Security, and Development.* Washington, DC, 2011.

Wright, Robin. *Dreams and Shadows: The Future of the Middle East.* New York: Penguin, 2008.

Wuthnow, Joel. "Beyond the Veto: Chinese Diplomacy at the UN." PhD thesis, Columbia University, 2011.

———. *Chinese Diplomacy and the UN Security Council: Beyond the Veto.* New York: Routledge, 2013.

Yee, Herbert, ed. *China's Rise: Threat or Opportunity?* New York: Routledge, 2011.

Young, Michael. *The Ghosts of Martyr Square: An Eye-Witness Account of Lebanon's Life Struggle.* New York: Simon and Schuster, 2010.

Zanotti, Laura. *Governing Disorder: UN, Peace Operations, International Security, and Democratization in the Post–Cold War Era.* University Park: Pennsylvania State University Press, 2011.

Zaum, Dominik, and Mats Berdal. *Political Economy of Statebuilding: Power After Peace.* Abingdon: Routledge, 2013.

Zimmermann, Warren. *The Origins of a Catastrophe.* New York: Times Books, 1996.

The Contributors

Alex J. Bellamy is professor of peace and conflict studies and executive director of the Asia Pacific Centre for the Responsibility to Protect at the University of Queensland, Australia. He is also a nonresident senior adviser at the International Peace Institute and fellow of the Academy of Social Sciences in Australia.

Mats Berdal is professor in the Department of War Studies and director of the Conflict, Security, and Development Research Group at King's College London. He was formerly director of studies at the International Institute for Strategic Studies in London.

David Bosco is assistant professor at American University and author of books on the Security Council and the International Criminal Court. He writes regularly for *Foreign Policy* magazine.

Markus E. Bouillon has worked for the United Nations since 2004 at headquarters and in three field missions in Nairobi/Mogadishu, Beirut, and Jerusalem/Gaza. A Middle East expert, he has advised a series of senior UN envoys on the Arab-Israeli conflict, Lebanon, and Syria, and has published widely on conflict dynamics in the region.

Arthur Boutellis is a nonresident adviser at the International Peace Institute. He has worked with the United Nations missions in Burundi (BINUB), Chad and the Central African Republic (MINURCAT), Haiti (MINUSTAH), and Mali (MINUSMA). He has also worked at NGOs, think tanks, and academia with a particular focus on the Middle East and Africa.

Tatiana Carayannis is deputy director of the Conflict Prevention and Peace Forum at the Social Science Research Council and was a visiting fellow at the Institute of Public Knowledge at New York University. She has written widely on the Congo wars and the role of the UN in conflict management in Africa.

Simon Chesterman is dean of the National University of Singapore Faculty of Law. He is also editor of the *Asian Journal of International Law* and secretary-general of the Asian Society of International Law.

Poorvi Chitalkar is program officer at the Global Centre for Pluralism, Ottawa, Canada. She holds an LL.M. from the University of Toronto.

James Cockayne is head of office at the United Nations for United Nations University. He has previously led the Transnational Crime Unit of the Australian attorney-general's department, the Center for Global Counterterrorism Cooperation, and the editorial committee of the *Journal of International Criminal Justice,* and was a senior fellow at the International Peace Institute.

Raghida Dergham is a columnist and UN bureau chief for *Al Hayat* and founder and executive chairman of Beirut Institute, an independent think tank for the Arab region.

Sue Eckert is senior fellow in international studies at the Watson Institute, Brown University, where she directs projects on targeted sanctions and terrorist financing. She has previously served as assistant secretary of export administration in the Clinton administration and on the staff of the House Foreign Affairs Committee.

Sebastian von Einsiedel is director of the Centre for Policy Research at the United Nations University. He is a longtime UN staffer who has worked, inter alia, in the Department of Political Affairs, the Secretary-General's office, and the UN mission in Nepal.

Richard Gowan is research director at New York University's Center on International Cooperation and senior policy fellow at the European Council on Foreign Relations. He is a regular writer and broadcaster on UN affairs.

Jeremy Greenstock has been chairman of UNA-UK since 2011. Previously he was a UK career diplomat from 1969 to 2004, including UK permanent representative to the UN from 1998 to 2003 and UK special envoy for Iraq from 2003 to 2004. He then was director of the Ditchley Foundation from 2004 to 2010.

Jean-Marie Guéhenno is president of the International Crisis Group and previously served as director of the Center for International Conflict Resolution at Columbia University. He was also deputy joint special envoy of the United Nations and the Arab League for Syria and, from 2000 to 2008, was UN under-secretary-general for peacekeeping operations.

John L. Hirsch's thirty-two-year foreign service career (1966–1998) included assignments in Somalia, South Africa, and Sierra Leone (as US ambassador) at moments of crisis and transformation. Since 1998, he has held senior positions at the International Peace Institute and has taught courses on UN peacekeeping, contemporary diplomacy, and African peace and security at Columbia University, the University of Konstanz, and Occidental College.

Patrik Johansson is a postdoctoral research fellow in the Department of Political Science, Umeå University, and the National Centre for Peace and Conflict Studies, University of Otago. He served with the European Union Monitoring Mission (EUMM) in Macedonia from 2001 to 2002 and with the Temporary International Presence in Hebron (TIPH) in the West Bank from 2003 to 2004.

Ian Johnstone is professor of international law and former academic dean at The Fletcher School, Tufts University, and previously served in the UN Secretary-General's office. He has written extensively on the UN, the Security Council, international law, and international relations.

Bruce D. Jones is deputy director for foreign policy at the Brookings Institution and a consulting professor at Stanford University. He has served in UN positions in Pristina, Jerusalem/Gaza, and New York, and was previously the director of the New York University Center on International Cooperation.

Colin Keating is an independent adviser on international affairs and from 2012 to 2014 was special envoy of the prime minister of New Zealand during the successful New Zealand campaign for election to the UN Security Council. Previously he had served as the founding executive director of Security Council Report and, at earlier stages, as the secretary for justice of New Zealand and as the ambassador to the UN during New Zealand's previous term on the Security Council from 1993 to 1994.

Leng Xinyu is associate professor at the Law School of the China University of Political Science and Law and chairperson of the Board of Advisers of the Chinese Initiative on International Criminal Justice.

Edward C. Luck served as assistant secretary-general and special adviser to the UN Secretary-General on the Responsibility to Protect from 2008 to 2012. A scholar, professor, and prolific author, as well as practitioner, he has held a wide range of leadership positions in academia, nonprofit organizations, think tanks, and the United Nations.

Kishore Mahbubani, one of Asia's leading public intellectuals, is dean and professor in the practice of public policy of the Lee Kuan Yew School of Public Policy at the National University of Singapore. He previously served for thirty-three years in Singapore's diplomatic service and, as ambassador to the UN in New York, represented his country in the Security Council from 2001 to 2002.

David M. Malone has been rector of the United Nations University in Tokyo and a UN under-secretary-general since 2013. Previously a Canadian public servant, occasional scholar, and think-tank maven, he has authored or edited fourteen books, of which five address in some way the Security Council, notably its powers, performance, and pathologies.

Francesco Mancini is adjunct associate professor at Lee Kuan Yew School of Public Policy, National University of Singapore, and at the School of International and Public Affairs, Columbia University. He is also nonresident senior adviser at the International Peace Institute.

Heiko Nitzschke currently covers Security Council issues at the German mission to the United Nations in New York, having previously served with the UN mission in Sudan and as deputy head of mission at the German embassy in Khartoum. He has written articles and book chapters on the political economy of civil wars and UN security issues.

Alexandra Novosseloff is research associate at the Centre Thucydide at the University of Paris–Panthéon-Assas and a senior expert in the Peace and Security Section of the Global Governance Institute in Brussels.

Connie Peck is founder of the UNITAR Programme in Peacemaking and Preventive Diplomacy, which she created to provide advanced training in negotiation and mediation to UN staff and diplomats. She is the author of numerous journal articles and book chapters as well as thirteen books, including *On Being a Special Representative of the Secretary-General.*

Adam Roberts is senior research fellow in international relations, Oxford University, and emeritus fellow of Balliol College, Oxford. He was president of the British Academy from 2009 to 2013, and is the author and editor of numerous articles and books on international relations.

Amanda Roberts is senior research analyst at Security Council Report, covering the Middle East.

Peter Romaniuk is associate professor of political science at the John Jay College of Criminal Justice, the City University of New York, and senior fellow at the Global Center on Cooperative Security. In addition to numerous articles, chapters and reports, he is the author of *Multilateral Counter-Terrorism: The Global Politics of Cooperation and Contestation.*

Herman Schaper, a former Dutch career diplomat, is the Peter Kooijmans Chair for Peace, Law, and Security at Leiden University. He served as the permanent representative of the Netherlands to both the UN and NATO, and has published widely on Dutch foreign policy, European security, transatlantic relations, NATO, and the UN.

Salman Shaikh is director of the Brookings Doha Center and fellow at the Center for Middle East Policy. His earlier career with the United Nations included postings as special assistant to the special coordinator to the Middle East peace process and political adviser to the Secretary-General's personal representative for Lebanon.

Waheguru Pal Singh Sidhu is a senior fellow with Brookings India in New Delhi and a nonresident senior fellow at New York University's Center on International Cooperation. His research focuses on addressing nuclear weapon and missile challenges, development challenges in fragile states, and the role of India in the evolving global order.

Bruno Stagno Ugarte is deputy executive director (Global Advocacy) at Human Rights Watch, and formerly executive director of Security Council Report (2011–2014), minister of foreign affairs of Costa Rica (2006–2010), ambassador to the United Nations (2002–2006), president of the Assembly of States Parties of the International Criminal Court (2005–2008), and co-president of the Comprehensive Test Ban Treaty Conference (2007–2009).

Stephen John Stedman is senior fellow at the Freeman Spogli Institute for International Studies at Stanford University. From 2003 to 2005 he served with the United

Nations, first as research director of the United Nations High-Level Panel on Threats, Challenges, and Change, and later as assistant secretary-general and special adviser to the Secretary-General.

Eran Sthoeger, a former legal clerk at the Supreme Court of Israel, is a research analyst for Security Council Report covering, inter alia, the working methods of the Security Council, international criminal justice, and the rule of law. He is also a member of several legal teams in interstate disputes, past and present.

Thierry Tardy is senior analyst at the European Union Institute for Security Studies in Paris. He is the coeditor of the *Oxford Handbook on UN Peacekeeping Operations.*

Dmitri Trenin is director of the Carnegie Endowment for International Peace's Moscow Center. During his earlier career as an officer in the Soviet and Russian armed forces, he served, inter alia, as a staff member of the delegation to the US-Soviet nuclear arms talks in Geneva from 1985 to 1991.

Francesc Vendrell has served as personal representative of the UN Secretary-General for Afghanistan (2000–2002) and special representative of the EU for Afghanistan (2002–2008).

Peter Wallensteen is senior professor of peace and conflict research, Uppsala University, Sweden (Dag Hammarskjöld professor from 1985 to 2012) and Richard G. Starmann Sr. Research Professor of International Peace Studies, Kroc Institute, University of Notre Dame. He leads the Uppsala Conflict Data Program and the Special Program on International Targeted Sanctions at Uppsala University.

Thomas G. Weiss is presidential professor of political science and director emeritus of the Ralph Bunche Institute for International Studies at The Graduate Center of the City University of New York. He was a director of the United Nations Intellectual History Project, and has written extensively about the UN and humanitarian action.

Christian Wenaweser has been the permanent representative of Liechtenstein to the United Nations since 2002, and served as president of the Assembly of State Parties of the International Criminal Court from 2008 to 2011.

Joanna Weschler is director of research and deputy executive director of Security Council Report. Previously, she was the UN representative for Human Rights Watch.

Teresa Whitfield is senior adviser to the president of the International Crisis Group. Her previous positions included senior fellow at the Center on International Cooperation, senior adviser to the Centre for Humanitarian Dialogue, and director of the Conflict Prevention and Peace Forum in New York.

Paul D. Williams is associate professor in the Elliott School of International Affairs at George Washington University. He is a nonresident senior adviser at the International Peace Institute.

Dominik Zaum is head of the School of Politics and International Relations at the University of Reading and a senior research fellow in conflict and fragility in the UK Department for International Development. He has written widely on the political economy of statebuilding and peacebuilding and politics of international organizations.

Zhu Wenqi is professor of international law at Renmin University School of Law in Beijing. He is a former legal adviser in the Chinese Foreign Ministry and previously served as legal adviser and appeals counsel in the Office of the Prosecutor of the International Criminal Tribunal for the former Yugoslavia.

Index

Abidjan attacks, 685, 691–692, 696*n*19
Abkhazia. *See* Georgia conflict
Abu Nidal, 280
Abyei conflict, 623–624, 627–630, 628, 630
ACABQ. *See* Advisory Committee on
    Administrative and Budgetary Questions
Accountability: Charter constraints for, 783–
    784; consistency issues for, 787–788,
    869–870; E10 re-election and, 207; human
    rights, 855–856; indirect judicial review
    for, 784–786; in military interventions,
    229; political checks for, 786–787; power
    dynamics and, 825–826; of Security
    Council, 783–787, 868–870; in Syria,
    728–731; working methods, 188, 199, 786
Accountability, Coherence, and Transparency
    (ACT) Group, 188, 199
Accra III Agreement, 685
Achille Lauro attack, 280
ACT. *See* Accountability, Coherence, and
    Transparency Group
Act of Chapultepec, 477
Activism, civil society, 764, 852–856. *See
    also* Protests
Advisory Committee on Administrative and
    Budgetary Questions (ACABQ), 462–463
Afghanistan: bin Laden in, 648; Bonn process
    on, 66, 437*n*11, 651–652, 654–655; Cold
    War era relations in, 644–645; conclusion
    on, 655–657; conflict origins, 643–644;
    death count in, 46*tab*; democracy
    promotion in, 243; drug trafficking from,
    114, 303–304, 649; electoral assistance in,
    243–244, 653–655; emerging powers
    intervention in, 797; Geneva Accords for,
    645; Geneva Initiative for, 648;
    humanitarian justification for intervention

in, 222; ISA territory of, 643; ISAF in,
    405–406, 651–652, 653; Islamic Emirate
    territory of, 643; Islamic State of, 643;
    Karzai representation of, 653, 659*n*39;
    London Compact of, 654; Luncheon
    Group talks on, 647; mujahidin of, 644–
    645; NATO in, 405–406, 652; Operation
    Enduring Freedom in, 108, 652;
    Resolution 1333 on, 303, 656; resolution
    count in, 46*tab*; sanctions on, 283, 290,
    291, 647, 655, 656; Six Plus Two talks on,
    647, 658*n*22; Soviet Union relations with,
    644–645; SRSG for, 647, 648–649, 650–
    651, 655; transitional authority in,
    651–652, 653–655; UNAMA in, 563,
    652–655; Uniting for Peace resolution on,
    644; UNSMA in, 643–648, 649; US
    invasion of, 12, 66, 108, 222, 652–655,
    860; use of force on, 66
AFISMA. *See* African-led International
    Support Mission to Mali
Africa: conflict management by, 838, 847–
    848, 847*fig*; economy of, 797; French
    interventionism in, 832; peacekeeping
    contributions from, 847; P5 relations with,
    838, 870; resolutions by region, 40, 41*fig*,
    42*fig*, 43, 54*n*22; stance towards ICC, 855-
    856; UN interventionism in, 838; UN
    peacekeeping deployments in, 847;
    Working Group on Conflict Prevention
    and Resolution in, 453, 464, 474*n*20
African Group: G4 proposal response of, 170,
    181, 192*n*32, 192*nn*28–29; membership
    expansion of, 134, 163, 167, 170, 181;
    membership reform interests of, 170, 181,
    192*n*32; S5 proposal response of, 186
African Union (AU): Constitutive Act of, 242,

604, 708; Côte d'Ivoire mediation by, 686–687, 690; in Darfur as UNAMID, 97, 484, 604, 624, 625, 630–631, 634–635, 755–756, 764, 852; democracy promotion in, 242; hybrid operations with, 43; ICC Darfur referral response of, 518, 855–856; ICC Kenya referral response of, 520, 856; Libya stance of, 160, 282, 701, 702, 708; in Mali as AFISMA, 482, 485, 781; police contributions by, 54n22; resource limitations of, 851–852; sanctions by, 424–425; Security Council relations with, 483–485, 603–604, 605–606, 629, 763, 851–852; in Somalia as AMISOM, 603–606, 608–609, 613n47; in Somalia as transition support, 601; in Sudan, 97, 484, 485, 621, 623, 626, 755. *See also* Organization of African Unity

African Union Mission in Somalia (AMISOM), 603–606, 608–609, 613n47

African-led International Support Mission to Mali (AFISMA), 482, 485, 781

An Agenda for Democratization (Boutros-Ghali), 241

An Agenda for Peace (Boutros-Ghali), 7, 9, 10, 62, 227, 375, 397–398, 399, 437n17, 450–451, 482–483, 493

Agreed Framework, 333

Agreed Minutes of 1964, 778

Ahmed, Sharif Sheikh, 601

Ahtisaari, Martti, 821

Aidid, Mohamed Farah, 63, 597, 598, 599

AIDS pandemic, 679n30, 783, 865–866

Ajello, Aldo, 467

Akashi, Yasushi, 585, 586

Albania, 508, 587–588

Albright, Madeleine: ambassadorship style of, 65; on Bosnia, 579–580; ICTY establishment approval by, 76; on Iraq sanctions, 555; on Rwanda withdrawal, 63; on Somalia, 598; on Sudan sanctions, 617

Algeria, 621, 622, 667

Allawi, Iyad, 562

Ambassadorship: committee chairmanship and, 148, 205, 208, 421–423, 835; E10 orientation to, 213n21, 213n24; junior, 147; Russia style of, 110; to SRSG, 467; US style of, 65

AMIS. *See* AU Mission in Sudan

AMISOM. *See* African Union Mission in Somalia

Amos, Valerie, 728

Angelo, Victor, 761

Angola: MONUA in, 266; sanctions on, 417tab, 420tab, 424, 427, 857; UNITA in, 306, 417tab, 427

Annan, Kofi, 14, 64, 304, 359, 620; appointment of, 445; Article 99 used by, 451; on Darfur crisis, 761; democracy promotion by, 241, 245; human rights institution changes by, 264–265; humanitarian rhetoric of, 223, 224, 404, 453, 590; on Iraq War, 823; *In Larger Freedom* by, 224, 245, 438n17, 484, 809, 813n42; membership reform proposal by, 809, 813n42; NATO relations with, 404; norm entrepreneurship of, 453; on peacekeeping failure, 398; on regional organizations, 484; sanctions reform by, 438n17; Syria mediation by, 70, 500, 720, 723–725, 742; *Uniting Against Terrorism* by, 289; on UNSCOM, 558; on use of force, 375–376, 391n7, 405

Annapolis Conference, 536

Apartheid, 238, 260, 326–327

Al-Aqsa intifada, 534–535

Arab League: on Darfur referral to ICC, 518, 626; on Friends of civilian protection, 499–500; Libya stance of, 701, 702–703, 707–708; in Palestine, 478–479; Security Council relations with, 43, 478, 852; Syria proposal by, 721, 722–723, 734tab, 742

Arab Spring, 244, 290, 839, 852; Lebanon protests, 541; Libya protests, 701; Syria protests, 717–718

Arab-Israeli conflict: al-Aqsa intifada as, 534–535; Camp David Accords for, 532; Cold War era of, 530–533, 794; conclusion on, 544–546; Gaza wars, 535–539; Lebanon relations in, 88tab, 532, 539–544, 749; P3 contention on, 534; peacemaking for, 533, 536; permanent armistice for, 530; precedents set by, 529, 530–531; Quartet role in, 534, 535–536, 538; recent crises of, 533–544; Six-Day War as, 531–532; Suez crisis as, 212n15, 374, 531–533; as unsolvable challenge, 529–530

Arafat, Yasser, 289

Argentina: in Falklands War, 481; Haiti troop contribution by, 759; OAS relations with, 479, 481

Arias, Inocencio, 288

Arias, Oscar, 288

Aristide, Jean-Bertrand, 239, 447

Armed Forces of the Democratic Republic of the Congo (FARDC), 380–382, 673–675

Arms embargoes, 416–418tab

Arnault, Jean, 468

Arraud, Gérard, 873n25

Arria formula, 151, 177, 199, 261, 268, 836, 854

Articles of UN Charter. *See* Charter

ASEAN. *See* Association of Southeast Asian Nations

Ashton, Catherine, 702

Asia: conflict management by, 797; Council

resolutions focused on, 40, 41*fig*, 42*fig*, 43; emerging power tensions in, 795, 804–805; peacekeeper count comparison in, 847*fig*; peacekeeping contributions from, 847; subregional office in, 461; UN interventions in, 838

Al-Assad, Bashar, 70, 98, 227, 717–718

Assassination: of Bernadotte, 279, 530; of Betancourt, attempted, 480; of Daoud Khan, 644; of Hariri, Rafik, 419, 446, 513, 540–541; of Kabila, Laurent, 671; of Mubarak, attempted, 54*n*27, 282, 617; of Shermake, 596

Association of Southeast Asian Nations (ASEAN), 481

Atomic Energy Commission. *See* UN Atomic Energy Commission

Atrocity Prevention Board, 223

AU. *See* African Union

AU Mission in Sudan (AMIS), 621, 623, 755

Australia: Campaign for Council membership by, 758; East Timor intervention by, 64, 752; penholder role of, 151; Syria proposal by, 728, 730, 736, 737

Austria: OHCHR consultation by, 264, 853; Vienna Group, 338

Aviation: flight bombings, 281, 784; travel sanctions, 416–418*tab*

Axworthy, Lloyd, 223

Backup force capacity, 387

Badme conflict, 46*tab*

Baker, James, 60, 553

Balkans: Macedonia, 88*tab*, 91, 161, 592*n*13; Slovenia, 571–574, 576. *See also* Bosnia-Herzegovina conflict; Croatia; Kosovo; Turkey; Yugoslavia

Ban Ki-moon: Article 99 used by, 451; on Darfur crisis, 626, 761; on Gaza wars, 537; on Goma crisis, 674; HRC involvement by, 265; on Libya resolutions, 408, 702, 711, 842; NATO relations with, 406, 409; norm entrepreneurship of, 453; R2P approach of, 224; on sanctions reform, 438*n*17; on Somalia transition support, 607–608; stance on peacekeeping by, 846–847; on Syria proliferation management, 745

Bangladesh, 88*tab*, 89*tab*

Barak, Ehud, 539

Barre, Siad, 597, 601–602

Baruch Plan, 325

Al-Bashir, Omar, 96–97, 617; arrest warrant for, 518, 626, 786, 855–856; overthrow call, 628–629; resolution rejection by, 623, 624; al-Turabi split from, 618, 619

Bédié, Aimé Henri Konan, 688, 696*n*23

Beirut bombing, 419, 446, 513, 540–541

Bellemare, Daniel, 541

Bemba, Jean-Pierre, 679*n*33

Benghazi massacre prevention, 701, 703, 706–707

Berdal, Mats, 90, 751

Bernadotte, Folke, 279, 530

Betancourt, Rómulo, 480

Biersteker, Thomas, 435

Bin Laden, Osama: in Afghanistan, 648; in Sudan, 282, 617, 618

Bir, Cevik, 599

Black Hawk Down, 9, 63, 595, 599

Black markets, 8, 556

Black September Organization, 279

Blair, Tony, 130, 535, 744, 821

Blix, Hans, 559

Bolton, John, 67, 340, 623

Bombing: Beirut, 419, 446, 513, 540–541; *Cole*, USS, 648; embassy, 280, 283, 419, 618, 646; flight, 281, 784; Hiroshima, 325; Kampala, 605; Khartoum, 616; Lockerbie, 281, 784; UNAMI headquarters, 561, 562

Bonn process, 66, 437*n*11, 651–652, 654–655

Bosnia-Herzegovina conflict: agreements overload in, 579; China stance on, 580–582; Dayton Accords for, 64, 359, 400, 402, 587; deadlock on, 574–575; death count in, 46*tab*, 47*tab*; ethnic mix and, 570–571; EU response to, 577–580, 585–586; hostage crisis, 584; human rights catastrophe of, 262–263; IDPs in, 592*n*18; indirect judicial review of, 784–785; investigation commission on, 269; membership of, 576; myths about, 584; NAM stance on, 578, 591*n*5, 592*n*26; NATO air strike in, 358–359, 400, 401–402, 583–586; P3 contention on, 140, 577–580; P5 contention on, 140, 572; refugee support in, 576, 579, 592*nn*17–18; regional organization assistance in, 482; Resolution 757 on, 576; Resolution 776 on, 576; Resolution 836 on, 361–362, 384, 578, 583; resolution count in, 46*tab*, 47*tab*; Russia stance on, 580–582, 585; safe areas regime in, 577–580; Srebrenica massacre in, 8, 9, 262–263, 358, 784–785; UNPROFOR in, 8, 9, 266, 361–362, 401, 576–577, 578–579, 583–586; US response to, 577–580, 585–586; use of force in, 358–359, 361–362, 582–586. *See also* International Criminal Tribunal for the Former Yugoslavia

Bouaké air strike, 685

Boulden, Jane, 366

Boutros-Ghali, Boutros, 444, 534, 585; *An Agenda for Democratization* by, 241; *An Agenda for Peace* by, 7, 9, 10, 62, 227, 375, 397–398, 399, 437*n*17, 450–451,

482–483, 493; Article 99 used by, 450–451; on Bosnia safe areas, 578; on Groups of Friends, 493; on military intervention, 397–398, 446–447; NATO relations with, 399; on nonbinding resolutions, 775; reappointment opposition for, 445, 447; on regional organizations, 482, 487; on Rwanda options, 446; on sanctions reform, 437*n*17; on Somalia priority level, 597, 610*n*4

Brahimi, Lakhdar: role in Iraqi transition, 561; as Syria SRSG, 725, 729, 743

Brahimi Report, 64–65, 262, 364, 375–376, 404–405, 409, 455n15, 461, 464, 760, 836, 847

Brammertz, Serge, 541

Brazil: in G4 reform proposal, 134, 162–163, 170, 180–181, 192*nn*28–32, 867; Haiti troop contribution by, 759; in IBSA, 737–738; Iran proliferation negotiations with, 337–338; Libya stance of, 704, 706, 710; permament membership consideration for, 806–808; OAS agreement with, 479; RWP proposal by, 226, 700, 711–712, 713; Syria stance of, 719, 720–721, 737–738; US relations with, 807

Brazil, Russia, India, and China (BRIC), 167, 794, 800, 807–808; Russia stance toward, 109, 116, 119

Brazil, Russia, India, China, and South Africa (BRICS), 830; Libya Resolution 1973 and, 710, 842; new Groups of Friends and, 498, 499; sanctions stance of, 858; Syria and, 741–742

Bremer, Paul, 561

BRIC. *See* Brazil, Russia, India, and China

BRICS. *See* Brazil, Russia, India, China, and South Africa

Brown, Mark Malloch, 566

Budget: committees, 462–464; dues payment reform for, 167; field visits, 190*n*11; global financial crisis and, 756; ISIS counterterrorism, 736; for peacekeeping operations, 7, 129*tab*, 133, 144, 462–463, 756, 760; piracy law enforcement, 314; for political missions, 463–464, 846; UNAMI, 563; UNCCT, 292. *See also* Costs

Bukavu crisis, 379–380

Bunche, Ralph, 374, 530

Burkina Faso, 688

Burma. *See* Myanmar

Burns, Nicolas, 813*n*42

Burundi, 47*tab*, 605, 672, 764

Bush, George H. W.: Operation Desert Storm authorized by, 553–554; Security Council relations under, 60–61, 75–76; UNITAF authorized by, 598

Bush, George W.: foreign policy of, 65–67, 76, 801–802; freedom agenda of, 242–243, 249; on Khartoum peace talks, 620; 9/11 response of, 12–13, 860–861; North Korea-US relations under, 333; Security Council relations under, 65–67, 76, 801–802

Butler, Richard, 558

Buttenheim, Lisa, 469

Cambodia, transitional authority in, 6–7, 90, 91, 239, 266

Cameron, David, 70, 607, 710, 726, 744

Cammaert, Patrick, 380

Camp David Accords, 532

Canada: Angola sanctions leadership by, 857; Friends of Haiti and, 496–497; Groups of Friends for children and, 502–503; Groups of Friends for civilians and, 503; ICISS established by, 11, 213*n*18, 221, 222–223, 224, 404; Sudan relations with, 619; Zaire support from, 665–666

Capstone Doctrine, 376–377

Carlsson, Ingvar, 267–268

Carrington, Peter, 572

Carter, Jimmy, 333, 575

Carter Doctrine, 597

Central African Republic: Chad and, 47*tab*, 130, 624, 755–756, 761, 764–765; human rights investigation commission on, 269; MINURCA in, 9; MINURCAT in, 130, 625, 756; sanctions on, 418*tab*, 420*tab*; trafficking in, 309

Central Intelligence Agency (CIA), 66, 479, 555

Chad conflicts, 47*tab*, 130, 624, 755–756, 761, 764–765

Chapters of UN Charter. *See* Charter

Chapultepec, Act of, 477

Charter: accountability constraints by, 783–784; amendment capability, 772, 773, 788*n*3; amendment process, 197, 202, 876*n*62; Article 1, 259; Article 2, 235, 251*n*2, 481, 772, 777; Article 10, 182; Article 21, 236–237; Article 23, 146, 203, 206; Article 24, 783–784; Article 25, 44, 160, 423, 775; Article 27, 206, 353–354; Article 29, 197; Article 30, 197; Article 33, 476; Article 34, 269; Article 36, 476; Article 39, 220, 353, 354, 779; Article 41, 414, 436*n*3; Article 51, 12, 66, 354, 395, 477, 778, 860; Article 52, 476; Article 52 decline, 481–487; Article 52 preeminence, 478–481; Article 53, 395, 476, 479–481; Article 57, 487*n*1; Article 94, 508; Article 96, 509; Article 98, 446; Article 99, 178, 443–444, 446, 448–452, 844; Article 103, 477, 479, 785, 788*n*2; Article 108, 197, 876*n*62; Article 109, 211*n*3; Chapter VI invocation, 4–5, 781; Chapter VII definition, 52*n*6, 375, 775; Chapter VII invocation, 3–4, 10, 29–33, 34*fig*, 227, 582–583, 750–751, 765–766; Chapter VII invocation, by region, 40, 42*fig*, 43; Chapter VII vetoes, 29*tab*, 30*fig*, 34*fig*; Chapter VIII, 40, 43, 399–400, 414; Chapter VIII internal contradictions, 475–478; collective security in, 353, 393; constitutive character of, 772, 773, 788*n*3; democracy language not in, 235, 236–237, 251*n*2; design of, 201; domestic jurisdiction clause in, 235, 251*n*2, 779–780; enemy clauses in, 214*n*26; force and intention of, 353–354, 374, 390*n*1, 393–394; ICJ in, 508–509, 773; lawmaking power from, 773, 774–777; League of Nations comparison to, 251*n*2; Military Staff Committee setup by, 374, 394, 408; NATO and, 395, 399–400; regional representation consideration in, 198, 211*n*6; regulative rules of, 772; Security Council constraints by, 783–784; Security Council powers by, 3–5, 142, 773–774; specialized agencies in, 487*n*1; threat defined by, 143–144, 220, 239, 779; use of force and intention of, 353–354, 374, 390*n*1, 393–394; violations outside of, 778

Chechnya conflict, 46*tab*, 114

Chemical weapons: Iraq use of, 327–328; Libya use of, 332; Syria use of, 70, 112, 338–339, 726–728, 743–745

Chemical Weapons Convention, 327, 339

Chernomyrdin, Viktor, 821

Chesterman, Simon, 241

Children and armed conflict, 267, 270, 436*n*4, 501, 502–503

Chile: Haiti troop contribution by, 759; use of force stance of, 874*n*30

China: Asian power tensions and, 804–805; Bosnia stance of, 580–582; in BRIC, 794, 800, 807–808; in BRICS, 498, 499, 710, 741–742, 830, 842, 858; civilian protection stance of, 798; counterterrorism response of, 92–93, 281–282; Dalai Lama talk with, 263; democracy promotion responses by, 239; economic rise of, 164–165, 794, 795, 829; electoral assistance from, 91; engagement transformation, 83–84, 86–91, 98–100; Eurasian Union and, 119; Five Principles of Peaceful Coexistence by, 84–85; foreign policy early years, 86–87; foreign policy post-Cold War, 85, 87, 90–91; foreign policy principles of, 84–85, 100*n*1; G4 reform opposition by, 163, 181; human rights abstention by, 95–98, 237, 263; human rights commissioner consultation with, 264; ICCPR response of, 237; India

relations with, 367; Iran relations with, 94–95, 437*n*15; Japan relations with, 163, 367, 805, 867; Libya conflict stance of, 361, 703–704, 706–707, 800; membership acquisition of, 86; membership preferences of, 53*n*15; membership reform interests of, 163, 181, 182, 813*n*42, 867; military capability of, 794; NAM relations with, 84, 85, 86; national interest exploitation by, 88*tab*, 90, 91, 102*n*51; North Korea relations with, 93–94, 273, 334, 360, 803, 863; One China policy of, 90–91; organized crime stance of, 305; peacekeeping involvement of, 91–92, 129*tab*, 848; proliferation management by, 93–95, 325; R2P stance of, 95–98, 800–801; resolution abstention by, 87, 90; ROC transfer to, 86; Russia convergence with, 38, 88–89*tab*, 97–98, 116–117, 829–830; S5 reform opposition by, 182; sanctions stance of, 87, 428, 437*nn*15–16, 858; Saudi Arabia relations with, 437*n*15; South Korea relations with, 805; Soviet Union relations with, 100*n*4; Sudan relations with, 96–97, 621, 623, 624, 632, 641*n*68; Syria stance of, 97–98, 720–722, 724, 730, 732, 742, 800–801; Taiwan relations with, 88*tab*, 90, 91, 102*n*51; US relations with, 795, 805; value and importance of, 99; vetoes by, 53*n*15, 86, 88–89*tab*, 90–91, 129*tab*, 830, 831*fig*. See also Permanent five members

Chirac, Jacques, 128

Choi Young-jin, 688, 762

Cholera, 362

Churchill, Winston, 171, 299

Churkin, Vitaly, 110, 629

CIA. See Central Intelligence Agency

CIRT. See Committee for the International Repression of Terrorism

Civil society activism, 764, 852–856

Civilian protection: China, India and Russia for, 798; Groups of Friends for, 501, 503; P5 cohesion on, 798; peacekeeping provision, 376, 388, 501, 705; resource limits on, 675; SRSG behavior in, 761–762. See also Responsibility to Protect

Claes, Willy, 401

Claude, Inis, 159, 277, 293

Clausewitz, Carl von, 387, 403

Clinton, Bill: on Bosnia, 579–580; on economic shift, 164–165; foreign policy of, 61–65; General Assembly speech by, 62–63; Security Council relations under, 61–65; on Somalia withdrawal, 599–600

Clinton, Hillary: on Khartoum, 627, 640*n*58; on Libya, 703; on Somalia, 607; on Syria, 742

Closet vetoes, 143, 158
CNDP. *See* National Congress for the Defense of the People
Coalitions of the willing, 9, 355–356, 808
Cockayne, James, 469, 471
Coercive protection, 228–229
Coffee Club, 162–163
Cold War era: Afghanistan relations in, 644–645; Arab-Israeli conflict in, 530–533, 794; counterterrorism, 278–281; democracy promotion, 238; France power status in, 121, 122–123; geopolitical fragmentation origins in, 816; human rights approach in, 259–260; humanitarian system origins in, 220–221; membership origins of power in, 139–140, 141–143; military interventions, 4; NATO establishment and, 394–395; peacekeeping invention in, 374, 397; peacekeeping operations, 4–5, 374; post-Cold War era resolutions compared to, 29, 29*tab*, 31, 33; proliferation management mistakes in, 326–328; regional organizations in, 478–481; sanctions, 4; Security Council origin in, 3–5, 201; UK power status in, 121, 122–123; US unilateralism in, 58–60; Yugoslavia and expectations of, 590. *See also* Post-Cold War era
Collective law enforcement, 311–313
Collective no-vote, 145–146, 202–203
Collective security, 3, 353, 393. *See also* Selective security
Colombia: death count in, 46*tab*; drug trafficking from, 304; OAS agreement with, 479; resolution count in, 46*tab*
Command and control: NATO dual key agreement and, 401–402, 585; strengthening, 767; of troop contributors, 760; unspecified, 408; use of force issues of, 363–364, 385–386
Committee for the International Repression of Terrorism (CIRT), 278
Committees: budget, 462–464; chairmanship and, 148, 205, 208, 421–423, 835; Counter-Terrorism, 12–13, 285–288, 419, 484, 861; 1540, 339–341, 864; Fifth, 462–463, 467, 760; Military Staff, 374, 394, 408; Red Cross, 219, 220, 221, 671; sanctions, 421–423, 428, 835; Special Committee on Peacekeeping Operations, 759
Communism: Afghanistan conflict origins and, 643–644; regional organizations against, 479–481
Compaoré, Blaise, 688
Compliance research, 53*n*9
Conflict management: by Africa, 838, 847–848, 847*fig*; by Asia, 797; categories of,

798–799; challenge factors, 839; democracy promotion motivation for, 799–801, 846; by emerging powers, 796–797, 799–801, 847–848; focus areas of, 838–839, 847*fig*; prevention as, 843–844; R2P motivation for, 799–801, 840–843. *See also* Peacekeeping
Conflicts: children in, 267, 270, 436*n*4, 501, 502–503; complexity and selectivity of, 365–366, 839–840; cultural understanding in, 817, 819, 826; by death count, 45, 46–47*tab*, 54*nn*25–29; decline of, 49, 50*fig*, 51, 351–352; by intensity level, 50*tab*; intrastate, 38, 39*fig*, 351, 352–353, 837–838, 872*n*10; postcolonial character and, 352–353; power division on, 799–801; power unification on, 798–799, 831; precedents for, 531; prevention of, 264–265, 701, 703, 706–707, 843–844; recurrence of, 839, 850; regional concentration of, 796–797, 847*fig*; by resolution count, 45, 46–47*tab*, 54*nn*25–29; use of force and change in, 351–353, 389–390, 850; veto trends by, 34*fig*. *See also* Military interventions; Peacekeeping
Congo. *See* Democratic Republic of the Congo
Consistency issues: accountability and, 787–788, 869–870; in international law, 787; on R2P, 271–273, 274, 787, 840–841, 870; on resolutions, 45, 46–47*tab*, 48–49; of Security Council, 787–788, 869–870; on selective security, 349–351
Constitutive Act, of AU, 242, 604, 708
Constitutive character, of UN Charter, 772, 773, 788*n*3
Contact Groups, 498–499, 818
Contingency planning, 464
Convention on the Safety of United Nations and Associated Personnel, 364
Core Group on East Timor, 493–494, 496
Corporations: human rights role of, 426; sanctions role of, 426, 433–434; trafficking law enforcement by, 305–307
Costa Rica, 641*n*68. *See also* Small five members
Costs: of AMISOM, 605–606; of ICTR and ICTY, 512–513; of Iran-Iraq War, 552; of sanctions, 419, 437*n*10, 438*n*22
Cot, Jean, 578
Côte d'Ivoire: Abidjan attacks, 685, 691–692, 696*n*19; Accra III Agreement nullification in, 685; arms embargo on, 685–686, 693; AU mediation on, 686–687, 690; Bédié presidency of, 696*n*23; conclusion on, 693–695; democracy promotion in, 240, 244; ECOWAS support of, 244, 382, 682–684, 690; electoral assistance in, 244,

382–383, 686–688, 694; enforcement challenge in, 682; Forces Nouvelles in, 682–683, 684–685, 691; France intervention in, 112, 244, 382, 383, 682–685, 691–693; Gbagbo arrest and removal from, 244, 383, 519, 682, 692; Gbagbo loyalist retaliation in, 683, 685, 691–693, 764; government air strikes in, 684–685; Group of Friends of, 682; HRC inquiry on, 684–685, 690, 697n34; human rights investigation commission on, 269; ICC referral for, 383, 519, 690, 692, 697n33; legalist and sovereignist split in, 689–690; Linas-Marcoussis Agreement for, 683, 684–685; MINUCI in, 683; Operation Licorne in, 682–683, 692; Ouagadougou Agreement for, 688; Ouattara presidency of, 244, 382–383, 688–689, 693, 696n26; post-electoral crisis in, 689–691; post-electoral crisis origin in, 682–684; protests in, 685; Resolution 1633 on, 687; Resolution 1721 on, 687; Resolution 1765 on, 688; Resolution 1962 on, 690; Resolution 2112 on, 693; Russia stance on, 383, 690; sanctions on, 270, 383, 417tab, 420tab, 421, 685–686; SRSG role in, 688, 689, 762; transitional authority in, 683; UNOCI in, 112, 244, 382–383, 684–685, 686, 691–693, 694; use of force on, 69, 112, 244, 382–383, 691–693, 694

Counterterrorism: Abidjan attacks, 685, 691–692, 696n19; adaptation to, 278; al-Aqsa intifada, 534–535; China involvement in, 92–93, 281–282; Cold War era, 278–281; to embassy bombings, 280, 283, 419, 618, 646; foreign fighters resolutions, 727, 735tab, 831, 862; GCTF for, 289–290, 292–293, 803, 861–862; Hamas, 535–538; Hezbollah, 281, 514, 540–544, 733, 749–750; to hostage-taking, 279–281, 448–449; human rights abuses by, 66, 861; humanitarian intervention ethics and, 222; Islam radicalization and, 601–603, 617–619; Khartoum, 617–619; lawmaking power for, 776–777; by League of Nations, 278–279; lessons from, 278; modern multilateralism in, 288–293; Mujahidin, 644–645; to open-door policy, 282; organized crime and, 286, 303–304; overview, 277–278, 293–294, 859–862; post-Cold War era, 281–283; P5 convergence, 799, 831; pre-9/11, 279, 280, 281, 859–860; Resolution 1267 for, 161, 271, 303, 419, 426, 430–431, 780, 786, 860; Resolution 1368 for, 12, 66, 284, 860; Resolution 1373 for, 12–13, 44, 76, 93, 107, 284–288, 304, 419, 776–777, 822, 860; Resolution 1540 for, 44, 339, 776–

777, 864; resolution trends by issue, 38, 39fig; Russia involvement in, 114, 283; sanctions regime 1267, 161, 271, 303, 426, 430–431, 780, 786, 860; sanctions regime 1373, 776–777; Security Council role in, 283–288, 859–862; Al-Shabaab, 601–603, 605, 607, 609; Syria, Council failure on, 741–746; Syria terrorist tactics and, 718, 726–728; UNCCT for, 291–292; use of force, 389; vetoes, 280–281; working methods, 285, 287. See also Taliban

Counter-Terrorism Committee (CTC), 12–13, 285–288, 419, 484, 861

Counter-Terrorism Committee Executive Directorate (CTED), 12–13, 288, 290–291

Counter-Terrorism Implementation Task Force (CTITF), 289–291, 292

Courts: ECJ, 161, 313, 524n3, 785–786; EU General, 785; Security Council role as, 777–780; Special Court for Sierra Leone, 508; UIC, 602–603. See also International Court of Justice; International Criminal Court

Cousens, Elizabeth, 467–468

Crime. See Organized crime

Crime against humanity. See Human rights

Crimea, 112, 829, 859

Crisis management. See Conflict management

CrisisWatch, 707

Croatia: ethnic mix in, 571; independence of, 571–574; membership of, 576; transitional authority in, 587; UNCRO in, 592n13; UNPROFOR in, 574, 592n13; use of force on, 584

CTC. See Counter-Terrorism Committee

CTED. See Counter-Terrorism Committee Executive Directorate

CTITF. See Counter-Terrorism Implementation Task Force

Cuba: human rights abstention by, 237; OAS relations with, 479, 480; sanctions on, 480

Cultural understanding, 817, 819, 826

Cunliffe, Philip, 751

Cyprus, 40, 398, 450

Dalai Lama, 263

Dallaire, Roméo, 363

Danforth, John, 621

Daoud Khan, Mohammed, 644

Darfur crisis: Annan stance on, 761; Ban stance on, 626, 761; Chad and, 625, 755–756, 761; civil society activists in, 764; deadlock on, 755–756; EU intervention in, 756; as genocide issue, 621; Germany response to, 620, 638n28; host state disruption in, 764, 765; ICC referral for, 96, 190n10, 269, 517–518, 622–623, 626, 855–856; inaction on, 841; international attention on, 615, 620–621; Khartoum peacemaking and, 619–627, 633–634, 639n37, 642n79; routine of, 630–631; Secretariat power dynamic in, 761; UNAMID for, 97, 484, 604, 624, 625, 630–631, 634–635, 755–756, 764, 852; US stance on, 518

Dayton Accords, 64, 359, 400, 402, 587–588

De Hoop Scheffer, Jaap, 406

De Mistura, Staffan, 738

De Soto, Alvaro, 492, 535

DEA. *See* Drug Enforcement Agency

Decentralized power, 771

Decisionmaking. *See* Penholders; Power dynamics; Working methods

Decolonization: character, 352–353; geopolitical fragmentation origins in, 816; institutions, 817

Democracy promotion: in Afghanistan, 243; by Annan, 241, 245; apartheid and, 238; in AU, 242; by Boutros-Ghali, 241; Charter language without, 235, 236–237, 251n2; China response to, 239; Cold War era, 238; conflict management motivated by, 799–801, 846; in Côte d'Ivoire, 240, 244; coups and, 242, 254n52; development agencies, 242–243; in DRC, 242, 248; in East Timor, 241, 243; effectiveness assessment, 246–248, 249–250, 255n76; emerging powers stance on, 799–801; EU organizations for, 256n93; factors, 237, 248–250; fraud in, 243–244; freedom agenda and, 242–243, 249; geopolitical change and, 249; in Haiti, 240; human rights and, 236–237, 246; in India, 238; in Indonesia, 238; institutional engineering for, 241; in Iraq, 243; jurisdiction and, 235, 251n2, 779–780; in Kosovo, 241; in Middle East, 244–245; new millennium, 242–245; opposition and skepticism toward, 241, 242–244; overview, 235–236, 248–250; P3 stance on, 248–249, 256n93; post-Cold War era, 238–242; power dynamics, 799–801; RCD, 662–663, 670, 672, 677n5, 678n23; resolution language of, 237, 240–241, 242, 251n6; role assessment of UN Security Council, 246–248; role of UN beyond Security Council, 245–246; sanctions for, 239–240; Santiago Declaration, 240; scholarship lacking on, 251n8; in Somalia, 239; threat redefining for, 239; training gap in, 239; use of force for, 239–240; Vienna Declaration, 237; Warsaw Declaration, 242; women and, 242

Democratic Forces for the Liberation of Rwanda (FDLR), 672, 678n16

Democratic People's Republic of Korea (DPRK). *See* North Korea

Democratic Republic of the Congo (DRC): assessment visits to, 467; Bukavu crisis in, 379–380; CNDP of, 673; conclusion on, 675–676; conflict background, 662–663; death count in, 46tab; democracy promotion in, 242, 248; electoral assistance in, 248, 380–381, 672–673; EU support in, 379, 380, 672, 695n6; FARDC coordination in, 380–382, 673–675; FDLR and, 672, 678n16; FIB in, 674–675, 757, 759, 849, 850, 874n29; Goma crisis in, 381, 674–675; human rights field trips to, 270; ICC referral for, 519; Ituri crisis in, 378–379, 672–673; Kampala Accord for, 672; Kisangani massacre and, 378; Lusaka agreement on, 662, 663, 668, 669; M23 insurrection in, 673–675, 850; MLC position in, 662–663, 677n5, 678n23, 679n33; MONUC for, 65, 378–380, 667–671, 672, 675, 754, 766; MONUSCO for, 242, 248, 381–382, 392n32, 674–675, 757, 766; Operation Artemis in, 379, 672, 695n6; Operation Turquoise impact on, 663–665; organized crime in, 306; origins of, 663; peacekeeping challenges in, 378–382, 392n32; RCD position in, 662–663, 670, 672, 677n5, 678n23; Resolution 1080 on, 665–666; Resolution 1234 on, 669; Resolution 1258 on, 669; Resolution 1279 on, 669; Resolution 1291 on, 670; Resolution 1355 on, 671; Resolution 2098 on, 410, 674, 778; resolution count in, 46tab; Rwanda occupation of, 378, 379, 381, 670–671, 672; SADC support in, 381, 485; sanctions on, 417tab, 420tab, 673; troop contributors to, 759; Uganda occupation of, 378, 670–671, 672; UNOC in, 4, 448; war, first, as Zaire, 665–667; war, second, 667–671; war, third, 672–673

Democratization: process, 247; waves, 238–239, 252n23

Deng Xiaoping, 84, 87

Department for Peacekeeping Operations (DPKO): civilian protection resources and, 675; DPA counterbalance to, 761; personnel casualties, 364; responsibility of, 458; Security Council cohesion with, 760–761; Security Council contention with, 761–762; size of, 408, 760

Department of Humanitarian Affairs (DHA), 221

Department of Political Affairs (DPA), 292, 305, 429; DPKO counterbalanced by, 761; meeting service by, 835; responsibility of, 458; SCAD of, 199, 212n17, 422, 835; size of, 761

DHA. *See* Department of Humanitarian Affairs

Diamond, Larry, 564
Diamonds: sanctions, 416–418*tab*, 857; trafficking, 306
Diarra, Seydou, 685
Disease, 362, 679*n*30, 783, 865–866
Dobbins, James, 358
Dodd-Frank Act, 306
Domestic interest. *See* Geopolitical fragmentation; National interest
Domestic jurisdiction, 235, 251*n*2, 313–314, 779–780
Dominican Republic, 479, 480–481
Doyle, Michael, 470
DPA. *See* Department of Political Affairs
DPKO. *See* Department for Peacekeeping Operations
DPRK (Democratic People's Republic of Korea). *See* North Korea
DRC. *See* Democratic Republic of the Congo
Drug Enforcement Agency (DEA), 310
Drug trafficking, 114, 301, 303–304, 305, 308, 310, 649, 864–865
Dual key agreement (UN-NATO), 362, 400, 401–402, 585
Due process, 303, 307, 313–314
Dumbarton Oaks conference, 123, 201
Dunant, Henri, 220

E10. *See* Elected ten nonpermanent members
East Timor: Australia intervention in, 64, 752; Core Group on, 493–494, 496; democracy promotion in, 241, 243; electoral assistance in, 241, 243, 496; UNTAET in, 241, 243, 464, 752–753
Eastern Slavonia, 587
Ebola, 783, 866
EC. *See* European Community
ECJ. *See* European Court of Justice
ECOMOG. *See* Economic Community of West African States Military Observer Group
Economic and Social Council, 875*n*55
Economic Community of West African States (ECOWAS): Côte d'Ivoire and, 244, 382, 682–684, 690; Liberia and, 481, 482, 484; Mali and, 384; Security Council relations with, 43, 481, 482, 483, 484
Economic Community of West African States Military Observer Group (ECOMOG), 752, 753
Economy: of Africa, 797; of China, 164–165, 794, 795, 829; of emerging powers, 159, 160, 164–165, 166–167, 794–795; global financial crisis, 756, 846, 871; of Japan, 795; membership reform and, 159, 160, 164–165, 166–167; of Russia, 795; of US, 164–165, 794
ECOWAS. *See* Economic Community of West African States

Ecuador, OAS relations with, 479
Eelam conflict. *See* Sri Lanka
Egeland, Jan, 471, 620
Egypt: Abu Nidal hijacking, 280; on Cuba-OAS relations, 480; in Gaza wars, 536, 537; Mubarak assassination attempt, 54*n*27, 282, 617; role in ending Operation Cast Lead, 536; in Six-Day War, 531; Sudan relations with, 617, 637*n*10; Suez crisis, 212*n*15, 374, 531–533; UNEF in, 374, 531–532
Eide, Kai, 243
El Baradei, Mohamed, 559
El Salvador, 6–7, 266, 492, 839, 853
Elected ten nonpermanent members (E10): human rights penholdership and, 272–273; marginalization of, 145–149, 272–273, 833–834; orientation workshops for, 213*n*21, 213*n*24; P3 and, 758; penholder power of, 151, 205–206, 272–273, 758; power improvements for, 149–152, 153, 205–206, 834–836; re-election of, 166, 168, 206–207; resolution abstention by, 834; role and expertise of, 203–206, 758, 834–836; sanctions committee chairmanship by, 421–422, 835; 7-7-7 reform formula for, 166, 168, 214*n*25; structure of, 204–205; Sudan contention of, 633; Syria approach by, 736–738; thematic issues headed by, 149–150, 178, 835
Electoral assistance: in Afghanistan, 243–244, 653–655; in Cambodia, 239; certification, 239, 244; challenges, 248; from China, 91; in Côte d'Ivoire, 244, 382–383, 686–688, 694; in DRC, 248, 380–381, 672–673; in East Timor, 241, 243, 496; effectiveness of, 248, 249–250; as exit strategy, 239, 249; in Haiti, 239–240; in Mali, 248; in Somalia, 607–608; staff, 239–241, 447; in Sudan, 243, 248. *See also* Democracy promotion; Transitional authority
Eliasson, Jan, 624
Embassy: bombings, 280, 283, 419, 618, 646; Tehran hostage crisis, 448–449, 552
Emerging powers: Afghanistan intervention by, 797; Asia contention in, 795, 804–805; conclusion on, 809–810; conflict management by, 796–797, 799–801, 847–848; cross-alliance of, 807; democracy promotion stance of, 799–801; economies of, 159, 160, 164–165, 166–167, 794–795; G4 convergence with, 180; membership consideration for, 135, 159, 162–171; military capability of, 794–795, 806–807; MINT as, 167, 498; noncompliance by, 160; Obama relations with, 68–69; oil production for, 797; P5 convergence with,

165; population underrepresentation of, 160, 166; R2P stance of, 799–801; regional organizations and, 498; resource development for, 797, 810; as troop contributors, 759, 873*n*22; win-win reform solution for, 166–171
Enemy clauses, 214*n*26
Energy security, 797, 810
Environmental threats, 875*n*55
Eritrea, 270, 306; death and resolution count in, 46*tab*; host state disruption in, 764; sanctions on, 416*tab*, 417*tab*, 420*tab*, 606; UNMEE in, 758, 764
Escovar-Salom, Ramón, 511
Ethics, of humanitarian intervention, 221–223
Ethiopia: death and resolution count in, 46*tab*, 47*tab*; host state disruption in, 764; Italy conflict with, 142; sanctions on, 417*tab*, 420*tab*; Somalia relations with, 597, 601, 603, 604, 608, 613*n*47; Sudan relations with, 617, 637*n*10; UNMEE in, 758, 764
EU. *See* European Union
EU4. *See* European Union Group of Four
Eurasian Union, 119
European Community (EC), 481, 571, 572–574
European Court of Justice (ECJ), 161, 313, 524*n*3, 785–786
European Union (EU): AMISOM support from, 606; in Arab-Israeli conflict Quartet, 534, 535–536, 538; Bosnia response of, 577–580, 585–586; Darfur intervention by, 756; democracy promotion organizations in, 256*n*93; DRC support from, 379, 380, 672, 695*n*6; General Court, 785; indirect judicial review of, 785; membership consolidation in, 134, 170–171; OSCE, 241; peacekeeping troop size in, 847*fig*; piracy response from, 312, 313; population misrepresentation by, 160, 170; reform challenge for, 170; regional organizations in, 481; resolutions by region, 40, 41*fig*, 42*fig*, 43; Russia relations with, 108–109; sanctions, regional comparison in, 424–425; sanctions mistakes response of, 271, 288, 785–786; Security Council relations with, 763; UK relations within, 821; Ukraine crisis avoidance by, 795–796; UNIFIL support from, 543; WEOG, 758
European Union Group of Four (EU4), 737
Executive policing, 309–310
Expert panels. *See* Panels of experts
Ezulwini consensus, 186, 192*n*32

Fabius, Laurent, 153, 213*n*19, 739
Falklands War, 481
Famine relief, 598

FARDC. *See* Armed Forces of the Democratic Republic of the Congo
FATF. *See* Financial Action Task Force
FCO. *See* Foreign and Commonwealth Office
FDLR. *See* Democratic Forces for the Liberation of Rwanda
Federal Republic of Yugoslavia. *See* Yugoslavia
FIB. *See* Force Intervention Brigade
1540 Committee, 339–341, 864
Fifth Committee (General Assembly), 462–463, 467, 760; assessment visits by, 467
Finances. *See* Budget; Costs; Economy
Financial Action Task Force (FATF), 286, 306
Financial crisis of 2008, 756, 846, 871
Financial sanctions, 416–418*tab*, 426–427, 782
Finland: Kosovo stance of, 821; membership aspiration of, 758
Fission, 352
Five Principles of Peaceful Coexistence, 84–85
Flight bombings, 281, 784
Force. *See* Use of force
Force Intervention Brigade (FIB), 674–675, 757, 759, 849, 850, 874*n*29
Forces Nouvelles, 682–683, 684–685, 691
Foreign and Commonwealth Office (FCO), 131–132
Foreign fighters campaign, 727, 735*tab*, 831, 862
Fowler, Robert, 424
Fox, Gregory, 239, 240
Fragmentation. *See* Geopolitical fragmentation
France: Africa interventions by, 832; Côte d'Ivoire intervention by, 112, 244, 382, 383, 682–685, 691–693; DRC intervention from, 379, 695*n*6; in EU4, 737; Friends of Haiti and, 496, 759; Friends of Western Sahara and, 495; G4 proposal support of, 181; humanitarian NGOs from, 220–221; Iraq War stance of, 823; Lebanon UNIFIL support by, 543, 749–750; Liberia stance of, 125*tab*; Libya stance of, 125*tab*, 702; Mali intervention by, 383–384, 781; membership acquisition by, 123; membership reform interests of, 133–135, 136, 182; membership removal of, 169, 171, 832; Ministry of Foreign Affairs, 132–133; NATO dual key issues viewed by, 401; 9/11 resolution 1368 and, 284; peacekeeping involvement of, 123–127, 128, 129*tab*, 130–131, 133; penholdership of, 128, 129*tab*, 131–133; power decline of, 121, 122–123, 159–160, 169; Rwanda Operation Turquoise by, 664; S5 reform engagement by, 182; sanctions involvement of, 130; Security Council

engagement level of, 127–128, 129*tab*, 130–131, 832; Security Council strategic importance for, 122–127, 125–126*tab*, 135–136; Syria stance of, 736; Tunisia blockade against, 449; UNAMID push by, 625; vetoes by, 124, 125–126*tab*, 128, *129*tab; voluntary veto restraint initiative by, 203, 213*n*19. *See also* Permanent five members; Permanent three members

Franck, Thomas, 237, 299, 303, 558, 784

Freedman, Lawrence, 574

Freedom: agenda, 242–243, 249; cultural gap in, 817; *In Larger Freedom* (Annan), 224, 245, 438*n*17, 484, 809, 813*n*42; Operation Enduring Freedom in, 108, 652

Freedom House, 246

Frozen files, 870–871

G4. *See* Group of Four

G77. *See* Group of Seventy-Seven

Gabon, 690

Galbraith, Peter, 243–244

Garang, John, 616, 625

Gaza wars, 535–539. *See also* Israel-Palestine conflict

Gbagbo, Laurent: arrest and removal of, 244, 383, 519, 682, 692; election postponement by, 687, 688; loyalist retaliation, 683, 685, 691–693, 764; Ouattara support over, 244, 382–383, 688–689; post-electoral crisis with, 689–691

GCC. *See* Gulf Cooperation Council

GCTF. *See* Global Counter-Terrorism Forum

General Assembly: annual reporting to, 199; budget subcommittee of, 462–464; Clinton speech at, 62–63; counterterrorism agenda addition for, 280; Deng speech at, 84; Economic and Social Council of, 875*n*55; Fifth Committee, 462–463, 467, 760; human rights reporting to, 266; membership amendment by, 197; membership reform framework in, 183, 184–186; Open-Ended Working Group by, 179, 180, 182, 183; Razali proposal in, 162, 179–180, 191*n*26; Secretary-General appointment by, 445; Security Council relations with, 144–145, 531; Special Committee on Peacekeeping Operations, 759; Syria action taken by, 722–723; thematic issues action of, 178; veto limitation proposal by, 153. *See also* Resolutions

Geneva 1973 peace conference, 533

Geneva Accords, 645

Geneva Initiative, 648

Geneva II communiqué, 500, 720, 724–725, 736*tab*, 742, 745–746

Genocide: Benghazi, 701, 703, 706–707;

Darfur, 621; prevention measures, 264–265; Rome Statute on, 190*n*1, 267, 308, 381, 515–517, 697*n*33, 855; Rwanda triggers, 599, 663–664; Srebrenica, 8, 9, 262–263, 358, 784–785

Geopolitical change: democracy promotion and, 249; membership reform and, 169, 806–809; within P5, 828–833, 831*fig*; in peacekeeping, 847–848, 847*fig*. *See also* Emerging powers

Geopolitical fragmentation: cultural understanding and, 817, 819, 826; on Iraq War, 822–823; on Kosovo, 821–822; on Libya, 823; member groupings and, 818; origins of, 815–816; post-Cold War era institutions and, 816–817; Security Council impacted by, 819–821; Security Council relevance despite, 824–826; on Syria, 823–824; in UN operations, 818–819

Georgia conflict, 108, 110; Group of Friends of, 493, 494–495

Germany: Bonn-Berlin sanctions process sponsored by, 857; Bonn Conference in, 66, 437*n*11, 651–652, 654–655; Darfur crisis response of, 620, 638*n*28; EU member consolidation and, 170–171; in EU4, 737; on G4 reform proposal, 134, 162–163, 170, 180–181, 192*nn*28–32, 867; in Geneva Initiative, 648; Iran proliferation management by, 94, 115, 336, 337, 498, 719, 808, 818; Libya stance of, 702, 703, 707, 714*n*27, 800; military capability of, 806; in P5+1, 94, 115, 337, 498, 719, 745, 808, 818; piracy response of, 313; role as nonpermanent member, 833; Syria stance of, 720, 737; Yugoslavia collapse and, 572

Ghouta attack, 726, 743

Global Counter-Terrorism Forum (GCTF), 289–290, 292–293, 803, 861–862

Global financial crisis, 756, 846, 871

Global Policy Forum, 199

Goldstone, Richard, 536

Goma crisis, 381, 674–675

Good offices operations, 458, 461, 645

Gorbachev, Mikhail, 5, 106, 552, 644

Gore, Al, 679*n*30, 865

Goulding, Marrack, 363, 400, 576

The Great Convergence (Mahbubani), 165, 166

Greenstock, Jeremy, 12, 285, 286, 287, 288, 562, 671

Group of Four (G4): L69 spin-off, 183; reform proposal, 134, 162–163, 170, 180–181, 192*nn*28–32, 867

Group of Seventy-Seven (G77), 11, 501

Groups of Friends: of Afghanistan, as Six Plus

Two, 647, 658*n*22; of children in armed conflict, 501, 502–503; conclusion on, 503–504; of Côte d'Ivoire, 682; of East Timor, 493–494, 496; of El Salvador, 492; formation factors, 492; of Georgia, 493, 494–495; of Guatemala, 492; of Haiti, 492–493, 494, 496–497, 759; historical overview of, 492–494; International Contact Groups and, 498–499; introduction to, 491; of Libya, 499–500; Luncheon Group, 647; of Madagascar, 499; new, 497–500; old, 494–497; P5 contention on, 498–500, 503; of Philippines, 499; of Syria, 500, 724, 742; thematic, 500–503; of Western Sahara, 493, 495–496; of women, 501, 502; working methods, 497, 503

Guatemala: CIA mercenary in, 479; Group of Friends of, 492; in ICC and Security Council relations, 520–521; MINUGUA, 88*tab*, 91; OAS and, 53*n*18

Guinea-Bissau, 310, 418*tab*

Gulf Cooperation Council (GCC): Libya and, 701–702, 707, 708; Syria and, 718–719; Yemen and, 485

Gulf of Guinea piracy, 315

Gulf War (1991): death and resolution count in, 46*tab*; NATO in, 399, 564–565; Operation Desert Fox of, 13, 555; Operation Desert Storm of, 553–554; Operation Provide Comfort after, 23*n*11, 554, 781; peacekeeping after, 6, 23*n*11, 161–162, 554–555; Resolution 660 on, 774, 775; Resolution 661 on, 6, 553, 774, 775; Resolution 678 on, 87, 553–554; Resolution 686 on, 7; Resolution 687 on, 555, 565, 774–775; Resolution 688 on, 10, 261, 554, 781; Resolution 689 on, 554; as success, 60

Habash, George, 280

Habyarimana, Juvénal, 510, 663

Haiti: cholera outbreak in, 362; democracy promotion in, 240; electoral assistance in, 239–240; Group of Friends of, 492–493, 494, 496–497, 759; MINUSTAH, 309, 496–497; OAS in, 496, 874*n*36; sanctions on, 416*tab*, 420*tab*, 447; troop contributors to, 759; UNMIH, 90, 239–240; US relations with, 240, 754

Hamas, 535–538

Hammarskjöld, Dag, 374, 397; appointment of, 445; Article 99 used by, 448, 449; death of, 4, 446; on Guatemala, 53*n*18; norm entrepreneurship of, 452; on Secretary-General neutrality, 444; UNOC led by, 4, 448

Hannay, David, 571, 580

Hariri, Rafik, 419, 446, 513, 540–541

Hariri, Saad, 541

Hassan, Abdikassim Salad, 601

Helms, Jesse, 822

Helsinki Final Act, 573

Hersh, Seymour, 555

Herzegovina. *See* Bosnia-Herzegovina conflict

Hezbollah, 281, 514, 540–544, 733, 749–750

Higgins, Rosalyn, 780

High-level Panel on Threats, Challenges, and Change, 134, 203, 213, 224, 233, 296, 436, 484, 490, 813, 872; *A More Secure World*, 813*n*42

Hijacking, 279, 280, 281

Hilterman, Joost, 563

Hiroshima bombing, 325

"Hitting the Ground Running" workshop, 213*n*21, 213*n*24

HIV/AIDS pandemic, 679*n*30, 783, 865–866

Hobson's choice, 157, 159

Holbrooke, Richard, 65, 170, 586, 593*n*46, 670, 822

Hollande, François, 70, 213*n*29, 744

Honduras, 479

Horizon scanning, 178–179, 268, 844

Host state consent, 763–765, 850

Hostages, 279–281, 532; Bosnia crisis, 584; Mazar-i-Sharif, 646; Munich Olympics, 279; Sierra Leone, 65; Tehran crisis, 448–449, 552; UNDOF, in Syria, 532

Howe, Jonathan, 63, 599

HRC. *See* Human Rights Council

Human rights: accountability, 855–856; advocacy groups, 426; apartheid violation of, 238, 260; approach in Cold War era, 259–260; approach in post-Cold War era, 260–264, 590; approach in recent years, 271–274; catastrophes, 262–263; for children, 267, 270, 436*n*4, 501, 502–503; China abstention from, 95–98, 237, 263; civil society role in, 852–856; corporate social responsibility and, 426; counterterrorist abuses of, 66, 861; democracy promotion and, 236–237, 246; field trips, 269–270; genocide prevention measures for, 264–265; horizon scanning meetings for, 178–179, 268, 844; institutional design changes on, 264–265; investigation commissions, 269–270; investigation opposition, 272–273; OHCHR position for, 263–264, 268, 853; P3 focus on, 272, 798; P5 contention on, 272–273; penholder contention on, 272–273; reporting, Arria formula for, 261, 268, 854; reporting, horizon-scanning for, 268; reporting, to General Assembly, 266; Resolution 688 shift in, 10, 261; sanctions for, 220, 270–271, 426; sexual exploitation and, 267, 270, 436*n*4; tools development, 265–271; trafficking and, 307; Universal Declaration of, 236–237, 260; vetoes, 272; violation determination, 778; working methods for, 261, 266, 268–269. *See also* Responsibility to Protect

Human Rights Council (HRC): Côte d'Ivoire inquiry by, 684–685, 690, 697*n*34; democracy law laid by, 237; establishment of, 265; Israel inquiry by, 534, 536; Libya inquiry by, 265, 701, 785; OHCHR before, 263–264, 268, 853

Human Rights Watch, 764

Humanitarian intervention: abuse of, 225–227, 230; ethical landscape of, 221–223; famine, 598; imperative or impulse-driven, 218; legal landscape of, 218–221, 782; military intervention bridged with, 406–408; military intervention justified by, 226–230; national interest exploitation and, 217, 222–223; NGOs, 220–221, 426, 853–854; oil-for-food, 14, 161–162, 447, 556; origins of, 220–221; overview on, 217–218, 230–231; political landscape of, 223–226; rhetoric on, 223–226, 404, 453, 590; Russia stance on, 111, 264, 273; sovereignty limits and, 11, 218–220, 223–224; spending, 221; threat level determination for, 219–220. *See also* Responsibility to Protect

Hussein, Saddam, 6, 64, 66, 108, 328, 329, 451, 822; Kuwait oil production and, 553; UNSCOM and, 555

Hutu Revolution, 524*n*12

IAEA. *See* International Atomic Energy Agency

IBSA. *See* India, Brazil, South Africa

ICAO. *See* International Civil Aviation Organization

ICC. *See* International Criminal Court

ICCPR. *See* International Covenant on Civil and Political Rights

ICISS. *See* International Commission on Intervention and State Sovereignty

ICJ. *See* International Court of Justice

ICRC. *See* International Committee of the Red Cross

ICTR. *See* International Criminal Tribunal for Rwanda

ICTY. *See* International Criminal Tribunal for the Former Yugoslavia

IDPs. *See* Internally displaced persons

IGAD. *See* Intergovernmental Authority on Development

IGC. *See* Iraqi Governing Council

Ignatieff, Michael, 222

IMF. *See* International Monetary Fund

Immunity, 517

Implied powers doctrine, 773, 781

In Larger Freedom (Annan), 224, 245, 438*n*17, 484, 809, 813*n*42

Independent Diplomat, 854

India: in BRIC, 794, 800, 807–808; in BRICS, 498, 499, 710, 741–742, 830, 842, 858; China relations with, 367; civilian protection stance of, 798; democracy promotion in, 238; DRC troop contribution by, 759; in G4 reform proposal, 134, 162–163, 170, 180–181, 192*nn*28–32, 867; in IBSA, 737–738; Japan compared to, 166–167; Kashmir conflict, 46*tab*, 160, 871; Libya stance of, 97, 704; membership consideration for, 80, 367, 758, 806–808, 867; military capability of, 806; NAM from, 100*n*2; noncompliance by, 160; piracy concern of, 315; proliferation management of, 326; Russia relations with, 115, 116; 7-7-7 reform formula for, 166–167; Syria stance of, 719, 720–721, 737–738; US relations with, 807

India, Brazil, South Africa (IBSA), 737–738

Indonesia: democracy promotion in, 238; in MINT, 167, 498

Informal interactive dialogue, 179, 191*nn*17–19, 199–200, 836–837

Informal Working Group on Documentation and Other Procedural Questions (IWGD), 176, 182, 183–184; chairmanship of, 192*n*37, 198–199

Informal Working Group on General Issues on Sanctions, 428, 432

Institutionalism: inherent failure of, 817; liberal, 15, 136

Interahamwe, 664–665, 678*n*16, 679*n*33

Intergovernmental Authority on Development (IGAD): Somalia mediation by, 600, 601, 603; Sudan mediation by, 619–620, 635

Interlaken process, 437*n*11, 857

Internally displaced persons (IDPs): in Bosnia, 592*n*18; in Iraq, 45, 562; in Sudan, 45; in Syria, 720, 746

International Atomic Energy Agency (IAEA), 326, 327, 330, 331, 332, 333, 336, 559

International Civil Aviation Organization (ICAO), 279, 281

International Commission on Intervention and State Sovereignty (ICISS), 11, 213*n*18, 221, 222–223, 224, 404, 711

International Committee of the Red Cross (ICRC), 219, 220, 221, 671

International Contact Groups, 498–499, 818

International Court of Justice (ICJ): advisory opinion request to, 775, 780, 784; indirect judicial review by, 784–785; lawmaking power and, 773, 774; P5 relations with, 158; role of, 508–509

International Covenant on Civil and Political Rights (ICCPR), 237, 252*n*13

International Criminal Court (ICC), 219, 266–267, 426; conclusion on, 521–523; Côte d'Ivoire referral to, 383, 519, 690, 692, 697*n*33; Darfur referral to, 96, 190*n*10, 269, 517–518, 622–623, 626, 855–856; DRC referral to, 519; drug trafficking in, 308; effectiveness challenges, 766; establishment of, 10, 515; hostility toward, 855–856; immunity in, 517; implied powers doctrine and, 773; informal interactive dialogue with, 179; Kenya referral to, 520, 856; Libya referral to, 519, 701, 786; referral right, 776, 855–856; Rome Statue of, 190*n*1, 267, 308, 381, 515–517, 697*n*33, 855; Security Council relations with, 517–523; selective targeting by, 144, 522; state cooperation refusal, 518–519; Syria referral to, 526*n*42, 729–730

International Criminal Tribunal for Rwanda (ICTR): China stance on, 90; costs and completion strategy for, 512–513; criticism of, 507; establishment of, 10, 76, 510, 776; prosecutor for, 511; Security Council relations with, 510–511, 512

International Criminal Tribunal for the Former Yugoslavia (ICTY): China stance on, 90; costs and completion strategy for, 512–513; cynicism toward, 507, 513, 523*n*2, 577; establishment of, 10, 76, 509–510, 577, 776; prosecutor for, 511; Security Council relations with, 510–512

International Crisis Group, 707, 764, 854

International Law Commission, 776

International Monetary Fund (IMF), 871

International Peace Institute, 53*n*9, 466

International Security Assistance Force (ISAF), 405–406, 651–652, 653

International Trade Organization, 871

Iran: China relations with, 94–95, 437*n*15; in Geneva Initiative, 648; Iraq chemical weapons against, 327–328; Mazar-i-Sharif hostage crisis in, 646; membership reform for, 808; proliferation management of, 69, 93–95, 115, 336–338, 437*n*15, 498, 719, 743, 745, 803, 808, 818, 863; sanctions on, 93–95, 336–337, 338, 418*tab*, 420*tab*, 424, 425, 863; Syria conflict and, 733; Tehran Declaration for, 337–338, 863; Tehran hostage crisis in, 448–449, 552

Iranian Revolution, 552

Iran-Iraq War, 5, 45, 450, 552

Iraq: Agreed Minutes of 1964, 778; chemical weapons of, 327–328; Coalition conflicts, 47*tab*; death and resolution count in, 46*tab*, 47*tab*; democracy promotion in, 243; human rights action in, 261; IDPs in, 45, 562; ISIS of, 718, 727–728, 736, 739; Israel Osiraq attack on, 327, 329; Kuwait invasion by, 46*tab*, 60, 329, 358, 552–553; legal-regulatory approach to, 553, 557–558; oil-for-food program, 14, 161–162, 447, 556; overview of, 551, 563–566; P5 cohesion on, 552, 554, 863; P5 contention on, 330, 555, 556–557, 559, 563–566, 862; proliferation management of, 13, 327–331, 333, 451, 555–558, 559; refugees from, 554, 562; sanctions on, 6, 14, 161–162, 416*tab*, 420*tab*, 447, 555–558; transitional authority in, 561–563; UNAMI in, 561, 562–563; US in, 6, 13, 60–61, 360, 553–554, 863. *See also* Gulf War

Iraq War (2003): events leading to, 12–13, 558–560; France stance on, 823; geopolitical fragmentation on, 822–823; initiation of, 13–14, 66, 72, 559–560; lessons, 564–565; previous assessment of, 827–828; Resolution 1441 on, 559, 565; Resolution 1483 on, 560–561, 823; resource limitations for, 564; Russia stance on, 108, 823; transitional authority after, 561–562; UNAMI bombing in, 561, 562; unilateral approach to, 62, 72; use of force for, 66, 358, 360, 553–554, 559–560. *See also* Gulf War

Iraqi Governing Council (IGC), 561

Ireland, on Kashmir, 160

ISA. *See* Islamic State of Afghanistan

ISAF. *See* International Security Assistance Force

ISIS. *See* Islamic State of Iraq and al-Sham

Islam radicalization, 601–603, 617–619

Islamic Emirate, 643

Islamic State of Afghanistan (ISA), 643

Islamic State of Iraq and al-Sham (ISIS), 718, 727–728, 736, 739

Israel: HRC inquiry on, 534, 536; Iraq Osiraq attack by, 327, 329; Lebanon relations with, 88*tab*, 532, 539–544, 749; Munich Olympics hostages from, 279; PFLP hijacking raid by, 280; proliferation management of, 327; Russia relations with, 534, 538; Suez occupation by, 212*n*15, 374, 531–533; Syria ICC referral and, 729–730; Syria relations with, 88*tab*, 343*n*14, 532, 732–733; United Red Army of Japan attack on, 279; US relations with, 732–733. *See also* Arab-Israeli conflict

Israel-Palestine conflict: al-Aqsa intifada as, 534–535; France stance on, 125–126*tab*,

126; Gaza wars as, 535–539; humanitarian intervention in, 536–538; Operation Cast Lead in, 536; Operation Protective Edge in, 537; Oslo Accords for, 533; Quartet role in, 534, 535–536, 538; Resolution 1397 on, 534; Resolution 1850 on, 536; Resolution 1860 on, 536; UK stance on, 125–126*tab*, 126; US stance on, 64, 77–78, 367, 534–539

Italy: Ethiopia conflict with, 142; in Geneva Initiative, 648; Lebanon UNIFIL support by, 543

Ituri crisis, 378–379, 672–673

IWGD. *See* Informal Working Group on Documentation and Other Procedural Questions

Izetbegovic, Alija, 572

Jackson, Jesse, 65

Jallow, Hassan Bubacar, 511

Janjaweed, 620–621, 623

Janvier, Bernard, 574–575, 585, 586

Japan: China relations with, 163, 367, 805, 867; economy of, 795; in G4 reform proposal, 134, 162–163, 170, 180–181, 192*nn*28–32, 867; Hiroshima bombing in, 325; India compared to, 166–167; Israel attack by, 279; membership consideration for, 80, 163, 166–167, 367, 867; military capability of, 806; Nagasaki bombing in, 325; North Korea compromise with, 334; S5 proposal engagement by, 182; United Red Army of, 279; US relations with, 805

Jarring, Gunnar, 532

Jen a, Miroslav, 465

Jeunes Patriotes, 685

Johnston, Robert, 598

Jonah, James, 597

Jones, Bruce, 529, 808–809

Jones Parry, Emyr, 192*n*38

Jordan: membership acquisition by, 737; Sierra Leone withdrawal by, 753; Syria proposal by, 728, 730, 736, 737. *See also* Small five members

Juba. *See* Khartoum conflict

Jurisdiction: democracy promotion and, 235, 251*n*2, 779–780; piracy law enforcement and, 313–314

Jus cogens (peremptory legal norms), 785, 788*n*2

Kabila, Joseph, 248, 380, 663, 671, 672–673

Kabila, Laurent, 662–663, 670, 671

Kadi, Yassin, 430, 785–786

Kadijevic, Veljko, 573

Kagame, Paul, 599

Kampala Accord, 607–608, 672

Kampala bombing, 605

Karadzic, Radovan, 509

Karlsrud, John, 762

Karzai, Hamid, 653, 659*n*39

Kashmir conflict, 46*tab*, 160, 871

Kay, Nicholas, 608

Kennedy, Paul, 401

Kenya: AMISOM support from, 605; ICC referral for, 520, 856; ICTR and fugitives in, 512; Nairobi Declarations, 675; Nairobi shooting, 520, 605, 609; Somali piracy response of, 313

Kenyatta, Uhuru, 520, 856

Kerry, John, 537, 539, 725

Khalilzad, Zalmay, 163

Khan, Abdul Qadeer, 332, 340, 864

Khartoum conflict: Abyei conflict and, 627–630; development of, 616–619; peacemaking, 619–627, 633–634, 639*n*37, 642*n*79. *See also* Darfur crisis

Al-Khatib, Abdelilah, 702

Khomeini, Ruhollah, 552

Khrushchev, Nikita, 444

Kidnappings, 364

Kim Jong-il, 335

Kim Jong-un, 335

Kimberley Process, 306, 857

Kisangani massacre, 378

Kordofan conflict, 627–628

Korean War, 4, 37, 350, 360, 396, 449, 824

Kosovo: Dayton Accords for, 587–588; democracy promotion in, 241; Finland stance on, 821; geopolitical fragmentation on, 821–822; Liberation Army attacks in, 588; Macedonia UNPREDEP and, 91; NATO in, 11, 64, 402, 403, 589, 821; organized crime in, 309; recognition of, 589–590; Resolution 1160 on, 588–589; Russia stance on, 821–822; transitional authority in, 752, 753; UNMIK in, 241, 309, 589, 752, 753. *See also* International Criminal Tribunal for the Former Yugoslavia

Kozyrev, Andrey, 581

Kubiš, Jan, 465

Kurdish refugees, 554

Kurdistan conflict, 46*tab*

Kuwait invasion, 46*tab*, 60, 329, 358, 552–553. *See also* Gulf War

Lahoud, Emile, 540

Landgren, Karin, 466

Lang, Jack, 314

Laos-Vietnam relations, 449

LAS (League of Arab States). *See* Arab League

Lasso, José Ayala, 263

Latin America Friends of Haiti, 496–497, 759

Lavrov, Sergey, 110, 703, 725, 742

Law, humanitarian. *See* Courts

Law, international: consistency issues in, 787; decentralized nature of, 771; democracy as human rights in, 236–237; domestic jurisdiction and, 235, 251*n*2, 313–314, 779–780; due process in, 303, 307, 313–314; enforcement, collective, 311–313; enforcement, fact-finding for, 307–309; enforcement, private, 305–307, 312; enforcement, Security Council role of, 780–782; enforcement by executive policing, 309–310; enforcement by military action, 309–310; enforcement obstacles, 301–303, 305, 313–314; humanitarian intervention and, 218–221, 782; indirect judicial review and, 784–786; interpretation of, 778–780; *jus cogens*, 785; liability determination, 778; norm entrepreneurship, 452–453; on organized crime, 301–310; overriding, 772, 773, 777; P5 exception to, 141–143; on piracy, 310–316, 804; *rechtsstaat*, 316; rules of conduct, 302–303; Russia advocacy of, 110–112; sanctions and, 414, 423, 429, 430–431, 782; sovereignty as obstacle in, 301–302, 305; sovereignty limits and, 10–11, 141–143, 218–220; on trafficking, 301–310; United States repudiation of, 65, 72; on use of force, 357, 778, 781

"Lawfare," 65

Lawmaking power, 772, 773, 774–777

League of Arab States (LAS). *See* Arab League

League of democracies, 77

League of Nations: counterterrorism by, 278–279; Italy-Ethiopia conflict and, 142; on regional organizations, 488*n*6; UN Charter comparison to, 3, 251*n*2; United Nations comparison to, 158–159; veto provision of, 368; weaknesses of, 142, 158–159

Lebanon: Beirut bombing, 419, 446, 513, 540–541; Israel relations with, 88*tab*, 532, 539–544, 749; Resolution 425 on, 539–540; Resolution 1559 on, 513, 540, 544; Resolution 1636 on, 541; Resolution 1701 on, 543–544, 749–750, 781; Resolution 1757 on, 514, 541; sanctions on, 418*tab*, 419, 420*tab*, 513; Special Tribunal for, 508, 513–515, 541–542; Syria relations with, 513–514, 540–542, 737; UNIFIL in, 532, 543–544, 749–750, 781

Legitimacy, 868–870. *See also* Accountability

Léotard, Francois, 401

Levitte, Jean-David, 671

Liberal institutionalism, 15, 136

Liberia: ECOWAS support of, 481, 482, 484; France stance on, 125*tab*; peacekeeping,

481, 482, 484, 754; sanctions on, 161, 416*tab*, 420*tab*; UK stance on, 125*tab*; UNOMIL in, 482, 484; US in, 754

Libya: Arab League response to, 701, 702–703, 707–708; AU stance on, 160, 282, 701, 702, 708; Benghazi massacre prevention, 701, 703, 706–707; Brazil stance on, 704, 706, 710; chemical weapons of, 332; China stance on, 361, 703–704, 706–707, 800; Cold War era terrorism by, 280, 281–282; conflict aftermath, 709–712; France stance on, 125*tab*, 702; GCC and, 701–702, 707, 708; geopolitical fragmentation on, 823; Germany stance on, 702, 703, 707, 714*n*27, 800; Groups of Friends of, 499–500; HRC inquiry on, 265, 701, 785; ICC referral of, 519, 701, 786; NATO in, 97, 111, 226–227, 290, 356, 359, 361, 406–408, 499, 699, 710–711, 841–842; no-fly zone in, 702–704, 707; OAU stance on, 97, 160, 282, 786; P3 negotiations on, 281, 282, 407; P5 contention on, 702–703; proliferation management of, 331–332, 334; protests in, 701; R2P controversy in, 222, 226–227, 700, 705, 711, 713, 800, 841–842; regional support for, 43; Resolution 1970 on, 270, 406, 421, 700, 701, 702, 707, 778, 782; Resolution 1973 on, 97, 135, 407–408, 421, 499, 699–712, 823; Russia stance on, 97, 361, 703, 800, 823; sanctions on, 270, 281–282, 290, 331–332, 416*tab*, 420*tab*, 426–427; South Africa stance on, 709–710; SRSG reports on, 465–466; Syria comparison to, 741, 742, 800, 823–824, 842–843; transitional authority for, 499–500, 701, 702; UK stance on, 125*tab*, 702; US in, 69, 111, 226–227, 332, 703, 707, 710; use of force on, 69, 111, 356, 361, 699–709

Lie, Trygve, 396, 445, 449

Liechtenstein. *See* Small five members

Linas-Marcoussis Agreement, 683, 684–685

Lippmann, Walter, 444

Lisbon Treaty, 137*n*19

Lockerbie bombing, 281, 784

Løj, Ellen, 461–462

London Compact, 654

L69 group, 183

Luck, Edward C., 453; membership reform proposal by, 206–209, 214*n*25

Lukabu Khabouji N'Zaji, 666

Luncheon Group, 647

Lusaka agreement, 662, 663, 668, 669

Luxembourg: membership of, 758; Syria proposal by, 728, 730, 736, 737

Macedonia, 88*tab*, 91, 161, 592*n*13

MacKenzie, Lewis, 363
Madagascar, 499
Madrid peace conference, 533
Mahbubani, Kishore, 165, 166, 214*n*25. *See also* 7-7-7 formula
Mahiga, Augustine, 466, 607, 608
Malaysia, 499
Mali, 130, 131; AU and AFISMA in, 482, 485, 781; counterterrorism in, 290–291, 384; ECOWAS support of, 384; electoral assistance in, 248; France intervention in, 383–384, 781; MINUSMA in, 309, 384, 392*n*28, 392*n*29; Resolution 2085 on, 392*n*29, 781; trafficking in, 309; troop contributors to, 759
Malta, Egypt Air hijacking raid in, 280
Mandates: appropriateness of, 464–467; contingency plans for, 464; design of, 458; renewal or amendment of, 459, 462; resources for, 459, 461–464, 467–468. *See also* Resolutions
Mandela, Nelson, 667
March 23 Movement (M23), 673–675, 850
Marcoussis. *See* Linas-Marcoussis agreement
Maritime security. *See* Piracy
MARO. *See* Mass Atrocity Response Operations
Marr, Phebe, 564
Martin, Ian, 463, 465–466
Masire, Ketumile, 668
Mass atrocity. *See* Bombing; Genocide
Mass Atrocity Response Operations (MARO), 229
Massoud, Ahmad Shah, 643, 660*n*46
Matheson, Michael, 77
Mazar-i-Sharif hostage crisis, 646
Mazowiecki, Tadeusz, 261, 262–263
Mbeki, Thabo, 626, 627, 629, 635, 686
McCain, John, 77
McChrystal, Stanley, 406
Media, relationship development with, 460
Medvedev, Dmitri, 108–109, 244
Meece, Roger, 462, 463, 467
Meetings: Arria formula, 151, 177, 199, 261, 268, 836, 854; DPA service of, 835; horizon-scanning, 178–179, 268, 844; informal interactive dialogue, 179, 191*nn*17–19, 199–200, 836–837; open thematic debate, 177–178; P5 dominance of, 148–149, 151–152; wrap-up sessions, 178. *See also* Reporting
Mehlis, Detlev, 540, 541
Membership: African Group expansion of, 134, 163, 167, 170, 181; Australia acquisition of, 758; Bosnia acquisition of, 576; Brazil consideration for, 807–808; China acquisition of, 86; China preferences on, 53*n*15; committee

appointments, 148, 205, 208, 421–423, 835; continuity importance of, 143; Croatia acquisition of, 576; emerging powers consideration for, 135, 159, 162–171; EU consolidation of, 134, 170–171; Finland consideration for, 758; France acquisition of, 123; France removal from, 169, 171; General Assembly amendment to, 197; groupings growth, 818; India consideration for, 80, 367, 758, 806–808, 867; Japan consideration for, 80, 163, 166–167, 367, 867; Jordan acquisition of, 737; Luxembourg acquisition of, 758; military capability for, 806–807; new category of, 153; Pakistan consideration for, 758; Palestine consideration for, 53*n*12, 78, 538–539; Russia preferences on, 118; Saudi Arabia declination of, 80, 737; Slovenia acquisition of, 576; Turkey consideration for, 808; UK acquisition of, 123; UK removal from, 169, 171, 832; US preferences on, 80; vetoes, 34*fig*, 35, 53*n*12, 53*n*15, 78, 88*tab*, 162–163; Vietnam consideration for, 53*n*12. *See also* Elected ten nonpermanent members; Membership reform; Permanent five members; Permanent three members
Méndez, Juan, 264
Menkerios, Haile, 606, 629
Mérimée, Jean-Bernard, 578
Mexico: Act of Chapultepec in, 477; human rights Arria briefing by, 268
Mexico, Indonesia, Nigeria, Turkey (MINT), 167, 498
Middle East: Carter Doctrine on, 597; conflict management focus on, 838; democracy promotion in, 244–245; new Groups of Friends and, 498; peacekeeping notoriety of, 529–530; resolutions by region, 40, 41*fig*, 42*fig*, 43; UNTSO in, 91, 397, 530, 547*n*11; US vetoes on, 64. *See also* Arab League; Arab Spring; Arab-Israeli conflict
Mikulaschek, Christoph, 469
Military capability: of China, 794; of emerging powers, 794–795, 805–806; of Germany, 806; of India, 806; of Japan, 806; membership and, 806–807; of NATO, 400, 402, 409–410
Military interventions: accountability in, 229; approval of, 227–228; Boutros-Ghali stance on, 397–398, 446–447; coercive protection doctrine of, 228–229; Cold War era of, 4; failed, overview of, 8–10, 227; humanitarian bridging of, 406–408; humanitarian justification of, 226–230; mission creep of, 9, 229, 230, 462; NGOs, 229; objectives in, 228; for organized crime, 309–310; out-of-area, 398–399;

peacekeeping compared to, 228–229, 354–357, 397–398; for piracy, 312, 313; restrictions on, 225; Secretary-General role in, 446–447; for trafficking, 309–310. *See also* Humanitarian intervention; North Atlantic Treaty Organization; Use of force

Military Staff Committee, 374, 394, 408

Millennium Declaration, 242

Miller, Laurel, 358

Milosevic, Slobodan, 509, 570, 573, 587–589, 821–822

Mineral trafficking, 306–307

MINT. *See* Mexico, Indonesia, Nigeria, Turkey

MINUCI. *See* UN Mission in Côte d'Ivoire

MINUGUA. *See* UN Verification Mission in Guatemala

MINURCA. *See* UN Verification Mission in the Central African Republic

MINURCAT. *See* UN Mission in the Central African Republic and Chad

MINURSO. *See* UN Mission for the Referendum in Western Sahara

MINUSMA. *See* UN Multidimensional Integrated Stabilization Mission in Mali

MINUSTAH. *See* UN Stabilization Mission in Haiti

Miqati, Najib, 541–542

Mission creep, 9, 229, 230, 462

Mitchell, George, 547–548n30

Mladic, Ratko, 509, 586

MLC. *See* Movement for the Liberation of the Congo

Mobutu Sese Seko, 665, 666–667

Mogadishu, 9, 63, 387, 597, 599, 600, 602–603, 605

Mohamud, Hassan Sheikh, 608, 609

Mongolia, 53n15

Monteiro, Antonio, 687

MONUA. *See* UN Observer Mission in Angola

MONUC. *See* UN Organization Mission in the DRC

MONUSCO. *See* UN Organization Stabilization Mission in the DRC

Mood, Robert, 723, 761–762

A More Secure World (Annan), 813n42

Moreno-Ocampo, Luis, 626

Morocco: Arab League proposal on Syria by, 721, 737; Western Sahara relations with, 495–496

Morris, Nicholas, 579

Moussa, Amr, 536

Movement for the Liberation of the Congo (MLC), 662–663, 677n5, 678n23, 679n33

Mozambique, 6–7

M23. *See* March 23 Movement

Mubarak, Hosni, 54n27, 282, 617

Mujahidin, 644–645

Murphy, Deborah, 621

Museveni, Yoweri, 607

Myanmar, 54n25, 88tab, 95–96, 858

Nagasaki bombing, 325

Nairobi Declarations, 675

Nairobi shooting, 520, 605, 609

Najibullah, Mohammad, 644–645

NAM. *See* Non-Aligned Movement

Namibia, 91, 492, 509, 775

National Congress for the Defense of the People (CNDP), 673

National interest: China-Taiwan relations and, 88tab, 90, 91, 102n51; humanitarian intervention and, 217, 222–223; membership reform case of, 161–162; Russia-Georgia relations and, 108, 110; sanctions for, 161–162; in Security Council decision-making, 15–16; UK exploitation of, 161; US exploitation of, 78–79, 161–162. *See also* Geopolitical fragmentation

National Union for the Total Independence of Angola (UNITA), 306, 417tab, 427

NATO. *See* North Atlantic Treaty Organization

Nehru, Jawaharlal, 211n11

Nepal conflict, 47tab, 463–464, 466

Netherlands, 313, 605, 758

New Zealand, 140, 145, 146

Ngongi, Namanga, 379

NGOs. *See* Non-governmental organizations

Nicaragua, 479, 508–509

Niger flight 772 bombing, 281

Nigeria: Côte d'Ivoire stance of, 690; Gulf of Guinea piracy and, 315; in MINT, 167, 498; 7-7-7 reform formula for, 167, 170; in Sierra Leone, 752, 753; South Africa compared to, 167

9/11 attacks: Bush, George W., response to, 12–13, 860–861; Resolution 1368 after, 12, 66, 284, 860; right to self-defense after, 778, 860; Sudan and, 617, 618; Taliban fall after, 650–652. *See also* Resolution 1373

Non-Aligned Movement (NAM): Bosnia stance of, 578, 591n5, 592n26; China relations with, 84, 85, 86; Cold War era counterterrorism response of, 279; criminal law enforcement stance of, 305, 311; democracy promotion opposition by, 241; establishment of, 84, 100nn2–3; humanitarian intervention stance of, 404; position on Rome Statute, 515; stance on thematic resolutions of, 854; use of force stance of, 376, 849; stance on peacekeeping doctrine of, 376; stance on piracy response of, 311; stance on Security Council role in addressing trafficking, 305, 865

Non-governmental organizations (NGOs): humanitarian, 220–221, 426, 853–854; lobbying by, 764; military intervention, 229; role in Security Council decisionmaking by, 854–855; sanctions role of, 426, 433–434; transparency supported by, 199, 837; for women, 502

Nonpermanent members. *See* Elected ten nonpermanent members

Non-Proliferation Treaty (NPT). *See* Nuclear Non-Proliferation Treaty (NPT)

Nonstate actors: accountability political checks on, 786; overall concern for, 859; proliferation management of, 339–341, 864; sanctions on, 427

Norm entrepreneurship, 452–453

Norms: entrepreneurship, 452–453; peremptory legal, 785, 788*n*2

North America: OAS, 53*n*18, 240, 477, 479–481, 496, 874*n*36; peacekeeping troop size in, 847*fig*; resolutions focusing on, 40, 41*fig*, 42*fig*, 43

North Atlantic Treaty Organization (NATO): in Afghanistan, 405–406, 652; Annan relations with, 404; Ban relations with, 406, 409; in Bosnia, 358–359, 400, 401–402, 583–586; Boutros-Ghali relations with, 399; Charter and, 395, 399–400; in Cyprus, 398; dual key agreement with, 362, 400, 401–402, 585; establishment of, 394–395; in Gulf War, 399, 564–565; in Korean War, 396; in Kosovo, 11, 64, 402, 403, 589, 821; league of democracies with, 77; in Libya, 97, 111, 226–227, 290, 356, 359, 406–408, 499, 699, 710–711, 841–842; military and peacekeeping capability of, 400, 402, 409–410; out-of-area interventions, 398–399; regional scope of, 43, 399–400; role constraint of, 410; Russia relations with, 105, 107–108, 109, 402, 403; Secretary-General coordination with, 407; Security Council cohesion with, 403–404, 406, 408–409; Security Council contention with, 401–402; Somali piracy response of, 312; UK stance on, 396

North Korea: Agreed Framework for, 333; China relations with, 93–94, 273, 334, 360, 803, 863; human rights investigation opposition on, 273; Japan compromise with, 334; in Korean War, 4, 37, 350, 360, 396, 449, 824; proliferation management of, 93–94, 116, 145, 332–336, 803, 863; Russia relations with, 116, 273, 863; sanctions on, 93–94, 418*tab*, 420*tab*, 424, 425, 863; South Korea recent attacks by,

335, 805; US relations with, 333–334, 360, 396

Norway: E10 marginalization and, 145

Note 507, 150–151, 182, 183–184, 192–193*nn*42–44, 192*n*39

NPT. *See* Nuclear Non-Proliferation Treaty

Ntganda, Bosco, 519

Nuclear Non-Proliferation Treaty, 115, 325, 328, 343*n*8

Nuclear Security Summit, 340, 802–803, 864

Nuclear Suppliers Group, 340, 343*n*9

Nuclear weapons. *See* Proliferation management

Al-Nusra Front, 727, 743

Oakley, Robert, 598

OAS. *See* Organization of American States

OAU. *See* Organization of African Unity

Obama, Barrack: Atrocity Prevention Board by, 223; Ebola addressed by, 866; emerging powers support from, 68–69; foreign fighters campaign of, 727, 735*tab*, 831, 862; foreign policy of, 67–71, 80, 802–803, 828–829; Gaza wars response of, 538; Global Counter-Terrorism Forum by, 289–290, 292–293, 803, 861; on Libya intervention, 703, 710; Nobel Peace Prize for, 393; Nuclear Security Summit by, 340, 802–803, 864; Russia reconciliation by, 68, 108–109; Security Council relations under, 67–71, 80, 802–803, 828–829; on Syria intervention, 726, 733, 736, 743, 744–745; Tehran Declaration support of, 337, 863

Obasanjo, Olusegun, 170

Office for the Coordination of Humanitarian Affairs (OCHA), 221

Office of Legal Counsel, 187, 194*nn*58–59

Office of the High Commissioner for Human Rights (OHCHR), 263–264, 268, 853

Ogata, Sadako, 576

OHCHR. *See* Office of the High Commissioner for Human Rights

OIC. *See* Organization of the Islamic Conference

Oil: in emerging powers countries, 797; in Kuwait, 553; sanctions, 14, 161–162, 416–418*tab*, 447, 556, 621; in Sudan, 619, 621, 625; Syria conflict and, 742

Oil-for-food program, 14, 161–162, 447, 556

Omar, Mohammed, 645, 648, 649

One China policy, 90–91

O'Neill, Jim, 167

ONUSAL. *See* UN Observer Mission in El Salvador

OPCW. *See* Organization for the Prohibition of Chemical Weapons

Open-door policy, 282

Open-Ended Working Group, 179, 180, 182, 183
Operation Artemis, 379, 672, 695*n*6
Operation Cast Lead, 536
Operation Deliberate Force, 358–359, 584–586
Operation Desert Fox, 13, 555
Operation Desert Storm, 553–554
Operation Enduring Freedom, 108, 652
Operation Infinite Reach, 618
Operation Iraqi Freedom. *See* Iraq War
Operation Licorne, 682–683, 692
Operation Lifeline Sudan, 616
Operation Protective Edge, 537
Operation Provide Comfort, 23*n*11, 554, 781
Operation Turquoise, 663–665
Operation Unified Protector, 699
Organization for Security and Cooperation in Europe (OSCE), 241
Organization for the Prohibition of Chemical Weapons (OPCW), 112, 332, 338–339
Organization of African Unity (OAU): DRC support from, 667, 668; in Falklands War, 481; Libya stance of, 97, 160, 282, 786; Sudan stance of, 617
Organization of American States (OAS), 53*n*18, 240, 477, 479–481, 496, 874*n*36
Organization of the Islamic Conference (OIC), 701, 707–708
Organized crime: atrocity crime compared to, 308; China stance on, 305; conclusion on, 316–317, 864–865; counterterrorism and, 286, 303–304; in DRC, 306; executive policing of, 309–310; fact-finding on, 307–309; international law on, 301–310; in Kosovo, 309; law enforcement obstacles for, 301–303, 305; military intervention for, 309–310; overview on, 299–301, 864–865; piracy compared to, 310–311; private enforcement against, 305–307; revenue and resources, 301, 302; in Russia, 114–115; Security Council role in, 864–865
OSCE. *See* Organization for Security and Cooperation in Europe
Osiraq attack, 327, 329
Oslo Accords, 533; PRIO in, 47*tab*
Otunnu, Olara, 502
Ouagadougou Agreement, 688
Ouattara, Alassane: Abidjan offensive by, 691–692; background of, 696*n*24; presidency of, 244, 382–383, 688–689, 693, 696*n*26

Pakistan: Bosnia safe areas role of, 578; death count in, 46*tab*; DRC troop contribution from, 759; Geneva Accords for, 645; Kashmir conflict, 46*tab*, 160, 871;

membership consideration for, 758; proliferation assistance from, 115, 332, 340, 864; resolution count in, 46*tab*; Somalia support from, 598, 599
Palestine: Arab League in, 478–479; Cold War era terrorism by, 279, 280; E10 role in, 834; membership consideration of, 53*n*12, 78, 538–539; Syria contention with, 478–479. *See also* Israel-Palestine conflict
Palme, Olof, 552
Panel of experts, 288, 290, 307–309, 335, 422–424, 433, 437*n*10, 438*n*22, 447, 600, 622, 673–674, 680*n*39, 686, 704, 766, 857–858
Panel on United Nations Peace Operations. *See* Brahimi Panel
Paris, Roland, 247
Pascoe, B. Lynn, 720
Peace Research Institute Oslo (PRIO), 47*tab*
Peacebuilding Commission, 245, 850–851
Peacebuilding phase, 470–472
Peacekeeping: accelerated growth of, 7, 24*n*16, 28–29; in Angola MONUA, 266; assessment visits for, 177, 466–467; authorization assessment of, 357–359; Ban views on, 846–847; bargaining and planning, 755–756, 845; in Bosnia UNPROFOR, 8, 9, 266, 361–362, 401, 576–577, 578–579, 583–586; Brahimi Report on, 64–65, 364, 375–376, 404–405, 409, 455*n*15, 461, 464, 760, 836, 847; budget, 7, 129*tab*, 133, 144, 462–463, 756, 760; Capstone Doctrine on, 376–377; in Central African Republic and Chad MINURCAT, 130, 625, 756; in Central African Republic MINURCA, 9; China involvement in, 91–92, 129*tab*, 848; civil components in, 6–7; civilian protection provision of, 376, 388, 501, 705; Cold War era, 4–5, 374; conflict decline and, 49, 50*fig*, 51, 351–352, 838–839; major trends in, 844–851, 845*fig*, 847*fig*; contingency planning for, 464; in Côte d'Ivoire ECOWAS, 244, 382, 682–684, 690; in Côte d'Ivoire MINUCI, 683; in Côte d'Ivoire UNOCI, 112, 244, 382–383, 684–685, 686, 691–693, 694; in Croatia UNPROFOR, 574, 592*n*13; in Cyprus, 40, 398, 450; in Darfur UNAMID, 97, 484, 604, 624, 625, 630–631, 634–635, 755–756, 764, 852; deaths per conflict and, 45, 46–47*tab*, 54*nn*25–29; in the DRC, MONUC, 65, 378–380, 667–671, 672, 675, 754, 766; in the DRC, MONUSCO, 242, 248, 381–382, 392*n*32, 674–675, 757, 766; in the DRC, ONUC, 4, 448; E10 role in, 758; in East Timor UNTAET, 241, 243, 464, 496, 752–753; in Egypt Suez crisis,

212*n*15, 374, 531–533; in Egypt UNEF, 374, 531–532; in El Salvador ONUSAL, 6–7, 266; era, boom and bust, 750, 752, 760, 844–845, 845*fig*; era, new, 757; era of expansion, 144, 362–363, 375, 483, 750–751; era of failure, 1–3, 8–10, 45, 46–47*tab*, 397–398, 483; era of recovery, 752–754, 767, 845; in Eritrea UNMEE, 758, 764; escalation ability, 387; in Ethiopia UNMEE, 758, 764; first innovations in, 529, 530–531; France involvement in, 123–127, 124, 128, 129*tab*, 130–131, 133; frozen files, 870–871; geopolitical change in, 847–848, 847*fig*; in Guatemala MINUGUA, 88*tab*, 91; after Gulf War, 6, 23*n*11, 161–162, 554–555; in Haiti MINUSTAH, 309, 496–497; in Haiti UNMIH, 90, 239–240; host state consent in, 763–765, 850; invention of, 4, 374, 397; in Iran-Iraq War, 5, 45, 450, 552; in Kosovo UNMIK, 241, 309, 589, 752, 753; in Lebanon UNIFIL, 532, 543–544, 749–750, 781; in Liberia, 481, 482, 484, 754; in Macedonia UNPREDEP, 88*tab*, 91, 161, 592*n*13; in Mali AFISMA, 482, 485, 781; in Mali MINUSMA, 309, 384, 392*n*28, 392*n*29; mandating, 458–459, 461–468; military interventions compared to, 228–229, 354–357, 397–398; mission creep of, 9, 229, 230, 462; in Mozambique, 6–7; NATO capability for, 400, 402, 409–410; non-UN contributions to, 43, 54*n*22, 54*n*23; P5 engagement comparison in, 129*tab*; personnel casualties, 364; police contributors to, 759–760; postcolonial character and, 352–353; power dynamics of, 751, 752–754; principles of, 354–355, 374–377, 848; regional organizations contradictions in, 475–478; regional organizations decline in, 481–487; regional organizations preeminence in, 478–481, 752–754, 762–763; resource limitations for, 363–364, 385–386, 387, 402, 462–463, 467–468, 756, 765–767, 846; robust, opposition to, 849; robust assessment by capacity, 387; robust assessment by crisis examples, 378–384; rules of engagement in, 361–362, 386; Russia involvement in, 112–113, 129*tab*; in Rwanda UNAMIR, 11, 63–64, 140, 262, 266, 446, 483, 510, 664, 677*nn*7–9; in Sierra Leone ECOMOG, 752, 753; in Sierra Leone UNAMSIL, 229, 752–753, 754; in Somalia AMISOM, 603–606, 608–609, 613*n*47; in Somalia UNOSOM I, 8, 222, 598; in Somalia UNOSOM II, 8–9, 63, 483, 598–600; in South Sudan UNMISS, 242, 243, 623–624, 628; sovereignty limits in, 10–12, 218–220; Special Committee on Peacekeeping Operations, 759; SRSG leverage in, 468–472, 761–762; SRSG relationships for, 459–461; success factors, 468; in Sudan AMIS, 621, 623, 755; in Sudan UNAMID, 97, 484, 604, 624, 625, 630–631, 634–635, 755–756, 764, 852; in Sudan UNISFA, 623–624, 628, 630; in Sudan UNMIS, 622, 623–624, 627–628; in Suez, 212*n*15, 374, 531–533; as symbolic, 374, 390; in Syria UNDOF, 532; in Syria UNSMIS, 723–725; task types, 257*n*98, 848; tools, 765–767; trends reshaping, 752; troop contributors to, 759–760, 767–768, 873*n*22; troop size by region, 847*fig*; UK involvement in, 123–127, 128, 129*tab*, 133; US involvement in, 129*tab*; in Western Sahara MINURSO, 266, 495–496; in Zaire, 665–667. *See also* Military interventions

Peacemaking: Accra III Agreement, 685; Act of Chapultepec, 477; Agreed Framework, 333; Agreed Minutes of 1964, 778; for Arab-Israeli conflict, 533, 536; Bonn process, 66, 437*n*11, 651–652, 654–655; Camp David Accords, 532; concept of, 387–389; Dayton Accords, 64, 359, 400, 402, 587–588; Five Principles of Peaceful Coexistence, 84–85; Geneva Accords, 645; Kampala Accord, 607–608, 672; for Khartoum conflict, 619–627, 633–634, 639*n*37, 642*n*79; Linas-Marcoussis Agreement, 683, 684–685; London Compact, 654; Lusaka agreement, 662, 663, 668, 669; Nairobi Declarations, 675; Oslo Accords, 533; Ouagadougou Agreement, 688; for Somalia, 601, 607–608; Tehran Declaration, 337–338, 863

Peacemonger (Goulding), 363

Pearson, Lester, 374

Penholders: E10 power as, 151, 205–206, 272–273, 758; France as, 128, 129*tab*, 131–133; human rights contention among, 272–273; Luck reform proposal for, 208; P3 power as, 272, 833–834; P5 power as, 129*tab*, 147–148, 205–206, 272–273, 834; Russia as, 833; UK as, 128, 129*tab*, 131–133

People's Liberation Army (PLA), 91–92

People's Republic of China (PRC). *See* China

Peremptory legal norms, 785, 788*n*2

Perestroika (Soviet reformation), 5

Pérez de Cuéllar, Javier, 5, 450, 552, 572, 573

Perle, Richard, 77

Permanent five members (P5): Africa relations with, 838, 870; Bosnia contention of, 140, 572; civilian protection cohesion of, 798;

committee chairs and, 148, 205, 208, 421–422, 835; convergence of, 831, 859; credibility or composition battle of, 157, 159–162; deference to, 23n1, 28; E10 power improvements with, 149–152, 153, 205–206, 834–836; E10 power marginalization by, 145–149, 272–273, 833–834; emerging powers convergence with, 165; failures and relevance of, 1–3; formation of, 123, 139–140; France removal from, 169, 171; G4 reform contention of, 163, 181; geopolitical change within, 828–833, 831fig; Groups of Friends contention of, 498–500, 503; human rights contention of, 272–273; ICJ relations with, 158; international law exception of, 141–143; Iran proliferation agreement by, 719; Iran proliferation contention of, 337–338; Iraq cohesion of, 552, 554, 863; Iraq contention of, 330, 555, 556–557, 559, 563–566, 862; legitimacy issues of, 870; Libya contention of, 702–703; Luck proposal on, 208; meetings determined by, 148–149, 151–152; national interest exploitation by, 161–162; North Korea proliferation contention of, 334, 863; Note 507 pushback by, 151, 182, 183–184; penholdership of, 129tab, 147–148, 205–206, 272–273, 834; population misrepresentation by, 160, 170; post-Cold War cooperation of, 5, 551; procedural power of, 146–149, 198; proliferation management contention of, 13, 93–94, 115–116, 330–331; proliferation management exception for, 323–324, 325, 345n6; R2P contention of, 840–843; regional organization contradictions within, 477; Rome Statute and, 515, 516–517; Rwanda contention of, 140; sanctions contention of, 425, 428, 437nn15–16; sanctions role of, 421, 424; Secretariat de facto addition to, 835–836; Secretary-General relations with, 445, 836; Security Council engagement comparisons of, 127–128, 129tab, 130–131; selective security and contention of, 367–368; Sudan contention of, 617, 622–624, 631–632, 755–756; Suez crisis contention of, 212n15; Syria contention of, 69–70, 88–89tab, 718–720, 724–725, 731–733, 734–735tab, 736; Tehran Declaration contention of, 337–338; troop contributions by, 759, 873n22; UK removal from, 169, 171, 832; use of force authorization power of, 773; use of force contention of, 367–368; veto trends of, 35, 36fig, 37–38, 53n12, 78, 129tab, 830,

831fig; voluntary restraint of, 202–203, 213nn18–19; win-win reform solution for, 166–171
Permanent five members plus Germany (P5+1), 94, 115, 337, 498, 719, 745, 808, 818
Permanent three members (P3), 10, 421, 428; Arab-Israeli conflict contention of, 534; Bosnia contention of, 140, 577–580; Côte d'Ivoire post-electoral stance of, 689–690; democracy promotion by, 248–249, 256n93; divisions on peacekeeping within, 755–756; E10 and, 758; human rights focus of, 272, 798; Iraq proliferation contention of, 328; ISIS stance of, 727; Libya negotiations with, 281, 282, 407; penholdership of, 272, 833–834; Syria cohesion of, 720, 722, 723, 731
Perry, Chris, 469
Petterson, Don, 641n71
P5. See Permanent five members
P5+1. See Permanent five members plus Germany
PFLP. See Popular Front for the Liberation of Palestine
Philippines, 499
Pillay, Navi, 200, 721, 729, 853
Piracy: analysis and lessons, 314–316; due process and, 313–314; law enforcement on, 310–316, 804; military intervention for, 312, 313; problem of, 310–311, 865; regional organizations fighting, 311–313, 804
PLA. See People's Liberation Army
Police contributors, 54n22, 759–760
Political checks, 787–788
Political missions: in Afghanistan UNAMA, 563, 652–655; in Afghanistan UNSMA, 643–648, 649; budget and resources for, 463–464, 846; effectiveness of, 846; in Nepal, 47tab, 463–464, 466; Secretary-General function in, 447, 448–452; in Somalia UNPOS, 600; in Somalia UNSOM, 608–609. See also Electoral assistance
Popular Front for the Liberation of Palestine (PFLP), 279, 280
Population representation, 160, 166, 170
Portugal: disease addressed by, 866; Syria stance of, 720, 737
Post-Cold War era: accelerated growth of Security Council activity, 7, 24n16, 28–29; China foreign policy in, 85, 87, 90–91; Cold War era resolutions compared to, 29, 29tab, 31, 33; conflict management focus, 838–839; counterterrorism, 281–283; deaths per conflict in, 45, 46–47tab, 54nn25–29; democracy promotion, 238–242; geopolitical fragmentation and

institutions of, 816–817; human rights approach in, 260–264, 590; P5 cooperation in, 5, 551; proliferation management in, 328–339; resolutions per conflict in, 45, 46–47*tab*, 54*nn*25–29; sanctions, 7–8; successes, 5–8; use of force selectivity during, 349–351; working methods of, 176–179

Powell, Colin, 283–284, 598, 621, 843

Power, Samantha, 703

PRC (People's Republic of China). *See* China

Presidential statements, 28, 147, 190*n*12, 205, 243, 254n52, 267, 283, 295*n*27, 304, 327, 470, 493, 497, 503, 534–543, 600, 645–646, 668, 727, 751, 765, 779

PRIO. *See* Peace Research Institute Oslo

Procedure: P5 power over, 146–149, 198; provisional rules of, 176, 198, 269. *See also* Working methods

Prodi, Romano, 484, 605

Proliferation management: 1540 Committee for, 339–341, 864; China involvement in, 93–95, 325; Cold War era mistakes in, 326–328; factors against, 329, 341–342; of India, 326; international law enforcement by, 782; of Iran, 69, 93–95, 115, 336–338, 437*n*15, 498, 719, 743, 745, 803, 808, 818, 863; of Iraq, 13, 327–331, 333, 451, 555–558, 559; of Israel, 327; lawmaking power in, 776–777; of Libya, 331–332, 334; of nonstate actors, 339–341, 864; of North Korea, 93–94, 116, 145, 332–336, 803, 863; NPT for, 115, 325, 328, 343*n*8; Nuclear Non-Proliferation Treaty, 115, 325, 328, 343*n*8; Nuclear Security Summit for, 340, 802–803, 864; Organization for the Prohibition of Chemical Weapons, 112; P5 contention on, 13, 93–94, 115–116, 330–331; P5 exception to, 323–324, 325, 345*n*6; of Pakistan, 115, 332, 340, 864; peaceful explosions and, 326, 343*n*8; post-Cold War era of, 328–339; pre-Cold War era of, 324–326; problem overview, 323–324, 341–342; resolutions on, 39*fig*, 44, 323; Russia involvement in, 112, 115–116, 324–325, 338–339, 726–727, 745; sanctions for, 323, 326–327, 330–331, 335–338, 414, 415, 416–418*tab*, 419; Security Council outside of, 802; Security Council role in, 862–864; of South Africa, 326–327; of Syria, 70, 112, 337–339, 726–727, 743–745; threat defined for, 328; US organizations for, 340; WMD definition for, 342*n*1

Proliferation Security Initiative, 340

Pronk, Jan, 761

Protests: in Côte d'Ivoire, 685; in Lebanon, 541; in Libya, 701; in Syria, 717–718

Provisional Rules of Procedure, 176, 198, 269

P3. *See* Permanent three members

Public opinion: peacekeeping leverage by, 469; on sanctions, 431; on use of force, 71

Pugh, Michael, 751

Puntland, 598, 607, 609–610

Putin, Vladimir, 108, 109, 743, 829

Qaddafi, Muammar: capture and execution of, 699, 842; Darfur crisis eruption and, 619; intentions of, 331, 359, 706; isolation of, 708; protests against, 701; resolution rejection by, 408, 702; warrant for, 519

Qaddafi, Saif al-Islam, 519

Al-Qaeda, 114, 222, 384; *Cole*, USS, attack by, 648; defeat of, 108; al-Nusra and, 743; Operation Enduring Freedom against, 108, 652; power unification against, 799; sanctions on, 161, 271, 291, 417*tab*, 420*tab*, 655, 860; US embassy bombing by, 618

Qatar, 541, 609, 624, 625, 743

Quartet (on Middle East peace process), 534, 535–536, 538

R2P. *See* Responsibility to Protect

Rabbani, Burhanuddin, 643

Rally for Congolese Democracy (RCD), 662–663, 670, 672, 677*n*5, 678*n*23

Razali Ismail, Tan Sri, 162, 179–180, 191*n*26

RCD. *See* Rally for Congolese Democracy

Rechtsstaat (rule of law), 316

Red Cross. *See* International Committee for the Red Cross

Reform: ACT Group for, 188, 199; adaptation or, 197–200; African Group on, 170, 181, 192*n*32; background, 175–176, 195, 197–200; China on, 163, 181, 182, 813*n*42, 867; conclusion on, 209–210, 866–868; by dues payment, 167; for E10, 7-7-7 formula for, 166, 168, 214*n*25; for E10, expertise and, 203–206; for E10, power dynamics and, 149–152, 153; economic consideration for, 159, 160, 164–165, 166–167; evolution of, 197–200; France on, 133–135, 136, 182; geopolitical change and, 169, 806–809; national interest exploitation and, 161–162; negotiation framework, 183, 184–186; Note 507, 150–151, 182, 183–184, 192–193*nn*42–44, 192*n*39; obstacles to, 162–165, 867–868; Open-Ended Working Group for, 179, 180, 182, 183; P5 and emerging powers convergence for, 165; population consideration for, 160, 166, 170; by privilege and responsibility balance, 167–168; proposal by Annan, 809, 813*n*42; proposal by G4, 134, 162–

163, 170, 180–181, 192*nn*28–32, 867; proposal by Jones, 808–809; proposal by L69, 183; proposal by Luck, 197, 206–209, 214*n*25; proposal by Razali, 162, 179–180, 191*n*26; proposal by S5, 78, 134, 181–188, 189, 192*n*33–194*n*62, 868; proposal of 7-7-7 formula, 166–171, 214*n*25; questions, 195; reasons for, 157–162, 196, 209–210; Russia on, 117–118, 181, 182; Security Council preservation points in, 196, 200–203, 212*n*16; troop contributors on, 767–768; UK on, 133–135, 136, 182; Unanimity Principle for, 201–203; US on, 79–80, 163, 182, 807–809, 813*n*42, 867; win-win solution to, 166–171

Refugees: Bosnian, 576, 579, 592*nn*17–18; Iraqi, 554, 562; largest number of, 45; Rwandan, 664–665, 678*n*17, 678*n*21, 679*n*33; Somali, 597, 605; Syrian, 720, 746; use of force for, 356–357; Western Sahara, 495

Regional organizations: Annan on, 484; anti-communist, 479–481; Article 33 on, 476; Article 51 on, 477; Article 52 on, 476, 478–487; Article 53 on, 476, 479–481; Article 103 on, 477, 479; Boutros-Ghali on, 482, 487; Cold War era, 478–481; conclusion about, 486–487; cross-purposes of, 486; CTC relations with, 484; emerging powers and, 498; growth and value of, 818–819, 851–852; League of Nations on, 488*n*6; piracy fought by, 311–313, 804; power contradictions on, 475–478; power decline of, 481–487; power preeminence of, 478–481, 752–754, 762–763; resolution precedents with, 482–483, 484–485; resource limitations for, 484; sanctions enforced by, 424–425, 482; specialized agencies and, 487*n*1; subsidiary status of, 477; temporary primary status of, 477; use of force cover by, 852

Regional scope: of conflicts, 796–797, 847*fig*; E10 expertise on, 204; of NATO, 43, 399–400; representation considerations by, 198, 211*n*6; resolution distribution by, 40, 41*fig*, 42*fig*, 43; SRSG coordination with, 460; subregional offices and, 461

Reporting: General Assembly annual, 199; human rights, 261, 266, 268, 854; proliferation, 287; by Secretary-General, 458, 465; by SRSG, 465–467

Republic of China (ROC). *See* Taiwan

Resolutions: accelerated growth of, 7, 24*n*16, 28–29; Chapter VI, 4–5, 781; Chapter VII vetoes on, 29*tab*, 30*fig*, 34*fig*; on children and armed conflict, 267, 270, 436*n*4, 501,

502; China abstention on, 87, 90; civilian protection, 376, 388, 501, 705; Cold War and post-Cold War comparison of, 29, 29*tab*, 31, 33; compliance, 53*n*9; conclusion on, 51–52; conflict deaths and, 45, 46–47*tab*, 54*nn*25–29; conflict decline and, 49, 50*fig*, 51; consistency issues on, 45, 46–47*tab*, 48–49; democracy language in, 237, 240–241, 242, 251*n*6; E10 abstention on, 834; Ebola, 783, 866; foreign fighters, 727, 735*tab*, 831, 862; HIV/AIDS, 679*n*30, 783, 865–866; on institutional matters, 44; intrastate, 38, 39*fig*, 838, 872*n*10; lawmaking power of, 774–777; length and complexity of, 751, 766, 781; leverage factors on, 469–470; on membership expansion, 162–163; nonbinding, 775–776; non-UN contributions to, 43, 54*n*22, 54*n*23; procedural evolution of, 146–148; progress assessment lack on, 212*n*12; on proliferation, 39*fig*, 44, 323; regional collaboration precedents on, 482–483, 484–485; regional distribution of, 40, 41*fig*, 42*fig*, 43, 54*n*22; by sanction type, 416–418*tab*; on sexual exploitation, 267, 270, 436*n*4; Six-Day War, 531–532; trend overview of, 28–29; trends, by issue areas, 38, 39*fig*; trends, by issue themes, 44–45, 149–150, 177–178; Uniting for Peace, 354, 644, 657*n*2, 723, 743; on women, 44, 242, 501, 502. *See also* Vetoes

Resources: Africa economy and, 797; AMISOM, 604, 608, 613*n*47; AU limits in, 851–852; civilian protection, 675; emerging powers, 797, 810; global financial crisis and, 756, 846, 871; Iraq War limits to, 564; mandate, 459, 461–464, 467–468; organized crime revenue and, 301, 302; peacekeeping limits on, 363–364, 385–386, 387, 402, 462–463, 467–468, 756, 765–767, 846; political mission limits on, 463–464, 846; regional organization limits on, 484; sanctions limits on, 429, 432–433

Responsibility to Protect (R2P): abuse of, 2, 11, 69, 225–227, 230, 787; Ban approach to, 224; China stance on, 95–98, 800–801; conflict management motivated by, 799–801, 840–843; consistency issues on, 271–273, 274, 787, 840–841, 870; definition of, 782; emerging powers stance on, 799–801; formation of, 98, 192*n*27, 224, 453, 705, 782; humanitarian rhetoric on, 223–226, 404, 453, 590; ICISS report on, 2, 11; Libya as test of, 222, 226–227, 700, 705, 711, 713, 800, 841–842; P5 contention on, 840–843; power dynamics,

799–801; Russia stance on, 111, 800–801; sovereignty limits and, 218–219, 224–226; Syria contention on, 800–801, 842–843; voluntary veto restraint and, 213n18. *See also* Humanitarian intervention
Responsibility While Protecting (RWP), 226, 700, 711–712, 713
Rhodesia, Southern, 53n8, 238, 260
Rice, Condoleezza, 229
Rice, Susan, 68, 629, 703
Richardson, Bill, 65
Right to self-defense, 395; authorization for, 778; categories, 219; 9/11 and, 778, 860; regional organization primacy in, 477; threat definition and, 143–144, 220, 239
Rights, human. *See* Human rights
Rising powers. *See* Emerging powers
Roberts, Adam, 218, 589
Robinson, Mary, 263, 675
Robust peacekeeping: assessment by capacity, 387; assessment by crisis examples, 378–384; trends toward and opposition to, 848–850
ROC (Republic of China). *See* Taiwan
Rød-Larsen, Terje, 534
Rome Statute, 190n1, 267, 308, 381, 515–517, 697n33, 855
Roosevelt, Franklin D., 201, 212n14, 299, *300*
Rothchild, Donald, 467–468
Rouhani, Hassan, 337, 863
Rousseff, Dilma, 711
Rowswell, Ben, 562
Ruggie, John, 434
Rule of law (*rechtsstaat*), 316
Rules of conduct, 302–303
Rules of engagement, 357–358, 361–362, 386
Russia: ambassadorship style of, 110; in Arab-Israeli conflict Quartet, 534, 535–536, 538; Bosnia stance of, 580–582, 585; in BRIC, 794, 800, 807–808; in BRICS, 498, 499, 710, 741–742, 830, 842, 858; Chechnya conflict and, 46tab, 114; China convergence with, 38, 88–89tab, 97–98, 116–117, 829–830; civilian protection stance of, 798; Côte d'Ivoire stance of, 383, 690; counterterrorism response of, 114, 283; drug trafficking in, 114; economy of, 795; EU relations with, 108–109; Eurasian Union and, 119; G4 reform opposition by, 181; Georgia conflict and, 108, 110, 493, 494–495; humanitarian intervention stance of, 111, 264, 273; ICTY criticism by, 513; India relations with, 115, 116; international law advocacy of, 110–112; Iraq War stance of, 108, 823; Israel relations with, 534, 538; Kosovo conflict stance of, 97, 361, 703, 800, 823; under

Medvedev, 108–109, 244; membership preferences of, 118; membership reform interests of, 117–118, 181, 182; national interest exploitation by, 108, 110; NATO relations with, 105, 107–108, 109, 402, 403; North Korea relations with, 116, 273, 863; Obama reconciliation with, 68, 108–109; organized crime in, 114–115; peacekeeping involvement in, 112–113, 129tab; penholdership of, 833; power status concern of, 105, 106, 581, 796, 829–830; predictions for, 118–119; proliferation management by, 112, 115–116, 324–325, 338–339, 726–727, 745; under Putin, 108, 109, 743, 829; R2P stance of, 111, 800–801; S5 reform opposition by, 182; sanctions stance of, 858; Soviet mindset legacy of, 106; Sudan relations with, 622, 628–629; Syria proliferation agreement with, 338–339, 726–727, 745; Syria stance of, 69–70, 97–98, 111–112, 718–725, 729–732, 741–746, 800–801, 823–824; Ukraine conflict and, 109, 112, 746, 795–796; US distrust by, 105, 107–108, 109, 718–719, 726–727, 743; US reconciliation with, 68, 108–109; use of force stance of, 107–108, 110–112, 383; vetoes by, 35, 36fig, 37–38, 116–117, 118, 129tab, 830, 831fig; Western integration of, 106–109; under Yeltsin, 107, 581. *See also* Permanent five members
Ruto, William, 520, 856
Rwanda: Boutros-Ghali options for, 446; Carlsson report on, 267; death count in, 47tab; DRC occupation by, 378, 379, 381, 670–671, 672; FDLR for, 672, 678n16; genocide triggers, 599, 663–664; as human rights catastrophe, 262, 263; human rights investigation commission on, 269; Hutu Revolution and, 524n12; Operation Turquoise in, 663–665; P5 contention on, 140; refugees, 664–665, 678n17, 678n21, 679n33; repercussions of, 9; resolution count in, 47tab; sanctions on, 417tab, 420tab; UNAMIR in, 11, 63–64, 140, 262, 266, 446, 483, 510, 664, 677nn7–9; withdrawal from, 8, 63–64, 664. *See also* International Criminal Tribunal for Rwanda
RWP. *See* Responsibility While Protecting

S5. *See* Small five members reform proposal
Saakashvili, Mikheil, 110
SADC. *See* Southern African Development Community
Sahnoun, Mohamed, 598, 667
Saleh, Ali Abdullah, 485

Salim, Salim Ahmad, 624

SAMs. *See* Sanctions assistance missions

San Francisco conference, 3, 139, 141–143, 201, 477, 784

Sanctions: on Afghanistan, 283, 290, 291, 647, 655, 656; analysis improvement on, 434; on Angola, 417*tab*, 420*tab*, 424, 427, 857; Annan reform of, 438*n*17; apartheid, 238; by AU, 424–425; authorization of, 780; Ban reform of, 438*n*17; black markets from, 8, 556; Boutros-Ghali reform of, 437*n*17; on Central African Republic, 418*tab*, 420*tab*; China stance on, 87, 428, 437*nn*15–16, 858; Cold War era, 4; committees, 421–423, 428, 835; compliance, 53*n*9, 766; corporation role in, 426, 433–434; cost of, 419, 437*n*10, 438*n*22; on Côte d'Ivoire, 270, 383, 417*tab*, 420*tab*, 421, 685–686; counterterrorism by Resolution 1267, 161, 271, 303, 426, 430–431, 780, 786, 860; criminal targeting, 300–301, 306–307, 309–310; on Cuba, 480; for democracy promotion, 239–240; diamond, 416–418*tab*, 857; on DRC, 417*tab*, 420*tab*, 673; E10 chairmanship on, 421–422, 835; effectiveness of, challenges, 427–431, 435, 435*tab*, 766, 858–859; effectiveness of, strengthening, 431–434, 435*tab*, 857; enforcement of, 424–425, 429–430, 433, 438*n*27, 439*n*28, 482; on Eritrea, 416*tab*, 417*tab*, 420*tab*, 606; on Ethiopia, 417*tab*, 420*tab*; evolution timeline of, 419, 420*tab*, 421; expansion of, 413–414, 425–426, 857; financial, 416–418*tab*, 426–427, 782; France involvement in, 130; frequency of, 856; on Guinea-Bissau, 418*tab*, 420*tab*; on Haiti, 416*tab*, 420*tab*, 447; for human rights, 220, 270–271, 426; implementation groups, 421–423, 437*n*11; implementation improvements, 432–433, 438*nn*25–26; implementation weakness, 428–430; innovations and trends, 423–427; international law and, 414, 423, 429, 430–431, 782; on Iran, 93–95, 336–337, 338, 418*tab*, 420*tab*, 424, 425, 863; on Iraq, 6, 14, 161–162, 416*tab*, 420*tab*, 447, 555–558; on Kuwait, 553; on Lebanon, 418*tab*, 419, 420*tab*, 513; on Liberia, 161, 416*tab*, 420*tab*; on Libya, 270, 281–282, 291, 331–332, 416*tab*, 420*tab*, 426–427; mistakes, 271, 288, 403–431, 785–786; monitoring of, 429–430, 433, 438*n*27, 439*n*28; on Myanmar, 88*tab*, 96, 858; for national interest, 161–162; need for, 413; NGO role in, 426, 433–434; on nonstate actors, 427; on North Korea, 93–94, 418*tab*, 420*tab*, 424, 425, 863; objectives,

414–415, 419, 436*nn*4–5, 857; oil, 14, 161–162, 416–418*tab*, 447, 556, 621; organizations, 421–423; overview of, 413–414, 856–859; panel of experts, 288, 290, 307–309, 335, 422–424, 433, 437*n*10, 438*n*22, 447, 600, 622, 673–674, 680n39, 686, 704, 766, 857–858; P5 contention on, 425, 428, 437*nn*15–16; P5 role in, 421, 424; post–Cold War era, 7–8; for proliferation management, 414, 415, 416–418*tab*, 419; public misunderstanding of, 431; on al-Qaeda, 161, 271, 291, 417*tab*, 420*tab*, 655, 860; regional role in, 424–425, 482; resource limitations for, 429, 432–433; Russia stance on, 858; on Rwanda, 417*tab*, 420*tab*; Secretariat role in, 422, 424, 429, 447; Secretary-General management of, 447; on Sierra Leone, 417*tab*, 420*tab*; on Somalia, 270, 306–307, 416*tab*, 420*tab*, 606–607; on South Africa, 238; on South Sudan, 418*tab*, 420*tab*; on Southern Rhodesia, 238; on Sudan, 282, 417*tab*, 420*tab*, 617, 621; on Syria, 418*tab*, 420*tab*, 720–721; on Taliban, 161, 283, 291, 417*tab*, 419, 420*tab*, 647, 655, 656, 860; targeting methods, 415, 426–427, 435*tab*, 857; trafficking, 306–307; travel, 416–418*tab*; TSC research on, 53*n*9, 424, 435; types of, 414–415, 416–418*tab*, 435*tab*, 436*n*5, 857; UK involvement in, 130; violations, 430; working methods for, 422, 428; on Yemen, 418*tab*, 420*tab*; on Yugoslavia, 416*tab*, 420*tab*, 482, 572; on Zimbabwe, 88*tab*, 96, 858

Sanctions assistance missions (SAMs), 433, 439*n*28

Sanctions Implementation Task Force (SITF), 438*n*26

Santiago Declaration, 240

Sarajevo siege, 358–359, 584–586

Sarkozy, Nicolas, 132, 692, 710, 760

Saudi Arabia: China relations with, 437*n*15; membership declined by, 80, 737; Syria stance of, 737, 743; UNCCT contribution by, 292

SCAD. *See* Security Council Affairs Division

Scowcroft, Brent, 60

SCSL. *See* Special Court for Sierra Leone

Searle, John, 772

Secretariat: briefing of, 465–466; horizon-scanning role of, 178, 268, 844; mandate resources role of, 464; permanent status of, 835–836; power dynamics, 760–762, 835; sanctions role of, 422, 424, 429, 447; thematic expansion role of, 150; transparency by, 199

Secretary-General: accountability political

checks on, 786; appointment and candidacy of, 445; Article 99 power of, 178, 443–444, 446, 448–452, 844; horizon-scanning by, 178; lineage, 444; military functions of, 446–447; NATO coordination with, 407; neutrality of, 444; norm entrepreneurship of, 452–453; P5 relations with, 445, 836; personalities of, 444, 454; political mission functions of, 447, 448–452; power dynamics with, 178, 443–444, 446, 448–452; reporting by, 458, 465; role overview of, 444–446; sanctions management by, 447; success challenges of, 445–446; tasks of, 446–448; thematic expansion by, 149–150. *See also* Special Representative of the Secretary-General

Security Council Affairs Division (SCAD), 199, 212*n*17, 422, 835

Security Council relations: Arab League and, 43, 478, 852; AU and, 483–485, 603–604, 605–606, 629, 763, 851–852; DPKO cohesion in, 760–761; DPKO contention in, 761–762; ECOWAS and, 43, 481, 482, 483, 484; EU and, 763; France engagement level and, 127–128, 129*tab*, 130–131, 832; France strategic importance of, 122–127, 125–126*tab*, 135–136; GCC and, 485; General Assembly and, 144–145, 531; ICC and, 517–523; ICTR and, 510–511, 512; ICTY and, 510–512; NATO cohesion in, 403–404, 406, 408–409; NATO contention in, 401–402; OHCHR and, 853; P5 engagement comparisons and, 127–128, 129*tab*, 130–131; Soviet Union boycott, 59, 101*n*11; UK engagement level and, 127–128, 129*tab*, 130–131, 832; UK strategic importance of, 122–127, 125–126*tab*, 135–136; US multilateralism and, 60–61, 65–69, 802–803, 822, 861–862; US under Bush, George H. W., 60–61, 75–76; US under Bush, George W., 65–67, 76, 801–802; US under Clinton, Bill, 61–65; US under Obama, 67–71, 80, 802–803, 828–829; US unilateralism and, 57–60, 62–65, 69–73, 78–79, 366–367, 560, 821–823, 827–828

Security Council Report, 199, 498, 837, 854

Security threats. *See* Threats to peace and security

Selective security: conflict complexity and, 365–366, 839–840; consistency issues on, 349–351; forms of, 365; legitimacy and, 368–369; P5 contention on, 367–368; US role in, 366–367; use of force and, 349–351, 365–369; vetoes and, 367–368

Self-defense. *See* Right to self-defense

Al-Senussi, Abdullah, 519

Seoul Plan of Action, 242

Serbia. *See* Kosovo

7-7-7 formula: advantages of, 169–170; challenges of, 166–169, 170–171; design of, 166, 214*n*25

Sexual exploitation, 267, 270, 436*n*4

Al-Shabaab, 601–603, 605, 607, 609

Shermake, Abdirashid Ali, 596

Sierra Leone: China stance on, 90; death and resolution count in, 46*tab*; ECOMOG in, 752, 753; hostages, 65; Jordan in, 753; Nigeria in, 752, 753; sanctions on, 417*tab*, 420*tab*; Special Court for, 508; UNAMSIL in, 229, 752–753, 754; withdrawal from, 753

Sinai conflicts, 212*n*15, 374, 531–533

Singapore. *See* Small five group

Siniora, Fouad, 541

SIPRI. *See* Stockholm International Peace Research Institute

SITF. *See* Sanctions Implementation Task Force

Six Plus Two group, 647, 658*n*22

Six-Day War, 531–532

Slaughter, Anne-Marie, 10

Slavonia, Eastern, 587

Slovenia: independence of, 571–574; membership of, 576

Small five group (S5) reform proposal, 78, 134, 192*n*33–194*n*62, 868; ACT Group replacement of, 188, 199; cancellation of, 187–188, 194*n*60; development of first, 181–182, 192*n*34; development of second, 184–186, 193*nn*46–53; early support and opposition for, 182, 186, 192*n*38; implementation lag, 183–184; Legal Counsel blocking of, 187, 194*nn*58–59; overview of, 189; voting on, 186–187, 193*nn*54–56, 194*nn*57–59

Smith, Mike, 290

Smith, Rupert, 575, 584, 585–586

Somalia: Al-Shabaab in, 601–603, 605, 607, 609; AMISOM for, 603–606, 608–609, 613*n*47; assessment mission to, 466–467; Barre rule of, 597, 601–602; Black Hawk Down in, 9, 63, 595, 599; Boutros-Ghali comments on, 597, 610*n*4; death count in, 46*tab*, 605; democracy promotion in, 239; electoral assistance in, 607–608; Ethiopia relations with, 597, 601, 603, 604, 608; famine relief, 598; future of, 609–610; humanitarian justification for, 222; IGAD mediation for, 600, 601, 603; independence of, 596; involvement overview, 595–596; Kampala Accord for, 607–608; Mogadishu, 9, 63, 387, 597, 599, 600, 602–603, 605; Mohamud presidency of, 608, 609; new government strategies, 608–609, 613*n*45; Pakistan support for, 598, 599; peacemaking for, 601, 607–608; piracy, 310–316, 804, 865; refugees from, 597, 605; Resolution 751 on, 606; Resolution 794 on, 222; resolution count in, 46*tab*; sanctions on, 270, 306–307, 416*tab*, 420*tab*, 606–607; Soviet relations with, 597; SRSGs for, 599, 608, 611*n*14; trafficking in, 306–307; transitional authority in, 601; UNITAF in, 8, 595, 598; UNOSOM I in, 8, 222, 598; UNOSOM II in, 8–9, 63, 483, 598–600; UNPOS in, 600; UNSOM in, 608–609; withdrawal from, 599–600

Somaliland, 598, 607, 609–610

Soro, Guillaume, 682, 684, 688

South Africa: apartheid in, 238, 326–327; in BRICS, 498, 499, 710, 741–742, 830, 842, 858; Côte d'Ivoire stance of, 690; in IBSA, 737–738; Libya stance of, 709–710; Mbeki of, 626, 627, 629, 635, 686; Nigeria compared to, 167; proliferation management of, 326–327; sanctions on, 238; Syria stance of, 719, 720–721, 737–738

South America: resolutions focusing on, 40, 41*fig*, 42*fig*, 43

South Korea: China relations with, 805; in Korean War, 4, 37, 350, 360, 396, 449, 824; North Korea recent attacks on, 335, 805; Seoul Plan of Action, 242

South Ossetia. *See* Georgia conflict

South Sudan: Abyei conflict for, 623–624, 627–630, 628, 630; sanctions on, 418*tab*, 420*tab*; UNMISS in, 242, 243, 623–624, 628

Southern African Development Community (SADC), 381, 485, 667, 669

Southern Rhodesia, 53*n*8, 238, 260

Sovereignty: China foreign policy principles of, 84; conflict decline and, 352; Côte d'Ivoire legalist split and, 689–690; criminal law enforcement obstacle of, 301–302, 305; defenders of, 224–225; fundamental rule of, 141–142; geopolitical fragmentation origins and, 816; ICISS on, 11, 213*n*18, 221, 222–223, 224, 711; international law on, 10–11, 141–143, 218–220; overview, 10–12; R2P and, 218–219, 224–226; rhetoric, 223, 224, 590; threat threshold and, 143–144, 220

Soviet Union: Afghanistan relations with, 644–645; China relations with, 100*n*4; Cold War era counterterrorism response of, 279; disarmament abstention by, 324–325; under Gorbachev, 5, 106, 552, 644; Iran-Iraq War and rise of, 552; under Khrushchev, 444; Korean War and, 396; mindset legacy, 106; NATO establishment

and, 395; OAS relations with, 479–481; *perestroika* reformation of, 5; Secretary-General power opposition of, 449–450; Security Council boycott by, 59, 101*n*11; Somalia relations with, 597; under Stalin, 212*n*16, 325; unilateralism, 60; vetoes by, 35, 36*fig*, 37–38, 53*n*12, 59; Warsaw Treaty Organization of, 477. *See also* Permanent five members

Special Committee on Peacekeeping Operations, 759

Special Court for Sierra Leone (SCSL), 508

Special Representative of the Secretary-General (SRSG): Afghanistan, 647, 648–649, 650–651, 655; ambassadors to, 467; assessment visits with, 466–467; Bosnia air strike authorization by, 585–586; civilian protection behavior of, 761–762; Côte d'Ivoire, 688, 689, 762; electoral certification by, 244; interviews with, 472; Libya, 465–466; mandate appropriateness and, 464–467; mandate resources and, 461–464; peacekeeping leverage of, 468–472, 761–762; peacekeeping relationships with, 459–461; peacekeeping success factors of, 468; personality and skills of, 461; reporting by, 465–467; selection of, 457–458; Somalia, 599, 608, 611*n*14; Syria, 725, 729, 743; transitional authority role of, 461; UNAMI bombing of, 561, 562

Special Tribunal for Lebanon (STL), 508, 513–515, 541–542

Specialized agencies, 487*n*1

Srebrenica genocide, 8, 9, 262–263, 358, 784–785

Sri Lanka, 705, 841; death and resolution count in, 46*tab*; informal interactive dialogue for, 179; meeting power dynamic on, 152

SRSG. *See* Special Representative of the Secretary-General

Stalin, Joseph, 212*n*16, 325

Stedman, Stephen, 467–468

STL. *See* Special Tribunal for Lebanon

Stockholm International Peace Research Institute (SIPRI), 92

Stockholm process, 437*n*11

Stoudmann, Gérard, 687

Sudan: Abyei conflict in, 623–624, 627–630, 628, 630; AMIS for, 621, 623, 755; AU in, 97, 484, 485, 621, 623, 626, 755; bin Laden in, 282, 617, 618; Canada relations with, 619; Chad tension with, 625; China relations with, 96–97, 621, 623, 624, 632, 641*n*68; death and resolution count in, 45, 46*tab*, 54*n*27; E10 contention on, 633; Egypt relations with, 617, 637*n*10;

electoral assistance in, 243, 248; Ethiopia relations with, 617, 637*n*10; IDPs in, 45; IGAD in, 619–620, 635; independence of, 616; Khartoum conflict development in, 616–619; Khartoum peacemaking implementation in, 622–627, 634; Khartoum peacemaking in, 619–622, 633, 639*n*37, 642*n*79; Kordofan conflict, 627–628; new war aversion in, 627–631; 9/11 attacks and, 617, 618; OAU stance on, 617; oil in, 619, 621, 625; Operation Lifeline, 616; overview on, 615–616; P5 contention on, 617, 622–624, 631–632, 755–756; Resolution 2046 on, 629; Russia relations with, 622, 628–629; sanctions on, 270, 282, 417*tab*, 420*tab*, 617, 621; transitional authority in, 627–628; UNISFA in, 623–624, 628, 630; UNMIS in, 622, 623–624, 627–628; US relations with, 618, 620, 621, 631–632, 641*n*71, 755. *See also* Darfur crisis; South Sudan
Suez crisis, 212*n*15, 374, 531–533
Sweden: SIPRI of, 92; Stockholm process sponsored by, 437*n*11
Switzerland: Geneva 1973 peace conference in, 533; Geneva Accords in, 645; Geneva II communiqué in, 500, 720, 724–725, 736*tab*, 742, 745–746; Geneva Initiative in, 648; Interlaken process of, 437*n*11, 857. *See also* Small five members
Swords Into Plowshares (Claude), 277, 293
Syria: accountability in, 728–731; Annan mediation for, 70, 500, 720, 723–725, 742; Arab League proposal for, 721, 722–723, 734*tab*, 742; Australia proposal on, 728, 730, 736, 737; Brahimi as SRSG for, 725, 729, 743; Brazil stance on, 719, 720–721, 737–738; BRICS and, 741–742; chemical weapons use by, 70, 112, 338–339, 726–728, 743–745; China stance on, 97–98, 720–722, 724, 730, 732, 742, 800–801; conclusion on, 738–739; cross-border aid access to, 728–731, 735*tab*; death count in, 46*tab*, 720, 726, 746; E10 approach to, 736–738; failure to help, 741–746; France stance on, 736; GCC and, 718–719; General Assembly circumvention on, 722–723; Geneva II communiqué on, 500, 720, 724–725, 736*tab*, 742, 745–746; Germany stance on, 720, 737; Ghouta attack in, 726, 743; Group of Friends on, 500, 724, 742; ICC referral for, 526*n*42, 729–730; India stance of, 719, 720–721, 737–738; Iran and, 733; Iran proliferation management and, 719, 743, 745; ISIS in, 718, 727–728, 736, 739; Israel relations with, 88*tab*, 343*n*14, 532, 732–733; Jordan proposal on, 728, 730, 736, 737; Lebanon relations with, 513–514, 540–542, 737; Libya comparison to, 741, 742, 800, 823–824, 842–843; Luxembourg proposal on, 728, 730, 736, 737; al-Nusra Front in, 727, 743; oil pipeline through, 742; overview of, 717–720; P3 cohesion on, 720, 722, 723, 731; P5 contention on, 69–70, 88–89*tab*, 718–720, 724–725, 731–733, 734–735*tab*, 736; Palestine relations with, 478–479; Portugal stance on, 720, 737; proliferation management of, 70, 112, 337–339, 726–727, 743–745; protests in, 717–718; Qatar stance on, 743; R2P contention in, 800–801, 842–843; refugees and IDPs from, 720, 746; regional support for, 43; Resolution 67/262 on, 740*n*9; Resolution 2042 on, 723, 734*tab*; Resolution 2043 on, 734*tab*; Resolution 2059 on, 724, 734*tab*; Resolution 2118 on, 338, 341, 726, 734*tab*; Resolution 2139 on, 728–730, 734*tab*; Resolution 2165 on, 730, 735*tab*; Resolution 2170 on, 727, 735*tab*, 862; Resolution 2178 on, 727, 735*tab*; Resolution 2191 on, 735*tab*; Resolution 2199 on, 727–728, 735*tab*; Resolution 2209 on, 735*tab*; resolution count in, 46*tab*, 734–735*tab*; Russia stance on, 69–70, 97–98, 111–112, 718–725, 729–732, 741–746, 800–801, 823–824; sanctions on, 418*tab*, 420*tab*, 720–721; Saudi Arabia stance on, 737, 743; South Africa stance on, 719, 720–721, 737–738; terrorist tactics in, 718, 726–728; transitional authority for, 500, 742, 743; UK approach to, 70, 720, 726, 736, 744; UNDOF hostage crisis in, 532; Uniting for Peace resolution for, 723, 743; UNSMIS in, 723–725; US approach to, 69–70, 718–719, 725, 726–727, 732–733, 736, 743–746, 843; use of force on, 69–70, 227; vetoes, 1st, 720–721, 734*tab*; vetoes, 2nd, 723–725, 734*tab*; vetoes, 3rd, 721–722, 734*tab*; vetoes, 4th, 730, 735*tab*

Taiwan, 35, 53*n*15, 86; China relations with, 88*tab*, 90, 91, 102*n*51
Taliban: drug trafficking by, 303–304; early attacks by, 646; early negotiations with, 646–650; fall of, 108, 114, 650–652; formation of, 645; resurgence of, 653; sanctions on, 161, 283, 291, 417*tab*, 419, 420*tab*, 647, 655, 656, 860. *See also* Islamic Emirate
Targeted Sanctions Consortium (TSC), 53*n*9, 424, 435
Taylor, Charles, 90
Tehran Declaration, 337–338, 863

Tehran hostage crisis, 448–449, 552
Terrorism. *See* Bombing; Counterterrorism; Taliban
Terrorist Financing Convention, 284, 285
Tévoédjrè, Albert, 683
Thant, U, 449–450
Thematic issues: E10 contribution to, 149–150, 178, 835; expansion, 44–45, 149–150; General Assembly action on, 178; Groups of Friends of, 500–503; NGO contribution to, 854–855; verbatim records on, 874nn29–30; working methods on, 177–178
Thomson, John, 5
Threats to peace and security: categories, 219, 415; defining, 143–144, 220, 239, 779; disease as, 362, 679n30, 783, 865–866; drug trafficking as, 304, 305, 864–865; enormity of, 827; environmental, 875n55; non-democracy as, 239; proliferation as, 328
Tickell, Crispin, 875n55
Timor-Leste. *See* East Timor
Tito, Josip Broz, 570
To End a War (Holbrooke), 593n46
Trafficking: diamond, 306; drug, 114, 301, 303–304, 305, 308, 310, 649, 864–865; executive policing of, 309–310; fact-finding on, 307–309; human rights and, 307; law enforcement obstacles for, 301–303, 305; military intervention for, 309–310; mineral, 306–307; piracy compared to, 310–311; private law enforcement for, 305–307; problem of, 114, 303–304, 864–865; US stance on, 303–304, 864–865; wildlife, 307, 309
Transitional authority: in Afghanistan, 651–652, 653–655; in Cambodia, 6–7, 90, 91, 239, 266; in Côte d'Ivoire, 683; in Croatia, 587; in East Timor, 241, 243, 752–753; in Iraq, 561–563; in Kosovo, 752; in Libya, 499–500, 701, 702; power to create, 776; in Somalia, 601, 607–608; SRSG role in, 461; in Sudan, 627–628; in Syria, 500, 742, 743; UNTAG, 91
Transparency, 150–151, 176, 182, 188, 199, 837. *See also* Accountability
Travel sanctions, 416–418tab
Treaty violation, 778
Tribal identity, 817, 819
Tribunal for Lebanon, 508, 513–515. *See also* International Criminal Tribunal for Rwanda; International Criminal Tribunal for the Former Yugoslavia
Trinidad and Tobago, 308
Troop contributors, 759–760, 767–768, 847fig, 873n22
Trujillo, Rafael, 479

TSC. *See* Targeted Sanctions Consortium
Tudjman, Franjo, 570, 573
Tunisia blockade, 449
Al-Turabi, Hassan, 617, 618, 619
Turkey: in Gaza wars, 537; Iran proliferation negotiations with, 337–338; Kurdistan conflict with, 46tab; Kuwait invasion and, 358; membership consideration for, 808; in MINT, 167, 498

UCDP. *See* Uppsala Conflict Data Program
Uganda: AMISOM support from, 604, 605; death and resolution count in, 46tab; DRC occupation by, 378, 670–671, 672; PFLP hijacking to, 280
UIC. *See* Union of Islamic Courts
UK. *See* United Kingdom
Ukraine conflict, 73, 109, 112, 746, 795–796
UN. *See* United Nations
UN Assistance Mission in Afghanistan (UNAMA), 563, 652–655
UN Assistance Mission in Iraq (UNAMI), 561, 562–563
UN Assistance Mission in Rwanda (UNAMIR), 11, 63–64, 140, 262, 266, 446, 483, 510, 664, 677nn7–9
UN Assistance Mission in Sierra Leone (UNAMSIL), 229, 752–753, 754
UN Assistance Mission in Somalia (UNSOM), 608–609
UN Atomic Energy Commission (UNAEC), 324, 325, 342n5
UN Centre on Counterterrorism (UNCCT), 291–292
UN Charter. *See* Charter
UN Commission for Conventional Armaments (UNCCA), 324, 325, 342n5
UN Commission on Global Governance, 220, 224
UN Confidence Restoration Operation in Croatia (UNCRO), 592n13
UN Development Fund for Women (UNIFEM), 502
UN Development Programme, 245
UN Disengagement Observer Force (UNDOF), 532
UN Charter. *See* Charter
UN Educational, Scientific, and Cultural Organization (UNESCO), 248–249
UN Emergency Force (UNEF), 374, 531–532
UN General Assembly. *See* General Assembly
UN High Commission for Refugees (UNHCR): Bosnia support by, 576, 579, 592n17; Rwanda support by, 664, 678n21, 679n33
UN Institute for Training and Research, 472
UN Integrated Mission in Timor-Leste (UNMIT), 241, 464, 496

UN Interim Force in Lebanon (UNIFIL), 532, 543–544, 749–750, 781
UN Interim Security Force in Abyei (UNISFA), 623–624, 628, 630
UN International Independent Investigation Commission (UNIIIC), 540–541
UN Iran-Iraq Military Observer Group (UNIIMOG), 552
UN Iraq-Kuwait Observer Mission (UNIKOM), 554
UN Mission for Ebola Emergency Response (UNMEER), 783, 866
UN Mission for the Referendum in Western Sahara (MINURSO), 266, 495–496
UN Mission in Côte d'Ivoire (MINUCI), 683
UN Mission in Ethiopia and Eritrea (UNMEE), 758, 764
UN Mission in Haiti (UNMIH), 90, 239–240
UN Mission in Kosovo (UNMIK), 241, 309, 589, 752, 753
UN Mission in South Sudan (UNMISS), 242, 243, 623–624, 628
UN Mission in Sudan (UNMIS), 622, 623–624, 627–628
UN Mission in the Central African Republic and Chad (MINURCAT), 130, 625, 756
UN Monitoring, Verification, and Inspection Commission (UNMOVIC), 330, 559
UN Multidimensional Integrated Stabilization Mission in Mali (MINUSMA), 309, 384, 392n28, 392n29
UN Observer Mission in Angola (MONUA), 266
UN Observer Mission in El Salvador (ONUSAL), 6–7, 266
UN Observer Mission in Liberia (UNOMIL), 482, 484
UN Office for West Africa (UNOWA), 461
UN Office on Drugs and Crime (UNODC), 301, 304
UN Operation in Côte d'Ivoire (UNOCI), 112, 244, 382–383, 684–685, 686, 691–693, 694
UN Operation in Somalia I (UNOSOM I), 8, 222, 598
UN Operation in Somalia II (UNOSOM II), 8–9, 63, 483, 598–600
UN Operation in the Congo (ONUC), 4, 448
UN Organization Mission in the DRC (MONUC), 65, 378–380, 667–671, 672, 675, 754, 766
UN Organization Stabilization Mission in the DRC (MONUSCO), 242, 248, 381–382, 392n32, 674–675, 757, 766
UN Political Office for Somalia (UNPOS), 600
UN Preventive Deployment Force (UNPREDEP), 88tab, 91, 161, 592n13

UN Protection Force (UNPROFOR): for Bosnia, 8, 9, 266, 361–362, 401, 576–577, 578–579, 583–586; for Croatia, 574, 592n13
UN Regional Center for Preventive Diplomacy for Central Asia (UNRCCA), 461
UN Regional Office for Central Africa (UNOCA), 461
UN Security Council. See Security Council; Security Council relations
UN Special Commission (UNSCOM), 13, 329–331, 333, 555, 558
UN Special Mission to Afghanistan (UNSMA), 643–648, 649
UN Stabilization Mission in Haiti (MINUSTAH), 309, 496–497
UN Supervision Mission in Syria (UNSMIS), 723–725
UN Transition Assistance Group (UNTAG), 91
UN Transitional Administration of Eastern Slavonia (UNTAES), 587
UN Transitional Authority in Cambodia (UNTAC), 6–7, 90, 91, 239, 266
UN Transitional Authority in East Timor (UNTAET), 241, 243, 464, 496, 752–753
UN Truce Supervision Organization (UNTSO), 91, 397, 530, 547n11
UN Trusteeship Council, 817
UN Verification Mission in Guatemala (MINUGUA), 88tab, 91
UN Verification Mission in the Central African Republic (MINURCA), 9
UNAEC. See UN Atomic Energy Commission
UNAMA. See UN Assistance Mission in Afghanistan
UNAMI. See UN Assistance Mission in Iraq
UNAMID. See UN-AU Mission in Darfur
UNAMIR. See UN Assistance Mission in Rwanda
UNAMSIL. See UN Assistance Mission in Sierra Leone
Unanimity Principle, 201–203
UN-AU Mission in Darfur (UNAMID), 97, 484, 604, 624, 625, 630–631, 634–635, 755–756, 764, 852
UNCCA. See UN Commission for Conventional Armaments
UNCCT. See UN Centre on Counterterrorism
UNCRO. See UN Confidence Restoration Operation in Croatia
UNDOF. See UN Disengagement Observer Force
UNEF. See UN Emergency Force
UNESCO. See UN Educational, Scientific, and Cultural Organization
UNHCR. See UN High Commission for Refugees

UNIFEM. *See* UN Development Fund for Women

Unified Task Force (UNITAF), 8, 595, 598

UNIFIL. *See* UN Interim Force in Lebanon

UNIIIC. *See* UN International Independent Investigation Commission

UNIIMOG. *See* UN Iran-Iraq Military Observer Group

UNIKOM. *See* UN Iraq-Kuwait Observer Mission

Unilateralism, 57–60, 62–65, 69–73, 78–79, 366–367, 560, 821–823, 827–828

Union of Islamic Courts (UIC), 602–603

UNISFA. *See* UN Interim Security Force in Abyei

UNITA. *See* National Union for the Total Independence of Angola

UNITAF. *See* Unified Task Force

United Kingdom (UK): DRC Operation Artemis led by, 379, 672, 695*n*6; EU relations with, 821; in EU4, 737; in Falklands War, 481; FCO of, 131–132; G4 proposal support of, 181; Iraq War initiation by, 13–14, 66, 559–560; Israel-Palestine conflict stance of, 125–126*tab*, 126; Liberia stance of, 125*tab*; Libya proliferation management by, 332; Libya stance of, 125*tab*, 702; membership acquisition by, 123; membership reform interests of, 133–135, 136, 182; membership removal of, 169, 171, 832; national interest exploitation by, 161; NATO stance of, 396; peacekeeping involvement of, 123–127, 128, 129*tab*, 133; penholdership of, 128, 129*tab*, 131–133; piracy response of, 313, 315–316; power decline of, 121, 122–123, 159–160, 169; S5 reform engagement by, 182; sanctions involvement of, 130; Security Council engagement level of, 127–128, 129*tab*, 130–131, 832; Security Council strategic importance for, 122–127, 125–126*tab*, 135–136; Six-Day War resolution of, 531; Syria approach by, 70, 720, 726, 736, 744; vetoes by, 124, 125–126*tab*, 128, *129*tab. *See also* Permanent five members; Permanent three members

United Nations (UN): as capital forum, 820–821, 824–825; democracy promotion role of, 245–246; formation of, 37, 59, 123, 201, 299, 300*photo*, 784, 816; geopolitical fragmentation in, 818–819; purpose of, 235, 818

United Red Army of Japan, 279

United States (US): in Afghanistan, 12, 66, 108, 222, 652–655, 860; ambassadorship styles, 65; al-Aqsa intifada stance of, 534; in Arab-Israeli conflict Quartet, 534, 535–536, 538; Atrocity Prevention Board, 223; Bosnia response of, 577–580, 585–586; Brazil relations with, 807; China relations with, 795, 805; in Côte d'Ivoire, 69; criminal law enforcement by, 305, 310; on Darfur and Bashir arrest, 518; in Dominican Republic, 480–481; Ebola addressed by, 866; economy of, 164–165, 794; embassy bombings, 280, 283, 419, 618, 646; embassy hostage crisis in Tehran, 448–449, 552; foreign policy conclusion, 71–73; foreign policy of Bush, George H. W., 60–61, 75–76, 242–243; foreign policy of Bush, George W., 65–67, 76, 801–802; foreign policy of Clinton, 61–65; foreign policy of Obama, 67–71, 80, 802–803, 828–829; G4 reform opposition by, 163, 181, 867; in Guatemala, 479; Haiti relations with, 240, 754; ICJ briefing opposition by, 158; India relations with, 807; international law repudiation of, 65, 72; in Iraq, 6, 13, 60–61, 360, 553–554, 863; Iraq War initiation by, 13–14, 66, 72, 553–554, 559–560; Israel relations with, 732–733; Israel-Palestine conflict stance of, 64, 77–78, 367, 534–539; Japan relations with, 805; in Korean War, 360, 396; leadership maintained by, 831–832; Lebanon UNIFIL support by, 749–750; in Liberia, 754; in Libya, 69, 111, 226–227, 332, 703, 707, 710; membership preferences of, 80; membership reform interests of, 79–80, 163, 182, 807–809, 813*n*42, 867; in Mogadishu, 9, 63, 387; multilateralist approach by, 60–61, 65–69, 802–803, 822, 861–862; national interest exploitation by, 78–79, 161–162; North Korea relations with, 333–334, 360, 396; peacekeeping involvement of, 129*tab*; proliferation security organizations of, 340; resolutions by region, 40, 41*fig*, 42*fig*, 43; Russia distrust of, 105, 107–108, 109, 718–719, 726–727, 743; Russia reconciliation with, 68, 108–109; in Rwanda, withdrawal, 63–64; scapegoating by, 62–64; Security Council authority expansion by, 75–77, 801–803; selective security role of, 366–367; Somalia and Persian Gulf recon by, 597; Somalia UNITAF led by, 8, 595, 598; Somalia UNOSOM I led by, 8, 222, 598; Somalia UNOSOM II led by, 8–9, 63, 483, 598–600; Sudan relations with, 618, 620, 621, 631–632, 641*n*71, 755; Syria approach by, 69–70, 718–719, 725, 726–727, 732–733, 736, 743–746, 843; Syria proliferation agreement with, 338–339, 726–727; terrorism in Cold War era

against, 280–281; trafficking stance of, 303–304, 864–865; unilateralist approach by, 57–60, 62–65, 69–73, 78–79, 366–367, 560, 821–823, 827–828; vetoes by, 35, 36*fig*, 37–38, 53*n*12, 60, 64–65, 77–78, 129*tab*, 158, 367, 534, 831*fig*; Western Sahara negotiations by, 495–496; in Zaire, 665–666. *See also* Permanent five members; Permanent three members
Uniting Against Terrorism (Annan), 289
Uniting for Consensus Group, 163, 181, 183
Uniting for Peace resolution: for Afghanistan, 644; failure and disuse of, 354, 657*n*2; for Syria, 723, 743
Universal Declaration of Human Rights, 236–237, 260
UNMEE. *See* UN Mission in Ethiopia and Eritrea
UNMEER. *See* UN Mission for Ebola Emergency Response
UNMIH. *See* UN Mission in Haiti
UNMIK. *See* UN Mission in Kosovo
UNMIS. *See* UN Mission in Sudan
UNMISS. *See* UN Mission in South Sudan
UNMIT. *See* UN Integrated Mission in Timor-Leste
UNMOVIC. *See* UN Monitoring, Verification, and Inspection Commission
UNOC. *See* UN Operation in the Congo
UNOCA. *See* UN Regional Office for Central Africa
UNOCI. *See* UN Operation in Côte d'Ivoire
UNODC. *See* UN Office on Drugs and Crime
UNOMIL. *See* UN Observer Mission in Liberia
UNOSOM. *See* UN Operation in Somalia I; UN Operation in Somalia II
UNOWA. *See* UN Office for West Africa
UNPOS. *See* UN Political Office for Somalia
UNPREDEP. *See* UN Preventive Deployment Force
UNPROFOR. *See* UN Protection Force
UNRCCA. *See* UN Regional Center for Preventive Diplomacy for Central Asia
UNSCOM. *See* UN Special Commission
UNSMA. *See* UN Special Mission to Afghanistan
UNSMIS. *See* UN Supervision Mission in Syria
UNSOM. *See* UN Assistance Mission in Somalia
UNTAC. *See* UN Transitional Authority in Cambodia
UNTAES. *See* UN Transitional Administration of Eastern Slavonia
UNTAET. *See* UN Transitional Authority in East Timor
UNTAG. *See* UN Transition Assistance Group

UNTSO. *See* UN Truce Supervision Organization
Uppsala Conflict Data Program (UCDP), 47*tab*
Urquhart, Brian, 405, 529
Uruguay, 379, 759
US. *See* United States
US Agency for International Development (USAID), 256*n*93
Use of force: on Afghanistan, 66; Annan stance on, 375–376, 391*n*7, 405; appropriateness of, 387–389; authorization assessment, 357–359; authorization power, 366, 773; on Bosnia, 358–359, 361–362, 582–586; Brahimi Report on, 375–376; Charter intention and, 353–354, 374, 390*n*1, 393–394; Chile stance on, 874*n*30; coercive protection and, 228–229; command and control issues in, 363–364, 385–386; conflict change in nature and, 351–353, 389–390, 850; conflict complexity and, 365–366; on Côte d'Ivoire, 69, 112, 244, 382–383, 691–693, 694; counterterrorism role in, 389; on Croatia, 584; for democracy promotion, 239–240; increase in, 356–357; international disagreement on, 350, 359–364; international law on, 357, 778, 781; interpretation broadness of, 360–361; Iraq War by, 66, 359, 360, 553–554, 559–560; legitimacy of, 363–364, 368–369; on Libya, 69, 111, 356, 361, 699–709; military and peacekeeping comparison in, 228–229; misconduct in, 362; NAM stance on, 376, 849; by non-UN agencies, 355–357; P5 contention on, 367–368; peacekeeping expansion by, 750–751; peacekeeping principles and, 354–355, 374–377, 848; peacemaking goal of, 387–389; personnel casualties and, 364; public opinion on, 71; R2P abuse for, 2, 11, 69, 225–227, 230, 787; reasons for, 349; reevaluation points, 351; refugee flow and, 356–357; regional organizations cover for, 852; rules of engagement problem in, 357–358, 386; Russia stance on, 107–108, 110–112, 383; RWP on, 226, 700, 711–712, 713; selectivity and, 349–351, 365–369; on Syria, 69–70, 227; types of, 354–357; unauthorized, 350–351; unintended disasters from, 362; US unilateralism and, 57–58, 69–73, 78–79, 366–367, 560, 821–823, 827–828; War Powers Act and, 71
USS *Cole* bombing, 648
UTA flight 772 bombing, 281

Van der Stoel, Max, 261

Van Kleffens, Eelco, 395
Vance, Cyrus, 572
Védrine, Hubert, 134
Venezuela: Betancourt assassination attempt, 480; Bosnia safe areas role of, 578; drug trafficking from, 304
Vetoes: abuse of, 158; Chapter VII, 29*tab*, 30*fig*, 34*fig*; by China, 53*n*15, 86, 88–89*tab*, 90–91, 129*tab*, 830, 831*fig*; closet, 143, 158; collective no-vote, 145–146, 202–203; counterterrorism, 280–281; by E10, 834; by France, 124, 125–126*tab*, 128, *129*tab; human rights, 272; League of Nations provision on, 368; limitation of, 153, 180, 202–203; membership, 34*fig*, 35, 53*n*12, 53*n*15, 78, 88*tab*, 162–163; political price of, 202–203; power dynamics of, 143, 145–146, 153, 202–203; Razali proposal on, 180; by Russia, 35, 36*fig*, 37–38, 116–117, 118, 129*tab*, 830, 831*fig*; S5 reform of, 78, 134, 184; Secretary-General appointment, 445; selective security and, 367–368; by Soviet Union, 35, 36*fig*, 37–38, 53*n*12, 59; on Syria, 720–722, 723–725, 730, 734–735*tab*; trend by conflict, 34*fig*; trend by P5 distribution, 35, 36*fig*, 37–38, 53*n*12, 78, 129*tab*, 830, 831*fig*; by UK, 124, 125–126*tab*, 128, *129*tab; unanimity principle of, 201–203; by US, 35, 36*fig*, 37–38, 53*n*12, 60, 64–65, 77–78, 129*tab*, 158, 367, 534, 831*fig*; value of, 158–159; voluntary restraint of, 202–203, 212*n*17–213*n*19
Vieira de Mello, Sergio, 561, 562
Vienna Declaration and Program of Action, 237
Vienna Group, 338
Vietnam: Laos relations with, 449; membership veto of, 53*n*12
Volcker Report, 558, 564

Waldheim, Kurt, 280, 445, 449, 450, 552
Walzer, Michael, 222
War crimes. *See* International Criminal Court
War Powers Act, 71
Warsaw Declaration, 242
Warsaw Treaty Organization, 477
Washington Treaty, 395
Watson Institute for International Studies, 435
Weapons of mass destruction (WMD), 342*n*1. *See also* Proliferation management
Wells, Melissa, 637*n*16
WEOG. *See* Western European and Others Group
West Africa: ECOMOG, 752, 753; trafficking in, 304, 306; UNOWA, 461. *See also*

Economic Community of West African States
Western European and Others Group (WEOG), 758
Western Sahara, 266, 493, 495–496
WikiLeaks, 59, 163
Wildlife trafficking, 307, 309
Withdrawal: host state disruption for, 765, 850; from Rwanda, 8, 63–64, 664; from Sierra Leone, 753; from Somalia, 599–600
WMD. *See* Weapons of mass destruction
Wolfensohn, James, 535
Women: democracy promotion and, 242; Groups of Friends of, 501, 502; NGOs for, 502; resolutions on, 44, 242, 501, 502; sexual exploitation of, 267, 270, 436*n*4
Working Group for Women, Peace, and Security (NGOWG), 502
Working Group on Children and Armed Conflict, 267
Working Group on Conflict Prevention and Resolution in Africa, 453, 464, 474*n*20
Working methods: accountability in, 188, 199, 786; ACT Group and, 188; Arria formula format of, 151, 177, 199, 261, 268, 836, 854; beginning of, 176; conclusion, 188–190; consistency dilemma, 787–788, 869–870; counterterrorism, 285, 287; evolution of, 198–200; field visits as, 177, 190*nn*8–11, 269–270; G4 proposal on, 180–181; Groups of Friends, 497, 503; horizon scanning as, 178–179, 268, 844; for human rights, 261, 266, 268–269; implementation obstacles, 183–184, 468; inclusivity in, 188, 199; informal interactive dialogue as, 179, 191*nn*17–19, 199–200, 836–837; IWGD on, 176, 182, 183–184, 192*n*37, 198–199; L69 proposal on, 183; legitimacy of, 869; need for, 175–176; negotiation framework, 183, 184–186; Note 507, 150–151, 182, 183–184, 192–193*nn*42–44, 192*n*39; Open-Ended Working Group for, 179, 180, 182, 183; post–Cold War innovations in, 176–179; power dynamics of, 148–149, 151–152; Razali proposal on, 162, 179–180, 191*n*26; S5 proposal on, 78, 134, 181–188, 189, 192*n*33–194*n*62, 868; sanctions, 422, 428; Secretary-General reporting, 458, 465; SRSG reporting, 465–467; thematic debates as, 177–178; transparency of, 150–151, 176, 182, 188, 199, 837; wrap-up sessions as, 178
World Bank, 871
World Summit: democracy promotion language in, 237; G4 reform at, 180;

organized crime issues in, 301; Peacebuilding Commission at, 245, 850–851; R2P adoption at, 98, 192n27, 224, 782; regional collaboration precedents at, 484
World War I, 220
World War II, 3, 139, 220, 248, 259, 299, 816
Wörner, Manfred, 400
Wrap-up sessions, 178

Yalta conference, 123
Yanukovych, Viktor, 112
Yeltsin, Boris, 107, 581
Yemen: GCC mediation with, 485; sanctions on, 418tab, 420tab

Yugoslavia: Cold War era expectations and, 590; collapse of, 570–574; ethnic mix of, 570–571; overview of, 569–570; sanctions on, 416tab, 420tab, 482, 572. See also Bosnia-Herzegovina conflict; International Criminal Tribunal for the Former Yugoslavia; Kosovo
Yusuf, Adbullahi, 601

Zahir Shah, Mohammed, 644
Zaire, 665–667
Zenawi, Meles, 617, 628
Zhou Enlai, 84
Zimbabwe sanctions, 88tab, 96, 858
Zuma, Jacob, 709

About the Book

AFTER GRAPPLING FOR TWO DECADES WITH THE REALITIES OF the post–Cold War era, the UN Security Council must now meet the challenges of a resurgence of great power rivalry. Reflecting this new environment, *The UN Security Council in the Twenty-First Century* provides a comprehensive view of the Council's internal dynamics, its role and relevance in world politics, and its performance in addressing today's major security challenges.

Sebastian von Einsiedel is director of the United Nations University Centre for Policy Research. **David M. Malone** is under-secretary-general of the United Nations and also rector of the United Nations University. **Bruno Stagno Ugarte**, most recently executive director of Security Council Report, now serves as deputy executive director for advocacy at Human Rights Watch.